UML Diagrams

Static Relationships

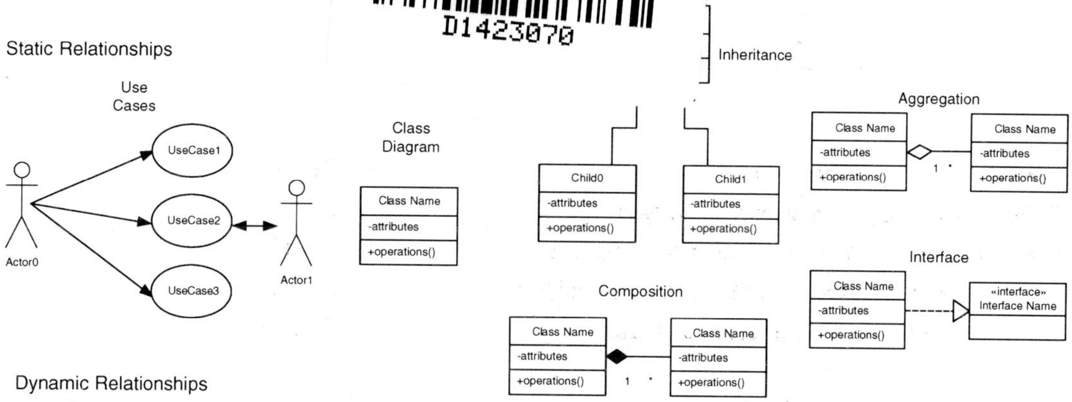

Dynamic Relationships

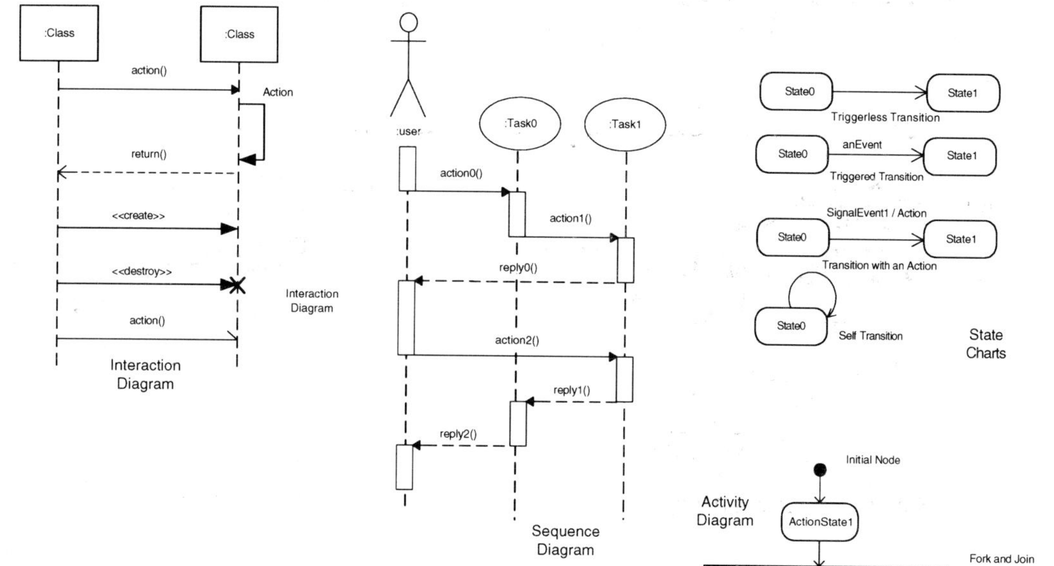

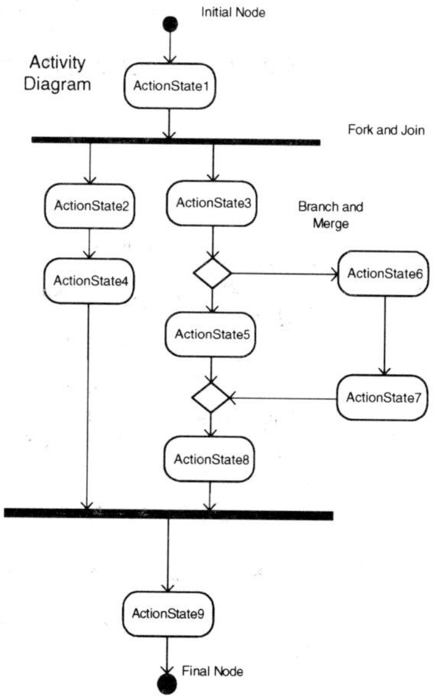

Data and Control Flow Diagrams

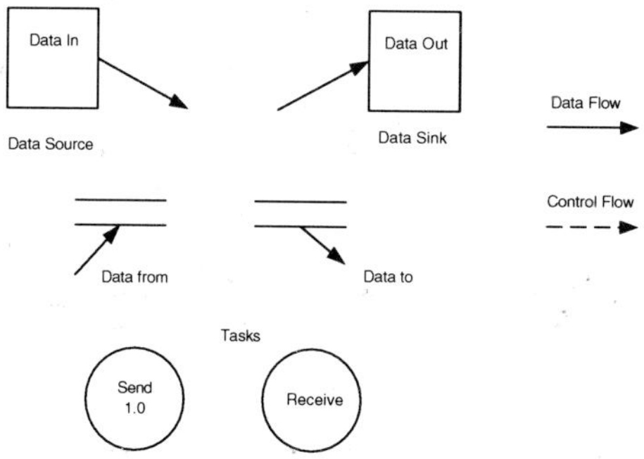

Embedded Systems

A Contemporary Design Tool

BICENTENNIAL 1807 WILEY 2007 BICENTENNIAL

THE WILEY BICENTENNIAL–KNOWLEDGE FOR GENERATIONS

Each generation has its unique needs and aspirations. When Charles Wiley first opened his small printing shop in lower Manhattan in 1807, it was a generation of boundless potential searching for an identity. And we were there, helping to define a new American literary tradition. Over half a century later, in the midst of the Second Industrial Revolution, it was a generation focused on building the future. Once again, we were there, supplying the critical scientific, technical, and engineering knowledge that helped frame the world. Throughout the 20th Century, and into the new millennium, nations began to reach out beyond their own borders and a new international community was born. Wiley was there, expanding its operations around the world to enable a global exchange of ideas, opinions, and know-how.

For 200 years, Wiley has been an integral part of each generation's journey, enabling the flow of information and understanding necessary to meet their needs and fulfill their aspirations. Today, bold new technologies are changing the way we live and learn. Wiley will be there, providing you the must-have knowledge you need to imagine new worlds, new possibilities, and new opportunities.

Generations come and go, but you can always count on Wiley to provide you the knowledge you need, when and where you need it!

WILLIAM J. PESCE
PRESIDENT AND CHIEF EXECUTIVE OFFICER

PETER BOOTH WILEY
CHAIRMAN OF THE BOARD

Embedded Systems
A Contemporary Design Tool

James K. Peckol, Ph.D.
University of Washington

John Wiley & Sons, Inc.

Executive Publisher	*Don Fowley*
Associate Publisher	*Dan Sayre*
Acquisitions Editor	*Catherine Shultz*
Project Editor	*Gladys Soto*
Editorial Assistant	*Chelsee Pengal*
Marketing Manager	*Chris Ruel*
Production Editor	*Lea Radick*
Cover Designer	*Michael St. Martine*
Cover Image	*©Megumi Takamura/Dex Image/Getty Images*
Bicentennial Logo Design	*Richard J. Pacifico*

This book was set in *Times Ten* by *Preparé* and printed and bound by *Hamilton Printing*. The cover was printed by *Phoenix Color*.

Library of Congress Cataloging-in-Publication Data

Peckol, James K.
Embedded system: a contemporary design tool / James K. Peckol.
p. cm.
ISBN 978-0-471-72180-2 (cloth)
1. Embedded computer system. 2. Object oriented methods (Computer science)
I. Title.
TK7895.E42P43 2008
004.16--dc22

2007017870

ISBN 978-0-471-72180-2

To order books or for customer service please call 1-800-CALL WILEY (225-5945).
Printed in the United States of America

10 9 8 7 6 5 4 3 2 1

Preface

INTRODUCING EMBEDDED SYSTEMS

Less than 150 years ago, shipping a new product, petroleum, down the Mississippi in barges was viewed with skepticism and fear of possible explosion. Fifty years later, electricity and electric lights were viewed as marvels of modern technology available only to a few. Another 50 years subsequent, someone suggested that the world would need at most three to four computers. Our views continue to change. Today we ship petroleum (still with concern) all over the world. Electricity has become so common that we are surprised if a switch is not available to turn on a light when we enter a room. The need for three to four computers has grown to hundreds of millions, perhaps billions, of installed computers worldwide.

This book presents a contemporary approach to the design and development of a kind of computer system that most of us will never see—those that we call embedded systems. The approach brings together a solid theoretical hardware and software foundation with real-world applications. Why do we need such a thing? A good question, let's take a look.

Today we interact with an embedded computer in virtually every aspect of our everyday life. From operating our car to riding an elevator to our office to doing our laundry or cooking our dinner, a computer is there, quietly, silently doing its job. We find the microprocessor—microcomputer—microcontroller—everywhere. Today these machines are ubiquitous. Like the electric light, without thought, we expect the antilock braking system in our car to work when we use it. We expect our mobile phone to operate like the stationary one in our home. We carry a computer in our pocket that is more powerful than the ones the original astronauts took into space.

Today we have the ability to put an increasingly larger number of hardware pieces into diminishingly smaller spaces. Software is no longer relegated to a giant machine in an air-conditioned room; our computer and its software go where we go. This ability gives engineers a new freedom to creatively put together substantially more complex systems with titillating functionality, systems that only science fiction writers thought of a few years ago. Such an ability also gives us the opportunity to solve bigger and more complex problems than we have ever imagined in the past—and to put those designs into smaller and smaller packages. These are definitely the most fun problems, the exciting kinds of things that we are challenged to work on. Okay, where do we begin?

The embedded field started almost by accident not too many years ago. In the early 70s Federico Faggin and many others at Intel and Motorola introduced the 4004, 8008, and 6800 microprocessors to the engineering world. Originally intended for use in calculators and in calculator-like applications, today, driven by evangelists like Faggin, the microprocessor has become a fundamental component of virtually everything we touch. With such widespread application, the ensured safety and reliability of such systems are absolutely essential.

The embedded systems field has grown virtually overnight from nonexistent several years ago to encompass almost every aspect of modern electrical engineering and computing science. Embedded systems are almost unique in this respect. Although certainly other disciplines within electrical engineering and computing science utilize the knowledge of other fields, it is essential for those studying and working with embedded systems to develop multidisciplinary skills, particularly in the areas of digital hardware and software. Electrical and computer engineers, working with embedded systems, contribute to all aspects of the development process from planning and design to manufacturing and marketing.

The embedded systems field is also a bit of an enigma. Unlike the fields of mathematics, physics, or chemistry, embedded systems have evolved from the engineer's workbench rather than from the scientist's research lab. Much of our formal theory has roots in the efforts of skilled engineers and computer scientists whose work has been quickly adapted to the factory floor. The field of embedded systems is more like a large umbrella. The systems designed under that umbrella require skills from many diverse fields. Without those skills, embedded systems cannot exist. Herein lies one of the dilemmas of trying to write a book on the field. Finding the right balance between depth and breadth can be a significant challenge. Hopefully, we have approached a good and useful balance.

This text is based on a vast store of theoretical and practical knowledge gained in developing safe, highly reliable embedded applications over the years for the aerospace, commercial, and medical industries. We endeavor to present the material in interesting, exciting, and challenging ways. We hope that we have succeeded and that this text will create lots of opportunities for you to explore and to learn further.

SELECTING A LANGUAGE AND TOOLS

This book contains a rich collection of real-world hardware and software examples. In both areas, we have a variety of ways through which we can turn our ideas and designs into real-world hardware and software components. Perhaps someday we will develop a universal language in which we can express all applications from business to science to engineering. Perhaps someday we will talk to our computer, and it will effortlessly perform our requests—maybe even making suggestions along the way. We're not there yet. The hardware and software concepts we study here are largely language independent. In this book, as we take the step from concept to realization, we will use the Verilog language as a modeling and synthesis tool to express the hardware implementation, the Unified Modeling Language (UML) and structured design to model the software designs, and the C language to affect the software implementation. Although beyond the scope of this text, modeling the hardware and software functions of our design is central to the developing field called hardware-software co-design. Moving to other implementation languages and tools should be rather straightforward. For those readers not fully versed in Verilog or C, we provide a good introduction to and overview of the fundamentals of both tools.

ORGANIZING THE BOOK

It is often all too easy to hack together a one-off embedded application that works. Trying to replicate a million or more copies of such a design (with tight time constraints) very quickly runs into the real-world gremlins that are waiting for us. A solid, robust, reliable design must always be based on the underlying theory and a disciplined design approach. Such methods are growing increasingly important as we continue to push the design envelop.

This book takes a developer's perspective to teaching embedded systems concepts. It examines, in detail, each of the important theoretical and practical aspects that one must consider when designing today's applications. These include the formal hardware and software development process (stressing safety and reliability); the digital and software architecture of the system; the physical world interface to external analog and digital signals; the debug and test throughout the development cycle; and finally improving the system's performance.

THE CHAPTERS

Introduction and Background

The *Foreword* gives an introductory overview, some of the vocabulary that is part of the embedded world, a bit of background and history, and a few contemporary examples.

Hardware and Software Infrastructure

With a preliminary background set, the next several chapters cover the essential aspects of the hardware and software necessary for the design and development of contemporary embedded systems. The Verilog hardware design language, Unified Modeling Language, and structured design models are introduced as tools in support of the development process.

Chapter 1 provides the first formal look at embedded systems and introduces some basic concepts, approaches, and vocabulary. The chapter begins with the hardware and computing core, which is usually manifest as a microprocessor, microcomputer, or microcontroller, and follows with an introduction to and discussion of the classic von Neumann and Harvard architectures.

Next, at the opposite end of the system hierarchy, methods by which the bits, bytes, and volts can be interpreted as the various and essential kinds of information (numbers, characters, addresses, and instructions) found inside of an embedded system are studied. Building on the instructions, the instruction set architecture (ISA) and register transfer (RTL) levels of the computer are introduced and studied.

Chapters 2 and 3 address a portion of the hardware side of embedded system design. The material provides a solid basis for practical aspects of working with digital circuits and systems in the embedded world. The Verilog hardware design language is used as a modeling tool in the design and synthesis of combinational and sequential logics. Time constraints and related issues at the hardware level are introduced as critical considerations in embedded applications. Difficulties with and solutions to problems of asynchronous system I/O are examined. Effective clocking schemes for the design of robust digital hardware move the reader into the synchronous world.

Embedded systems work and sometimes fail in the real world. As part of a recurring emphasis on the need for safe, robust, and reliable designs, several of the more common failure modes in combinational and sequential hardware as well as methods for testing for such failures are presented. Those who already have a good background in digital design or hardware design languages can still benefit from going over the material on timing, time constraints, and the effects of parasitic devices or reviewing the Verilog examples.

Chapter 4 looks at how memory is used in embedded systems. This section begins with an examination of registers and cache and studies several of the more commonly used cache organizations and schemes. Next, the static and dynamic allocation of memory and their impact on performance in real-time embedded designs are studied. Finally, the stack data type and how it is used in multitasking design is examined.

Chapter 5 presents the major UML modeling diagrams that are relevant to the material subsequently presented in the text and later moves to the data and control flow diagram from the structured design approach to system modeling and development. The chapter introduces UML-based static and dynamic models of the software. The static view, which begins from outside the system, is refined to increasing levels of detail to capture the comprising modules, their relationships, and their communication paths.

The dynamic view expresses the behavior of the system while it is performing its intended tasks and provides information about interactions among tasks. Concurrent task operation and persistence are introduced and discussed as two of the more important dynamic considerations in anticipation of subsequent studies of tasks, intertask communication, scheduling, and the operating system.

Chapters 6 and 7 provide a review of the core elements of the C language as well as of several of the more commonly used data structures and algorithms necessary for developing embedded applications. Whether you are an experienced programmer or know just enough to get into trouble, this material guides you through developing software for an embedded environment. The chapters introduce the C basics with specific coverage of variables, storage types, scopes, addresses, pointers, and structs. Bit operations are presented as an essential tool for working with hardware signals. Functions, function calls, and pointers to functions are introduced and discussed in the context of embedded applications.

Developing the Foundation

The next few chapters present the embedded system development process based on the need to deliver a safe and reliable design. The development section closes as it does in the real world with the debug and test processes.

Chapter 8 introduces the basic concepts of safety, reliability, and robustness in embedded applications, formulates definitions for each, and identifies their differences. Several real-world examples in which minor oversights have led to either significant or potentially significant and costly failures are examined. After establishing some of the relevant vocabulary and the need for robust and reliable applications, several design approaches are presented to help to ensure those needs are met. The chapter concludes with the introduction of some tools and techniques that can be used to detect and manage problems that may occur during system operation.

Chapter 9 formalizes the embedded systems design and development process. Several different manifestations of the development life cycle are presented, studied, and analyzed. The reader is introduced to several traditional approaches to system design. Such approaches utilize models and model-based development, both of which are becoming increasingly critical in the design of today's highly complex systems. The primary tools in such discussions will be Verilog models, structured design techniques, and UML. Approaches for assessing and criticizing the quality and robustness of a design are presented and discussed. The chapter concludes, as the design must also, with an examination of the core elements in a design release package.

Chapter 10 contains concepts and material that are always relevant. Though certainly no substitute for a sound design process, debug, test, and troubleshooting are essential components throughout the process of developing embedded systems. This chapter begins by motivating the need for testing in both hardware and software. Then, starting with the pre-debug phase of a project, the presentation moves through module, subsystem, and system debug and test. Included are discussions of test process and associated specifications, test case design, alpha and beta testing, then production test as well as self-test and agency-driven testing.

Doing the Work

The next chapters build on the foundation established earlier to develop the application as a collection of interacting tasks under the management of a real-time operating system. Deadlock problems arising from such designs are examined. Prior to moving outside of the microprocessor in the following section, methods for analyzing and optimizing the performance of an embedded application are presented.

Chapters 11 and 12 provide an introduction to and motivation for tasks, multitasking, and the control of an embedded application. Beginning with the necessary terminology, the material examines the critical role of time in developing and deploying many embedded applications, and presents a first look at time-based and reactive systems. The chapter identifies the central responsibilities of an operating system, examines the characteristics and capabilities that distinguish a Real-Time Operating System (RTOS), and then examines the core set of requirements of the OS as embodied in the kernel.

Study then shifts to the fundamentals of flow of control, communication, and detailed timing in embedded applications. The discussion begins with event-driven control schema based on simple polling, interrupts, and associated handling mechanisms. Topics of interest include intertask communication, data and resource sharing, and task synchronization through semaphores and monitors. Scheduling, scheduling algorithms, and methods for evaluating scheduling algorithms in a real-time context round out the topic.

Chapter 13 continues the study of schedulers by examining the problem of deadlocks and starvation in multitasking embedded applications. Several methods for avoiding, preventing, identifying, and resolving deadlocks, as well as ensuring progress through the system, are described and discussed.

Chapter 14 examines performance and the quantification and evaluation of performance in embedded designs. To begin the study, several different metrics are introduced and discussed. An analysis of several important metrics—response times, time loading, and memory loading in embedded applications—follows. The chapter also studies the evaluation and optimization of time and power consumption aspects of performance. By looking at the opposite side of performance, several common errors in analysis of performance measures are explored and evaluated.

Interacting with the Physical World

Continuing the design and development of an embedded application, the scope is expanded first to local peripheral devices and then to more remote ones. The next several chapters move outside of the processor and into the physical world that includes working with a wide variety of different kinds of signals. First, a model of the interaction is developed as an extension of that developed earlier in Chapter 12, and then specific applications are examined in the context of that model.

Chapters 15 and 16 open the study by exploring how an embedded application can interact with the external world. The internal interprocess and communication model developed earlier is expanded to include information, control and synchronization, and addressing in the external world and is extended to include a transport component. Following the introductory discussion, each component is studied in detail from the points of view of a shared variable (local) and a message-based (remote) model of information exchange. The objective of these chapters is to establish the basic infrastructure and various implementation architectures for both the local and remote models of external world interaction.

Chapter 17 focuses on the typically local analog and digital I/O interface to the external world. The chapter begins with several different methods for generating analog output signals and then looks at how various physical world analog input signals can be converted into a digital form. Three specific conversion algorithms—dual slope, successive approximation, and voltage to frequency—are studied. Because the outputs of the various sensors and transducers are often nonlinear, the problem of working with such signals is examined.

The chapter next introduces the topic of generating digital signals as control inputs to several different kinds of small motors, including stepper and servo motors, and as information that must be displayed. The discussion of digital I/O concludes by studying how time and frequency parameters of digital signals can be measured.

Chapter 18 examines the world in which interaction with the external world devices takes place via a network. The chapter introduces four different, commonly used network-based input/output designs. The study of each begins with the problems that motivated the development of the interface. Analysis of each design includes the transport mechanism, the control and synchronism scheme used, and the identification of message senders and receivers in the context of the model of intertask communication and synchronization developed earlier.

The chapter opens with the traditional RS-232 standard asynchronous serial interface, follows with a synchronous approach utilized by the Universal Serial Bus, and then examines the I^2C bus and the CAN bus. The objective is to establish the basic infrastructure and various implementation architectures for both local and remote models of external world interaction.

Chapter 19 provides an introduction to programmable logic devices (PLDs). The chapter begins with a brief discussion motivating the use of such devices in embedded systems and then examines the underlying logical concepts that have led to their development and widespread use. Next, the commonly used technologies for implementing programmable devices are examined. The basic structure of the components, variations on I/O configurations, and the fundamental architectures for the Complex Programmable Logic Device (CPLD) and the field programmable gate array (FPGA) are then presented.

As representative examples of PLD architectures, two of the more commonly used components—the CPLD and the Gate Array—as well as a more general-purpose device called a Programmable System on a Chip are presented. The chapter concludes with a look at several applications.

Supporting and Background Material

The first appendix is an introductory Verilog tutorial. The second provides a number of laboratory projects of increasing complexity that can be used to reinforce the practical application of the theory underlying the design of embedded systems.

Appendix A introduces the Verilog language and presents the important features and capabilities it then used in this book. The material begins with the basic components and organization of a Verilog program; examines the behavioral, dataflow, and gate-level or structural models for combinational logic circuits, and follows with similar models for sequential circuits. Design is only one element of the product development; each design must also be tested to confirm that it meets specified requirements. To that end, each section also discusses how one can formulate test suites to verify the proper operation. The material on testing will lay the foundation to guide the developer in building test cases for performing testing to the desired level. It is beyond the scope of this text to present a comprehensive treatise on testing.

Appendix B, found on the text's companion website, www.wiley.com/college/peckol, gives a number of lab exercises that are classified into three categories: *Getting Started, Developing Skills,* and *Bringing It Together*. The exercises in the first category suggest some basic projects that introduce some of the fundamental requirements of an embedded system such as bringing information into the microprocessor, using that information in an application, and producing some outputs. Projects in the second category are more complex. Many of these require a multitasking implementation, although they do not require an operating system. They utilize many of the peripheral devices commonly found in an embedded microprocessor, microcomputer, or microcontroller-based design. Projects in the third category represent simplified examples of real-world applications. These projects cover the complete product development life cycle from identifying requirements through design and test.

Additional Materials

A great variety of additional support material is available on the book's companion website, www.wiley.com/college/peckol. This includes information freely available to everyone such as the latest errata and additional background tutorials covering the basics of digital design and the C language fundamentals.

On the instructor's portion of the site, among other things, we include Power Point slides of all of text's figures and Appendix B which was described previously.

THE AUDIENCE

The book is intended for students with a broad range of background and experience and also serves as a reference text for those working in the field. The core audience should have at least one quarter to one semester of study in logic design, facility with a high-level programming language such as C, C++, or Java, and some knowledge of operating systems, and should be an upper-level junior or senior or lower-level graduate student.

NOTES TO THE INSTRUCTOR

This book can be a valuable tool for the student in the traditional undergraduate electrical engineering, computer engineering, or computer science programs as well as for the practicing engineer who wishes to review the basic concepts. Here the student may study the five essential aspects of the development of contemporary embedded systems, and is notably given a solid presentation of hardware and software architecture fundamentals, a good introduction to the design process and formal methods (including safety and reliability), the study of contemporary real-time kernel and operating system concepts, a comprehensive presentation of the interface to local and distributed external world devices, and finally debug and test of the designs.

Key to the presentation is a substantial number of worked examples illustrating fundamental ideas as well as how some of the subtleties in application go beyond basic concepts. Each chapter opens with a list of *Things to Look For* that highlight the more important material in the chapter and concludes with review questions and thought questions. The review questions are based directly on material covered in the chapter and mirror and expand on the *Things to Look For* list. They provide the student a self-assessment of their understanding and recall of the material covered. Though based on the material covered in the chapter, the thought questions extend the concepts as well as provide a forum in which the student can synthesize new ideas based on those concepts. Most chapters also include an extensive set of problems to permit the student to begin to apply the theory. These do not require laboratory support; however, they could be easily extended into basic lab projects. Included in *Appendix B*, found on the text's companion website, www.wiley.com/college/peckol, are 23 in-depth laboratory exercises.

The text is written and organized much as one would develop a new system, from the top down, building on the basics. Ideas are introduced and then revisited throughout the text, each time to a greater depth or in a new context. Busses may appear in the first few paragraphs to introduce the idea, later used to interconnect system components, and analyzed at a detailed level as the concepts of critical timing and data movement are studied. Safety and reliability are absolutely essential components in the development of any kind of system today. Such material is placed near the front of this text to emphasize its importance. The goal is to have the student think about such issues as he or she learns about and designs embedded applications.

As we stated in the opening of this Preface, finding a good balance between depth and breadth in an embedded systems text is a challenge. To that end, a couple of decisions were made at the outset. First, the text is not written around a specific microprocessor. Rather, the material is intended to be relevant to (and has been used to develop) a wide variety of applications running on many different kinds of processors. Second, the embedded field is rapidly changing even as this sentence is being typed and read. In lieu of trying to pursue and include today's latest technologies, the focus is on the basics that apply to any of the technologies. It is the underlying philosophy of this book that the student well grounded in the fundamentals will be comfortable working with and developing state-of-the-art systems utilizing the newest ideas. Ohm's law hasn't changed for many years; the field of electrical engineering has.

The core material has been taught as a one-quarter senior-level course in embedded systems development for approximately nine years. Roughly two-thirds of the material has been successfully taught for several years as a three-quarter on-site and distance learning outreach program to a population of students with rather diverse backgrounds. The outreach students have typically been working in industry for at least five years post-bachelor's degree.

Based on student background, the text is sufficiently rich to provide material for a two- to three-quarter or two-semester course in embedded systems development at the junior to senior level in a traditional four-year college or university. Beyond the core audience, the sections covering the assumed foundation topics can provide a basis on which the student with a limited hardware or software background can progress to the remainder of the material. The logic and software sections are not sufficiently deep to replace the corresponding one- or two-quarter courses in the topics. For those with adequate background in such areas, the material can either be skipped or serve as a brief refresher. Students with a Java background may find the material on pointers, bitwise operators, and structs to be particularly useful. The same holds for portions of the material on operating systems; such material is not intended to replace a formal, in-depth operating systems course. As deemed appropriate, the material may be skipped, used as a good refresher, or serve to introduce topics unique to embedded applications.

THE AUTHOR

The author's background spans over 40 years as an engineer and educator in the field of software, digital, and embedded systems design and development. As an engineer in the aerospace, commercial, and medical electronics industries, the author has worked on test systems for military aircraft navigation systems and radar systems, the *Apollo* color camera, various weather satellites, the Mars *Viking Lander*, flight control systems for a number of commercial aircraft, production of high-quality electronic test instruments and measurement systems, and several defibrillation systems. Academic experience spans more than 20 years of developing and teaching software, digital design, networking, and embedded systems design courses for students with experience ranging from limited hardware or software background to those at the junior, senior, and graduate levels.

ABOUT THE COVER

The umbrella on the cover is based upon an original photograph by Megumi Takamura. The image was chosen because it expresses the idea that the embedded systems field covers applications that utilize knowledge and skills from almost every discipline in engineering and computing science. Like the cover on this book, if we open the cover of most contemporary products, we will find embedded designs being used as tools to enhance their features and capabilities.

ACKNOWLEDGMENT

Over the years, as I've collected the knowledge and experiences to bring this book together, there have been many, many people with whom I have studied, worked, and interacted. Our discussions, debates, and collaborations have led to the ideas and approach to design presented on the pages that follow.

While there are far too many to whom I owe a debt of thanks to try to list each here, I do want to give particular thanks to David L. Johnson, Corrine Johnson, Greg Zick, Tom Anderson, David Wright, Gary Anderson, Patrick Donahoo, Steve Swift, Paul Lantz, Mary Kay Winter, Kasi Bhaskar, Brigette Huang, Jean-Paul Calvez, Gary Whittington, Olivier Pasquier, Charles Staloff, Gary Ball, John Davis, Patrick F. Kelly, Margaret Bustard, and Donna Karschney for all they've done over the years. William Hippe and Alex Talpalatskiy, who spent many hours proofreading, commenting, and making valuable suggestions to improve the early versions of the text, deserve a special thank you.

From John Wiley, I want to thank Bill Zobrist who supported the original idea of publishing this text and especially Gladys Soto, the Project Editor who carried the development forward, the Production Editors Lea Radick and Lisa Wojick who brought everything together, and the unknown copyeditors, compositors, and others whose efforts on and contributions to this project have been invaluable.

In any project, design reviews are an essential part of producing a quality product. I wish to express my appreciation and thanks to this project's many reviewers for their evaluations and constructive comments, which helped guide its development.

John Acken	Oklahoma State University, Stillwater
Farrokh Attarzadeh	University of Houston
Saad Biaz	Auburn University
Phillip De Leon	University of Colorado-Boulder
Michael Eastman	Rochester Institute of Technology
Richard Fryer	Cal Poly, San Luis Obispo
Subra Ganesan	Oakland University
Adam Hoover	Clemson University
Kenneth Jacker	Appalachian State University
Phillip Laplante	Pennsylvania State University
Al Liddicoat	Cal Poly, San Luis Obispo
Tulin Mangir	California State University, Long Beach
Michael Morrow	University of Wisconsin-Madison
Brad Naegle	US Naval Postgraduate School
Kamesh Namuduri	Wichita State University

Kimberly Newman	University of Denver
Mitchell Nielsen	Kansas State University
Dan Phillips	Rochester Insuitute of Technology
HR Shih	Jackson State University
Tom Stuart	University of Toledo
Jindong Tan	Michigan TechnologicalUniversity
Richard Wall	University of Idaho-Moscow
Hong Zhao	Embry Riddle Aeronautical University
Peixin Zhong	Michigan State University

Finally, I extend a thank you to my many teachers, friends, colleagues, and students who I've had the pleasure of knowing and working with over the years.

James K. Peckol, Ph.D.

To my family: Near and Extended, Close and Distant,
Present and Departed, So Similar,
So Different, So Known, So Surprising . . .
especially to our youngest brother Karl,
taken from us out of season during the last voyage
of the Edmund Fitzgerald.

Contents

Part Two Developing the Foundation

Part Three Doing the Work

Part Four Interacting with the Physical World

Foreword

THINGS TO LOOK FOR . . .

- The definition of an embedded system.
- The need for embedded applications.
- Some of the vocabulary of the field.
- Philosophy for the development of embedded applications.
- The major hardware and software components in an embedded system.
- The design and development process of an embedded system.
- Some of the basic architectures and how they evolved.

0.1 INTRODUCING EMBEDDED SYSTEMS

This foreword begins with some personal philosophy about the development of embedded systems. It also gives an overview of what an embedded system is and how such things are structured, and it concludes with a high-level view of the development process for an embedded system.

0.2 PHILOSOPHY

The approach and views on solving engineering problems in general taken in this work are my views and my approach; yours will probably be different, particularly as you learn and develop your skills and as the technology changes. This stuff is fun and challenging. At the same time, it is also important to recognize that not everyone feels the same way. If you have a different view, put this book down as quickly as you can, go out, and explore other vistas; go to the top of that next hill and then over it, until you find the things that are exciting and challenging for you.

As we begin, let's hop on a time machine and pop back, say 10,000 years or so to the shores of some beautiful lake somewhere. In the distance, we see some people walking along, picking up stones or rocks, or perhaps some sticks. Imagine what they might be thinking. Look, one person sees something. It's a small roundish flattish sort of rock—"ah ha," he says, " I'll bet I can make this rock skip five or even ten times over that lake if I throw it just right. In fact, I can make it skip more times than you." Another picks up a larger one—a round one too but more like a basketball. This could make a great chair (they probably didn't really say chair since the word hadn't been thought of yet). Yet another sees a long, stout stick—perfect for helping his mom walk since she's getting older. In each case, they saw the object from the outside. That's what first drew their interest—size, shape, color, and possible uses. Later, it was curiosity that drove them to learn more, to understand, to find out what was inside of something or what made it work. It's the drive to throw the rock further, make it skip more times, or make it shinier than the next guy that pushes us to constantly improve our designs.

Perhaps sometime during your early years someone told you that necessity was the mother of invention. Perhaps it was even your mother. Unfortunately, they lied. Necessity is not the mother of invention: laziness is. That's right, laziness. Our ancestors digging in the garden with sharpened sticks didn't say "I think I need a shovel." They more likely said, "this is hard work and I'm sick of it. Why do I have to do all the work? I'd rather be relaxing under that tree over there. I think I'll invent a shovel so I can get this job done quicker. If I could invent gasoline, I'd invent a tractor and a plow and get this done even faster."

We see here the two main themes that will be interwoven through each of the chapters ahead. With each new design, our first look should be from the outside. What are we designing? How will people use it—*what is its behavior*? What effect will it have on its operating environment—*what are the outputs*? What will be the effect of its operating environment—*what are its inputs*? How well do we have to do the job—*what are the constraints*? We want to look at the high-level details first and then go on to the lower. We can borrow the idea of the public interface (an outside view) to our system from our colleagues working on object-centered designs.

As technology advances, we are able to do more and more. Today, we can put several very powerful computers in the space that a single vacuum tube occupied several years ago. Keeping track of the behavior of a single vacuum tube offers minimal challenge. Orchestrating the information flow and managing the computation schedules of several high-performance microprocessors is a much more interesting problem.

To address such problems, we must have tools—tools to help us attack the complexity of the designs we are undertaking today; tools to help us get the job done more quickly and more efficiently. Hey, sitting under that tree is not too bad of an idea. Philosophy is fun, but now it's time to get to work. Unfortunately, today we don't have any tools that will automatically get this knowledge into our head. Yet, where do we go in the next 20 to 50 years? What tools will we have then? Let your imagination go free—that's now your job as tomorrow's engineers and scientists.

0.3 EMBEDDED SYSTEMS

We'll open by exploring embedded systems. Remember, as we start, embedded systems are not a standalone field. We use the tools, techniques, and knowledge from just about every discipline in electrical engineering and computing science.

0.3.1 What Is an Embedded System?

Embedded systems are a combination of hardware and, software parts, as well as other components that we bring together into products such as a cell phone, a music player, a network router, or an aircraft guidance system. They are a system within another system as we see in Figure 0.1.

VLSI—Very Large-Scale Integrated Circuits

Embedded systems techniques allow us to make products that are smaller, faster, more reliable, and cheaper. They allow us to bring features and capabilities to everyday things that could only be dreamed about just a few years ago. *VLSI—Very Large-Scale Integrated Circuits*—are the key component in enabling all of this to happen. Yesterday, we talked about individual transistors or tens of transistors. Today, with VLSI we think in terms of millions of transistors collected into a single integrated circuit. Without VLSI,

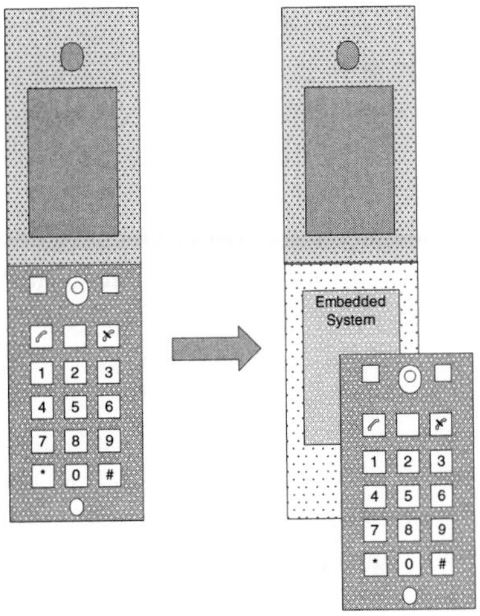

Figure 0.1 A Simple Embedded System

embedded systems would not be feasible, and without embedded systems, VLSI would serve little purpose.

When we develop an application program such as this word processing software or the latest video game, we want people to see it, to like it, and to buy it. If that does not happen, we have failed. In contrast, we intend our embedded designs to do their job reliably, quietly, efficiently, and out of sight inside some larger system such as the fuel control system in our car. We become aware that they are there only when they don't work.

Embedded systems present a variety of challenges as we bring the hardware, the software, and vagaries of the world outside of the microprocessor together. Seeing our design sending a rover across the plains, conducting experiments on Mars or photographing some planet in a distant galaxy, saving lives as a part of the latest heart monitoring system, or working as the core of the newest entertainment system—these are all the reasons we are in this business.

A few years ago when microprocessors and Programmable Read Only Memories (PROMs) first appeared as new tools, developing applications—firmware as it became known—was rather undemanding. Armed with a teletype, a simple assembler, and a host minicomputer, we were ready to go. "Sophisticated" applications of several hundred lines of code transformed rather complex, discrete, logic designs into simple, yet powerful, state-of-the-art systems. Today, we are designing embedded applications comprising thousands of lines of code, multiple microprocessors, Very Large Scale Integrated (VLSI) components, and array logics that may be distributed around an office or around the world. The complexity of today's problems has increased manyfold. To successfully attack such problems, we must develop and learn new tools to replace those we've grown comfortable with.

Unlike the desktop PC, an embedded computer must interact with a wide variety of analog and digital devices. The skilled embedded developer must know and understand the operation of sensors and transducers, analog-to-digital conversion (and vice versa), networks and their many protocols, motors, and other processors, as well as the more traditional peripherals. As we make our systems smaller and smaller, dozens of dead physicists are lurking. Our old friends Maxwell, Faraday, Gauss, and Lenz are there to quickly point out when we've violated one of their laws. Solving problems arising from signal coupling, noise, electromagnetic interference, or propagation delays is challenging indeed—but necessary.

0.3.2 Building an Embedded System

system bus

Address, Data, Control

As we begin to study embedded applications, we will find that, in addition to a wide variety of other hardware components, we embed three basic kinds of computing engines into our systems: microprocessors, microcomputers, and microcontrollers. The microcomputer and other hardware elements are connected via the *system bus,* which provides an interconnecting path for electrical signals to flow. The system bus is actually subdivided into three busses, segregated by the information they carry: *Address*, *Data*, and *Control*.

firmware

We'll examine each of these elements of the system in greater depth in the coming chapters. For now, we see that a typical embedded system comprises hardware and software, and is designed and optimized to solve a specific problem very efficiently. The microprocessor controls the whole system, and ultimately the application, by executing a set of instructions called *firmware* that is stored in ROM in the memory subsystem.

fetches, decodes, executes

instruction cycle

To run the application, when power is first turned on, the microprocessor addresses a predefined location and *fetches, decodes,* and *executes* one instruction after another. As each instruction is completed, the processor fetches the next one. The *instruction cycle* repeats forever, unlike a typical application program which eventually terminates. At the top level, an embedded program is structured as an infinite loop, as illustrated in the code fragment in Figure 0.2.

```
while(1)
{
        Embedded Program
}
```

Figure 0.2 Top-Level Embedded Program

instruction set

The program never executes a return; there is no place to return to. The specific set of instructions that a microprocessor knows how to execute is called its *instruction set.* Included are instructions that bring data in from the outside world, output signals to the external world, and provide a means to exchange data with the memory subsystem.

embedded system, embedded

The term *embedded system* refers to a system that is enclosed or *embedded* in a larger system. Such a system often continually interacts with its surrounding environment as it monitors and controls some set of processes. A good example is the automobile, which may contain as many as 100 embedded microprocessors and microcontrollers for managing engine ignition and firing, transmission shifting, power steering, the antilock braking system, security system, or the passenger entertainment system.

watchdog timer

When operating in electrically harsh environments such as the engine compartment of an automobile or the cockpit of an aircraft, there is a high probability that electromagnetic noise may cause the system to behave erratically. Similar behavior on our desktop machine is easily remedied by simply reaching over and resetting the system. We do not have that luxury with an embedded application that may be flying along at 40,000 feet. To address the problem, we add what we call a *watchdog timer.* Such a timer is not much more than a fancy alarm clock. Periodically, the microprocessor must reset the timer. If it fails to do so, the timer will reset the microprocessor, which generally solves the problem. In Figure 0.3, the signal from the watchdog timer comes in to the processor as a nonmaskable interrupt (NMI)—that is, an interrupt that cannot be ignored.

real-time

Time is often an essential constraint in an embedded application, in contrast to what one finds in a typical desktop application, for example. Stating that a system is *real-time* demands that the system must respond to designated external or internal events within a specified time interval. The expected response is typically the execution of the task associated with the triggering event.

We identify three kinds of real-time systems based on the urgency of meeting the required time constraint. A system is considered to be a *soft real-time system* if failure to meet the time constraint results only in degraded performance. If a time constraint is not met in a *hard real-time system,* the system is said to have failed. Such a failure may be seen as catastrophic if it can result in considerable risk to people, to the environment, or to a system being monitored or controlled. A *firm real-time system* falls in between with a mix of the two kinds of tasks.

soft real-time system

hard real-time system

firm real-time system

When an operating system is used in an embedded microcomputer, typically it is a real-time operating system, or RTOS. An RTOS is specifically designed and optimized to predictably handle the strict time constraints associated with events in a real-time context.

microprocessor

The implementation of a *microprocessor*-based embedded system combines the individual pieces into an integrated whole as we see in Figure 0.3, which presents the architecture for a typical embedded system and identifies the minimal set of necessary components.

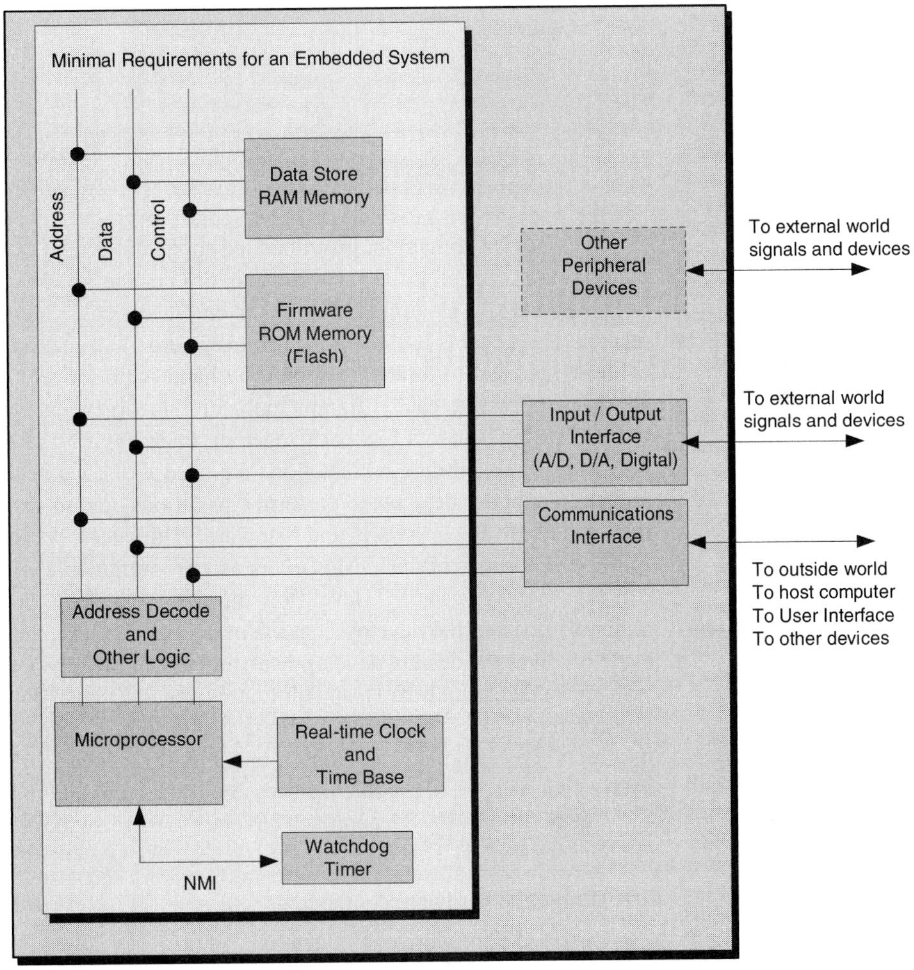

Figure 0.3 A Microprocessor-Based Embedded System

0.4 THE EMBEDDED DESIGN AND DEVELOPMENT PROCESS

Not too many years ago, we began the design of a new embedded application with some thought about the problem, wrapped some registers, logic, and busses around the microprocessor, wrote a few lines of assembly language code, downloaded the assembled object file to the development environment, debugged it, and shipped it—or so it seemed. Such an approach worked great when all we had to be concerned about was the microprocessor, a handful of inputs and outputs, a few Small-Scale Integrated (SSI) or Medium-Scale Integrated (MSI) gate packs, and firmware that fit into a couple of PROMs as we see in the simple drawing in Figure 0.4. Today, delivering robust, reliable, and well-designed embedded applications to our customers is not quite that easy.

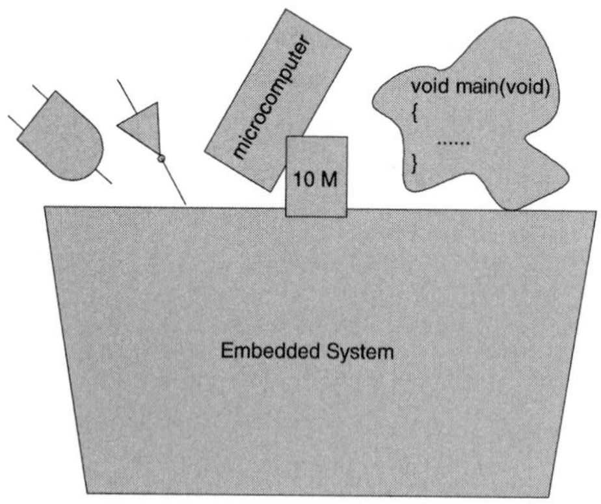

Figure 0.4 Building an Embedded System

We find that contemporary embedded applications tend to fall into two groups: the simple ones that run the toaster, microwave, or children's video game, and the sophisticated ones that control a jet aircraft, manage an entertainment system, or help to control a nuclear reactor. The systems in the second group are orders of magnitude more complex than any of those we used to build. Designing by hand is no longer feasible. Utilizing an ad hoc approach tailored to each different application is too expensive and too fraught with error. We can't simply wire a few parts together, hack out a bit of software, and spend days or weeks trying to debug the collection. We need tools; we need formal methods. We need tools to model our designs, to perform simulations, and to simplify and interactively optimize the hardware, software, and firmware. Ultimately, we need tools that we can use to synthesize portions of that design either as a programmable logic device or a VLSI circuit.

Figure 0.5 gives a high-level flow through the development process and identifies the major elements of the development *life cycle*. Specifically, the hardware portion of the life cycle involves the design, development, and test of the physical system architecture, packaging, printed circuit boards, and ultimately, the individual components. The software portion entails the tasks or algorithmic portion of the application. Such software may be written in a high-level language, assembler, or a mixture of the two. Work in assembly requires detailed knowledge of the microprocessor architecture and its register structure.

life cycle

The traditional design approach has been to traverse the two sides of the accompanying diagram separately. That is,

- Design the hardware components.
- Design the software components.
- Bring the two together.
- Spend time testing and debugging the system.

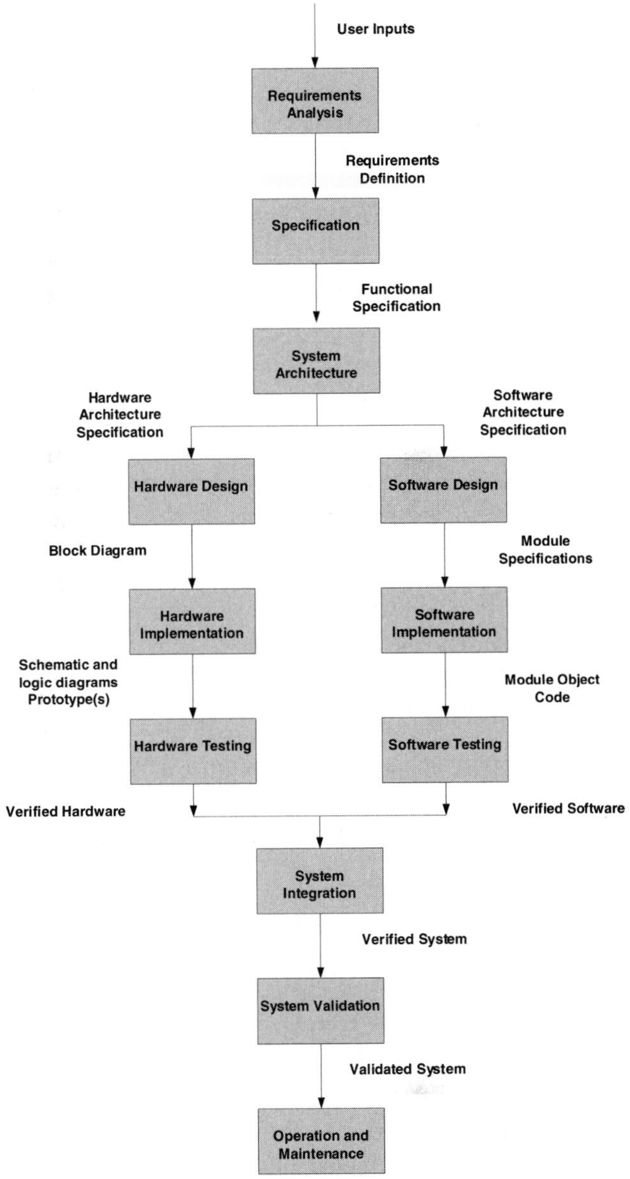

Figure 0.5 The Embedded System Life Cycle

Contemporary methodologies favor the combined and "simultaneous" design of both the hardware and the software components, with the objective of meeting system-level requirements through trade-offs between these two. The key points in such an approach are to specify and (iteratively) design and develop both aspects of the system concurrently with the goals of increased productivity—reduced design cycle time—and improved product quality.

Such an approach focuses on the major areas of the design process:

- Ensuring a sound hardware and software specification and input to the process
- Formulating the architecture for the system to be designed
- Partitioning the hardware and software
- Providing an iterative approach to the design of hardware and software

Each of the issues we have identified is listed in Figure 0.6 and will be addressed in detail during our studies of the development of modern embedded systems

Major Aspects in the Development of Embedded Applications

- Digital hardware and software architecture
- Formal design, development, and optimization process
- Safety and reliability
- Digital hardware and software/firmware design
- The interface to physical world analog and digital signals
- Debug, troubleshooting, and test of our design

Figure 0.6 Considerations When Developing an Embedded System

The contemporary creative design and development process begins with an abstracted notion of the system to be built and moves through an iterative series of transformations to the final product. Computer-based tools are essential to that process. To be able to effectively use such tools today, as engineers we must understand how to develop accurate hardware and software models of the systems we intend to design and build. As an integral part of embedded systems development, we continually trade off speed, size, power, cost, weight, or time constraints to meet specified constraints or to improve performance. Tools can help us to make those trade-offs more efficiently.

A comprehensive study of the design process and all related modeling tools and methodologies could easily take up several volumes—and does. Here, we take a first step and lay the groundwork on which people may build with future work. We will introduce, study, and apply the basic concepts of formal methods and tools. We learn that good system designers and designs proceed using a minimum of five steps. These steps are listed in Figure 0.7.

- Requirements definition
- System specification
- Functional design
- Architectural design
- Prototyping

Figure 0.7 Important Steps in Developing an Embedded System

In today's world, we see that the contemporary design process must also take into consideration design reuse and intellectual property at every design stage. Through hierarchical modeling and functional decomposition, we will become familiar with and work with formal design methodologies. In our studies, we will use the Verilog HDL—Hardware Design Language—as our hardware modeling and simulation tool. We will study the software life cycle in depth; the Unified Modeling Language (UML) and structured methods are presented and will become our software modeling tools.

A good, solid, and reliable design always begins with a firm foundation (Figure 0.8). Without that, everything we add later is fragile. Today, engineering students who want to work in the embedded field must have a sound understanding of the basics of digital hardware and software architecture as well as facility with more complex systems. Thus, we will begin our studies by revisiting the basics; we will build on that knowledge as we move to new topics.

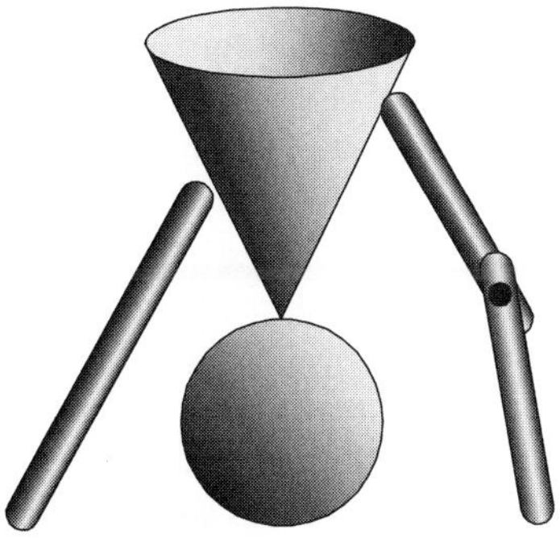

Figure 0.8 The Essential Foundation

We will open with the high-level structure and components coupled with an introduction to the von Neumann and Harvard architectures that comprise the hardware and computing core of an embedded application. That core is usually manifest as a microprocessor, microcomputer, or microcontroller. At the opposite end of the system hierarchy, we will take our first look at the bits, bytes, and volts as we study how the various and essential kinds of information (numbers, characters, addresses, and instructions) are represented inside of a digital system.

Next, we examine control and data flow in such machines and discuss how each is manifest as a microprocessor, microcomputer, or microcontroller. Analog and digital peripheral devices are incorporated to extend the basic architecture into the world of embedded applications. The programmer's view of the machine is introduced through a discussion of register transfer level (RTL) and instruction set architecture (ISA) models. The system designer's view brings the hardware and software together. With the high-level view in place, we proceed with a solid review of logic fundamentals and C language basics essential to developing robust embedded firmware.

Today's embedded systems are used in many applications that can affect people's lives, result in significant environmental impact, or cost millions of dollars in the event of failure. One of our goals in the design of embedded applications is to provide the highest performance at the lowest cost while still delivering a safe and reliable system. The design process does not stop with the first cut at a design; performance evaluation, like testing, must occur at every stage in the development. This book integrates the philosophy of safe and reliable design methodologies throughout. As a lead-in to the design cycle, we examine many of the considerations necessary for the execution of a safe, robust, and reliable design. We study both hardware and software methods to address the problems.

Design is the process of translating a customer's requirements into a working system. Working from the specification, we partition the system into its major functions and then map those functions onto an architectural structure. The application itself is generally manifest in software and sits on top of the hardware infrastructure.

A colleague once commented that hardware is merely a vehicle for software to express itself. His statement has some validity. Certainly, an essential component of any embedded system is the software/firmware. Early systems utilized an infinite loop to continuously cycle through the various jobs in the application. Such an approach is still effective in a number of today's simpler designs. For the more complex designs, more powerful methods are needed; such methods organize the required jobs into formal *tasks* or *processes* and carefully schedule when each is executed. The schedule becomes more complex as various constraints are added. Tasks will often need to share information: to *cooperate* and to *communicate* with each other with the world outside of the processor in well-controlled ways.

tasks, processes

cooperate

communicate

polling, event-driven

In the chapters ahead, we will introduce the fundamentals of the control and management of embedded applications by beginning with the simple *polling* and *event-driven* schemes. These ideas will be extended first to nonpreemptive and then to preemptive task-based systems. Time-based and reactive systems will lead to the development of simple scheduling algorithms. Building from these concepts, the real-time kernel will be introduced, studied in depth, and extended to include multitasking and multithreaded control. A comprehensive presentation of intertask communication methods and problems will lead to the need to coordinate and synchronize data exchange, the concept of critical sections, and the semaphore and monitor as tools for addressing such needs.

The concept of a real-time operating system as an extension to the basic kernel concepts will provide the next level of sophistication and power. The notions of task priorities and scheduling criteria will lead to a formal discussion of several fundamental scheduling algorithms, which include first-come first-served, round robin, and rate monotonic. Once again, addressing the need for safe and reliable systems, priority inversion, deadlocks, and starvation will be presented as potential problems in multitasking systems. Approaches for identifying and resolving such difficulties will be studied in some depth.

Embedded applications are intended to work with the physical world, sensing various analog or digital signals while controlling, manipulating, or responding to others. The study of the interface to the external world extends the I/O portion of the von Neumann machine (see Figure 0.9) with a detailed study of busses, their constituents, and their timing considerations. Local exchange is extended to include distributed and remote systems. The study of basic transaction management, consistency models, idempotent systems, and error management continues the thread of designing safe and reliable systems.

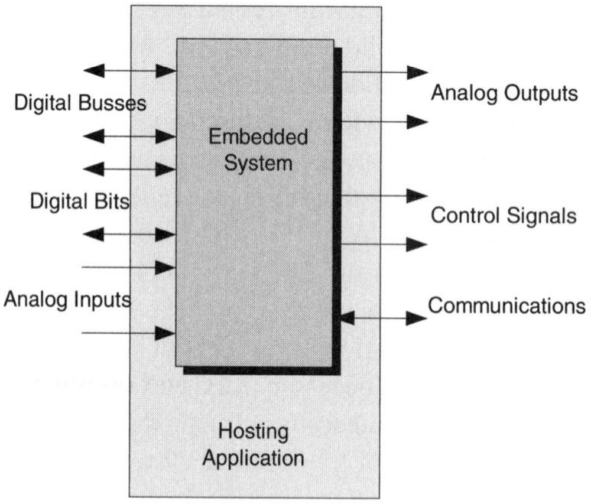

Figure 0.9 Interfacing to the Outside World

A substantial presentation of the development of interfaces for a variety of the more familiar serial and parallel hardware devices provides a solid set of tools on which to build. The discussion expands to the sensing and transducing elements (and their associated problems) with which the typical embedded application must deal.

A design is not complete when the first prototype is delivered; the system must also be tested once the design is released to manufacturing. However, the need for testing does not start with the release to manufacturing. We test at different times for different reasons; testing and debugging, like modeling, must be interwoven with the development process.

Let us look back at the good old days one more time. Once we built the hardware and firmware for our system, confirming that it worked was generally a straightforward task. A handful of switches, hardwired signals, a good emulator, an oscilloscope, and a logic analyzer, peppered with a little ingenuity, would generally suffice as a comprehensive test system. Today that is not even close. We're now working with dozens of simultaneously changing high-speed signals, on dozens of components that may exhibit failures based on infrequently occurring patterns in the data. Further complicating the problem is the simple fact that we have little visibility into the processors, VLSI circuits, or array logics with which we're working. Complicating the task even further, we must now deal with state-of-the-art operating systems, timing constraints measured in nano- or pico seconds, multiple processors, and systems scattered all over the world.

As with modeling, the literature, tools, and techniques in the field of test are extensive. Nonetheless, having a solid grounding in test and basic test techniques is essential, yet this knowledge is missing from the toolkit of most contemporary undergraduates and many working engineers. An even more significant tool missing from many young engineers' tool chests is an understanding of basic debugging techniques, in particular, when confronted with the complexity of today's systems. All too often, magic replaces critical problem analysis skills. "*This circuit only operates properly in the afternoon when the sun is out and I work on this bench . . . by the window.*" Gee, why? "*I don't know, it just does . . . I tried other places or times and it never works.*" Could it be the warmer temperature that's affecting your system's behavior, or shall we stay with magic as the answer?

The philosophy espousing the need to test is integral to each section of this book. We endeavor to provide such a basis for critical analysis by first introducing some simple debugging techniques, motivating the need for test, and then showing how we can design circuits and systems so that they can be easily debugged and tested. We will study fundamental methods for analyzing basic digital hardware and software systems. The goal of such study will be to learn to develop tests and methods of test for many of the more common failures and to learn how to extend such concepts to more complex designs.

In today's world, we continuously strive to make our designs faster, smaller, and cheaper, and to consume less power. As engineers, we always believe that we can make our design just a little bit better. We can purchase a ticket, hop a plane, and be in Asia, Europe, or just about any other part of the world in a few hours. With pockets filled with batteries, we may manage to nurse our laptop through most of the trip. We're pushing Moore's law (processing power doubles approximately every two years) daily and may be nearing the wall; yet we have to make things better.

In this book, we introduce several measures of system performance and discuss a number of methods and trade-offs for optimizing a design. In our discussions, we devote significant coverage to methods for analyzing and optimizing the performance of embedded systems in time, in size, cost, and power consumption.

0.5 SUMMARY

The text provides a valuable tool for the student in the traditional undergraduate electrical engineering, computer engineering, or computer science programs as well as for the practicing engineer who wishes to review the basic concepts. We present five essential aspects of the development of contemporary embedded systems: hardware and software architecture fundamentals, the design process and formal methods (including safety and reliability), contemporary real-time kernel and operating system concepts, interface to the local and distributed external world, and debug and test of the designs.

Our goal in designing embedded systems is to help to solve problems for people. Our designs can affect people's lives. Always do your best to make your designs as safe and as reliable as you can for each application. Remember, too, that the cost of a product is not limited to the cost of the parts that make it up. We also have to consider the costs of building, selling, supporting, and adding new features to your design. Finally, remember that our responsibility for a design does not end with design release. Good luck and have fun.

0.6 REVIEW QUESTIONS

Embedded Systems

0.1 What is an embedded system?

0.2 What is the difference between VLSI and embedded systems?

0.3 What are the three kinds of computing engine that are utilized in embedded systems?

0.4 How are an embedded microcomputer and supporting hardware elements interconnected?

0.5 An embedded system bus is typically made up of three separate busses; what are these?

0.6 What is an instruction cycle?

0.7 An instruction cycle comprises several steps; what are these steps?

0.8 What is an instruction set?

0.9 What is the purpose of a watchdog timer in an embedded application?

0.10 What does the term *real-time* mean?

0.11 What is the difference between hard, firm, and soft real-time?

Embedded System Design and Development

0.12 Briefly describe the major elements of the embedded system development life cycle.

0.13 What are the major elements of the design process?

0.14 The chapter identifies five steps that good designers usually take when designing a system. Identify and briefly describe each step.

0.15 What are the major categories of signals through which an embedded system interfaces with the external world?

0.7 THOUGHT QUESTIONS

Embedded Systems

0.1 Some pundits suggest that embedded systems will form the basis for ubiquitous computing tomorrow. Do you agree or disagree? Please elaborate.

0.2 Give two examples of a system that might be considered to be soft real time; hard real time: firm real time.

0.3 Discuss the advantages and disadvantages of having multiple specialized busses rather than a single generic bus interconnecting the various components within an embedded system.

0.4 Discuss the pros and cons of interconnecting the various components within an embedded system using a network scheme such as a miniaturized version of the Internet rather than a traditional bus.

0.5 Would there be any benefit to having multiple watchdog timers in an embedded application? Explain your answer.

0.6 Give several examples of analog and digital signals with which an embedded system might interface.

0.7 Give several examples of analog and digital devices with which an embedded system might interact.

Embedded System Design and Development

0.8 Today, in the typical embedded system development cycle, hardware design precedes software design. Discuss the advantages and disadvantages of developing the hardware and software components of the system at the same time.

0.9 An embedded system is made up of hardware and software components. What things should be considered when deciding whether to implement a piece of functionality in hardware or software?

0.10 What are some of the more difficult problems that today's embedded systems designers face? Consider such examples as a very popular consumer product, an intelligent robot system to be sent on a mission to Mars, or an automatic landing system on a commercial jet airliner.

0.11 What do you think might be some of the more important performance considerations that one should take into account when designing an embedded system?

PART 1 HARDWARE AND SOFTWARE INFRASTRUCTURE

Chapter 1

The Hardware Side—Part 1: An Introduction

THINGS TO LOOK FOR . . .

- The differences between microprocessors, microcomputers, and microcontrollers.
- The four major functional blocks of a computer and their interconnecting busses.
- How to represent numbers, characters, addresses and instructions in a digital system.
- Different instruction formats and addressing modes.
- Data and control flow through a computer.
- The instruction set architecture level (ISA) model of a computer.
- The computer instruction cycle.
- The register transfer level (RTL) model of a computer.

1.0 INTRODUCTION

Our brief introduction to embedded systems in the Foreword shows that hardware, software, and firmware are essential elements in today's embedded systems. The digital hardware provides the platform from which the three can synergistically perform amazing tasks. What is to be implemented in hardware and in software or firmware changes with every design—perhaps even within a single design as the requirements and the development evolve. Hardware brings a variety of strengths and weaknesses to the design; software and firmware do the same. As we learn to develop embedded applications, we will learn all their strengths and weaknesses. We will also learn when and how to choose which to use in a design.

In this chapter we will begin with the high-level structure and components: the hardware and computing core of an embedded application. That core is usually manifest as a microprocessor, microcomputer, or microcontroller. At the opposite end of the system hierarchy, we will take our first look at the bits, bytes, and volts as we study how the various and essential kinds of information (numbers, characters, addresses, and instructions) are represented within a digital system. Building on the instructions, we will introduce and study the instruction set architecture level (ISA) and register transfer level (RTL) of the computer. Throughout the remaining chapters of this book, we will develop and study each of these parts of an embedded design in detail. That study will also include the hardware and software interaction, for without both we cannot build any kind of system today.

VLSI *FPGAs* *(C)PLDs, ASICs* *MSI* *SSI*

In today's high-tech and changing world, we can put together a working hierarchy of hardware components. At the top, we find *VLSI* (Very Large-Scale Integrated) circuits comprising significant pieces of functionality: microprocessors, microcontrollers, *FPGAs* (Field Programmable Gate Arrays), *(C)PLDs* ((Complex) Programmable Logic Devices), and *ASICs* (Application Specific Integrated Circuits). Perhaps we could include memories as well. At the next level down, we find *MSI* (Medium-Scale Integrated) circuits, which bring smaller, yet complete, pieces of functionality. Going down one more step, we have *SSI* (Small-Scale Integrated) circuits. At the very bottom, we have the electrical signals we use to represent our data and control information and the other signals that come into our system as noise or other unwanted signals. We will develop the hardware side of the design according to that hierarchy.

glue logic

Today, we collect components in the last two categories of integrated circuits (MSI and SSI) into what we call *glue logic*. As we continue to make significant advances in the design and development of more complex digital components, one must wonder about the remaining lifetime of the glue logic components. Tomorrow, the AND and OR gates, as standalone entities, may only be available at the Smithsonian or the British or Deutches museums.

We will start at the core microprocessor level and then look inside the hardware components through a review of the fundamentals of Boolean algebra, finite state machines, as well as arithmetic and logical circuits. In our study of the hardware side, we will study good design practices and some important considerations when developing hardware foundations that are robust, reliable, and maintainable. The complexity of today's systems precludes many of the approaches we used yesterday. Building a breadboard of a design comprising 500,000 gates is neither feasible nor reasonable. At the same time, building a computer model of such a system is entirely practical. Throughout our studies on the hardware side, we will utilize the Verilog modeling language to enable us to test, confirm, and demonstrate the viability of our designs prior to committing to hardware. The language will enable us to work at various levels of detail—at the top or behavioral level, we can confirm high-level functionality, and at the lower level or structural level, we can confirm details of timing, scheduling, and control. Facility at both levels is essential today.

If you already feel comfortable with hardware design and developing hardware systems, take a few minutes to scan through the next several chapters and perhaps review the material on good design practices. If hardware design is new to you, working through the material in this chapter should get you started on the road to digital proficiency. Good luck and have fun.

1.1 THE HARDWARE SIDE—GETTING STARTED

Our study of the hardware side of embedded systems begins with a high-level view of the computing core of the system. We will expand and refine that view to include a detailed discussion of the hardware (and its interaction with the software) both inside and outside of that core. Figure 1.0 illustrates the sequence we will follow.

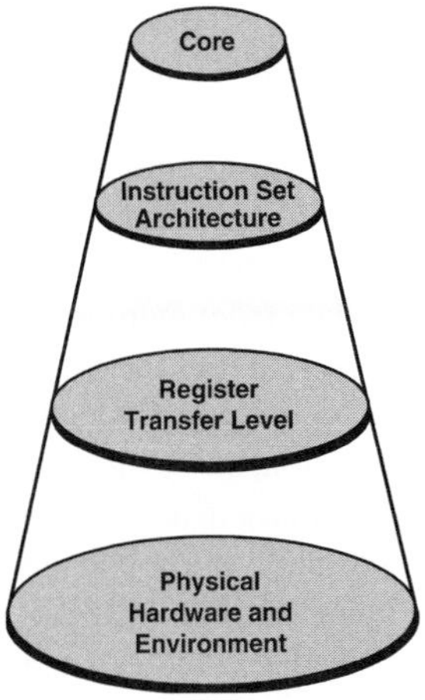

Figure 1.0 Exploring Embedded Systems

The computing core is the central hardware component in any modern embedded application. It often appears as a microprocessor, microcomputer, or microcontroller. Occasionally, it may appear as a custom-designed VLSI circuit or FPGA. It interacts with and utilizes the remaining components of the system to implement the required application. Such actions are under the control of a set of software and firmware instructions. Information and data come into the system from the surrounding environment and from the application. These data are processed according to the software instructions into signals that are sent back out of the system to the application. The software and firmware instructions, as well as signals coming into or going out of the system, are stored in memory.

1.2 THE CORE LEVEL

input, output, memory, datapath, control

At the top, we begin with a model comprising four major functional blocks (*input, output, memory,* and *datapath* and *control*) depicting the embedded hardware core and the high-level signal flow. These are illustrated in Figure 1.1. While there is nothing inherent in the model that demands a microprocessor, typically, one is used for the computation and control function.

memory
software, firmware
input

The *memory* block serves to hold collections of program instructions that we call *software* and *firmware* as well as to provide short-term storage for input data, output data, and intermediate results of computations. Data as well as other kinds of signals come into the system from the external world through the *input* block. Once inside of the system, they

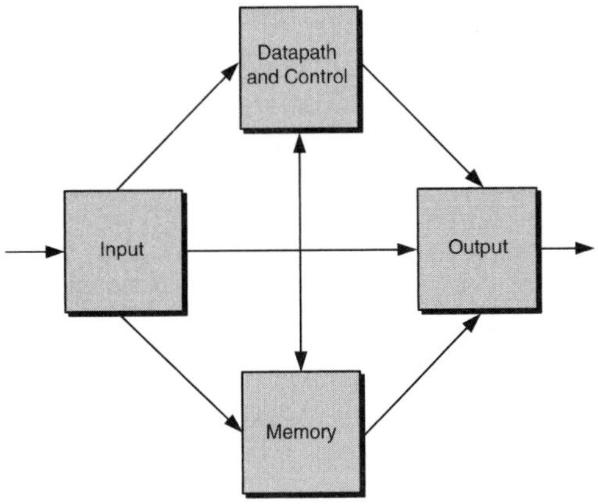

Figure 1.1 Four Major Blocks of an Embedded Hardware Core

output ***datapath and control*** ***CPU*** ***central processing unit***

may be directed to any number of destinations. The *output* block provides the means to send data or other signals back to the outside world. The *datapath and control* block, more commonly known as the *CPU* or *central processing unit*, coordinates the activities of the system as well as performs computations and data manipulation operations necessary to executing the application. In performing its responsibilities, the CPU fetches instructions from memory, interprets them, and then performs the task indicated by the instruction. In doing so, it may retrieve additional data from memory or from the input block. Often, it will also produce information that is sent out of the system.

busses ***address, data, control***

We move signals into, out of, or throughout the system on paths called *busses*. In their most common implementation, busses are simply collections of wires that are carrying related electrical signals from one place to another. We use the term *bus* so that we can speak of such a collection or group as a single entity. Signals flowing on the wires making up the busses are classified into three major categories: *address, data,* and *control*. The data are the key signals that are being moved around; the address signals identify where the data is coming from and where it is going to; and the control signals specify and coordinate how the data is transported.

Think of the arrangement as being similar to your telephone. The number you dial is the *address* of where your conversation will be directed, and the ring is one of the *control* signals indicating to the person you are calling that a call is coming in. Finally, your voice or text message is the *data* that you are moving from your location to the person on the other telephone. As with your telephone, the medium carrying the signal may take many forms: copper wire, fiber-optic cable, or electromagnetic waves.

bits

In the digital world, signals are expressed as collections of binary of 0's and 1's; the elements of such collections, the 0's and 1's, are called *bits*. A bit is simply a variable that takes on either of two values. At the hardware level, a bit may be represented by an electrical signal: a binary 0 as 0 volt and a binary 1 as 5 volts. In an optical communications channel, a bit may also be expressed by the presence or absence of light.

width

The *width* of a bus, that is, the number of signals or bits that it can carry simultaneously, provides an indirect measure of how quickly information can be moved. Transferring 64 bits of data on a bus that is 32 bits wide requires two transfers to move the data. In contrast, a bus that is only 8 bits wide will require eight transfers. Figure 1.2 illustrates moving such a set of data over an 8-bit bus from a source module to a destination module. In the model, each transfer requires one time unit; the process begins at time t0 and completes at time t7. Time increases to the left.

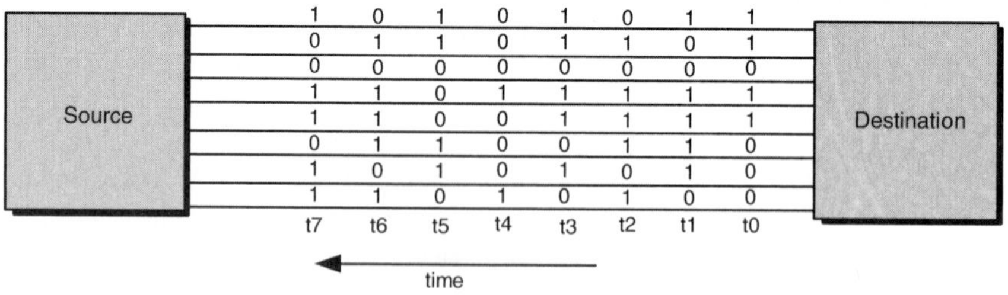

Figure 1.2 Data Movement over an Eight Bit Bus

The following C code fragment might produce such a pattern,

```
for (i = 0; i < 8; i++)
{
    printf("%i", a[i]);
}
```

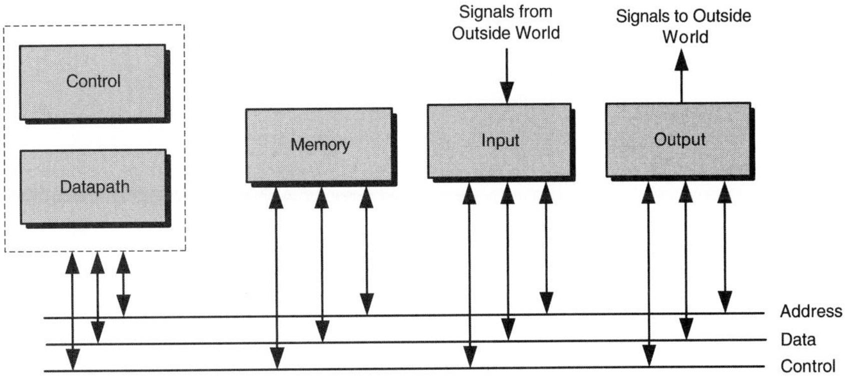

Figure 1.3 A Typical Bus Structure Comprising Address, Data, and Control Signals

The source of the transfer is the array of eight bit values; the destination is perhaps a display. In Figure 1.3, we refine the high-level functional diagram to illustrate a typical bus configuration comprising the address, data, and control lines.

None of the busses is required to have the same number of lines. To avoid cluttering a drawing by including all of the signals or conducting paths that make up a bus, we will often label the bus width using the annotation */ bus width* as illustrated in Figure 1.4. In this example, the *address bus* is shown to have 18 signals, the *data bus* 16, and the *control bus* 7.

bus width, address bus, data bus, control bus

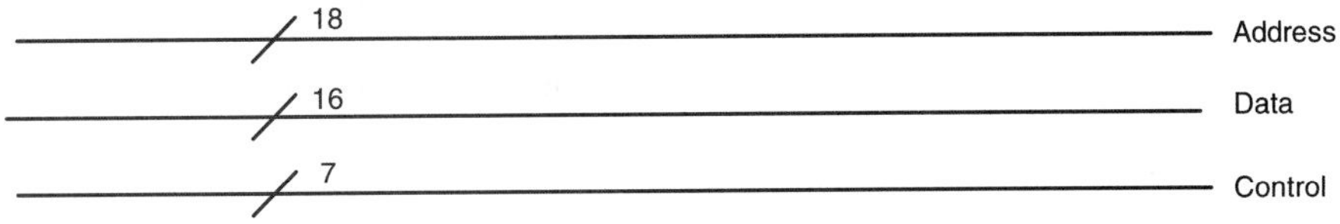

Figure 1.4 Identifying the Number of Signals in a Bus

In practice, such a block diagram will be implemented using a microprocessor, microcomputer, or microcontroller. Let's look at each of these, beginning with the microprocessor, with the goal of understanding the high-level structure of each and the differences among them.

1.2.1 The Microprocessor

A *microprocessor* is an integrated implementation of the central processing unit portion (control and arithmetic and logical unit) of the machine; it is often simply referred to as a CPU or datapath. Microprocessors differ in complexity, power consumption, and cost. Today, microprocessors range from devices with only a few thousand transistors at a cost of a dollar or less to units with 5 to 10 million transistors and a cost of several thousand dollars.

internal registers

registers

One may also find differences in the internal architecture of the machine, including the number of *internal registers*, the overall control structure of the machine, and the internal bus structure. *Registers* are small amounts of high-speed memory that are used to temporarily store frequently used values such as a loop index or the index into a buffer. Increasingly, the internal single-memory scheme that characterizes the von Neumann machine is giving way to the Harvard architecture and the benefits of simultaneous instruction and data access.

To implement a complete (embedded) computer system, we must still include the input/output subsystems and the external (to the microprocessor) memory system. We also include a clock or timing reference as the basis for timing, scheduling, or measuring elapsed

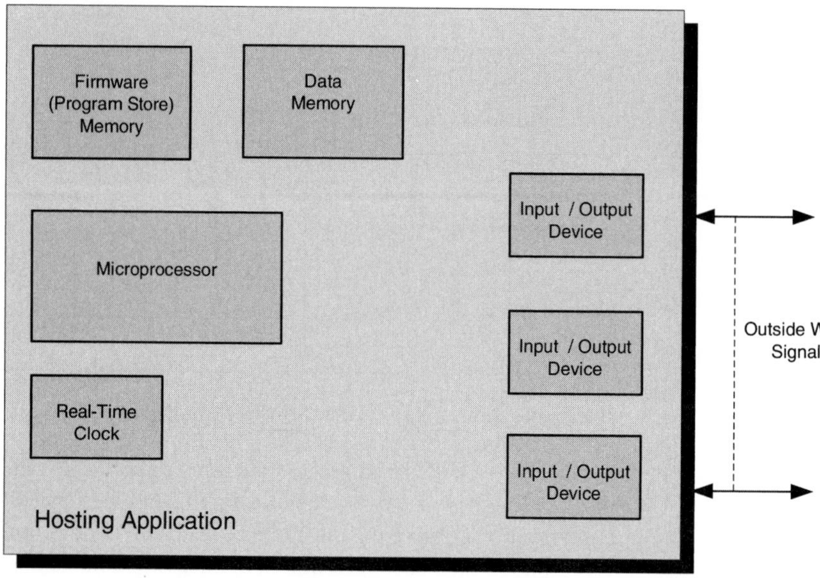

Figure 1.5 A Block Diagram for a Microprocessor Based System

time. All such components are connected via a system bus or busses. Figure 1.5 depicts a high-level block diagram of a microprocessor-based system.

firmware
data store
Read Only Memory
ROM
Random Access Memory (RAM)

External to the microprocessor, we see two different memory blocks. The *firmware*, or program store, contains the application code, and the *data store* contains data that is being manipulated, sent to, or brought in from the external world. In the embedded world, we refer to the application code as firmware because it is generally stored in a *Read Only Memory* (ROM), rather than on a hard drive as one might do for a desktop application. The data memory is usually made up of *Random Access Memory* (RAM).

> ***Caution:*** The two separate pieces of memory do not change the architecture from von Neumann to Harvard unless two separate busses are connecting them to the processor.

1.2.2 The Microcomputer

microcomputer

The *microcomputer* is a complete computer system that uses a microprocessor as its computational core. Typically, a microcomputer will also utilize numerous other large-scale integrated (LSI) circuits to provide necessary peripheral functionality. As we saw with the microprocessor, the complexity of microcomputers varies from simple units that are implemented on a single chip along with a small amount of on-chip memory and elementary I/O system to the complex that will augment the microprocessor with a wide array of powerful peripheral support circuitry. Costs, of course, are commensurate with capability.

1.2.3 The Microcontroller

microcontroller

The *microcontroller*, as illustrated in Figure 1.6, brings together the microprocessor core and a rich collection of peripherals and I/O capability into a single integrated circuit. Such additions typically include timers, analog-to-digital converters, digital-to-analog converters, digital I/O, serial or parallel communications channels, and direct memory access

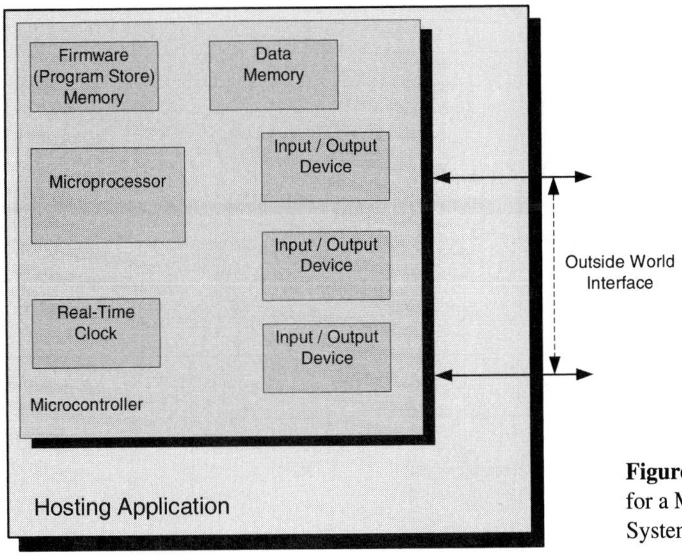

Figure 1.6 A Block Diagram for a Microcontroller-Based System

(DMA). A memory subsystem may or may not be included. If the memory is not included, the designer must add such capability outside of the microcontroller. Microcontrollers find great utility in basic embedded applications where low cost is a significant constraint.

We see that we have the same components as we found in the microprocessor-based system; however, now they are integrated into a single unit.

1.2.4 The Digital Signal Processor

digital signal processor (DSP)

In addition to the three different types of general-purpose computing engines that we have discussed, a special-purpose microprocessor called a *digital signal processor* (DSP) is becoming increasingly common in embedded applications. The DSP is typically used in conjunction with a general-purpose processor to perform specialized tasks such as image, speech, audio, or video processing. A representative block diagram for a DSP is given in Figure 1.7.

The tasks performed by the digital signal processor often require it to interface with the analog world. Real-world analog signals are captured through an analog-to-digital converter, processed, and returned through a digital-to-analog converter. One of the major strengths of the DSP is its ability to perform basic arithmetic computations such as multiply, add, and shift at the rate of millions of operations per second. To support high-speed arithmetic, the device will often implement a multiply-accumulate (MAC) primitive in which a multiply and add to the accumulator is performed in a single operation, which is useful in matrix operations. Its arithmetic operations often utilize saturation arithmetic in which overflows (underflows) remain at the maximum (minimum) value rather than wrapping around. In further support of high-speed signal processing, the DSP device is architected as a Harvard rather than the von Neumann machine and incorporates multiple computational units, a large number of registers, and wide high-bandwidth data busses.

Before proceeding to the next level of detail in our study of the hardware, let's move to the opposite end of the hierarchy and examine some of the signals that we are moving among the various components as well as into and out of the system.

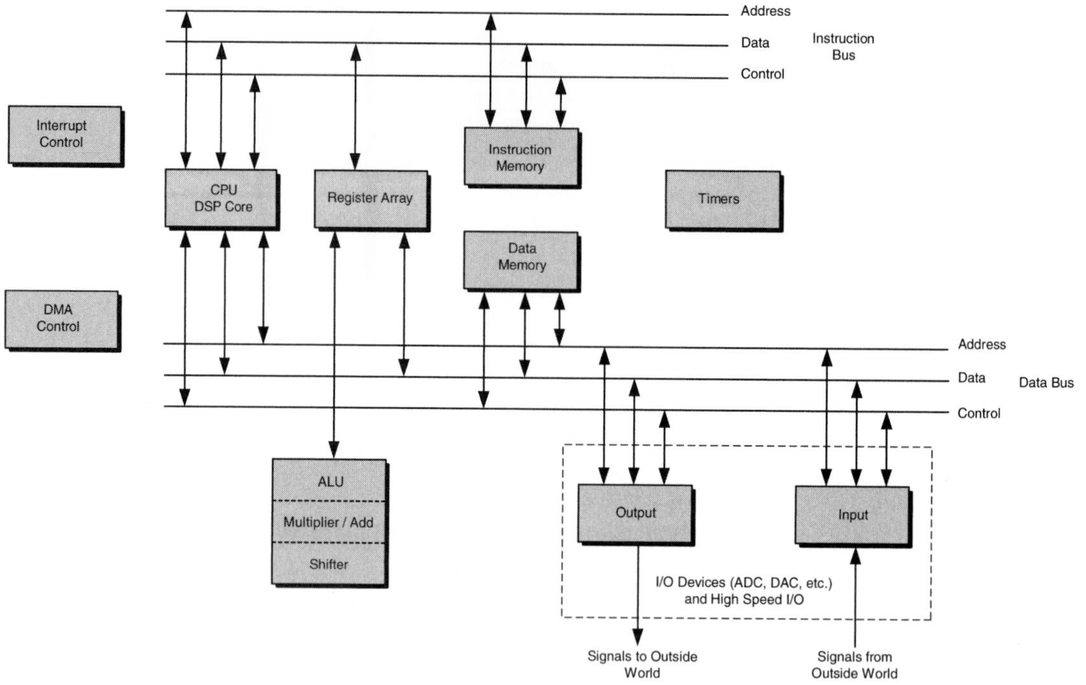

Figure 1.7 A Block Diagram for a Digital Signal Processor

1.3 REPRESENTING INFORMATION

In any embedded application, in addition to the expected numbers and symbols or characters, we must be able to represent both firmware instructions and the data that such instructions may be operating on. Because these instructions are stored in memory, we also need to be able to represent addresses in memory where the data and instructions are stored. In the next several sections, we will briefly examine how we can represent these different kinds of information and with such representations, what limitations we will encounter.

1.3.1 Word Size

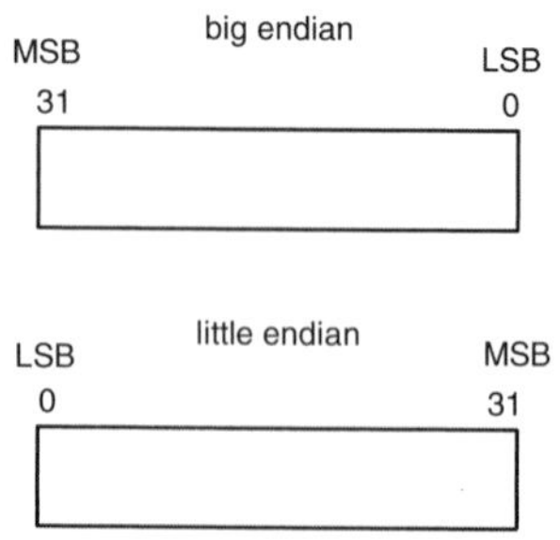

Figure 1.8 Big Endian vs. Little Endian Notation

One of the terms that we use to characterize a microprocessor is its word size. Generally, the word size in a microprocessor refers to the size of an integer. We will assume for the remainder of this study that we are working with a microprocessor that is using a word size of 32 bits. Such a processor is called a 32-bit machine. For such a system, we can interpret an unsigned integer, for example, according to either of the representations that we see in Figure 1.8.

We know that the data bus will be 32 bits wide and that each transfer on the bus will take one unit of time. If we examine the format of the word, several things are evident. The word consists of four bytes. The bits can be interpreted so as to place the most significant byte on the left and the least significant on the right, or vice versa.

Important Point

The interpretation of the order of the bits is just that, an interpretation. There is nothing inherent in the construction of a number that dictates which end has the most or least significant bits.

big endian
little endian

A word interpreted as in the top part of Figure 1.8 is said to be written in *big endian* format, and one written as in the lower figure is said to be written in *little endian* format. Different microprocessors, operating systems, and networks interpret such words in different ways. When executing a design, it is absolutely essential to determine which format each of these components in the system uses. In this text, we will assume a big endian interpretation unless specified otherwise.

1.4 UNDERSTANDING NUMBERS

We have seen that within a microprocessor, we do not have an unbounded number of bits with which to express the various kinds of numeric information that we will be working with in an embedded application. The limitations of finite word size can have unintended consequences for the results of any mathematical operations that we might need to perform. Let's examine the effects of finite word size on resolution, accuracy, errors, and the propagation of errors in these operations. In an embedded system, the integers and floating point numbers are normally represented as binary values and are stored either in memory or in registers—small pieces of memory. The expressive power of any number is dependent on the number of bits in the number. Although it is certainly true that, in the extreme, a number can be stored and transferred as a collection of words of size one, such an implementation is neither practical nor efficient. At the end of the day, we have memory limitations as well.

1.4.1 Resolution

To begin to understand the problem, let's consider a four-bit word. If the word is used to hold a number, the bits comprising the word can be interpreted in several ways as presented in Table 1.0.

Table 1.0 Interpreting a Four-Bit Number

Interpretation	Expressive Power
Integer	0–15
Real	
xxx.x	0–7.5
xx.xx	0–2.75
x.xxx	0–1.6875

If the bits are interpreted as expressing an unsigned integer, that integer may range from 0 to 15; the resolution is 2^0. Interpreting the number as a real with two bits devoted to the fractional component provides *two digits of resolution*. That is, we can express and resolve a binary number to 2^{-2}. The meaning of such a limitation is seen in the following example.

two digits of resolution

EXAMPLE 1.1

To represent the number 2.3 using a 4-bit binary number with 2 bits of resolution, the best that one can write is either (10.10) 2.5 or (10.01) 2.25. The error in the expression will be either +0.2 or –0.05. All that can be resolved is ± 0.25.

Because word size limits one's ability to express numbers, eventually, we are going to have to either round or truncate a number in order to be able to store it in internal memory. Thus, faced with truncation or rounding, one can ask which provides the greater accuracy, and which will give the best representation of a measured value? Which alternative is more or less accurate?

Let's consider a real number, N. Following either truncation or rounding of the original number to fit the microprocessor's word size, the number will have a fractional component of *n* bits. The value

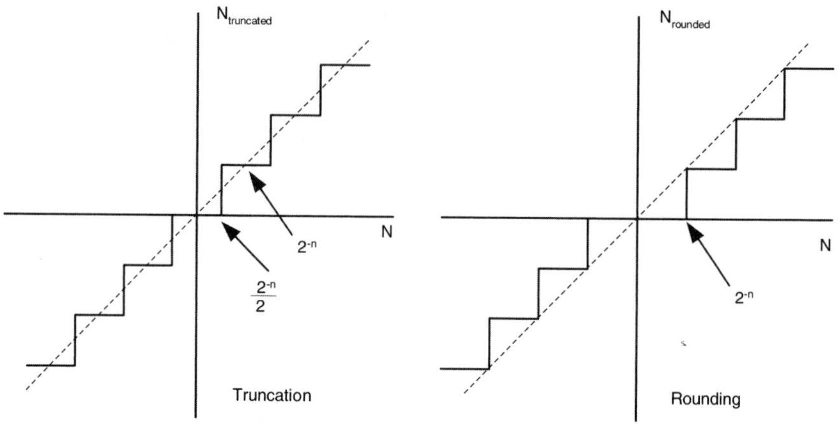

Figure 1.9 Truncation vs. Rounding

of the least significant bit is 2^{-n}. Whether we round or truncate, the resulting number will have an error. The graphs in Figure 1.9 plot the original number versus the truncated or rounded number.

The error following the operation is computed as

$$E_R = N_{rounded} - N \quad (1.1)$$

$$E_T = N_{truncate} - N \quad (1.2)$$

and given in Table 1.1.

Table 1.1 Truncation vs. Rounding Error

	N	$N_{rounded}$	$N_{truncated}$	Error
Truncation	0		0	0
	2^{-n}		0	-2^{-n}
Rounding	0	0		0
	$\frac{1}{2}\,2^{-n}-$	0		$\frac{1}{2}\,2^{-n}-$
	$\frac{1}{2}\,2^{-n}+$	2^{-n}		$\frac{1}{2}\,2^{-n}$

As the graph and table illustrate, the operations produce the following ranges of errors

Truncation

$$-2^{-n} < E_T \le 0$$

Rounding

$$-\tfrac{1}{2}2^{-n} < E_R \le \tfrac{1}{2}2^{-n}$$

Observe that the full range of the error is the same; however, for the case of rounding, the error is more evenly distributed and the maximum error is less.

1.4.2 Propagation of Error

Next, we analyze how the errors propagate under processing. We begin with two perfect numbers, N_1 and N_2. Under truncation, the error is less than 1 least significant bit.

1.4.2.1 Addition

We can express the numbers with an error as

$$N_{1E} = N_1 + E_1 \tag{1.3}$$

$$N_{2E} = N_2 + E_2 \tag{1.4}$$

$$\begin{aligned} N_{1E} + N_{2E} &= (N_1 + E_1) + (N_2 + E_2) \\ &= N_1 + N_2 + E_1 + E_2 \end{aligned} \tag{1.5}$$

The error in the resulting sum is in the range

$$2 \bullet 2^{-n} < E_T \leq 0 \Rightarrow 2^{1-n} < E_T \leq 0$$

Observe that the resulting error is the (algebraic) sum of the original errors.

1.4.2.2 Multiplication

We can express the numbers with an error as

$$N_{1E} = N_1 + E_1 \tag{1.6}$$

$$N_{2E} = N_2 + E_2 \tag{1.7}$$

$$\begin{aligned} N_{1E} \bullet N_{2E} &= (N_1 + E_1) \bullet (N_2 + E_2) \\ &= (N_1 . N_2) + (N_2 . E_1 + N_1 . E_2) + (E_1 . E_2) \end{aligned} \tag{1.8}$$

If we neglect $E_1 . E_2$, the resulting error is

$$(N_2 . E_1 + N_1 . E_2) < E_T \leq 0$$

Observe that the magnitude of the error now depends on the size of the numbers.

To further illustrate the propagation of error in basic calculations, consider the measurement system in Figure 1.10 that is designed to determine power in a resistive load. The power in the resistor is computed from measurements of the voltage drop across the resistor and the current flow through the part. Those measurements are given as

$$E = 100 \text{ VDC} \pm 1\%$$

$$I = 10 \text{ A} \pm 1\%$$

$$R = 10\ \Omega \pm 1\%$$

The power dissipated in the resistor, R, can be calculated in three ways. In theory, they should produce identical results.

In each of the three computations, lower order terms are neglected; however, doing so will have minimal effect on the final results.

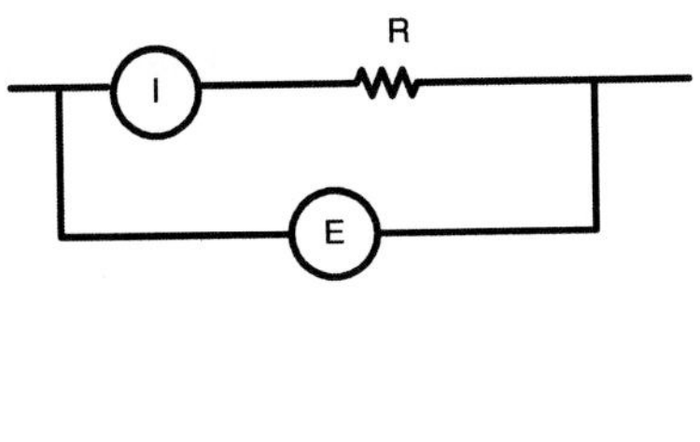

Figure 1.10 A Simple Measurement System

$$\begin{aligned} EI &= (100V \pm 1\%) \bullet (10A \pm 1\%) \\ &= ((1000 \pm 10 \bullet 1\%) \pm ((100 \bullet 1\%) \pm (1\% \bullet 1\%))) \\ &= (1000 \pm 1.1) \\ EI &\Rightarrow 998.9 \rightarrow 1001.1 \end{aligned} \tag{1.9}$$

$$\begin{aligned} I^2R &= (10A \pm 1\%) \bullet (10A \pm 1\%) \bullet (10\Omega \pm 1\%) \\ &= (100 \pm (20 \bullet 1\%) \pm (1\% \bullet 1\%)) \bullet (10 \pm 1\%) \\ &= (100 \pm 0.2) \bullet (10 \pm 1\%) \\ &= ((1000 \pm 2) \pm ((100 \bullet 1\%) \pm (0.2 \bullet 1\%))) \\ &= (1000 \pm 3) \\ I^2R &\Rightarrow 997 \rightarrow 1003 \end{aligned} \tag{1.10}$$

$$\begin{aligned} \frac{E^2}{R} &= \frac{(100V \pm 1\%) \bullet (100V \pm 1\%)}{(10\Omega \pm 1\%)} \\ &= \frac{(10000 \pm 2) \bullet (1\% \pm 1\%)}{(10 \pm 1\%)} \\ \frac{E^2}{R} &\Rightarrow 908.9 \rightarrow 1111.3 \end{aligned} \tag{1.11}$$

The results of the three calculations not only yield three different answers, but, depending on which formula is used, have substantially differing error magnitudes as well.

These simple examples illustrate rather graphically that when one is performing mathematical computations, it is important to understand where errors can arise, how they can propagate under mathematical operations, and how such phenomena can affect any calculations. Such errors can have serious consequences for the safety of any applications if we are not careful.

1.5 ADDRESSES

In the earlier functional diagram as well as in the block diagram for a microprocessor, we learned that information is stored in memory. Each location in memory has an associated address much like an index in an array. If an array has 16 locations to hold information, it will have 16 indices. If a memory has 16 locations to store information, it will have 16 addresses. Information is accessed in memory by giving its address. As we found with encoded characters, each address has a unique binary pattern. Addresses begin at binary 0 and range to the maximum value the word size will permit.

For a word size of 32 bits, the addresses will range (in hex) from 00000000 to FFFFFFFF. Thus, with 32 bits, we have up to 4,294,967,296 unique combinations and therefore that same number of possible addresses. Of course, we may not use them all, but they are there. Figure 1.11 illustrates how a word might look if the bits are interpreted as expressing an address. In fact, an address does not look any different from an unsigned integer, which, in reality, it is. It is important that it is not a signed integer. The microprocessor does not support negative addresses.

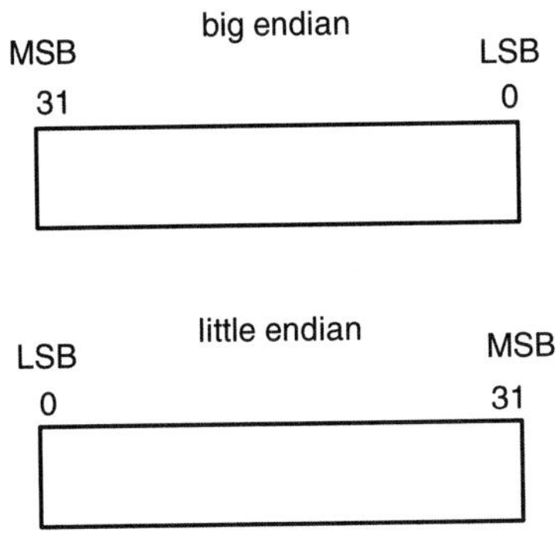

Figure 1.11 Expressing Addresses

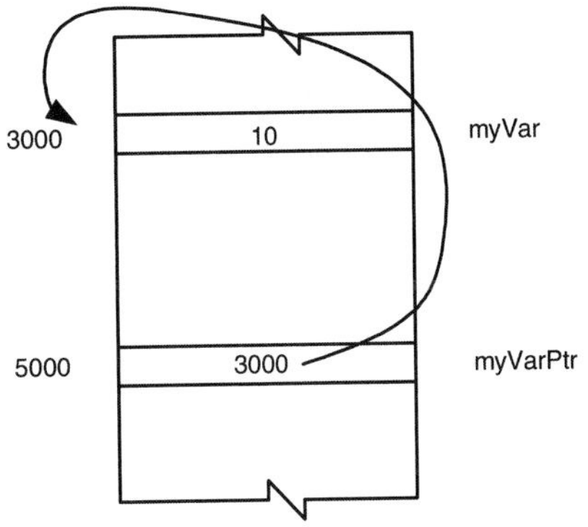

Figure 1.12 Using the Value of One Variable to Hold the Address of Another Variable

The following C or C++ declarations place the integer value 10 in binary into some location in memory. Let's say at address 3000.

```
int myVar = 10;
int* myVarPtr = &myVar;  // take the address of myVar
                         // assign it to the pointer variable myVarPtr
```

myVar
value

When interpreted by the system, the code fragment directs the system to set aside another memory word to hold the address of the signed integer, *myVar* (let's say at address 5000) and puts 3000 into that address. The *value* at address 5000 points to address 3000. The accompanying diagram in Figure 1.12 illustrates such an arrangement.

1.6 INSTRUCTIONS

The last view that we want to take on a word is as an instruction. Our examination at this stage of our study will be at a very high level. As we proceed with our studies, we will examine instructions in greater detail.

actions
operations

To start, we stipulate that the purpose of an instruction is to direct the hardware of the microprocessor to perform a series of *actions*. Such actions can include the following: perform an arithmetic or logical calculation, assign or read the value of a variable, or move data from one place to another such as from input to memory or from memory to output. In the parlance of instructions, such actions are called *operations*.

operands
arity

The entities that instructions operate on are denoted *operands*. The number of operands that an instruction operates on at any time is called the *arity* of the operation.

Let's look at the following code fragment:

```
x = y + z;
```

binary

Here we have two operations, the addition operation and the assignment operation. First, the addition operation: that operation is performed on two operands, y and z. The addition operator is said to be a *binary* operator—its arity is two. Now, the assignment operator: the operation is performed by giving x the value returned by the addition operation. It also is performed on two operands, the result of the addition and the operand x—its arity is two as well.

binary operators
unary operators

In C and C++, both operators are referred to as *binary operators*. Operators taking only a single operand have an arity of one and are referred to as *unary operators*. With one exception, all operators in C and C++ are either unary or binary.

operation
operands

We see, then, that an instruction must contain at least two components, the *operation* and the *operands*. Depending on the arity of the operation, the instruction may have one or two operands. Let's look at several common C or C++ instructions.

1. `x = y;`

   The instruction expresses the basic C/C++ assignment *operation* in which the value of the *operand* y (the source operand) is assigned to the *operand* x (the destination operand).

   two operands
   binary operator
   two-operand instruction,
   two-address instruction

   Analyzing the format of the instruction, we see that we have *two operands,* x and y, thus making the *operator* a *binary operator*. Such an instruction is thus referred to as a *two-operand or two-address instruction*.

2. `z = x + y;`

   The code fragment is adding the two operands, x and y; the result is assigned to the operand z. Analyzing, we see that we have two *operations*: an addition operation and an assignment operation. Both are binary.

   For the addition operation, the *operands* x and y are the sources, and the (temporary) result is the destination. Moving to the assignment operation, the result (destination) of the addition is the source of the assignment operation. The operand z is the destination of the assignment.

   three operands
   three-operand instruction,
   three-address instruction

   If we ignore the transient intermediate result, we see that for the code fragment, we have *three operands*, x and y are sources and z is a destination. Such an instruction is designated a *three-operand or three-address instruction*.

3. `x = x + y;`

   The code fragment is adding the two operands, x and y. The result is assigned to the operand x. Analyzing, once again, we see that we have two *operations*: an addition operation and an assignment operation. Both are binary.

   As before, for the addition operation, the *operands* x and y are the sources, and the (temporary) result is the destination. Moving to the assignment operation, the destination of the temporary result from the addition is the source of the assignment operation. The operand x, in addition to being one of the source operands, is also the destination of the assignment.

   We see that one operand serves the dual role of source and destination. In that role, the value that it held as the source is lost as a result of the assignment.

   two operands
   two-operand instruction,
   two-address instruction

   If we ignore the transient intermediate result as before, we see that for the code fragment, we have *two operands*, x and y are sources and x is also a destination. Such an instruction is designated a *two-operand or two-address instruction*.

4. `++x or x++;`

   operation
   one-operand
   one-operand instruction
   one-address instruction

   In the code fragment, the requested *operation* is to increment the value of the variable. In this case, the variable x is both the source and the destination of the operation; we have only *one operand*. Such an instruction is designated as a *one-operand or one-address instruction*.

one-, two-, three-operand instruction

The previous code fragments have illustrated three classes of instructions we might find in the system software or firmware. These classes are the *one-*, *two-*, or *three-operand instruction*. Let's now see how we can interpret the bits in a 32-bit word to reflect such instructions. Any such interpretation will have to support the ability to express both operands and operations as seen in Figure 1.13.

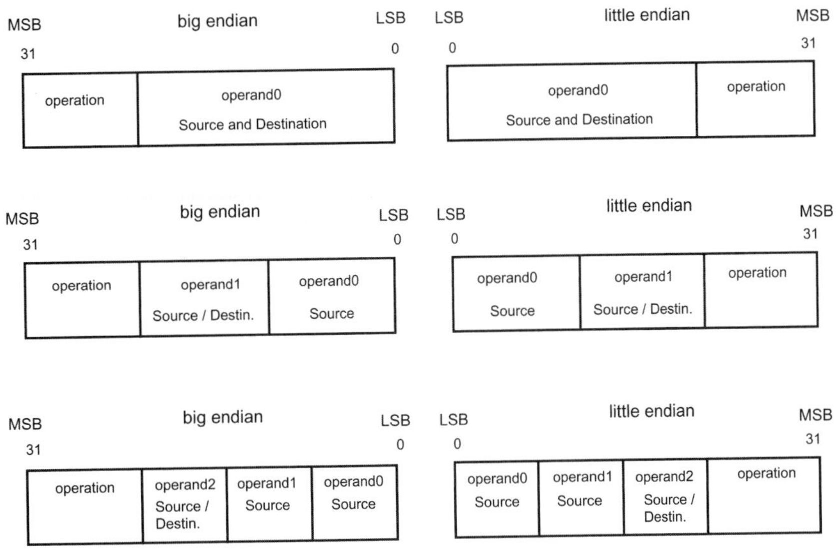

Figure 1.13 Expressing Instructions

groups
fields, operation
operands

In Figure 1.13, we see that within the 32-bit word, the bits are aggregated into *groups* or *fields*. Some of the fields are interpreted as the *operation* to be performed, and others are seen as the *operands* involved in the operation. At this juncture, we have not specified how many bits comprise each field. Such a determination is made during the early stages of the development of the architecture and design of the microprocessor.

The field used to identify the operation is the easiest one to specify the size of. The first step in specifying the size is to decide how many different instructions the microprocessor is to support. Such instructions can include arithmetic operations (e.g., add, subtract, multiply, or divide), logical operations (e.g., and, or, shift, or invert), data movement, or flow of control (e.g., jump, function call, or branch). Once the number of instructions is determined, then each is assigned a unique code, exactly as was done earlier when encoding characters. Such a code is called the *operation code* or *op-code*. If the microprocessor is to support 128 instructions, a minimum of 7 bits will be necessary. The designer may elect to allocate 8 bits to permit room to incorporate additional instructions at a later time or in support of an enhanced version of the microprocessor.

operation code, op-code

1.7 REGISTERS—A FIRST LOOK

The size of the fields allocated to the operands is not much more complex. Before answering the question, however, we must make a slight digression. For those readers who have begun to anticipate a small problem, you are correct. We have been discussing how we can interpret a 32-bit word as various types of data (operands) that can be operated on by user-selected operations. If an instruction, containing even a single operand, in addition to the op-code, is 32 bits, a 32-bit piece of data will not fit into any of the field(s) allocated to hold the operand.

register

To solve this seemingly intractable problem, we utilize a hardware component that is called a *register*. A register is a special kind of memory that is large enough to hold a single data word. A register is a piece of short-term memory that temporarily holds the operands during the execution of an instruction.

Prior to executing the instruction, the operand(s) are moved from memory into registers and then back to memory if the data value is not going to be needed in the immediate future. While such continual movement of data words into and out of memory and into and out of registers seems to involve a lot of extra work, the higher speed of registers compared with the memory we have discussed so far can significantly improve system performance.

Complex Instruction Set Computers (CISC)

Reduced Instruction Set Computers (RISC)

Depending on the architecture of the microprocessor, it may have a few registers—16 to 256 or so—or it may have over 1000. Those microprocessors in the former category are referred to as *Complex Instruction Set Computers* (CISC), and those in the latter are called *Reduced Instruction Set Computers* (RISC). While the number of registers is not the only (or most significant) difference between the two architectures, their effect on system performance can be significant.

We can now examine the role that registers play in the format of an instruction. The contents of the operand field within an instruction is not the operand; rather, it is a binary number indicating which of the microprocessor's registers contains the operand.

Let's assume a hypothetical microprocessor with 144 instructions. To permit each instruction to be uniquely identified, we will have to specify that the op-code contains 8 bits since $2^7 < 144 < 2^8$. Let's further assume that the microprocessor is designed to include 256 registers. To permit each register to be uniquely identified will also require 8 bits.

Our earlier diagram for the various instruction formats can now be modified to reflect the new interpretation of the operand fields as illustrated in Figure 1.14.

The operand fields in the two-and one-operand instructions are large enough to provide more than 256 combinations as register designators; most of the combinations will remain unused.

Figure 1.15 summarizes the big endian interpretations of a word in a microprocessor system. The little endian interpretations follow naturally.

Note

It is important to understand that an aggregate of bits has no inherent meaning.
Meaning comes from our interpretation of those bits, and this is what is defined as type information.

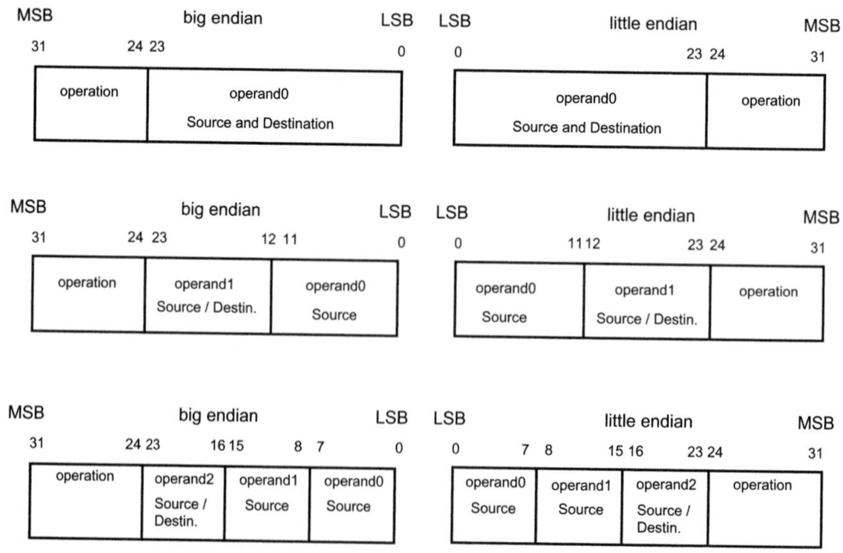

Figure 1.14 Expressing Instructions

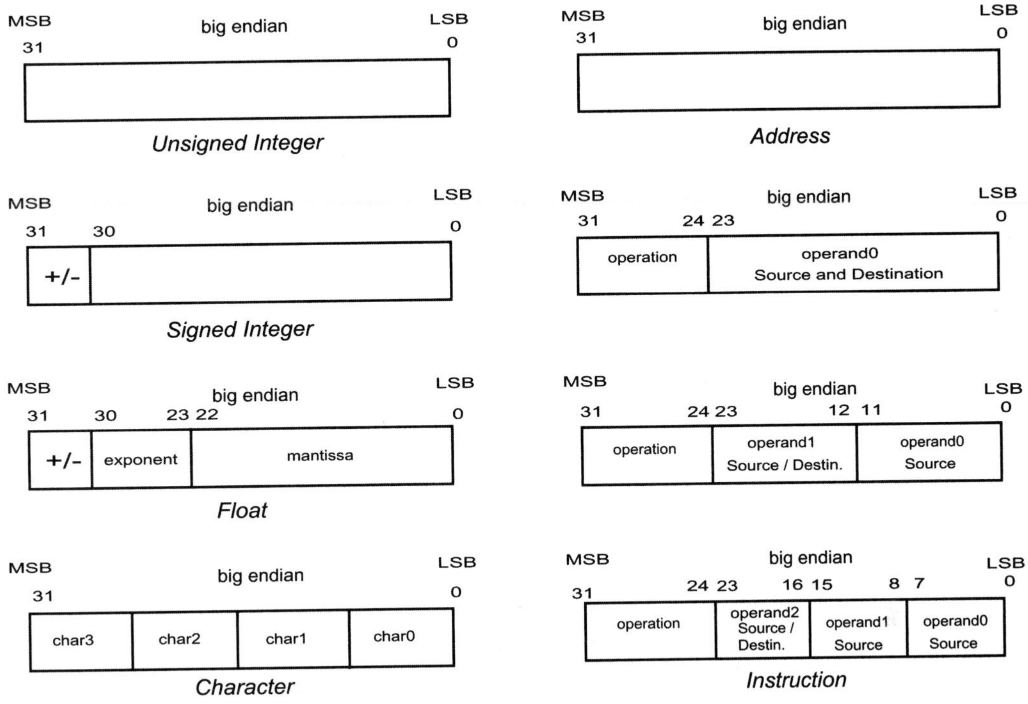

Figure 1.15 Possible Interpretations of a Set of Bits as Big Endian representation. Little Endian follows similarly.

1.8 EMBEDDED SYSTEMS—AN INSTRUCTION SET VIEW

assembly language

The software (firmware) in an embedded system is generally written in a high-level language such as C or C++. In other cases, it may be written in what is called the *assembly language* for the machine on which the application is to run. Sometimes combinations of the two are used, as is the case when portions of programs must be optimized for speed or size.

machine language
instruction set
instruction set architecture

When working with assembly language, we are working one step removed from the microprocessor's *machine language*—the collection of 0's and 1's that control the hardware components in the execution of an instruction. At the assembly language level, we are working with the set of instructions that the machine supports—its *instruction set*. Such a set drives the architecture, the design of the underlying hardware of the processor. That architecture, the *instruction set architecture (ISA)*, thus provides to the programmer the public interface for the underlying hardware.

machine code
assembler
IEEE Standard for Microprocessor Assembly Language

At the assembly language level, mnemonic names are given to binary patterns expressed by the op-codes to make them easier to work with. A program written in the machine's assembly language is translated into *machine code* by a software tool called the *assembler*. Thus, the machine code reflects binary encoding of the machine's instructions or op-codes. Such a set of op-codes for an ISA can be viewed as the machine language for that particular architecture. For the discussion that follows, the assembly language instructions are taken from the *IEEE Standard for Microprocessor Assembly Language*—IEEE Std. 694-1985.

The complete list of assembly language instructions and how to work with them is given in the support manuals for the specific processor. These will be provided by the developer of each processor.

1.8.1 Instruction Set—Instruction Types

transfer
store, operate, make decisions

A microprocessor's instruction set specifies the basic operations supported by the machine. From the earlier functional model, we see that the objectives of such operations are to *transfer* or *store* data, to *operate* on data, and to *make decisions* based on the data values or outcome of the operations. Corresponding to such operations, we can classify instructions into the following groups:

- Data Transfer
- Flow of Control
- Arithmetic and Logic

Data transfer instructions provide the means and mechanism for moving data within the system and for executing exchanges with external devices, including memory. The flow of control instructions determine the order in which instructions comprising the embedded application are executed. Such instructions often respond to the side effects resulting from the arithmetic or logical operations. The arithmetic and logical instructions provide the majority of the computational capabilities and useful functionality of a microprocessor.

1.8.2 Data Transfer Instructions

data, location of the data,
source, destination

Data transfer instructions are responsible for moving data around inside the processor as well as for bringing data in from the outside world or sending data out. Each such instruction must have three pieces of information: the *data*, the *location of the data*—the *source* of the transfer, and where the data is to be sent—the *destination* of the transfer.

The source and destination can be any of the following:

- A Register
- Memory
- An Input or Output Port

as is illustrated in Figure 1.16.

Some of the more common instructions used in support of such data transfers include those presented in Figure 1.17. A processor design will not implement both the *MOVE* and the *LD/ST* pair. For completeness, both are illustrated in the figure.

addressing mode

Data transfer is supported by instructions using any of the three different address formats we discussed earlier. The op-code portion of each instruction identifies the operation to be performed on the operands. The path to the actual selection of the operands is controlled by the *addressing mode* specified for the operand.

1.8.2.1 Addressing Modes

Typically, a microprocessor design will implement four to eight different addressing modes. A portion of each operand field is designated as a specification to the hardware as to how to interpret or use the information in the remaining bits of the associated address field. That

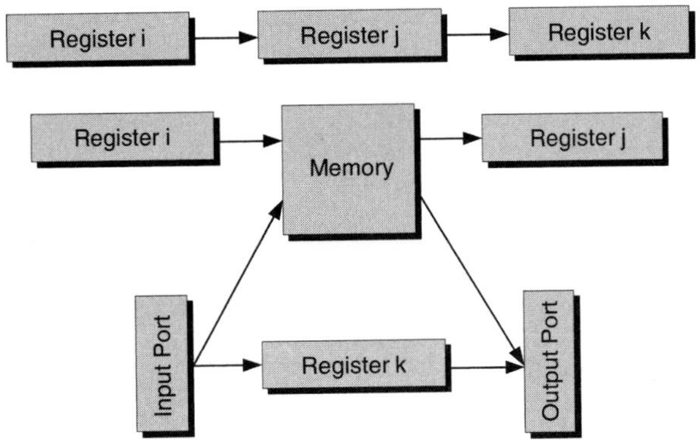

Figure 1.16 Transferring Data

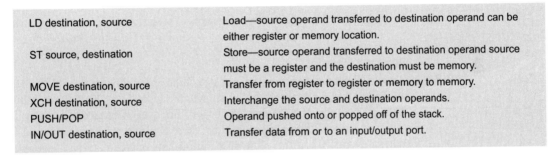

LD destination, source	Load—source operand transferred to destination operand can be either register or memory location.
ST source, destination	Store—source operand transferred to destination operand source must be a register and the destination must be memory.
MOVE destination, source	Transfer from register to register or memory to memory.
XCH destination, source	Interchange the source and destination operands.
PUSH/POP	Operand pushed onto or popped off of the stack.
IN/OUT destination, source	Transfer data from or to an input/output port.

Figure 1.17 Data Transfer Instructions

addressing mode ***effective address*** specification is called the *address mode* for the operand. The address that is ultimately used to select the operand is called the *effective address*.

Addressing modes are included in an instruction in order to offer the designer greater flexibility in accessing data and controlling the flow of the program as it executes. However, some of the address variations can impact flow through a program as well as the execution time for individual instructions. We will discuss this issue in greater detail when we examine methods for optimizing the performance of an application. Each is identified by a unique binary bit pattern that is interpreted. The drawings in Figure 1.18 refine our earlier expression of each instruction format to reflect the inclusion of the address mode information.

Some of the more commonly used addressing modes include

- Immediate
- Direct and Indirect
- Register Direct and Register Indirect
- Indexed
- Program Counter Relative

address mode field, ***operand address*** We will examine each of these modes in the upcoming paragraphs. To support the five modes plus the direct/indirect selection, the *address mode field* associated with each *operand address* will have to be 4 bits wide. Let's now examine each of these addressing modes and identify their strengths and weaknesses.

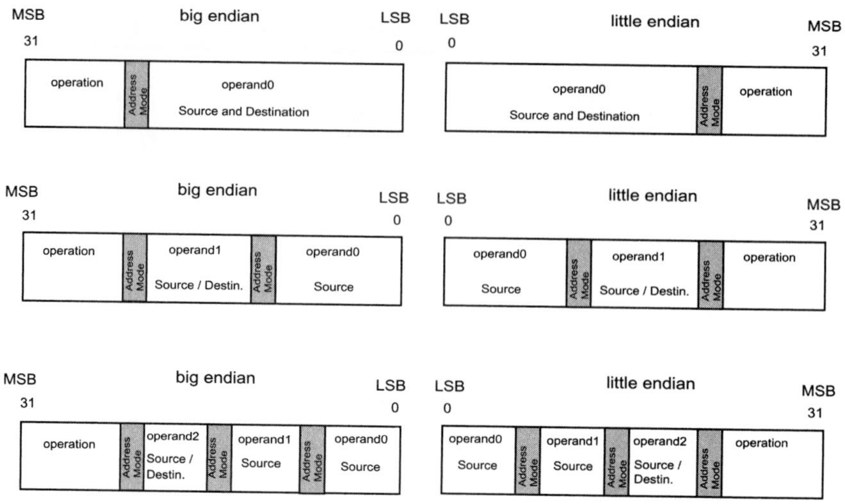

Figure 1.18 Instruction Types Enhanced to Include Address Mode Information

IMMEDIATE MODE

immediate

An *immediate* mode instruction uses one of the operand fields to hold the value of the operand rather than a reference to it, as shown in Figure 1.19. The major advantage of such an instruction is that the number of memory accesses is reduced. Fetching the instruction retrieves the operand at the same time; there is no need for an additional access. Such a scheme works well if the value of the immediate operand is small, as might be found for loop indices or initializing values.

arithmetic and logic unit (ALU)

The immediate instruction might appear as a one- or two-operand instruction as illustrated in Figure 1.19. The one-operand version contains only the immediate value. Without an explicit destination, the target must be implied. Typically, that is the accumulator in the *arithmetic and logic unit (ALU)*. The two-operand version illustrates the operation at both the C or C++ level and the assembly language level. In the former case, the variable y is declared and initialized to the hex value 0xB. Such an expression is compiled into an assembly language statement of the kind shown.

The immediate value in the assembly language expression is intended to be a hex number and is so designated by the H suffix on the number. The first form of the instruction has the accumulator in the arithmetic and logic unit, *ALU* as an implied destination; there is no

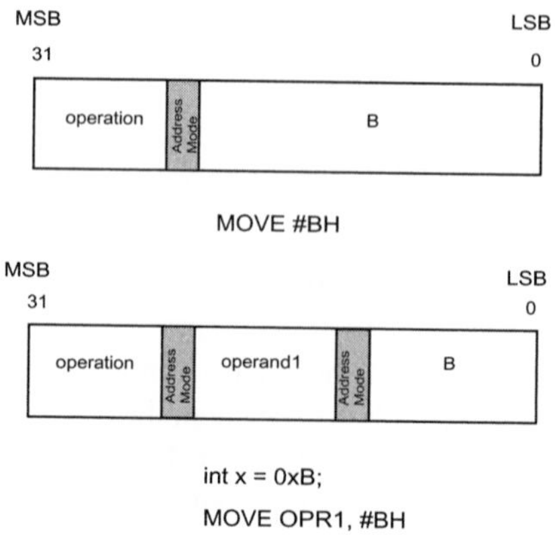

Figure 1.19 Immediate Mode Instruction Formats

C or C++ level equivalent. After all, the developer is not supposed to be aware of the accumulator at such a level. The second form sets the value of operand1 to the hex value B.

On some processors, the instruction mnemonic designates that the operation is to use an immediate operand. In such cases, the instruction may be written as illustrated in Figure 1.20.

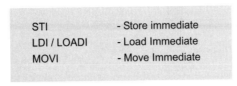

STI	- Store immediate
LDI / LOADI	- Load Immediate
MOVI	- Move Immediate

Figure 1.20 Variations on the Immediate Mode Instruction

DIRECT AND INDIRECT MODES

direct, indirect

When using the *direct* and *indirect* addressing modes, we are working with operand addresses rather than operand values. In both cases, the first level of address information is contained in the instruction. The difference between the two modes is that, in the direct mode, the contents of the operand field in the instruction are the address of the desired operand, whereas in the indirect case, the field contains the address of the address of the operand. In the latter case, the operand is fetched through one level of indirection.

Because of the limited size of an operand field, the range of memory locations that can be addressed is less than what is possible with the register direct and indirect modes discussed next. With either mode, the major disadvantage is the additional memory accesses necessary to retrieve an operand.

direct, yPtr
xPtr

In the following figure, Figure 1.21, two different data transfer operations are shown. For the *direct* operation, at the C/C++ level, the value pointed to by one variable, *yPtr,* is assigned to a second variable pointed to by *xPtr*. At the assembly language level, the *MOVE* instruction directs that the contents referenced by operand1 be copied to the location referenced by operand0.

indirect
yPtrPtr
xPtrPtr

For the *indirect* operation, at the C/C++ level, the value of one variable, stored in memory and pointed to by the pointer variable *yPtrPtr,* is assigned to a second variable pointed to by a second pointer variable, *xPtrPtr*. At the assembly language level, the *MOVE* instruction now directs that the contents of one memory location serve as the address in memory of the operand that is to be assigned to the location in memory identified by the second operand.

The double ** symbols preceding the operands in the indirect access mode indicate that two levels of indirection are necessary to reach the final operand in memory.

The flow and two representative instructions at the assembly and the C and C++ levels are illustrated in Figure 1.21.

REGISTER DIRECT AND REGISTER INDIRECT MODES

register direct, register indirect

The distinction between the *register direct* and *register indirect* modes lies in the content of the referenced register. In the former case, the register contains the value of the operand and in the latter case, the address (in memory) of the operand. The register indirect mode provides the means to easily implement pointer-type operations that are commonly used in C and C++.

The major disadvantage of indirect addressing is that an additional memory access is necessary to retrieve the operand's value. In contrast, when utilizing direct addressing, the value of the operand is found in the register.

register direct

In Figure 1.22, two different data transfer operations are shown. For the *register direct* operation, at the C/C++ level, the value of one variable, *y*, is assigned to a second variable, *x*. At the assembly language level, we assume that the values for *x* and *y* have previously been stored in registers R2 and R3, respectively. The *MOVE* instruction directs that the contents of R3 be copied to R2.

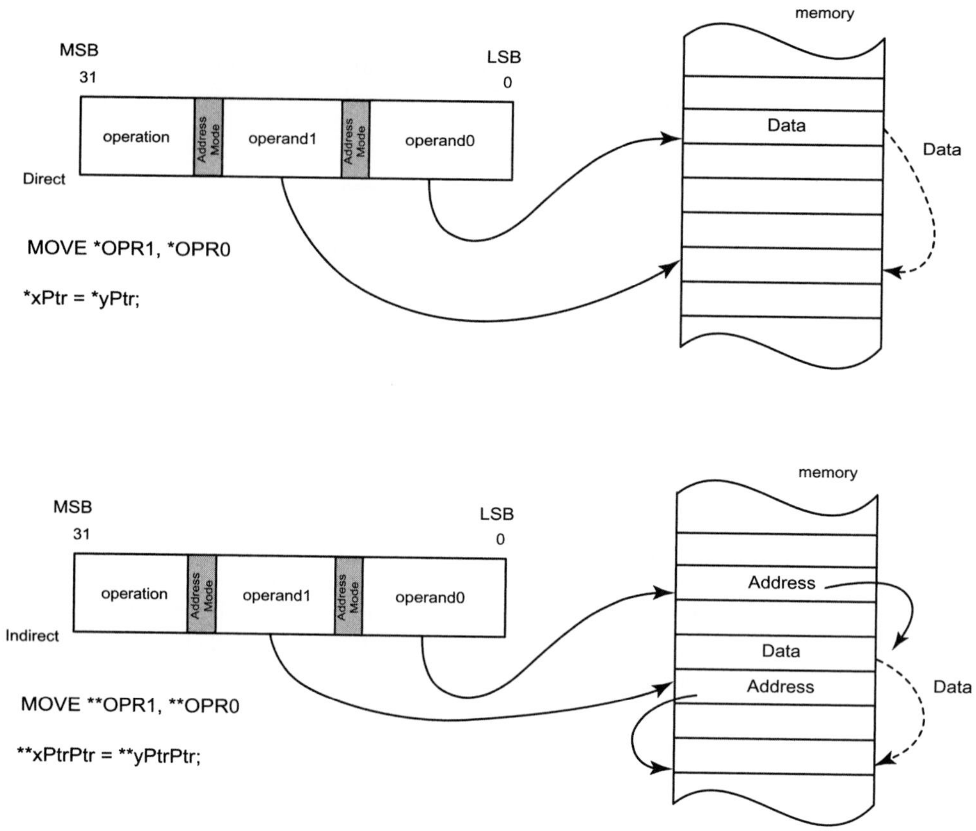

Figure 1.21 Register Direct and Register Indirect Instruction Formats

register indirect
yPtr, x

For the *register indirect* operation, at the C/C++ level, the value of one variable, stored in memory and pointed to by the pointer variable *yPtr,* is assigned to a second variable, *x*. At the assembly language level, once again we assume that the values for *x* and *yPtr* have been previously stored in registers R2 and R3, respectively. The *MOVE* instruction now directs that the contents of R3 serve as an address into memory; the value of the variable at that address is to be retrieved and to be copied into R2.

If the values and address modes of the two operands are interchanged, the data transfer would be from R2 into the location in memory pointed to by the contents of R3.

The flow and two representative instructions at the assembly and the C and C++ levels are illustrated in Figure 1.22.

The * preceding the second operand in the indirect instruction indicates that the assembler is to set the indirect addressing mode for the instruction.

INDEXED MODE

indexed, displacement

The *indexed* or *displacement* addressing mode provides support for accessing container-type data structures such as arrays. The effective address is computed as the sum of a base address and the contents of the indexing register. It is important to note here that following the execution of the instruction, neither the base address nor the index values are changed.

The major disadvantage of indexed addressing is the time burden associated with computing the address of the operand and then retrieving the value from memory. Indexing adds a greater burden to system performance than does indirect addressing.

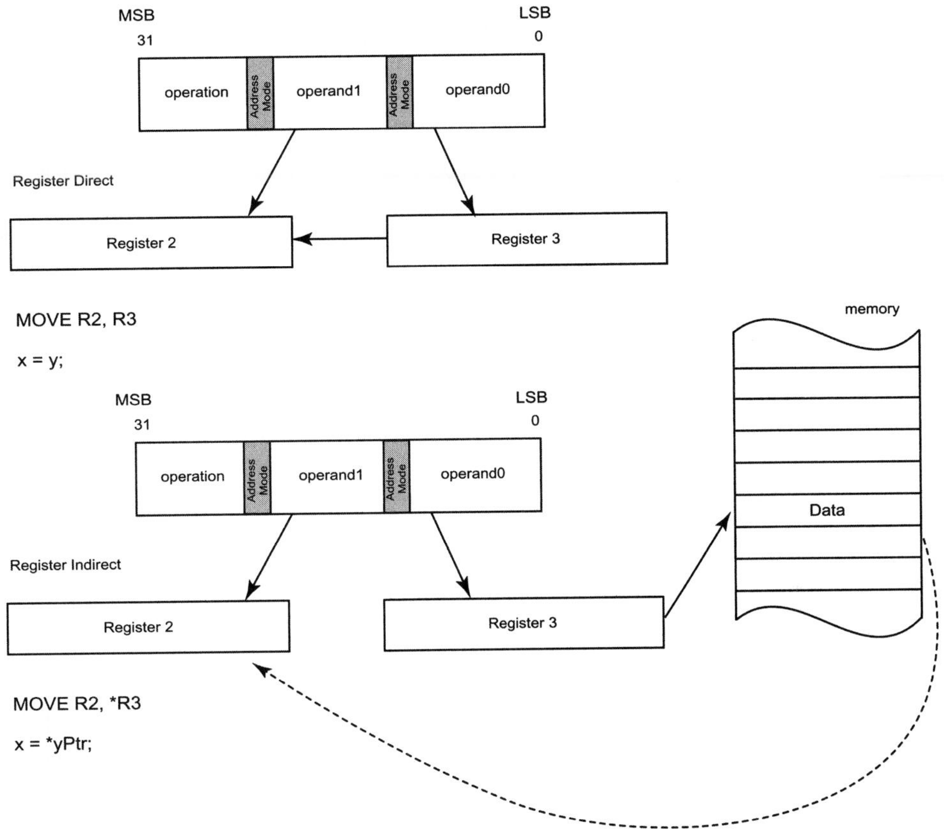

Figure 1.22 Register Direct and Register Indirect Data Transfer Operations

Figure 1.23 illustrates the retrieval of an indexed variable using code fragments written at the assembly and the C or C++ levels.

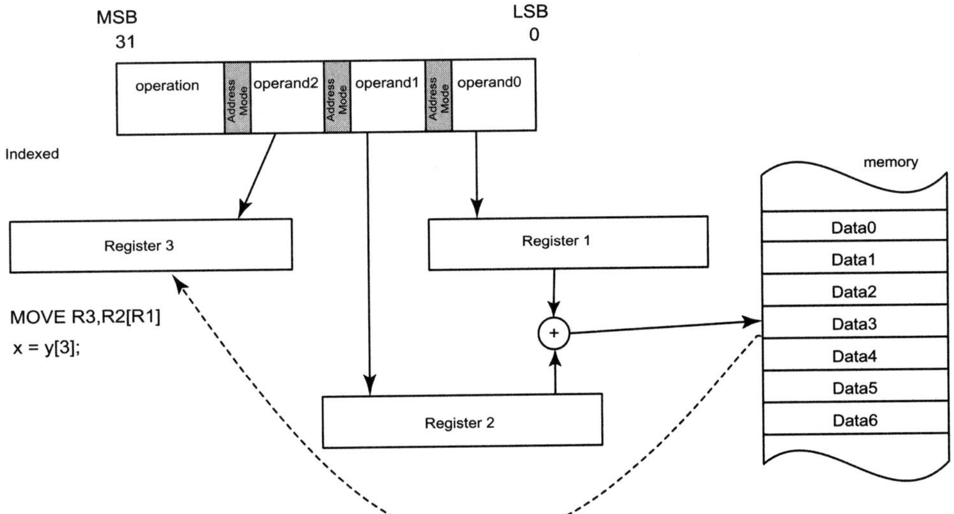

Figure 1.23 Indexed Mode Data Transfer Operations

Starting at the C/C++ level, we have an array variable named *y* and an integer variable *x*. The variable *x* is to be assigned the value contained in the fourth element of the array.

At the assembler level, the C/C++ fragment gets translated into a three-operand instruction. The base register, R2, will hold the starting address of the container in this case, the address of the 0th element of the array named *y*. The value of the variable *y* contains the address of the variable *Data0*, the start of the array. Register R1 will serve as the index register—that is, provide the offset. At the assembly level, we assume that the register R1 has already been initialized to the value 3, the offset into the container.

When the instruction is executed, the contents of R1 are added to the contents of R2, giving an address in memory. The value of the data stored in memory at the computed address is retrieved and written into register R3.

PROGRAM COUNTER RELATIVE MODE

program counter relative

Recall that the program counter contains the address in memory of the next instruction to be executed. That said, *program counter relative* addressing is mechanically almost identical to the indexed addressing mode. Nonetheless, there are several important differences. First, the value in the program counter serves as the base address, and second, the program counter is assigned the value of the computed effective address; that is, the contents of the program counter are modified as a result of executing the instruction. Finally, the offset that is added to the program counter is a signed number. Thus, the PC contents following the addition of the offset may refer to an address that is higher (the offset was positive) or lower (the offset was negative) than the original value.

Figure 1.24 illustrates the flow of the instruction. For this instruction, operand0 is serving as the index register and is holding a value that has already been stored in it. The effective address is computed by adding the contents of the register identified by operand0 (R1

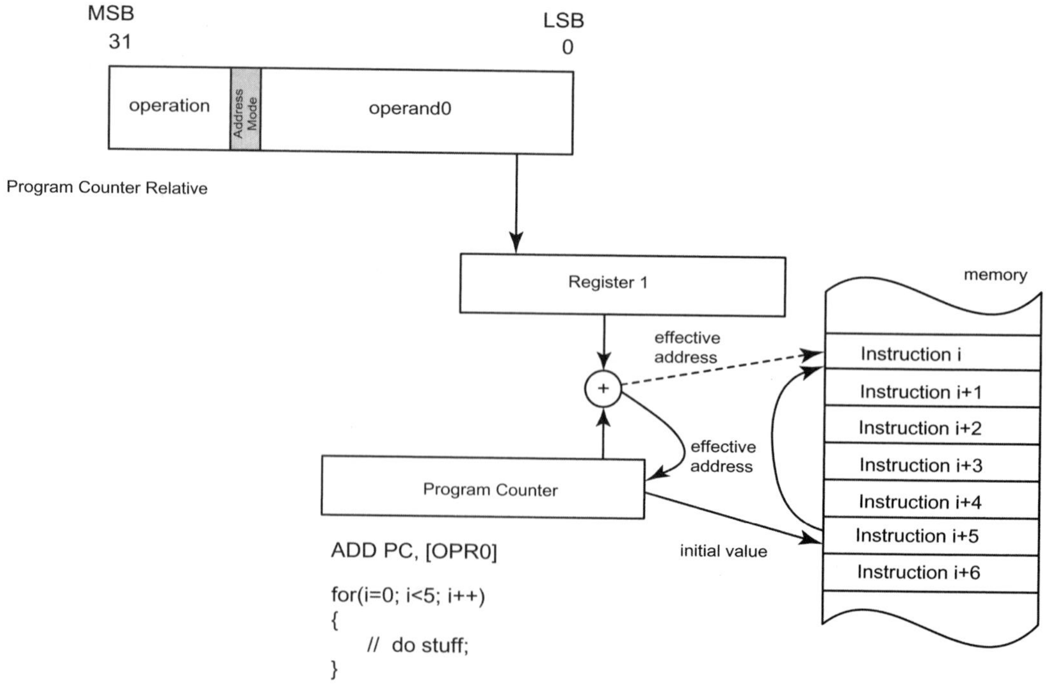

Figure 1.24 Program Counter Relative Operations

in this case) to the contents of the program counter. The program counter contents are then updated to the new value and now refer to the instruction at the computed address.

for

The C/C++ code fragment illustrates a simple *for* loop. Following the execution of the body of the loop, the flow must move back to the top of the loop and test the loop variable once again. A negative offset would have to be added to the contents of the PC to effect that movement.

The disadvantages of the PC relative mode are similar to those found in the indexed mode. There can be potential degradation of system performance.

1.8.3 Execution Flow

The execution flow or control flow captures the order of evaluation of each instruction comprising the firmware in an embedded application. We identify these as

- Sequential
- Branch
- Loop
- Procedure or Function Call

and will now examine each in turn.

1.8.3.1 Sequential Flow

Sequential control flow describes the fundamental movement through a program. Each instruction contained in the program is executed in sequence, one after another. A significant amount of the total code in an application is evaluated and executed in sequential order, although the individual sequences may be rather short. We capture that notion in the accompanying diagram in Figure 1.25, in the following C/C++ code fragment in Figure 1.26, and in assembler code in Figure 1.27.

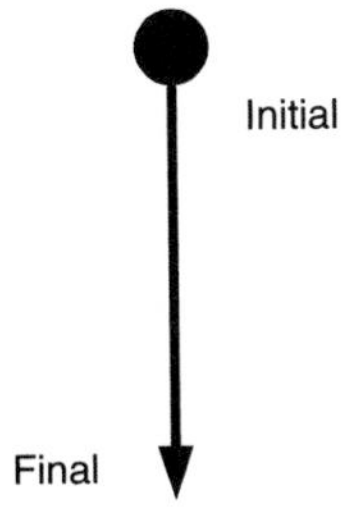

Figure 1.25 Sequential Flow

```
a = 10;
b = 20;
c = a + b;
```

Figure 1.26 C / C++ Sequential Flow

```
MOVE R1, #AH;     // puts 10 – hex A – into R1
MOVE R2, #14H;    // puts 20 – hex 14 – into R2
ADD R3, R1, R2;   // computes R1 + R2 and puts result into R3
```

Figure 1.27 Assembler Sequential Flow

The execution first assigns values to several variables and, then performs an arithmetic operation on the two variables.

1.8.3.2 Branch

Figure 1.28
The Branch Construct

A branching construct terminates a sequential flow of control with a decision point. At such a point, one of several alternate paths for continued execution is taken based on the outcome of a test on some condition. Graphically, such a construct is seen in Figure 1.28. The branch construct is used to implement an *if else, switch,* or *case* statement.

if else, switch, case

The branch may be executed unconditionally, in which case the contents of the PC are replaced by the effective address specified by the operand. Alternately, the branch may be taken conditionally based on the side effects of operations performed on data or on several different kinds of comparisons between two variables such as equality, a greater than or less than relationship, a carry from an arithmetic operation, or a variable being equal to or not equal to zero.

flag register
condition code register

The conditional information is temporarily held as a collection of bits in a *flag register* or *condition code register*. The state of each bit in the register is evaluated and potentially changed following the execution of every instruction. Figure 1.29 lists some of the possible conditions that may be supported in a microprocessor.

E, NE	Operand1 is *equal/not equal to* Operand2.
Z, NZ	The result of the operation is *zero/not zero.*
GT, GE	Operand1 is *greater than/greater than or equal* to Operand2.
LT, LE	Operand1 is *less than/less than or equal* to Operand2.
V	The operation resulted in an *overflow*—the result is larger than can be held in the destination.
C, NC	The operation produced a *carry/no carry.*
N	The result of the operation is *negative.*

Figure 1.29 Typical Condition Codes

Branching alternatives that may be supported in a particular microprocessor are given in Figure 1.30.

BR label	unconditional branch to the specified label
BE label, BNE label	branch to the specified label if the equal flag is set or not set
BZ label, BNZ label	branch to the specified label if the zero flag is set or not set
BGT label	branch to the specified label if the greater than flag is set
BV label	branch to the specified label if the overflow flag is set
BC label, BNC label	branch to the specified label if the carry flag is set or not set
BN label	branch to the specified label if the negative flag is set

Figure 1.30 Typical Branching Instructions

The if-else construct is illustrated with the following C/C++ code fragment in Figure 1.31 and with assembler code fragments in Figure 1.32.

```
if (a == b)
    c = d + e;
else
    c = d - e;
```

Figure 1.31 C / C++ if-else Construct

```
CMP R2, R1              // compare the contents of R1 and R2, will set the equal flag
BE $1                   // if the equal flag is set jump to $1
                        // $1 is a label created by compiler
SUB R3, R4, R5          // compute d – e and put results in c
BR $2                   // $2 is label created by compiler
$1: ADD R3, R4, R5      // compute d + e and put results in c
$2: ...
```

Figure 1.32 Assembler if-else Construct

1.8.3.3 If-else Construct

In the C code fragment in Figure 1.31, the two variables are compared. If they are equal, one arithmetic operation is performed; otherwise a second one is executed.

The code fragment in Figure 1.32 illustrates the construct in assembler. We assume that the variables a–e have been placed into registers R1–R5.

The compiler will create labels $1 and $2 if the original source was written in a high-level language or by the designer if the original source was assembler code.

1.8.3.4 Loop

entry condition
exit condition
do, repeat, while, for

The loop construct permits the designer to repeatedly execute a set of instructions either forever or until some condition is met. As Figure 1.33 illustrates, the decision to evaluate the body of the loop can be made before the loop is entered (*entry condition* loop) or after the body of the loop is evaluated (*exit condition* loop). In the former case, the code may not be executed, whereas in the latter, the code is executed at least once. The loop type of construct is seen in the *do, repeat, while,* or *for* statements.

The following C/C++ and assembler code fragments in Figure 1.34 and Figure 1.35, respectively, illustrate a *while* loop construct.

The body of the loop is continually evaluated as long as the loop variable is less than a specified value. This code fragment implements an entry condition loop.

myVar, index

Assume that the variables *myVar* and *index* have been placed in R2 and R3, respectively.

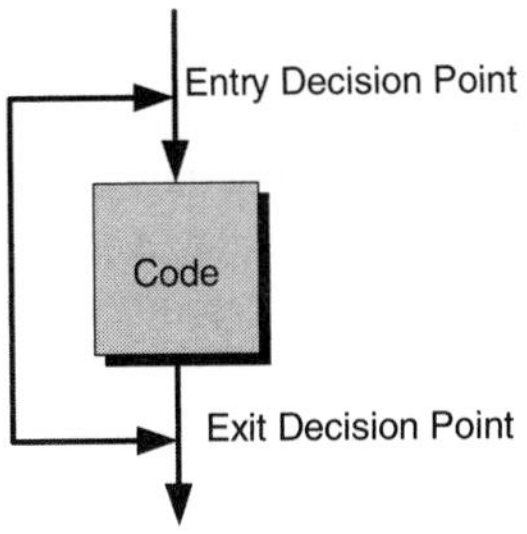

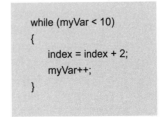

Figure 1.33 The Looping Construct

```
while (myVar < 10)
{
    index = index + 2;
    myVar++;
}
```

Figure 1.34 C / C++ Looping Construct

```
$1: CMP R2, #AH     // test if R2 < 10
BGE $2              // if R2 greater than or equal to 10 branch to $2
ADD R3, #2H         // compute index + 2 put result in index
ADD R2, #1H         // add 1 to myVar
BR $1               // continue looping
$2: ....
```

Figure 1.35 Assembler Looping Construct

1.8.3.5 Procedure or Function Call

The procedure or function invocation is the most complex of the flow of control constructs. It is not more difficult; it is simply more involved.Such an invocation requires that the control flow leave the current context, execute a set of instructions, and then return to the original context as we see in Figure 1.36. Such a construct is seen for a procedure or subroutine call, an interrupt handler, or co-routine.

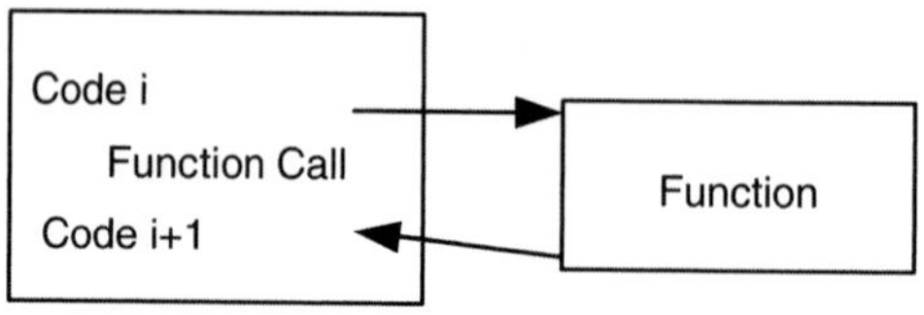

Figure 1.36 The Procedure Call

The operation is supported by the instructions given in Figure 1.37.

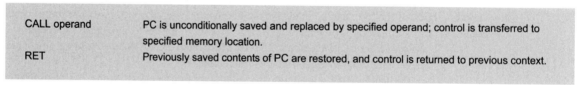

CALL operand	PC is unconditionally saved and replaced by specified operand; control is transferred to specified memory location.
RET	Previously saved contents of PC are restored, and control is returned to previous context.

Figure 1.37 Common Procedure Call Instructions

stack Before we examine the CALL process, we need to introduce a data structure called a *stack*.

STACK

The stack is a data structure that occupies an area in memory. It has finite size and supports several operations. Its structure is similar to an array except that, unlike an array, data can be entered or removed at only one location called the *top*. The top of the stack is equivalent to the 0th index in an array. When a new piece of data is entered, everything below is pushed down like a stack of trays in a cafeteria or like the last card in a discard pile in a card game. When a piece of data is removed, all data below moves up, again, like a stack of plates or the new top card.

top

Figure 1.38 illustrates a model for the operations for several pieces of data. Data entry is called a *push* and data removal is called a *pop*. In reality, such a model is impractical because of the time burden in moving every piece of data each time a new entry is made. A more practical implementation adds or removes data at the open end of the structure.

push, pop

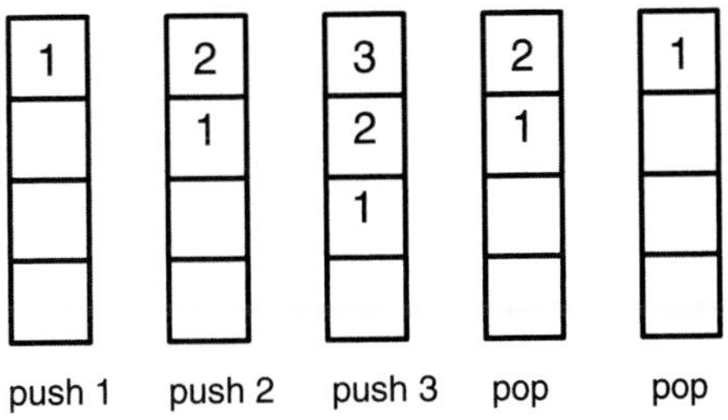

Figure 1.38 Stack Operations

The memory address reflecting the current top of the stack is remembered and modified after each addition or removal. Such an address is called a *stack pointer*.

stack pointer

Figure 1.39 presents a modified version of the previous diagram and illustrates how the stack pointer is properly managed.

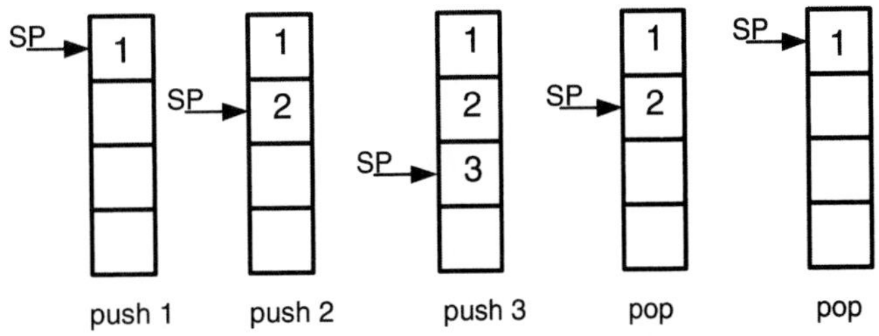

Figure 1.39 Managing the Stack Pointer

PUSH

The push operation puts something onto the top of the stack where it is held for later use. Mechanically, the push operation increments the address that is held by the stack pointer to refer to the next empty spot (the new top of the stack) and then writes the data to be stored into the address in memory designated by that address. As we see in Figure 1.39, for ease of implementation, the address contained in the stack pointer is typically incremented from a lower memory address to higher memory address.

POP

The pop operation takes something off the top of the stack by first retrieving the value in the memory location designated by the stack pointer and then decrementing the address that is held by the stack pointer to refer to the next lower address (the new top of the stack). The retrieved value is returned as the result of the pop operation.

PROCESS

Let's now return to the function call. From a high-level point of view, code execution proceeds in a sequential manner until the function call is encountered. Flow of control switches to the function, the code comprising the function body is executed, and flow returns to the original context as seen in Figure 1.40.

Let's now examine the process in somewhat greater detail. In the following code fragment, the program is initially loaded into memory and begins executing from address 3000. Code is executed until the flow reaches address 3053, at which point the function call is encountered. At this point, the sequence of operations shown in Figure 1.41 will occur.

```
3000 Code
3053 CALL F1(3)
3054 pop R2
3055 More Code
....
5000 code            // Function Body....
5053 Return
```

Figure 1.40 Function Call Construct

1. The return address and parameters are pushed onto the stack.
   The address saved is 3054.
   The parameter saved is 3.
2. Address of function body 5000 is put into PC.
3. Instruction at 5000 begins executing.
4. Execution continues until 5053.
5. Return encountered
   Stack gets
      Return values
   Stack loses
      Return address
6. Return address is put into PC.
7. Flow returns to address 3054, and the top of stack is popped and put into register R2.
8. Execution continues at 3055.

Figure 1.41 Function Call Flow of Control

Had an additional function call been encountered in function F1, an identical process would have occurred. The process can be repeated multiple times; however, we must be aware that stack can overflow. If too much is pushed onto the stack, we begin to lose information, particularly the return address.

1.8.3.6 Arithmetic and Logic

Arithmetic and logical operations are essential elements in affecting what the processor is to do. Such operations are executed by any of several hardware components comprising the ALU (arithmetic and logic unit). Figure 1.42 presents a block diagram for a possible functional ALU architecture.

Data is brought into the ALU and held in local registers. The op-code is decoded, the appropriate operation is performed on the selected operand(s), and the result is placed in another local register.

ARITHMETIC

add, subtract, multiply, divide

Typically, the processor will support the four basic arithmetic functions: *add, subtract, multiply,* and *divide*. Simpler processors will only implement the first two, relegating the last two to a software implementation by the designer. The add and subtraction operations may be supported in two versions, with and without carry and borrow.

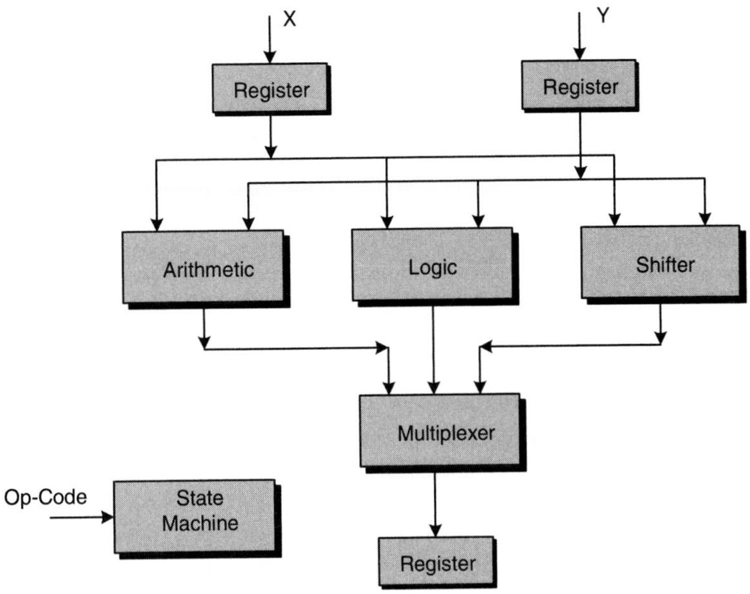

Figure 1.42 An ALU Block Diagram

The last two versions are intended to support double-precision operations. Such an operation is performed in two steps: the first computation holds any carry (borrow) and then utilizes that value as a carry in (borrow in) to the second step. Most such operations are implemented to support integer-only computations. If floating point mathematics is supported, a separate floating point hardware unit may be included. In addition to the four basic functions, the processor may also implement hardware increment and decrement operations.

At the instruction set level, a typical complement of arithmetic support will comprise the function listed in Figure 1.43.

LOGICAL OPERATIONS

Logical operations perform traditional binary operations on collections of bits or words. Such operations are particularly useful in embedded applications where bit manipulation is common. Such operations are discussed in detail in our studies of the software side of

ADD2, ADD3	// Two or three operands addition
ADDC	addition with carry
SUB2, SUB3	// Two or three operands subtraction
SUBB	subtraction with borrow
MUL	multiplication
DIV	division
INC	increment
DEC	decrement
TEST	operand tested and specified condition set
TESTSET	atomic test and set

Figure 1.43 Typical Arithmetic Instructions

embedded systems. Typical operations included in the set of logical instructions are illustrated in Figure 1.44.

AND	bitwise AND
OR	bitwise OR
XOR	bitwise Exclusive OR
NOT or INV	complement
CLR or SET	clear or set
CLRC, SETC	carry manipulation

Figure 1.44 Typical Logical Instructions

SHIFT OPERATIONS

logical, arithmetic, rotate

Shift operations typically perform several different kinds of shifts on collections of bits or words. The major differences concern how the boundary values on either side of the shift are managed. Typically, three kinds of shift are supported: *logical, arithmetic,* and *rotate*. Any of the shifts may be implemented as a shift to the left or to the right.

A *logical* shift enters a 0 into the position emptied by the shift; the bit on the end is discarded. An *arithmetic* shift to the right propagates (and preserves) the sign bit into the vacated position; a shift to the left enters 0's on the right-hand side and overwrites the sign bit. The *rotate* shift circulates the end bit into the vacated bit position on the right- or left-hand side based on a shift to the left or to the right.

Typical operations in the set of shift instructions include those listed in Figure 1.45.

SHR operand, count	logical shift right
SHL operand, count	logical shift left
SHRA operand, count	arithmetic shift right
SHLA operand, count	arithmetic shift left
ROR operand, count	rotate right
ROL operand, count	rotate left

Figure 1.45 Typical Shift Instructions

1.9 EMBEDDED SYSTEMS—A REGISTER VIEW

transfer
store, operate,
make decisions

At the ISA level, the instruction set specifies the basic operations supported by the machine—that is, the external view of the processor from the software developer's perspective. During the early stages of design, it plays a significant role in the formulation of the architecture of the machine. The instruction set expresses the machine's ability to *transfer* data, *store* data, *operate* on data, and *make decisions,* all of which are necessary for the machine to be able to perform its ultimate task of aiding in solving problems.

control unit
datapath
microoperation

Underlying the instruction set is the physical hardware necessary to implement the operations directed by the instructions. The core hardware comprises a *control unit* and a *datapath* as illustrated in Figure 1.46.

The datapath is a collection of registers and an associated set of *microoperations* on the data held in the registers. The control unit directs the ordered execution of the microoperations so as to effect the desired transformations of the data. Thus, the system's behavior (execution of the ISA level instructions) can be expressed by the movement of data among those registers, by operations and transformations performed on the register's con-

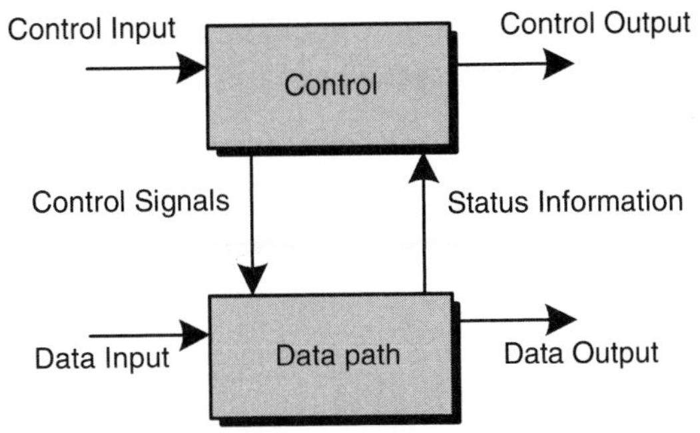

Figure 1.46 A Control and Datapath Block Diagram

tents, and by the management of how such movements and operations take place. The operations on data found at the instruction level are paralleled by a similar, yet more detailed, set of operations at the register level or *register transfer level* (RTL). When we study modeling of the hardware components of an embedded application, we will find that working initially at the RTL level is natural and convenient. Such an approach easily segues into the *hardware design language* (HDL) implementation.

register transfer level

hardware design language (HDL)

1.9.1 The Basic Register

A register is a storage device that is capable of holding the collection of one or more bits. Based on the level of detail we need, we take several views of a register as we see in the accompanying drawings in Figure 1.47 and Figure 1.48.

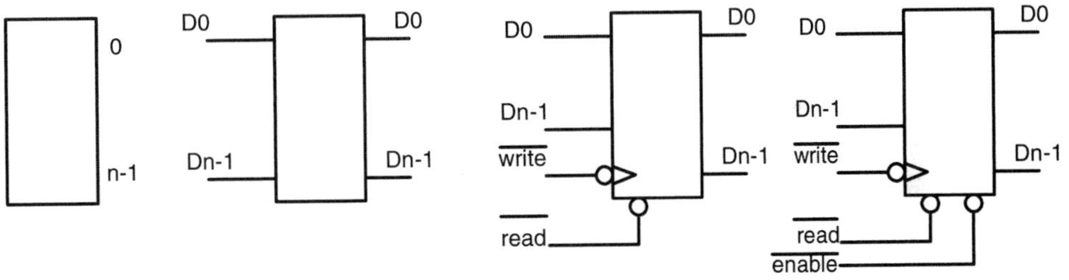

Figure 1.47 The Register at Several Levels of Abstraction—Parallel Data Entry

The abstract view on the left in Figure 1.47 shows a simple box with the bits numbered to reflect the size and outputs of the register. More refined/detailed views show inputs and outputs; those views may be further elaborated to include some control signals. Data is entered into the registers in parallel, as shown in Figure 1.47, or in serial as illustrated in Figure 1.48.

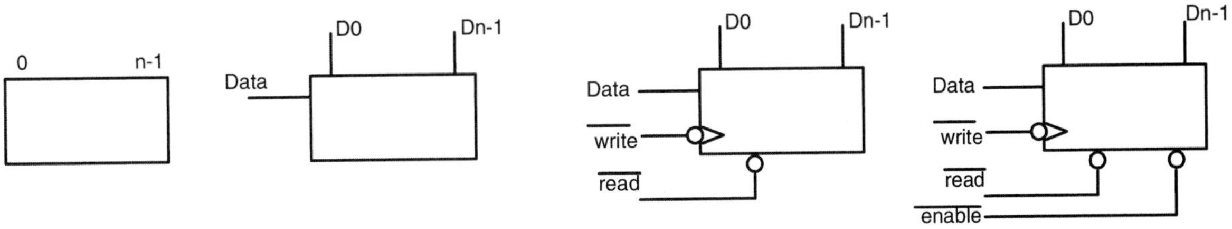

Figure 1.48 The Register at Several Levels of Abstraction—Serial Data Entry

1.9.2 Register Operations

Registers support two basic operations:

Read
Write

incrementing/decrementing
counting, shifting

These operations are illustrated in the timing diagrams shown in Figure 1.49; all other operations are built on these. Such higher level operations include *incrementing/decrementing, counting,* or *shifting.*

Write to a Register

parallel write
write
serial write, write

A *parallel write* operation begins when the data is placed onto the inputs of the register. Following a delay to allow the data to settle on the bus, the *write* signal is asserted. For a *serial write* operation, a *write* signal must accompany each data bit that is entered. In the drawings shown in Figure 1.49, the *write* signal is asserted low—which is typical.

Following each write operation, the contents of the register are changed to reflect the new values of the input data.

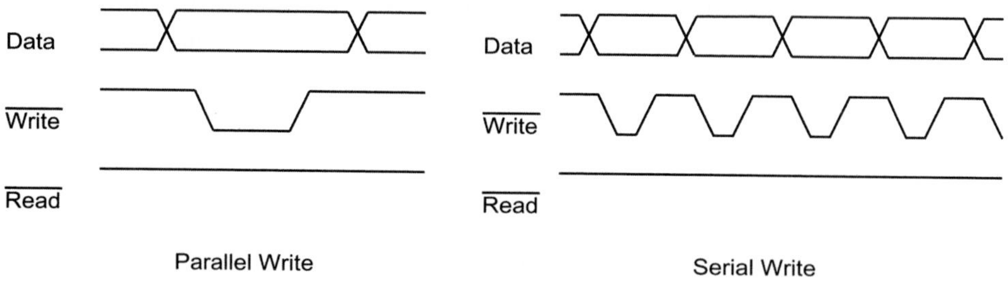

Figure 1.49 Writing to a Register

Read from a Register

read

The *read* operation is executed as shown in Figure 1.50 and Figure 1.51. The *read* signal is issued; following some delay, the data appears on the register output. In this illustration, the read signal is shown as asserted low.

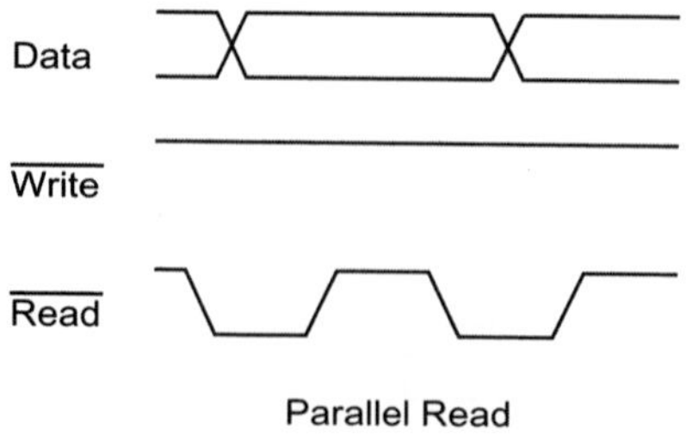

Figure 1.50 Parallel Read

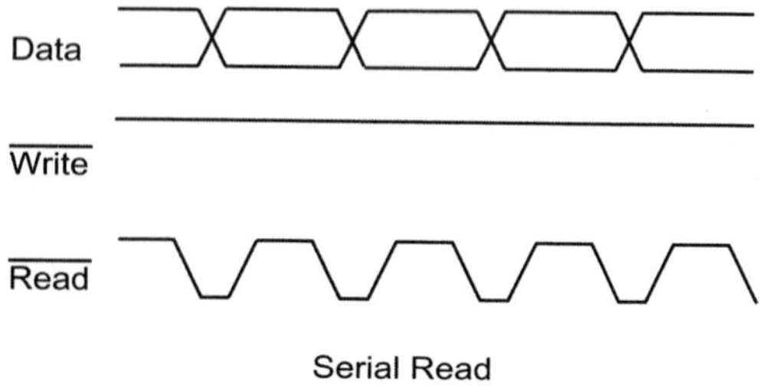

Figure 1.51 Serial Read

The output data will be a copy of the contents of the register; the state of the register is unchanged by the read operation.

read
enable

In some designs, when the *read* signal is not asserted, the data output from the register is disabled; in others, output is disabled by an *enable* control signal.

1.10 REGISTER TRANSFER LANGUAGE

register transfer language
register transfer notation (RTN)

At the register transfer level, data transfers, operations on data, and control flow are described/specified using a *register transfer language*. Within the language, individual operations and transfers are expressed using *register transfer notation* (RTN). Table 1.2 summarizes the RTN notation that we will use in the remaining discussion. Such a notation has a direct equivalent in contemporary hardware design languages (HDLs) such as Verilog or VHDL, thereby facilitating the transformation from design to implementation.

Table 1.2 Register Transfer Notation

Operator	Operation
←	Transfer from Right-Hand Side to Left-Hand Side
→	If-then operation
[index]	Select word from memory at index
< index >	Select bit or bits from register at index or range
i..j	Index range
:=	Text substitution
#	Concatenation
:	Separator for parallel operations
;	Separator for sequential operations
@	Replication
{ }	Information about operation
( )	Grouping
= ≠ < ≤ > ≥	Comparison operators
+ − × ÷+	Arithmetic operators
∧ ∨ ¬ ⊕ ≡	Logical operators

Table 1.3 illustrates how representative operations from the ISA level can be expressed using RTN.

1.11 REGISTER VIEW OF A MICROPROCESSOR

We will now examine the datapath and control for a simple microprocessor at the RTL level. We will begin by looking at the components that comprise the datapath from a register point of view. From there, we will look at the control of such a datapath by studying the instruction cycle for such a machine.

Table 1.3 Instruction Set Architecture Operations Expressed in Register Transfer Notation

Type	Instruction	ISA Level	Register Transfer Level
Data Transfer	Move register	MOVE R1, R2	R1 ← R2
	Move from memory	MOVE R1, memadx	R1 ← (memadx)
	Move to memory	MOVE memadx, R1	(memadx) ← R1
	Move immediate	MOVE R1, #DEAD	R1 ← #DEAD
Control Flow	Unconditional branch	BR $1	PC ← $1
	Conditional branch	BNE $1	cond (PC ← $1) if(cond) PC = $1
Logic	Complement accumulator	CMA	A ← ¬A
	AND register	AND R1, R2	R1 ← R1∧R2
	OR register	OR R1, R2	R1 ← R1∨ R2
	Shift register	SHL R1, #3	R1<31..0> ← R1<31-n..0>#(n@0) Contents of R1 get replaced by bits in range of 31–n..0, where n is number of bits to shift and n 0s get extended on right
Arithmetic	ADD register with carry	ADDC R1, R2	R1← R1 + R2 + C
	Clear carry	CLRC	C ← 0
Program Control	Don't execute an instruction	NOP	PC ← (PC + 1)
	Stop executing instructions	HALT	PC ← PC

1.11.1 The Datapath

Figure 1.52 expresses the architecture of the datapath and the memory interface for a simple microprocessor at the register transfer level.

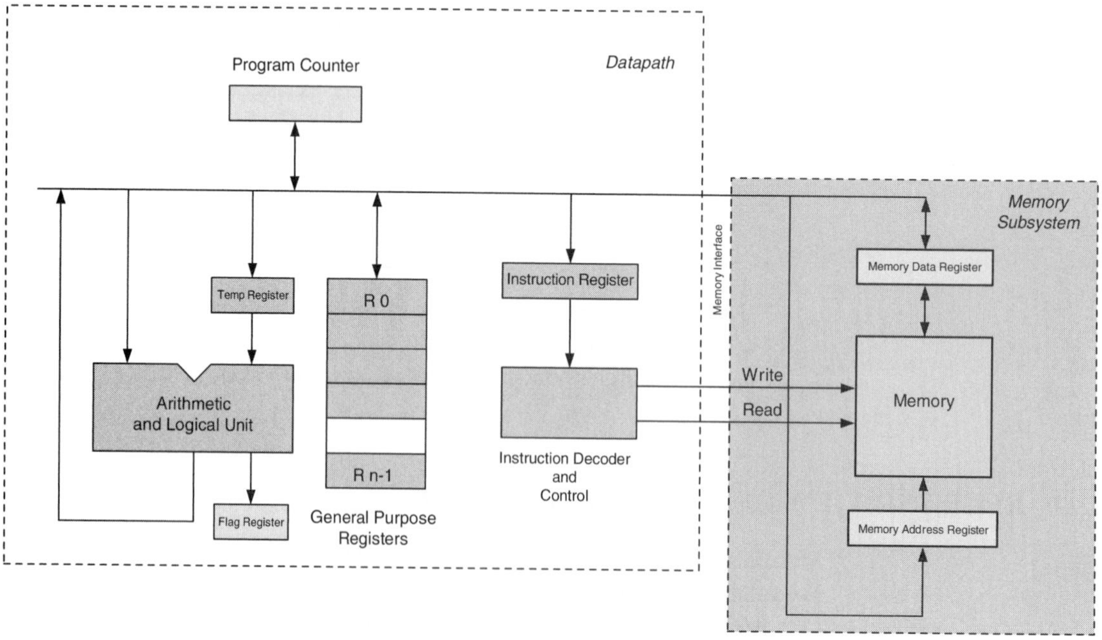

Figure 1.52 RTN Model for a Microprocessor Datapath and Memory Interface

Program Counter – PC	Hold next instruction address
Instruction Register – IR	Hold current instruction
General Purpose Registers – R0-Rn-1	Temporary data store
Memory Address Register – MAR	Hold address during read or write operation
Memory Data Register – MDR	Hold address during read or write operation
TR0	Hold operand during ALU operation
TR1	Hold the result of an arithmetic operation

Figure 1.53 Typical Microprocessor Register Set

In the diagram, we can identify the minimal set of registers, as listed in Figure 1.53.

1.11.2 Processor Control

instruction cycle The control of the microprocessor datapath comprises four fundamental operations defined as the *instruction cycle*. These steps are identified in Figure 1.54, and are further described according to state diagram in Figure 1.55.

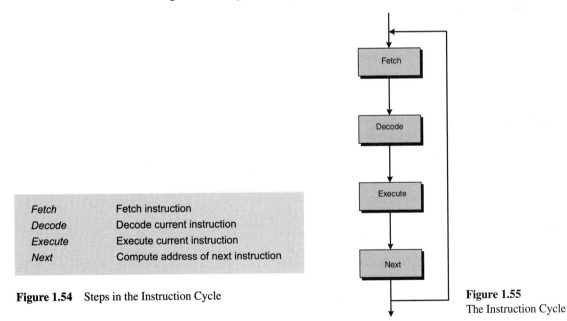

Fetch	Fetch instruction
Decode	Decode current instruction
Execute	Execute current instruction
Next	Compute address of next instruction

Figure 1.54 Steps in the Instruction Cycle

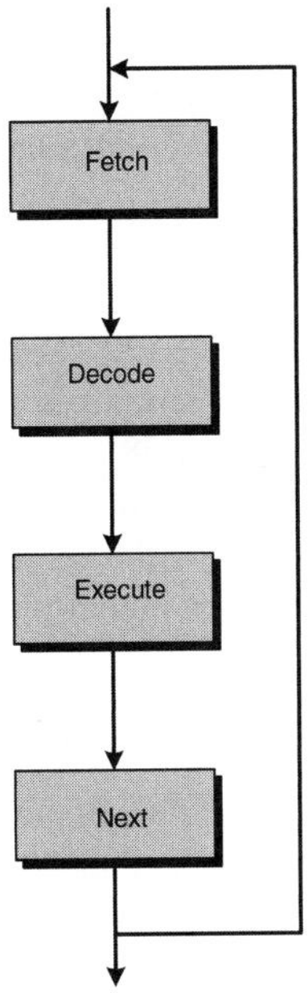

Figure 1.55
The Instruction Cycle

Fetch

fetch The *fetch* operation retrieves an instruction from memory. That instruction is identified by its address, which is the contents of the program counter, PC. Thus, at the ISA level, the *fetch* operation is written as

```
MOVE IR, *PC;
```

Move the memory word identified by the address contained in the program counter into the instruction register.

fetch
Memory Address Register
Read
Memory Data Register
Instruction Register, fetch

The first step in the *fetch* operation places the contents of the program counter (which identifies the address of the next instruction) into the *Memory Address Register* (MAR). A *Read* command is issued to the memory, which retrieves the instruction stored in the addressed location and places it into the *Memory Data Register* (MDR). The contents of the MDR are then transferred to the *Instruction Register* (IR). At the RTL level, the *fetch* decomposes into the sequence of steps given in Figure 1.56.

```
MAR←PC;                  // PC enabled out to bus, MAR captures value
MDR ← Memory[MAR];       // contents of specified memory location placed into MDR
IR ← MDR;                // MDR enabled out to bus, IR captures value
```

Figure 1.56 Components of the fetch Instruction

READ
read

The second step in this sequence executes a *READ* operation from the specified memory location. The underlying hardware will generate the *read* control signal and manage the underlying timing.

Decode

decode
Instruction Decoder
control logic, execute

The *decode* step is performed when the op-code field in the instruction is extracted from the instruction and decoded by the *Instruction Decoder.* That information is forwarded to the *control logic*, which will initiate the *execute* portion of the instruction cycle.

Execute

control logic
execute

Based on the value contained in the op-code field, the *control logic* performs the sequence of steps necessary to *execute* the instruction. Two examples are given in Figure 1.57 and Figure 1.58.

Store the contents of a register in a named location in memory.

Add the contents of a register to a piece of data stored in memory and place the result back into memory, but at a different location.

Next

The address of the next instruction to be executed is dependent on the type of instruction to be executed and, potentially, on the state of the condition flags as modified by the recently completed instruction. At the end of the day, most reduce to algebraically adding a value to

```
// C Instruction
    *xPtr = y;
// ISA Level Instruction
    ST *R1, R2;
// RTL Level Instructions
    MAR ← R1;                // R1 enabled out to bus, MAR captures value
    MDR ← Memory[MAR];       // contents of specified memory location placed into MDR
    R2 ← MDR;                // MDR enabled out to bus, R2 captures value
```

Figure 1.57 An Execute Sequence

```
// C Instruction
      *zPtr = x + *yPtr;
// ISA Level Instruction
      ADD *R3, R1, *R2;
// RTL Level Instructions
// Assume that R2 and R3 already contain the desired addresses in memory
      TR0 ← R1;                 // R1 enabled out to bus, TR0 captures value
      MAR ← R2;                 // R2 enabled out to bus, MAR captures value
      MDR← Memory[MAR];         // contents of specified memory location placed into MDR
      TR1← TR0 + MDR;           // MDR enabled out to bus, ALU adds TR0 and MDR
                                // places result in TR1
      MAR ← R3;                 // R3 enabled out to bus, MAR captures value
      MDR ← TR1;                // TR1 enabled out to bus, MDR captures value
      Memory[MAR] ← MDR;        // contents of MDR placed into specified memory location
```

Figure 1.58 An Execute Sequence

the PC. For short jumps, the displacement may be contained in one of the operand fields of the instruction; for longer jumps, the value may be contained in the memory location following the instruction.

next Thus, at the ISA level, the several versions of the *next* operation are written as

```
ADD PC, offset;
```

Algebraically modifying the PC is best accomplished by using one of the arithmetic functions in the ALU. The operation begins when the control logic places the desired offset into the ALU's temporary register. Next, the output of the PC is directed to the other ALU input. The ADD instruction is executed, and the result is entered into the PC. Placing a specific value into the PC can be done directly by the control logic since the target address is generally contained in the instruction.

next At the RTL level, the *next* step decomposes into the sequence of steps given in Figure 1.59.

```
// Assume the offset is contained in the instruction
TR0 ← IR<n..m>;          // offset field of instruction enabled out to bus, TR0 captures value
TR1 ← TR0 + PC;          // PC enabled out to bus, ALU adds TR0 and PC
PC ← TR1                 // TR1 enabled out to bus, PC captures value
```

Figure 1.59 The Next Sequence

The Verilog program in Figure 1.60 implements a behavioral model of a portion of the datapath and control for the simple CPU presented at the start of this section. The number of registers has been reduced, only two instructions are implemented, and the address mode field supports four different modes. Nonetheless, the architecture implements a working system. Included are the test bench and the tester for the CPU.

```
`define TRUE        1'b1
`define FALSE       1'b0
/*
 instruction format 32 bit word
        31..24          op-code
        23..22          address mode field operand 1
        21..12          operand 1
        11..10          address mode field operand 0
        9..0            operand 0
 all registers are 32 bits
*/

// Build a test bench to test the design
module testBench;

wire [31:0]         pc;                             // connect the pc
wire [31:0]         ir;                             // connect the ir
wire                clock;                          // connect the clock
hal0                aComputer (pc,ir, clock);       // build an instance of the computer
testIt              aTester(clock, pc, ir);         // build a tester

endmodule

// Test module
module testIt(clock, pc, ir);
// declare the input and output variables
input [31:0]        pc;                             // program counter
input [31:0]        ir;                             // instruction register
output              clock;                          // system clock
reg                 clock;                          // system clock

parameter halfPeriod = 1;

initial
clock = 0;

// manage the clock
always
begin
#(halfPeriod) clock = ~clock;
end

// manage the display and look for changes
always @(posedge clock)
begin
        $monitor ($time,, "pc = %h \t ir = %h", pc, ir);    // record only changes
        #(10*halfPeriod);                                   // let clock cycle a couple of times
        #(halfPeriod);                                      // needed to see END of a simulation
        $stop;                                              // stop so user can look at waveform
        $finish;                                            // exit
        end
endmodule
```

Figure 1.60 Model of the Datapath and Control for a Simple CPU

```
// The Computer - Hal0
module hal0 (pc, ir, clock);

// declare the I/O and registers
input            clock;
output [31:0]    pc;
output [31:0]    ir;

reg [31:0]       m [0:15];       // 16 x 32 bit memory
reg [31:0]       pc;             // 32 bit program counter
reg [31:0]       acc;            // 32 bit accumulator
reg [31:0]       ir;             // 32 bit instruction register
reg [31:0]       r[0:7];         // 8 32 bit general purpose registers

reg              notDone;        // flag to end program

integer          i;

// define op-codes

parameter add    =  8'h01;       // 8 bit add op-code
parameter move   =  8'h05;       // 8 bit move op-code
parameter done   =  8'hff;       // 8 bit done op-code

// define address mode field values

parameter dir    =  2'b00;
parameter ind    =  2'b01;
parameter imm    =  2'b10;
parameter pcr    =  2'b11;

// define registers

parameter r0     =  32'h0;
parameter r1     =  32'h1;
parameter r2     =  32'h2;
parameter r3     =  32'h3;
parameter r4     =  32'h4;
parameter r5     =  32'h5;
parameter r6     =  32'h6;
parameter r7     =  32'h7;
```

Figure 1.60 Model of the Datapath and Control for a Simple CPU *(Cont.)*

```
// initialize the system

    initial                          // initialize the pc and the accumulator
        begin
            pc = 0;                  // pc <- 0
            acc = 0;                 // acc <- 0

            notDone = `TRUE;         // initialize notDone flag

    // define the instruction rom
    // enter some instructions into memory
            m[0] = 'h05000803;       // r0 <- 0x3
            m[1] = 'h05001802;       // r1 <- 0x2
            m[2] = 'h01001000;       // r1 <- r1 + r0
            m[3] = 'hFFFFFFFF;       // done - end of program
            m[4] = 'h00000000;
            m[5] = 'h00000000;
            m[6] = 'h00000000;
            m[7] = 'h00000000;

            ir = m [pc];             // fetch operation - get first instruction
end
```

Figure 1.60 Model of the Datapath and Control for a Simple CPU *(Cont.)*

```
// run the program
    always
        while (notDone == `TRUE)
        begin
            @(posedge clock)                        // control system timing
            case(ir[31:24])                         // decode operation
                move:                               // move op-code
                begin
                    $display("\nMove");             // annotate execution

                    case(ir[11:10])                 // check address mode
                        dir:    $display("\ndirect");
                        ind:    $display("\nindirect");
                        imm:                        // implement immediate mode move
                        begin
                            $display("\nimmediate");     // execute operation
                            r[ (ir[21:12]) ] = ir[9:0];  // rx <- aValue

                            $display("\n register value %h", r[ (ir[21:12]) ]);
                        end

                        pcr: $display("\n pc relative");
                    endcase
                end
                add:                                // add op-code
                begin
                    $display("add\n");
                    case(ir[11:10])
                        dir:                        // register direct
                        begin
                            $display("\ndirect");   // execute operation

                            // rx <- rx + ry
                            r[ (ir[21:12]) ] = r[ (ir[21:12]) ] + r[ (ir[11:0]) ];
                            $display("\n register value %h", r[ (ir[21:12]) ]);
                        end

                        ind:  $display("\nindirect");
                        imm: $display("\nindirect");
                        pcr:  $display("\npc relative");
                    endcase
                end
                default:  $display("illegal op-code trap\n");  // identify illegal op-codes
            endcase
            pc = pc+1;                              // next operation compute next address
            ir = m [pc];                            // fetch operation
            if ( ir[31:24] == done )                // check for end of program
                notDone =`FALSE;                    // done
        end
```

Figure 1.60 Model of the Datapath and Control for a Simple CPU *(Cont.)*

1.12 SUMMARY

We introduced a high-level view at the computing core of an embedded application and then refined that core through several levels of increasing detail. We observed that such a core is usually manifest as a microprocessor, microcomputer, or microcontroller. We briefly examined each, identified the basic elements of each, and learned how they differ. We introduced and studied the architecture of the computing core beginning with the functional level, which comprises the four major blocks—input, output, memory, and CPU—as well as the bus as a means of interchanging information among the four blocks.

We then moved to the opposite end of the spectrum to learn how various essential kinds of information (numbers, characters, addresses, and instructions) are represented inside of a digital system. Building on the instructions, we learned that the instruction set drives or defines the architecture of the computer and how that architecture is refined and subsequently expressed at the register level. We designated these two levels as the instruction set architecture level (ISA) and register transfer level (RTL) of the computer.

At the ISA level, we examined how data and information are expressed within the machine, the different instruction formats, and the different addressing modes commonly supported by contemporary computing engines.

At the RTL level, we introduced the register, basic register operations, and the register transfer notation (RTN) used for expressing operations at the register transfer level. We then decomposed the CPU into the control and datapath components. We introduced the instruction cycle and examined how its fetch, decode, execute, and next constituents can be expressed at both the ISA and RTL levels.

We concluded with a behavioral level Verilog implementation of a simple datapath.

1.13 REVIEW QUESTIONS

The Hardware Side

1.1 Beginning with the computing core and moving to the complete system and its environment, the chapter identified a hierarchy of views of an embedded system. Please identify and briefly describe each of these views.

1.2 Identify and briefly describe the major functional blocks that comprise the computing core.

1.3 How are the major blocks of the computing core interconnected?

1.4 What are the major categories of signals flowing among the major blocks in the computing core?

1.5 What is meant by the term *bus width*?

1.6 Describe what is meant by the term *microprocessor*. Please be specific.

1.7 Describe what is meant by the term *microcomputer*. Please be specific.

1.8 Describe what is meant by the term *microcontroller*. Please be specific.

Representing Information

1.9 What kinds of information must we be able to represent in an embedded application?

1.10 What are the two basic classifications of numbers with which we are concerned in an embedded application?

1.11 How do we distinguish a signed integer from one that is unsigned?

1.12 What do the terms *little endian* and *big endian* mean? Why are they important?

1.13 When expressing a floating point number, what are the essential components that must be captured?

1.14 What do we mean when we say that the representation of a binary number has four bits of resolution?

1.15 A number that exceeds a microprocessor's word size may be truncated or rounded. Which of these will produce a greater error?

1.16 When arithmetic is performed on numbers with an error, the error will be reflected in the result of the calculation. How will that error affect the result if the numbers are added (subtracted), multiplied, or divided?

1.17 How are alphanumeric characters and symbols represented inside of a microprocessor?

1.18 How is an address expressed in a microprocessor word?

Instructions

1.19 An instruction is used to direct a microprocessor to perform some action. What are the major pieces of a microprocessor instruction?

1.20 What is meant by the *arity* of an instruction?

1.21 Please explain the terms *one-*, *two-*, or *three-operand instruction*.

1.22 Please explain the terms *one-*, *two-*, or *three-address instruction*.

1.23 What is the meaning of the term *op-code*?

1.24 What is the purpose of an *op-code*?

An Instruction Set View

1.25 Please explain the terms *instruction set* and *instruction set architecture*.

1.26 What is the purpose of the software tool called an *assembler*?

1.27 What is meant by the term *machine code*?

1.28 Microprocessor instructions can be classified into three major groups. What are these groups? Please describe what characterizes instructions in each of the groups.

1.29 Identify the hardware components that may be the source or destination of a data transfer instruction.

1.30 What information does the *addressing mode* of an instruction convey?

1.31 Please identify and briefly describe the more commonly used addressing modes discussed in the chapter.

1.32 How is the addressing mode information incorporated into an instruction?

1.33 Please explain the meaning of the term *execution* or *control flow*.

1.34 What are the four major categories of execution flow through an embedded program? Briefly describe what each means.

1.35 What is the purpose of a *flag* or *condition code register*?

1.36 What is the difference between an entry condition loop and an exit condition loop?

1.37 Please identify and describe the necessary steps for executing a function or procedure call. Please be precise.

1.38 What is a stack?

1.39 What are the major access operations that can be performed on a stack?

1.40 What is the purpose of the variable called the stack pointer?

1.41 What is the function of the ALU?

A Register View

1.42 Underlying the microprocessor's instruction set is the implementation hardware. What are the core components of that hardware?

1.43 What is meant by the expression *register transfer level*? How does the register transfer level view of a microprocessor relate to the instruction set architecture level view?

1.44 What is a register, and what is its purpose in a microprocessor?

1.45 What basic operations can be performed on a register?

1.46 What is the purpose of a register transfer language and register transfer notation?

1.47 Please identify and briefly describe the registers that one will typically find in a microprocessor's datapath.

1.48 The control of a microprocessor's datapath is made up of four operations called the instruction cycle. Please identify and describe each of these operations.

1.14 THOUGHT QUESTIONS

The Hardware Side

1.1 Three kinds of computing engine are utilized in embedded systems. What are the advantages and disadvantages of each?

1.2 Under what circumstances should one consider using a microcontroller? microcomputer? microprocessor? Please explain your answer in detail.

1.3 Discuss the advantages and disadvantages of a wide versus narrow internal system bus.

1.4 Is it necessary for the address and data portions of the system bus to have the same number of bits? What are the pros and cons of a wider address bus? data bus?

1.5 In some designs, the address and data signals are multiplexed onto the same set of bus lines. What are the advantages and disadvantages of such a scheme?

1.6 Discuss the benefits gained from and the disadvantages of a von Neumann versus Aiken Machine.

Representing Information

1.7 What are the limitations on the amount of information that can be stored in a data word?

1.8 What are the trade-offs of a wide versus narrow word size?

1.9 If the system bus is 1 byte wide, how can a 32-bit word be transferred over the bus?

1.10 If an embedded system is designed around a 16-bit word, is it possible to support 32-bit floating point numbers? If so, how and if not, why not?

1.11 Identify several reasons for using unsigned integers.

1.12 If the word size in an embedded system is 16-bits, why would one ever use bytes? Unsigned bytes?

1.13 If an embedded core is implemented as a *big endian* machine, how can one communicate with a peripheral device that is *little endian*?

1.14 Why is type information necessary for data words?

1.15 The hidden bit format for floating point numbers provides an extra bit of resolution for free. Someone has suggested applying the same technique to gain two extra bits. What do you think of the idea? Are there any problems with it?

Instructions

1.16 The essential components of an instruction are the op-code and the operand(s) on which the operation is to be performed. Is it necessary that the op-code always contain the same number of bits? Why or Why not?

1.17 The chapter discussed one-, two-, and three-address instructions. Is it possible to have a zero-address instruction? What are the benefits of such a design?

1.18 How can double indirection be implemented in an instruction?

An Instruction Set View

1.19 What are the four major pieces of information that an instruction must convey? How are these done?

1.20 In the chapter, several different addressing modes were discussed. Can you think of others that might be useful?

1.21 Are the bits in the *machine code* representation of an instruction arbitrary, or do they have a specific meaning? If they have meaning, what might it be?

1.22 Microprocessor instructions can be classified into three major groups. What are these groups? Please describe what characterizes instructions in each of the groups.

1.23 If an instruction contains the address of an operand in memory, how can the source or destination of an operation be conveyed if the source or destination is an input or output port on the microprocessor?

1.24 If one has an assembly code listing for an embedded program that has been running on a Motorola processor, will that program run on an Advanced Micro Devices (AMD) processor?

1.25 If one has a C code listing for an embedded program that has been running on a Motorola processor, will that program run on an AMD processor?

1.26 Please explain how a branch type of instruction works from an instruction set point of view.

1.27 How does an instruction know how or where to access a *flag* or *condition code register*?

1.28 Discuss ways of managing the case of the instruction decoder finding an op-code in an instruction that it does not recognize.

A Register View

1.29 A RISC architecture frequently incorporates many more registers than does a CISC design? Why is this?

1.30 Explain why a register access is generally faster than a memory access.

1.31 Explain how an indexed type of instruction might be implemented at the register level.

1.32 How can data from multiple sources be transferred into the same register?

1.33 Discuss the advantages and disadvantages of building a register from latches versus flip-flops.

1.34 What are the advantages and disadvantages of tristate gates versus a traditional multiplexer gate for transferring data from one register to another?

1.15 PROBLEMS

1.1 Express the following decimal numbers in the bases indicated.

Decimal: 1011, 23.4, 207, 111.439

(a) Binary
(b) Octal
(c) Hexadecimal
(d) Binary Coded Decimal (BCD)

1.2 Express the following binary numbers in the bases indicated.

Binary: 101101011, 1101.11001, 1001001110, 111.001

(a) Decimal
(b) Binary Coded Decimal (BCD)
(c) Hexadecimal

1.3 Express the following hexadecimal numbers in the bases indicated.

Hexadecimal: B3D9, CA.43, 1234, 5D.06F

(a) Decimal
(b) Binary Coded Decimal (BCD)
(c) Binary

1.4 Express the following decimal numbers in the bases indicated.

Decimal: 12.34, 9503.313

(a) Binary
(b) Hexadecimal

1.5 Express your given name and your family name as ASCII characters in the following format:

givenName familyName

The ASCII characters should be written in their binary form and stored so as to use the smallest number of 16-bit words. Check the Web site asciitable.com for the set of ASCII characters.

1.6 We have the following data stored in the first 32 locations of a memory as shown.

Memory Address	Value
00000	0000010
	0101001
	1000001
	0101111
	0001111
	0000011
	1100101
	1101001
	1111101
	0001111
	0011101
	0010111
	0001011
	0000001
	0101111
	0101001
	0100011
	0000010
	0001101
	0000111
	0111101
	0111001
	1101001
	0011101
	0000011
	0001111
	0011111
	0010001
	0111101
	1001101
	1001101
11111	1010101

(a) Please identify the words at the following hexadecimal addresses.

12, F, 1E, 7, 1C

(b) Please give the hexadecimal addresses for the following words in memory.

1100101, 0010111, 0100011, 0111101

1.7 We have the following C code fragment:

```
unsigned char a = 0xD3;
char b = 'A';
int c = 6;
int d = 9;
int e = -31564;
unsigned int f = 0xFAD7;
float g = 3.1;
float h = 0.0345;
int j;
int* cPtr = &c;
int* dPtr = &d;
int** cPtrPtr = &cPtr;
int** dPtrPtr = &dPtr;
float* gPtr = &g;
float* hPtr = &h;
```

Variable	Memory Address	Value
00000	1000	
	1001	
	2000	
	2001	
	3000	
	3001	
	4000	
	4001	

(a) Please put the values, in binary, for all of the variables into memory. Assume 16-bit words and big endian notation.

(b) How do the values in memory change after the following code fragment is executed?

```
e = e + f;
*gPtr = *gPtr + *hPtr;
j = **cPtrPtr - **dPtrPtr;
```

1.8 Convert each of the following floating point numbers into binary. Assume a 16-bit word for which the weight of the least significant bit is 2^{-4}. Following the conversion, what is the error for each number?

(a) E = 72.23
(b) F = 121.034
(c) G = 98.6
(d) H = 43.612

1.9 Using the numbers and errors from Problem 1.8, perform the following calculations. What is the worst case error for each calculation?

(a) E+F+G+H
(b) E*F
(c) G*H
(d) (G*H) / (E+F)

1.10 Please show the contents of the stack, the position of the stack pointer (SP), and the contents of the indicated registers after the execution of each of the following instructions. The instructions are executed in sequence.

Initially, the registers contain the following values `R0 = 1234, R1 = 2345, R2 = 4567, R3 = 8901.`

For two-operand instructions, assume that the left-hand operand is also the destination.

PC	Instruction
FACE	ADD R3, R1
FACF	PUSH R2
FAD1	POP R3
FAD6	ADD R1, R2

Registers		Stack
R0		
R1		
R2		
R3		
PC		

Registers		Stack
R0		
R1		
R2		
R3		
PC		

Registers		Stack
R0		
R1		
R2		
R3		
PC		

Registers		Stack
R0		
R1		
R2		
R3		
PC		

Registers		Stack
R0		
R1		
R2		
R3		
PC		

1.11 Using the assembly language instructions introduced in the chapter, write a program to solve the following problem.

$$\left(\frac{(A \cdot B)}{(C-D)}\right) \cdot E$$

The variables A–E are already stored in the registers R1–R5. The result is to be placed into register R6. You may not change what is stored in registers R1–R5.

1.12 How does your program in Problem 1.10 change if the registers contain the addresses of the variables rather than the values of the variables?

1.13 Given the memory locations, values below, and a one-address machine with an accumulator (the accumulator is the default destination), what values do the following instructions load into the accumulator?

Assume that R1 and R3 contain the values 0x5000 and 0x3000, respectively.

Memory Location	*Contents*
1000	2000
2000	3000
3000	FACE
4000	5000
5000	1000

Accumulator

```
MOVE     R1 5000
LOADI    0x5000
MOVE     *R1
LOADI    0xFACE
MOVE     *R2 3000
```

1.14 A partial set of specifications for a typical embedded processor are given as follows.

- 16-bit architecture—16-bit-wide data words
- 20-bit instructions.
- 8 general-purpose registers.
- One-, two-, and three-address instructions.
- Each address field is qualified by a 2-bit field to identify any of the following four different addressing modes: *register direct, register indirect, pc relative, indexed.*

(a) Please give the format for a one-, two-, and three-address instruction for this machine. Observe that the width of the instruction is different from the width of the data. This is not a problem.

(b) Please show how the following instructions would be implemented using the format you designed.

```
ADD2, SUB2, MUL, DIV
opcodes: 00001, 00010, 00011, 00100
respectively
```

add, subtract, multiply, divide two operands.

```
MOVE          opcode: 00101
```

Move a word from memory into a register.

Move a word to a memory address location that is contained in a register.

```
JUM           opcode: 00110
```

Jump to a location.

```
BR, BE        opcodes: 00111, 01000
```

Load a 16-bit integer into a register.

```
CMP           opcode: 01001
```

Compare two operands and set the appropriate condition code.

```
CALL, RET     opcodes: 01010, 01011
```

PC is replaced by a specified address, and control is transferred to the address.

Control is returned to the calling context.

1.15 We have the following requirements for a microprocessor. Assume that the processor has 32-bit instructions. Let each register operand address be specified by a 5-bit field for the address and qualified by a 2-bit field to identify any of the following four different addressing modes: *register direct, register indirect, pc relative, indexed.*

Assume there are K two-operand instructions and L zero-operand instructions (e.g., HALT) required.

(a) What is the maximum number of one-address instructions that can be provided in the computer?

(b) Give the format for zero-, one-, and two-address instructions. How are these distinguished?

(c) How would the following instructions be expressed using your format:

- Move a word from memory into a register.
- Move a word to a memory address location that is contained in a register.
- Jump to a location.
- Add, subtract, multiply, divide two operands.
- Load the integer 59 into a register.
- Read from the keyboard.

1.16 Consider the following state of a computer:

```
Register R1 contains 800
Register R2 contains 3000
Memory location 1000 contains 2000
Memory location 2000 contains 3000
Memory location 3000 contains 1000.
```

All numbers are expressed in hex notation.

For the following three instructions, each is executed from the above initial state.

(a) What is the effect of executing each instruction?

(b) How many words does each instruction occupy?

(c) How many memory accesses does the fetching and execution of each instruction require?

Assume each instruction is independent of the others

```
MOVE *R2, R1        // move R1 to what R2 is
                    // pointing at
MOVE *R2,1800(R1)   // move the contents of the
                    // memory location indexed
                    // by R1 to what R2 is
                    // pointing at
MOVI *R2, #DEAD     // move the constant DEAD to
                    // what R2 is pointing at.
```

1.17 An embedded application executing on the microprocessor in Problem 1.15 is required to perform the following computation:

$$Z \leftarrow W_1 \bullet Y_1 + W_2 \bullet Y_2 + W_3 \bullet Y_3$$

on the contents of memory locations Z_1, W_1, Y_1, W_2, Y_2, W_3, and Y_3. None of the contents of locations W or Y may be destroyed.

(a) Write a straight-line program for the task described above.

(b) Write a loop program for the same task on the same computer.

(c) Calculate the number of main memory accesses (Read or Write operations) required for each program. Include all accesses required or fetching and executing the instructions. For example, the instruction:

```
MOVE Ri, Rj
```

requires two memory accesses: one for reading the instruction from main memory into the microprocessor and one for reading the operand from main memory location contained in R_i into the microprocessor.

1.18 In some computers, subroutine linkage is implemented in the following way. The call subroutine instruction stores the return address (the next instruction in the calling program) in the first location of the subroutine, and then branches to the second location, where the execution of the subroutine begins.

(a) Define a suitable instruction for returning from the subroutine.

(b) How would you pass parameters between the calling program and the subroutine?

(c) Would the above linkage support nesting of subroutines? Why or why not?

(d) Would the above linkage support recursion? Why or why not?

1.19 Based on the RTL model of a microprocessor datapath given in Figure 1.52 and the RTL operations given in Table 1.3, please identify the necessary steps that comprise each phase of the instruction cycle in order to perform the following instruction on that microprocessor:

```
// add the contents of the value contained in
// the register R3 to the contents of the
// memory location pointed to by R2 and put
// the results into R4.

add R4, R3, *R2;
```

1.20 We have the following C code fragment that adds one to each element of an array.

```
int a[4] = {1, 2, 3, 4};      // declare an array
                              // of integers
int i ;
for (i = 0; i < 4; i++)
a[i] = a[i] + 1;              // add 1 to each
                              // element of the array
```

(a) Using the instructions you developed in Problem 1.15 translate the given code fragment into assembler.

(b) Using the RTL operations given in Table 1.3, translate the assembler to RTL level.

(c) Using the instructions you developed in Problem 1.15 and the assembler from part (a), translate the code fragment into machine code.

1.21 The architecture known as the Aiken or Harvard architecture uses a separate data memory and a separate instruction memory.

(a) Please give two advantages and two disadvantages of the Harvard architecture in comparison to the Princeton architecture. Be precise in your answer.

(b) For the following C++ code fragment. Which memory, the instruction or the data memory, should contain the values for x and y? Please explain why.

```
int x = 3;
int y = 4;
x = x + y;
```

(c) Using the following memory diagrams, please place the values for x and y into locations in the appropriate memory.

Instruction Memory		
Memory Location	*Memory Address*	*Contents*

Data Memory		
Memory Location	*Memory Address*	*Contents*

(d) Are the following assembly code instructions one-, two-, or three-address instructions? Please explain your answer.

```
LOADI Ri, #constant     // load the constant into
                        // Ri
LOADI *Ri, #constant    // load the constant into
                        // what Ri is pointing to
ADD2 Ri, Rj             // add the contents of Ri
                        // to Rj and place the
                        // result in Ri
ADD2 *Ri, *Rj           // add the contents of what
                        // Ri is pointing to what
                        // Rj is pointing to and
                        // place the result in what
                        // Ri is pointing to
```

(e) Using the instructions above, complete the following code fragment to implement the addition operation in part (b).

LOADI		
LOADI		
ADD2		

(f) Using the following memory diagrams, please place the instructions you wrote in part (e) into locations in the appropriate memory.

Instruction Memory		
Memory Location	*Memory Address*	*Contents*

Data Memory		
Memory Location	*Memory Address*	*Contents*

(g) Please provide a format for the `add` instruction given above. Explain the purpose of each field in your implementation.

(h) Please identify all of the steps necessary to execute the `add` instruction in part (e) above on the Harvard machine. Refer to the specific parts of the architecture diagram in your descriptions.

1.22 A computer is designed that uses a set of special registers, RS0–RS3, rather than the stack to pass data into and out of a subroutine. The stack is only used to hold the return address. The stack pointer is held in the special register SP and the program counter in register PC.

The machine has four general-purpose registers R0–R3.

The machine has a status flag, equal, that is appropriately set or reset for each instruction execution as indicated below.

Write a routine exp (num, pow) that will compute num^{pow} for such a machine and return that value.

(a) Please write the detailed level pseudocode for invoking such a routine assuming that it is called from some higher level function. Be certain to identify ***all*** the steps.

(b) Please write the sequence of assembly language steps necessary to implement such a sequence using the following instructions.

```
LOAD Ri, Rj      // Ri ← Rj, sets the equal
                 // flag true if Ri contains 0
LOAD Ri, #val    // Ri ← #val, sets the
                 // equal flag true if Ri
                 // contains 0
BE @Ri           // jumps to address
                 // contained in Ri if the equal
                 // flag is true
BNE @Ri          // jumps to address
                 // contained in Ri if the equal
                 // flag is false
```

```
MUL Ri, Rj          // Ri ← Ri * Rj, sets the
                    // equal flag true if Ri
                    // contains 0
DIV Ri, Rj          // Ri ← Ri / Rj, sets the
                    // equal flag true if Ri
                    // contains 0
ADD2 Ri, Rj         // Ri ← Ri + Rj, sets the
                    // equal flag true if Ri
                    // contains 0
SUB2 Ri, Rj         // Ri ← Ri - Rj, sets the
                    // equal flag true if Ri
                    // contains 0
INC Ri              // Ri ← Ri + 1
DEC Ri              // Ri ← Ri - 1, sets the
                    // equal flag true if Ri
                    // contains 0
PUSH R   i          // stack ← Ri
POP Ri              // Ri ← stack
```

(c) Using a value of 20 for num and 3 for pow, please indicate the contents of each of the following registers at the execution points indicated assuming the sequence of steps you have identified was executed. Also indicate the top of the stack.

Assume the original function call is at memory address 3050 and that the subroutine is at memory address 5000.

Prior to Function Call

PC	

GP Registers	
R0	
R1	
R2	
R3	

SP Registers	
RS0	
RS1	
RS2	
RS3	

Stack	

After the Function Call

PC	

GP Registers	
R0	
R1	
R2	
R3	

SP Registers	
RS0	
RS1	
RS2	
RS3	

Stack	

Prior to the Return

PC	

GP Registers	
R0	
R1	
R2	
R3	

SP Registers	
RS0	
RS1	
RS2	
RS3	

Stack	

After the Return

PC	

GP Registers	
R0	
R1	
R2	
R3	

SP Registers	
RS0	
RS1	
RS2	
RS3	

Stack	

Chapter 2

The Hardware Side—Part 2: Combinational Logic—A Practical View

THINGS TO LOOK FOR . . .

- Output topology for logic devices.
- Real-world considerations—Logic levels, drive capability, rise and fall times, and propagation delays.
- Effects of the real world.
- Race conditions and hazards.
- Understanding and modeling of parasitic components and their effects on digital circuit.
- Common faults in combinational logic circuits.

2.0 INTRODUCTION

The previous chapter introduced the hardware side of an embedded application from a top-down view of the computing core and from a bottom-up view of the bits and bytes expressing the information used by that core. Another view of that hierarchy is from the perspective of the physical components that turn the high-level design concepts and the bits and bytes into a working application. The digital hardware is an essential component in the design of all embedded systems. At the same time, in today's systems the hardware is of little use without the accompanying software and firmware. The goal of this chapter and the next is to provide a solid basis for the practical aspects of working with digital circuits in the embedded world. Later chapters will augment and complement the hardware side with the software/firmware side and then merge the two into safe, reliable real-world applications.

When we are focusing on digital hardware, software, and firmware, we sometimes forget that underneath all of our 0's and 1's is also an analog world. It is a world in which the voltages and currents that we work with and that we turn into software bits and bytes are not always stable or accurate. It is a world in which signals are delayed going through gates, flip-flops, array logics, and microprocessors. To be able to design and build robust, production-quality applications that work in a wide variety of real-world applications, it is essential that one understand how that world affects the components and the designs.

Modeling and simulation are essential steps in the process of designing systems today. One often hears the alternative view, which suggests that with the rapid growth of powerful programmable logic elements we will soon be able to quickly synthesize a design and then just try it out rather than waste time simulating. After all, don't we do this already with software? An important point to remember is that if all we had to do was complete a design and get it working with one set of parts, such an approach might be reasonable. Unfortunately, not all parts (even from the same manufacturer—even with the same date code) are identical; each is slightly different. Parts and subsystems can interact in many unexpected ways. Software does not age. It is not affected by manufacturing tolerances, humidity, temperature, or electromagnetic radiation. Modeling and simulation allow us to subject the critical (here, often hardware) parts of our designs to such real-world phenomena quickly and cheaply. We introduced modeling at the register transfer level in the last chapter. In this chapter and the next, we will move closer to the gates and flip-flops that make up the RTL devices and control. Our discussions of the physical level of embedded systems will assume a solid understanding of Boolean algebra and logic reduction techniques as well as familiarity with the basic small-scale and medium-scale logic devices and families.

We open the chapter with an examination of physical world logic signal levels, their variability, and the effects of noise on those signals. Such an understanding is essential when trying to design and mass produce a new system. The ability of a logic device to drive other devices is studied next. We routinely use such knowledge when we are interconnecting components within a module as well as when we are interfacing with other modules or systems.

We then move from the static world to the dynamic as we learn that logic signals do not change state instantly and that they propagate through a system at different rates. Using the Verilog hardware design language, we learn to model (portions of) our designs at different levels of abstraction in order to permit such real-world effects to be studied and taken into consideration during the design life cycle. Delving deeper into the real world, we explore the first-order effects of passive parasitic components—the resistor, capacitor, and inductor—on our designs. We conclude by studying common faults in combinational logic circuits and how we begin to test such circuits.

2.1 A LOOK AT REAL-WORLD GATES—PART 1: SIGNAL LEVELS

When we start to use logic gates to realize our designs, the first view is of the function that they are performing. Our next view must be of their electrical and mechanical characteristics: how large they are, how much heat they dissipate, how much power they consume, how fast they are, their ability to drive other parts, the kind of load they present to other parts, the amplitude of their output, and the requirements on input signals.

In the world of philosophy and logic, it is reasonable to talk about the concepts of truth and falsity. Ultimately, if we are going to build circuits and systems to implement logical relationships, we must be able to express such concepts in terms of measurable real-world quantities such as photons, voltage, or current. In addition, we must be able to design and manufacture devices that accept those quantities as the values of input variables, implement a desired logical function, and present the quantities as output variables.

2.1.1 Logic Levels

In our equations, we deal with a logical 0 or logical 1. In physical parts, those values are represented by different voltage or light intensity levels (or any of several other measures). Today, normally we define, as

```
Logical 0 as 0 volts
Logical 1 as +5 volts
```

Newer logics, including those we call green logics (which help the environment by consuming less power), are starting to use lower-voltage-level signaling.

Now the problem of interfacing between different logic devices is becoming increasingly complex because of the wide variety of devices and logic families that are being used in embedded applications today. For the discussion here, we will assume signal levels of 0.0 or 5.0 VDC. The concepts discussed easily scale to any levels.

```
Logical 0 as 0 volts
Logical 1 as +1.5 or 3.0 volts
```

Higher speed systems that must also tolerate potential electrical noise contamination will utilize differential signaling. In these cases, the signal levels may follow some national or international standard or be unique to the design.

On paper, the logic levels are always exactly at their defined values and are never affected by the environment or by the manufacturing process. When working with real parts, however, a logical 1 is never precisely 5.0 VDC and a logical 0 is never exactly 0.0 V. If a logical high-voltage level gets too low, it could be interpreted as logical 0. Similarly, if a logical low voltage gets too high, it could be interpreted as logical 1. As a result, the vendors will specify minimum (maximum) values for logical 1's (logical 0's). Integrated circuits are manufactured in large quantities on a production line. Because no production line produces all identical parts, there will always be slight variations in the values of each of the different parameters among parts that are produced on different days, by different vendors, or different production lines by the same vendor. Such variations have to be taken into account in any design; specifications for and the range in the variation of the values for such parameters are given in the vendor's data sheets.

typical
minimum, maximum

Because the parameter values vary, the vendor will specify a *typical* value and a *minimum* or *maximum* value based on the nature of the parameter. To see how this works, let's assume that the variations in the values of the parameters have a Gaussian or normal distribution. From the vendor's data sheet, we take the information given in Table 2.0 for a 74LS04 inverter.

Table 2.0 Logic Signal Levels

	Min	Typical	Max
VOH	2.5	3.4	
VOL		0.2	0.4
VIH	2.0		
VIL	0.8		

Let's now connect two of the inverters into the simple circuit in Figure 2.0 such as we might find on a signal path on a system bus.

Observe that the positions of the bubbles on the gates are used to reflect the state of the logic signals on each device. The figure on the left illustrates the range of vendor-specified values for the high-level output voltage, V_{OH}, and corresponding high-level input voltage, V_{IH}—those values to the right of the arrow. The figure on the right illustrates the range of specified values for a low-level output voltage, V_{OL}, and corresponding low-level input voltage, V_{IL}—those values to the left of the arrow.

The figure on the left illustrates the typical value for the high-level output voltage, VOH_{typ}, to be 3.4 VDC, with the guarantee that a logical 1 will never be lower than

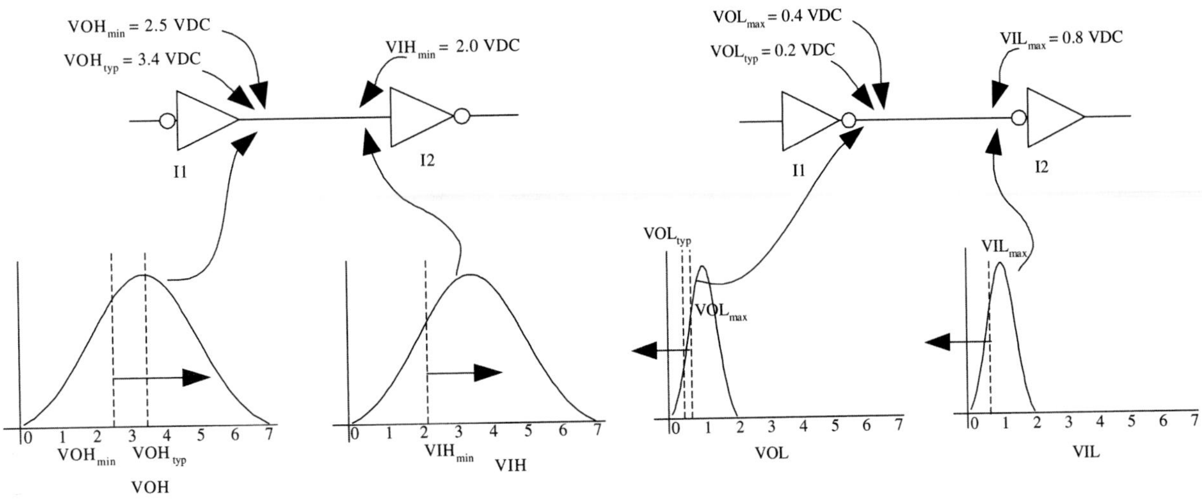

Figure 2.0 Variation of Logic Signal Levels on Device Inputs and Outputs

greater

2.5 VDC, VOH_{min}. Thus, all values *greater* than VOH_{min} are to be interpreted as valid high-level outputs. We also see that the device is guaranteed to interpret all voltage as low as 2.0 VDC, VIH_{min}, as valid high-level inputs.

higher
less

The figure on the right illustrates the same relationships for a low-level output and corresponding input. A logical 0 out of the left-hand inverter has a typical value for a low-level output voltage, VOL_{typ}, of 0.2 VDC and a guaranteed logical 0 that will never be *higher* than 0.4 VDC, VOL_{max}. Therefore, all values *less* than VOL_{max} are to be interpreted as valid low-level outputs. For inverter I2, we see that the device is guaranteed to interpret any voltage as high as 0.8 VDC as valid low-level inputs, VIL_{max}.

high-level noise immunity
noise margin
low-level noise immunity
noise margin

The difference between the minimum guaranteed output high voltage and the minimum acceptable input high voltage is called the *high-level noise immunity* or *noise margin* of the part. The difference between the guaranteed maximum output low voltage and the maximum recognized input low voltage is called the *low-level noise immunity* or *noise margin*. These specifications ensure that with a minimum output signal of 2.5 VDC from a driving device, the receiving device will tolerate up to 0.5 VDC of noise on its input and still interpret the signal as a logical 1.

With a maximum output signal of 0.4 VDC from a driving device, the receiving device will tolerate up to 0.4 VDC of noise on its input and still interpret the signal as a logical 0. From the values in the vendor's data sheet information, we calculate

```
0.5 V of high noise margin
0.4 V of low noise margin
```

The region between the minimum input high-level voltage and the maximum input low-level voltage is an unknown region. A vendor will make no guarantees about the behavior of the part in this region.

We can express these values graphically as illustrated in Figure 2.1.

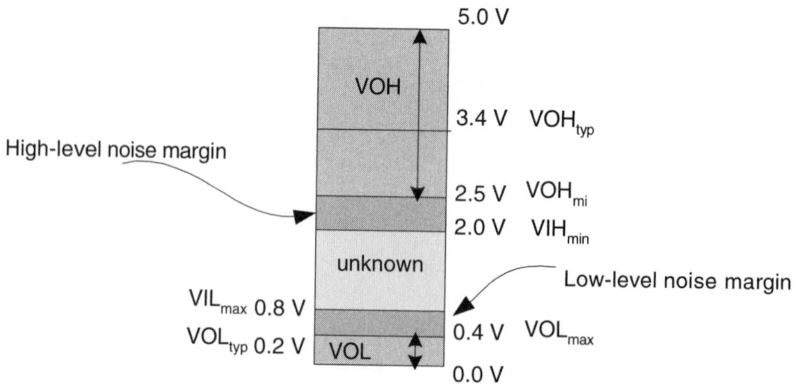

Figure 2.1 Min and Max Values of Logic Signal Levels

2.1.2 A First Look Inside the Logic Gate

bipolar technology
MOS technology
Transistor-Transistor Logic (TTL)
Field Effect Transistors (FETs)
Metal Oxide Semiconductors (MOS)
Complementary Output Symmetry MOS (CMOS)
totem pole

Today's integrated circuits implement the various logical devices using several different technologies and device architectures. One of the more significant differences among the various devices arises from the two primary semiconductor technologies that are used: *bipolar technology* and *MOS technology*. The former utilizes bipolar transistors to implement what is called *Transistor-Transistor Logic* (TTL), and the latter utilizes *Field Effect Transistors* (FETs) to implement *Metal Oxide Semiconductors* (MOS) and *Complementary Output Symmetry MOS* (CMOS) logic.

We can model the inverter as two switches connected in series as we see in Figure 2.2. Moving inside of the device, we see that the logical behavior modeled by these switches arises from the configuration of the output portion of the implementation logic. Logic gates implemented utilizing either technology employ output nets structured in a *totem pole* pattern. Such a configuration is illustrated in the following drawings presenting the output network for each technology.

The basic output structure for the family of devices built utilizing TTL is given in Figure 2.3. Although there are many variations on the basic implementation technology (standard TTL [as shown], Schottky, low-power Schottky, plus minor derivatives), the architecture remains the same.

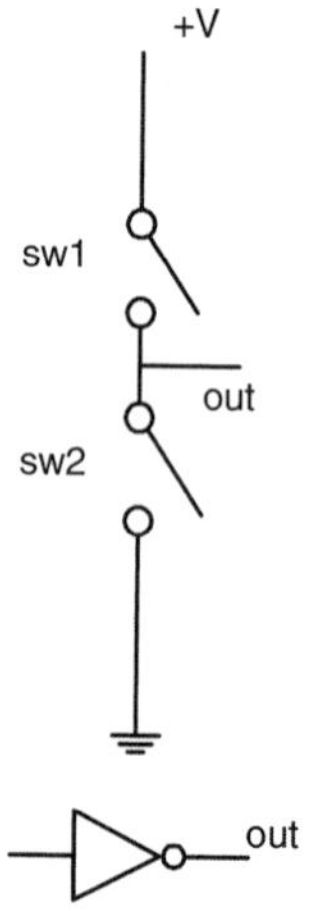

Figure 2.2 Inverter Model

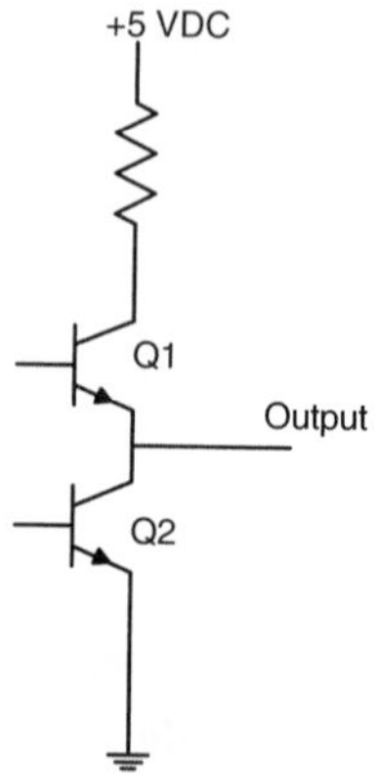

Figure 2.3 TTL Totem Pole Output Configuration

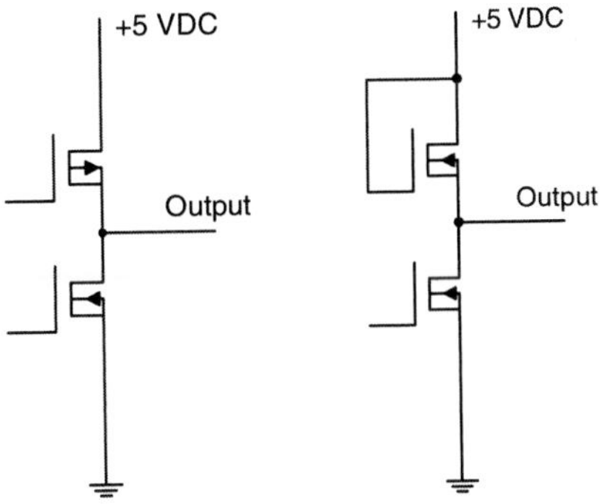

Figure 2.4 CMOS and NMOS Totem Pole Output Configuration

In Figure 2.4, the circuit on the left presents the CMOS configuration. The architecture remains a totem pole structure. The upper transistor is a PMOS device and the lower an NMOS device. The NMOS device, presented in the circuit on the right, is a simple modification of the CMOS device. The upper transistor is replaced by a second NMOS transistor implemented as a load device. They are short hand for P channel and N channel.

The ability of the top transistor to source current when the output of the device is a logical 1 and the bottom transistor to sink current when the output is a logical 0 is called the *drive capability* of the device.

drive capability

2.1.3 Fan-In and Fan-Out

fan-out
source
sink, fan-in
sources
sinks

The number of devices that a typical gate can drive without degrading its specified minimum and maximum output logic levels is called the *fan-out* of the device. The fan-out of a device specifies how much current the device can *source* to other devices in logic high state and *sink* from other devices in the logic low state. *Fan-in* is a measure of a device's input current requirements. It specifies how much current the device *sources* to other devices when the input is in the logical 0 state and *sinks* from other devices when the input is in the logical 1 state.

sourcing current
sinking current

When current is leaving the device (driver or receiver), it is said to be *sourcing current*; when current enters the device (driver or receiver), it is said to be *sinking current*. We define current leaving the device as negative and current entering the device as positive. This is an arbitrary, but consistent, labeling. We can see these in Figure 2.5.

In the first case, inverter Inv1 is sourcing current to Inv2, which is sinking that current. With respect to Inv1, the current, I, will be negative, and with respect to Inv2, it will be positive. In the second case, the roles are reversed; Inv1 is sinking current (which will be viewed positive) that is being sourced by Inv2 (which will be viewed as negative). Once again, we use the bubbles on the gate to indicate the logical 0 state.

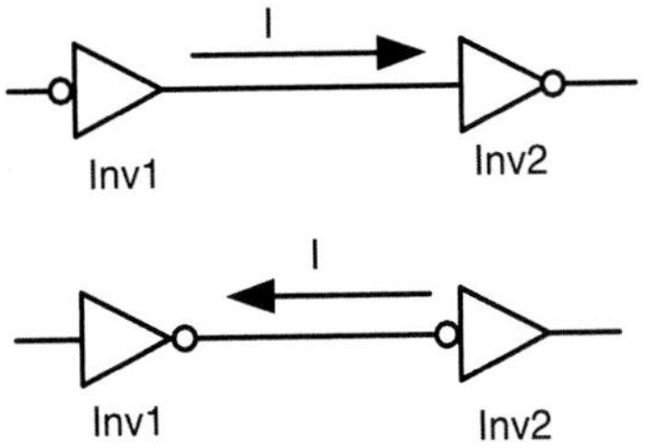

Figure 2.5 Sourcing and Sinking Current

The data sheet for the device will give the specifications in Table 2.1.

Table 2.1 Source and Sink Currents for an SN74LS04

	Current	Voltage
IOL	8 mA (entering)	@V_{OL} = 0.5 VDC
IOH	–400μA (leaving)	@V_{OH} = 3.4 VDC
IIL	–400μA (leaving)	@V_{IL} = 0.4 VDC
IIH	–20μA (entering)	@V_{IH} = 2.7 VDC

Starting from the data sheet, one can compute the fan-out for the SN74LS04 device. Two cases must be considered when computing the fan-out for the device, when the output is in the logical 0 state and when it is in the logical 1 state. When specifying the fan-out for the device, we always use the lower of the two values.

Logic 0 State

output ***input*** When the *output* is at a logical 0 level, the data sheet specifies that the device can sink 8mA, and when an *input* is at a logical 0 level, it sources –400 μA.

Thus, when its output is in the logical 0 state, an SN74LS04 can sink the current from 20 similar devices.

$$\text{fan-out} = \left|\frac{8\text{mA}}{-400\mu\text{A}}\right| = 20 \tag{2.0}$$

Logic 1 State

When the output is in the logic 1 state, the data sheet specifies that the device can source –400μA, and when an input is at logic 1, it sinks 20 μA.

$$\text{fan-out} = \left|\frac{-400\mu\text{A}}{20\mu\text{A}}\right| = 20 \tag{2.1}$$

Thus, when its output is in the logical 1 state, an SN74LS04 can source current to 20 similar devices.

In this case, the fan-out for the two configurations is the same. If the values were different, we would select the lower value as we see in the following example.

EXAMPLE 2.0

In the circuit in Figure 2.6, the device identified as the *Driver* has an output that is connected to a light-emitting diode (LED) circuit and is also fanning out to a number of other gates.

Driver When the output of the device is a logical 0, the warning LED is to be illuminated leading to current flow as shown by the arrow in Figure 2.6. When the output of the *Driver* gate is a logical 1, the warning LED is off and no current flows through the LED.

The devices have the following specifications:

Inverter	I_{IL} = –400 μA		
	I_{IH} = 20 μA		
Driver	I_{OL} = 24 mA	for	V_{OL} = 0.2V
	I_{OH} = –15 mA	for	V_{OH} = 3.5V
LED current	10 mA		

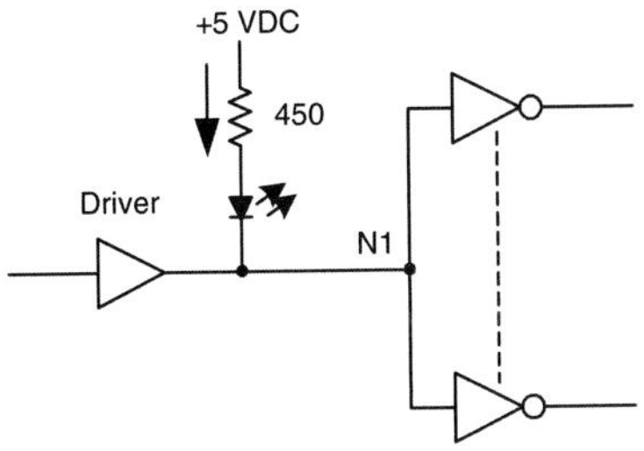

Figure 2.6 One Device Driving Several Different Kinds of Loads

To compute the fan-out for the driving device, we apply Kirchhoff's current law at node N1 for both logic states.

Logical 1

If the output of the Driver is in the logical 1 state, the currents will appear as in the drawing in Figure 2.7. Summing currents at node N1 gives the results shown in the figures.

$$i1 + i2 - i3 = 0 \tag{2.2}$$

Since the LED is specified as OFF under the current conditions:

$$
\begin{aligned}
i3 &= i1 \\
i3 &= 15\text{mA} \\
\text{fan-out} &= \frac{i3}{i4} \\
&= \frac{5\text{mA}}{20\mu\text{A}} \\
&= 750
\end{aligned}
$$

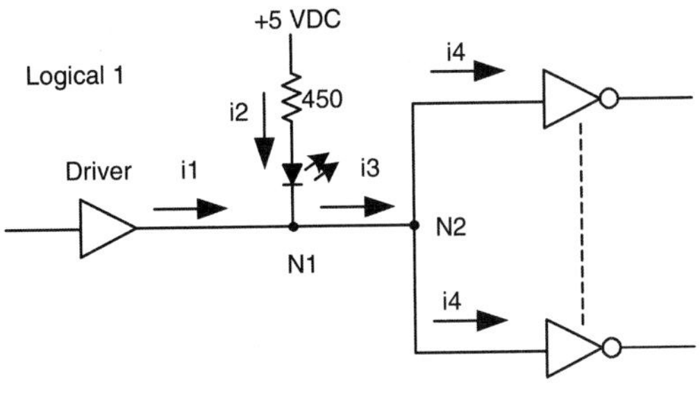

Figure 2.7 Driving to the Logical 1 State

Logical 0

If the output of the Driver is in the logical 0 state, the currents will now appear as in Figure 2.8. Observe that bubbles on the logic symbols are altered to reflect the logical 0 values on the respective gates.

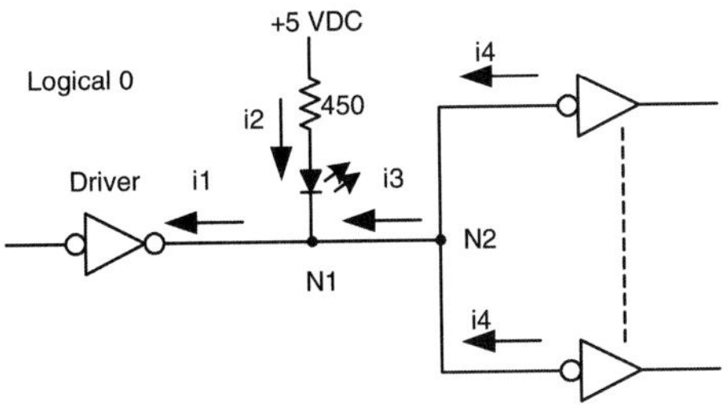

Figure 2.8 Driving to the Logical 0 State

Once again, summing currents at node N1 gives,

$$-i1 + i2 + i3 = 0 \tag{2.3}$$

For this case, i2 is not 0 and must be taken into account.

$$i3 = i1 - i2$$
$$i3 = 15mA - 10mA$$
$$\text{fan-out} = \frac{i3}{i4} = \frac{5mA}{20\mu A} = 250$$

In the logical 0 case, the driver must be able to sink the current from the LED as well as that from the collection of inverters. After the LED current has been taken into account, substantially less remains available for the inverters. As this analysis illustrates, in the logical 0 case, the fan-out is reduced to 250. Thus, we must use the smaller of the two figures in any design. The fan-out for the circuit is determined to be 250.

We now extend our two-switch device output model to incorporate the nonideal output signal levels by adding two resistors as shown in Figure 2.9. The resistors will model the ON resistance of the top and bottom transistors in the totem pole output configuration. When the device is sinking current, from Ohm's law, there will be a voltage drop across R2, giving an increase in the output voltage from the ideal case of 0.0 VDC. Similarly, when it is sourcing current, we will see a drop across R1 and a corresponding decrease in the output voltage from the ideal value of +5.0 VDC. The device input interface can also be modeled as a resistor network and voltage source as shown in the right-hand figure.

When the device is sourcing current, that is, the input signal is a logical 0, from Ohm's law, there will be a voltage drop across R3. Under normal operation conditions, the worst case current draw will occur when the input is at 0.0 VDC. The output signal level from the driver, V_{OL}, is generally going to be higher. Lowering the input signal level below 0.0 VDC can potentially damage the part.

Similarly, when the device is sinking current, there will be a drop across R4. Forcing the device to exceed the specified limit, once again, can damage the part.

2.2 A LOOK AT REAL-WORLD GATES—PART 2: TIME

In the ideal world, signal levels change from one state to another in zero time, and the effect of an input change on a device output is immediate. There is no delay. In the real world, signals take time to change state, and their effect on the output of a device will occur some time in future. Such delays and delayed behavior must be taken into consideration during design, particularly if signaling paths have tight time constraints. Under such constraints, one must carefully analyze the part's data sheet to understand the delays as well as to consider how any variations may affect the system behavior.

2.2.1 Rise and Fall Times

rise time
fall time

We define the time for a signal to change from one state to another as its *rise time* if the change is from a logic 0 state to a logic 1 state and as its *fall time* if the change is from logic 1 to logic 0. These times are specified as τ_{rise} and τ_{fall}. In real-world parts, these two values are generally not the same. In fact, there can be as much as a two to one difference.

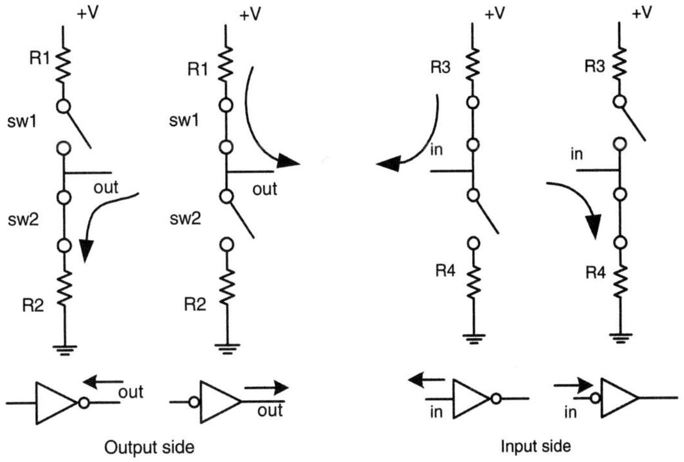

Figure 2.9 A First-Order Model for Device Input and Output Circuitry

The parameters, how we measure them, and their asymmetry are illustrated in Figure 2.10. Observe that we measure the rise and fall time at the 10% and 90% points of the signal.

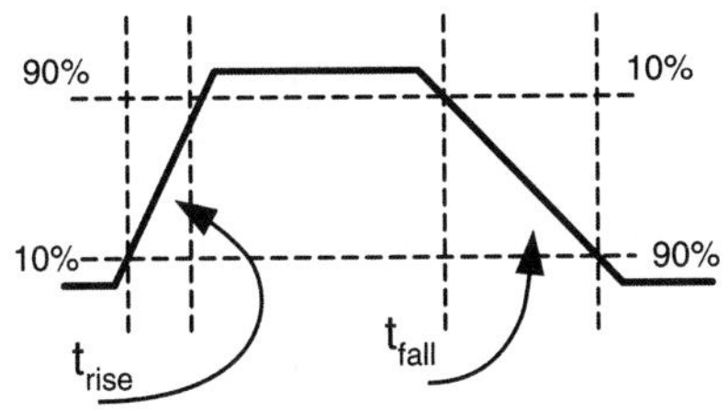

Figure 2.10 Digital Signal Rise and Fall Times

Rise and fall times that are too long can create problems. Under such conditions, the gate no longer acts as a switch; instead, it becomes a rather poor amplifier and enters what ***metastable*** is called a *metastable* region. We'll discuss this shortly.

The syntax for including rise and fall times in a Verilog device model is given as,

```
Syntax
  # (riseTime, fallTime) deviceInstance
```

The following code fragment illustrates the inclusion of such parameters in a part model.

```
parameter riseTime = 1;
parameter fallTime = 2;
not #( riseTime, fallTime) myNot (sigOut, sigIn);
```

2.2.2 Propagation Delay

The time required for the effects of an input signal to be reflected in a corresponding change ***propagation delay*** in a device's output is called the *propagation delay* of the part. In response to an input signal, the time for the output to change from a logical 0 to a logical 1 is often different from a state change in the opposite direction. The two different propagation delays are designated τ_{pdLH} and τ_{pdHL}.

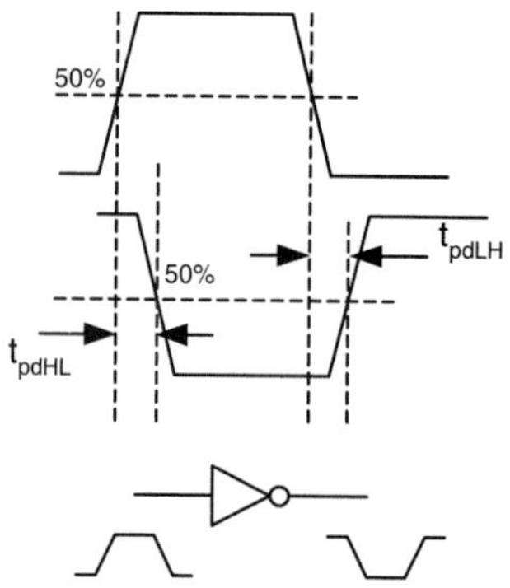

Figure 2.11 Digital Signal Propagation Delay

Propagation delay can easily be observed in an inverter. If a high going signal is set as the input into the device, the output will change to low sometime later. We measure that time at the 50% point of two signals. The parameters, how we measure them, and their asymmetry are illustrated in Figure 2.11.

In real-time embedded applications, one of the major design concerns is meeting time specifications. Although in some cases the concern is about a signal arriving too quickly, generally the focus is on trying to ensure that the signal arrives before a specified deadline. Thus, when modeling a combinational circuit, we use the longer of the two delays, specifying that value as simply, τ_{pd}.

The syntax for modeling such a delay in Verilog is given by

```
Syntax
  # delay LHS = RHS;    // RHS changes and is assigned to LHS after
                        // delay
```

The following code fragment illustrates the inclusion of a delay of two time units in a part model.

```
parameter propagationDelay = 2;
not #propagationDelay myNot (sigOut, sigIn);
```

Verilog also supports the inclusion of device rise time, fall time, and delay. The syntax is given as

```
Syntax
  # (rise time, fall time, delay) device;
```

The code fragment in Figure 2.12 illustrates the inclusion of a rise time of one time unit, a fall time of two time units, and a delay of three time units in a part model.

```
parameter riseTime = 1;
parameter fallTime = 2;
parameter propagationDelay = 3;
not #(riseTime, fallTime, propagationDelay)
myNot (sigOut, sigIn);
```

Figure 2.12 Modeling Rise Time, Fall Time, and Propagation Delay

When modeling temporal behavior in combinational logic, one must pose the following question: if a signal is entered into a combinational net and the state of the signal changes several times before the initial value can propagate through the net, what is the effect on the output?

transport delay
inertial delay

Two different propagation delay models can be used to study the behavior of combinational devices. These are defined as *transport delay* and *inertial delay*. The circuit's behavior is the same in both cases if the input makes a single state change (and no others) before the output propagates to the output. Under the *transport delay* model, the changes in input are seen by the output following the specified delay. The *inertial delay* model refines the notion of delay to attempt to account for the physical movement of electronic charge within a device. As discussed earlier, the voltage level within a device must reach a specified minimum level before it is recognized as a logical 0 or logical 1. The inertial delay model states that if the duration of a signal is less than a specified minimum, the signal state change will not be reflected in the device output. Such a duration is typically set to be less than or equal to the propagation delay of the device.

Figure 2.13 illustrates the two types of delay models in a simple device. Observe that the short-duration state change does not appear in the output waveform for the inertial model.

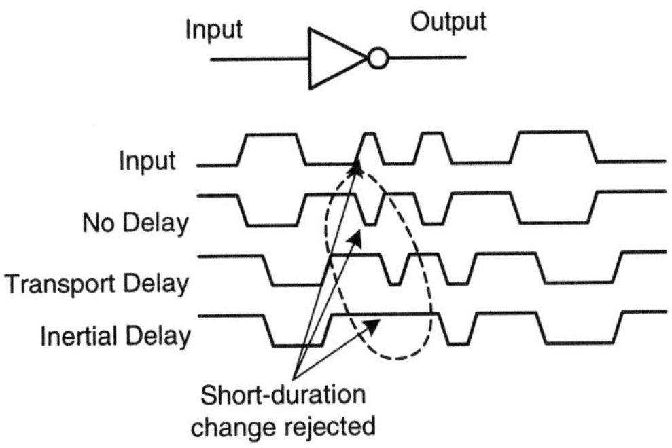

Figure 2.13 Two Models for Propagation Delay

2.2.3 Race Conditions and Hazards

A race condition occurs when several signals arrive at a circuit's inputs or common decision point (AND gate, OR gate, etc.) at different times. The different arrival times result from delays in through a circuit or system because of the different path lengths that a signal may traverse before reaching the decision point.

critical
noncritical
hazard, decoding spike, glitch
static, dynamic

A *critical* race occurs when the state or output of the circuit depends on the order in which several associated inputs arrive at the decision point. A *noncritical* race occurs when the state or output of circuit does not depend on the order in which several associated inputs arrive at the decision point. A *hazard* (called a *decoding spike* or *glitch* in the jargon of the field) exists in any circuit that has the possibility of producing an incorrect output. Two types of hazards, *static* and *dynamic*, are defined.

2.2.3.1 Static Hazard

static-0

A static hazard exists when there is a possibility that a glitch will appear on a circuit's output as a result of a race between two or more input signals when it is expected to remain at a steady level based on a static analysis of the circuit function. A *static-0* hazard occurs when

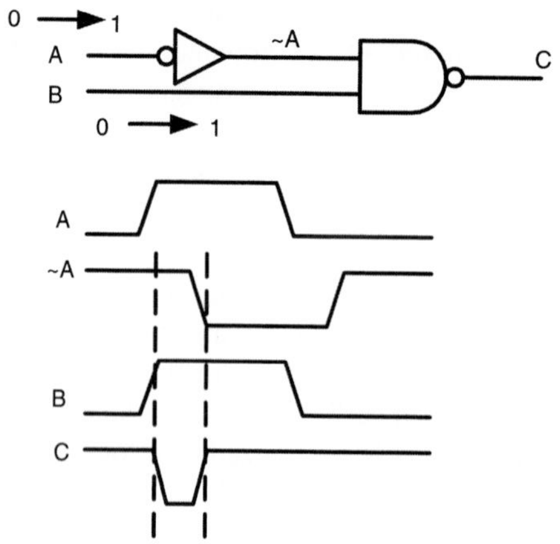

Figure 2.14 A Static-1 Hazard

the circuit can produce an erroneous logical 1 output when the output should be a constant logical 0. A *static-1* hazard occurs under the opposite condition.

static-1

Let's look at a simple example. The circuit in Figure 2.14 has a static-1 hazard. The circuits in Figure 2.15 give additional examples of static hazards.

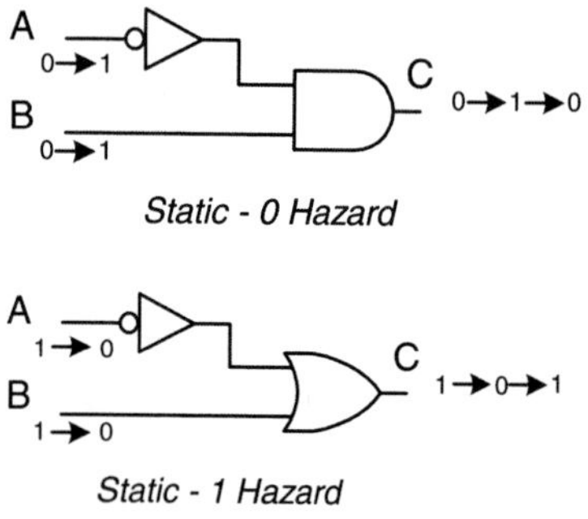

Figure 2.15 Logic Circuits Producing Static-0 and Static-1 Hazards

The Verilog modules in Figure 2.16 model the static-0 and static-1 hazards. We use such models to reflect real-world behavior when testing and verifying a design.

In the models, the extra delay through the path with the inverter leads to the hazards. The problem cannot be fixed by inserting additional buffers to try to match path lengths.

```
// Modeling a Static 0 Hazard
// A simple circuit comprised of an and gate and an inverter
module Static0 (o0, i1, i2);
// declare the inputs and outputs
    input i    1, i2;
    output  o0;
    parameter delay = 6;
// build logic functions
    not #delay inv0(ni1, i1);
    and and0(o0, ni1, i2);
endmodule
```

```
// Modeling a Static 1 Hazard
// A simple circuit comprised of an or gate and an inverter
module Static1 (o0, i1, i2);
// declare the inputs and outputs
    input     i1, i2;
    output  o0;
    parameter delay = 6;
// build logic functions
    not #delay inv0(ni1, i1);
    or or0(o0, ni1, i2);
endmodule
```

Figure 2.16 Modeling Static-0 and Static-1 Hazards

The natural variation in the values of electrical parameters across large part lots makes such an approach ineffective in mass-produced products.

2.2.3.2 Dynamic Hazard

dynamic

A *dynamic* hazard exists when the circuit output may erroneously change more than once as the result of a single input transition. The circuit in Figure 2.17 contains a dynamic hazard.

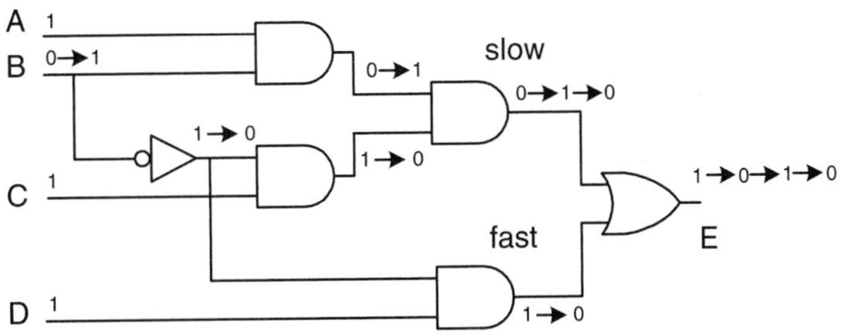

Figure 2.17 A Digital Circuit with a Dynamic Hazard

Observe that the path through a portion of the circuit is slow; that is, the propagation delay through the gates is at the high end of the specification. A second path comprises gates that have a delay at the low end of the specification. The remaining devices are assumed to have typical delays (which fall between the short and long delays) and to all be of the same value.

The quiescent conditions on the input signals are specified. We assume that the signals have been stable for a time that is much greater than the propagation delay through the circuit. The signal on input B is then changed from a logical 0 to a logical 1. The diagram illustrates the propagation of that signal though the logic. Observe that the output signal makes three state changes before it finally settles.

The Verilog module in Figure 2.18 models a dynamic hazard.

```
// Modeling a Dynamic Hazard
module Dynamic0 (E, term0, term1, term2, A, B, C, D);
// declare the inputs and outputs
    input      A, B, C, D;
    output     E, term0, term1, term2;
    parameter delay0 = 10;
    parameter delay1 = 5;
// build logic functions
    not #delay0 inv0(nB, B);
    and #delay0 and0(term0, A, B);
    and #delay0 and1(term1, nB, C);
    and #delay0 and2(term2, term0, term1);
    and #delay1 and3(term3, nB, D);
    or #delay1 or0(E, term2, term3);
endmodule
```

Figure 2.18 Modeling a Dynamic Hazard

2.3 A LOOK AT REAL-WORLD GATES—PART 3: THE LEGACY OF EARLY PHYSICISTS

Let us now look at a third factor that can affect the behavior of real-world devices. When we work with ideal devices, we are working at the macro level: we are taking a high-level, abstracted view of the device and its behavior. When we move to real-world hardware, we must begin to take a micro-level view; that view and that world are analog—at the end of the day, it's an analog world.

As the operating frequency of our embedded applications increases, our focus must increasingly shift toward a solid understanding of passive components, where they are, and how they affect the behavior of our systems. Such components include current, voltage, resistors, capacitors, inductors, wire (a special case of a resistor), and the behavior of each of them in both the time and frequency domains. Understanding the basic laws of electronics such as Ohm's and Kirchhoff's laws as well as the fundamental models given by Théve-nin and Norton is essential.

We know from Ampère's law that current flowing in a wire will produce a magnetic field. From Faraday's and Lenz's work, we have learned that a wire moving in a magnetic field has an induced current. From the work of Gauss and others, we recognize that charge and the potential difference between two conducting surfaces are related by a quantity called capacitance. From these, we see that Mother Nature and our physics colleagues are conspiring against us.

When we have adjacent conducting paths, capacitive and inductive physics couples signals from one circuit to the other. Any time we have two circuits, we have a mutual capacitance. Voltages in one circuit create electric fields; such fields affect the surrounding circuits. Any time we have two loops, we have mutual inductance. Current in one loop creates a magnetic field; such fields affect other loops.

Let's look at each of these fundamental elements and understand their effects on the behavior of the signals within a combinational logic network.

2.3.1 Resistors

We begin with the resistor. At the physical level we have a piece of resistive material such as that shown in Figure 2.19. The resistive material may be a physical resistor, a printed circuit trace, a wire, a pin on an integrated circuit package, a run of doped silicon or metal inside of an integrated circuit, or any number of other components or devices in our circuit. The resistance of the device is given in Eq. 2.4 by the basic formula from physics:

$$R = \frac{\rho}{A} \cdot L \tag{2.4}$$

where

R	Resistance
ρ	Resistivity of the material
L	Length of the material
A	Cross-sectional area of the material

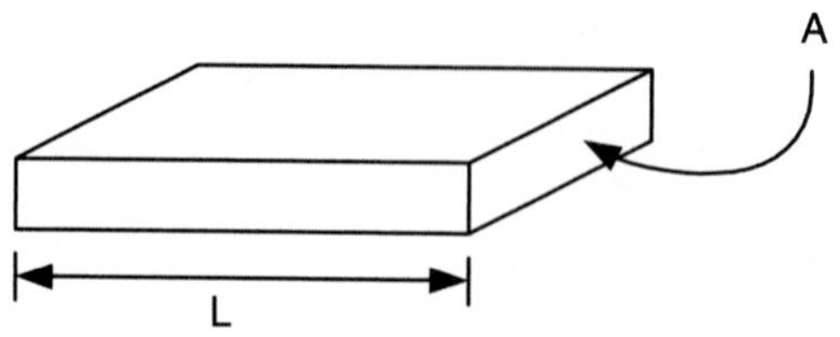

Figure 2.19 A Piece of Resistive Material

The key point expressed by the formula is that as the length L increases or decreases, R increases or decreases and that as A increases or decreases, R decreases or increases.

What such behavior means in the implementation of our designs is that as we make the printed circuit traces, for example, smaller and smaller, the cross-sectional area, A, of the current path correspondingly decreases, thereby increasing the resistance of the conduction path. When such behavior is coupled with the continuing effort to lower signal levels within the circuits, suddenly an increased voltage drop along a conduction path can begin to seriously affect the noise margin of signals throughout the digital system.

Routing a long signal trace through a microprocessor, gate array, or programmable logic device can have the same effect. As the length of the path increases, so does the resistance along that path.

2.3.1.1 A First-Order Resistor Model

parasitic devices

lumped system

distributed model

The network shown in Figure 2.20 gives a first-order model of the resistor. The inductor and capacitor are inherent *parasitic devices* (such as stray capacitance or the resistance and inductance in a piece of wire) with the typical values given. Using such a model assumes that the circuit as a whole can be treated as a *lumped system*. That is, a state change in any signal appears "instantly" throughout the system. If such is not the case, a *distributed model* must be used; all components in the model shown in the figure must then be expressed as a function length—R(x)dx, L(x)dx, C(x)dx.

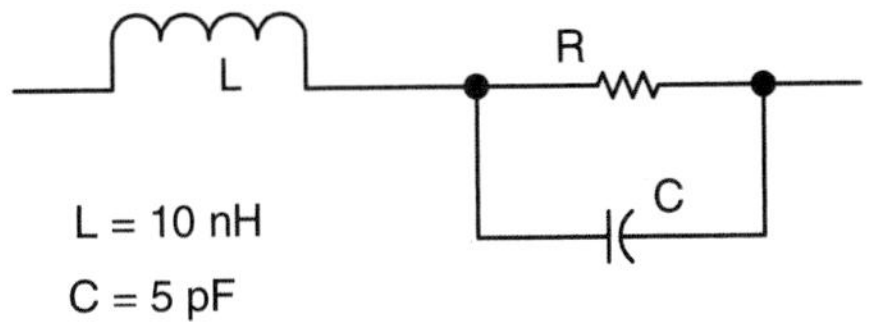

Figure 2.20 A Lumped Resistor Model

A quick analysis of the model for DC signals treats L as a short circuit and C as an open circuit. The circuit looks like a resistor. For time-changing signals, L now has finite nonzero impedance and C has finite impedance.

The impedance of the inductor and capacitor are given as

$$|Z_L(\omega)| = L\omega \tag{2.5}$$

$$|Z_{LC}(\omega)| = \frac{1}{C\omega} \tag{2.6}$$

Observe that if the frequency is increased, the impedance of the inductor will increase and that of the capacitor will decrease. As the frequency is increased further, the capacitor will eventually form a low-impedance path across the resistor, and the impedance of the inductor will then dominate that of the resistor. What had been a wire or resistor at low frequencies has suddenly become a frequency-dependent impedance.

The problem is actually more complex. If we write the transfer function for the network as a Laplace transform, we have:

$$\begin{aligned} Z(s) &= Ls + R||\frac{1}{Cs} \\ &= \left(Ls + \frac{R}{RCs + 1}\right) \end{aligned} \tag{2.7}$$

Evaluating the expression for s = jω and solving for the impedance and phase angle of the transfer function, we have:

$$|Z(\omega)| = \sqrt{\frac{R^2(1 - LC\omega^2)^2 + (L\omega)^2}{1 + (RC\omega)^2}} \tag{2.8}$$

$$\phi = \phi_1 - \phi_2$$

$$\phi_1 = \tan^{-1}\left(\frac{L}{R}\left(\frac{\omega}{1 - LC\omega^2}\right)\right) \tag{2.9}$$

$$\phi_2 = \tan^{-1}(RC\omega)$$

Checking the boundaries for the impedance, for $\omega = 0$, $|z(\omega)| = R$ and for $\omega \to \infty$, $|z(\omega)| = L$. These values are consistent with those that we estimated earlier. Because of the inductive and capacitive elements, we also get a phase shift through the path. The simple wire or resistor has suddenly become more complex.

If we now plot Z(ω) versus frequency for several values of R, we get the three graphs depicted in Figure 2.21. The values of R are given as 10K, 1K, and 0.1K, respectively.

The three graphs once again confirm our earlier analysis. As frequency increases, the impedance begins to roll off as the capacitor shorts out the resistor. At approximately 10 GHz, the inductor becomes the dominant factor and the impedance of the network begins increasing again.

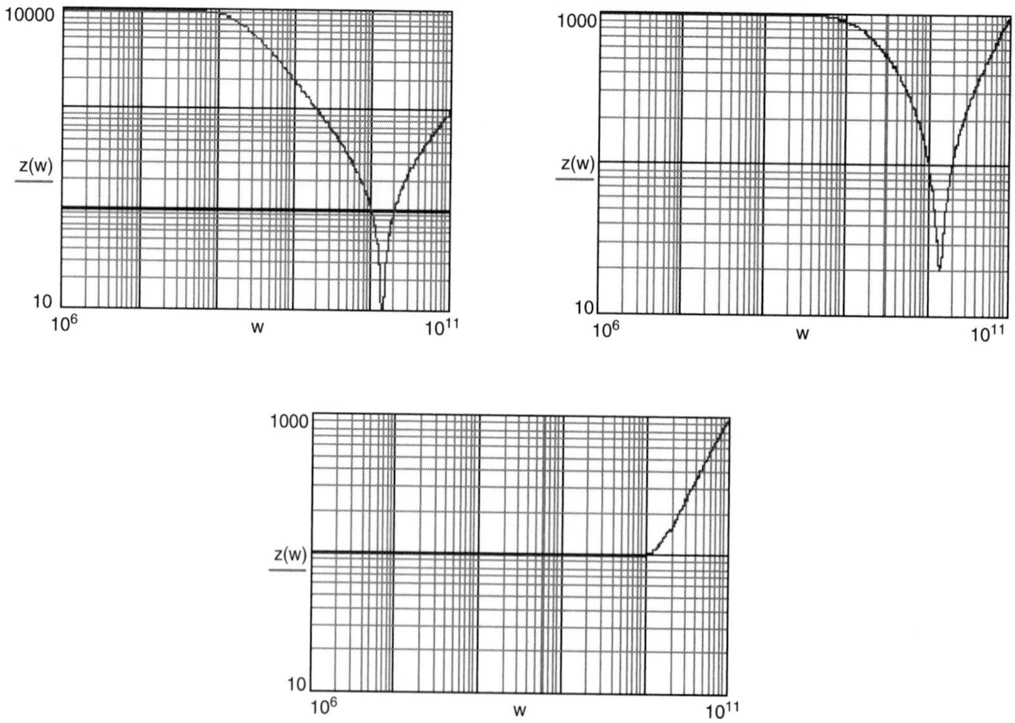

Figure 2.21 Plots of the Change in Value as a Function of Frequency for a 10K, 1K, and 0.1K Resistor

Such a phenomenon will have a significant impact on any logic circuits as the frequency at which the system is operating continues to increase and as the voltage levels at which it is operating continue to decrease.

2.3.2 Capacitors

Working next with a capacitor, at the physical level we have a device configured as two parallel plates separated by a dielectric medium as illustrated in Figure 2.22.

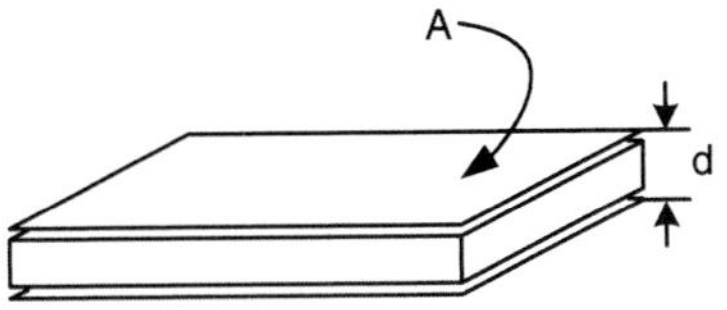

Figure 2.22 A Parallel Plate Capacitor

The capacitor may be a conventional capacitor, the device formed by the power and ground planes on a printed circuit board, the device formed by two parallel circuit board traces, parallel wires, adjacent pins on an integrated circuit package, P and N material inside of an integrated circuit, or any number of other devices in our circuit. The capacitance of the device is given by the standard formula from physics, Eq. 2.10.

$$C = \frac{\varepsilon A}{d} \tag{2.10}$$

where

C	Capacitance
A	Cross-sectional area of the capacitor
ε	The permittivity of the dielectric material between the plates
d	The separation of the plates

As with the resistor, the key point to understand from the formula is that as d increases or decreases, C decreases or increases and as A increases or decreases, C increases or decreases.

In a printed circuit, two signal traces can form the two plates of a capacitor. That capacitor appears as a parasitic device between the two signal traces we see in the drawing in Figure 2.23. As we continue to reduce the size of a design, those traces are moved closer and closer together; the distance between the plates decreases, thereby increasing the associated capacitance. Because the voltage across a capacitor cannot change instantaneously, a portion of the signal originating at the logic gate on the left will be coupled into the lower trace as noise. Routing any signal trace through a microprocessor, gate array, or programmable logic devices is going to produce the same effect to varying degrees.

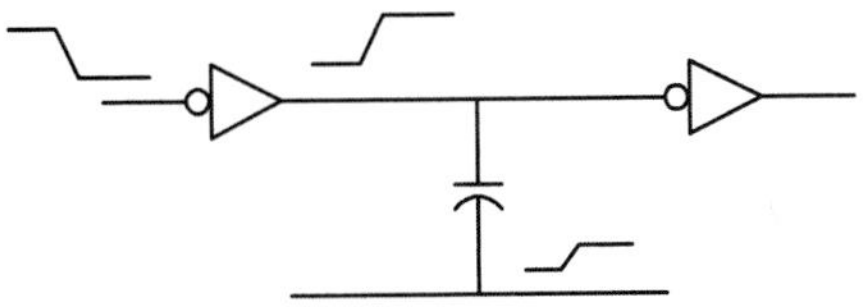

Figure 2.23 A Parallel Plate Capacitor from Two Signal Traces

2.3.2.1 Discrete Component Model

We can express a first-order model of the capacitor as the network in Figure 2.24. As we saw in the earlier resistor model, the inductor and the resistor are inherent parasitic devices with typical values given. The lumped model assumption we made for the resistor holds for the capacitor as well.

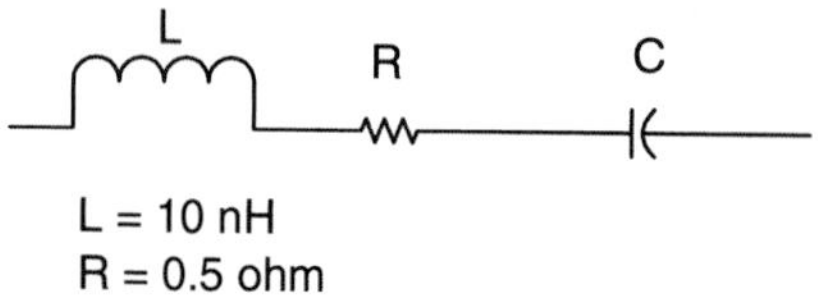

Figure 2.24 A Lumped Capacitor Model

A quick analysis of the model for DC signals treats L as a short circuit and C as an open circuit. The circuit looks like a capacitor should at DC. For AC signals, L now has finite nonzero impedance and C behaves like a capacitor.

As the frequency of an AC signal is increased, the impedance of the inductor will increase and that of the capacitor will decrease. We expect this latter change. As the frequency is increased further, the impedance of the inductor will dominate that of the resistor and the capacitor (whose impedance is decreasing with frequency). The component that initially behaved as a capacitor at low frequencies now behaves as an increasing impedance at higher frequencies.

Writing the transfer function for the network as a Laplace transform, we have:

$$Z(s) = \frac{1}{Cs} + Ls + R \tag{2.11}$$

Evaluating the transfer function for $s = j\omega$ and then finding the magnitude and phase angle for the expression, we have:

$$|Z(\omega)| = \sqrt{\frac{(1 - LC\omega^2)^2 + (RC\omega)^2}{(C\omega)^2}} \tag{2.12}$$

$$\begin{aligned} \phi &= \phi_1 - \phi_2 \\ \phi_1 &= \tan^{-1}\left(\frac{RC\omega}{1 - LC\omega^2}\right) \\ \phi_2 &= \frac{\pi}{2} \end{aligned} \tag{2.13}$$

The phase angle for the transfer function has been modified by the effects of the parasitic components from the expected value of $\pi/2$ from the capacitor.

Plots of $|Z(\omega)|$ versus ω for C = 1 μf, 0.1 μf, 0.01 μf are, respectively, given as illustrated in Figure 2.25.

Once again, the dominating effect of the inductor on the circuit impedance at higher frequencies is evident.

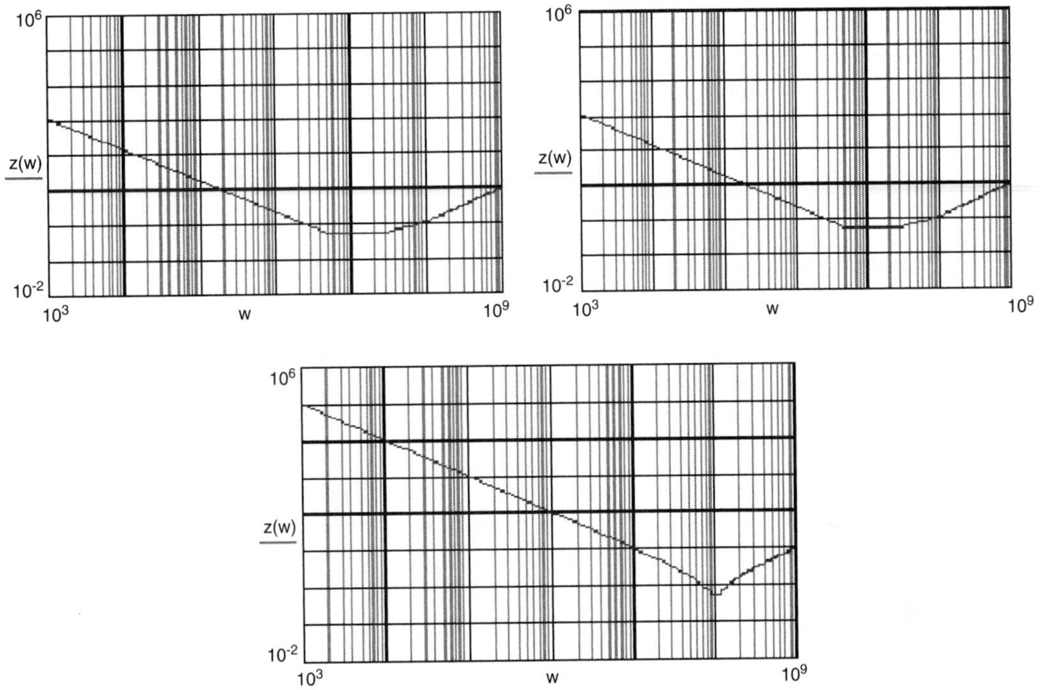

Figure 2.25 Plots of the Change in Value as a Function of Frequency for a 1-μf, 0.1-μf, and 0.01-μf Capacitor

2.4 LOGIC CIRCUITS AND PARASITIC COMPONENTS

Let's now examine the effect of parasitic components on the behavior of a logic circuit. We will use the basic logic circuit in Figure 2.26 for this analysis; the results extend naturally to more complex circuits.

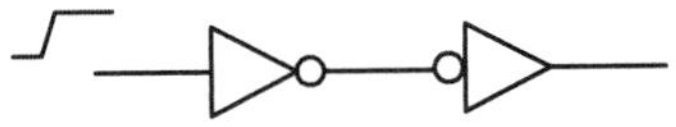

Figure 2.26 A Model to Study Parasitic Components

Our digital system comprises two logic devices that we model using two inverters. The source produces a typical digital signal such as one might find originating from a logic gate, a bus driver, or the output of a more complex device such as an FPGA or microprocessor. The receiver of the signal is any similar such device.

2.4.1 First-Order RC Circuits

We will begin with a first-order model for the devices, the environment, and the wire interconnecting the two devices as shown in Figure 2.27.

This basic model plays a significant role in first-order analyses of typical digital circuit behavior.

The resistor models the resistive component of the interconnecting path. The capacitor includes the contribution from the logical device, the wire, the integrated circuit package, and the coupling capacitances to other devices. The system can now be modeled as in Figure 2.28.

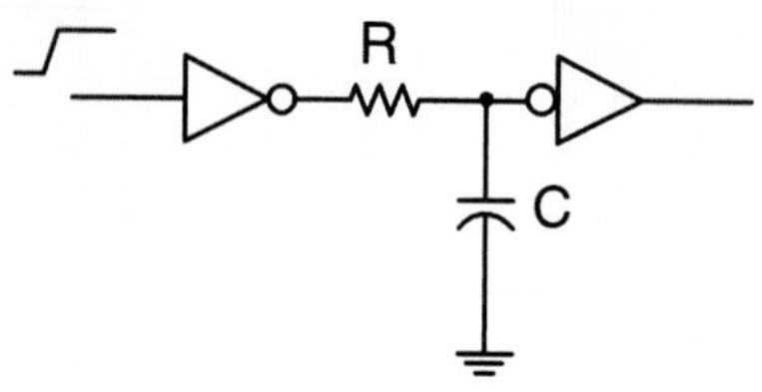

Figure 2.27 A First-Order Model for a Wire Interconnect

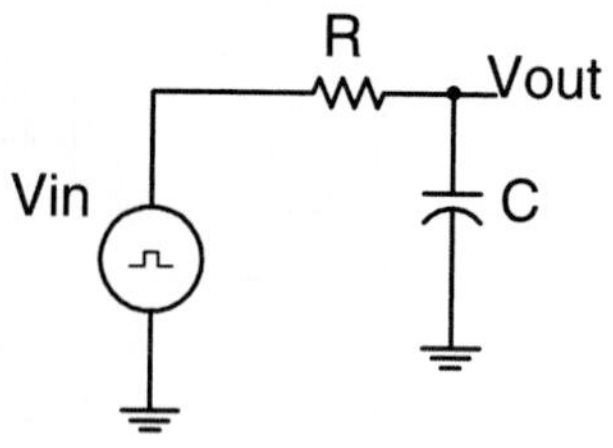

Figure 2.28 A First-Order Model for a Wire Interconnect and Driver

The signal generator serves as the source of the transmitted digital signal. The values Vin and Vout are related by the voltage divider formed by the capacitor and the resistor. The relationship between the input and output voltages, as a function of *s*, is given as

$$V_{out}(s) = \left(\frac{\frac{1}{Cs}}{R + \frac{1}{Cs}}\right) V(s)_{in}$$

$$= \left(\frac{1}{RCs + 1}\right) V(s)_{in} \tag{2.14}$$

If V_{in} is a step, as it will be for most digital signals, we have:

$$V_{out}(s) = \frac{V_{in}}{s}\left(\frac{1}{RCs + 1}\right) \tag{2.15}$$

Following a partial fraction expansion,

$$V_{out}(s) = \frac{V_{in}}{s}\left(\frac{1}{RCs + 1}\right) \tag{2.16}$$

Taking the inverse Laplace transform,

$$V_{out}(t) = V_{in}\left(1 - e^{-\frac{t}{RC}}\right) \tag{2.17}$$

The consequences of the two passive parasitic components are evident in Figure 2.29.

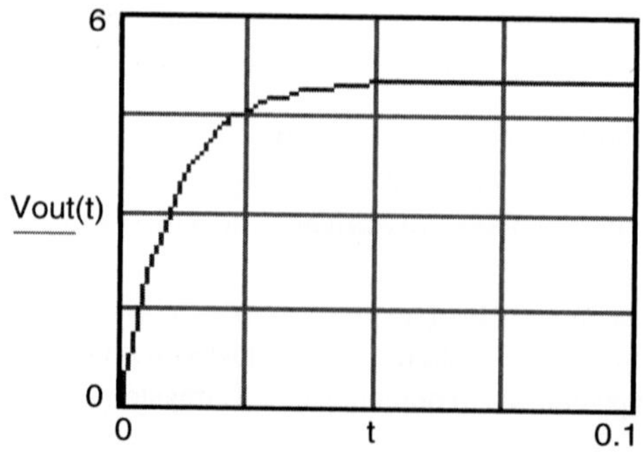

Figure 2.29 Plot of the Effect of the Parasitic Components on Signal Rise Time

The parasitic resistor and capacitor combine to slow the rise and fall times of the digital signal. The graph reflects the increase in rise time; the fall time will be similarly affected. With increased rise and fall times, there is a reasonable possibility that the logical device will enter a metastable state. The consequences of metastability include damaged components or a significantly reduced data transfer rate. We also note that the circuit under discussion is a first-order circuit; therefore, it cannot oscillate. Let us now examine three common situations in which the parasitic capacitor can have a significant impact on the behavior and performance of an application.

2.4.1.1 Tristate Drivers

The tristate driver is commonly used in bus-based applications to enable multiple different data sources onto a system bus. Let's analyze one signal of such a bus and examine how the parasitic device can affect performance.

The bus signal is presented in Figure 2.30. The capacitor models the bus, package, and adjacent path parasitic capacitances. This value will be approximately 50pf, and the typical pull-up resistor is 10K for TTLS logic. The parasitic contributions from the interconnecting wire do not contribute in this analysis.

When the sending device is enabled and is transmitting data, bus capacitance and wire parasitics contribute, as discussed earlier. In the circuit in the diagram, the driver has been disabled and is entering the tristate region. We model that turn-off as we did earlier.

When the driving device is disabled, the driven bus is now under the control of the pull-up resistor. We model that circuit in Figure 2.31.

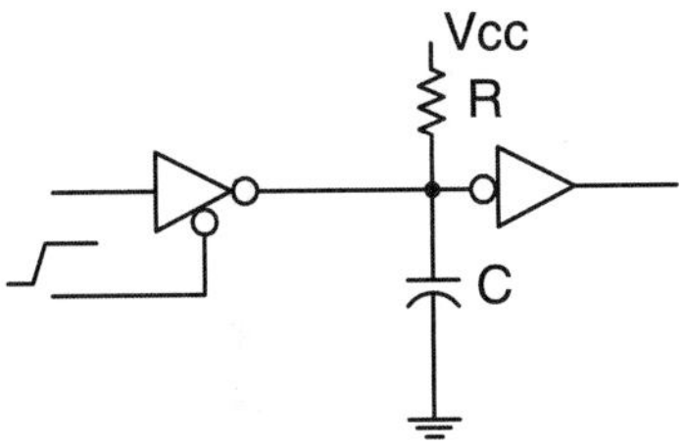

Figure 2.30 Parasitic Components on a Tristate Line

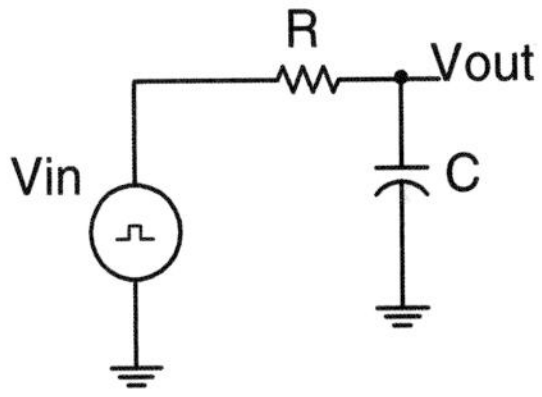

Figure 2.31 A First-Order Model of Parasitic Components on a Tristate Line

If the state of the bus was a logical 0 when the tristate device was disabled, the resistive pull-up voltage acts as a step input into the circuit. The signal, Vout—input to the driven device—will increase according to the earlier equations. The equation and timing diagram are given in Eq. 2.18 and Figure 2.32.

$$V_{out}(t) = V_{in}(t)\left(1 - e^{-\frac{t}{RC}}\right) \tag{2.18}$$

The consequences of the parasitic capacitor are evident in Figure 2.32.

Our earlier analysis concluded that if the signal degradation becomes too severe, the receiving device can enter a metastable region, potentially resulting in significant oscillation on the device's output.

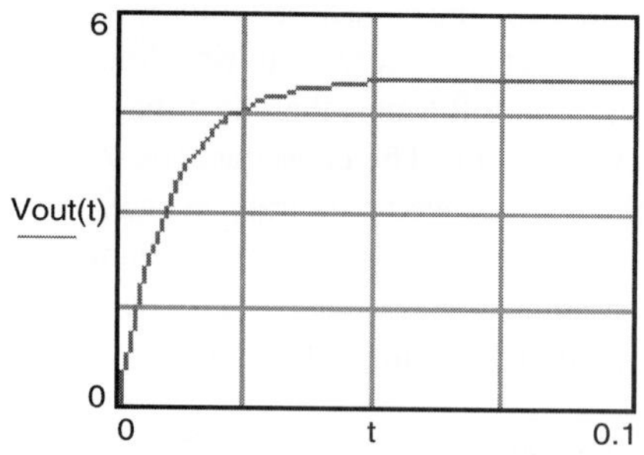

Figure 2.32 Plot of the Effect of the Parasitic Components on Signal Rise Time

2.4.1.2 Open Gate Inputs

floating

One should never leave gate inputs open or *floating*. How we define the state of unused inputs is as important as not leaving them floating. To understand why, let's consider a design that requires a two-input AND gate. Rather than add another component, the designer opted to use a spare three-input AND gate. The third unused input on the device can be managed in several ways. Figure 2.33 presents three alternatives. In theory, all three designs should be equivalent. Let's take a look at a more detailed model. In doing so, we will focus on the critical parasitic capacitors.

Figure 2.34 now adds those components.

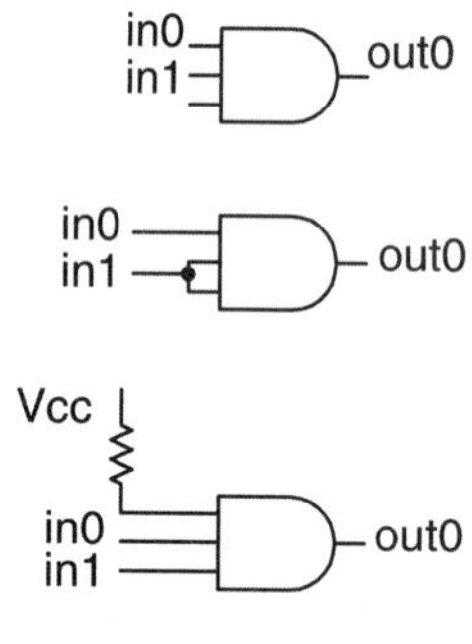

Figure 2.33 Managing Unused Inputs

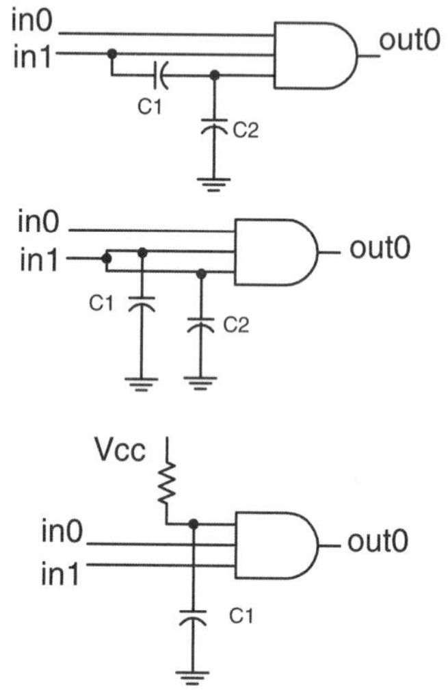

Figure 2.34 Unused Gate Inputs with Parasitic Components Added

The circuit in the first diagram has left the unused input open. The two parasitic capacitors, C1 and C2, form a voltage divider as shown in the circuit in Figure 2.35.

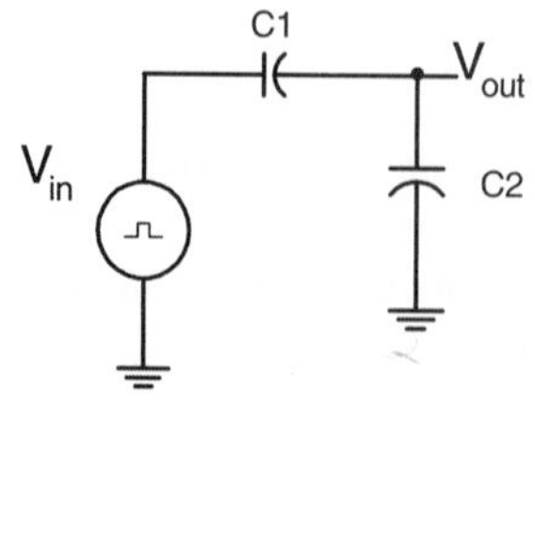

Figure 2.35 A First-Order Model for the Parasitic Components on Unused Gate Inputs

The resulting voltage on C2 is now given as

$$V_{out}(s) = \left(\frac{\frac{1}{C_2 s}}{\frac{1}{C_1 s} + \frac{1}{C_2 s}}\right) V(s)_{in}$$
$$= \left(\frac{C_1}{C_1 + C_2}\right) V(s)_{in} \tag{2.19}$$

If the voltage on C2 is sufficiently high, the AND gate will function as expected. If the voltage drops below VIH_{min}, the device will hold a constant logical 0 as its output state. Sometimes the circuit may work and sometimes it may not.

In the design of the second circuit, two of the inputs are connected together, thereby eliminating the floating input. Logically, such a practice will give the desired result. However, the two parasitic capacitors are now in parallel. Since parallel capacitors add, the net value is now C1 + C2. The voltage going into the device on the combined pins is now given as

$$V_{out}(t) = V_{in}(t)\left(1 - e^{-\frac{t}{RC}}\right) \tag{2.20}$$

where the value of C in the time constant is now C1 + C2. If the two capacitors have the same value, the time constant has doubled, thereby substantially slowing the rising or falling edge of the input signal. Doing so can induce metastable behavior when the device switches and can potentially damage the part.

In the third circuit, the design uses a pull-up resistor to define the state of the unused input. Although the parasitic capacitance associated with the unused input is still there, the value of the voltage stored on the capacitor is held at the supply voltage. It will cause no problems.

2.4.2 Second-Order RLC Circuits

Let's now extend the first-order interconnect model and add the parasitic inductance. With the introduction of the inductor, we now have a second-order system, as shown in Figure 2.36.

The driver and interconnect network can now be modeled as in Figure 2.37.

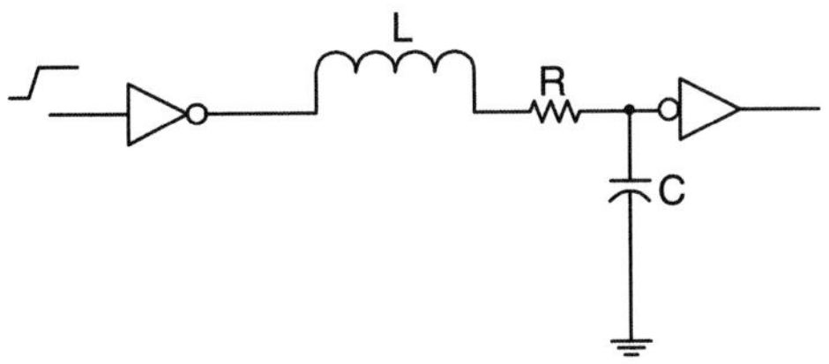

Figure 2.36 Extended First-Order Model, Including Parasitic Inductance

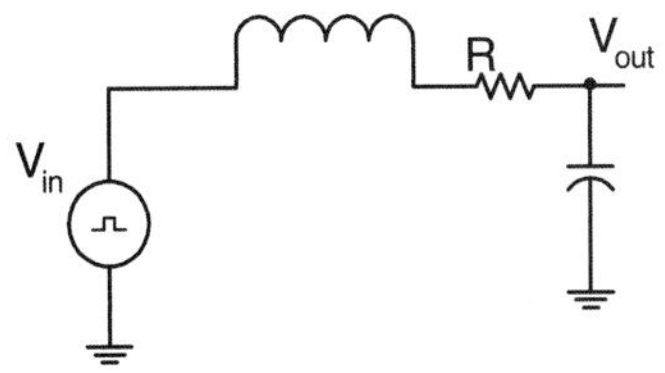

Figure 2.37 Extended First-Order Model of Driver and Parasitic Components

Once again we use a simple voltage divider to compute V_{out}.

$$V_{out}(s) = \left(\frac{\frac{1}{Cs}}{R + Ls + \frac{1}{Cs}}\right)V(s)_{in}$$
$$= \frac{V_{in}(s)}{LC}\left(\frac{1}{s^2 + \frac{R}{L}s + \frac{1}{LC}}\right) \tag{2.21}$$

The expression in the denominator on the right-hand side of the equation can be written in the form of the standard characteristic equation. Thus,

$$V_{out}(\omega) = \frac{V_{in}(\omega)}{LC}\left(\frac{1}{s^2 + 2\xi\omega_n s + \omega_n^2}\right) \tag{2.22}$$

The natural frequency and damping factor for the circuit are given as in the following.

$$\omega_n = \frac{1}{\sqrt{LC}} \tag{2.23}$$

$$\xi = \frac{R}{2}\sqrt{\frac{L}{C}} \tag{2.24}$$

underdamped
critically damped,
overdamped

The value of the damping factor, ξ, determines whether the circuit is *underdamped* ($\xi < 1$), *critically damped* ($\xi = 1$), or *overdamped* ($\xi > 1$). For a digital system, we want neither underdamped (possible oscillation and noise) nor overdamped (possible metastability) behavior. Critical damping permits the signal to reach full magnitude following a state change, the fastest of the alternatives with minimal overshoot.

The Q of a circuit is a measure of a circuit's ability to support oscillation. Good oscillators have high Q and vice versa. For this circuit, the Q is given as

$$Q = \frac{\sqrt{\frac{L}{C}}}{R} = \frac{\omega_n L}{R} = \frac{1}{2\xi} \tag{2.25}$$

If V_{in} is a 5.0 V step input and we solve for $V_{out(t)}$ in the time domain, we arrive at

$$V_{out}(t) = 5 - 5e^{-\left(\frac{\omega t}{2Q}\right)}\left(\frac{\sin\left(\frac{\sqrt{4Q^2-1}}{2Q}\omega t\right)}{\sqrt{4Q^2-1}}\right) - 5e^{-\left(\frac{\omega t}{2Q}\right)}\left(\cos\left(\frac{\sqrt{4Q^2-1}}{2Q}\omega t\right)\right) \tag{2.26}$$

Although the previous equation may seem a bit overwhelming at first blush, it is actually rather straightforward. Let's first look at its general form, which is given as

$$V_{out}(t) = V_{in}(t)\left(1 - e^{-\frac{t}{\tau}}\right) \tag{2.27}$$

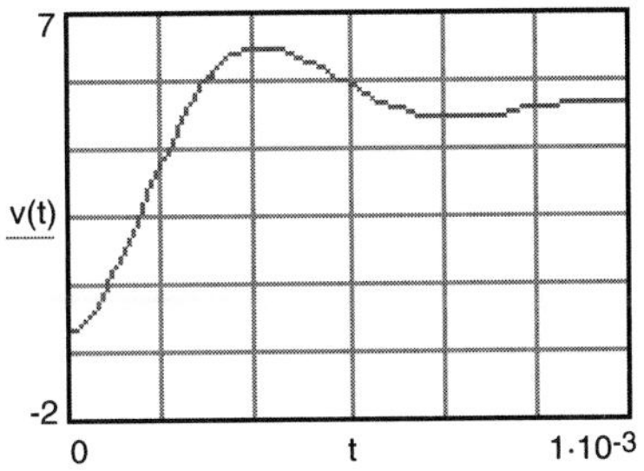

Figure 2.38 Plot of Step Response of Extended First-Order Model of Driver and Parasitic Components

That is, we have a damped exponential as a signal envelope. Within that envelope, there is an oscillatory behavior as given by the two sinusoidal terms. Thus, we have an exponentially decaying sinusoidal oscillation, as we see in the following plot of Eq. 2.26 in Figure 2.38.

2.5 TESTING COMBINATIONAL CIRCUITS—INTRODUCTION AND PHILOSOPHY

debugging
troubleshooting, testing

Debugging is the process of identifying errors in a new or modified circuit or system, and *troubleshooting* is identifying failures in a previously working system. *Testing* is verifying that any hardware or software modules, prototypes, subsystems, collections of subsystems, or the final integrated system performs as it was specified.

Once the initial functionality is confirmed, testing efforts shift to ensuring that the completed system meets all requirements and design specifications. Any system will change and grow with time as modifications are made or as new features and capabilities are added to satisfy new and changing customer requirements. As with the original design, one must make certain that the completed system, with all its new features and capabilities, also satisfy all specifications. Meeting all specifications means making certain that the original behavior of the system has not been modified in unintended or unexpected ways as a result of the changes. Finally, because no manufacturing process is perfect yet, we must make certain that the system functions properly after being built.

When we are thinking about testing and when we are putting test suites together, a good way to think about them is in terms of the amount of information that can be gained with each step. When a step within a test fails, what is it saying? What is the maximum amount of information that can be gained from the failure? When a test succeeds, what does it say about the circuit or system being tested? Are we closer to proving that it performs as we desire? If yes, then good. If not, then why did we include that step?

2.6 MODELING, SIMULATION, AND TOOLS

As we have seen in our studies so far, modeling and simulation play a critical role in the design of modern-day digital circuits and systems. We have learned about several different kinds of tools as well as how and when we apply them. When we move to test, those tools should follow; they are just as important during the test portion of the development as they were during the design portion. Today one would not think about attacking a complex design without modeling tools like Spice, VHDL, or Verilog. Test problems should be attacked with the same formal methods.

One can use models to break a problem down into parts that are simpler and easier to manage. During the early stages in the design of a circuit or system, models can serve as aids to understanding and dealing with the complexity of the problems to be solved. During test, models serve as aids in understanding the behavior of the hardware or software under faulted conditions and as guides in developing a solid testing strategy and the subsequent tests.

Faults and errors in the original design or those introduced during its manufacture are no different in their effects on the behavior of the circuit or system than the components that are designed into the system. We will look at how to begin to model such faults and the role such models play during debug and test of a design.

intermittent, transient faults

fault, failures

errors

Before we begin, however, let's look at the scope of our problem. The analysis and understanding of *intermittent* (existing only occasionally) or *transient* (occurring only once) *faults* require detailed statistical information characterizing how they occur and special tools for analyzing the collected data. We will begin with some of the relevant vocabulary before we proceed. A *fault* is any unsatisfactory system condition or state. *Failures* and *errors* are different kinds of faults. A failure is an (undesired) dynamic event occurring at a specific time. An error is static. An error is an inherent characteristic of a system resulting, for example, from a design mistake or oversight. A fault can affect a system in many different ways.

Faults may be random or systematic, and failures are typically random. When a failure occurs in a system, we now have a system that once functioned properly that no longer does so. Failures usually occur in the field when a hardware part breaks or wears out. Random faults can only occur in physical things such as an electrical component. We cannot design them away. Such is not the case for errors. Errors are inherent in the system as the result of a design oversight or mistake. They surface (generally at the most embarrassing times—frequently in front of our best customer) under situations such as unexpected combinations of inputs. Through careful design and thorough testing, one can catch most errors. One further tries to identify potential failure conditions through stress testing.

logical fault models

structural faults

functional faults

A design is characterized as static or dynamic; one does the same with faults in the system. Static faults are independent of time; dynamic faults appear as the result of transients and/or changing signals such as races. As we did in earlier work, we begin by modeling the physical faults. To do so, we develop *logical fault models* as abstract representations of the effect of a real world or physical faults on our system. With such models, one can identify those that affect the logical behavior of the system and those that affect its performance. One can identify the source of faults as originating from the interconnections among components, the *structural faults*, and those arising from within a component, the *functional faults*.

single-fault assumption

The *single-fault assumption* allows one to assume that when studying structural faults one is working with good components—those that are fault free and vice versa.

2.7 STRUCTURAL FAULTS

2.7.1 Stuck-at Faults

net

stems, branches

Within a circuit or system, a *net* is defined as a signal or collection of signals connecting two or more elements. Signal paths are made up of *stems* and *branches*. A stem is the origin of a signal, usually the output of a logic device. A branch is one or more signal paths that may fan out off a stem. A branch usually terminates at the input of a logic device.

stuck-at fault model

Structural faults arise from defects in the net interconnecting the components in the system. Such faults may originate at the stem of the net or at one of its branches. One of the models commonly used to study such faults is called the *stuck-at fault model*. In such a

stuck-at-one (s-a-1) ***stuck-at-zero (s-a-0)*** ***open*** ***short***

model, a signal is interpreted as either permanently held to the logical one state, *stuck-at-one* (s-a-1), or to the logical zero state, *stuck-at-zero* (s-a-0).

An *open* is a signal line that is designed to be connected to a circuit element or other signal line that is not connected. A *short* is a signal line that is not intended to be connected to a circuit element or other signal line that is connected.

Stuck-at faults generally occur because of missing or unintended connections of one kind or another. Examples might include an open circuit, an incorrectly connected wire, or a sliver of printed circuit trace material connecting a signal in a net to one of the power rails or to another signal in the net. In the latter two cases, one can assume that all components of the net are at the same logic level. In the first case, one cannot make that assumption.

An open circuit represents a special kind of stuck-at fault. The open may be the result of a broken wire, damaged printed circuit trace, or bad solder joint. The difficulty with such faults is that they can appear as a stuck-at-0 or a stuck-at-1, depending on parasitic connections to neighboring components or the physical characteristics of the device. Let's now see how such faults will appear in a design and how they can be modeled.

In the accompanying figures, we will use logic gates to model any conjunctive (AND) or disjunctive (OR) type of relationship and to illustrate the effects of stuck-at faults in each context. We assume a single-fault model; thus, faults such as a stuck-at fault on a stem accompanied by an open on a branch on that same net represent two faults and thus will not be considered.

2.7.1.1 Stuck-at-Zero Faults

Let's begin with stuck-at-zero faults. In Figure 2.39, we consider the simple cases of a logical AND, Circuit 0, and a logical OR function, Circuit 1. In the presence of the fault, neither circuit implements its intended logic function.

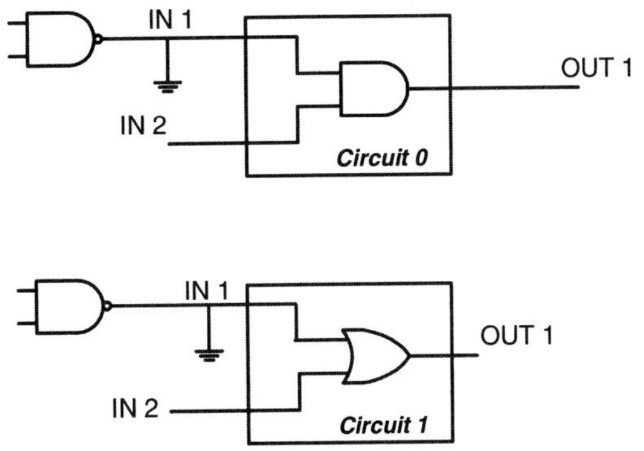

IN 1	IN 2	OUT 1
0	0	0
0	1	0
1	0	0
1	1	1

IN 1	IN 2	OUT 1
0	0	0
0	1	1
1	0	1
1	1	1

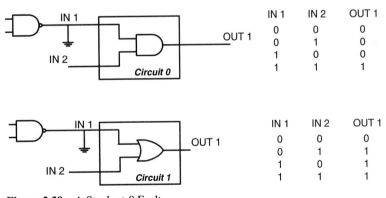

Figure 2.39 A Stuck-at-0 Fault

For Circuit 0, the fault has changed the implemented function from a logical AND to a constant logical zero while blocking the passage of any other signal through the gate. In Circuit 1, in the presence of the fault, the logic function has changed from an OR to a simple buffer; OUT1 is independent of IN1, and the circuit merely copies IN2 to the output.

Within the circuit, a net has two ends—its input side and its output side. Although apparently obvious (we can ignore the difference most of the time), such a distinction can be important for certain kinds of faults, as we will see later.

s-a-0 The *s-a-0* fault on a circuit input is modeled by opening the associated input line at the logical device then, as in Figure 2.40, replacing that connection with a short to ground.

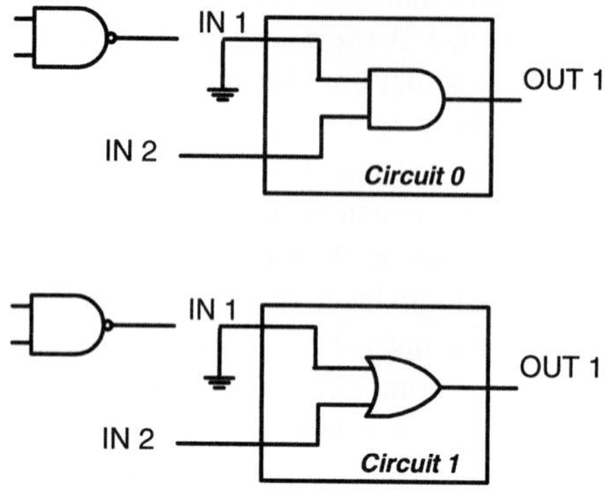

Figure 2.40 Modeling a Stuck-at-0 Fault

A stuck-at-0 condition on a circuit output (on a system internal net rather than on a board edge) can be modeled as a stuck-at fault on the following circuit input. The same fault on a board edge is modeled as a short to ground on the circuit output.

2.7.1.2 Stuck-at-One Faults

A circuit or system with a stuck-at-1 fault appears as in Figure 2.41.

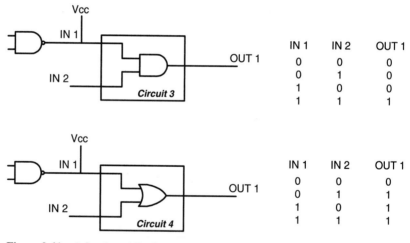

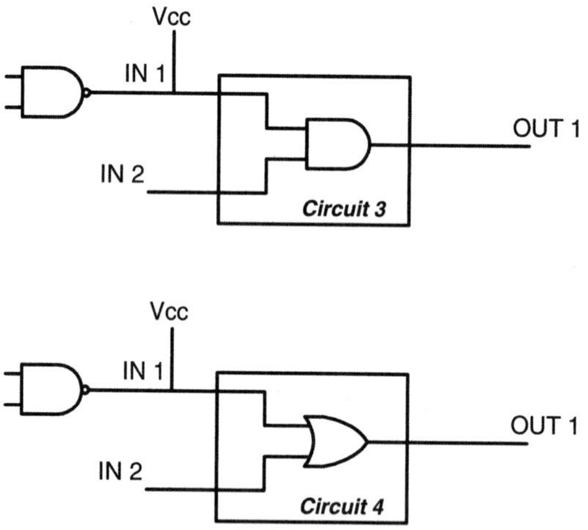

IN 1	IN 2	OUT 1
0	0	0
0	1	0
1	0	0
1	1	1

IN 1	IN 2	OUT 1
0	0	0
0	1	1
1	0	1
1	1	1

Figure 2.41 A Stuck-at-1 Fault

In the presence of a stuck-at-1 fault, the AND gate, Circuit 2, now functions as the OR did with a stuck-at-0, that is, as a simple buffer. It passes all signals that appear on the input IN 2. The stuck-at-1 on the OR in Circuit 3 is the dual of the stuck-at-0 on the AND. The signals on IN2 are blocked, and the output of the system remains a constant logical 1.

The model for the stuck-at-1 is similar to that for the stuck-at-0 and is shown in Figure 2.42.

The model for stuck-at-1 condition on a circuit output follows naturally from the stuck-at-0 model.

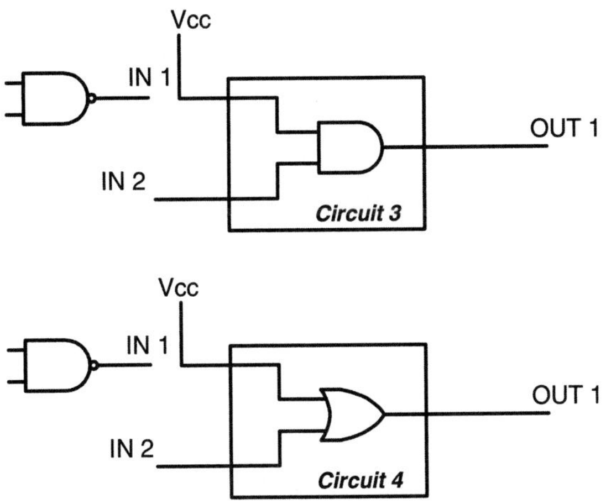

Figure 2.42 Modeling a Stuck-at-1 Fault

2.7.2 Open Circuit Faults

Let's now look at how an open circuit fault may appear in the circuit. We will use a standard CMOS logic gate driven by two different signals. The circuit includes the parasitic capacitor, C1, connected to IN2 as in Figure 2.43. The capacitor models the input capacitance of the package as well as any coupling to other traces.

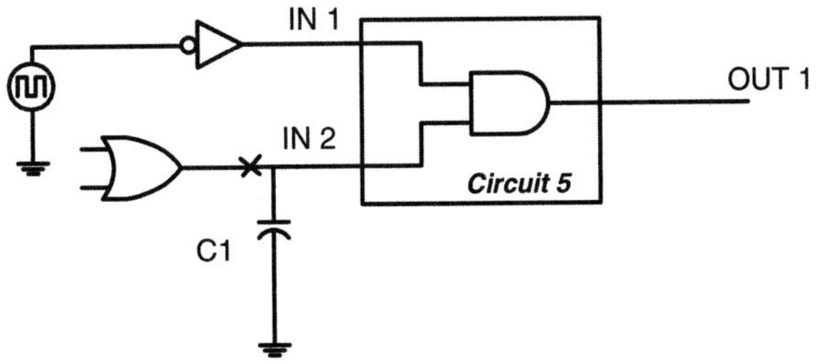

Figure 2.43 An Open Circuit Fault

If IN2 is a logical one, the signal on IN1 will pass through the gate. Next, hypothesize an open circuit in the signal trace connecting the output of the OR gate to IN2 and mark that with an x in the figure.

If the capacitor C1 can accumulate sufficient charge through parasitic coupling to enable the voltage on IN2 to rise above the threshold for a logical 1, the signal on IN1 will appear on the output, OUT1. The open appears as a stuck-at-1 on the IN2 net. On the other hand, once again, through parasitic coupling, if sufficient charge can be removed from C1, then IN2 appears as a logical 0 and the signal IN1 is blocked. The fault now appears as a stuck-at-0 on the net.

Identifying and isolating such faults can be a very difficult problem. The simple process of probing the signals during troubleshooting can affect the amount of charge stored on the parasitic device. After probing, all signals may appear to be correct. Only after some time will the circuit output return to a faulted state.

2.7.3 Bridging Faults

bridging faults *Bridging faults* add the next level of complexity to the fault models. As the name might suggest, a bridging fault forms a connection between two (or more) signal lines where none was originally intended. Bridging faults arise from bad solder connections or flakes from a printed circuit trace that may have been undercut during etch or an errant piece of wire. When a circuit trace has been undercut as shown in Figure 2.44, it is not difficult for the thin edge to break off.

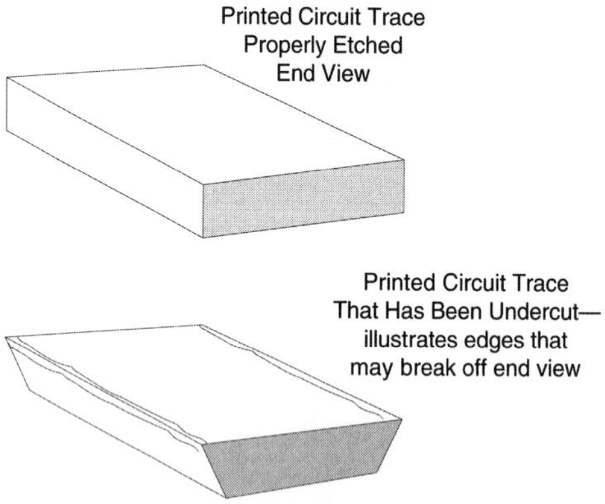

Figure 2.44 Bridging Faults

Bridges are typically defined as occurring between logic device (or subsystem) outputs, between inputs, or between an output and input. One can model such faults, as is done in the circuit fragments in the following logic circuits in Figure 2.45. The circuits illustrate a possible bridge on an input net and two possible bridged outputs.

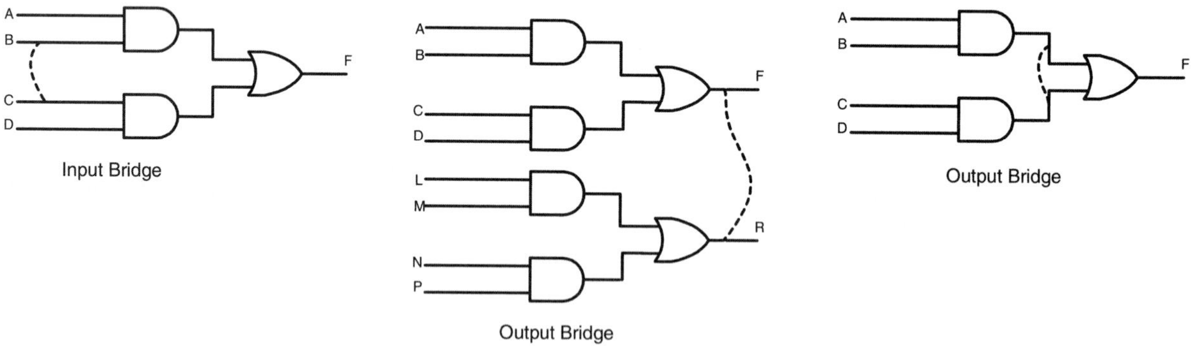

Figure 2.45 Common Input or Output Bridging Faults

The next two circuits in Figure 2.46 illustrate different possible feedback bridge configurations.

We will now look at both kinds of bridge fault.

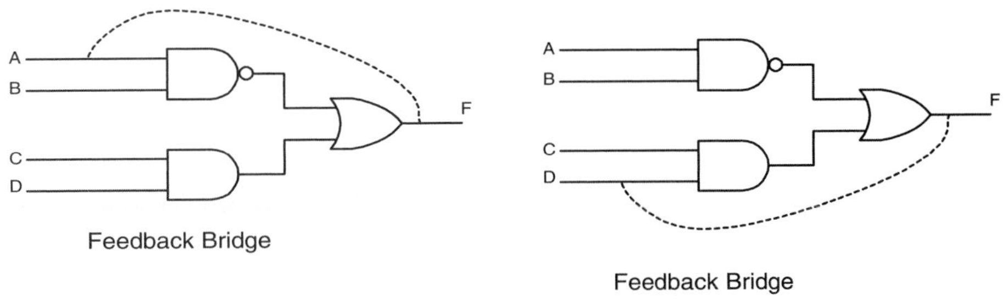

Figure 2.46 Common Feedback Bridging Faults

2.7.3.1 Nonfeedback Bridge Faults

Let's begin with nonfeedback bridge faults. These are the easiest to understand and to model. The simplest nonfeedback faults are those that bridge between a component input or output and a power rail (the supply or ground). Such faults are modeled using the stuck-at model as was done earlier.

The next level of complexity arises when the fault occurs between several signal traces or logic gate pins; the model becomes a bit more involved. Two cases must be considered. The first case is a bridge between two or more circuit inputs on a connector pin or card edge, and the second reflects an internal bridge between two or more signal traces or a bridge between several output signals on a card edge.

A bridge fault on an input signal on a card edge will only affect another card edge input. Such a fault can be modeled as a common signal going to both inputs. A bridge fault that is internal to the circuit involves the interconnection of several device outputs. Under such a condition, those outputs will be battling furiously. Devices with outputs in the logical one state will be trying to pull the signal high, while those in the logical zero state will be trying to do the opposite. The result of the fight depends strongly on the device and logic family. The more powerful (ability to source or sink current) device(s) will generally be more successful.

We can formulate a first-order model for such a fault by starting with the Thévenin equivalent circuit for the driving and receiving devices. Using TTLS parts, we will assume that only two devices are bridged. The model can easily be extended to other logic families and to additional devices comprising the bridge as necessary (with two more, we could have a foursome, but that's another game).

Here, in Figure 2.47, we show the Thévenin equivalent circuits for the two device outputs. Let's now assume that the device on the left is driving $Output_0$ high, and that on the

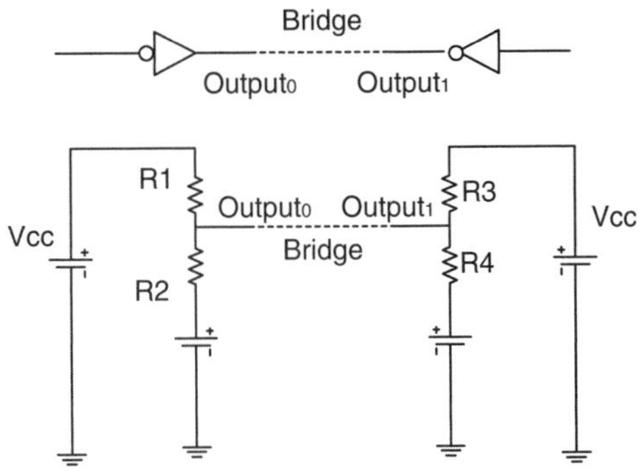

Figure 2.47 A Bridge Model

right is driving $Output_1$ low. Under such a configuration, R2 and R3 will be out of the circuit, and current will flow through R1 and R4 to ground. Using vendor data sheet specifications, we have a short-circuit output current of about 20 mA for a 74LS04. Furthermore, we can compute R4 to be close to 100Ω. As a first-order approximation, we can then compute the voltage at the bridge to be about 2.0 volts.

Such a fault can be modeled as a voltage source. The value of the source will be a function of the number of logical devices connected into the bridging net, the state(s) to which they are trying to drive, and the drive capability of each. Assuming only two devices are joined, one can use the value of 2.0 volts just calculated as a reasonable approximation.

A minor caveat should be given here. The value to which a combined output is driven when the device inputs are of opposite values strongly depends on the logic family(ies) involved. The value of the signal on a bridge between a TTL and a CMOS part will most likely be determined by the TTL part. In general, it is assumed that the more powerful part will win.

2.7.3.2 Feedback Bridge Faults

Feedback bridge faults are a bit more complex to analyze and model. Such a bridge transforms a circuit that begins life implementing a combinational logic function into one that behaves as a sequential circuit.

We will redraw the earlier two circuits in Figure 2.48 to illustrate the different possible feedback bridges.

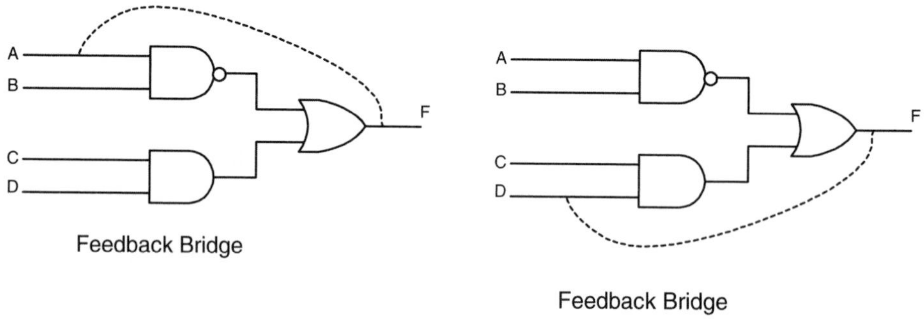

Figure 2.48 Feedback Bridges

The circuit on the left contains an odd number of inversions around the bridged path; consequently, it may oscillate. Such faults are difficult to model and to detect for several reasons. If the delay around the bridged path is short, the frequency of oscillation can potentially be quite high. At higher frequencies, the comprising devices may not be able to reach a full, valid logic level.

In general, the bridged input will also have its intended connection from the output of some other logic function. With the feedback bridge, once again, there are two outputs in conflict. We now have a situation that is similar to that discussed earlier for bridged device outputs.

The circuit on the right contains an even number of inversions and most likely will not oscillate. One can often analyze such faults using a stuck-at model. As with the inverting path feedback bridge, one can also have the situation in which several device outputs are in contention.

2.8 FUNCTIONAL FAULTS

Let's change the focus from static to dynamic faults. Dynamic faults are those that arise from the inherent manufacturing variations in the timing parameters of the parts as well as from the operating environment. Were all of the parts identical, one might stand a chance at being able to design dynamic faults out of the system. Such is not the case as we saw earlier. Even with identical parts, different (parasitic impedance) loading in the circuit is going to affect the propagation of signals through the system.

Hazards and Race Conditions

In ideal digital circuits or those operated at very low frequencies, propagation delays through the logic devices are nonexistent or are sufficiently small that they can be ignored. For such circuits, we look at a circuit's output only after the inputs have been stable for a long time relative to the delays in the circuit's electronics. Because of circuit delays, however, the higher speed transient behavior of a digital circuit may differ from what is predicted by a steady-state analysis.

race conditions, hazards

We learned about *race conditions* and *hazards* in our earlier studies in this chapter. The study of functional faults means thoroughly understanding both of these phenomena. One can model a hazard type fault in a number of different ways. One approach is to consider the gates to be delay free and then add a spike generator to the output circuit as we see in Figure 2.49.

Such an approach gives the ability to control the width, polarity, and timing of the hazard, independent of the model of the logic gates.

A second approach is to add delay elements to each conjunctive or disjunctive path. By using such an approach, one can closely approximate the propagation delays that each signal will experience as it travels from its source and through the net. Such a model is given in Figure 2.50.

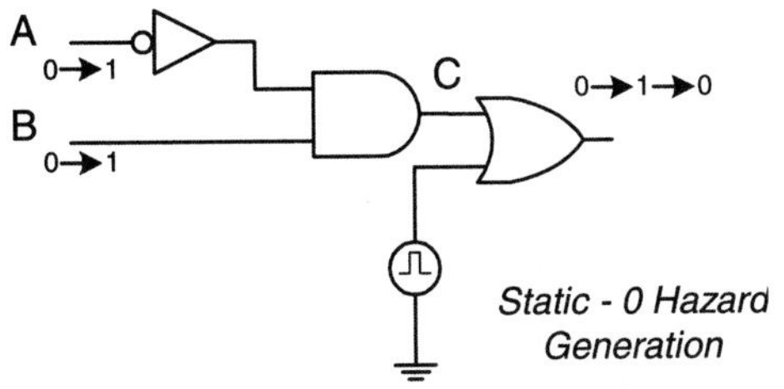

Figure 2.49 Static-0 Hazard Generation

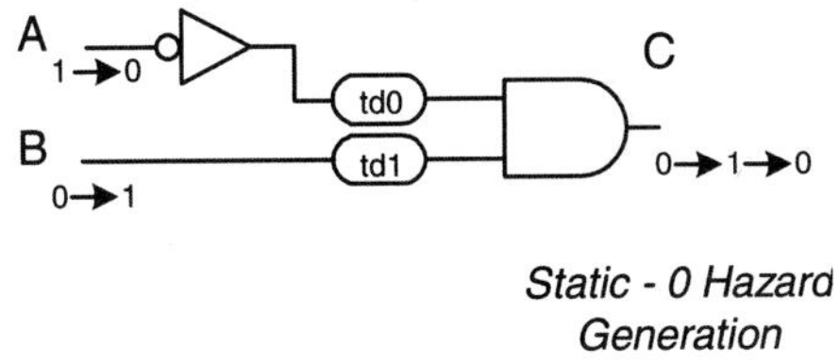

Figure 2.50 Static-0 Hazard Generation

Once again, we assume perfect parts. The two delay elements, td0 and td1, are inserted to model the path delays. By making td0 – td1 > 0, one can easily produce the decoding spike; by controlling the magnitude of the difference between the two delays, the width of the spike can be controlled.

At the end of the day, through proper design, we can eliminate most hazards. As we begin to push the speed envelope of today's parts, eliminating hazards through design becomes a bit more difficult project.

2.9 SUMMARY

We opened the chapter with an examination of real-world logic signal levels, their variability, and the effects of noise on those signals. We then studied the capability and limitations of one logic device driving other devices.

We moved from the static world to the dynamic where we learned that logic signals do not change state instantly and that they propagate through a system at different rates. Using the Verilog hardware design language, we modeled (portions of) our designs at different levels of abstraction to study such real-world effects. Delving deeper into the real world, we explored the first-order effects of passive parasitic components—the resistor, capacitor, and inductor—on our designs. We concluded by studying common faults in combinational logic circuits and how we begin to test such circuits.

2.10 REVIEW QUESTIONS

Real-World Gates—Signal Levels

2.1 What voltage levels typically define a logic 0 and a logic 1 today?

2.2 What voltage levels typically define a logic 0 and a logic 1 in the newer logics today?

2.3 What is meant by VOH? VOL? VIH? VIL?

2.4 Are the values for VOH, VOL, VIH, and VIL always the same for all parts in the same logic family?

2.5 What is meant by VOH_{typ}? VOH_{min}? VOL_{typ}? VOL_{max}? VIH_{typ}? VIH_{min}? VIL_{typ}? VIL_{max}?

2.6 What is meant by high-level noise immunity or noise margin? low-level noise immunity or noise margin?

2.7 Why is noise immunity important?

2.8 How is noise margin computed?

A Look Inside the Logic Gate

2.9 What are the major semiconductor technologies used in making integrated circuits today?

2.10 What is the output configuration commonly used in today's logic devices called?

2.11 What is the major difference between TTL logic and CMOS logic?

Fan-In and Fan-Out

2.12 What does the term *fan-out* mean? *fan-in*?

2.13 What is the difference between sinking current and sourcing current?

2.14 How do we compute fan-out? fan-in?

Real-World Gates—Time

2.15 What is meant by the term *rise time*? *fall time*?

2.16 How do we measure rise time? fall time?

2.17 Are the values for the rise time and fall time for all devices within a particular logic family the same?

2.18 Can we incorporate rise time and fall time values into a Verilog model? How?

2.19 What is meant by the term *propagation delay*?

2.20 How do we measure propagation delay?

2.21 Are the values for the propagation delay through a device the same for a signal making a transition from a logical 0 to a logical 1 as for a state change in the opposite direction?

2.22 Can we incorporate delay values into a Verilog model? How?

2.23 What is meant by the term *transport delay*? *inertial delay*?

2.24 What is the difference between *transport delay* and *inertial delay*?

2.25 What is meant by the term *race* in a logic circuit?

2.26 What is meant by the term *critical race* in a logic circuit? *noncritical race*?

2.27 What is a hazard in a logic circuit?

2.28 What is a static-0 hazard? static-1 hazard?

2.29 What is a dynamic hazard?

2.30 Why do we care about hazards?

Real-World Gates—The Legacy of Physics

2.31 How does the resistance of a piece of resistive material such as a wire or printed circuit board trace vary with length? diameter?

2.32 What is a parasitic device in a logic circuit?

2.33 What components make up the first-order model of a resistor? Which of these are consider to be parasitic devices?

2.34 What is meant by the term *lumped model*? *distributed model*?

2.35 What are the major effects of the parasitic devices in the first-order resistor model?

2.36 How does the capacitance between two parallel plates such as two printed circuit board traces or the power and ground planes in a logic circuit vary with the separation of the plates? the cross-sectional area of the plates?

2.37 What components make up the first-order model of a capacitor? Which of these are considered to be parasitic devices?

2.38 What are the major effects of the parasitic devices in the first-order capacitor model?

2.39 A wire can be modeled by the first-order circuit in Figure 2.27. Based on such a model, how is a digital signal transmitted through the wire affected?

2.40 What is meant by a floating gate input?

2.41 What is the best way to manage floating gate inputs?

2.42 A wire can be modeled by the second-order circuit in Figure 2.36. Based on such a model, how is a digital signal transmitted through the wire affected?

2.43 What is meant by the term *underdamped*? *critically damped*? *overdamped*?

Testing Combinational Circuits

2.44 What do we mean by the term *debugging*? *troubleshooting*? *testing*?

2.45 What are the main reasons we test an embedded system or its components?

2.46 What is a fault?

2.47 What is the difference between a failure and an error?

2.48 What are intermittent or transient faults?

2.49 What is a logical fault model, and why do we develop such a thing?

2.50 What are structural faults? functional faults?

2.51 What is the single-fault assumption?

2.52 What is the stuck-at fault model, and how do we use it?

2.53 What is a bridging fault, and what are some the things that may cause them?

2.54 Identify and describe several different kinds of bridge fault.

2.11 THOUGHT QUESTIONS

Real-World Gates—Signal Levels

2.1 Can an embedded design use logic devices from different families, for example, CMOS and TTL? If not, why not? If so, what important factors should one consider?

2.2 The minimum high-output logic level is specified by VOH_{min} and the maximum low output logic level is specified by VOL_{max}. What are the consequences of violating these specifications?

2.3 The minimum high-input logic level is specified by VIH_{min}, and the maximum low input logic level is specified by VIL_{max}. Will a logic device work if the input signal is lower than VIH_{min} or higher than VIL_{max}?

2.4 If a logic device operates properly under the conditions described in Question 2.3, can such behavior be assumed for all devices in that family? Why or why not? If not, why did the device operate correctly?

2.5 If a sample of 15 logic devices operates properly under the conditions described in Question 2.3, can such behavior be assumed for all devices in that family? Why or why not? If not, why did the devices operate correctly?

2.6 Can an embedded system be considered to be properly designed if a lower value of noise immunity than computed from the data sheet information is accepted? Why or why not?

2.7 Under what conditions would a decision such as that described in Question 2.6 be acceptable?

A Look Inside the Logic Gate

2.8 In an open drain or open collector device, the top transistor in the output totem pole is left off. Why would we want to use such a device?

2.9 What is the major difference between an open drain/collector device and a tristate device?

2.10 What are the pros and cons of using an open drain/collector device versus a tristate device?

2.11 Can an open drain/collector device be used on a tristate bus? Why or why not?

Fan-In and Fan-Out

2.12 Can the calculated fan-out of a logical device be exceeded? If not so, why? If so, what are the consequences of doing so?

2.13 Can a design such as that described in Question 2.12 be considered to be a good design? If not, why not and if so, why?

2.14 Where on a device data sheet would one look to find information supporting a decision such as that described in Question 2.12 and the consequences of such a decision?

2.15 How do we compute fan-out for devices from one logic family driving a different logic family? fan-in?

Real-World Gates—Time

2.16 What are the consequences of increasing the rise time or a logic signal? the fall time?

2.17 Do the consequences of the situation described in Question 2.16 change as the frequency of the input signal changes?

2.18 What are the consequences on the output of a logical device of the rise time of an input signal being longer (shorter) than the fall time?

2.19 Do the consequences of the situation described in Question 2.18 change as the frequency of the input signal changes?

2.20 What are the effects on the output of a logical device of propagation delay through the device?

2.21 How do the effects of propagation delay through a logical device change with increasing (decreasing) frequency?

2.22 How is the output of a device affected if the propagation delay through the device is longer (shorter) for a signal making a transition from a logical 0 to a logical 1? Under the same circumstances, how is the output affected, for a state change in the opposite direction?

2.23 If a logical circuit has a critical race condition, can that race be corrected by using additional logic gates to match the lengths of the delay paths causing the race? Why or why not?

2.24 How can one correct a critical race condition without matching delay path lengths?

Real-World Gates—The Legacy of Physics

2.25 How does the resistance of a piece of material such as a wire or printed circuit board trace affect the temporal behavior of a signal passing through the material?

2.26 Using the first-order RC model of a wire described in Figure 2.27, what is the effect on the temporal behavior of a signal being driven from an open drain/collector device?

2.27 Using the first-order RC model of a wire described in Figure 2.27, what is the effect on the temporal behavior of a signal being driven from a tristate device?

2.28 Using the first-order RC model of a wire described in Figure 2.27, what is the effect on the temporal behavior of a signal being driven into that wire from a device with a totem pole output configuration?

2.29 What are some of the possible effects on the output of a logic gate if one (or more) of the device input(s) is floating?

2.30 Do the effects described in Question 2.29 change if the logical device is implemented using CMOS technology? TTL technology?

2.31 Do the effects described in Question 2.29 change if the frequency of the input signal is increased? decreased?

Testing Combinational Circuits

2.32 When we are troubleshooting an embedded subsystem or system, what fundamental assumptions can we make?

2.33 When we are testing an embedded subsystem or system, what fundamental assumptions can we make?

2.34 When we are debugging an embedded subsystem or system, what fundamental assumptions can we make?

2.35 Consider that we are debugging a circuit of subsystem and we encounter an intermittent or transient fault. We replace one or two parts and the problem goes away. Can we assume that the parts that we replaced were bad? If not, why not?

2.36 If we have been debugging two modules and have now concluded that both are working perfectly, it is now time to integrate them into a larger subsystem. Can we assume that the subsystem will work as intended? Why or why not?

2.37 If, as a result of the debugging process, we conclude that a newly integrated system has no structural faults, can we assume that it also contains no functional faults? Why or why not?

2.38 Is the single-fault assumption reasonable in most cases? When might it not be valid?

2.39 When troubleshooting a failed system, is it reasonable to assume that there are no stuck-at faults? bridge faults?

2.12 PROBLEMS

Digital Signals—Levels and Parasitics

2.1 A friend has shown you his clever new design for turning on lamps remotely. He plans to build and sell hundreds of these and has asked you what you think of his design shown in Figure P2.51.

He describes its operation as follows: When the *Lamp ON* signal is a logical 0, the relay closes and the lamp turns ON. When the *Lamp ON* signal is a logical 1, the relay opens and the lamp turns OFF.

He says the circuit works well, but that his vendor is supplying some bad parts and that sometimes the relay will not close.

(a) Using the data that follows, you analyze the circuit and discover that there is a problem with the design. Use the results of your analysis to explain what it might be.

SN 74LS04	$I_{OL} = 8\ mA\ @\ V_{OL} = 0.2V$
	$I_{OH} = -400\ \mu A\ @\ V_{OH} = 3.5V$
Relay	$I_{CLOSE} = 375\mu A \pm 10\%@\ V = 3.5V$

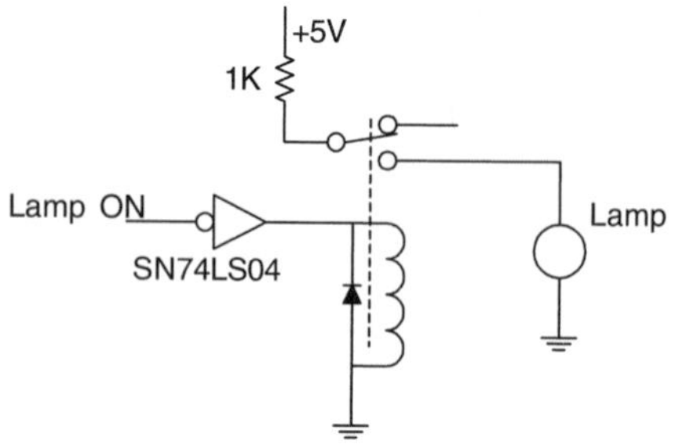

Figure P2.51

(b) Based on your analysis, propose a way to correct the design. Explain why your modification fixes the design error.

2.2 A colleague designed the circuit in Figure P2.52 in which an inverter is used to drive a single light-emitting diode (LED) as a component in an annunciation subsystem of a project currently under development. At the moment, she is in Paris talking with the customer about new features to be incorporated into the project.

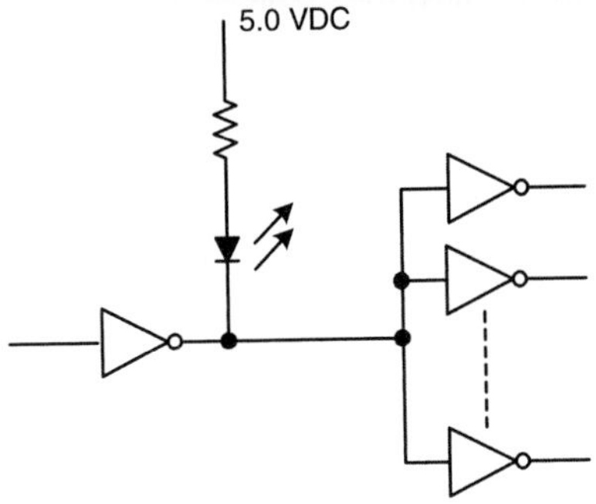

Figure P2.52

As part of the process of designing the circuit, she was considering several different logic families, but she did not get the chance to complete her analysis and so has asked if you would help while she was gone. Her notes indicate that she was considering the following logic families and configurations:

Driver	Receiver
74LS04	74LS04
74LS04	74HC04
74S04	74HCT04
74HCT04	74ALS04

Her notes also specify the LED currents as

LED	ON	3.0 mA	V_{OL} on the cathode
	OFF	50 μA leakage	V_{OH} on the cathode

To complete her analysis,

(a) Identify and label all of the currents in the circuit above if the input signal to the circuit above is a logical 1.

(b) Identify and label all of the currents in the circuit above if the input signal to the circuit above is a logical 0.

(c) For each of the combinations she has listed above, based on vendor data sheets, what is the maximum number of gates we can drive and still meet the vendor's specifications if the input signal is a logical 1? logical 0?

(d) What is the worst case noise margin for each configuration and for each logic state?

2.3 As part of a design review of a larger system, you decide to analyze the circuit shown in Figure P2.53. The design review package includes the following information from the vendor's data sheets:

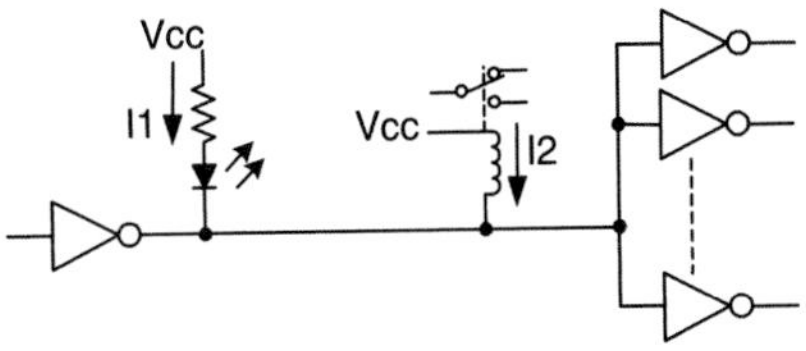

Figure P2.53

I_{OH}	–400 μA	@ V_{OH} = 3.4 V
I_{OL}	4.0 mA	@ V_{OL} = 0.4 V
I_{IH}	20 μA	@ V_{OH} = 3.4 V
I_{IL}	–500 μA	@ V_{OL} = 0.4 V
LED	ON	1.25 mA
	OFF (leakage)	1 μA
Relay	ON	1.5 mA
	OFF	0 μA

The design specifications require that, in addition to the relay and LED, the circuit must be able to drive four other gates. Determine if the design meets the specified requirements.

2.4 A warning annunciator is needed in a design that you are working on. In a discussion with several of your colleagues, several say the two circuits given in Figure P2.54 are equivalent, others say that the one on the left is better, while the remainder recommend the one on the left.

Assume that the driver is an SN74LS04 and that the diode requires 1.25 mA to turn on. To settle the debate, you decide to do a complete analysis of the circuit.

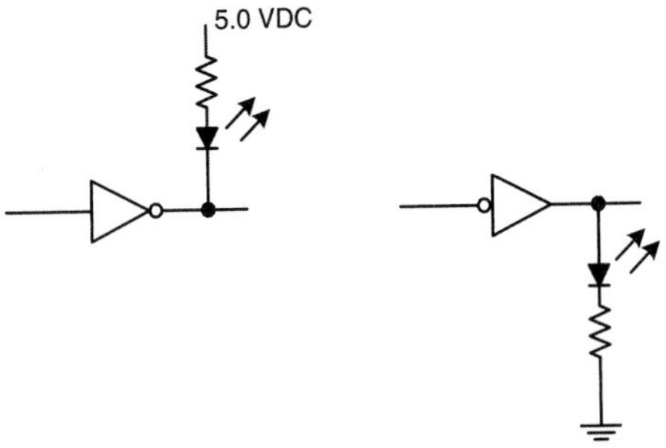

Figure P2.54

(a) Based on your analysis, which configuration will give the brighter light?

(b) Which configuration will consume more power?

(c) What are the noise margins for the two configurations if one additional SN74LS04 device is to be driven?

2.5 When using tristate bus drivers, one must ensure that the circuit being driven is never left with a floating or open input. The following two bus fragments in Figure P2.55 illustrate two of the commonly used ways to ensure that the state of the bus is defined when the driver is disabled.

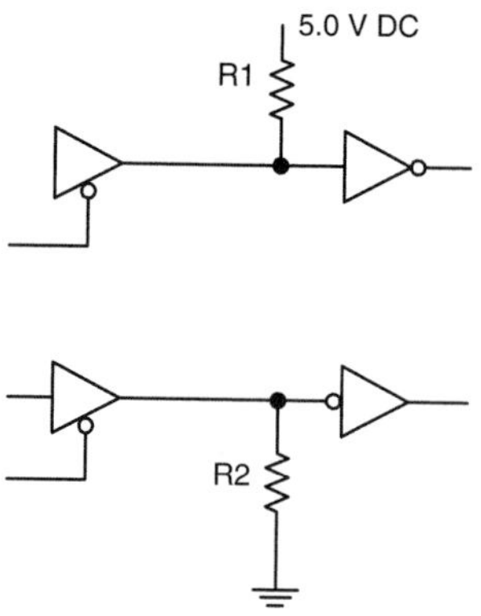

Figure P2.55

Assume that the driver is a 74LS244 and the inverter is a 74LS04. Analyze the two circuits and select the values for the two resistors to

(a) Minimize power dissipation in the resistor when the signal from the driver is in the high state, low state, and tristate.

(b) Maximize the noise margin when the signal from the driver is in the high state, low state, and tristate.

2.6 Using the first-order model for a bus wire discussed in the text and your values for the resistors from Problem 2.5, determine the following:

(a) For the design in the top figure, assume that the bus signal is in the logical 0 state and the driver is disabled. What is the time required for the state of the bus to reach a minimum logical 1 state?

(b) For the design in the bottom figure, assume that the bus signal is in the logical 1 state and the driver is disabled. What is the time required for the state of the bus to reach a minimum logical 0 state?

2.7 Repeat Problem 2.6 if the driver fans out to 10 other devices.

2.8 Using the first-order model for a bus wire discussed in the text and your values for the resistors from Problem 2.5, determine the following:

(a) For the design in the top figure, assume that the bus has been disabled for a sufficiently long time that the state of the signal has reached its maximum. The driver is now enabled and is driving the bus to the logical 0 state. What is the time required for the state of the bus to reach a maximum logical 0 state?

(b) For the design in the top figure, assume that the bus has been disabled for a sufficiently long time that the state of the signal has reached its maximum. The driver is now enabled and is driving the bus to the logical 0 state. What is the time required for the state of the bus to reach a maximum logical 0 state?

2.9 Repeat Problem 2.5 if the receiver is an MC74HC04 rather than an SN74LS04.

2.10 Repeat Problem 2.5 if the receiver is a 74ACT04 rather than an SN74LS04.

2.11 Using the first-order model for a bus wire discussed in the text, determine

(a) The time required for a state change from a typical TTLS logic 0 level to V_{IH} min

(b) The time required for a state change from a typical TTLS logic 1 level to V_{IL} max

(c) How do your answers to parts (a) and (b) change if the time constant is doubled? tripled?

2.12 The two alternate designs in Figure P2.56 for driving each line of a system bus have to be analyzed.

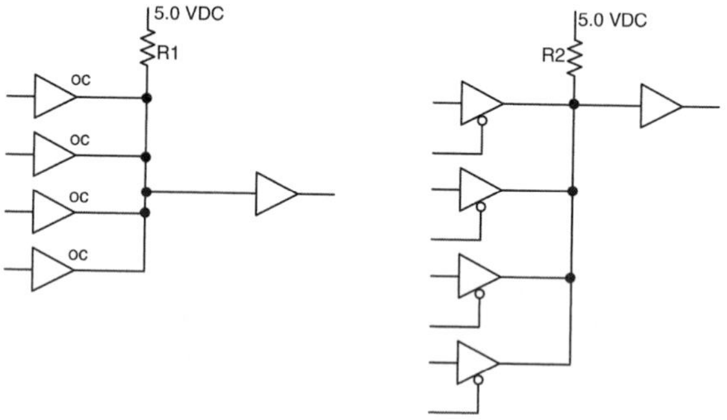

Figure P2.56

The design on the left utilizes an open collector driver, 74LS05, to gate a data stream onto the bus; the design on the right utilizes a tristate driver, 74LS244.

(a) Using the first-order model for a bus wire discussed in the text, determine the maximum switching speed of a bus line in both cases for a pull-up resistor of 1 KΩ, 10 KΩ, and 100 KΩ.

(b) Determine the worst case power dissipation for each pull-up resistor value.

(c) Determine the worst case noise margin for each pull-up resistor value.

2.13 The circuit fragment and control in Figure P2.57 have been proposed as an element of a system bus in a new applica-

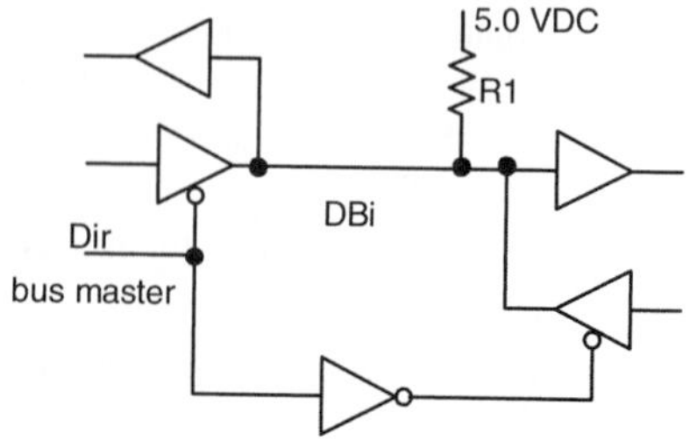

Figure 2.57

tion. The bus master sets the direction of communication using the *Dir* line.

(a) Can you see any problems with the design?

(b) Are there any possibilities for bus contention? If so, can you suggest a modification to the circuit to remove any contention?

2.14 A designer has come up with a logic expression for a portion of a larger system. He has written the equation in minterm form as

$$out = \Sigma\,(m4, m5, m6)$$

(a) Reduce the equation for the circuit output to its simplest sum of products form.

(b) The reduced equation in part (a) should give you three different, but logically equivalent, equations. Give the logic diagram for each. Assume a delay for each gate as five time units. Analyze the three circuits, commenting on and comparing the different path delays through each and the susceptibility of each to both static and dynamic hazards.

2.15 Repeat Problem 2.14, using the min-typical or typical-max delay ranges from the vendor's data sheets for the parts you are using.

2.16 The circuit fragment in Figure P2.58 implements the basic RS latch.

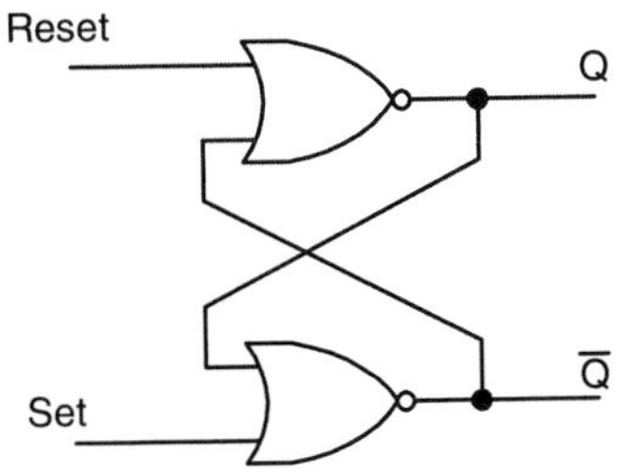

Figure P2.58

(a) Analyze the circuit and draw a detailed timing diagram. Assume that there is a delay of five time units for each gate and that the Q output and the R and S are initially 0. Base your analysis on the following input sequence: (R,S) = (0,0), (0,1), (0,0), (1,0), and (0,0).

(b) Repeat the analysis, using the min-typical or typical-max delay ranges from the vendor's data sheets for the parts you are using.

(c) Verify your analysis using a Verilog structural model for the circuit and the vendor's data sheets.

Digital Signals—A Dynamic View

2.17 The circuit in Figure P2.59 has been proposed for turning a level into a pulse.

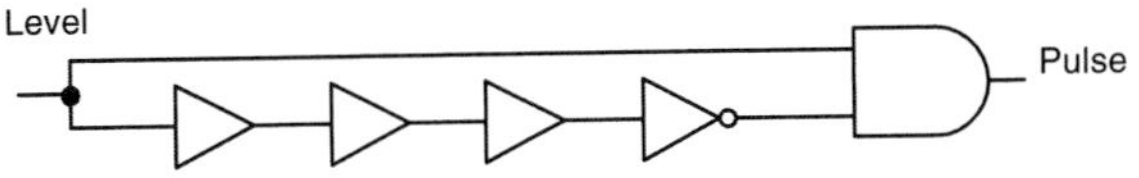

Figure P2.59

(a) Analyze the circuit using the min-typical or typical-max delay ranges from the vendor's data sheets for the parts you are using.

(b) What is the worst case variation on the width of the pulse based on your analysis?

(c) What are your thoughts on the design?

2.18 A junior engineer has proposed the design in Figure P2.60 for a portion of a circuit she is working on. She has said the design works perfectly, but has asked you to review it anyway. She gives you the information shown in the figure from the vendor's data sheet.

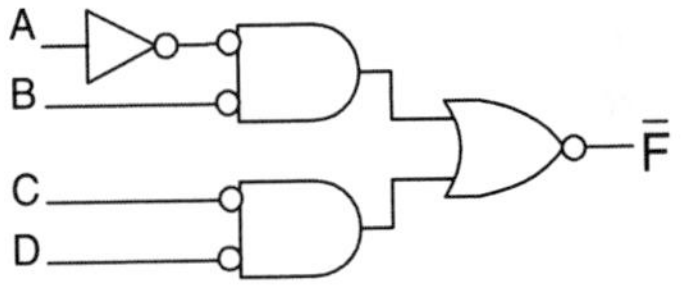

Figure P2.60

$\tau_{pdHL} = 10ns$ // Propagation delay from a high input to a low output

$\tau_{pdLH} = 15ns$ // Propagation delay from low input to a high output

(a) Using the information from the data sheets, complete the timing diagram in Figure P2.61 for the identified signals based on the conditions shown.

Assume each square is 10 ns.

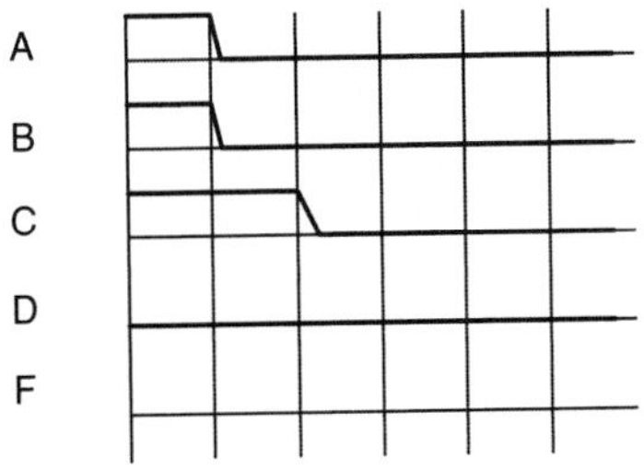

Figure P2.61

(b) Based on your analysis, what can you tell her about the design?

2.19 For the circuit in Figure P2.62:

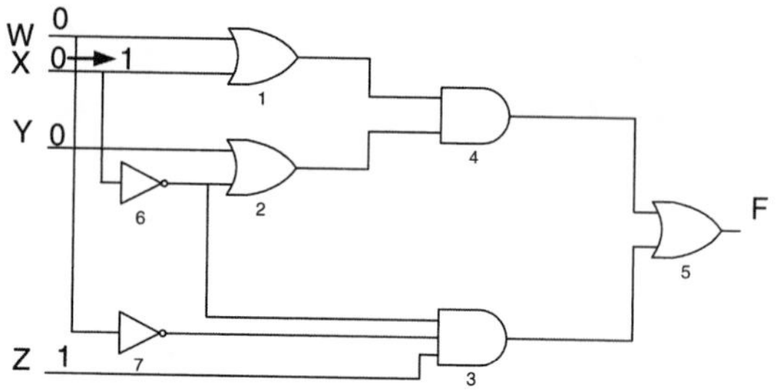

Figure P2.62

(a) Draw the theoretical signals on the output of each of the seven gates as a result of the indicated change on the input to gate 1. Assume no delay.

(b) Draw the signals on the output of each of the seven gates as a result of the indicated change on the input to gate 1 assuming the delays given.

Gate 1:	$\tau_{pHL} = \tau_{pLH} = 5\text{–}10$ ns
Gate 2:	$\tau_{pHL} = \tau_{pLH} = 10\text{–}15$ ns
Gates 3–7:	$\tau_{pHL} = \tau_{pLH} = 5\text{–}7$ ns

2.20 A circuit such as that seen in the accompanying diagram in Figure P2.63 is occasionally used to provide a clock in a low-cost embedded application. Assuming that the logic gates are SN74LSXX types of devices, analyze the circuit and identify any possible problems.

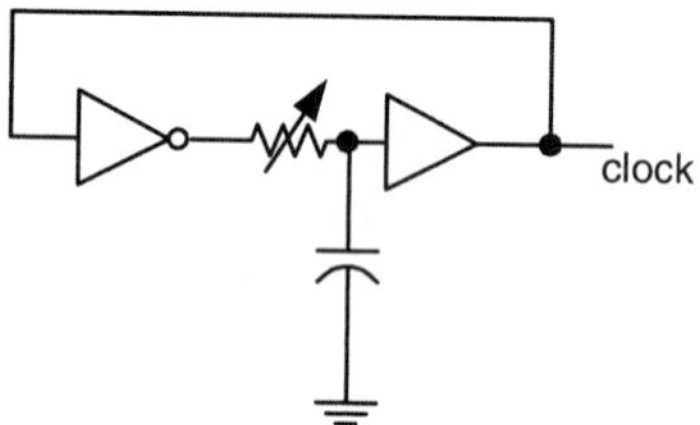

Figure P2.63

Consider the circuit's ability to start oscillating by itself when power is applied, behavior under lower voltage conditions, variations in propagation delay based on different parts, slow rise and fall times, and potential metastability problems.

2.21 In the chapter, circuits of the form shown in Figure P2.64 were identified as possibly producing static hazards. Someone suggested that the problem could easily be solved by simply adding a buffer with the same delay as the inverter to the bottom leg of the gate.

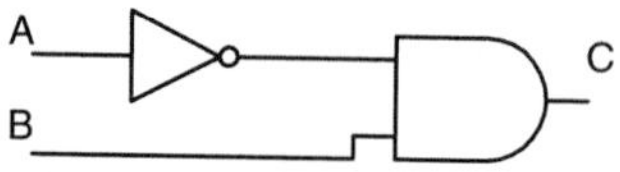

Figure P2.64

(a) Will such a change solve the problem? Why or why not?

(b) If the answer to part (a) is yes, can the modification be incorporated with confidence into a product that will be selling over 100,000 units each year? Why or why not.

2.22 Design, implement, and verify a full adder using structural Verilog. Use the vendor's data sheets for the propagation delay for each logic device in your circuit.

(a) What is the longest path and worst case delay through your full adder?

(b) Does your design have any static or dynamic hazards? If so, please identify.

2.23 Using the full adder from Problem 2.22, design, implement, and verify a 4-bit carry save adder using structural Verilog. Use the vendor's data sheets for the propagation delay for each logic device in your circuit.

A carry save adder uses a full adder to add two numbers one column at a time starting with the least significant column. The carry out from the addition of the ith column is saved and becomes the carry in to the addition in the i+1th column.

(a) What is the longest path and worst case delay through your 4-bit adder?

(b) What is the shortest path and shortest case delay through your 4-bit adder?

(c) Does your design have any static or dynamic hazards? If so, please identify.

2.24 Using your full adder from Problem 2.22, design, implement, and verify a 4-bit ripple carry adder using structural Verilog. Use the vendor's data sheets for the propagation delay for each logic device in your circuit.

(a) What is the longest path and worst case delay through your 4-bit adder?

(b) What is the shortest path and shortest case delay through your 4-bit adder?

(c) Does your design have any static or dynamic hazards? If so, please identify.

2.25 Using your full adder, from Problem 2.22 design, implement, and verify a 4-bit look ahead carry adder using structural Verilog. Use the vendor's data sheets for the propagation delay for each logic device in your circuit.

(a) What is the longest path and worst case delay through your 4-bit adder?

(b) What is the shortest path and shortest case delay through your 4-bit adder?

(c) Compare the results with those for the carry save adder and the ripple carry adder.

(d) Does your design have any static or dynamic hazards? If so, please identify.

2.26 Design, implement, and verify a 2-bit by 2-bit multiplier using the shift and add algorithm. For the addition, use the highest performance (shortest time to compute the sum) adder from your previous designs. Use the vendor's data sheets for the propagation delay for each logic device in your circuit.

What is the worst case execution time for your design?

2.27 Signals being transmitted over a bus in any embedded system are going to experience delays as they traverse that bus. At lower frequencies, the effects of those delays are generally negligible. As the transmission rate of the bus signals increases, the consequences of the delays become more significant. Under such circumstances, the following must be considered in higher performance systems:

- The delay for each individual bus signal is going to be different. That is, each signal on the bus is going to arrive at an individual module at a slightly different time.
- As the collective signals propagate down the bus from source to destination, the set will experience a (different) delay along the bus. Thus, signals arriving at modules close to the source will see the signals at different times from those at greater distance.

The following circuit fragments in Figure P2.65 illustrate one line of a system bus interconnecting three modules and a basic first-order model for a segment of that path. The buffer B0 isolates the segments in the model and has no delay.

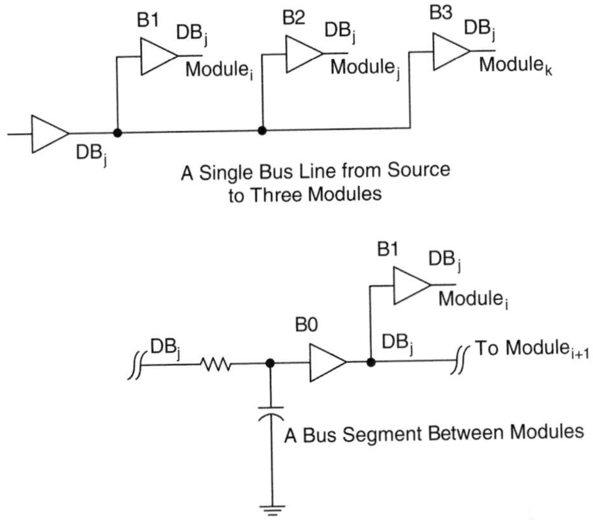

Figure P2.65

(a) Using the segment model given to model the bus between each module, build a model of a 4-bit bus interconnecting three modules.

(b) Place the bit patterns 0101 1010 successively onto the bus at the source. Draw a detailed timing diagram showing the propagation of the wave front down the bus. That is, show how the signals appear, in time, at the outputs of buffers B1–B3 on each of the respective modules. Make certain that you take into account the variation in delay through each of the module buffers B1–B3.

Chapter 3

The Hardware Side—Part 3: Storage Elements and Finite-State Machines—A Practical View

THINGS TO LOOK FOR . . .

- The concepts of state and time in digital systems.
- Formal model for the finite-state machine.
- Design of registers and shift registers.
- Design of counters and dividers.
- Modeling of memory devices and simple finite-state machines in Verilog.
- Real-world behavior of memory devices and finite-state machines.
- Design of clock systems and time bases.
- Use of homing sequences, scan path, and boundary scan to test FSMs.

3.0 INTRODUCTION

sequential circuits finite-state machines

Chapters 1 and 2 introduced the hardware side of an embedded application from a topdown view starting with the computing core and then moving to the opposite end of that hierarchy with the study of the combinational devices and things to consider when designing real-world applications. This chapter extends that study of practical considerations to *sequential circuits—finite-state machines* (FSMs).

latches, flip-flops

The logic devices that we have studied so far are combinational. The outputs of such circuitry are a function of inputs only; they are valid as long as the inputs are true. If the inputs change, the outputs change. Computers and other kinds of digital systems need the ability to store data and information and to perform mathematical or logical operations on that data. Devices that play a significant role in these tasks are called, in the jargon of the field, *latches* and *flip-flops*.

registers, shift registers

Our discussion in this chapter assumes an understanding of the basic latch and flip-flop types (R-S, J-K, D) as well as of sequential circuits built from these devices. Thus, our study of finite-state machines will focus on several specific applications and on how the real-world affects the behavior of memory devices used in such circuits. We will open with a short review of the concepts of state and time in digital systems because of the significant role these concepts play in the design and modeling of both the hardware and software components of an embedded system. Building on these notions, we will evolve a formal finite-state machine model. We will then briefly examine basic *registers* and *shift registers,* which are fundamental to the RTL model of most contemporary computing cores and to error-detecting and -correcting systems. Next, we will revisit fundamental *counters* and *dividers* and the critical role they play in the design of clock and time-base subsystems commonly used in embedded designs. Building on this theoretical basis, we will then examine the effects of nonideal behavior in real-world applications.

counters, dividers

As we did with our studies of combinational circuits, we will conclude with an introduction to testing sequential circuits. Many of these techniques will subsequently be applied in our studies of debugging embedded designs in Chapter 10. Because they are built around memory devices, sequential systems are significantly more complex to test than combinational circuitry. Their behavior is time dependent and governed by the values of their input signals and the order in which they appear. Compounding the test problem in FSMs is the inherent cyclic nature of such systems. We will introduce and study several different methods for attacking the problems unique to sequential circuitry.

3.1 THE CONCEPTS OF STATE AND TIME

We begin the discussion of finite-state systems by examining the concepts of time and state.

Time

A combinational logic system has no notion of time or history. The present (static) output does not depend in any way on how the output values were achieved. Neglecting delays through the system, we find that the output is immediate and a direct function of the current input set. In contrast, the current output of a finite-state system depends both on the path the system took to reach the current state and, potentially, the present values of the input set. Time is an integral part of the behavior of such systems.

State

In an analog circuit, we define branch and mesh currents and branch or node voltages. The values these variables assume over time characterize the behavior of that circuit. If we know the values of the specified variables over time, we know the behavior of the circuit.

state variables, state of a system

Such variables are called *state variables*. We define the *state of a system* at any time as a set of values for such variables; each set of values represents a unique state. Figure 3.0 illustrates a collection of example states. When the value of any variable changes, the state of system changes.

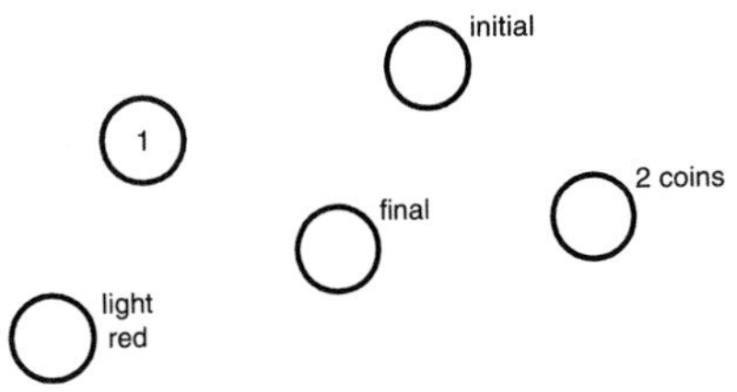

Figure 3.0 A Collection of States

State Changes

In traditional logic, a simple memory device, represented by a single variable, has two states, binary 0 and binary 1. The device will remain in the state until changed. For a set of state variables, the state changes with time are called the *behavior of a system*. For simple

behavior of a system

systems, one can exhaustively name each state. For more complex systems, some form of algorithm or formula is often more efficient.

3.2 THE STATE DIAGRAM

state diagram, graph

node, vertex

In the embedded world, the *state diagram*, or more formally a *graph*, is one means used to capture, describe, and specify the behavior of a system. In a state diagram, each state is represented by a circle, *node*, or *vertex*. We label each node to identify the state. The label should be simple and descriptive. A memory device has two states—its output is a logical 1 or a logical 0; thus, to express its behavior we will need two nodes as shown in Figure 3.1.

arc, edge

directed graph, head

final state, tail

initial state

We show the transition between two states using a labeled directed line or arrow called an *arc* (or *edge* in graph theoretic language) as illustrated in Figure 3.2. Because the line has a direction, the state diagram is referred to as a *directed graph*. The *head* or point of the arrow identifies the *final state*, and the *tail* or back of the arrow identifies the *initial state*. Special arcs, such as the one labeled *initial*, reflect an external, overriding asynchronous event, such as a reset, which places the system into a designated state, here *state a*.

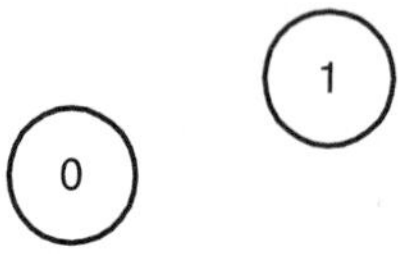

Figure 3.1 States of a Digital Memory Device

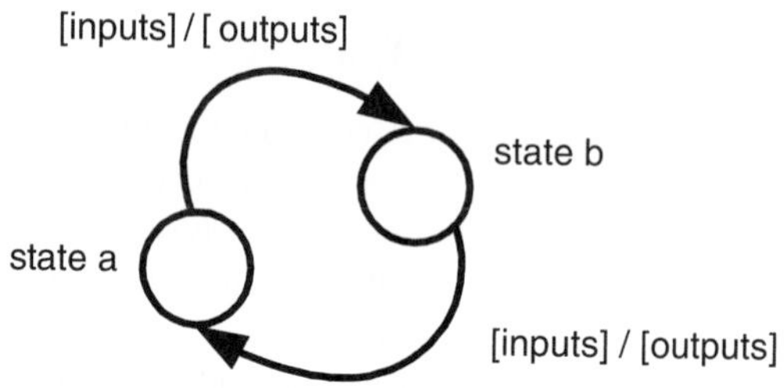

Figure 3.2 Transitions Between States in a Digital Memory Device

cyclic graph

Because the graph can contain cycles, it is further qualified as a *cyclic graph*. The label on each identifies what caused the change and the output(s) of system, if appropriate.

EXAMPLE 3.0

We can use a state diagram such as that in Figure 3.3 to describe an evening's entertainment.

The diagram graphically expresses the same behavior that is described textually in Figure 3.4.

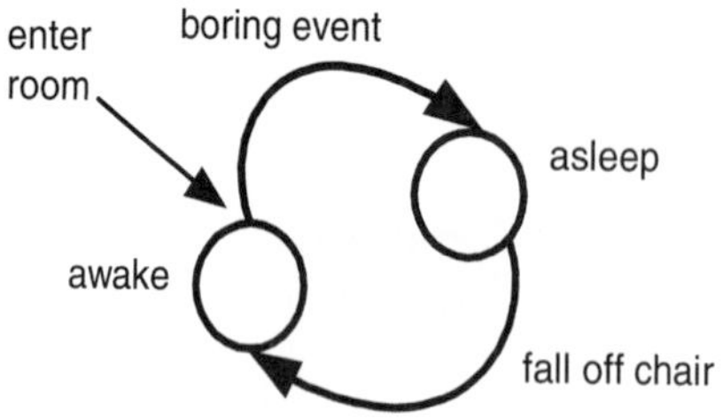

Figure 3.3 An Example State Diagram

enter room
If in state ***awake***
    Input ***boring event***
    Change to state asleep
else if state ***asleep***
    Input ***fall off chair***
    Change to state ***awake***

Figure 3.4 Textual Description of the Behavior Expressed in the State Diagram

In the embedded world, the state diagram is a very powerful tool for specifying and modeling the behavior of many different kinds of hardware and software systems from a high-level, abstract point of view and, as the design progresses, from a detailed point of view.

3.3 FINITE-STATE MACHINES—A THEORETICAL MODEL

Unified Modeling Language (UML)

finite-state machine

We can (in theory) express the behavior of an arbitrarily complex digital system using a state diagram. The diagram captures the states, the system inputs and outputs, and the transitions among those states in response to the inputs. Extensions to the basic diagram, such as we find in hardware/software co-design tools or the *Unified Modeling Language* (UML) state charts, support a rich set of system-modeling capabilities.

A sequential circuit, or more formally, a *finite-state machine*, is the means by which we ultimately transform the behavior expressed in the state diagram into a hardware and/or software implementation. Such circuits also form the basis for the sophisticated computation and control algorithms that one finds at the core of most modern digital systems.

A hardware implementation of such machines can be affected utilizing

- LSI or VLSI
- Arrayed logic
- PLDs or CPLDs
- ROMs
- Discrete logic

A software implementation will typically appear as the firmware that executes on any of the various pieces of hardware.

autonomous clocks

Simple finite-state machines as shown in Figure 3.5 have no inputs other than a clock and have only primitive outputs (we generally don't show the clock). Such machines are referred to as *autonomous clocks*. As we move to more complex designs, we will introduce inputs as well as more sophisticated outputs. A high-level block diagram for a finite-state machine begins with the diagram in Figure 3.6.

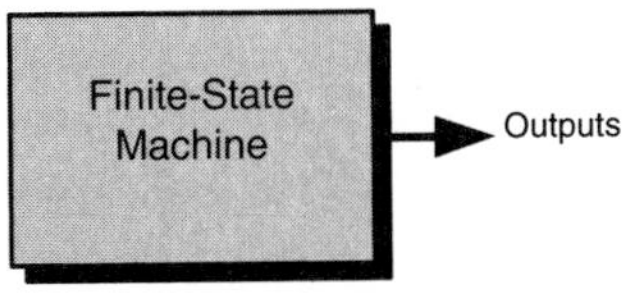

Figure 3.5 An Autonomous Clock

Figure 3.6 A High-Level Block Diagram for a Finite-State Machine

The outputs shown in the diagram may be the values of the state variables (as they will be in counting-type designs), combinations of the state variables, or combinations of the state variables and the inputs.

Refining the level of detail the block diagram for the state machine appears as shown in Figure 3.7.

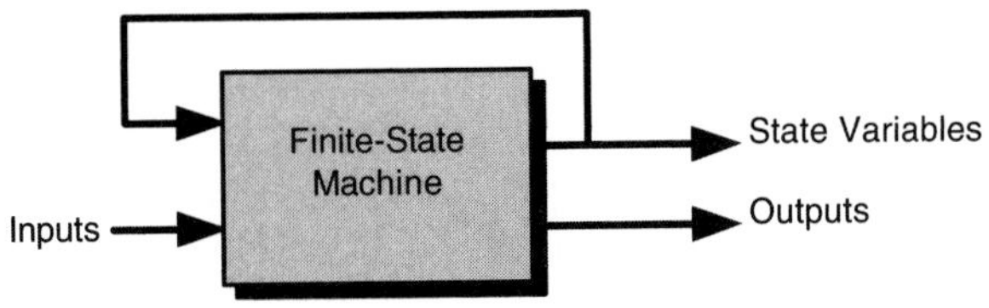

Figure 3.7 A High-Level Block Diagram for a Finite-State Machine

We see first that the signals out of the finite-state machine decompose into two sets: *state variables* and *outputs*. Observe that the state variables are fed back as inputs to the system. The diagram illustrates the essence of the strength of the machine. It has the ability to recognize the state that it is in and then to react based on the values of the state variables and (potentially) to the inputs to the system. The decision as to which state to go to next is determined from the current input and the state that the machine is currently in. The present state of a finite-state machine inherently encodes the history of the path taken to get there.

state variables, outputs

If we continue increasing the level of detail in the model, we now include the storage elements comprising the machine and the combinational logic that implements the output functionality and the input equations to the storage elements. The block diagram now becomes that in Figure 3.8.

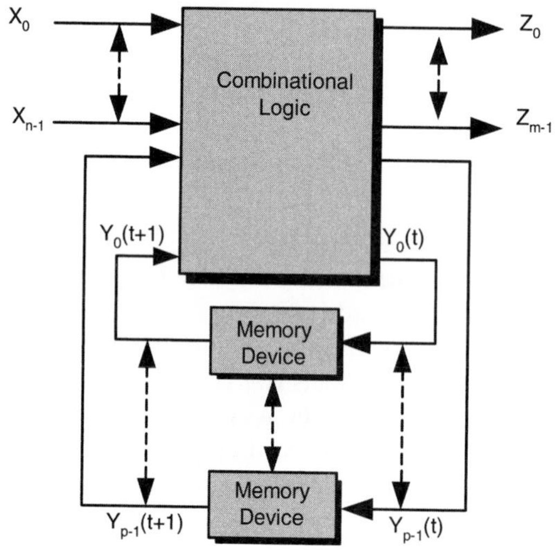

Figure 3.8 A High-Level Block Diagram for a Finite-State Machine

n inputs, m outputs, p state variables

The model has *n inputs, m outputs,* and *p state variables*. A memory device is associated with each state variable, and each state variable is associated with a memory device. At this point no particular type of memory device is specified.

Working from this block diagram, we can begin to formalize our model of the finite-state machine. That model must reflect the inputs, outputs (which may be a function of the inputs and the state variables or the state variables alone), the state variables, and the movement between states.

We specify the set of variables X_i to represent the n inputs to the system; Z_j to represent the m outputs from the system; and Y_k to represent the p internal state variables. We define our finite-state machine as a quintuple.

```
M = (I, O, S, λ, δ)
    I - Finite nonempty set or vector of inputs
    O - Finite nonempty set or vector of outputs
    S - Finite nonempty set or vector of states
    δ - Mapping I x S → S
    λ1 - Mapping I x S → O - Mealy Machine
    λ2 - Mapping S → O - Moore Machine
```

Cartesian, cross product

The operator in the mappings δ and λ_1 is the *Cartesian* or *cross product*. The Cartesian product of two vectors gives a matrix of all possible pairs among the element's two vectors.

To reflect the different ways of expressing the output of such a machine, we define the Mealy and Moore machines.

```
Mealy machine - λ1
    The output is a function of the present state and inputs
Moore machine - λ2
    The output function of the present state only
```

In the next several sections, we will review two practical implementations of the theoretical finite-state machine model. We will begin with the basic register and then examine several different counting/dividing circuits.

3.4 DESIGNING FINITE–STATE MACHINES—PART 1: REGISTERS

register

A single latch or flip-flop can store a single bit of information—a single logical 1 or logical 0. A collection of such devices, treated as a single entity, is called a *register*. We encountered such devices in our earlier studies of the microprocessor datapath.

3.4.1 Storage Registers

for, while

width

Registers are used to hold data; they form one small component of the memory system in a microprocessor. Often they are used for temporary storage of frequently used values such as a control variable in a *for* or *while* loop. No restrictions are placed on the size (number of flip-flops or latches) of a register. However, it is common practice to design binary-sized groups: 4; 8; 16; or 32-bit registers. The size of a register is often more appropriately called its *width*. The devices comprising a register

- Have a common clock or gate
- May have common reset (and preset)
- Work as a single unit

latch, register

Common parlance refers to the device as a *latch* if it consists of gated latches and a *register* if the member devices are flip-flops. The following logic diagram in Figure 3.9 illustrates a 4-bit latch and a similar-sized register.

Any values placed on the inputs to the device are clocked or gated to the outputs. With a simple inversion, the sense of gate or clock can be modified. The register is sometimes implemented with a common reset signal as well. The important point here is that the set of devices comprising the part are treated as a group.

3.4.2 Shift Registers

shift register

Like the basic register, a *shift register* is a collection of flip-flops that can store data. The shift register has the additional capability of shifting the stored data to the left or to the right. As with the basic register, it is common practice to design the shift register in binary-sized groups. The devices comprising a shift register

- Have a common clock to effect the shift operation
- May have a common reset
- Work as a single unit

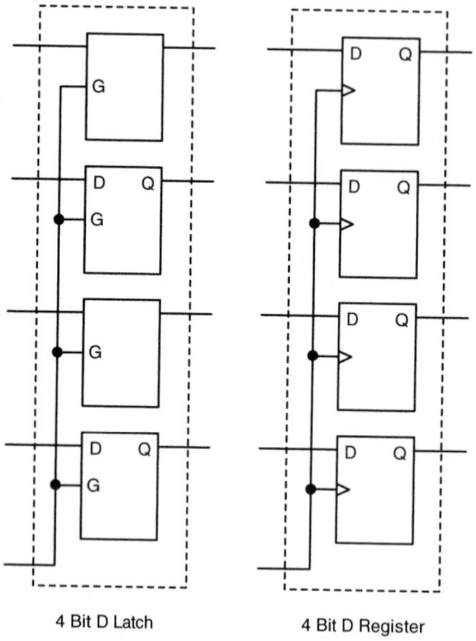

Figure 3.9 The Basic Latch and Register

Why don't we use gated latches as the building block for a shift register?

3.4.2.1 Shift Right Shift Register

4-bit shift right shift register

Four D flip-flops in the configuration shown in Figure 3.10 implement a *4-bit shift right shift register* and illustrate the basic architecture for the family of devices.

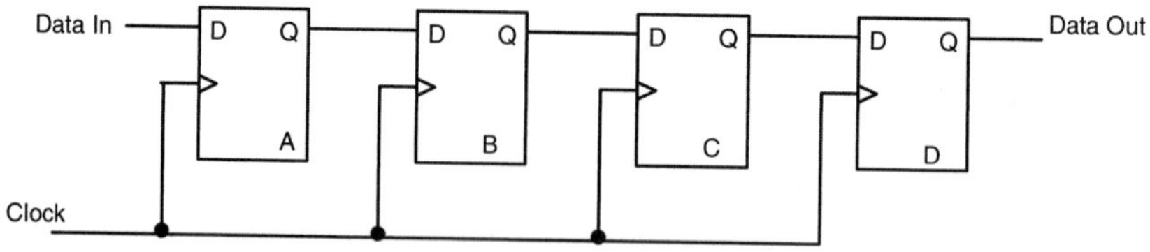

Figure 3.10 A 4-Bit Shift Register

Assume that the initial state of all devices is logical 0. At time t_0 we put a logical 1 on the data input and issue one clock pulse. The state of the flip-flops is given in Figure 3.11.

Time	Data	Q_A	Q_B	Q_C	Q_D
t_0	1	0	0	0	0
t_1	0	1	0	0	0

Figure 3.11 Shift Register Following One Clock Pulse

After the clock pulse, the input data bit has been stored into the first flip-flop.

At time t_1 we put a 0 on the data input and issue another clock pulse. The state of the flip-flops now appears as in Figure 3.12.

Time	Data	Q_A	Q_B	Q_C	Q_D
t_0	1	0	0	0	0
t_1	0	1	0	0	0
t_2	0	0	1	0	0

Figure 3.12 Shift Register Following Two Clock Pulses

After the clock pulse, a logical 0 has been stored into the first flip-flop and the logical 1 from the first flip-flop has moved to the second.

At time t_2, we leave the 0 on the data input and issue another clock pulse. The state of the flip-flops is given in Figure 3.13.

Time	Data	Q_A	Q_B	Q_C	Q_D
t_0	1	0	0	0	0
t_1	0	1	0	0	0
t_2	0	0	1	0	0
t_3	0	0	0	1	0

Figure 3.13 Shift Register Following Three Clock Pulses

After the clock pulse, a logical 0 has propagated to the second flip flop. The logical 1 from the second flip-flop has moved to the third.

At time t_3, we leave the 0 on the data input and issue another clock pulse. The state of the flip-flops appears as shown in Figure 3.14.

Time	Data	Q_A	Q_B	Q_C	Q_D
t_0	1	0	0	0	0
t_1	0	1	0	0	0
t_2	0	0	1	0	0
t_3	0	0	0	1	0
t_4	0	0	0	0	1

Figure 3.14 Shift Register Following Four Clock Pulses

After the clock pulse, a logical 0 has propagated to the third flip-flop. The logical 1 from the third flip-flop has now moved to the fourth. With each clock pulse, the stored data is shifted one position to the right, and the new data bit is entered into the first flip-flop. Data entered into the device will appear on the output after N clock pulses. The output stream is thus a delayed version of the input stream, making it an effective tool whenever an embedded application requires a well-controlled delay.

Based on these observations, two equations formalizing behavior of the device can be written:

For the 0th flip flop,

$$D_0 = \text{data}$$

For the ith D flip flop

$$D_i = Q_{i-1}$$

right shift by one 4-bit shift register

The design implements a *right shift by one 4-bit shift register.*

The Verilog model for such a device is given in the following code modules. We begin with the RTL model, given in Figure 3.15.

```
// RTL Model - Four Bit Shift Right Shift Register
module ShiftRegister4(dataOut, dataIn, clk, por);
    // declare the inputs and outputs
    input dataIn, clk, por;
    output dataOut;

    reg [3:0] data;     // implements the shift register
    reg dataOut;

    // build the shift register
    always@ (negedge por or posedge clk)
    begin
        // reset the register
        if(por==0)
        begin
            data<= 4'b0;
            assign dataOut = 0;
        end
        // implement shift operation
        else
        begin
            assign dataOut = data[3];
            data <= {data[2:0], dataIn};
        end
    end
endmodule
```

Figure 3.15 RTL Implementation for a 4-Bit Shift Right Shift Register

POR—Power On Reset

The design implements a master reset called *POR—Power On Reset.* Such a reset is essential in any embedded application to ensure that the system will always start in a known state; typically, that state is the all-zeros condition. The most significant bit, D3 or data[3], is on the right. Data enters on the left.

The RTL implementation utilizes a Verilog array-type data structure to express the functionality. The structural implementation for the design is given in the code module in Figure 3.16.

```
module DFF(q, qBar, D, clk, rst);
    input D, clk, rst;
    output q, qBar;

    parameter delay0 = 2;   // delay reset to q
    parameter delay1 = 3;   // delay clock to q
    parameter delay2 = 2;   // delay for qBar with respect to q

    reg q;

    not #delay2 n1 (qBar, q);
    always@ (negedge rst or posedge clk)
    begin
      if(rst==0)
          #delay0 q = 0;
      else
          #delay1 q = D;
    end
endmodule

// Structural Model - Four Bit Shift Right Shift Register
module ShiftRegister4(dataOut, dataln, clk, por);
    // declare the inputs and outputs
    input dataln, clk, por;
    output dataOut;

    // bulid the shift register
    DFF ff3(dataOut, q3Bar, q2, clk, por);
    DFF ff2(q2, q2Bar, q1, clk, por);
    DFF ff1(q1, q1Bar, q0, clk, por);
    DFF ff0(q0, q0Bar, dataln, clk, por);
endmodule
```

Figure 3.16 Structural Implementation for a 4-Bit Shift Right Shift Register

The D flip-flop model is included and has been simplified to only support a reset signal. The propagation delay parameters are implemented through the underlying flip-flop implementation rather than in the shift register itself.

3.4.2.2 Parallel In/Serial Out—Serial In/Parallel Out Left Shift Registers

The shift register is also a convenient means for converting between serial and parallel data. The first diagram, in Figure 3.17, implements a simple 4-bit serial to parallel converter.

Data A 4-bit word is entered into the shift register, in serial, through the input labeled *Data*. After four clock pulses, the word appears on the four output lines labeled *D3–D0*.

One common extension to the basic design is to use a tristate buffer on the outputs to permit the outputs of several such devices to be multiplexed onto a common bus.

As implemented, one must count the number of bits entered to ensure that the register is not overrun. The addition of one flip-flop to incorporate a marker bit into the design can provide an alternate approach, as is illustrated in Figure 3.18.

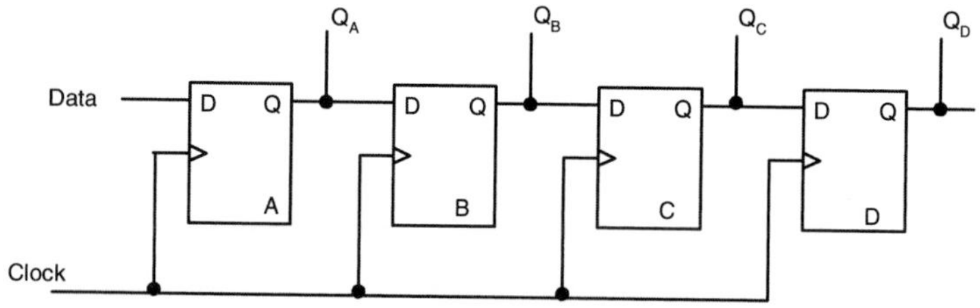

Figure 3.17 4-Bit Serial In/Parallel Out Shift Register

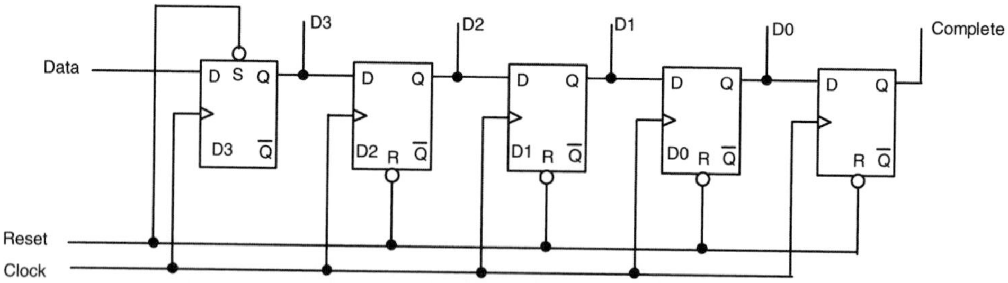

Figure 3.18 4-Bit Serial In/Parallel Out Shift Register with a Marker Bit

Reset Prior to entering the data word, the *Reset* input is asserted. Following the reset, the 0th stage is in the logical 1 state and all others are at logical 0's. After four shifts, the logical 1 is in the last state, and the *Complete* signal is now asserted. ***Complete***

Implementing a parallel in/serial out shift register entails adding a two-to-one multiplexer on the input of each stage and a selector control input to select between loading and shifting. Such a design is presented in Figure 3.19.

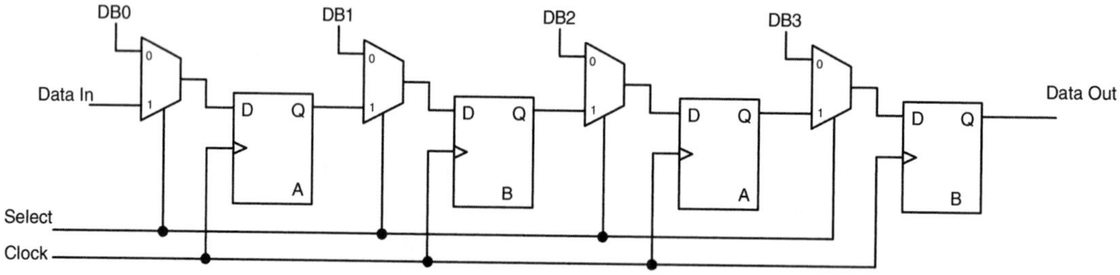

Figure 3.19 4-Bit Parallel In/Serial Out Shift Register

Select When the *Select* input is in the logical 1 state, the circuit acts like a 4-bit shift right shift register. When it is in the logical 0 state, the parallel input data can be stored on the next clock rising edge.

3.4.3 Linear Feedback Shift Registers

A linear feedback shift register (LFSR) finds wide application in any embedded applications that utilize pseudorandom sequences. Such applications include random noise generation, the development of "random" vectors in test systems, encoding and encryption, or wireless telecommunication systems utilizing code division multiple access (CDMA) or spread spectrum techniques.

One cannot generate truly random numbers using a finite-state machine. The finite number of states ensures that any path through the sequence of states must eventually repeat. The best that can be expected is that the period of the machine is "very long"; thus, such a machine is called *pseudorandom*. The upper limit to the length of any such sequence is given by $2^n - 1$, where n is the number of flip-flops in the shift register. Such a sequence is called a *maximal length sequence,* and the producing shift register configuration is described as a *maximal length shift register*. The upper bound is not 2^n as one might expect with *n* stages because the all-zero state is not permitted. Once the generator enters the all-zero state, it will not be able to exit. Because of their application to noise generation, maximal length LFSR sequences are often termed *pseudo-noise sequences* or *PN sequences*.

pseudorandom

maximal length sequence

maximal length shift register

pseudo noise sequences, PN sequences

The high-level block diagram for such a design is called a *linear feedback shift register* (LFSR) and is given in Figure 3.20.

linear feedback shift register (LFSR)

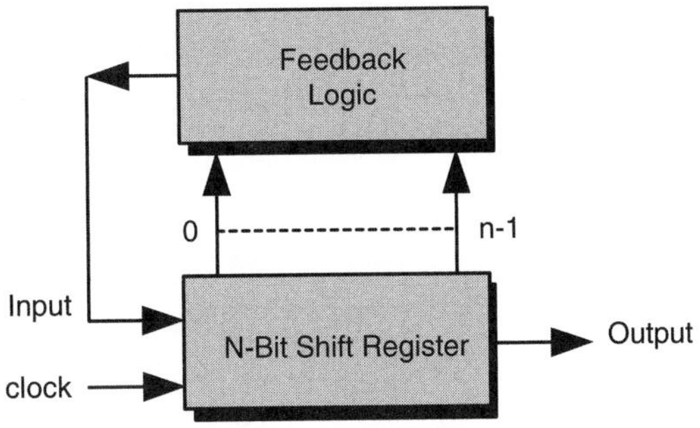

Figure 3.20 A Block Diagram for a Linear Feedback Shift Register

A subset of the outputs from the shift register are fed back as input data according to the polynomial given in Eq. 3.0.

$$\text{input} = v_0 + v_1X + v_2X^2 + \ldots + v_{n-1}X^{n-1} \quad (3.0)$$

$v_i = 0$ or 1

+ implemented as an exclusive OR

X^i represents the flip-flop outputs

The length of the generated sequence, appearing on the output as a series of 0's and 1's, is determined by the starting value in the shift register and by which outputs are fed back as specified by the values for the v_i. The generator will produce a maximal length sequence if the connection polynomial is irreducible; that is, it cannot be factored. Such a polynomial is called a *primitive polynomial*. Equation 3.1 expresses one such polynomial.

primitive polynomial

$$\text{input} = 1 + X + X^4 \quad (3.1)$$

The structural Verilog model for the design of the LFSR is given in the code module in Figure 3.21.

The D flip-flop used in the implementation has both an asynchronous *set* and an asynchronous *reset* input. Since only the *reset* input is used, the *set* input must be defined; that is, it cannot be left floating. The variable *pullUp* serves that purpose.

set

reset

pullUp

An LFSR configured according to the given polynomial is illustrated in Figure 3.22.

```
module LFShiftRegister4(q3, q2, q1, q0, feedBack, clk, por);
    // declare the inputs and outputs
    input   clk, por;
    output  q3, q2, q1, q0, feedBack;

    reg  pullUp;

    initial
        pullUp = 1;.

    xor  xr0 (feedBack, q2, q3);
    // bulid the shift register
    DFF  ff3(q3, q3Bar, q2, clk, por, pullUp);
    DFF  ff2(q2, q2Bar, q1, clk, por, pullUp);
    DFF  ff1(q1, q1Bar, q0, clk, por, pullUp);
    DFF  ff0(q0, q0Bar, feedBack, clk, por, pullUp);
endmodule
```

Figure 3.21 Structural Verilog Code Module for a Linear Feedback Shift Register

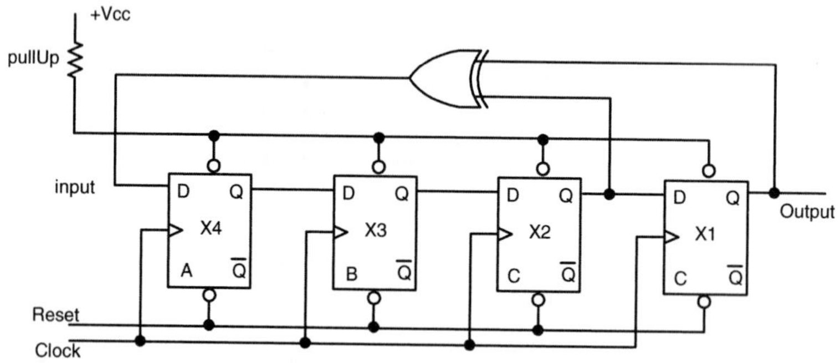

Figure 3.22 A Linear Feedback Shift Register Implemented According to Eq. 3.1

3.5 DESIGNING FINITE-STATE MACHINES: PART 2—COUNTING AND DIVIDING

Sequential machines and finite-state automata form the theoretical models of computation on which we base most of the computation and control capability found in modern digital systems. Counting and dividing are essential tasks in a wide variety of contemporary embedded applications. The designs implementing such capability represent some of the simpler sequential machines we will encounter. We find such capability supported inside of the microprocessor through a number of user programmable counters/timers and outside of the microprocessor with the implementation of specialized MSI or LSI timing and counting functions.

We employ counters to accumulate events, count bits, or determine when or if a specified number of events have occurred. We use timers (a simple variant on a counter) to measure elapsed time between events in an application or to delay an operation for a specified time after an event. Dividers are used primarily to develop a lower from a higher frequency.

In the ensuing discussions, we will base most designs on the D flip-flop simply because it finds common application in most of the implementation mediums: VLSI, FPGAs, CPLDs. It is attractive because it is easy to implement and because it presents a very small footprint in integrated implementations.

3.5.1 Dividers

Dividers find frequent application in designs where we must produce a lower frequency signal from a higher one.

Divide by Two

The simplest such circuit accepts an input frequency and produces one-half of the frequency as output. The implementation of a divide by two circuit is rather straightforward as we see in Figure 3.23. We begin with a D flip-flop and connect the $\overline{Q}$ output back to the D input. From the truth table for the flip-flop we see that it will alternate between states if configured as shown and then clocked.

Neglecting delays, the output of the device will appear as in the timing diagram given in Figure 3.24.

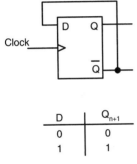

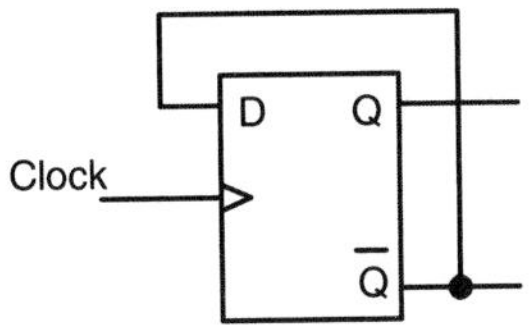

D	Q_{n+1}
0	0
1	1

Figure 3.23 A Divide by Two Divider

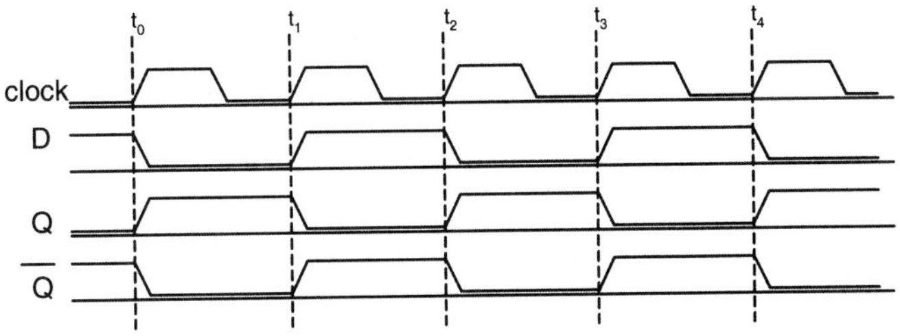

Figure 3.24 Timing Diagram for a Divide by Two Divider

On each rising edge of the clock, the flip-flop changes state. At each such occurrence, the new state of the $\overline{Q}$ output is fed back into the input of the flip-flop and will thus affect the value of the next state via the D input. After several cycles of the clock, it is clearly evident that the frequency of the signal at the Q output is one-half that of the clock. The input frequency has been divided by two.

3.5.2 Asynchronous Dividers and Counters

Let's extend the circuit as shown in Figure 3.25. The second flip-flop, B, is clocked by the $\overline{Q}$ output of the first flip-flop, A. When the Q output of A changes state from logical 1 to logical 0, the $\overline{Q}$ output will change state from logical 0 to logical 1. On such a transition, flip-flop B will change state. Thus, B will be clocked every other time A changes state, or at one-fourth the frequency of the clock.

Observe how we label the output signals on the flip-flops. The timing diagram is now given as seen in Figure 3.26.

divide by four
asynchronous divide by four

The circuit is called by several names. It is called a *divide by four* circuit because the output is one-fourth of the input frequency. It is qualified as an *asynchronous divide by four*

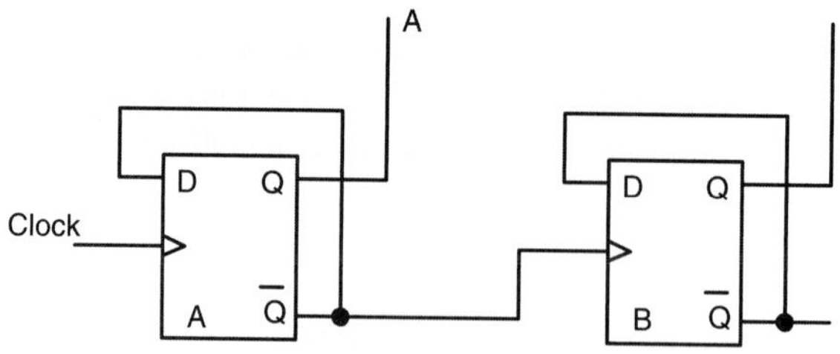

Figure 3.25 Logic Diagram for a Divide by Four Divider

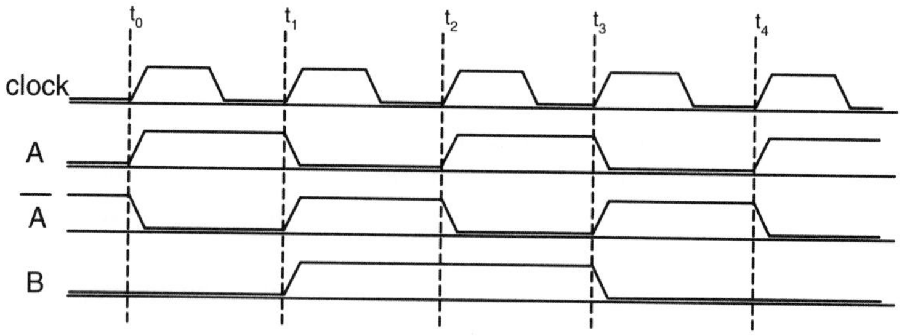

Figure 3.26 Timing Diagram for a Divide by Four Divider

circuit because the two flip-flops are not clocked by the same signal. Based on the sequence of states through which the circuit transitions, {B,A = 00, 01, 10, 11}, the circuit is also referred to as an *asynchronous, 2-bit, binary up counter*. It is counting up from the initial state of 00, and the counting sequence is in binary.

asynchronous, 2-bit binary up counter

The state diagram and state table for the circuit are given in Figure 3.27.

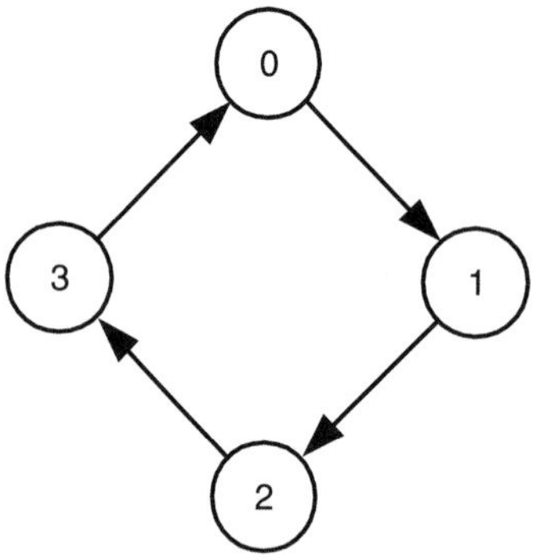

Present State $t = t_n$	Next State $t = t_{n+1}$
B A	B A
0 0 0	1 0 1
1 0 1	2 1 0
2 1 0	3 1 1
3 1 1	0 0 0

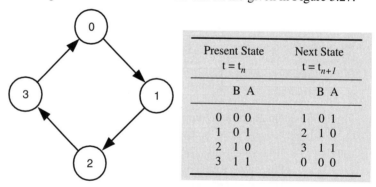

Figure 3.27 State Diagram and State Table for a Divide by Four Divider

The edges in the state diagram are not labeled because there is no input signal causing the state change (other than the clock which is not shown). The nodes or states are labeled to reflect the binary value of the two state variables, A and B. The left-hand column, labeled *Present State*, illustrates successive current states, and the right-hand column, labeled *Next State*, identifies the successor or next states—the state the system will be in at the next time tick.

Present State, Next State

Observe that because of the way logic drawings are commonly presented with the signal flow from left to right and top to bottom, the least significant bit of the counter appears on the left-hand side—little endian notation.

Configured as it is, flip-flop B cannot change state until after flip-flop A changes. As long as all we are doing is dividing, we have no problem. If many such stages are cascaded, we will encounter significant delay as each stage changes state, much like so many dominoes falling over. Like the series of dominoes, the last stage cannot change state until all preceding stages have changed. Such a design is called *asynchronous* because the clocking of successive stages is not synchronized to a master clock. It is also called a *ripple counter* because a change in the first stage ripples through the intermediate stages, eventually reaching the last. We cannot decode any of the state variable patterns without running the serious risk of both static and dynamic hazards.

asynchronous

ripple counter

To see the significance of the effects of delay, assume that each device has a clock to Q propagation delay of *m* time units. Let the first flip-flop be clocked at time t_0.

- The first stage output will appear at time $t = t_0+m$.
- The second stage output will appear m time units after the output of the first or at $t = t_0+2m$.
- For n stages, the final output will appear at $t = t_0+2mn$ worst case.
- Let m have a value of 10ns
- The output of the last stage of a 10-stage ripple counter, for example, will change states 200 ns after the initial clock edge.

The previous analysis illustrates why ripple counters typically do not find wide application as general-purpose counters or timers. They can, however, be very effective for dividing a higher frequency signal down to a lower one.

Caution: Decoding combinations of the state variables in a ripple counter can (and will) potentially lead to both static and dynamic hazards on the outputs of any combinational network. Such a practice is best avoided.

3.5.3 Synchronous Dividers and Counters

synchronous

Synchronous design is the preferred choice for a counter or timer. All stages are synchronized to a common clock. Each flip-flop output signal changes at approximately the same time. The state diagram and state tables will remain unchanged.

Working with the characteristic equation and truth table for the D flip-flop and the state table for the counter, we can develop the D input equations for the two flip-flops. From the definition of the D flip-flop, as expressed by either the truth table or characteristic equation, we conclude that for the state of the device to be a logical 1 at time t_{n+1}, the D input must be a logical 1 at time t_n; otherwise the state will be a logical 0. The state table for the 2-bit binary up counter is repeated in Figure 3.28 for convenience.

Present State $t = t_n$		Next State $t = t_{n+1}$	
	B A		B A
0	0 0	1	0 1
1	0 1	2	1 0
2	1 0	3	1 1
3	1 1	0	0 0

Figure 3.28 State Table for a 2-Bit Binary Up Counter

From the specified state table, we determine that

- From state 0, the counter must transition to state 1. In doing so, flip-flop A must change state from logical 0 to logical 1; flip-flop B must remain unchanged. Therefore, D_A must be a logical 1.
- From state 1, the counter must transition to state 2. In doing so, flip-flop A must change state from logical 1 to logical 0, and flip-flop B must change state from logical 0 to logical 1. Thus, D_A must be a logical 0, and D_B must be a logical 1.
- From state 2, the counter must transition to state 3. In doing so, flip-flop A must change state from logical 0 to logical 1; flip-flop B must not change state. Thus, D_A and D_B must both be a logical 1.
- Finally, from state 3, the counter must transition to state 0. Both flip-flops must transition to logical 0; both D inputs must be logical 0.

We conclude that D_A must then be a logical 1 in states 0 and 2 and D_B must be a logical 1 in states 1 and 2. The following D input equations result.

$$\begin{aligned} D_A &= \bar{A} \bullet \bar{B} + \bar{A} \bullet B \\ &= \bar{A} \end{aligned} \tag{3.2}$$

$$\begin{aligned} D_B &= \bar{A} \bullet B + A \bullet \bar{B} \\ &= A \oplus B \end{aligned} \tag{3.3}$$

The logic diagram follows in Figure 3.29.

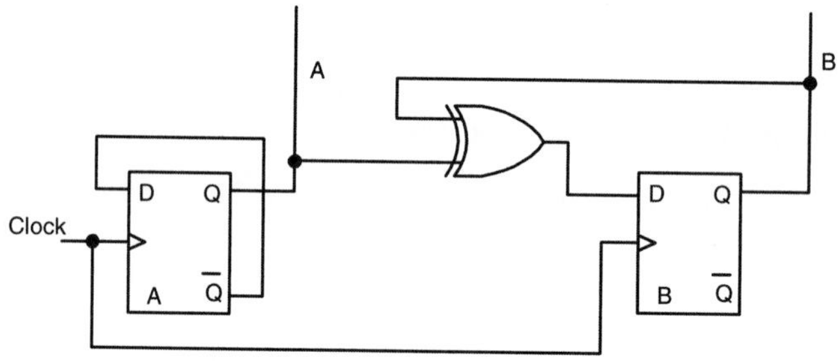

Figure 3.29 Logic Diagram for a Synchronous 2-Bit Binary Up Counter

3.5.4 Johnson Counters

Johnson counters

Johnson counters are an interesting and useful subset of counters. They find significant utility in designing time bases for embedded applications as well as for other digital systems. Their design is based on a classic shift register, with the $\bar{Q}$ output of the last stage fed back as the data input to the first stage.

3.5.4.1 Two-Stage Johnson Counter

The two-stage or 2-bit Johnson counter executes the state table and has the state diagram given in Figure 3.30.

The structural Verilog model for the design is given in the code module in Figure 3.31.

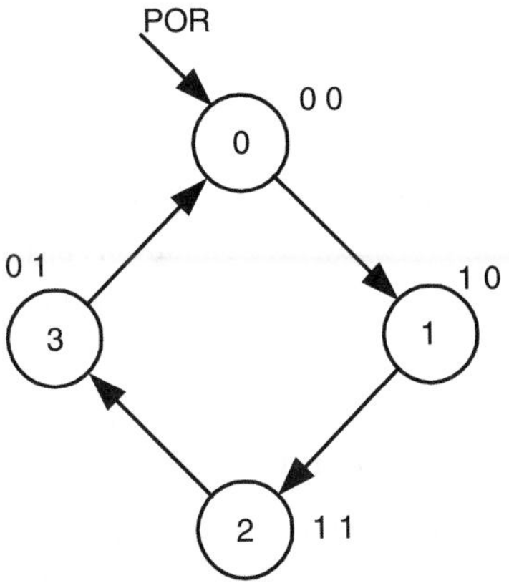

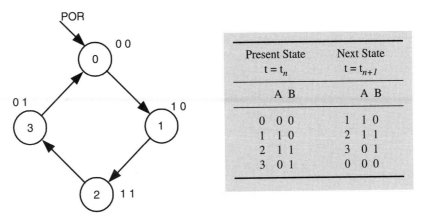

Present State $t = t_n$		Next State $t = t_{n+1}$	
	A B		A B
0	0 0	1	1 0
1	1 0	2	1 1
2	1 1	3	0 1
3	0 1	0	0 0

Figure 3.30 State Diagram and State Table for a 2-Bit Johnson Counter

Based on the Verilog code, the logic diagram is given in Figure 3.32.

```
module JohnsonCounter(qF1, qF0, clk, por);
    input   clk, por;
    output qF1, qF0;

    reg    pullUp;

    initial
        pullUp = 1;
    // Build the counter

    DFF f1(qF1, qBarF1, qF0, clk, pullUp, por);
    DFF f0(qF0, qBarF0, qBarF1, clk, pullUp, por);
endmodule
```

Figure 3.31 Verilog Code Module for a 2-Bit Johnson Counter

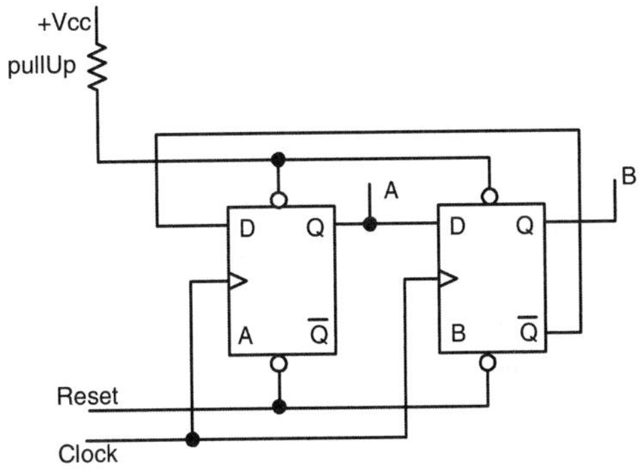

Figure 3.32 Logic Diagram for a 2-Bit Johnson Counter

The timing diagram for the counter is given in Figure 3.33.

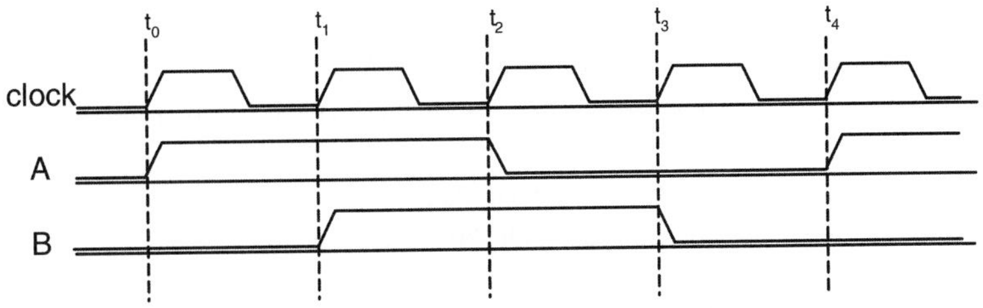

Figure 3.33 Timing Diagram for a 2-Bit Johnson Counter

Observe the following key points about the two-stage or 2-bit Johnson counter.

- The states change in a Gray sequence—there is only a single variable change between successive states.
- Because the count sequence is Gray, any state can be decoded, using combinational logic, and there will never be any race conditions or hazards (decoding spikes).
- With two state variables, there are 2^2 combinations; all are used in the count sequence.

3.5.4.2 Three- or Greater Stage Johnson Counter

The three-stage Johnson counter has the state diagram and executes the state table in Figure 3.34. Those with more than three stages simply extend the pattern.

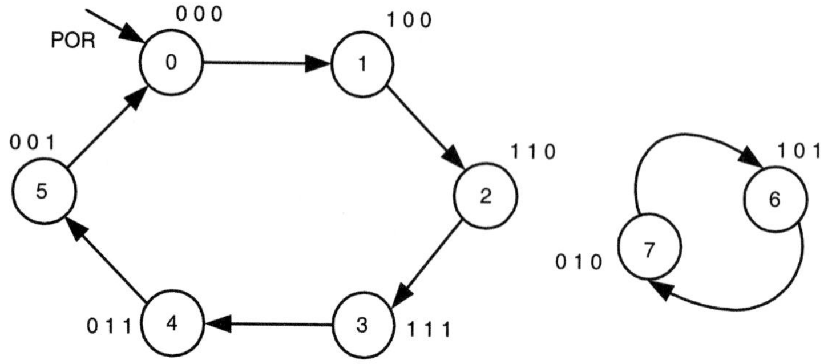

Present State $t = t_n$		Next State $t = t_{n+1}$	
	A B C		A B C
0	0 0 0	1	1 0 0
1	1 0 0	2	1 1 0
2	1 1 0	3	1 1 1
3	1 1 1	4	0 1 1
4	0 1 1	5	0 0 1
5	0 0 1	0	0 0 0

Figure 3.34 State Diagram and State Table for a 3-Bit Johnson Counter

The state table for the three-stage Johnson counter has two distinct components; this is also seen in the state diagram or graph, which is made up of two disconnected subgraphs. The desired state diagram subgraph is given on the left. However, if the counter ever enters the second-state subgraph shown on the right because of noise in the system or some other external causes, it cannot exit. It is stuck.

Such a situation is not acceptable from either a reliability or a safety point of view. The problem must be corrected. Such a correction can be implemented by specifying the inputs to each of the D flip-flops so as to ensure that the system returns to a valid state within the count sequence. Possible solutions will be explored as an exercise at the end of the chapter.

Observe the key points in Figure 3.35 about Johnson counters with more than two stages.

- The states change in a Gray sequence—there is only a single variable change between successive states.
- Because the count sequence is Gray, any state can be decoded, using combinational logic, and there will never be any hazards (decoding spikes).
- With n stages or state variables, there are 2^n combinations; however, not all are used in the count sequence.
- The period of any Johnson counter is 2n; the remaining $2^n - 2n$ states form a disconnected subgraph of illegal states. These must be identified and managed.

Figure 3.35 Designing a Multistage Johnson Counter

3.6 PRACTICAL CONSIDERATIONS—PART 1: TIMING IN LATCHES AND FLIP-FLOPS

For combinational logic devices, the major timing concerns focused on the delay of signals propagating through the devices. The timing relationship between the input data and the gate in latches and the clock in flip-flops introduces the notions of *setup time* and *hold time*.

setup time, hold time

Setup time specifies how long input signals must be present and stable before the gate or clock changes state. *Hold time* specifies how long an input signal must remain stable (i.e., cannot be changed) after a specified gate or clock has changed state.

3.6.1 Gated Latches

Gate

The setup and hold time relationships are illustrated in Figure 3.36 for a gated latch that is enabled by a logical 1 on the *Gate*. The specification for the times is given at the 50% point of each signal.

setup time, hold time

The *setup* and *hold times* permit incoming signals to propagate through any input logic and to initiate and complete the appropriate state changes for any internal memory elements. These times are designated as

$$\tau_{setup} \quad \text{or} \quad \tau_{su} \quad \text{and} \quad \tau_{hold}.$$

If the setup time constraints are not met—that is, if the input data changes within the setup window—the behavior of the circuit is undefined. The input may or may not be recognized, or the output may enter a metastable state in which it oscillates for an indeterminate time such as we might see in Figure 3.37 as the device's internal components attempt to reach a stable state. Such oscillation can persist for several nanoseconds.

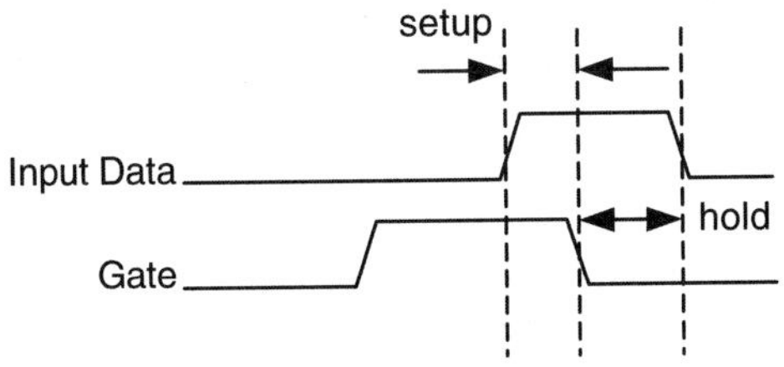

Figure 3.36 Setup and Hold Times for a Gated Latch

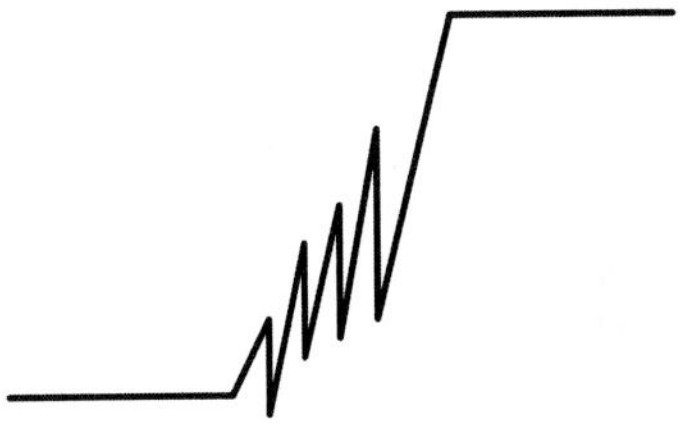

Figure 3.37 Typical Metastable Behavior

3.6.2 Flip-Flops

setup time
hold time

The accompanying diagram in Figure 3.38 graphically illustrates the *setup* and *hold time* relationships for a positive edge–triggered flip-flop. The specification for the times is given at the 50% point of each signal.

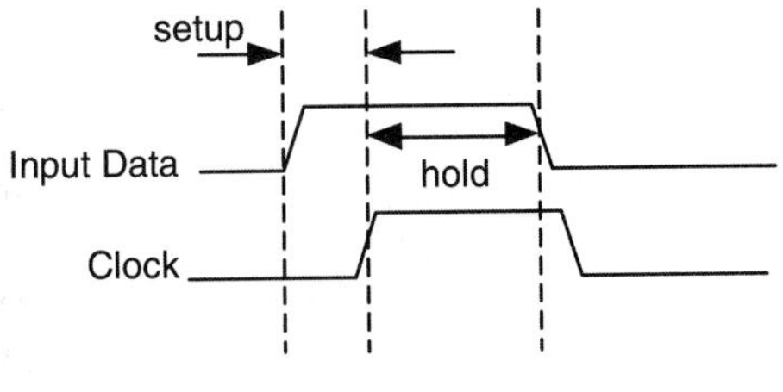

Figure 3.38 Setup and Hold Times for a Positive Edge Triggered Flip-Flop

The need for and consequences of violating the setup and hold time constraints in the flip-flop are the same as those for the gated latch.

3.6.3 Propagation Delays

In combinational circuits, propagation delay specifies the interval following a change in state of an input signal to the device and the effect of that change appearing on the output of the device. Such an interval is characterized by *minimum, typical,* and *maximum* values. In flip-flops, the measurement is made with respect to the *causative edge* of the clock.

minimum, typical

maximum, causative edge

The timing diagram in Figure 3.39 illustrates the minimum and maximum clock to Q output propagation delays for a low to high and a high to low transition on the flip-flop output.

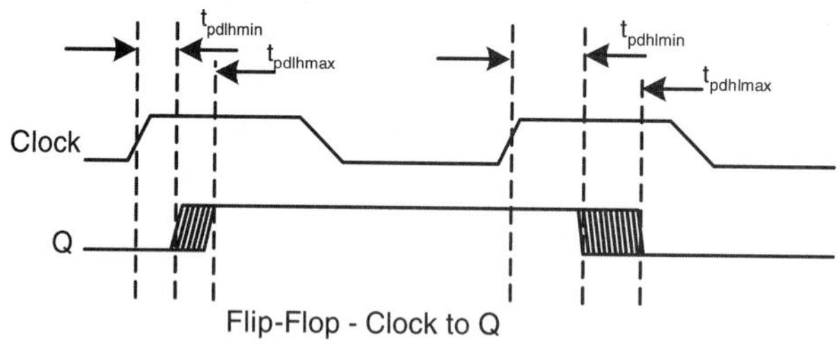

Figure 3.39 Clock to Q Propagation Delays for a Positive Edge Triggered Flip-Flop

As with combinational logic, the delays are measured at the 50% point, between the causative and consequent edges of the signals; the two delays are generally not symmetric.

The propagation delay specification for latches is slightly more complex. In addition to the delay from the causative edge (or level) of the gate, latch transparency requires that the delay from input to output when the *Gate* is enabled be specified as well.

Gate

The timing diagram in Figure 3.40 illustrates the delay from the leading edge of the *Gate* to the Q output of the device.

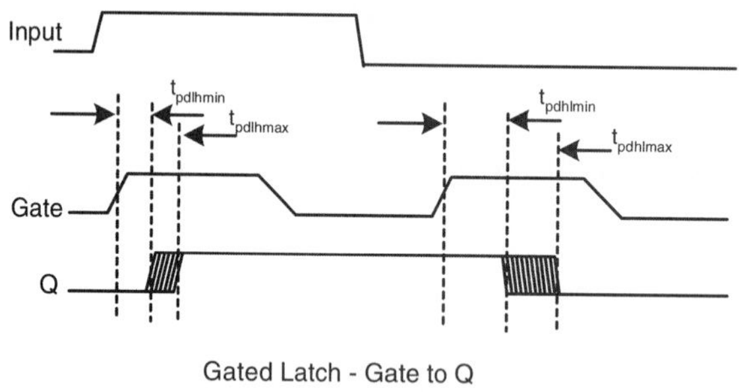

Figure 3.40 Gate to Q Propagation Delays for a Gated Latch with an Active High Gate

The delay to the latch Q output resulting from a state change in the input follows naturally.

3.6.4 Timing Margin

timing margin

To study the concept of *timing margin*, we will analyze the Johnson counter timing in greater detail. The two-stage implementation is redrawn in Figure 3.41 for reference.

If we clock the circuit, we will get the pattern {...0011001100...} on the output of either flip-flop. If we continually increase the frequency, the pattern will repeat until at some fre-

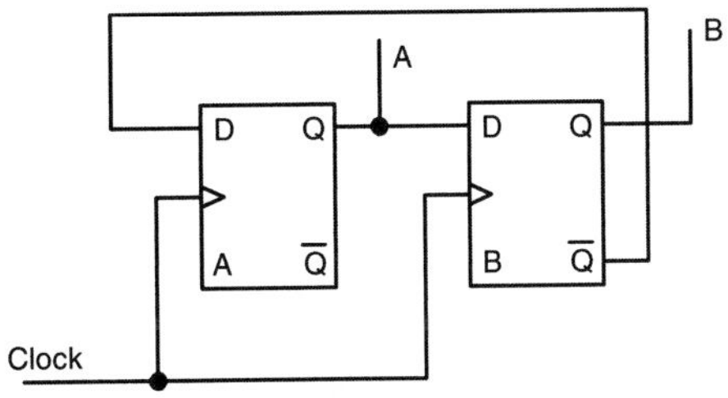

Figure 3.41 A Two-Stage Johnson Counter

quency it fails. Why? Let's analyze the timing of the circuit to understand what and where problems might originate. The essential specifications on the 74ALS74 D-type flip-flop are given as

$$\tau_{PDLH} = 5 - 16\text{ns}$$
$$\tau_{PDHL} = 7 - 18\text{ns}$$
$$\tau_{su} = 16\text{ns}$$

The timing diagram in Figure 3.42 illustrates the clock and the Q output of the A flip-flop for two changes in the value of the state variable.

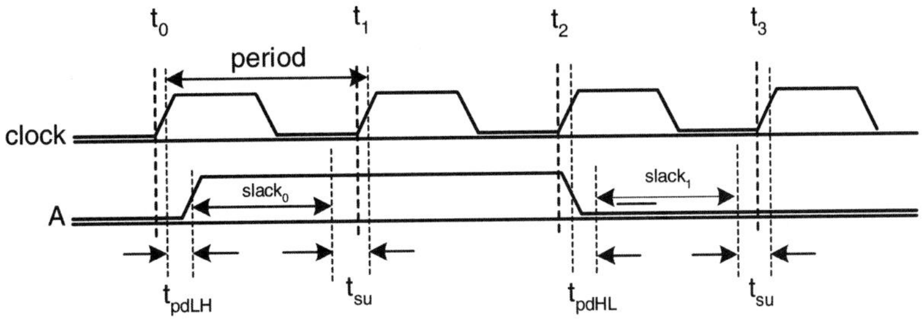

Figure 3.42 Timing Diagram Illustrating Propagation Delays in One Stage of a Two-Stage Johnson Counter

As we discussed earlier, when the setup time is violated, the circuit will not behave as designed and may behave in unpredictable ways. To understand the circuit timing constraints, let's consider two cases. The foregoing analysis assumes no signal delay caused by either parasitic devices or the board layout.

CASE 1 *Low to High Transition of Q_A*

From the timing diagram:

$$\text{clock period} = \tau_{pdLH} + \tau_{su} + \text{slack}_0$$

In the limit, as slack_0 approaches 0, the clock period approaches a minimum:

$$\text{clock period} = \tau_{pdLH} + \tau_{su}$$

Under such a condition and with the minimum value for τ_{pdLH}, the maximum frequency for the counter will be:

$$F_{max} = \frac{1}{(5 + 16)\text{x}10^{-9}\text{sec}}$$
$$= 48\text{MHz}$$

If τ_{pdLH}, is at its maximum value, the maximum frequency for the counter will be:

$$F_{max} = \frac{1}{(16 + 16)\text{x}10^{-9}\text{sec}}$$
$$= 31.3\text{ MHz}$$

CASE 2 *High to Low Transition of Q_A*

From the timing diagram:

$$\text{clock period} = \tau_{pdHL} + \tau_{su} + \text{slack}_1$$

In the limit, as slack_1 approaches 0, the clock period approaches a minimum:

$$\text{clock period} = \tau_{pdHL} + \tau_{su}$$

Under such a condition and with the minimum value for τ_{pdHL}, the maximum frequency for the counter will be:

$$F_{max} = \frac{1}{(7 + 16)x10^{-9}\text{sec}}$$
$$= 43.5 \text{ MHz}$$

If τ_{pdHL}, is at its maximum value, the maximum frequency for the counter will be:

$$F_{max} = \frac{1}{(18 + 16)x10^{-9}\text{sec}}$$
$$= 29.4 \text{ MHz}$$

Based upon these calculations, the maximum clock frequency that can be used for the circuit is 29.4 MHz to ensure reliable operation with any individual SN74ALS74 device. When designing, one must always consider worst case values and then make an educated evaluation of how far to carry such analysis. If carried too far, it is possible to prove that no design will ever work properly.

3.7 PRACTICAL CONSIDERATIONS—PART 2: CLOCKS AND CLOCK DISTRIBUTION

3.7.1 The Source

The clock system or time base in a digital system is an essential component in ensuring proper operation. For certain hard real-time applications, having the proper time base is critical to meeting the timing specifications.

Four fundamental parameters should be considered when designing or selecting a clock system or time base. For the basic clock, these parameters are

- Frequency and frequency range
- Rise times and fall times
- Stability
- Precision

Frequency

Often we start out with a clock source that is a higher frequency than necessary. We then can use ripple counters to divide down the higher frequency to a number of lower frequencies. Remember: because ripple counters are asynchronous, one should never decode any of the state variable combinations to generate a specific frequency. Decoding spikes will occur and will have enough energy to clock flip-flops and latches at the wrong times.

phase locked loop (PLL)

Building a higher frequency from a lower one is done using a *phase locked loop* (PLL). The basic block diagram appears as drawn in Figure 3.43.

voltage-controlled oscillator (VCO)

The feedback signal is the output of a *voltage-controlled oscillator* (VCO) that is controlled by the output voltage. When the phase difference between the input signal and the

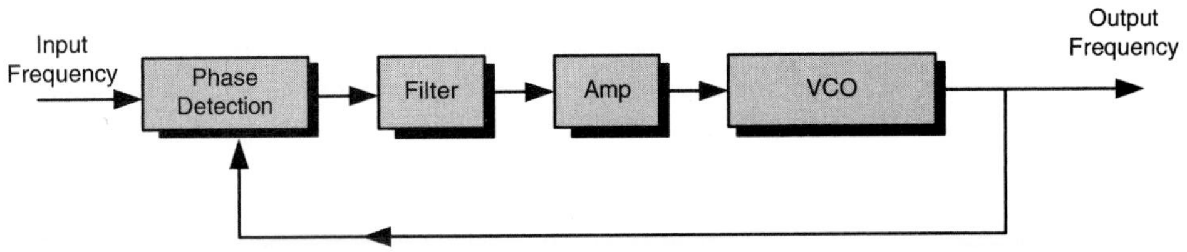

Figure 3.43 Block Diagram for a Basic Phase Locked Loop

output of the VCO is zero, the system has *locked* onto the input frequency. The output of the phase detector will be zero. A difference in phase appears as an error voltage that is filtered by the low-pass filter shown, amplified, and used to provide an input voltage to the VCO. The output of the VCO can now serve as the clock to the system time base.

rate multiplier A scheme to select a fractional portion of a clock signal is called a *rate multiplier*. The block diagram for such a circuit is given in Figure 3.44.

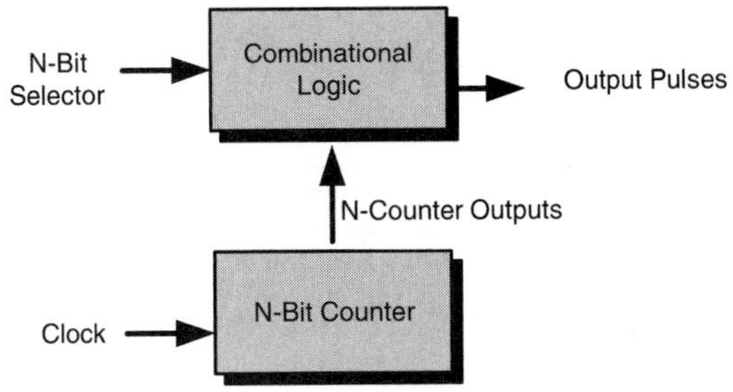

Figure 3.44 Block Diagram for an N-Bit Rate Multiplier

A rate multiplier is simply a combinational logic block combined with an N-bit counter. The period of the counter will be 2^N; that is, the counter will cycle through all of its states every 2^N clock pulses. The N-bit selector also permits 2^N combinations. For each ***selector*** of the 2^N combinations on the *selector* input, the device will output that many pulses. Thus, if N is 4, the counter will be 4 bits and there will be 4 *selector* lines. If the counter is a binary counter, and the selector pattern is 0101, binary 5, then for every 16 clock pulses coming ***output*** into the counter, there will be 5 *output* pulses. The output frequency will be 5/16 of the input frequency. The design of the rate multiplier is such that the selected number of output pulses is evenly distributed across the period of the clock, as illustrated in the timing diagram in Figure 3.45 for a selector pattern of binary 5.

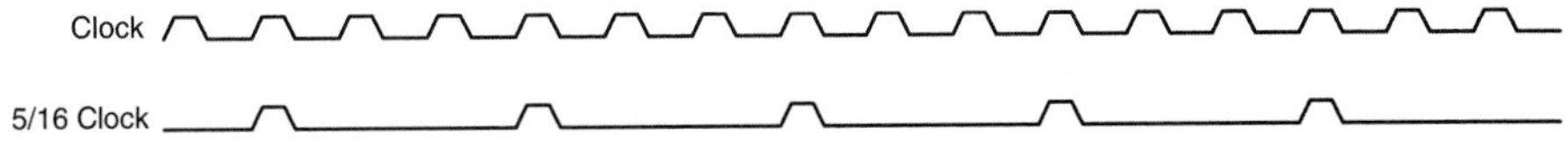

Figure 3.45 Timing Diagram Illustrating the 5/16 Output Frequency for a 4-Bit Binary Rate Multiplier

If one is using a high-frequency oscillator as the primary clock source in a design but a portion of the application requires a significantly lower frequency, a ripple counter can provide a very effective means of developing such a signal. Twelve- to fourteen-stage ripple counters are commonly found as a single MSI part. By using such a counter, one can easily divide the high-frequency source by as much as 16K. When doing so, however, one must be aware that there will be a substantial skew between the edge of the input signal and the resulting edge of any of the lower frequency signals coming out of the counter because of the ripple delay through the device. The application of such a divider is illustrated in the following logic diagram. The effect of the edge skew is reflected in the subsequent timing diagram in Figure 3.46 for an asynchronous binary up counter.

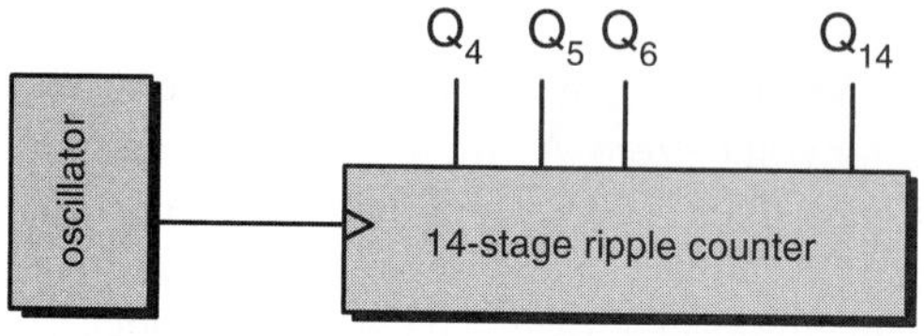

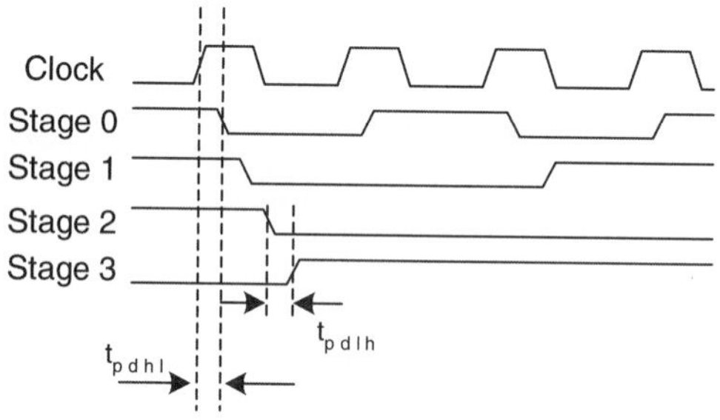

Figure 3.46 Timing Diagram Illustrating the Accumulation of Delays in an Asynchronous Ripple Counter

The timing diagram illustrates the propagation delay for the first four stages as the counter changes from a count of binary seven to binary eight. Observe that the interstage delay accumulates as subsequent flip-flops change state. In this example, the change in state of the third stage is delayed by four propagation delays following the causative event in the first stage. It doesn't take too much imagination to visualize the situation in which the least significant stage may have changed states twice before the *n*th stage is able to change.

Precision and Stability

The simplest kinds of clock sources use resistor and capacitor combinations to set their output frequency. Although such devices may be perfectly reasonable for controlling windshield wipers or a door bell, they should never be used in critical hard real-time applications. Capacitors have wide tolerances and are subject to humidity, brownout, or low-voltage levels, as well as a number of environmental effects.

Crystal-based sources are generally the best solution for stable and accurate timing signals. When using such devices, one can either start with the basic crystal, and then design the analog electronics necessary to implement the desired oscillator or buy a prepackaged oscillator. Each crystal or oscillator has different stability and accuracy specifications. If the application demands greater accuracy and stability than are available with standard devices, the next step is to use temperature-compensated designs. Such sources utilize a small heater to minimize the effects of temperature variation of the oscillator.

3.7.2 Designing a Clock System

3.7.2.1 Single-Phase Clocks

A single-phase clock should start with the crystal oscillator. Such an approach gives stability and repeatability to any clocking and timing that need to be in the embedded application.

Variations on the circuit in Figure 3.47 should never be used.

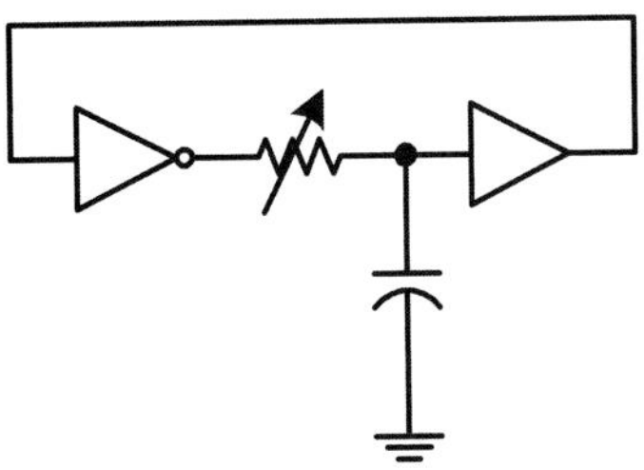

Figure 3.47 A Simple Clock Generator

The design is trying to do a digital job with analog parts. Adding the R and C as shown can significantly affect the rise and fall times of the input signals to the buffer. As the transition times increase, so does the probability of the circuit becoming metastable.

3.7.2.2 Multiple-Phase Clocks

Contemporary digital systems frequently require more precise resolution in time than can be achieved with a single-phase clock. Consider the basic clock waveform in Figure 3.48.

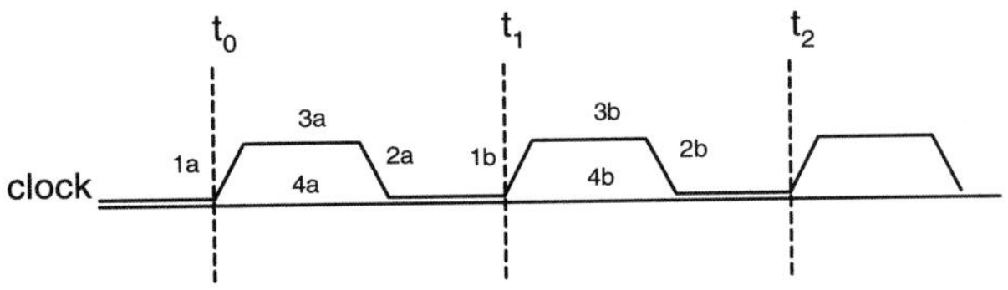

Figure 3.48 Decision Points in a Basic Clock Waveform

A decision can be made in four places within a single clock period:

1. The rising edge
2. The falling edge
3. The high level
4. The low level

One cannot tell the difference in time between the edge at 1a and that at 1b. The best resolution we have is a half period.

The simplest multiple-phase clock generator is given in Figure 3.49. The circuit generates two nonoverlapping clock signals as output. The structural Verilog model for the clock generator is given in the code module in Figure 3.50.

The timing diagram for the generator is given in Figure 3.51.

We can now see that over a two clock-cycle interval, we have eight different places that a logical decision can be made. Furthermore, the edge at t_0 is distinguishable from the edge at t_1; the same holds true for the remaining edges and levels along the two phases.

Using such a scheme, we can now use P2 as a causative edge and P1 as a sampling edge for example. P2 will affect an event or state change. The interval between P2 and P1 should

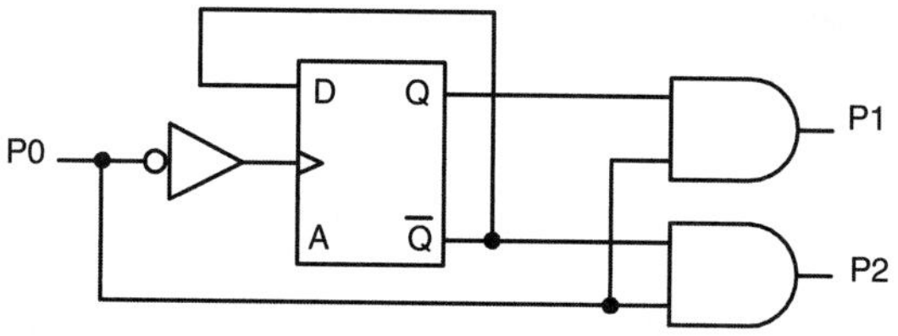

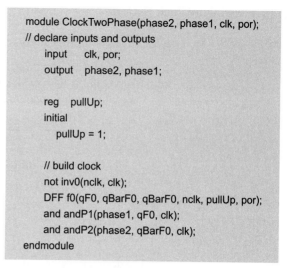

Figure 3.49 A Basic Two-Phase Clock Generator

```
module ClockTwoPhase(phase2, phase1, clk, por);
// declare inputs and outputs
    input    clk, por;
    output   phase2, phase1;

    reg  pullUp;
    initial
        pullUp = 1;

    // build clock
    not inv0(nclk, clk);
    DFF f0(qF0, qBarF0, qBarF0, nclk, pullUp, por);
    and andP1(phase1, qF0, clk);
    and andP2(phase2, qBarF0, clk);
endmodule
```

Figure 3.50 A Structural Verilog Code Module for the Two-Phase Clock Generator

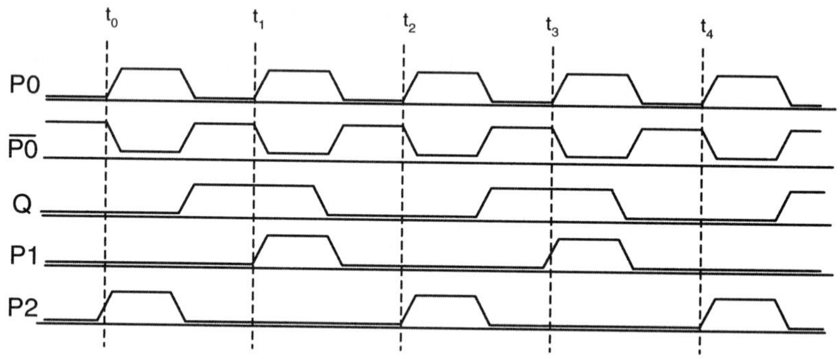

Figure 3.51 Timing Diagram for the Two-Phase Clock Generator

be sufficient for all changing and propagating signals to settle before they are acted upon by the logic clocked by P1.

Although the circuit contains a race as illustrated in the logic diagram in Figure 3.52, the race is biased toward path2 so that there can never be a decoding spike on either of the two AND gates generating P1 and P2.

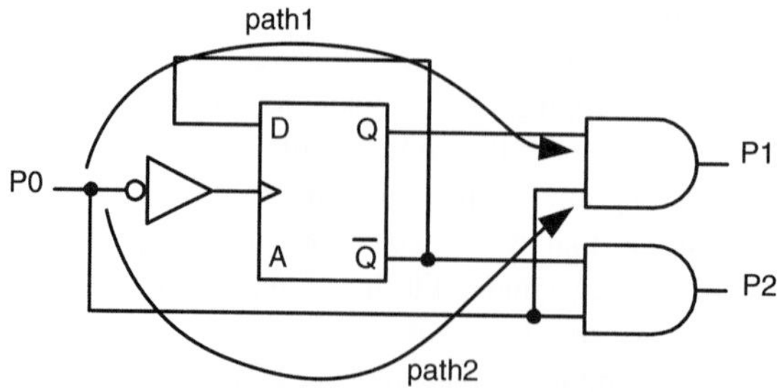

Figure 3.52 Critical Timing Paths in the Two-Phase Clock Generator

Another effective and flexible way to produce a multiple-clock phase time base is to use a Johnson counter. The two-stage counter is repeated and extended in the logic diagram

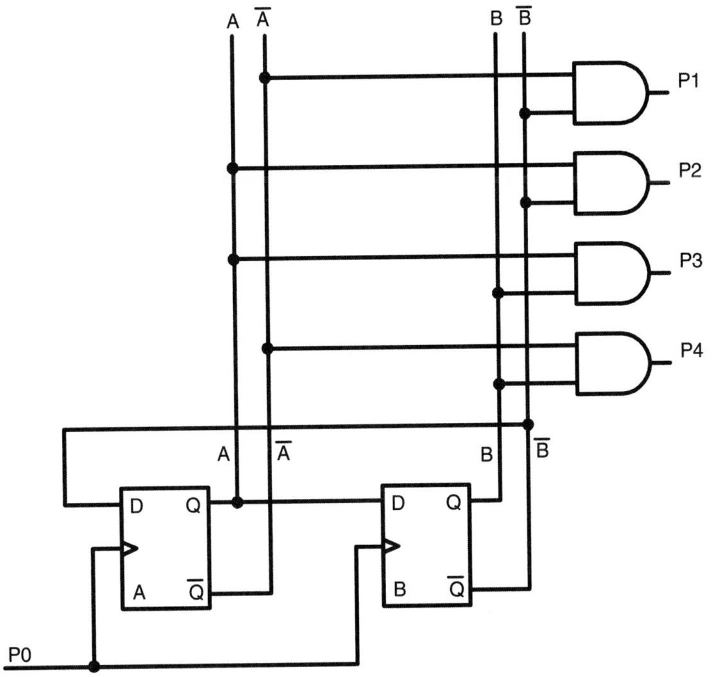

Figure 3.53 Logic Diagram of a Four-Phase Clock Generator Using a Johnson Counter

shown in Figure 3.53. By decoding each of the four states in the counting sequence, we can generate four different phased clocks as we see in the figure.

The structural Verilog model follows in Figure 3.54.

```
module ClockFourPhase(phase4, phase3, phase2, phase1, clk, por);
// declare inputs and outputs
   input    clk, por;
   output   phase4, phase3, phase2, phase1;

   reg  pullUp;

   initial
      pullUp = 1;
   // build clock
   not inv0(nclk, clk);
   DFF f0(qF0, qBarF0, qBarF1, nclk, pullUp, por);
   DFF f1(qF1, qBarF1, qF0, nclk, pullUp, por);

   // build the four phases
   and andP1(phase1, qBarF0, qBarF1);
   and andP2(phase2, qF0, qBarF1);
   and andP3(phase3, qF0, qF1);
   and andP4(phase4, qBarF0, qF1);
endmodule
```

Figure 3.54 Structural Verilog Code Module for a Four-Phase Clock Generator Using a Johnson Counter

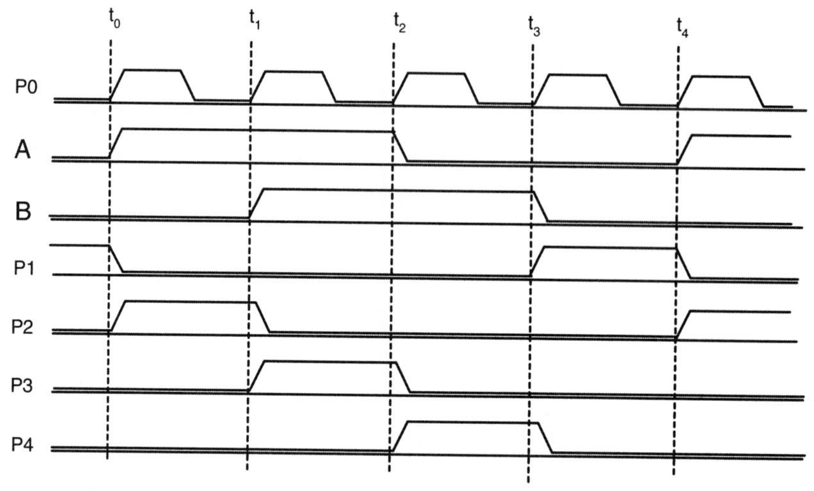

Figure 3.55 Timing Diagram for a Four-Phase Clock Generator Using a Johnson Counter

The timing diagram in Figure 3.55 illustrates the four different clock phases.

By incorporating additional phases, we have increased our control over the placement or sampling of events in time.

3.7.2.3 More than Four Phases

Expanding the time base beyond four phases, we can continue to build on the Johnson counter. If such a design is utilized, the disconnected subgraph for each case will have to be managed. An alternative approach is to utilize a delay-based scheme such as a tapped delay line. The advantage of such an approach is that one can use a lower frequency clock. The Johnson counter used in the previous design requires a base clock that has a frequency that is four times the frequency of the phases.

3.7.2.4 Multiple Clocks versus Multiple Phases

The major advantage of multiple phases when compared to multiple clocks is that all phases are derived from the same fundamental frequency. Clock noise can be filtered out much more easily. With multiple clocks, although all may be using the same frequency, they are all running asynchronous to each other.

3.7.2.5 Gating the Clock

The general rule of thumb is that gating the clock should never be done because of the high potential for hazards. If gating becomes essential, one should thoroughly understand the timing and change the control logic only when the clock in such a state that it cannot result in a change on the gate output. An example is the two-phase clock discussed earlier.

3.8 TESTING SEQUENTIAL CIRCUITS

Testing sequential circuits is much more complex than testing combinational circuitry. Sequential machines have memory; their behavior is determined by the values and the order in which the input signals occur. Combinational circuits can be tested very effectively by using PN (pseudo noise) sequence generators of the type we studied earlier. Such an approach is not feasible in a circuit with potentially cyclic behavior. Testing in the sequential world brings a whole new set of interesting opportunities.

3.8.1 The Finite-State Machine Model Revisited

As a first step toward addressing the test problem, we will briefly review the basic model for the finite-state machine given in Figure 3.56.

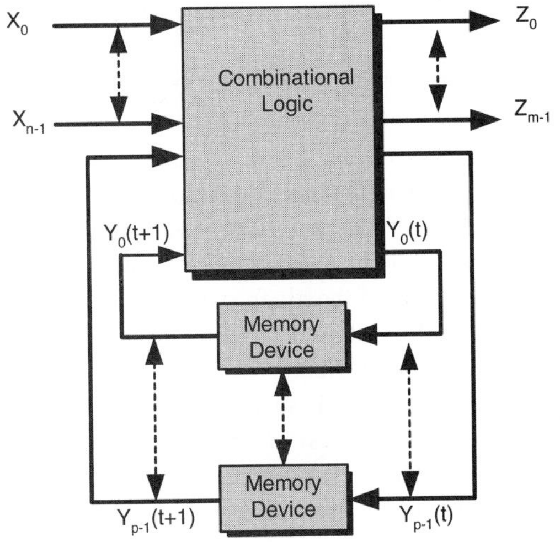

Figure 3.56 Model for a Finite-State Machine

The essential components of a sequential machine and its behavior comprise the combinational circuitry, the memory devices, and their combined operation. Faults in the combinational circuitry can be modeled using the methods that have been discussed earlier. Such techniques extend naturally to the memory devices as well. We will examine these devices in greater detail shortly. Modeling the behavior of the complete system is a bit more complex.

The objectives when developing tests for a sequential machine are similar to those established for strictly combinational systems. Each path through the circuit must be verified, the proper operation of each comprising element must be ensured, and the proper operation of the system must be confirmed.

3.8.2 Sequential Circuit Test—A First Look

One can attack the complexity of testing sequential circuits in a number of ways. We will begin with a rather basic approach and then explore some ways by which the more complex problems can be simplified—basic doesn't necessarily mean efficient or fast. Remember the linear search algorithm? It's rather simple (look at each case until the target is found) but most definitely not fast.

test vector
Unit Under Test (UUT)
test pattern

A *test vector* is a collection of 0's and 1's that is applied to the input of a *Unit Under Test* (UUT) to verify some aspect of its functionality by producing a signal (or set of signals) on a specified output or outputs. A *test pattern* is a sequence of test vectors that is applied to a UUT to test a series of input/output combinations or to test the temporal behavior of the UUT.

A first, high-level view of the problem is illustrated in Figure 3.57.

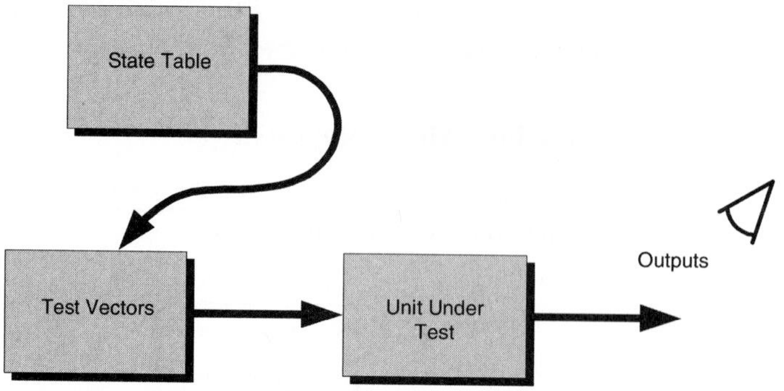

Figure 3.57 A High-Level View of Testing a Finite-State Machine

Beginning with a sequential circuit (the unit under test—UUT), a state table describing its behavior, and a series of test vectors, the test pattern is applied to the primary circuit inputs and the responses on the primary circuit outputs are observed. The observed behavior is then compared with that of the given state table. If it matches *and* if the test is a good test, one can assume that the system is functioning properly. Otherwise, there has been a failure and the cause must be identified.

The test is rather simple. If such tests are examined in greater detail, it is evident that each is made up of two pieces: an initializing sequence that will take the machine to a desired starting state and a testing sequence that will take the machine from the initial state through each of its possible transitions to the proper final state. Such a structure is shown in Figure 3.58. A complete test suite comprises a sufficient number of such tests to ensure the proper behavior of the machine.

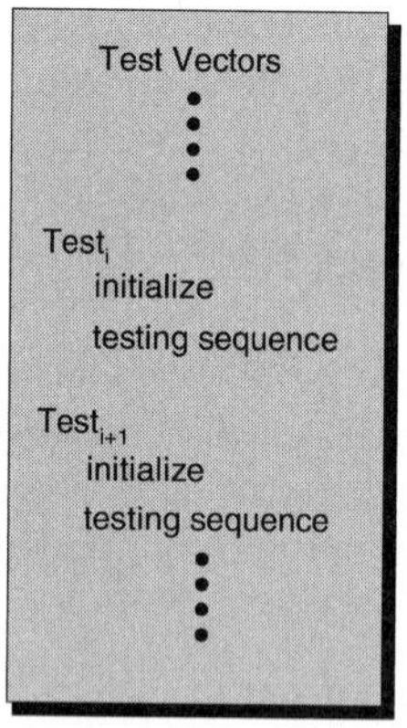

Figure 3.58 Test Cases for Testing a Finite-State Machine

strongly connected ***transfer sequence*** ***weakly connected***

Let's now start to formalize our approach; we will begin with some vocabulary. A finite-state machine is said to be *strongly connected* if and only if, for *any* ordered pair of states $\{S_i, S_j\}$, there is an input sequence $\{I_m \ldots I_n\}$ that will take the machine from S_i to S_j. The shortest such sequence is called a *transfer sequence,* $T\{S_i, S_j\}$. Real-world machines are not strongly connected. Clearly, such is the case for any machines with terminal states. For the purposes here, we define a *weakly connected* machine as one in which there exists an ordered pair of states, $\{S_{initial,} S_j\}$ and a finite input sequence, I, such that if the machine is in state $S_{initial,}$ the machine can reach state S_j if the sequence I is applied. If such is not the case, then the system has an unreachable state as the result of a design error or oversight. That problem must be corrected.

The notion of a weakly connected machine presupposes that the machine is able to reach each such initial state. This can be accomplished in several ways. If access to the machine is restricted to its primary inputs, then a sequence of inputs must be defined that will place the system in the desired initial state, $S_{initial}$. Such a sequence is called an *initialization sequence*, $I_{initial}$. Developing such a sequence can be a nontrivial task. Further compounding the difficulty is the possibility that the sequence may be quite long. One of the goals in production testing is to keep the cost of tests to a minimum while ensuring a quality product. In production, time is money.

initialization sequence

An alternative technique is based on recognizing that the objective in a production test is to identify defects introduced during manufacturing. One must begin with the initial assumption that the design of the UUT is correct. Thus, we have the option of placing the system in the desired initial state through adjunct circuitry that can be included solely for that purpose. Such a method is called *scan design*; we will discuss the approach in greater detail a bit later. The shorter initialization sequence applied via scan design will still be referred to as $I_{initial}$.

scan design

In a properly operating machine, once the system is in the desired initial state, the *test sequences*, $\{I_{test}\}$, will take it to the desired *terminal states*. A *homing sequence* for a finite-state machine is defined as an input sequence that will produce a unique destination state (from any initial state) after the sequence is applied. If the notions of a homing and a transfer sequence are coupled with the weakly connected machine, one can conclude that a complete test sequence for a sequential machine begins with an initialization (homing) sequence, followed by a transfer sequence: $I_{testSequence} = I_{initial} + I_{transfer}$. The test suite can now consist of the necessary set of all such sequences that are needed to confirm the proper behavior of the circuit.

test sequences
terminal states
homing sequence

From linear system theory, it is known that two systems are equivalent if their output behavior is identical for all combinations of inputs. It is just this recognition that allows one system to be replaced by another perhaps simplified or less expensive version. Although such an ability is beneficial during design, it can be rather troublesome during testing of the system.

A fault condition in a finite-state machine will alter its logical structure. When a given test sequence is applied to a system, the underlying assumption is made that the observable output behavior for the faulted circuit will be distinguishable from that of the fault-free version for applied sequence. Such a sequence is called a *distinguishing sequence*. Such an assumption depends, in part, on the machine being fully specified and reduced.

distinguishing sequence

Defining Homing and Transfer Sequences

Let's now take a look at formulating a homing (initialization) sequence and a transfer sequence for the simple state machine described in this section. We will work with the machine specified by the state table in Figure 3.59.

Present State $t = t_n$	Next State $t = t_{n+1}$		Output	
	x = 0	x = 1	x = 0	x = 1
A	C	D	0	0
B	B	A	1	0
C	A	C	1	1
D	D	B	0	1

Figure 3.59 A Basic Finite State Machine

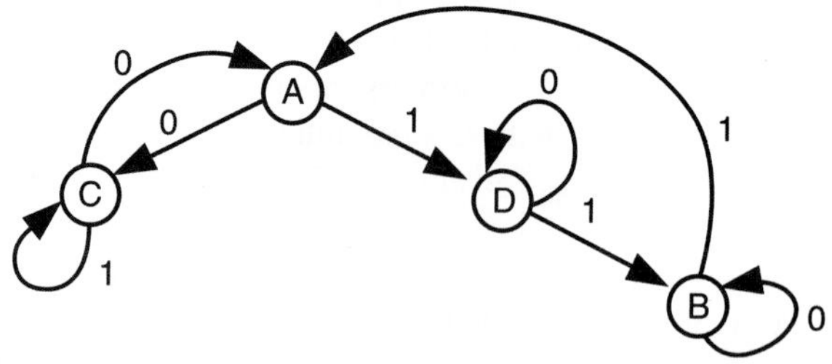

Figure 3.60 A State Diagram for the Example Finite-State Machine

We will assume that the system is initially in state A. The state diagram in Figure 3.60 is extracted from the state table. Based on the state diagram, one can easily formulate a transfer sequence to get from any initial state to any other state. Thus, if *state D* is selected as the initial state, the input sequence {1, 1} will take the machine to *state A* and {1,1,0} will take it to *state C*.

successor tree

A homing sequence for the state machine can be built using a simple binary tree called a *successor tree*. A homing sequence has been defined as a set of input values that will take the state machine from any initial state to a unique final state. Therefore, if the state machine is viewed as a black box, initially one does not know which state it is in. We have maximum uncertainty. With each input value that is applied, the uncertainty about the state of the machine is reduced. After the full homing sequence is complete, the machine will be in one of the comprising states (and have perfect knowledge or zero uncertainty).

For the example machine, we begin with maximum uncertainty; that is, all that is known is that it is in one of the states in the set {A,B,C,D}. If a logical 0 is applied as an input data, and the output is observed, if the system was initially in *state A* or *state D,* then the output must be a logical 0. If the machine was in either *B* or *C* initially, the circuit output must be a logical 1. The initial uncertainty has been reduced.

Prior to applying the first input, the machine could have been in any of four states. By observing the output value, one now knows that the machine was in either of two sets of two states. Similarly, if a logical 1 is applied to the input, the system output will be a logical 0 if the initial state was *state A* or *state B* and a 1 if the system had started in *state C* or *state D*.

Thus, after the application of just one input value, the initial uncertainty is cut in half. Prior to applying the first input, the best one could say was that the machine was in one of four states; now it is in one of two. We continue applying 0's or 1's until either no new information is gained or we have perfect knowledge. The successor tree in Figure 3.61 illustrates the process.

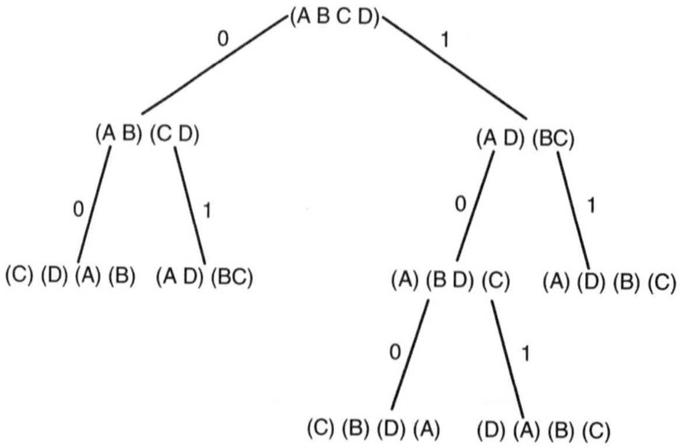

Figure 3.61 A Successor Tree for the Example Finite State Machine

Present State $t = t_n$	Next State / Output $t = t_{n+1}$		Sequence (0,0)		Sequence (1,1)		Sequence (1,0,0)		
	x = 0	x = 1	T_0	T_1	T_0	T_1	T_0	T_1	T_2
A	C/0	D/0	C/0	A/1	D/0	B/1	D/0	C/0	D/0
B	B/1	A/0	B/1	B/1	B/0	D/0	A/0	D/0	A/1
C	A/1	C/1	A/1	C/0	C/1	C/1	C/0	A/0	C/0
D	D/0	B/1	D/0	D/0	B/1	A/0	B/1	B/1	B/1

Figure 3.62 A State Table Illustrating the Response of the Example Finite-State Machine to Several Homing Sequences

Observe that each of the input sequences {0,0}, {1,1}, and {1,0,0} results in a unique final state, as we see in the state table in Figure 3.62.

The specific final state is based on the original starting state. Each sequence constitutes a homing sequence. No new information is gained beyond that shown if the sequence {0,1} is applied. Notice further that there is a unique output sequence for each of the different starting states.

One can now apply any of the homing sequences as an initialization sequence to establish any of the states as an initial state; from there, one can then apply the proper transfer sequence to reach any other state. A fault will alter the physical structure of the machine, forcing it to follow a different pattern in response to any of the three input sequences.

All reduced state machines have at least one homing sequence. In the previous example, any of the three sequences will take the machine to one of the four possible states, based on the starting state. However, such is not always the case; a specific sequence may always lead to the same state, independent of the initial state, as the following example for a simple pattern recognizer shows.

EXAMPLE 3.1

The system, illustrated in the state diagram and state table in Figure 3.63, is designed to recognize the pattern 1010 in a continuous serial stream of data. The output signal, Z, will indicate a logical 1 if the pattern is found.

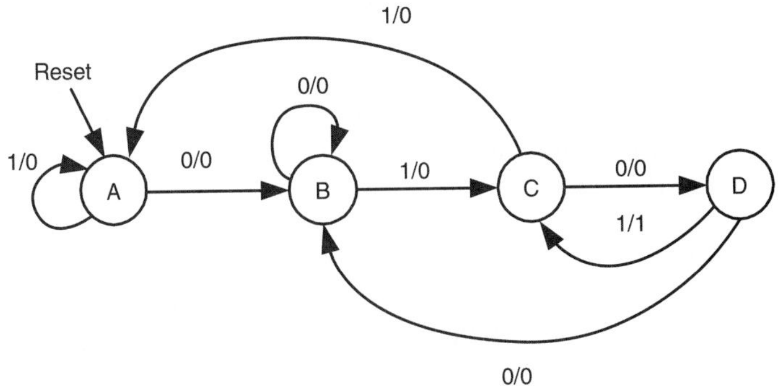

Present State $t = t_n$	Next State $t = t_{n+1}$	
	x = 0	x = 1
A	B/0	A/0
B	B/0	C/0
C	D/0	A/0
D	B/0	B

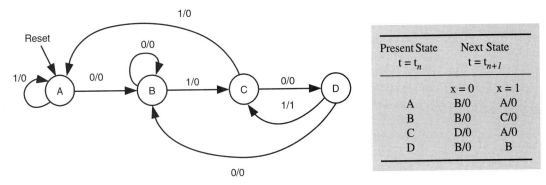

Figure 3.63 A State Diagram and State Table for a Simple Pattern Detection Circuit

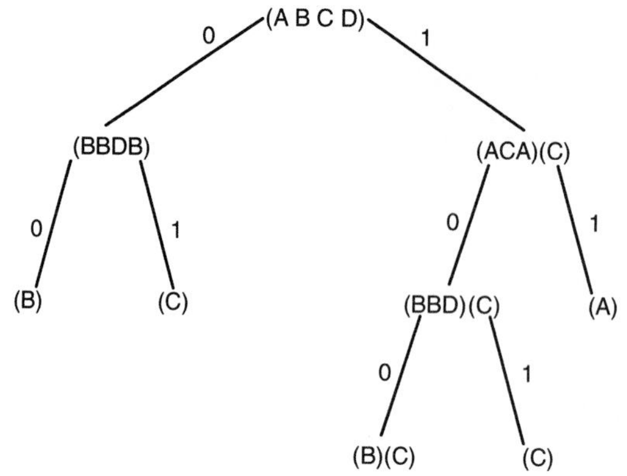

Figure 3.64 A Successor Tree and Homing Sequences for a Simple Pattern Detection Circuit

The successor tree in Figure 3.64 can now be built.

Starting from a state of complete uncertainty, observe that on application, each of the different sequences will take the machine to a unique state. However, one cannot deduce the initial state by observing the state of the system after application of a single homing sequence.

3.8.3 Scan Design Techniques

Earlier we observed that a finite-state machine can be decomposed into a combination logic block and a flip-flop block. If each piece can be tested separately, then the task will be a lot easier. The combinational portion can be tested using techniques introduced earlier. The flip-flops can be verified much more easily if one does not have to worry about long sequences or cyclic behavior. There are two minor problems, however: how can one segregate the two portions of the circuit, and how can one gain visibility of the flip-flop states from the primary outputs?

Recall that in the earlier designs of counters and shift registers several different pieces of functionality (count up/count down, shift left/shift right) were combined into a single circuit and used a selector input to choose between them. Let's reexamine that idea. Reuse of designs is always a good plan. We begin by identifying the pieces of functionality that we will need.

To verify the proper operation of the flip-flops, one must show that each device can be placed into the logical 0 or logical 1 state. If all the flip-flops can be configured into a shift register and a pattern of logical 0's and 1's shifted through, that task can be accomplished. Thus, we have the first piece of functionality—a shift register. Next, the combinational logic must be confirmed. Confirmation can take either of two directions. One can test for any stuck-at faults, or one can confirm that all of the state transitions can be executed. Either path requires that known values be placed on the inputs to the combinational logic block.

The values $\{X_n\}$ can be entered through the circuit's primary inputs. It is known how to configure our flip-flops as a shift register. When so configured, it is possible to shift in any desired pattern. Specifically, one can shift in a pattern that can place any of the needed values on the variables $\{Y_m(t+1)\}$ from the model. The values $\{Z_k\}$ can be confirmed through the primary outputs. What remains to confirm are the values of the variables $\{Y_m(t)\}$. These, too, can be accessed through the shift register. The second piece of functionality is to configure the shift register to support a parallel load. This, however, is no different from the normal behavior of the flip-flops.

The test can be executed by appropriately choosing between the shift register functionality and the normal operation of the system. To implement the strategy, the original circuit

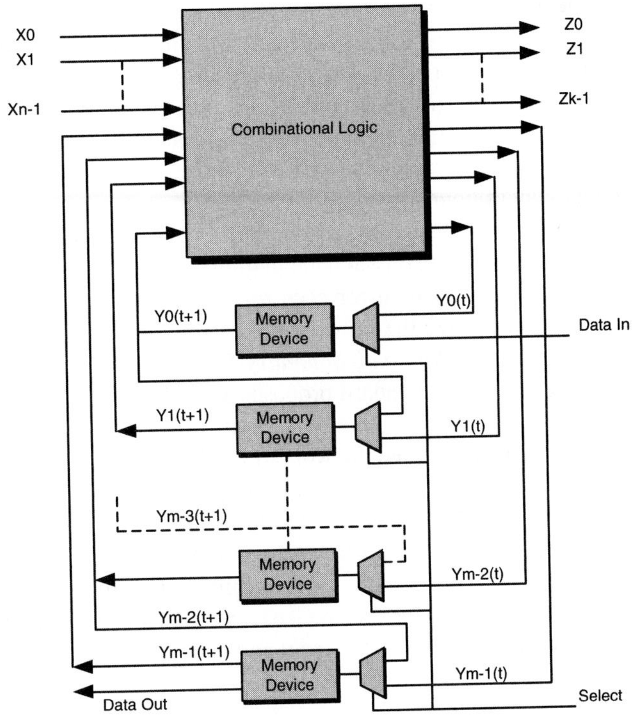

Figure 3.65 A Finite-State Machine with Supporting Scan Path

must be modified to allow one to select between the two modes. Such a reconfiguration can be controlled through a simple multiplexer as seen in Figure 3.65.

scan path, scan in
scan out

The shift register is called a *scan path*; the serial data in and out are called *scan in* and *scan out*, respectively. The multiplexer control permits one to select between normal operation and test. These signals are brought to connector pins to provide easy access and connection to a test fixture. A clock to the machine is included in the set of signals that are brought to the outside. Although one could use the internal system clock, the tests can be executed more effectively if the internal clock can be disabled and a test clock provided to control the machine.

scan in, scan out

When the test mode is selected, the memory devices are configured as a shift register. Data can be entered through the *scan in* port and read from the *scan out* port. In the normal mode, the values $\{Y_m(t)\}$ will appear on the flip-flop inputs and can be stored when the devices are clocked. We can then switch back to the test mode to shift the values out.

Using a scan path now gives some visibility into and control over the test of a finite-state machine. What if there are two or three such machines? Are separate input and output paths, separate clocks, and separate test mode control required for each machine? These are good questions.

3.8.4 Boundary Scan—Extending Scan-Path Techniques

The growth, changes, and technological advances that have occurred during the last 20 to 30 years have been remarkable; they have been the stuff of science fiction. Today changes continue at an ever-increasing pace. Are these changes always good? That is sometimes difficult to say. Nonetheless, each change presents new levels of complexity and new challenges to discover ways to deal with that complexity. Not too many years ago, all the test equipment needed were a good scope and a bit of intuition. This is no longer so. Today's ASICs, CPLDs, Array Logics, custom VLSI circuits, or Systems on a Chip make design and test much more interesting. How can we test? How can we see what we can't see?

Let's begin where we left off. Once again, let's reuse a design idea. A scan path can provide visibility into the internals of a state machine. Without much work, the idea can be extended to an entire chip or system. The scan-path concept forms the basis for what is known today as *boundary scan*.

boundary scan

In the mid- to late 1980s, a group of international electronics firms recognized that a common means for testing and debugging complex systems and integrated circuits would be economically essential for each to remain competitive in today's fast-paced market. Together they formed the Joint Test Advisory Group (JTAG), and they developed a *Standard Test Access Port and Boundary-Scan Architecture* for such systems. Commonly known as JTAG, the standard proposes a simple four-wire serial interface through which test vectors and test results can be entered into and read from a system or integrated circuit. In 1990, the IEEE adopted the work of the Joint Test Advisory Group as a standard (IEEE 1149.1), which defines a common protocol and boundary-scan architecture. Today IEEE 1149.1 has become accepted as an industry standard.

Standard Test Access Port and Boundary-Scan Architecture

A boundary scan provides a software method to control and observe the values on connector or I/O pins on any circuit board or integrated circuit that is compatible with the JTAG standard. Let's take a look at the basic components and architecture for a boundary-scan system. We will begin with the input and output pin structure, as illustrated in Figure 3.66.

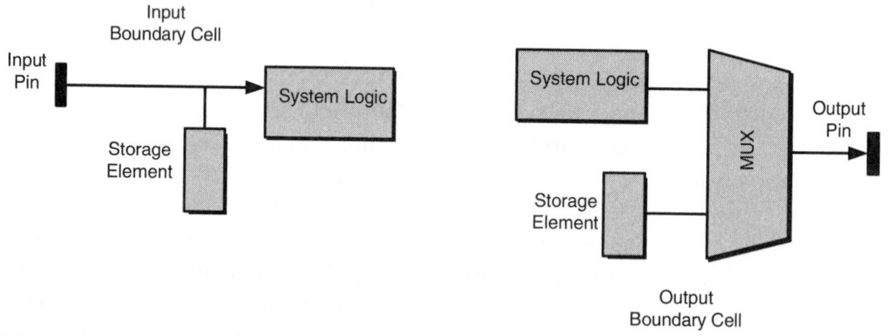

Figure 3.66 Input and Output Pin Structure in a Boundary-Scan Architecture

During normal operation, the boundary cells are disabled and the I/O signals pass into or out of the system normally. In the test mode, input signals are shadowed in the associated storage elements, and output signals are set to selected test values that are propagated down the scan path to test other devices. The scan cells are controlled through the *Test Access Port* (TAP) and *Instruction Register*, as shown in Figure 3.67.

Test Access Port (TAP)
Instruction Register

The TAP Controller is a simple state machine with up to 16 possible states. It is used to control the actions associated with the boundary-scan cells. The system uses four signals, *Test Mode Select* (TMS), *Test Data In* (TDI), *Test Data Out* (TDO), and *Test Clock* (TCK), to manage the operation of the boundary-scan system. TDI and TDO signals are used to introduce data into the system or to propagate test signals or data out.

Test Mode Select
Test Data In
Test Data Out
Test Clock
Test Mode Select

The boundary-scan system can easily be extended to multiple integrated circuits or boards within a system simply by connecting the TDO signal from one portion to the TDI signal of the next ciruict. By activating the Bypass Register, one can sidestep the scan path on selected components while testing others.

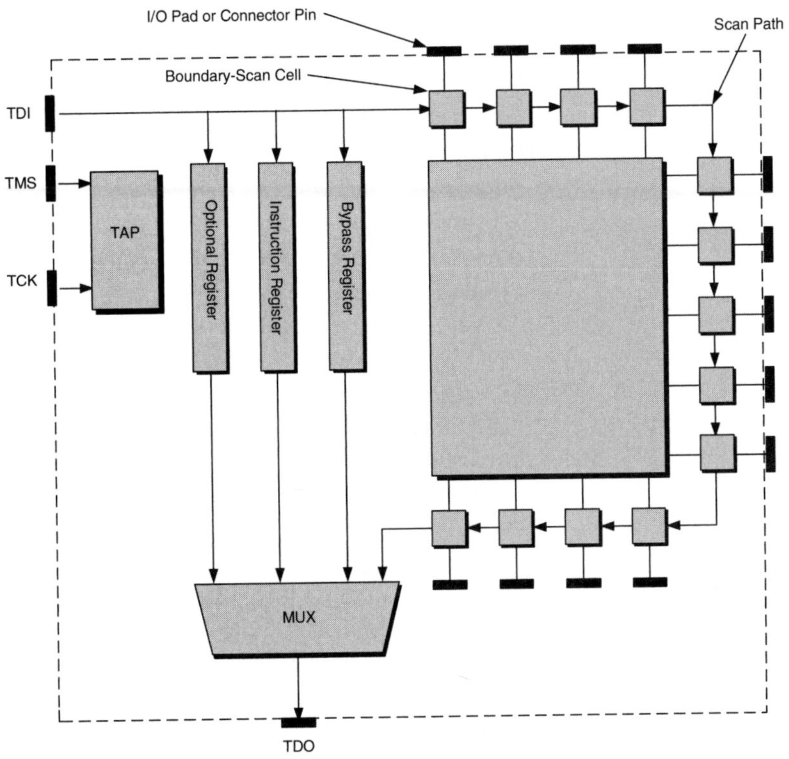

Figure 3.67 The Boundary-Scan Architecture and Unit Under Test

Instruction Register

A test operation is initiated when a command is sent by a tester on the *Test Mode Select* (TMS) input directing the *Instruction Register* (IR) to load a sequence of bits appearing on the Test Data In (TDI) input. The data received by the IR identifies which type of test the system is to perform. The latest version of the specification, IEEE 1149.1-2001, dictates that all devices must support the following four required instructions:

EXTEST: The EXTEST instruction places the device into an external boundary test mode and connects the boundary-scan register (BSR) between the TDI and TDO pins. On execution, the output boundary-scan cells are loaded with test patterns to send to downstream devices. The input boundary-scan cells are configured to shadow the input data.

BYPASS: The Bypass instruction directs that a device's scan path is to be bypassed and that the TDI input data is to be routed directly to the TDO output without interfering with the ongoing operation of the device.

SAMPLE: The SAMPLE instruction allows the device to remain in a functional (rather than a test) mode and connects the BSR between the TDI and TDO pins. During execution, the boundary-scan register can be read to monitor data entering the device.

PRELOAD: The PRELOAD instruction is also used to load known data values into the BSR. We can use such values for initialization, for example.

Both the PRELOAD and SAMPLE instructions are used as a prelude to future activity.

In addition to the required instructions, the Standard specifies several optional instructions. These are given as follows.

INTEST: The INTEST instruction is used to activate the BSR for tests of a device's internal logic.

IDCODE: The IDCODE instruction accesses a device's (optional) internal identification register that contains manufacturer and part-specific information. That data is returned through the TDO register.

USERCODE: The USERCODE instruction permits user identification data to be loaded into the device's identification register. Such information is useful if a device has an original generic function such as a gate array and a value-added identification such as a high-speed graphical manipulator.

BIST: The BIST instruction is used to invoke user-defined built-in self-test functionality. It is assumed that the built-in capability does not need any external initialization. Once the built-in tests have been completed, the results are sent to the outside world via the TDO output path.

CLAMP: Working in conjunction with PRELOAD, the CLAMP instruction drives the device's output lines with the values that have been entered during PRELOAD and then enables the BYPASS functionality. The CLAMP instruction can be used to ensure that the device's outputs are held in a desired state. Such a capability can be used to avoid conflicts between several different devices sharing a common bus.

HighZ: HighZ works like the CLAMP instruction to ensure that specific device outputs are placed into the high-impedance state.

The IEEE 1149.1 Standard also provides for an optional input pin, TRST, which can be used to asynchronously reset the TAP controller.

3.9 SUMMARY

In this chapter, we began with the idea of state and time, two key aspects that distinguish sequential from combinational circuits, and presented a theoretical model for the finite-state machine.

We introduced registers and shift registers as elementary examples of a finite-state machine. We expressed the concepts of state and time using the state diagram and state table, two of the basic tools for characterizing and working with sequential circuits. We then used the state diagram and state table to describe the behavior of basic counting and dividing circuits. We looked at clocking systems and time-base designs that are useful for accurately controlling the digital hardware in embedded applications.

We then moved from the theoretical to the practical world when we examined how real-world issues encountered earlier with combinational logic circuits, as well as several new ones, are also present in sequential designs.

We concluded our study of sequential circuits with the problem of how to test finite-state systems. Possible tools and alternatives included homing sequences, scan-path, and boundary-scan techniques as methods for attacking the problems unique to testing sequential circuitry.

3.10 REVIEW QUESTIONS

The Concepts of State and Time

3.1 What are state variables, and what do they tell us?

3.2 When we say *state of the system*, what do we mean?

3.3 What is a state diagram?

3.4 What is the purpose of a state diagram, and what information can we derive from it?

3.5 What are the basic elements of a state diagram?

3.6 What is a finite-state machine, and what is its purpose?

3.7 In the text, a finite-state machine was defined as a quintuple. What are the elements that comprise the quintuple, and what is the purpose of each?

3.8 What is the difference between a Mealy and a Moore finite-state machine?

Designing Finite-State Machines—Registers

3.9 What is a register?

3.10 What do we mean by the width of a register?

3.11 What is a shift register?

3.12 Describe the characteristic behavior of a shift register.

3.13 What do we mean by a parallel in/serial out or serial in/parallel out shift register?

3.14 What do we mean by the term *transparent latch*?

3.15 What is a linear feedback shift register?

3.16 What do we mean by the term *maximal length* shift register?

3.17 What is a PN sequence?

Designing Finite-State Machines—Counting and Dividing

3.18 For what purposes do we use counters and dividers in embedded applications?

3.19 What is the major difference between an asychronous counter/divider and a synchronous one?

3.20 What is a ripple counter?

3.21 What characteristic makes Johnson counters different from the other counters studied in this chapter?

3.22 What is the general expression for the period of a Johnson counter?

Practical Considerations—Timing in Latches and Flip-Flops

3.23 What does the term *setup time* mean? *hold time*?

3.24 Why is setup time an important parameter? hold time?

3.25 What is the difference between setup time in a latch versus a flip-flop? hold time?

3.26 What does the term *metastable* mean?

3.27 How do we measure propagation delay in a latch? flip-flop?

3.28 How is propagation delay different in a latch or flip-flop from that in combinational logic?

Practical Considerations—Clocks and Clock Distribution

3.29 What is a time base?

3.30 What are the four fundamental parameters that one should consider when selecting or designing a clock system or time base?

3.31 What is a phase locked loop?

3.32 What is the purpose of a phase locked loop?

3.33 What is a rate multiplier? What is its purpose?

Testing Sequential Circuits

3.34 What is the major difficulty when testing sequential circuits versus combinational logic systems?

3.35 What is a test vector?

3.36 What do we mean when we say that a finite-state machine is strongly connected? weakly connected?

3.37 What does the term *transfer sequence* mean?

3.38 What is an initialization sequence?

3.39 What is a terminal state?

3.40 What is a homing sequence, and what purpose does it serve in testing finite-state machines?

3.41 What is a test sequence, and what purpose does it serve in testing finite-state machines?

3.42 What is a distinguishing sequence?

3.43 What is a successor tree, what is its purpose, and how do we construct one?

3.44 What is a scan path, and how is it used in testing finite-state machines?

3.45 What does the term *boundary scan* mean? Describe how it is used in testing finite-state machines.

3.11 THOUGHT QUESTIONS

The Concepts of State and Time

3.1 For larger systems, the state diagram can become unwieldy rather quickly. Suggest ways by which the underlying concept can be modified to accommodate such problems.

3.2 The *state of the system* can convey important information about a system. Can you think of situations in which the state of a system can be a problem. Consider cases in which the system has failed and is recovering.

3.3 Why is the concept of time important in an embedded system?

Designing Finite-State Machines—Registers

3.4 Propose some situations in which a latch rather than a register would be the preferred storage device. Explain the reasoning behind your choices.

3.5 Propose some situations in which a register rather than a latch would be the preferred storage device. Explain the reasoning behind your choices.

3.6 How can the shifting function be implemented without a storage element?

3.7 What advantages can you think of for a design such as that proposed in Question 3.6?

3.8 Propose several uses for a parallel in/serial out shift register? for a serial in/parallel out shift register?

3.9 Can a latch be used instead of a flip-flop to implement a shift register?

3.10 Propose several uses for a linear feedback shift register?

3.11 Can a linear feedback shift register be used as a counter? timer? What would be the pros and cons of such design?

Designing Finite-State Machines—Counting and Dividing

3.12 Why is a *Power On Reset* control signal important in the design of finite-state machine-based designs?

3.13 Is a *Power On Reset* control signal subject to fan-out restrictions?

3.14 What are the major problems that one encounters with a ripple counter? How does the frequency of the input clock affect these problems?

3.15 Are there cases for which the ripple counter is preferred to a comparable synchronous counter? Explain your choice(s).

3.16 Are there cases for which the synchronous counter is preferred to a comparable ripple counter? Explain your choice(s).

3.17 What is the major difference between a counter and a timer?

3.18 For a timing application, what determines the temporal resolution of your timer?

3.19 One problem with a long synchronous counter or divider chain is the rapid increase in the complexity of the flip-flop input equations. Can you propose a possible solution to this problem?

3.20 Can a latch be used instead of a flip-flop as the basic storage element in a counter or divider? Why or why not?

3.21 Is it necessary that the clock input to a counter, timer, or divider be a square wave?

Designing Finite-State Machines

3.22 Give several examples in which a Mealy state machine is preferred to a Moore machine? Explain your choice.

3.23 Give several examples in which a Mealy state machine is preferred to a Moore machine? Explain your choice.

3.24 As the complexity of a design increases, the finite-state machine used to implement a solution can become large rather quickly. Propose several solutions to such a problem.

3.25 Give several examples in which we might use a finite-state machine as the underlying control mechanism.

3.26 Must a finite-state machine always be implemented in hardware?

3.27 Please give several examples of embedded applications for which a pattern recognition system would be required.

3.28 Cite several examples showing when a sliding window recognizer would or would not be an appropriate solution. Explain your choices.

3.29 Why or under what circumstances might a one hot state assignment scheme be appropriate for a Moore machine?

3.30 Why or under what circumstances might a Gray-code-based state assignment be appropriate for a Mealy machine?

Practical Considerations—Timing in Latches and Flip-Flops

3.31 What are the consequences of failing to meet the *setup time* specifications for a storage device? *hold time* specifications?

3.32 Setup time in a storage device is based on what factors in the design of the device?

3.33 What are some of the factors that limit the operating speed in a counting, dividing, or timing circuit?

3.34 What are some of the factors that one must consider when generating control or clocking signals by decoding the states of a finite-state machine?

3.35 Why is generating control or clocking signals by decoding the states of a ripple counter generally discouraged? Under what circumstances might such a technique be considered reasonable?

Practical Considerations—Clocks and Clock Distribution

3.36 Discuss the pros and cons of utilizing multiphase versus a single-phase clocking scheme or time base for an embedded application.

3.37 What problems might arise in a clocking scheme that utilizes the rising edge of a timing signal to clock some flip-flops in a system and the falling edge to clock others?

3.38 Are timing signals subject to fan-out restrictions?

3.39 When routing timing signals throughout a system, not all paths may be of equal length. Is this a potential problem?

3.40 What potential problem might arise from including a timing signal such as a clock on a system bus?

3.41 What problems might arise in a clocking scheme from parasitic R, L, C components in a system? How can these be addressed?

3.42 What are some of the factors that limit the frequency at which the embedded hardware in a system may be clocked?

3.43 Normally, for high-performance systems we strive to have signals change state quickly. What are some of the consequences of very small rise and fall times in clocking and timing signals?

Testing Sequential Circuits

3.44 What are some of the things that can be done to facilitate the test of sequential circuits?

3.45 Is it necessary to test all possible combinations of inputs to a finite-state machine?

3.46 What combinations of signals should be included in the set of test vectors for a sequential machine?

3.47 Why are synchronous designs easier to test than asynchronous?

3.48 What purpose does the *Power On Reset* control signal play in the test of sequential circuits?

3.49 What does the expression "break the feedback loop" mean in the test of sequential circuits?

3.50 When testing sequential machines, how should we deal with the machines for which the associated state diagram has loops or cycles?

3.51 What is a homing sequence, and what purpose does it serve in testing finite-state machines?

3.52 Can you think of an easy way to test shift registers?

3.53 How can a long counting, timing, or dividing chain be tested without having to traverse all states? Discuss any caveats with your proposed approach.

3.54 Must a counting, timing, or dividing chain be tested at its intended operating frequency? What are the consequences of not doing so?

3.12 PROBLEMS

Flip-Flops, Latches, and Shift Register Designs

3.1 For the two devices in Figure P3.68 and their inputs, data and sigIn, please draw the corresponding output signals, QA and QB. Be sure to explain your answer.

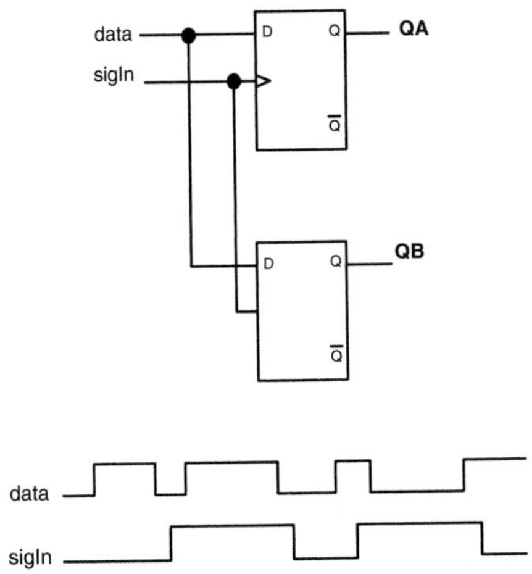

Figure P3.68

3.2 Design and implement an 8-bit shift register that can shift 1 or 2 bits to the left or right based on the states of two input control lines.

3.3 You have just won a contract to design and implement a high-speed logical shifter. The specification you have been given requires the design of a circuit that will shift a 16-bit word to the right or to the left by 1-, 2-, 3-, or 4-bit positions in a single clock time.

The input to your system is a 3-bit word that is to be interpreted as follows:

B 2 - 0 shift right
1 shift left

B1	B0	Meaning
0	0	Shift by 1
0	1	Shift by 2
1	0	Shift by 3
1	1	Shift by 4

(a) Draw a top-level block diagram for your system.

(b) Assume you decide to build the shifter using 16 D flip-flops. Write the logic equations for the D inputs.

(c) Explain how your design works.

(d) Confirm your design by writing and testing a structural Verilog model.

3.4 Extend the design in Problem 3.2 by incorporating the ability to load the contents of the shift register in parallel. Confirm your design by writing and testing a behavioral Verilog model.

3.5 An N-bit circular shift register, as shown in Figure P3.69, operates as follows:

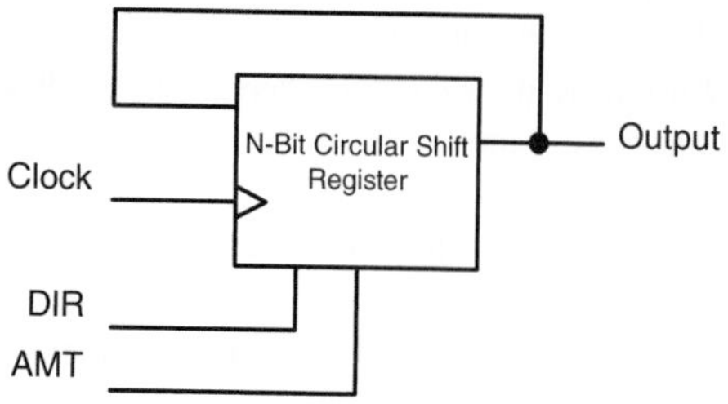

Figure P3.69

Dir	Amt	Meaning
0	0	Shift right by 1
0	1	Shift right by 2
1	0	Shift left by 1
1	1	Shift left by 2

Assuming that the shift register is implemented using D flip-flops, write the input equation for the 0th flip-flop.

(a) Write the input equation for the ith flip-flop.

(b) It's just days away from first shipment and the customer requests a simple addition to the design. They would now like to be able to load the shift register in parallel (all bits at once). What additional signals, if any, will we have to add to the design and how would they be used? Be specific.

(c) Rewrite the input equation for the ith flip-flop to incorporate the design change in part (c).

3.6 The purchasing department in your company, *Storage Stuff, Ltd.*, has just gotten a great deal on 100,00 74LS175 quad D flip-flops. These devices have an internal logic diagram as shown in Figure P3.70.

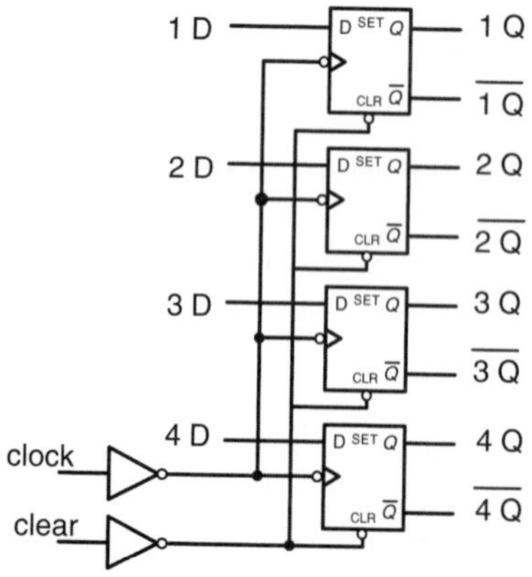

Figure P3.70

Using the 74LS175, and any other parts you need, design an 8-bit shift register that can be loaded, in parallel, from two different sources and then enabled to shift the data to the right or to the left.

(a) From the vendor's data sheet, we have the following information:

$$\tau_{setup} = 5 \text{ ns}, \tau_{hold} = 0 \text{ ns},$$
$$\tau_{pLH} = 15 \text{ ns and } \tau_{pHL} = 10 \text{ ns for each flip flop.}$$

(b) What is the maximum rate that data can be reliably shifted through the shift register? Explain how you arrived at your answer.

Counters

3.7 Design and implement a synchronous BCD counter using D flip-flops that will count up or down based on the state of an input control line, UP-DOWN.

3.8 Design and implement a 3-bit synchronous counter using D flip-flops that counts according to the following sequence:

A	B	C
0	0	0
1	0	0
0	1	1
1	1	0
0	1	0

3.9 The following circuit is designed to provide an output signal on QC with an input clock frequency of 12 MHz. The system containing the circuit has been in production for several months, but now sometimes it works and sometimes it does not.

(a) Draw the theoretical timing diagram for the circuit showing the signals at points A, B, and C with respect to the clock.

(b) After a little bit of research, you find from the vendor's data sheets that the flip-flops have the following characteristics:

$\tau_{dHL} = 25$ to 40 ns

$\tau_{dLH} = 13$ to 25 ns

$\tau_{SU} = 25$ ns

and the exclusive OR gate has the following characteristics:

$\tau_{dHL} = 20$ to 30 ns

$\tau_{dLH} = 13$ to 20 ns

(c) Draw the actual timing diagram for the circuit showing the signals at points A, B, and C with respect to the clock when the practical circuit parameters are considered.

(d) Can you explain why the circuit behavior has suddenly changed? Use your real-world timing diagram as necessary for illustration.

(e) Can you determine the maximum frequency at which the circuit can be safely operated?

3.10 For the following circuit in Figure P3.71

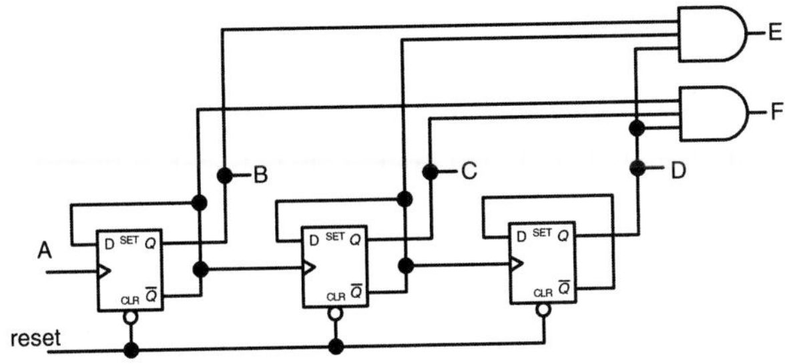

Figure P3.71

please give a detailed timing diagram for signals A–F. You have the following specifications:

Input clock 1 MHz
Flip Flops

$$\tau_{\text{setup}} = 10 \text{ ns}$$

$$\tau_{\text{hold}} = 0 \text{ ns}$$

$$\tau_{\text{pdhl}} = 15 \text{ ns}$$

$$\tau_{\text{pdlh}} = 10 \text{ ns}$$

Gates

$$\tau_{\text{pdhl}} = 7 \text{ ns}$$

$$\tau_{\text{pdlh}} = 11 \text{ ns}$$

At what input clock frequency will the circuit fail to properly generate the output signals E and F?

3.11 You have been asked to do a detailed analysis and design review of the counting circuit in Figure P3.72.

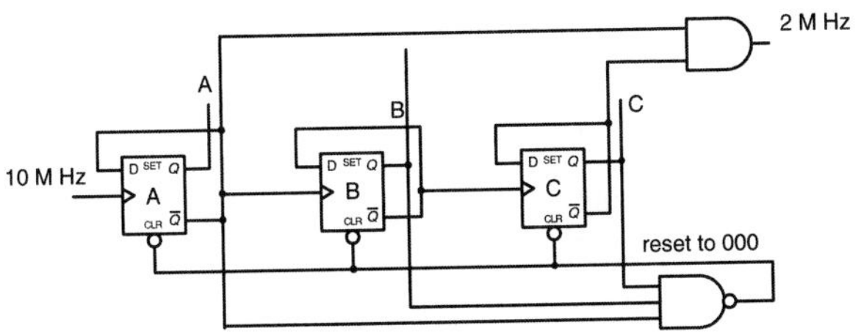

Figure P3.72

(a) As part of the review you decide to determine the counting sequence for the circuit. Give a table showing the complete sequence of states the machine goes through starting at the initial state of 000.

(b) As a next step toward analyzing the design, you draw the ideal timing diagram (no delays) for the circuit showing the signals at points A, B, C, the reset line, and the 2-MHz output—all with respect to the clock.

(c) You next move to the vendor's data sheets for the flip-flops containing the following characteristics:

$$\tau_{\text{pdhl}} = 15 \text{ ns}$$

$$\tau_{\text{pdlh}} = 30 \text{ ns}$$

$$\tau_{\text{su}} = 35 \text{ ns}$$

The AND and NAND gates have the following characteristics:

$$\tau_{\text{pdhl}} = 10 \text{ ns}$$

$$\tau_{\text{pdlh}} = 5 \text{ ns}$$

Draw the actual timing diagram for the circuit showing signals at points A, B, C, the reset line, and the 2-MHz output with respect to the clock when the practical circuit parameters are considered.

(d) Concluding your analysis, are there any states of flip-flops A, B, and C, the reset, or the 2-MHz clock that could be a problem? If so, what are they and why are they a problem? It is important to be specific in a design review.

(e) Can you recommend a change to the design to correct any problems you have discovered?

3.12 Design a four-stage Johnson counter.

(a) Detect any of the illegal states and force the counter back to the 0000 state. You cannot do this by using the master reset or clear signal.

(b) Detect all of the illegal states and force the counter back to the 0000 state. You cannot do this by using the master reset or clear signal.

(c) Discuss the pros and cons of the two designs.

(d) Under what circumstances would you select the first design? the second design?

3.13 A counting circuit has the output waveforms given in Figure P3.73.

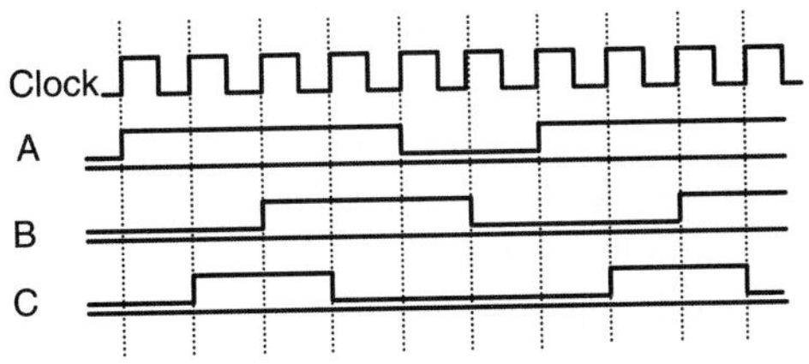

Figure P3.73

(a) Give the state table for a 3-bit counter that operates according to the timing diagram given in Figure P3.73. Assume that the machine starts in an initial state of 000.

(b) What is the period of such a counter in input clock cycles? Why?

(c) Design and draw the logic diagram for a counter, using D flip-flops, that operates according to the timing diagram and state table from part (a). Your flip-flops must reflect on which edge of the clock the transitions occur. Be sure to take into account any don't cares.

(d) The vendor's data sheets show that the flip-flops and gates have the following characteristics:

$$\tau_{pdhl} = 20 \text{ to } 30 \text{ ns}$$

$$\tau_{pdlh} = 10 \text{ to } 20 \text{ ns}$$

$$\tau_{su} = 20 \text{ ns}$$

Draw the actual timing diagram, based on the data from the data sheet, for the circuit showing the signals at points A, B, and C with respect to the clock.

Assume a 10-MHz clock.

Timers and Time Bases

3.14 An application requires a timing signal with a 1-ms period. A 10-MHz crystal oscillator, from which the required signal can be derived, is available in the system.

(a) Design the timing chain that will produce the required signal. Consider using a cascade of a ripple counter prescaler followed by a synchronous chain in your design.

(b) Discuss the difficulties of designing the timer chain as a fully synchronous circuit.

(c) Discuss the problems that can arise if the timer chain is fully asynchronous.

(d) What is the error in the period of the 1-ms period contributed by the timer chain, excluding the oscillator error?

(e) If the frequency of the oscillator is increased to 20 MHz, what is the effect on the error in the 1-ms period.

3.15 Design a timer that meets the following specifications:

The timer supports the timing of two intervals, A and B. While in interval A, a high true output signal is generated signifying the interval. At the end of interval A, interval B starts, the interval A output goes false, and the interval B output goes true. At the end of interval B, both outputs go false.

The two intervals can be set independently and can be set to count from 1 to 255 input clock pulses.

The input clock is a 20-MHz oscillator.

The timer supports the modes *Time*, *Stop*, and *Hold*. When in the *Time* mode, the system is timing as specified. When in the *Stop* mode, the timer is held in its initial state. When in the *Hold* mode, the timer is not advancing and is holding its current state.

3.16 An embedded application that you have been working on requires a timing generator that produces three periodic signals specified according to the timing diagram in Figure P3.74. Time units are in nanoseconds. The signals T0–T2 are not necessarily the Q outputs of flip-flops.

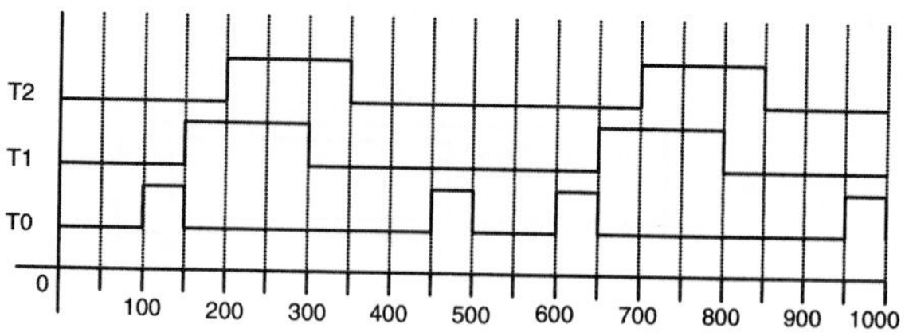

Figure P3.74

In addition to the waveform specification, the specification requires that the time base will only generate the waveforms T_0–T_2 if the *Enable* input to the system is high.

In executing the design,

(a) What frequency do you choose for the clock? Why?

(b) What is the period of your time-base unit? Why?

(c) Please give the flip-flop equations for your time-base unit if it is implemented using D flip-flops.

(d) Please give the logic output equations for the time-base unit to generate output signals T_0–T_2.

(e) Develop and test a structural Verilog model of the time base you designed.

(f) The vendor's specifications for the 74ALS74 D-type flip flop are given as

$$t_{pdlh} = 15 \text{ ns}$$

$$t_{pdhl} = 20 \text{ ns}$$

$$t_{su} = 15 \text{ ns}$$

The logic gates have the following delays.

$$t_{pdlh} = 9 \text{ ns}$$

$$t_{pdhl} = 15 \text{ ns}$$

Please give a timing diagram for the signals T_0–T_2 that reflect the flip-flop and gate delays.

3.17 An embedded application requires a time base that produces a four-phase nonoverlapping periodic clock output. Each clock output must have a frequency of 10 MHz.

(a) What input frequency do you choose? Why?

(b) Design the time base that will produce the four outputs.

(c) Develop and test a behavioral Verilog model of the time base for the design.

(d) Select the components for the design, and from the vendor's data sheets, identify all of the appropriate delays. Using the vendor information, give a timing diagram reflecting the operation of your design.

3.18 A technique called pulse width modulation (PWM) is commonly used in embedded applications as a method for controlling small motors. The PWM signal for driving the motor has a fixed frequency and a variable duty cycle. At a duty cycle of close to 0%, the motor is running at a slow speed; with a duty cycle close to 100%, the motor is running at close to full speed.

(a) Design such a timer that can control the duty cycle of the output waveform in ± 5% increments.

(b) What frequency have you selected for the PWM signal? Why?

3.19 You have completed the design of most of a new embedded application; only the time-base unit remains to be designed. The time base has two inputs: *select* and *clock* and 1 output: *sync*. The unit has the following specifications:

The input signal *clock* has a frequency of 1 MHz.

When *select* is a logical 0, the output signal, *sync*, is a 1-μsec-wide pulse with a period of 3 μsec. When *select* is a logical 1, the output signal, *sync*, is a 1-μsec-wide pulse with a period of 7 μsec.

(a) Please draw a timing diagram for the output of the time-base unit showing its behavior when *select* is a logical 0.

(b) Please draw a timing diagram for the output of the time-base unit showing its behavior when *select* is a logical 1. Be certain to label time units on your diagram.

(c) Please give the flip-flop input equations if the time base is to be implemented using D flip-flops.

(d) Please write and test a behavioral Verilog model for your design.

(e) Please show the logic diagram for your time-base unit based on your equations.

Finite-State Machines

3.20 As part of a satellite system for locking on to an incoming data stream, we must design a synchronizer that operates as follows: A system accepts a serial data stream (one bit at a time) on its input and produces two outputs, Z_1 and Z_2. The two outputs are normally *high*.

The synchronizer is to operate as follows: If two consecutive input bits arriving at times t_i and t_{i+1} have the values (01 or 10), output Z_1 is to be in the logical 0 state. If the two consecutive input bits arriving at times t_i and t_{i+1} have the values (11 or 00), output Z_2 is to be in the logical 0 state. Otherwise, both outputs are to be in the logical 1 state.

When either pattern is detected, the system enters and remains in a locked state.

(a) Draw a state diagram for such a system using a Mealy model.

(b) Give the state and output table for such a system based on your state diagram and using a Mealy model.

(c) Reduce the state and output table for such a system to their simplest form.

(d) Provide a state assignment based on your reduced state and output table.

(e) Give the equations for the two output signals, Z_1 and Z_2.

(f) Write and test a behavioral Verilog model for the synchronization system.

3.21 A system has two inputs, serial data (DI) and a control signal (SEL), and a single output (Z) as shown in Figure 3.75.

Figure P3.75

The system has the following specifications:

- If the control input SEL is a logical 0, the system is to produce a logical 1 on the output Z at time $t = t_2$ if the previous three input data bits had been the pattern 110. Otherwise it is to produce a logical 0 on the output.
- If the control input SEL is a logical 1, the system is to produce a logical 1 on the output Z at time $t = t_2$ if the previous three input data bits had been the pattern 011. Otherwise it is to produce a logical 0 on the output.
- Draw a state diagram for such a system.
- Give the state and output table for such a system.
- Provide a state assignment for such a system.
- Write and test a structural Verilog model for your design.

3.22 An error management system is needed as a subsystem in a new telecommunication system. As a proof of concept, we will design and build a prototype that works with 4-bit serial words. A partial block diagram for the subsystem is shown in Figure P3.76.

Figure 3.76

It operates as follows:

- 3 bits of data are loaded into *Register A* using a *load* signal.
- A *start* signal is sent to the *encoder*.
- Following the *start* signal, the *encoder* outputs a logical 0.
- The *encoder* sends an *enable* signal to *Register A* to tell it to shift data out of the *serialData* line one bit at a time.
- The *encoder* accepts each data bit from the *serialData* line and outputs (transfers) that data to the *serialOut* line.

- After 4 data bits have been transferred, the encoder outputs a parity bit to the *serialOut* line.
- The parity bit should be a 1 if the 4 data bits contained an odd number of 1's and a 0 if the number of 1's was even.
- Following the parity bit, the *encoder* outputs a logical 1 to the *serialOut* line and returns to its initial state.
- The total number of bits sent to the *serialOut* line is 6.

(a) Draw a complete, *unreduced*, state diagram for such a system expressing all combinations of inputs and states.

(b) Give the state and output table for such a system.

(c) Give a *reduced* state and output table for such a system. Be certain to show how you reduced the number of states.

(d) Provide a state assignment for the reduced system.

(e) Give the reduced transition table for such a system.

(f) Give the input equations for each of the D flip-flops and for the output in the reduced system. Be certain to take into account any don't cares.

(g) Write and test a behavioral Verilog model for your design.

Applications

3.23 You have just developed a new toy in a small black box that we see in the picture in Figure P3.77 and are showing it to your grandmother.

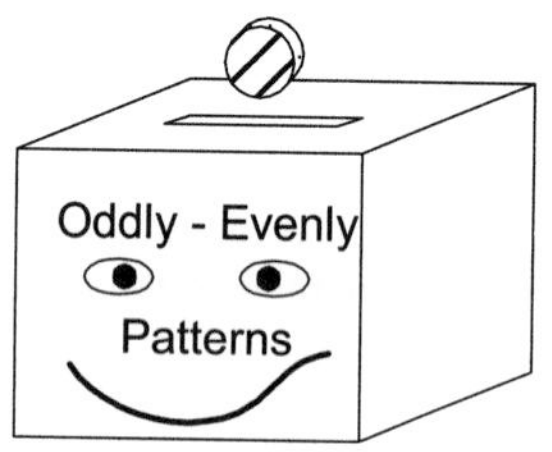

Figure P3.77

You tell her that she should put in three coins, one after the other. You tell her that a coin can be either a dime or a penny.

Then you say, if she puts in zero or two pennies, the *ODDLY* eye will turn on and if she puts in one or three pennies, the *EVENLY* eye will turn on. She wants you to explain how it works.

(a) Give her an exhaustive (unreduced) state diagram that will describe the behavior of the toy (she's a smart grandmother).

(b) Give her a state and output table for the system.

(c) Reduce your state table to its simplest form.

(d) Give a state assignment for the system.

(e) Write and test a structural Verilog model for your design.

3.24 A new temperature monitoring system that utilizes an analog-to-digital converter to collect data at various points in a yogurt production process is to be designed. The control logic accepts the input signals shown and generates the output signals as specified in Figure P3.78.

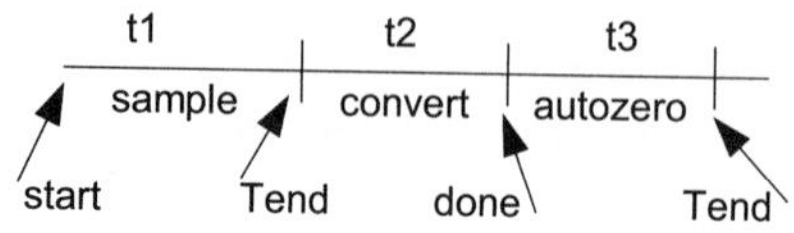

Figure P3.78

- Upon receipt of a *start* signal, the system must cycle through the three time intervals—t1, t2, and t3—and command the following operations to take place: *Sample*, *Convert*, and *Autozero*.
- The system is to respond to the input signals as shown in the diagram. At the end of time t3, as signaled by the T_{end} input, the system must return to its initial state and wait for a *start* input.
- The times, t1–t3, are not inputs to the system; they merely identify the length of each interval.
- The signals *start*, *done*, and t_{end} are inputs to the system. They identify the start or end of the intervals as indicated.
- The system must have several output signals to control the electronics doing the conversion. The control logic is in one room, and the analog-to-digital converter is in another. There is a limit to the number of wires in the cable connecting the two portions of the system.

For the system, develop the following:

(a) A block diagram for the system

(b) The minimum number of output control signals, explaining why your answer is correct.

(c) The state diagram

(d) The state table

(e) The output table

(f) The state assignment

(g) The transition diagram

(h) A behavioral model for the control block

(i) Once the behavior is verified from the model, the complete design of the system

(j) Specification of the minimum number of flip-flops and an explanation of why your answer is correct

(k) The input equations for a D flip-flop

3.25 A colleague has developed the block diagram in Figure P3.79 for an instrument for measuring frequency.

Accompanying the drawing are the following description and specifications.

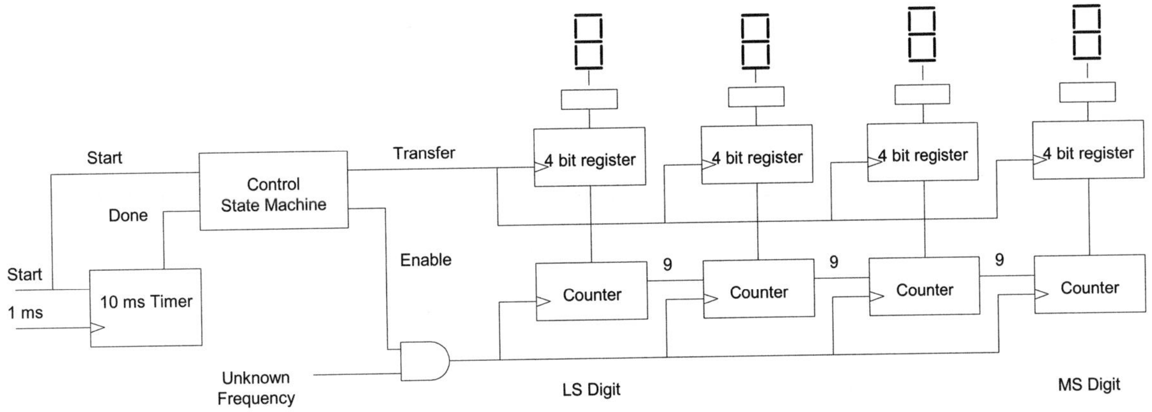

Figure P3.79

Measure

When a *Start* signal is received, the timer will start timing and the control state machine will put the *Enable* output into the logical 1 state.

While the *Enable* signal is in the logical 1 state, an unknown frequency will be used as the clock to a decade counter chain.

After 10 ms, the timer will output the *Done* signal.

Store

In response to the *Done* signal, the control state machine will place the *Enable* signal into the logical 0 state and place the *Transfer* signal into the logical 1 state.

After one clock pulse, the control state machine will place the *Transfer* signal into the logical 0 state and return to idle awaiting another *Start* signal.

When the *Enable* returns to the logical 0 state, the decade counter chain will contain a value equivalent to the measured frequency.

The value contained in the counters in a decade counter chain is then transferred to the 4-bit register (in response to the transfer signal), where it is displayed on the readout. Provide:

(a) A high-level timing diagram for the system

(b) A complete design for the *timer* block

(c) A complete design for one of the *counter* blocks

(d) A state diagram for the *control* state machine

(e) A state table for the *control* state machine

(f) A state assignment for the *control* state machine

(g) A structural Verilog model for the *control* state machine

3.26 You have been hired by *Let There Be Lyght—Signals Abound, Ltd.* to design a traffic control system. The design your predecessor proposed failed at a critical time while he was in the middle of the intersection testing it.

The intersection you must control is shown in Figure P3.80. Your design must meet the following specifications:

- Each light, L1 and L2, has two states, ON or OFF

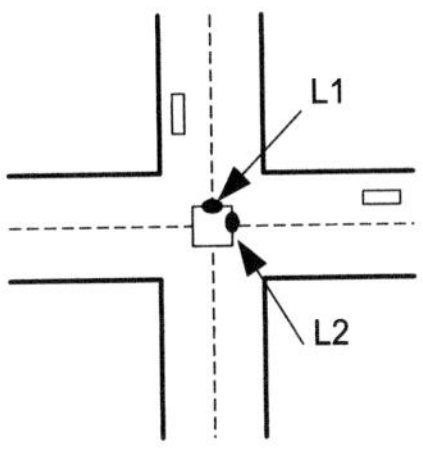

Figure P3.80

- If a car arrives at the intersection and the light in its direction is OFF, it may proceed through the intersection.
- If a car arrives at the intersection and the light in its direction is ON, the car must stop. A timer, *Timer1*, is started. At the end of six time units, the light is turned OFF, a second timer *Timer2* is started, and the car may proceed. After 12 time units have elapsed on the second timer, the light is turned ON again.
- The cars must not collide.

Please design the following:

(a) The input and output equations for the two timers, *Timer1* and *Timer2*

(b) An implementation for the two timers

(c) A state diagram showing the behavior of the traffic control system

(d) The state and output table for the traffic control system

(e) The flip-flop input and system output equations for the traffic control system

3.27 An embedded system that you are working on has a system bus with the following specifications:

Data	2 bits
Address	2 bits
Control	

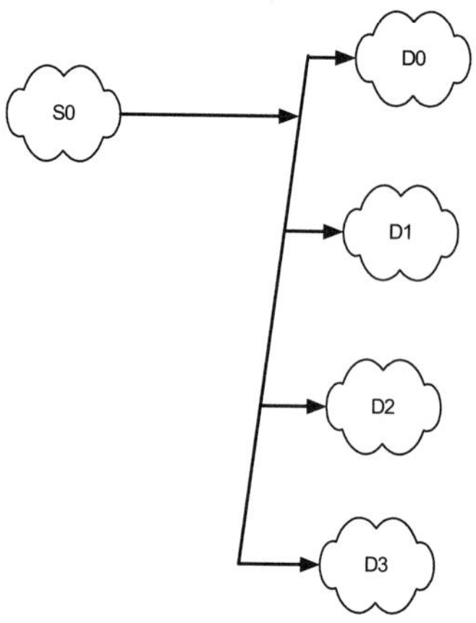

Figure P3.81

You are responsible for the system bus and bus interface that manages transfers of data from the source, S0, to the four destinations, D0–D3, as shown in Figure P3.81. Data can be transferred from the source to only one destination at a time.

You have an unlimited number of the following part types available:

L2B	2-Bit latches
R2B	2-Bit Registers
BD2	2-Bit Bus Drivers—noninverting—similar to inverter but with greater drive capability
BR2	2-Bit Bus Receivers—noninverting—similar to inverter but no inversion
NG2–NG4	2-, 3-, and 4-input NOR gates

Provide the following:

(a) A block diagram for the system

(b) The signals contained in the Control Bus

(c) A top-level timing diagram of the design showing how data is transferred from the source to a single destination

(d) A detailed logic diagram of your design using only the part types listed above.

(e) A description of the operation of your design.

Be sure to state any assumptions.

For this portion of the design, you are only designing the bus and bus interface.

The source of the data and its use after it is on the board are not relevant to the design. However, it must be handled properly when accepted from the bus.

3.28 Your team is working on the audio portion of a larger home entertainment system. The system combines a mix of new and legacy components that must be understood and integrated into a high-quality system.

The volume control for the system is marked with the decimal digits 0–5. Based upon the input selection, the selector outputs the single BCD digit corresponding to the level selected. Selection 0 outputs BCD 0, selection 1 outputs BCD 1, and so on.

Our gain stage, however, requires a value in the range of 0–15. Thus, we must design a circuit that will multiply that single digit BCD number by 3 to give us the proper value as shown in the following block diagram in Figure P3.82.

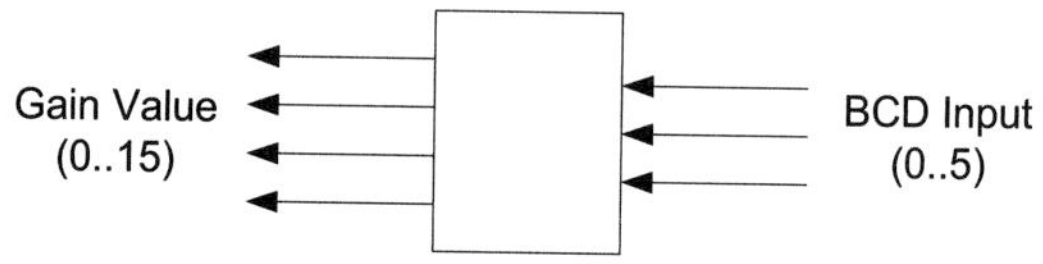

Figure P3.82

(a) Please provide a design and logic diagram for such a circuit. Because this is to be a commercial product, simplicity and low cost are very important.

The input to the system may come from any of four different sources: a CD player, a DVD player, a Tuner, and a Joystick. Each of these devices produces a stream of data 4 bits wide.

Consequently, it is necessary to design a circuit that will select any of these data streams and route it into the system bus as shown in the following block diagram in Figure P3.83.

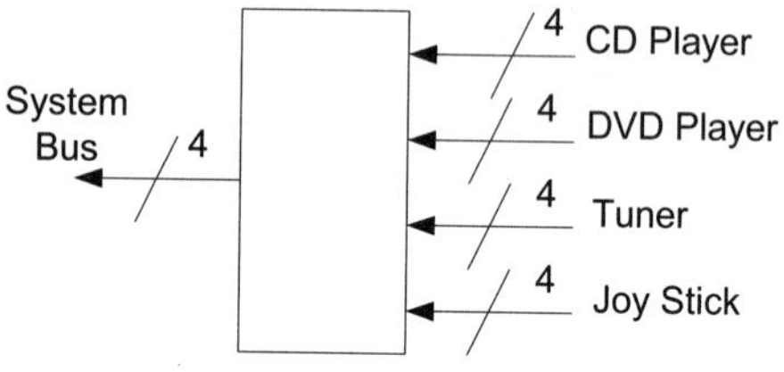

Figure P3.83

(b) Design the logic to go inside the block.

The output from the system may be sent to any of four different devices: a digital-to-analog converter, a digital display, a memory, and a glitzy graphic output.

Each of these devices requires a stream of data 4 bits wide. We must design a circuit that will route data from the system bus to any of these devices as shown in the following block diagram in Figure P3.84.

(c) Design the logic to go inside the block.

Although the system bus is 4 bits, internally, the system controller uses an 8-bit word. Thus, data must be brought into the controller 4 bits at a time and assembled into an 8-bit word. We must design a *Data Assembler* as an interface between the sys-

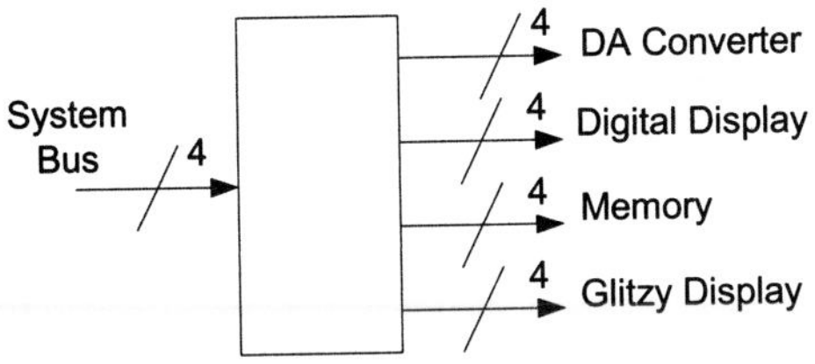

Figure P3.84

tem bus with the system controller as shown in the block diagram in Figure P3.85.

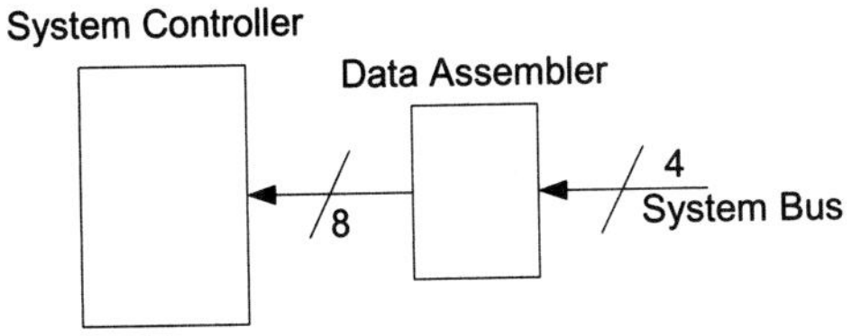

Figure P3.85

The *Data Assembler* must operate according to the following algorithm:

- The first 4 bits appear on the bus accompanied by a *DV–Data Valid* signal.
- The *DV* transitions from a logical 0 to a logical 1 to signify that the data on the bus is valid.
- The 4 bits of data are loaded, in parallel, into the *most* significant 4 bits of an 8-bit shift register.
- The *DV* transitions from a logical 1 to a logical 0.
- An output signal, *Shift Left*, is generated to enable the shift register to be clocked four times.
- The second 4 bits appear on the bus accompanied by a *DV–Data Valid* signal.
- The *DV* transitions from a logical 0 to a logical 1 to signify that the data on the bus is valid.
- The 4 bits of data are stored into the *most* significant 4 bits of the 8-bit shift register, thereby building up the complete 8-bit word.
- The *DV* transitions from a logical 1 to a logical 0.
- A *Load Complete* output signal is generated to signify that the data has been captured.

(d) Give a state diagram for the bus interface system. Identify any additional control signals that you may need.

(e) Provide a detailed block diagram for the *Data Assembler* by showing the major blocks and all of the input and output signals, including any that you have added.

(f) The system needs a clock source that has a 0.5-μs period as part of the system time base. An 18-MHz clock source is the only one available in the system, and you must now design and implement the clock source using D flip-flops.

Chapter 4

Memories and the Memory Subsystem

THINGS TO LOOK FOR . . .

- The general categories of memory devices.
- The general and specific interfaces to different memory devices.
- Caching and how it is used in an embedded context.
- Direct mapped, associative, and block-set associative caching schemes.
- Memory maps and their role in embedded design.
- Test of RAM- and ROM-type memories.

4.0 INTRODUCTION

For smaller embedded applications, the memory on board the microprocessor or microcontroller is sufficient. Larger applications require substantially larger amounts and must move outside of the processor to a full-memory subsystem to meet those needs.

The memory subsystem is the place within an embedded system where instructions and data are stored. The architecture and design of that subsystem can have a significant impact on the behavior of the system. During design, the major concerns include the effects of the memory and memory management on the execution times of the various modules making up the application, the predictability of those execution times, the amount of memory needed during runtime, and the amount necessary and available to ultimately hold the firmware. An improperly designed memory subsystem and access scheme can be a leading contributor to a failed system.

memory management

static,
dynamic allocation

In embedded applications, *memory management* is concerned with managing the process stack(s) and the *static* and *dynamic allocation* of memory. Static allocation addresses the partition of memory into the code and data segments used by both the application and the system. Dynamic allocation addresses the allocation and management of memory resources for the processes at runtime.

When managing memory in embedded systems, the major concerns are avoiding dangerous allocation and minimizing or reducing overhead during memory allocation. Improper allocation can result in the loss of deterministic behavior and potentially create deadlock situations at runtime.

In this chapter, we will introduce and discuss the various kinds of devices utilized to implement memory subsystems in embedded applications. We will begin with the two

read only memory, ROM
random access memory, RAM

general categories, *read only memory* or *ROM* and *random access memory* or *RAM*. To gain an understanding of how to interact with memory, we will study the general memory interface, then discuss the commonly used memory storage devices in detail, and work through the designs of representative memory systems utilizing such devices.

direct mapped, associative
block-set associative

The concept of caching in the context of embedded systems is introduced and discussed. Several different caching schemes, *direct mapped, associative,* and *block-set associative*, are developed and studied. The strengths and weaknesses of each of these approaches are analyzed.

memory maps
dynamic allocation

Discussion moves to the system level with the introduction of *memory maps* and simple *dynamic allocation* in an embedded context. The topic of memory test closes the chapter. Several approaches for testing RAM and ROM memories are introduced and studied.

4.1 CLASSIFYING MEMORY

read only memory, ROM
random access memory, RAM
static, dynamic

As a first step in studying memory systems, it is important to recognize that the term *memory* is generic. There are many different kinds of memory, each with its strengths and weaknesses. Understanding the characteristics of each and how to design with them can lead to more robust and effective design solutions. We begin by classifying memory into two general categories: *read only memory* or *ROM* and *random access memory* or *RAM*. We further subdivide RAM into *static* RAM, SRAM, and *dynamic* RAM, DRAM. These classifications lead to a number of different subcategories of both ROM and RAM. Some of the more common subclassifications are described in the following list.

RAM—*Random Access Memory*. As the name suggests, any location in memory is visible for immediate access rather than having to sequence through predecessor locations. The times for a read operation and a write operation are comparable. A RAM may be organized as bits, bytes, or words.

DRAM—*Dynamic RAM*. A simple memory cell design with bit storage implemented using a stored charge mechanism. The stored charge can leak away if it is not repeatedly restored. These devices are used for larger memory systems. I/O is asynchronous with respect to any external system clocks.

SRAM—*Static RAM*. A more complex memory cell design with bit storage implemented using a latch-type mechanism. The stored data does not have to be refreshed. These devices are used for higher speed memory systems because they are faster than DRAM designs. I/O is asynchronous with respect to any external system clocks.

Semistatic RAM. The periphery is clock activated (dynamic). Only one memory cycle is permitted per clock. The periphery circuitry must be allowed to reset after each active memory cycle for minimum pre-charge time. No refresh is required.

SDRAM—*Synchronous DRAM*. SDRAM synchronizes all addresses, data, and control signals to the system clock and allows much higher data transfer rates than asynchronous transfers.

ROM—*Read Only Memory*. During normal operation, ROM can only be read. Like RAM, any location in memory is visible for immediate access rather than having to sequence through predecessor locations. The read operation is orders of magnitude faster than a write operation. The write is typically referred to as *programming* the ROM. Like a RAM, the ROM may be organized as bits, bytes, or words.

PROM—*Programmable ROM.* A PROM is typically programmed using a programming device of one form or another. The device can only be programmed one time.

EPROM—*Erasable PROM.* Like the PROM, an EPROM is typically programmed using a programming device. Erasure, so that it can be reprogrammed, is done by placing the device under ultraviolet light for a specified time interval.

EEPROM—*Electrically Erasable PROM.* EEPROM is similar to EPROM in that it can be reprogrammed. Rather than requiring a UV light for erasure, the operation is done electrically via a programming device.

FLASH—A kind of EEPROM. Its advantage is that it can be reprogrammed *in situ.* The device does not have to be removed from the circuit for reprogramming although it can be.

4.2 A GENERAL MEMORY INTERFACE

As a first-level model of memory, we can view the device as an array. A value can be assigned to a location in an array and the value of a piece of data that has been stored there can be read. For an array, we identify where the data is stored by an index number. Figure 4.0 illustrates a simple array with eight entries. For each index that is accessed, the corresponding stored value appears on the output. Conversely, if one provides an index and an input value, the data will be stored at the corresponding indexed location.

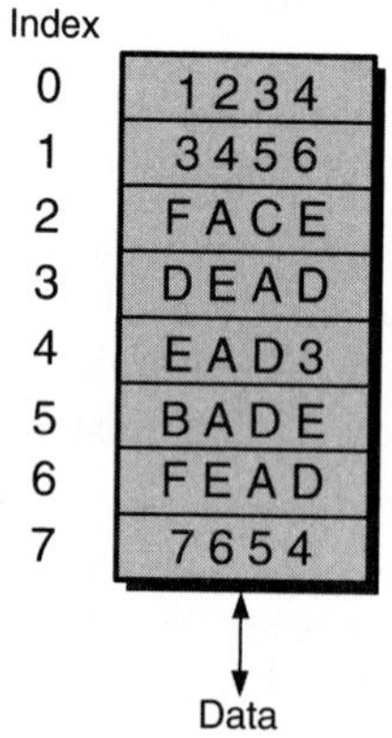

Figure 4.0 The Array as a Simple Memory Model

One could seamlessly carry this mathematical model into a physical implementation. In doing so, however, one finds rather quickly that several difficulties arise. First, using one index value for each entry will very quickly lead to a substantial number of input signals. That problem can be solved by encoding the index value as a binary number that is defined as an *address*. The binary encoded address can now easily be decoded into the corresponding index value. In the mathematical model, a *read access* at a specified index automatically returns the stored value and a *write access* stores a new value.

address
read access
write access

The physical model requires a bit more work. One must *control* the *data* lines going into and out of the memory. One must also *control* when the *read* and *write* operations take place. The diagram in Figure 4.1 illustrates how such capabilities might be added to the array model.

control, data
read, write

The three-to-one-of-eight decoder converts the incoming address patterns into the equivalent in index numbers. The read and write signals perform the associated operations.

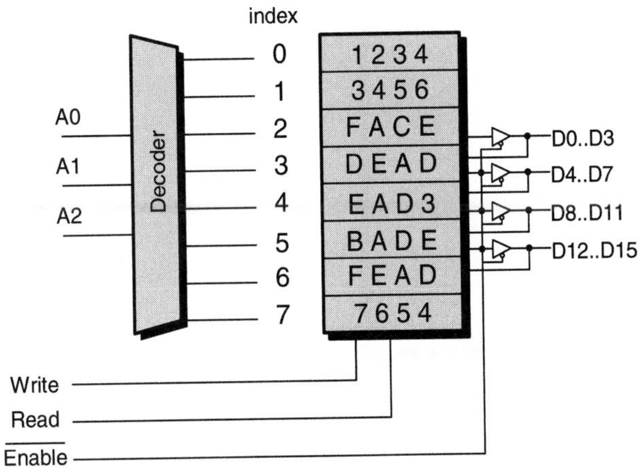

Figure 4.1 The Array as a Simple Memory Model

Prior to writing, the output drivers for the memory must be placed into the high-impedance state so that there is no conflict with the incoming data words. For this simple model, the data is entered into or read from the memory as a 16-bit word.

address, data, control

Thus, we see that a memory interface generally requires three categories of signals: *address*, *data*, and *control*. *Address* signals are inputs to the memory, *data* can be either an input or an output, and the *control* signals are generally inputs. All of the different memory types require both address and data signals. They differ in the number and the nature of the necessary control signals.

In Table 4.0, we identify some of the more common control signals.

Table 4.0 Common Memory Control Signals

	Chip Select —CS	Output Enable—OE	Read—R	Write—W	Column Address Strobe—CAS	Row Address Strobe—RAS
ROM	X	X				
SRAM	X	X	X	X		
DRAM	X	X	X	X	X	X

- Chip Select—CS—Enables a memory device for reading or writing. Generally low true.
- Output Enable—OE—Memory device output tristate control. Generally low true.
- Read—R—Signify a read operation on the memory device.
- Write—W—Signify a write operation on the memory device.
- Column Address Strobe—CAS—Signify that the signals on the address inputs represent a column address for the memory device.
- Row Address Strobe—RAS—Signify that the signals on the address inputs represent a row address for the memory device.

4.3 ROM OVERVIEW

Although there are exceptions, the ROM is generally viewed as a read only device. A high-level interface to the ROM given in Figure 4.2. Moving inside the ROM, we find that the adjacent diagram illustrates several bits in a ROM fragment. When the ROM is implemented, positions in the array that are to store a logical 0 have a transistor connected as shown in the figure. Those positions intended to store a logical 1 have none.

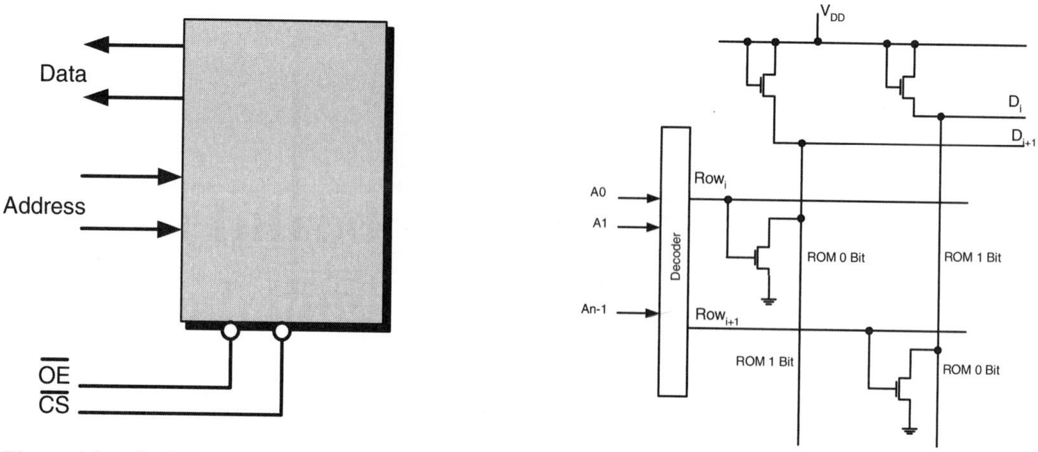

Figure 4.2 The ROM—Outside and Inside

4.3.1 Read Operation

A value is read from a ROM by asserting one of the row lines. Those rows in which there is a transistor will be pulled to ground thereby expressing a logical 0. Those without the transistor will express a logical 1.

Typical timing for a ROM read operation is given in Figure 4.3.

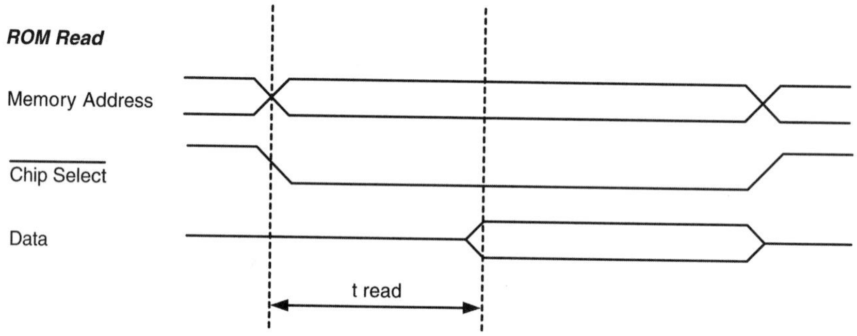

Figure 4.3 The ROM—Read Operation Timing

4.4 STATIC RAM OVERVIEW

A high-level interface to the SRAM is very similar to that for the ROM. The major differences arise from support for write capability. Figure 4.4 presents the major I/O signals and a typical cell in an SRAM array.

Observe that there are six transistors per cell (two in each of the buffers and the two pull-up transistors); two access transistors enable the cell for read and write.

4.4.1 Write Operation

A value is written into the cell by applying a signal to b_i and $\overline{bi}$ through the write/sense amplifiers. Asserting the word line causes the new value to be written into the latch.

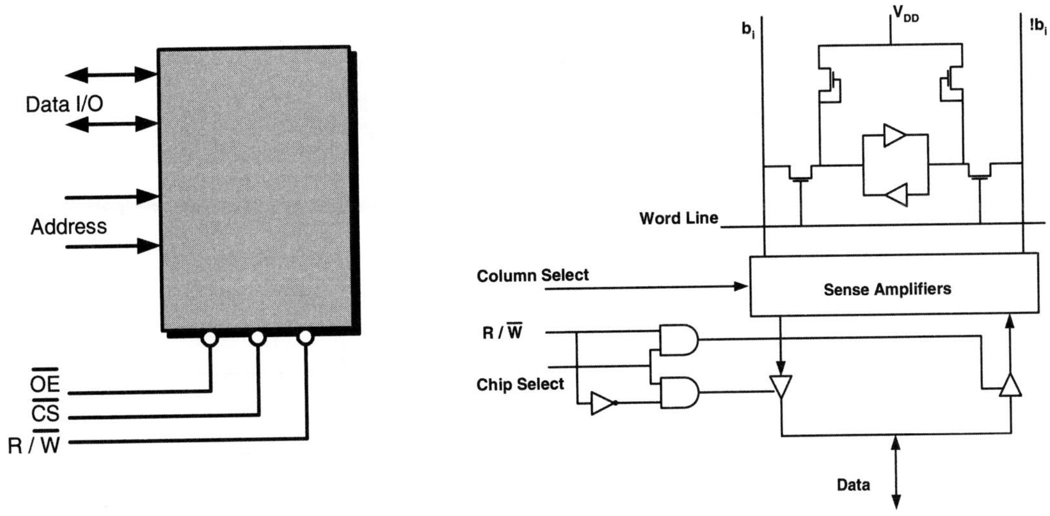

Figure 4.4 The SRAM—Outside and Inside

4.4.2 Read Operation

A value is read from the cell by first precharging b_i and $\overline{bi}$ to a voltage that is halfway between a 0 and a 1. Asserting the word line drives b_i and $\overline{bi}$ to high and low or low and high depending on the value that has been stored. The values are sensed and amplified by the write/sense amplifier.

Typical timing for a read and a write operation is shown in Figure 4.5.

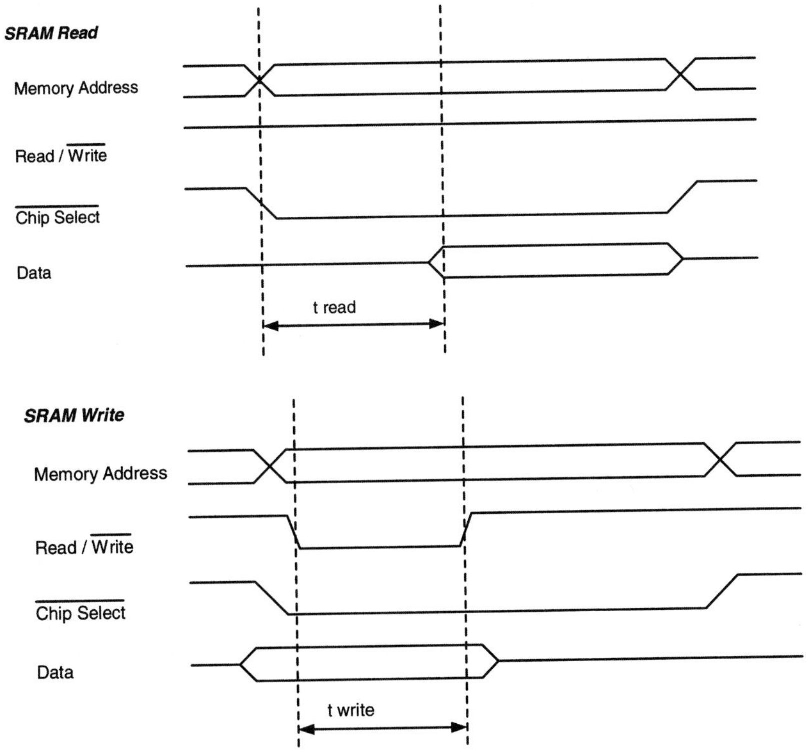

Figure 4.5 Timing for the SRAM—Read and Write Operations

4.5 DYNAMIC RAM OVERVIEW

A typical cell in a DRAM array appears as illustrated in Figure 4.6. Observe that in contrast to the configuration of the SRAM cell, in the DRAM, there is only one transistor per cell. The read and write operations use a single bit line.

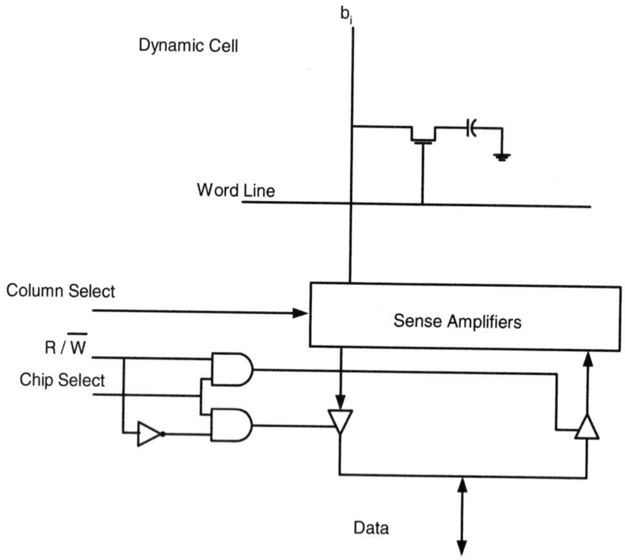

Figure 4.6 The DRAM Inside

4.5.1 Read Operation

A value is read from the cell by first pre-charging b_i to a voltage that is halfway between a 0 and a 1. Asserting the word line enables the stored signal onto b_i. If the stored value is a logical 1, through charge sharing, the value on line b_i will increase. Conversely, if the stored value is a logical 0, charge sharing will cause the value on b_i to decrease. The change in value is sensed and amplified by the write/sense amplifier. The read operation causes the capacitor to discharge. The sensed and amplified value is placed back on to the bit line. This is called a *restore* or *rewrite* operation.

restore, rewrite

4.5.2 Write Operation

A value is written into the cell by applying a logical 0 or logical 1 to b_i through the write/sense amplifiers. Asserting the word line charges the capacitor if a logical 1 is to be stored and discharges it if a logical 0 is to be stored.

4.5.3 Refresh Operation

Dynamic memories only store data for short periods of time on the parasitic capacitor associated with a MOS transistor. If the charge stored on the capacitor is not replaced periodically, it will leak away, thereby losing the data stored in the memory. Replacement is implemented by executing a read operation followed by a rewrite of the data back into the cell. Such replacement is referred to as *refresh* or a *refresh cycle*. The time between two refresh operations is called the *refresh time interval*. The interval is determined by the vendor's specification and the system in which memory is operating. A high-level interface to the DRAM is given in Figure 4.7.

refresh, refresh cycle
refresh time interval

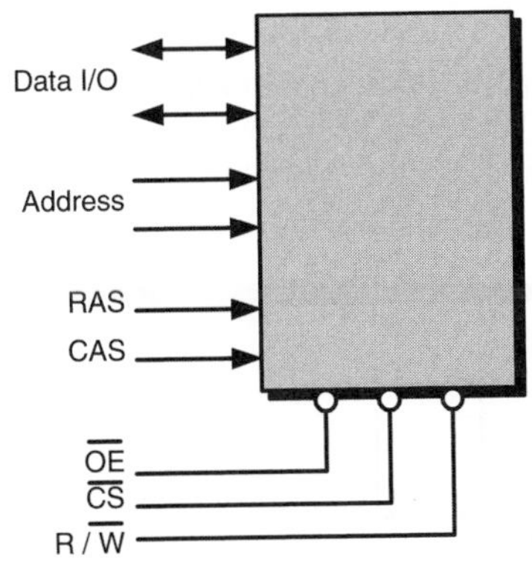

Figure 4.7 The DRAM Outside

Column Address Strobe
Row Address Strobe

CAS or *Column Address Strobe* is a clock used in dynamic memories to control the input of column addresses to the memory. RAS or *Row Address Strobe* is a clock used in dynamic memories to control the input of row addresses to the memory.

Typical DRAM read and write timing is given in Figure 4.8.

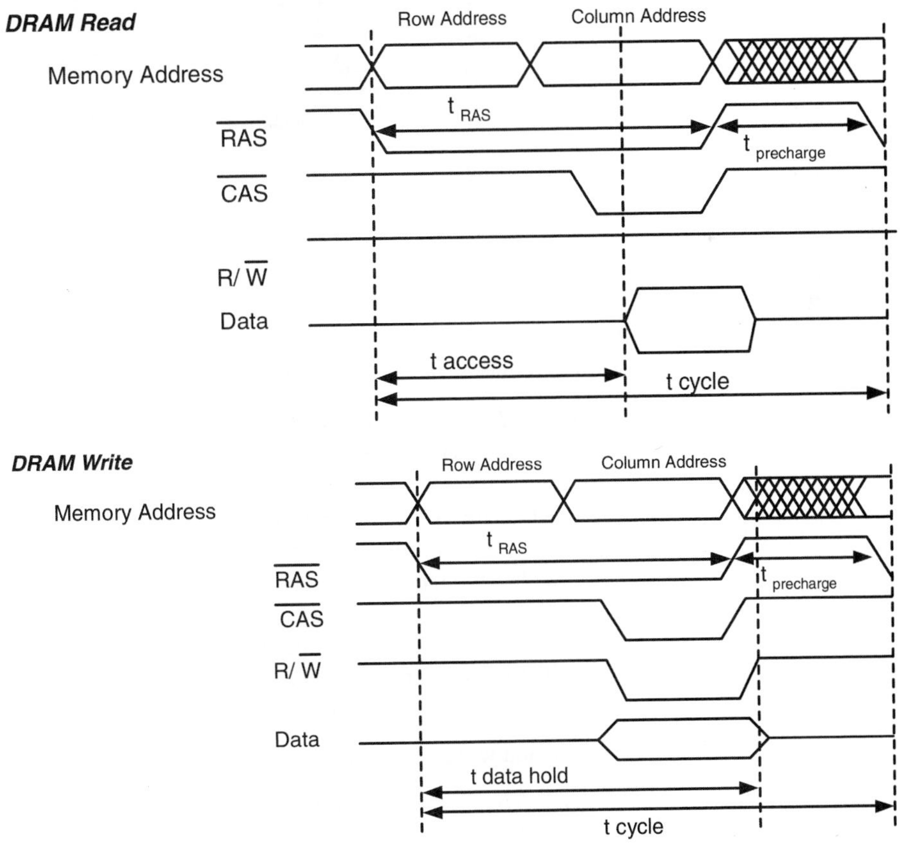

Figure 4.8 Timing for the DRAM Read and Write Cycles

4.6 CHIP ORGANIZATION

Independent of type of internal storage, the typical memory chip appears as is shown in Figure 4.9.

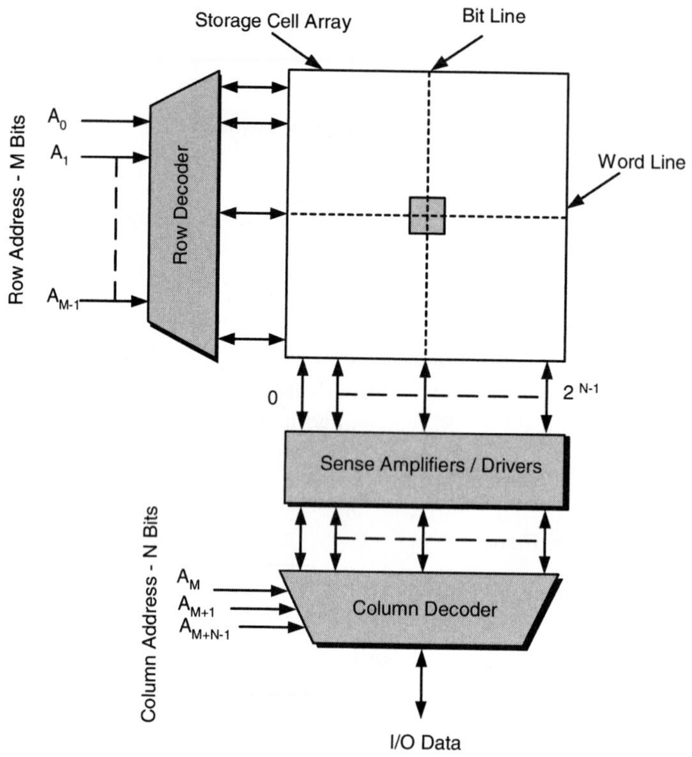

Figure 4.9 Typical Memory Chip Internal Architecture

4.7 TERMINOLOGY

Prior to delving into the detailed design and application of memory systems, it is appropriate to introduce some of the vocabulary.

Access Time—The time to access a word in memory.

Access time specifies to perform a read or a write operation. Note that the times for these two operations may be different. The time is measured from the point at which the access commences (as defined by the application of the address) until the operation is complete. For a read operation, that time will be when the data appears at the output port of the device. For a write operation, that time will be when the data is successfully written into the memory.

write

In the following timing diagram for the write operation, it is assumed that the internal write process commences on the transition from high to low on the *write* line and completes sometime later.

The read and write operations are illustrated in the timing diagram in Figure 4.10.

Cycle Time—The time interval from the start of one read or write operation until the start of the next.

Cycle time is a measure of how quickly the memory can be repeatedly accessed. It is illustrated in the timing diagram in Figure 4.11.

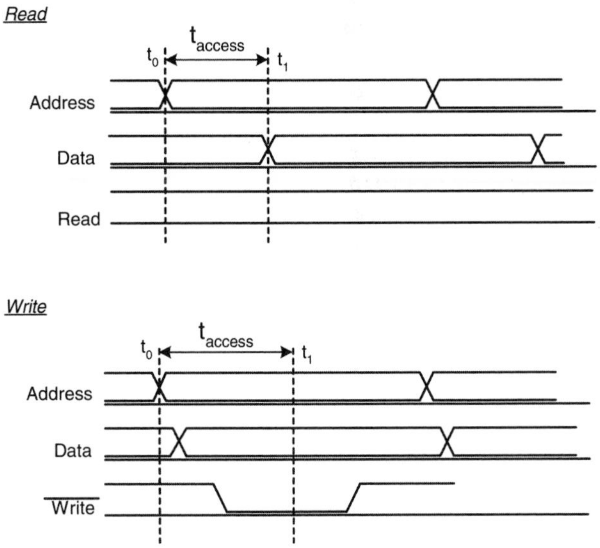

Figure 4.10 Memory Access Time

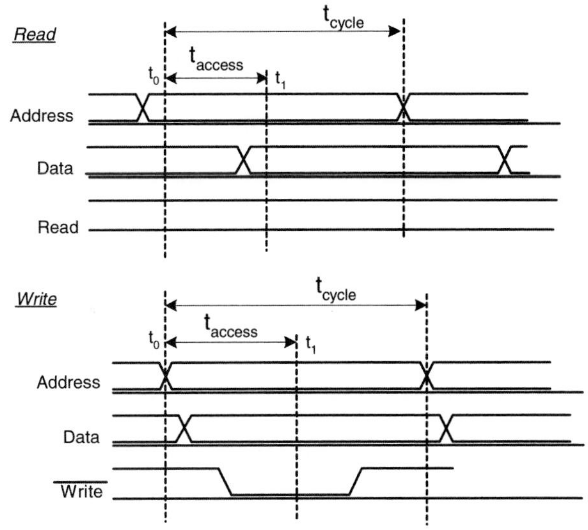

Figure 4.11 Memory Cycle Time

logical

blocks

Block Size—A block is a *logical* view placed on a collection of words in memory.

When quantities of data are transferred within a system, the units of transfer are called *blocks*. The block size specifies the number of words in such a collection. Figure 4.12 illustrates a memory organized into blocks.

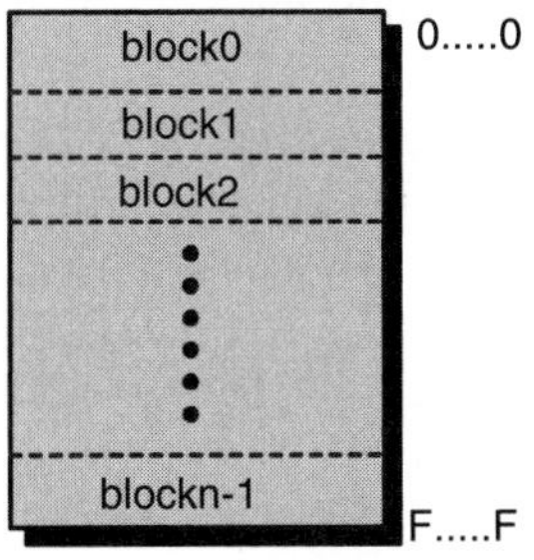

Figure 4.12 Memory Organized into Blocks

Bandwidth—Memory bandwidth is a measure of the word transmission rate to and from memory via the memory I/O bus.

Consider a memory in which the stored data words are a pattern of alternating 0's and 1's such as is illustrated in Figure 4.13.

When the data is read from memory, the pattern on each data line will be a square wave. The highest frequency of that square wave is the memory bandwidth.

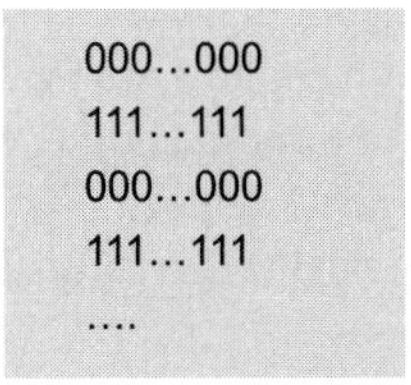

Figure 4.13 Memory Storing Alternating 0's and 1's

Latency—Latency is the amount of time required to access the first of a sequence of words.

Latency measures the time necessary to compute the address of that sequence and then locate its first block of words in memory.

Block Access Time—Block access time gives a measure of the time to access an entire block from the start of a read.

Block access time will include the time to find the 0th word of a block and then to transfer the remaining words.

Page—A page is a logical view placed on larger collections of words in memory.

Pages are generally comprised of blocks; the size of a page can be given in words or in blocks.

4.8 A MEMORY INTERFACE IN DETAIL

If a single ROM or RAM chip is large enough and the address and data I/O are wide enough to satisfy system memory requirements, then the interface is rather straightforward. Often, however, one or the other of the requirements is not satisfied. Let's look at implementing a memory system in which neither of the requirements is met.

We will look first at an SRAM system and then at a DRAM design. A ROM implementation is identical to an SRAM design minus the write capability.

4.9 AN SRAM DESIGN

A system specification requires an SRAM system that can store up to 4 K 16-bit words. However, the largest memory device available is 1 K by 8. That is, it can store up to 1024 8-bit words. Consequently, the design will require eight of the smaller memory devices: two sets of four.

In the worst case, to support 4 K 16-bit words, 12 address lines and 16 data lines are required. If sufficient I/O lines are available on the microprocessor, the design is straightforward. Let's assume that such is not the case and that only 8 address lines and 8 data lines are available. Under such a restriction, two address transfers and two data transfers will be necessary to complete a single transaction. The architecture of such a system is given in Figure 4.14.

THE MEMORY ARRAY

memory array

Let's look at the various pieces of the design starting with the *memory array*. The requirements specify support for 4 K 16-bit words. The available memory chips only support 1 K 8-bit words. We can use two 1 K by 8 memory chips to hold 1 K 16-bit words.

One memory chip will store the upper byte, and the other memory chip will store the lower byte, as we see in Figure 4.15. By duplicating such a configuration four times, we will have sufficient storage for the 4 K 16-bit words.

chip select

output enable

Ten address bits will enable us to identify each location in a 1 K block since 10 bits gives us 2^{10} or 1024 combinations. Next, one must be able to identify which of the 1 K by 16-bit blocks to read from or write to. Two additional address bits enable such a selection to be made. These four combinations can be used to activate the *chip select* (CS) control input for the appropriate 1 K block. The *output enable* (OE) control inputs for the individual RAMs must be placed in the logical 1 state during a write cycle and in the logical 0 state during a read cycle.

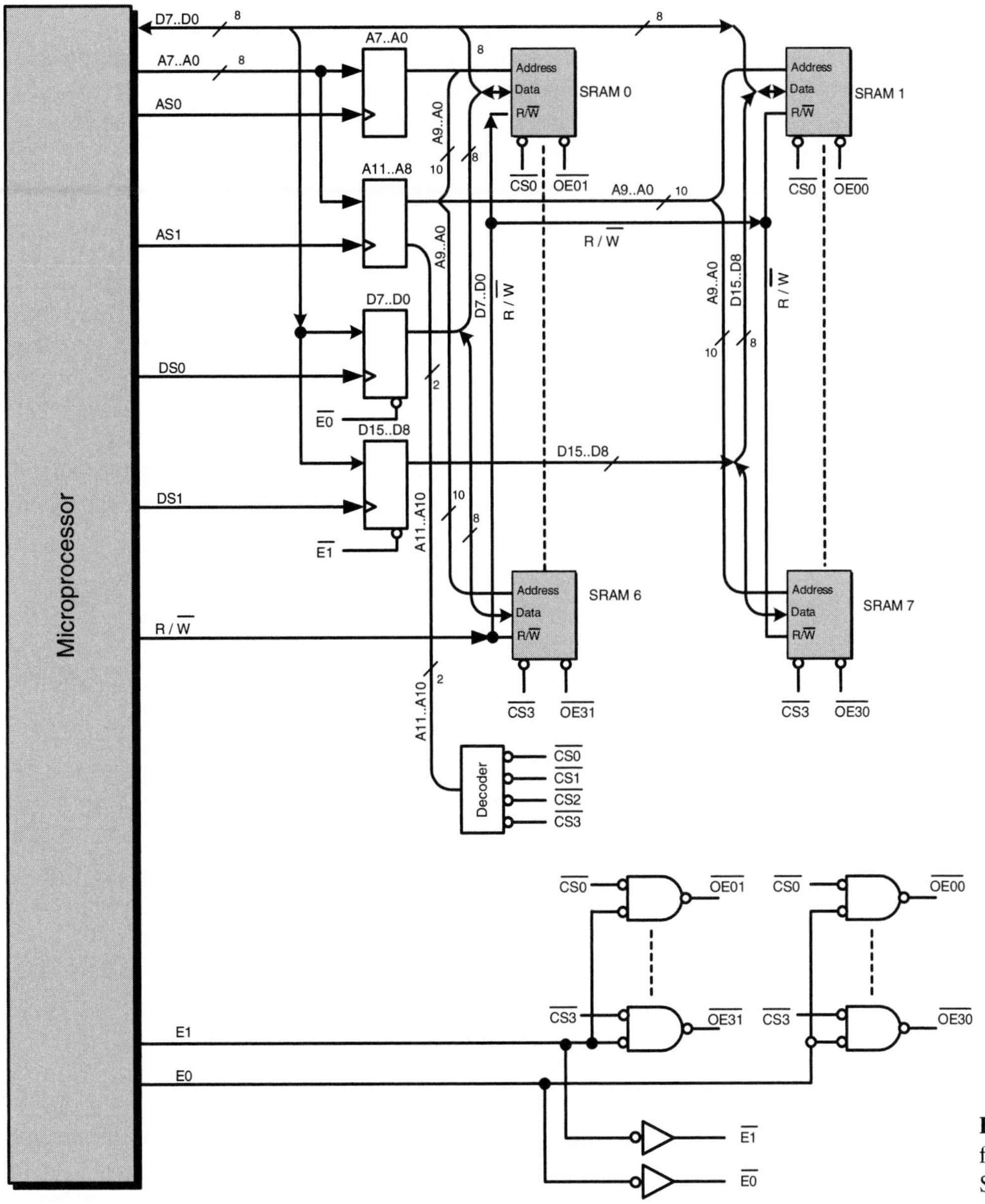

Figure 4.14 Design for a 4 K x 16 SRAM System

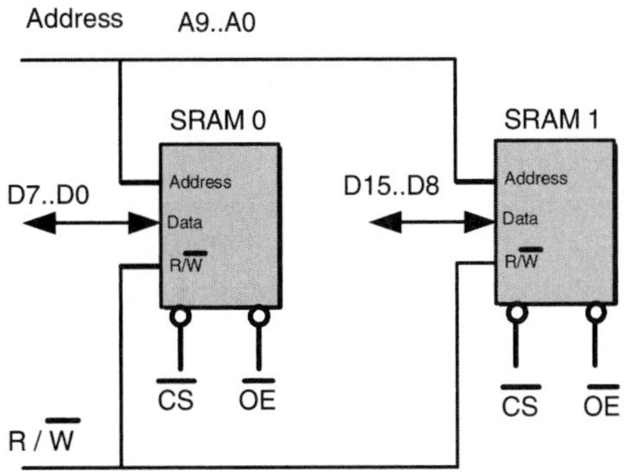

Figure 4.15 Using Two 8-Bit SRAMs to Store 16-Bit Words

READING AND WRITING

Since the microprocessor only supports eight address lines, the full address is built up in two transfers on the address bus. Each address byte is stored in a register; the register is clocked by a strobe accompanying each transfer. Only 12 address bits are required; therefore, the upper 4 bits from the second transfer are not used.

WRITE

Data transfers to and from memory are managed using a technique similar to that used for addresses. For a write operation, each data byte is first stored in a register. To execute a write operation, the memory address and the data to be written to that address are placed onto their respective busses, 8 bits at a time. Each transfer is accompanied by a strobe that will be used to store the address and data values in 16-bit address and data registers. After
write the data has been stored in the data latches, the *write* command is issued.

When writing to the memory, one must ensure that its output drivers are turned off; otherwise there will be a bus contention. The high-level timing diagram for the write operation is given in Figure 4.16.

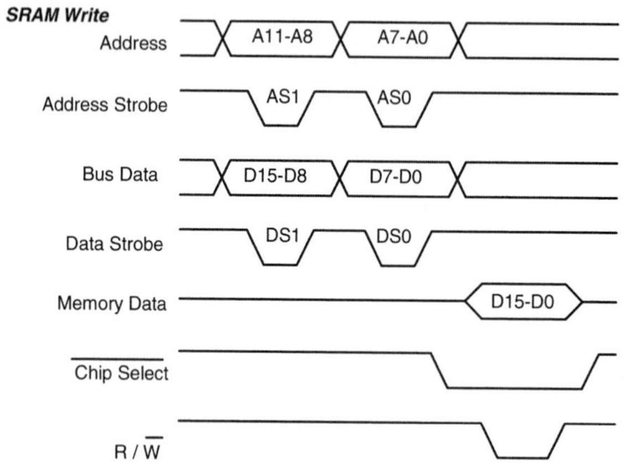

Figure 4.16 SRAM System Write Timing

READ

For a read operation, one must disable the outputs of the data latches and enable the memory output drivers. To accommodate the 8-bit microprocessor bus, data is transferred from the memory array 8 bits at a time. To execute a read operation, the desired memory address is selected, as was done during the write operation. The proper chip select signal, combined with the state of the read line, begins the read process on the selected memory block. The output enable signals shown in the logic diagram in Figure 4.17 are successively asserted to first place the upper and then the lower data bytes onto the data bus as depicted in the timing diagram in Figure 4.18.

There are a number of variations on the design that we have just completed. One of the major differences between applications and designs is the number of I/O lines that the processor has available to support the interface. On the one extreme, there are sufficient lines to support full address and data busses. If each bus comprises 12, 16, 32 bits, or more, such a luxury is rare in an embedded application. On the other extreme, signals must be multiplexed onto busses and stored in registers until all information is collected.

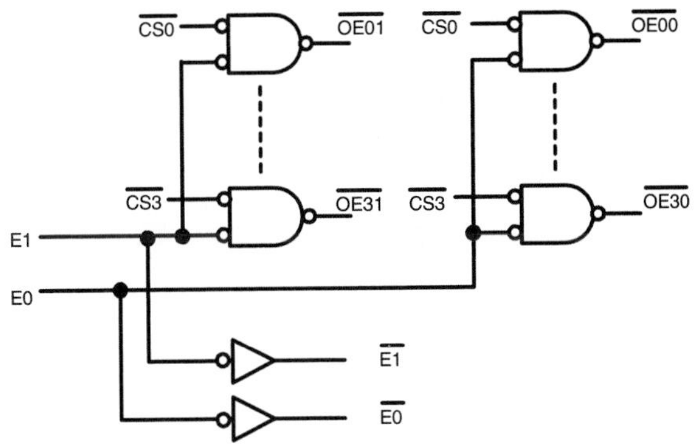

Figure 4.17 SRAM System Read Control Logic

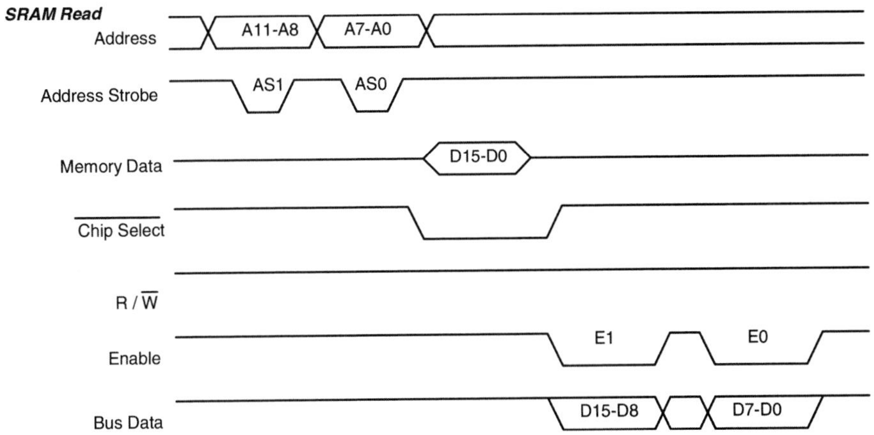

Figure 4.18 SRAM System Read Timing

A multiplexed implementation is the more common architecture: sharing one set of bus lines between the two functions (address and data). Under such circumstances, the address and data registers are necessary for temporary storage. One finds such registers referenced in the literature as a memory address register—MAR—and a memory data (buffer) register—MD(B)R. The design of such a system will closely parallel what we have done here.

4.10 A DRAM DESIGN

Let's now explore the design and implementation of an interface to a DRAM system. The DRAM system will utilize an architecture that duplicates most of the previous SRAM system. One of the major differences is the potential need to manage the refresh function. A second difference results from a memory size versus IC package size difficulty.

EDO (Extended Data Output) ***SDRAM (Synchronous DRAM)*** ***FPM (Fast Page Mode)***

Today one can easily find numerous variations on the basic DRAM architecture (*EDO—Extended Data Output*; *SDRAM—Synchronous DRAM; FPM—Fast Page Mode*). At the end of the day, all of these different types are simply DRAMs. The differences appear in the way that they are organized and how they are accessed. At the root of the differences is the need to accommodate the ever increasing speed of contemporary processors. Thus, the DRAM access is synchronized to the system clock, block access addressing is improved, or pipelined access is permitted. Today the basic DRAM is referred to as the

regular, conventional

regular or *conventional* DRAM. The newer devices incorporate refresh management inside the device and support a number of other useful features as well.

In the SRAM design, insufficient pins were available on the microprocessor to permit all the necessary address bits to be controlled in parallel. The problem was solved by multiplexing the desired address onto a smaller bus and then demultiplexing them into a full-width address register.

The ability to store large quantities of information in today's DRAMs presents a similar conundrum. Current integrated circuit package technology does not support a sufficient number of I/O pins to simultaneously accommodate the necessary number of address bits. We solve the problem by multiplexing the address into the chip as a row segment and a column segment and then demultiplexing them once they are inside. As we did with the SRAM design, each segment of the address is accompanied by a strobe; for the DRAM these are identified as the *Row Address Strobe* (RAS) and the *Column Address Strobe* (CAS).

Row Address Strobe (RAS)

Column Address Strobe (CAS)

As a basis for understanding contemporary variations on the DRAM, let's abstract away the performance-enhancing modifications and examine the operation of the basic DRAM core. For the current analysis, we will use a 4 M by 16-bit device—a RAM that will store 4 million 16-bit words.

4.10.1 DRAM Timing Analysis

Core Components

To begin the study of the DRAM core and the critical timing elements, some new vocabulary is necessary.

• ***RAS—Row Address Strobe***	Asserts that the row segment of the address is on the input address bus.
• ***CAS—Column Address Strobe***	Asserts that the column segment of the address is on the input address bus.
• ***RAS Cycle Time***	Specifies the period of RAS.
• ***RAS to CAS Delay***	Specifies the separation between the start of a row address strobe and the start of a column address strobe.
• **Refresh Period**	Specifies the maximum period in which all memory cells must be refreshed to ensure that no data is lost.

The relative timing for some of these signals in the base case is illustrated in Figure 4.19.

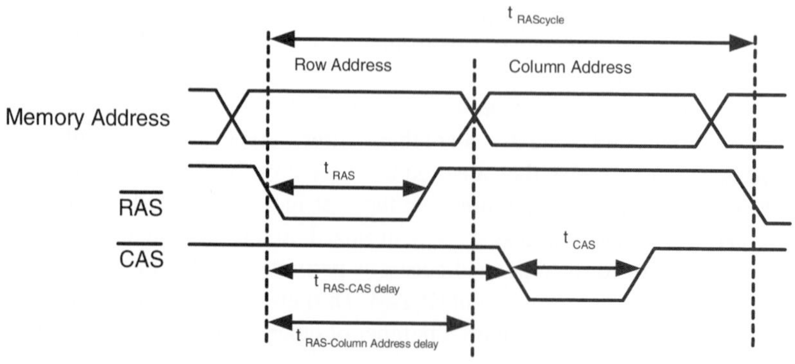

Figure 4.19 Basic DRAM Timing

The timing of the row or column address with respect to the RAS or CAS signals permits either the leading or trailing edge of the strobe to capture the address information.

EDO—Extended Data Output

For illustration, the basic cycle is extended in the next timing diagram to illustrate a DRAM that supports *EDO—Extended Data Output*. Rather than returning to the deasserted state following the row address capture, the RAS signal is reinterpreted to include the row address portion followed by one or more column address portions. In Figure 4.20, three successive column accesses use the same row address. With such a scheme, two row address cycles have been eliminated, thereby substantially reducing the amount of time to perform the read or write operations.

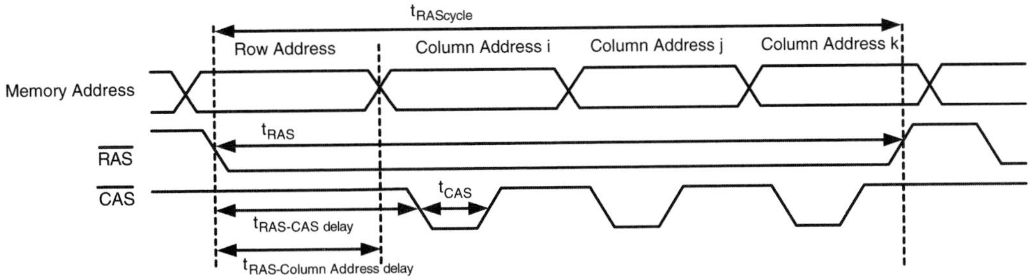

Figure 4.20 EDO DRAM Timing with Successive Column Accesses using a Single Row Address

With such a modification, row address information must be captured on the leading edge of RAS. We see that the time interval t_{RAS} now comprises the RAS interval and one or several subsequent CAS intervals.

4.10.2 DRAM Refresh

Refresh management can be accomplished in several ways. It is important to remember that the refresh operation is overhead; normal read and write operations are the intended purpose of the memory. Consequently, it is desirable that the refresh have minimal impact on the normal operations.

Although a normal read or write operation will refresh the addressed row, one cannot depend on such operations to ensure that each row in the memory is accessed or that such accesses occur frequently enough to meet the maximum refresh period specification. Periodically performing a burst refresh in which normal operations are suspended while all rows are refreshed can potentially affect real-time performance. An alternative approach is to refresh one row at a time according to a schedule that ensures that all rows are visited at least once within the maximum refresh period. Such an approach seeks to evenly distribute the refresh burden.

The various DRAM chip designs typically support a variety of different refresh schemes. The major differences center on whether the refresh is controlled externally or internally and where the refresh addresses originate, again, externally or internally.

4.11 THE DRAM MEMORY INTERFACE

From the microprocessor's point of view, the interface for normal read and write operations to the DRAM replicates much of that which has already been designed for the SRAM. Let's now add the refresh component.

For this design, we will implement a scheme that refreshes one row at a time and will implement the refresh management outside of the chip. We will assume a 4M word memory chip organized as 4 K rows and 1 K columns, and we will posit that each row must be refreshed every 64 ms. The organization will require a total of 22 address bits comprising 12 row address bits and 10 column address bits. The memory chip will support 12 address input pins; 10 of the pins will be shared between the row and column address bits.

We will further assume that the timing will utilize a two-phase clocking scheme that is derived from a 50-MHz source shown in Figure 4.21.

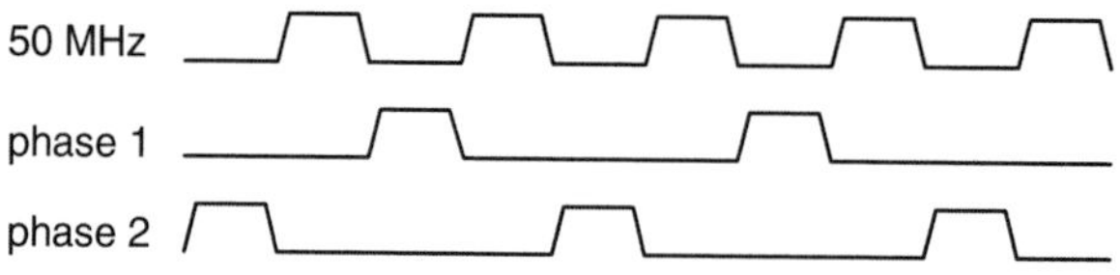

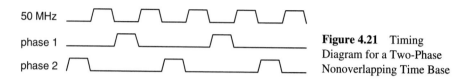

Figure 4.21 Timing Diagram for a Two-Phase Nonoverlapping Time Base

A two-phased clock design gives greater flexibility in time than is possible with a single-phase clocking scheme. See the earlier discussion of clocks and time bases in Chapter 3.

4.11.1 Refresh Timing

To meet the refresh timing constraint, one row must be refreshed every 16 μsec. Four hundred counts from a 9-bit counter incremented from either phase of the clock (25 MHZ) will provide the 16-μ sec interval. Decoding the two most significant bits of such a counter will produce a signal that occurs at count 384 or after 15.36 μsec. Executing a refresh 16 counts early provides some timing margin. That design for the refresh interval timer is given in Figure 4.22.

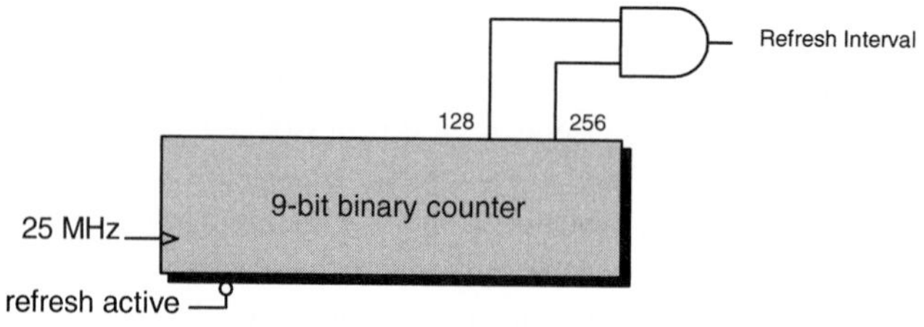

Figure 4.22 Refresh Interval Timer

4.11.2 Refresh Address

The refresh address is not the same address as is used by the normal read or write operations. To provide the address, a 12-bit binary counter is used. The counter should be incremented following the completion of each row refresh operation. The address counter appears in Figure 4.23.

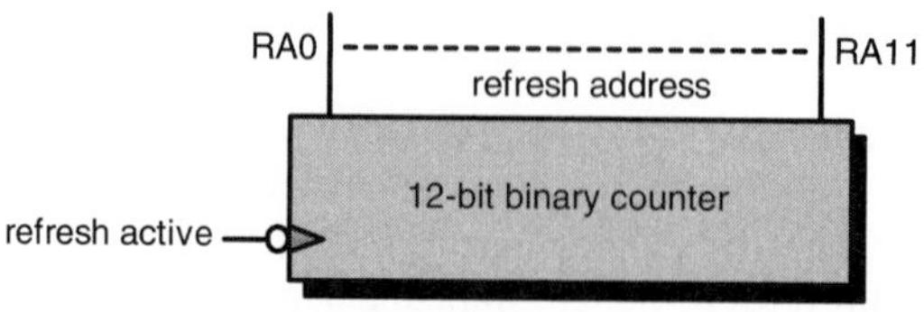

Figure 4.23 Refresh Address Generator

During a normal read or write operation, the row addresses to the DRAM are provided by the source executing the operation. During a refresh, they are given by the refresh address counter. Thus, the DRAM address lines must provide row, then column addresses during normal operation and refresh row addresses during the refresh cycle.

Selection among the three alternatives is shown in Figure 4.24.

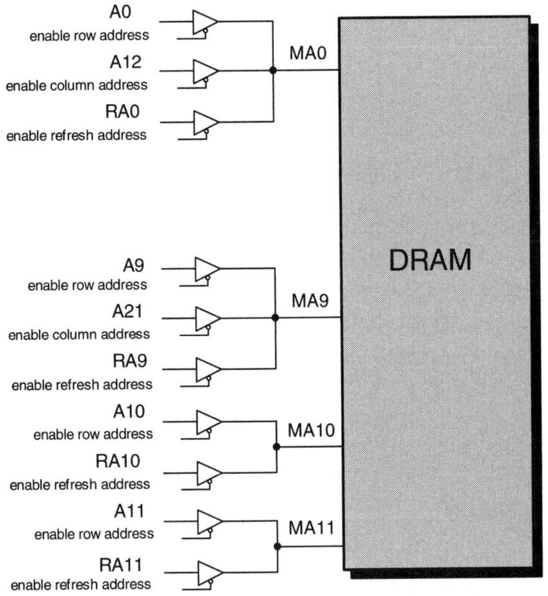

Figure 4.24 Address Source Control

Note that only 10 address bits are needed for the column address since the memory has 1 K columns. The timing of the normal row and column address enable signals is given in Figure 4.25.

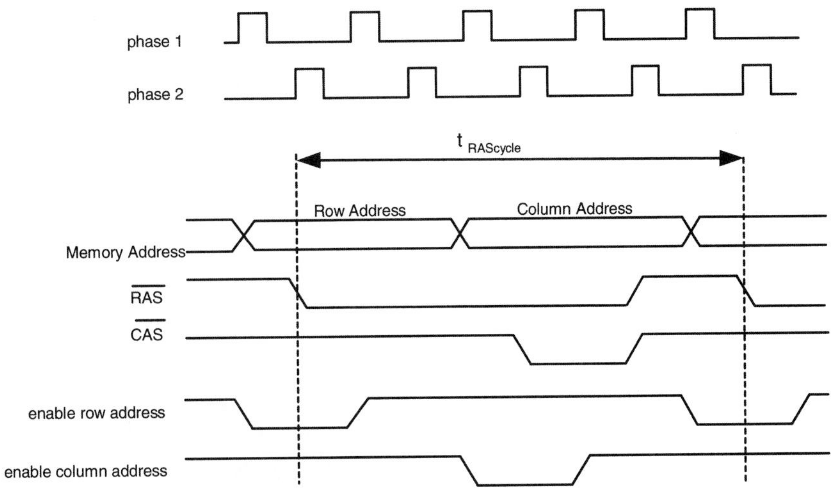

Figure 4.25 Row and Column Address Timing

The signal timing is set such that the addresses are generated on phase 1 of the clock. The row and column address enable signals are asserted on the same phase. RAS and CAS are generated on phase 2 of the clock. The two enable signals can be generated using the state machine in Figure 4.26.

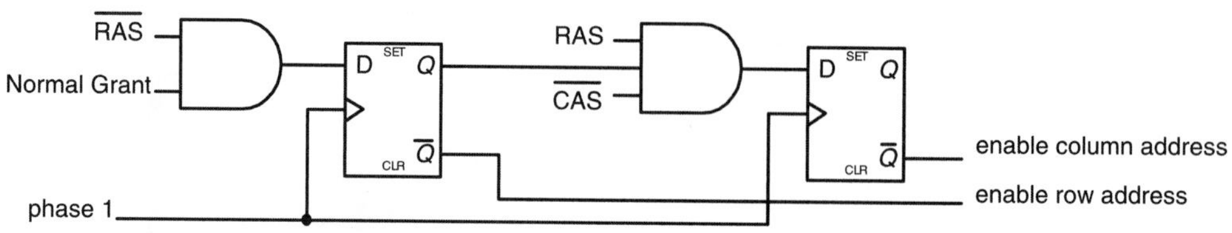

Figure 4.26 Row and Column Address Enable

4.11.3 Refresh Arbitration

The refresh address is independent from that used by the normal read or write operations. Consequently, there is a nonzero probability that either a refresh or normal read or write operation may be in progress when the other is requested or that there may be a collision in which both are simultaneously requested. All three cases must be accommodated; we set the following rules:

1. If a normal read or write operation starts, it is allowed to complete.
2. If a refresh operation has started, the normal operation is remembered.
3. In the case of a tie, the normal operation is given priority.

The following signals are defined:

Read-Write	Indicates that a normal read or write operation has been initiated on the microprocessor bus.
Refresh Interval	Indicates that the refresh time interval has elapsed.
Normal Request	Indicates that a normal read or write operation is requested by the arbitration logic.
Refresh Request	Indicates that a refresh operation is requested by the arbitration logic.
Normal Grant	Indicates that a normal read or write operation is granted by the arbitration logic.
Refresh Grant	Indicates that a refresh operation is granted by the arbitration logic.
Normal Active	Indicates that a normal read or write operation has commenced.
Refresh Active	Indicates that a refresh operation has commenced.

Read-Write, Operation Complete, Normal Active, Refresh Active

The specific implementation of several of these signals will be application and processor dependent. These include *Read-Write, Operation Complete, Normal Active,* and *Refresh Active*. In any case, they are not difficult to build. For the current design, they will be assumed to exist.

The logic diagram, presented in Figure 4.27 implements the arbitration circuitry as a two-level design—the request portion followed by the grant portion.

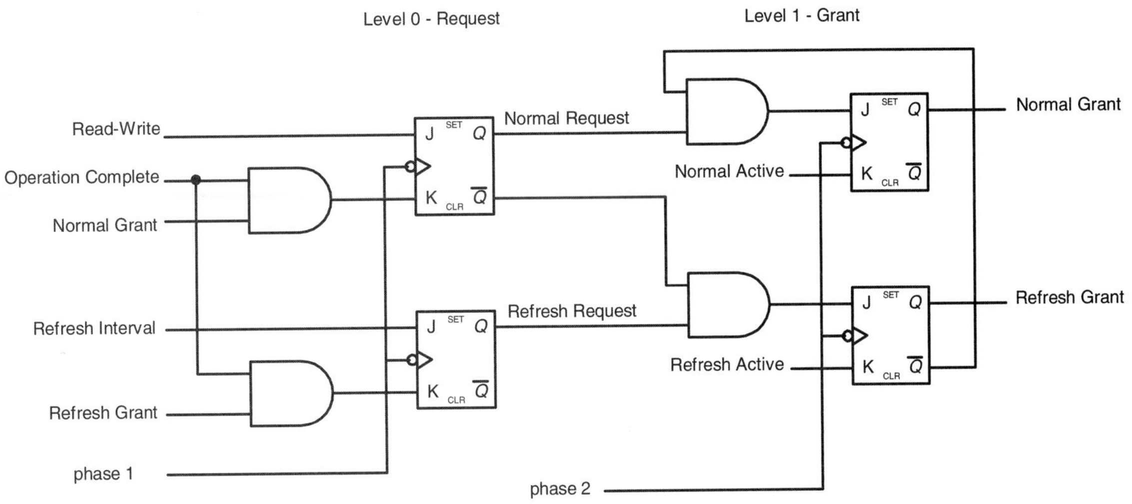

Figure 4.27 Normal vs. Refresh Access Arbitration

We now bring the major pieces of the DRAM addressing and refresh management together in the block diagram shown in Figure 4.28.

The data read and write operations to the DRAM will generally follow the timing diagrams presented earlier. They are repeated in Figure 4.29 for reference.

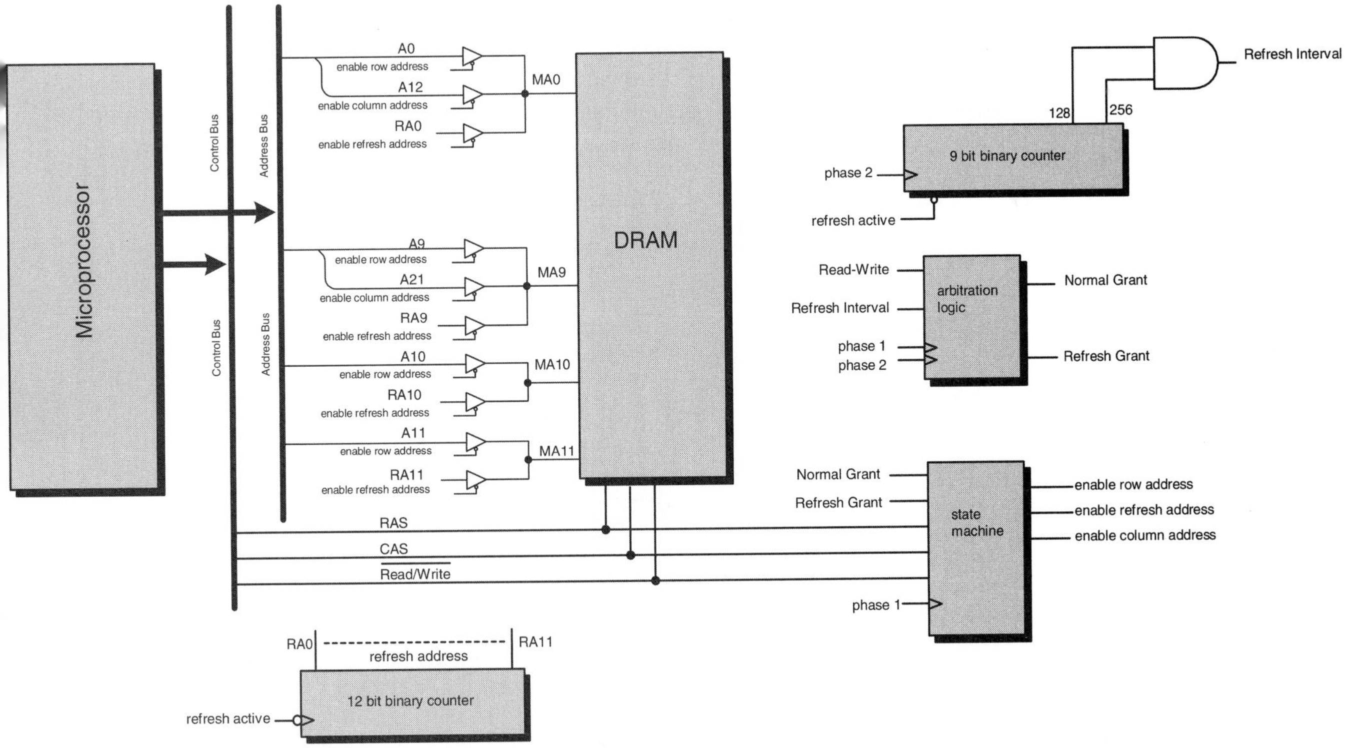

Figure 4.28 Block Diagram—DRAM Memory System

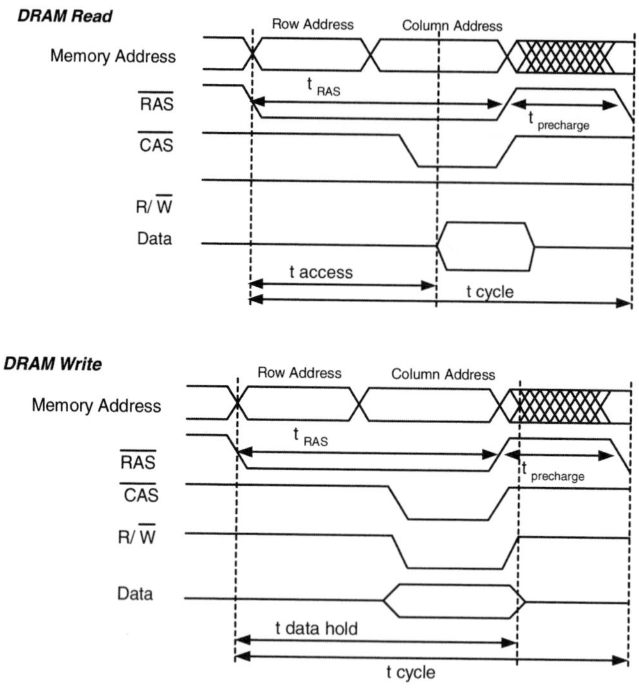

Figure 4.29 Timing Diagrams—DRAM Memory System Read and Write Access

4.12 THE MEMORY MAP

memory map

As a first step toward understanding the memory subsystem in an embedded application, we begin with a *memory map*. Formulating a memory map is a useful early step in the design of the core system. The map specifies the allocation and use of each location in the physical memory address space. At a bare minimum, the memory map should identify the data and code space. A typical memory map for a small 16-bit machine is presented in Figure 4.30.

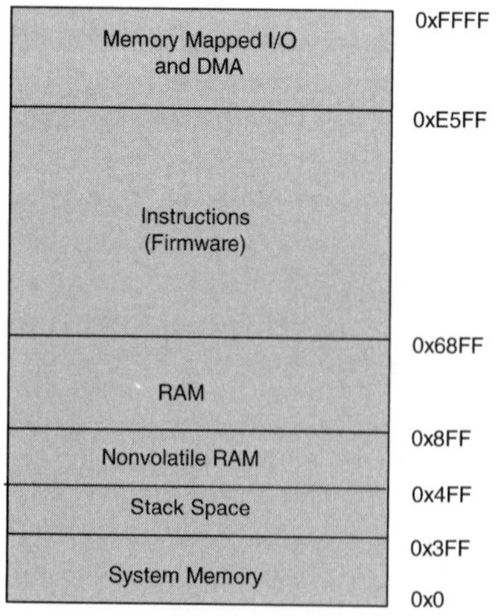

Figure 4.30 Basic Memory Map

As illustrated, the memory map lists the addresses in memory allocated to each portion of the application. Note that this is primary physical memory. From a high-level perspective, the memory subsystem is comprised of two basic types: RAM and ROM. ROM is used to hold words that are not expected to change at runtime. This will be the space available to the application firmware. RAM is used to hold words that may change at runtime. This will be the space available to hold data among other things. A portion of the RAM memory may be allocated for nonvolatile RAM that is be used for data that needs to be retained if power is removed from the system. If the design is using memory mapped I/O, then all of physical memory will not be available for data or code.

virtual memory
overlays

Note that it is possible for the required code and data space to exceed total available primary memory. Under such circumstances, one must use techniques called *virtual memory* and *overlays* to accommodate the expanded needs.

4.13 MEMORY SUBSYSTEM ARCHITECTURE

We have looked at several different kinds of memory, how one can design and build an interface to them, and how one might allocate subsets of the physical memory address space to meet the different requirements of the application. We now bring a number of those pieces together in a memory system. The block-labeled memory in the diagram for a von Neumann machine is actually comprised of a number of memory components of different kinds, sizes, and speeds arranged in a hierarchical manner and designed to cooperate with each other. Such a hierarchy is given in Figure 4.31.

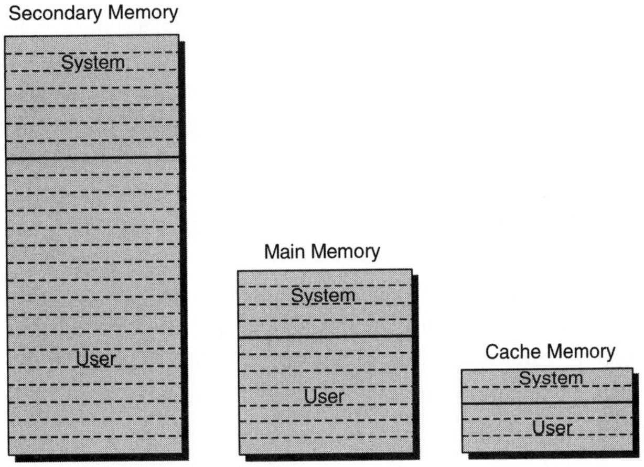

Figure 4.31 Typical Memory Hierarchy Utilizing a Variety of Memory Types

secondary
cache
main, primary

The commonly used hierarchical metrics for relating the different kinds of memories are speed and storage capacity. At the top are the slowest, largest, and least expensive memories. These are known as *secondary* memory and are shown in the diagram by the block on the left. At the bottom are the smallest, fastest memories called *cache* memory; these are typically higher speed SRAMs. These devices also tend to be the most expensive. In the middle of the hierarchy is *main* or *primary* memory. These are either lower speed SRAM devices or, more commonly, DRAM memories. CPU registers are sometimes included in the ranking as higher speed memory than cache.

The motivation for building a memory system as a hierarchical collection of different kinds of memories is that we would prefer an application program to execute as quickly as possible. Accessing memory takes time; each access contributes to the time required to execute an instruction that can have a significant negative impact on real-time performance in an embedded application.

We will not consider secondary storage; the typical embedded applications will not use this. The discussion here will focus on main memory and cache, the last two blocks on the right. These can be implemented using (variations on) the designs presented in the previous sections.

4.14 BASIC CONCEPTS OF CACHING

Cache is a small, fast memory that temporarily holds copies of block data and program instructions from the main memory. The increased speed of cache memory over that of main memory components offers the prospective for programs to execute much more rapidly if the instructions and data can be held in cache. Many of today's higher performance microprocessors, implemented around the Harvard architecture, will internally support both an *icache* (instruction cache) and a *dcache* (data cache). We will now examine the concept of caching in greater detail. We will look first at the ideas behind caching, what cache is, why it works, and some of the potential difficulties encountered in embedded applications. We will then examine several alternative caching schemes and, later, the effect of caching on performance in Chapter 14.

icache, dcache

4.14.1 Locality of Reference

Time is a critical constraint in many embedded applications. Time burdens arising from memory accesses and memory access speeds can have a significant impact on meeting those constraints. Thus, in executing a design, among the many goals two are to reduce the number of memory accesses and make each access as short (in time) as possible. Ideally, one would like to make all memory as fast as technology allows. There is an associated cost, however. High-speed memories are expensive and complex to design; support circuitry can be rather expensive as well. As the speed demands and the requirements for additional support circuitry increase, a growing stress will be placed on the system's power supplies. Let's look at an alternate approach.

Almost all embedded software today is written using a procedural paradigm and is often written in the C language. Many years ago IBM analyzed how such programs are designed and execute and discovered an interesting phenomenon. Execution generally occurs either sequentially or in small loops with a small number of instructions. Such behavior means that the overall forward progress through a program is proceeding at a much lower rate than the access times of the fastest memory. Put another way, with respect to the entire program, actual execution takes place within a small window that moves forward through the program. This is shown in Figure 4.32.

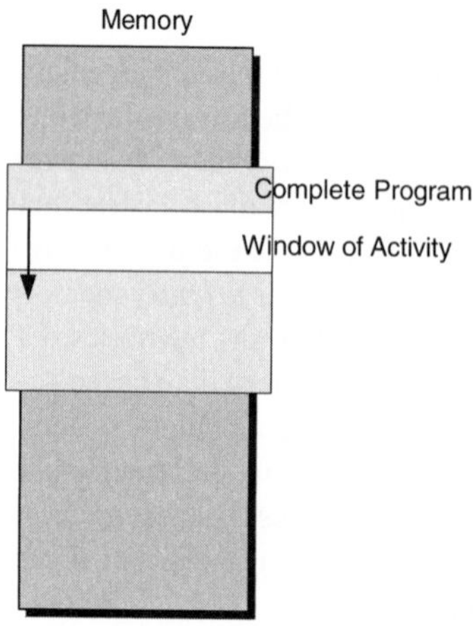

Figure 4.32 Locality of Reference

sequential locality of reference

Formally, such a phenomenon is called *sequential locality of reference*. Because the program is executing only a few instructions within a small window, if those few instructions can be kept in fast memory, the program will appear to be executing out of that memory. Through such a scheme, we can gain the benefits of higher speed at a reduced cost. An important point to remember is that the approach works if the area within the program in which the application is currently executing is in the local window. The method can easily be defeated with large loops or repeated branches outside of the window. Two other types of *locality of reference*, *spatial* and *temporal*, are also defined. Spatial locality suggests that a future access of a resource, a memory address in this case, is going to be physically near one previously accessed. Temporal locality suggests that a future access of a resource, again, a memory address, is going to be temporally near one recently accessed. Using locality of reference knowledge can significantly improve memory access time performance.

locality of reference, spatial, temporal

A major caveat for real-time applications that utilize a caching scheme is that demand for the movement of blocks of instructions or data from or to main memory to or from cache is driven by the execution path taken through the program. Such a path is often governed by results of computations, external events, and/or any of a variety of other factors. Which path of a branch is taken, for example, may determine whether or not the application has to bring in data/instructions from cache.

Although it is important to keep in mind that any such schemes can have significant negative impact on real-time systems, it is also important to remember that, when properly used, they can have a significant positive impact on system performance. It is evident, then, that using caching schemes is sometimes appropriate. If caching must be used, it is essential to understand the problem and the caching algorithm completely, to determine an upper bound on context switching, and to leave plenty of time margin in the application.

4.14.2 Cache System Architecture

When using a caching scheme, the goal is to operate out of cache memory—typically SRAM—to the greatest extent possible. When program execution needs an instruction or data that is not in the cache, it must be brought in from main memory—typically DRAM.

The block diagram for the architecture appears as shown in Figure 4.33.

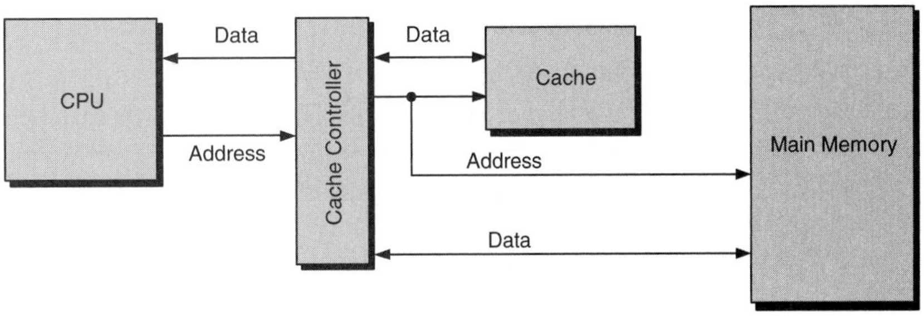

Figure 4.33 Cache System Architecture

4.15 DESIGNING A CACHE SYSTEM

Caching requires a certain amount of higher speed memory. The size of that memory determines how much information can be stored locally. In larger modern processors, several levels of cache internal to the processor can be enabled or disabled. The cache under discussion here is external to the CPU.

4.15.1 A High-Level Description

The application program begins executing and encounters a need for a piece of data or an instruction. To locate that item, first the cache is checked. If the item is found, there is a *cache hit*. The data or instruction is retrieved and used. If the item is not found, there has been a *cache miss* and the item must be obtained from somewhere else. For the current discussion that location will be main memory.

cache hit ***cache miss***

The block containing the data or instruction is brought into the cache from main memory. If there is room left in the cache, the block is stored; otherwise room must be made. That task is accomplished by overwriting or removing an existing block. On one hand, if the contents of the block have been modified, the changes must be saved. On the other hand, if there have been no modifications to any data in the old block, that block can simply be discarded and the new block written in its place.

Several questions arise immediately.

- How do we know when something is not in the cache?
- Where do we go to find something if it is not in the cache?
- What if it's not there?
- How do we know if there is room left in the cache?
- How do we know if information in the cache was modified?
- How do we select the block to replace?

4.16 CACHING—A DIRECT MAPPED IMPLEMENTATION

direct mapping

The first cache management strategy that we will study is called *direct mapping*. As we examine the design, we will address each of these questions. First the specifications:

- The cache and main memory will store 32-bit words.
- The cache size will be 64 K words.
- The cache will be organized as 128 0.5 K word blocks.
- The cache will implement a *direct mapped* replacement algorithm.
- Memory addresses will be 32 bits.
- Main memory size will be 128 M words.
- Main memory will be organized as 2 K pages; each page will hold 128 blocks.

The core hardware components of the cache are given in the following diagrams. These comprise the cache memory array, the Memory Address Register (MAR) used to hold the address being accessed, and the Memory Data Register (MDR) used to hold data being read from or written to cache. The diagram on the right in Figure 4.34 gives the software view of the cache, which is logically divided into 128 blocks. Each block will contain 512 words.

The cache will now logically appear as we see in Figure 4.34.

During normal operation, an instruction or data fetch from memory or data write to memory proceeds as discussed earlier. The address (and data as appropriate) is provided, and the read or write operation is executed. When the target address is not found in the cache, a *cache miss* occurs. Under such circumstances, the required data or instruction must be copied into the cache from main memory.

cache miss

Rather than bring a single word into the cache, when such a transfer is needed, the complete block containing the required word is brought in. The destination to where the new

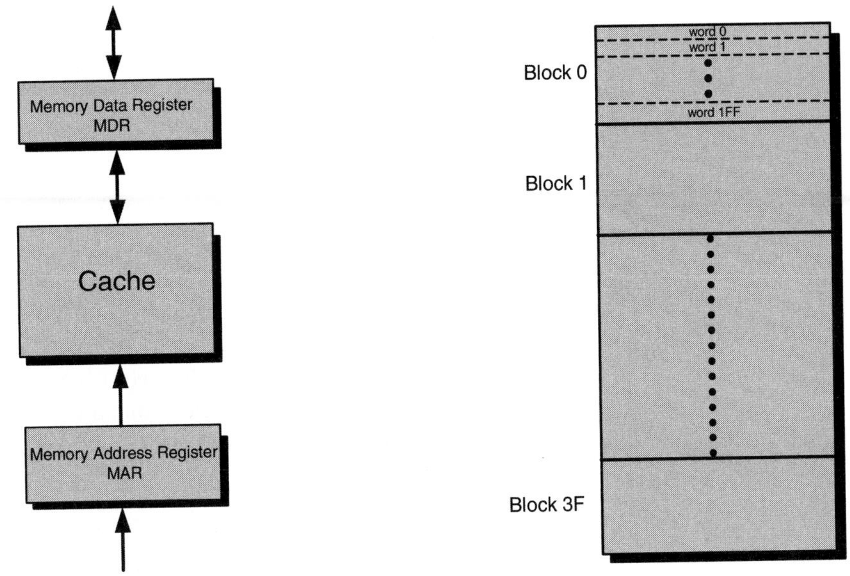

Figure 4.34 Cache System Architecture in Greater Detail

block is copied is determined by the replacement algorithm designed into the cache. The design under discussion will use the *direct mapping* algorithm. This algorithm is one of the simpler ones.

direct mapping

The main memory page size is set equal to the cache size; therefore, each page will contain a corresponding number of blocks. Thus, main memory will contain $size_{main\ memory}$ mod $size_{cache}$ pages. Consequently, each main memory page will contain a block 0, block 1, and so on.

When a block is brought into the cache from main memory, it is placed into the corresponding numbered block in the cache. Thus, a main memory *block 0* will always be placed (or directly mapped) into the cache *block 0* slot, a main memory *block 1* will always be placed into the cache *block 1* slot, and so forth. The mapping is illustrated in Figure 4.35.

block 0, block 1

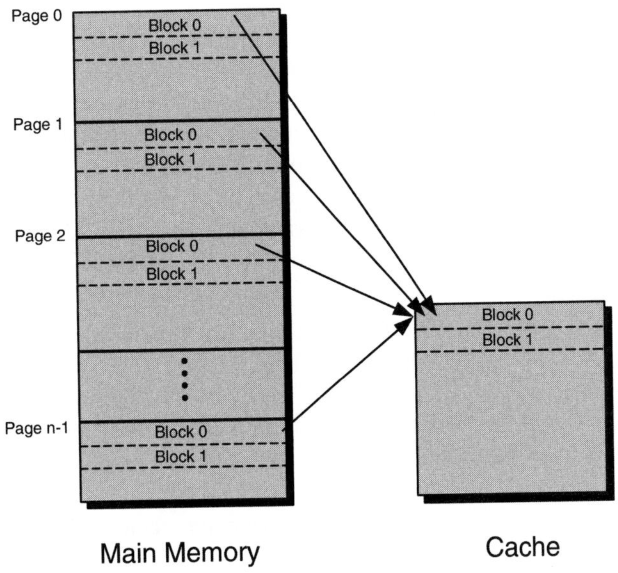

Figure 4.35 Main Memory to Cache Mapping

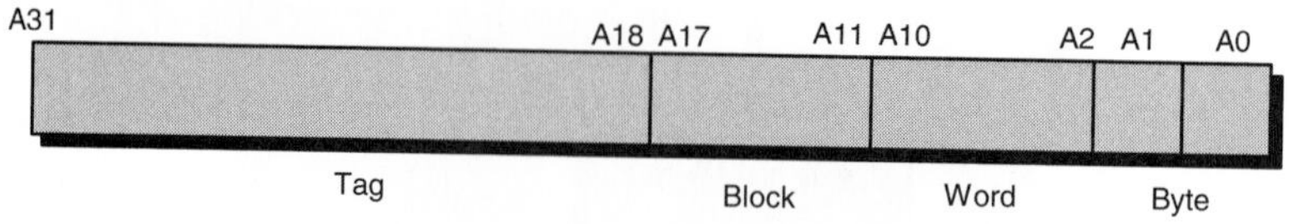

Figure 4.36 Address Interpretation in the Cache Context

The system memory address is 32 bits; only 18 of them will be needed for the cache address (if byte addressing is supported). The 18 cache address bits are interpreted as presented in Figure 4.36.

- Bits A1–A0 — Each data or instruction word is 32 bits or 4 bytes long. Bits A1 and A0 identify a byte within a word.
- Bits A10–A2 — Each block contains 512 words. Address bits A10–A2 identify a word in a block.
- Bits A17–A11 — The block address within the cache is identified by address bits A17–A11. These bits are called the *index* into cache and also correspond to the block's address within a main memory page.

  Thus, any main memory address with address bits A17–A11 having the values [000 0000] will be mapped into block 0 in cache.
- Bits A31–A17 — Identify which main memory page the block came from. This value is called the *tag*. These values will be stored in a data structure called a *tag table* and are used when testing to see if the needed word is in a cache.

  The current design will use 11 of these bits; the remainder will be 0.

tag table The *tag table* is a data structure that contains information essential to the proper management of the cache. The *tag table* contains one record for each block in the cache. For the current design the tag table will therefore contain 128 entries. Typical information contained in each record includes:

Tag — A subset of bits from the main memory address identifying the page (in main memory) where the block originated.

Valid Bit — A flag indicating whether the corresponding block contains valid data.

valid bit When an application starts, the cache contains no relevant information. All blocks allocated to the application are empty. The *valid bit* associated with each block is set to FALSE. When a block is brought into the cache, the valid bit is tested. If FALSE, the new block is copied to the target location and the valid bit is set. If the valid bit is TRUE, the block must be checked for changes.

Dirty Bit — A flag indicating whether the corresponding block contains data that has been modified.

coherent When a new block is first brought into the cache, the copy in the cache and the copy in main memory are identical or *coherent*. If a change is made to any piece of data in the cache, the two blocks are no longer the same.

write through There are two main schemes for addressing the issue. The first, called *write through*, propagates any data change immediately to main memory,

delayed write

thus ensuring that the two remain consistent. The second, called *delayed write*, assumes that if a piece of data changed once, it may change again in the near future. Thus, time can be saved by not performing (potentially) multiple write operations to the same data. To identify that the data has changed, the *dirty bit* is set to TRUE.

dirty bit, valid bit

When a new block is brought into memory and the *valid bit* is TRUE, the *dirty bit* associated with the block is checked. If the bit is FALSE, the new block overwrites the old. If the bit is set, then the old block must be copied back to main memory before the new one is brought in.

Time — Time of day information may be stored with a tag entry indicating when the block was brought into the cache or when it was last accessed.

Time information is used in other replacement algorithms. The direct mapping scheme does not require it.

4.17 CACHING—AN ASSOCIATIVE MAPPING CACHE IMPLEMENTATION

Although simple, the direct mapped algorithm can have some negative effects on system performance, particularly if real-time constraints must be satisfied. It is easy to imagine a situation in which different portions of an algorithm are in different block 0's in main memory. In such a circumstance, the two blocks would be repeatedly interchanged.

associative search

An alternative approach lets a new block be placed anywhere in the cache. An *associative search* is then executed to locate it. Such an algorithm searches by content rather than by address. The associative search asks, "given a target, is it in memory and if so, where?" The traditional access says, "here is an address; return the contents of that address."

A mapping from main memory may now appear as illustrated in Figure 4.37.

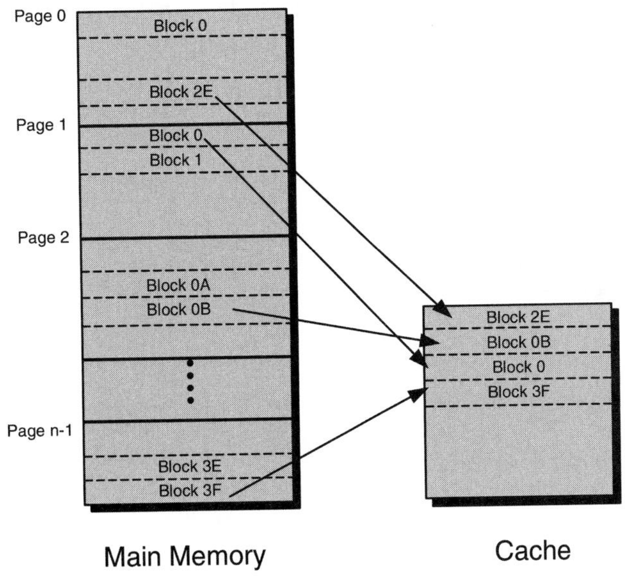

Figure 4.37 Block Mapping from Main Memory to Cache Memory

A new main memory block can be placed anywhere in the cache. As with the direct mapping algorithm, the tag table entry corresponding to the cache block will contain the address information identifying the main memory origin. However, a linear search of the tag table to locate a required block is not feasible.

A cache miss using an associative mapping scheme is handled in much the same way as was done in the direct mapping scheme. The two differ in how the new block is brought into the cache and in which block is to be replaced. Since the new block is not constrained to a specific location, replacement offers more opportunities and becomes a bit more interesting. Any of three schemes are commonly used. Each has advantages and disadvantages; the choice for implementation is often governed by the requirements of the application.

Least Recently Used (LRU)
Most Recently Used (MRU)

With an associative mapping algorithm, time is added as one of the components of the tag table record. Two of the more commonly used algorithms applying temporal locality of reference as a metric are *Least Recently Used* (LRU) and *Most Recently Used* (MRU). The former is also called a FIFO—first-in-first-out scheme. The latter is referred to as LIFO—last-in-first-out. A third algorithm selects and removes a block at random.

The FIFO algorithm is based on the assumption that the oldest block in the cache is the one that is least likely to be used in the future; thus, it should be the one to be replaced. The LIFO algorithm takes a different tack and assumes that the newest block is the least likely to be used in the future since it was just used. Therefore, that one should be removed.

The tag table in an associative mapping scheme uses an associative memory as illustrated in the high-level block diagram in Figure 4.38.

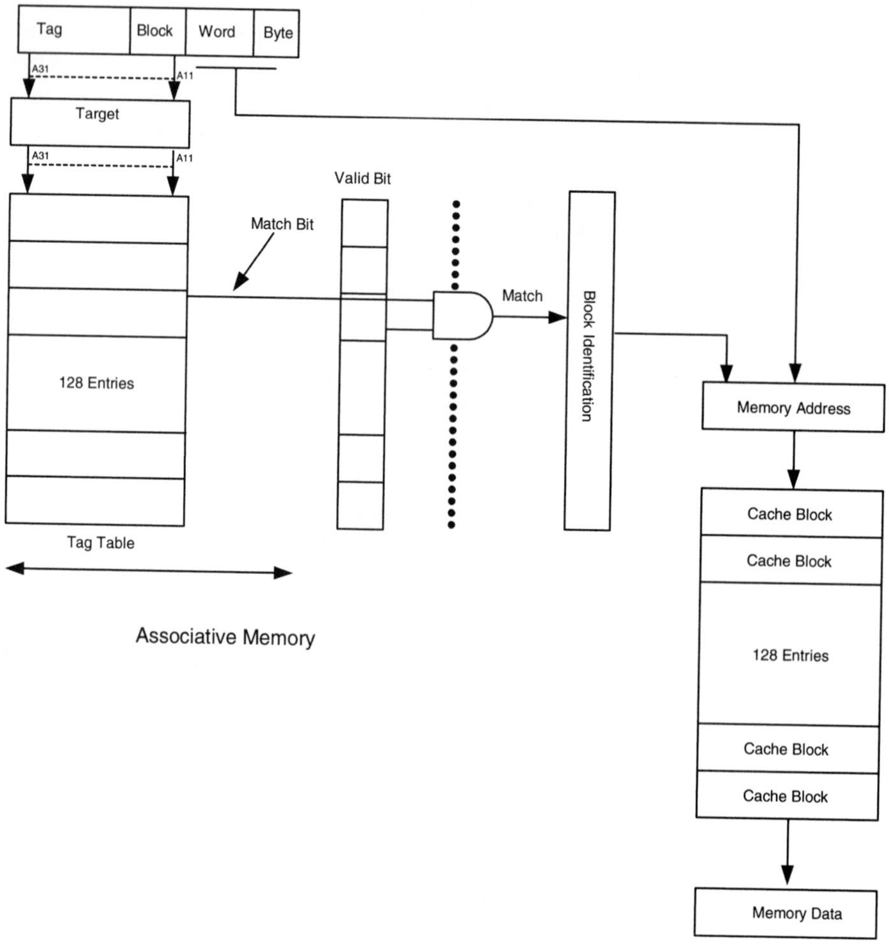

Figure 4.38 Tag Table Block Lookup in an Associative Mapping Scheme

To find a word in the cache, the tag and block portions of the memory address specify the target for the associative search. All entries in the tag table are searched in parallel. If a match is found, the tag table location identifies the block in the cache containing the target word. That information, combined with the remainder of the memory address, is used to retrieve the needed word.

The problems with fully associative caches are the long search times, which can potentially slow down the application, and the complexity and cost of the underlying logic.

4.18 CACHING—A BLOCK-SET ASSOCIATIVE MAPPING CACHE IMPLEMENTATION

block-set associative

set

two-way set associative scheme

A third algorithm for storing and retrieving data and instructions into and out of the cache, called *block-set associative,* combines some of the simplicity of the direct mapping algorithm with some of the flexibility of the associative algorithm. Under the block-set associative scheme, the entry at a specific index is expanded from a single block to multiple blocks. Such a collection is called a *set*. The number of blocks in each set is determined by the specific implementation. The design to be implemented will be a *two-way set associative scheme*; thus, each set will have two blocks. Similarly, a four-way implementation would support sets containing four blocks. The cache for a two-way implementation takes on the form illustrated in Figure 4.39 for a cache size of n sets.

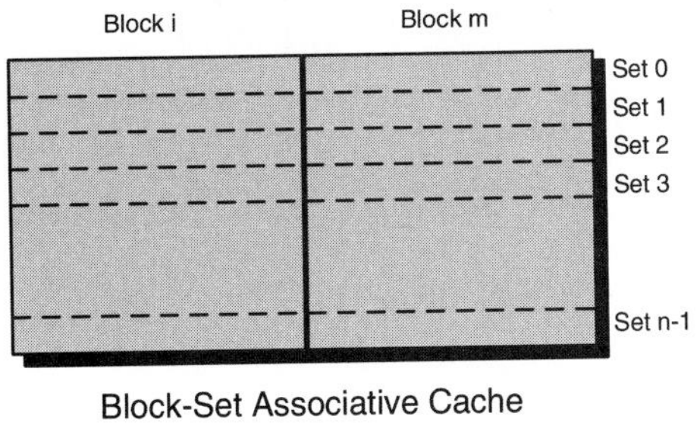

Figure 4.39 Two-Way Set Associative Cache Implementation

Main memory address space is first organized as a collection of m blocks. The m blocks are then organized as a collection of n groups. The group number to which each block is assigned is computed as

groupNumber = m mod n

The set number in the cache corresponds to the main memory group number. Any block from main memory group j can be placed into cache set j. A set is now searched associatively; the search is far less complex because we are dealing with much smaller search space.

For our current system,

Cache	64 K with 128 0.5 K blocks organized as 64 two-block sets.
Main Memory	256 K words organized as 512 blocks. The resulting groups are given in Table 4.1.

The tag table will have 128 entries. Table 4.2 illustrates how the main memory addresses are mapped to the cache addresses.

Table 4.1 256 K Main Memory Organized into 64 Groups Comprising 512 Blocks

Block						Group
0	64	128	• • •	384	448	0
1	65	129		385	449	1
2	66	130		386	450	2
•						
•						
63	127	192		447	511	63

Table 4.2 Main Memory to Cache Mapping

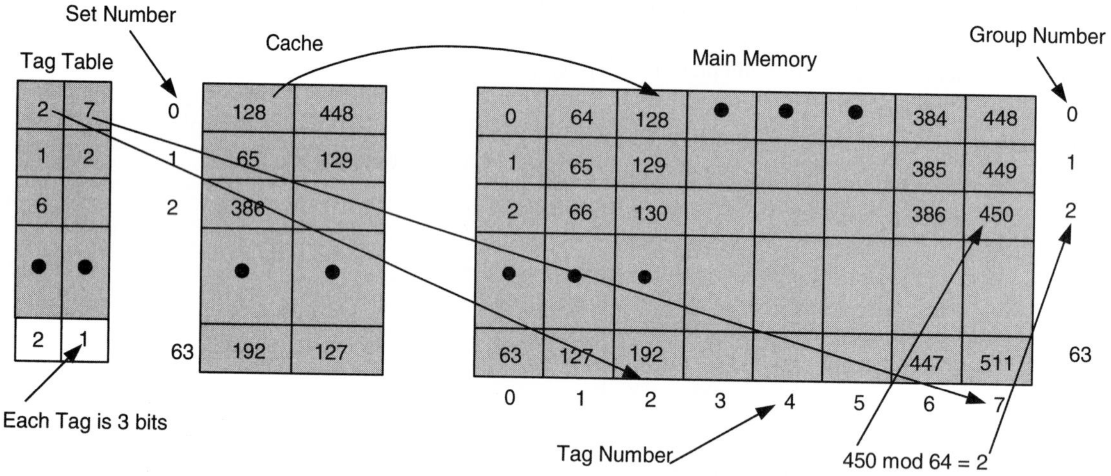

4.19 DYNAMIC MEMORY ALLOCATION

Dynamic memory allocation is usually interpreted as the process of allocating memory at runtime associated with some extensible data structure such as a linked list or heap. The linked-list-based scheme works well for an embedded system. The C malloc and C++ new operators are examples of routines that are used in conjunction with the heap.

Remember: in embedded systems we generally use two kinds of memory, ROM and RAM (which may be cache or main memory). Here we are more concerned with managing main memory to accommodate

- Programs larger than main memory
- Multiple processes in main memory
- Multiple programs in main memory

Traditional virtual memory schemes are completely nondeterministic and thus are rarely used in real-time systems, particularly those systems with hard deadlines.

Let's look at several schemes for dynamic memory allocation that can work well in embedded systems.

4.19.1 Swapping

swapping

Remember that memory in our system is segregated into two portions: that designated as system memory and that allocated to code and data space for user programs as we see in Figure 4.40. The simplest method for accommodating multiple programs in memory is called *swapping*. With such a scheme, the system remains resident in memory and further assumes that only a single-user program is resident in memory at a time. The same holds true for tasks; typically there is only a single task in memory at any one time.

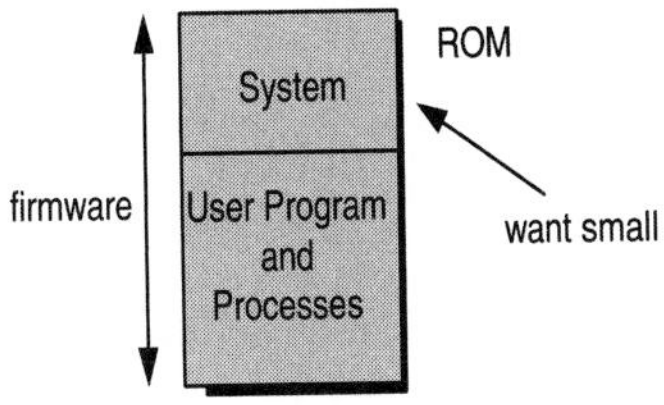

Figure 4.40 Typical Memory Segregation into User and System Allocations

We assume that a program consists of several tasks. The first task is executing when a second must be run. We now have a situation that is similar to a subroutine call only slightly more complex. We proceed as follows. The first task is suspended and swapped to a secondary storage device. Here we will use the word "secondary" to refer to nonruntime memory. In an embedded system, typically we do not have a large hard drive mounted anywhere that might be convenient. Secondary storage could also be in ROM somewhere since we are dealing with firmware. We also save our context; we could be working out of a cache and execute a swap to main.

Next, the second process, with its context, is loaded into user space and activated by the dispatcher. Note that such a scheme can be deadly in time-critical systems. At the same time, the timing can be deterministic if the program/task/thread is well understood. If such a scheme is used, one should ensure that the task/program execution time is long compared to the swap time. Such processes might be those associated with chemical processing or thermal control.

4.19.2 Overlays

overlays

An overlay is a poor man's version of virtual memory. The overlay will be in ROM and used to accommodate a program that is larger than main memory. The program is segmented into a number of sections called *overlays*. Usually, there is one main section plus several remaining overlays. The main section usually contains the following as is reflected in Figure 4.41.

- Top level routine
- Code to perform overlay process
- Data segment for shared data
- Overlay segment

When the overlay process is executed, a new overlay segment replaces the current one in main memory. Care must be taken in designing such systems. Specifically, the code in each overlay must be selected carefully; we cannot just cut the program into pieces that fit. Two halves of a loop may land in different overlays, which can result in thrashing. Usually the segmentation is hand tailored.

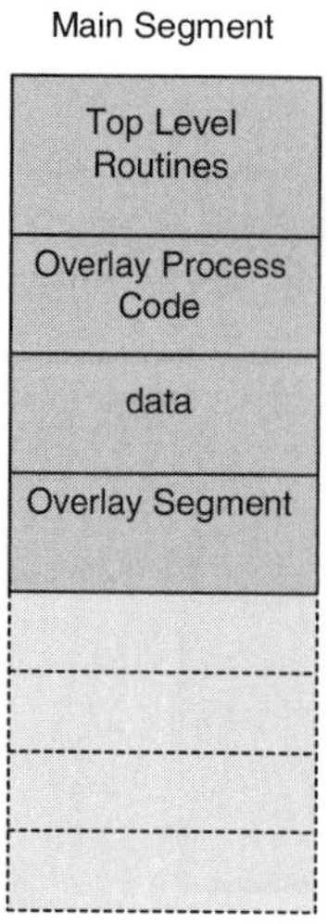

Figure 4.41 A Program Segmented into Overlays

4.19.3 Multiprogramming

As the name suggests, multiprogramming permits one to run multiple programs in the same memory space (RAM). Here we consider two versions: programs in which the number of tasks is fixed and programs for which the number of tasks is variable.

Fixed

Designs with a fixed number of tasks/threads look very similar to paging systems. Such a scheme is useful when the number of tasks is known in advance. Certainly, this is true for many embedded systems. To implement the design, the user space is divided into a number of fixed size partitions and is presented in Figure 4.42. The tasks must reside in contiguous partitions; linking becomes extremely difficult otherwise.

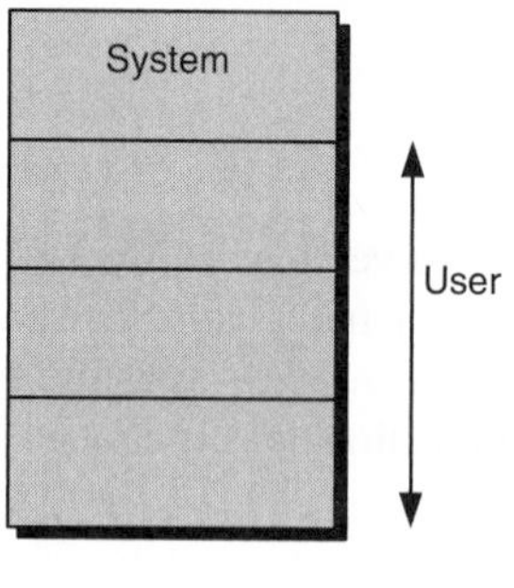

Figure 4.42 User Space Divided into Fixed Size Segments

When preempted, a partition is swapped to disk or (in the case of most embedded systems) to slower memory or RAM, or the code portion address is saved. As is common in virtual memory schemes, using fixed-size partitions can lead to memory fragmentation. Fragmentation can happen in several ways. Consider a system using fixed-size partitions of 2 K. Let three jobs be brought into memory:

J1–1.5 K

J2–0.5 K

J3–2.1 K

Let these jobs be allocated to successive partitions in memory. We see that four partitions are required. Now, let J2 finish and be swapped out. What does this mean? We immediately see the following problems:

J2—Leaving has left a hole that can only be filled by job ≤ 2 K. The task consumes a 2 K partition leaving three-fourths of it unused.

J3—Requires 2 partitions, one of size 2 K and one of size 0.1 K; this is very wasteful of memory. If these three jobs consume the last of the memory, a new job of size 1 K cannot enter, although it will fit.

Variable Number

Programs with a variable number of tasks are treated in a similar manner to segments in a traditional virtual memory scheme. Memory allocation for a variable number of tasks is similar to a paged virtual memory scheme. Allocation is determined by the process's requirements when it is loaded into memory. Such an approach works well when the number of tasks is unknown or variable. Wasted memory arising from a misfit into a partition size is virtually eliminated. Holes remain but can be eliminated by using compaction schemes. Compaction moves pieces of used memory into contiguous locations. It is important to keep in mind that any such schemes can have significant negative impact on real-time systems. If they must be used, then one needs to understand them and the application context completely. One should also determine an upper bound on context switching and leave plenty of margin in the application.

4.20 TESTING MEMORIES

Let's now look at the problem of testing memories. As we learned in earlier studies, a wide variety of different kinds of memories can be incorporated into a design. On the one hand, the amount of memory (ROM or RAM) that can economically be included in a contemporary system seems to grow daily. On the other hand, trying to test that memory as a part of production test has become more costly and complex. Exhaustive testing of all possible combinations of data values is not a practical approach. Moreover, it is logical to assume that in production, the object of a memory test is not to confirm the individual memory chips themselves, but rather to ensure that the installation and interconnection of the devices are defect free.

To address the memory test problem, as with any other problem, we begin by decomposing it into the basic pieces. The high-level diagrams for a RAM or ROM memory system are redrawn in Figure 4.43. Looking first from an external point of view, we see that both types of memory are similar, the major difference being the R/$\overline{W}$ line and bidirectional data flow for the RAM. Each memory block shown may be comprised of a number of memory chips interconnected via the address, data, and control busses.

At the system level, memory is no different from any other component we have dealt with. The manufacturing defects that one encounters are much the same as well—shorted, open, or bridged lines. Such faults may show up as either stuck-at or bridging type defects on the address, data, or control lines. Based on the anticipated kinds of faults, one can begin to formulate a test strategy. Internal to each memory chip are variations on the architecture in Figure 4.44. With a ROM memory, in most cases, all of the data lines would be strictly outputs.

Defects internal to a memory device arising from its manufacture may appear in the cell array itself, in the row or column address decoding logic, or in the read/write logic and

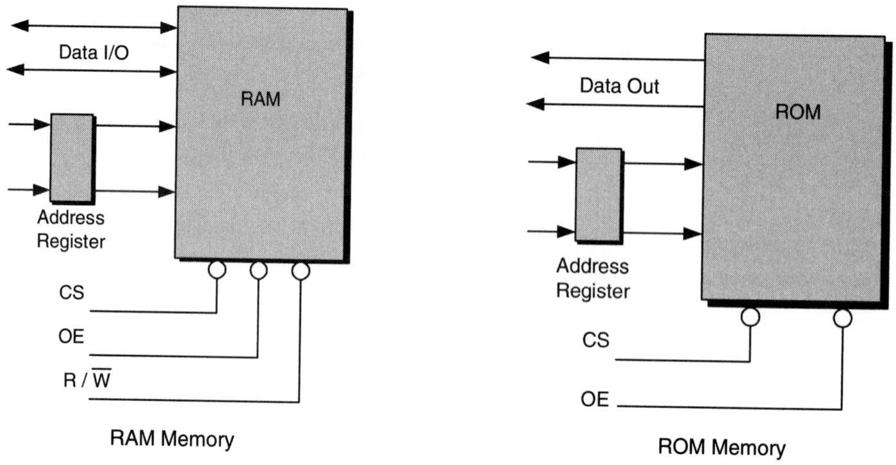

Figure 4.43 A System-Level View of Memory

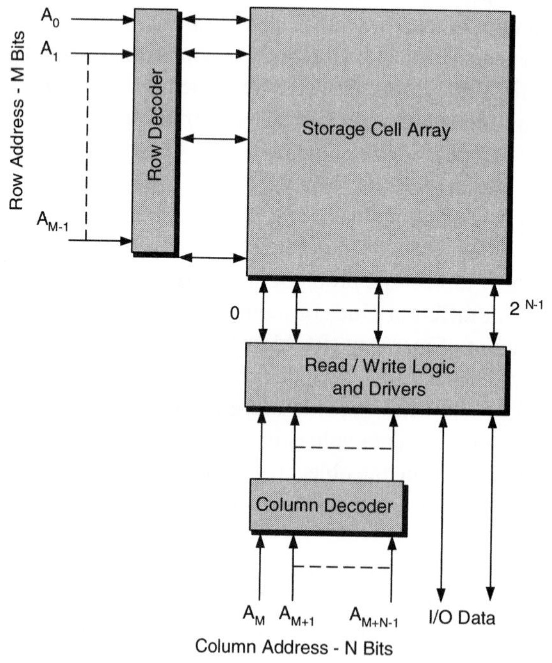

Figure 4.44 Basic Memory Architecture

drivers. The entire category of what are called soft errors will not be considered. Such errors include those resulting from alpha particles, thermal effects, or transient-type errors. Dealing with soft errors is more of a design issue than a test problem. In addition, it will be further assumed that the memory devices themselves are defect free.

4.20.1 RAM Memory

Let's first examine a RAM fault model. We base the analysis on the assumption that the design of the RAM chips is correct and that they contain no internal manufacturing defects. We begin with faults on the data lines. Stuck-at faults prevent the intended data from being

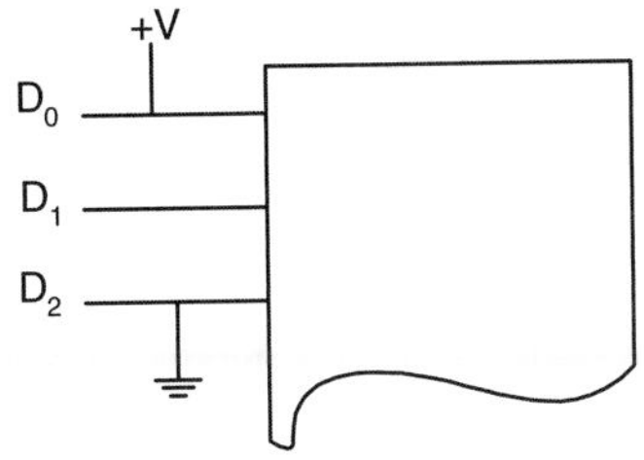

Figure 4.45 Memory Data Line Faults

correctly written to or read from the memory. The models for such faults follow directly for those that were used in the discussion of faults in combinational logic; these are shown in Figure 4.45.

A stuck-at-1 fault results in a logical 1 being written to the affected bit for all memory addresses. Similarly, a stuck-at-0 fault yields a logical zero written to the affected bit for all device addresses. The effects of the faults provide the basis for testing.

To test for the stuck-at-1 condition, a pattern of all 0's is written to a memory address and followed by a read operation from the same address. For a stuck-at-0 condition, the pattern of all 1's is written and then read. If the same data is read as was written, then a stuck-at fault does not exist on any of the data lines. It should be sufficient to perform the write and the read at a single address. For such faults, no further information is gained by testing additional locations.

A bridge fault, as illustrated in Figure 4.46, connects two (or more) data lines. As was noted in the earlier discussion of bridge faults in combinational logic, the actual voltage level appearing on the signal lines comprising the faulted net depends on the relative strengths of the driving signals. The assumption here is that each of those signals (D_0 and D_1 in this case) will share a common value. Thus, the test consists of writing a ....101010... pattern to all the data lines going to memory, executing a read, writing a ....010101... pattern and executing a read. In the presence of a bridge fault, one can expect to see the same value on two adjacent data lines for the two reads. The different patterns should enable a dominant driver to be identified.

Let's now look at similar faults on the address lines. The fault model for a stuck-at condition on an address line is identical to that on any of the data lines as shown in Figure 4.47. The tests, however, are slightly different. In the presence of a stuck-at address line fault, two different memory addresses are mapped to the same location.

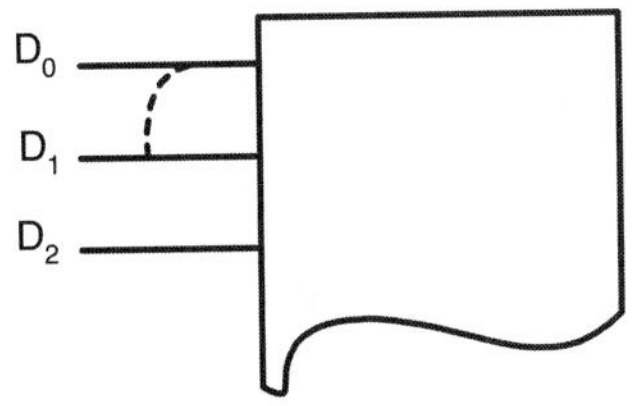

Figure 4.46 Bridged Data Line Faults

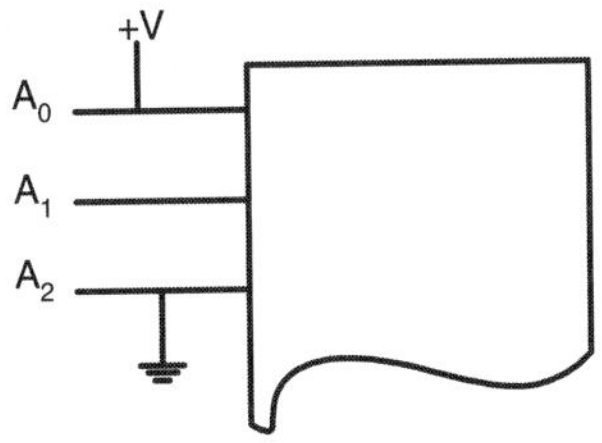

Figure 4.47 Address Stuck-at Faults

To identify such faults, one must prove that each address bit can be driven to the logical 0 and logical 1 state and that data can be properly written to and read data from each such memory location. Stated the opposite way, one must show that if data is written to a specific test address, that data is not also written to the address with the bit under test complemented.

The test is performed as follows. An address bit, A_0, is selected as the bit under test. Next, a data pattern, ...0000, for example, is chosen and that data is written to memory address ... xxx0. A different data pattern, say ....1111, is then selected and written to memory address ... xxx1.... The contents of the two locations are then read. If there is a stuck-at fault on A_0, both addresses will be mapped to the same location and the same data will be read from the two different addresses.

Like a bridge fault on the data bus, such a fault on the address bus will constrain two (or more) address lines to the same value. Once again, several addresses have been mapped to a single address. Such a fault is depicted in Figure 4.48. The motivation for and method of test for bridges is similar to that used for stuck-at faults. The tests are only slightly more complex. Data is written to one address and read from a second. If there is no bridge fault, the proper data will be read.

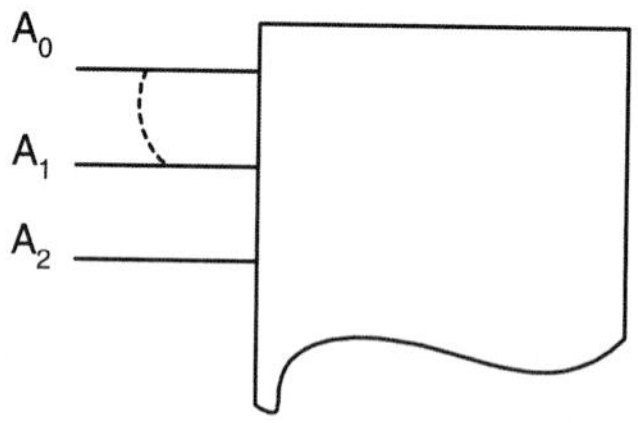

Figure 4.48 Bridged Address Lines

Assume that a test for a bridge between address bits A_0 and A_1 is conducted. As the test address, any address of the form: ... xxxx01 is selected. Next, a background data pattern (...1111, for example) is written to the two possible aliased addresses: ... xxxx00 and ... xxxx11. A different data pattern (... 0000, for example) is then written to the test address. Finally, all three addresses are read.

The test may have any of four possible outcomes. If there is no bridge fault, the correct data will be read from each address. If there is a bridge fault, one must consider three cases: the logical 1 in the test address dominates, or the logical 0 dominates, or neither dominates. For the first case, the data written to the alias address ... xxxx11 will be contaminated, and for the second, the data written to the alias address ... xxxx00 will be corrupted. The third case is a bit more difficult (probably several bits, actually). If neither address bit dominates, then the data in any of the three addresses may be affected.

So far, the analysis of bridging faults has assumed a voltage/current model in which one of the constituent signals in the bridge dominates and thereby affects the logical behavior of our system. If a resistance model is considered instead, the task becomes a bit easier. With such a model, how the component operates is not important; rather, the resistance between the pins of interest is simply measured.

When formulating tests for bridging faults, one can use either a black box or a white box model. In the black box model, all possible pairs of faults must be considered. With a little knowledge about the pin out of the memory and the layout of the printed circuit board, most of the possible combinations can be eliminated. If the device pins or the bus layout are such that a bridge between two address or data lines is physically impossible, there is no need to test those combinations for such a fault.

groupNumber = m mod n

4.20.2 ROM Memory

From an external point of view, the ROM fault model is no different from that used for the RAM. In addition, the underlying assumptions on which the analysis is based are similar. For the RAM, it was assumed that the devices contained no manufacturing defects. On one level that same assumption can be made for ROMs. However, the ROM (which may be manifest as a programmable device) is intended to have a particular set of data stored. If the stored pattern is incorrect, the device is considered to have a failure. Thus, the strategy for testing ROMs must address the stuck-at and bridging faults as well as ensuring that the correct data has been stored.

CRC, cyclic redundancy check, signature analysis

An effective method for testing ROM memories that can address all of these issues is based on the *CRC* or *cyclic redundancy check* and is known as *signature analysis*. Signature analysis uses an LFSR to compress a data stream into a K-bit pattern. The testing algorithm is rather straightforward and follows the approach commonly used for error management in inter- and intrasystem communication.

Design Note
Observe that in developing a method for testing ROMs, ideas are being utilized from several different areas, areas that are completely unrelated to test. Whenever approaching a design, keep the initial options wide open and alternatives unrestricted.

One can model the contents of a ROM as an $N \bullet M$ bit data stream where N is the number of addresses in the ROM and M is the number of bits stored at each address or word size. To test the ROM, a CRC or signature is computed for the known data stream. A similar signature is generated for the ROM under test. If the signatures agree, the correct data has been stored; otherwise there is a data fault.

A block diagram for a simple system is given in Figure 4.49.

Data is read from the ROM into the Parallel In/Serial Out shift register. The stored data is then sent through the LFSR. In this implementation, a comparison can be made either after each word or after the complete contents of the ROM have been read.

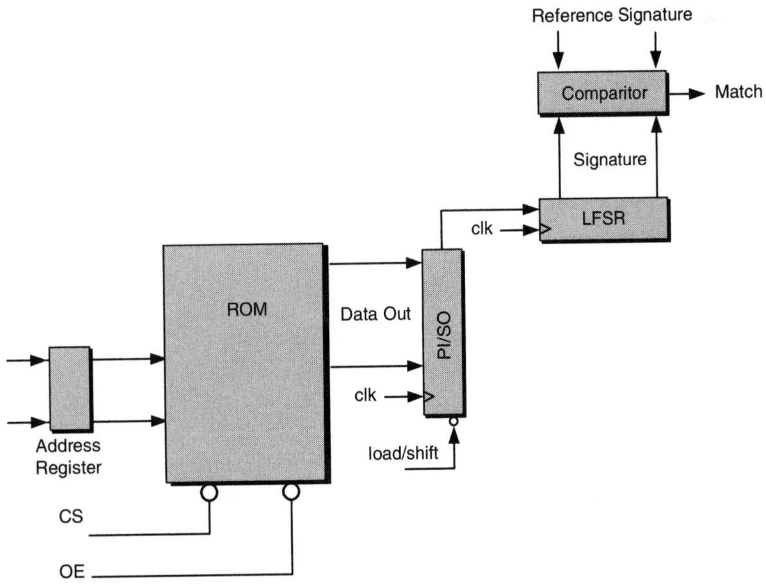

Figure 4.49 CRC Generation and Test of a ROM Signature

Comparison after each word has the advantage that stuck-at faults can be quickly identified. The disadvantage is the cost in time of the additional comparisons. If such comparisons are made at hardware speeds, however, the cost can be small.

The signature test in the above design can also be used to help identify, but not necessarily isolate, bridge faults. Once again, taking a page from coding theory, a word read from the ROM under a bridge fault condition can be modeled as a word with multiple bit errors or with a burst error. By choosing an irreducible polynomial that can detect such errors, one can then configure the LFSR accordingly as we see in Figure 4.50.

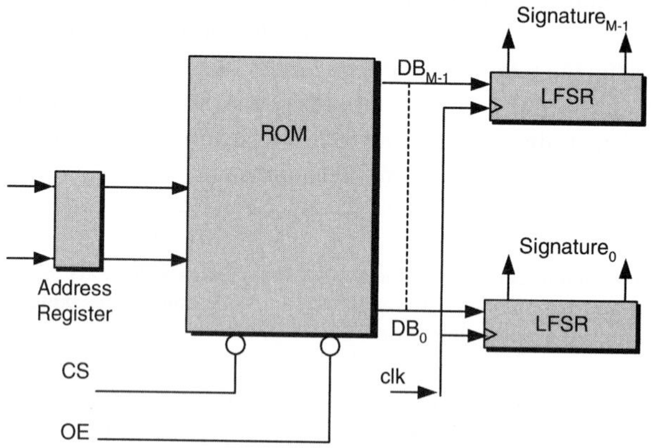

Figure 4.50 Using Data Signatures to Identify ROM Faults

In this design, a signature is computed for each data bit stream. Such a configuration provides greater flexibility for isolating both stuck-at and bridged faults. Bits with the same (incorrect) signature can be assumed to be bridged, for example.

4.21 SUMMARY

We began with an introduction to and discussion of the various kinds of memory devices utilized in embedded applications. We studied the general memory interface and discussed commonly used memory devices in detail. We then worked through the designs of representative SRAM- and DRAM-based memory systems, which can form the infrastructure for a typical caching scheme.

The concept of caching in the context of embedded systems was introduced and discussed. Several different caching schemes, *direct mapped, associative,* and *block-set associative*, were developed and studied. The strengths and weaknesses of each approach were presented.

Discussion then moved to the system level with the introduction of *memory maps* and simple *dynamic allocation* in an embedded context. Finally, several approaches for testing RAM and ROM memories were introduced and studied.

4.22 REVIEW QUESTIONS

Introduction

4.1 In embedded applications, what are the major responsibilities of a memory management system?

4.2 What do the terms *static* and *dynamic allocation of memory* mean?

4.3 What are the two major categories of memory devices that are utilized in embedded applications?

Classifying Memory

4.4 We use the terms *ROM* to identify read only memory and *RAM* to designate random access memory. What is the major difference between the two kinds of memory?

4.5 Does ROM memory support random access?

4.6 What do the terms *SRAM* and *DRAM* mean, and what are the major differences between the two types of RAM?

4.7 What are the major differences between the following types of read only memory: ROM, PROM, EPROM, EEPROM, and FLASH?

Memory Overview

4.8 What are the major interface signals in a basic memory system? What is the purpose of each?

4.9 Are the major interface signals in a basic memory system the same for both ROM and RAM?

4.10 Explain the terms t_{access} and t_{cycle}. Why and when are they important?

4.11 In a DRAM, what is the restore or rewrite operation?

4.12 In a DRAM, what is refresh and the refresh cycle? Why is it necessary?

4.13 In a DRAM, what is the difference between a restore operation and a refresh operation?

4.14 In a DRAM, what is the refresh time interval? What are the consequences of not meeting the time interval?

4.15 In a DRAM, what are the purposes of the Row and Column Address Strobes?

4.16 What do the terms *block* and *block size* mean? What role do they play in memory access?

4.17 What are latency and block access time? How are they related, and why are they important in reading from or writing to a memory?

4.18 What is memory bandwidth, and why is it important in reading from or writing to a memory?

Memory Map

4.19 What is a memory map?

4.20 How is a memory map used in the design of embedded systems?

4.21 What kinds of information are typically identified in a memory map?

Memory Subsystem Architecture

4.22 In the chapter, we discussed the memory system hierarchy and the types of memory that are typically included. What are these?

4.23 What kinds of memory devices would one typically find in each of the categories in the memory hierarchy discussed in the chapter?

4.24 Three types of locality of reference were discussed in the chapter. What were these, and what are their differences?

4.25 What is a caching scheme, and what is its role in a memory subsystem hierarchy?

4.26 Describe, in detail, how a caching scheme works.

4.27 In the chapter, we discussed three caching schemes. What were these? Briefly describe how each operates.

4.28 In a caching scheme, what is the *tag table,* and what is its purpose?

4.29 What are some of the kinds of information stored in a *tag table*? What is the purpose of each?

4.30 Describe how a *tag table* is used.

4.31 What do the terms *write through* and *delayed write* mean?

4.32 What is an *associative search*?

4.33 Explain the *least recently used* algorithm when applied to cache memory management.

4.34 Explain the *most recently used* algorithm when applied to cache memory management.

4.35 Explain the terms *block-set associative* and *two-way set associative* with respect to cache memory management.

Dynamic Memory Allocation

4.36 In the context of an embedded application, what do we mean by dynamic memory allocation?

4.37 In an embedded application, when might one consider using a dynamic memory allocation scheme?

4.38 In the chapter, swapping was described as one of the simpler dynamic memory management schemes; describe how the scheme works.

4.39 Describe how the overlay scheme works to support programs larger than will fit in main memory.

4.40 How does the dynamic memory management scheme called multiprogramming work?

4.41 What are the major differences among the dynamic memory management schemes discussed in the chapter?

Testing Memories

4.42 Describe how one might test for a stuck-at-1 condition on a data line in a RAM-type memory? a stuck-at-0 condition?

4.43 Describe how one might test for a stuck-at-1 condition on a data line in a ROM-type memory? a stuck-at-0 condition?

4.44 Describe how one might test for a stuck-at-1 condition on an address line in a RAM-type memory? a stuck-at-0 condition?

4.45 Describe how one might test for a stuck-at-1 condition on an address line in a ROM-type memory? a stuck-at-0 condition?

4.46 Describe how one might test for bridged data lines in a RAM-type memory?

4.47 Describe how one might test for bridged data lines in a ROM-type memory?

4.48 Describe how one might test for bridged address lines in a RAM-type memory?

4.49 Describe how one might test for bridged address lines in a ROM-type memory?

4.50 Describe how to construct a CRC-based algorithm to test the validity and integrity of data stored in a ROM.

4.23 THOUGHT QUESTIONS

Introduction

4.1 Discuss the pros and cons of static and dynamic allocation of memory in embedded applications. Be certain to address the circumstances under which there may be potential problems.

4.2 What are the advantages and disadvantages of storing information in ROM memory? RAM memory?

Memory Overview

4.3 Discuss the benefits of using SRAM versus DRAM; DRAM versus SRAM.

4.4 What types of systems would benefit from an SRAM-based memory system? a DRAM-based memory system?

4.5 Would a high- or low-speed system gain the most from an SDRAM-based memory subsystem?

4.6 Why are some memory devices designed and specified as *nbits* x *1*? That is, n rows and one column. What kinds of applications might benefit from such a configuration?

4.7 In what kinds of embedded systems should the following types of Read Only Memory be used: ROM, PROM, EPROM, EEPROM, and FLASH?

Memory Map

4.8 What are some of the factors that should be considered when designing a memory map for an embedded design?

4.9 Why is a memory map necessary in the design of embedded systems?

Memory Subsystem Architecture

4.10 The address and data signals are among the interface signals in a basic memory system. In a memory system design, is it required to connect the least significant address bit to the pin designated as A0, etc. and the least significant data bit to the pin designated as D0, etc.? Why or why not?

4.11 Can a memory be accessed faster than the rate specified by t_{access} and t_{cycle}? Why or why not?

4.12 Can a memory be accessed slower than the rate specified by t_{access} and t_{cycle}? Why or why not?

4.13 In a DRAM, what are the consequences of violating the refresh and the refresh cycle time specifications?

4.14 Can a DRAM be refreshed more quickly than the refresh cycle time specifications?

4.15 What are some of the factors that should be taken into consideration when specifying the block size in a memory subsystem design?

4.16 Can you think of ways that latency and block access time can be reduced within a single memory device?

4.17 If a memory device is bandwidth limited, can you think of ways to increase block access time in a memory system as a whole?

4.18 Why is a caching scheme of limited utility in certain kinds of embedded system?

4.19 What kinds of embedded system might significantly benefit from a memory system design utilizing a virtual memory and caching scheme?

4.20 In the chapter, we discussed three caching schemes. What are the pros and cons of each design?

4.21 What are the trade-offs between the *write through* and *delayed write* update algorithms?

4.22 What are the advantages and disadvantages of a caching scheme utilizing an *associative search*-based architecture?

4.23 What kinds of applications would benefit from a *least recently used* algorithm when applied to cache memory management?

4.24 What kinds of applications would benefit from a *most recently used* algorithm when applied to cache memory management?

4.25 Discuss the trade-offs between cache designed to utilize a four-way and one designed to employ a two-way set associative scheme.

Dynamic Memory Allocation

4.26 In the context of an embedded application, what potential problems might we encounter when utilizing dynamic memory allocation? What are some of the benefits?

4.27 For what kinds of applications might one consider using a dynamic memory allocation scheme?

4.28 The C language uses malloc and free; the C++ and Java languages use new to allocate and delete and a garbage collector, respectively, to return unused memory to the system. What impacts might these three schemes have on an embedded system with hard real-time constraints? soft real-time constraints? firm real-time constraints?

4.29 For what kinds of embedded systems would swapping be a useful technique. Why?

4.30 For what kinds of embedded systems would swapping not be recommended. Why?

4.31 For what kinds of embedded systems would overlays not be recommended. Why?

Testing Memories

4.32 Propose some simple tests that might form the basis of a built-in self-test for a RAM memory system. For a ROM memory system?

4.33 In a design for an embedded system utilizing a built-in self-test scheme to verify memory, how can the test be executed if the memory is defective?

4.34 Discuss the pros and cons of using a CRC-based algorithm to test the validity and integrity of data stored in a ROM.

4.24 PROBLEMS

Building Basic Components

4.1 A memory system is needed in a new design to support a small amount of data storage outside of the processor. The design is to be based on the 16 K bit CY7C128A SRAM organized as 2 K x 8.

(a) Provide a high-level block diagram for such an interface.

(b) Provide a high-level timing diagram for the interface to the SRAM from the microprocessor, assuming that separate address and data busses are available. Define any control signals that may be necessary.

(c) Design the interface based on the timing diagram from part (a).

(d) Analyze the memory performance for a write and a read operation of 1, 10, and 100 bytes.

4.2 Repeat Problem 4.1 with the restriction that data and address use a shared bus.

4.3 An upgrade to the memory system in Problem 4.1 is necessary to support higher performance. The word size is doubled. Repeat Problem 4.1with the new requirements.

4.4 An upgrade to the memory system in Problem 4.3 is necessary to support higher performance. The storage capability of the memory is doubled. Repeat Problem 4.3 with the new requirements.

4.5 Repeat Problem 4.3 with the restriction that data and address signals use a shared bus.

4.6 Repeat Problem 4.3 for a memory system implementing separate data and instruction memories. Instructions are to be held in a ROM memory with the same organization and specifications as the SRAM. For part (d), only the read operations are appropriate for the ROM component.

4.7 Extend the architecture of the memory system designed in Problem 4.1 to include support for a peripheral device that performs read only operations from the memory.

(a) Provide a high-level block diagram for the modified design.

(b) Provide a high-level timing diagram for the interface to the SRAM from the microprocessor, assuming that separate address and data busses are available. Define any control signals that may be necessary.

(c) Identify any possible bus or access contentions, your proposed solution, and why your solution solves the problem.

(d) Design the interface based on the timing diagram from part (a).

(e) Analyze the memory performance for a write and a read operation of 1, 10, and 100 bytes.

4.8 Repeat Problem 4.7 to include support for a peripheral device that performs read and write operations from and to the memory.

(a) Provide a high-level block diagram for the modified design.

(b) Provide a high-level timing diagram for the interface to the SRAM from the microprocessor, assuming that separate address and data busses are available. Define any control signals that may be necessary.

(c) Identify any possible bus or access contentions, your proposed solution, and why your solution solves the problem.

(d) Design the interface based on the timing diagram from part (a).

4.9 Please explain the term *cache* and why we use it in a computer memory.

4.10 Please give a top-level design for a *direct mapped cache* between the CPU and main memory.

(a) Let the main memory contain 16 K words (requires a 14-bit address) and the cache contain 4 K words. Be sure to explain your reasoning for any choices you make. The cache must have more than one block.

(b) Pease explain, in detail, how the word at main memory address 356D is read if it is in a cache.

(c) Please explain, in detail, how the word at main memory address 356D is read if it is not in a cache.

4.11 Repeat Problem 4.10 for a *four-way block-set associative* design. Compare the performance of your design with the *two-way block-set associative* design presented in the chapter.

Timing Considerations

4.12 The memory subsystem designed in Problem 4.4 has the capability of storing 4 K words. The lower device (addresses 0–2 K) will store the first 2 K words and the upper device (addresses 2 K–4 K) will store the second 2 K.

If successive read operations cross the physical address boundary between devices, the output drivers from the lower device will have to be turned off and those for the upper device will have to be turned on. Under such circumstances, there is the potential for bus contention.

Taking parasitic components into consideration, what is the maximum time after the OE (output enable) signal on the lower device has disabled its SRAM output that the upper device can be enabled onto the bus without contention?

4.13 Under the constraint that contiguous memory words are to be read as fast as possible, propose either a design change or an access algorithm that will prevent possible contention arising from the shared bus described in Problem 4.5.

4.14 A distributed embedded application utilizes a memory subsystem as a buffer between the main processor and a high-speed peripheral device. The peripheral device produces data in 1 K word, 10-μsec bursts. The memory devices have a minimum read or write access time of 40 ns. The interval between bursts can be controlled; however, the word transfer rate to memory cannot. The processor is able to transfer data from memory at a 10-MHz rate.

(a) Give a block diagram for the design of a system that will implement the buffer interface between the two portions of the system.

(b) Give a data and control flow diagram reflecting the data transfers between the two components.

(c) How many memory devices does your design use?

(d) What is the minimum time between bursts from the peripheral device?

4.15 The microcontroller in a low-end embedded system has an 8-bit word size and the memory system in Problem 4.1. The cross compiler defines char data types as one byte, integer and instruction data types as two bytes, and floating point data types as four bytes.

A statistical study of the application shows that char data types are used in 20% of the operations, integer data types in 40%, instructions in 37%, and floating point types in 3%.

How many memory accesses will be required for a program with 100, 1000, 10,000 instructions?

4.16 Repeat Problem 4.15 for the memory system design in Problem 4.2.

Applications

4.17 A home entertainment system is designed to utilize a caching scheme to improve system performance. An application in such a system attempts to fetch the instruction at cache address 3000 and has a miss.

(a) Describe the sequence of operations that would be necessary to retrieve the 512-word block containing that instruction from primary memory.

(b) Draw a theoretical timing diagram showing the address, data, and control signals necessary to execute such a transfer. Assume a separate address and data bus.

(c) The following information is contained in the hardware manual for the system microprocessor and memory system:

Register delay, $\tau_{rd,}$	25 ns max
Delay from internal processor register to output port	
Register set up time, $\tau_{su,}$	15 ns min
Time data must be settled on register input prior to clocking	
MAR counter propagation delay, $\tau_{ard,}$	10 ns max
Time required for counter input to propagate to the output following clocking	
Primary memory read/write access time, $\tau_{paccess,}$	100 ns min
Delay to Read or Write from/to memory	
Cache memory read/write access time, $\tau_{caccess,}$	50 ns min
Delay to Read or Write from/to memory	
Primary memory—Cache Data Bus propagation delay, $\tau_{bd,,}$	10 ns max
Delay from time signal placed on bus until reaching destination	

Based on the data given here, please modify your theoretical timing diagram in part (e) to reflect the real-world address, data, and control signals necessary to transfer such a block.

(d) Based on your analysis, what is the highest frequency that such a transfer could be executed?

4.18 A certain program contains two nested loops. The general structure of the program is as shown in Figure P4.51. The decimal addresses shown delineate the locations of the two loops as well as the beginning and end of the complete program. Other than the two loops, all remaining portions of the program execute in a straight-line sequence.

The program is executed on a computer with a cache. The cache uses a direct mapping scheme and the important memory parameters are:

Main	64 K words
Cache	1 K words
Block	128 words

The cycle time (minimum time between consecutive accesses) for main memory is 10 τ sec and that for the cache is 1 τ sec.

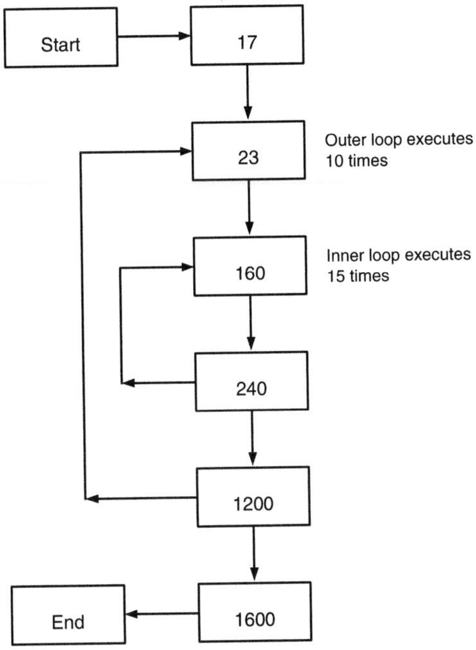

Figure P4.51

(a) Please specify the number of bits in the Tag, Block, and Word fields of a main memory address.

(b) What is the total time for fetching instructions for this program?

4.19 A presentation system is to be designed and installed in a new convention center that is being built. The system will have the ability to provide all forms of high-performance video display.

To the performance of the system, the video memory subsystem is implemented using a hierarchical scheme as shown in Figure P4.52. Video data is transferred from main memory to the cache in blocks.

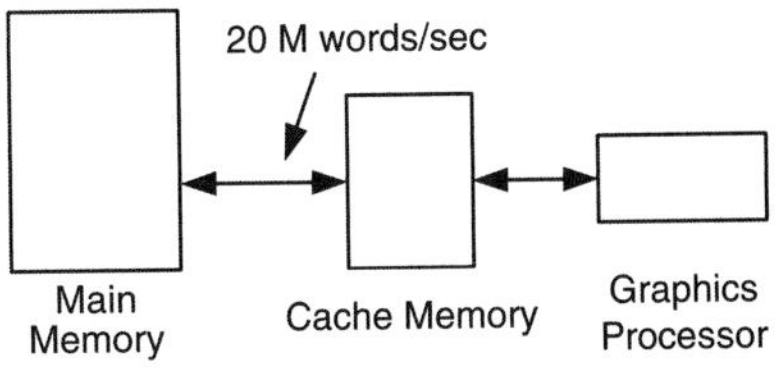

Figure P4.52

As you design the system, using specifications from the memory vendor's data sheets, you specify for the memory system as follows:

Main memory latency	4.0 μsec
Data transfer bandwidth	20.0 M words/sec
Block size	256 words

Based on these specifications, what should the speed of the graphics processor be to ensure that the processing and transfer rates match?

4.20 A memory subsystem that is to be utilized by four different independent subsystems, S0–S3, to store information is needed in a new design. The memory design is to be based on the 16 K bit CY7C128A SRAM organized as 2 K x 8.

By design, each subsystem is allocated 500 words of the memory. Nonetheless, there may be conflicts if more than one subsystem tries to access the memory at the same time.

(a) Provide a textual description of how one subsystem will be prevented from accessing memory that has been allocated to another subsystem.

(b) Provide a textual description of how bus conflicts will be avoided.

(c) Provide a high-level block diagram for the memory interface.

(d) Provide a high-level timing diagram for the interface to the SRAM assuming that separate address and data busses are available. Define any control signals that may be necessary. Your diagram should illustrate a bus contention and resolution.

4.21 Modify the design in Problem 4.20 to provide 100 words of shared memory locations between S0 and S1, S1 and S2, S2 and S3, S3 and S0.

Testing

4.22 Design a built-in self-test that could be conducted on the memory design in Problem 4.1 to identify any address bits that are stuck low or high. Explain how your algorithm works and how it is assured of finding the fault.

Your test must be designed to ensure that if it passes, the contents of the memory are left unchanged.

If your test fails, what statement can you make about the contents of the memory?

4.23 Repeat Problem 4.22 for any data bit.

4.24 The memory design in Problem 4.5 uses a shared address and data bus. Design a self-test to identify if one of the bus lines is stuck low or high. Can you devise a test that will further isolate such stuck-at faults to the address or data component of the bus?

4.25 Devise a simple test that can be used to ensure that a ROM contains the correct data. Consider the bitwise operators. Can such a test be used to test a RAM as well? If so, what are the constraints on the test?

Chapter 5

An Introduction to Software Modeling

THINGS TO LOOK FOR . . .

- Unified Modeling Language overview and diagrams.
- Major static modeling diagrams in UML and the utility of each.
- UML class diagrams and use cases.
- Diagrams for expressing intermodule relationships.
- The need for dynamic modeling.
- Major dynamic modeling diagrams in UML and the utility of each.
- UML state, timing, sequence, and activity diagrams.
- The philosophy behind the Structured Design methods.
- The purpose and utility of the data and control flow diagram.

5.0 INTRODUCTION

Unified Modeling Language
Structured Design

As we begin our studies of the design and development of the software side of embedded systems, it is appropriate that we start to learn about some of the tools that can help us with that portion of the job. On the hardware side, we used the Verilog language to model and to analyze the behavior of the modules prior to physical implementation. In this chapter, we will introduce UML—the *Unified Modeling Language*—and several tools taken from the *Structured Design* approach to system design for that same purpose. A common theme with both approaches to software modeling is the heavy use of graphics as a first step in dealing with the complexity of many contemporary software systems.

We will begin our studies with a brief history of some of the work that led up to the UML. We will then present and discuss the different diagrams that comprise the UML approach. Our initial goal will be to learn techniques by which we can express and model the static structure of a system. We will then work to capture and model its dynamic behavior.

The static view of a system begins from the outside. Such a view is initially captured by seeking to identify and to express how the user (which may be another system or peripheral device) expects to interact with the system. As the system is analyzed and modeled at increasing levels of detail, the comprising modules, their relationships, and their communication paths are identified, defined, and included.

concurrent
persistence

Dynamic models capture the behavior of a system while it is performing its intended tasks, as well as provide information about interactions among tasks. *Concurrent* task operation and *persistence* are two of the more important dynamic considerations.

In the design of embedded applications, we work with collections of cooperating objects. These objects may be software entities such as tasks or processes or hardware modules such as processors or various peripheral devices. Some of these objects may be *active*, that is, centers of independent activity, whereas others may be inactive. *Concurrency* expresses the ability of a system to handle many such activities simultaneously. It is the property of objects that models parallel operations through an implementation based on time sharing a single processor or multiple processors.

active

concurrency

The *sequential* execution of a set of instructions in a task or process in an embedded application is called a *thread* or *thread of control.* Systems supporting concurrent operation will have multiple threads of control. Some of the threads may be transitory, and others may last the lifetime of the system execution. Concurrency focuses on the notions of abstraction, coordination, and synchronization among those threads. Understanding and modeling this aspect of system behavior is essential in the design of multitasking and multiprocessing embedded systems.

sequential

thread of control

A software object takes up space, and it exists for a finite period of time. *Persistence* is the property of an object that describes its existence in space and in time. For instance, a temporary variable may only exist during the evaluation of an expression. Local variables exist only while control flow is within their scope and then vanish when the scope is exited. Global variables, for example, may have a lifetime that extends beyond their scope. Other variables persist between executions of a program, and between versions of a program, or may outlive the program.

persistence

In this chapter, our study of the dynamic aspects of the system will focus on variables and on tasks, whose lifetime falls into the first three categories listed earlier. Persistence, however, is concerned with more than just data lifetime; the state of the object must also be considered. Values must be consistent, particularly in situations such as physically or temporally distributed systems. The type of an object must be considered. In a distributed application, every element of the system must interpret the data in the same way.

We will conclude our introduction of software modeling with a brief look at some of the Structured Design methodologies. Structured Design, which has been around for over 30 years, provides another rich set of tools for attacking the complexities of contemporary designs. In our studies, we will introduce two of the dynamic modeling tools that are useful for conveniently expressing the flow of data and control within a system. Like the UML, a key aspect of Structured Design is that it is graphical.

5.1 AN INTRODUCTION TO UML

The approach that we will use to introduce UML will be to bring in the pieces as we need them. In this section, we will provide some initial background, terminology, and vocabulary.

As we mentioned earlier, a wide variety of tools are available to help with the design, development, and test of software. Each tool has its strengths and weaknesses. There are times and places where they should be used and times when they should not be used.

Part of creativity and of design is the ability to see things where perhaps they "don't belong" or in ways that were not originally intended. We introduce UML in a software context; the underlying ideas and approach, however, have much broader application as we will see when we study more formal design.

UML evolved from the work of a great many people who were looking for better ways to design and develop object-oriented models and systems. By the mid-1990s, the number of credible approaches was reduced to three. Continuing efforts developed and refined these approaches until by 1997 the *Object Management Group* (OMG) submitted and accepted version 1.1 of UML. OMG is an international body that defines standards in many areas of

Object Management Group OMG

computer science. The current version of UML is 1.3—which, of course, will be outdated by the time this text gets into print.

As its history suggests, UML evolved with the goal of making object-centered design easier; consequently, much of the vocabulary and approach centers around objects. Nonetheless, we can extend those ideas to a wide variety of both software and hardware applications. Frequently in the ensuing discussions, we will use the words *class* and *object*. The intention here is to describe or refer to an abstract entity (or group of entities) rather than either the intrinsic Java or C++ classes.

class, object

Many of the tools that we will introduce are graphical in nature. We, as human beings, often find it easier to grasp a new concept when it appears as a picture rather than in pages of text. The use of graphics, however, does not eliminate the need for clear, concise, and understandable textual descriptions. A good graphic can quickly capture high-level concepts; we still rely on text to express the details.

5.2 UML DIAGRAMS

UML uses diagrams and models as a first step toward expressing static and dynamic relationships among objects. While an important part of the standard, the authors do not see such diagrams as the main thrust of the approach. Rather, a philosophy of a *Model-Driven Architecture (MDA)*, in which UML is used as a programming language, is more common. The high-level goal is to create an environment in which tool vendors can develop models that can work with a wide variety of other MDA tools. On the user side, designers who work with UML range from those who are putting together a "back of the envelop" sketch to those who utilize it as a formal (high-level) design and programming language. UML provides a very good mechanism for quickly exchanging ideas with other designers and for capturing the critical elements of a design.

Model-Driven Architecture (MDA)

This discussion notwithstanding, the current standard recognizes 13 different classes of drawings. As a design evolves, these different perspectives offer a rich set of tools whereby we can formulate and analyze potential solutions. Such tools enable us to model several different aspects of a design. It is rare that all of the types are used in a single design. The different diagram types are presented in Table 5.0.

Table 5.0 Common UML Diagrams

- Class
- Use Case
- Component
- Communication

- State Chart
- Timing
- Sequence
- Activity

- Object
- Package
- Composite Structure
- Interaction
- Deployment

As is suggested by their names, diagrams in the first four categories provide the means for developing a static or structural view; the next four add dynamic analysis; and the final five bring the pieces together.

We will begin with several of the static components and relationships; these will be sufficient to get us started. We will spend only limited time on the diagram types in the last category.

5.3 USE CASES

use case The first diagram we will look at is the *use case,* which gives us an outside view of the system. It describes the public interface for the module or system and answers the questions, "What is the behavior that the user sees?" "What is the behavior the user expects?" The use case repeatedly poses the question, "What?" until the external view of the system has been satisfactorily captured.

The use case diagram presents the main components of the system and shows how the user interacts with those components. Like many of the diagrams we will work with, the use case diagram can be hierarchical. From the top-level drawing, one can expand each use case into subuse cases as necessary.

system, actor(s), use case(s) The use case diagram has three components: the *system,* the *actor(s),* and the *use case(s).* The meaning of system is self-evident; after all, that is what is being designed. It is expressed in the diagram as a box—we will often leave this off the diagram. The actor(s), drawn as simple stick figures, represent any one or any thing that might be using the system. They are viewed as being outside of the system. The use cases, represented as a solid oval, identify the various behaviors of the system or ways that it might be used. They encapsulate the events or actions that must occur to implement the intended behavior of the system and are stated or expressed from the point of view of the user. Accompanying each use case is a textual component fully describing it. Use case diagrams can be a very powerful tool during the early stages of a project when one is trying to identify, define, and capture the requirements for the system.

As we construct the diagram, we place the actor that executes the use case on the left-hand side. Supporting actors appear on the right-hand side. Supporting actors are not restricted to human users; an actor can be a computer or other system as well. The set of use cases appears in the center of the drawing, with arrows indicating the actors involved in the use case.

A generic use case diagram is given in Figure 5.0. We see that the system comprises three use cases. Actor0 is using the system and appears on the left-hand side; Actor1 is supporting UseCase2 and is placed on the right-hand side.

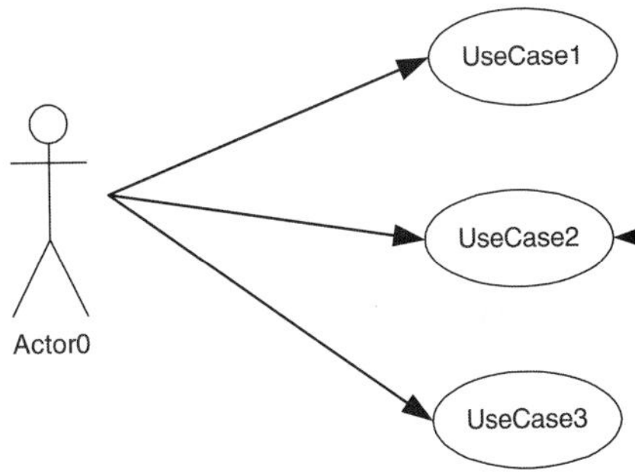

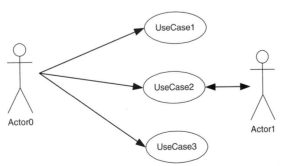

Figure 5.0 The UML Use Case Diagram

One should keep things simple when putting the use case diagram together. If a system being designed is showing 25 to 50 use cases on the top-level drawing, then it is time to rethink the design.

In this next example, we are working on a simple data acquisition system.

EXAMPLE 5.0

A basic data acquisition system that has the ability to measure voltage and temperature is to be designed. The use case diagram for the system begins with the user shown as Actor0. After the data has been collected, it needs to be analyzed for trends, alarm conditions, or other specific patterns. In addition, because the temperature sensor is a nonlinear device, a linearization operation must be performed.

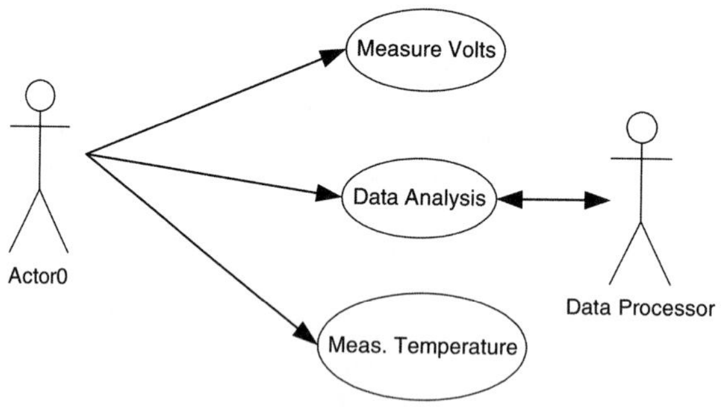

Figure 5.1 Use Case Diagram for a Simple Data Acquisition System

The data is collected at very high speed from a number of measurement points; as a result, hardware co-processing capability is probably going to be necessary. That entity is included as a second actor and is labeled *Data Processor.* A possible use case diagram for the data acquisition system is given in Figure 5.1.

Data Processor

WRITING A USE CASE

The use case diagram captures a graphical representation of the public interface to the module or system. Associated with each use case is a textual description of what actions the actor is to perform and how the system is expected to respond. Such a description can be decomposed into two pieces: the *normal activity* of the use case and how *exceptional conditions* are to be handled.

normal activity, exceptional conditions

Let's examine the *measure volts* use case for the data acquisition system. We specify how the user is to select the task, any options associated with the task, and how exceptions are handled as is done in Figure 5.2. Do not forget: a use case description is not intended to be *War and Peace*.

measure volts

5.4 CLASS DIAGRAMS

Once we have identified how the user intends or expects to interact with the system, the next step is to begin to identify and to formulate the modules that give rise to that external behavior. That process begins with the *class diagram.* This diagram gives a description of the objects in a system coupled with the relationships that exist among them. Such a description is frequently found among the foundation elements of most modeling tools. The class diagram enables one to specify the *public interface* to the object, the interface expressed in the use cases. Such a description includes the properties and the operations that instances of the object can perform and identifies any constraints the application imposes on those opera-

class diagram

public interface

User

Select measure volts mode

Select measurement range or autorange

System

If range specified

Configure to specified gain

Make measurement

If in range—display results

If exceed range—display largest value for range and flash the display

If auto range

Configure to midrange gain

Make measurement

If in range—display results

If above or below range—adjust gain to next range and repeat the measurement

If exceed range—display largest value for range and flash the display

Figure 5.2 Writing a Use Case Description

tions. The public interface should always be one of the earlier views one takes of any design. We want to see the design from our user's point of view.

associations *name* *properties* *operations*

The class diagram presents the various kinds of objects in the system and identifies the relationships called *associations* among them. Objects are expressed as a rectangle, subdivided into three areas as illustrated in Figure 5.3. The top area gives the *name* of the class or object, and the middle section identifies all of the *properties* of the object. These will generally be declared inside the module implementation and thereby hidden from the casual user. The third pane identifies the *operations* that the object is intended to perform. These operations establish the external behavior of the object; they provide the public interface to the object.

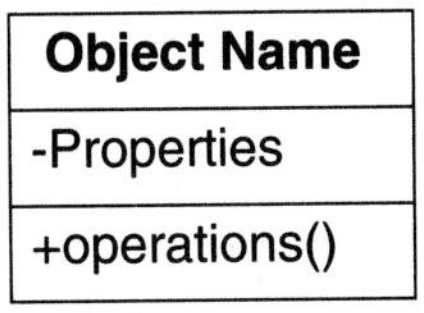

Figure 5.3 UML Class Diagram

attributes, associations *multiplicity*

The *properties* of an object provide a mechanism to capture the structural features of that object. A property may be further elaborated as *attributes* or *associations*. Attributes describe a particular characteristic of a property such as the address of an output port, whereas associations capture how the object relates to other objects within the system. A property can be quantified by a *multiplicity* attribute identifying how many objects may fill the property. The wheel on an automobile has a *multiplicity* of 4.

CLASS RELATIONSHIPS

We can define a number of different relationships among classes, including

- Parent–child or inheritance or generalization
- Containment or aggregation

5.4.1 Inheritance or Generalization

inheritance We express *inheritance* using a solid line terminating in a hollow arrow. Figure 5.4 presents a portion of the design of an external world communications interface in an embedded system. ***Driver*** Therein, we represent the relationship between the parent–*Driver* and two children— ***Serial, Parallel, a kind of (AKO)*** *Serial* and *Parallel*. We say that Serial or Parallel are *a kind of (AKO)* Driver.

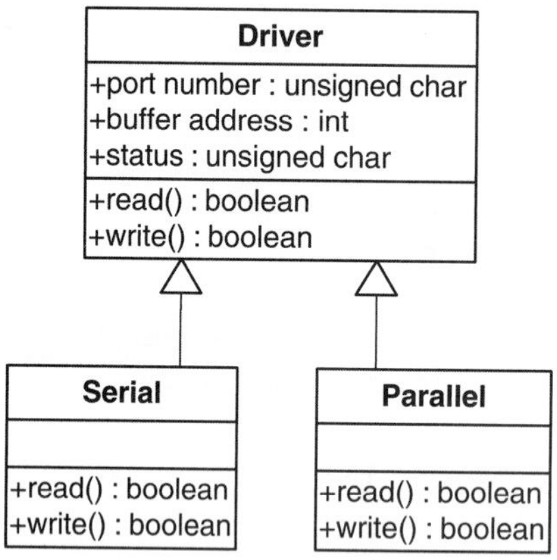

Figure 5.4 UML Inheritance Diagram

The diagram captures the requirement (through the parent interface) that each of the different types of interface must support a common subset of capabilities. Specifically, a port number must be associated with each interface, the driver must provide the address to ***read(), write()*** an I/O buffer, it must manage a status flag, and it must implement the *read()* and *write()* functions to execute the transfer. The + sign in the diagram indicates that each of the corresponding elements is publicly visible.

We generally think of inheritance as supported by the Java or C++ languages; the concept naturally applies as we begin the design of an I/O interface and its associated drivers. It seems reasonable that there should be a common way of communicating with each driver. Although the C language does not formally support inheritance, such a limitation should not preclude using the concept as a hardware or software design tool.

5.4.2 Interface

interface An *interface* is a wrapper around one piece of functionality that allows us to present a different set of capabilities as a public view. We express an interface in a manner that is similar to that which we use for inheritance. We use a dashed line terminating in a hollow arrow.

In Figure 5.5, we illustrate the concept of an interface with a standard laboratory instrument. We will apply the same concept shortly when we are working with several different data structures.

measurePressure ***convert()*** In the diagram, the interface, *measurePressure*, gives the underlying voltmeter the public appearance of a pressure meter. The hidden operation, *convert()*, performs the necessary math to transform the raw voltage reading from a transducer into the corresponding and proper pressure reading.

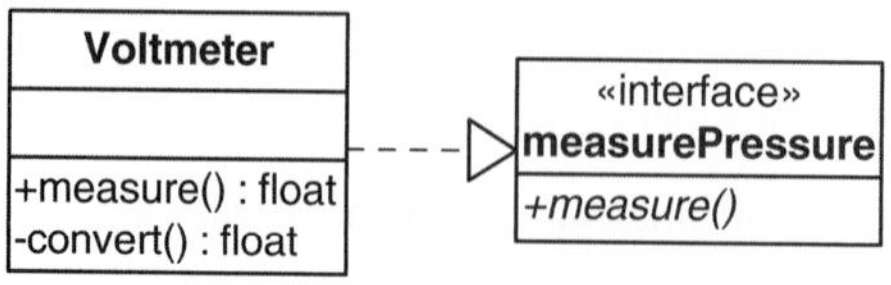

Figure 5.5 Representing an Interface

5.4.3 Containment

containment **aggregation** **composition**

Containment conveys the idea that one object is made up of several others, that is, a whole–part relationship. Under UML, we can express two different forms of containment, *aggregation* and *composition.*

5.4.3.1 Aggregation

aggregation, whole–part relationship

Aggregation expresses a *whole–part relationship* in which one object or module contains another module. A key characteristic of an aggregation is that the owned module may be shared with other modules outside of the aggregation. Under such conditions, rules must be established to ensure proper management of the shared module.

pressure

Continuing with the voltmeter system, let's assume that one of the design requirements specifies that, in addition to executing *pressure* measurements, it must also perform several different kinds of analyses on the data that it collects. In partial support of such analysis, we design an algorithm that performs a series of statistical computations, such as trend, mean, limits test, or rate of change, on the collected data.

To perform the necessary computations, the algorithm utilizes a number of different library functions. Although the individual functions may be collected under the umbrella of the analysis package in the design, they can exist without that module and certainly could be used by other modules within the system as well.

aggregation

The statistical analysis algorithm is an *aggregation* of many specific algorithms. The UML diagram for the aggregation relationship, shown in Figure 5.6, presents both the whole and its parts connected via a solid line that originates at an open diamond on the end associated with the whole and terminates on the end associated with the part.

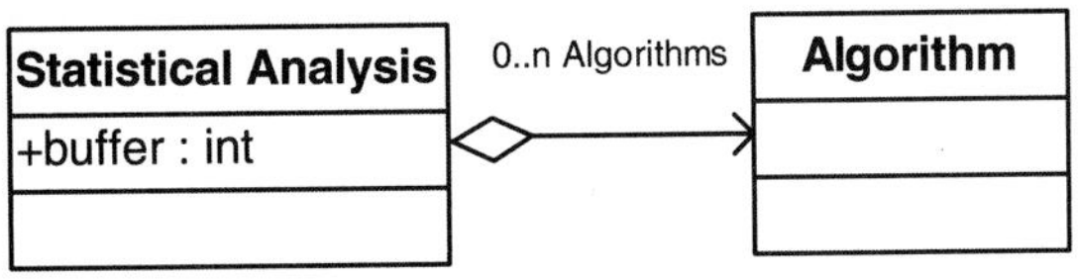

Figure 5.6 Representing the Aggregation Relationship

5.4.3.2 Composition

composition

The *composition* relationship is similar to aggregation, but the notion of ownership of the parts by the whole is much stronger. The elements of the composition cannot be part of another object and, unlike the aggregation relationship, they cannot exist outside of the whole object. Although this may sound a little strange, at the core of the issue is the proper management of memory. The idea is loosely analogous to local variables in a function. Once one leaves the scope of the function, the local variables disappear.

In an embedded system, we often build an application as a collection of tasks. Each of these tasks executes according to a designated schedule. The schedule is made up of a number of intervals. Without the schedule, the intervals have no meaning. We express such a relationship in a composition diagram as shown in Figure 5.7.

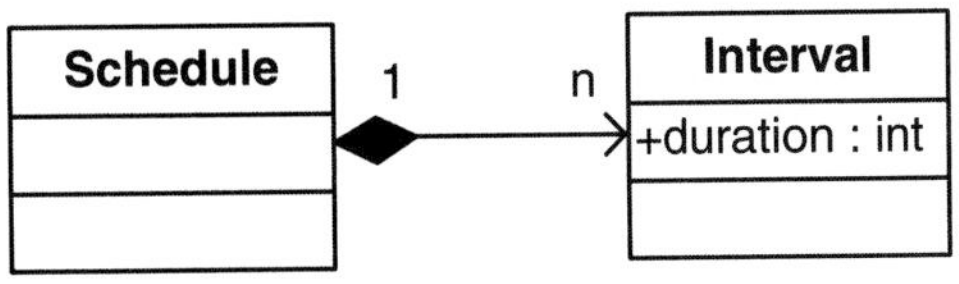

Figure 5.7 Representing the Composition Relationship

The schedule is composed of 1 to n intervals. Observe that the diagram is similar to that for the aggregation. The connecting line now originates in a solid rather than an open diamond. We annotate the relationship as a 1 to n composition.

5.5 DYNAMIC MODELING WITH UML

Dynamic modeling provides the means to capture, understand, and design the intended behavior of a system. The static structure gives an architecture; the dynamic aspects of the design get the real work done. Important elements of a dynamic model include

- Recognizing intermodule interaction and communication
- Ensuring the proper order of task execution
- Understanding what activities can be done in parallel
- Selecting alternate paths of execution
- Identifying which tasks are active and when they are not

In the next several sections, we will study UML diagrams that will enable us to explore, express, and make trade-offs on these elements of a design.

5.6 INTERACTION DIAGRAMS

interaction diagram

The first diagram that we will study is the *interaction diagram.* For embedded design, understanding and modeling the dynamic behavior of the system is essential. Dynamic behavior gives information about the lifetime of a task, identifies when that task is active or inactive, and models interactions among tasks. Such interaction often takes the form of messages. A message is a means of communication between two or more tasks. It can take several forms:

- Event
- Rendezvous
- Message

Generally, the receipt of a message results in the initiation of one or more actions. Such actions are executable functions within the task and result in a change in the values of one or more attributes associated with the task.

UML explicitly supports five kinds of actions:

- ***Call and Return***

  The *call action* invokes a method on an object and the *return action* returns a value in response to call.
- ***Create and Destroy***

  The *create action* creates an object; the *destroy action* does the opposite.
- ***Send***

  The *send action* sends a signal to an object.

Each of these actions is directly applicable to later work with tasks. These actions are shown in the following diagrams. The dashed line emanating from each object or class is called a *lifeline*. The lifeline captures the notion of the persistence of the object.

lifeline

5.6.1 Call and Return

call action
return action

A *call action* is expressed by a solid arrow from the calling object to the receiving object and the *return action* by a dashed, open arrow from the receiving object to the calling object. Such an interaction is shown in Figure 5.8.

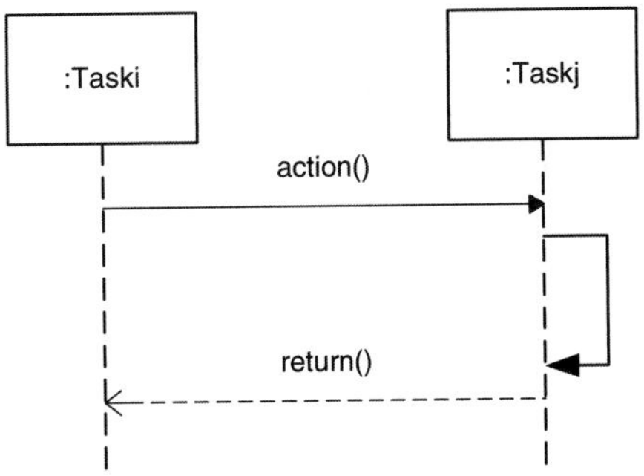

Figure 5.8 The Call and Return Interaction Diagram

5.6.2 Create and Destroy

create action
destroy action

The *create action* is represented by a solid arrow from the creating object to the created class instance, and the *destroy action* by a solid arrow from the destroying object to the destroyed class instance. This relationship is presented in Figure 5.9.

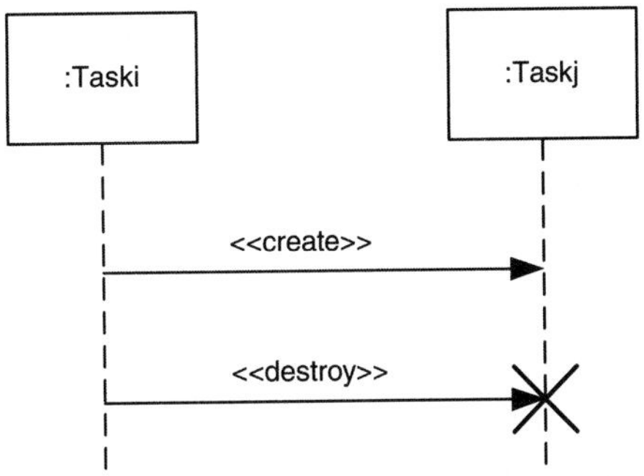

Figure 5.9 The Create and Destroy Interaction Diagram

5.6.3 Send

send action

The *send action* is captured by a solid arrow with an open half arrow head from the sending task to the receiving task as seen in Figure 5.10.

The sender does not expect a response.

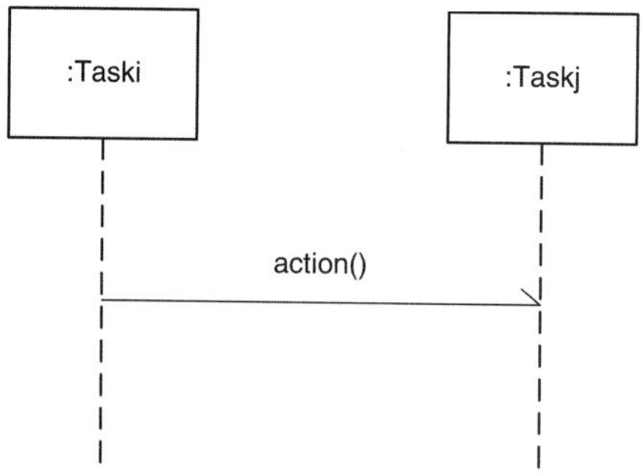

Figure 5.10 The Send Interaction Diagram

5.7 SEQUENCE DIAGRAMS

sequence diagram

The purpose of a *sequence diagram* is to express the temporal ordering of a series of message exchanges between objects. The diagram comprises the four principal components presented in Figure 5.11.

- ***Objects***

  Objects appear along the top margin of the diagram as they did in the interaction diagrams. In our designs, these will be the tasks.
- ***Lifeline***

  The *lifeline,* drawn as a dashed line leaving the object, captures the notion of object persistence.
- ***Focus of Control***

  The *focus of control* reflects the durations in the object's life during which it is considered to be active. It is expressed as a thin rectangular box that straddles the object's lifeline and indicates the time during which the object is in control of the flow, that is, executing a method or creating another task. This is the time when a task has the CPU.
- ***Messages***

  The *messages* show the actions that objects perform either on themselves or on each other.

Figure 5.11 Principal Components of the UML Sequence Diagram

sequence diagram
measure
execute measurement
convert
display

Figure 5.12 gives a *sequence diagram* for making, converting, and displaying a time interval measurement in a simple counter design. The initial selection of the specific function spawns the *measure* task. The measure task retrieves the range and measurement edge information from an internal buffer and sends these to the *execute measurement* task. The execute task returns the raw reading to the measure task, which spawns the *convert* task to process the raw reading into a format that can be displayed. The convert task will also perform the bounds check on the reading and return the bounds exceeded value if necessary. Finally, the measure task sends the measurement to the *display* task, which presents it to the user via the front panel display.

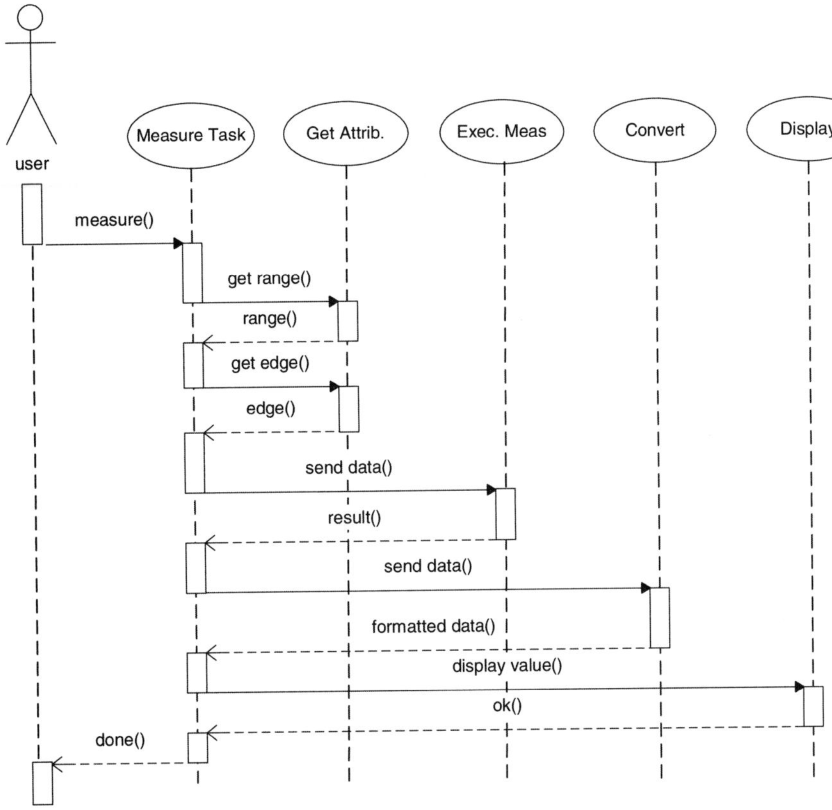

Figure 5.12 Sequence Diagram for Making a Time Interval Measurement

5.8 FORK AND JOIN

When working with a multitasking embedded system, a common sequence of operations is for a parent process to start and then spawn several child tasks to do the real work. The child tasks complete their jobs and terminate and then the parent class follows. The process of splitting the control flow into two or more flows of control or subtasks is called a *fork*. Each subtask represents a separate, independent thread of control. When the subtasks are brought back together or resynchronized, it is called a *join*.

fork

join

fork and join

Such behavior of tasks and subtasks is modeled using a *fork and join* diagram as reflected in Figure 5.13.

synchronization bar

The tasks are represented by a cartouche or rounded rectangle. Sequential flow is given by a solid arrow. Forks and joins are represented by a thick bar or rectangle called a *synchronization bar*. The fork occurs after the first parent activity or action completes. Following such an action, we see that the task spawns subtasks and then suspends itself until subtasks have completed. Once all subtasks have completed, the join occurs, and the parent task resumes its activities.

In Figure 5.13, the parent spawns two child tasks. One child performs its task and completes; the second similarly finishes its task and then spawns a second. When all activity completes, the child tasks terminate and the parent continues.

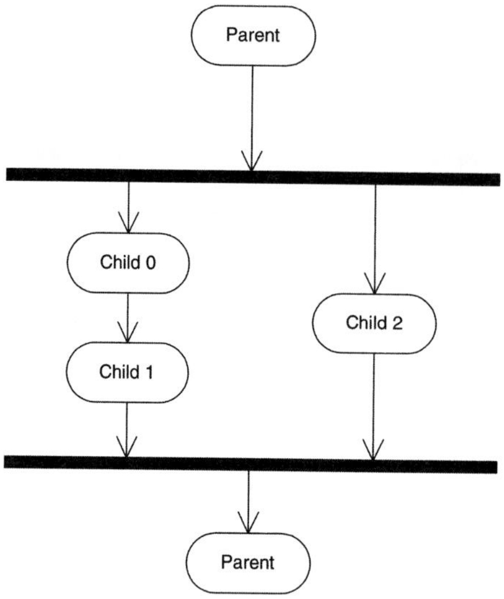

Figure 5.13 The UML Fork and Join Diagram

5.9 BRANCH AND MERGE

branch Another form of flow of control is the *branch* in which the thread of execution is determined by the value of some control variable. Such a structure permits one to model alternate ***merge*** threads of execution. A *merge* brings the flow back together again. Each is represented by the diamond symbol, which is commonly found in the familiar flow chart. Sequential flow is shown by a solid arrow, and individual tasks or activities are shown using a rounded rectangle.

A simple diagram with two alternate paths of execution for a portion of the overall task is given in Figure 5.14.

Following the completion of the activities in the right-hand path, the flow of control merges back to a single path. At each branch point one can associate a guard condition to stipulate under what conditions the branch is to be taken. The guard condition is shown in square brackets on the transition arrow.

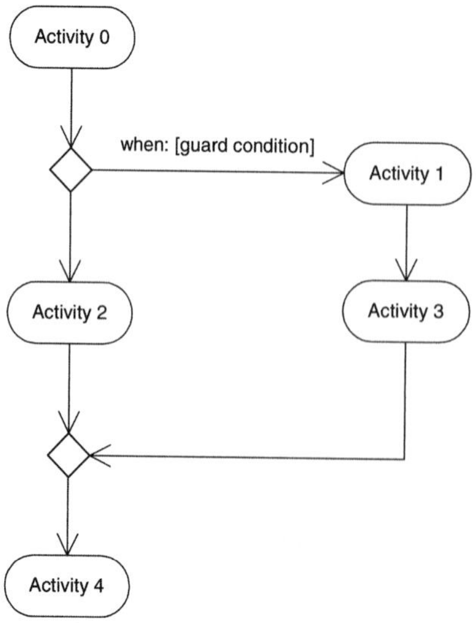

Figure 5.14 The UML Branch and Merge Diagram

5.10 ACTIVITY DIAGRAM

activity diagram An *activity diagram* permits the capture of all the procedural actions or flows of control within a task. Such actions may be a branch and merge, a fork and join, or a simple transition from state to state.

The initial node in the diagram is given by a solid black circle; the final node is a solid black circle surrounded by a second circle. The accompanying diagram in Figure 5.15 shows how we might combine our earlier activities into a larger task. Conversely, one can show how a larger task is decomposed into its components.

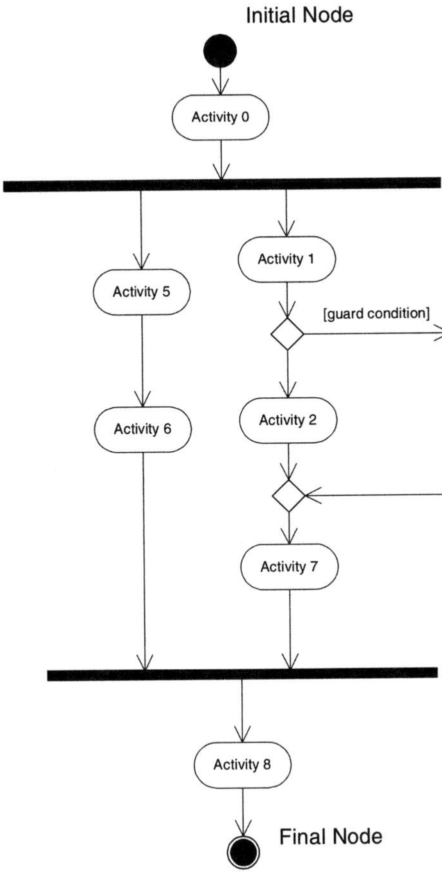

Figure 5.15 The UML Activity Diagram

5.11 STATE CHART DIAGRAMS

state chart diagram The *state chart diagram*, like the familiar state diagram, finds its roots in the mathematics of graph theory. Using the diagram, we can begin to capture and to model the state behavior of the (software) system as well as the myriad external and internal events that are affecting that behavior.

5.11.1 Events

Any embedded application must interact with the world around it. The system will accept inputs and produce outputs. Inputs generally result in some associated action, and the actions may or may not lead to an output. Such inputs, outputs, and actions are known by ***events*** various names. Under the UML umbrella, they are collected under the name *events*. An event is any occurrence of interest to the system, more specifically and typically to one of the tasks in the system.

UML supports the four kinds of events given in Figure 5.16.

- ***Signal***
  A *signal* is an asynchronous exchange between tasks.
- ***Call Event***
  A *call event* is a synchronous communication that involves sending a message to another task or sending a message to self.
- ***Time Event***
  A *time event* occurs after a specified time duration has elapsed following another event.
- ***Change Event***
  A *change event* occurs after some designated condition has been satisfied.

Figure 5.16 UML Events

5.11.2 State Machines and State Chart Diagrams

(FSMs) *state machine*

We have studied and used the finite-state machines (FSMs) to model and to implement a system's behavior in time. The term *state machine* is used to describe

- The states that a system can enter into during its lifetime
- Events to which the system can respond
- Possible responses the system can make to an event
- Transitions between possible states

Because of its simplicity, the FSM gives a good first-order model of a system's behavior. UML supports and extends the traditional notion of state machines.

5.11.2.1 UML State Chart Diagrams

state chart diagram *state*

A *state chart diagram* is nothing more than the familiar state diagram with some extensions/modifications under UML. The diagram begins with the notion of a state. A *state* is written as a cartouche—a rectangle with rounded corners as illustrated in Figure 5.17. Transitions between states reflect a change in system from one state to another and are expressed as an arrow directed from the source state to the destination state.

Figure 5.17 UML State

Mathematically, the UML state chart is a directed graph. Because cycles are permitted, it is a cyclic directed graph.

5.11.2.2 Transitions

transition *triggerless*

A *transition* between states occurs when an event of interest to the system takes places or when the system has completed some action and is ready to move to the next state. The former is called a triggered transition and the latter transition is called a *triggerless* transition. One may associate an action with the transition, and a transition to self is permitted. All four types of transition are illustrated in Figure 5.18.

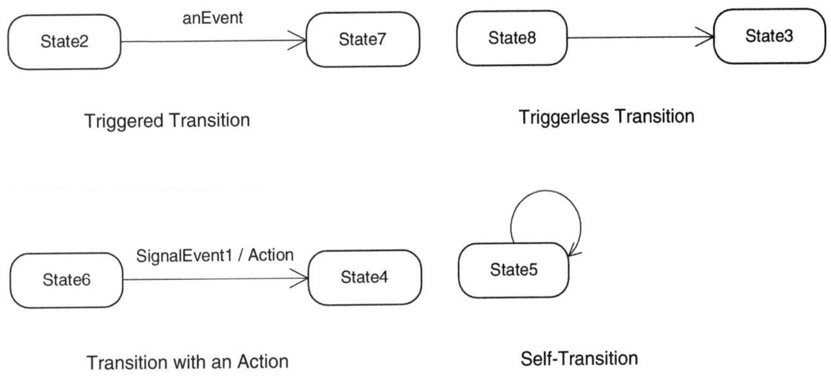

Figure 5.18 Possible Transitions in a UML State Chart

5.11.2.3 Guard Conditions

guard condition A *guard condition* can be associated with a transition. A guard condition is a Boolean expression that must evaluate to true before the transition can fire. As was done in the branch and merge diagram, a guard condition is shown in square brackets on the transition arrow. UML supports several different kinds of guard.

- An event and a guard condition are written as

  EventName [*guardCondition*]

  on the state transition edge. If the *guardCondition* evaluates to false, the transition will not be taken.
- An event, guard condition, and action triple appear as

  EventName [*guardCondition*]/*Action*

  on the state transition arrow. If the *guardCondition* evaluates to false, the action is not executed and the transition not taken.
- A guard condition by itself is described as

  [*guardCondition*]

  Under such a condition, there is a repeated transition to self until the guard condition is met. Through such a mechanism, one can model the polling operation or blocking on an event or a variable's state.

In the following diagram, a solid circle represents the initial state, and a solid circle with a surrounding open circle represents the final state. Illustrated in Figure 5.19 is a transition with an action and a guarded event.

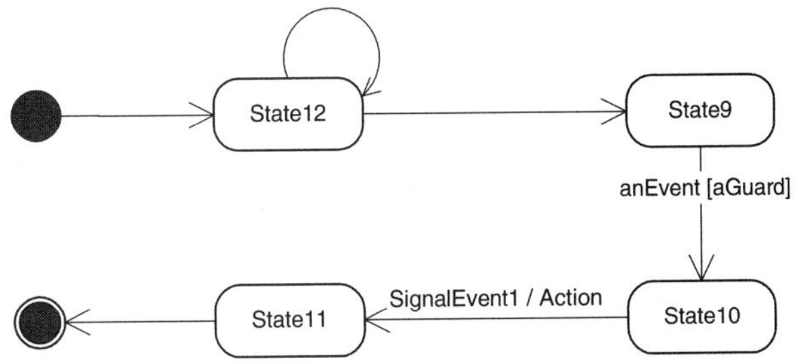

Figure 5.19 Transitions with Guard Conditions in a UML State Chart

UML also makes the following definitions,

entry action

- An *entry action* is an action that the system always performs immediately upon entering a state. The requirement appears as *entry/actionName* within the state symbol

exit action

- An *exit action* is an action the system always performs immediately before leaving the state. The constraint appears as *exit/actionName* within the state symbol

deferred event

- A *deferred event* is an event that is of interest to the system. Handling the event is deferred until the system reaches another state. The deferred event appears as *eventName/defer* within the state symbol. Such events are entered into a queue that is checked when the system changes to the new state.

5.11.2.4 Composite States

composite states

The states that we have looked at so far are called simple states. UML extends the notion of a simple state to include multiple nested states called *composite states*. These come in several different varieties.

SEQUENTIAL STATES

sequential states

If the system exists in a composite state and in only one of the state's substates at a time, such substates are called *sequential substates*. Transitions between such substates are permitted as expected. Using sequential substates, the behavior of a state can be decomposed into smaller components as shown in Figure 5.20.

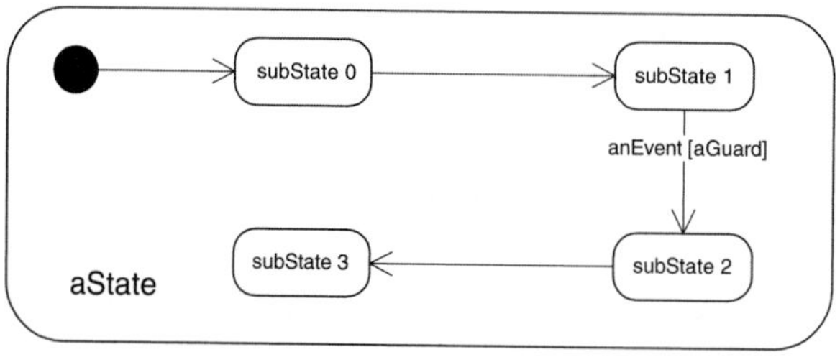

Figure 5.20 Composite States in a UML State Chart

HISTORY STATES

history substate

When a system makes a transition into a composite state, typically the flow of control will start in the initial substate. However, it may be desirable or necessary to begin in some other state. UML includes the concept of a *history substate* to support such a capability. The history substate, shown in the state chart in Figure 5.21 by a small circle enclosing the letter "H," will hold the last state that the system was in before leaving the composite state at an earlier time.

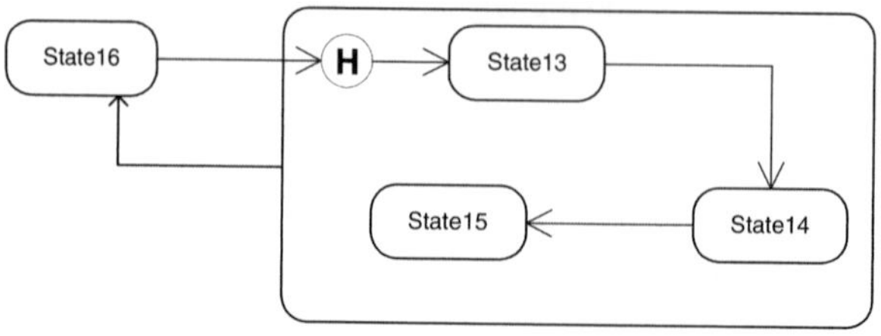

Figure 5.21 Expressing a History Substate in a UML State Chart

Such a state can be useful when modeling interrupt behavior or if one encounters a situation in which it is necessary to temporarily switch to another context to perform some operation prior to continuing. In either case, the present state is temporarily exited. Some time in the future, flow of control will return to that same state.

CONCURRENT SUBSTATES

A system may be in a composite state and also in more than one of the substates. Such is the situation in which the system may have two or more sets of substates representing parallel flows of control. When a system enters a composite state with *concurrent substates*, it enters into an initial state of both flows. Resynchronization is achieved by showing a final state for each flow as in Figure 5.22.

concurrent substates

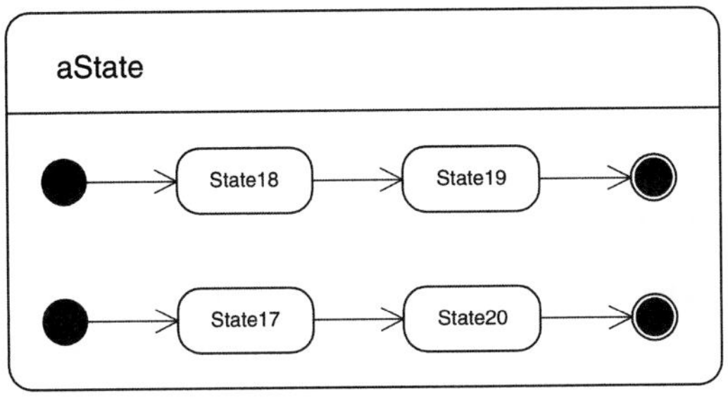

Figure 5.22 Expressing Concurrent Substates in a UML State Chart

We have only touched on some of the capabilities of the static and dynamic UML diagrams. This will be sufficient for our present work. A vast amount of literature is available for those interested in more detailed study.

5.12 DYNAMIC MODELING WITH STRUCTURED DESIGN METHODS

The next tool that we will study is taken from the Structured Design approach to software modeling. The structured design methodologies, as we noted in our brief study of the UML approach, provide a far richer and more expansive set of tools that we will present here. Our focus will be solely on capturing a high-level view of the flow of data and control within a design.

5.12.1 Brief Introduction to the Structured Design Philosophy

Structured Design methodologies provide another tool for attacking the complexities of today's designs. The approach has been around in one form or another for over 30 years. It provides one of the fundamental bases from which many of the modern tools, including UML, grew. A key aspect of the approach is that it is graphical. Its goals are rather simple. The design philosophy presented in this text is an outgrowth of many of its concepts. From top to bottom these goals are as follows:

- To reduce the number of errors made during initial design
- To make it easy to find and fix those errors that do occur
- To develop robust, reliable, safe software

Its approach, comprised of five fundamental ideas, is equally simple:

1. Use the definition of the problem to guide the definition of solution.
2. Attack problem complexity by partitioning the problem into modules and then organizing the modules into hierarchies.
3. Use tools to help to make complex systems understandable.
4. Develop the solution from a well-defined statement of the problem.
5. Identify criteria for evaluating the quality of a design.

Many of the static and philosophical approaches to design have already been manifest in earlier discussions and in earlier tools; they are not relevant to the material here. The data and control diagram, however, provides a very simple tool for quickly and easily capturing a high-level view of the dynamic structure of a design.

5.12.2 Data and Control Flow Diagrams

data and control flow (DFD) diagram

The *data and control flow (DFD) diagram* is used to partition a system into its active components and the data and control interfaces between them. The diagram is also sometimes known as a bubble chart.

5.12.2.1 The Elements

The data flow diagram comprises four graphic elements:

- The data and control flows
- The processes or tasks and threads
- The data sources and sinks
- Any data stores

Let's look at each of these elements.

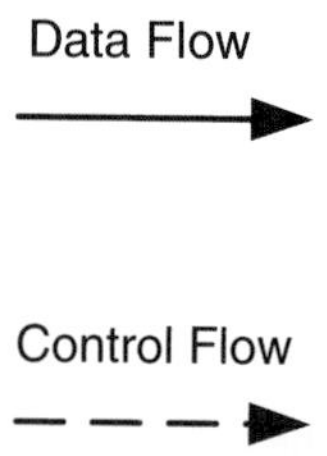

Figure 5.23 The Notation for Expressing Data and Control Flows

DATA AND CONTROL FLOWS
Data and control flows are expressed using notation that is similar to what we see in many UML diagrams. Data flow is indicated by a closed, solid arrow and control flow by a closed dashed arrow. As Figure 5.23 indicates, data or control flow in the direction of the arrow.

PROCESSES OR TASKS
The processes, modules, functions, or tasks are where the significant work in the application is being accomplished. Using a notation similar to that used in UML for states, these are expressed in a data and control flow diagram by labeled circles. The label identifies the name of the process or task and the level in the hierarchy at which the process resides.

- Level 0—1.0, 2.0, 3.0, etc.
- Level 1—1.1, 1.2, 1.3; 2.1, 2.2, 2.3; 3.1, 3.2, etc.
- Level 2—1.1.1, 1.1.2; 1.2.1, 1.2.2, etc.

The communications portion of an embedded system may contain tasks for managing the send and receive operations in the system. They would be expressed as is drawn in Figure 5.24.

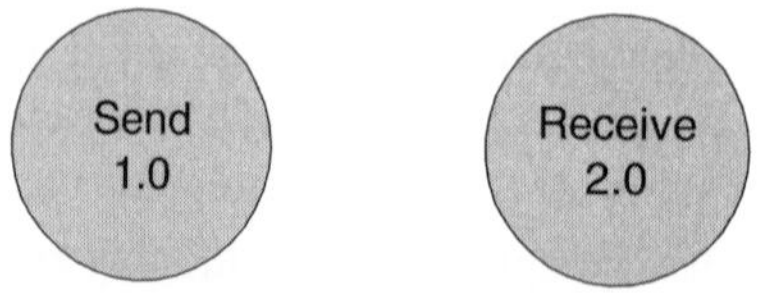

Figure 5.24 The Structured Design Notation for Expressing Processes or Tasks

DATA SOURCES/SINKS

source
sink

As the name implies, the *source* identifies where the data originates, for example, from an input port, and a *sink* indicates where data goes to, for example, to an output port. The

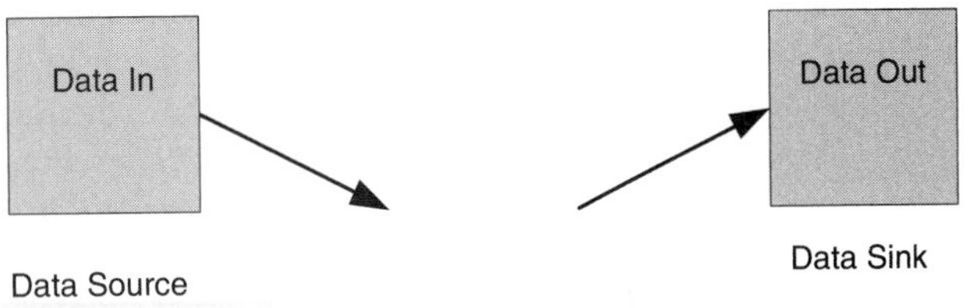

Figure 5.25 Expressing a Data Source or Sink

source or sink is drawn as a labeled box with an arrow to indicate the direction of data flow, as seen in Figure 5.25.

The source or sink are usually entities that are outside of the system.

DATA STORES

data storage The final element is *data storage*. The data store reflects the temporary storage of data or a time-delayed repository of data. The data store is represented by two parallel lines or two parallel lines that are closed on the left-hand side. To our electrical engineering students, this should look just like a capacitor—and does much the same job. The graphic is accompanied by a labeled arrow to indicate the direction of the data flow as we see in Figure 5.26.

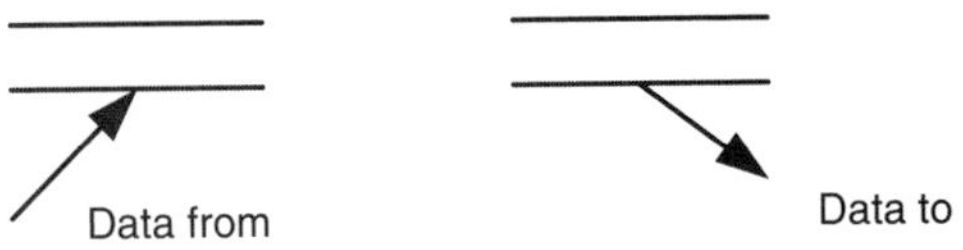

Figure 5.26 Expressing a Data Store

Let's look at a simple example.

EXAMPLE 5.1

Figure 5.27 presents a level 0—top-level—data and control flow diagram for a system that accepts commands from a remote source; collects image data at a local site; and then sends the information back to the remote site.

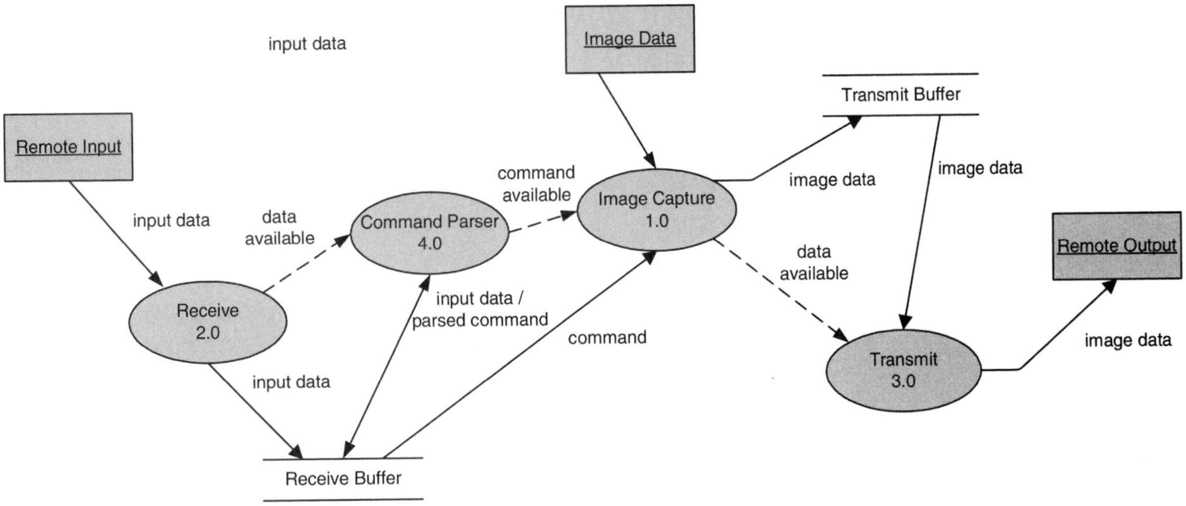

Figure 5.27 Capturing the Data and Control Flow in an Imaging System

Command data comes into the system from the remote site. This input is shown as a data source. The reception is managed by the *Receive* task, which brings the information into the system and stores it in the *Receive Buffer*. Once the *Receive* task accepts a compete message, it sends a control message to the *Command Parser* task, which parses the data and interprets the command. When it finishes, the *Command Parser* writes the command back into the buffer and sends a message to the *Image Capture* task to execute the capture. The *Image Capture* task collects the data from an external source and stores it into the transmit buffer. When the capture is complete, it signals the *Transmit* task to send the collected data back to the remote site.

Receive ***Receive Buffer*** ***Command Parser*** ***Image Capture*** ***Transmit***

Figure 5.28 illustrates a hierarchical decomposition of a data flow diagram through three levels. At each level, greater detail is provided.

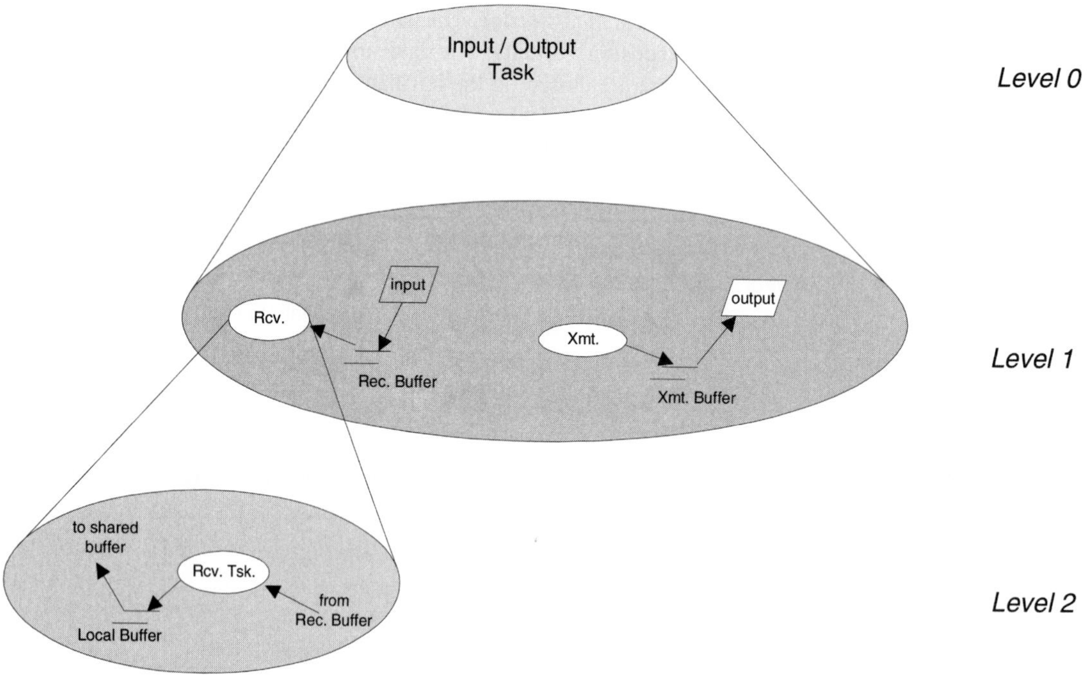

Figure 5.28 A Hierarchical Data and Control Flow Diagram in an Input/Output Task

5.13 SUMMARY

In this chapter, we have taken our first steps into basic software design. In doing so, we started to learn about some of the tools that can help us with that job. Specifically, we opened the chapter with a presentation of some of the tools that we take from UML—the *Unified Modeling Language*. We have introduced several different UML diagrams and one Structured Design diagram as tools that can be used to capture and model the static and dynamic relationships in a typical embedded application. We learned that the static models are essential for capturing the structure of the system and the dynamic models are important for expressing the desired behavior of system while it is performing its designated tasks and for providing information about interactions amongst those tasks. Finally, we found that the understanding of the concurrent operation of modules within the application and the persistence of software entities comprising the system are among the more important considerations when designing a system.

5.14 REVIEW QUESTIONS

Introduction

5.1 Why do we use the UML and Structured Design methodologies when developing embedded systems?

5.2 What information does a static view of an embedded system provide? a dynamic view?

5.3 In an embedded application, what does the term *concurrency* mean?

5.4 Explain the terms *thread* or *thread of control*.

5.5 What does the term *persistence* mean in an embedded software application?

5.6 Are there different forms of *persistence*? If so, briefly describe what these might be.

An Introduction to UML

5.7 Where did UML originate, and why was it developed?

5.8 In the context of the work in this text, what is the interpretation of the terms *class* and *object*?

5.9 Why are many of the tools used in UML graphical?

UML Diagrams

5.10 What is the purpose of UML diagrams?

5.11 What are the major classes of UML diagrams or drawings? Give a one- or two-sentence description of the purpose of each type of drawing.

5.12 In the text, the UML diagrams were segregated into three major groupings. What are these?

Use Case Diagrams

5.13 What does a *use case* diagram provide for us?

5.14 What are the major components of a *use case* diagram? Briefly describe each.

5.15 Are the *actors* in a *use case* diagram always people?

5.16 A textual description is typically associated with a *use case* diagram. What information should that description contain?

Class Diagrams

5.17 What information should we include in a *class diagram*?

5.18 When we say that the *class diagram* presents the public interface to an object, what do we mean?

5.19 A *class diagram* is expressed as a rectangle subdivided into three components. Identify these components and briefly describe the information contained in each.

5.20 The properties of an object can be decomposed into associations and attributes. Briefly describe what each of these means.

5.21 What are the different kinds of relationships that can be defined among classes or objects?

5.22 What kind of information should be captured in an *inheritance diagram*?

5.23 For what kind of relationship should an *inheritance diagram* be used?

5.24 What is the purpose of an *interface diagram*?

5.25 What kind of relationship do we express with an *aggregation diagram*?

5.26 What kind of relationship do we express with a *composition diagram*?

5.27 What is the difference between an *aggregation* and a *composition diagram*?

Dynamic Modeling with UML

5.28 What information does a dynamic model give us about a design?

5.29 What are the major elements that should be included in a dynamic model?

5.30 Three different forms of message can be expressed in an *interaction diagram*. What are these?

5.31 What are the different kinds of actions supported in a UML *interaction diagram*? Briefly describe each action.

5.32 What is the purpose of a UML *sequence diagram*?

5.33 What are the major elements of a *sequence diagram*.

5.34 What is a *fork and join* diagram? When should such a diagram be used?

5.35 What kind of activity does a *branch and merge diagram* allow us to express?

5.36 For what purpose do we use an *activity diagram*?

5.37 In the context of the Unified Modeling Language, what is an *event*?

5.38 What kinds of events are supported by UML? Briefly describe each event.

5.39 A UML *state chart diagram* is an extension to the familiar state diagram for expressing the behavior of a finite-state machine. What is a state diagram intended to describe?

5.40 The UML *state chart* specifies four kinds of transitions between states. Please identify each of these and briefly describe what each means.

5.41 What is the purpose of a *guard condition* in a UML *state chart*?

5.42 What kinds of *guard conditions* does UML support? Briefly describe what each such condition means.

5.43 What is a *composite state* in a UML *state chart*?

5.44 What kinds of *composite states* does UML support? Briefly describe each one and its intended purpose.

Structured Design Methodologies

5.45 What are the major goals of the Structured Design methodology?

5.46 The Structured Design approach to software modeling consists of five fundamental ideas. What are these?

5.47 What is the purpose of a *data* and *control flow* diagram?

5.48 What are the four major elements in a *data* and *control flow* diagram? What information does each capture?

5.15 THOUGHT QUESTIONS

Introduction

5.1 Why is the modeling of both a static and a dynamic view of an embedded system essential throughout the design process?

5.2 When designing the software for a multitasking embedded system, why is the understanding of and the ability to model concurrency important?

5.3 Why is the ability to model persistence in an embedded software application necessary?

Use Case Diagrams

5.4 The *use case* diagram provides the ability to capture and model the external view of a system. Why is such a view important in the early stages of the design of an embedded system?

5.5 Is the *use case* diagram limited to a top-level/external view of the system?

5.6 Discuss possible benefits of developing a use case analysis for each module comprising a system.

5.7 Is the *use case* diagram limited to the software components of a system?

5.8 Why is a textual description an important component of a *use case* diagram?

Class Diagrams

5.9 What is the purpose of developing a *class diagram*?

5.10 When we say that the *class diagram* presents the public interface to an object, how is this different from a *use case diagram*?

5.11 The *class diagram* provides the name of the class, its properties and its operations. Why is it important to capture this information during the early stages of the design of class?

5.12 What role can the class diagram play during the system-level definition of an application?

5.13 The properties of an object can be decomposed into *associations* and *attributes*. Why is this information important?

5.14 Why are the different kinds of relationships that can be defined among classes or objects important to understand in the early stages of system definition?

5.15 Why might an *inheritance diagram* be useful even if an object-oriented language is not being utilized for implementation?

5.16 What information should be expressed in an *interface diagram*?

5.17 Why do we distinguish an *aggregation* and a *composition* diagram?

5.18 What assessments do the *aggregation* and a *composition* diagrams enable us to capture about the elements of the corresponding collections?

Dynamic Modeling with UML

5.19 Why is the information about a system that is captured in a dynamic model critical to the design of a modern embedded system?

5.20 What kinds of information should we include in a dynamic model?

5.21 The event, rendezvous, and message quantify the exchange in an *interaction diagram*. Characterize the nature of the information in each of these exchanges.

5.22 Is the applicability of an *interaction diagram* restricted to inside the system?

5.23 Why do we distinguish the three types of information exchanged between entities in a system?

5.24 Please give an example from an embedded application that you are familiar with for each type of action modeled in an *interaction diagram*.

5.25 What information are we trying to understand and model using a UML *sequence diagram*?

5.26 Should we consider creating a *sequence diagram* for a complete system?

5.27 For what kinds of systems is a *fork and join diagram* going to provide useful information?

5.28 When should we be using a *branch and merge diagram*?

5.29 For what purpose do we use an *activity diagram*?

5.30 Several kinds of events are supported by UML. Give an example from a commercially available embedded application with which you are familiar where each such type of event might occur.

5.31 A UML *state chart diagram* is an extension to the familiar state diagram for expressing the behavior of a finite-state machine. Give several examples from a commercially available embedded applications with which you are familiar for which the behavior on the software side of the system can be modeled by a *state chart*.

5.32 The UML *state chart* specifies four kinds of *transitions* between states. Give an example from a commercially available embedded applications with which you are familiar in which each such type transition might occur.

5.33 Give several examples of commercially available embedded applications with which you are familiar that might use *composite state(s)* as an effective aid in expressing and modeling certain aspects of system behavior? Explain how the use of *composite state(s)* has helped.

5.34 Give several examples of commercially available embedded applications with which you are familiar that might use *history state(s)* as an effective aid in expressing and modeling system behavior? Explain how the use of *history state(s)* has helped.

Structured Design Methodologies

5.35 Give several examples of commercially available embedded applications with which you are familiar for which a *data and control flow diagram* might provide a simpler and more appropriate model of behavior than a UML state chart, interaction diagram, or activity diagram. Explain why the *data and control flow diagram* is the preferable alternative.

5.16 PROBLEMS

UML Modeling—Basic Containers

For each of the data types that one might use in an embedded application, please provide the following diagrams.

- *Use Case Diagram* and textual description of each use case
- *Class Diagram* for each top level module

5.1 A link in a linked list

5.2 A linked list

5.3 A queue

5.4 A stack

5.5 A FIFO container

5.6 A LIFO container

5.7 A circular list

UML Modeling—Applications

For the following embedded applications, please provide each of the following diagrams as appropriate.

- *Use Case Diagram* and textual description of each use case
- A first-level decomposition of the application into top-level modules
- *Class Diagram* for each top-level module
- An *Activity Diagram* identifying the major activities in the application
- A *State Chart* (or State Charts as appropriate) identifying the state behavior of the application
- An *Interaction Diagram/Sequence Diagram* (or Diagrams as appropriate) identifying the interaction and temporal behavior of the high-level modules within the application

5.8 Creating an embedded application

5.9 A digital watch

5.10 A Tic Tac Toe or naughts and crosses game

5.11 A cell phone

5.12 A cell phone with three-way calling

5.13 A coffee pot

5.14 An iPod™

5.15 An automobile

5.16 An automobile cruise control

5.17 A television with VCR/DVD player

5.18 A digital camera

5.19 A washing machine

The controls must include the ability to set water temperature, washing start times, modes (presoak, normal, permanent press, delicate), and annunciation of temperature, times, and mode.

5.20 An intrusion detection with three doors and timers on each door

If a door is left open too long, the intruder alarm is initiated.

5.21 An oven control

The controls must include the ability to set temperatures, cooking start and stop times, modes (bake, broil, clean), and annunciation of temperature, times, and mode.

5.22 A seat belt—engine—door lock interlock

The engine cannot start if the seat belt is not fastened. The doors automatically lock when the engine is started.

5.23 An entertainment system

> The entertainment system should support the ability to program and control a stereo, television, in-home movie theater, and gaming console, and to route music to any of six rooms in the house.

5.24 A television

5.25 A television remote control

5.26 A VCR/DVD record and playback device

5.27 A stereo

5.28 A gaming console

5.29 A module implementing a four-seat passenger entertainment system on a commercial aircraft

> The entertainment system should support the ability of each of the four passengers to program and control.

Movie selection
Audio selection
A gaming console

5.30 An automatic process for filling and capping bottles of juice on an assembly line

Structured Design Concepts—Data and Control Flow

For the following aspects of an embedded application, provide a data and control flow diagram.

5.31 Reading/writing from/to a USB port and a general parallel port

5.32 Accessing and reading a mouse

5.33 Accessing and reading keys from a keyboard

5.34 Controlling and accessing a digital-to analog converter

5.35 Controlling and accessing analog-to-digital converter

5.36 Burning a CD

5.37 Transferring data from an external device to memory and then to a display

5.38 Managing and controlling a video on demand system in a motel or hotel

5.39 An automatic process for filling and capping bottles of juice on an assembly line

Chapter 6

The Software Side—Part 1: The C Program

THINGS TO LOOK FOR . . .

- The structure of an embedded C program.
- The C program build process.
- C variables—Their type, storage class, and scope.
- The structure of a C program.
- Working with multiple files.

6.0 INTRODUCTION

Software and firmware, like digital hardware, are essential elements in today's embedded systems. In this chapter and the next we will cover the elements of the C language that are essential to developing today's embedded systems. We will begin with a top-level look at an embedded C program as we examine its structure and learn how to build a multiple-file program. We will study good programming style and some important considerations when developing programs that are robust, reliable, and maintainable.

We will then look inside the program through a review of the fundamentals of the C language, specifically variables, their type, scope, and storage class. We will conclude with a look at the structure of a C program itself and learn the details of working with multiple-file programs, a necessity for larger applications. In the next chapter, we will introduce bit operators, pointers, functions, and structs.

If you already feel comfortable with the C language and developing programs, take a few minutes to scan through this chapter and the next. If programming in C is new to you, working through the material in this chapter and the next should get you started on the road to C proficiency. Good luck and have fun.

6.1 SOFTWARE AND ITS MANIFESTATIONS

A colleague once commented that the hardware is merely a vehicle for allowing the software to express itself. Clearly, this is a software fellow; yet, to some extent, this observation is right. In an embedded application, the hardware is an integral part of the job. Without the hardware, there is no place for the software to do any expressing. Both pieces are necessary.

As the early computer developers showed, by rewiring the computer appropriately they could configure it to solve their particular problem. Originally, all the mathematical operations used integer rather than floating point numbers. The early developers were all mathematicians; they felt that everyone knew how to scale numbers.

Continually rewiring the computer is hard work. To make programming the computer easier, smart people have been developing increasingly sophisticated and powerful languages. These languages hid the lower layers of the machine. We now write in more comfortable terms, and the tools we have developed figure out how to translate our directions into signals that manipulate the underlying hardware to solve our problem. We do no more rewiring. We express the whole idea in Figure 6.0, a diagram we call an onion model.

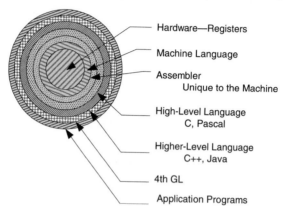

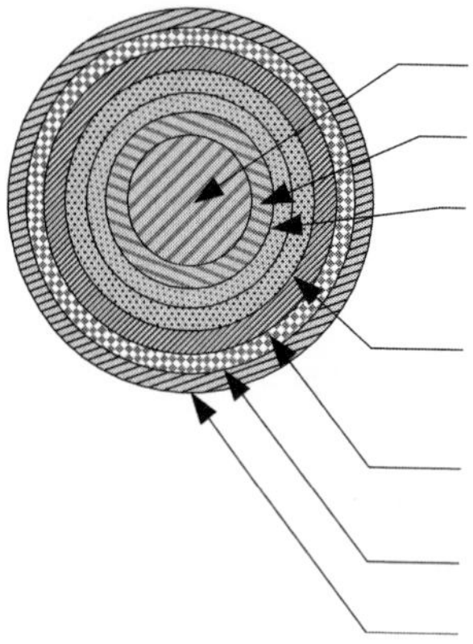

Figure 6.0 From Hardware to Applications

6.1.1 Combining Hardware and Software

We see then that an embedded application is simply a tool to make solving problems easier. Let's follow the process from the original problem statement to see how the hardware and software can work together.

> ***Problem***
>
> Let's begin with a very simplified version of an automated landing system
>
> *As the plane approaches the runway, continually decrease the velocity until the aircraft is at an altitude of 20 meters. At that altitude, activate the final approach profile and flare the plane onto the runway. If the aircraft descends too quickly, increase the thrust.*

The original problem is stated in a natural language as part of a customer requirement. From a software perspective, we can see several familiar things: the need for variables to express altitude and velocity, a basic loop construct—*repeat until* and a conditional *if* construct. We also see the need to bring information into the system from external sensors. What form does that information take? What types of variables are we going to use? But we are getting a little ahead of ourselves.

Today's computers, embedded or not, cannot accept a problem stated in a natural language. Thus, the first step must be:

> **Step 1.** Translation of the problem statement into a more computer-compatible form.

6.1.2 High-Level Language

We will see that all our design activities simply involve translating the problem from one form into another until we achieve a representation the computer hardware can accept and respond to. In the current case, we translate into the C language. This translation is done by hand today, although times are changing.

program
high-level language

This translation process is what we call software design or programming, and the result of the translation is a *program*. The program is written in what is called a *high-level language*. At this point, a variety of different translations are possible; they are not unique. They differ with the problem's constraints and with the person performing the translation. This is also the stage during which we have the most creative freedom.

With the program in hand, additional levels of translation are still necessary.

Step 2. More translation.

object code

The program, expressed in a high-level language, must be translated into a form that the microprocessor can understand, a collection of 0's and 1's that is called *object code*. At this stage, the object code is incomplete and thus cannot be used by the microprocessor without further processing. Now the problem becomes a little more complex. More questions need to be answered, however. Namely, how are different versions of the target language accommodated if necessary? Can the object code execute on different target machines or run on different operating systems? The first high-level model of the next translation process looks like the block diagram in Figure 6.1.

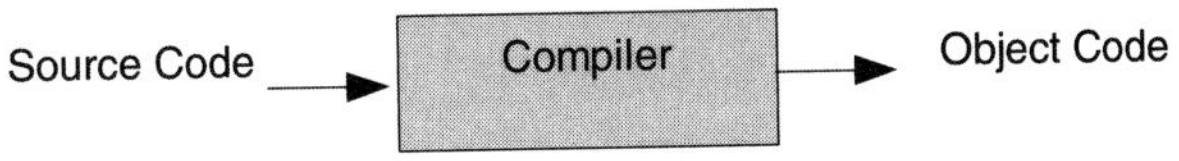

Figure 6.1 Translating from Source Code to Object Code

Let's now look inside the block.

6.1.3 Preprocessor

preprocessor
compiler

At this stage, we can bring in some tools to help in the process. The first such tool, called a *preprocessor*, performs several mechanical operations to prepare a source file for the *compiler*. Such duties include macro processing, selecting source text for compilation, or incorporating different shared files into the file that will ultimately be compiled.

The block diagram now takes on the expanded view shown in Figure 6.2.

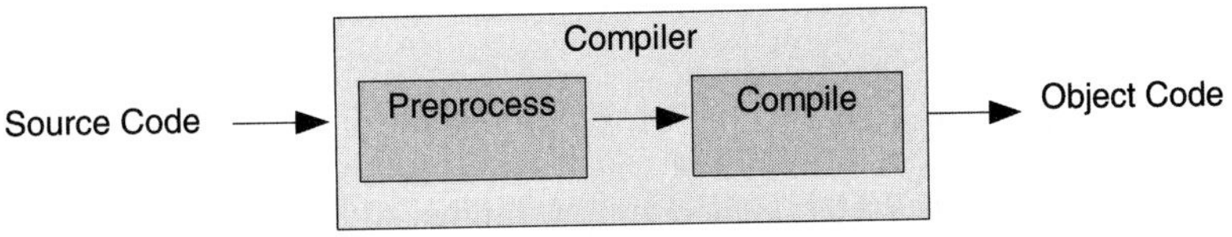

Figure 6.2 Translating from Source Code to Object Code—An Expanded View

6.1.4 Cross Compiler

cross compiler
assembly language

The compiler (more specifically here, a *cross compiler*—more on this shortly) is a tool for translating programs into a variety of forms. One such form is *assembly language.*

We note that prior to this stage, the program is independent of the target microprocessor. If the program is written well, in theory, one should be able to compile any program written in a high-level language (C in our case, which is portable) into an assembly language program that executes on any specific target microprocessor architecture.

cross compiler
development platform
target machine

Enter the cross compiler. A *cross compiler* is a compiler that runs on one machine, typically the *development platform*, and generates code for a different machine, typically, the *target machine*.

6.1.5 Assembler

assembler
machine language

The *assembler* is the next tool we use for continuing the series of translation steps. The assembler converts the collection of assembly language steps into *machine language.* Machine language represents each of the program's instructions as a specific collection of 0's and 1's that the machine is designed to understand. We are not finished yet.

The level of detail in the block diagram is increased one more time as illustrated in Figure 6.3.

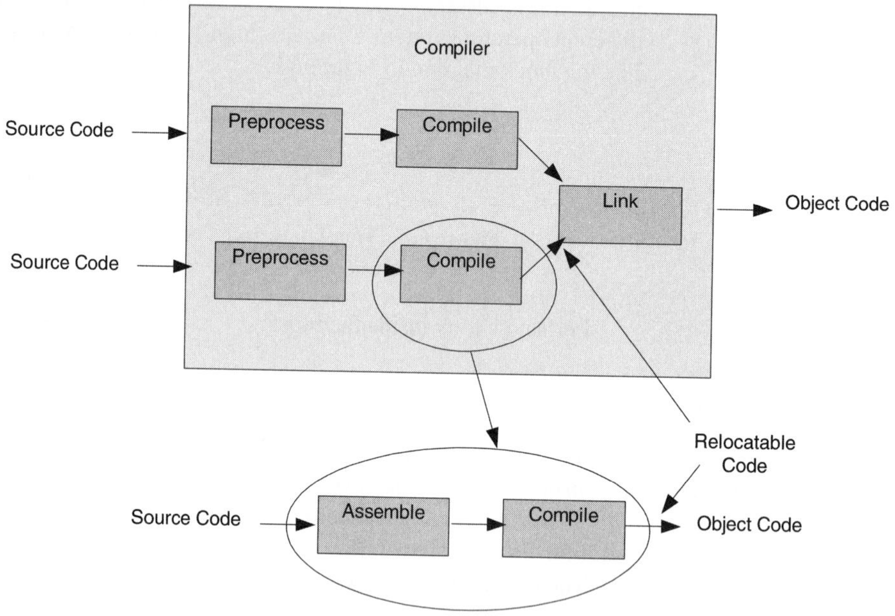

Figure 6.3 Translating from Source Code to Object Code—More Detail

6.1.6 Linker and Loader

linker and loader

The *linker and loader* now follow. Although the program is now in machine language, it is not ready to be executed. The problem is that all variables and data structures used in the program must reside in computer memory, and each needs an address in memory. The next question we can ask is, which address should be used? To solve this problem, the assembler

relocatable code

generates *relocatable code*—code that can be placed anywhere in memory. A second question now arises.

When developing software solutions, it is beneficial to be able to use existing code. By reusing code, we can reduce development time as well as costs. Such code may be from previous projects or be purchased as specialized pieces of functionality. How can such code be incorporated into the program without retyping everything? The tool called the *linker-loader* can help with both problems.

linker-loader

The linker-loader tool does two jobs: it links a collection of program modules together, and it resolves (or identifies) address problems. To see how this works, consider the following two diagrams. The first, in Figure 6.4, shows the movement through the tools involved in the translation sequence, and the second shows some of the changes to the modules comprising the program in greater detail. There are others, but we will pass over them for the moment.

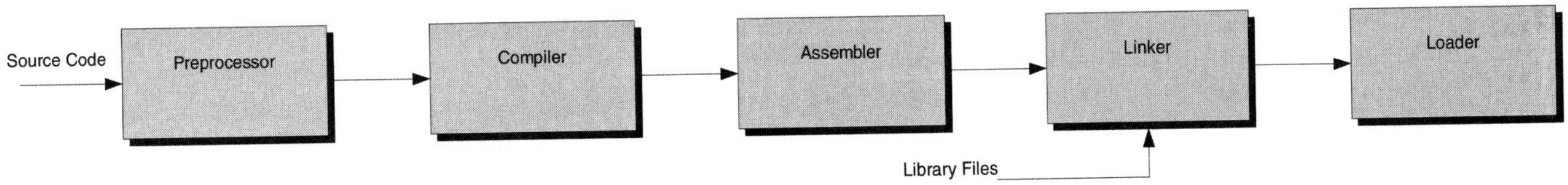

Figure 6.4 Translating from Source Code to Object Code—Flow Through the Tools

The original program contains two user-written modules and one library module. In the diagram in Figure 6.5, it is assumed that the preprocessing step has been completed.

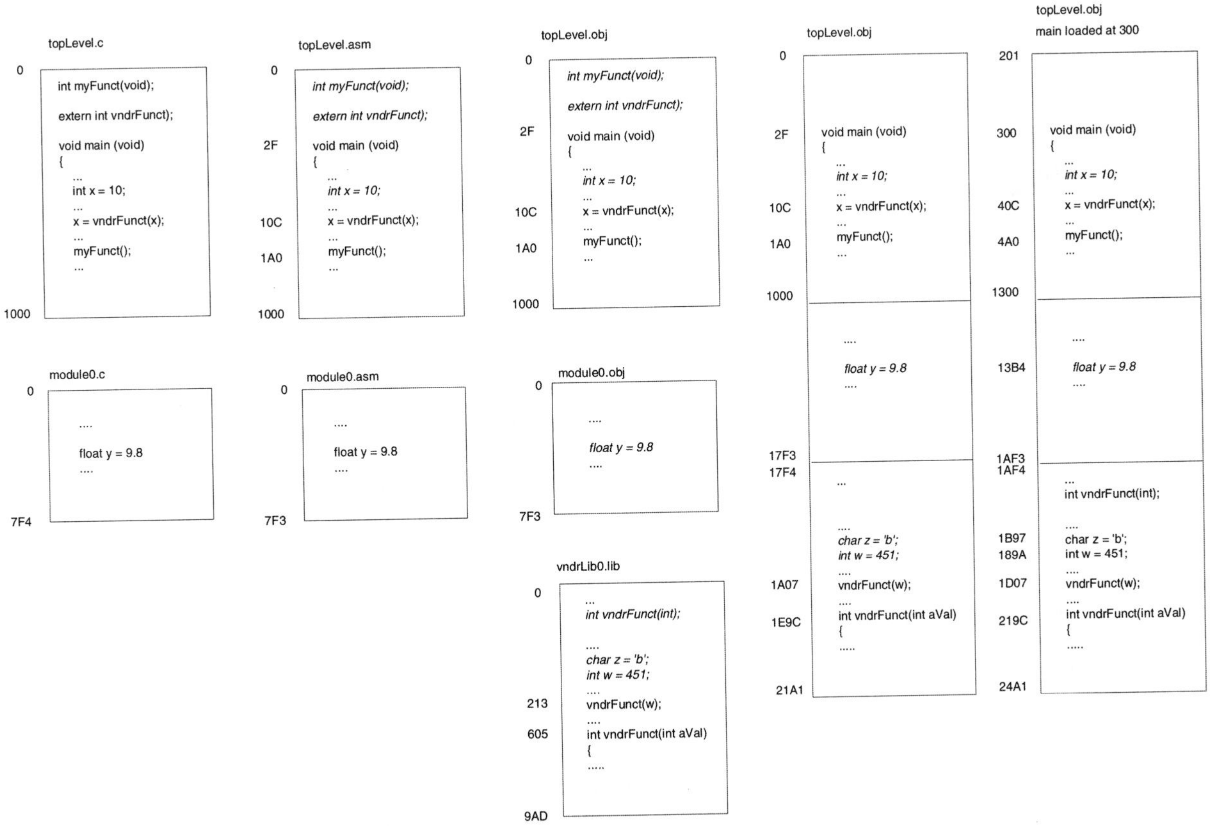

Figure 6.5 Translating from Source Code to Object Code Flow Through the Tools Expanded

The sizes of each module and the location of several of the variables and functions, with respect to the start of the module, are shown. Note that the function prototypes and external declarations do not become part of the final code and are therefore not assigned addresses.

The compiler translates each of the two C modules into the assembly language for the target machine. During that process, the names of all variables are identified, and an entry for each is made in a table called the *symbol table*. If the compiler is able to identify an address within the module for each variable, that information is associated with the variable in the symbol table. If it cannot, and it hasn't been told that the variable is defined in some other module (via the extern directive), it cites the variable as being undefined.

symbol table

If the extern directive is present to tell the compiler to defer concerns about the definition, that it has been taken care of, and if when the linker arrives and the linker cannot find that definition, the process ends with a *link error*.

link error

Note that the locations of each variable are still with respect to the start of the module wherein it was defined.

relocatable

The assembler translates the assembly language program into what is called *relocatable* object or machine code, leaving the variable locations unchanged. In the diagrams, the variables that will ultimately go on the stack are shown in italics. The linker accepts the two object modules from the assembler, and the library file then links the three together.

Linking involves combining all of the machine code into a single file and re-referencing all addresses to the start (address 0) of the new module. When the C program begins execution, it is looking for the location of *main()*. The location of *main()* in instruction code space is dependent on the machine on which it is executing. It is the job of the loader to modify all variable addresses to reflect the start of the program.

main()

Step 3. Into Memory.

6.1.7 Storing

The process is not yet complete; several more stages remain. At this point, the linker and loader have prepared the program to go into memory. For an embedded application, this means going into some form of nonvolatile memory such as a flash-type ROM. Once the program begins to run, the instructions and data will be taken into RAM, cache, and various registers. Adding these, we complete the job. We have now seen how to take the problem, expressed in a natural language, and turn it into something that can be solved by a computer. It sounds easy—take the problem, add some knowledge, imagination, and creativity, bring them together, and we have it.

We will now look at the pieces of the C language that make all this possible, and we will also describe some of the mechanical steps that are necessary to bring the complete program together.

6.2 AN EMBEDDED C PROGRAM

6.2.1 A Program

We begin with the program. Whether embedded or running on a desktop computer, a program is a sequence of instructions that directs the computer hardware and software to solve a problem. One can immediately ask, "Is any set of instructions satisfactory?" "Are some instructions better than others?" "If some are, what defines a good set of instructions and what defines a bad set?"

Starting with the machine, the computer, we recognize that it is simply that—a machine. Some of the fun science fiction movies notwithstanding, today's machine is a rigid, dispassionate pile of silicon and wires designed and built to react in precise ways. The program directing its operations is a large collection of instructions organized as algorithms and computational procedures to perform some task. The difference between the hoped for performance and the actual performance is evidence of human failure to instruct the computer properly. Nonetheless, who gets the blame for the bugs or errors in the machine's operation? The computer, of course.

1. Performance
2. Robustness
3. Ease of change
4. Style

Figure 6.6 Program Design Goals

Our mission as designers of embedded software programs is to write programs that solve a problem and that are bug free and, of course, to have fun doing it. We approach the first of these goals asymptotically; specifically, they are listed in Figure 6.6.

performance ***robust*** ***ease of change*** ***style***

Quantifying each goal, we find that *performance* must begin with solving the problem. It is then measured by assessing certain characteristics or attributes of that program such as its size, speed, or utility to name a few. A *robust* program is tolerant of failure conditions, misuse, unexpected inputs, side effects, or boundary conditions on inputs or computed data. *Ease of change* demands modularity and support for modification, reuse, or addition of new features. Good design and coding *style* include clarity in the algorithms and control flow through the code, modularity, readability, proper use of indentation and white space, and documentation.

6.2.2 Developing Embedded Software

specification, design

Software can be developed from the top down, the bottom up, or a combination of both. Major pieces in the process begin with formulating a good specification, then executing the design, doing the coding, and debugging the code, and finally testing the product. There are two key points here. First, one should devote most of one's attention to the top of the list—the *specification* and the *design*. Second, no amount of debugging and testing can turn a poorly specified and designed application into a good one. Too often, people do the reverse. Comments such as "We have to get the product out, we don't have the luxury to spend time designing" or "We have to get coding done because there's a lot of debugging to do" are sure steps to project and product failure. Specification and design should be about 70 to 80% of the job, while code and test should be the remainder—not the reverse.

Let's now look at a couple of terms and concepts that we will encounter throughout the design and development process.

Abstraction

All computer programming involves working with real-world things; this is even more the case with embedded applications. Inputs, outputs, and algorithms come from real-world things: motors, sensors, communications ports, switches, and other systems. When we write a program, the focus is on those aspects of that information necessary for the application; the rest is discarded. The real world is abstracted from volts, current, or other quantities to ints, floats, chars, or more complex data structures.

Abstraction is the ability to minimize or eliminate details that are unimportant or nonessential while focusing on those that are important. With abstraction, the focus is on the essential elements of the problem; details that are not immediately important are ignored.

levels

Different *levels* of abstraction are possible. At the higher *levels*, the concern focuses on the major elements of the design; at the lower levels, it turns to the detailed elements of the design. As we study the design and development of embedded applications, the concept of abstraction will come up time and time again. To be successful at designing embedded systems, one must learn to change how one thinks about problems and how the real world is viewed.

Let's now take a look at some of the elements of the C language that will be of use as we learn to design embedded systems. For those of you already comfortable with C, it is okay to briefly skim over the highlights. A more extended review of the material on basic pointers and pointers to functions might prove beneficial.

6.3 C BUILDING BLOCKS

With an understanding of the general structure of an embedded C program, we will next examine, to a much greater depth, the fundamental pieces that we use to build such a program. We will begin with the data types that are specified as part of the C language. These are known as the *intrinsic* (or built-in) types.

intrinsic

6.3.1 Fundamental Data—What's in a Name?

Identifiers in C

variable, function, identifier

The name of a *variable* or a *function* in C is called an *identifier*. Although any combination of symbols could be used, the ANSI/ISO C standard establishes some restrictions as to what constitutes a legal identifier.

- An identifier is case-sensitive.

  As we noted earlier, this means that main() and MAIN() are two different functions.
- The first character of an identifier must be an alphabetic character or an underscore.

  While some compilers permit a $, this is nonstandard and should be avoided.

  Some vendors prefix proprietary identifiers with one or two underscores. The ANSI/ISO C standard has specific rules allowing vendors to do this. Consequently, it is best to avoid using identifiers that begin with a single or double underscore; otherwise, the local variable identifiers may conflict with some in a library file, for example.
- Typically, variable and function identifiers begin with a lower case letter, and symbolic constants are written with all upper case letters, although neither is required.
- Identifiers cannot be a C keyword.

  return or *int* cannot be used as identifiers, for example.
- Identifiers should be as descriptive as possible.

  Using descriptive identifiers makes any program easier to read and less prone to errors if someone else is trying to modify or upgrade it.
- ANSI/ISO standard identifiers have no length limit.

> ***Caution:*** Several compilers claim unlimited length identifiers and yet specify that identifiers must be unique only in the first 32 bytes. This requirement is not standard; refer to the compiler documentation to be certain.

EXAMPLE 6.0

Consider the following declarations,

```
int t1 = 98.6;
int temperature1 = 98.6;
```

Both are legal identifiers. Which conveys more information?

6.3.2 Defining Variables—Giving Them a Name and a Value

declare, define
declared, namespace

The C language permits one to *declare* and *define* different kinds of variables. When a variable is *declared*, that variable's name is brought into the *namespace* of the program. It can now be referred to by other entities within the program. However, no memory is allocated.

defined

When a variable is *defined*, memory *is* allocated. The definition automatically specifies how much memory is needed to store the variable, quantifies the characteristics of that storage, and associates the name (identifier) for the variable with that piece of storage. The word *type* is used to denote the information expressed in a declaration.

type

EXAMPLE 6.1

The expression

```
int age;
```

declaration, definition
identifier, age
integer

is a *declaration* and a *definition* for a variable. The line of code says that the name of the variable, its *identifier*, is the word *age* (the declaration) and that sufficient memory is to be allocated to hold an *integer*-type variable (the definition).

---

limits.h, float.h
include
initialize

At this point, without knowing the target machine, one cannot know the size (number of bits) of the variable. The system files *limits.h* and *float.h* specify the sizes for integral and floating point types, respectively, for the specific machine. Generally, these files will be found in the *include* subdirectory where the compiler was installed.

One should always *initialize* a variable with a value at the point that it is defined:

```
int age = 21;
```

assigned

A new value may be *assigned* anytime thereafter:

```
age = 40;
```

assignment operator
initialize, assign

using the *assignment operator:* =

Observe that one can *initialize* a variable only once; one can *assign* to it as often as needed.

equality
gets, equals

We will talk more about *equality* shortly. For now, it is sufficient to know that the equality operator is ==; that is, *two* equal signs. It is very easy to confuse these two operators, so be very careful when you are coding. To emphasize the difference between assignment and equality, we pronounce = as *gets* and == as *equals*.

When one declares and defines a variable in C, it is not automatically assigned a value. The variable does have a value, however; that value is whatever the current state of the bits in the memory location assigned to the variable. That value will most likely be different each time the system is powered up. This is why it is important to always assign an initializing value when the variable is defined.

Important Points

- The *declaration* of a variable or function makes its name visible to the program. *No* memory is allocated.
- The *definition* of a variable or function directs the compiler to allocate memory to hold the variable or the body of the function.
- Finally, initialization occurs one time only, when a variable is defined. Thereafter, a value is assigned to the variable.

6.3.3 Defining Variables—Giving Them a Type, Scope, and Storage Class

type, scope, storage class

Each variable in a C program is characterized by its *type*, *scope*, and *storage* class. We have already introduced the notion of type; scope and storage class further characterize the identifiers. These all must be taken into consideration as one designs both the hardware and software portions of an embedded application.

6.3.3.1 Type

name, type

A variable is a piece of memory used in a program to hold data. Each variable also has an associated identifier, its *name,* by which it is referred to in a program. Each also has a *type* that specifies its size, that is, how much memory is needed to store it. It's a bit like barrels—we have a number of different types or sizes of barrels. These are 10-, 20-, 50-, 100-, or 500-liter containers. Obviously, each holds a different amount of stuff. Also, it is pretty obvious that trying to put the contents of a 100-liter barrel into a 10-liter barrel is going to be a problem. Furthermore, putting salt in a container labeled sugar can give the user of either product some rather unexpected reactions.

INTRINSIC TYPES

intrinsic types
fundamental types
integral types,
floating point types

As we look around the real world, we see that we measure things by a number of different units: inches, feet, yards, miles, centimeters, meters, kilometers, grams, kilograms, and so on. These are standards; they are intrinsic units of measure. C does the same thing. The language specifies a number of standard numeric types. These are predefined types of variables with known sizes. Such numeric types are called the *intrinsic types* or are sometimes also called *fundamental types.* The language classifies intrinsic types into two major groups: *integral types* and *floating point types.* We studied each of these earlier from a hardware point of view when we learned how to represent information in a computer. Let's now take a look at them from a software perspective.

INTEGRAL TYPES

integral types, integer

Integral types are whole numbers; they have no fractional part. The *integer* is probably the most familiar of the integral types. Others differ in the number of bits of required storage. The number of bits of memory space occupied by an integral variable depends on its type and the architecture of the machine for which the program is to be run on. In the embedded world, typical word sizes for different microprocessors are 4, 8, 16, or 32 bits. As a user, we must always refer to and work with the hardware and software documentation accompanying our tools and target environment.

unsigned, signed

The ANSI/ISO C language standard defines integral types listed in Figure 6.7. Integral types may be either *unsigned* or *signed.* By default all the types identified here are signed—yes, chars are signed by default. A signed integer can express either a positive or a negative

chart
short
int
long

Figure 6.7 ANSI/ISO C Integral Types

value; an unsigned integer can only be positive. Unsigned integral types are specified by using the C keyword *unsigned* in the definition.

EXAMPLE 6.2

To define an unsigned integer with a value of 25, we write

```
unsigned int aNotherNumber = 25;
```

On a number line, an unsigned integer has the expressive power shown in Figure 6.8, where n is the number of bits in the word.

On a 16-bit machine, the format for an unsigned integer is given in Figure 6.9.

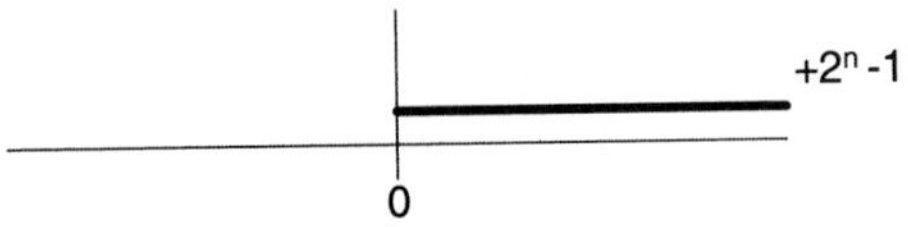

Figure 6.8 Expressive Power of an Unsigned Integer

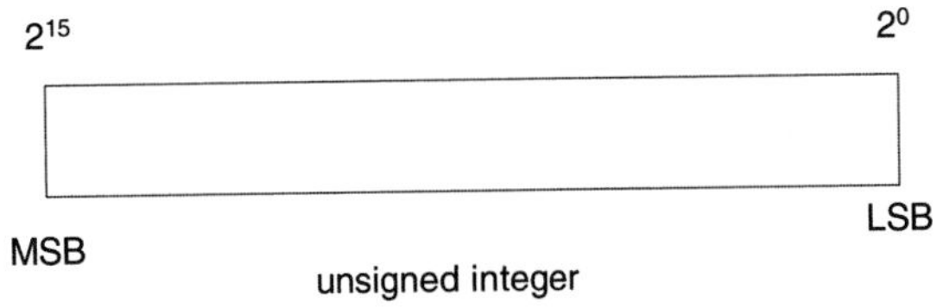

Figure 6.9 Format of a 16-Bit Unsigned Integer

EXAMPLE 6.3

To define a signed integer with a value of –25 in a program, one writes

```
signed int aNumber = -25;
```

or simply

```
int aNumber = -25;
```

---

signed The second form is permitted because the language standard stipulates that all integers are *signed* by default. When a signed integer is specified, the number line shifts to the left and the expressive power is modified as shown in Figure 6.10.

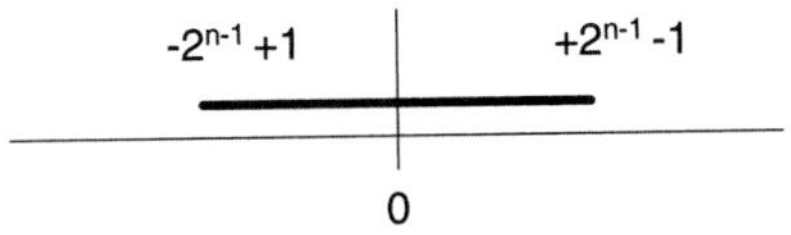

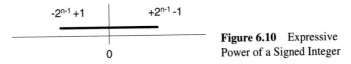

Figure 6.10 Expressive Power of a Signed Integer

Inside the microprocessor, if the Most Significant Bit of an unsigned number is reinterpreted as a sign bit, then, for a 16-bit machine, the format for a signed integer is given as in Figure 6.11.

Binary 0 is used to indicate a positive sign and binary 1 a negative sign.

Based on such a format, the expressive power for these two variable types is given as

unsigned integer	$0..2^{15}-1$
signed integer	$\pm\ 0..2^{14}-1$

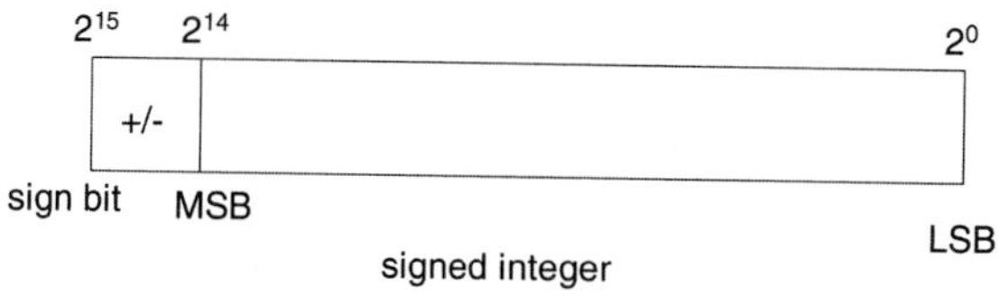

Figure 6.11 Format of a 16-Bit Signed Integer

Observe that we have lost one number using the signed notation. There are now two representations for the number 0, a positive version and a negative one.

The numbers, expressed as hex numbers, will appear in memory, as illustrated in Figure 6.12.

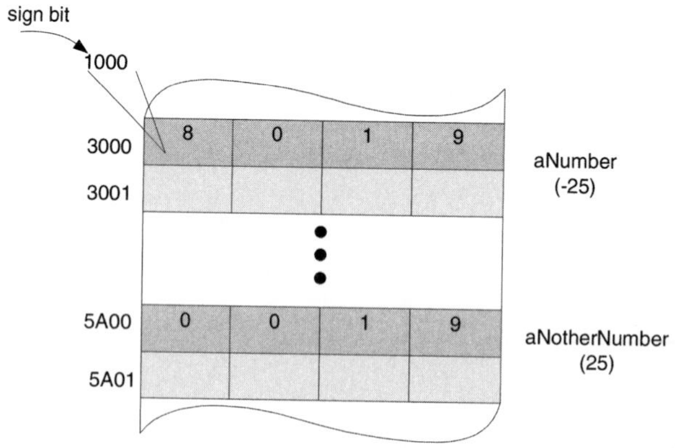

Figure 6.12 Two 16-Bit Signed Integers in Memory

aNumber
nibble

For the (negatively) signed integer *aNumber*, the sign bit (the most significant bit of the number) results in a most significant *nibble* (4 bits) with hex value 0x8. The unsigned integer has a most significant nibble with value of hex 0x0.

> ### *For Future Reference*
>
> Observe that each of these numbers resides at an address in memory. We can identify the variable either by its name (which is not stored) or by its address (where it has been stored).

Interpret the MSB as the sign of the number
Use the full expressive power of the type

Why use an unsigned integer anyway? This is a very good question. Numbers are stored in the microprocessor memory as binary bits. For signed numbers, one of the bits is used to indicate polarity of number—typically the most significant bit. Writing signed or using the default says to the compiler: *Interpret the MSB as the sign of the number.* Writing unsigned tells the compiler: *Use the full expressive power of the type.* We want all of the bits in the word to be interpreted as part of the data.

In an embedded design, the microprocessor's I/O ports are used to send signals to or to read from various kinds of external devices as we see in Figure 6.13. If a word is read from a digital imager and written into memory, for example, all of the bits contain relevant pixel information. The bits should not be interpreted as a negative value if the MSB is a 1.

CHAR INTEGER TYPE

char

The integral type *char* has historically been used to represent characters. By assigning a value to a char, we are, in effect, assigning a character to that variable. Today, there are two different sizes of char. The traditional char is 8 bits, 1 byte. The Unicode char, used for expressing Asian, Middle Eastern, or similar types of characters, is 16 bits, 2 bytes.

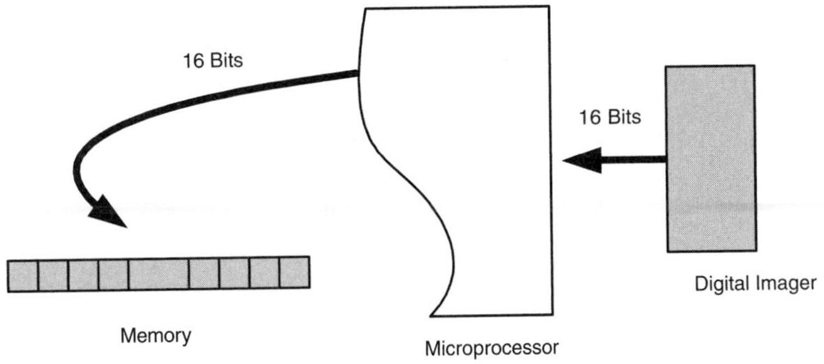

Figure 6.13 Reading from an External Device into Memory

The format for these char integer types, expressed in a 16-bit word, is depicted in Figure 6.14.

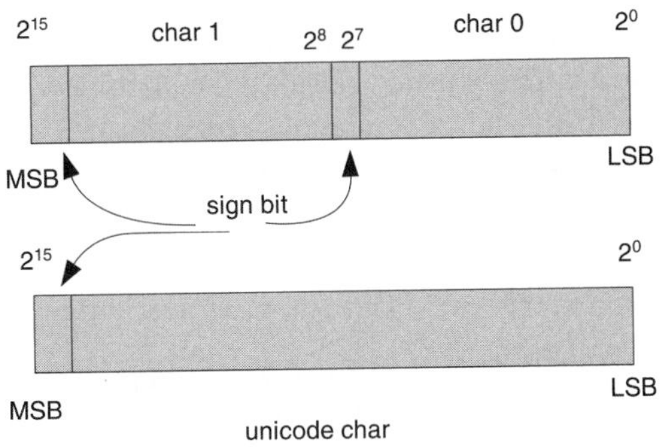

Figure 6.14 Format of the Character Integral Type

Because the char is an integral type, it is signed by default.

EXAMPLE 6.4

ASCII

American Standard Code for Information Interchange

If one is using the *ASCII* code (ASCII is the acronym for *American Standard Code for Information Interchange*), then

```
char x = 'A';
char y = 65;
```

both of the above lines of code do the same thing since the integer 65 *is* the decimal value of the ASCII character A.

---

null character

Note that there is a difference between the integer 0 and the character 0. Failure to notice the difference can result in a difficult to find program bug. The integer zero is written as 0. That is, all bits are 0. A char integer with a value of zero is often referred to as a *null character*. On the other hand '0' has a value of 48 in the ASCII character set. If the objective is to compare something to zero but we use '0', we are actually comparing to the integer 48. When working with integers and characters, always make certain which one is intended, the integer interpretation or the character interpretation.

SHORT INTEGER TYPE

short

The *short* integral type, as the name suggests, is a short integer. It was commonly used in the early days of computing (when memory was expensive) to express small integer values.

Typically, it is one-half the size of the integer. In embedded applications, memory is still expensive. Consequently, it is not unusual to use either chars or shorts to express integer numbers. In embedded applications, one typically selects the smallest type that will suffice for the task at hand.

LONG INTEGER TYPE

long

The *long* integral type is the opposite of a short integral type and probably evolved in the same way. The long is used when an integral type is needed, but the size of the integer on the machine is too small to express the magnitude of the number and floating point numbers are either not available or not preferred. Typically, it is twice the size of the integer.

FLOATING POINT TYPES

We have seen how to use integral types to express information in a microprocessor. With integral types, the size of a number one can express is determined by the number of bits in an integer for the target machine. The microprocessor in the early PCs expressed integers as 16-bit words; therefore, the largest positive integer number that could be expressed was 65,536. Although one seldom has to work with and manage the national debt, in an embedded application, there are times when it is necessary to represent larger numbers. To do so, one must use a different data type called the *floating point* type.

floating point type

Because mathematical operations using floating point numbers are more complex, slower, and consume more memory than those using integral types, most compilers for embedded targets do not automatically load the floating point math packages. It is up to the user to specifically request that they be included in the build.

Note

Whenever we work with floating point numbers, we are going to lose precision. Some floats are irrational, and we generally don't have sufficient memory to be able to store an unlimited number of bits.

So that we can fit it into available storage, we either round or truncate the number. The error is the same in either case but is more evenly distributed, and the maximum error is less if we round rather than truncate.

The representation for a floating point number is a bit more complex than that for an integral type. It is important, however, to recognize that the bits are the same (although there may be more of them); it is the *interpretation* of those bits that becomes more complex.

interpretation

In a 16-bit machine, a float is typically expressed using 32 bits. This means that a floating point number will occupy two consecutive words of memory, twice as much as is required for a basic integer. To see how the number is expressed in the computer, first remember how floating point numbers are written using scientific notation. For the number

```
+11.287593
```

the conversion algorithm is:

- Move the *decimal point* immediately to the left of the leftmost digit.
- Multiply the resulting number by the appropriate power of 10 to retain the original value.

Thus, we write:

$$+0.11287593 \times 10^{+2}$$

The same rule applies when we are working with binary numbers. The rules are now:

- Move the *binary point* immediately to the left of the leftmost one.
- Multiply the resulting number by the appropriate power of 2 to retain the original value.

sign, number, exponent, sign of the exponent

When a number is expressed in scientific notation, four important pieces of information must be stored: the *sign* of the number, the *number* itself, the *exponent*, and the *sign of the exponent*.

A floating point number can now be represented as shown in Figure 6.15.

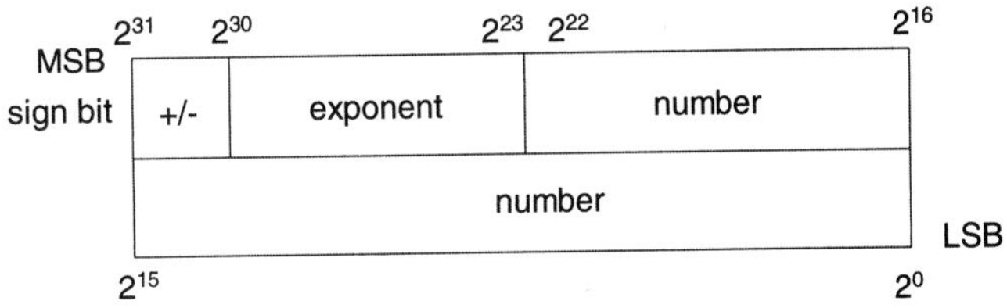

Figure 6.15 Format of the Floating Point Type

and the expressive power given as

$$\pm(2^{22} - 1) \times 2^{(2^8 - 1)}$$

With 8 bits allocated to the exponent, one can either accommodate positive exponents or support exponents in the range of ± 7.

To avoid having to store the sign, 127 is added to the exponent to move it from the range ± 127 to the range +0.255 as is evident from the graphic in Figure 6.16. (Please see Chapter 1 for a discussion of the IEEE Hidden Bit Format standard for increasing the expressive power of floating point numbers.)

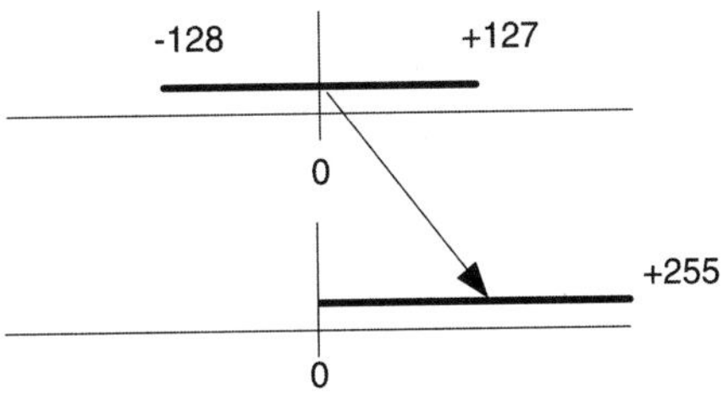

Figure 6.16 Representing the Floating Point Type Exponent

The ANSI/ISO C language standard specifies two floating point types:

float

double

significant figures

Each of these types contains the same maximum exponent; the double allows for more *significant figures*—more bits to the right of binary point. There is even a long double that contains even more significant bits.

6.3.3.2 The const Qualifier

The *const* qualifier is now a part of ANSI/ISO C where it is used to declare or specify a constant. One immediate application of the const qualifier is as a replacement for the #define preprocessor directive. The major advantage of such a replacement is that #define statements are handled by the preprocessor; therefore, there is no type checking. The const qualifier is interpreted by the compiler and therefore has all of the associated benefits of type checking and optimization.

The const semantics gives the programmer the means to specify that a particular object should not be changed. The compiler will enforce that requirement.

The declaration

```
const int speed = 60;
```

speed transforms the symbolic variable, *speed,* into the symbolic constant, *speed,* within the scope of speed. Now writing

```
speed = 70;
```

is illegal.

Similarly,

```
const int speed;
speed = 60
```

is illegal. One must always assign an initializing value at the time the const is declared and defined.

6.3.3.3 Variable Names Revisited

Consider the following declarations:

```
unsigned int i = 3;                                      // set i to 3
unsigned char x = 0xC;                                   // initialize x to hex C
unsigned int maxTemperatureLimitOnStarboardEngine = 500; // set temperature limit
```

The first two declarations give no indication as to the purpose of either variable. The comments do nothing to improve the situation. To complicate matters further, choosing 'i' as a variable name makes searching for it in a large file rather difficult. The third declaration certainly explains the purpose of the variable. However, now there is too much information. Searching for that variable begins with trying to type in the name.

Now let's try

```
unsigned int maxTempEngine1 = UPPER_LIMIT;     // UPPER_LIMIT is 500
```

The name is shortened, and we are using a symbolic constant rather than a magic number. The comment provides a reminder of the actual value that had been defined as a symbolic constant earlier in the program.

Coding Style

When we are declaring variables in our code, we should always select names that are meaningful and reflective of the intent of the variable. In addition, any annotation associated with the variable should add information rather than repeating the obvious.

6.3.3.4 Type Conversions

casting, implicit

We have now learned about the primitive data types supported by the C language. As we work with those types, we will find that at times we have to convert from one type to another. Such a process is called *casting*. We begin by looking at *implicit*-type conversions.

IMPLICIT-TYPE CONVERSIONS

intrinsic type

safe, promotions

doubles, floats, long, long double

An implicit-type or side-effect conversion occurs when the compiler needs to convert data from one *intrinsic type* to data of another *intrinsic type*. Such conversions take place silently without the programmer's knowledge. Implicit conversions that preserve values are said to be *safe* and are commonly called *promotions*. Before an arithmetic operation is performed, integral promotion is used to create *int*s out of shorter integral types and floating point conversions to make *doubles* out of *floats*. Promotions will not promote to a *long* or to a *long double*.

The integral promotions are as follows:

```
char, signed char, unsigned char, short int, or unsigned short int →
int.
bool   → int
false  → 0
true   → 0
true   → 1
```

Let's look at several example conversions.

INTEGRAL PROMOTIONS

EXAMPLE 6.5

Let's look at the simple program in Figure 6.17.

```
#include <stdio.h>
// Execution on a 32 bit machine
void main(void)
{
    // declare some variables
    short myShort = 2;
    int myInt = 3;
    myInt = myShort;
    printf("myInt %i\n", myInt);            // prints 2

    myInt = 3;
    myShort = myInt;
    printf("myShort %i\n", myShort);        // prints 3

    myInt = 32767;
    myShort = myInt;
    printf("myShort %i\n", myShort);        // prints 32767

    myInt = 100000;
    myShort = myInt;
    printf("myShort %i\n", myShort);        // prints -31072
    return;
}
```

Figure 6.17 Integral Promotions

The assignment of myShort to myInt is safe

```
myInt = myShort
```

short, int

because a *short* (typically 16 bits on a 32-bit machine) can fit inside an *int* (32 bits on a 32-bit machine). The conversion takes place as a side effect of the assignment operation.

The first assignment of *myInt* to *myShort* will work because the value of the integer, 3, can be expressed in fewer than 16 bits, but the assignment will probably generate a compiler warning.

myInt, myShort

In the next assignment, *myInt* could have an integer as large as 32767, and the assignment would still give the correct results since 2^{16} is 65536.

```
myShort = myInt;
```

What will display if the integer is first assigned the value 65536 and then assigned to the short as shown above? If the value 100000 is assigned to the integer, what will print?

Both of these assignments will create a problem. The value that is being assigned exceeds the expressive power of the type. What if such a line of code was included in a design and the variable myInt was subsequently permitted to take on the range of values that have been described?

> ***Caution:*** We must be extremely careful in making such implicit or side-effect casts. By using them, we are creating a situation in which the program will work sometimes and not others, or will give erroneous results based on the magnitude of the data values. Such problems are extremely difficult to debug.

FLOATING POINT CONVERSIONS

Because floating point conversions cannot be guaranteed to preserve values, they are not called promotions. Converting a float to a double is safe, but converting a double to a float is safe only if the value in the double will fit in the float. If it won't, the results are not defined.

As with all implicit conversions, the compiler is not obligated to issue a warning. Floating point conversion to an integer works fine as long as the integer variable is large enough to hold the resulting value. The decimal portion of the floating point number is truncated. If the truncated value is too large to be represented by the integer type, the conversion is undefined.

EXPLICIT TYPE CONVERSIONS

implicitly, casting
explicitly

We have seen that type conversions can occur automatically, or *implicitly*. *Casting* is a way to *explicitly* convert data from one type to another. When an explicit cast is used, we state to the compiler, "make this type change; I know what I am doing."

The cast is specified using the following syntax:

> **Syntax**
> `(targetType) sourceExpression`

EXAMPLE 6.6

The code fragment

```
unsigned int anInt = 0;
unsigned char aChar = 'b';
anInt = (unsigned int) aChar;
```

makes a copy of aChar that is of type unsigned int using an explicit cast. It then assigns the value (98—the hex representation of the character b in ASCII) of the copy to anInt.

As noted earlier, some argue that using a cast suggests an error in the original design. In general, this is probably true. However, shortly we will see several cases where the ability to cast from one type to another is a powerful and essential tool.

> ***Caution:*** When using an implicit or explicit cast, be careful and thoroughly understand what you are doing and the consequences of your actions.
>
> When you make a narrowing conversion (a conversion from a larger to a smaller type), make absolutely certain that you perform a boundary check on the value of the data prior to the assignment.
>
> Look in the header files limits.h and float.h to see the maximum and minimum legal values for any of the types you are using.

6.3.3.5 Scope

function, variable
variable or function

Let's now examine the scope of a variable or function. In this section, rather than repeating the words or *function* every time, the word *variable* is used, and complicating the issue, assume they are there. When you see *variable*, think *variable or function*.

Scope specifies a variable's visibility within the program. What does this mean? Let's present a brief digression first. The structure or architecture of a program describes how a program is organized. Certainly, a number of interesting and perhaps creative alternatives are available. On the one hand, one can have one rather large main function containing the entire program. While such a model, such as formatting a program into a single line several kilometers in length, is legal (at least theoretically), it certainly makes debugging and future modifications more of a challenge.

all-in-one

For those who find the *all-in-one* model underwhelming at best, there is the multiple module single-file approach. If designed properly, each comprising module contains related functions and subroutines. Debugging and maintenance drastically simplify things.

A more reasonable approach is to decompose the program into multiple files, each of which may contain multiple modules. The individual implementation files can be compiled and linked either at the same time or at different times.

Most contemporary designers will use the latter model. Beyond the immediate benefits of ease of maintenance, extension, and simplified development, one adds the further benefit of being able to subcontract or simply buy standard pieces of functionality that we may not have the resources to develop.

The immediate questions that arise include, "How is information and data shared among all the different pieces?" "Can the same variable name be used in multiple files?" Furthermore, if different variables can have the same name in different modules, when the program is compiled and linked together, "How does the compiler know about or sort out the identifier and storage requirements for a variable defined in one module and used in several others?"

scope

Now to the issue at hand. These questions all relate to what is defined as the *scope* of the variable's name. Scope establishes how widely a variable name is known within an application.

ANSI/ISO C specifies the three primary scopes listed in Figure 6.18.

- Program or Global
- Local
- File

Figure 6.18 ANSI/ISO Scopes

The name of each scope suggests the visibility of any variables defined therein. Visibility extends beyond simply reading the variable's value to enabling operations in other parts of the program to change that value. The three scopes in C can be modeled as the three nested boxes presented in Figure 6.19. Those inside can see out, but no one can see in.

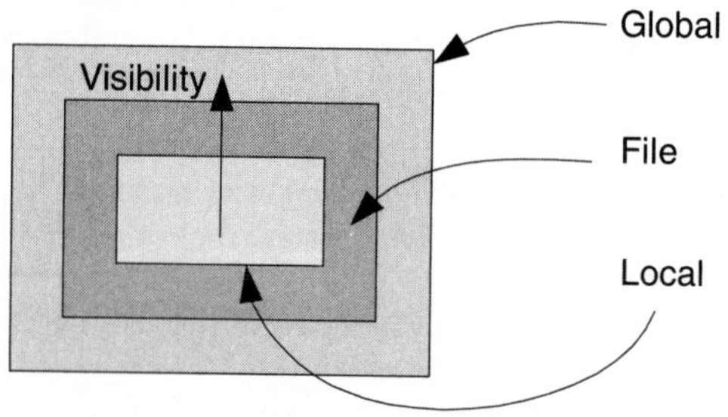

Figure 6.19 Modeling the ANSI/ISO Scopes

LOCAL

local scope

Local scope is the most restricted. Local variables are only visible within the block in which they have been declared and defined. For C, this means within the function or procedure in which they were declared. Variables in a local scope *are not initialized* upon declaration unless special provisions are made.

are not initialized

> ***Caution:*** Although a local variable is not assigned an initializing value by default—they do have a value. That value is whatever happens to be in the location in memory where the variable has been stored.

Local variables and their values exist only while program execution is within the function body where the variables are declared. Furthermore, they do not persist across invocations of the enclosing function.

FILE SCOPE VARIABLES

file scope variables, file

The visibility of *file scope variables* is limited to the *file* in which they are declared. We will discuss these in greater detail shortly in the context of storage class.

GLOBAL SCOPE AND GLOBAL VARIABLES

Before beginning any discussion of global variables, it is important to understand that such variables should only be used with extreme care and parsimony.

> ***Caution:*** *Global variables,* as their name suggests, are visible from the point of declaration until the end of the program. They are visible to every function within the program, all comprising C source files. Such visibility means that *any* function within the program can access and potentially change these variables.
>
> Problems arise because functions may change a value that others depend on.

Cautions are duly noted. As we commented earlier, in embedded applications global variables can be very useful. When they are declared, they are initialized to 0 by default in most compilers. They provide a means to share data between functions or tasks without the overhead of physically moving that data (or a reference to it) from one place to another. We save the time burden and complexity of a function call. The obvious visibility of global variables dictates that one must ensure strictly controlled access when multiple users (task or function) are supported. We will discuss such problems and alternative solutions in much greater detail when we study intertask communication a bit later.

6.3.3.6 Storage Class

- auto
- extern
- static
- register
- typedef
- volatile

Figure 6.20 ANSI/ISO Storage Classes

Storage class determines a variable's lifetime or persistence and storage location within the program. ANSI/ISO C specifies six possible storage classes/qualifiers as listed in Figure 6.20. Formalizing what we have already seen, we find that the syntax for declaring a variable is given as

Syntax
```
storage-class type variable-name
```

Let's look at each of these classes and understand their significance in an embedded application. There are three important considerations here: the variable's scope, persistence, and access privileges.

AUTO

auto
stack

The storage class *auto* is the default storage class in C. It specifies that the variable so designated is to be stored on the *stack*, that it will be local to the function using it, and that the compiler will automatically destroy it when the enclosing scope is exited.

Syntax
```
auto type variable-name
```

Because auto variables are created on the stack, one cannot declare an auto variable outside of a function; remember: main() is a function too. Furthermore, since it is the default storage class, it is not necessary to include the keyword auto as part of a declaration.

Auto variables assume the scope in which they were declared—global, file, or local. An auto variable is created and stored on the stack when program execution enters the scope in which the variable has been declared and is destroyed when execution leaves that scope.

> ***Caution:*** In embedded applications, the size of the stack is generally limited and can be exceeded if too many variables are entered.

EXTERN

declared, defined, declaration definition, extern

Every variable in a C program must be *declared* and *defined*. A *declaration* introduces the name of the variable into the namespace of the implementation file in which it was specified. A *definition* allocates memory to hold that variable. Variables declared as *extern* provide a first tool for working with multiple-file programs. As was just identified, the auto variables are local to the block or file in which they are declared and defined. The extern storage class gives the means to declare and define a variable in one implementation file (or standard or custom library) and then to use it in another. Qualifying a variable as extern prevents the compiler from generating unresolved external reference errors during individual file compilation. Rather, the unresolved external reference is marked and (hopefully) resolved by the linker later.

Syntax
```
extern type variable-name
```

The extern qualifier introduces a variable name (and hence the variable) into the namespace of a file other than the one in which it was originally declared. The named variable is now shared between the two files. Such data sharing is a common means of communication within an embedded application.

> ***Caution:*** The type specifier in an extern declaration is important. Consider the following:
>
> ```
> file0.c
>    char myVar = 'a';
> file1.c
>    extern myVar;
> ```
>
> Without the type specifier, myVar in file1.c will be treated as an integer rather than the intended char. This misinterpretation occurs because the compiler will assume the type to be an int when none is specified.

declarations *definition*

Although such a variable may be declared (and thus used) in several places throughout a program, only one piece of memory is allocated to it. The C language permits multiple *declarations* but only a single *definition*—only a single place where memory is allocated. Memory allocation is at the heart of the distinction between declaration and definition.

defined, declaration

As the compiler is building each file within a program, it is tracking all of the identifiers within the file and making sure they are *defined.* The extern *declaration* tells the compiler that the definition–allocation of memory is in another file and that the compiler is not to flag an error. All declarations, internal and external, get resolved when the linker combines all modules.

Because the external declaration brings a variable name into a file without allocating memory, the notions of scope and persistence are not relevant.

STATIC

static

We have seen that auto variables exist only as long as the program is actively executing within the scope in which they have been defined. There are times when one would like to have a variable persist for a longer time—for example, a variable in a function that indicates if a function is called and if so, how many times. A variable qualified as *static* enables one to implement such functionality. A static variable persists across multiple invocations of the containing function. The memory for such a variable is allocated in the static memory pool and initialized *once* (to 0 by default) when the program starts, and yet it lives as long as the program containing it does. The scope of static variables is local to the more restricted of the block or file in which they were declared.

The syntax is specified as

> **Syntax**
> ```
> static type variable-name
> ```

EXAMPLE 6.7

The program module in Figure 6.21 comprises one file in which two variables are declared and defined, one of which is qualified as static, and a second file in which they are used. Despite declaring them both as extern variables (thereby bringing their names into the namespace of main()) in the main file, only the nonstatic one is visible. Attempting to use the static variable results in a compile error.

```
// staticData0.c
#include <stdio.h>

// make the function name available in this file
extern unsigned int myData0;
extern unsigned int myData1;

void main (void)
{
	printf ("myData0 is: %i \n", myData0);

// results in compile error - the variable name
// is not visible
// printf ("myData1 is: %i \n", myData1);
	return;
}
```

```
// containData0.c

#include <stdio.h>

unsigned int myData0 = 3;

static unsigned int myData1 = 4;
```

Figure 6.21 Scope of the Static Storage Classes

REGISTER

Registers are the fastest type of hardware storage and are the closest to the CPU of all the memory in the microprocessor. Ideally, therefore, one would like to be able to store all the variables in registers, particularly in designs with very tight time constraints.

recommend

To take advantage of the speed that such registers offer, one can *recommend* to the compiler that it place certain variables into registers. Such a recommendation tells the compiler that the variable may be heavily used and that, by placing it in a register, its access time is minimized. The goal is faster and smaller programs. In certain embedded applications with tight time constraints, such an advantage in time can mean the difference between meeting and not meeting the specification.

Such a qualification, however, is only a recommendation; the compiler does not have to follow it. It may be the case that the compiler does not have a register available at the time the request is made, so it may not be granted.

One of the more powerful features in RISC architectures is that they include a large number of registers, sometimes as many as 1000. In contrast, in CISC architectures one typically finds 8 to 128. Using the register qualification for large numbers of variables may be counterproductive. Frequently, today, using the qualification with highly optimizing compilers may have little effect. Such compilers typically allocate variables to register as necessary without recommendation.

The syntax is specified as

Syntax

```
register type variable-name
```

A register variable can only have local scope or be declared a function parameter. Registered global variables are not permitted. In addition, such variables are restricted to those types that can fit into a register on the microprocessor. Because they are in a physical hardware register, not in the larger RAM memory, one cannot take the address of a register variable.

The persistence of a register variable is the same as that for an auto variable. The best place to use them is in tight loops where access speed is important in minimizing the loop time and they are not going to change often. Access to a registered variable is limited to their scope.

TYPEDEF

typedef The final storage class is the *typedef*, which is not actually a new storage class. The typedef qualifier permits the user to define synonyms for an existing type. It provides new data type ***names*** *names*. It does not actually create a new type—it can only create a new name for an existing type. The new name acts like an alias for an existing data type. That data type can be either simple or complex.

The syntax is specified as

Syntax

```
typedef type synonym
```

The typedef is in scope from the time of its definition. The notion of persistence is not applicable, and access to or utilization of a typedefed variable is limited to the scope of the original variable. The typedef is similar to the preprocessor #define macro. The difference is that typedef's are managed by the compiler (with appropriate type management) rather than the preprocessor, which merely substitutes text.

EXAMPLE 6.8

uint The following typedef allows us to define *uint* as a synonym for an unsigned int. Thereafter, the alias can be used as one would use any other type qualifier.

```
typedef unsigned int uint;
uint myVar = 0x56;
```

One should be careful when using typedefs. It is easy to redefine and thereby completely obfuscate and transmogrify the language. One should use the typedef to clarify code and make it more readable.

VOLATILE

volatile Like the typedef, the keyword *volatile* is not a storage class; rather, it is a qualifier. Volatile is not something that one encounters in routine desktop applications. It is more likely to appear in embedded applications involving asynchronous internal or external tasks or specific memory locations used by hardware devices. Volatile is also used in system programming involving multiple processes and threads.

The volatile qualifier tells the compiler that the variable so qualified can be modified by processes outside of the current process or program. Therefore, it should be excluded from any attempts by the compiler to optimize it in any way because its value may change at any time. Its value needs to be read every time even if the value was just read by the previous instruction. The volatile qualifier can be viewed as the opposite of const.

6.4 C PROGRAM STRUCTURE

At the start of the chapter, we studied the process of how an embedded application, written in the C language, is designed, built, and ultimately turned into machine code that becomes the firmware that is stored in the system and executed by the embedded microprocessor. We will now analyze the structure of the C program itself. Generally, such a program is built from multiple implementation files; many of the files will be proprietary, and others will be available only in binary form from a specific vendor. Of particular interest is how to share variables and functions among the project files and how to compile each of the separate files and then link them to create an executable object module.

6.4.1 Separate Compilation

Today's embedded applications are still rather small compared to the large desktop or server software systems that have become so common. Nonetheless, an embedded project will still frequently have a large number of people involved in developing both hardware and software modules for the program. In such cases, each individual works on only a portion of the program. Typically, each piece is developed as a separate implementation file or files, each with its associated header files. While developed as individual pieces of functionality, software modules may share common information with other parts of the system. The final program will bring together all of the implementation files, header files, legacy files, library files, and any other information that may comprise the build.

Although a large operating system might contain 100,000 implementation files, a large embedded application still counts its files using much smaller numbers. In either case, each person working on the project must be able to compile his or her implementation file(s) independent of all of the other implementation files. Ultimately, the linker that was discussed earlier combines or links the compiled files into the executable program. The entire

build

process is called a *build,* which is illustrated in Figure 6.22. Observe that each implementation file is processed separately.

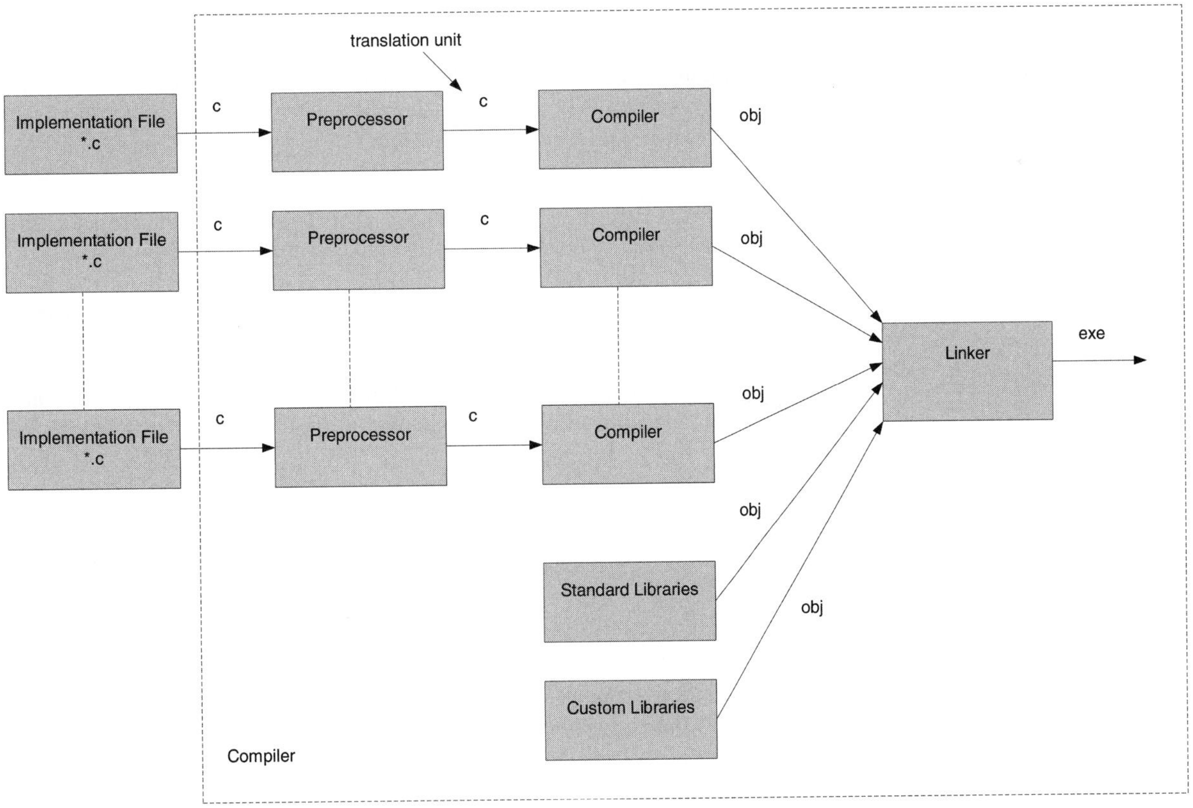

Figure 6.22 Building a C Program

6.4.2 Translation Units

translation unit Each file is read by the preprocessor and is used to build a temporary file called a *translation unit.* The translation unit is what the compiler ultimately compiles to produce an object file. To start, the preprocessor locates each header file and places a copy into the translation unit, ***#include*** replacing the *#include* directive for that header file. The preprocessor then processes any ***#ifndef, #define*** other directives such as *#ifndef* and *#define*. After the translation unit is compiled to create the object file, the translation unit is deleted; it is no longer necessary.

Each translation unit is self-contained. It cannot use variables or functions that are part of another translation unit. Calling *functionA()* when the code for *functionA()* is outside the translation unit produces an error. The same is true for variables declared outside the trans- ***unresolved external reference*** lation unit. When this happens, the translation unit has an *unresolved external reference.* Unless instructed otherwise, the build will fail at this point. Instructions needed to complete the build are usually contained in a header file. These instructions allow us to defer resolution of such problems to the link process after compiling all of the translation units.

6.4.3 Linking and Linkage

In our studies, we have learned that an embedded program usually comprises a number and variety of different files and that variables and functions are often shared among those files. At the end of the day, all of the files must be brought together, and the identifiers from each must be checked to ensure proper visibility and memory allocation.

6.4.3.1 Linking

As noted, each implementation file is separately compiled to produce an object file. A pro- ***linker*** gram called the *linker* reads each object file and copies it to the executable program. At this time, all unresolved external references are resolved.

EXAMPLE 6.9

printf

Suppose the object file uses *printf*. The code for *printf* is not in the object file, and the compiler has marked *printf* as an unresolved external reference. The linker will check the other object files for *printf.*

If *printf* is not found, standard libraries and custom libraries will be checked using a list the programmer supplies to the linker. These are the include files. When the (compiled) code for *printf* is found, it is copied to the executable.

All references to *printf* in the object file connected to the code are copied into the executable. When all unresolved external references for all object files are resolved, the executable program is complete.

---

unresolved external reference When the linker fails to resolve an external reference, it generates an *unresolved external reference* error and does not create the executable program. The object files remain.

6.4.3.2 Linkage

linkage *Linkage* relates to sharing variables and functions among implementation files. A variable ***external linkage, extern*** or function has *external linkage* when it uses the *extern* storage class. For example:

```
extern unsigned int myData;
extern void myFunction(void);
```

Such directives instruct the compiler to look for the definition of the variable or function in another file or in a library. The compiler is told that *myData* is an *unsigned int,* and as long as it is used that way no error should be generated. Similarly, the body of *myFunction()* is defined in another file, and as long as its use in the current file is consistent with the prototype, once again, no error should be generated. This is the real meaning of function prototyping: Advising the compiler not to worry when no *definition* (in this case, the code comprising the body of the function) is found in this file.

myData, unsigned

myFunction()

definition

Let's look at several variables that are shared among two files.

```
myFile1.c
unsigned int myData;
++myData;
```

```
myFile2.c
++myData;
```

myData

extern

In myFile1.c, the use of the variable *myData* is correct and legal. However, in myFile2.c, the variable is not defined; no storage is allocated, and an error results during compile. With the inclusion of the keyword *extern*, we solve the problem.

```
myFile1.c
unsigned int myData;
++myData;
```

```
myFile2.c
extern unsigned int myData;
++myData;
```

Now in myFile2.c, the compiler is told that the variable is defined elsewhere in the program; still no storage is allocated in the second file. This is a key point: It is important that the storage only be allocated in one place.

Coding Style

Generally we would place the line extern unsigned int myData in a header file and include the header in myFile2.c.

Be careful when you are trying to use static external variables; statics are local to the file that declares them:

```
myFile1.c
static unsigned int myData;
++myData;
```

```
myFile2.c
extern unsigned int myData;
++myData;
```

In the first case, use of the variable myData is correct and legal. In the second case, however, there is a problem. The variable myData is static—it is local to myFile1.c, and it has *internal linkage*. It cannot be seen outside of myFile1.c.

internal linkage

The same access mechanism works with functions. To be able to call a function that was declared and defined in another implementation file, we include the function prototype qualified by the keyword extern in our file. Such an approach works provided the function *is not static*. This is why one can call or invoke functions in libraries.

is not static

Caution: Static variables and static functions have internal linkage—they are local to the implementation file that declares or defines them. You cannot use extern to gain access to static variables and functions.

6.4.4 Where C Finds Functions

When you make a function call, C locates the function according to the following decision logic.

- If the function is local or static, use the function definition in this implementation file.
- Otherwise, use the definition from another object file.
- Otherwise, use a library definition.

When your function prototype matches the function prototype of a library function, your function will be preferred (override) to the library function. That is, your function will always hide a library function with the same name and signature.

printf()

We use such capability to our advantage in developing embedded applications. The function *printf()*, for example, writes to standard out, usually the display, in a desktop application. For an embedded system, there is no display. If we write a proprietary version of *printf()* that uses a serial port, then we can use the function transparently in the program and we will get the behavior we want.

> ***Caution:*** When you write functions that have the same prototype as a library function, make absolutely certain to clearly document what you have done, why you have done it, and what the current programmer must do to be certain your program is compiled correctly.

6.4.5 Makefiles

makefile
make
project file

The process for building a program as described requires a place to contain the instructions that specify what files to compile, lists of standard and custom libraries, the name of the executable program, and perhaps whether or not debugging information should be included in the executable. Such a place is called a *makefile*; the instructions in the makefile specify the build or *make* process. The utility that reads the makefile and invokes the preprocessor, compiler, and linker appropriately is called the *make* utility. The name and format of the make utility vary among different environments. Some compiler vendors provide an integrated development environment (IDE) that automates the generation and execution of the make file. That process is masked by the *project file,* which provides a convenient tool for synthesizing the makefile.

A makefile is simply a file comprising a collection of rules and directions of the general form:

```
targetName    Dependencies or Components of the form x.c, y.obj, z.h
that make up the target and Rules for building targetName such as the
compiler and compiler options

Components Subcomponents comprising each component
Rules for building each subcomponent
...
```

The syntax and rules for building a makefile to direct the compile process may seem a bit arcane and inflexible, and to a large extent they are. Nonetheless, a little study removes most of the mystery.

make

An example of a very simple makefile is given in Figure 6.23. The makefile uses the GNU C compiler to build an executable module from the implementation file hw.c. In this example, the makefile and the implementation file must be in the same directory. Typing the keyword *make* will run the makefile and produce the file hw.exe. To run the first rule, the hw.o is required. If that does not exist, the second rule must be executed to produce it.

```
A very simple makefile
    To make hw.exe (the .exe is implied) use hw.o and
        Use the gcc compiler with the identified input, flag, and output

    To make hw.o use hw.c and
        Use the gcc compiler with the identified input and flag
hw: hw.o
    gcc hw.o -o hw

hw.o: hw.c
    gcc -c hw.c

// Simple classic C program hw.c
#include <stdio.h>
int main(void)
{
    printf("hello world\n");
    return 0;
}
```

Figure 6.23 A Simple Makefile

6.4.6 Standard and Custom Libraries

.lib A library contains compiled code and may have a file extension of *.lib*. Compiler vendors provide libraries as part of the implementation of the C programming language. These are the *standard libraries*. As a C developer, one may write his or her own libraries to contain functions that have been written specifically for the current project or those that may have been found useful in earlier developments. These are the *custom libraries*. As part of the makefile, one may specify a list of libraries that the linker is to search for functions.

standard libraries

custom libraries

Libraries are distributed with a header file and a binary file containing the compiled code. The header file may be included in the implementation file, and one may include the name of the library in the makefile. Then one may make calls to library functions.

6.4.7 Debug and Release Builds

A build can include, or not include, information that is used by a debugging tool or that has been added to the code to provide additional insight into the software (and hardware) operation during development. If the debugger information is excluded, the executable can certainly be much much smaller, but debugging is more difficult. On the other hand, if the debugging information is included, the executable can be substantially larger and slower as well as issue surprising information that the customer may not have been expecting.

One can include debugging code in several ways. One method is to use preprocessor directives as we discussed earlier. Depending on which compiler is used, it may support a switch to select between including and not including debug information. Be careful here. When you perform a debug build, you must be certain that you use debug libraries in the build. Conversely, with a release build, you must be certain to use release libraries. The reason for this is that the memory allocation may be different between the two builds. Using inappropriate or different allocation schemes on different parts of the build can cause unexpected behavior.

Always be certain that the libraries you use are compatible with the compiler settings. If you are using an IDE (Interactive Development Environment), the makefile is usually automatically generated with the correct libraries. If you are doing this manually, you must read the documentation for your compiler to locate the names of these libraries.

6.5 SUMMARY

In this chapter we opened with a high-level look at an embedded C program, its structure, and an introduction to the mechanics of building a multiple-file program. We discussed good programming style and some important considerations when developing robust, reliable, and maintainable programs.

We then moved inside the program through a review of the fundamentals of the C language, specifically variables, their scope and storage class. We concluded with a detailed look at the structure of a C program itself and working with multiple-file programs.

6.6 REVIEW QUESTIONS

Software and Its Manifestations

6.1 What is the purpose of the software tool called the preprocessor?

6.2 What is a cross compiler, and how is it different from the basic compiler?

6.3 What is the function of the assembler?

6.4 Please explain the purpose of the software tool called the linker and briefly describe its operation.

6.5 What is relocatable code?

6.6 What is a link error, and how can it occur during the compile process?

6.7 What is the purpose of the software tool called the loader?

An Embedded C Program

6.8 What are the four major goals to strive for when developing an embedded software application? Briefly describe each one.

6.9 Why is the return type for the top-level function, main(), in an embedded C program void?

6.10 Is it necessary to put each statement in an embedded C program on a separate line?

6.11 What is boot code, and what is its purpose?

C Building Blocks

6.12 What does the term *identifier* mean in the C language?

6.13 Are C language identifiers case sensitive?

6.14 What do the terms *declare* and *define* in the C language mean? What is the difference between them?

6.15 How can one find out the sizes, in terms of bits or bytes, for each of the intrinsic types for a specific target machine?

6.16 Why is it important to initialize each variable when it is declared and defined? How many times can a variable be initialized?

6.17 What is the difference between assigning a value to a variable and initializing that variable?

6.18 How many times can we assign a value to a variable?

6.19 What is the difference between the C operators = and ==?

6.20 The C language classifies built-in or intrinsic types into two major groups. What are these? What are the major differences between entries in each group?

6.21 What is the purpose of the const qualifier?

6.22 Is it possible to convert a variable from one type to a different type?

6.23 What is the difference between a cast and a promotion?

6.24 Within an embedded C program, what does the term *scope* mean?

6.25 The C language specifies three primary scopes. Please identify each of these classes and briefly describe what each means.

6.26 Within an embedded C program, what does the term *storage class* mean?

6.27 The C language specifies six primary storage classes. Please identify each of these classes and briefly describe what each means.

6.28 What is the difference between a variable's scope and its storage class?

C Program Structure

6.29 Why is it good practice to design an embedded C program as a number of individual files?

6.30 What is a translation unit, and what is its purpose?

6.31 What does the term *external linkage* mean when applied to a C variable?

6.32 What does the term *internal linkage* mean when applied to a C variable?

6.33 What is the difference between internal and external linkage when applied to a C variable?

6.34 When a C function is called, where does the language find the definition of that function, that is, the function's body?

6.35 What is a makefile, and what is its purpose?

6.36 What is a make utility? What is its purpose?

6.37 What is the difference between a debug and a release build for an embedded application?

6.7 THOUGHT QUESTIONS

Software and Its Manifestations

6.1 Identify and discuss each of the steps that are necessary to convert a problem statement into the bits and bytes that can be run on an embedded microprocessor.

6.2 Why do we use relocatable code?

6.3 Why is relocatable code useful in an embedded application?

6.4 What is a symbol table? Please identify the information that is stored in the symbol table. What is the purpose of the symbol table?

6.5 Why is a link error difficult to find when debugging a program?

6.6 Why do we use the software tool called the loader in an embedded application?

An Embedded C Program

6.7 The chapter identifies four major goals to achieve when developing an embedded software application. What is the purpose for setting each of these as a goal? Discuss possible consequences of not considering such goals.

6.8 What is the purpose of annotating an embedded software program?

6.9 Briefly describe the essential information that should be included in a program's annotation.

6.10 What are preprocessor directives, and what is their purpose?

6.11 What is the purpose of function prototypes? Where, within an embedded C program, should they be placed?

6.12 What is the purpose of a while(1) loop in the top-level function, main(), in an embedded C program.

6.13 We will often suggest using pseudo code as a tool during the design process. What role can pseudo code play in annotating the final program?

6.14 Why is it important to cite the source for any algorithms that may have been used or adapted from the literature in a program's annotation?

6.15 How can the preprocessor be an effective tool during the debug process?

6.16 What is the purpose of a header file in a C or C++ program?

6.17 Why should variable or function definitions never be included in a header file?

6.18 Does the C language automatically protect from writing beyond the end of an array?

6.19 Can a program write to storage that is beyond the end of a C array?

6.20 The while(1) construct is one way to create an infinite loop in an embedded C program. Are there other ways?

6.21 Is the following code fragment legal in C? If not why not?

```
int x = 2;
float y = 3.7;
x = y;
char z = 'a';
```

C Building Blocks

6.22 Why do we declare certain variables as unsigned?

6.23 How may times can a C identifier be declared?

6.24 Why can a C identifier be defined only once?

6.25 If a pointer variable has been declared and defined, what will happen if the pointer is dereferenced but never been initialized or assigned to?

6.26 Can one array be assigned to a second one using the = operator? Why or why not?

6.27 Can two arrays be compared using the == operator?

6.28 Why would we wish to qualify a variable that is being passed into a function as const? Please give a specific example of when such a practice might be particularly useful in an embedded application.

6.29 The C language supports converting from a variable of one type to a different type; what precautions must be taken when doing so?

6.30 What is the value for the variable x in the following code fragment?

```
int x = 2;
float y = 3.7;
x = y;
```

6.31 What will the following code fragment print?

```
int x = 2;
char y = 'a';
x = y;
printf("the value is %i", x);
```

6.32 The following code fragment contains several ill-advised practices. What are these?

```
int x = 2;
char y = 'a';
x = y;
printf("the value is %i", x);
```

6.33 The C language specifies three primary scopes. Give an example of when each might be used.

6.34 The C language specifies six primary storage classes. Give an example of when each might be used.

6.35 Can a variable declared in one function be returned by reference to another function? Why or why not?

6.36 Can a pointer variable declared and assigned to refer to a variable in one function be returned and dereferenced in another function? Why or why not?

C Program Structure

6.37 What are the major kinds of files that will typically be compiled and linked together in an embedded C software application? Briefly describe the information that might be contained in each such file.

6.38 Give examples of several different types of declarations for which external linkage might be useful?

6.39 How can the identity of a C variable declared in one file in a program be hidden from other files in the program? Why would we want to do such a thing?

6.40 How can the identity of a C function declared in one file in a program be hidden from other files in the program? Why would we want to do such a thing?

6.41 Can a function be declared on one file and defined in another? If so, how and why would we want to do such a thing?

6.42 Why do we distinguish between a debug and a release build for an embedded application?

6.43 How do we create a debug version of a program? a release build?

6.44 How can we ensure that debugging code be preserved and available for future revisions and yet not impact the size of the code used for the embedded application?

6.45 How can we make a test suite available for future revisions without impacting the size of the code used for the embedded application?

6.8 PROBLEMS

Using the Preprocessor

6.1 Starting with the program given in Figure P6.24, write two functions with the prototypes

```
int incrementItem(void)
int decrementItem(void)
```

that will increment or decrement the variable count by 2.

Using the preprocessor, conditionally include either the original or the new functions based on whether the variable TWO is defined.

```
// Top level program, demo0.c, used to generate demo. It is made up of demo0.c
#include <stdio.h>

// function prototypes
    int incrementItem(void);
    int decrementItem(void);

// a global static variable
    static int count = 0;

// global variables
    int gVar0 = 0;
    int myArray[10];

void main(void)
{
    // local declaration
    int number = 0;
    // assign a value to the global variable i
    gVar0=3;
    // This line will print 3
    printf ("The value of gVar0 is %i\n", gVar0);
// Three values are entered into the array myArray[] and printed
    for (gVar0=0; gVar0< 3; gVar0++)
    {
        myArray[gVar0]=gVar0;
    }
    for (gVar0=0; gVar0< 3; gVar0++)
    {
        printf ("the value of myArray is %i\n", myArray[gVar0]);
    }
```

Figure P6.24a

```
        // The function incrementItem is called to increment the variable count the results are printed

        for (gVar0=0; gVar0< 3; gVar0++)
        {
            number = incrementItem();
        }

        printf ("The total number of items is: %i\n", number);
        // The function decrementItem is called to decrement the variable count and the results are printed
        for (gVar0=0; gVar0< 3; gVar0++)
        {
            number = decrementItem();
        }
        printf ("The value of number is: %i\n", number);
        printf ("The value of count is: %i\n", count);
        return;
}

int incrementItem(void)
{
        count += 1;
        return count;
}

int decrementItem(void)
{
        count -= 1;
        return count;
}
```

Figure P6.24b

6.2 Starting with the program given in Figure P6.24 and using the preprocessor, convert the functions `incrementItem()` and `decrementItem()` to macros.

6.3 Starting with the program given in Figure P6.24, write macro versions of the functions `incrementItem()` and `decrementItem()`. Using the preprocessor, build the program such that the two functions are compiled either as functions or macros based on whether the variable MACROS is defined. How can you verify that the desired version of the build has occurred?

Multiple Files

6.4 Starting with the program given in Figure P6.24, move the functions and global static variable to one .c and global variables to a second.

C Scope

6.5 Starting with the program in Problem 6.4, add debug code to the two functions to print out the value of the variable *count* each time the function is called. Using the preprocessor, conditionally include the debug code whenever the variable DEBUG is defined.

6.6 A colleague has come to you with the code fragment in Figure P6.25. He claims that sometimes he gets the correct results and for other times he does not. Can you explain to him what is happening and why?

6.7 You find the code fragment in Figure P6.26 in a legacy application that you are working on to incorporate some new features. The current application works with no problems. After you add your modifications, the data in the array sometimes gets corrupted. When you remove your code, everything works properly again. Can you identify and correct the problem?

6.8 A colleague has written a simple function shown in Figure P6.27 to prompt the user to make a selection as part of a new application you both are working on. Somehow the correct data does not seem to be returned properly, even though it prints correctly in the prompting function. Can you explain to him what the problem is and how to correct it?

```c
#include <stdio.h>
#define max(a,b) ((a) > (b) ? (a) : (b))

void main(void)
{
        int i = 0;
        int j = 0;
        int a = 3;
        int b = 4;
        int c = 6;
        int d = 5;

        i = max (a, b);
        j = max (c, d);
        printf ("i = %i, j = %i\n", i, j);

        i = max(a++, b++);
        printf ("a = %i, b = %i\n", a, b);
        j = max(c++, d++);
        printf ("c = %i, d = %i\n", c, d);
        return;
}
```

Figure P6.25

```c
#include <stdio.h>
void main(void)
{
        int i = 0;
        unsigned char j = 0;
        char myArray[5];                          // declare a character array

        for (i = 0; i <= 5; i++)                  // fill array with characters
        {
                // fill with the ascii characters A..F
                // 65 is the ascii value for A
                myArray[i]= 65+(j++);
        }
        for (i = 0; i <= 5; i++)                  // display the array
        {
                printf("the value is: %c\n", myArray[i]);
        }
        return;
}
```

Figure P6.26

```
#include <stdio.h>
// get data from the user
char* getSelection();

void main (void)
{
        // declare variable to store the selection and a pointer to it
        char myValue;
        char* myPtr = &myValue;

        // get selection from the user
        myPtr = getSelection();

        // display the selection
        printf("the selection is: %c \n", *myPtr);

        return
}

// prompt the user to make a selection then return a pointer the variable holding that selection
char* getSelection(void)
{
        // declare a temp place to store the selection
        char tempValue;
        char* valuePtr;

        // let valuePtr point to it
        valuePtr = &tempValue;

        // prompt for selection
        printf("Please enter a choice between 0..9: ");

        // get the data
        *valuePtr = getchar();

        // display its value
        printf ("you selected: %c\n", *valuePtr);
        return valuePtr;
}
```

Figure P6.27

Chapter 7

The Software Side—Part 2: Pointers and Functions

THINGS TO LOOK FOR . . .

- Pointers to variables and functions.
- C functions—Passing and returning by value or reference.
- How and when to pass by information value or by reference.
- Writing and working with pointers to function pointers.
- The struct data type—declaration, initialization, and accessing.
- Pointers to structs and passing structs to functions.
- Interrupting events and interrupt control flow.
- Understanding the interrupt vector table and Interrupt service routines.
- Managing interrupts—enabling, disabling, and masking.

7.0 INTRODUCTION

In the early days, the software for embedded applications was written either in machine code or in assembler. The C language was developed to expedite and to simplify the design and development process. Consequently, several of the features and capabilities we find in the language were targeted specifically for such applications. In this chapter, we will examine four of these: *bitwise operators, functions, pointer variables,* and *structs*. We will also look at two important uses of pointers: *pointers to functions* and *interrupting events.*

bitwise operators, functions, pointer variables, structs

pointers to functions, interrupting events

Bitwise operators work naturally with embedded hardware by permitting the test and modification of individual signals coming into or going out of the embedded processor. *Functions* provide the means to share a block of code among a number of tasks within a program rather than requiring each to provide and maintain its own copy. *Pointer variables* enable data or instructions to be accessed through their memory address. When used properly, such an ability can be a very powerful tool. The *struct* data type provides the ability to mix different data types in the same container and to treat that collection as a single entity.

interrupts

Pointers to functions are a powerful mechanism that enables a function to be passed to another block of code and evaluated in the local context. *Interrupts* provide support for accepting and managing asynchronous events originating from inside or outside of the system.

7.1 BITWISE OPERATORS

Bitwise operators in C are more commonly found in the embedded systems developer's tool box than in that of the traditional application developer's. Such operators are intended for work at the hardware level—that is, with the registers and input or output ports on a target machine.

The bitwise operators are summarized in Table 7.0.

Table 7.0 Bitwise Operators

	Operator	Meaning	Description
Shift			
	>>	Logical shift right	Operand shifted positions are filled with 0's
	<<	Logical shift left	Operand shifted positions are filled with 0's
Logical			
	&	Bitwise AND	
	|	Bitwise inclusive OR	
	^	Bitwise exclusive OR	
	~	Bitwise negation	

unsigned integral type, unsigned char unsigned short, unsigned int

When working at the bit level, often *all* of the bits in a word are important because they generally represent the state of some signal in the hardware of the machine. Consequently, the underlying operand type should be an *unsigned integral type* such as an *unsigned char*, *unsigned short*, or *unsigned int*. We don't want one of the bits to be interpreted as a sign.

Common operations that one might perform include

- Setting or resetting bits on a microprocessor or microcontroller output port
- Testing status bits on input lines or in registers
- Setting or resetting status bits as the result of some operation
- Making comparison operations
- Quickly performing certain multiplication or division operations

The application of each operator is rather straightforward and follows naturally from the logical operators. Let's examine some examples of these to see how they might apply in our designs. We will first look at some simple bit manipulation operations.

7.1.1 Bit Manipulation Operations

each of the individual bits

The logical bitwise operators are binary operators that return the result of the logical AND, OR, or XOR of *each of the individual bits* in the two operands. The code module in Figure 7.0 illustrates how each of these works.

EXAMPLE 7.0

```
// we are working with byte sized pieces in this example

unsigned char a = 0xF3;      // a = 1111 0011 – note this is not a negative number
unsigned char b = 0x54;      // b = 0101 0100 – note this is not a positive number

unsigned char c = a & b;     // c gets a AND b
                             // a 1111 0011
                             // b 0101 0100
                             // c 0101 0000

unsigned char d = a | b;     // d gets a OR b
                             // a 1111 0011
                             // b 0101 0100
                             // d 1111 0111

unsigned char e = a ^ b;     // e gets a XOR b
                             // a 1111 0011
                             // b 0101 0100
                             // e 1010 0111

unsigned char f = ~a;        // f gets ~a
                             // a 1111 0011
                             // f  0000 1100
```

Figure 7.0 Working with Bitwise Operators

7.1.2 Testing, Resetting, and Setting Bits

We can use the logical bitwise operators to determine whether a specific bit within a word is set or reset—that is, has a value of logical 1 or logical 0.

EXAMPLE 7.1

We have executed the following code to read the state of an I/O port on a microprocessor, and we wish to test whether bit 5, a status bit, is set. If it is, we wish to reset it, acknowledging the event flagged by the status bit, and we set bit 3 to initiate some action in the external device.

setPort()

We will assume that the port comprises 8 bits, 1 byte. We further assume that we have the I/O support function, *setPort()*, which we can use to perform the necessary operations on the microprocessor's I/O ports. Such functions are found on most microprocessors that support I/O port-type operations.

portShadow

The code module in Figure 7.1 illustrates several interesting techniques.

First, notice that we are using a variable *portShadow*. We use such a variable to mirror or shadow the state of all bits on an I/O port. We do this for several reasons.

As we did in the argument to the *if* clause:

```
if (portShadow & testPattern0) // if bit 5 is set, the AND will give a
                               // nonzero result
```

The state of the port can be tested without the time cost of actually reading the state of the port—reading from memory can be much faster.

```
unsigned char testPattern0 = 0x40;        // testPattern0 = 0010 0000
unsigned char setPattern0 = 0x8;          // setPattern0 = 0000 1000

// assume portShadow holds 1010 0110
if (portShadow & testPattern0)            // if bit 5 is set, the AND will give a nonzero result
{
        // set bit3 reset bit 5 and update portShadow
        // portShadow = (1010 0110 & ~(0010 0000)) | (0000 1000)
        // portShadow = (1010 0110 & 1101 1111) | (0000 1000)
        // portShadow = 1000 1110

        portShadow = (portShadow & ~testPattern0 ) | setPattern0;
        setPort(portShadow);
}
```

Figure 7.1 Using the Bitwise Operators to Test and Modify I/O Port Signals

If the shadow had been stored in an internal register, the operation could be even faster. In some microprocessor implementations, the state of a port may not be able to be read, only written.

When bit 5 is reset, rather than declaring a separate variable to hold a pattern that could be used to reset the bit, the pattern used to test the bit is simply inverted.

```
// portShadow = (1010 0110 & ~(0010 0000)) | (0000 1000)
// portShadow = (1010 0110 & 1101 1111) | (0000 1000)
```

The first line in the code fragment shows the starting pattern. The second line shows the bitwise inversion of the right-hand operand to the bitwise AND. The result of the AND will be to reset bit 5 giving the intermediate result

```
1000 0110
```

As the final step, we simply OR a logical 1 into bit position 3 giving

```
1000 1110
```

Coding Style

When using the bitwise operators, it is good practice to use parentheses to ensure that the desired operations are being implemented.

Let's now see how the left shift operator can be used to aid in this task. Remember that the shift operators are binary operators. Their two operands comprise the operand to shift and the amount to shift. The operator implements a logical shift and, unless steps are taken to the contrary, the shift applied to the operand is only temporary.

EXAMPLE 7.2

Let's begin with two 8-bit numbers and shift one four places to the left and the other two places to the right as we see in the code fragment in Figure 7.2.

Note that, the values of the two operands will remain unchanged.

```
unsigned char a = 0x3;                                   // a = 0000 0011
unsigned char b = 0xC5;                                  // b = 1100 0101
printf (" a shifted 4 places left is %x\", a << 4);      // prints...0011 0000
printf (" b shifted 2 places right is %x\", b >> 2);     // prints ...0011 0001
printf (" a is %x\", a );                                // prints...0000 0011
printf (" b is %x\", b );                                // prints ...1100 0101
```

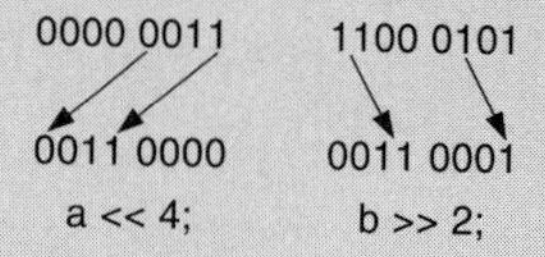

Figure 7.2 Using the Bitwise Operators to Set and Reset Bits Within a Data Word

EXAMPLE 7.3

Let's repeat the earlier example now using the left shift operator as shown in Figure 7.3.

```
unsigned char bitPattern0 = 0x1;            // bitPattern0 = 0000 0001

// assume portShadow holds 1010 0110
if (portShadow & (bitPattern0 << 5)         // if bit 5 is set, the AND will give a nonzero result
{
    // set bit3 reset bit 5 and update portShadow
    // portShadow = (1010 0110 & ~(0010 0000)) | (0000 1000)
    // portShadow = (1010 0110 & 1101 1111) | (0000 1000)
    // portShadow = 1000 1110

    portShadow = (portShadow & ~(bitPattern0 << 5) ) | (bitPattern0 << 3);
    setPort(portShadow);
}
```

Figure 7.3 Using the Bitwise Operators to Set and Reset Bits Within a Data Word

Now, let's look at a slightly more complex problem.

EXAMPLE 7.4

getPort(), setPort()

The data is to be read in from a microprocessor port using an access function *getPort()* and then tested for the pattern 0001 1010. Like *setPort()*, such a function is typical on most microprocessors supporting port I/O. The function reads the port and returns the state of the port signals.

In this example we execute the following,

- Read in the data from the port.
- Reset all bits, except those of interest to zero.

We implement the reset operation by defining a mask with 1's in the positions of interest and 0's elsewhere and then ANDing the mask with the data.

Bits with a value of 1 in the pattern will appear as 1's in the result. All other bits will appear as 0's. The mask operation is important to ensure that the subsequent pattern match is restricted to the relevant bits.

```
unsigned char getPort(void);                   // port access function prototype

unsigned char testPattern0 = 0x1A;             // testPattern0 = 0001 1010
unsigned char mask = 0x1E;                     // mask = 0001 1110
unsigned char portData = 0x0;                  // working variable

// assume port holds 1101 1011
portData = getPort();                          // read the port

if !((portShadow & mask) ^ testPattern0)       // will give a zero result if pattern present
{
    printf( "pattern present \n";
}
```

Figure 7.4 Using the Bitwise Operators to Test for a Pattern Within a Data Word

Next, we form the bitwise exclusive OR (^) between the word under test and the desired pattern. If the pattern is present, the result should be all 0's.

These steps are illustrated in the code fragment in Figure 7.4.

7.1.3 Arithmetic Operations

We can take advantage of the bit shift operations to improve system performance on certain arithmetic operations. Recognizing that binary multiplication by two is simply a left shift and that division by two is a right shift, one can perform such operations when necessary rather than using the corresponding operations in the math package.

Some basic operations can be implemented as in Figure 7.5.

EXAMPLE 7.5

```
Multiply by x where x is 2, 4, 8, ...
result = number << x;

Divide by y where y is 2, 4, 8, ...
result = number >> y;
```

Figure 7.5 Using the Bitwise Operators to Perform Arithmetic

Some slightly more complex examples can be implemented as given in the code module in Figure 7.6.

EXAMPLE 7.6

```
Multiply by x where x is a simple number such as 5, 6, 9, 10, 12,...
result = (number << 2) + number;               // multiply by 5, ...0101
result = (number << 2) + (number << 1);        // multiply by 6, ...0110
result = (number << 3) + number;               // multiply by 9, ...1001
result = (number << 3) + (number << 1);        // multiply by 10, ...1010
result = (number << 3) + (number << 2);        // multiply by 12, ...1100
```

Figure 7.6 Using the Bitwise Operators to Perform Arithmetic

Little is gained by more complex operations.

7.2 POINTER VARIABLES AND MEMORY ADDRESSES

7.2.1 Getting Started

We have been looking at variables that hold different types of data with different values.

```
int myAge = 39;
float mySpeed = 54.52;
char myAnswer = 't';
```

We know that those variables are stored in memory somewhere and that the different types require different amounts of memory. At this point, we should be asking several questions. How does one know *where* the variables are stored? How does one know *how* the variables are stored? Are large data objects stored the same way as smaller ones? How should one pass a large data object into a function? These questions are more relevant to embedded applications than to those on the desktop because often in embedded applications, one is trying to optimize the amount, organization, and use of memory in the system. The desktop application typically does not have such concerns. Let's see how to begin to answer these questions.

where, how

defined

Each variable that is *defined* has a storage place somewhere in memory and a value in that location independent of whether the variable is initialized or assigned. That place has an address. As each of the program's variables is stored, the system memory will begin to look like that in Figure 7.7.

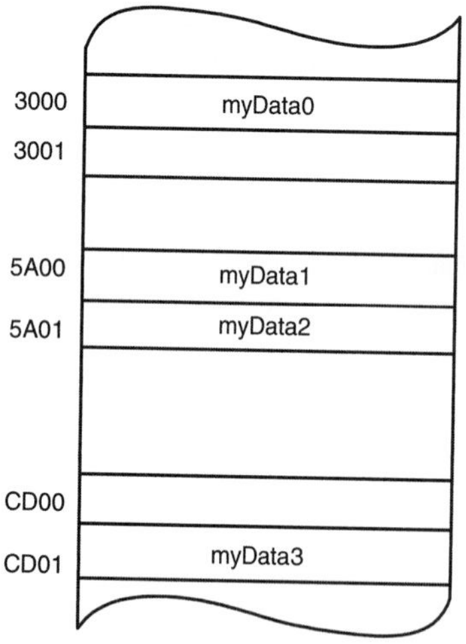

Figure 7.7 A Typical View of Data Storage in Memory

When one works with data, that is, variables, one can read their values, modify their values, or ask where they are stored. We have learned that variables hold different types of values, integers, floats, chars, and so on. In C, the type of the value of a variable can be a memory address as well. An address is just another variable with a value. Up to that point, it is nothing special. However, now some confusion can potentially arise.

As we learned when we first started working with the intrinsic types, they are simply a collection of bits in memory. It was not until a type was associated with the collection that it took on a meaning as an integer or char or float. If we look at the 16-bit quantity, 0xFE89, there is nothing to distinguish it as a variable's value or a variable's address. The compiler is no smarter. Therefore, to reduce the confusion, each variable that holds an address is *pointers* given a distinguishing name and type—*pointers*. Thus, a pointer is a variable whose values are addresses in memory—nothing more and nothing less.

Consider the standard C declaration, definition, and initialization in the context of the memory fragment given above.

```
unsigned int myData0 = 0x3;
```

In response to such a declaration, the compiler

myData0

- Allocates 16 bits of memory to hold the variable *myData0*, assuming that we are working with 16-bit integers in our microprocessor. This is both a declaration and a definition.
- Places value 3 (0x3) into those 16 bits.
- Associates an address such as 0x3000 in memory where the data is stored with the variable *myData0*.

myData0

address of

Subsequently, when we write *myData0*, we are actually referring to the data at location 0x3000. If we wish to know where data is stored, that is, at which address in memory, we simply ask. We use the *address of* operator &, and the compiler responds with the appropriate information. If we write

```
&myData0; // read address of myData0
```

the compiler returns 0x3000 as the place where data is stored. Now, if we write

```
int *myData0Ptr = &myData0;
```

the following occurs. The compiler

myData0Ptr

myData0

- Allocates 16 bits of memory to hold the (pointer-type) variable *myData0Ptr*.
- Finds the address of *myData0* (which is 0x3000) and places that value into the 16 bits at that address.

We use the symbol * to tell the compiler that this variable is a pointer. We use a distinguishing name such as *myData0Ptr* to tell us (or people working with the code) that this variable is a pointer. This is good coding style.

When we are dealing with pointers and pointer declarations, knowing how to read them sometimes helps to make their role a little more clear.

EXAMPLE 7.7

Starting with the declaration and assignment,

```
int *myData0Ptr = &myData0;
```

the code fragment on the left of the assignment operator is read in several steps from right to left:

1. *myData0Ptr*—the first part
2. *is a pointer*—* the second part
3. *to an integer*—int the third part
4. myData0Ptr is a pointer to an integer

One more time,

```
float* anOtherPtr = &myFloatVar;
```

we read

1. *anOtherPtr*—the first part
2. *is a pointer*—* the second part
3. *to a float*—float the third part
4. anOtherPtr is a pointer to a float

If we assume that the compiler put the pointer variable *myData0Ptr* (remember, it's just another variable) at memory address 0xCD00, we now have the picture shown in Figure 7.8.

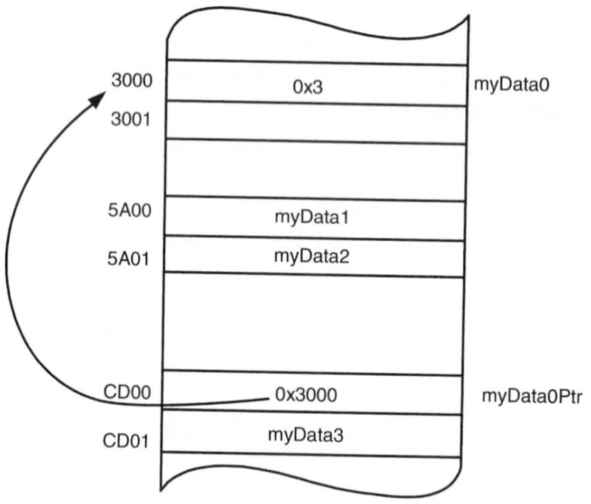

Figure 7.8 A Pointer Refers to a Variable in Memory

myData0Ptr, dereference operator

We can retrieve the value that *myData0Ptr* refers to by using the *dereference operator*, *, preceding the pointer variable. Thus, if we write

```
int myData1 = *myData0Ptr;
```

myData1

The value 0x3 is assigned to *myData1* using the steps shown in Figure 7.9.

Similarly, if we write

```
myData3 = 0x4;
*myData0Ptr = myData3;
```

myData0Ptr

The value 0x4 is assigned to the memory location referred to by the pointer variable *myData0Ptr* using the steps listed in Figure 7.10.

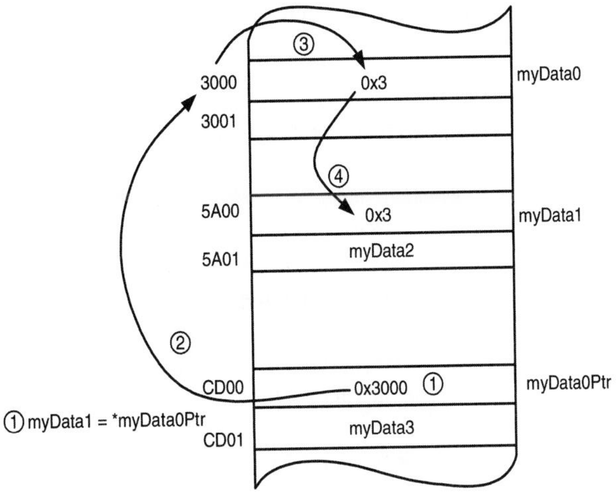

① Get the value contained in the pointer variable *myData0Ptr*, 0x3000.

② Go to the address (0x3000) specified, pointed, or referred to by that value.

③ Get the value of the variable, *myData0*, at memory address 0x3000 – this will be the value 0x3.

④ Assign that value (0x3) to the variable *myData1*.

Figure 7.9 Using a Pointer to Retrieve the Value of a Variable in Memory

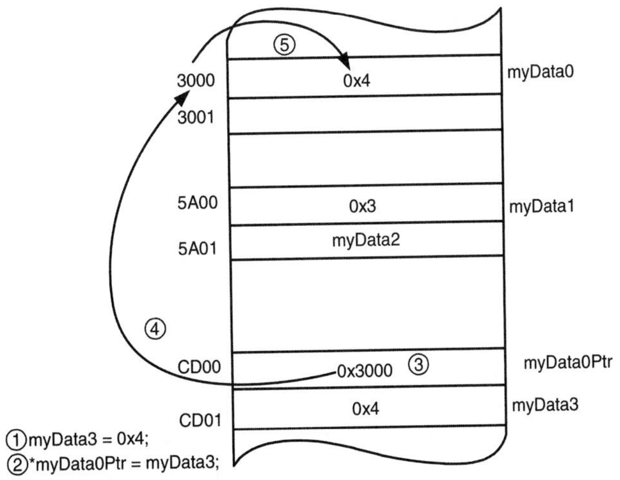

① Assign the value 0x4 to the variable *myData*3.

② Get the value contained in the variable *myData3* – 0x4.

③ Get the value of the pointer variable *myData0Ptr*, 0x3000.

④ Go to the address (0x3000) specified or pointed to by that value.

⑤ Assign the value contained in the variable, *myData3* to the variable at memory address 0x3000, *myData0*—this will be the value 0x4.

Figure 7.10 Using a Pointer to Change a Variable in Memory

EXAMPLE 7.8 Let's try this (see Figure 7.11).

```
/*
 * A First Look at Pointers
 */
#include <stdio.h>
void main(void)
{
      int myData0 = 0x3;
      int myData1 = 0;
      int myData2 = 0;
      int myData3 = 0;

      int *myData0Ptr = &myData0;        // myData0Ptr is a pointer to int
                                         // initialized to point to myData0
      myData1 = *myData0Ptr;             // myData1 now contains the value 3

      printf ("The value of myData1 is: %d\n", *myData0Ptr);
      myData3 = 0x4;                     // myData3 now contains the value 4
      *myData0Ptr = myData3;             // myData0 now contains the value 4 as well

      printf ("The value of myData3 is: %d\n", *myData0Ptr);
      return;
}
```

Figure 7.11 Working with Pointers

This program will print

```
The value of myData1 is: 3
The value of myData3 is: 4
```

7.2.2 Simple Pointer Arithmetic

We have learned that a variety of arithmetic operators can be applied to a C variable. It is reasonable to ask if those same operators can be applied to a pointer variable. The answer is yes and no. Let's first see what cannot be done.

Pointers *cannot* be added, multiplied, or divided. With a little bit of thought, these restrictions make sense. Pointers *cannot* be added, multiplied, or divided by a scalar. These, too, make sense. In both cases, one has to ask: If such operations were legal, does the result of the arithmetic operation give a meaningful answer?

On the other hand, a pointer variable and a scalar *can* be added. The result is a pointer variable—specifically, a pointer variable that refers to a memory address that is offset from the original address by the size of the offset in bytes. Conversely, two pointers can be subtracted; the result is a scalar. The value of the scalar is the size of the offset (in bytes) separating the two pointers.

On the surface, all this appears to be rather straightforward. Below the surface, it is still straightforward as long as one recognizes that there is some minor pointer magic going on. Let's see what that magic is and, at this point, if it really is only minor.

As we have learned, different variable types occupy different amounts of memory. The number of bytes required to store a type can be determined by applying the C *sizeof* operator to that type.

```
sizeof(type)
```

The application of the operator returns the number of bytes required to store an operand of the specified type. The operand may be an intrinsic type or a user-defined type.

What is happening under the hood when the following expression is written

```
myPointer0 = myPointer1+ anInteger
```

is that the compiler actually computes

```
myPointer0 = myPointer1+ anInteger * sizeof(type of myPointer1)
```

Such an operation gives a new pointer value that refers to a memory location that is separated from the original by *aScaler* number of variable instances of the specified type. Let's take a look in memory.

EXAMPLE 7.9

Let myPointer1 be of type pointer to integer and placed at memory location 0x3000. Let's further assume that an integer is 16 bits – 2 bytes on the machine. If we write

```
int* myPointer0 = myPointer1 + 4;
```

the code fragment is interpreted as

```
int* myPointer0 = myPointer1 + 4 * (sizeof ( int ) );
                = 0x3000 + 4*2
                = 0x3008
```

The variable myPointer1 will now refer to the address 0x3008.

EXAMPLE 7.10

Let's repeat the previous example; only now we will use a negative integer. Once again, let myPointer1 be of type pointer to integer and placed at memory location 0x3000. We write

```
int* myPointer0 = myPointer1 - 4;
```

the code fragment is interpreted as

```
int* myPointer0 = myPointer1 - 4 * (sizeof ( int ) );
                = 0x3000 - 4*2
                = 0x2FF8
```

The variable myPointer1 will now refer to the address 0x2FF8.

Returning to the problem of subtracting pointers, we should now see that the difference between two pointers is computed by the compiler as

$$\text{pointer}_1 - \text{pointer}_0 \ / \ \text{sizeof(type)}$$

Remember that when we write the name of a variable—in this case, a pointer— it is synonymous with writing its value and that value is an address.

The meaning and result of any of the following code fragments should now start to become clear.

```
int* myPtr = anAddress;
myPtr + 1;
myPtr++;
myPtr + 3;
myPtr - 1;
--myPtr;
```

Each of the operations algebraically adds a scalar value to a pointer. However, one must be careful when using the auto increment (decrement) operator and know when the pointers are dereferenced. For the auto increment (decrement) operator, prefix placement says to do the arithmetic and then evaluate the pointer variable, while postfix placement says to evaluate the pointer variable and then do the arithmetic.

The code fragments in Figure 7.12 do not all accomplish the same thing, nor do they leave the value of the pointer in the same state. Let's assume that the value of the pointer starts out at 0x3000, that the value 0x3 is stored at location 0x3000, and that we are working with 16-bit integers.

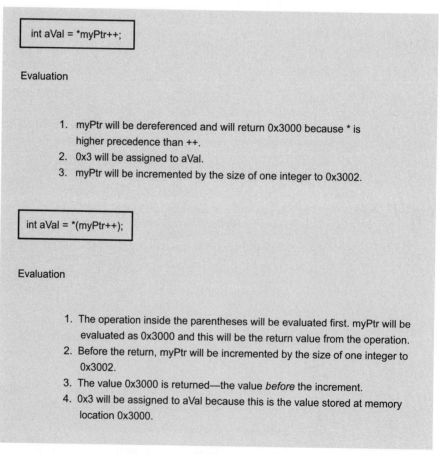

```
int aVal = *myPtr++;
```

Evaluation

1. myPtr will be dereferenced and will return 0x3000 because * is higher precedence than ++.
2. 0x3 will be assigned to aVal.
3. myPtr will be incremented by the size of one integer to 0x3002.

```
int aVal = *(myPtr++);
```

Evaluation

1. The operation inside the parentheses will be evaluated first. myPtr will be evaluated as 0x3000 and this will be the return value from the operation.
2. Before the return, myPtr will be incremented by the size of one integer to 0x3002.
3. The value 0x3000 is returned—the value *before* the increment.
4. 0x3 will be assigned to aVal because this is the value stored at memory location 0x3000.

Figure 7.12a Precedence with Pointers and Pointer Operations

```
int aVal = *myPtr+1;
```

Evaluation

1. myPtr will be evaluated as 0x3000 and dereferenced.
2. The value at memory location 0x3000 will be returned.
3. 1 will be added to the value returned from memory location 0x3000 to yield 0x4.
4. 0x4 will be assigned to aVal.

```
int aVal = *(myPtr+1);
```

Evaluation

1. myPtr will be evaluated as 0x3000.
2. 1 will be added to 0x3000 to give 0x3002.
3. The value at memory location 0x3002 will be returned and assigned to aVal.

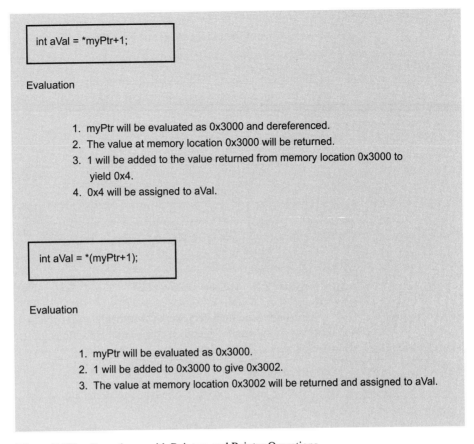

Figure 7.12b Precedence with Pointers and Pointer Operations

Pointer Comparison

Another form of arithmetic on pointers is comparison. In reality, what is being compared are addresses. Such a comparison is meaningful only if the addresses are in the same address space.

Legal comparisons are as follows.

```
==, !=
The two pointer values are or are not the same address
< , <=, >=, >
The two pointer values are or are not referring to higher or lower
addresses
```

7.2.3 Const Pointers

The const qualifier applied to pointers can be somewhat confusing. This confusion occurs because there are three different interpretations based on placement of the const keyword,

Pointer is const

Pointer is const

Value of the pointer cannot be changed and must be initialized at the time of declaration.

Thing pointed to is const

Thing pointed to is const

Value of the object cannot be changed.

Both are const

Both are const

as illustrated in Figure 7.13. Stated alternatively, if the keyword const appears to the left of the *, the object pointed to is constant; if the keyword appears to the right of the *, the const pointer is constant.

char myChar = 'a';

Object is Constant		*Pointer is Constant*
char	*	ptr = &myChar
const char	*	ptr = &myChar
char	*	const ptr = &myChar
const char	*	const ptr = &myChar

Figure 7.13 Pointers and const

Reading a pointer declaration from right to left helps to lessen the confusion a bit. Looking at the second and third entries in the previous table, we have

```
const char* ptr = &myChar;
```

Read this as

```
ptr is a pointer to a character constant - the character is constant,
it can't be changed.
```

```
char* const ptr = &myChar;
```

Read this as

```
ptr is a constant pointer to a character - the pointer is constant, it
can't be changed.
```

EXAMPLE 7.11

The simple program in Figure 7.14 illustrates how we work with pointers and the const qualifier.

```
#include <stdio.h>

void main(void)
{
    // declare some working variables

    const char myChar0 = 'a';
    char myChar1 = 'b';
    const char* ptr0 = &myChar0;
    char* const ptr1 = &myChar1;

    // *ptr0 = 'c';          // illegal ptr0 points to a constant
    *ptr1 = 'd';             // ok, the pointer not the object is const

    ptr0 = &myChar0;         // ok, the object is const not the pointer
    // ptr1 = &myChar1;      // illegal, the pointer is const
    return;
}
```

Figure 7.14 Working with Pointers and const

One can initialize a pointer to a const object with the address of a nonconst object. Doing so states we will not change an object that can legally change. We cannot assign the address of const object to a pointer to a nonconst object. The object may be changed through the pointer. One can cast the address of a const object to a pointer to a nonconst object. This can be dangerous. It is defeating the intent of the const.

EXAMPLE 7.12

```
const int a;
int * aPtr = &a;          // illegal
int* aPtr = (int*) &a;    // legal but dangerous
```

7.2.4 Generic and NULL Pointers

7.2.4.1 Generic Pointers

The pointer variables that we have been working with must always refer to a variable that is of the same type as the pointer. Such a restriction is imposed to ensure that the compiler returns the proper number of bytes from memory whenever the pointer is dereferenced. It is occasionally convenient to be able to use the same pointer to refer to a variable of any type.

generic pointer

*void, void**

To support such a capability, ANSI/ISO C introduces the *generic pointer*. The generic pointer is a pointer variable that can hold the address of a variable of any type. Such a pointer is said to be a pointer of type *void* or a *void* * pointer. Traditionally, this was done by casting the pointer to a variable of type pointer to char, then casting back to the proper type before dereferencing. The void* pointer was introduced to mitigate the obvious confusion that can result from using a char* pointer.

The void * pointer is guaranteed to be large enough to hold a pointer to any type of object, except a function type. A pointer to a variable of any type can be converted to a void* pointer and back again without losing any information.

An assignment to a void* pointer requires the use of the cast operator to remove the type information from the variable. To be able to dereference the value contained in the void* pointer, the process must be reversed; that is, the void* pointer must be cast back to a pointer of the original type. Because all of the type information has been taken away, a void* pointer cannot be dereferenced directly.

EXAMPLE 7.13

Assigning to a generic pointer

```
unsigned int* myIntPtr;               // declare a working pointer
void * myGenericPtr;                  // declare a generic pointer
unsigned int myValue = 3;             // declare an integer variable
myGenericPtr = (void*) (&myValue);    // find the address of myValue and
                                      // cast to a void*
```

To dereference the generic pointer, it must be cast back to a pointer of the original type.
Dereferencing the generic pointer

```
myIntPtr = (unsigned int*) myGenericPtr;   // recast myGenericPtr back
                                           // to original type
```

7.2.4.2 Null Pointers

Recall that when a variable in C is declared and defined, no default value is automatically assigned. One certainly *can* dereference a pointer that has not been initialized or to which no specific value has been assigned. Dereferencing treats the pointer's value as an address; however, what the address is referring to is not known. It could refer to another part of the program, the operating system, or some other piece of code. Such bugs can be very difficult to find because, generally, the system will crash shortly after the errant dereference. Initializing values for global or static pointers vary with compiler vendor. The value 0 is typically used. Dereferencing such a value usually gives a runtime error followed by program termination. This is never a desirable result, but it is particularly unpleasant for embedded applications.

null pointer

ANSI/ISO C offers a solution with the definition of a special pointer, the *null pointer*, whose value is guaranteed not to point to any object or function. That value is given as

```
(void*)0
```

<stddef.h>

and is defined as a macro in the header file *<stddef.h>,* where it is given the name *NULL.* Good programming style recommends that all pointers have the value NULL when not assigned to any object or function. The pointer must be assigned a valid address to some value before dereferencing.

7.3 THE FUNCTION

library functions

user defined

A C program is simply a collection of functions. A special set of these called *library functions* are predefined and are found in the Standard C Libraries. Most functions, however, are *user defined.* These will be our first focus.

main()

We have already written one function, *main().* As we write larger programs, we will need to write more and sophisticated functions. We will also comment later on the general rules for writing functions; the principal rule will be to keep things simple.

We talked earlier about the desirability of decomposing a program into modules. The modules we write are further decomposed into functions. If we are careful with the designs and if we document everything well, future designers working with the code will be able to use those modules and functions without ever needing to know the details of their internal implementation. If we are very clever, we will be able to change and improve (reduce the required amount of memory, increase speed, lower power) these functions and still maintain the same external behavior. Our goal is to design our functions to have a robust and persistent public interface so that those utilizing them will never have to modify the internal code.

defining

function header, function body

We create a function by *defining* it. Defining a function entails specifying and designing a *function header* and a *function body.*

FUNCTION HEADER

function name, return type, parameter list, prototype

The function header specifies the *function name*, the *return type*, and a *parameter list.* The header is also called a *prototype.*

FUNCTION NAME

referred to, invoked, called

The function name is a C identifier. As we learned in our study of variables, the function's identifier is how it is *referred to* or *invoked* or *called* when needed in the application.

ARGUMENTS OR PARAMETER LIST

argument or parameter list
signature

The arguments comprise a comma-separated list, enclosed in parentheses, that appears after the function name. The parentheses and the arguments are called the *argument or parameter list.* The number, type, and order of the arguments are called the *signature* of function. The parameters are given values when the function is invoked, called, or executed. The arguments can be used to

input arguments
output arguments

- Send data into the function; such arguments are *input arguments.*
- Retrieve data from a function; such arguments are *output arguments.*

RETURN

return
return value
return type
void

Another method by which data can be returned from a function is to use its *return* statement. When a value is returned from a function in such a way, the function is said to have a *return value*. The type of data returned is called the *return type*. One can think of the function's return value as replacing the function call at the place in the program where the function was invoked. Sometimes functions have nothing to return; they have a return value of *void.*

THE FUNCTION BODY

function body

A function is simply a series of C instructions enclosed in curly braces. That collection of instructions expresses the *function body.* This is where the real work gets done. Both the general form of a function and a specific instance are presented in Figure 7.15.

Syntax

```
    returnType functionName ( arg0, arg1...argn-1 )
    {
        body
    }

int multiply(int first, int second)
{
    // this is the function body
    return first * second;
}
```

Figure 7.15 The Function Syntax

7.3.1 Using a Function

executing, evaluating, invoking, calling, function call, calling function, called function

By itself, a function may be interesting or even elegant, but it is of little use unless one does something with it. Using a function is called *executing, evaluating, invoking,* or *calling* the function. The function is executed by performing a *function call*. The function performing the function call is called the *calling function,* and the function being executed is called the *called function.* All functions are created equal; any function can call any other function, including itself.

Consider the arithmetic function that performs the multiplication of two integers as we have described earlier. One can write the function body such that it is able to multiply the first and second arguments and return the product. Questions to think about include

- How do we call the function?
- How do we pass in the numbers to be multiplied?
- How do we use the product that is returned?

Let's step inside the function and see what happens when the function is called. We will

- Call the function
- Pass variables into the function
- Perform a computation in the function
- Return from the function
- Return a variable from the function

The code fragment in Figure 7.16 defines a simple function, *computeArea( )*, that computes the area of a specified rectangle.

```
#include <stdio.h>
// function prototype
int computeArea (length, width);
void main(void)
{
    // declare and initialize some variables
    int  length =10;
    int  width=20;
    int  area=0;

    area = computeArea(length, width);  //  this is the function call

    printf("the area is: %d\n", area);        //  displays 200
    return;
}

int computeArea(int first, int second)
{
    int  answer;
    answer =first *second;
    return answer;
}
```

Figure 7.16 Working with Functions

To get a function to execute the lines of code contained in the body, one must *call* the function. The call is affected by writing the name of the function followed by the argument list, enclosed in parentheses, as a line of code in a program. This is shown in the following line:

```
area = computeArea(length, width); // this is the function call
```

computeArea(), first, second, length, width, main()

Observe that the arguments of *computeArea()* are not *first* and *second,* but are *length* and *width*. The names *length* and *width* are in the scope of the *main()* function; they are not visible to *computeArea()*. The names *first* and *second* are in the scope of the *computeArea()* function and are not visible outside of that function. To get data into the function so that it can be assigned to the function's internal variables, it has to be passed in through the function's arguments. Recall that the exchange takes place via the stack. The operation is illustrated in Figure 7.17.

make a copy, length first, width second, passes arguments

When the *computeArea()* function is called, the compiler will *make a copy* of *length,* name the copy *first,* and place that variable onto the stack. Similarly, a copy of *width* will be created, be named *second*, and placed onto the stack. We say such a process *passes arguments* to the function.

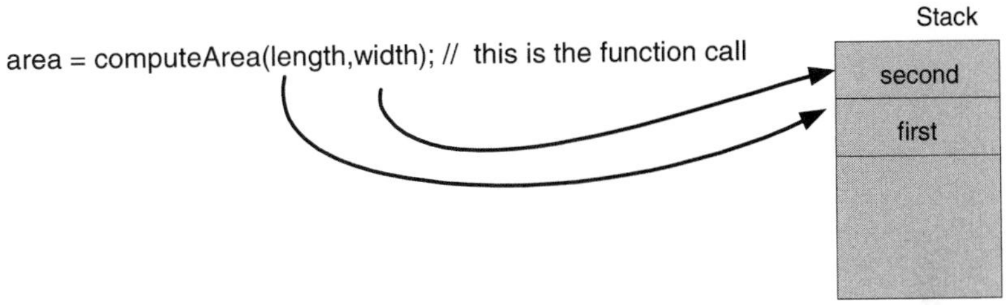

Figure 7.17 Passing Data to a Function via the Stack

area main() computeArea(), context switch, context

Thus, when the C program reaches the line given above, it determines that a value is to be assigned to the variable *area.* However, the value does not exist; it must be calculated. At this point, the compiler stops executing in *main(),* and flow of control is passed to the *computeArea()* function. The change in flow of control is called a *context switch.* Instruction execution moves from the *context* in which the call was encountered to that which contains the block of instructions intended to perform the specified operation.

For designers of embedded applications, it is important to understand how function calls are managed. In most cases, it is sufficient to let the compiler take care of the details. However, there are times when it is necessary to get involved. Understanding the mechanics of the process can provide an understanding of how the program works, what the bottlenecks might be, how to optimize the flow if necessary, and if it is is not working, perhaps why.

stack frame activation record

We know that variables are local to a function, but exactly where are they stored in memory? The answer is that they are stored in a *stack frame,* which is also sometimes called an *activation record.* The stack frame is dynamically allocated and populated when the function is called. It contains

- Copies of all the variables used as arguments.
- Copies of any local variables from the original context as necessary, which saves the existing context. These will be restored on return.
- A place for the return value.
- The address in the calling function where execution is to jump when the call is complete. This is known as the *return address*. The return address is always the address of the next machine instruction after the call.

return address

As long as the function is executing, the stack frame remains in memory, on the stack. This means that if a function calls another function or itself, a new stack frame is created and added to the top of the stack. When a function exits, the values of all variables in the original context are restored, any return value from the called function is assigned as designated in the calling function, flow of control returns to the original context, and its stack frame is removed from the stack. Removal occurs by modifying the top of stack pointer. The old stack frame is *not* erased. As a result, it should be very obvious why one should never return the address of a local variable. Returning a local variable is permissible, however, because that value can be retrieved prior to deleting the stack frame of the called function.

stack overflow

In embedded applications, one does not have the luxury of unlimited memory; thus, if too many stack frames are added to the stack, the result is a *stack overflow*. Under such a condition, the stack frame and all its contents can be lost. Such a loss means that variables in the original context cannot be restored, but, worse, the return address is gone.

length, width, first, second
computeArea()
allocating a variable on the stack

It should now be evident that when *computeArea()* is encountered in a code module, the compiler makes the copies of *length* and *width,* names them *first* and *second*, pushes them onto the stack, and jumps to the opening brace of the *computeArea()* function. It should now be understood that the phrase *allocating a variable on the stack* simply means the variable is stored in the stack frame associated with the function that declared that variable.

The function body for *computeArea()* is now given as

```
int computeArea(int first, int second)
{
     int  answer;
     answer = first*second;
     return answer;
}
```

computeArea()
first, second

When invoked, the *computeArea()* function will retrieve the two variables from the stack and assign the values to the internal variables *first* and *second*. Execution entails evaluating each line of (machine code) in the *computeArea()* function to calculate the result: *answer.*

answer

Answer, however, belongs to—is in the scope of—the *computeArea()* function. When the line

```
return answer;
```

copy of answer, main()

is executed, a temporary *copy of answer* is made and returned to *main()*. Like the incoming variables, that copy is placed onto the stack as we see in Figure 7.18.

The return statement in *computeArea()* is the end of the function. After this statement executes, all of the copies of variables made for *computeArea()* to use and pushed onto the stack earlier are destroyed. All that is left is the *copy* of *answer* (which is a constant). Execution resumes in *main()* where the copy of *answer* is now assigned to *area.* After the assignment is made, the copy of *answer* is no longer valid.

When the program is compiled, the body of the function will be stored in memory much as is seen in Figure 7.19. The key point here is that the code comprising the body of the function has an address and, in this example, that address is 0x6FAC. We will work more with such addresses shortly.

Observe that only the implementation portion of the function is stored. The parameters passed in, and, thus, the local variables are stored on the stack.

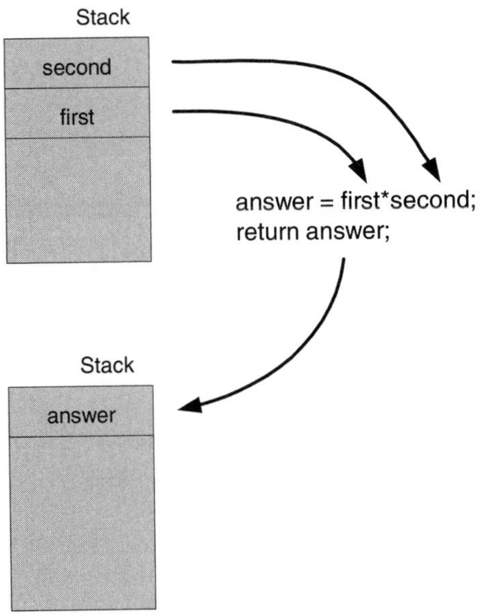

Figure 7.18 Returning Data from a Function via the Stack

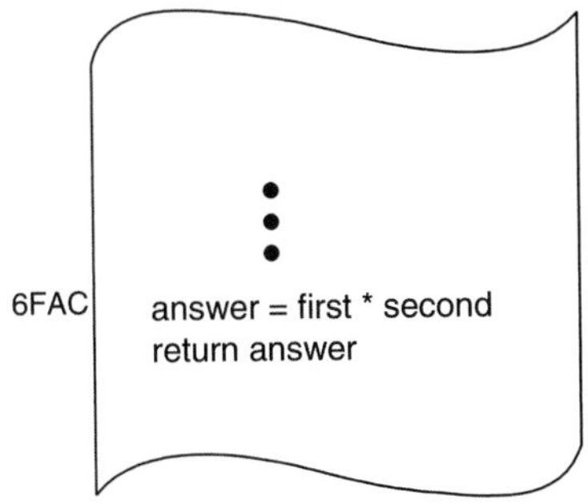

Figure 7.19 The Function Body in Memory

7.3.2 Pass by Value

pass by value

In the program just described, we stressed that the variables passed into and returned from the function were copies of the original variables. The C language is called a *pass by value* language. This means that although the variables inside the body of the function have the same values as the originals, they *are not* the original variables. Consequently, any changes made to those values while in the function body are not reflected in the original variables; the original variables are in a different local scope.

The same is true for any variables declared within the function body; such variables cannot be accessed in the original calling function. Once again, the local scopes are different. If we return such a variable, we are only returning its value. Any variables declared within the function body are not valid as soon as the enclosing scope is exited.

The pass by value semantics of the C language is a very good source of programming bugs. The common lament is, "I made a change to the variable, I can see the change, but, it still has the original values back here. . . . I don't understand this." The code module in Figure 7.20 will illustrate the problem.

EXAMPLE 7.14

```
#include <stdio.h>
/*
      Demonstrate pass and return by value in C
*/
int myFunction(int aValue);
void main(void)
{
      // declare and initialize some working variables
      int myValue = 5;
      int aReturnVal = 0;
      myFunction(myValue);

      // will show myValue as 5...no change
      printf("main(): myValue is: %i\n", myValue);

      // will show aReturnValue as 0...no change
      printf("main(): aReturnVal is: %i\n", aReturnVal);

      // by assigning to aReturnValue, we copy the returned value
      aReturnVal = myFunction(myValue);

      // will show aReturnValue as 9
      printf("main(): aReturnVal is: %i\n", aReturnVal);
      return;
}
int myFunction(int myValue)
{
      // declare and initialize a working variable
      int aReturnValue = 0;
      // change the value of the input parameter
      // this change will not appear in main
      myValue = myValue + 4;

      // will show myValue as 9
      printf("myFunction: aValue is: %i\n", myValue);
      aReturnValue = myValue;
      return aReturnValue;
}
```

Figure 7.20 Passing to a Function by Value

myFunction() As is evident, any changes made to the variables passed in to *myFunction()* are visible only while within the scope of that function, even if the same names are used as in the calling function.

7.3.3 Pass by Reference

pass by reference

Although C is a pass by value language by default, it is sometimes necessary to be able to pass the original variables into a function, operate on those variables, and have the results persist outside of the function. Under such circumstances, *pass by reference* semantics are required.

Such a capability is not difficult to achieve. If one knows where the variable to be modified is stored in memory, one can simply go to that location and perform the desired operations. Thus, it is possible to change the original object. How does one find out where the object is stored within a function? The address in memory of where the data is stored is passed into the function through a pointer variable.

Let's modify the previous example to work with the original data. Note that when using pass by reference, one does not have to return the modified value. That change is already reflected in the value of the variable as seen in the following code module in Figure 7.21. Thus, we save the time to copy the value onto the stack as well as the time to copy the stack value to a local variable in the calling routine.

EXAMPLE 7.15

```
#include <stdio.h>
/*
    Demonstrate pass by reference in C
*/
void myFunction(int* aValuePtr);

void main(void)
{
    // declare and initialize a working variable
    int myValue = 5;
    // pass in the address of the data
    myFunction(&myValue);
    // will show myValue as 9...the original has been changed through the pointer
    printf("main(): myValue is: %i\n", myValue);
    return;
}

void myFunction(int* myValuePtr)
{
    // change the value of the input parameter this change will appear in main
    *myValuePtr = *myValuePtr + 4;
    // will show myValue as 9
    printf("myFunction(): myValue is: %i\n", *myValuePtr);
    return;
}
```

Figure 7.21 Passing to a Function by Reference

7.3.4 Function Name Scope

extern

information hiding

static

Without additional qualification, the visibility of the name of a function is restricted to the scope in which it was declared. However, the name of the function declared in one file may be made visible to other files through the qualifier *extern,* as was discussed earlier. Using such a qualifier, one can make the name—the identifier—of the function known to the linker and thus make it available for use in other contexts.

There are also times when one wants to restrict the function name from general use. This is what is called *information hiding*. The C++ and Java languages make widespread use of such capability, although the implementation in those languages is a bit different. In C, one can accomplish information hiding by putting the function name into a separate file and qualifying it with the keyword *static* as is seen in Figure 7.22.

```
// staticFunct0.c

#include <stdio.h>
// make the function name available
// in this file
extern void myFunct0(void);

// this name will not be available
extern void myFunct1(void);
void main (void)
{
     myFunct0();

// results in compile error -
// the function name is not visible
     myFunct1();
     return;
}
```

```
// containFunct0.c

#include <stdio.h>
// function prototypes
void myFunct0(void);

// function not visible outside of this file
// ...remove static to make visible
static void myFunct1(void);

// define the functions
void myFunct0(void)
{
     int x = 3;
     printf("x is %i\n", x);
     return;
}
// remove static to make visible
static void myFunct1(void)
{
     int y = 4;
     printf("y is %i\n", y);
     return;
}
```

Figure 7.22 Controlling the Visibility of a Function Name with the Static Qualifier

With such a qualification, the name is not exported—made visible to—the linker. Even with the extern qualifier, the name remains hidden and thus is not available for use by other functions, as we saw with static variables.

7.3.5 Function Prototypes

function prototype

In the example program, the line near the top that looks like a function header is called a *function prototype;* it provides some useful information to the compiler.

```
// function prototype
int computeArea (int length, int width);
```

Initially, this appears to be duplicate information; it seems that the compiler should be able to get the necessary information from the function header. One problem arises, however. It is not uncommon to define a function, that is, provide the header and then provide the actual implementation, later in the program (often in another file), following some other function such a *main()* that uses it. To ensure that a function call is correct, the compiler examines

main()

- The expected return type
- The order, number, and type of arguments provided by the caller
- The function identifier

It then tries to match these against the name, signature, and return type for functions that it knows about. If there is no match, the compiler does not know which function body to associate with the call, so it guesses—it is preferable that guessing by the compiler be limited. Such guessing can lead to runtime errors because, without the prototype, the compiler cannot do any type checking.

What happens if a prototype is not provided? If the function is defined before being called, there is no problem. The compiler has sufficient information to perform all of its checks. Otherwise the compiler starts guessing again.

To keep the compiler happy and to enable full-type checking through the prototype, it is sufficient to simply declare the function. The declaration is done by listing the return value (type), the function name, and the function's signature at the top of the program. In the prototype, it's only necessary to specify the parameter types; the specific variable names are not necessary.

Coding Style

Although the variable names are never used by the compiler, they can provide additional information about the intent of each parameter to users of the function.

Good coding style strongly recommends including the names.

Which is more useful as the prototype for computing the area of a rectangle?

```
int f1(int, int);
```

or

```
int computeArea(int length, int width);
```

Although both are syntactically correct, the second, using a descriptive function name as well as meaningful parameter names, can significantly improve the readability of a program, mitigate against possible errors, and simplify future enhancements to the function. Often, all of the function prototypes will be placed into a common header file, which can then be included when needed.

The only function that does not require a prototype is *main()* because there is only one such function in the program. It is the same function prototype in all C programs, so the compiler already knows everything about it.

Coding Style

When we write a function, we follow the same general guidelines that we did for variables. Always select meaningful and relevant names. Because functions can sometimes be rather complex or may be visible only from their calling interface, good annotation becomes very important. We provide such documentation in a function header.

As one gains experience in designing and writing functions and their documentation, each person will probably evolve his or her own style and preferences. The template shown in Figure 7.23 is a good place to start.

```
/*
 *  Function Name with Signature
 *  Short Description of intent/purpose of the function
 *  Input Parameters with short description and range of legal values
 *  Return Values with short description and range of legal values
 *  Side effects of the Function—What it might change that could affect other parts of the program.
 *  Invariants—Things the function should not change
 *  Revision History—Identify who, when, and what changes have been made to the function.
 *  Citation of Code Source or Reference if developed by another author
*/
```

Figure 7.23 A Template for a Function Documentation Header

7.3.6 Nesting Functions

nesting When one function is used inside of a second function, it is called *nesting*. A fair question is, "How deeply can functions be nested?" The question has a relative answer. The compiler makes copies of the variables used for arguments in the function, pushes them onto the stack for use in the function, and then destroys the copies when the function completes. It seems reasonable that all the copies should hang around until the most deeply nested function call completes.

stack A simple model of such a situation is a collection of airplanes "stacked up" waiting to land. When the system runs out of the *stack* memory the executing program will crash. The amount of stack memory varies with operating systems and is usually adjustable if needed. In embedded applications, because of memory limitations, this limit is reached sooner rather than later.

Some compilers will try to estimate the amount of stack space required by looking at first level function calls within a function and trying to adjust the necessary stack size. Detecting recursion, or two or more functions calling one another, is a much more complex problem. As designers, it's our responsibility to anticipate and manage the stack size. We do this through information provided by the compiler vendor in the documentation for the compiler.

7.4 POINTERS TO FUNCTIONS

data pointers ***function pointers*** The pointer variables we have discussed so far have held the addresses of variables or data. We refer to them as *data pointers*. Since the value of a pointer variable is an address and the body of a function has an address in memory, there is no reason one cannot use a pointer variable to hold the address of a function body. Such pointers are called *function pointers*.

The syntax for a function pointer, given in Figure 7.24, is a little more complex and, perhaps, more confusing than that for the data pointer. With a little practice, the complexity will disappear.

> ***Syntax***
> return type (* functionPointer) (<arg_0, arg_1...arg_n>)
> arg list may be empty

Figure 7.24 Declaring a Pointer to a Function

Let's look at a couple of examples to see what this means.

EXAMPLE 7.16

We make the following function pointer declaration:

```
int (* intfunctPtr) (void);
```

We read the declaration in several steps:

intFunctPtr

1. is a pointer to a function.
2. the function takes no arguments.
3. the function returns an int.

intFunctPtr

The parentheses enclosing the pointer, *intFunctPtr*, are important and necessary. Without them, we would have a prototype for a function that takes no arguments and returns a pointer to an integer. Let's try another one,

```
double (* doublefunctPtr) (int, char);
```

We read the declaration in several steps:

doubleFunctPtr

1. is a pointer to a function.
2. the function takes two arguments, one of type integer and the other of type char.
3. the function returns a double.

As with the variables in C, the name of a function is equivalent to its address in memory. More specifically, for a function that address is the location where the body of the function is stored. Thus, to initialize or assign to a function pointer, one simply writes the function's name on the right-hand side of an assignment operator.

EXAMPLE 7.17

We first declare a function pointer and then a function to point to. After that, we simply make the assignment.

```
int (* intFunctPtr) ();      // declare a function pointer
int myFunction(void);        // declare a function

intFunctPtr = myFunction;    // point to the function
```

Observe that in assigning the function address to the pointer variable, we only use the function's name. It is not necessary to give the function's signature or return type.

A function pointer can be dereferenced in several ways. The syntax is given in Figure 7.25.

```
syntax
    (* functionPointer) (<arg0, arg1...argn>)
        or
    functionPointer (<arg0, arg1...argn>)
        arg list may be empty
```

Figure 7.25 Dereferencing a Pointer to a Function

EXAMPLE 7.18

The code fragment in Figure 7.26 illustrates how we declare, assign a value to, and dereference function pointers.

```
unsigned int anInt = 3;                     // declare some working variables
unsigned char aChar = 'a';

int (* intFunctPtr) ();                     // declare a function pointer
double (*doubleFunctPtr)(int, char);        // declare another function pointer

int myFunction(void);                       // declare a function
double yourFunction (int, char)             // declare another function

intFunctPtr = myFunction;                   // point to the first function
doubleFunctPtr = yourFunction;              // point to the second function

(*intFunctPtr)();                           // dereference the first pointer
(*doubleFunctPtr)(anInt, aChar );           // dereference the second pointer
```

Figure 7.26 Working with Pointers to Functions

Using a function, one can encapsulate a piece of functionality that can be used in several places throughout our application. We have a single implementation and multiple calls to that function. Such a capability is powerful and can substantially reduce the size of an application if the body of such a function is moderately sized and is used in a number of places. Of course, we are trading off reduced code size for additional overhead in making the function call.

When we use pointers to functions, we gain an additional level of capability and flexibility. By using a pointer to refer to a function, we have the ability to pass the functionality to another function with the same ease that we did a simple variable. In the same way that we use a single pointer to refer to a number of different variables, it is possible to use the same function pointer to refer to a number of different functions.

With that kind of capability, one can design a computational module, for example, that takes as input a pointer to a mathematical function, the arguments to that function, and returns the result of the computation. The computational module does not have to know anything about the internal design of the functions it is evaluating.

Let's see how this works with the simple program in Figure 7.27.

EXAMPLE 7.19

```
//  Pointers to Functions used as Function Arguments
#include <stdio.h>

// function prototypes
int add(int a1, int a2);
int sub(int a1, int a2);

// myFunction has a three parameters,
// a pointer to a function taking 2 ints as arguments and the argument values, and returning an int.

int myFunction (int (*fPtr)(int, int), int, int);

void main(void)
{
    // declare some working variables
    int sum, diff;

    // Declare fPtr as a pointer to a function taking 2 ints as arguments and returning an int
    int (*fPtr)(int a1, int a2);

    // assign fPtr to point to the add function
    fPtr = add;                                  // fPtr points to the function add
    sum = myFunction(fPtr, 2, 3);                // pass fPtr to myFunction()
    printf ("The sum is: %d\n", sum);            // prints The sum is: 5

    // assign fPtr to point to the sub function
    fPtr = sub;                                  // fPtr points to the function sub
    diff = myFunction(fPtr, 5, 2);               // pass fPtr to myFunction()
    printf ("The difference is: %d\n", diff);    // prints The difference is: 3

    return;
}
// perform requested binary computation and return result
int myFunction (int (*fPtr)(int a1, int a2), int aVar0, int aVar1)
{
    // variables a1 and a2 are placeholders - they are not used
    // dereference the pointer and return value
    return (fPtr(aVar0, aVar1));
}

// add two integers and return their sum
int add(int a1, int a2)
{
    return (a1+a2);
}

// subtract two integers and return their difference
int sub(int a1, int a2)
{
    return (a1-a2);
}
```

Figure 7.27 Working with Pointers to Functions

Let's look at the code fragment in Figure 7.28 from the program above.

```
// Declare fPtr as a pointer to a function taking 2 ints as arguments and returning an int
int (*fPtr)(int a1, int a2);

// assign fPtr to point to the add function
fPtr = add;                              // fPtr points to the function add
sum = myFunction(fPtr, 2, 3);            // pass fPtr to myFunction()
printf ("The sum is: %d\n", sum);        // prints The sum is: 5
```

Figure 7.28 Working with Pointers to Functions

add(int,int)

The first line declares a pointer to a function. That pointer can then be used to refer to the function *add(int,int)* that had been declared earlier. One does so by simply assigning the address of the function to the pointer. One can now pass the pointer, along with a couple of numbers to be added, to a second function where the function pointer is dereferenced and the result is computed, returned, and then assigned to the variable sum.

In the code fragment in Figure 7.29, the process is repeated, only now the function pointer is used to refer to the subtract function.

```
// assign fPtr to point to the sub function
fPtr = sub;                                   // fPtr points to the function sub
diff = myFunction(fPtr, 5, 2);                // pass fPtr to myFunction()
printf ("The difference is: %d\n", diff);     // prints The difference is: 3
```

Figure 7.29 Working with Pointers to Functions

myFunction()

The same pointer has been used to refer to two different functions. In neither case does *myFunction()* know anything about the computation it is performing; it simply dereferences the pointer.

The function pointer will play a significant role in building an operating system kernel. We will introduce that topic shortly. Several additional pieces of information are necessary first.

7.5 STRUCTURES

structure
heterogeneous

The final intrinsic C language data type that we will study is the *structure*. We learned earlier that an array or a string is a homogeneous collection of variables grouped under the same name and treated as a single entity. The *structure* data type permits one to form a *heterogeneous* collection of variables that can be grouped under a single name and treated as a single object. The semantics are similar to the C++ or Java class. Through the structure data type, one can also define new data types that allow the basic C language to be extended.

The newly defined types are first-class types—they are treated exactly as any of the intrinsic types. We will begin with the basic concept.

7.5.1 The Struct

point

From a mathematical perspective, a point in a Cartesian coordinate system can be described by two integers, as illustrated in Figure 7.30. However, we don't think of the point that way. We simply think of it as a point. We are accustomed to treating those two variables as a single object and to referring to different points in space. We think of a variable of type *point.*

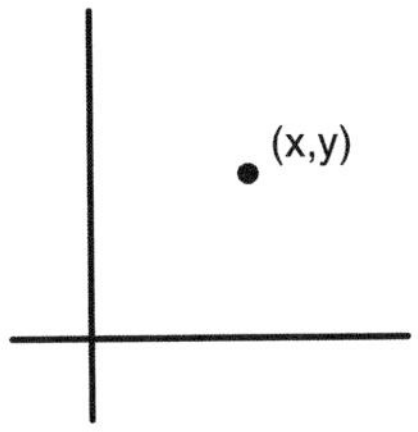

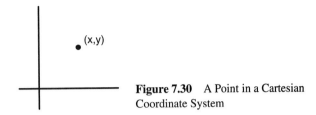

Figure 7.30 A Point in a Cartesian Coordinate System

struct *point*

In C, we can capture that concept and express the two attributes of a real-world point in the data type called a *struct.* Thereafter, we can refer to and work with entities of the type *point.* We will see an example of how we do this shortly. Let's first examine the struct.

typedef

The syntax and general format for a struct are given in Figure 7.31. We see that the declaration of a structure in C begins with the keyword *struct,* which must precede the identifier. We will learn how to use a *typedef* shortly to make such a declaration more readable. Once the struct is declared, we can create instances of it just as is done with any of the intrinsic types.

```
syntax
    struct StructTag
    {
        struct body;
    };
    struct StructTag anInstance;
```

Figure 7.31 Syntax and General struct Format

anonymous *data members*

The structure tag, which is optional, is used as an identifier for the structure. If we choose not to use an identifying name, the struct is designated as *anonymous.* The body of the struct is enclosed in curly braces and comprises a heterogeneous collection of variables that are called *data members.* Each line in the body is terminated with a semicolon. The body cannot contain functions, but can include pointers to functions. The closing brace for the struct is terminated with a semicolon. This is in contrast to other blocks in the language such as a looping construct.

Like the declarations of intrinsic variable types, the declaration of a struct *does not* allocate any memory. It simply brings the identifier name into the namespace. Memory for the data members is not allocated until an instance is created. The declaration simply says: "*The following variables will be grouped together; that grouping will be known by this identifier. An instance of the data type will be created later if necessary.*" Such treatment of the type is no different from any of the intrinsic types. Naming of the type integer simply specifies the characteristics of the type when one is eventually created.

Coding Style

We generally make the first letter of the structure tag upper case to distinguish a structure type from a variable name (usually lower case first letter) and from a symbolic constant (usually all upper case letters).

One can express the struct using a UML object diagram as shown in Figure 7.32.

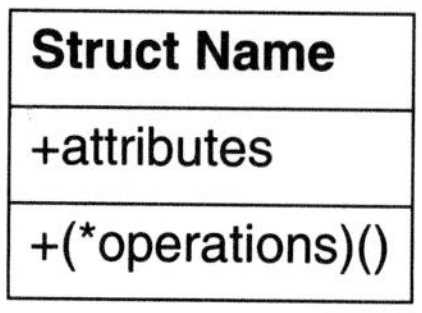

Figure 7.32 The struct Expressed as a UML Object Diagram

Because the struct data type in the C language does not support functions, if such capability is required, one must use pointers to functions. This should not present any problem.

EXAMPLE 7.20

Point, data members

To express the point in Cartesian space using a struct, we will select the tag name *Point*. The *data members* will be the two integers defining the point in two-dimensional space as in Figure 7.33. The UML diagram is presented first followed by the C declaration.

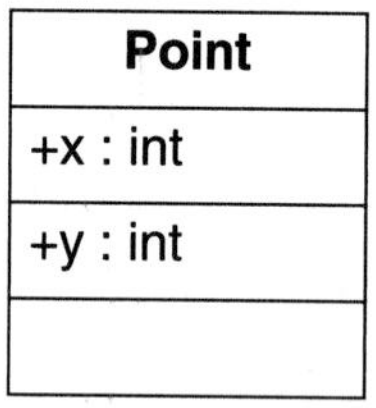


```
struct Point
{
    int x;
    int y;
};
```

Figure 7.33 A UML Object Diagram for the *Point* Data Type and the Corresponding struct Declaration

Point

Such a declaration has created a new type called *Point*. One can now create instances of a *Point*:

```
struct Point aPoint1;
struct Point aPoint2;
```

---

struct

Writing the keyword *struct* for each declaration becomes tedious quickly. One can use the typedef construct to fix this problem, as we see in the code fragment in Figure 7.34.

```
typedef struct
{
    int x;
    int y;
} Point;
```

Figure 7.34 Using a typedef to Simplify the struct Type Specification

Now we have it. The identifier Point is an alias for the struct declaration.

EXAMPLE 7.21

Point

Following the typedef, one can now create several instances of a *Point*.

```
Point aPoint1;
Point aPoint2;
```

7.5.2 Initialization

Like the array, one can initialize the data members of a struct by following the declaration with a list of initializing values as given in Figure 7.35. There is a one-to-one correspondence between each of the data members and the initializing values.

syntax

```
struct StructTag
{
        struct body;
};

struct StructTag anInstance = (initializer list);
```

Figure 7.35 Initializing a struct Instance

EXAMPLE 7.22

The following code fragment creates an instance of a *Point* that has the initial coordinates of 100 and 200.

```
typedef struct
{
    int x;
    int y;
} Point;
Point pt = (100, 200);
```

7.5.3 Access

One can access each of the data members in an instance of the struct by using a fully qualified name. That is, we give the instance name followed by the member name using a construct of the form

```
structureName.member
```

EXAMPLE 7.23

The following code fragment creates an instance of a *Point* that has the initial coordinates of 100 and 200 and then prints the values of the two coordinates.

```
typedef struct
{
    int x;
    int y;
} Point;

Point pt = (100, 200);
printf("x = %i y=%i\n", pt.x, pt.y);
```

The identifier, pt, designates the specific instance of the struct Point in the same way *im aVar* that *int aVar* might designate an instance of the type int. The x or y designates which data member of the instance pt we are interested in.

As with a function, the body of a struct represents a distinct local scope. Variables declared within the body of a struct are in the scope of that struct. In the preceding example, we could not, for example, simply write

```
x = 50;
```

because we have no way of distinguishing a variable with the identifier x in the struct versus one with the same name elsewhere in the program. By specifying the context in which the *Point* variable exists, pt.x—in this case within the *Point* instance variable pt—the identifier ambiguity is resolved.

7.5.4 Operations

The only legal operations on a struct are

- Copying
- Assignment to as a unit
- Taking address, using the address of the operator, &.

Structs cannot be compared. Operations such as the following

```
Point{…};
Point pt1, pt2;

if (pt1 == pt2)
{
}
```

are illegal.

7.5.5 Structs as Data Members

7.5.5.1 Accessing Members

Since a struct is a user-defined type and since one can declare instances of that type, there should be no reason that a data member of a struct could not be an instance of another struct. *Point* Such is, in fact, the case. Continuing with the *Point* example, a rectangle is fully specified by naming its opposite vertices. Expressing this concept graphically gives the diagram in Figure 7.36.

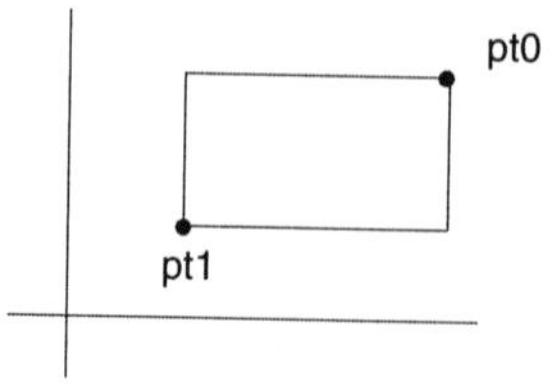

Figure 7.36 A Rectangle Is Specified by Two Points

We start with the UML object diagram for the rectangle. One can also say that the Rect- *composed* angle is *composed* of two points. Such a relationship can be expressed in the composition diagram shown in Figure 7.37.

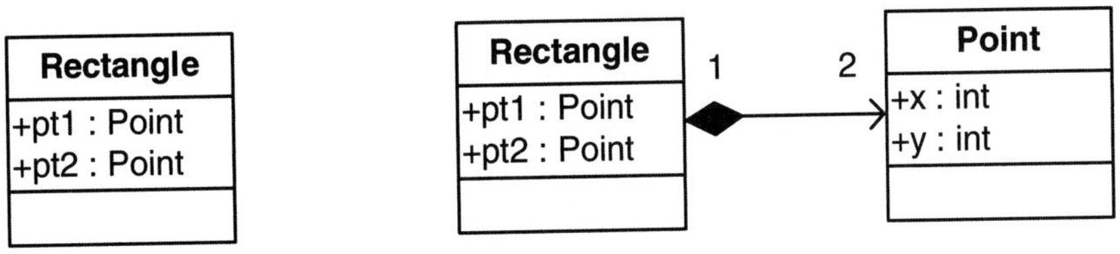

Figure 7.37 Expressing the *Rectangle* as a Composition of *Points*

The Point and the Rectangle can be defined as C structs shown in Figure 7.38. Once again, we will use the typedef in the declaration to simplify matters.

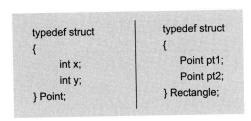

```
typedef struct
{
    int x;
    int y;
} Point;
```

```
typedef struct
{
    Point pt1;
    Point pt2;
} Rectangle;
```

Figure 7.38 Using a typedef to Simplify the Type Specification of a *Point* and a *Rectangle*

The order in which the two structs are declared is significant. Recall what we learned about function prototypes earlier. Since the declaration of a struct defines a new data type, one must make certain that it has been declared before it is used in a subsequent declaration. If the Rectangle was declared prior to the declaration of the Point, any attempt to compile the code fragment would have resulted in an error.

Accessing a data member of struct type within a struct is a simple extension of what we have done so far.

Given the declaration:

```
Rectangle r1;
r1.pt1.x
```

Refers to x coordinate of pt1

```
r1.pt1.y
```

Refers to y coordinate of pt1

7.5.5.2 Initialization and Assignment

The initialization of a data member of struct type within a struct is a bit trickier. One cannot initialize an instance of a Rectangle with bracketed list of points

```
Rectangle r1 = {pt1, pt2};
```

Values for the data members can be assigned, however. The following code fragment will provide values for the two data members.

```
Point p1 = {10, 20};
Point p2 = {20, 30};

Rectangle r1;
r1.pt1 = p1;
r1.pt2 = p2;
```

7.5.5.3 Functions

Let's now see how to put the struct to work. Some of the things that one might like to know about a Rectangle are its area and its perimeter. Since the C struct does not support functions, we will use pointers to functions. First the UML diagram and then the C definition are presented in Figure 7.39.

The object diagram shows that the Rectangle has two data members of type Point and two members that are pointers to functions. Each function takes two parameters of type Point and returns an int.

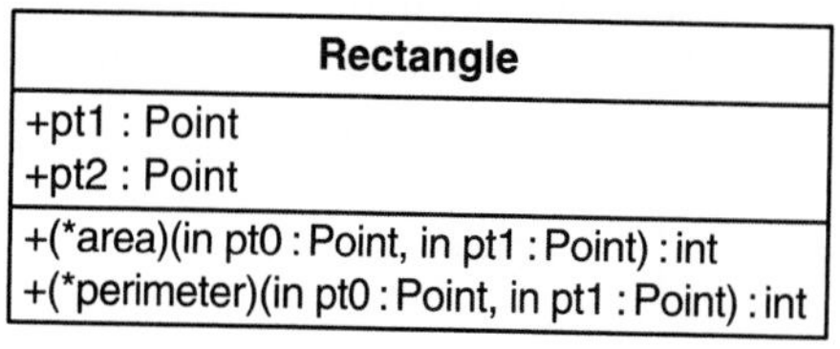

Rectangle
+pt1 : Point
+pt2 : Point
+(*area)(in pt0 : Point, in pt1 : Point) : int
+(*perimeter)(in pt0 : Point, in pt1 : Point) : int


```
typedef struct
{
    Point pt1;
    Point pt2;
    int (*area)(Point pt0, Point pt1);
    int (*perimeter) (Point pt0, Point pt1);
} Rectangle;
```

Figure 7.39 Adding Function Capability to a struct

The design can now be turned into C code.

For this example, we will build the project from three separate files:

header file
included
Points, Rectangles

- A *header file* containing the struct definitions and the function prototypes—rect.h as identified in Figure 7.40. The header will be *included* in the two other files because they must know about *Points* and *Rectangles.*

```
typedef struct
{
    int x;
    int y;
} Point;

typedef struct
{
    Point pt1;
    Point pt2;
    int (*area)(Point pt0, Point pt1);
    int (*perimeter) (Point pt0, Point pt1);
} Rectangle;
int computeArea(Point pt0, Point pt1);
int computePerimeter(Point pt0, Point pt1);
```

Figure 7.40 Writing Header File for the struct Declarations

implementation file
linked

- An *implementation file* containing the definitions of the functions used to compute the rectangle's area and perimeter is given in Figure 7.41. This is a C source file and will be *linked* into the project.

```
#include "rect.h"
// Rectangle area function
int computeArea(Point pt0, Point pt1)
{
      int area = (pt1.x - pt0.x) * (pt1.y - pt0.y);
      return area;
}

// Rectangle perimeter function
int computePerimeter(Point pt0, Point pt1)
{
      int perimeter = 2*(pt1.x - pt0.x) + 2*(pt1.y - pt0.y);
      return perimeter;
}
```

Figure 7.41 Writing the Implementation File for the struct Definitions

- The *main implementation file* appears in Figure 7.42. This is a .c source file and the place where the work gets done.

```
#include <stdio.h>
// bring in struct definitions and function prototypes
#include "rect.h"

void main (void)
{
      // declare and instance of Rectangle
      Rectangle myRectangle;
      // declare some working variables
      int myArea = 0;
      int myPerimeter = 0;

      // assign values to instance data members
      myRectangle.pt1.x = 5;
      myRectangle.pt1.y = 10;
      myRectangle.pt2.x = 10;
      myRectangle.pt2.y = 20;

      // assign values to instance function pointers
      myRectangle.area = computeArea;
      myRectangle.perimeter = computePerimeter;

      // compute the area and perimeter
      myArea = myRectangle.area(myRectangle.pt1, myRectangle.pt2);
      myPerimeter = myRectangle.perimeter(myRectangle.pt1, myRectangle.pt2);

      printf("the area and perimeter are: %i, %i\n", myArea, myPerimeter);
      return;
}
```

Figure 7.42 Writing the Main Implementation File

Observe how the area and perimeter functions are invoked and in particular, how the parameters were passed in.

7.5.6 Pointers to Structs

A struct has an address in memory; therefore, one can use a pointer variable to refer to it exactly as was done with pointers to any of the other variables we have studied. One can write:

```
typedef struct
{
    int pt1;
    int pt2;

} Rectangle;

Rectangle myRect;
Rectangle* rectPtr;
rectPtr = &myRect;
```

This code fragment declares an instance of a Rectangle and an instance of a pointer to a Rectangle; then it assigns the address of the instance to the pointer variable. Now let's look at accessing members of the rectangle.

7.5.6.1 Accessing Members

Since

```
*rectPtr
```

identifies the struct, the code fragment

```
(*rectPtr).pt1
```

refers to the member pt1. The parentheses around the pointer must be included because the . has higher precedence than * .

Without the parentheses,

```
*rectPtr.pt1
```

is interpreted as

```
*(rectPtr.pt1)
```

which is illegal since pt1 is not a pointer.

Because such pointer operations are so common, the C language defines a special shorthand symbol, ->. That notation allows one to replace the construct

```
(*ptr).member
```

with

```
structPtr -> member
```

The -> symbol is typed as the two characters: - followed by >.

Using the shorthand notation, one may write

```
rectPtr -> pt1;
```

The notation says that

- `rectPtr` is pointer to a struct
- `pt1` is a member

Thus if one has

```
Rectangle r1;
Rectangle *r1Ptr = &r1;
```

the following are equivalent

```
r1.pt1;
r1Ptr -> pt1;
```

7.5.7 Passing structs and Pointers to structs

Passing an instance of a struct or a pointer to such an instance to a function is the same as any of the simpler intrinsic types. Let's look at an example.

EXAMPLE 7.24

In this example, we will declare two functions as given in Figure 7.43. One will accept an argument of type struct by value and the other by reference using a pointer. We access the data members exactly as was done outside of the function.

```
// Passing Structures to Functions

#include <stdio.h>
// declare the struct
typedef struct
{
    int aVar0;
    int* aVar1Ptr;
}Data;

//   Declare the function prototype
void funct0(Data aBlock);
void funct1 (Data* aBlock);

void main(void)
{
    Data myData;

    // Declare and define a variable
    int varData0 = 20;

    // assign values to the struct data members
    myData.aVar0 = 10;
    myData.aVar1Ptr = &varData0;

    // Will print on execution:
    // The variables values are: 10, 20

    // Pass the struct to the function by
    // value then by reference
    funct0(myData);
    funct1(&myData);

    return;
}
```

```
void funct0(Data aBlock)
{
    // Retrieve the data from the struct
    // Using the member selector
    printf ("The variables values are: ");
    printf ("%i, %i\n",    aBlock.aVar0,
                           *(aBlock.aVar1Ptr));

    return;
}

void funct1(Data* aBlockPtr)
{
    // Retrieve the data from the struct
    // Using the pointer to member selector

    printf ("The variables values are: ");
    printf ("%i, %i\n",    aBlockPtr->aVar0,
                           *(aBlockPtr->aVar1Ptr));

    return;
}
```

Figure 7.43 Passing structs to Functions

Unlike arrays, the struct is passed by value in C by default. In an embedded application, passing a large struct by value can potentially cause the stack to overflow, thereby leading to unexpected system crashes. The problem is made significantly worse if one or more of the data members is an array.

Coding Style

Passing a struct to a function by value is generally not efficient.
Passing by reference is the preferred way.

Coding Style

It is not considered good practice to declare an array as a struct data member and then to pass that struct into a function.

7.6 THE INTERRUPT

synchronous
asynchronous

An interrupt is very similar to a function call. The major difference between the two is that the function invocation is *synchronous* to the normal program flow of control; the interrupt invocation originates with some event either inside or outside of the system and is *asynchronous* to the normal program flow of control. Among the minor differences, we find that variables can be passed into and returned from a function; one can neither pass a variable into nor return a variable from an interrupt. The reason will become clear shortly. First let's look at the structure of the interrupt control flow.

7.6.1 The Interrupt Control Flow

An interrupt scheme is used so that one can be working on one job and then, when an important issue arises, immediately be notified. It is not necessary to continually check to see if the event has happened. A good simple model for an interrupt is the telephone. It is not necessary to sit by the telephone all day waiting for a call to come in—although, perhaps some people do. The ring provides notification that new information is arriving.

There are three major pieces to the interrupt structure:

- The interrupt event and source
- The interrupt service routine
- The interrupt vector table

7.6.2 The Interrupt Event

An interrupt event can originate from a variety of sources. These sources may be in one of the many pieces of hardware in the system or in some piece of software. The interrupt is used to signify that some event of interest has occurred and that it must be dealt with. Potential events can include a timer expiring, an external signal changing state, or the result of a calculation or measurement exceeding a prespecified value.

Different microprocessors and microcomputers permit different numbers and kinds of interrupts. Some may be designated as software interrupts, whereas others are relegated to signaling hardware events. The number of interrupts may range from as few as 1 to as many as 12 to 16. One typically does not have the luxury of assigning any interrupt to any arbitrary event. Some are designated to signal specific events; one for each different timer in the system, one for detecting a bad or illegal op-code, or one to signify that an analog-to-digital conversion is complete are several examples.

We also often find that interrupts are assigned different priorities. The processor manufacturer may specify that a timer interrupt has a higher priority than the conversion complete signal from the A/D or the bad op-code interrupt higher than both. Such a priority scheme is used to handle the cases of several interrupts occurring at the same time or an urgent condition occurring while we are working on a less critical one. Interrupts are generally numbered, in order of decreasing priority, from 0 to n-1, if we have n interrupts.

7.6.3 The Interrupt Service Routine—ISR

interrupt service routine (ISR)

When an interrupt occurs, it is necessary to do something, and to be able to do something, one must know what one is supposed to do. In a software program, one knows what needs to be done, and that is accomplished by executing a series of instructions. With a function, the task to be accomplished comprises the body of the function. For the interrupt, that body of code is called the *interrupt service routine* (ISR).

The structure of an ISR is no different from the functions with which we have been dealing. With no other contextual information, one could not tell them apart. The template for an ISR is given in Figure 7.44.

```
void ISRName(void)
{
    body
}
```

Figure 7.44 A Template for an Interrupt Service Routine (ISR)

Observe that the return type is specified as void and that the function's signature is similarly specified as void.

One must write an ISR for each interrupt that will be used in a system; the reason will become clear very shortly.

> **Coding Style**
>
> When we write an ISR, our goal should be to make that routine as short and simple as possible. While we are in the routine, we are spending time away from the main line code, which is typically our primary focus. An ISR that exceeds 15 to 20 lines of C code is probably too long.

7.6.4 The Interrupt Vector Table

When one writes and uses a function, one specifies the prototype and defines the function body. To invoke the function, one enters the name of the function, with the appropriate arguments, as a line of code in the program. When the program flow reaches the line of code containing the call, a context switch to the code comprising the function body is made and the code is executed, as was discussed earlier.

The interrupt presents a more interesting challenge. Since the interrupt is asynchronous to the normal flow in the program, there is no place to put the call. There must be another scheme, and this is where the interrupt vector table comes in.

To see how this works, remember that the code comprising the body of the function resides in memory somewhere. That memory location has an address. Using a pointer to a function and assigning the address of the body of the function to that pointer then dereferencing that pointer evaluates the function code. Herein lies the secret.

Let's build a table. In its basic implementation, this table is no more complex than an array. If we have eight interrupts, we will have an array with eight rows and one column. Let's declare our array as follows,

```
void (*isrFunctionPtr)(void) aTable[8];
```

That is, we have an array of eight pointers to functions; those functions take no arguments and return no value. In each array entry, we put the address of the body of each ISR.

Here are the mechanics. As noted earlier, each interrupt has a number; in this case those numbers will be 0–7. One can use these values as indices into the array. Thus, for example, if we put the address of the ISR for interrupt 2 into index position 2 of the array and write

```
aTable[2]();
```

we will evaluate the function body for that interrupt.

interrupt vector table

The table so created is called an *interrupt vector table*. The vector table is built automatically by the microprocessor's internal control logic. It is still up to the designer to make certain that the proper address for each ISR is entered into the correct position in the table.

handled

Again, based on the microprocessor's control logic, when the event assigned to each of the interrupts occurs, then flow of control automatically "vectors" to the index in the table associated with that interrupt. The contents of that location are interpreted as the address of the corresponding ISR. Flow of control is automatically redirected to that location. The interrupt is said to be *handled*. If a specific address had not been entered or if an incorrect one was entered, the process does not care. The redirection proceeds to that erroneous address. This is why, if one is going to use a specific interrupt, an ISR must be written to handle the interrupt and the address of the ISR must be entered into the vector table.

We can now use the graphic presented in Figure 7.45 to see how this process works.

In the graphic, the program is executing the mainline code. That process is interrupted by an event on interrupt 1. That interrupt is recognized by the system, and the system finds the pointer at index 1 in the interrupt vector table. The pointer is dereferenced, causing a context switch to the ISR associated with interrupt 1. Execution continues in the ISR until a return is encountered. At that time, control returns to the point in the original code that was interrupted when the event occurred, the original context is restored, and execution continues.

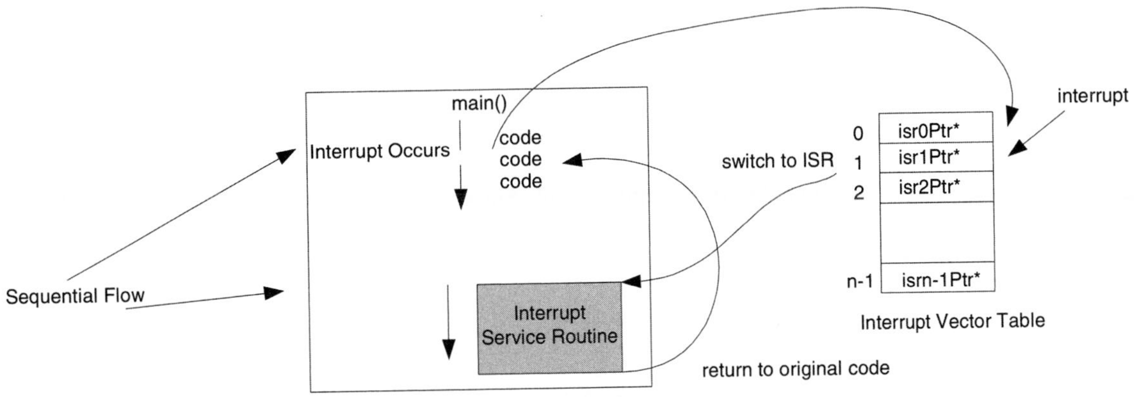

Figure 7.45 Following an Interrupt

The sequence of steps involved in the context switch to the ISR is exactly like the sequence we encountered in the context switch to the body of a function. That is, the current state of the system is saved on the stack, the return address is saved on the stack as well, and the address of the first line of the ISR (as determined by dereferencing the function pointer in the interrupt vector table) is put into the program counter. The only difference is that we do not have to save any parameters to pass into the ISR or any values to return onto the stack.

At this point one should ask, "How does one get the address of the ISR into the vector table?' This is a very good question, to which the answer is not obvious. The method that one uses depends on the compiler or assembler that one is using to write and to build the firmware for the application to run on the processor. At the assembler level, each vendor has an instruction to enter the address into the vector table. These are typically wrapped (a standard high-level language technique) in a function call that is part of one of the support libraries the compiler vendor will provide.

7.6.5 Control of the Interrupt

At this point, we have examined the basic operation and flow of control of the interrupt process. We have noted the similarities and some of the differences between a function call and an interrupting event. There remain several additional differences in how we control an interrupt versus a function invocation. Let's look at these now.

7.6.5.1 Enable–Disable

The flow of control process under interrupts can be enabled or disabled. We do not have such an ability with a function invocation. What such a capability means is that by using the proper control instruction, one can choose to permit or prohibit interrupts from affecting the normal flow of control through the program. There are several occasions when such capability is useful.

The most obvious time to use such a capability is when there is no need to use any interrupts. We do not want an extraneous (noise or error) signal generating an interrupt when we have made no provisions to handle such a thing. Another occasion occurs when we have a critical task that we must perform in a timely manner and cannot afford to devote time away from the job.

Many systems will force all interrupts to be disabled immediately following the occurrence of an interrupting event. They will remain disabled (by the system) for one instruction after the context switch has occurred to give the user time to disable them for a longer time if necessary. Such a situation would be similar to getting a telephone call in the middle of responding to a telephone call. Since the interrupting events are all asynchronous with respect to each other, such a thing can easily happen.

7.6.5.2 Recognizing an Interrupting Event

When an interrupting event occurs, the microprocessor is most likely in the middle of executing some instruction. Most processors will complete the current (machine-language level) instruction before responding to the interrupt. Once the instruction has completed, the interrupt process continues. One of the early steps in the handling sequence is to acknowledge the interrupt. How and when this is done is processor specific.

7.6.5.3 Interrupting and Masking an Interrupting Event

The disable and enable capability provides global control over interrupt behavior; we would often like much finer-grained control. For most microprocessors, such capability comes in at least two forms, both of which are executed through what is called a

masking process *masking process*.

In the same manner that we can call a second function from within a first, an interrupt that has a higher priority than the current level can occur. The first form of masking utilizes the different priorities of the interrupts. With this form, the microprocessor supports the ability to disable all interrupts below a certain level or priority. Thus, if the system is responding to an interrupt at levels (or with priority) 5, one can block all interrupts below level 2, for example. Since those at levels 3 and 4 are higher priority than the current one, we may not want to allow them to be recognized during the time that we are handing the level 5 interrupt. However, an event at level 2 may be sufficiently critical that we should not ignore it. The microprocessor compiler or assembler will provide the appropriate instruction to set the mask if the processor supports such capability.

The second form of mask provides for an even finer-grained management. This form gives control over the individual interrupts. Associated with the set of interrupts that the

interrupt mask register processor supports is what is called an *interrupt mask register*. The mask register is a vector of bits, one for each supported interrupt as we see in the graphic in Figure 7.46 for a system with four interrupts.

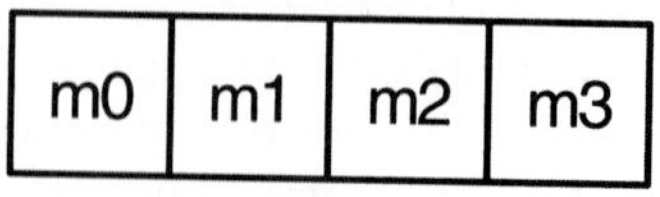

Figure 7.46 Following an Interrupt

The register is typically implemented at the hardware level in the processor. Each mask bit can be independently set to either a logical 1 or 0. If the bit is set to a logical 1, the interrupting event will be recognized by the interrupt subsystem; otherwise it will be ignored.

Because most interrupting events are transient, if we choose to ignore an event, it is most often the case that we cannot later come back and look at it. Once again, the means to set or reset the individual bits is a processor-specific operation and instruction.

7.7 SUMMARY

In this chapter, we covered four elements of the C language—*bitwise operators*, *functions*, *pointer variables*, and *structs*—that are essential to the development of the software side and interfacing with the hardware side of embedded systems. In addition, we looked at two important uses of pointers: *pointers to functions* and *interrupting events.*

We have now covered the major elements in the C language that are necessary for our remaining studies of embedded systems.

7.8 REVIEW QUESTIONS

Bitwise Operators

7.1 What is the difference between a C language logical operator and the bitwise operator with the same name?

7.2 What are some of the applications for which one might use a bitwise operator?

7.3 What is a shadow variable, and why might we use such a thing?

Pointer Variables and Memory Addresses

7.4 What is the difference between a pointer variable and a typical data variable, for example?

7.5 Following declaration and definition, a variable is stored somewhere in memory. How can one find out where the variable has been stored?

7.6 If a pointer variable holds the address of a variable in memory, how do we retrieve the value of that variable?

7.7 Can the value of a variable be changed through a pointer to that variable? If so, how?

7.8 Can two pointer variables be added or multiplied in the same way as nonpointer variables? If so, what is the result?

7.9 Can a pointer variable and a scalar be added? If so, what is the result?

7.10 Are the expressions myPtr + 1 and myPtr++ equivalent?

7.11 Are the expressions *myPtr++ and *(myPtr++) equivalent? Why or why not?

7.12 Can two pointer variables be compared using the standard C logical operators? If so, what is the meaning in each case?

7.13 The const qualifier may be applied to a pointer variable. Explain how the interpretation of the const and the pointer change based on where the const is placed in a declaration.

7.14 What is a generic pointer?

7.15 Can a generic pointer be dereferenced? Why or why not?

7.16 What is a NULL pointer?

7.17 What is the difference between a NULL pointer and a generic pointer?

Functions

7.18 What is a function header, and what are its major components?

7.19 What is the purpose of a function's parameter list?

7.20 What is the purpose of a function's return type?

7.21 How many data variables can be returned through a function's return-type variable?

7.22 What is the signature of a function, and why is it important?

7.23 What is the purpose of a function's body?

7.24 Describe how data is passed into a function.

7.25 Describe how a data variable can be returned from a function.

7.26 What is a stack frame or an activation record?

7.27 Identify all of the steps that typically occur when a function is called. Be specific.

7.28 What is meant by the expression *pass by value* with respect to passing data in to a function?

7.29 What is meant by the expression *pass by reference* with respect to passing data in to a function?

7.30 Can a function declared and defined in one file be used in another? If so, how?

7.31 Can functions be nested?

7.32 Can functions call other functions?

7.33 Can a function call itself?

Pointers to Functions

7.34 Why would one wish to use a pointer to a function?

7.35 What is the general syntax for declaring a pointer to a function?

7.36 How does one assign a pointer to a function?

7.37 If a pointer to a function is declared and assigned to point to a specific function, to what is it pointing?

7.38 Can a pointer to a function be used to point to different functions at different times?

7.39 How can one dereference a pointer to a function?

7.40 Can one pass data into a function that is invoked via a pointer? If so, how?

Structures

7.41 What is the major difference between a C struct and other C containers?

7.42 Can a C struct contain both data members and function members?

7.43 What is a structure tag, and what is it used for?

7.44 Can one create an instance of a struct?

7.45 When a struct is declared, is memory allocated to hold the member variables?

7.46 When is memory allocated to hold a struct's member variables?

7.47 How can the member variables in a struct be initialized?

7.48 Can the member variables in a struct also be structs?

7.49 Can the member variables in a struct be arrays?

7.50 How can we access member variables within a struct?

7.51 Can we declare and define a pointer to a struct?

7.52 How can we access member variables in a struct through a pointer to the struct?

7.53 What are the only legal operations that can be performed on a struct?

7.54 Can one struct be assigned to another?

7.55 Can a struct be passed as a data variable into a function? returned from a function?

Interrupts

7.56 What is the major difference between a function call and an interrupt?

7.57 What are the major pieces of an interrupt structure?

7.58 What is an interrupt event?

7.59 What is an interrupt service routine? Why is it necessary?

7.60 What is the difference between an interrupt service routine and a function body?

7.61 What is an interrupt vector table? What is its purpose?

7.62 What do we mean when we say that an interrupt has been handled?

7.63 Identify and briefly describe the steps necessary to handle an interrupt.

7.64 Explain what it means to enable or disable an interrupt.

7.65 Explain what it means to mask an interrupt.

7.66 What is the difference between enabling/disabling and masking/unmasking an interrupt?

7.9 THOUGHT QUESTIONS

Bitwise Operators

7.1 Without writing any code, describe how two binary numbers can be compared using bitwise operators?

7.2 Without writing any code, describe how a specific bit pattern within a binary word can be identified using bitwise operators?

Pointer Variables and Memory Addresses

7.3 Discuss the advantages and disadvantages of using pass by reference versus pass by value in an embedded C program. Be specific with your points.

7.4 Which data structure(s) is(are) automatically passed by reference in a C program? Why do you think such to be the case?

7.5 When two pointers are compared using the = operator, what is actually being compared?

7.6 When two pointers are compared using the == operator, what is actually being compared?

7.7 Can we assign one array to another using the = operator? Why or why not?

7.8 Explain, in detail, elaborating on the underlying process, why the following can be written and evaluated with the correct results.

```
int x[2] = {0, 1, 2};
float y[2] = {1.1, 2.2, 3.3};
int* xPtr = x;
float* yPtr = y;
xPty++;
yPtr++;
```

7.9 What is the result of evaluating the steps in the following code fragment.

```
int x = 2;
float y = 3.7;
int xPtr = &x;
float yPtr = xPtr;
```

Can the pointer variable yPtr be dereferenced? If so, what will be returned?

7.10 What values of y and z result from evaluating the following code fragment.

```
int w;
float x = NULL;
int wPtr = &w;
float xPtr = &x;
int y;
float z;
y =*wPrt;
z=*xPtr;
```

7.11 A two-dimensional array in C is built using one-dimensional arrays and pointers. Explain how this can be done. Illustrate using a simple drawing.

7.12 Describe how to extend the design in Question 7.11 to an arbitrary number of dimensions.

7.13 Why do we use generic pointers? Give several examples in practical embedded applications for which such use might be appropriate?

7.14 Does the value of a pointer variable always have to refer to an address in ROM or RAM? If not, to what other entities can it refer?

Functions

7.15 Identify and describe each of the steps involved in a function call. Be specific about any registers, data structures, or addresses that may be involved. How can we return several values, of different types, from a function?

7.16 Can a pointer to an array be passed to a function? Why would we wish to do so? Can you cite several real-world examples illustrating why such a thing might be useful?

7.17 Can a C function call itself? If so, is there a limit on the number of times? If so, how is the limit set?

7.18 If a C function can call itself, discuss the possible consequences.

7.19 When are the variables local to a C function declared? defined? initialized?

7.20 How many data variables can be returned through a function's return-type variable?

7.21 How can we return multiple variables of the same type from a function?

7.22 How can we return multiple variables of different types from a function?

7.23 How can we return multiple variables of different types from a function if the return type is void (not void*)?

7.24 When a pointer to a local variable that was declared in a called function is returned to the calling function, can that pointer be dereferenced in the calling function? Explain why or why not? If the pointer can be dereferenced, will the result be the value of the local variable.

7.25 To what memory address does control flow return to when the function is complete—the address that it was at when the function call occurred, the address following, or the address preceding?

Pointers to Functions

7.26 Are the following declarations equivalent? Why or why not?

```
int (*myFunction)(char val0, int val1);
int *myFunction(char val0, int val1);
```

7.27 Can a pointer to a function be passed as an argument into a function?

7.28 Should a pointer to a function be initialized? If so, what should that value be? If not, why not?

7.29 Pointers support several different arithmetic operations such as the addition of a scalar to the pointer. Are these operations supported on a pointer to a function? If so, please explain the results of applying each such operation.

Structures

7.30 How can we include a function in a struct?

7.31 Can a struct have more than one function member?

7.32 Can we declare an array of structs? Are there any constraints?

7.33 Can we compare structs using the == operator? If not, why not?

7.34 Can we assign one struct to another using the = operator? If not why not?

7.35 Why is including arrays in a struct data type ill advised in an embedded C program if an instance of that struct may be passed as an argument to a function?

7.36 Can one declare an array of structs in which the data members for each struct are of different types; for example, one struct containing ints, a second floats, and a third chars? If not, why not and if so, how?

7.37 Can one declare an array of structs containing both data and function members in which the struct members in each struct are of different types? If not, why not and if so, how?

Interrupts

7.38 If an interrupt service routine is not assigned to a particular interrupt and the interrupt occurs, what will happen?

7.39 Identify and describe each of the steps involved in handling an interrupt. Be specific about any registers, data structures, or addresses that may be involved. How can we return several values, of different types, from a function?

7.40 Why do interrupt service routines typically accept no arguments and have no return value?

7.41 Describe the structure and contents of a typical interrupt vector table?

7.42 To what memory address does control flow return to when the interrupt is complete: the address that it was at when the interrupt occurred, the address following, or the address preceding?

7.43 An interrupt may be enabled or disabled under program control. Why do we wish to be able to do such a thing?

7.44 If interrupts have been disabled, will the interrupts still occur? Please explain your answer.

7.45 What are some of the possible side effects of disabling interrupt?

7.46 An interrupt may be masked under program control. How is masking different from disabling?

7.47 Under what circumstances might we wish to mask versus disable an interrupt? Explain your answer.

7.48 If interrupts have been masked, will the interrupts still occur? Explain your answer.

7.49 Some interrupts are said to be nonmaskable. What might this mean, and why might we wish to so designate certain interrupts?

7.50 Give some examples of situations under which we would want to preclude interrupt masking.

7.10 PROBLEMS

Bit Manipulation

Using the bit manipulation operators, develop and test C programs to perform the following.

7.1 Starting with the word 0xF0A6, reset bit 3, set bit 6, set bit 8, reset bit 13.

7.2 Starting with the word 0xCB43, determine if the word contains the pattern 0x43 in the least significant byte.

7.3 Starting with the word 0xCB43, determine if the word contains the pattern 0xB4 anywhere in the word.

7.4 Starting with the word 0x7C5E, determine if bit 7 is reset and bit 14 is set. If so, complement bits 6 and 12.

7.5 Develop a C program that will accept a pointer to an array of 16 unsigned chars and return an unsigned char that is the result of exclusively ORing the contents of the array using the bitwise exclusive OR.

The value being retuned is called a Block Check Sum and is used in error management schemes, which will be discussed in a later chapter.

Data Types

Containers are a commonly used data type in many embedded applications. Please provide the *Use Case* and *Class Diagrams* for each of the following containers. Next, provide the C code for each container data type. Verify that your implementation is consistent with your model.

7.6 A link in a singly linked list

7.7 A singly linked list

7.8 A link in a doubly linked list

7.9 A doubly linked list

7.10 A queue

7.11 A priority queue—the highest priority stored item is always returned.

7.12 A stack

7.13 A FIFO container

7.14 A LIFO container

7.15 A circular list

Tools and Algorithms

7.16 Using nested ifs, write a function *min3* that returns the smallest of three int values passed to it as parameters. Also write a function *max3* that returns the largest of its three int parameters.

7.17 Formulate a decimal to binary conversion program in C as a subroutine. Any program that invokes the subroutine passes two addresses through main memory locations. The first of these is the address of a 3-byte main memory buffer that the clients are to use for storing input decimal digit characters. The second address is the location of the converted binary number.

Draw a data and control flow diagram for the design.

7.18 Formulate a binary to decimal conversion program in C as a subroutine. Any program that invokes the subroutine passes two addresses through main memory locations. The first of these is the location of the binary number to be converted. The second is the address of a 3-byte main memory buffer from which the clients retrieve converted decimal digit characters.

Draw a data and control flow diagram for the design.

7.19 Using the routine from Problem 7.17, design a program that converts a three-digit BCD (binary coded decimal) number to ASCII.

Draw a data and control flow diagram for the design.

7.20 Write a function *tableInit ( )* that sets every element of an array of integers to a particular value. The function takes three parameters: the array, its size, and the initial value.

7.21 Write a function *tableFill( )* that generates random integer values in the range of 0–100 to fill an array. Note: this is different from *tableInit( )* in Problem 7.20. The function takes two parameters: the array and its size. Make certain that you check the array boundaries.

7.22 Write a function *tableAverage( )* that computes and returns the average of a subset of N elements of an array of ints. Test with a small program that uses *tableFill()* to fill the array with values.

7.23 Using the function *tableFill( )* to fill an array, use selection sort to sort the array. In selection sort, we first find the largest element in the array and exchange it with the first element's value. We then find the next largest element in the array and exchange it with the second element's value. We continue the process until the array is sorted.

7.24 Repeat Problem 7.23 using the bubble sort algorithm.

7.25 Repeat Problem 7.23 using the C library function QSort.

7.26 Write a C program that accepts two points and computes the distance between them. Given two points (X_1, Y_1) and (X_2, Y_2), the distance between them is:

$$\sqrt{(X_1 - X_2)^2 + (Y_1 - Y_2)^2}$$

7.27 The values for the coordinates are integers, and the result must be expressed as an integer. What is the worst case error resulting from the calculation?

7.28 The following program to average a collection of values produces incorrect results if the number of values is greater than INT_MAX, if any input value is greater than INT_MAX, or if the sum is greater than LONG_MAX. Rewrite the program to avoid these problems.

7.29 Write a program that is part of an automatic screening system on a factory assembly line. The module accepts integer data representing a parameter on the component being manufactured, places each into the appropriate category, and returns the tag for the category and the number of entries in the category. For this design, the categories are: 100–90, 89–80, 79–70, 69–60, and 59–0.

7.30 Define a probe that can be inserted into a function as a test coverage device. The probe is to track if the function is called and if so, how many since the program was started. For a function, the probe is to track how many times the function is called.

The probe is to respond with the appropriate tracking information when the function containing the probe is queried. It will be necessary to figure out the best way to present the query. Demonstrate your probe on several different functions.

Applications

7.31 In the C language, the struct cannot hold function members; thus, we include functions by using pointers to functions. Combining data and the functions that operate on that data can be a very powerful tool in developing embedded applications.

(a) Give the class diagrams for three structures. The three structures will share a common data variable called *sharedData* through pointers to that data. The three functions will be *getData()*, *compute()*, and *outputData()*.

The function *getData()* will bring data into the system, *compute()* will multiply the data by 2, and *outputData()* will send the data out of the system.

(b) Give the data and control flow diagrams for such a system.

7.32 Write the C code corresponding to each of the structures that were modeled in Problem 7.31.

7.33 Design an array containing each of the structures in Problem 7.32. Design a C program that will continually walk through the array and evaluate the function contained in each struct.

Software is a significant component in an embedded system. The following problems address that portion of application development. For each of these designs, your complete package should include, as appropriate:

- A use case diagram for your design
- A class diagram for each of your modules
- A sequence diagram for your design
- A data and control flow diagram for your design
- A tested C implementation of your design

7.34 Design and implement an automatic coffee pot with the following capabilities.

The controls must include the ability to set the start time on a 24-hour clock, reduce the temperature to warming, and annunciate when the brew cycle is complete, and stop water flow if the pot is removed from its receptacle.

7.35 Design and implement a digital watch with the following capabilities.

The controls must include a 12-hour time expressed in hours, minutes, and seconds, AM and PM tracking and annunciation, alarm, and the ability to set the alarm and time values.

7.36 Design and implement a washing machine with the following capabilities.

The controls must include the ability to set water temperature, washing start times, modes (presoak, normal, permanent press, delicate), and annunciation of temperature, times, and mode.

7.37 Design and implement an oven control with the following capabilities.

The controls must include the ability to set temperatures, cooking start and stop times, modes (bake, broil, clean), and annunciation of temperature, times, and mode.

7.38 Design and implement a module implementing a four-seat passenger entertainment system with the following capabilities on a commercial aircraft.

The entertainment system should support the ability for each of the four passengers to program and control

Movie selection

Audio selection

A gaming console

7.39 Design and implement a seat belt–engine–door lock interlock with the following capabilities.

The engine cannot start if the seat belt is not fastened. The doors automatically lock when the engine is started.

PART 2 DEVELOPING THE FOUNDATION

Chapter 8

Safety, Reliability, and Robust Design

THINGS TO LOOK FOR . . .

- The definitions of reliability and safety.
- The need for good specifications.
- The need for reliable and safe hardware and software designs.
- The definitions of and difference between faults, failures, and errors.
- The need for context when measuring reliability and safety.
- Guidelines and approaches for developing safe, robust, and reliable designs.
- How to use failure modes analysis to help to identify potential problems in a design.
- Identification of runtime faults using built-in tests.

8.0 INTRODUCTION

As we have learned, embedded systems are universal; from a handful of computers a few years ago, we now literally count them in the billions. The days of ubiquitous computing are not too far in the future and may even be here now. We are encountering embedded computers in our daily lives at an increasing rate. Microprocessors, microcontrollers, and the like are found in systems ranging from the complex to the mundane. Among the complex systems, we have aircraft flight control systems and sophisticated medical equipment. On the mundane side, we see the familiar washing machine and, of course, children's toys. Failures in such systems can have a significant and resounding impact. As embedded computing becomes more widespread, safety and reliability in such systems are becoming correspondingly more important considerations. Today, reliability and safety are an integral part of the design of any embedded system. People often confuse safety with reliability and robustness; all are important issues, but they are distinct concepts.

In this chapter we will introduce the basic concepts of safety, reliability, and robustness in embedded applications, formulate definitions for each, and identify their differences. We will examine several real-world examples in which minor oversights have led to either significant or potentially significant and costly failures. We will establish the need for robust and reliable hardware and software and some of the relevant vocabulary. We will then examine several approaches that may be taken to the design of the major hardware and software subsystems in order to help ensure a safe, reliable, and robust embedded system. Finally, we will conclude with some tools and techniques that can be used to detect and manage problems that may occur during system operation.

8.1 SAFETY

We will begin with a discussion of safety. Once again, we note that safety is distinct from reliability. Nonetheless, both are interrelated or perhaps interdependent. A risk is *any* event or condition that is deemed to be undesirable. Risks can be small or they can be large. A safe system is one that is ideally free from risk. In reality, a safe system is one that has been carefully and fully analyzed to identify all potential risks. Each risk is then evaluated and assessed to ensure that, should it occur, it does not present unacceptable consequences to people or to equipment.

One can relate safety and reliability through the following simple relationships.

Risk = Probability of Failure • Severity
Increased Risk → Decreased Safety

Safety appears indirectly on the left-hand side of the first relationship. The second expression above suggests an abductive relationship between risk and safety. Increasing the risk associated with an embedded application implies that the safety of the system decreases; however, it is not guaranteed to be so. Risk can be effectively managed if the system is designed to operate in a safe and reliable manner using good engineering practices.

probability of failure
severity

Reliability affects the *probability of failure* component on the right-hand side of the equation which, combined with the *severity* component (small or large), give us the risk. Building a prototype chemical processing plant with an innovative, yet not thoroughly tested, control system (probability of failure) in the middle of a populated area (high severity) rather than far out in the country side (low severity) poses different levels of risk. Although the control system's probability of failure may be the same in both cases, the consequences are not. In any event, neither is a reasonable thing to do.

Among the list of potentially undesirable conditions comprising risk, we can include

- Interference with life support functions
- Supply of misleading information to safety personnel and to control systems
- Release of energy
- Release of toxins
- Failure to alarm when hazardous conditions arise

Safety hazards can occur in a system through misuse, improper or unsafe specifications, or failures in some component of the system.

8.2 RELIABILITY

Let's look at the reliability component of the equation. One must remember that designing a system is one thing; designing a reliable system is another. One measure of reliability is a measure of up time or the availability of a properly operating system. Today the expression five or six 9's in reference to the reliability of many applications is commonly used. With such a statement, one demands that the system be up and available 99.999 or 99.9999% of the time. This constraint translates to a down time of 3 to 31 seconds per year.

Reliability is becoming increasingly important in the design of many of today's systems for a variety of reasons. We are becoming the victims of our own successes—hoist with our own petard, as they say. Embedded systems are finding their way into areas where the typical user knows very little about the proper operation of the products they buy. Consequently, future designs must become increasingly tolerant of unexpected or improper inputs or (un)intentional misuse. A few years ago, the computer lived a relatively comfortable life in an air-conditioned room with good, clean power systems feeding it. Today, embedded systems need to be road warriors. Their operating environment is hot, dirty, electrically noisy, humid, and interconnected via poor power distribution systems; it has perhaps a dozen other difficulties as well. We must keep such conditions in mind as we develop tomorrow's systems.

An embedded application that has been sent to Saturn or put on the bottom of the ocean is a bit difficult to pop over and repair. Systems today must be able to operate for extended periods with little or no chance for repair. Not too many years ago, anyone with a screwdriver, wrench, and a hammer was an expert auto mechanic. Today, typically one needs a garage full of sophisticated test equipment to perform even a basic tune-up. The same trend is occurring in all of the systems that we are designing. Yesterday's telephone had a simple dial, and one made telephone calls with it. Today's cell phone supports pictures, games, music, e-mail, text messages—and, almost as an afterthought, even does telephone calls too. The complexity of today's systems is bringing increasingly larger numbers and varieties of components into the design, and these designs are being forced into smaller and smaller containers. Each hardware component that we include in a system has a failure rate. The failure rate of each component can potentially contribute to the overall reliability of the system.

Let's look at how to begin solving the problem. To start, one must recognize that a reliable system begins at the specification and design stage, not at the preproduction stage. Reliability (and quality) cannot be tested into a product no matter how good the test suite is or how many times it is executed. It requires little effort for one to design a test suite that will ensure that a system with known errors or failure modes will pass even the most stringent test.

The goal should be to identify *all* faults before a product ever arrives at a customer's site. It is also recognized that with the complexity of today's systems this goal is approached asymptotically. Today, one will often utilize statistical-based methods to analyze a design to make assessments as to how many bugs remain. On occasion, and after considered thought, a product will be released if the estimated number of bugs is below a certain threshold.

At the end of the day, reliability is somewhat of a soft measure—not soft in the sense that it cannot be measured but soft in the sense of its meaning. Several common-sense descriptors may apply in the general case.

- The product consistently performs in a manner that the customer expects.

  For many embedded systems, this mainly means meeting all performance constraints. Moving and processing high-quality video and audio cannot tolerate delays. Such delays produce distortion in the delivered image or sound.

- The mean time between failures (MTBF) is long.

  All physical things fail eventually; one wants the time before/between failures to be as long as is reasonable. When monitoring signals during nuclear testing or when performing experiments using an atomic accelerator, a long time can be measured in fractions of second. On the other hand, today's automobile manufacturers are quoting guarantees of 100,000 miles or more on certain parts.

A better objective is to ensure that the MTBF is long in the context of the useful life of product. At a recent meeting, a colleague who works in the research department of a major company said, "long term is if the demo keeps working until the director has approved the funding for the next phase of the research." This colleague knows his context . . . perhaps too well.

- The system responds in a deterministic way.

  People have grown accustomed to having a product respond the same way each time they use it. Customers lose their sense of humor if, each time they use a product, it responds in a different, and perhaps, unpredictable way. An excellent book, *The Design of Everyday Things* by Donald A. Norman (Doubleday (1988)), explores this problem within a more general scope.

  The Design of Everyday Things

- The system responds or fails gracefully in response to out-of-bounds or unexpected inputs and recovers if possible. When the system fails, it fails gracefully and safely.

  When people are using a product, they are going to try to do things that perhaps had not been anticipated during design. While certainly one cannot think of everything, one must consider how a design will respond under such conditions. It is important to understand and to safely manage the behavior of a system in response to an input that was expected to be a particular value and within a certain range that suddenly becomes significantly larger or smaller. Such was the case recently in a European space program. We will look at this problem in greater detail shortly.

Failing gracefully

Failing gracefully and safely is often of critical and life-saving importance. Every recent model automobile on the road has a number of embedded microprocessor-based systems controlling everything from the radio to the fuel flow and braking systems. Though annoying, an abrupt failure in the radio is certainly less disturbing than having the fuel system shut down while in the process of passing a truck just ahead of an even bigger truck coming the opposite direction. Consider, too, our modern aircraft. Many passengers would die if they were flying at 35,000 feet and the system controlling cabin pressure and oxygen flow suddenly quit and had to be reloaded on the ground. Good engineering practice demands graceful failure; it demands that a backup system be ready if failure occurs.

8.3 FAULTS, ERRORS, AND FAILURES

fault
transient
soft, intermittent
periodic, aperiodic
permanent
hard

A *fault* is any system condition or state deemed to be incorrect or unacceptable. Faults can be characterized in time by duration and frequency. A fault may be *transient* as the result of some temporary external event such as the effect that sun spots may have on a telecommunication satellite. Such faults are referred to as *soft*. A fault may be *intermittent,* occurring as the result of some unstable hardware or a marginal design. An intermittent fault may be either *periodic* or *aperiodic*. My coffee grinder that turns on when the door on a running microwave is opened or an aperiodic confluence of signals leading to hazards in combinational logic are examples. A fault may be *permanent,* as might result from an incorrect design, but more often arises from a failed hardware component. Permanent faults are known as *hard* faults.

errors
failures

Based on their nature and origin, faults are classified into two major categories: *errors* and *failures*. An *error* is considered to be static, an inherent characteristic of the system such as the result of a design error or an incorrect or misunderstood specification, for example.

Included in this category are faults that occur because of some incorrect or improper user action. This position is taken because the fact that it was permitted to occur (rather than blocked) indicates a breakdown in the design path somewhere.

failure

A *failure* is viewed as a dynamic event, as something that occurs at a specific time, generally while the system is operating. When a fault occurs, the system can be affected in a number of different ways. Some of the more common consequences of a fault include the following.

- Action—an inappropriate action taken or an appropriate action not taken
- Timing—actions taken at an inappropriate time, either too early or too late
- Sequence—an action that is skipped or is executed out of sequence
- Quantity—an inappropriate amount of energy or reagent used

When a system fails, we have a system that once functioned properly and now no longer does so. Failures usually occur in the field when some hardware component breaks or wears out. Software, on the other hand, does not break or wear out through or from use.

Faults that occur in an electrical or a mechanical component in the system cannot be designed away. Problems originating in the hardware can be addressed in a number of different ways; one common approach is to design into the system multiple instances of critical components.

8.4 ANOTHER LOOK AT RELIABILITY

It is relatively easy to find volumes of material written on reliability. While it is beyond the scope of this text to cover the field of reliability in any significant depth, the goal is to stress the importance of both reliability and safety in the design of embedded systems and to try to introduce some of the important considerations. Thus, in this section, we will present some of the fundamental ideas, identify the potential problems that one should think about in any solid design, and propose some alternate solutions by which these issues can be addressed.

What is reliability?

The first question that should be answered is: "*What is reliability*?" One simple, formal definition suggests that reliability means that the probability that a system will fail is less than some threshold. Is this reasonable? What does fail mean? There are systems that fail regularly and yet are considered highly reliable, from a user's point of view. To see such a system, one does not have to look much beyond the Internet or the telephone system. We use each of these systems every day, and yet we are unaware of the routine failures of individual pieces.

It is evident that proposing a workable definition of reliability needs a bit more thought. The task of ensuring the reliable (and safe) operation of embedded systems occurs at several places during its lifetime. At the start of a new project, the main objective is to ensure a proper and *safe design*. We endeavor to design the system in such a way that potential faults are identified early and avoided or eliminated during the later stages of development.

safe design

Once the design is complete and the product is in the customer's hands, we assume that, to the best of our knowledge and ability, the design is correct and that the product has been manufactured properly (or that any manufacturing defects that did occur have been identified during production test and then corrected). The focus now shifts to *detecting any faults* that might occur in the field. Such faults may originate either from inside the system or from without. We do not want to just let them happen. Once a fault has been detected, efforts shift to *managing the fault*. Management can range from a graceful and safe shutdown to limiting

detecting any faults

managing the fault

the damage, to issuing a warning and continuing with decreased capability, to activating redundant components.

Modern intelligent and self-diagnosing/correcting systems can detect anomalous conditions and potentially reconfigure themselves (if they support multiple configurations) or work around problems. Failures may occur but never be detected. On communication networks such as the Internet, packet transfers *fail* continuously but recover through retransmission or other means on a regular basis. Such systems are said to be *fault tolerant*.

fail

fault tolerant

With this recognition, we can define reliability in an embedded system as

> The probability that a failure is *detected* by the user is less than a specified threshold.

8.5 SOME REAL-WORLD EXAMPLES

A solid understanding of the system requirements, a good specification, and a well-executed design form the foundation for developing a safe, reliable, and robust embedded systems. Nonetheless, these *do not* eliminate the need for comprehensive testing. We cite three cases in point. All of these are space-borne applications; one resulted in complete loss of the system and two came very close. Each has at least one fundamental flaw that should have been identified either during design or test.

BIG WORD . . . SMALL REGISTER

The first case involves the rocket designed and developed by the European Space Agency that was mentioned earlier. The Ariane 5 was designed and built over a 10-year period at a cost of over $7 billion. Within less than a minute following its initial launch, the rocket was gone; the problem was register overflow.

At the heart of the guidance and control system on the rocket were an inertial guidance computer, a steering computer, and an array of sensors to collect the data needed for the flight control computations. The sensors produced a 64-bit data word; the guidance system used a 16-bit word. The root of the problem lay in the guidance system. That system had a long history of successes on previous versions of the rocket. It made good sense to reuse a system with a proven track record. On launch, the path of the earlier rockets was straight, whereas that of the Ariane 5 had a slight dogleg. The sideways movement of the rocket was naturally reflected in the output data from the ship's sensors. The inertial guidance system's computer assigned that 64-bit data value to one of its own 16-bit words—the root of the problem.

Earlier, the engineers had dismissed the difference in word sizes as a potential problem because that particular piece of velocity data "would never get that large, particularly since it never had on the previous rockets." The new engine, however, was faster than the older models. When the abrupt sideways movement occurred, the sensor data overflowed the (16-bit) word in the guidance computer, thereby yielding an erroneous, out-of-range result. The computer responded by shutting itself down and passing control to the backup unit. The backup unit, with identical hardware and software, produced the same incorrect result (we will discuss the caveats with identical designs shortly). When it received the erroneous data from the guidance system computers, the onboard steering computer assumed that a course correction was necessary and issued the command to execute that correction. The abrupt change caused the rocket to swerve off course and begin disintegrating. Self-destruction was automatically triggered; that part of the design worked as required.

IT'S MY TURN—NOT YOURS

The next example presents a problem that will be examined more fully in our study of operating systems and how to schedule and coordinate tasks within an application. The Mars Pathfinder arrived on Mars in 1997 about midyear. It was widely proclaimed as a nearly perfect mission. After a few days of executing its task of collecting meteorological data, the system began resetting itself. Accompanying each reset was a loss of the collected data. Of course, the onboard computer got the blame. The "software glitches" occurred because "the computer was trying to do too many things at once," according to the newspapers.

In reality, the root cause of the problem was that lower priority tasks were able to acquire and hold resources that were needed by the higher priority, more important tasks, thereby effectively blocking them. Let's examine what happened.

Involved in the problem were three tasks that had to be executed. The first was a management task that ran the internal information bus to move certain kinds of data (including the meteorological data) within the space craft; it was assigned a high priority. The communications task, which did not need the information bus but took a long time to execute, was assigned medium priority. Finally, the task-collecting meteorological data was assigned a low priority. It ran rather infrequently, but it used the information bus to broadcast its data.

Now the problem. The first task was not doing anything, so the meteorological task would run to dispatch its information. The high-priority bus manager, now seeing that data needed to be sent to the various parts of the system that required it, got ready to run. Unfortunately, the meteorological task was using the bus. Therefore, the higher priority task had to wait until the bus was available. In the meantime, the communication task had to run occasionally. Since it had a higher priority than the meteorological task and did not need the information bus, it could preempt the lower priority task and run with no problem. Because the communication task was quite slow, the watchdog timer, doing its job, would notice that the information bus task had not run for quite a while and conclude that something had gone terribly wrong. Once again, doing its job, it would reset the system.

We will discuss this problem and potential solutions in greater detail in our discussion of operating systems and scheduling.

WHERE DO I PUT MY STUFF?

For our last example, let's look at another Mars mission. Shortly after landing on Mars early in 2004, the rover *Spirit* suddenly went silent. As with many such problems, the root cause was to be found much earlier in the mission. While the craft was in route, the team on the Earth recognized that some serious problems existed with the software package that had been launched with the rover. The problems were identified and corrected; a new image was compiled and sent on its way to the spacecraft and installed on the rover.

The computer system on board the rover has a memory system comprising both RAM and flash memory. The flash memory stores the executable code images that get loaded into RAM when the system is booted. At runtime, then, the real-time operating system and all other executable code is resident in the RAM memory.

In addition to the code bits, the flash memory also holds other files (including image data from the system's cameras) that contain data collected by the rover's subsystems prior to transmission to Earth. Such files are held until a communication window opens, at which point the data is downloaded. The communication protocol dictated that all such files be held until it had been confirmed that the data had been fully and correctly received on Earth. At that time, the system is commanded to delete them. In addition to the files just mentioned, the flash memory also held other miscellaneous data associated with the initial software (that had been updated) but never deleted.

Sometime before the rover went silent, a script was uploaded to identify and delete all such extraneous files. Part of the upload failed; the old information remained. Somewhat later, the data collection tasks needed additional file space, and the rover's computer attempted to perform the allocation. The attempt exceeded the number of files that the RAM space allowed, and an exception was raised. The task attempting the allocation was suspended and a reboot commenced. The operating system, a UNIX™ derivative, attempted to rebuild the directory structure to include the additional space. Unfortunately, there was insufficient RAM to do so and a reboot commenced . . . and commenced . . . and commenced. Eventually, the problem was recognized on the ground, and a command was sent to reboot without mounting the flash file system. That succeeded and, one by one, the old files were manually deleted. When complete, the system was rebooted with the flash file system, and all was right on Mars once more.

The problems that occurred in each of these three cases are safety, reliability, and quality issues. They should have been recognized and corrected during the design phase of the projects. Their discovery should not have been delayed until after the systems had been delivered. The problems were neither complex nor obscure. As we design and develop today's embedded applications, it is incumbent upon us to always pay attention to the low-level details of our design.

8.6 SINGLE-POINT AND COMMON MODE FAILURE MODEL

Before we can discuss designing safe and reliable systems, we must establish a base and a context. A number of years ago, a noted researcher and scientist was lecturing about intelligent systems. He raised the question, "Is a system intelligent if it can cross a busy street without getting hit by a car?" "What if the car is going really fast?" "What if the car is going really really fast?" "What if it's a stealth car and it is going so fast you can't see it?" The point here is that it is always possible to hypothesize situations in which a system might fail and that there may be cases in which the fault is not recognized until it is too late. One *must* understand the context in which the system is to operate; only then can one begin to design and assess the safety and reliability of the system accordingly. For the current studies, we will establish the following base line.

> A safe system design is one that will ensure that the failure of a single component or the failure of multiple components due to a single failure event does not lead to an unsafe condition.

The first step toward achieving such an objective must begin with the specification and the design.

8.7 SAFE SPECIFICATIONS

identify the hazards

Without knowing and understanding the possible potential hazards, one cannot proceed with the design. To *identify the hazards*, one must first identify the context in which the system is to operate. The hazards encountered by a space craft are different from those seen by a pacemaker and are different again from what a cell phone might encounter. Once the hazards that must be dealt with are known and understood, the design process can proceed. However, knowing the potential hazards is only part of the problem. A second part of the *potential risk* operating context is the *potential risk* to the environment. Risk assessment must include effects on people, equipment, and the natural environment.

Focus then shifts to the system being designed. If the initial analysis has determined that the potential risks are minimal, then it is probably not necessary to incorporate additional or extraordinary *safety measures* into the design. If such is not the case, then methods to mitigate the risk must be added. On the space station, failure of the system that provides a breathable atmosphere for the astronauts represents significant risk. Alternatives outside of the system such as a space suit may be a reasonable safety measure. Others might include an emergency oxygen generator that is activated immediately on failure of the controller for the primary system.

safety measures

With the preliminary analysis completed, the results of that analysis must be incorporated into the specification of the systems requirements. Every specification that we write should include a list of agencies, safety standards, and proprietary guidelines with which the system complies.

A very small sampling of such agencies around the world includes the following.

In the United States

- The Underwriters' Laboratory
- The Federal Communications Commission
- The Food and Drug Administration
- GMP—Good Manufacturing Practices
- The Federal Aviation Agency
- The Atomic Energy Commission
- NASA

In Canada

- The Canadian Standards Agency

In Germany

- TUV—Test agency that certifies products for the European Community International
- ISO—International Standards Organization
- International Atomic Energy Agency

8.8 SAFE AND ROBUST DESIGNS

The next step in the process of developing safe and robust designs is to focus on the design itself. We will start with considerations at the project level, move on to the high-level design of the system, examine potential failures in the major functional components of the system, and finally, propose methods by which those failures can be addressed.

8.8.1 Understanding System Requirements

Requirements definition is the process of identifying and understanding what the needs of all interested parties are and then documenting those needs as written definitions and descriptions. The focus is on *what* problem the system has to solve. The emphasis is on the world in which the system will operate, not on the system itself. The process of identifying and specifying requirements will be covered in detail in Chapter 9 on design. Here, the

what

emphasis is on the role that such specifications play in the safety and reliability of an embedded system.

The design of an embedded application is made up of a series of translations that begin with the customer's requirements and lead to the system hardware and machine code that runs on that hardware. Errors arise whenever any one of these translations fails to accurately reflect the initial intention. The single largest cause of such errors, and ultimately of unreliable systems, is simply one of translation or misunderstanding—meters to feet, for example.

At each step through the development process, it is important that the current deliverables be critically reviewed for conformance with requirements as well as for proper and improper operation.

8.8.2 Managing Essential Information

Good documentation management is essential to developing reliable, high-quality hardware and software. At the outset, a project directory structure should be formulated and set up. All of the sources, tools, drawings, and documentation should be under a version control system. A number of very good commercial packages are available. On the software side, two that are included with the various UNIX™ and LINUX™ releases are *RCS—The Revision Control System*, and *CVS—The Concurrent Versioning System*. However, source control is not just for the traditional software side of the project. With the increasing use of modeling tools and hardware design languages, the hardware side of the project can generate as many source code modules as the software side.

RCS—Revision Control System

CVS—Concurrent Versioning System

A typical project directory might have a high-level structure something like that given in Figure 8.0.

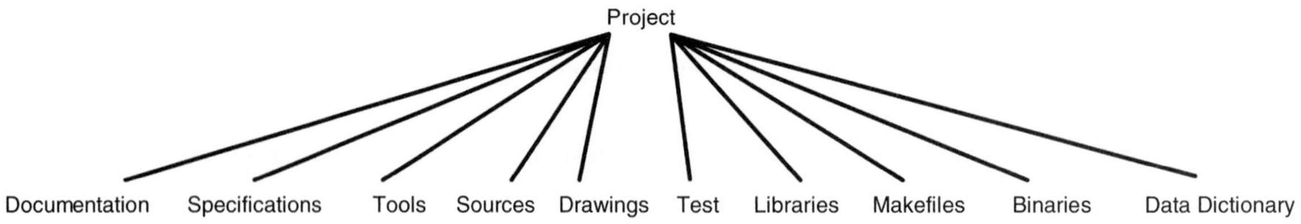

Figure 8.0 Typical Project Directory Structure

Proper management of the version control system is an important part of hardware or software source management. With most version control systems, the source is checked in to a vault or repository. To make changes to a particular module, the designer checks the module out. Such a process gives the designer a *copy* of the original and then locks the original. The original can now only be checked out to another designer as a read only document.

copy

The designer next makes the desired modifications to the source and tests the changes with the rest of the modules. Such testing ensures that the changes operate as intended and have not broken any other functionality of the system. The next step now depends on the project.

If this is the only module being changed, it can safely be checked back into the vault. However, if other modules are in a state of flux as well, the module should be checked in to a holding area within the vault awaiting completion of modifications on all the other modules. Once there is agreement among the team, a system build should be executed and tested. Only after that should all modules be moved from the holding area into the main archival area.

8.8.3 The Review Process

Once the requirements are identified and formalized, they should be reviewed with the customer. One must make certain that understanding and concurrence have been achieved prior to starting the detailed design. The review process is not complete at this point, however.

Several times during the course of the development, design reviews are essential. Generally, these reviews occur toward the latter part of each phase as the deliverables begin to take shape. During the early stages of the project, the reviews are necessarily high level. The review focuses on functional descriptions and decomposition, high-level interface definitions, and gross parameters and signal flow. The goal is to identify errors in understanding or conception, standards violation, or safety issues.

As the design progresses and system-level issues are resolved, the level of detail addressed by the design reviews should similarly increase. On the hardware side, emphasis should be on the major hardware blocks and the components from which they are built. Of significant importance are critical timing issues, potential data flow bottlenecks, possible electromagnetic interference (EMI) susceptibility, and likely failure modes and their consequences. On the software side, the initial focus is on the algorithms, races, potential critical sections, thread management, and so on. The objectives are to identify lockup conditions, the potential for data corruption, or software impacts on any time constraints. Later in the process, the software emphasis shifts to the actual code (called *code inspections* and *code walkthroughs*). During the reviews, one must ask hard questions of and about the design and insist on answers.

code inspections
code walkthroughs

The pre-review analysis should be done by teams of people and should not include the designer(s) of the hardware or software under review. Once the analysis is complete, everyone should walk though the design as well as the specific hardware and software components, resolving any questions that have come up during the analysis.

A typical review process would look like the one illustrated in Figure 8.1.

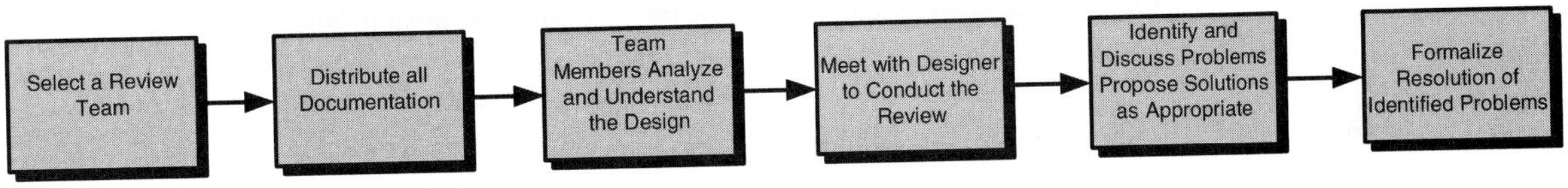

Figure 8.1 Typical Review Process

As engineers, we are and should be proud of our work. That pride is good; however, as one proceeds through a development, to be successful and deliver a quality product, one *must* practice what is called *egoless design*.

egoless design

Satisfying specified requirements is just part of executing the design. Safe operation of the design outside of those specified boundaries must be verified as well. During development, one *must* try to break the design. Verifying system behavior at boundary conditions cannot be avoided; one cannot assume that just because the system behaves as expected and specified for the proper inputs, that it will do so for all inputs and critical input combinations.

8.8.4 Bug Lists

As the development proceeds and moves into the module, subsystem, and system debug, test, and integration, one should maintain an active bug list. The accepted view is that bugs are only found on the software side. Such is no longer the case. Software underlies most contemporary hardware designs. The bug list should identify each bug in detail. It should also, as much as possible, provide a set of steps whereby the bug can be duplicated. As each bug is fixed, the root cause of the problem as well as a brief description of the fix should be noted and documented. It should then be checked off the list, but not removed. Sometimes the little guys have a way of reappearing. Furthermore, such information is always good for a postmortem analysis of the project.

8.8.5 Errors and Exceptions

errors ***exceptions*** *Errors* are static events that arise as the result of a design miscalculation or oversight or from an incorrect or misunderstood specification. *Exceptions* are unexpected and undesirable events that occur at runtime and are distinguished from errors because the system has the possibility of recovering from these situations. Exception handling is intended to enable the program to deal with such problems in a constructive way.

Too often, error and exception handling is left as something to do when the job is completed. For the most part, the obvious errors are caught at compile time; most of the others are handled when they arise as the development progresses through the debug and integration phases. Finally, and to our embarrassment, one must deal with the insidious ones that arise at trade shows or after the product has been released and is in the hands of the first customer.

phase of the moon errors The last-named errors are those that, humorously, we can call *phase of the moon errors*. These seem to have a certain mythical quality about them. They only happen occasionally and can never (or almost never) be reproduced. Nonetheless, they are real and are extremely difficult to track down. When they do surface, too often the typical response is, "let's reset the system and see if it happens again." It never does (at least not immediately), and they are dismissed as imagination. They will always return sometime. One should never take this approach; everything should be done to try to recreate the error.

> ***Good Design Practice***
>
> One should never deal with bugs by resetting the system and hoping that they go away.

The complexity of today's systems is increasing the demand for a more proactive approach to error management. Exceptions as well as exception handling and recovery need to be addressed more formally. The problem of exception management must be considered from the initial stages of the design rather than as something that gets incorporated after the job is complete. Bruce Eckel, a noted expert and writer on the C++ and Java languages, points out that one of the most powerful ways to improve program robustness is through the proper handling of exceptions.

assert, goto, setjmp, longjmp Traditional exception handling in C ranges from none to immediate mode handling—*assert*—or an error handler of some sort—*goto;* C library functions—*setjmp* and *longjmp*; or returning an error value or code from a function.

The assert macro is a standard C library macro. It evaluates its argument and, if the argument is nonzero, it does nothing. Otherwise, the program terminates. Assert is an all or nothing approach that was originally intended for use during the debugging phase of a project. When used, it is often disabled using #define statements before the code is delivered. Forcing an embedded application to abort and terminate is not robust exception management.

assert The syntax for the *assert* macro is given in Figure 8.2. The code fragment shown in Figure 8.3 illustrates the use of the assert macro to ensure that a pointer is not NULL prior to dereferencing it.

```
syntax
    void assert( int anExpression)
```

Figure 8.2 Assert Macro Syntax

```
void aFunction(int* aPtr)
{
    #ifdef DEBUG
        assert(aPtr);        // test for a NULL pointer during debugging
    #endif
    printf("The value is: %d \n", *aPtr);
    return;
}
```

Figure 8.3 Using the *assert* Macro

setjmp, longjmp

The C library functions *setjmp* and *longjmp* are intended to implement an elementary form of jump and can be used to handle abnormal or exceptional conditions. Each of these functions is implemented as a macro in the language. Their syntax is given in Figure 8.4.

```
syntax
    int setjmp (jmp_buf environment);
    int longjmp(jmp_buf environment, int status);
```

Figure 8.4 Syntax for the setjmp and longjmp Functions

The flow of control proceeds as follows:

setjmp
jmp_buf
longjmp

- *setjmp* stores the caller's context or environment in what is called a jump buffer—a buffer of type *jmp_buf* –, which is a C implementation specific array.
- Before executing a *longjmp*, *setjmp* must have been executed to save the environment; *setjmp* returns a 0.
- When a subsequent *longjmp* is executed, the environment stored in the *jmp_buf* is restored and execution resumes after the *setjmp*. The value of the status variable is returned.

We can see how this works in Figure 8.5.

divider()
longjmp

If the denominator is not zero, the *divider()* function takes a normal exit; otherwise, the exit is through the *longjmp*. The status variable gets set as a side effect, and the program attempts to recover.

One should be very careful using this mechanism in an embedded application. If recovery fails, the system is stuck in an infinite loop. The design must address such a possibility and implement a more graceful failure management scheme.

Languages like C++ and Java have much more sophisticated and powerful exception handling mechanisms than does the C language. Those, however, are outside the scope of this text. If one is working with them, it is important to understand how exceptions are handled in those languages and to take advantage of the methods.

```
#include<setjmp.h>
#include<stdio.h>
#include <stdlib.h>
// test function
int divider(jmp_buf env, int num, int denom)
{
    if(0==(denom))
        // we have an exception - return status as 1
        longjmp(env,1);
    else
        // normal return
        return num/denom;
}
int main(void)
{
    // set up jump buffer
    jmp_buf env;

    // declare some working variables
    int status, num, denom, quotient;

    // prompt for input
    printf("Enter two integers numerator and denominator please\n");
    scanf("%d%d",&num,&denom);

    // save the environment
    status=setjmp(env);

    // on first pass status is 0 - flow will skip the if
    // longjmp will return here and set status
    if(status!=0)
    {
        // we have an exception
        printf("Divide by zero - status is: %i\n", status);

        // try to recover
        printf("Enter two integers numerator and denominator please\n");
        scanf("%d%d",&num,&denom);
    }
    // normal return
    quotient = divider(env,num, denom);
    printf("The quotient is: %i\n", quotient);}
```

Figure 8.5 Using setjmp and longjmp

8.8.6 Use the Available Tools

Some of the most powerful steps that one can take toward improving the safety and reliability of designs are very often the simplest. On the software side, one of those steps begins with the compiler. Most compilers support various warning levels. The levels typically range from no warnings to treating any warnings as errors. Set the warning level high; warnings should not be ignored. They are generated for a reason. Understand and resolve each one as it occurs. The goal should be to identify any errors at compile time rather than at runtime.

weak, strong, none

Variable typing is another area in which the available tools can be used to advantage. Three different kinds of typing are defined: *strong*, *weak*, and *none*. With strong typing, type conformance is strictly enforced. Operations cannot be called on an object unless the exact signature of the operation is defined by the object's type. A violation of the type is detected at compile time. With no type enforcement, an object of any type can be used as an object of any other type at any time. Type violations may not be known until runtime—with potentially disastrous consequences, one might add. On the other hand, weak typing is a mix of strong and no typing. C and C++ fall into this category. C++ and Java tend toward stronger typing and C toward the weaker. With weak typing, it is possible to ignore, suppress, or be unaware of type information.

8.9 SAFE AND ROBUST DESIGNS—THE SYSTEM

The typical embedded system core comprises a microprocessor, a memory subsystem, a time base, a collection of peripheral devices, a watchdog timer, a bus system, a power system, and a reset system. In Figure 8.6, we repeat an earlier block diagram of such a system for reference.

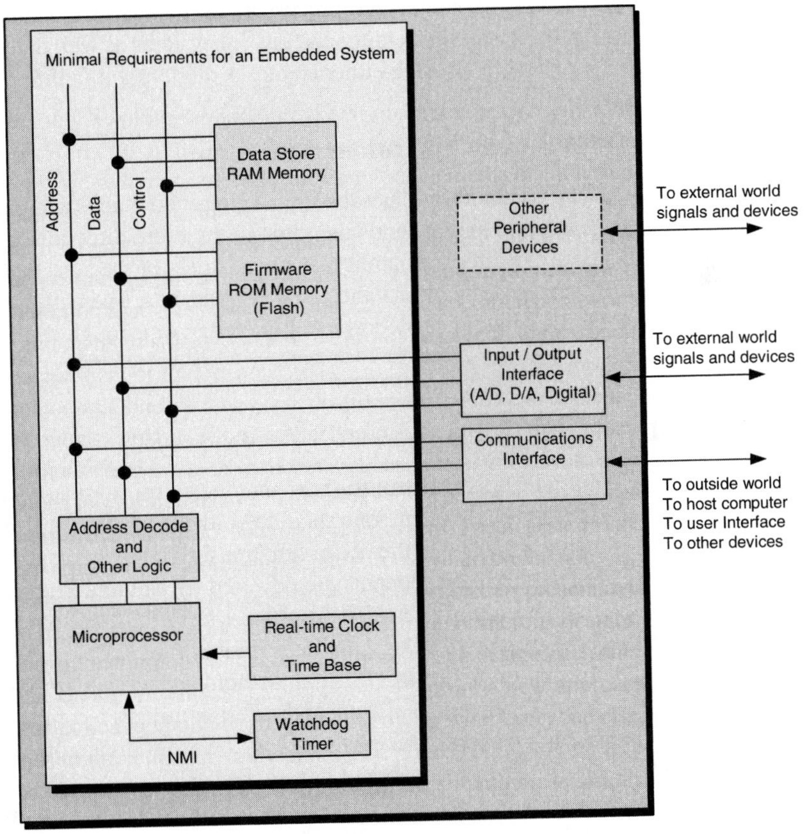

Figure 8.6 Typical Embedded System Block Diagram

8.10 SYSTEM FUNCTIONAL LEVEL CONSIDERATIONS

Faults can occur in any one of the pieces that make up the embedded system core. We will utilize this core in a control application. A risk assessment has determined that failure of the control function poses a moderate risk. To manage the risk, an alarm component will be added to the core. In addition, the system is interacting with a remote application that requires reliable and secure data exchange.

8.10.1 Control and Alarm Subsystems

Both the main control function and the alarm subsystem (which may include system shutdown responsibility) require computational capability. One should avoid designing the system to utilize the same microprocessor for both the command and the alarm functions. If the microprocessor fails in the control task, it will be unable to invoke alarms or shut the system down. If possible, the safety components should be designed as a separate subsystem. Failure of either the main microprocessor or that managing the safety elements does not constitute a single-point failure that will lead to system failure. We make the assumption that the failure of either microprocessor is an independent event. Both failing (nearly) simultaneously constitutes multiple failures that violate the original assumption of a single-point failure.

8.10.2 Memory and Bus Subsystems

Utilizing separate microprocessors for the alarm and control subsystems without also dedicating separate memory and bus subsystems as well defeats the gains from segregating the processors. Sharing either creates a single-point failure potential.

8.10.3 Data Faults and the Communications Subsystem

The communications subsystem brings commands and data into the system from the external world and/or sends the same in the other direction. Corrupted information can jeopardize the safety, reliability, and robustness of the system. Of initial concern is the ability to distinguish between valid and corrupted data. Thereafter any erroneous information must be dealt with either by correcting the error or through the exchange protocol or an encoding algorithm.

8.10.4 Power and Reset Subsystems

Both the main control function and the alarm subsystem require power to operate. As with the alarm subsystem, one should avoid designs that utilize the same power system for both the command and the alarm functions. Often, when designing a safety critical system, the safety/alarm components are powered by an uninterruptible power supply (UPS). Thus, if the power subsystem for the main system fails, the alarm capability remains operational. One could also design an alarm monitoring system into the main system. Failure of the power supply for the alarm and shutdown subsystem could trigger a compromised state alarm via the main system. If the design utilizes a common power system, the potential for a single-point failure exists and can be a significant problem.

Power On Reset (POR)

Every system should have a *Power On Reset* (POR) capability to ensure that all the comprising storage elements start in a known state. A common reset to the two major blocks of the system prevents either from doing its job. The main block and the safety critical block should each have a POR from its own supply.

8.10.5 Peripheral Device Subsystems

Hard or soft failures in any of the peripheral devices can affect the operation of the application in a number of ways. A hard failure in any device eliminates the services it was intended to provide. A soft failure, in which the device appears to be functioning but is actually returning incorrect data or performing an incorrect operation, potentially raises a higher safety risk. Either failure presents two problems: identifying the occurrence of the fault and dealing with the consequences. Identifying the fault can be addressed through built-in self-test functions running in the background. Coping with the loss of a (critical) device is a design phase issue that is dealt with in the same manner as the control and alarm faults.

8.10.6 Clock Subsystem

System designs that utilize the same clock or time base for both command and alarm functions have a potential common point for failure. In the system described earlier, both the main control function and the watchdog subsystem require a clock to operate. A watchdog timer is like the *dead man's throttle* on a train. If not reset on a regular basis, it forces the system into a fail-safe state. If a shared clock is used, failure of the clock prevents the microprocessor from resetting the watchdog timer. At the same time, such a failure also prevents the timer from advancing. Independent clocks, similar to independent microprocessors, mitigate the effect of the simultaneous failure of two clocks.

dead man's throttle

We will now examine each of these pieces of functionality and present system-level alternatives for supporting robust and reliable designs while reducing safety risks. One must bear in mind that the incorporation of any of the design alternatives must take into consideration the context and requirements of the specific application.

8.11 SYSTEM ARCHITECTURE LEVEL CONSIDERATIONS

Let's now look at some possible hardware architecture alternatives for addressing the control and alarming subsystems. Highly reliable systems fall into three classes, based on their capabilities following failure. The first are called *fail operational*^{2} (read as *fail operational squared*). Such systems can tolerate two single-point failures and continue to operate with full capability. Those in the second group are called *fail operational*. These systems will tolerate one single-point failure and still continue to operate with full capability. Following failure, those in the third group can continue to operate but at diminished capability.

fail operational*^{2}, *fail operational

Based on such classifications, one can build safety into a design at a number of different levels. How that is done generally involves trading off increased cost for reduced risk. At the one extreme, *fail operational*^{2} capability often entails incorporating fully redundant paths of control and separate safety critical elements or error detection-correction capability into the architecture. At the opposite extreme, sufficient capability is added to the design to ensure minimum capability or, at the very least, annunciation and graceful failure.

8.11.1 Fail Operational^2/Fail Operational Capability

At the component level, *fail operational*^{2} capability commonly involves some form of voting scheme. The implementation comprises an odd number of channels of control and a voting protocol to decide on the validity of incoming signals and outgoing controls. The basic case is denoted *triple module redundancy* (TMR) and is shown in Figure 8.7. In this figure, we are focusing on potential failures in the three channels, not in the voter or alarm. Clearly, both the voter and alarm are vulnerable to single-point failures.

***fail operational*^{2}**

triple module redundancy (TMR)

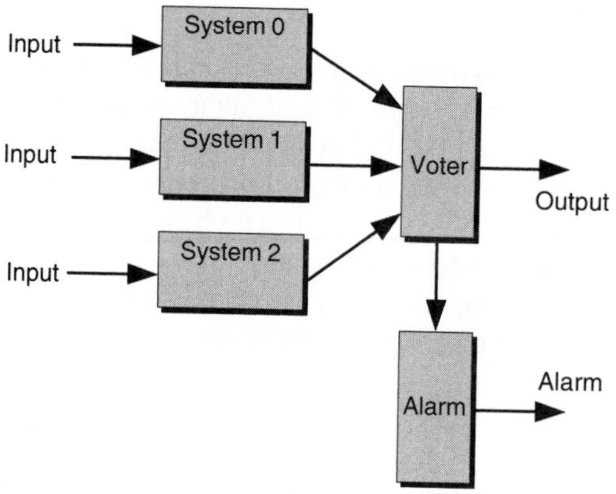

Figure 8.7 Triple Module Redundancy

The design we have illustrated uses three separate sensors, one for each system. A reduced alternative would be to use a single sensor and bus the output to all three systems. Such a modification can be made if it is known that the reliability of the sensor is very high. For this design, all three systems are on line and making decisions. The voter examines each of the outputs and selects the value on which two (or more) agree. With such a design, the best one can do is fail operational capability. The decision must be made at design time as to how the system should behave should two units fail. Alarm capability is added to announce the first failure and then, if necessary, the occurrence of a second.

N module redundancy
majority (NMR)

By adding two more systems, one can achieve fail operational[2] capability. Such a configuration, as shown in Figure 8.8, is called *N module redundancy* (NMR). The voter is slightly more complex. The output is now determined based on the results of the *majority*. N must always be an odd number to ensure that there cannot be a tie.

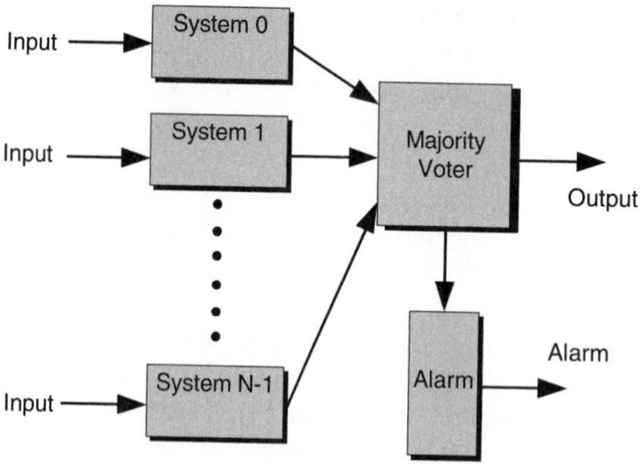

Figure 8.8 N Module Redundancy

The next variation on the approach is driven by the design of the individual systems. The systems may be implemented with the same or with different designs.

8.11.1.1 Same Design

In the first alternative, all of the individual designs are physically identical. One must ensure that single-point failure will not affect all channels. The advantage of such a scheme is that it gives improved robustness to the system at minimal design cost. Additional systems are simply copies of the original design. The disadvantage is that a common failure mode, for example, a design flaw, can appear in all systems. If the design has a susceptibility to certain kinds of input errors, when one system is affected, the error affects all systems. Recall the Ariane 5 rocket.

8.11.1.2 Alternative Designs

The use of alternative designs implements redundancy by replicating systems. Each design is physically different and yet has the same public interface, that is, implements the same functionality. The advantage of such an approach is that a common failure or design flaw has a low probability of being replicated in all of the systems used for control. The system can detect/respond to certain kinds of input errors. The disadvantage, of course, is cost. The scheme is implemented in several different ways. One approach is to make all elements functionally the same. That is, all channels implement same behavior. This can be done in different ways, although generally the implementation uses different hardware and software. Such a design is the most expensive of the three alternatives. For added reliability, the input sensors may be duplicated or, if deemed necessary, these may be different as well. One of the major commercial aircraft manufacturers, for example, uses microprocessors from several different vendors in their cabin pressure management system to guard against a common design error or fault susceptibility in any of the processors.

8.11.2 Reduced Capability

The next approach gives somewhat reduced capability under failure.

8.11.2.1 Lightweight Redundancy

lightweight redundancy

As an alternative to full operational capability under failure, the design may support a critical subset of the output signals and add alarm capability. Such a scheme is called *lightweight redundancy*. A secondary system with alarm, annunciation, and some control capability accepts a subset of the inputs. It then calculates a subset of the outputs while monitoring the actions taken by the primary channel. If there is a difference in the calculated output values and the primary outputs are out of bounds, a warning is issued.

The intent is to identify gross failures and to focus on fault detection rather than tolerance. The secondary system can provide a subset of critical functionality and outputs as necessary but cannot completely fill in for the main system in the event of failure. The block diagram for such a system appears in Figure 8.9.

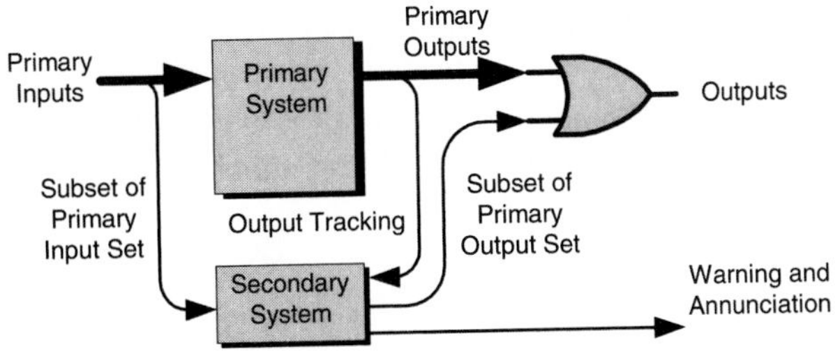

Figure 8.9 Lightweight Redundancy

8.11.2.2 Monitor Only

An alternative to lightweight redundancy, with somewhat less capability, implements a primary system with a separate monitoring function. The monitoring subsystem does not support any of the primary functionality.

The primary system is charged with implementing the necessary actions while the monitor subsystem is responsible for keeping track of what actions need to be taken. The monitor channels also track the physical environment to ensure that the results of the actions are appropriate and correct. The sensing utilized by the monitor subsystem is separate from that of the primary system. The sensors for the primary system are strictly dedicated to that job, although a subset may be directed to the secondary subsystem.

The objective of such an approach is to have the monitor subsystem identify primary system failures and inform the appropriate fault-handling mechanisms. It is clear that a failure in the monitor subsystem does not affect the primary system. Nonetheless, we must still identify, and eliminate, points of single failure. The two channels exchange messages to ensure proper and continuing operation of each. The block diagram is now refined as illustrated in Figure 8.10.

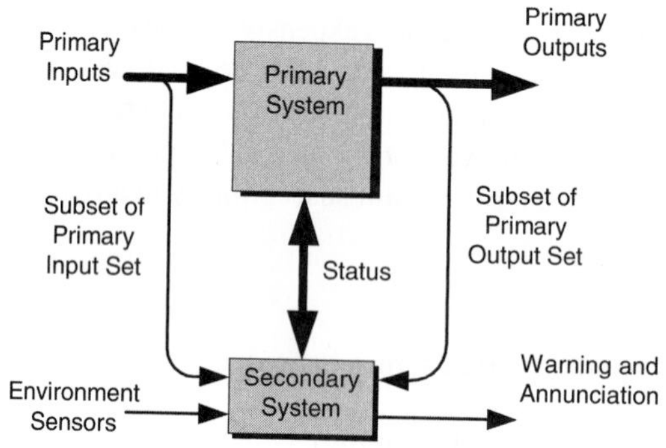

Figure 8.10 Monitor Only System Configuration

8.12 BUSSES—THE SUBSYSTEM INTERCONNECT

star, ring, multidrop

The various components in the system are interconnected by one or more bus structures. These busses comprise the address, control, and data signals necessary for proper operation of the system. The embedded world commonly utilizes variations on three general configurations: the *star*, the *ring*, and the *multidrop* bus. Each has certain advantages and certain disadvantages. We will discuss the detailed operation of each in a subsequent chapter. For now, the intent is to examine each from a reliability perspective.

8.12.1 The Star Configuration

star, master-slave

The *star* configuration, shown in Figure 8.11, implements a *master-slave* arrangement. Device-to-device communication must go through the master device. During the transmit operation, the master device at center directs all of the activities and message exchange with all of the other devices. During the slave's receive operation, the master transmits to the desired destinations.

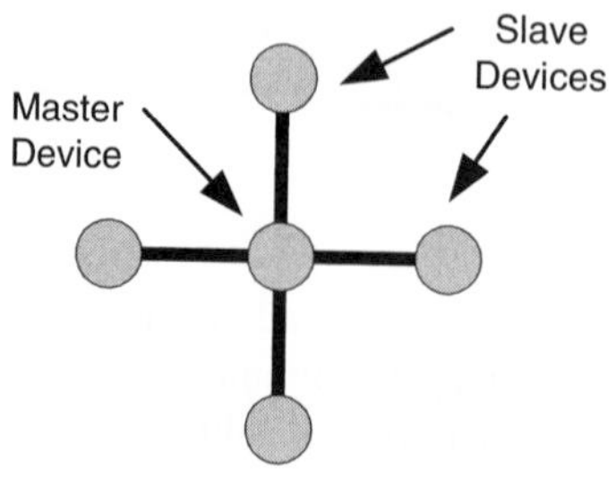

Figure 8.11 Star Bus Configuration

If there is a link or slave device failure, communication with the other devices can continue. While a portion of the functionality is lost, the system can still be operated at a reduced level. Loss of the master device will, of course, result in a permanent or hard failure.

8.12.2 The Multidrop Bus Configuration

The multidrop bus is a variation on the star architecture as the diagram in Figure 8.12 shows. There may or may not be a bus master. This simple bus is probably one of the more commonly used architectures. Devices may be designed with several different levels of capability: all can transmit or receive; some can transmit only, while others may receive only. Failure of the link at a single device will not compromise the entire net. A severed net, however, can prevent communication beyond the severed point.

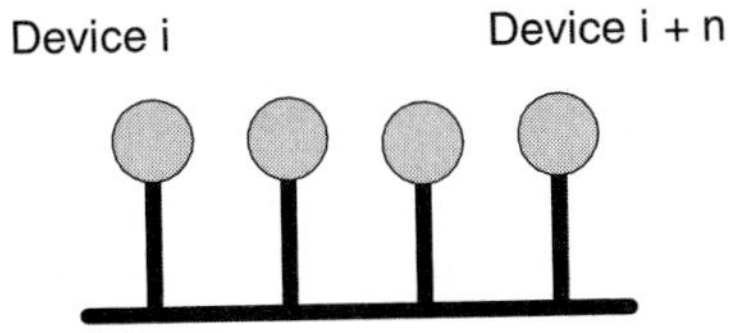

Figure 8.12 Multidrop Bus Configuration

8.12.3 The Ring Configuration

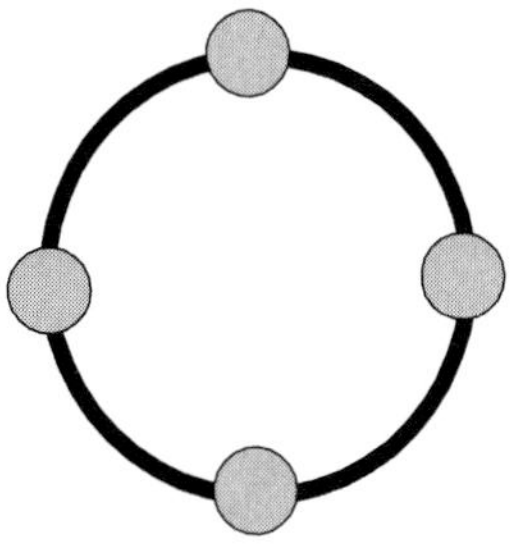

Figure 8.13 Ring Bus Configuration

The basic ring structure is shown in Figure 8.13. The ring configuration also serves as the basis for token ring type networks. There is typically no bus master (on some occasions, one of the nodes is designated as lord). Each device accepts all of the messages circulating within the ring. If a device receiving the message is the addressed device, the message is accepted; otherwise, the message is passed on to the next device. Such a configuration has been utilized for many years as the basis for IBM's token ring. When configured with one node designated as lord, people have gotten into the hobbit of referring to the architecture as a tolkien ring. Variants on the ring architecture are common in communication networks in automotive or aircraft applications.

Failure of the link in the basic ring configuration still permits full interconnection of all comprising nodes. If one of the links is lost, the architecture reduces to the multidrop bus configuration. A variant on the ring adds a second inner ring, as we see in the leftmost network in Figure 8.14.

Traffic flows in one direction on the outer ring and in the opposite direction on the inner ring. On failure, the loss of a single link on either ring still leaves one of the rings intact as we see in the center drawing, which shows two alternate failures. If both links are severed between any adjacent nodes, as in the rightmost drawing, a single ring remains intact.

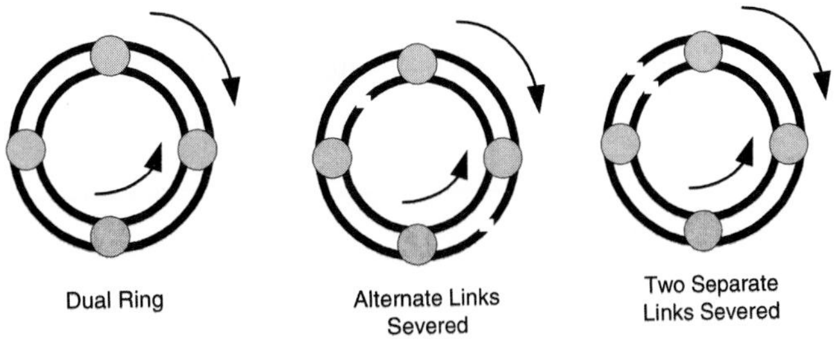

Figure 8.14 Multiring Bus Configuration

8.13 DATA AND CONTROL FAULTS—DATA BOUNDARY VALUES

type, range

One of the essential steps during the early phases of a design is the definition of the interface signals among the system functions and then the modules. This process involves specifying the *type* and *range* of each signal. As each of those decisions is made, one must further consider how the system will behave/respond if the input data either does not match the expected type or exceeds the specified range. In addition to deciding what to do if the signal exceeds the specified range, one must also consider the proper course of action if (and when) the signal returns to the proper values.

The problem can be addressed from both the design and operational sides. During design, one must ensure that the input data is in bounds prior to incorporating it in any calculations or before making any irrevocable decisions. Furthermore, one must decide how to treat out-of-bounds values at runtime.

Under no circumstances should an out-of-bounds piece of input data ever be mapped into one that is in bounds without warning. That said, boundary tests must be incorporated into the runtime code to confirm that input data has values (and types) that are within the specified upper and lower bounds. Furthermore, one needs to decide what to do if such bounds are exceeded. Alternatives include the following.

- Hold at max or min value
- Alarm
- Combination

8.13.1 Type Conformance

The task of ensuring type conformance for input signals is somewhat easier in an embedded application because we have greater control over inputs and their characteristics than one might find in the typical desktop application. Runtime type mismatch should not be a major issue.

When new features are added to a legacy design, one must be sure that existing functions are invoked with the proper signature. Extra care must be taken when the application is written in a language such as C++ that supports overloaded functions.

8.13.2 Boundary Values

Figure 8.15 illustrates a typical signal and a specified range or limits on that signal. At points A and B, the signal is at the low and high boundaries, respectively; at these two points, the signal value remains in range.

At C_1, the signal exceeds the specified range in the negative direction and continues decreasing. It reaches a negative peak and begins increasing, crossing the lower bound at C_2. The increase continues until the upper bound is crossed at D_1. The behavior at the lower bound is repeated at the upper bound, and eventually the signal crosses back into the specified range at D2.

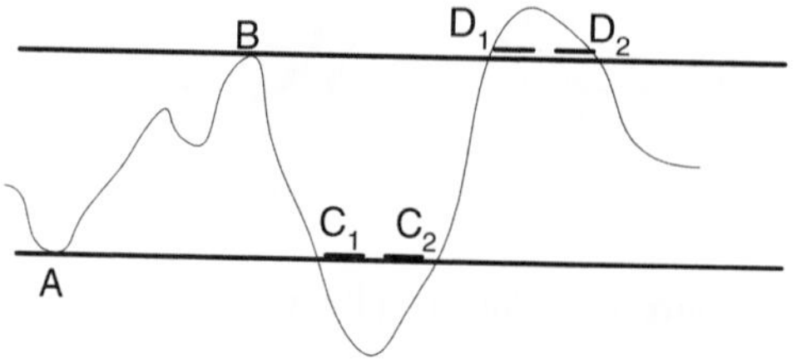

Figure 8.15 Signal Illustrating Possible Range and Limits

The signal values at points A and B are valid and must be accepted as proper inputs. The design and subsequent tests should confirm that behavior. The signals at points C and D, however, exceed the specifications. At both sets of points, we have several choices:

- Ignore the out-of-range values.
- Detect the out-of-range values, issue a warning, and continue operating. When or if the signal returns to the proper range, continue operation with annunciation of the original fault.
- Detect the out-of-range values, issue a warning, and terminate operation.

There are also several choices as to what values to assign to the signal at these points.

- Accept the actual value of the signal.
- Map the actual value into the maximum or minimum value but do not use the value other than for annunciation.

Whatever the choice, the system must be thoroughly tested at such values to ensure proper operation.

8.14 DATA AND CONTROL FAULTS—THE COMMUNICATIONS SUBSYSTEM

To be useful, any embedded application must interact with the outside world, and the internal modules must interact with each other. Such interaction necessarily involves the exchange of data. During the course of that exchange, the data can become corrupted. What should be done?

8.14.1 Damaged Data

At runtime, it is always possible that data will be damaged by noise, electromagnetic interference (EMI), or crosstalk within the system. One can ask several questions about such faults. Are the aberrant data detectable? Detectable faults are those that can be distinguished from legitimate data, whereas undetectable faults masquerade as legitimate data. What is the extent of the damage? Is it a single bit, several bits, a group of bits, or substantial—the complete loss of an input channel? What is the appropriate or best response? Alternatives range from ignoring the problem to attempting complete recovery.

Let's examine each of these alternatives, starting with being able to detect the faulty data.

8.14.1.1 Detectability

distance

Hamming distance

Faulty data contains a detectable error if it can be distinguished from legitimate data. One measure of the ability to detect corrupted data is related to the *distance* between legitimate words in the language. That is, the number of bits that must be changed to map one valid data word into another. Such a difference is denoted as the *Hamming distance* after R. W. Hamming who first proposed the idea. Put another way, the Hamming distance is given by the number of bits that must be changed before one valid data word is converted into another. The larger the Hamming distance between legitimate words, the greater must the extent of the damage be before an error is incorrectly interpreted as correct.

Consider a 3-bit piece of data. With 3 bits, there are eight possible combinations as illustrated on the vertices of the labeled cube in Figure 8.16.

unit distance

Each edge represents a *unit distance*. Between any two adjacent nodes, only a single bit needs to change to convert one pattern into the next. Within any of the faces of the cube,

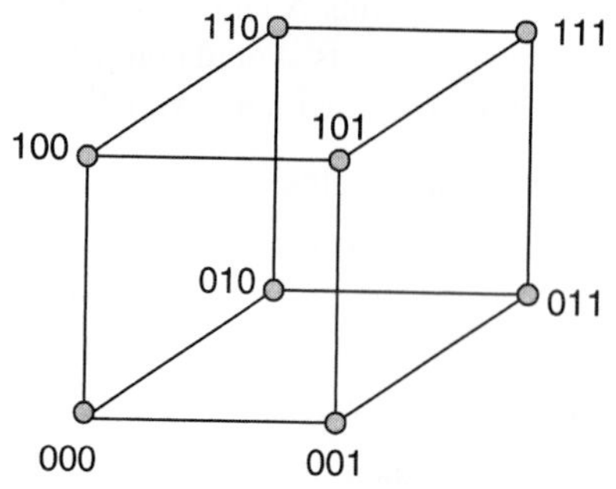

Figure 8.16 Graphical Illustration of Distance Between Data Words

2 bits must change to convert patterns on diagonally opposite edges from one to the other. They are separated by a Hamming distance of two. Finally, on the full cube, 3 bits must change to convert patterns on diagonally opposite vertices—a Hamming distance of three. Thus, if valid data words have a Hamming distance of two, for example, a data word must sustain two faults before one valid piece of data is converted into another.

To try to minimize the possibility that corrupted data will be interpreted as valid data, we try to maximize the Hamming distance between valid data words. Doing so, however, reduces the number of combinations available for a specified word size.

For the 3-bit word, specifying a Hamming distance of three permits only three different sets of two valid data words each: {(000, 111), (010, 101), (001, 110)}. A Hamming distance of two gives four possible sets of four valid data words each.

It can be shown that a minimum Hamming distance of two is required to be able to *detect* any single-bit error in a transmitted data word. It can also be shown that minimum distance of three is necessary to be able to *correct* any single-bit error. Generalizing, for a block of code words with a minimum Hamming distance of 2m +1, it can be shown that up to *m bit* errors can be corrected. Furthermore, if the minimum Hamming distance is 2m + n + 1, then it is possible to *correct* up to *m bit* errors and to *detect* up to *n bit* errors.

detect
correct
m bit
correct, m bit, detect, n bit

8.14.1.2 Extent

From the outset, data is subject to the vagaries of the environment. Such errors may comprise single/several bits; these errors occur when a bit is dropped/added to a data stream or when 1 bit is transformed from one state to another. Group-bit errors occur when a group of spatially close bits are corrupted. Such errors are referred to as *burst errors*. Substantial bit errors occur when there is a major loss of integrity in the physical link. We can address errors in the first two categories in a number of ways. Little can be done for those in the third.

burst errors

8.14.1.3 Response

When data is corrupted, one can detect the damaged bits and signal that an error has occurred, or one can detect and then correct the problem (depending on the extent of the error). However, the cost (time and added bits) of the correction algorithm must be considered.

8.14.2 Managing Damaged Data

There are several alternatives for dealing with data that has been corrupted. The choices are simple: ignore it, detect it, or detect and correct it. For either of the last two alternatives, additional information must be incorporated into the data object. The amount of additional information that is needed depends on the kinds of faults to be detected and the intended response.

8.14.2.1 Parity

parity *odd parity* The simplest form of detection is called *parity*. The basic scheme appends a single bit to each data word or block. When using *odd parity*, the total number of one bits (including the parity bit) must be odd. If the data word has an odd number of one bits, a 0 is added; if the data word has an even number of one bits, a 1 is added.

even parity For *even parity*, the total number of 1 bits (including the parity bit) must be even. If the data word has an odd number of one bits, a 1 is added; if the data word has an even number of one bits, a 0 is added.

Before the data is used, the parity is recomputed and compared with the expected. A mismatch indicates an error. If there is no mismatch, the best that can be said is that either there are no errors or there has been an even number of errors.

The advantage of such a scheme is that it is simple and detects all odd numbers of errors. The simplicity of the approach, however, also gives rise to several problems. Even numbers of errors are undetectable, for example. The approach does not work reliably for burst errors, and finally, it is a detection only scheme.

The basic parity codes have a Hamming distance of two. That is, 2-bit changes are required before one valid data word is changed into another.

EXAMPLE 8.0

Three-bit words will be used in Figure 8.17 to illustrate how to compute and check the parity bit for each of the schemes.

When checking for errors in this example, only single-bit errors are assumed to have occurred.

Generating		
Original Data	Odd Data Parity	Even Data Parity
000	000 1	000 0
001	001 0	001 1
010	010 0	010 1
011	011 1	011 0
100	100 0	100 1
101	101 1	101 0
110	110 1	110 0
111	111 0	111 1

Checking		
Data Received	Odd Parity Result	Even Parity Result
0000	Error	Valid
0001	Valid	Error
0010	Valid	Error
0011	Error	Valid
0100	Valid	Error
0101	Error	Valid
0110	Error	Valid
0111	Valid	Error
1000	Valid	Error
1001	Error	Valid
1010	Error	Valid
1011	Valid	Error
1100	Error	Valid
1101	Valid	Error
1110	Valid	Error
1111	Error	Valid

Figure 8.17 Generating and Checking Parity for a 3-Bit Data Word

8.14.2.2 Linear Codes

linear codes

encoding

Hamming codes

Implementing data error detection using the basic parity scheme is sufficient for many applications. If greater detection as well as correction capabilities are necessary, then a more sophisticated approach is appropriate. A good first step toward adding greater capabilities to a fault management scheme utilizes an encoding scheme that generates a family of codes called *linear codes*. Such codes are designated linear because the arithmetic combination of two existing words gives a third word that is also in the set of valid code words.

The term *encoding* in the current context refers to the process of adding parity bits to the data word to provide enhanced detection and correction capabilities. Code, code word, or encoded word specifies the data word with the additional parity bits. The first types of linear codes that we will look at are called the *Hamming codes.*

HAMMING CODES

A strategy developed by Hamming demonstrated a method for encoding data words with a minimum distance of three. Following encoding, data could be transmitted with the assurance that on reception, any single-bit error could be corrected and any double-bit error could be detected.

To execute the encoding process, one must specify the number of data bits and the number of parity bits. These two are related as follows.

Encoded word length	$= 2^p - 1$
Number of parity bits	$= p$
Number of data bits	$= 2^p - p - 1$

The approach requires that the parity bits be inserted into the data field in a particular way. Starting with the first bit position, any position that is a power of 2 should contain a parity bit; all remaining positions are used to store data bits. Thus, positions 1, 2, 4, 8, . . . will hold parity bits. The approach also specifies the bits over which each of the parity bits computes parity. The assignment works as follows.

Numbering begins from the least significant bit, which is labeled bit 1.

1. Parity bits are placed in bit positions: 1, 2, 4, 8, 16. . . Data bits are placed in the other positions.
2. The parity bits are chosen such that they provide even parity over the following groups of bit positions:
   - **a.** P0: 1, 3, 5, 7, … P0 will be in position 1
   - **b.** P1: 2,3, 6,7, 10,11, … P1 will be in position 2
   - **c.** P2: 4,5,6,7, 12,13,14,15 … P2 will be in position 4

The encoded word appears as in Figure 8.18.

Upon reception, the parity bits are recomputed. If the recomputed set of parity bits is all zero, the received word contained no errors; otherwise, the binary value of the bits in the

7	6	5	4	3	2	1
D3	D2	D1	P2	D0	P1	P0

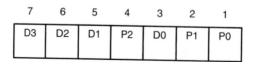

Figure 8.18 Hamming Encoding Scheme for a 4-Bit Data Word

recomputed set identifies the bit that is in error. At that point, the designated bit can simply be inverted.

The data word is illustrated in Figure 8.19.

4	3	2	1
1	1	0	1

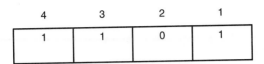

Figure 8.19 Sample Data Word

The encoding is given as in Figure 8.20.

7	6	5	4	3	2	1
1	1	0	0	1	1	0

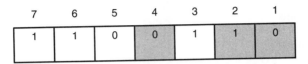

Figure 8.20 The Data Word Is Encoded

Assume that the encoded word shown in Figure 8.21 is received.

7	6	5	4	3	2	1
1	0	0	0	1	1	0

Figure 8.21 Corrupted Received Data Word

Each of the parity bits is computed as

P0: {1, 3, 5, 7} parity is 0

P1: {2, 3, 6, 7} parity is 1

P2: {4, 5, 6, 7} parity is 1

The check is showing a value of 110, binary 6. Indeed, bit 6 is the one that is incorrect. Had the check number been 0, the received word would have been correct.

BLOCK CODES

block codes

block check codes

block check sum

Block codes are the subset of linear codes in which error management is performed over blocks of data words rather than individual words. Among the simpler implementations of such codes are the *block check codes*. Encoding data using such codes begins with computing parity for each individual word as we did earlier. Next, a group of words is aggregated into a block or frame, and a parity *word* called a *block check sum* is computed over the entire block. The block check sum is a simple extension of the single parity bit idea, and it applies to a complete block or frame of data. The block check sum is computed according to the following rules.

1. The parity of each individual word is computed as in the base case; this is now referred to as a lateral or row parity bit.
2. A parity word is computed for the block as follows.

   Bit 0—Parity of bit 0 of all words in the block

   Bit 1—Parity of bit 1 of all words in the block

   Bit n—Parity of all lateral parity bits in the block

This word is called longitudinal or column parity.

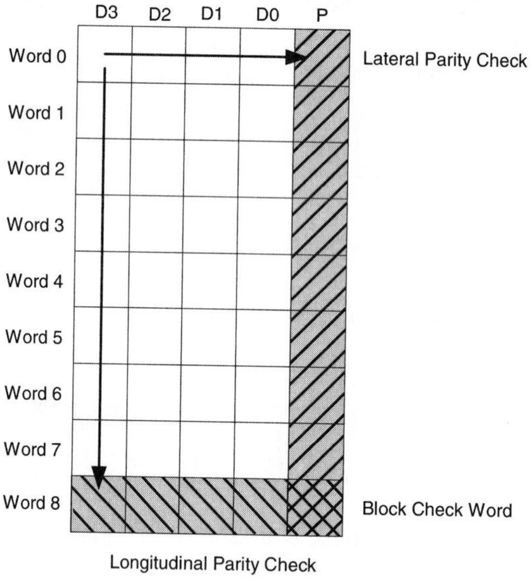

Figure 8.22 Computing Lateral and Longitudinal Parity in a Block Check Scheme

Figure 8.22 schematically illustrates a block of data (made up of 4-bit words) and the two parity checks for the data block.

As a variation on the scheme, one may elect to use odd parity in one direction and even parity in the other. Under such a variation, the parity bit in the lower right-hand corner of the block is ignored. The advantages of the block check sum are that it is simple and detects all single-bit errors as well as many double-bit errors. Nonetheless, some simple errors can still escape detection. Like the single-parity bit scheme, it does not work reliably for burst errors; also, it is a detection-only algorithm.

EXAMPLE 8.1

In this example, a block size of eight data words is defined. Each data word will comprise 4 bits. We will use even parity for each word and odd parity for each column in the block (see Figure 8.23).

	D3	D2	D1	D0	P
Word 0	1	1	0	0	0
Word 1	0	1	1	1	1
Word 2	0	1	1	0	0
Word 3	0	1	0	1	0
Word 4	1	1	1	0	1
Word 5	0	1	1	0	0
Word 6	1	0	0	1	0
Word 7	0	0	1	0	1
Word 8	0	1	0	0	0

Figure 8.23 Computing Lateral and Longitudinal Parity in a Block Check Scheme

CYCLIC ENCODING

cyclic encoding

The next level of sophistication utilizes a scheme called *cyclic encoding*. Such codes are a subset of linear codes and are quite effective at both error detection and correction. They are designated cyclic because a new code word is obtained from a circular shift of an existing one. Recall that the linear block codes accomplished the same thing by adding valid code words (a shift by two). Their very nature makes cyclic encoding quite easy to implement in hardware, particularly using FPGA or VLSI circuitry.

Much of the material introduced in this section is based on the work of Evariste Galois, an accomplished mathematician who lived in France in the early 1800s. His work has made significant contributions to many of the encoding and encryption methodologies we have today. It seems, however, that he was more skilled with mathematics than he was with a pistol. He died in a duel in Paris at the young age of 21.

cyclic redundancy check (CRC)

Of the cyclic codes, the *cyclic redundancy check* (CRC) encoding (commonly used in various memory systems) is probably the best known. The full details of the underlying theory of cyclic encoding are well beyond the scope of this text. The following discussion is intended to introduce some of the vocabulary and general concepts but does not have sufficient depth to permit one to design a complex system from scratch. It is recommended that the interested reader explore any of the numerous excellent texts on communication and coding theory that are available.

At the root of the approach is the notion of a polynomial associated with a binary sequence of bits. The polynomial, over a Galois Field of two elements—GF(2), is written in terms of a dummy variable, usually x, and is of the form

$$f(x) = \sum_{i=0}^{n-1} a_i x^i \tag{8.0}$$

The associated sequence of n – 1 bits is then given as: $[a_{n-1}, a_{n-2}, \ldots a_1, a_0]$. Note that the polynomial will be of order n – 1 when the sequence is of length n.

For the set of bits [1011], we will have,

$$a3 = 1, \quad a2 = 0, \quad a1 = 1, \quad \text{and} \quad a0 = 1$$

and the corresponding polynomial:

$$f(x) = x^3 + x + 1 \tag{8.1}$$

Furthermore, according to Galois Field arithmetic, we can define addition and multiplication as shown in Figure 8.24.

Addition	Multiplication
0 + 0 = 0	0 • 0 = 0
0 + 1 = 1	0 • 1 = 0
1 + 0 = 1	1 • 0 = 0
1 + 1 = 0	1 • 1 = 1

Figure 8.24 Galois Field Addition and Multiplication

As with the other encoding methods, the goal is to add sufficient redundant information to an encoded word that we are able to detect or detect and correct a specified number of bit errors in a received word. The more redundant information that is added, the greater the extent of the damage that can be repaired will be. As we learned with the linear Hamming codes, properly selecting the redundant bits is where the real work comes in.

Let's look at the math first. Start with a binary sequence of length k and append n-k additional parity bits. The result will be an n-bit word; that word now has the form

$$[d_{k-1}, d_{k-2}, \ldots d_1, d_0, r_{n-k-1}, r_{n-k-2}, \ldots r_1, r_0]$$

which can be written in polynomial form as

$$m(x) = \sum_{i=n-k}^{n-1} d_i x^i + \sum_{i=0}^{n-k-1} r_i x^i \tag{8.2}$$

or equivalently as

$$M(x) = x^n D(x) + R(x) \tag{8.3}$$

where M(x), D(x), and R(x) represent the three polynomials.

We can take advantage of such an equation as follows.
First, let

- n and k be integers, k > n
- D(x) be a k bit binary number expressed in polynomial form
- G(x) be an (n-k) bit number expressed in polynomial form
- R(x) be an (n-k) bit number expressed in polynomial form

Observe:

1. D(x) is shifted to the left by n places.

$$D(x) \bullet 2^n \tag{8.4}$$

2. Then it is divided by G(x) to give a quotient and a remainder:

$$\frac{D(x) \bullet 2^n}{G(x)} = Q(x) + \frac{R(x)}{G(x)} \tag{8.5}$$

3. Next, the remainder portion is added to both sides of the equation.

$$\frac{D(x) \bullet 2^n}{G(x)} + \frac{R(x)}{G(x)} = Q(x) + \frac{R(x)}{G(x)} + \frac{R(x)}{G(x)} \tag{8.6}$$

4. Finally, simplify:

$$\frac{D(x) \bullet 2^n + R(x)}{G(x)} = Q(x) \tag{8.7}$$

According to Galois Field arithmetic, the two remainder expressions on the right-hand side of the equation in line 3 (both expressing the same binary number) will cancel, giving the equation in line 4. Consequently, it is clear that if the polynomial given by the expression

$$F(x) = D(x) \bullet 2^n + R(x) \tag{8.8}$$

is divided by G(x), there will be no remainder. The binary sequence associated with F(x) represents the encoded data word that is transmitted.

In operation, the data is encoded according to the steps outlined above, and the resulting binary sequence is sent. When the received word is divided by G(x), a remainder of zero will indicate that there was no error. The upper k bits will be the data. If the result of the division is not zero, an error has occurred. The remainder can then be used to identify which bit(s) are in error.

The magnitude of n-k, the number of parity bits added, determines the extent of the code's ability to detect and correct errors. The number G(x) is called a generator polynomial. It is not arbitrary—it represents what is called a primitive or irreducible or unfactorable polynomial. Care must be taken in its selection to ensure the desired error management. The choice determines the number and type of errors that can be detected. The remainder bits indicated above are called the *frame check sequence*.

frame check sequence

The encoding can be executed using a simple circuit such as the one given in the block diagram in Figure 8.25.

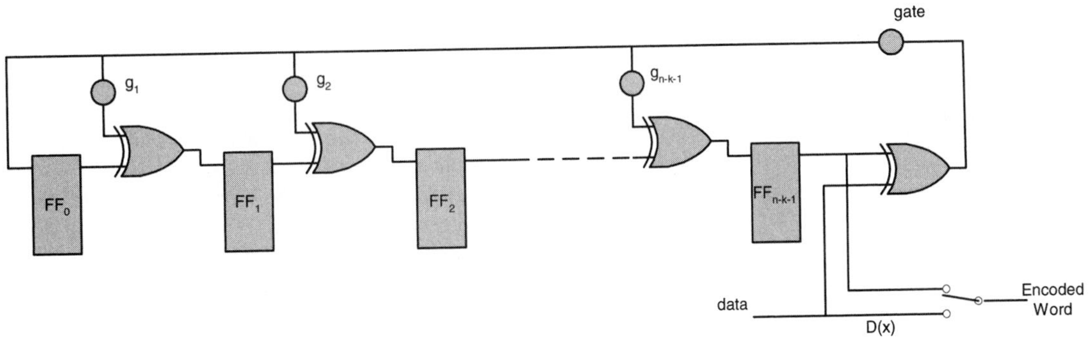

Figure 8.25 An n-k Stage Shift Register Encoder

In the diagram, the gate, g_i, indicates a connection or logical 1 if the corresponding coefficient in G(x) is present and a logical 0 otherwise. The encoding operation proceeds as follows. The message is shifted into the encoder and to the output, MSB first. After all the bits of the message are shifted out, the switch is placed in the upper position, the feedback is broken by disabling the feedback gate, the encoder is reconfigured as a shift register, and its contents (the remainder bits) are sent to the output as well.

The received message may have been corrupted during transmission; the goal of the receiver is to recover the original data. When the encoded word is received, it is processed by a circuit similar to that on the encoding side as shown in Figure 8.26. The circuit computes what is called the *syndrome* of the received message.

syndrome

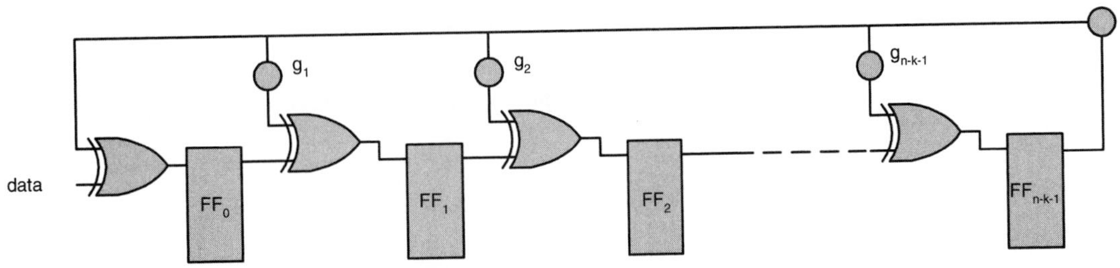

Figure 8.26 An n-k Stage Syndrome Calculator

syndrome After the entire encoded word has been received, if the *syndrome* is 0 (all flip-flops contain logical 0), the word was received correctly. There is no remainder; otherwise, there was an error. To identify the bit in error, the input to the decoder is connected to logical 0 and clocked. Starting with the MSB of the received message, successive bits are examined. When the contents of the decoder contain the value: 0000 . . . 01, the current bit of the message is in error. After all the bits have been shifted through, if the decoder does not contain all 0's, an uncorrectable error has occurred.

With the proper choice of generator, one can detect

- All single-bit errors
- All double-bit errors
- All odd numbers of bit errors
- All error bursts $< n + 1$
- Most error bursts $\geq n + 1$

Similar techniques can be used to detect and correct multiple-bit as well as certain families of burst errors. Typically, error correction relies on detection and re-transmission rather than computation by the receiver.

EXAMPLE 8.2

In this example, once again, the design will utilize a 4-bit data word. This sets the value of k to 4. If we wish to correct all single-bit errors, then the Hamming distance must be three. Three additional bits will be sufficient; thus, the encoded word length, n, will be 7. From a table of generator polynomials (which can be found in any of the references on coding theory cited at the end of the text), we select the following polynomial. The generator is implemented as given in Figure 8.27,

$$G(x) = 1 + x + x^3 \tag{8.9}$$

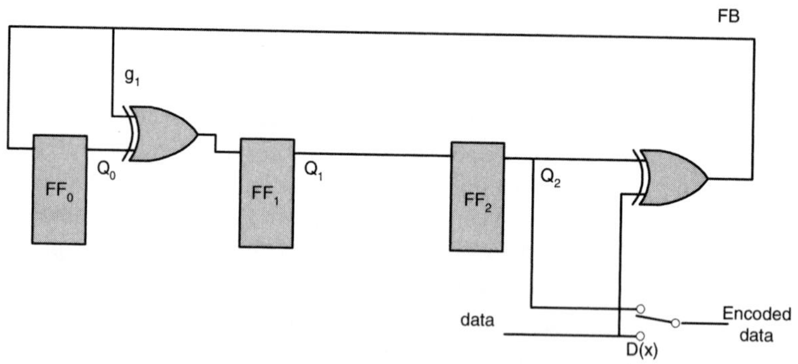

Figure 8.27 A (7-4) Stage Shift Register Encoder

Let's begin with the data word 0101. Expressing this as a polynomial in x

$$D(x) = x + x^3 \tag{8.10}$$

we will build the encoded word as illustrated in Figure 8.28 that follows. For the encoding process, the switch in the encoder is in the down position. Starting from the MSB (on the right-hand side), each bit is simultaneously sent into the encoder and out of the system.

Time	FB	Q0	Q1	Q2
0	1	0	0	0
1	0	1	1	0
2	0	0	0	1
3	1	1	1	0
4	0	0	1	1
5	0	0	0	1
6	0	0	0	0
7	0	0	0	0

Time							
0							
1	1						
2	0	1					
3	1	0	1				
4	0	1	0	1			
5	0	0	1	0	1		
6	1	0	0	1	0	1	
7	1	1	0	0	1	0	1

Figure 8.28 Encoding the Data Word 0101

After four time periods, the parity check bits are in the encoder. During the next three time intervals, the contents of the encoder are shifted out.

The properties of the cyclic codes make them very useful for incorporation into error-detection schemes associated with the transmission of large frames of data as might be found in memories. Three of the most commonly used generator polynomials are those identified as CRC-16, CRC-32, which are fifteenth and thirty-first-order polynomials, respectively, and CRC-CCITT, which is also a fifteenth-order polynomial.

These polynomials are given in Figure 8.29.

CRC - 16

$$f(x) = x^{16} + x^{2} + 1$$

CRC- - CCITT

$$f(x) = x^{12} + x^{5} + 1$$

CRC - 32

$$f(x) = x^{32} + x^{26} + x^{23} + x^{22} + x^{16} + x^{12} + x^{11} + x^{10} + x^{8} + x^{7} + x^{5} + x^{4} + x^{2} + x + 1$$

Figure 8.29 Several Standard Commonly Used Generator Polynomials

8.15 THE POWER SUBSYSTEM

As we have seen, there are a number of levels on which safety and reliability can be addressed and ensured. We can see this if we analyze the power subsystem. On the one extreme, the design specification can stipulate that on loss of power the system will continue to operate at full capability for some specified length of time. The power source used in such applications is called an *uninterruptible power source or supply* (UPS). On the opposite extreme, the specification may simply require ensuring a graceful shutdown.

uninterruptible power source or supply (UPS)

8.15.1 Full Operation

triple module redundancy (TMR)

The duration of full operation following power loss is the critical factor here. If the duration is "unlimited," then a source of power comparable to that which was lost must be provided. One approach is to implement a redundant power subsystem based on an architecture analogous to that which was used in the *triple module redundancy* (TMR) system architecture.

The block diagram for such a system is given in Figure 8.30.

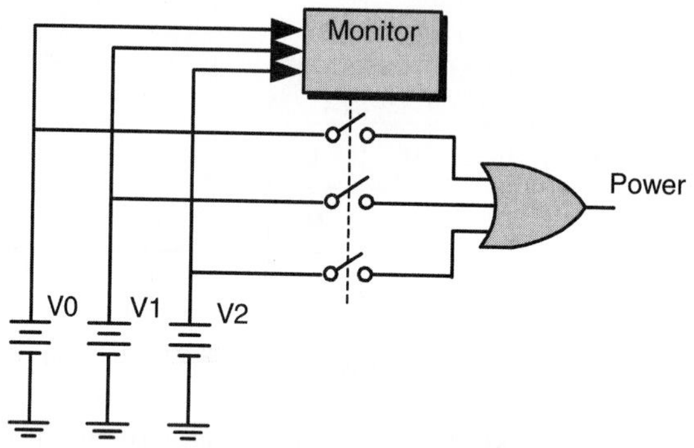

Figure 8.30 A Triple Module Redundant Power System

In this configuration, one of the three power sources will be connected to the system. The monitor is tracking the output of the selected source. There is no need for voting since the required voltage is known; it is also clear when the level is not at the proper value. If the selected supply output falls out of specification, it is switched off and one of the two remaining is selected as the main supply. A second failure repeats the process.

A number of variations on this scheme are possible. As we learned with the TMR approach, the designs of the supplies can be identical or different. The implementation can be simplified by reducing the number of supplies from three to two.

8.15.2 Reduced Operation

To ensure continued operation of a subset of the system's capabilities, the previous design can be modified to supply power to only the critical portions of the system as illustrated in the next block diagram in Figure 8.31.

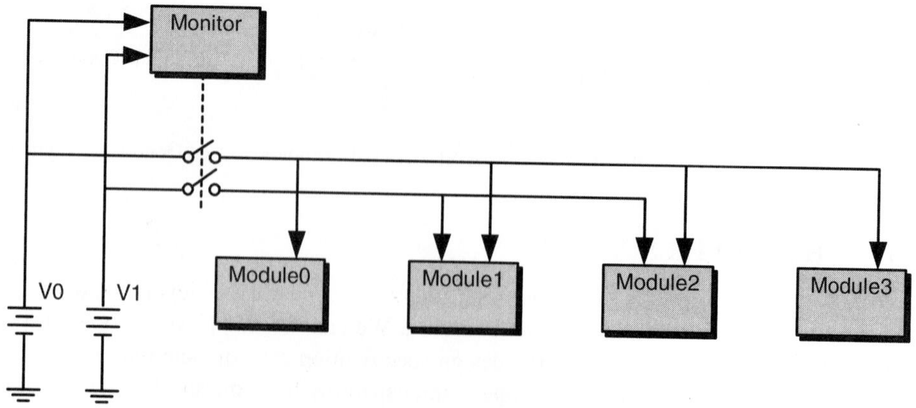

Figure 8.31 A Power System with Double Module Redundancy Supporting Critical Subsystems

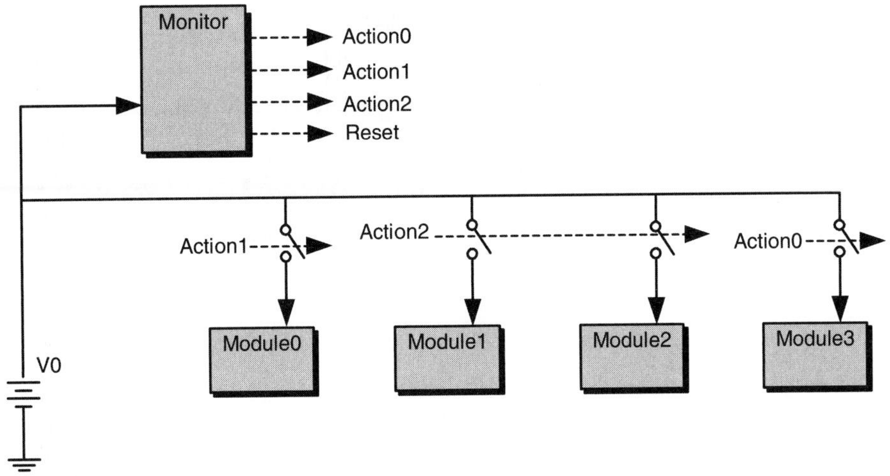

Figure 8.32 A Power System Implementing Multiple Trip Points

A variation on the scheme in Figure 8.31 assumes a single supply with a series of set points that trip with a decrease or fluctuation in the supply voltage, as seen in Figure 8.32.

Such an approach works well if the system's operating environment is subject to occasional brownout or other low-voltage conditions. Associated with each trip point is a set of actions that must be taken to reduce the load on the supply and to back up critical data. The final trip point causes a systemwide reset action to occur and thereby ensure that the logic voltages that have come out of regulation cannot cause erratic behavior in the microprocessor or other logic circuitry. In addition to unburdening the power system as power falls, the actions can also initiate backup sequences and place modules into a low-power mode as appropriate and as needed.

8.15.3 Backup Operation

The previous schemes assume that none of the power sources are batteries. Two final simple schemes are intended merely to hold critical data or settings until normal system power returns.

The first design, illustrated in Figure 8.33, utilizes a backup battery that has a voltage large enough to hold the module in a low-power mode. The battery voltage must also be lower than that of the main supply; otherwise it, rather than the main supply, will be supplying power to the system. A trickle charge circuit could also be added to charge the battery from the primary source during normal operation.

The second circuit utilizes a large capacitor as a temporary power source. During normal operation, the capacitor is charged from the primary source. When primary power fails, the capacitor voltage can be used to hold system power for a very short time. A circuit such as that shown in Figure 8.34 is most appropriate under transient conditions rather than for extended periods.

8.16 PERIPHERAL DEVICES—BUILT-IN SELF-TEST (BIST)

Ultimately, all the hardware and software come together in the application. If we have executed the design and test of the system well, then the probability that it will perform reliably, according to its specification, in the customer's hands will have improved substantially.

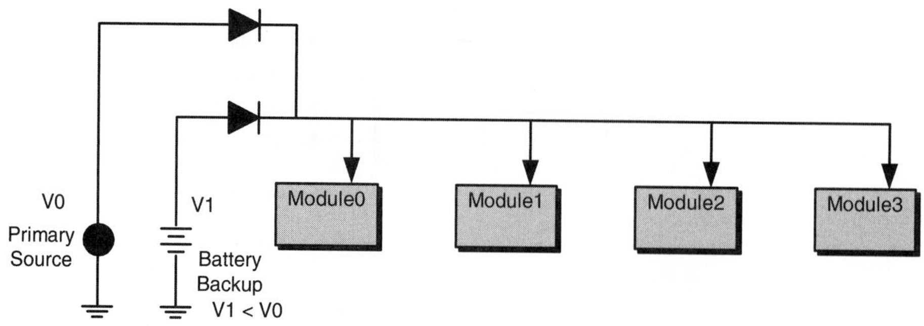

Figure 8.33 A Power Subsystem Implementing Battery Backup

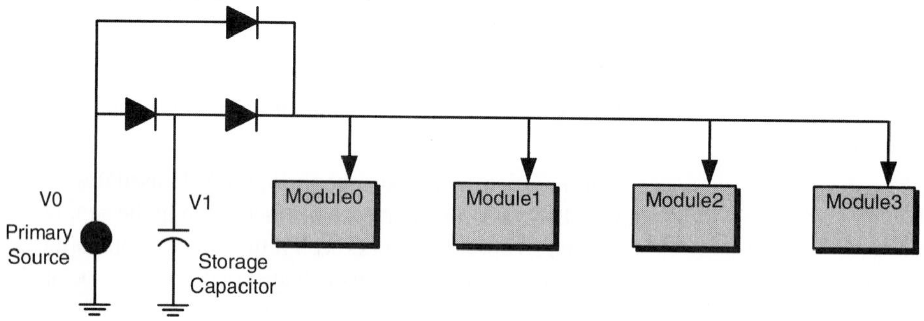

Figure 8.34 A Power System Implementing Short-Term Power Loss Protection

Nonetheless one will always have to deal with component failures. In addition, during operation, one has little control over the actual specific values of signals that come into the system. These two concerns provide the basis for a two-pronged approach to addressing runtime issues. To address data and control faults, one utilizes the bounds or limits on values or rates of change incorporated during the design as we discussed earlier. To deal with failures, one relies on built-in self-test hardware and software.

8.16.1 Self-Tests

basic Self-tests are a set of *basic* tests the system can execute. In developing and incorporating such tests into a design, the goals are to ensure that critical elements of the system are working and to establish a basis for action if the system fails or locks up.

on demand ***background*** Self-tests fall into two general categories: those invoked *on demand* and those running in the *background*. Such built-in tests target the major components of the system hardware. The focus is on the hardware because it is the hardware, not the software, that is going to fail. Any such tests should be as unobtrusive as possible so as to not impact the performance of the primary tasks of the system.

demand Self-tests invoked on *demand* are a sanity check to ensure that the system's core components are functioning properly. In an embedded application, these are often initiated at power up and then their status is reported on completion. Like the time spent compiling a program, the time spent testing prior to runtime only occurs once. Thus, although it is desirable that the system power up quickly, the time is not critical.

Background tests can be as simple as a watchdog timer that must be periodically reset by the CPU or as complex as a test suite running in the background. The consequences of a watchdog timer reset failure can be as extreme as a complete system reset or as benign as a warning or error message.

A periodic test suite can check the system busses for stuck lines, ROM memory for a signature (CRC check), or RAM for failed or stuck bits. In addition, one may check math processing, built-in A/D accuracy by measuring a known reference, or the D/A integrity by executing a conversion at the cardinal points. Power supply voltages can be easily monitored as well. The power supply tests identified earlier in this chapter are most definitely appropriate here and will not be repeated. The next few paragraphs discuss further tests that one might consider incorporating into a design.

8.16.2 Busses

Address, data, and control busses interconnecting all of the major components in an embedded system are essential elements for its normal operation. A failure on any of these components can cripple or severely restrict system operation. The major difficulty in performing a self-test on the busses is that the instructions and data fetched from memory must also use those busses. In the presence of a bus failure, the ability to execute a test suite may be severely limited. Consequently, if one is to implement such tests, an alternate way of acquiring test instructions and storing working data must be provided.

We can accomplish this in several ways. The key to any such scheme, however, is that there must be a way by which the test can be automatically invoked and terminated; otherwise, the problem is simply being moved or exacerbated.

The most straightforward approach is to have a small amount of memory available that does not sit on the main bus. There are a number of microcontrollers and microcomputers that have several thousand bytes of ROM and RAM onboard. The remainder of the firmware and RAM comprises an offboard memory system. The system memory map can be configured such that the test suite is in the onboard component. A system timer (set to an appropriate priority) can be configured to interrupt periodically. The associated ISR—interrupt service routine—(in internal ROM) can then execute a quick bus test.

Many of today's larger integrated circuits have incorporated JTAG ports that are intended for testing the device. As a second approach, one can consider using that port at runtime to bring instructions into the processor in support of the bus test portion of the built-in suite. Without onboard memory, the download sequence would have to be triggered and executed by offboard means.

If the main processor does not support onboard memory, a third alternative introduces a small auxiliary microcontroller into the design. In the simplest manifestation, the job of the test processor could be to confirm the integrity of the main busses. At the opposite extreme, it could be charged with the task of executing the complete test suite. Once again, its invocation would have to be automatic.

stuck-at faults, bridge faults

Presuming that a means has been devised to get the tests started, we find two categories of faults are of interest: *stuck-at faults* and *bridge faults*. With any testing, one should always start with the simplest tests first and, generally, with a known answer. The easiest way to know the answer is to set it up in advance. We will come back to this.

First, in a typical, well-designed bus, each of the system modules is isolated from the bus by buffers and tristate drivers as seen in the bus fragment shown in Figure 8.35. The initial visibility, therefore, is of the main bus—up to the inputs of the buffers. A stuck-at fault or bridge fault will be affecting one or more signals in that context.

The initial objective is to try to define a known quiescent state for the bus. That step begins with ensuring that no modules are driving the bus, which can be accomplished by "disabling" all of the tristate drivers. All modules should be only listening, and each of the

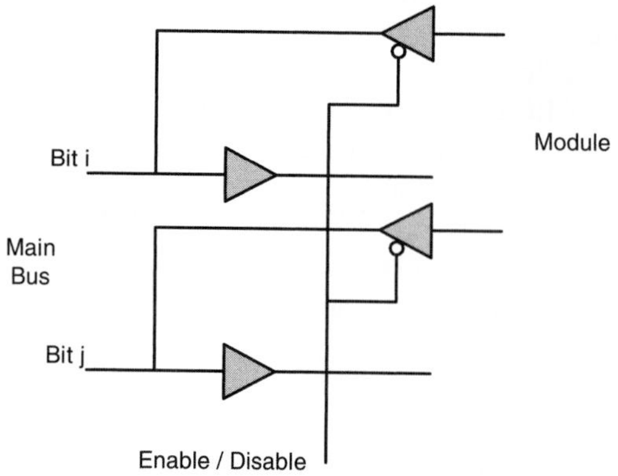

Figure 8.35 A Buffered Bidirectional Bus

bus lines should be in a known state; that state should be defined either by pull-up resistors or by some other means—this is part of the basic design of the bus.

A known pattern is placed onto the bus and then read back. The process is repeated with the complemented pattern. Perhaps one of the better patterns is alternating 0's and 1's followed by alternating 1's and 0's. If this test succeeds, it is confirmed that each bus line, individually, can be driven to either logic state and that no two logically adjacent signal lines are shorted.

Certainly, such patterns can be provided in a variety of ways. One interesting method entails implementing a "data source" that is independent of the test firmware. The bus fragment in Figure 8.36 gives one means to do so. The two enable signals used to select either of the two patterns are controlled by the source of the test.

Once the state of the system bus has been confirmed, some of the peripherals on that bus can be tested. The memory system is probably the next logical thing to test.

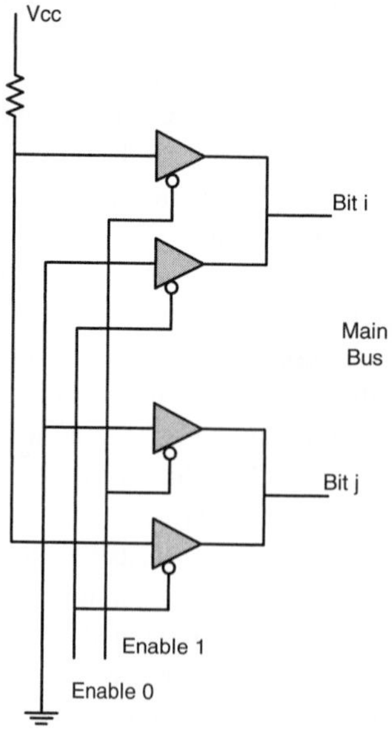

Figure 8.36 A Hardware-Based Bus Data Generator

8.16.3 ROM Memory

Presumably, the contents of the ROM have been confirmed at start-up via a CRC test or similar means. The underlying assumption at runtime is that those contents are not going to change and the focus is on accessing the device.

Thus, two kinds of tests can be conducted to confirm performance. The first entails storing a known set of patterns in the memory. Ideally, one would want to ensure that each individual address bit is working and that none is shorted to one another. A simple confidence test would require that a known pattern be stored at the set of locations that has each of the address bits in the logical 1 state and all others in the logical 0 state. Programming such a pattern and then controlling normal firmware accesses make this scheme somewhat tricky. A test that confirms only the data signals and a small subset of the addresses dictates storing known patterns in a more restricted set of addresses and then reading that pattern back. As with the bus test, selecting a pattern that can confirm that each individual data line can be asserted and deasserted and that no two are shorted should be sufficient.

8.16.4 RAM Memory

Executing a confidence test is somewhat easier on RAM than on ROM. The simplest test for RAM begins by reading a memory location to save the data currently stored there. Next, a known pattern is written to that location and read back. The pattern is complemented and the process is repeated. The original data is then restored to its proper location. The data and address patterns are chosen to exercise each of the signal lines in either state and to confirm that they are not shorted.

8.16.4.1 Peripheral Devices

Tests for confirming the operation of each peripheral device comprising the system are typically specific to that device. Trying to propose tests for each could take up the rest of this text. Thus, substituting general philosophy for specifics, let's look at some things that can be done.

For measurement devices, provide a known source that can be measured. For stimulus devices, provide a known stimulus and a way to measure that value and then compare the measurement against the known value. Confirm that any timing devices will expire after a known duration. If the system includes both measurement and stimulus devices, try to devise a test that permits one to test the other.

8.16.4.2 What to Do If a Test Fails?

Devising self-tests is easy. Deciding what to do if the test fails is more difficult, and controlling shutdown, if necessary, can be even more difficult. Spend time thinking this portion of the problem through. Several alternate architectures and approaches have been proposed in the opening of the chapter. These are certainly not the only alternatives, and they may not be the best alternatives for a specific system.

However the self-tests are formulated, they should be kept simple and be incorporated into the design in such a way that a failure within the testing subsystem will not cause the entire system to fail.

8.17 FAILURE MODES AND EFFECTS ANALYSIS

Failure Modes, Effects, and Criticality Analysis

Before concluding the current studies of reliability and safety in embedded applications, we will introduce one analysis tool that can be used to assess the vulnerability of a design to real-world faults. The tool is a *Failure Modes, Effects, and Criticality Analysis*; it is also known simply as a *Failure Modes Analysis*. Such an analysis was first utilized in the aerospace industry to identify potential problems or failures (and their effects) with an aircraft, spacecraft, or satellite system in the early stages of the design. The basic approach is to try to first identify the possible failure modes, that is, try to hypothesize what might go wrong with a system. Once such a set is collected, each possible failure mode is examined, it is hypothesized that it occurs, and the consequences of such a failure are assessed. Although it is not feasible to anticipate every possible failure, the analysis enables us to identify and to design out many common failure modes.

In practice, a failure modes analysis can be conducted at any level or phase of the design cycle. At the system level, the top-level functions are analyzed to try to identify which of the major pieces of functionality of the system might fail and where such a failure may occur, and to prioritize which are the most critical. At a lower level, concerns move to the subsystems and the components that make them up. We hypothesize how each of the inputs (outputs) may fail, and we study the consequences of such a failure on overall system behavior. The same analysis can be conducted with a focus on manufacturing. In each case, the goal is to anticipate failures and to take preemptive actions to eliminate those failures or to mitigate their effects if the failure mode(s) cannot be designed out.

A failure modes analysis is performed utilizing the following steps. Remember that these steps are intended as a guide, not a checklist.

1. Ensure that those performing the analysis have a clear and complete understanding of the system.
2. Have a set of drawings appropriate to the level at which the analysis is to be performed. Work at the system level should be guided by a high-level functional diagram or a block diagram. At lower levels, a schematic or logic diagram is essential.
3. Walk through each component (subsystem to logic gate) of the system and make note of the possible failure modes of each.
4. Identify the effects of each of the identified failure modes.
5. Identify the severity, risk, and probability of occurrence of each identified failure mode.
6. Prioritize the list and identify how each will be handled.

The following example performs a failure modes analysis on the serial communications subsystem of the core implementation.

EXAMPLE 8.3

An EIA232 Interface subsystem is shown in Figure 8.37.

The system accepts serial data, converts it to parallel, does a parity check on the data, and transmits it over a parallel bus to some other subsystem. The interface also accepts data, in parallel from the other subsystem, converts it to serial, adds a parity bit, and sends the word back over the serial port.

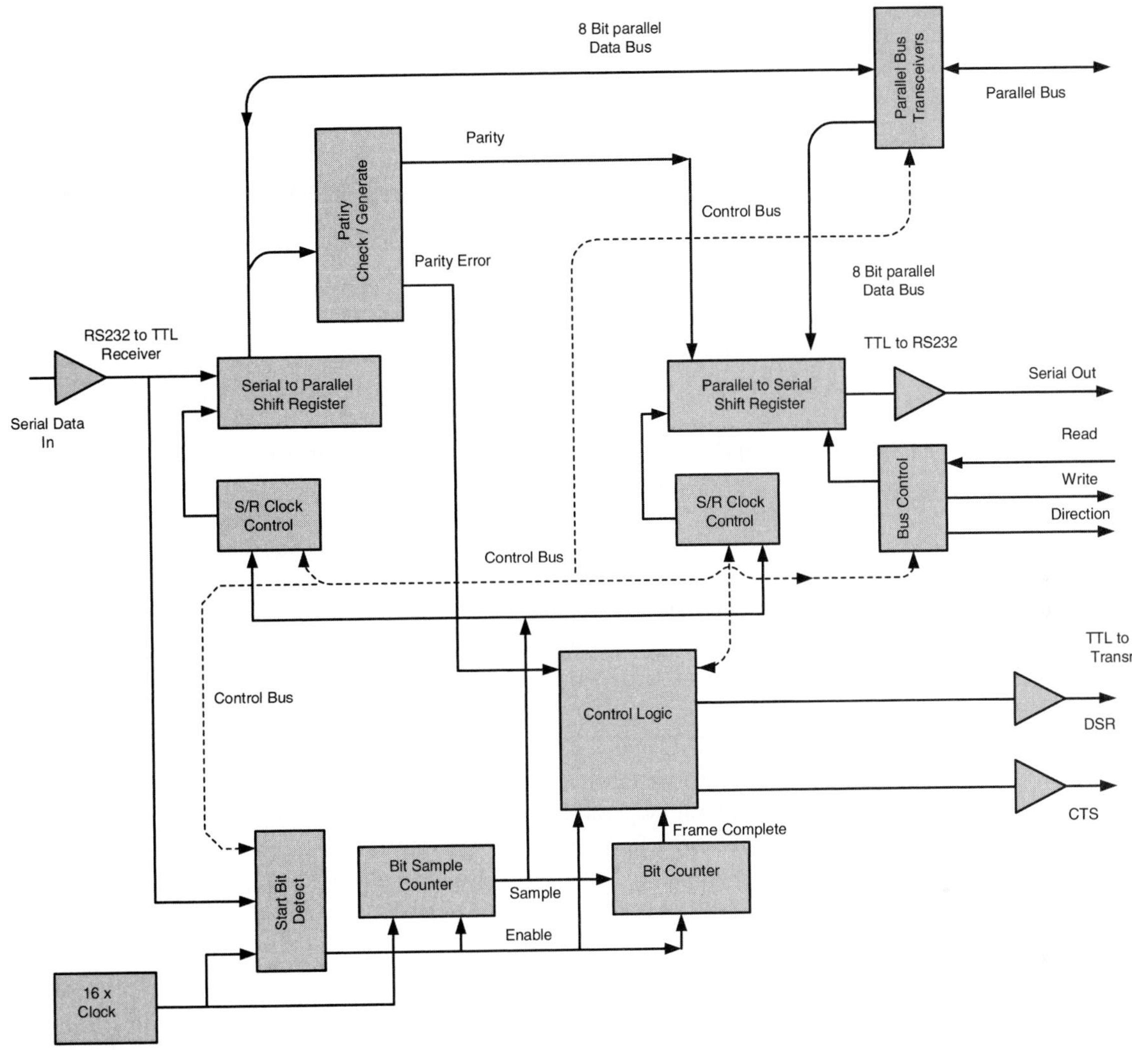

Figure 8.37 EIA232 Interface subsystem

At the system level, we will focus on static faults—those identified as stuck-at type faults. Dynamic, or hazard-type, faults tend to be dependent on implementation and must be included in a failure analysis at the design level.

Table 8.0 illustrates how the analysis might proceed. For each component, each failure mode is identified, the effect of each such failure is analyzed, the probability of such a failure occurring is determined, and the severity of the effects if it does occur is assessed.

Additional information can easily be included if deemed necessary. The final analysis should be included in the complete documentation package for the system.

The remainder of the table would be entered in a similar way. The probability numbers shown are for illustration only. All have been assigned the same value based on the assumption that these are all of the same logic family and that there will not be a significant variation across the family. In practice, the failure probabilities would come from the component vendor, from extensive testing and characterization of the part, or from field failure data for

Table 8.0 High-Level Failure Modes and Effects Analysis

Component	Failure	Effect	Probability/ Severity
RS 232 to TTL Receiver	Input or output stuck at 1	Start bit or data never recognized	0.00075/1
	Input or output stuck at 0	Continuous start bit or constant data assumed	0.00075/1
16 X clock	Output stuck	With no clock, data cannot be received or transmitted	0.00075/1
Start Bit Detect	Data Input stuck	See RS 232 to TTL Receiver failure modes	0.00075/1
	Clock input stuck	Cannot detect start bit	0.00075/1
	Control input stuck	Cannot detect end of frame	0.00075/1
Bit Sample Counter	Clock input stuck	Cannot determine sample point for incoming data	0.00075/1
	Enable input stuck	Either counter cannot be started or cannot be stopped	0.00075/1
	Sample output stuck	Bit counter will not advance, and data cannot be shifted into serial to parallel register	0.00075/1
Bit Counter	Sample input stuck	Cannot count number of incoming bits	0.00075/1
	Enable input stuck	Either counter cannot be started or cannot be stopped	0.00075/1
	Frame complete output stuck	Either cannot detect end of frame or continuously signal end of frame	0.00075/ 10.00075/1

similar parts. The severity value of 1 assumes that failure of any of these elements of the subsystem would render it inoperable, and thus each is critical to its proper operation.

By identifying such faults early in the design process, one can ensure that they are effectively dealt with as the design progresses. Suddenly finding a critical failure mode as the project is ready to be released to production or in the field can be expensive.

8.18 SUMMARY

We have taken a first small step toward designing and developing safe, robust, and reliable embedded systems. We have established the need for reliable hardware and software, introduced some of the vocabulary, and looked at several of the hardware and software approaches we may take at the system and architectural levels to help to ensure that we develop a reliable product. We have also presented some approaches we can use at runtime to detect problems. As we have noted in the discussions, we believe that the detailed concerns, more in-depth analysis, and possible solutions to specific issues are better dealt with closer to where those hardware and software concepts are introduced and discussed.

8.19 REVIEW QUESTIONS

Safety and Reliability

8.1 What is safety?

8.2 What is reliability?

8.3 What is the difference between safety and reliability?

8.4 What role does context play in the definitions of safety and reliability?

8.5 Why are safety and reliability important concerns in the design of an embedded application?

8.6 What role do specifications play in safety and reliability?

8.7 What is the difference between a fault, a failure, and an error? Give several examples of each that are different from those in the text.

The Design Process

8.8 What is the purpose of keeping bug lists?

8.9 What is the purpose of a design review?

8.10 What is *Fail Operational Capability*? *Fail Operational*^{2} *Capability*? Give several examples of each. Explain why such capability is important in each of your examples.

8.11 What is lightweight redundancy?

Busses

8.12 Explain the benefits of the star, ring, and multidrop bus configurations.

8.13 Explain some of the disadvantages of the star, ring, and multidrop bus configurations.

Dealing with Data

8.14 What is type conformance? Why is it important?

8.15 What are boundary values on data that comes into a system?

8.16 Give several ways by which data coming from an outside source into an embedded system can be damaged.

8.17 Give several alternative approaches that can be utilized in an embedded application to deal with damaged data.

8.18 What is Hamming distance?

8.19 If another designer tells you that her code has a Hamming distance of three, what is she telling you?

8.20 What is parity?

8.21 What are linear codes? block codes?

8.22 What are cyclic codes?

8.23 What is a burst error?

8.24 What are some of the possible causes of burst errors?

The Power System

8.25 Give several examples of possible failures in the power system of an embedded application.

Self Testing

8.26 What are built-in-self-tests?

Failure Modes Analysis

8.27 What is failure modes analysis?

8.28 What are some of the benefits of conducting a failure modes analysis?

8.20 THOUGHT QUESTIONS

Safety and Reliability

8.1 Are safety and reliability concerns more or less important in an embedded application when compared to a nonembedded system? Why or why not?

8.2 What is risk? Give several examples of low- and high-risk embedded applications. Identify several embedded applications that may either be high or low risk depending on their operating context.

The Design Process

8.3 Identify the major system-level functional considerations that help to ensure a safe and reliable design.

8.4 What are some of the architectural-level considerations that help to ensure a safe and reliable design?

8.5 What are some of the major hardware and software issues that should be examined during a design review?

8.6 What does *Fail Gracefully* mean? Give several examples and explain why such capability is important in each of your examples.

Busses

8.7 Explain some of the advantages of the star, ring, and multidrop bus configurations. Give several examples where each might be used. Explain the benefit(s) in each case.

8.8 Give several examples where the star, ring, and multidrop bus configurations might not be the best choice. Explain your reasoning in each case.

8.9 Discuss the reliability aspects of the star, ring, and multidrop bus configurations and possible causes and consequences of failure in each.

Dealing with Data

8.10 Who specifies the boundary values on data coming into the system? Why is it important to test program input data against such values?

8.11 What possible actions can be taken by an embedded application for data values that are within specifications, at specifications, outside of specifications? When do such actions become required rather than optional? Give several examples of data values in each category. For each of your examples identify when the actions you have specified are required or optional.

8.12 Explain the difference between odd and even parity. Why would one use one scheme over the other?

8.13 What are the limitations of a basic parity scheme? What are the advantages?

8.14 What is the maximum amount of information that we can gain if a simple parity check shows no error? shows an error?

8.15 If the computed parity on a received code word agrees with the value that was received, what do we know about the correctness of the received data?

8.16 If the computed parity on a received code word disagrees with the value that was received, what do we know about the correctness of the received data?

8.17 What advantages do block codes have over a basic parity scheme? When would one use a block coding scheme instead of a basic parity scheme? What are the additional costs of a block code scheme?

8.18 How do cyclic codes compare with basic, linear, and block encoding schemes? Consider factors such as ease of implementation, complexity, and runtime complexity.

8.19 When should one consider using an error-detection/correction scheme as part of a data exchange? Give several examples.

8.20 What major costs does one incur when using an error-detection/correction scheme?

The Power System

8.21 Identify possible design solutions to address possible failures in the power system of an embedded application. Discuss the advantages and disadvantages of each of your proposed solutions.

Self-Testing

8.22 Discuss several advantages and disadvantages of built-in self-tests.

Failure Modes Analysis

8.23 During what stage of the development life cycle should failure modes analysis be used? Why?

8.24 What kinds of failures should be considered?

8.21 PROBLEMS

8.1 The chapter discussed the loss of the Ariane 5 rocket and attributed the failure to a mismatch between the word size in the sensors and the word size in the guidance system. Propose a series of tests that might have identified the problem prior to launch.

8.2 Propose an addition or a modification to the guidance and control system in the Ariane 5 that would have managed the data in such a way as to have prevented the loss of the rocket without modifying the existing register sizes.

8.3 The chapter introduced a problem that occurred on the Mars Pathfinder in which a lower priority task was able to indefinitely block a higher priority task. Propose a series of tests that might have identified the problem prior to launch.

8.4 Propose a software or hardware modification that might prevent the blocking problem on the Pathfinder.

8.5 Provide a detailed hardware block diagram for the design of the voting block for the fail operational^2 system architecture using different designs as presented in the chapter.

8.6 Develop a UML sequence diagram expressing the necessary activities and responses to three failures in a fail operational^2 system architecture.

8.7 Provide a detailed software pseudo-code design of the voting block for the fail operational^2 system architecture using different designs as presented in the chapter.

8.8 Compare the strengths and weaknesses of the hardware and software voters discussed in Problems 8.5 and 8.7. Would your analysis change if the same design was used for each of the redundant systems? If so, how?

8.9 As an alternative to the fail operational^2 system architecture, the chapter proposes a design utilizing lightweight redundancy. Develop a UML sequence diagram expressing the necessary activities and responses to a failure in the system architecture utilizing lightweight redundancy.

8.10 In the system architecture utilizing lightweight redundancy, propose a detailed hardware block diagram or software pseudo-code design that identifies when a problem has occurred and affects the assumption of the reduced control responsibility and the warning and annunciation.

8.11 Propose a hardware or software strategy for detecting, annunciating, and managing a node or link failure in a system utilizing a star bus configuration.

8.12 Repeat Problem 8.11 for a system utilizing

(a) A multidrop bus configuration

(b) A single ring bus configuration

8.13 Using an array as the model for a typical data container for storing unsigned integers,

(a) Identify all of the boundary conditions that should be tested for.

(b) Write a software program that will implement the tests identified in part (a).

8.14 Design an algorithm that accepts data from an external source. Data values that fall in the range of ±4.0 are considered to be valid; data values exceeding the range are considered invalid. If the data is within range, it is to be displayed. If values fall outside of the valid range, a warning is to be issued and displayed and no additional data accepted until the warning is acknowledged. Use sinusoidal data in the range of ±5.0 to verify the performance of your algorithm.

8.15 Extend the design in Problem 8.14 to issue the warning and display the ceiling and floor values of the data but continue to accept input data. If the input data value returns to the specified range, the warning annunciation is to continue until acknowledged, but the current incoming data values are to be displayed.

8.16 Give a Verilog design for a system that will accept an 8-bit word, in parallel, append an odd parity bit, and output the resulting 9-bit word.

8.17 Repeat Problem 8.16 by writing a software algorithm to accomplish the same task.

8.18 Give a Verilog design for a system that will accept an 9-bit word, in parallel, check for odd parity, and output the 8-bit data word if the received parity is correct; otherwise issue an error.

8.19 Repeat Problem 8.18 by writing a software algorithm to accomplish the same task.

8.20 Give a Verilog design for a system that uses a Hamming code for error management. The system should accept an 8-bit data word, in parallel, encode the data, then output the resulting code word.

8.21 Repeat Problem 8.20 by writing a software algorithm to accomplish the same task.

8.22 Give a Verilog design for a system that will accept a 16-bit word that has been encoded using a Hamming code. The system should then check and output the corrected 8-bit data word.

8.23 Repeat Problem 8.22 by writing a software algorithm to accomplish the same task.

8.24 Give a Verilog design for a system that uses a block code for error management. The system should accept a 15-word block of 8-bit data words one word at a time, generate odd parity over the individual words, and even parity over the block, output each of the 15 9-bit data words, followed by the block check character.

8.25 Repeat Problem 8.24 by writing a software algorithm to accomplish the same task.

8.26 Give a Verilog design for a system that will accept a block of data words encoded as specified in Problem 8.24; then check the parity for each data word and for the block. The system should output each of the 8-bit data words, issue a word error if the parity is incorrect for any word, and issue a block error if the block check word is in error.

8.27 Repeat Problem 8.26 by writing a software algorithm to accomplish the same task.

8.28 Give a Verilog design for a system that uses cyclic encoding based on the following generator polynomial for error management.

$$g(x) = x^8 + x^7 + x^6 + x^4 + 1$$

(a) Use your design to encode the word 1011001.

(b) Verify that your design can detect a single-bit error in a received code word.

8.29 Repeat Problem 8.28 by writing a software algorithm to accomplish the same task.

8.30 Implement the design for the monitoring and control system for the full-operation 15.0 VDC redundant power supply system discussed in the chapter. You can assume that values of the supply voltages are acquired through an analog-to-digital converter.

8.31 Implement the design for the monitoring and control system for the reduced-operation 15.0 VDC power supply system that utilizes four set points discussed in the chapter. You can assume that values of the supply voltages are acquired through an analog-to-digital converter. Choose the set point to be in the range of 4 to 14 VDC. Explain the reasoning behind each of your choices.

8.32 Design a built-in self-test for a 256 K by 8 SRAM. You must ensure that no data is ever corrupted as a result of your test. Your test must be able to operate while normal memory operations are taking place. Is your design done in hardware, software, or a combination? Explain your choice.

8.33 Design a power up self-test for a 256 K by 8 ROM that utilizes a block check scheme. Is your design done in hardware, software, or a combination? Explain your choice.

8.34 Give the pseudo code for an algorithm that verifies the operational integrity of an embedded application at power up. State any assumptions.

8.35 Perform a failure modes and effects analysis on the fail operational^2 system architecture developed in Problem 8.5. State any assumptions.

8.36 Perform a failure modes and effects analysis on a system utilizing a star bus configuration. State any assumptions.

8.37 Provide a detailed block diagram for an alarm clock that also provides day and month annunciation. Perform a failure modes and effects analysis on such a system. State any assumptions.

8.38 Provide a detailed block diagram for an entertainment system that includes a television, stereo, DVD recorder and player, PC, and Internet connection. Perform a failure modes and effects analysis on such a system. State any assumptions.

Chapter 9

Embedded Systems Design and Development

THINGS TO LOOK FOR . . .

- Things to consider in a design.
- The product life cycle.
- The five steps to design.
- The need to understand the environment and the system being designed.
- The difference between requirements definition and specification.
- Motivation for and objective when partitioning a system.
- Coupling and cohesion and why they are important.
- The differences between functional and architectural models of a system.
- Motivation for and timing of static and dynamic analysis of a design.
- Capitalization and reuse of designs.
- Requirements traceability.

9.0 INTRODUCTION

In this chapter, we will study the major phases of the development process for embedded systems. The more detailed aspects of that process will be explored in conjunction with the design and test of the specific hardware and software elements of the system.

We will learn that design is the process of translating customer requirements into a working system and that the complexity of contemporary systems demands a formal approach and formal methods. Working from a formal specification of a problem, we will look at ways of partitioning the system as a prelude to developing a functional design. We will then examine the process of mapping a functional model on to an architectural structure and ultimately to a working prototype. To help ensure the robustness of the ultimate product, we will illustrate how to critically analyze the design both during and after development.

We will also examine several other important considerations in the design life cycle, including intellectual property, component/module reuse, and requirements management and the archival process.

As we begin to think about a new product or as we add new features to an existing one, we must look at things from many different points of view. The most important of these perspectives is the customer's since he or she finances the development of the product either directly through an agreed upon contract or indirectly through a purchase. The best design is of little value if no one is willing to buy it. So, we pose the question: What kinds of things should be considered?

costs, features
real, perceived needs

If we look at products, we must know how to measure *costs* and *features*. We must be able to identify and distinguish between *real* and *perceived needs*. Too often when we talk with customers about new products, the essential "requirement" in the next generation product is that which was missing when a problem arose this morning.

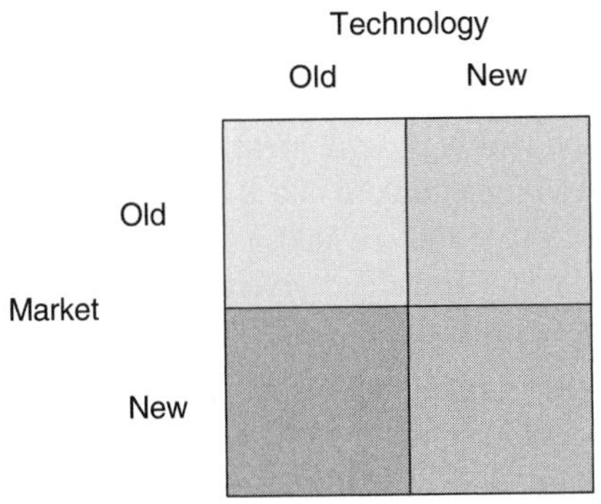

Figure 9.0 Market–Technology Trade-off

old technology
old markets
new technology, new markets
new, existing

It is important to learn how to make market and technology trade-offs. Several years ago the very simple table shown in Figure 9.0 was proposed. Taking *old technology* into *old markets* is a reasonable and safe strategy. These are the niche markets and often provide support and evolutionary growth for products that are no longer in a vendor's mainstream offering. Taking *new technology* into *new markets* is difficult and risky. At the same time, the rewards can be very high. The personal computer is a very good example. Xerox and Apple both had limited success with their early offerings. The people and the full technology were simply not ready. Taking *new* technology in to an *existing* area or *existing* technology in to a *new* area is easier. At least one portion of the problem—the market or the technology—is well understood and well developed.

deadlines, costs

We must understand the importance of *deadlines* and *costs*. Product development is based on a (directly or indirectly) negotiated contract between us and the customer(s). Failure to respect development and delivery costs or schedules leads to loss of sales, market share, and credibility.

reliability, safety, quality
robust

We also must always consider *reliability*, *safety*, and *quality* in the products we design. We learned about these in Chapter 8. Beyond an obvious need to work properly, the product must be *robust*. Simply put, "Does it do what it's supposed to?" and "How does it behave with unexpected inputs?" Robust means much more than this, however. Robust also implies that the system performs even if it is partially damaged, or under extreme temperature conditions, or if it is dropped. If a product does what it is supposed to do but is fragile and buggy, the product is not robust.

documentation
post-sales support

The *documentation* we produce to accompany the product must be clear and understandable. The product must be easy to use—intuitive rather than counterintuitive. *Post-sales support,* including the correction of bugs, is very important. Lack of quality has two costs. The first is obvious and immediate—the cost to repair, which is often small. The second is a hidden cost—the loss of customer confidence and sales—and it can be very large. Once confidence lost, it is very difficult to regain.

> ***A Simple Example***
>
> Years ago, when developing some of the early microprocessor-based embedded systems, we would encounter problems as we debugged the hardware and software. At that time, tools were few and far between. This was a new field.
>
> One very powerful tool for helping to track down such problems is called a logic analyzer. It allows one to follow which instructions the processor is executing (in real time) and learn why stuff goes in and never comes out. We had to have one, so, our company purchased two of them from two different vendors.
>
> The analyzer from vendor A arrived, was out of the box, on the bench, connected to the system, and making useful measurements within 10 to 15 minutes. Only several days later did anyone think to take a look at the manual. The analyzer from vendor B had a user interface that rivaled a 1040 tax form. Its one-inch thick manual was equally cryptic and demanded several hours of study before even the simplest measurements could be made.
>
> Guess which instrument always has a queue of people waiting to use it and guess which vendor sold us many more instruments?

9.1 SYSTEM DESIGN AND DEVELOPMENT

System design and development is a challenging problem. What makes it fun and exciting is its very large creative component. There are no rules, no steps to follow to make one creative. There are, however, a large collection of rules to ensure the opposite. Consider a new child. Each comes into this world, eyes wide open with a million questions. Why is the sky blue? Why is the sun yellow? Why can't we see the air? Where does air come from anyway? What do we do? We put them in school. We teach them the rules. Walk into any group of little ones and ask, how many of you can sing? How many of you can draw? Almost every tiny hand leaps up. Go into any similar group of adults and ask the same questions. Everyone is suddenly fascinated with their shoes. One hand may slowly come up. Why? We place too many restrictions on our thinking. Sure, we may need 10 million dollars worth of electronic equipment to give our voice perfect pitch, but so what. We need to remove artificial restrictions that we impose on our thinking.

Look at the little ones drawing or coloring. What do we tell them? No, people aren't purple. Cows can't fly. Fish don't have legs—anymore. Oh, and by the way, always color in the lines. . . . and let's also learn how to be creative.

9.1.1 Getting Ready—Start Thinking

Okay, let's start. Driving is always a good place to begin. The rules are easy. Keep the yellow line on your left and the white on your right—except in Britain and several other places. Now the chance to be creative. In the autumn in the northern parts of the world, the days are warm, but the nights start getting colder. Often there is a bit of fog that makes an appearance as well. By the morning, the fog and chill have combined to give a very fine glaze of ice on the road. We call this black ice; it gives us the opportunity to be creative. Hop in the car and race out onto the road. What's this nonsense about staying in the lines?

Now that perhaps we have decided that maybe we can be just a little creative, let's begin to explore. As we begin thinking about a new design, we will discover that there are a lot of things to be considered. The problem may not always be what it seems at first blush.

A Whack on the Side of the Head

Roger van Oech in *A Whack on the Side of the Head*, Warner Brooks (1983), says "Always

Figure 9.1 Old Woman—Young Woman

Figure 9.2 Goblet or Statue

look for the second right answer." He's right. As we begin, it is important to understand the problem to make sure that we are solving the right problem. Consider the illustration in Figure 9.1. Which one is the correct image? Is it the old lady or the young one?

When we begin trying to solve a problem, it is important to talk with everyone involved; to listen to different opinions; to see how the design might affect the people who have to work with it. We have to take the time to look at different views of the problem, to look at it from both the inside and the outside. Based on our view, we can have a couple of different interpretations of the problem presented in Figure 9.2. Are we building a goblet, or are we building two statues?

There will always be occasions in which we have too much information, too many opinions, or too many details. Remember the old expression of not being able to see the forest for the trees. The same holds true as we begin trying to understand a problem during the early stages of a design. Look at this next drawing in Figure 9.3. What do you see? This interesting design looks perhaps like a snowflake. This is a case in which we have too much information.

Let's remove some of the information as in Figure 9.4; if we take a more abstract view of the problem, the solution is easier to see.

Now that we have a start, let's look at the design problem. Let's look at each design as a chance to explore.

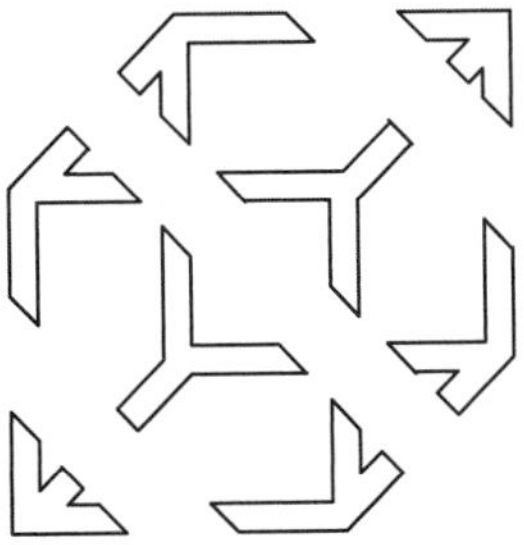

Figure 9.3 Too Much Information

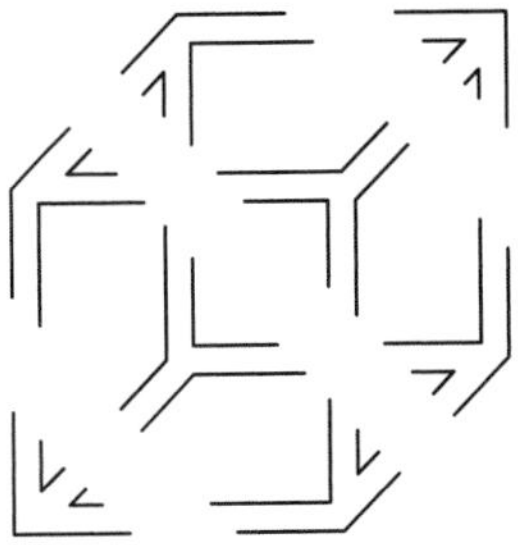

Figure 9.4 Remove Some Information

9.1.2 Getting Started

Designing and developing embedded systems does raise some interesting challenges and does require a large number of decisions. Some of those decisions require knowledge about the problem, others require knowledge about the tools and techniques that may be available, and still others choose methods for approaching the solution. There will often be still more

product life cycle

things to think about that are not related to the technical part of the problem at all. The collection of things we do as we move from requirement to application is often called the *product life cycle*.

Like so many other things in life, there are probably as many different product life-cycle models as there are people designing these systems. Who said there isn't any creativity? Each of these models has its supporters, and each also has its group of detractors. The goal in the next few pages is to introduce some of the more important things one should think about when executing a design, to present several of the more common life-cycle models, and to present some guidelines for things that have worked on successful projects. Despite what they tell you, there are no hard and fast rules—well, perhaps there are a few: learn a lot with each project, have fun, and do the job right, to the best of your ability. Let's get started.

9.2 LIFE-CYCLE MODELS

design process model, the life-cycle model

The product life cycle of an embedded application is purely a descriptive representation. It breaks the development process into a series of interrelated activities. Each activity plays a role of transforming its input (specification) into an output (a selected solution). The steps are organized according to a *design process model—the life-cycle model*. Formality in design provides the structure for a development that lets us creatively explore the design while using the tools to manage some of the more mechanical issues. We use the structure as an aid rather than as something that encumbers design.

As we have commented already, the related literature presents a variety of proposed approaches and models. At the end of the day, all have the same basic goal, however: they all have similar phases. Perhaps we could more accurately say that they all have similar needs or goals or objectives. These needs are very simple, as shown in Figure 9.5.

Several of the historically more common models or approaches are listed in Figure 9.6,

- Find out what the customers want.
- Think of a way to give them what they want.
- Prove what you've done by building and testing it.
- Build a lot of the product to prove that it wasn't an accident.
- Use the product to solve the customer's problem.

Figure 9.5 Fundamentals of Design

- Waterfall
- V Cycle
- Spiral
- Rapid Prototype

Figure 9.6 Common Life-Cycle Models

Today, we are continually developing new models. But whichever model we choose, the most important point is to understand the meaning and intent or objective of each phase or step in the process. Understand the deliverables for each step as well as the necessary outputs and inputs that are required to move, conclude, or enter each phase in the selected model. Then follow those and don't take shortcuts. We will look briefly at each of these four models momentarily. Before we do so, let's look at another model that fits just about any phase of engineering; it looks something like the one shown in Figure 9.7.

hockey stick model

This is called the *hockey stick model* or curve; its shape is strongly suggestive of where the name originated. We have talked about how important it is to address reliability and safety early in the requirements specification and design phases of the life cycle. The hockey stick curve, shown in Figure 9.7, provides an intuitive feel as to why. If we label the horizontal axis as time and the vertical one as cost, and apply it here, we see that the longer

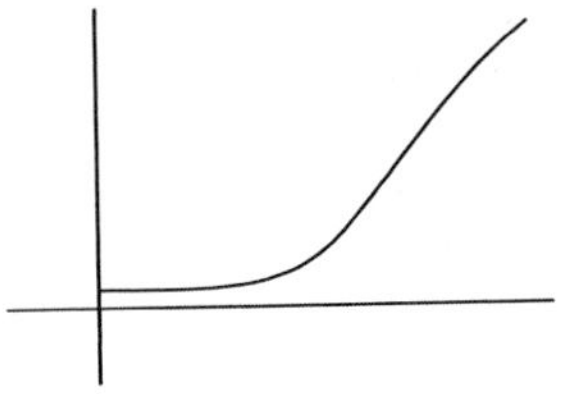

Figure 9.7 The Hockey Stick Curve

we delay in addressing those issues, the greater the cost will be. Cost is not limited to money alone.

Waterfall model Let's begin with the *Waterfall model*. Use your artistic creativity here. Its name evokes its sound, which evokes the philosophy and approach engendered in the model.

9.2.1 The Waterfall Model

Waterfall model The *Waterfall model* represents a cycle—specifically, a series of steps appearing much like a waterfall, sequentially, one below the next as we see in Figure 9.8.

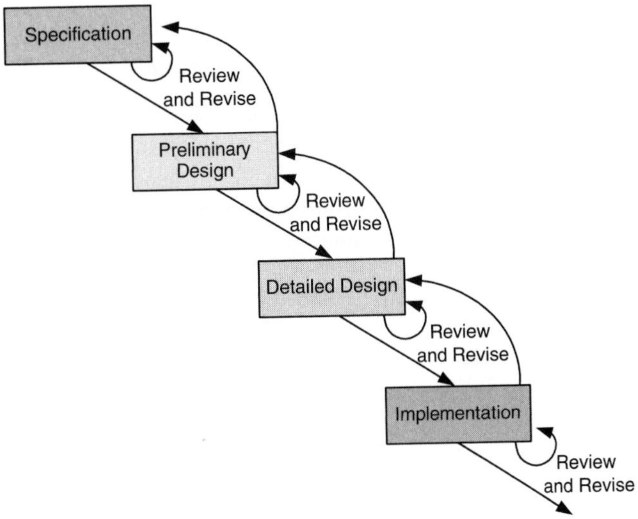

Figure 9.8 The Waterfall Life-Cycle Model

The steps are:

- Specification
- Preliminary design
- Design review
- Detailed design
- Design review
- Implementation
- Review

Complete this phase and go on to the next

Together, these capture each of the needs we identified earlier. Successive steps are linked in a chained manner. Such a linking tends to say: *Complete this phase and go on to the next.*

Observe that each phase is also connected to the previous phase. That reverse connection provides an essential verification link backwards to ensure that the solution (in its current form) agrees with and follows from the specification. With the Waterfall model, the recognition of problems can be delayed until later states of development where the cost of repair is higher (the hockey stick curve). The Waterfall model is limited in the sense that it does not consider the typically iterative nature of real-world design.

9.2.2 The V Cycle Model

V Cycle

The *V Cycle* is similar to the Waterfall model except that it places greater emphasis on the importance of addressing testing activities up front instead of later in the life cycle. Each stage associates the development activity for that phase with a test or validation at the same level. Each test phase is identified with its matching development phase as we see in Figure 9.9.

In the diagram, we have

- Requirements ↔ System/Functional Testing
- High-level Design ↔ Integration Testing
- Detailed Design ↔ Unit Testing

We identify the major phases of a project life cycle across the top of the drawing. These phases extend from specification to customer delivery and postdelivery support. If one follows the sequence down the left-hand side of the drawing, one can see that the specification and design procedure utilizes a top-down model, whereas implementation and test proceed from a bottom-up model as is reflected on the right-hand side of the drawing.

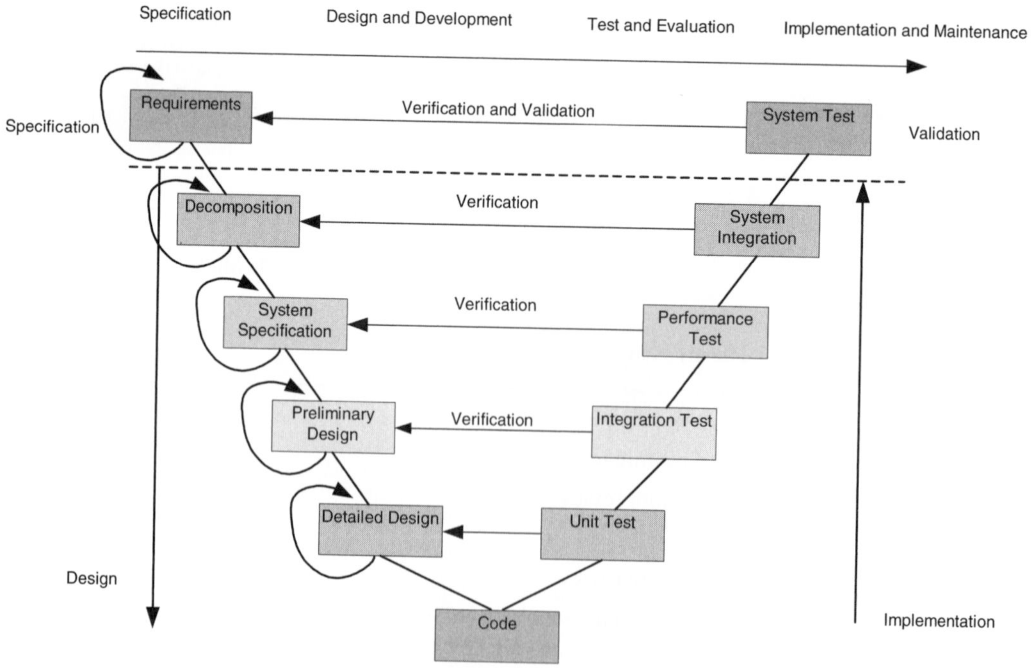

Figure 9.9 The V Life-Cycle Model

It is evident that each development activity builds a more detailed model of the system and that each verification step tests a more complete implementation of the system against the requirements at that phase. The development concludes the design and design-related test portion of the development cycle of the system with both a verification and a validation test against the original specification.

9.2.3 The Spiral Model

Spiral model, A Spiral Model of Software Development and Enhancement

The *Spiral model* was proposed and developed by Barry Boehm in *A Spiral Model of Software Development and Enhancement* (Computer, May 1988). A simplified version of that model is presented in Figure 9.10,

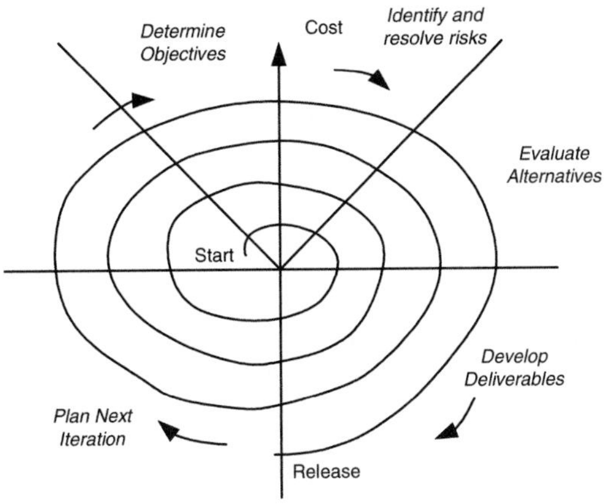
Determine
Objectives
Cost
Identify and
resolve risks
Evaluate
Alternatives
Start
Develop
Deliverables
Plan Next
Iteration
Release

Figure 9.10 The Spiral Life-Cycle Model

The model takes a risk-oriented view of the development life cycle. Each spiral addresses the major risks that have been identified. After all the risks have been addressed, the Spiral model terminates, as did the Waterfall and V models, in the release of a product.

Like the earlier models, the Spiral model begins with good specification of the requirements. It then iteratively completes a little of each phase. Its philosophy is to start small, explore the risks, develop a plan to deal with the risks, and commit to an approach for the next iteration. The cycle continues until the product is complete. Boehm's model contains a lot more detail than the one presented in Figure 9.11. In both cases, each iteration of the spiral involves six steps.

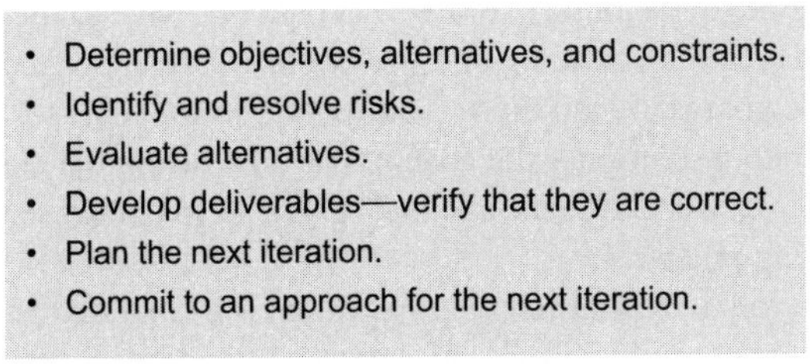
• Determine objectives, alternatives, and constraints.
• Identify and resolve risks.
• Evaluate alternatives.
• Develop deliverables—verify that they are correct.
• Plan the next iteration.
• Commit to an approach for the next iteration.

Figure 9.11 Spiral Life-Cycle Model Steps

The Spiral model is an improvement on the Waterfall and V models because it provides for multiple builds as well as several opportunities for risk assessment and customer involvement. On the negative side, it is elaborate, difficult to manage, and does not keep all developers occupied during all of the phases.

9.2.4 Rapid Prototyping—Incremental

Rapid Prototyping model

The *Rapid Prototyping model* is intended to provide a rapid implementation (hence the name) of high-level portions of both the software and the hardware early in the project. The approach allows developers to construct working portions of the hardware and software in incremental stages. Each stage consists of design, code and unit test, integration test, and delivery. At each stage through the cycle, one incorporates a little more of the intended functionality.

The prototype is useful for both the designer and the customer. For the designer, it enables the early development of major pieces of the intended functionality of system. By doing so, it helps to establish and verify the structural architecture as well as the control flow through the system. Such an approach permits one to identify major problems early (the hockey stick curve again).

The customer benefits by having the opportunity to work with a functional unit much earlier in the development cycle than with any of the three previous models. The customer can use the prototype in the intended context to provide feedback to the designers about any problems with the design.

Such feedback is a critical aspect of the approach because it encourages backwards or reverse flow through the process. It can be used to refine or change the prototype in order to correct the identified problems and to ensure that the design meets the real needs of the customer.

evolutionary, throwaway

The prototype can be either *evolutionary* or *throwaway*. It has the advantage of having a working system early in the development process. As noted, problems can be identified earlier, and it provides tangible measures of progress. To be effective, however, the rapid prototyping approach requires careful planning at both the project management and designer levels.

Be careful how the prototype is used:

> ***Caution:*** The prototype should never turn into the final product.

Let's now move into the design process. Design begins with the real world where we are trying to solve problems in order to make our lives easier.

9.3 PROBLEM SOLVING—FIVE STEPS TO DESIGN

When we begin the design of a new product or have to incorporate several new features or capabilities into an existing one, we begin with a set of requirements usually stated in text form. The goal is to map those requirements—the real world—through a series of transformations into a solution—the abstract world. During the design process, we move from the concrete, real world into the abstract. These steps comprise what we describe as good design engineering practices.

Hopefully, we learned years ago that the first step to design is not to grab the nearest keyboard or processor and start hacking out code or wiring parts together. With today's complex systems, planning and thought before starting are essential to any successful design. If one takes the central elements from each of the life-cycle models, one finds that good system designers and successful projects generally proceed using a minimum of five steps (see Figure 9.12).

- Requirements definition
- System specification
- Functional design
- Architectural design
- Prototyping

Figure 9.12 Five Steps to a Successful Design

The formality of each step depends on the complexity of the end product. If you are working alone or with several others in your own company on a smaller project, a white board in the center of the garage can often suffice. If you are orchestrating a project that includes developers, manufacturers, and regulations in several countries around the world (which is becoming increasingly common today), the need for formality increases. When working with each of these phases of a product life cycle, we must remember that they are guidelines—collective best practices. They are not a checklist to a successful project, and they are not exhaustive.

IP (intellectual property)

Today the contemporary design process must also enforce *IP (intellectual property)*, capitalization, and reuse at every design stage. The days of Bob Widler (the father of the op amp) lecturing about integrated circuit design in the bars of Silicon Valley are long gone. One must also consider traceability in both the forward and reverse directions. Traceability captures the relationships between requirements and all subsequent design data and helps in managing requirements changes.

9.4 THE DESIGN PROCESS

As we begin to explore the product development cycle, we will walk through each of these five steps. Rather than focus on how one particular model approaches the interpretation of these steps, we will try to identify the essential elements of each step. The approach that we will present is top down and iterative.

The first two steps focus on capturing and formalizing the external behavior of the system. The remaining three move inside the system and repeat the process for the internal implementation that gives rise to the desired and specified behavior. As we will do from the outside and on the inside, we will move from the general to the specific, capturing and specifying each aspect of the design.

A major task, once we move inside the system, will be to decompose and refine the design from a nebulous entity that someone needs into the product that implements that need. We will first decompose (organize) the collection of customers' wishes into functional blocks, which are then mapped into an architecture. That architecture provides the aggregate of hardware and software modules that will make up the ultimate system. The final step in the design cycle is to bring the design together into a prototype and ultimately into production.

Because there is not one right answer, the problem represents a challenge and an opportunity to be creative. A colleague who worked on numerous designs of a particular piece of measurement technology once said, "although each design performs exactly the same function, each also represents an opportunity to explore a new approach that is better than the old." That colleague built a career around doing what everyone else, including some of the top names in the industry, said couldn't be done.

One of the best ways to learn how to do something is simply to do it. So, let's get started. As we walk through each of the steps in the design process that we have identified, we will see how they apply to the following design. We begin with a textual description.

EXAMPLE 9.0

Designing a Counter

Stating the Problem

As a senior development engineer at *Your Time Is Our Frequency, Ltd.com*, you've just finished one project and are now getting ready to head off to the next. As part of the early planning of that project, you and one of the marketing folks are traveling around the country talking with people from a number of different engineering firms. You are trying to determine what features your customers would like to see in the next generation product.

You've been on the road with this guy for a couple of weeks now and are anxious to get home. All the cities are beginning to look exactly alike. Tuesday, this must be Cleveland . . . hmmm, looks just like the last three cities. Oh well. This is the last customer for this trip. This morning, you're talking with *High Flying Avionics, Inc.* They're interested in a new counter that can be used on several of their avionics production lines.

Following several hours of discussion with one of the manufacturing managers, you identify most of their requirements. Your discussion with them follows.

Business is a little slow right now and money is tight, so we don't have a large budget to purchase a lot of different new instruments. In fact, ideally, we'd like to be able to use the same instrument on several of our lines.

Today, we have our technicians running most of the tests manually, but, in future, we'd like to be able to automate as many of these tests as we can. As we upgrade our systems, we'd like to be able to operate several of these counters remotely from a single PC. Here are some of the other things that we'd like to be able to do.

As part of our ongoing efforts to improve production and flow through our lines, we monitor the rate at which units arrive into each of the major assembly areas. To do that, we need to be able to track how many of our navigation radios come down a production line each hour. Because we support small-quantity builds of different kinds of radios, the rate at which the units come past the monitoring points is not constant. As each radio arrives at an entry point, it breaks an IR beam. On most of the lines, breaking the beam generates a 1-μsec-wide, negative going 5.0 V pulse. However, we do have several older lines that we must still support. On these, the pulse is positive going.

On several of the newer lines, we have to measure frequency up to 150,000 MHz. We also have several tests for which we must measure frequencies in the range of 50 KHz ± 0.001 KHz and 100 Hz with 0.001 Hz resolution. On another line, we have several instruments with output signals that have a duration up to 1.0000 ± 0.0001ms and others that have a duration of up to 9.999 to 10.000 ms and up to 1.000 ± 0.001sec. These signals are not periodic. Finally, we have several periodic signals on those same units that we must be able to measure with the same accuracy and resolution.

9.5 IDENTIFYING THE REQUIREMENTS

The development of a well-conceived and well-designed system must begin with a requirements definition. Such a need holds, independent of the life-cycle model that one chooses to work with. Unlike the people in the drawing in Figure 9.13 paraphrased from an unknown author, we cannot begin a design until we know what we are supposed to be designing.

The goal of the requirements identification process is to capture a formal description of the complete system from the customer's point of view and then to document these needs as written definitions and descriptions. Such documentation forms the subsequent basis for the formal design specification.

Very often, we use the natural language of the customer and of the application context. We do so because such a formal expression of the requirements forces the early discussion and resolution of many complex problems, involving a variety of people with expertise in many different areas, particularly those who are knowledgeable in the application domain. We express the role that the requirements definition plays between the customer and those who execute the design with the accompanying simple graphic in Figure 9.14.

Figure 9.13 Starting a New Project

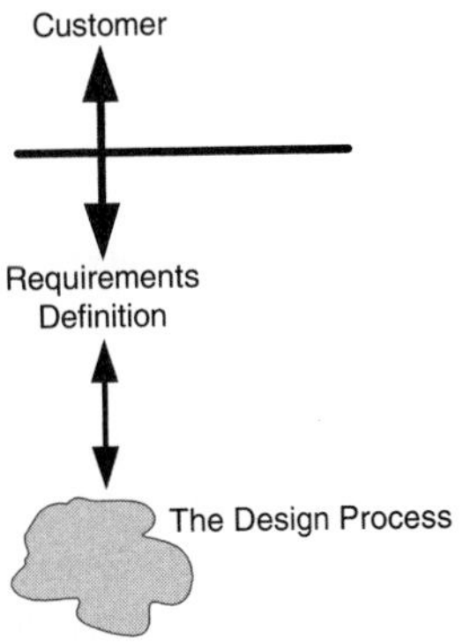

Figure 9.14 The Interface Between the Customer and the Design Process

The requirements definition provides the interface between the customer and the engineering process. It is the first step in transforming the customer's wishes into the final product. One can see, then, that the requirements definition is a description of something that is wanted or needed. It identifies and captures a set of required capabilities or operations. As one begins to identify all the requirements, it is important to consider *both* the system to be designed *and* the environment in which it is to operate.

At this early stage in the product life cycle, the goal is to capture and express purely external views of the environment, the system, and their interaction. With respect to the system, one refers to such a view as its public interface. One tries to identify *what* needs to be done (and *how well* it needs to be done) starting with the user's needs and requirements.

what

how well

The first view of the environment and of the system takes the form shown in Figure 9.15. It is evident that the environment surrounds the system. The inputs to and outputs from the system can come from or go to anywhere in the environment. As one begins, one should make no assumptions about the extent of either.

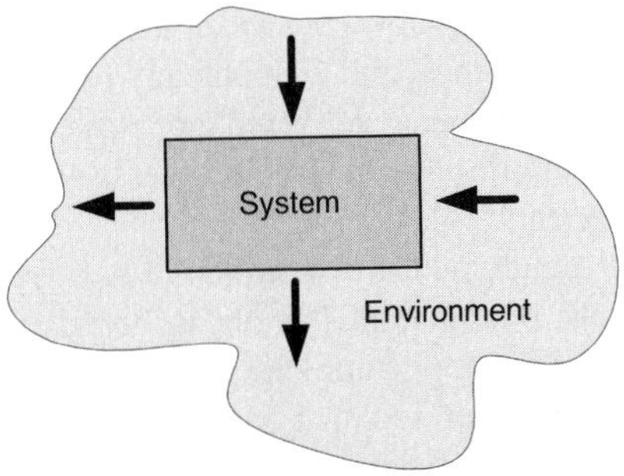

Figure 9.15 The System and Its Environment—Step 0

The first step is to abstract and consolidate that view so that both appear as the black boxes seen in Figure 9.16.

The initial focus must be on the world or environment (the application context) in which the system is to operate. Next, one follows with an increasingly detailed description of the role played by the system in that environment, and at each step one adds to and refines the requirements.

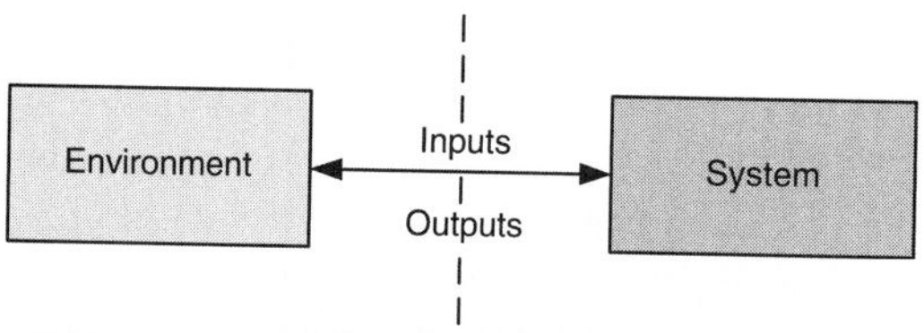

Figure 9.16 The System and Its Environment—Step 1

From the perspective of the environment, one can see that the requirements definition must include a specification for the containing environment, a description/definition of the inputs and outputs to and from that environment, a description of necessary behavior of the system, and a description of how the system is to be used.

From the system's point of view, one starts at a high level of abstraction with an *outside* view. One develops the definition(s) that are appropriate for that level. As was done when specifying the environment, through progressive refinement, one moves to lower levels of abstraction and a more detailed understanding and definition.

At this stage in the development life cycle, as the definition of the requirements solidifies and is ultimately formalized into a specification, one should be unencumbered by plans for implementation. The focus should be on the high-level behavior of the system. The complete, accurate, and internally consistent specification must be available before one can start formal design. Ideally, it should be executable and thereby able to work in conjunction with a modeling tool suite. Such an executable specification ultimately serves as the basis for validation of the system.

Although an executable specification is a laudable goal, achieving that goal can become difficult when one must include support for nonfunctional constraints, integrate legacy components into an abstract model, and potentially combine different domain-specific languages and semantics.

9.6 FORMULATING THE REQUIREMENTS SPECIFICATION

Let's now examine some of the things that one should think about when starting to identify and capture the requirements and when trying to define them in a formal specification. The form, extent, and formality of such a specification depends on the project on which one is working, the target audience, and the company for which one is working. Remember, too, that it is a product that is being delivered, not a pile of paper. As a rule of thumb, the specification should be the absolute minimum necessary to capture and clearly identify all of the necessary requirements.

requirements
specification

In capturing requirements, one strives to be very specific about the details from the user's point of view. Bear in mind that one is identifying and formalizing the *requirements.* One still cannot begin to design until the *specification* has been completed and the customer has agreed to it. Remember, too, that one should not be discussing microprocessors, memory, peripheral chips, or software modules at this point in the development process.

As one begins the designs, one usually has some general ideas, casual discussion, and thoughts but nothing firm. One can use these as a guide in directing the steps, but one cannot design from them. It is important to be careful, however, not to rely too heavily on preconceived ideas; one should always be open to alternative approaches. Starting to code or draw logic diagrams at this point is inviting major problems as the project proceeds. In all likelihood, the project will fail.

For the environment, one must establish a description of all relevant entities and of the behaviors of all activities. One must know how the environment is interacting with the system and the effects on the environment by the outputs from the system. For the system, one requires a description of all inputs and outputs as well as a complete description of the functional and operational behaviors and technological constraints.

At this juncture we can naturally ask: how can one get such information about (let alone model) the system and the environment without describing or knowing implementation of the system? The internals are inherently unknown at this point. How does one capture the desired behaviors?

9.6.1 The Environment

A reasonable first step begins with defining and describing the environment, the world in which the system must operate. The environment is a temporal world; it is a heterogeneous collection of entities of one form or another. It comprises the collection of physical devices to which the system is interconnected as well as any physical world attributes that the system intends to measure or control or that can have an effect on the system. The initial goals in understanding the environment are to identify all relevant entities, then characterize their effects on the system, and vice versa. When the requirements specification has been completed, one should have all the necessary information about such entities, with sufficient detail to support solving the problem.

9.6.1.1 Characterizing External Entities

Each entity that makes up the environment is characterized by a name and an abstracted public interface. That interface consists of the entity's inputs and outputs as well as its functional behavior. The specification of the external environment should contain the following for each entity.

- *Name and Description of the Entity*
  The name should be suggestive of what the entity is or does. The description should present the nature of the entity. Is it data, an event, a state variable, a message? An entity may be something that is to be controlled—for example, the rudder on an aircraft or the clear air turbulence that must be accounted for in such a control system.
- *Responsibilities—Activities*
  What activities or actions is the environment expected to perform? The hydraulic system moving the rudder is part of the environment. Its action or responsibility is to move the rudder in response to the signal coming from the system being designed.
- *Relationships*
  What are the relationships between the entity and its responsibilities or activities? Is that relationship causal or responding? Is it a producer or a consumer?
- *Safety and Reliability*
  Safety and reliability issues must be included early in the specification process. With respect to the environment, at the requirements stage, the focus is primarily on safety. The goal is to identify all safety critical issues and hazards so that they can be addressed in detail in the system design specification. One should also identify any regulatory agencies under whose auspices the system will operate.

9.6.2 The System

The focus next shifts to the system's point of view. The same questions posed for the environment are now asked about the system. As with the characterization of the environment, the initial goals are to identify all the aspects of the public interface of the system and then characterize their effects on the environment and vice versa.

9.6.2.1 Characterizing the System

Characterization of the system begins with identifying inputs and outputs.

- *System Inputs and Outputs*
  The system interacts with the real world through the entities described and defined in the environmental characterization. The inputs to the system are the outputs from environmental entities, and the outputs from the system are the inputs to the environmental entities. One can easily see that the system I/O has already been characterized in environmental entity specification.

  For each such I/O variable, the following information is already available:
  - The name of the signal
  - The use of the signal as an input or output
  - The nature of the signal as an event, data, state variable, and so on

  Working with the environment specification, one can write the structure, domain of validity, and physical characteristics of each signal. To these, one can add any technical or technological constraints that are identified.

- *Responsibilities—Activities*
  As was done with the specification of the environment, focus now turns to the function that the system is intended to perform. Before it is designed, the system appears as a black box. It can only be viewed from an external point of view. A section on functional behavior is now included in the specification.

  The functional description defines the external behavior of the system. It characterizes the effects of the system outputs on the environmental entities and the system's intended response to inputs from the environmental entities. It elaborates on how the system is used and to be used by the user. Such a specification is equivalent to developing a model of the system.

  The functional description can be captured in a variety of ways. One effective approach is to use the UML tools discussed earlier. One can construct one such view through use case and class diagrams. Another view can be gained through high-level state charts and activity diagrams; data and control flow diagrams commonly used in structured design methodologies give a third view.

  As one formulates these diagrams and the specification, care must be taken to ensure that the specified (and ultimately modeled) states are appropriate to the application. One must make certain that the actions that are captured in the specification accurately reflect the desired (external) behavior of the system as perceived and intended by the customer. In the specification, one must ensure that the conditions or constraints on its behavior are only a function of the inputs coming into the system, the specified states, the internal events, and the appropriate time demarcation (relative or absolute).

- *Safety and Reliability*
  In formulating the safety and reliability requirements for the system, the focus is on the high-level objectives of each and on the strategy for achieving those goals.
  The safety considerations should address
  - Safety guidelines, rules, or regulations under the governing agencies identified under the environment portion of the specification.

  With respect to reliability, one can specify
  - The system uptime goals
  - Potential risks, failures, and failure modes
  - Failure management strategy

EXAMPLE 9.0

Designing a Counter (Cont.)

Identifying the Requirements

Starting from the trip report from *High Flying Avionics, Inc.*, which discussed their needs for a new counter, let's put the requirements specification together.

As a first step in the thought process, one extracts and summarizes the essential information from the trip report. By doing so, one can begin to focus on what should be included in the requirements specification. From the discussions with the customer, a high-level sketch of the system and the environment captures the essential parts of the problem. The next step is to begin to formalize the model of the system and the environment as illustrated in Figure 9.17.

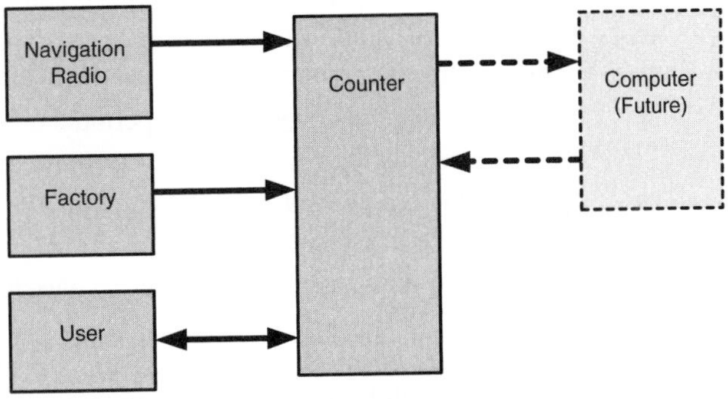

Figure 9.17 The System and Its Environment—Step 2

In its initial configuration, the environment contains:

- A set of navigation radios that are to be tested
- The user who is doing the testing
- The factory

Signals flow from the navigation radio to the counter, but not the reverse. The factory has inputs to the counter as well; these include the power system and the ambient environment in the factory. The user's interaction is bidirectional. The user must select and configure the measurement to be made and then view the results once the measurement is complete. For the computer, the signal interchange with the counter similarly occurs in both directions.

In the developing model, the factory can be viewed as an aggregation of test lines and the radios to be tested. Later, the remote computer is to be added. The system to be designed, that is, the counter, interacts with all three entities. Such an interaction is reflected in Figure 9.18.

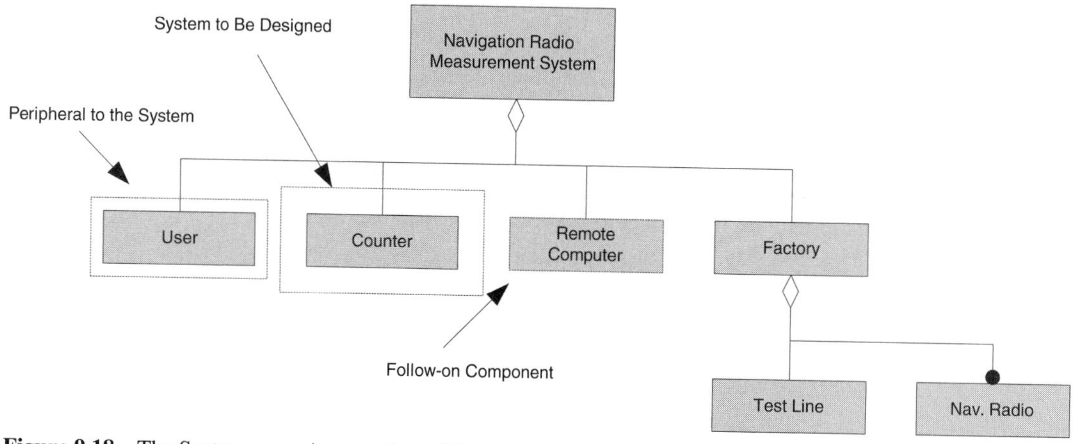

Figure 9.18 The System as an Aggregation of Components

Now let's move to the next level of detail.

ENVIRONMENT

- The customer has stated that the counter is to operate in a factory environment on any of several productions lines. Based on such an understanding, one can make certain assumptions about temperature, power, and ambient lighting.
- Time intervals and frequencies on the navigation radios and events from equipment monitoring the production line are to be measured.
- The time intervals may be either periodic or aperiodic but cannot be both.
- The polarity of the event signal to be counted can be either positive or negative going.
- The data display and the annunciation for mode and range are the only outputs expected from the counter.
- The assumption is made that the signals to be measured are independent of one another.
- In future, commands will be sent from a computer to the counter to direct its operation. Data will be sent from the counter to the computer.

COUNTER

- The counter must have the ability to measure time intervals and frequencies and to count events.
- The frequencies are fixed but span a range of values.
- The time intervals span a range of values and may be either periodic or aperiodic, but they cannot be both.
- The counter will support the user's ability to manually select mode and measurement range for all input signals.
- The counter will continue to make and display the selected attribute of the signal until power to the system is turned off or until the user makes another selection.
- The counter will measure only one signal at a time.
- An event can be modeled as an aperiodic time signal.
- The design will be sufficiently flexible to allow future inclusion of the ability to send commands from a computer to the counter to direct its operation.

- The response of the counter to remote commands will be the same as its response to front panel selections, with the exception that measured data will be sent from the counter to the computer as well as to the front panel display.

System Requirements Specification

The next step is to formalize, in a specification, what is known about the system to be designed. The document, the *System Requirements Specification*, opens with a summary of the design.

System Requirements Specification for a Digital Counter

System Description

This specification describes and defines the basic requirements for a digital counter. The counter is to be able to measure frequency, period, time interval, and events. The system supports three measurement ranges for each signal and two for events. The counter is to be manually operated with the ability to support remote operation in future. The counter is to be low cost and flexible, so that it may be utilized in a variety of applications.

Specification of External Environment

The counter is to operate in an industrial environment in a commercial grade temperature and lighting environment. The unit will support either line power or battery operation.

System Input and Output Specification

System Inputs

The system shall be able to measure the following signals.

Frequency in three ranges

• High range up to	150.000 MHz
• Midrange up to	50.000 KHz
• Low range up to	100.000 Hz

Period in three ranges

• High resolution up to	1.0000 ms
• Midresolution up to	10.000 ms
• Low resolution up to	1.000 sec

Time interval in three ranges

• High resolution up to	1.0000 ms
• Midresolution up to	10.00 ms
• Low resolution up to	1.000 sec

Events—up to 99 events in 1 minute

All signal inputs will be

- Digital data
- Voltage range 0.0 to 4.5 VDC

System Outputs

The system shall measure and display the following signals using a 6-digit display.

Frequency in three ranges

- High range up to 200.000 ± 0.001 MHz
- Midrange up to 200.000 ± 0.001 KHz
- Low range up to s200.000 ± 0.001 Hz

Period in three ranges

- High resolution up to 2.000 ± 0.0001 ms
- Midresolution up to 20.00 ± 0.01 ms
- Low resolution up to 2.000 ± 0.001 sec

Time interval in three ranges

- High resolution up to 2.0000 ± 0.0001 ms
- Midresolution up to 20.00 ± 0.01 ms
- Low resolution up to 2.000 ± 0.001 sec

Events in two ranges

- Fast up to 200 events in 1 minute
- Slow up to 2,000 events in 1 hour

User Interface

The user shall be able to select the following using buttons and switches on the front panel of the instrument.

Mode
- Frequency, Period, Time Interval, Events
- Range
  - Frequency, Period, Time Interval—High, Mid, Low
  - Events—Fast, Slow

Trigger Edge
- Frequency, Period, and Events
  - Rising or falling edge
- Time Interval
  - Rising to rising edge
  - Falling to falling edge
  - Rising to falling edge
  - Falling to rising edge
- Reset
- Power ON/OFF

The measurement results shall be presented on a 6-digit display; leading zeros will be suppressed. The display shall be readable in direct sunlight and from any angle.

The front panel will appear as follows.

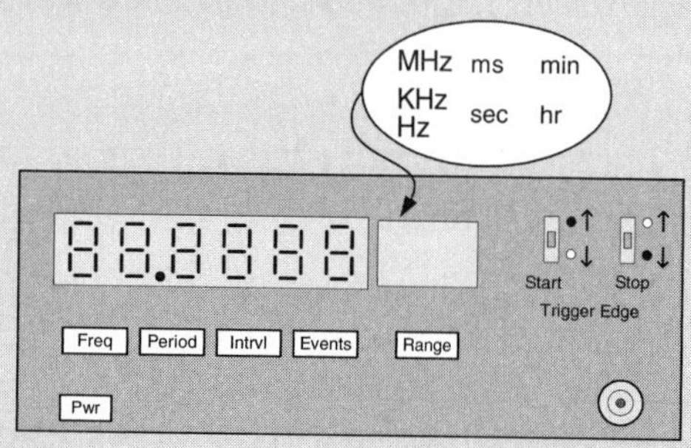

Use Cases

The use cases for the counter are given in the following two diagrams.

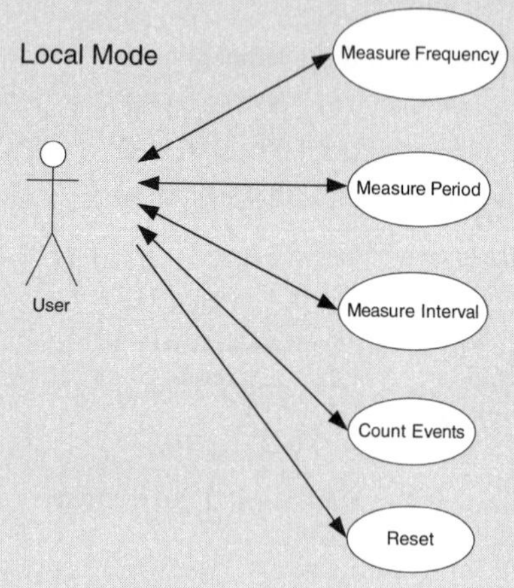

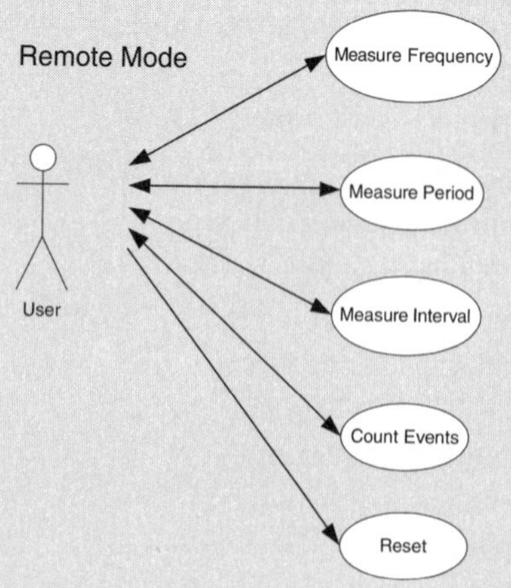

The first indicates manual operation through the front panel, and the second through a remote connection to a computer.

The remote option will not be included in the initial model, but will be incorporated in a later release. The time of that release is to be determined.

Execution of the selected measurement function will not depend on how (local or remote) that function was selected.

At power ON, the default mode is to measure frequency. All ranges will default to their highest value.

Measure Frequency The counter will continuously measure and display the frequency of the input signal on the currently selected range as long as the *Frequency* mode is selected.

If the frequency of the input signal exceeds the maximum allowable value on the selected range, the display will present the full-scale reading and will flash.

If the frequency of the input signal is below the minimum allowable value on the selected range, the display will present a zero reading.

If the input signal returns to a value within the bounds of the range, the value of the frequency will be displayed.

The range may be changed at any time by depressing the *range select* pushbutton.

The user may elect to measure frequency starting on the positive or negative edge of the signal by depressing the *start trigger edge* pushbutton.

Measure Period The counter will continuously measure and display the period of the input signal on the currently selected range as long as the *Period* mode is selected.

If the period of the input signal exceeds the maximum allowable value on the selected range, the display will present the full-scale reading and will flash. If the period of the input signal is below the minimum allowable value on the selected range, the display will present a zero reading.

If the input signal returns to a value within the bounds of the range, the value of the period will be displayed.

The range may be changed at any time by depressing the *range select* pushbutton.

The user may elect to measure period starting on the positive or negative edge of the signal by depressing the *start trigger edge* pushbutton.

Measure Interval The counter will continuously measure and display the duration of the selected portion of the input signal on the currently selected range as long as the *Interval* mode is selected.

If the duration of the selected portion of the input signal exceeds the maximum allowable value on the selected range, the display will present the full-scale reading and will flash.

If the duration of the selected portion of the input signal is below the minimum allowable value on the selected range, the display will display zero.

If the input signal returns to a value within the bounds of the range, the value of the duration of the selected portion of the input signal will be displayed.

The range may be changed at any time by depressing the *range select* pushbutton.

The user may elect to commence measuring the interval on the positive or negative edge of the signal by depressing the *start trigger edge* pushbutton.

The user may elect to terminate the measurement interval on the positive or negative edge of the signal by depressing the *stop trigger edge* pushbutton.

Note that the signal duration from positive edge to positive edge or negative edge to negative edge is the same as the period of the signal.

Events The counter will continuously count and display the number of occurrences of the input signal on the currently selected range. The accumulated count will be reset to 0 at the end of the select count duration.

The range may be changed at any time by depressing the *range select* pushbutton.

The user may elect to increment the count on the positive or negative edge of the input signal by depressing the *start trigger edge* pushbutton.

If the number of accrued counts exceeds the maximum allowable value on the selected range, the display will present the full-scale reading and will flash.

System Functional Specification

The system is intended to make four different kinds of digital measurement in the time and frequency domains comprising frequency, period, time interval, and events. The activities associated with the *measure frequency* mode are shown in the following diagram.

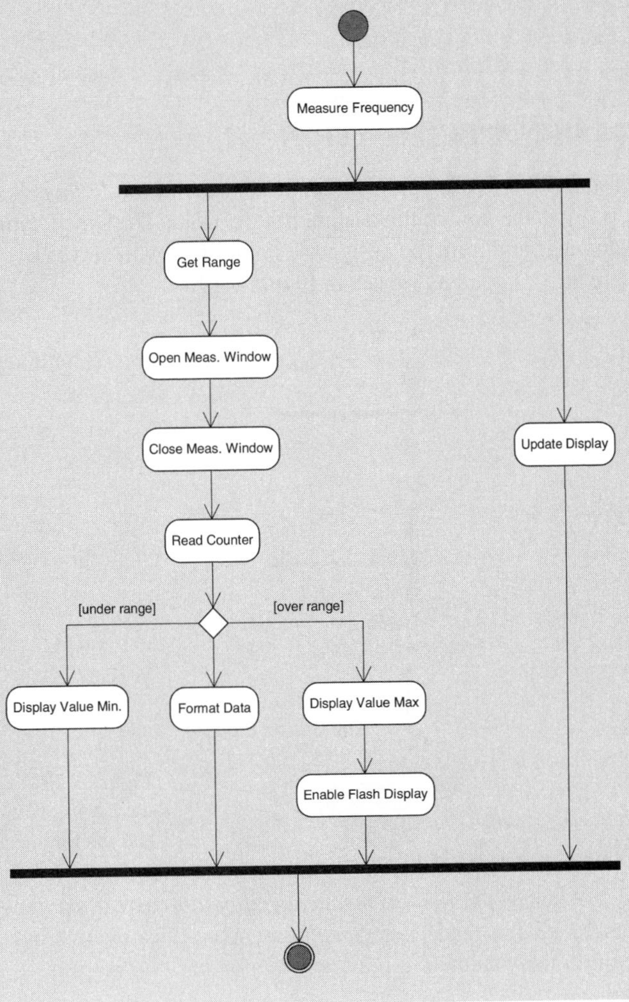

The time and frequency measurements will be implemented to provide three user selectable resolution ranges: high frequency range/shorter duration signals, a second for midrange frequency/midrange duration signals, and a third for low frequency/longer duration signals. The events measurement capability will support two selectable counting durations, shorter and longer.

For frequency, period, and events measurements, the user will be able to select either a positive or negative edge trigger. For interval measurements, the user will be able to select the polarity of the start and stop signals independently.

Operating Specifications

The system shall operate in a standard commercial / industrial environment

Temperature Range 0–85C

Humidity up to 90% RH noncondensing

Power 120–240 VAC 50 Hz, 60 Hz, 400 Hz, 15 VDC

The system shall operate for a minimum of 8 hours on a fully charged battery

The system time base shall meet the following specifications.

Temperature stability 0–50 C

$< 6 \times 10^{-6}$

Aging Rate

90 day	$< 3 \times 10^{-8}$
6 month	$< 6 \times 10^{-7}$
1 year	$< 25 \times 10^{-6}$

Reliability and Safety Specification

The counter shall comply with the appropriate standards

Safety: UL-3111-1, IEC-1010, CSA 1010.1

EMC: CISPR-11, IEC 801-2, -3, -4, EN50082-1

MTBF: Minimum of 10,000 hours

9.7 THE SYSTEM DESIGN SPECIFICATION

System Design Specification, System Requirements Specification

The *System Design Specification* is based on the *System Requirements Specification* and specifies the *how* of the design, not the *what.* The specification is written in the designer's language and from the designer's point of view. It serves as a bridge between the customer and the designer, as we see in Figure 9.19.

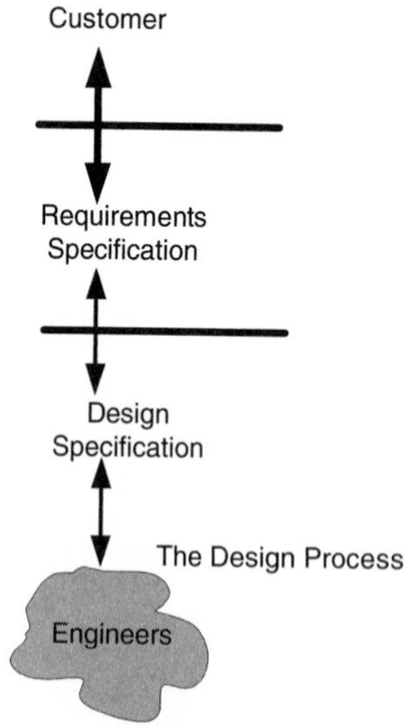

Figure 9.19 The Customer, the Requirements, the Design, and the Engineer

Requirements Specification Design Specification

Whereas the *Requirements Specification* provides a view from the outside of the system looking in, the *Design Specification* provides a view from the inside looking out as well. Notice also that the *Design Specification* has two masters:

- It must specify the system's public interface from inside the system.
- It must specify *how* the requirements defined for and by the public interface are to be met by the internal functions of the system.

Requirements Specification
Design Specification

We have seen that the *Requirements Specification* is written in less formal terms with the intent of capturing the customer's view of the product. The *Design Specification* must formalize those requirements in precise, unambiguous language. Putting the inevitable changes that occur during the lifetime of any project aside for the moment, we find that the design specification should be sufficiently clear, robust, and complete that a group of engineers could develop the product without ever talking to the author of the specification.

Design Note
A good litmus test of the viability of a design specification is the question, "If I send this to my colleague (who is working for one of our subcontractors), will he or she understand this?" If the answer is no, the specification should be reexamined.

9.7.1 The System

As part of formalizing and quantifying the system's requirements, one must attach concrete numbers, tolerances, and constraints to all of the system's input and output signals. All timing relationships must be defined. The system's functional and operational behaviors are described in detail.

9.7.2 Quantifying the System

The quantification of the system's characteristics begins with the inputs and outputs, based on the specified requirements. The necessary technical details are added to enable the engineer to accurately and faithfully execute the actual design.

- *System Inputs and Outputs*
  For each I/O variable, the following are specified.
  - The name of the signal
  - The use of the signal as an input or output
  - The nature of the signal as an event, data, state variable, and so on.

  Starting with the requirements specification, we provide detailed descriptions as necessary and incorporate any additional technical or technological constraints that may be needed.
  - The complete specification of the signal, including nominal value, range, level tolerances, timing, and timing tolerances
  - The interrelationships with other signals, including any constraints on those relationships
- *Responsibilities—Activities*
  - Functional and Operational Specifications
    The functional and operational specifications that will quantify the dynamic behavior of the system are now formulated. The functional requirements specification identifies the major functions that the system must perform from a high-level view. The operational specification endeavors to capture specific details of how those functions behave within the context of the operating environment.

The manner in which a particular function must operate, the conditions imposed on the operation, and the range of that operation are now captured. The specification must consider concrete numbers—precisions and tolerances.

All variables in the functional specification, all operating conditions, and all ordinary and extraordinary operating modes must be quantified. The specification may include domain-specific knowledge that is proprietary or heuristically known to the customer. Such knowledge can be very important to the design.

In stating the specific design requirements for the system, one can use tables, equations or algorithms, formal design language, or pseudo code, flow diagrams, or detailed UML diagrams such as state charts, sequence diagrams, and time lines. Schematics, codes, or parts lists are not included, except in limited circumstances.

- Technological (and Other) Specifications

  The technological portion includes all detailed and concrete specifications that are relevant to the design of the system hardware and software. Five areas that should be considered can easily be identified.

1. Geographical constraints

   Distributed applications can span a single room, can expand to include a complete factory, or can encompass several countries. Consequently, one must address both the technical items such as interconnection topologies, communications methods, restrictions on usage, and environmental contamination as well as nontechnical matters such as costs associated with the physical medium and its installation.

2. Characterization of and constraints on interface signals

   The assumption is made that signals between the system and the external world are electrical, optical, or wireless or that they can be converted into or from such a form. The necessary physical characterization of each is obviously going to depend on the type of signal. That is, an electrical signal is specified differently from an optical signal.

   Since many of the interface signals may be driven by the external environment, potentially they are beyond the designer's control. Therefore, it is important to gain as much information about them as possible.

3. User interface requirements

   If the system interfaces to such external world devices as medical or instrumentation equipment, how information is presented and whether any relevant and associated protocols exist must be considered. There may also be standards that govern how such information must be presented.

   Consider the significant risk that would arise if each avionics vendor presented critical flight information and controls to the aircraft pilot in a different way. The near disaster at Three Mile Island in 1979 arose, in part, because of the confusion caused by too much information.

4. Temporal constraints

   The system may have to perform under hard or soft real-time constraints. Such constraints may specify delays on signals originating from external entities, responses to system outputs by external entities, and/or internal system delays.

5. Electrical Infrastructure considerations

   There must be a specification for the electrical characteristics of any electrical infrastructure. Included in this portion of the specification are power consumption, necessary power supplies, tolerances and capacities of such supplies, tolerance to degraded power, and power management schemes.

- *Safety and Reliability*

  In formulating the design requirements for the safety and reliability of the system, the focus shifts to the detailed objectives of each and to the strategy for achieving those goals.

  Safety considerations should address

  - Understanding and specifying any environmental and safety issues

  The reliability specification should include

  - Requirements for diagnostic tests, remote maintenance, remote upgrade, and their details
  - Concrete numbers for MTTF and MTBF of any built-in self-test circuitry
  - Concrete numbers for MTTF and MTBF of the system itself
  - Consideration of system performance under partial or full failure

Let's now bring everything together.

EXAMPLE 9.0

Designing a Counter (Cont.)

Design Specification
Requirements Specification

Quantifying the specification

We will now continue with the development of the counter. The system *Design Specification* will follow, but extend, what has been captured in the *Requirements Specification*. The focus will now be on providing specific numbers, ranges, and tolerances for signals that are within the system.

Once again, we will put together any thoughts about the environment and the system prior to writing the specification.

Environment

Specifications relating to the environment have been discussed earlier. There are no changes here.

Counter

- When specifying measurement and stimulus equipment, the specifications for that equipment are generally 10 times (one order of magnitude) better than those for the signals that must be measured or generated.
- That margin is provided when specifying the range and tolerances on the counter's measurement capabilities.
- Specifications on counting events are based on the granularity of the timing of the interval during which the events are counted.
- The values to be displayed at the measurement boundaries are now defined.

The next step is to provide any additional detail that may be needed and to fully quantify the counter specifications.

System Design Specification for a Digital Counter

System Description

This specification describes and defines the basic requirements for a digital counter. The counter is to be able to measure frequency, period, time interval, and events. The system supports three measurement ranges for each signal and two for events. The counter is to be manually operated with the ability to support remote operation in future. The counter is to be low cost and flexible so that it may be utilized in a variety of applications.

Specification of External Environment

The counter is to operate in an industrial environment in a commercial grade temperature and lighting environment.
The unit will support either line power or battery operation. Specific details are included under Operating Specifications.

System Input and Output Specification

System Inputs

The system shall be able to measure the following signals

Frequency in three ranges

- High range up to 150.000 MHz
- Midrange up to 50.000 KHz
- Low range up to 100.000 Hz

Period in three ranges

- High resolution up to 1.0000 ms
- Midresolution up to 10.000 ms
- Low resolution up to 1.000 sec

Time interval in three ranges

- High resolution up to 1.0000 ms
- Midresolution up to 10.00 ms
- Low resolution up to 1.000 sec

Events

- Events to 99 per minute
- Signal level 0–4.0 V ± 0.5 V
- Transition time $10ns \le t_{rise} t_{fall} \le 50ns$

Voltage Sensitivity

- 50 mV RMS to ± 5.0 V ac signal + dc signal

All signal inputs will be

- Digital data
- Voltage range 0.0 to 4.5 VDC

System Outputs

The system shall measure and display the following signals using a 6-digit display

Frequency in three ranges

- High range
  - Measure: 0 – 200 ± 0.0001 MHz
  - Display: 0 – 200.000 MHz
- Midrange up to 200.000 KHz
  - Measure: 0 – 200 ± 0.0001 KHz
  - Display: 0 – 200.000 KHz
- Low range up to 200.000 Hz
  - Measure: 0 – 200 ± 0.0001 Hz
  - Display: 0 – 200.000 Hz

Period in three ranges

- High resolution up to 2.0000 ms
  - Measure: 0 – 2.00000 ± 0.00001 ms
  - Display: 0 – 2.0000± 0.0001 ms
- Midresolution up to 20.00 ms
  - Measure: 0 – 20.0000 ± 0.0001 ms
  - Display: 0 – 20.000± 0.001 ms
- Low resolution up to 2.000 sec
  - Measure: 0 – 2.0000 ± 0.0001 sec
  - Display: 0 – 2.000 ± 0.001 secUser Interface

Time interval in three ranges

- High resolution up to 2.0000 ms
  - Measure: 0 – 2.00000 ± 0.00001 ms
  - Display: 0 – 2.0000± 0.0001 ms
- Mid resolution up to 20.00 ms
  - Measure: 0 – 20.0000 ± 0.0001 ms
  - Display: 0 – 20.000± 0.001 ms
- Low resolution up to 2.000 sec
  - Measure: 0 – 2.0000 ± 0.0001 sec
  - Display: 0 – 2.000 ± 0.001 sec

Events in two ranges

- Fast up to 200 events in 1 minute
  - Measure: 0 – 200 ± 1 event
  - Display: 0 – 200 ± 1 event
- Slow up to 2000 events in 1 hour
  - Measure: 0 – 2000 ± 1 event
  - Display: 0 – 2000 ± 1 event

User Interface

The user shall be able to select the following using buttons and switches on the front panel of the instrument.

Mode

Frequency, Period, Time Interval, Events

Range

Frequency, Period, Time Interval—High, Mid, Low

Events—Fast, Slow

Trigger Edge

Frequency, Period, and Events

Rising or falling edge

Time Interval

Rising to rising edge

Falling to falling edge

Rising to falling edge

Falling to rising edge

Reset

The reset button will clear the display to all 0's and reset the internal timing/counting chain.

The counter will be placed in the *frequency* mode with the *range* set to KHz, and the *trigger edge* set to *rising*.

Power ON/OFF

The measurement results shall be presented on a 6-digit LED display; leading zeros will be suppressed.

The decimal point will move to reflect the proper value for the range selected as the range pushbutton is pressed.

The front panel will appear as follows.

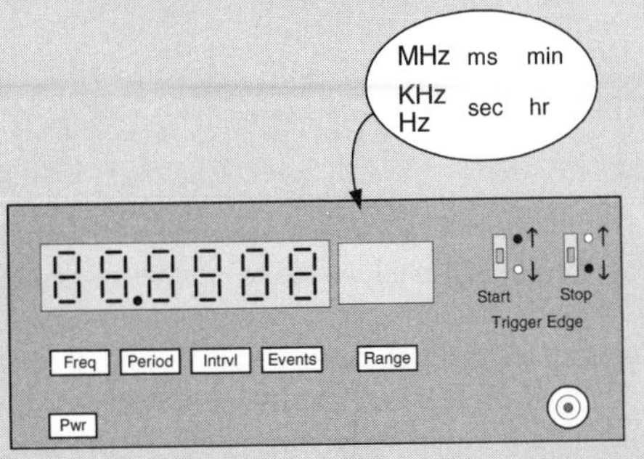

Use Cases

The use cases for the counter are given in the following two diagrams.

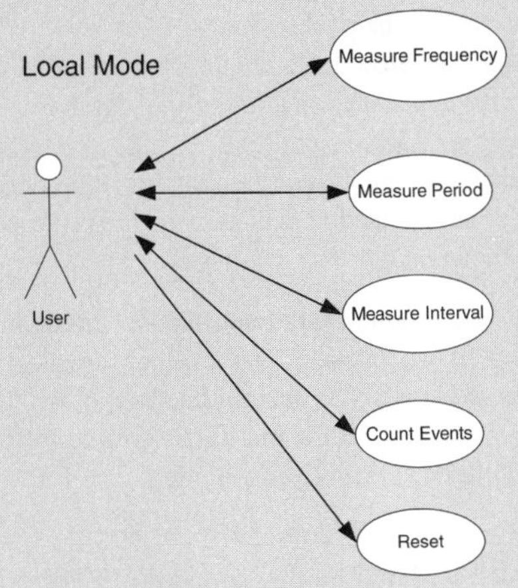

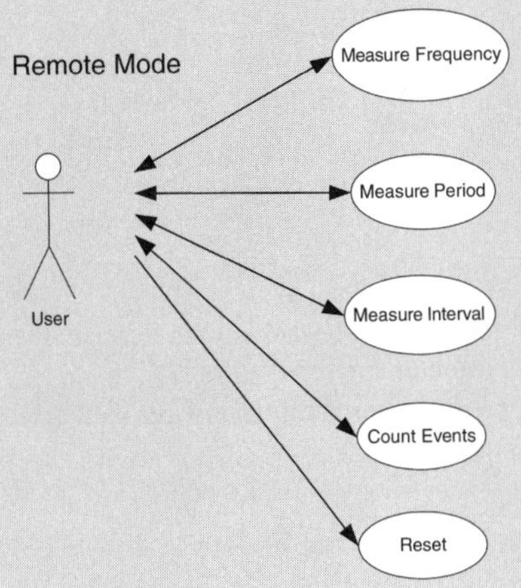

The first indicates manual operation through the front panel, and the second through a remote connection to a computer.

The remote option will not be included in the initial model but will be incorporated in a later release. The time of that release is to be determined.

Execution of the selected measurement function will not depend on how (local or remote) that function was selected.

At power ON, the default mode is to measure frequency. All ranges will default to their highest value.

Measure Frequency The counter will continuously measure and display the frequency of the input signal on the currently selected range as long as the *Frequency* mode is selected. The following use cases are defined for the *Frequency* mode.

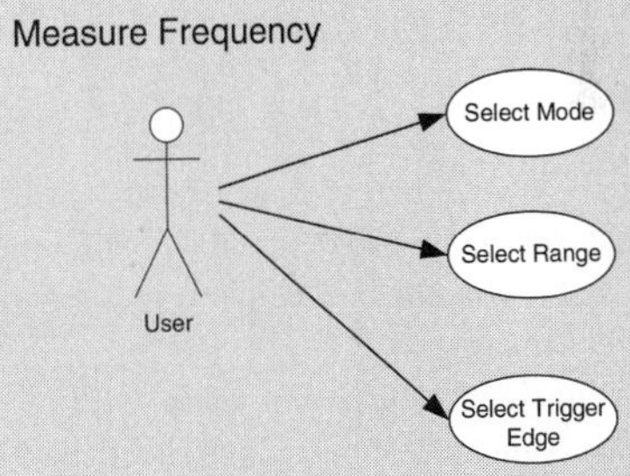

If the frequency of the input signal exceeds the maximum allowable value on the selected range, the display will flash and will present one of the following values based on the selected range,

- 200.000 MHz
- 200.000 KHz
- 200.000 Hz

If the frequency of the input signal is below the minimum allowable value on the selected range, the display will present a zero reading.

If the input signal returns to a value within the bounds of the range, the value of the frequency will be displayed.

The range may be changed at any time by depressing the *range select* pushbutton.

The user may elect to measure frequency starting on the positive or negative edge of the signal by depressing the *start trigger edge* pushbutton.

Measure Period The counter will continuously measure and display the period of the input signal on the currently selected range as long as the *Period* mode is selected. The following use cases are defined for the *Period* mode.

Measure Period

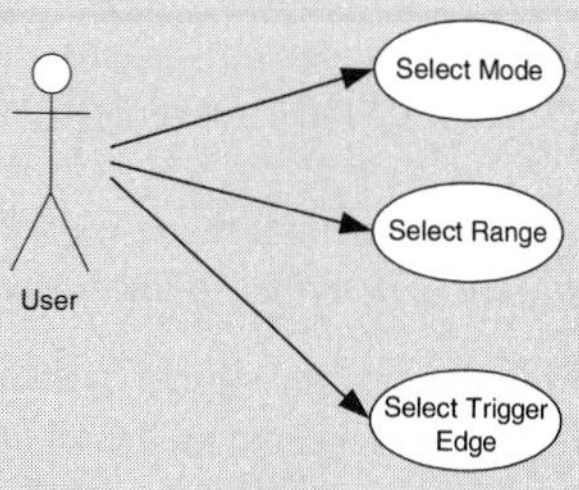

If the period of the input signal exceeds the maximum allowable value on the selected range, the display will flash and will present one of the following values based on the selected range:

- 2.0000 ms
- 20.000 ms
- 2.000 sec

If the period of the input signal is below the minimum allowable value on the selected range, the display will present a zero reading.

If the input signal returns to a value within the bounds of the range, the value of the period will be displayed.

The range may be changed at any time by depressing the *range select* pushbutton.

The user may elect to measure period starting on the positive or negative edge of the signal by depressing the *start trigger edge* pushbutton.

Measure Interval The counter will continuously measure and display the duration of the selected portion of the input signal on the currently selected range as long as the *Interval* mode is selected. The following use cases are defined for the *Interval* mode.

Measure Interval

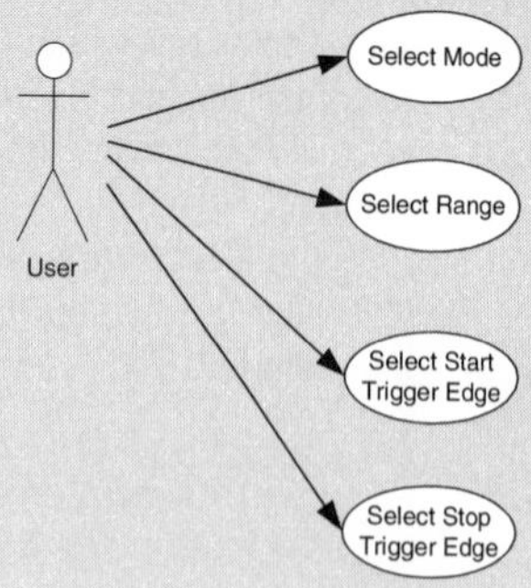

If the duration of the selected portion of the input signal exceeds the maximum allowable value on the selected range, the display will flash and will present one of the following values based on the selected range.

- 2.0000 ms
- 20.000 ms
- 2.000 sec

If the duration of the selected portion of the input signal is below the minimum allowable value on the selected range, the display will display zero.

If the input signal returns to a value within the bounds of the range, the value of the duration of the selected portion of the input signal will be displayed.

The range may be changed at any time by depressing the *range select* pushbutton.

The user may elect to commence measuring the interval on the positive or negative edge of the signal by depressing the *start trigger edge* pushbutton.

The user may elect to terminate the measurement interval on the positive or negative edge of the signal by depressing the *stop trigger edge* pushbutton.

Note that the signal duration from positive edge to positive edge or negative edge to negative edge is the same as the period of the signal.

Events The counter will continuously count and display the number of occurrences of the input signal on the currently selected range. The accumulated count will be reset to 0 at the end of the select count duration. The following use cases are defined for the *Events* mode.

Count Events

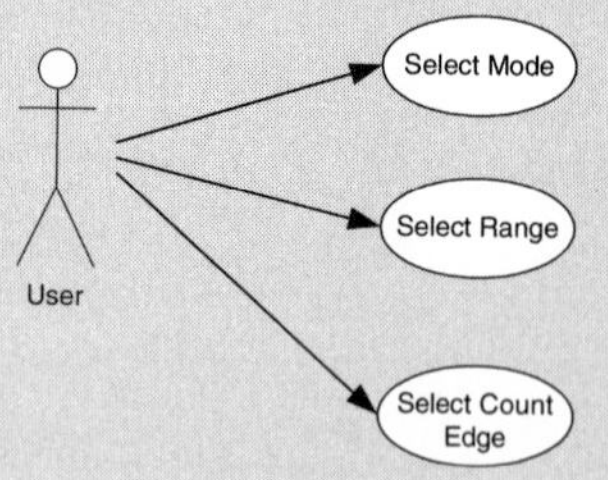

If the number of accrued counts exceeds the maximum allowable value on the selected range, the display will flash and will present one of the following values based on the selected range,

- 200 min
- 2,000 hr

The range may be changed at any time by depressing the *range select* pushbutton.

The user may elect to increment the count on the positive or negative edge of the input signal by depressing the *start trigger edge* pushbutton.

System Functional Specification

The system is intended to make four different kinds of digital measurements comprising frequency, period, time interval, and events.

The time and frequency measurements will be implemented to provide three user selectable resolution ranges: high frequency range/shorter duration signals, a second for midrange frequency/midrange duration signals, and a third for low frequency/longer duration signals. The events measurement capability will support two selectable counting durations, shorter and longer.

For frequency, period, and events measurements, the user will be able to select either a positive or negative edge trigger. For interval measurements, the user will be able to select the polarity of the start and stop signals independently.

The system will be designed so as not to preclude the incorporation of a remote access option in future.

The system comprises six major blocks as given in the following block diagram

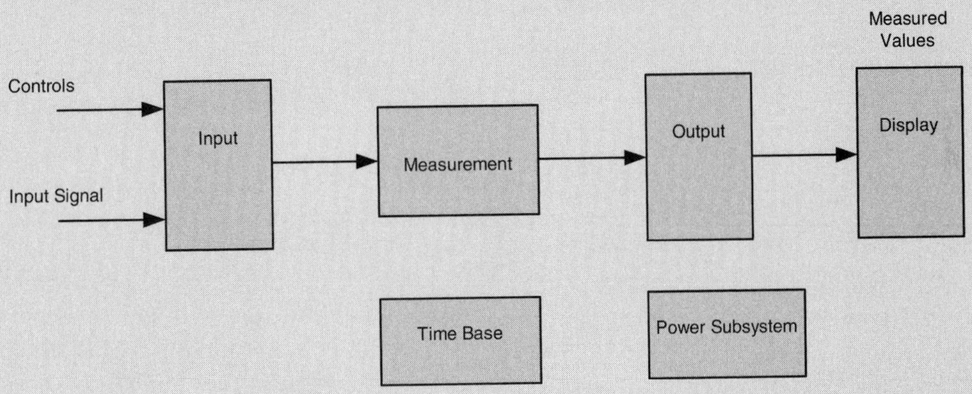

Input Subsystem The input subsystem shall provide the ability for the user to select any of the measurement functions, ranges, and triggering polarities. The subsystem also selects and routes the input signal to the appropriate portion of the measurement subsystem.

Output Subsystem The output subsystem implements the range, edge selection, control information, and data formatting for proper presentation on the front panel display.

Time Base The time-base subsystem is a phase locked loop and divider chain driven from a 100-MHz crystal oscillator. This subsystem will provide two clock phases to drive the internal control and decision logic. Each phase will be 200.0000 ± 0.0001 MHz.

The time base will also provide the following frequencies that are used to define the measurement windows for the events and frequency measurements and provide the counting frequencies for the time interval and period measurements.

- Frequency—200.0000 ± 0.0001 MHz
- Period—100.0000 ± 0.0001 MHz
- Time Interval—100.0000 ± 0.0001 MHz
- Events—10.00 ± 0.01Hz

Measurement Subsystem The measurement subsystem provides the logic and control to execute the measurements of time and frequency.

- The frequency measurement will be implemented by opening a window for 1.00 ± 0.01 seconds. During the time the window is open, the measurement subsystem will gate the unknown input frequency into a 7 stage binary coded decimal (BCD) counter. When the window closes, the counter will contain the value of the unknown frequency.

The activities necessary to execute a frequency measurement are given in the following diagram.

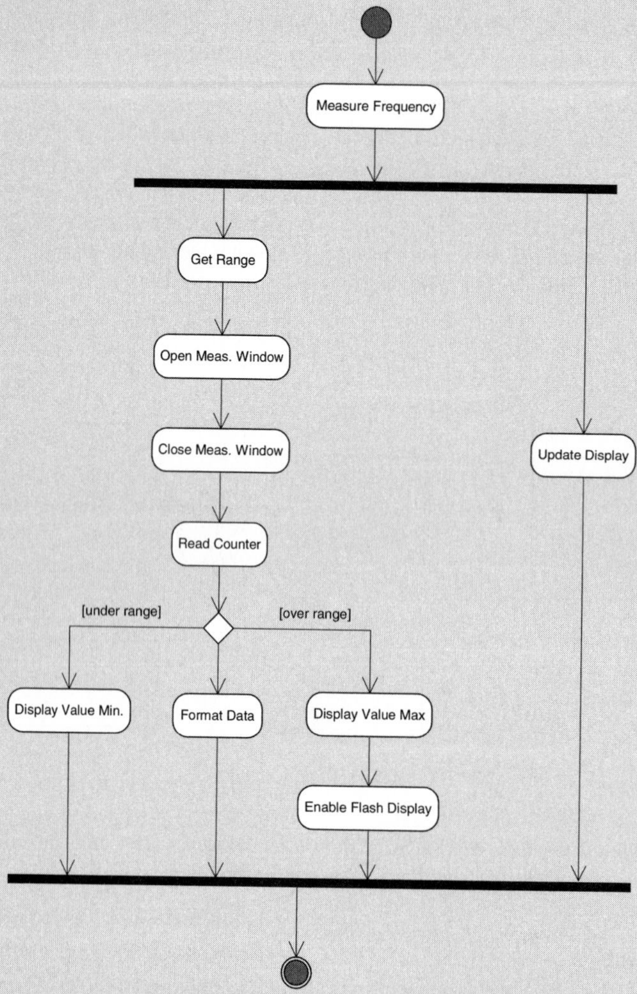

- The period and time interval measurements will be made by opening a window on the specified signal edge. While the window is open, a frequency of 100.0000 ± 0.0001 MHz will be gated into a 7 stage BCD counter. When the window closes, the counter will contain the values of the unknown time interval.
- The counter will contain the number of events that occurred during the measurement interval.
- The events measurement will be made by opening a window for 1.00 ± 0.01 seconds for the fast mode and 3600.0 ± 0.1 seconds for the slow mode. During the time the window is open, the measurement subsystem will gate the unknown input to a 4 stage BCD counter. When the window closes, the counter will contain a measure of the number of events that occurred during the time interval.

Power Supply Subsystem The power supply subsystem will provide the following voltages at the specified current levels to the internal logic.

```
+5.0 ± 0.01 VDC @ 10 A
+15.0 ± 0.01 VDC @ 500 mA
-15.0 ± 0.01 VDC @ 500 mA
```

At power on, there shall be a negative going reset signal. That signal shall remain in the low state for a minimum of 10 ms and shall have the ability to sink up to 1A.

Display The instrument display shall display the results of the selected measurement on a 6-digit, 7-segment red LED display. The layout of the major features and functions is given in the earlier diagram.

Operating Specifications

The system shall operate in a standard commercial/industrial environment.

Temperature Range 0–85C

Humidity up to 90% RH noncondensing

Power Automatic line voltage selection

- 100–120 VAC ± 10% 50, 60, 400 Hz ± 10%
- 220–240 VAC ± 10% 50, 60 Hz ± 10%

The system shall operate for a minimum of 8 hours on a fully charged battery.

Net weight/size 2.75 kg, H: 90 mm x W: 200mm x D: 300 mm

The system time base shall meet the following specifications.

Temperature stability 0–50 C

$< 6 \times 10^{-6}$

Aging Rate

90 day	$< 3 \times 10^{-8}$
6 month	$< 6 \times 10^{-7}$
1 year	$< 25 \times 10^{-6}$

Reliability and Safety Specification

The counter shall comply with the appropriate standards

Safety: UL-3111-1, IEC-1010, CSA 1010.1

EMC: CISPR-11, IEC 801-2, -3, -4, EN50082-1

MTBF: Minimum of 10,000 hours

9.8 SYSTEM SPECIFICATIONS VERSUS SYSTEM REQUIREMENTS

System Design Specification, System Requirements Specification

Examining the different steps that have been outlined up to this point, we find a lot of duplication. It would seem that the *System Design Specification* and *System Requirements Specification* are just different names for the same thing. But they are not; requirements and specifications are fundamentally different types of descriptions.

> ***Requirements*** Give a description of something wanted or needed. They are a set of needed properties.

what
how well, how,
System Design Specification

Generally, requirements come from the marketing or sales department, and they represent the customer's needs. The requirements definition and specification is not concerned with the internal organization of the system. Rather, it is intended to describe *what* a system must do and *how well* it has to do it, not *how* it does it. The *System Design Specification* is generated by engineering as an answer to and a description of how to implement the requirements. Then the two groups negotiate and iterate until the requirements and specifications are consistent.

> ***Specification*** is a description of some entity that has or implements those properties.

The system specification is a means of translating the description of needs into a more formal structure and model.

System Design Specification
Hardware, Software Specifications

Nonetheless, every part of the design needs another specification. Specifications can and do exist at various levels as the design is refined and elaborated. Different things must be quantified and at different levels of detail during different phases of the product development. The *System Design Specification* may require that an intersystem communication channel transfer data at the rate of 10,000 bytes per second at a specific bit error rate. The detailed *Hardware* and *Software Specifications* establish the requirements and constraints on their respective components to be able to meet those specifications.

A specification is a precise description of the system that meets stated requirements. Ideally, a specification document should be

- Complete
- Consistent
- Comprehensible
- Traceable to the requirements
- Unambiguous
- Modifiable
- Able to be written

System Specification

The specification should be expressed in as formal a language or notation as possible, yet readable. Ideally, it should also be executable. A *System Specification* should focus precisely on the system itself. It should provide a complete description of its externally visible characteristics, that is, its public interface. External visibility clearly separates those aspects that are functionally visible to the environment in which the system operates from those aspects of the system that reflect its internal structure.

9.9 PARTITIONING AND DECOMPOSING A SYSTEM

System Design Specification

At this point in the design cycle, all of the system requirements have been identified, captured, and formalized into the *System Design Specification*. The next step is to move inside the system and begin the process of specifying and designing the functionality that gives rise to the external behavior.

Throughout all of the previous discussions, modularity and encapsulation have been repeatedly stressed. We will look first at why such an approach is recommended and then at what should be considered as the process of decomposing and ultimately partitioning the system into hardware and software modules proceeds.

9.9.1 Initial Thoughts

So, let's get to the first question, "Why do we do this?" Reuse is one important reason. With each new design, one should always look to the previous project as well as the next one. What can be used from the last project to expedite the development of this one? How can the current design be implemented to support a future feature? Can parts of this design be used in future projects?

Second, many compilers generate object code in segments, one for each module. Such actions may place size restrictions on the individual modules. Poor module builds can significantly affect memory accesses, increase cache misses, promote thrashing, and significantly reduce performance.

Third, often, work assignments are made on a module-by-module basis. Module boundaries should be defined so as to minimize interfaces among different parts of the system. Such a practice simplifies the process of subcontracting some of the work as well. Security issues also play a role when subcontracting is considered. Whether working for a toy company or on a sensitive government project, one needs to consider what information to make available to outside vendors. By properly decomposing a system, the portions that can be outsourced and those for which control over should be retained can be more easily identified.

Fourth, the modules should be packaged with the goal of stabilizing the module interfaces during the early part of the design.

Fifth, partitioning the system into well-defined, loosely coupled modules helps to ensure a safe and robust design. Such an approach helps to prevent a failure in one part of the system from propagating into and affecting another.

progressively refines

The importance of partitioning a new design should be evident; the next step is to examine the process for doing so. The process starts with the top-level system and then *progressively refines* that model into smaller and more manageable pieces that can more easily be designed and built.

Initially, the focus is on a functional view of the system rather than on specific pieces of hardware and software. It is important first to understand and to capture the behavior at a high level. The next step is to map those functions, that functionality, onto the hardware and software as necessary to satisfy the constraints identified during the initial phases of the design. Partitioning is important during the early stages of the development of the system first as an aid in attacking the complexities of a large system and later as a guide in arriving at a sound physical architecture.

As we begin to think about organizing the system into the collection of pieces that will implement the customer's requirements, one should look at the problem from both a high-level view *and* a more detailed view. It is important to remember that developing a partition is not a one-time process; it is not necessary to be perfect the first time. The partitioning process will probably need to be done several times before a satisfactory and workable decomposition is achieved.

Prior to beginning the system partition, keep some general thoughts in mind.

1. Remember that with every rule or guideline, there must always be room for exceptions.
2. Each module should solve one well-defined piece of the problem.
3. Mixing functionality across modules makes all aspects of the development and support process much more difficult. By doing so, one can easily create noodle hardware and spaghetti code. Future changes to such modules will be very difficult to implement and can easily lead to unexpected side effects and unrelated pieces of the system suddenly not working.

   Although it is desirable to have well-defined modules, with simple interfaces, that solve nicely encapsulated pieces of the problem, in embedded applications sometimes one is not able to do so because of performance or economic constraints.

   The system should be partitioned so that the intended functionality of each module is easy to understand.

   If other parties can understand the design, then they will be able to maintain it and to extend it as necessary throughout the product's lifetime. Remember, over half of the engineers involved in embedded systems design do not do new designs; they maintain and enhance existing designs.

   During development, easy to understand designs will lead to fewer surprises as the design nears completion. All interested parties should be able to follow the design and comment as the process unwinds. A design that is too complex quickly discourages early criticism. People will not take the time to learn what the system is to do. Unfortunately, such early acceptance often is replaced by later rejection and potentially major redesign efforts. Although it is important to be proud of one's work, one should always seek out other constructive ideas.
4. Partitioning should be done so that connections between modules are only introduced because of connections between pieces of problem.

   One should not put a piece of functionality into a module just because there is nowhere else for it to go.

5. Partitioning should ensure that connections between modules are as independent as possible.
6. Once again, like things should be kept together. Such a practice helps to reduce errors. Partitioning is also done to help meet the economic goals of the design.

When forming partitions, the process must be considered from a number of viewpoints. Taking only a single point of view or neglecting any one can have significant long-term effects. At the end of the day, the system may meet neither the customer's expectations nor the performance specifications.

functional

coupling, cohesiveness

loosely coupled, highly cohesive modules

As the decomposition process proceeds, the design should first be considered from a *functional* point of view. The outcome from the decomposition steps is a functional model and that can be used to define the system architecture. Among the many things that should be considered, two that should appear early in the process are the *coupling* and the *cohesiveness* of the modules into which the system is being decomposed. The goal is to develop *loosely coupled, highly cohesive modules*. Let's see what these mean.

9.9.2 Coupling

coupling

Coupling is a heuristic that provides an estimate of how interdependent the modules are. Tightly coupled modules will generally utilize shared data or interchange control information. As module interdependence increases, so does the complexity of managing those modules, and the more difficulty one will have in

- Debugging the design during development
- Troubleshooting the system in the event of field failures
- Maintaining the modules and system
- Modifying the design to add features or capabilities

The major goal is to make the system's modules as independent as possible and to reduce or minimize coupling.

> ***Design Heuristic*** The lower the coupling, the better job that has been done during partitioning.

During the early stages of the design, think about the following to help to reduce coupling:

1. Eliminate all unessential interaction between modules.
   If a particular piece of functionality or shared parameter is not part of the intended task of two modules, then eliminate it.
2. Minimize the amount of essential interaction between modules.
   While this sounds the same as the previous point, it is not. If an early analysis establishes that some interaction with another module is necessary, effort should be made to reduce the complexity of that required interface. The goal is to keep things simple.
   Some of the ways to help to reduce complexity include:
   a. Reduce the number of interconnections between modules and thereby reduce the number of pieces of data that must flow between modules.
   b. Try to take the most direct route to a signal or piece of data as appropriate. In some cases the best implementation is to use a proxy as an interface to a signal or piece of data. In general, however, it is best to reduce the number of modules involved.

c. In general, avoid using shared global variables. A better method is to pass data into a module via its parameter list or calling interface.
With embedded applications, however, at times such sharing is critical to meeting time constraints.

d. Avoid arcane interconnections between or among modules. A guiding principle underlying all design is to keep things simple.

e. Don't hard code values into a module's parameter list or calling interface unless absolutely necessary. We must do so on occasion when an interface module or port must be at a specific address location; do not make this a general practice.

3. Loosen the essential interaction between modules, if possible.
Unless the environment demands a high degree of coordination between several modules to accomplish a task or to ensure error-free communication, simply pass the module the information necessary to get the job done. Thereafter, wait for an indication that the task has completed. Execute some other part of the task.

9.9.3 Cohesion

coupling, cohesion

An idea related to *coupling* is *cohesion.* The notion of coupling addresses the partitioning of a system; cohesion addresses bringing the pieces together. Cohesion is a measure of strength of the functional relatedness of elements in a module. The goal is to create strong, highly cohesive modules whose elements are genuinely and tightly related to one another. Conversely, elements should not be strongly related to elements in another module. We want to *maximize* cohesion and *minimize* coupling.

maximize, minimize

The use of cohesion as a reliability and quality metric has been around since the mid-1960s. A number of years of refinement and integration of the ideas of many people studying various designs and design approaches led Constantine and Yordon, *Structured Design*, Prentice-Hall (1979), to formulate a cohesion scale based on an ease of maintenance metric.

Let's look at several different kinds of cohesion.

Functional Cohesion The module implements a single task, and all comprising elements contribute to the execution of that one task.

Sequential Cohesion The module implements a task as a sequential set of procedures. The output data of each procedure becomes the input data to the next. All of the comprising elements are involved in one of those procedures.

Communicational Cohesion The module implements a task that has a number of procedures working on the same set of input data such as an image processing task.

Procedural Cohesion The module implements a number of procedures that may or may not be related to a common activity. Control, rather than data, flows from one procedure to the next.

Temporal Cohesion The module implements a number of unrelated procedures or activities that are sequentially ordered in time.

Logical Cohesion The module implements a number of procedures that are possible alternative methods for accomplishing a task. A subset of those alternatives is selected by an outside user to actually execute the task.

Coincidental Cohesion The module aggregates a number of unrelated procedures. Such cohesion, or lack thereof, should not be used.

We compare the different kinds of cohesion and coupling from several different perspectives in Table 9.0. The ranking is Excellent/Easy = 5 . . . Poor/Difficult = 1.

Table 9.0 Comparison of Coupling and Types Cohesion from Different Perspectives

Cohesion	Coupling	Ease of Modification	Ease of Understanding	Ease of Maintenance
Functional	5	5	5	5
Sequential	4	4	4	3–4
Communicational	3	3	3	3
Procedural	2–3	2–3	2–3	2
Temporal	1	3	3	2
Logical	1	1	2	1
Coindicental	1	1	1	1

Cohesion and coupling analyses provide a good set of metrics by which to begin to assess the high-level architectural aspects of a design. Remember, however, that both are guidelines. The work to ensure that the design is solid and that it is thoroughly tested still needs to be done.

There are plenty of good designs that require tightly coupled modules; CDMA cell phones are a good example. One can have tightly coupled multiprocessor designs as well as designs based on message passing. The implication is not that one design is right or wrong, or better than the other; it is just how it was done to meet the requirements.

9.9.4 More Considerations

spatial

resource

With today's systems, a *spatial* point of view is often essential. This is an external view of the system, and it yields a distributed functional architecture. With such a view, performance and communication costs are taken into consideration. Closely associated with the spatial viewpoint is that of *resource* allocation; again, this is an external view. Such efforts result in a "resource architecture." Once again, performance, costs, and dependability are factors that must be considered.

hardware

software

Finally, one must consider the *hardware* and the *software*. Decomposition becomes a design process that leads to a hardware architecture as was discussed earlier. Now performance must be considered. As embedded developers, we are playing a direct role in the design and selection of the hardware platform as well as the software environment. Making trade-offs intelligently in these two areas can take us a long way toward developing a safe, robust, and high-quality/high-performance system.

9.10 FUNCTIONAL DESIGN

functional

The purpose at this stage of the design is to find an appropriate internal *functional* architecture for the system. We are beginning to formulate *how* the requirements that have been identified can be implemented. The current focus is on analyzing the problem. Through such analysis, a somewhat loose understanding of the design can be transformed into a precise description. The result of such a process is a detailed textual or graphical description of the system. The end result is a complete consistent functional definition of the required tasks.

take-off, fly, land

To establish an appreciation of a functional model of a system, consider an aircraft. If an aircraft is the system to be designed, the top-level functional model should probably not consist of more than three major functions: *take-off, fly,* and *land.* With such a view, we make no statements about such issues as the support structure for the aircraft (wheels, skies, pontoons), the propulsion system (jet, rocket, propeller), or the method of lift (wings, conventional aircraft or blade, helicopter). Early on, these are not important; such decisions can be postponed until later. The advantage of such an approach is early flexibility—time to explore before beginning to constrain the system. A functional description simply formalizes the intended behavior of the design.

The functional description should be written to be understood by those knowledgeable in the application domain and by those who will do the hardware and software development. The specification must also be such that it can be reviewed by the many diverse and interested parties and tested against reality. If it is too complex to read and understand, no one will read it. When the completed project is delivered, it is too late to discover that the customer's view and developer's view of reality are totally different.

A first functional decomposition is carried out based on a search of essential internal variables and events in the system. The design process then consists of successive refinements or decompositions for each function (using exactly the same process) until elementary or leaf functions are obtained. Such decomposition forms a *functional model* of the system. The model expressed by the collection of such functions should be sufficient to verify the design quality and to evaluate system behavior and performance.

functional model

During modeling and verification, the system's operations and associated performance requirements can be allocated to the internal functions and the relations between such functions can be defined. Such a process also allows one to estimate the expected performance of the system.

As with the requirements specification, ideally, the functional model should be executable so as to permit verification with respect to the specification. There are tools today that will allow us to do this. One such tool is a behavioral Verilog model. UML is also beginning to make executable models a reality.

The functional model is different from the specification and also from the physical architecture that will be developed next. The specification describes the *external* behavior of the system; the functional model targets the *internal* behavior that will lead to the external. The architectural model addresses the physical hardware and software components onto which the functions are mapped.

external

internal

In Figure 9.20, we illustrate a first-level decomposition of a simple input/output task. The system must receive data from and transmit data to the outside world. Associated with the task is a code conversion to ASCII.

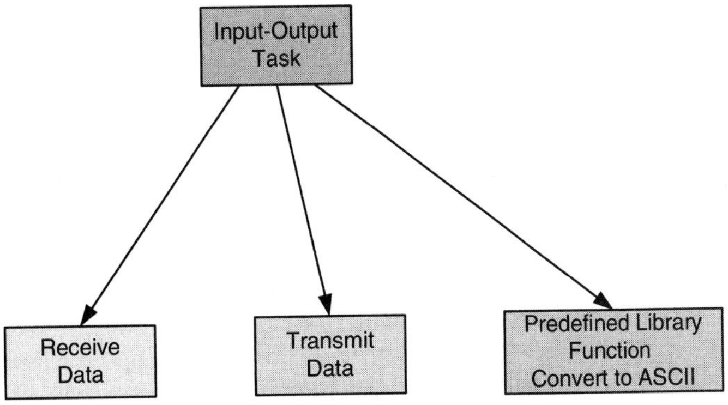

Figure 9.20 First-Level I/O Task Decomposition

Each of these functions may be further decomposed as necessary. If required, the second-level functions may also be successively refined to give the detail needed to understand and to execute the design.

The next step in the analysis is to identify the messages that flow between the user or other active external objects and the system as well as the internal signals that flow between the major functional blocks. We identify how the user will interact with the system in order to make it do what it is intended to do.

Let's now apply our understanding of partitioning to the functional design of counter system. First and foremost, we must continue to postpone the idea of working with the specific data structures, bits, bytes, microprocessors, or array logics for a while longer. Though important later in the process, at the moment, they limit exploration and can bias the functional decomposition of the system

EXAMPLE 9.0

Designing a Counter (Cont.)

Identifying the Functions

The first diagram, in Figure 9.21, presents an aggregation of the objects in the system. That aggregation includes both the environment and the counter being designed.

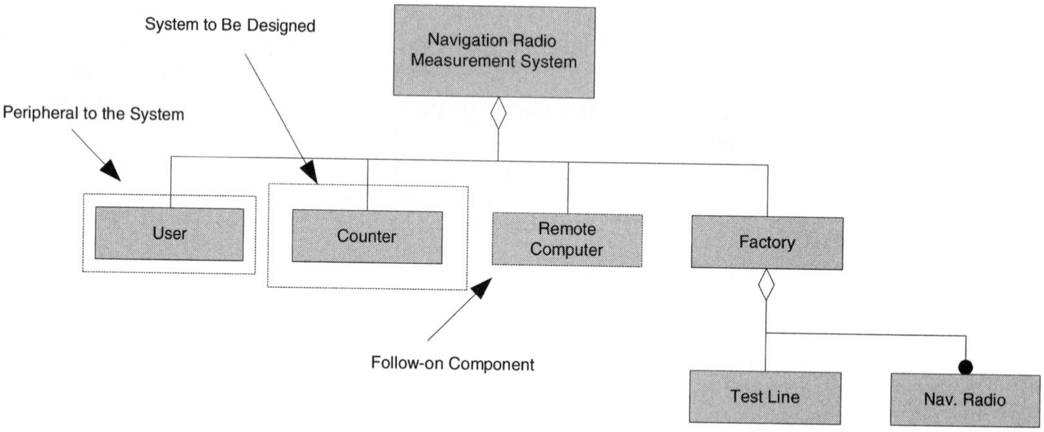

Figure 9.21 A Model of the Environment and the Counter as an Aggregation of Objects

The model of the measurement system is expressed as a collection of

- The user
- The factory
- The future remote computer
- The counter

aggregation, composition

The factory is an aggregation of test lines and numbers of navigation radios that must be tested. Note that we are using the looser term *aggregation* rather than *composition* here.

The design specification provided a high-level block diagram of the system. For this problem, such a diagram provides a good starting place for the initial hierarchical decomposition of the system. Figure 9.22 elaborates on the counter component and gives one possible decomposition for that system.

presentation of information, bringing in information

The interface to the outside world is segregated into two functional blocks. The first is associated with the *presentation of information* to the user. The second is charged with *bringing in information* from the user and other tasks necessary to support the measurement. Both functional blocks are further decomposed into local operations versus remote operations.

Such a choice is made in the first case because the display is considered to be an output function and control to be an input function. In the second case, two different sets of functionality and different

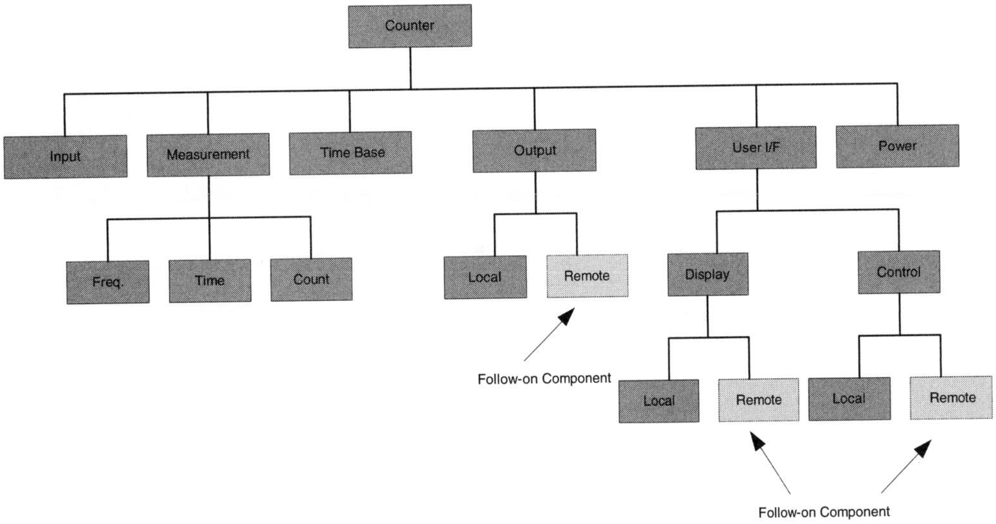

Figure 9.22 A Possible Hierarchical Decomposition of the Counter System

grammars for expressing the user's commands are anticipated. Front panel operations tend to be rather straightforward; remote operations can be a bit more involved. Certainly, these are not the only choices. The drawing in Figure 9.23 captures the interface between the counter and the surrounding environment.

The next drawing, in Figure 9.24, expresses a functional partitioning and the signal flow between the major functional blocks.

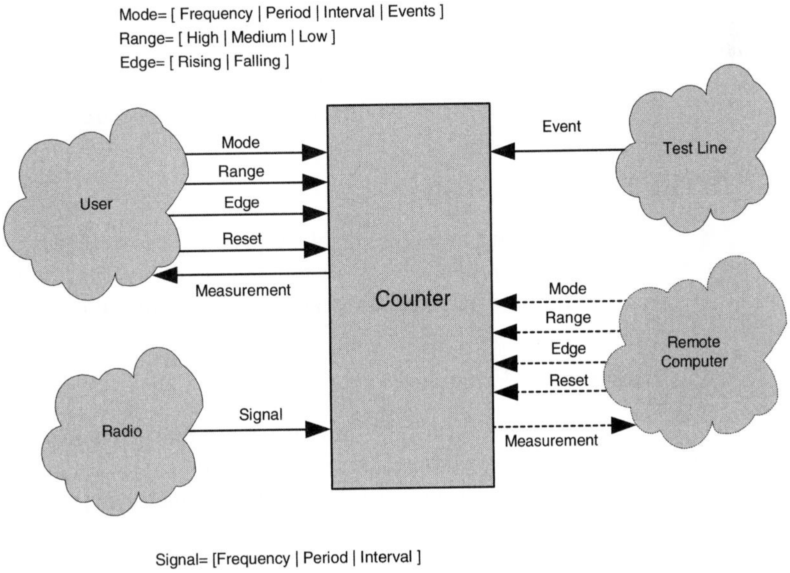

Figure 9.23 The Counter–Environment Interface

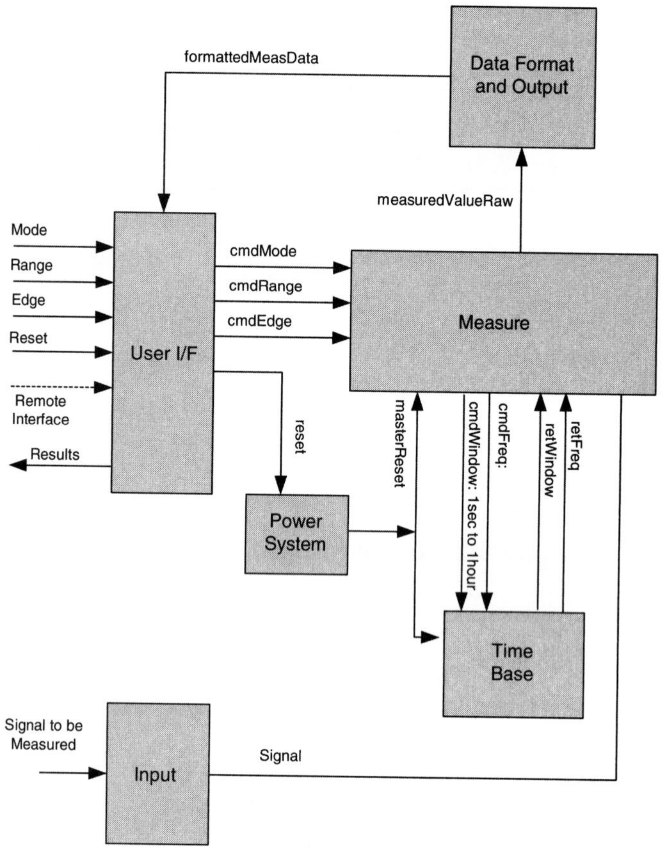

Figure 9.24 A Functional Partition of the Counter System

Next the system architecture is formulated, and functions are mapped onto the hardware and software blocks comprising that system.

9.11 ARCHITECTURAL DESIGN

In executing an architectural design, the goal is to select the most appropriate solution to the original problems based on exploration of a variety of architectures and the choice of the best-suited hardware/software partitioning and allocation of functionality.

9.11.1 Mapping Functions to Hardware

mapping

The view of a partition now changes to reflect a more detailed understanding of the system and involves the *mapping* or allocation of each functional module onto the appropriate physical hardware or software block(s). Such a mapping completely describes the hardware implementation of the system.

As noted earlier, one should always endeavor to broaden the scope of the architectural design so as not to preclude possible future enhancements. Certainly, this involves a balancing act between generality and practicality as well as simultaneously satisfying other specified requirements. Nonetheless, the plan should be for a system that evolves over its lifetime; if this is done well, add-ons, which are inevitable in today's systems, will be much easier.

The major objective of the architectural design activity is the allocation or mapping of the different pieces of system functionality to the appropriate hardware and software blocks. Work is based on the detailed functional structure. The performance requirements are analyzed, and finally the constraints that are imposed by the available technologies as well as those that arise from the hardware and software specifications are taken into consideration.

The important constraints that must be considered include such items as

- The geographical distribution
- Physical and user interfaces
- System performance specifications
- Timing constraints and dependability requirements
- Power consumption
- Legacy components and cost

Such constraints are strong factors for deciding which portions of the system should be implemented in software and which portions should be done in hardware.

The proper allocation of the pieces of functionality is generally obvious for a significant part of the system. For those, it is easy to say, "this part must be hardware or this part must be software." The power supply, display, communications port, and the package containing the system are necessarily hardware. The operating system and associated drivers, it is generally agreed, are necessarily software.

The situation is expressed graphically as in Figure 9.25. There is a gray area between the hardware and software where the implementation approach is not precisely defined. In selecting the components that make up this area, one is making engineering decisions or trade-offs of speed, cost, size, weight, as well as many other factors.

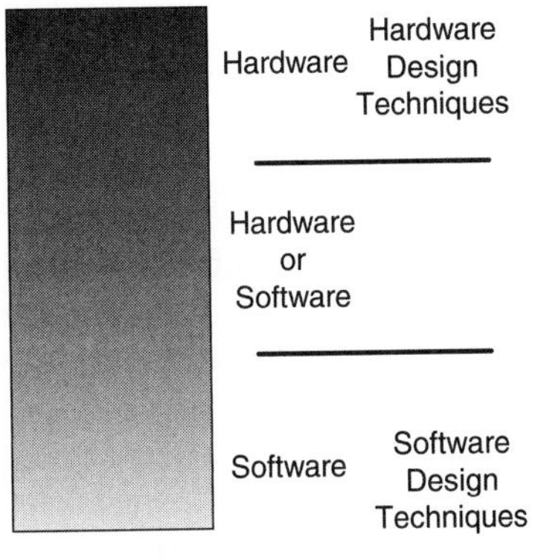

Figure 9.25 The Hardware-Software Continuum

mapping

The *mapping* onto such an architecture completely defines the hardware implementation of the system. The hardware portion of the system is specified by a physical architecture that may comprise one or more microprocessors, complex logical devices or array logics, or/and custom-integrated circuits. It is important to remember that with today's systems, these microprocessors and microcontrollers can take on a variety of personalities: (CISC) Complex Instruction Set, (RISC) Reduced Instruction Set, or (DSP) Digital Signal Processer.

For most applications, a substantial portion of the software can be easily separated from the hardware and thereby permit its concurrent development. The remaining part, that in the boundary, is more difficult to partition and falls under what is called *co-design.*

co-design

9.11.2 Hardware and Software Specification and Design

The system specification gives a detailed quantification of the system's inputs, outputs, and functional behavior based on our original requirements. The functional decomposition is analogous to those steps taken in defining the requirements. As the architecture of the design now begins to take shape, the objective is to determine, as fully as possible, the specifications for each of the physical components in the system and the interfaces between them. The specification of the hardware for the entire system is decided by defining the hardware architecture and all its properties. The specification of the software is obtained by defining the software implementation or block diagram (using any of a variety of methods) for each software component of the architecture.

Each functional subset to be implemented in software is described by a detailed software specification that expresses the priority of each task and the spatial (data coupling) and temporal dependence relations between tasks. UML diagrams, including detailed state charts, timing diagrams, sequence diagrams, activity diagrams, and collaboration diagrams, can all be very useful at this stage in the design.

A software implementation may or may not use a real-time kernel. With an off-the-shelf real-time kernel, the development time is reduced, but not the factory cost or time-based performance specifications. For systems that do not use a real-time kernel (which represents 80 to 90% of small and medium systems), one can achieve a better optimization of the design when addressing high-speed, hard real-time constraints. Under such circumstances, the solution is being hand tailored to the specific problem rather than adapting a general-purpose solution to a specific case.

For the software design, the following must be analyzed and decided:

- Whether to use a real-time kernel
- Whether several functions can be combined in order to reduce the number of software tasks and if so, how?
- A priority for each task
- An implementation technique for each intertask relationship

When it is appropriate, a real-time kernel or the services of an operating system can be used. In general, the main objective is to reduce the complexity of the organizational part in order to reduce the size and complexity of the software and the resulting development, testing, and debugging times.

Rate-Monotonic Scheduling

Under such circumstances, a frequent choice is the *Rate-Monotonic Scheduling* policy (this will be discussed shortly; more frequently executed tasks are assigned a higher priority). Permanent functions (those that run continuously without an activating event) and some cyclic functions without timing constraints are usually implemented within a background task.

For the implementation of intertask relationships, it is desirable to use procedure calls as much as possible, thereby simplifying the organizational part and reducing the intertask overhead. Such an implementation is only possible between functions with increasing relative priorities. Tasks triggered by hardware events are invoked through the processor interrupt or polling systems.

For each specific subpart of the system in which the partition is not obvious, a detailed specification is written; the final hardware/software partition is determined through a process of successive refinements, as was done in the earlier decomposition process. Each hardware/software partition must also include the hardware interfaces and the software drivers to support any intercomponent communication.

The result is a complete mapping of all remaining functions and functional relations onto the hardware architecture. Among the important criteria that we strive to optimize are:

- Implementation (or factory) cost
- Development time and cost
- Performance and dependability constraints
- Power consumption
- Size

EXAMPLE 9.0

Designing a Counter (Cont.)

Developing the Architecture

The next step in developing the counter begins with formulating the hardware architecture; the software architecture follows. We then map each of the functions identified earlier onto the architecture. The following diagram, in Figure 9.26, presents the hardware components.

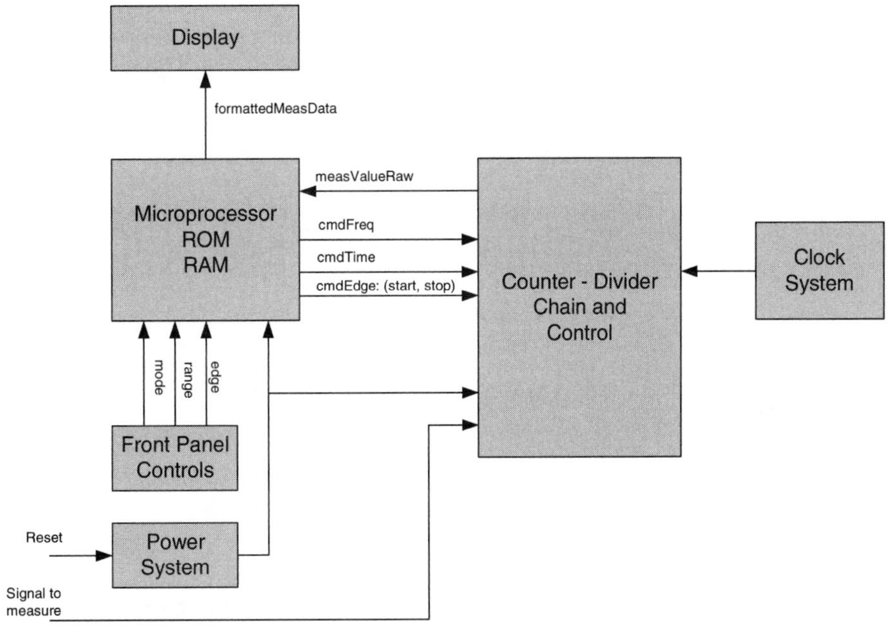

Figure 9.26 The Hardware Architecture of the Counter

In the design, the microprocessor, the display, the front panel controls, and the power system are clearly hardware. In theory, the clock system as well as the counter-divider chain and associated control could be implemented in software. However, the frequency at which the counter is intended to operate (200 MHz) biases the decision toward a hardware solution.

front panel task
display task
measurement task
counter-divider chain control block, output task

Figure 9.27 identifies the major software tasks, shared data, and I/O in a data and control flow diagram. The *front panel task* is continually checking (directly by polling or indirectly by interrupt) the state of the front panel for user input. A change in input is captured and passed to the *display task* (which will update the display accordingly) and to the *measurement task.* The *measurement task* issues the appropriate commands to the external *counter-divider chain control* block. At the end of each measurement, the raw data is read from the counter-divider and passed to the *output task.*

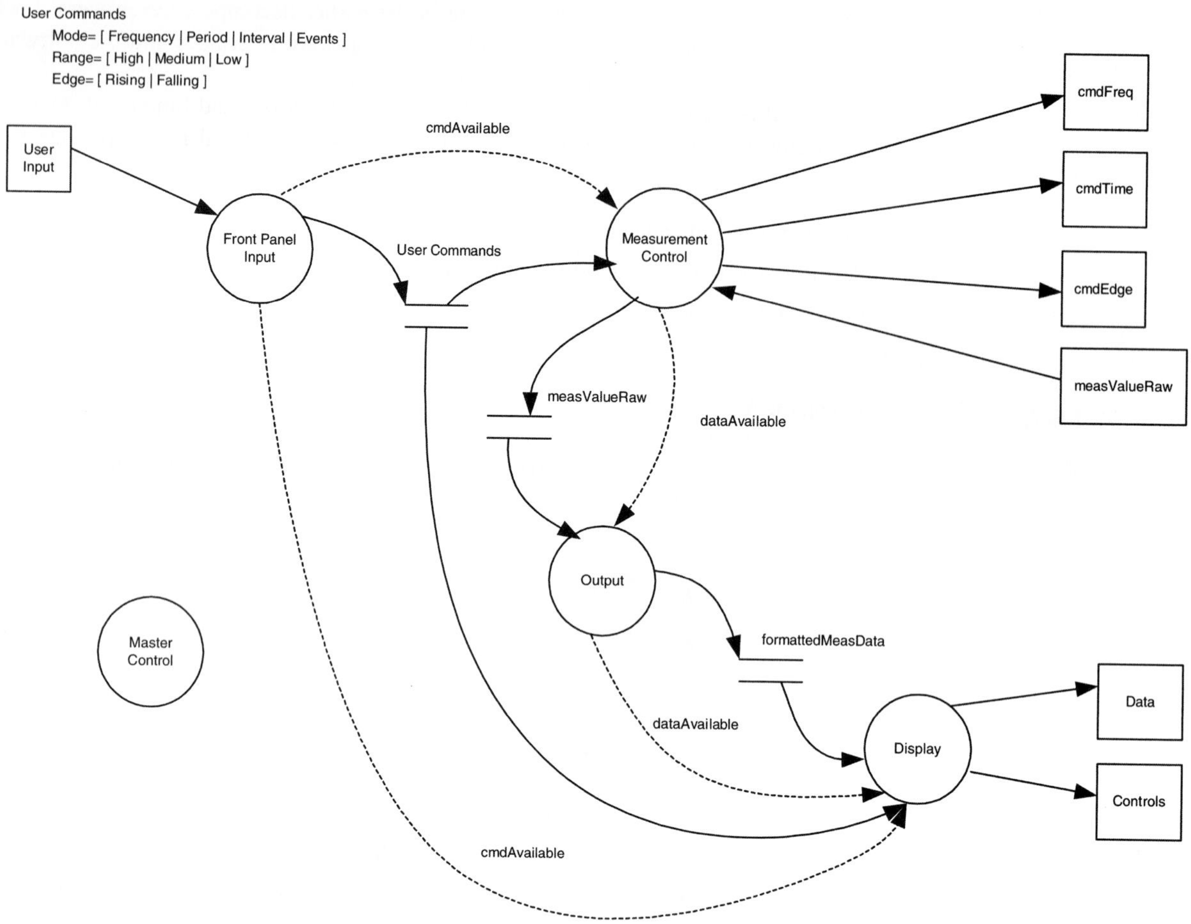

Figure 9.27 A Data and Control Flow Diagram for the Counter System

output task, display task
master control task

The *output task* properly formats the data and sends it to the *display task* for display on the front panel. The *master control task* manages the scheduling of all tasks and performs any necessary housekeeping or other duties as necessary.

9.12 FUNCTIONAL MODEL VERSUS ARCHITECTURAL MODEL

functional, architectural

A good question that one might ask at this stage is, "Why is it necessary to design a functional model and an architectural model?" We start by looking at any system—hardware, software, a mix—it doesn't matter. It quickly becomes evident that the internal organization of a system is based on a collection of components and interconnections among them. An appropriate model has to include elements both at the *functional* level and at the *architectural* level to be able to represent and evaluate hardware/software system.

9.12.1 The Functional Model

interacting functional elements

The functional model describes a system through a *set of interacting functional elements.* The design proceeds at a high level without initial bias toward any specific implementation. We have the freedom to explore and to be creative. The behavior of a functional element is best described with a hierarchical and graphical model. The functional modules will interact using one of the following three types of relations:

shared variable

- The *shared variable relation*—which defines a data exchange without temporal dependencies

synchronization

- The *synchronization relation*—which specifies temporal dependency

message transfer

- The *message transfer* by port—which implies a producer/consumer kind of relationship

We will discuss each of these relations when we study processes and interprocess communication. All of them are critical in the design and development of today's embedded systems.

9.12.2 The Architectural Model

physical architecture

The architectural model describes the *physical architecture* of the system based on real components such as microprocessors, arrayed logics, special-purpose processors, analog and digital components, and the many interconnections between them.

9.12.3 The Need for Both Models

mapping, functional

architectural configuration

These two views, when considered separately, are not sufficient to completely describe the design of contemporary systems. It is necessary to add the *mapping* between the *functional* viewpoint and the *architectural* one. Such a mapping defines a (functional) partition and the allocation of functional components to the hardware elements. This is also called *architectural configuration.*

functional model

The *functional model,* located between specification model and architectural model, is suitable for representing the internal organization of a system. It explains all necessary functions and the couplings between them—expressed from the point of view of the original problem. Using such a scheme leads to a technology-independent solution. In particular with this kind of model, all or part of the description can be implemented in either software or hardware.

architectural structure

The functional model is the basis for a coarse-grain partitioning of the system. Such a partitioning leads naturally to the selection of which functions to implement in hardware or software. The *architectural structure* is finer grained and generally follows from the functional model; the architecture may also be imposed *a priori.*

9.13 PROTOTYPING

The prototype phase leads to an operational system prototype. A prototype implementation includes:

- Detailed design
- Debugging
- Validation
- Testing

Prototyping is naturally a bottom-up process because it consists of assembling individual parts and fleshing out more and more of the abstract functionalities. Each level of the implementation must be validated. That is, it must be checked for compliance with the specifications on the corresponding level in the top-down design.

Hardware and software implementations can be developed simultaneously and involve specialists in both domains, hopefully reducing the total implementation time. Often this does not happen in reality. Typically, the software leads hardware. Nonetheless, a complete solution can be generated and/or synthesized for both hardware (in the form of ASICs and standard cores, etc.) and software (in the form of hardware/software interfaces). The resulting prototype can then be verified.

9.13.1 Implementation

Activities in this step are highly dependent on the technology used. Remember, the prototype is a tool for understanding and confirming system design. It is a proof of concept. A word of caution: one should not rush the analysis or design to get to the prototype. Also, one should not be afraid to throw the prototype away. For small projects, it sometimes works to try to transform the prototype into the final product. For large projects, it is usually more of a proof-of-concept that almost never can be migrated.

Those who hurry through the design and coding because a lot of testing needs to be done are going to be spending long nights getting things to work and even longer nights with unhappy customers. For some reason, customers do not seem to have much of a sense of humor when the failure of a product they have purchased has just cost them several million dollars. If you are selling to a general market, *your company* has just lost several million in R&D costs and you still do not have a product to take to market. So now, it is even worse, because you have missed an opportunity for sales revenue with a product that you cannot sell because it is poorly conceived, or it still is not ready.

9.13.2 Analyzing the System Design

We have been studying the system design process while moving from requirements to a design. Now that the first-level design is in place, it must be critically analyzed. This step provides several important checks on the design. First and foremost, it verifies that the solution meets the original requirements and specifications. At this stage in the design flow, it may also be necessary to trade off different architectural and functional aspects of the design. Such trade-offs must be made according to criteria identified in the original specification.

The first step entails a static analysis of the system. At this stage, the architecture of the system is examined. Of immediate interest is *not* how the system will behave at runtime. Rather, the major objectives are to have a system that is easy to understand, build, test, and maintain. All too often new designers (and, unfortunately, some who should know better), proclaim "but it works!!!" For systems that we are proud to put our name on, getting it to work is only one very small part of the job. Moreover, it is easy to make a one-off version of any system to work. Making one or ten million of the same design in production that will ultimately work safely and reliably is a much larger challenge.

The main goal in any design is to work ourselves out of a job. We want the design to be so reliable and so well documented that any future modifications and extensions will be effortless. The caveat, of course, is that one must also know what sufficient reliability is and when to stop documenting. Well-documented means just enough so that people can easily understand the design, but not so much that it becomes the primary deliverable.

9.13.2.1 Static Analysis

Static analysis should consider three areas:

1. Coupling
   We have examined this aspect of a design already. Coupling is related to the number and complexities of the relationships that exist among the various system modules. It also gives a measure of the implications of a change. The goal is loose coupling.

2. Cohesiveness
Another issue that is worth stressing again is cohesiveness, which is a measure of the functional homogeneity of elements that comprise the modules. This applies to both the components and the relations. One must consider both external and internal views. External cohesion begins with the appropriate naming and meaning for elements. Internally, the structure and relationships among components is analyzed. For example, coupling through shared data is more cohesive than messages. Messages imply a temporal dependency.

3. Complexity
functional, behavioral
Two kinds of complexity are identified: *functional* and *behavioral*.

Functional complexity is characterized by:

- The number of internal functions and relational components
The goal is to keep these small. Generally, as the number of functions and relations decreases, so does the complexity of the design. Note: this does not mean to sacrifice clarity.
- Interconnections among elements comprising each module
The earlier discussion of coupling applies here as well. Keep things simple.

Behavioral complexity is characterized by:

- The number of inputs and outputs
Once again, the target is a smaller number.
- The length and ease of reading and understanding the description of the module
If several paragraphs or a page of written text (in sub 6 point font) are required to describe the function of one of the modules, that module is probably too complex. To simplify such descriptions, use tables, logical equations, or pseudo code.
- The flow control through the module and the number and structure of state variables
Have a single major thread of control through the module and keep the number of states small.

9.13.2.2 Dynamic Analysis

The objective in performing a dynamic analysis on the system is to determine how it will behave in a context that closely approximates the ultimate working environment. Dynamic analysis considers the following:

- Behavior Verification
operational
The goal is to ensure that the behavior of the system, in its operating environment, meets the *operational* specification. That is, does it perform the functions it was intended to perform? This verification includes behavior at the boundaries of those functions. To be able to do so, of course, we need a good specification in the first place.
- Performance Analysis
performance
Performance Analysis ensures that the system, in its operating environment, meets the *performance* specification. The focus is on specific values for inputs and outputs. We'll talk about this in a later chapter.
- Trade-off Analysis
A trade-off analysis is necessary to determine the optimal solution for the given constraints and objectives. Such an analysis, based on only a small set of performance criteria, may affect the ultimate success or failure of the product.

9.14 OTHER CONSIDERATIONS

The two additional complementary and concurrent activities that need to be considered in today's business world are capitalization and reuse and requirements and traceability management. Let's look briefly at capitalization. Design reuse is one of the central threads in this text.

9.14.1 Capitalization and Reuse

Capitalization

Capitalization and reuse are activities that are essential to the contemporary design process. Proper and efficient exploitation of intellectual properties (IPs) is very important today. Intellectual properties are designs, often patented, that can be sold to another party to develop and sell as (a part of) their product. The company MIPS, for example, designs computer architectures. It does not actually do any implementation itself; the design is its product.

Reuse

Any consideration of component reuse is an activity to be performed during the functional and architectural design phases of the project. Note: one can sometimes consider these during prototyping as well.

present, future

One of the main purposes of reuse is to help designers shorten the development life cycle. Component reuse is facilitated in two ways: *present* and *future*. Reuse is supported in the present by identifying a set of external (existing) functional or architectural components that can satisfy some parts of desired functionality. Future reuse is supported by identifying components in the system under design that will be reusable in other projects or products.

To be reused, a component needs to be

- Well defined
- Properly modularized
- In conformance to some interchange standard

A well-thought-out, well-designed module will be much easier to adapt to a new situation than one that someone pieced together for some ad hoc purpose and barely got working. The same is true for a portion of a well-modularized system.

If, during the design phase, one makes decisions with an eye to modules that could be reused, the chances of such reuse are greatly enhanced. Finally, if the goal is for a module to have wider applicability than a local venue, then the designs must accommodate existing national and international standards. With today's international market growing daily, it is incumbent upon us to design to such standards.

Once again, the real-world intrudes, and trade-offs are part of the process. When designing for reusability or striving for a modular design, other factors need to be considered. If there is not enough ROM space for the code if it is designed to be completely modular, the design may be modified to be very application specific. While the decision might create problems in the future, we will end up with a noncompetitive product if the budget is exceeded.

9.14.2 Requirements Traceability and Management

Requirements Traceability

Requirements traceability refers to the ability to follow the life of a requirement (from the original specification) in both the forward and reverse directions through the entire design process and the design. Traceability is potentially a one-to-many relationship between a requirement and the components it relates or traces to (or that implement it). An accurate and complete record of traceability between requirements and system components provides several important pieces of information through the product life cycle. Among these are the following.

- The means for the project manager and (potentially) the customer to monitor the development progress.
- A path that can be used during the verification and validation of the product against the original specification. Knowing where and how a specified requirement has been implemented facilitates confirming that the requirement has been faithfully implemented.
- A means of identifying which hardware or software modules are affected if a requirement changes.

Requirements Management

Requirements management addresses

- Requirement modifications
- Changes
- Improvements
- Corrections

During the design, such changes are difficult to avoid for many reasons. Therefore a clear procedure that facilitates a way to accommodate such modifications has to be used during the whole design process.

9.15 ARCHIVING THE PROJECT

When the product has finally been released to production, some work remains to be done. During development, a tremendous amount of important design information has been produced. Most of that information must be retained for a variety of reasons. If the product follows the typical life cycle, bugs that must be fixed will be discovered as customers use the product; there will be future revisions; new features will be expected and added; and the next generation product will build on the current, to name just a few. The obvious question is, What must be saved?

The problem of dealing with what to archive is no different from confronting the original design. That said, we use the same approach and start at the top. The typical project will have had many contributors. A basic list can include

- Product planning
- Design and development
- Test
- Manufacturing
- Marketing
- Sales

Each group will have information, knowledge, documentation, and tools that will be important in the future. Let's focus on the technical subset of these: design and development, test, and manufacturing. In earlier studies of safe and robust design, we identified a typical software project directory structure. That diagram is presented in Figure 9.28 for reference.

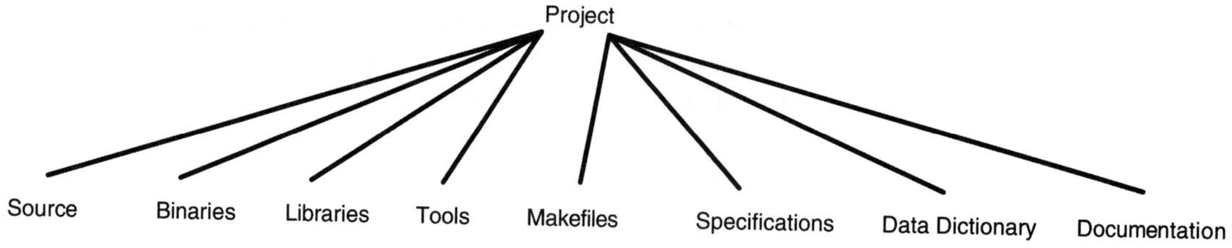

Figure 9.28 A Typical Project Software Directory

Each of the groups participating in the development should have a similar directory documenting their portion of the project. The project directories and all their contents are one of the main items that must be archived. These are obvious.

Now, let's consider the less obvious. Today, software, firmware, *and* software tools are essential to the design and development of any embedded system. If the source code or the ability to rebuild from sources is lost, any future work on the project will be seriously impaired. Today, source code no longer means just the C, C++, Java, or assembler listing in electronic form or on magnetic media.

In previous years, hardware was generally supported by hand-drawn hard-copy documentation. If a drawing was lost, it could be regenerated by skilled designers by reverse engineering the existing part. Today a rich set of CAD (computer-aided design), CAM (computer-aided manufacturing), and IC and FPGA modeling and synthesis tools have supplanted the old methods.

All of those tools run on a computer and are routinely modified or updated by their vendor. All of those tools also have a product life cycle and ultimately will no longer be supported. If the archived tools will not execute on today's computer running today's operating system, they are of little use. Today, in addition to archiving the end product, archiving the complete development environment—computer, hard drive, operating system, and so on—is well worth considering. The documentation for the tools should be included in that list as well.

virgin build

An essential step, once the collected archive has been set, is to conduct what is called a *virgin build.* A virgin build begins with a completely new environment or context. Next, the archived tools are installed and set up. The tools are run, as appropriate, and tested to see if the designated components of the product can be recreated. If the process fails, the missing components must be identified, added to the archive, and the process repeated.

Too often, over the span of the product development we build simple special-purpose tools to help manage the tasks of developing and building the system, and when creating the archive we forget that they are an essential part of the build or synthesis. The virgin build quickly reveals when those tools are missing.

Today, the financial investment in all aspects of a project development is significant. Retaining and protecting that investment for future use is an important closure to the cycle.

9.16 SUMMARY

In this chapter, we have introduced and studied the major phases of the development process for embedded systems. The more detailed aspects of that process are covered in conjunction with the study of the design and test of the specific hardware and software elements of the system.

We have seen that design is the process of translating customer requirements into a working system. We have learned that the complexity of contemporary systems now demands a more formal approach and more formal methods. Following a formal specification, we look at ways of partitioning the system as a step in developing a functional design. We formulate a functional model and then develop and refine it. Eventually, we map our functional model on to the architectural structure. We conclude with a working prototype, meanwhile, analyzing the system design both during and after development.

We have looked at several other important considerations in the design life cycle. These include intellectual property, component/module reuse, and requirements management and the archival process.

9.17 REVIEW QUESTIONS

Introduction

9.1 The chapter opened with a discussion of several kinds of things that should be considered when beginning the design of a new product. Please identify and briefly discuss each of these.

9.2 Why are deadlines and cost important when developing a product?

9.3 Why is it important to consider reliability, safety, and quality in an embedded design?

9.4 Why is product documentation important?

The Product Life Cycle

9.5 What is a product life cycle?

9.6 The chapter introduces and discusses several different product life-cycle models. What are the basic goals that each model shares?

9.7 What are the four life-cycle models presented in the chapter?

9.8 Identify and briefly discuss the steps that comprise the Waterfall life-cycle model.

9.9 Identify and briefly discuss the steps that comprise the V life-cycle model.

9.10 Identify and briefly discuss the steps that comprise the Spiral life-cycle model.

9.11 What is the underlying motivation of the rapid prototyping life-cycle model?

9.12 The chapter identified five steps usually found in successfully completed projects. Identify and briefly discuss the intent and purpose of each of these.

9.13 What is intellectual property?

The Design Process—Requirements Identification

9.14 An essential first step in designing a product is identifying the requirements. What are the major goals of this step?

9.15 For whom is the requirements documentation written?

9.16 Why is it important to consider the system's operating environment when identifying requirements?

9.17 Why should requirements identification not consider the detailed hardware and software components of the design?

9.18 What are some of the important things to identify when considering and specifying the system's operating environment?

9.19 What are some of the important things to identify when considering and specifying the system?

The Design Process—Design Specification

9.20 The requirements specification provides an external view of a system. What view does the design specification provide?

9.21 What is the primary purpose of the design specification?

9.22 For whom is the design specification written?

9.23 The chapter identified three major areas that should be examined and considered when formulating a design specification. What are these?

9.24 The chapter identified five sets of constraints that should be examined and considered when formulating a design specification. What are these?

9.25 What are the major differences between system requirements and design system specifications?

The Design Process—Partitioning a System

9.26 What is the major reason for partitioning a system?

9.27 The chapter outlines several general guidelines for partitioning a system. What are these, and why is each important?

9.28 What is the meaning of the term *coupling* with respect to partitioning a system?

9.29 What is the meaning of the term *cohesion* with respect to partitioning a system?

9.30 The chapter identifies several different kinds of cohesion. Identify and briefly describe each of them.

The Design Process—Functional Design

9.31 What are the purpose and goals of a functional design?

9.32 For whom is the functional description written?

9.33 What is one of the first steps that should be undertaken when starting a functional design of a system?

9.34 What is the difference between a specification and a functional model of a system?

The Design Process—Architectural Design

9.35 What are the purpose and goals of an architectural design?

9.36 For whom is the architectural design developed?

9.37 What are some of the major constraints that should be considered when formulating a system architecture?

9.38 What is the relationship between the functional design of a system and the architecture of the system?

9.39 What are some important criteria that should be considered when mapping a functional design onto an architecture?

The Design Process—The Prototype

9.40 What is the purpose of the prototype phase of a product design?

9.41 What steps are included in the prototype phase?

9.42 For whom is the prototype phase conducted?

The Design Process—The Analysis

9.43 What are the goals and objectives of the analysis phase of a product design?

9.44 The analysis process should entail both a static and a dynamic analysis. What are the major objectives of each?

9.45 A static analysis of a system design should consider three areas. Identify and briefly describe each of these.

9.46 A dynamic analysis of a system design should consider three areas. Identify and briefly describe each of these.

The Design Process—Other Considerations

9.47 Why should capitalization and reuse be considered to be important activities in the development of any product?

9.48 What is the purpose of requirements traceability and management? Why is it important?

9.49 What are some of the essential parts of a product development process that should be archived at the end of that process?

9.18 THOUGHT QUESTIONS

Introduction

9.1 The chapter opened with a discussion of several kinds of things that should be considered when beginning the design of a new product. Identify and briefly discuss each of these.

9.2 Deadlines and cost are important when developing a product. Discuss why, citing several real-world examples to illustrate your point.

9.3 What are the short- and long-term consequences of ignoring or not paying sufficient attention to reliability, safety, and quality in an embedded design? Give several real-world examples to illustrate your point.

9.4 Documentation is an important part of any embedded product. Give several examples of the kinds of documentation that are necessary to support a product.

The Product Life Cycle

9.5 The chapter identified five steps usually found in successfully completed projects. Discuss the possible consequences of skipping or reducing any of these steps.

9.6 Discuss the reasoning behind and the benefits of developing a new product according to one of the life cycles discussed (or one that was not covered that you may be aware of).

9.7 Why is the intellectual property content of a product important today?

9.8 What kinds of things can be considered to be intellectual property?

9.9 Identify and elaborate on the consequences of not protecting the intellectual property content of a product.

The Design Process—Requirements Identification

9.10 Why is identifying the requirements of an embedded system an essential first step in the design?

9.11 Discuss the consequences of not identifying the requirements prior to beginning design.

9.12 What factors about the system's operating environment should be taken into consideration when identifying system requirements? Please give specific examples of environmental factors that should be considered, coupled with the kinds of products for which such considerations might apply.

9.13 How would you answer someone who tells you that they can keep all the requirements in their head, that there's no need to write all of them down?

9.14 What role does the requirements specification play in the debug and test of an embedded design?

The Design Process—Design Specification

9.15 What role does the design specification play in the debug and test of an embedded design?

9.16 Please give specific examples of the kinds of information that should be included in a design specification. Explain your choices of information.

9.17 How much detail should be specified when describing and quantifying the system's behavior and input and output signals? the environment?

9.18 The design specification is considered to be a living document. What does this mean? Why is this important?

9.19 A version control system is generally used to manage code revisions on most embedded designs. Should the requirements and design specifications be managed in a similar manner? Explain your thinking.

The Design Process—Partitioning a System

9.20 During which stage of the design of a system should partitioning occur?

9.21 Discuss possible trade-offs that one might consider when formulating a system partition. What are the pros and cons of each of the items that you suggest?

9.22 Once a partition has been achieved, is there ever any reason to revisit the process? Please explain your answer and your reasoning?

9.23 What are some of the consequences of designing modules that are highly interdependent?

9.24 What are some of the steps that one can take to reduce coupling in a design? Explain the specific benefits gained from each.

9.25 What are some of the consequences of designing modules that are loosely cohesive?

9.26 What are some of the steps that one can take to improve cohesion in a module? Explain the specific benefits gained from each.

The Design Process—Functional Design

9.27 What are some of the primary aspects of an embedded system design that are captured through a functional design?

9.28 To what level of detail should a functional decomposition of a stem proceed?

9.29 Why is it important to retain links between the system requirements specification and the functional modules identified during the functional decomposition process?

The Design Process—Architectural Design

9.30 What are the purpose and goals of an architectural design?

9.31 For whom is the architectural design developed?

9.32 What are some of the major constraints that should be considered when formulating a system architecture?

9.33 What is the relationship between the functional design of a system and the architecture of the system?

9.34 What are some important criteria that should be considered when mapping a functional design onto an architecture?

The Design Process—The Prototype

9.35 What is the purpose of the prototype phase of a product design?

9.36 What steps are included in the prototype phase?

9.37 For whom is the prototype phase conducted?

9.38 In the chapter, the designer was cautioned that prototypes should never turn into a final product. Discuss the pros and cons of such a statement.

The Design Process—The Analysis

9.39 What are the goals and objectives of the analysis phase of a product design?

9.40 The analysis process should entail both a static and a dynamic analysis. What are the major objectives of each?

9.41 A static analysis of a system design should consider three areas. Identify and briefly describe each of these.

9.42 A dynamic analysis of a system design should consider three areas. Identify and briefly describe each of these.

The Design Process—Other Considerations

9.43 Why should capitalization and reuse be considered to be important activities in the development of any product?

9.44 What is the purpose of requirements traceability and management? Why is it important?

9.45 What are some of the essential parts of a product development process that should be archived at the end of that process?

9.19 PROBLEMS

Designing Systems

In the problems in this chapter, we will begin to put the formal design methodologies that we have learned into practice. In several of the earlier chapters, we approached these systems from either the hardware or the software side. We will now bring those together.

Let's now take each of those systems and apply the methods that we have studied in this chapter. For each of these systems, we will begin with identifying requirements and move to the architectural stage. Certainly, any of these can easily be carried into the laboratory as more extensive projects.

For each system, consider that you have started your own company and are going to specify, design, and manufacture the product. Thus, you are the one establishing the formal design specifications.

For each system

(a) Identify the requirements. Be sure to identify any safety and reliability requirements that might be appropriate.

(b) Write a basic requirements specification. Refer to the example in the chapter.

(c) Formalize the requirements in a design specification. Refer to the example in the chapter.

(d) Develop a functional design for the system. Identify the major functional elements of the system and the intercommunication between each function. Be certain to include the interaction with the environment with your design.

(e) Execute the architectural design. Map each of the functions onto the hardware and software.

9.1 Design an automatic coffee pot with the following capabilities.

The controls must include the ability to set the start time on a 24-hour clock, reduce the temperature to warming and annunciate when the brew cycle is complete, and stop water flow if the pot is removed from its receptacle.

9.2 Design a digital watch with the following capabilities.

The controls must include 12-hour time expressed in hours, minutes, and seconds, AM and PM tracking and annunciation, alarm, and the ability to set the alarm and time values.

9.3 Design a washing machine with the following capabilities.

The controls must include the ability to set water temperature, washing start times, modes (presoak, normal, permanent press, delicate), and annunciation of temperature, times, and mode.

9.4 Design an automatic oven control with the following capabilities.

The controls must include the ability to set temperatures, cooking start and stop times, modes (bake, broil, clean), and annunciation of temperature, times, and mode.

9.5 Design a module implementing a four-seat passenger entertainment system with the following capabilities on a commercial aircraft.

The entertainment system should support the ability for each of the four passengers to program and control

- Movie selection
- Audio selection
- A gaming console

9.6 Design a seat belt—engine—door lock interlock with the following capabilities.

The engine cannot start if the seat belt is not fastened. The doors automatically lock when the engine is started.

9.7 Design a new toy bank that we see in Figure P9.29.

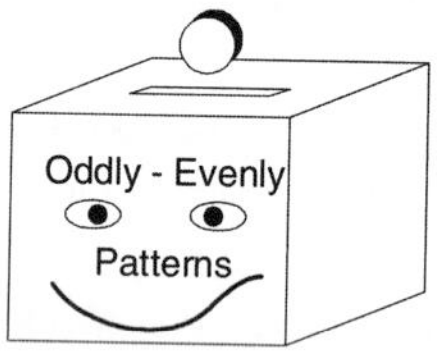

Figure P9.29

The toy is intended to let children have fun while learning to save money.

When the child puts in 0 or 2 coins—pennies, nickels, dimes, or quarters—the *ODDLY* eye will flash according to how much money was put in. If the little one puts in 1 or 3 coins, the *EVENLY* eye will similarly flash.

9.8 A new temperature monitoring system that utilizes an analog-to-digital converter to collect data at various points in a yogurt production process is to be designed. The control logic accepts the input signals shown and generates the output signals as specified in Figure P9.30.

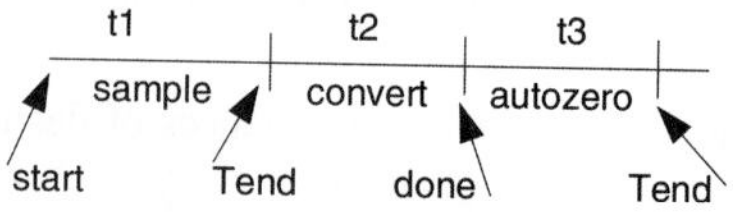

Figure P9.30

Upon receipt of a *start* signal, the system must cycle through the three time intervals—t1, t2, and t3—and command the following operations to take place: *Sample*, *Convert*, and *Autozero*.

The system is to respond to the input signals as shown in the diagram. At the end of time t3, as signaled by the T_{end} input, the system must return to its initial state and wait for a *start* input.

The times, t1–t3, are not inputs to the system; they merely identify the length of each interval.

The signals *start*, *done* and t_{end} are inputs to the system. They identify the start or end of the intervals as indicated.

The system must have several output signals to control the electronics doing the conversion. The control logic is in one room, and the analog-to-digital converter is in another. There is a limit to the number of wires in the cable connecting the two portions of the system.

The system must accept analog signals from eight different points around the tank where the yogurt is fermenting.

9.9 You have been hired by *Let There Be Lyght—Signals Abound, Ltd.* to design a traffic control system. The design your predecessor proposed failed at a critical time while he was in the middle of the intersection testing it.

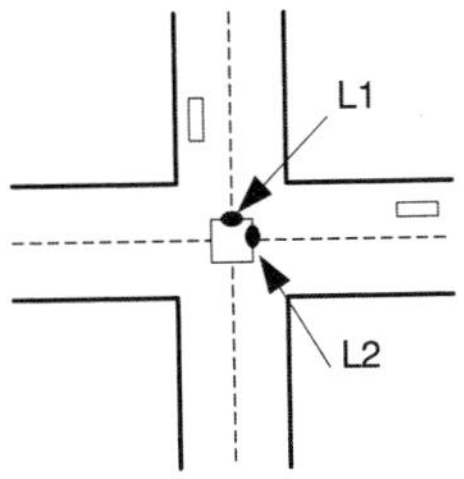

Figure P9.31

The intersection you must control is shown in Figure P9.31. Your design must meet the following specifications:

(a) Each light, L1 and L2, has two states, ON or OFF.

(b) If a car arrives at the intersection and the light in its direction is OFF, it may proceed through the intersection.

(c) If a car arrives at the intersection and the light in its direction is ON, the car must stop. A timer is started. At the end of six time units, the light is turned OFF, a second timer is started, and the car may proceed. After 12 time units have elapsed on the second timer, the light is turned ON again.

(d) The cars must not collide.

9.10 Your team is working on the audio portion of a larger home entertainment system. The system combines a mix of new and legacy components that must be understood and integrated into a high-quality system.

The volume control for the system is marked with the decimal digits 0–5. Based upon the input selection, the selector outputs the single BCD digit corresponding to the level selected. Selection 0 outputs BCD 0, selection 1 outputs BCD 1, and so on.

Our gain stage, however, requires a value in the range of 0–15. Thus, we must design a circuit that will multiply that single-digit BCD number by 3 to give us the proper value as shown in the block diagram in Figure P9.32.

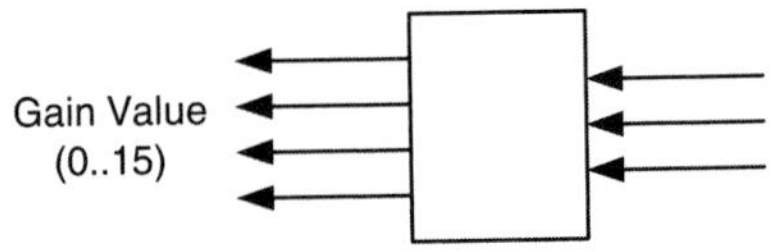

Figure P9.32

The input to the system may come from any of four different sources, a CD player, a DVD player, a Tuner, and a Joystick. Each of these devices produces a stream of data 4 bits wide.

Consequently, it is necessary to design a circuit that will select any of these data streams and route it into the system bus as shown in the block diagram in Figure P9.33.

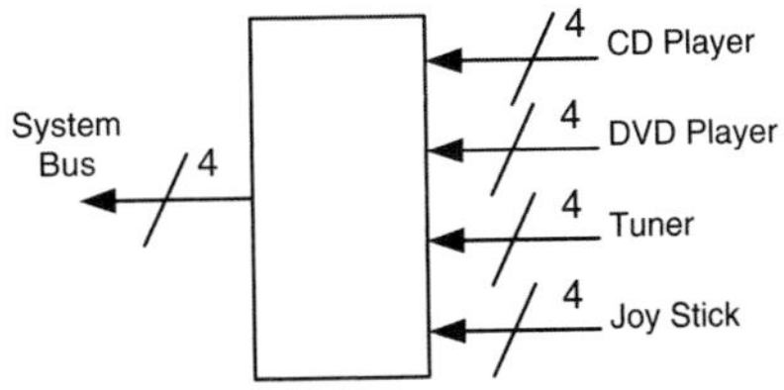

Figure P9.33

The output from the system may be sent to any of four different devices: a digital-to-analog converter, a digital display, a memory, and a glitzy graphic output.

Each of these devices requires a stream of data 4 bits wide. We must design a circuit that will route data from the system bus to any of these devices as shown in the block diagram in Figure P9.34.

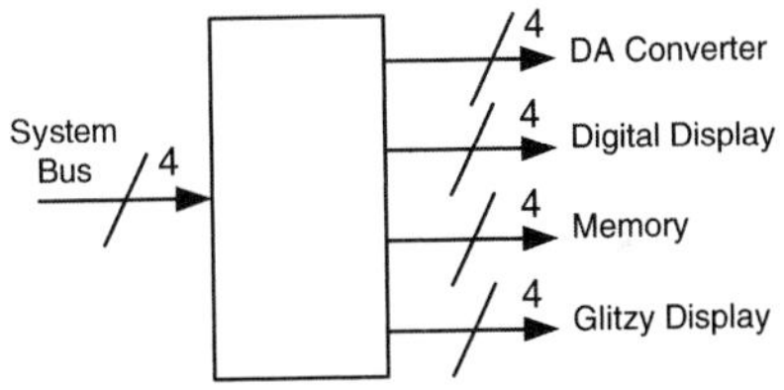

Figure P9.34

Although the system bus is 4 bits, internally the system controller uses an 8-bit word. Thus, data must be brought into the controller 4-bits at a time and assembled into an 8-bit word. We must design a *Data Assembler* as an interface between the system bus with the system controller as shown in the block diagram in Figure P9.35.

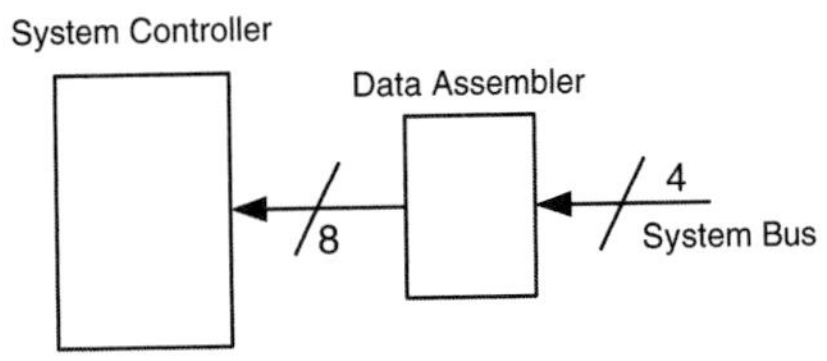

Figure P9.35

The *Data Assembler* must operate according to the following algorithm:

The first 4 bits appear on the bus accompanied by a *DV—Data Valid* signal.

The *DV* transitions from a logical 0 to a logical 1 to signify that the data on the bus is valid.

The 4 bits of data are loaded, in parallel, into the *most* significant 4 bits of an 8-bit shift register.

The *DV* transitions from a logical 1 to a logical 0.

An output signal, *Shift Left*, is generated to enable the shift register to be clocked four times.

The second 4 bits appear on the bus accompanied by a *DV—Data Valid* signal.

The *DV* transitions from a logical 0 to a logical 1 to signify that the data on the bus is valid.

The 4 bits of data are stored into the *most* significant 4 bits of the 8-bit shift register, thereby building up the complete 8-bit word.

The *DV* transitions from a logical 1 to a logical 0.

A *Load Complete* output signal is generated to signify that the data has been captured.

The system needs a clock source that has a 0.5-μs period as part of the system time base. An 18-MHz clock source is the only one available in the system.

9.11 Choose a system of your own.

Chapter 10

Hardware Test and Debug

THINGS TO LOOK FOR . . .

- The vocabulary of testing.
- The reasons for debugging, troubleshooting, and testing.
- The need for planning, specifications, test procedures, and test cases.
- Steps and heuristics for the debugging process.
- Identification and isolation of common faults in combinational and sequential circuitry.
- Tests for the designer and for the customer.

10.0 INTRODUCTION

Formulating a testing, debugging, or troubleshooting strategy should occur early in the design and development process. Ideally, it should be concurrent with the hardware and software development.

Most often, when we come up with an idea for any new design, we begin with a plan. We think about what the system will do; we think about its features, its capabilities, and its functionality. Debugging, troubleshooting, and testing are no different. We must have a plan. Without a plan, we can't be sure what we are looking for, or what it might look like if we find it, or when we are finished.

We will begin the study of test by introducing some of the relevant vocabulary. Understanding the terminology facilitates understanding the requirements of a test or test strategy, as well as the capabilities and limitations of the equipment utilized to execute the strategy. Earlier discussions of the effects of microprocessor word size on real numbers and subsequent computations now provide a basis for understanding, formulating, and interpreting measurements during the test process. We will then present a high-level model for a testing strategy; examine and motivate the need for planning, specifications, test procedures, and test cases; and examine several views, ranging from black to white box models, for approaching test. Finally, we will move into testing during the different stages of the product life cycle.

10.1 SOME VOCABULARY

As a prelude to the study of debugging and testing, it is important to understand some of the vocabulary of the area. Making measurements or generating signals is rather straightforward. Doing so properly is more of a challenge. In part, the vocabulary will illustrate where the challenges lie. As we do so (philosophy aside), it is important to recognize that physical entities exist, they have attributes, and, based on fundamental physics, those attributes have values independent of any ability to measure them or to replicate them. Herein lie most of the challenges.

True Value	The actual or inherent value of a physical quantity.
UUT / DUT	Unit or Device Under Test.
Accuracy	The measure of an instrument's capability to approach a true or absolute value.
Resolution	Measure of ability to discern the value of a measurement. Expression of the value measurement to 1, 2, or 3 decimal places provides three levels of resolution of the true value of the measured value.
Variance	Has no unit of measure. Variance provides an indication of the relative degree of repeatability of a set of measurements; that is, how closely the values of series of repeated measurements agree with each other.
Mean	Measure of the central value of a set of measurements and is given by the following equation. m_i is the value of an individual measurement. $$\text{mean} = \frac{1}{N}\sum_{i=0}^{N-1} m_i$$
Root Mean Square	The square root of the average of the squares of a set of values and given by the following equation. m_i is the value of an individual measurement. $$\text{rms} = \sqrt{\sum_{N} \frac{(y_i)^2}{N}}$$
Bias	Measure of how closely the mean value in a series of repeated measurements approaches the true value.
Residual	Measured value minus the mean.
Golden Unit	Unit whose behavior is completely known used as a standard.
Statistical Tolerance Interval	Estimate of the amount of measurement variability due to the test system, excluding the UUT variability. Test limits must be outside the STI limits.
Test Limits	Upper and Lower physical limits of the measurement.

With some of the basic vocabulary in hand, we begin by formulating a high-level strategy.

10.2 PUTTING TOGETHER A STRATEGY

debugging, testing, troubleshooting

Although the words *debugging*, *testing*, and *troubleshooting* all have the same general objectives, they represent three different tasks; they are undertaken at different times during the product's lifetime and with different underlying assumptions. Debugging is done during the early phases; testing is done before delivery; and troubleshooting afterwards. Debugging does not assume that the design has ever worked. *Debugging* is a process utilized to identify the cause of problems that occur in the design and implementation of a system as it is incrementally made to work. *Testing* begins with the assumption that the design is correct. It is a process charged with identifying any faults that may have been introduced during the manufacture of the system and ensuring that a properly working product is delivered to the cus-

troubleshooting

tomer. *Troubleshooting* begins with the premise that the design is correct and that the product worked at one time. The troubleshooting process seeks to identify which hardware component(s) have failed. The focus is on the hardware because, as was stated earlier in the discussion of safety and reliability, software components do not wear out and fail during use.

During the early stages of product development, any debugging plan is likely to be less formal. Most of it will probably be in the designer's head. Normally, the person who designed the circuit or the software *should* have a good idea of what to look for in terms of both Unit Under Test (UUT) functionality and the potential cause(s) of any anomalous or unintended behavior. Such is not always the case, however, so outlining a well-reasoned and orderly strategy is an excellent first step to help to focus the process.

As the design evolves and progresses through the development cycle, the need for a more formal approach becomes essential. In production, formal test procedures, based on a formal test plan, are required. In the field, troubleshooting procedures for the customer or the field service personnel are an essential part of a product's deliverables.

test plan, test specification, test procedure, test cases

In the ensuing discussion, the terms *test plan, test specification, test procedure,* and *test cases* are used in a generic sense. They apply equally to debug, test, and troubleshooting; only the initial presumptions and focus will differ for each. Although the main focus of the chapter is on the hardware side, the vocabulary, strategy, and philosophy apply equally well to the software side.

10.3 FORMULATING A PLAN

Testing in industry is not taken lightly. In companies that know what they are doing, it is a very serious task. For example, let's consider the approach of a very large manufacturer of electronic test and measurement equipment. For many large companies, there is a full, highly qualified test group. For smaller companies, the approach may be to take several senior engineers off design projects and have them thoroughly test a (new) product with the intention of finding problems before the design is approved for release to production.

stress testing

In some cases, the engineers have no knowledge of the specifics of the software or hardware inside of the box; they simply try to break it. Such testing is also called *stress testing* because the idea is to try to stress the software or hardware to break it or to find potential problems before they surface in a delivered product.

With a high-level overview, it is possible to begin to see how to put the high-level concepts to use. It is important to remember that testing is an integral part of all phases of product development, including design. Testing is done for four main reasons, as shown in Figure 10.0.

- To verify that any of the following performs as intended:
  - Code module or hardware prototypes
  - Subsystem or collection of subsystems
  - System interfaces
- To ensure that the system meets specification
- To ensure that any changes to the system work
  - Do not alter other intended functionality.
- To ensure that the system functions properly after being built

Figure 10.0 Principal Reasons to Test

System Test Plan
Test Specification

Each of these reasons has a different objective and scope and tests different aspects of the design. All such requirements should be found in the *System Test Plan* and subsequent *Test Specification.* Remember: like the System Requirements Document that was discussed earlier in the context of original design, the Test Plan identifies what tests need to be carried out. It describes in general terms the following information:

- What is to be tested?
- The testing order within each type of test
- Assumptions made
- Algorithms that may be used

Testing formality increases as the system moves toward the latter stages of development. Testing to ensure functionality can be reasonably informal; we still should have some form of plan. As the system begins to come together, formality must increase. Today's systems are becoming too complex. It is becoming too easy to miss critical, yet subtle, points.

Test Plan, what
Requirements Specification
how

A *Test Plan* begins the process. It describes in general terms *what* must be tested. Such a plan is based on the initial requirements captured in the *Requirements Specification.* It may specify *how* the testing will be carried out, the testing order within each general category of test (input, output, processing), as well as any assumptions that are made.

EXAMPLE 10.0

Consider a simple AND gate as a Unit or (device) under test UUT/DUT (see Figure 10.1).

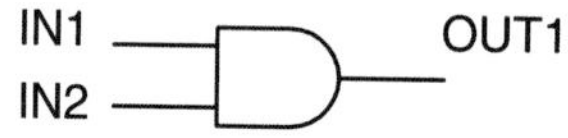

Figure 10.1 Unit Under Test

A test plan might be similar to the following,

> First verify the following static behavior of the device
>
> **a.** Ensure that the circuit functions as a logical AND gate according to its specified truth table.
>
> **b.** Verify the following signal values: V_{OHmin}, V_{OLmax}, V_{IHmin}, V_{ILmax}.
>
> Then verify its dynamic behavior.
>
> **a.** Confirm the following parameters: τ_{PDHL}, τ_{PDLH}, τ_{rise}, τ_{fall},

When putting an informal or formal test plan together, remember that the goal is to capture the essence of what must be tested. Keep things simple, precise, and to the point. The plan is not intended to be the next great novel.

The test plan establishes a strategy. During debugging, an informal test plan guides the process. During this phase, the behavior of the design is examined from a high level. Does a 5-volt signal appear on this pin? Does the counter work? Is the proper sequence of control signals being generated? Once again, informality, yet precision, is appropriate. As the design matures, testing must be based on concrete values and tolerances.

10.4 FORMALIZING THE PLAN—WRITING A SPECIFICATION

Test Specification
Requirements Specification,
Design Specification
what
how

The *Test Specification* evolves from and formalizes the test plan in a manner analogous to the relationship between the *Requirements Specification* and *Design Specification* studied earlier. The test specification includes a description of and specification for each test. As with the test plan, its focus remains on *what* is being tested. Analogous to the design specification studied earlier, the test specification also begins to establish *how* the tests are to be carried out and what the appropriate test stimuli and test limits should be. The test specification assigns specific values, limits, and tolerances to all of the parameters to be tested based on what was stated in the design specification. These values ultimately lead to constraints, requirements, and specifications for the test equipment to be utilized in creating and conducting the tests.

The test specification that is used during the design phase will often serve as a base on which to build the production test strategy. The full complement of tests utilized during the design phase to ensure compliance with the system specifications is generally not needed once the product is in production. Upon release to production, the design is assumed to be correct. A specific subset to confirm continued compliance is definitely appropriate.

The test specification for the UUT will now take on a more formal appearance as we see in the next example.

EXAMPLE 10.1

Verify the following static behavior of the device.

a. Ensure that the circuit functions as a logical AND gate according to its specified truth table.

IN1	IN2	OUT1
0	0	0
0	1	0
1	0	0
1	1	1

b. Verify the following signal values and limits:

V_{OHmin}	$2.4 \pm 0.003\ V_{DC}$
V_{OImax}	$0.4 \pm 0.001\ V_{DC}$
V_{IHmin}	$2.0 \pm 0.003\ V_{DC}$
V_{IImax}	$0.8 \pm 0.001\ V_{DC}$

Next, we must verify its dynamic behavior.

Confirm the following parameters:

τ_{PDHL}	15.0 ± 0.05 ns
τ_{PDLH}	15.0 ± 0.05 ns
τ_{rise}	5.0 ± 0.001 ns
τ_{fall}	5.0 ± 0.001 ns

The test specification provided a quantified description of what must be tested. Now, those tests must be carried out. During the debugging phase, the procedures and approaches may be based primarily on heuristic experience. In production, such an approach gives way to more formal methods.

10.5 EXECUTING THE PLAN—THE TEST PROCEDURE AND TEST CASES

Test Procedure, Test Cases, how

The *Test Procedure* and *Test Cases* specify *how* the test plan and specification are to be implemented and must provide the detailed lists of the necessary equipment and the steps for each test. These documents first decompose the plan into a series of blocks in much the same way we first decomposed the overall design into functional modules. Each block has a specific behavior, parameter, or set of related parameters in the system that it is testing. It gives the order of the test steps, values, and ranges of stimuli to be applied to the UUT during each test step. It specifies the values and ranges of the resulting measurements for each step. A series of (related) test cases is called a *test suite*.

test suite

Test case design is essential for testing at any level. The content of test cases will of course vary with the specific nature and intent of each individual test. During the early stages of test, one must test the design for behavior with following three kinds of values:

- Expected values
- Unexpected values
- The boundaries of expected values, inside, outside, and at the boundary

Recall the earlier comments in the chapter on safety and reliability.

The test values may be randomly generated test vectors or statistically based patterns. Such an approach is reasonable for combinational logic; however, it falls down on sequential types of relationships. See the earlier discussions of testing sequential circuits.

test coverage

To describe the efficacy of a test, the phrase *test coverage* is used. Test coverage provides the percentage of hardware, software, or system tested in a specific test or series of tests. When putting the test cases together, one must ensure that every path through the system is traversed at least once with signals of both polarities for the hardware cases and with variables of nominal and extreme values for the software cases.

During test, the emphasis is primarily on the system's behavior as manifest through various hardware signals. The purpose of the underlying firmware is to produce the intended or specified hardware behavior. Access to such hardware signals is gained through test points and/or test connectors. Access to software-driven results comes indirectly through those same signals. These are a signal or sets of signals, internal to the UUT, that can be observed directly via a probe point or connector that is incorporated into the circuit or system during design. When direct access to signals (inside of a complex component) is not available, boundary scan or similar techniques are used.

The test suite must evolve with testing. As faults are found and fixed, further tests are often suggested that may find similar faults that were not in the original test design.

The details of the test procedures strongly depend on the test system being used. Often such systems are a combination of commercial instruments such as power supplies, function generators, or digital word generators and proprietary circuits designed specifically for the test system. During debugging, one may use more sophisticated analysis equipment such as data generators and logic analyzers or oscilloscopes to help to verify the design. In production, it is assumed that the design is good; testing serves to identify defects introduced during manufacturing.

10.6 APPLYING THE STRATEGY—EGOLESS DESIGN

Let's now follow the test process from the initial stages of testing prior to release to manufacture. The process commences with testing for ourselves and then moves to testing for our customer.

egoless design

A key element of debug and testing during the early phases of the development life cycle is *egoless design*. What does design have to do with test? At this stage, testing begins with the initial specification as the basis for evaluating the preliminary designs. As we discussed in Chapter 8, such evaluation occurs through design reviews, code walkthroughs, and code inspections. One cannot let the belief that the best widget ever witnessed by humankind has just been designed to get in the way of an unbiased assessment of that design to determine if it is really the case. It is essential that ego not be part of the review process.

Design reviews, code walkthroughs, and code inspections must be done by someone else. As is often the case when proofreading one's own writing, schematics, or code, our brain ensures that they appear exactly the way we want them to rather than as it is actually written or designed.

10.7 APPLYING THE STRATEGY—DESIGN REVIEWS

During the early stages of product design, we are really testing for ourselves. That testing does not start when the first few pieces are on a lab bench or a couple of high-level algorithms have been coded up. In reality, it must begin much earlier during the design process.

A good first step in this direction is to hold design reviews as the design of the system progresses. Initially, such a review can ensure that everyone understands the high-level specifications and functionality of the system. Thereafter, a design review preceding the architectural phase can confirm detailed functionality. As the design progresses, at least one review prior to moving to prototype can ensure that the mapping from function to processors, FPGAs, or ASICs is sound. The formality of such reviews can vary with need. They can range from a simple exchange of drawings and code among the team members to detailed reviews with reviewers who are not directly involved with the project.

No matter how one chooses to proceed, it is important that the review be conducted in a constructive manner. All participants should recognize that a good review helps to ensure a more robust product at the end of the day.

10.8 APPLYING THE STRATEGY—MODULE DEBUG AND TEST

smoke test
debugging

As the design moves along the development cycle, the first prototypes of the individual modules are built and ready for a *smoke test* as the jargon goes. The phase now entered is called *debugging*. During this phase, the goal is to identify all of the different kinds of errors and faults that might have occurred in the development of a new or modified circuit, software module, or system.

> ***Caution:*** When running a smoke test. There is strong scientific evidence that most electronic circuits have an embedded smoke demon whose presence is essential to keeping the circuit working. Empirical evidence seems to support the theory since we can show that once the smoke demon is released from the circuit, it no longer works.

On both sides, we have design errors and oversights that have escaped earlier analysis, modeling, and reviews. On the hardware side we have implementation issues such as wiring errors (which often lead to stuck-at types of faults) and incorrect or incorrectly installed parts that have occurred during the prototype build.

To effectively debug the design, it is essential to know what behavior is being tested, how the necessary and appropriate stimuli are going to be produced, and how the results are going to be analyzed.

Black Box, White Box
Gray Box

The debug and early test of the design begins with the individual hardware and software modules. Once it is confirmed that these are operating as intended, they are integrated into larger and larger pieces; the process is repeated at each step. When debugging and testing modules, we generally recognize three kinds of testing, distinguished by the level of available knowledge of the internals of what is being tested: *Black Box*, *White Box,* and *Gray Box*. Such classifications and methods of test apply equally to hardware and software.

10.8.1 Black Box Tests

Although the more information one has available prior to formulating the test cases and test suite the better, complete and detailed information is not always available. The module may have a design that is proprietary to a particular vendor. Under such circumstances, complete information as to what signals the device required to effect the necessary outputs and the detailed characteristics of those output signals (both static state and dynamic state transition) is absolutely necessary. Without such information, one cannot ensure the proper or most efficient test of the module.

black box testing strategy

When debugging or testing such modules, we use what is called a *black box testing strategy*. Black box tests are data driven. Each module is tested from an external point of view. The method assumes no knowledge of system or subsystem internals. Consequently, black box testing requires that module interfaces be well thought out, clearly defined, and well understood.

Based on knowledge of the behavior of the module as expressed through its public interface, test cases can be generated and then applied. If a test case fails, the test process is aborted; the cause of the fault is identified and fixed. Continuing the test suite under a failed condition can yield results that in all likelihood are invalid. Depending on the rigidity of the test constraints, one may find it necessary to begin the test suite from the beginning rather than from the point of failure following a failure.

EXAMPLE 10.2

Consider the following system and its accompanying truth table in Figure 10.2.

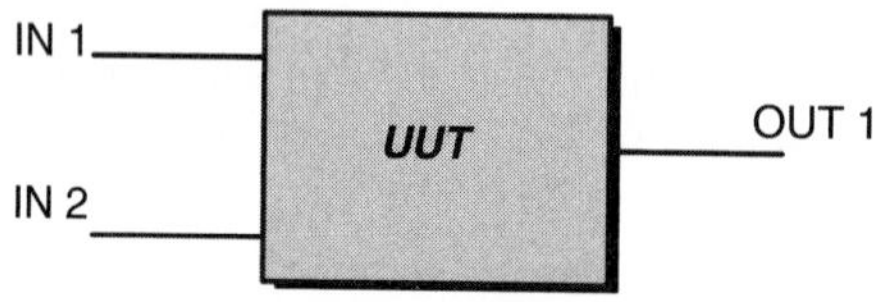

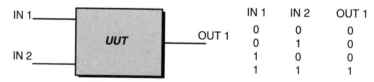

IN 1	IN 2	OUT 1
0	0	0
0	1	0
1	0	0
1	1	1

Figure 10.2 Basic System—Black Box View

If the relationship expressed in the truth table in the figure is the extent of the information that is available, then to ensure that the system is functioning properly, it is necessary to apply each of the input patterns and confirm the proper output. This is the best that can be done, or to put it another way, this is the minimum that must be done.

One of the significant weaknesses with black box testing is that, potentially, the test must be exhaustive. Such a test can be very time consuming, and it may miss certain paths or dead code inside the black boxes.

10.8.2 White Box Tests

white box testing strategy

When complete information about the internals of a module is known, we can use what is called a *white box testing strategy*. White box tests are logic driven. Each module is tested from the public interface as well as the internal point of view.

White box testing assumes perfect knowledge of system or subsystem internals. Test cases and the test suite are designed, generated, and applied to exercise every internal path and code segment. Like black box testing, a test case failure aborts testing until the fault is identified and fixed. Once again, potentially testing may resume from the beginning.

EXAMPLE 10.3

Let's now consider a somewhat different view of the system in Figure 10.3 with its accompanying truth table. The inside of the box is now visible.

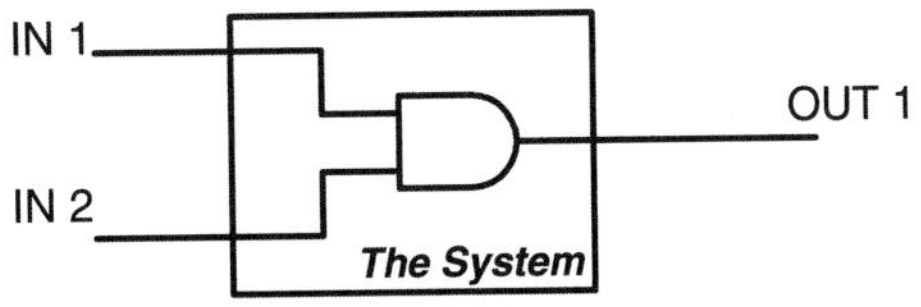

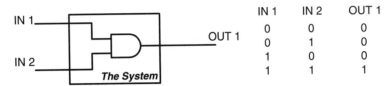

IN 1	IN 2	OUT 1
0	0	0
0	1	0
1	0	0
1	1	1

Figure 10.3 Basic System—White Box View

Based on complete knowledge of the internals of the system, one can now see that testing can be 25% simpler—and cheaper. Now, one can easily confirm the effect on the output when either input is in the logical 1 or logical 0 state. All that must be added is the one test to establish behavior when both inputs are logical 1. There is no need to test the condition that both inputs are logical 0. With complete knowledge, one can eliminate one test. The savings can be significant when a large number of units must be tested.

10.8.3 Gray Box Tests

gray box testing strategy

A *gray box testing strategy* is a mix of white and black box testing. Such an approach applies when the system includes modules designed by an outside vendor. Examples include complex LSI or gate arrays on the hardware side and library modules or canned algorithms on the software side.

10.9 APPLYING THE STRATEGY—THE FIRST STEPS

Never wait until a module or subsystem is completely built and coded before beginning to test. Never build or code the entire system and then try to debug it. This is a sure path to disaster. Start slowly, get individual modules working first, and then combine them into larger and larger pieces of the system.

As part of a strategy, one should give some thought to the order in which debugging and testing should proceed. Some of the major areas that one might want to think about include

- The parts
- The power system (power supplies and ground)
- The reset system
- The clocks and timing
- The system/component's inputs and outputs

10.9.1 The Parts

Check clocking (orientation) on all parts, and make certain that they have been installed in the board properly. Different kinds of parts are marked in different ways. Examine the semiconductor devices first; such devices include integrated circuits, transistors, and diodes.

Dual Inline Packages (DIP)

Figure 10.4 illustrates two 14-pin *Dual Inline Package's* (DIP). On such packages, usually either a small dot or a semicircle is used to identify pin 1. With the orientations shown, pin number 1 is on the upper left. The pin numbers increment and wrap around the end as illustrated.

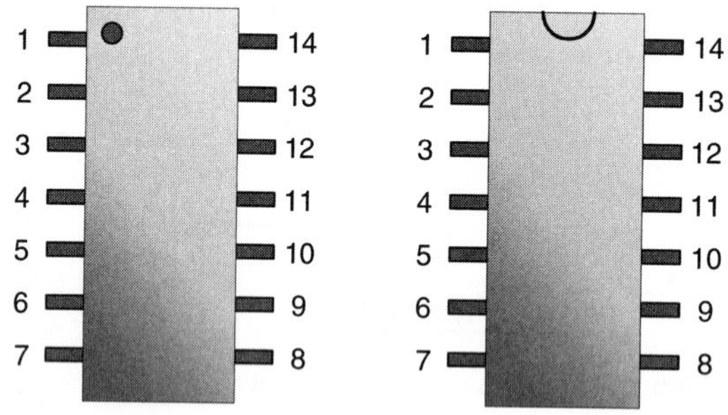

Figure 10.4 Top View—Dual Inline Package with Pin Numbers

Usually, the pin opposite from pin 1 is the VCC (voltage supply) pin where a +5V DC power supply is to be connected. Diagonally across the power pin is the GND (ground) pin. These two pins are placed as far from each other as possible to prevent any accidental shorting between the two, which may damage the whole chip in an instant.

It is important to remember that as ICs become more complex, so do the packages. For each device, it is always safest to refer back to the vendor's data sheets.

When using transistors, look for the emitter, base, and collector for bipolar devices and the gate, source, and drain for MOS devices. Several different possibilities are given in Figure 10.5, which illustrates two common configurations for bipolar devices.

When working with diodes, one should be able to identify the anode and the cathode. For the small signal diodes (which is what are commonly used), the cathode end of the diode is marked with a small ring. A typical diode package will appear as shown in Figure 10.6.

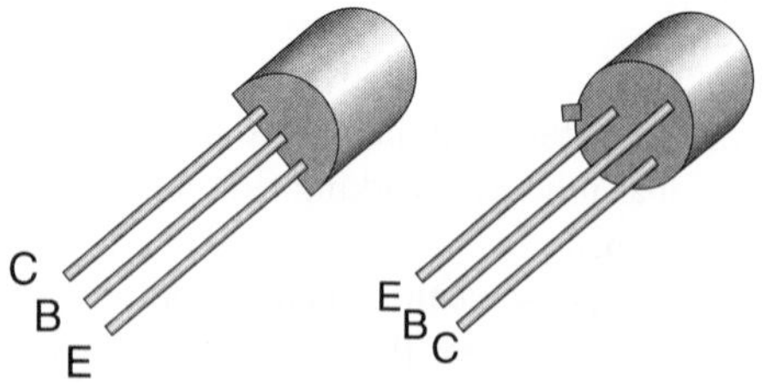

Figure 10.5 Transistor Packages

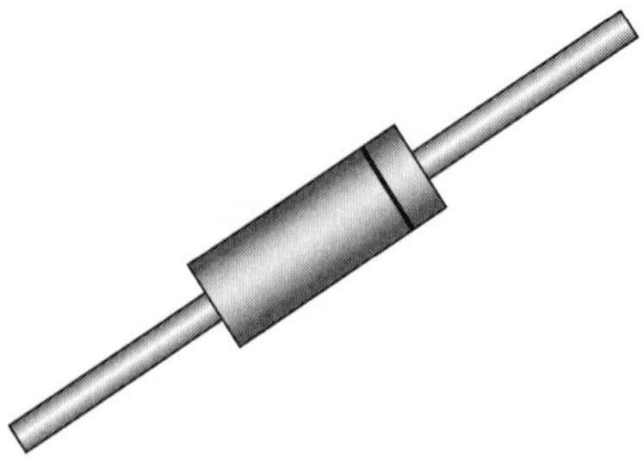

Figure 10.6 Diodes

When working with passive electronic parts such as resistors, inductors, or small valued capacitors, one is generally not concerned with part orientation. Of major concern with these devices is making certain that the part with the correct value and correct power rating for the application is installed.

During design, make certain to do a wattage calculation in addition to a value calculation for each part. One must go beyond the familiar I^2R calculation. A check of the vendor's data sheets will reveal that there are specifications for AC power, DC power, and pulsed power. These are different, and one must use the appropriate specifications for the specific application.

Electrolytic capacitors are polarized; it is very important that they be installed in the circuit with the correct orientation. However, installing them backwards is definitely more interesting. Under such circumstances, and with a sufficiently high voltage applied, they will explode. Such a mistake generally does not impress people who are working around you. However, prior to exploding they are known to give off some marvelous smoke, the color of which depends on the type of dielectric used.

Electrolytic capacitors are marked with a + on the positive lead or a series of rings, or indentation near the negative end. Some of the larger devices will have a small cross on the top. Don't confuse this with the plus sign. This is a blowout hole in case the device has been installed improperly and the smoke demon manages to extricate itself. The capacitor internals vent through this port rather than allowing the device to send shrapnel throughout the lab or factory, which is even less impressive.

Make certain that the proper current limiting is provided for all LEDs used in the system. Without the proper current-limiting resistors, the devices may burn out shortly after power is applied.

10.9.2 Initial Tests and Measurements—Before Applying Power

We are almost ready to apply power to the circuit for the first time. Before doing so, however, we should check a couple of more things. It is assumed that before the circuit was actually built the impedance between any of the power rails and ground was measured and that these all showed open. That measurement is repeated after the parts have been installed.

One may get several possible results. The measurement could still yield an open or very high-valued measurement. If such is the case, power has not been properly connected to the components; that must be corrected before proceeding. If the measurement shows less than 5 Ω, then there is a strong possibility of a short or very low-impedance path between the two rails. Once again that must also be corrected prior to moving on.

Applying the voltage and raising the current limit in hopes that the short will go away are challenging to the smoke demon. Don't do it. The measurement should be greater than approximately 10 to 15 Ω and less than 10 K Ω.

When making such a measurement, one may encounter an interesting phenomenon. The impedance initially reads 10 to 15 Ω and then begins to increase. Such behavior is easily explained. Most modern multimeters measure resistance by injecting a known current into the circuit and then making a voltage measurement across the port. By properly selecting the magnitude of the injected current, the voltage that is read corresponds directly to the resistance. An increasing resistance value is reflecting the result of the measurement current charging capacitors inside of the system.

Finally, when using bench supplies while debugging, remember to check the current limit and voltage settings on the supplies.

10.9.3 Initial Tests and Measurements—Immediately after Applying Power

Power is now on the system. What to look for first is smoke or fire, of course. If some wiring problems have escaped early scrutiny and are now causing problems, turn the power off quickly. With smoke or fire, there is generally a good indication of the source of the problem. Put the fire out and get the problem fixed first before proceeding.

Next, check the current that is being drawn. Use either the meter on the bench power supply or a separate instrument. The amount of current the circuit is consuming gives a strong early indication of potential problems with the system. What should be a reasonable level?

"Reasonable" depends on the kind of logic being used (TTL or CMOS), how many parts are in the system, the voltage level, and whether or not there are floating (unused) inputs among other things. Let's establish a base line. Assume that the system has approximately 25 to 30 ICs comprising a mix of SSI, MSI, and a couple of small programmable logic devices. For a TTLS design, the current should be in the range of 1 to 2 Amps. For a CMOS design, one should measure less than 1 Amp. If the measurement shows a very low value (close to 0 Amp), then it can be assumed that power is not properly connected to the system. On the other hand, an excessive value indicates a potential wiring error, an improper part, or a part installed incorrectly.

For CMOS logic in particular, one should always define the inputs of unused gates. If the inputs are not defined, the unused gates may be partially turned on and actually draw more current than the remainder of the circuit. If the circuit includes a number of LEDs or seven segment displays, each LED is going to draw about 5 to 15 mA. So, each seven-segment LED display may contribute around 100 mA or more to the power budget.

If the amount of current the circuit is drawing is within the range of what is expected, one should next check the temperature of the components. Feel the board and look for hot spots. These are an indication of incorrect wiring, incorrect parts, or a part that is improperly installed. Once again, it is important to have a heuristic feel for what the temperature of the components should be.

If you are working with a TTL board and it is cold, then there is a problem. It is most likely not powered or does not have power connected to all parts of the circuit. If a component feels as hot as a 20 to 40 watt light bulb, then, it is too hot. A normal CMOS board should feel about the same temperature as the surface of the lab bench. A TTL board should be a bit cooler than a morning coffee or tea cup.

10.10 APPLYING THE STRATEGY—DEBUGGING AND TESTING

The module or system now has power applied, and we can begin to execute our various test cases to confirm its operation. In the next several sections, we will begin by identifying some of the places to start to look for gross problems. Then we will move through some strategies for debugging combinational and sequential logic circuits.

10.10.1 The Reset System

Every system should incorporate a Power ON Reset (POR) signal. Starting any system in a known state is simply good engineering practice. During the debugging phase, every prototype module should provide manual access to and control of the POR signal. On initial application of power, the unit being tested should be held in the reset state, and the initial values of the available state variables should be confirmed prior to further testing and debugging. Such a practice enables one to always start the process from a known point.

As testing starts to progress, the first step in debugging nonfunctioning sequential logic is to confirm that the POR signal is in the non-reset state.

10.10.2 The Clocks and Timing

During the debug phase, one may be using a bench function generator or an oscillator that is built into the system. When using a bench source, prior to connecting it to the circuit, make sure that it is configured properly. Always check the level and offset of the signal. One should always do this with an oscilloscope. The first measurement should be to verify where ground is set on the scope.

In either case, make certain that the clock is operational and that the frequency and amplitude are correct. Remember that a current limit (fanout) applies to the clock as well. Check the rise and fall times to verify that they are within the desired limits. If the clock is too heavily loaded, the rise and fall times will be long and the risk that the parts will enter a metastable region during switching will increase. Finally, make certain that the clock is connected to all the appropriate parts.

10.10.3 The Inputs and Outputs

The next step is to move to the heart of the testing and debugging process, confirming the behavior of the system. The key to confirming system behavior is to fully understand what the behavior should be. Although such a statement may seem obvious to the system designer, this simple statement gives most people the greatest difficulty when debugging. What is meant here is that one must know what output value to expect for each selected input combination.

One cannot know whether or not the set of input signals accomplished anything meaningful without knowing what they were intended to demonstrate. Furthermore, any disagreement between the anticipated and actual results can provide the first clue towards identifying the root cause of the discrepancy.

Although the heuristic holds throughout the testing and debugging phase, the initial steps in particular should start with a small portion of the system using as simple an input or set of inputs as possible. Ideally, the input set should be DC signals, a repeating time-varying signal, or a known transient. One should remember that a failure during the debugging process should lead to a shift in strategy from ensuring behavior of the design to identifying the root cause of the fault.

The set of input and corresponding output signals combined with the order in which they are applied form the basis for the test cases in the test procedure. While mainly informal during early testing and debugging, the set is culled and formalized during the later phases of the design cycle.

As the process now unfolds, we will look first at testing and debugging of combinational and then sequential logic. But first we will have a short digression.

10.10.4 Sudden Failure during Debugging

Let's now assume that we have been working on the circuit for some time and have been approaching debugging and integration tasks methodically, adding and debugging one functional subcomponent at a time. So far, three of the five modules in the system have been debugged and integrated, and now the fourth is added. The new module does not work (although it worked as a standalone component). Furthermore, the first three modules now fail to work properly. If module 4 is disconnected from the circuit, the original components once again work properly. Repeated tests on module 4 alone fail to identify any possible faults. What could the problem be?

Consider a simple model. A Thévenin equivalent circuit can be developed for each of the five components in the system. As each one is integrated, the system can be modeled as in the sequence of drawings shown in Figure 10.7.

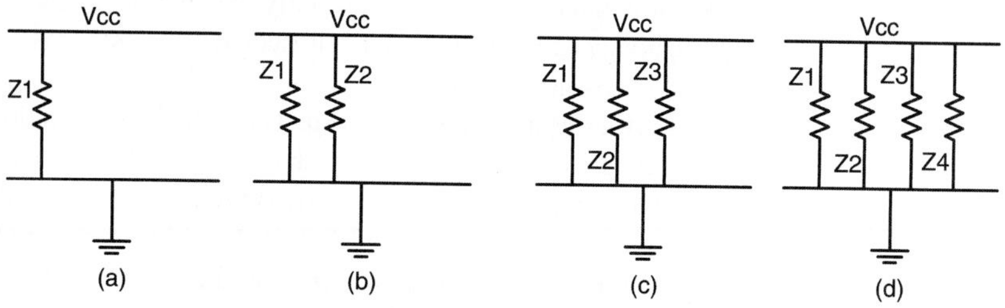

Figure 10.7 Modeling a System as Components Are Added

For the current discussion, assume that the Thévenin equivalent impedance of each module is the same. Initially, the current demand is given as

$$I_1 = \frac{VCC}{Z} \tag{10.0}$$

The second module is now added. Since the impedances are in parallel, the current requirement is now

$$I_2 = \frac{2 \bullet VCC}{Z} = 2 \bullet I_1 \tag{10.1}$$

As modules are continuously added, the equivalent impedance continues to decrease. After the fourth module is added, the current required is now

$$I_4 = \frac{4 \bullet VCC}{Z} = 4 \bullet I_1 \tag{10.2}$$

The Thévenin model for the power supply is given in Figure 10.8.

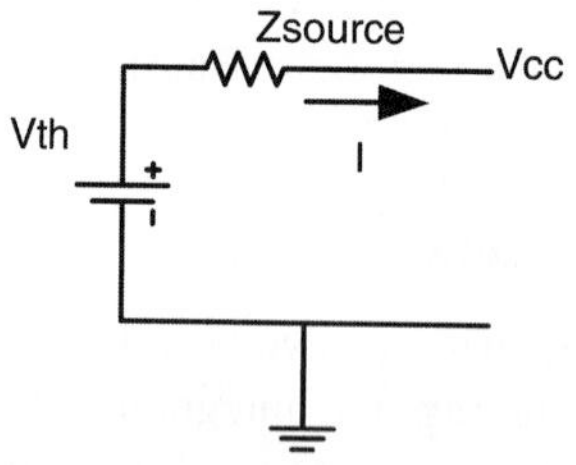

Figure 10.8 Power Supply Basic Model

It is now evident that as the current demand increases, there will be an increasingly larger drop across the internal impedance of the power supply, with a consequent decrease in the output voltage. To remedy the problem, one must increase the current limit if a bench supply is being used or modify the design of the supply if that is required to provide a greater drive capability.

In the next several sections, we will apply some of the concepts that we learned earlier in our discussions of testing combinational and sequential logic to the problem of debugging new designs. We will find that the problems of test and debug are very similar and that we can utilize much of the same strategy.

10.11 TESTING AND DEBUGGING COMBINATIONAL LOGIC

One objective of the early test cases is to show that the circuit and software modules, or subsystem and system, meet the core behavioral requirements. Boundary condition testing occurs later in the process. The test stimuli should reflect the basic requirements and should, in theory, yield the anticipated output signals. One should not exhaustively apply all input patterns. Rather, another early goal is to ensure that all possible paths from input to output are verified.

When a test fails, the debugging process starts. At this stage, it is not known if the design for the module being tested is correct. Sherlock Holmes, the fictional detective, proposed an interesting strategy that can easily be applied to debugging and troubleshooting: *eliminate everything that is not causing the fault and what's left is the culprit*. Thus, when debugging, one should use test stimuli that can eliminate circuit paths that are not contributing to a fault being isolated. Such knowledge derives from the clear understanding of the behavior of the module being tested—white box testing.

eliminate everything that is not causing the fault and what's left is the culprit

In contrast, in formal test, one begins with the assumption that the circuit is good, and the objective is to prove such is the case by confirming that each path can pass the necessary signals properly. The test vectors used in test are often a subset of those used during debugging.

10.12 PATH SENSITIZING

To be able to effectively test or debug a circuit, one must apply the appropriate test signals (test vector) and observe the consequences of such signals on the circuit. A signal is said to be *directly observable* if its behavior can be seen (tested) directly at card edge or test point and *indirectly observable* if it can only be seen through some intermediate component.

directly observable
indirectly observable

One simple and effective approach for determining the necessary stimuli for both test and troubleshooting is based on what is called *path sensitizing*. With such an approach, first identify a path from the signal under test (or fault) to an observable circuit output. Next choose values for the remaining signals, as appropriate, such that any changes in the circuit output under test are only a function of the signal being tested.

path sensitizing

We will begin with the following two basic logic gates in Figure 10.9 as a first model. Although we are using logic gates to illustrate the method, they can easily model more general conjunctive or disjunctive relationships between inputs and output in either hardware or software.

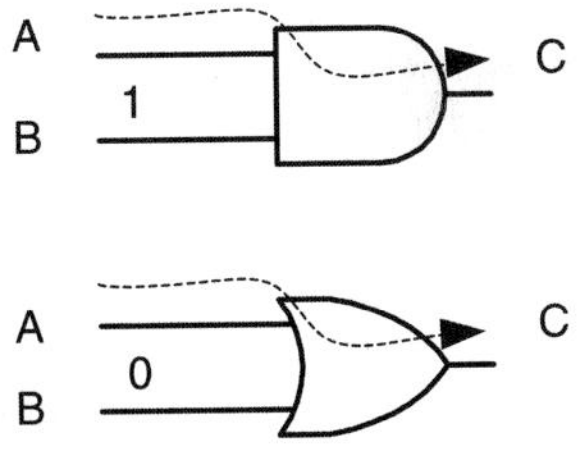

Figure 10.9 Path Sensitizing

For an AND (conjunctive) function, one must ensure that all inputs, except the one under test, are in the logical 1 state. Assume that we wish to test the behavior of input signal A. We place the input signal B into the logical 1 state. Under such a condition, any changes to the output, C, are only a function of changes in the input, A. Thus, a stuck-at condition on A is directly observable on C. That is, if the signal A is changed and the corresponding change is not reflected on C, one can conclude that a stuck-at condition exists on A. We state that the *fault has been forwarded* to an observable output.

fault has been forwarded

For an OR (disjunctive) function, we sensitize the path by placing all nets not on the path in the logical 0 state. Once again, changes in the output reflect only those on input A, and a stuck-at condition on A appears on C.

10.12.1 Single Variable–Single Path

Path sensitizing can be used to test and debug the accompanying circuit in Figure 10.10.

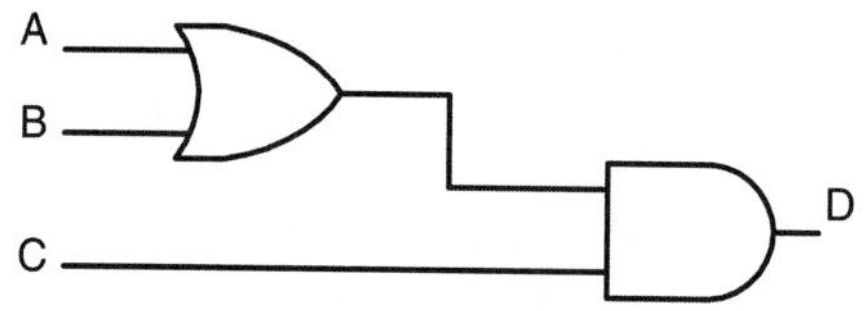

Figure 10.10 Basic Combinational Logic Circuit

Testing

To test the circuit, one must show that signals A, B, and C will propagate to D or are blocked subject to the logical constraints of the circuit. Input C is a logical choice to start with since it is the simplest. If debugging is necessary, hypothesize a stuck-at state on the output D and work backwards.

Going forward for the moment to test C, one must ensure that the upper leg of the AND gate is in the logical 1 state, thereby sensitizing the lower path to the signal C. The required system state can be achieved by assigning either A or B a value of logical 1. The state of the other input does not matter.

That condition is represented with the don't care value on B in Figure 10.11.

Now the output D is solely a function of the input C. We test by first applying a logical 0 and then a logical 1 to C and confirming the proper behavior for the signal D and indirectly partially confirming the correct operation of the output AND gate.

A and B are tested by reversing the roles. To test A, sensitize that path first by making C a logical 1 and then by making B a logical 0. Now the output D is solely a function of the input A. Testing B follows similarly as reflected in Figure 10.12. As a side effect of the two test cases, the correct logical operation of the AND and OR gates is now confirmed.

Observe that six of the eight possible combinations of the three inputs are sufficient to confirm the proper logical operation of the circuit.

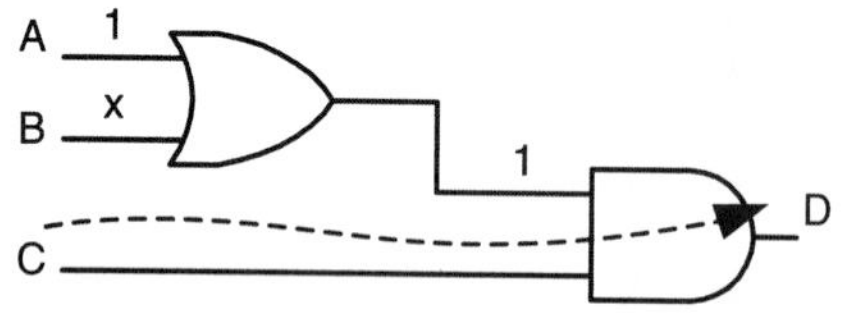

Figure 10.11 Basic Combinational Logic Circuit

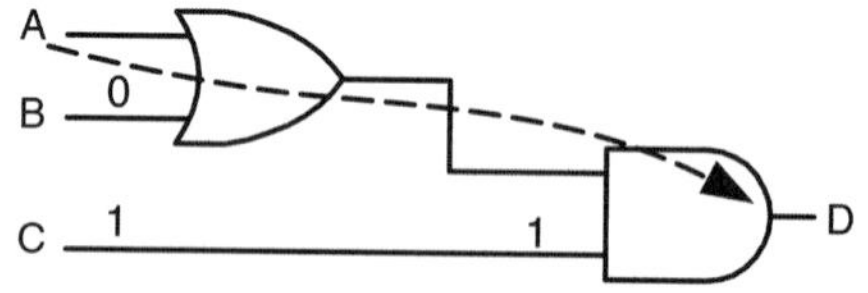

Figure 10.12 Basic Combinational Logic Circuit

Debugging

Debugging or troubleshooting a fault in the circuit follows naturally. As noted, first hypothesize a stuck-at fault on signal D. The root cause of the problem can be either direct via a fault on the output or indirect via one of the inputs to the AND gate. To isolate the fault, choose the test vector that sensitizes path C since it is the simpler.

One must first confirm that the net A+B is in the logical 1 state. If not, pursue that path. Otherwise, the reasoning process proceeds as follows.

> One knows how the output should behave if C is changed.
>
> - If the desired changes are evident on D, move to the left and troubleshoot the A+B net.
> - If the behavior of both of the AND gate inputs is correct, follow the D net.
> - If AND gate input nets are not functioning properly, work backwards following the signal path that is not behaving properly.

10.12.2 Single Variable–Two Paths

In the logic circuits discussed earlier, the two paths are independent; that is, they do not share any common signals. At the next level of complexity the two paths share a common signal. Consider the configuration in Figure 10.13 as a simplified model of a more general circuit or system architecture.

In reality, this fragment is not much more complex than the previous one. If the signal B is held at a logic 1, then one can easily verify the paths from A or C to the output as in Figure 10.14 for the path from A. The path from C follows in a similar manner.

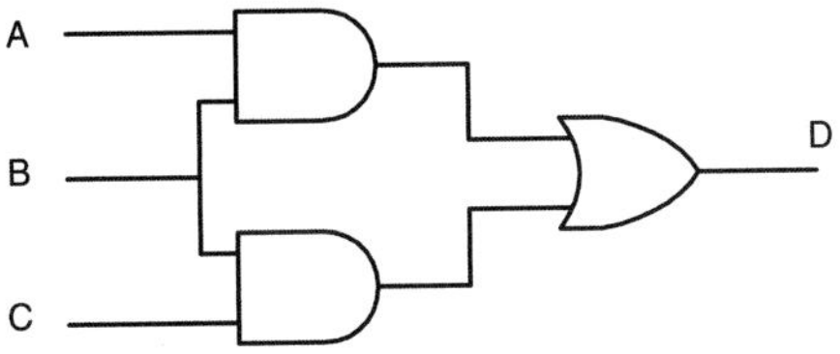

Figure 10.13 Basic Combinational Logic Circuit with Two Independent Signal Paths and Shared Common Signal

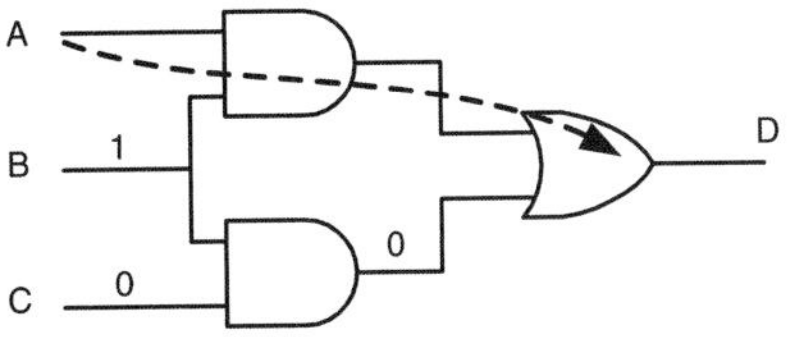

Figure 10.14 Basic Combinational Logic Circuit with Two Independent Signal Paths and Shared Common Signal, One Path Sensitized

Verifying the effects of the common signal, B, is not much more complex. By holding first A to a logical 1 and C to a logical 0, one can verify the upper path. Reversing the values on A and C gives visibility through the lower path as can be seen in Figure 10.15. Once again the path through C follows naturally. To debug or troubleshoot such a configuration, the same reasoning is followed as is used in developing the test cases.

A slight modification is made to the circuit. The output OR gate is replaced with an AND as in the drawing in Figure 10.16.

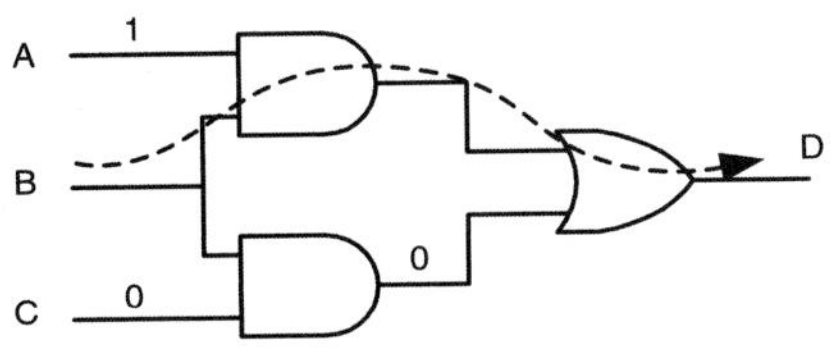

Figure 10.15 Basic Combinational Logic Circuit with Two Independent Signal Paths and Shared Common Signal, One Path Sensitized

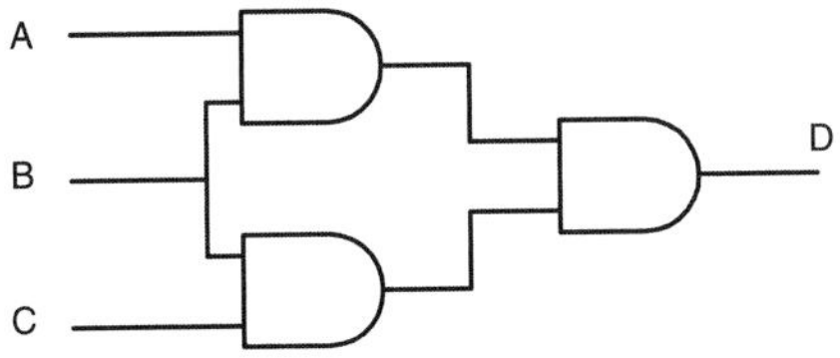

Figure 10.16 Basic Combinational Logic Circuit with Two Independent Signal Paths and Shared Common Signal

With the altered output configuration, one can no longer use a single sensitized path to confirm proper full logical operation. One can still use a single path to confirm the behavior of signal flow from A or C. However, to test signal flow from B, one must send signals through both paths to D as in Figure 10.17.

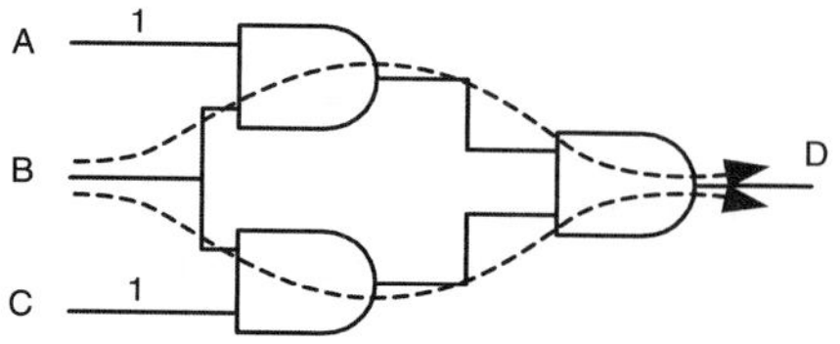

Figure 10.17 Basic Combinational Logic Circuit with Two Independent Signal Paths and Shared Common Signal, Both Sensitized

First, the two paths are sensitized with logical 1 values on the A and C inputs. Observe that to test the function properly, one must execute the two single-path tests from A and C to the output first. Otherwise, one will be unable to determine if a stuck-at condition on either of the two interior AND outputs results from A (C) or B.

10.13 MASKING AND UNTESTABLE FAULTS

The circuit in Figure 10.18 contains a static 1 hazard associated with the signal B. Under the proper conditions, a 1→ 0 transition on B can produce a transient 1 on the output D.

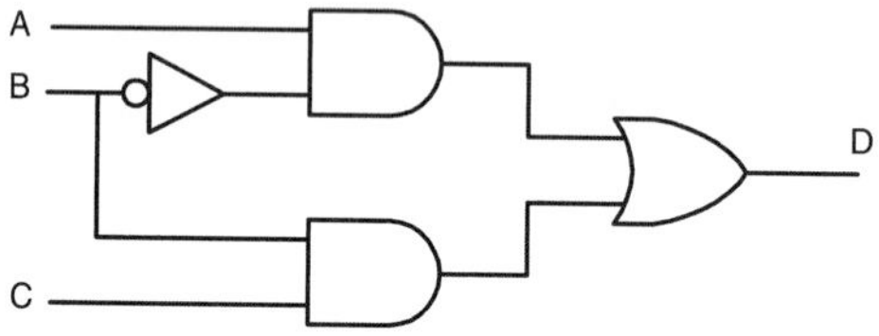

Figure 10.18 Basic Combinational Logic Circuit with a Static Hazard

mask

untestable

As we learned earlier, to eliminate the hazard, one can *mask* the change by including the extra conjunct, AC, as illustrated in Figure 10.19. One side effect of making such a change is that we now have a circuit with an *untestable* potential fault. If the output of the bottom AND gate is stuck-at-1, then the fault will be indistinguishable from a proper logical 1 on the same signal line.

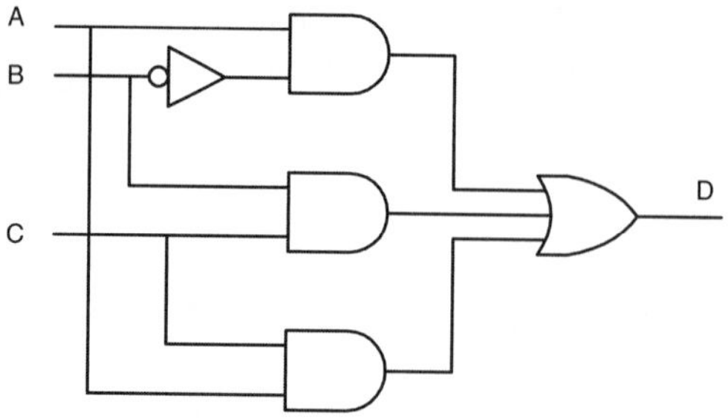

Figure 10.19 Basic Combinational Logic Circuit with Redundant Paths of Control

Such a situation occurs because the term AC is redundant as can easily be shown by plotting the expression on a Karnaugh map. That is, one can show that the circuit output, D, is independent of the added term.

Since single faults are being considered, we will not consider that a stuck-at-1 fault on any of the AND gates above will also mask a stuck-at-0 fault on any of the remaining nets feeding the OR gate. Such a fault will also prevent one from effectively testing the remaining nets.

When a logic circuit has redundant literals or terms such as is seen here, then a fault in such an expression (here the stuck-at-1 condition) can be masked by others (here $\mathbf{A\bar{B}C}$ or **ABC**) in the circuit implementation. Such faults are said to be untestable; they can only occur in circuits to which we have incorporated redundancy.

The circuit fragment presented here models the more general problem that is encountered in systems with redundant paths of control. In such systems, one must find a way to disable the redundant paths during test. The best way to accomplish this is strongly dependent on the specific design.

With redundant paths of control, the strategy for debugging and troubleshooting changes from that of getting exact information to that of maximizing what can be gained from the circuit. Once again, maximizing the knowledge gained from a failure depends directly on how well the correct operation of the module is understood.

For the current module, the initial objective should be to confirm that one can set the signal D to a logical 0. Failing that, the most that can be learned is that one of the inputs (or the output) is stuck-at-1. One can then backtrack and test each of the input nets. If each of the member inputs can be driven to either state, then one concludes that it is the output that is stuck. Otherwise, the appropriate diagnostic process is to work slowly backward from the suspect input(s).

10.14 SINGLE VARIABLE–MULTIPLE PATHS

In practice, systems are rarely limited to a single output. With multiple outputs, it is often found that several have one or more variables or logical expressions in common. Such a situation can be modeled with the circuit fragment given in Figure 10.20.

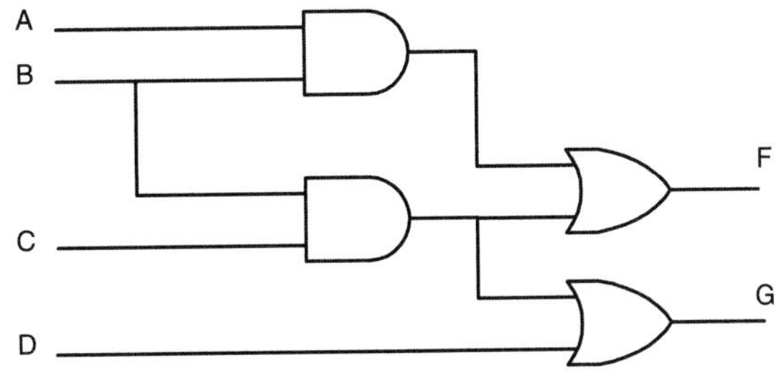

Figure 10.20 Basic Combinational Logic Circuit with Multiple Outputs

Observe that both outputs share the net that carries the conjunction of signals *B and C*.

The test is started by sensitizing the portion of that path carrying the signal B, as seen in Figure 10.21. Note that both outputs must be examined to verify the complete BC net.

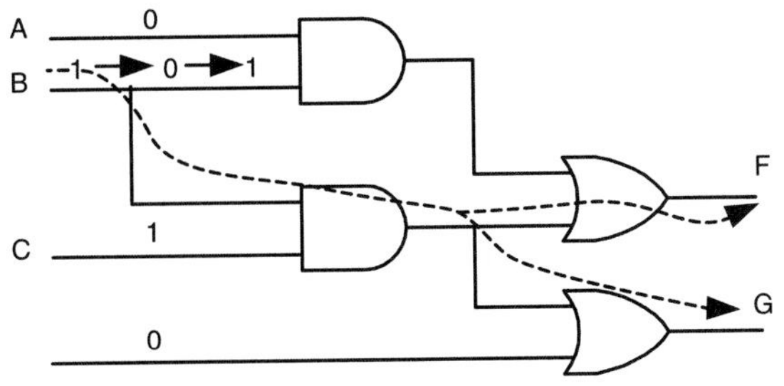

Figure 10.21 Basic Combinational Logic Circuit with Path to Multiple Outputs Sensitized

C can be tested in a similar manner, and the remaining paths to the two outputs are tested as before. By holding B to a logical 1 and C to a logical 0, we sensitize the path for A. The same set of inputs also sensitizes the path for D.

To debug or troubleshoot, assume a stuck-at fault on the output of either E or F. To begin, A and D are placed in the logical 0 state and C in the logical 1 state. The net expressing the conjunction of A and B should be in the logical 0 state.

Exercising input B through a 1-0-1 sequence should cause corresponding changes in both outputs. A change in only one provides two pieces of information: the net expressing the conjunction of B and C is functioning properly, and most likely the fault is with the output of the unchanging OR gate.

The diagnosis is confirmed by placing signal C in the logical 0 state and the signal B in the logical 1 state, thereby disabling the lower AND gate (and the corresponding output nets) and sensitizing the path from A. Either A or D can then be toggled as appropriate.

10.15 BRIDGE FAULTS

Recall that a bridge fault occurs when a connection among two or more signals exists where none had been originally intended. Generally, such faults will be identified during a good manufacturing defects test that would detect the unintended low-impedance path. During debugging, without the aid of such a test, one must fall back on one or more variants of a functional test.

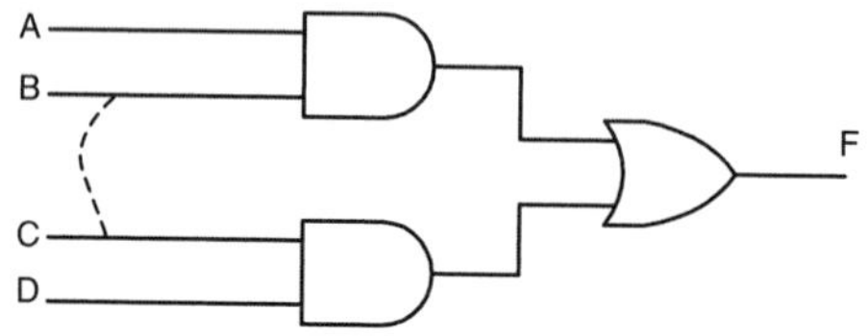

Figure 10.22 Bridge Fault

A card edge input bridge fault such as the one in Figure 10.22 can be tested using a path sensitization scheme coupled with a test using complementary values for signals B and C. We debug or troubleshoot the fault in a similar way, testing whether first one and then the other (B or C) can propagate the intended value to the circuit output.

An approach to identifying an (internal or card edge) output bridge fault such as those in the next two circuit fragments in Figure 10.23 begins with the same approach used for stuck-at faults.

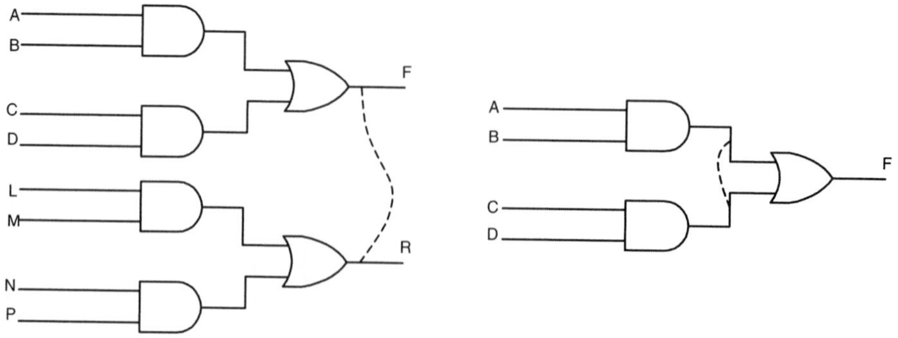

Figure 10.23 Bridge Faults

The objective is to propagate a signal via either path to the corresponding output. For the circuit on the left, we initially test for the ability to drive the signals R and F to opposite states. Failing to do that, we debug by confirming that the disjunctive inputs (the outputs of the individual AND gates) can be placed individually into the desired states. Success suggests a problem with the OR gate outputs, in particular a bridge based on the single-fault assumption. Failure initiates a trace backward along the path of the signal that could not be controlled.

For the circuit on the right, the objective is to propagate both logic states through one path while disabling the other. If one path dominates, any attempts to propagate signals to the output on the other path will fail. If both paths are equal, attempts to alter the output state via either path will fail. We debug or troubleshoot by confirming that the signals on the two disjunctive paths can be altered.

A feedback bridge fault, such as those illustrated in the two circuit fragments in Figure 10.24, presents a more interesting challenge. Starting with the pieces, the first step is to determine what is known.

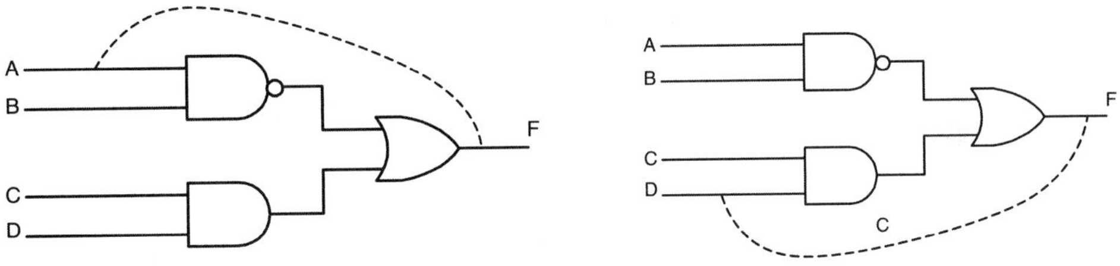

Figure 10.24 Feedback Bridge Faults

If the signals coming into the logic block are on the card edge, one can generally assume that the tester or data generator will have sufficient capability to overdrive the fed back output signal. For the circuit on the left, the input pattern [0→1→0, 1, 0, x] on the respective inputs [A, B, C, D] will identify the fault. Similarly, the pattern [1, 1, 0, 0→1→0] on the respective inputs [A, B, C, D] will identify the problem in the circuit fragment on the right. Observe that for the right-hand circuit, the output should never change because C should block forward signal propagation. However, the feedback fault also provides the means to overdrive the output and force a signal change.

If the signals driving the logic block are from an internal net, then one must assume that at least two outputs are fighting: signal F and the output of the device driving either A or D. We test and troubleshoot as was done with the "outputs tied" bridge fault in the earlier discussions.

10.16 DEBUGGING—SEQUENTIAL LOGIC

Turning on, debugging, and troubleshooting the sequential machines provide the opportunity to apply engineering creativity, imagination, and intuition. Sequential logic introduces time as a variable, which somewhat complicates the test and debug process. With combinational logic, the desired (or perhaps undesired) output appears shortly after the inputs are applied. In contrast, in a sequential system, getting to the desired state often involves a specific (and sometimes tedious) series of input patterns. (Refer back to the earlier chapters on finite-state machines.)

Efficiently debugging sequential circuitry requires a bit of forethought and planning. As discussed earlier, the first step in debugging is taken during design. In any system, one should always provide a master reset input to any latch or flip-flop based logic. The signal provides the means by which to place the machine into a known initial state. Of course, if that fails, we have a place to begin troubleshooting. Moreover, that is a combinational problem, and we have just studied those.

verify the truth table strategy

At this point, one can take a variety of paths. One good approach is to verify the state machine's truth table—we call this strategy *verify the truth table strategy*. Two tools are essential to begin the task: a data generator and a logic analyzer. The first gives the ability to write and produce a series of test vectors that can be applied to the circuit's input to produce the desired transitions. The second provides the means to monitor and collect the values of the machine's outputs for each input vector.

We will use the simple pattern recognition circuit studied earlier to illustrate the approach. The state diagram and truth table for the system are presented in Figure 10.25.

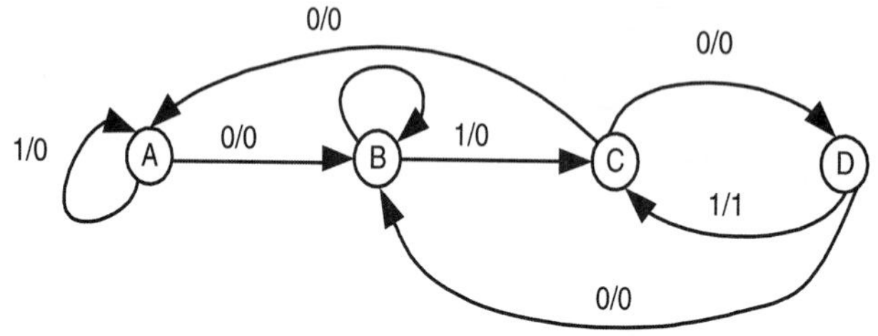

Present State	Next State / Output	
	X=0	X=1
A	B/0	A/0
B	B/0	C/0
C	D/0	A/0
D	B/0	C/1

Figure 10.25 Simple Pattern Recognition State Machine

For this example, we will use a simple binary assignment for the state variables, which will yield the excitation table given in Figure 10.26.

Present State	Next State / Output	
	X=0	X=1
A 0 0	B/0 0 1 / 0	A/0 0 0 / 0
B 0 1	B/0 0 1 / 0	C/0 1 0 / 0
C 1 0	D/0 1 1 / 0	A/0 0 0 / 0
D 1 1	B/0 0 1 / 0	C/1 1 0 / 1

Figure 10.26 Excitation Table

The first step is to write a test vector that will apply the master reset and thereby force the system to its initial state, A, the {00} state. The next step is to select a state transition to be verified and write a homing or initialization sequence that will send the machine to the state just before the transition. For this example, we elect to test the transition from state C {1,0} to state D {1,1}.

Starting from state A, we create the data generator pattern: {Reset, X} = {(0,0), (1, 0), (0,1)}. If the machine is functioning properly, it should be in state C. Next, we write a vector to effect the transition. The new vector is added to the data generator pattern: {Reset, X} = {(0,0), (1,0), (1,1), (1,0)}.

The logic analyzer is connected to the circuit, and the set of test vectors is entered into the data generator. Following application of the suite of vectors, the following sequence for the state variable and output variable transitions should be captured on the logic analyzer as {M, N, Z} =.

```
0 0 0
0 1 0
1 0 0
1 1 0
```

One additional input vector will now confirm the output logic for Z as well. This process is repeated for each transition to be verified.

Recall that in the formal model of the finite-state machine, the next state is given by the mapping

$$\delta: IxS \rightarrow S \tag{10.3}$$

All this equation states is that the output of a flip-flop comprising the FSM depends on the combinational logic providing the input. Thus, if a failure occurs, the data generator can be used to debug the combinational logic portion of the machine exactly as was done with a pure combinational logic system earlier.

In order for the test just completed to succeed, there must have also been successful transitions from A to B and then to C. From the results of one test, we have confirmed a significant portion of the logic. A failure also lays the groundwork for a debugging strategy. In such an event, we split the state transition sequence in half—do a binary search. We ask: "Did we get to state C?" If not, we explore the early transitions; otherwise we examine the later ones.

10.17 SCAN DESIGN TESTING

The strategy for debugging sequential machines using scan design techniques is rather straightforward. The flip-flops are at the heart of the circuit and the technique, so it is best to ensure that they are functioning properly first. We repeat the drawing of a state machine with scan design support in Figure 10.27.

select, test
scan in
scan out

Initially the *select* input is placed into the *test* mode. With the flip-flops configured as a shift register, a pattern of alternating 0's and 1's is entered on the *scan in* input and monitored on the *scan out* output. If the pattern that has been entered appears properly on the output, we assume that the devices are working correctly and can proceed.

If the output appears as a constant 0 or 1, then we infer that one of the devices (or its input) is malfunctioning. If manual access to the individual flip-flop pins is possible, we debug by probing those signals. If such access is not available, little can be done.

Assuming that the necessary access is available, the first debugging step is to verify the reset signal (if it is present) to ensure that the machine is not being held in the reset state. The same is done with the preset signal. Next the presence of the clock on each device is

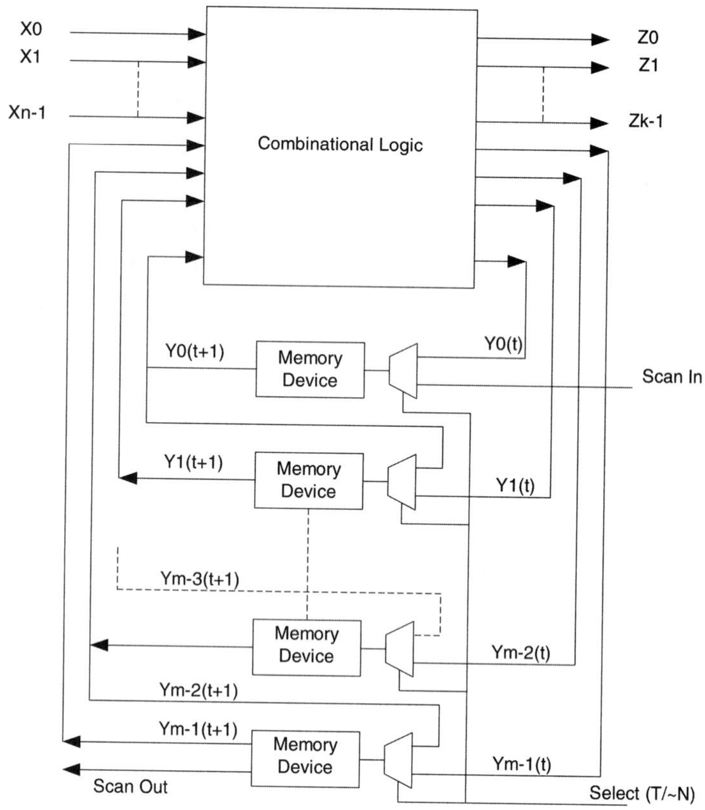

Figure 10.27 Basic State Machine with Scan Path Logic

confirmed. If those signals are operating properly, the flip-flop outputs are examined to determine how far through the register the test pattern has correctly propagated.

Once the flip-flops are confirmed to be functioning correctly, the combinational logic is addressed. If one is using a *test for stuck-at strategy*, then the *test* mode is selected and the shift register and the primary inputs $\{X_n\}$ are used to enter the test vectors to be applied to the combinational net. The logic is switched to *normal* mode, and the state of the $\{Y_m(t)\}$ signals is strobed into the flip-flops. Going back to the *test* mode once again allows the state of the combinational logic to be shifted out through the *scan out* line where it and the $\{Z_k\}$ values are compared with the proper values.

test for stuck-at strategy, test, normal, test, scan out

A *verify the truth table strategy* is not much more complex. Let's repeat the previous exercise and see how scan design now applies. As a first step, select a state transition to be verified. Next, select the *test* mode, shift in the values for $\{Y_m(t)\}$ that will cause the transition, enter the *normal* mode, execute the transition, go back to *test,* and clock out and confirm the flip-flop state. This process is repeated for each transition to be verified. The truth table is redrawn in Figure 10.28 for reference.

verify the truth table strategy, test, normal

Once again, a simple binary assignment for the state variables is used, which will yield the excitation table given in Figure 10.29.

The test begins by placing the machine into state A, the {00} state. The initialization is accomplished by placing the FSM into the test mode and entering the pattern {00} on the scan in line. The X input is placed in the logical 0 state and the state machine into the normal mode. The output, Z, is confirmed to be in the logical 0 state. Next the machine is clocked one time to execute the transition to state B, the {01} state. The test mode selection is reas-

Present State	Next State / Output	
	X=0	X=1
A	B/0	A/0
B	B/0	C/0
C	D/0	A/0
D	B/0	C/1

Figure 10.28 UUT State Machine Transition Table

Present State	Next State / Output	
	X=0	X=1
A 00	B/0 01/0	A/0 00/0
B 01	B/0 01/0	C/0 10/0
C 10	D/0 11/0	A/0 00/0
D 11	B/0 01/0	C/1 10/1

Figure 10.29 UUT State Machine Transition Table

serted, and the contents of the flip-flops are shifted out and examined to ensure that the proper transition occurred.

Table 10.1 illustrates the test sequence for the first two rows of the state table.

Table 10.1 Test Sequence

Step	Select	Action	State	Scan In	Scan Out	Input	Output
1	Test	2 clocks, enter starting state {0,0}	00	00	-	-	-
2	Normal	Enter Input / Read Output	00	-	-	0	0
3	Normal	1 clock, enter next state	01	-	-	0	0
4	Test	2 clocks, shift out current state shift in next starting state {0,0}	01	00	01	-	-
5	Normal	Enter Input / Read Output	00	-	-	1	0
6	Normal	1 clock, enter next state	00	-	-	1	0
7	Test	2 clocks, shift out current state shift in next starting state {0,1}	00	01	00	-	-
8	Normal	Enter Input / Read Output	01	-	-	0	0
9	Normal	1 clock, enter next state	01	-	-	0	0
10	Test	2 clocks, shift out current state shift in next starting state {0,1}	01	01	01	-	-
11	Normal	Enter Input / Read Output	01	-	-	1	0
12	Normal	1 clock, enter next state	10	-	-	1	0
13	Test	2 clocks, shift out current state shift in next starting state {1,0}	10	01	00		
14-19		Continue with remaining states					

If a failure occurs, the combinational logic is debugged exactly as was done with a pure combinational logic system earlier. The one difficulty may be limited visibility into the internal nodes of the circuit.

10.18 BOUNDARY-SCAN TESTING

The approach one takes to debugging larger parts of the system is often directed by the technologies that have been used to execute the designs. Today we frequently are working with ASICs, CPLDs, array logics, or custom-designed integrated circuits. These are VLSI class components. In such a context, boundary-scan methods can provide a very powerful tool.

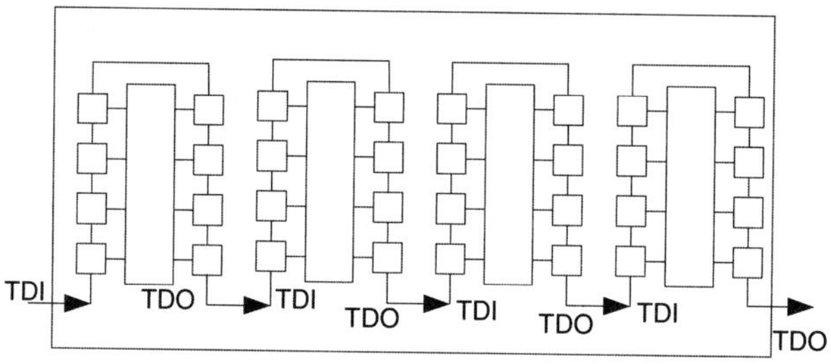

Figure 10.30 Boundary-Scan Circuit Configuration

If the system has been designed to support boundary-scan capability, the high-level architecture appears as in Figure 10.30. From here, testing is based on a three-point strategy:

- Test the tester.
- Test the device interconnect.
- Test the devices.

test the tester

Starting with the *test the tester* heuristic in the initial step ensures that the boundary-scan infrastructure is functional. One simple way to do this is to force each device in the system to connect its instruction register between its TDI and TDO pins. There is now a path from the TDI signal on the input side of the system, through all the devices to the TDO signal on the output side of the system. Each device in the chain can be directed to place a 1-0 pattern into the IR. The combined pattern, which will propagate through all devices in the chain, can be detected at the output. If the appropriate number of 1-0 pairs does not appear, one can assume that there is a problem in the system.

Next the interconnections between the devices in the system are verified. Generally, the system uses a bus structure to exchange commands or data between the constituent devices. These interconnections can easily be checked using the input/output capabilities of the boundary-scan cells on the various scan paths.

To see how this might work, consider the circuit fragment in Figure 10.31. Three kinds of faults have been incorporated.

Next the EXTEST (refer back to Chapter 4) instruction is used to propagate various test patterns through the scan register. A reasonable choice is to begin with all 0's and then all 1's. With such patterns, the stuck-at (including open) faults are identified. These faults will appear as a bit with the opposite value of the test pattern—for a stuck-at 0 and a pattern of 1's, the 0 will appear and vice versa. Testing follows with an alternating 0-1 test pattern to identify the bridge-type faults: two consecutive bits appearing with the same value.

Finally, we might use the RUNBIST instruction to command the individual devices to execute their self-test sequences or some version of INTEST to test the device's internal logic. After completing the self-tests, the following will have been confirmed: the boundary-scan infrastructure is working, the most common manufacturing faults (stuck-at, open, or bridge) have been detected, and each of the devices that supports boundary-scan in

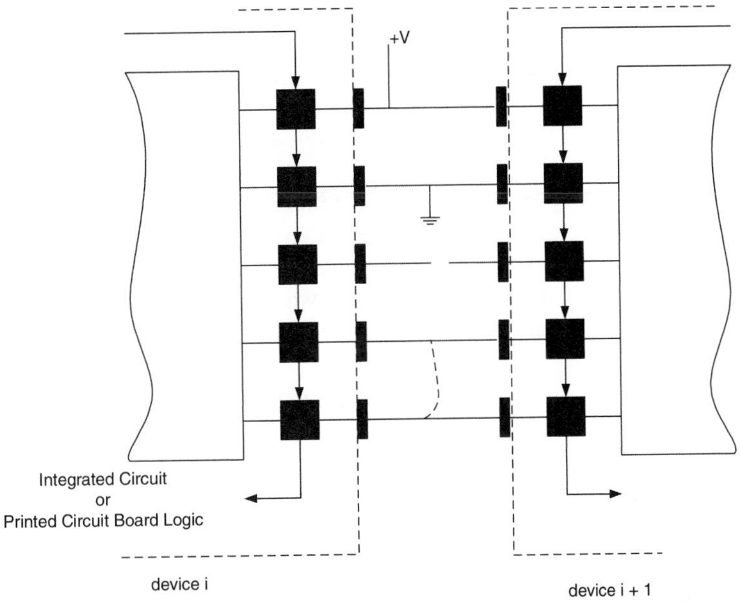

Figure 10.31 Boundary-Scan Interface Configuration

the system is present and has a basic level of functionality. One must include other nonboundary-scan tests in the test suite to cover the remaining untested devices. Additional, more detailed tests can be included as deemed necessary.

As with the scan design approach, if a failure is detected, debugging can be a bit complex. Generally, when using scan design or boundary-scan tools, the system is made up of mainly VLSI class devices. Once again, we are going to have only limited visibility into the internals of the devices. Such a restriction is not as severe as it may first appear long term. Remember, in production the objective is to identify manufacturing defects, and such defects are going to be external to the devices.

10.19 MEMORIES AND MEMORY SYSTEMS

The strategy for debugging memories and memory systems follows directly from the techniques discussed in Chapter 4, Section 4.20, for testing memories and will not be repeated here.

10.20 APPLYING THE STRATEGY—SUBSYSTEM AND SYSTEM TEST

Once the individual modules are tested and their behavior has been confirmed, they are integrated and tested in larger subsystems until the complete system comes together. Many of the techniques used at the module level still apply.

Of critical concern as subsystems are built and tested are the more insidious dynamic and interaction problems that frequently occur as larger and larger portions of the system are integrated. Designing and building individual modules that perform a desired function is rather straightforward. Ensuring that several such modules function properly together when signal delays, noise, temperature, and other aberrations from the real world are at play is a more complex and challenging problem. Bringing all of the system modules together into a properly functioning product offers one the opportunity to use a myriad of engineering tools and skills. Once again, a full understanding of the design forms an essential basis on which this phase of the process is built.

As the remaining modules and subsystems are integrated, one must now also consider several additional things: estimating how many bugs remain in the product and developing tests that grow with the product. In large complex systems there is always the potential that some unthought-of combination of signals will produce an undesired behavior.

During testing, the engineers may keep a log of the defects that turn up and rank them on a scale of 1 to 5, for example, with 5 being critical (system crashes), 4 being serious (lost functionality), and so on down to 1. A product may be considered to pass if no 4 or 5 level defects are logged against it in 40 hours of testing. If a defect is found, the clock starts over again.

10.21 APPLYING THE STRATEGY—TESTING FOR OUR CUSTOMER

Alpha and Beta Tests, Verification Tests, Validation Tests

Remember that testing for the customer begins at the specification stage of design. At this phase, we need to distinguish between production tests and ongoing testing for product support. Testing comprises a three-pronged attack comprised of *Alpha and Beta tests, Verification Tests,* and *Validation Tests.*

10.21.1 Alpha and Beta Tests

The intent of alpha and beta tests is to gain real-world experience with the system. Early versions of the product are given to selected customers or internal users. The goal is to have the product used as it is intended and expected to be used.

Alpha tests

Alpha tests occur shortly after system design. We assume that the first implementation has been completed and a comprehensive internal test suite has been conducted and passed. Alpha testing is usually done by an in-house group of QA (quality assurance) testers when hardware and software development teams release the product.

Beta Tests

Beta tests follow the incorporation of the fixes for bugs or unwanted features discovered during alpha tests. Beta testing is usually done by a group of friendly users from outside the company.

Both the alpha and beta tests series may be repeated any number of times until the required level of confidence in the new product is reached. These tests are very important because they give us the first look at how the design will operate in a real-world environment.

10.21.2 Verification Tests

Verification testing is designed to prove that the product meets its specification. These tests are not as comprehensive as some of the earlier system testing that was conducted. Remember that the efficacy of this test suite is only as good as the original specifications. When thinking about putting a verification suite together, it might be useful to consider developing a reduced regression suite.

10.21.3 Validation Tests

The intent of validation testing is to prove that the verification test suite is testing what it is supposed to test, that it is making the required measurements within the required tolerance, and that it can identify faults. The validation suite is executed prior to releasing tests to production and whenever a product or its tests are modified.

10.21.4 Acceptance Tests

The acceptance test suite is a set of tests the customer uses when accepting a product. Such a suite may include any or all verification and validation tests. Later, during production acceptance tests may be randomly applied to ensure that quality standards are being maintained.

10.21.5 Production Tests

Once a product has been released to production, one assumes that the system is designed correctly and that it meets all specifications. Production tests are not developed to verify the integrity of the design. Often, they are a subset of the verification tests. In writing these tests, we imply a twofold goal:

1. Test the system the least amount necessary to ensure a quality system—that it meets specifications and will not be dead on arrival at the customer site.
2. Test as quickly as possible.

Production testing does not add any value to the product; it is a cost. If one could guarantee the quality of the component parts and the quality of manufacturing, such tests could go away.

10.22 SELF-TEST

Self-tests were discussed in some detail in the chapter on reliability and safety. The following paragraphs provide a brief summary of that discussion.

Self-tests are a series of built-in tests the system can execute. In developing and incorporating such tests into a design, the goals are to ensure that the system is working and to use the test results as a basis for action if the system fails or locks up. Self-tests fall into two general categories: those invoked *on demand* and those running *in background*.

on demand, in background

10.22.1 On Demand

Self-tests invoked on demand are a sanity check to ensure that the system is basically operational. These tests are often done at power up and report a status on completion.

> ***Caution:*** When developing such tests, the process of simply executing the test often requires that most of the system be working.

10.22.2 In Background

Background tests can be as simple as a RAM read/write test or as complex as a test suite to check the system busses for stuck lines, memory for ROM signature, or RAM for failed or stuck bits. In addition, one may check math processing, built-in A/D accuracy by measuring a known reference, or the D/A integrity by executing a conversion at the cardinal points.

> ***Caution:*** Anything added to a system for testing can fail as well.

10.23 SUMMARY

In this chapter we began the study of test by introducing some of the relevant vocabulary. We then formulated a high-level model for a testing strategy and motivated the need for planning, specifications, test procedures, and test cases. We followed with the main reasons for debugging, test, and troubleshooting, and we learned how the modeling and simulation tools studied earlier in the context of original design can apply to the test problem as well.

We examined test and the test process from several perspectives that ranged from black to white box models. We moved into the various kinds of testing that take place during the different stages of the product life cycle. We began with the early phases of the test and debug strategy by examining the debugging process, and we studied how to isolate common faults in combinational and in sequential logic. We concluded with a brief look at testing for the customer and some of the various kinds of tests that one performs in production.

10.24 REVIEW QUESTIONS

Defining a Strategy

10.1 Debugging, troubleshooting, and testing have similar goals, but occur at different times during a product's lifetime with a different set of premises. When does each of these occur?

10.2 What are the underlying assumptions about the design at the start of debugging? troubleshooting? testing?

Formulating a Plan

10.3 What are the four main reasons for testing a design?

10.4 What is stress testing, and what is its purpose?

10.5 What is a test plan, and what is it based on?

10.6 What is the purpose of a test plan?

10.7 What is a test specification, and what is it based on?

10.8 What is the purpose of a test specification?

Executing the Plan

10.9 What is a test procedure? What is its purpose?

10.10 What is a test case, and what is it based on?

10.11 What is the purpose of a test case?

10.12 What is a test suite?

Applying the Strategy—Egoless Design

10.13 What is egoless design?

Applying the Strategy—Design Reviews

10.14 What is the purpose of a design review?

10.15 During what stage of the development life cycle should a design review be held?

10.16 Who should participate in a design review?

Applying the Strategy—Module Debug and Test

10.17 What is a smoke test?

10.18 During the early stages of debugging, what kinds of problems are typically identified?

10.19 What is a black box test? gray box test? white box test?

10.20 What do the expressions *directly observable* and *indirectly observable* mean in the context of debug and test?

10.21 What is *fault forwarding*?

10.22 What is *path sensitizing*?

Applying the Strategy—Subsystem and System Test

10.23 What kinds of problems are likely to occur at the subsystem and system test level?

10.24 When is a system test process complete?

Applying the Strategy—Testing for the Customer

10.25 What is an *alpha test*? *beta test*?

10.26 What are the goals and objectives of alpha tests? beta tests?

10.27 What are the goals and objectives of verification tests? validation tests?

10.28 What are the goals and objectives of acceptance tests? production tests?

10.29 What are the goals and objectives of self-tests?

10.30 What is the difference between on demand and background self-test?

10.25 THOUGHT QUESTIONS

Defining a Strategy

10.1 We have found that the processes of debugging, troubleshooting, and testing have similar goals, but occur at different times during a product's lifetime, processes with a different set of premises. How do the strategies and goals for each of these differ?

10.2 Why is a sound strategy essential for effective debugging, troubleshooting, or testing?

10.3 How does testing strategy change with product type, for example, a video game, a medical device, or a robot control system?

10.4 Some say that design should be a top-down process while debug and test should be bottom up. What do they mean?

10.5 When formulating a self-test strategy, what things should one consider? Explain each of your choices.

10.6 Discuss the pros and cons of *fault seeding* as a test strategy.

Formulating a Plan

10.7 The chapter cites four main reasons for testing a design. Can you propose others?

10.8 Beyond testing the functionality of the hardware and software components in an embedded design, what other kinds of tests should be performed? Explain your thinking behind your proposal.

10.9 What information should be included in a test plan?

10.10 What information should be included in a test specification?

Executing the Plan

10.11 How does a test procedure differ from a test specification?

10.12 What kinds of signal values should be tested under a test suite?

10.13 What range of signal values should be utilized during debugging and prior to release to production?

10.14 What range of signal values should be utilized following release to production?

10.15 Is it necessary to apply all combinations of input signals to test a system? Why or why not?

10.16 When a debugging test fails, what kind of information should be recorded and kept? Please explain each of your recommendations.

10.17 What is test coverage? Why is it important?

10.18 What should be the next steps following a test failure during debug? during stress testing? during production test? during alpha or beta test?

Applying the Strategy—Egoless Design

10.19 Why is egoless design considered to be part of test?

Applying the Strategy—Design Reviews

10.20 Design reviews should be held several times during a product's development cycle. What aspects of the product design should be examined during each of those design reviews?

Applying the Strategy—Module Debug and Test

10.21 When formulating a debugging strategy, what are some of the major areas that one should consider?

10.22 What is *fault masking*? Why is it a potential problem?

10.23 On the software side of test, what is *dead code*?

Applying the Strategy—Subsystem and System Test

10.24 What kinds of problems are likely to occur at the subsystem and system test level?

10.25 Propose and discuss capabilities that can be incorporated into a hardware design that can facilitate debug and test; a software design.

10.26 When can one say, prior to release to production, that the system test process is complete?

Applying the Strategy—Testing for the Customer

10.27 What should one do following completion of an alpha test phase? beta test phase?

10.28 Can sufficient testing ensure the quality of a product?

10.29 Why is production testing considered a burden rather than a benefit?

10.30 If a failure has occurred either on the system bus or within the memory subsystem, how can a self-diagnostic program be executed?

10.31 Discuss some of the benefits of an on-demand self-test?

10.32 Are there circumstances under which it is reasonable to release and ship a product that has known bugs? Explain your thinking.

10.26 PROBLEMS

Debugging and Testing Systems

In the problems in this chapter, we will take the next steps in the product development life cycle. In earlier chapters we looked at the formal approaches to design, the detailed design of the hardware side and the software side. In this chapter, we have examined two aspects of that process: debug and test. In the first, we assume that the first cut at the design of the hardware and software modules that comprise the design is complete. In the second, the product is ready to go into production.

As we learned in the chapter, a strategy, a plan, is essential in both endeavors. We will now address each of those parts of the process.

For the systems designed in Problems 9-1 to 9-10 at the end of Chapter 9:

(a) *Formulate a debugging strategy.* What module should be debugged first, what inputs should you use, what outputs should you expect to see? How should you begin to integrate the modules? What should you do on failure?

(b) *Formulate a test plan.* Tie this plan back to the original requirements. What should be tested? How extensively? How can you generate test inputs, outputs? Should you do boundary condition testing? Is running/testing the system at full operating speed important?

PART 3 DOING THE WORK

Chapter 11

Real-Time Kernels and Operating Systems

THINGS TO LOOK FOR . . .

- Understanding of tasks and threads.
- The motivation for multitasking and multiprocessing.
- Understanding of the basic concepts and vocabulary of multitasking and multiprocessing.
- The definition of an operating system kernel.
- Meaning of foreground-background systems.
- Understanding of task control blocks.
- The description of an operating system and its responsibilities.
- The major responsibilities and architecture of an operating system.
- Characteristics that distinguish a real-time operating system.
- The meaning of and differences between soft and hard real-time systems.
- The different kinds of stacks in a system and their role in context switching.

11.0 INTRODUCTION

multitasking
exchanging/sharing, synchronizing, scheduling, sharing resources
operating system
real-time

A typical embedded system solves a complex problem by decomposing it into a number of smaller, simpler pieces called *tasks* that work together in an organized way. Such a system is called a *multitasking* system. Several important aspects of a multitasking design include *exchanging/sharing* data between tasks, *synchronizing* tasks, *scheduling* task execution, and *sharing resources* among the tasks. The piece of software that provides the required coordination is called an *operating system*. When the control must ensure that task execution satisfies a set of specified time constraints, the operating system is called a *real-time* operating system.

This chapter provides an introduction to and motivation for implementing tasks and multitasking as a design strategy for an embedded application. We will introduce some of the necessary terminology and examine the critical role of time in developing and deploying many embedded applications.

We will start by examining the tasks themselves and look at some of the problems that arise when we seek to build, operate, and control a system made up of a number of independent tasks. We will introduce the operating system as one means to coordinate and control the task execution so as to ensure that the higher level application performs as we desire. We will identify the major responsibilities of an operating system, examine the characteristics and capabilities that distinguish an *RTOS—Real-Time Operating System*, and then study the core set of requirements of the *OS* as embodied in the kernel. We will identify the central responsibilities of and the basic architecture for various control strategies. Finally, we will look at different kinds of stacks and their role in managing context switches associated with task state changes, task preemption, or interrupts.

RTOS—Real-Time Operating System

11.1 TASKS AND THINGS

Let's open the discussion with an invitation to a small group of special friends. We invite them over for an evening filled with music, a gourmet meal, and perhaps some congenial philosophical discussions while dining. For our friends, it is important that everything be perfect. We want each of the dishes that are being prepared to finish at the same time so that they are cooked to perfection and can all be presented at the table together. As we plan the meal, we have to decide when we must start cooking the meat, the fish, the vegetables, the rice or potatoes or noodles. If we have scheduled everything properly, they will all finish together and culminate in a marvelous banquet; if not, we order out and then rely on the music and conversation.

At some point, all of the different dishes are cooking together. We have broken the main task—cook the meal—down into a number of smaller ones, subtasks, that can be done at the same time. However, since there is only one of us, we cannot devote all of our attention to each of the subtasks all the time. Therefore, we continually check one dish and then the next to make sure that everything is proceeding smoothly—add a little salt here, adjust the flame a bit there, add a little wine to that sauce, adjust the seasoning on this one, start that one. We can capture the meal preparation in a high-level UML activity diagram as shown in Figure 11.0.

The common approach to designing an embedded application follows the same pattern. The application comprises a number of tasks that must be completed in order for the intended application to be completed. In the preparation of the meal, we are working on several of the tasks at the same time; in the application, the CPU is being shared among the tasks so that each can progress.

In the earlier studies of design, as with the meal, we learned to partition the application first into major functions and then into smaller pieces. Ultimately, we mapped those pieces onto the hardware and software modules. Each of the software modules that comprise the embedded program is simply a collection of instructions—the firmware—that direct the system's central processing unit, the CPU, to carry out a prescribed job. If the partitioning is done well, each of the smaller modules will naturally become one of the tasks that make up the application.

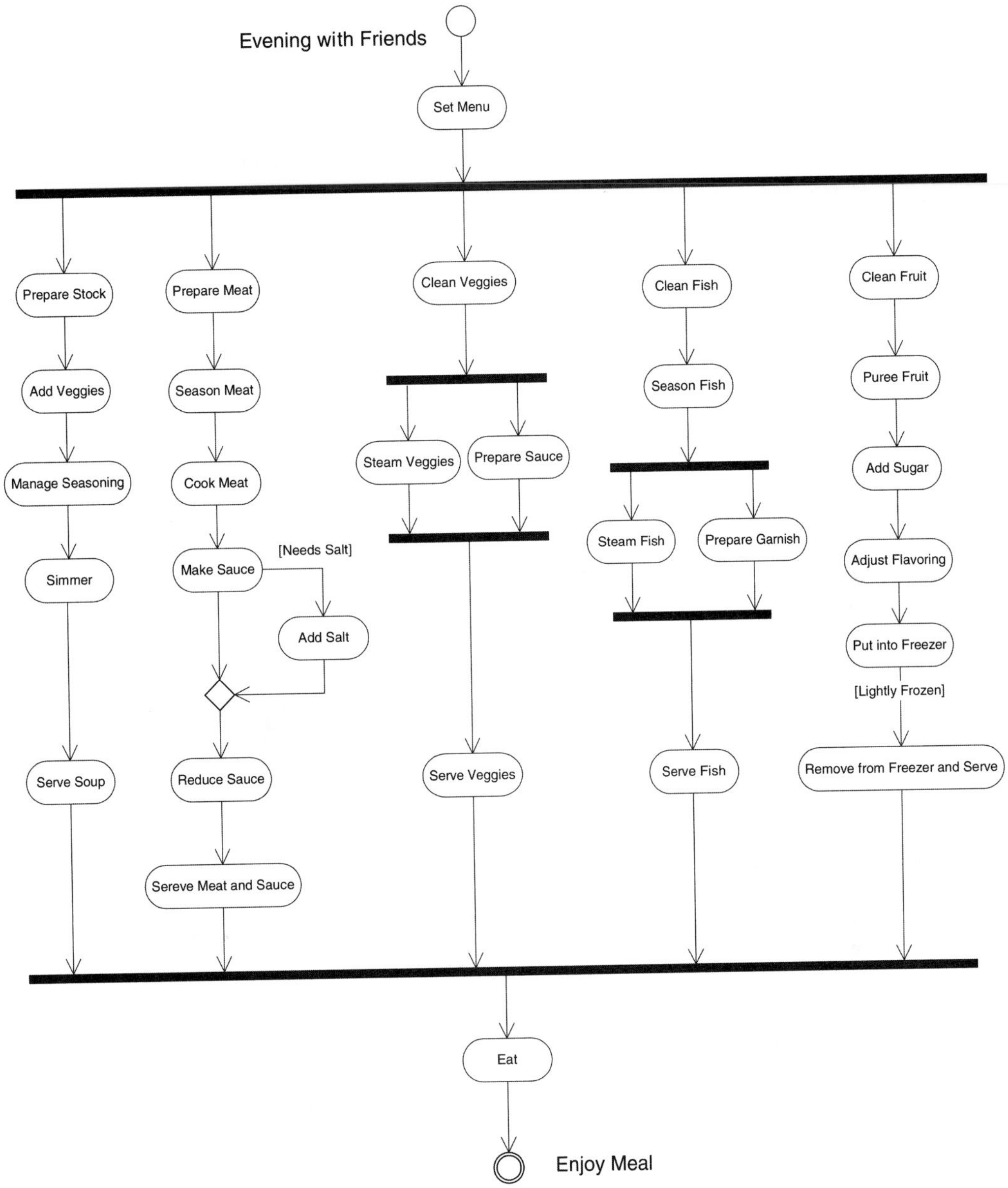

Figure 11.0 Activity Diagram for Preparing a Meal for Friends

11.2 PROGRAMS AND PROCESSES

running, executing

process, task

An embedded program, made up of a collection of firmware modules, is a static entity. It can do no useful work unless it is *running* or *executing*. When a firmware module is executing, it is called a *process* or *task*. These words are often used interchangeably. When a process is created, it is allocated a number of resources by the operating system. These can include a process stack, memory address space, registers (through the CPU), a program counter, I/O ports, network connections, file descriptors, and so on. These resources are generally not shared with other processes.

During execution, the contents of the program counter are continually changing as the process moves from instruction to instruction within the program, reading, manipulating, and writing *data*. That data may be produced by the application, read from the system's memory, or entered into the system from some external source such as sensors, switch closures, or remote applications. The currently executing instruction (identified by the value of the program counter) and the present values of the associated data in memory or in registers are collectively known as the *process state*. The process state may contain the values of a large number of other pieces of information as well.

data

process state

11.3 THE CPU IS A RESOURCE

program

The traditional view of computing focuses on the *program*. One says that the *program*, or more specifically a task within the program, is running on the computer. In an embedded application, we change the point of view to that of the microprocessor. Viewed with respect to the microprocessor—more specifically, the CPU—the CPU is being used to execute the firmware. The CPU is another resource that is available for use by the task to do its job as illustrated in Figure 11.1.

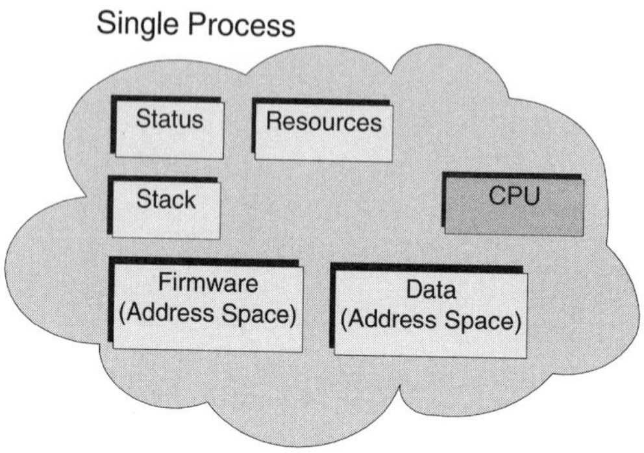

Figure 11.1 A Model of a Single Process (The CPU is a resource)

execution time, terminates
persistence

As is evident from this figure, when a task enters the system it takes up space—memory—and uses other system resources. The time that it takes to complete is called its *execution time*. The duration from the time when it enters the system until it *terminates* is called its *persistence*. If there is only a single task in the system, there will be no contention for resources and no restrictions on how long it can run.

If a second task is added to the system, potential resource contention problems arise. Generally, there is only one CPU, and the remaining resources are limited. The problem is resolved by carefully managing how the resources are allocated to each task and by controlling how long each can retain the resources.

appearance, multitasking
concurrently

The main resource, the CPU, is given to one task for a short while and then to the other. If each task shares the system's resources back and forth, each can get its job finished. If the CPU is passed between the tasks quickly enough, it will appear as if both tasks are using it at the same time. We will thus have a system that models parallel operations by time sharing a single processor. The execution time for the program will be extended, but the operation will give the *appearance* of simultaneous execution. Such a scheme is called *multitasking*; the tasks are said to be running *concurrently*. The concept can easily be extended to more than two tasks as Figure 11.2 illustrates.

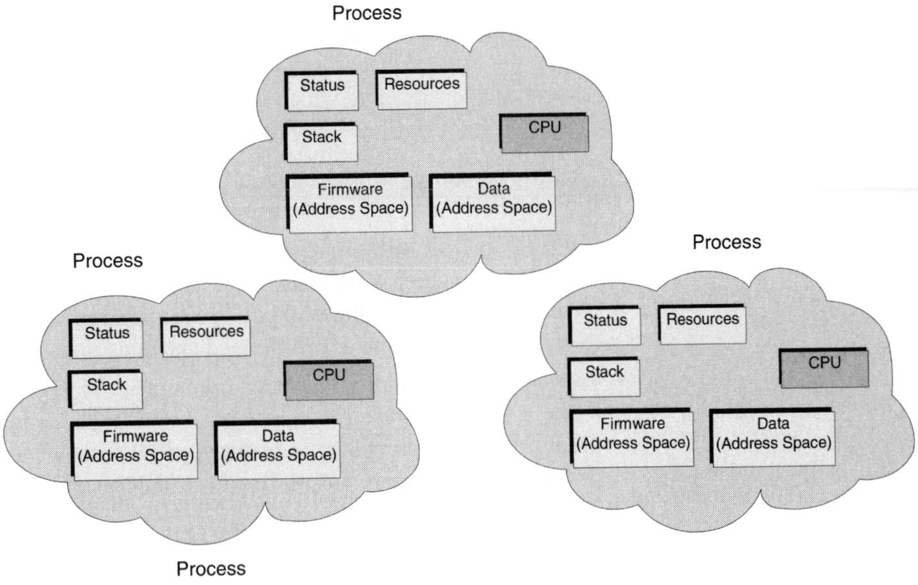

Figure 11.2 Multiple Processes

11.3.1 Setting a Schedule

Under such a scheme, in addition to the CPU, the processes are sharing other system resources as well such as timers, I/O facilities, and busses. Despite the illusion that all of the tasks are running simultaneously, in reality, at any instant in time, only one process is actively executing. That process is said to be in the *run* state. The other process(es) is/are in the *ready waiting* state. Such behavior is illustrated in the state and sequence diagrams in Figure 11.3 for a system with three tasks. One task will be running while the others are waiting to be given the CPU. With the ability to share the CPU among several tasks, the problem of deciding which task will be given the CPU and when arises.

run
ready waiting

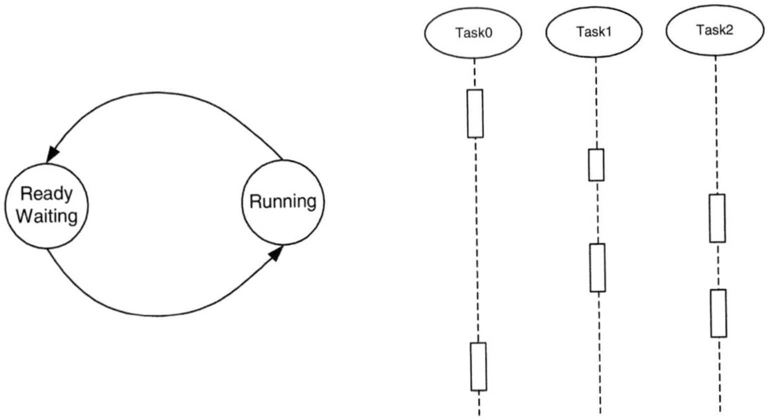

Figure 11.3 State Chart and Sequence Diagram for a System with Three Tasks

schedule

As with many similar such problems in real life, a *schedule* is set up to specify when, under what conditions, and for how long each task will be given use of the CPU (and other resources).

scheduling strategy

The criteria for deciding which task is to run next are collectively called a *scheduling strategy*. Such strategies generally fall into three categories:

- *Multiprogramming* in which the running task continues until it performs an operation that requires waiting for an external event (e.g., waiting for an I/O event or timer to expire).
- *Real-Time* in which tasks with specified temporal deadlines are guaranteed to complete before those deadlines expire. Systems using such a scheme require a response to certain events within a well-defined and constrained time.
- *Time sharing* in which the running task is required to give up the CPU so that another task may get a turn. Under a time-shared strategy, a hardware timer is used to *preempt* the currently executing task and return control to the operating system. Such a scheme permits one to reliably ensure that each process is given a slice of time to use the operating system.

preempt

11.3.2 Changing Context

context
preempted, blocked
ready, switch, context
restored

A task's *context* comprises the important information about the state of the task such as the values of any variables (held in the CPU's registers), the value of the program counter, and so forth. Each time that a running task is stopped—*preempted* or *blocked*—and the CPU is given to another task that is *ready*, a *switch* to a new *context* is executed. A context switch first requires that the state of the currently active task be saved. If the task that is scheduled to get the CPU next had been running previously, its state is *restored* and it continues where it had left off. Otherwise, the new task starts from its initial state. As is evident, a context change entails a lot of work and can take a significant amount of time.

The earlier state diagram is now extended in Figure 11.4 to reflect a task entering the system, being preempted, and terminating.

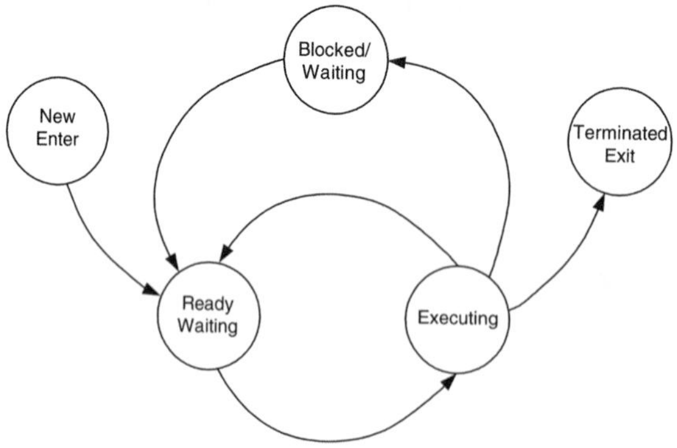

Figure 11.4 A Basic Diagram of Possible Task States

11.4 THREADS—LIGHTWEIGHT AND HEAVYWEIGHT

As we learned earlier, a task or process is characterized by a collection of resources that are utilized to execute a program. The smallest subset of these resources (a copy of the CPU registers including the program counter and a stack) that is necessary for the execution of

thread *lightweight thread* *heavyweight thread*

the program is called *thread*. Think about the basic Turing machine. Sometimes the subset of resources is also called a *lightweight thread,* in contrast to the process itself which may be referred to as a *heavyweight thread.* A thread can be in only one process, and a process without a thread can do nothing.

11.4.1 A Single Thread

thread of execution, thread of control *physical* *single process–single thread design*

The sequential execution of a set of instructions through a task or process in an embedded application is called a *thread of execution*, or *thread of control*. Recall that the thread has a stack and status information relevant to its state and operation and a *copy* of the (contents of) the physical registers. During execution the thread uses the code (firmware), data, CPU (and associated *physical* registers), and other resources that have been allocated to the process. Figure 11.5 presents a single task with one thread of execution. The model is referred to as a *single process–single thread design.*

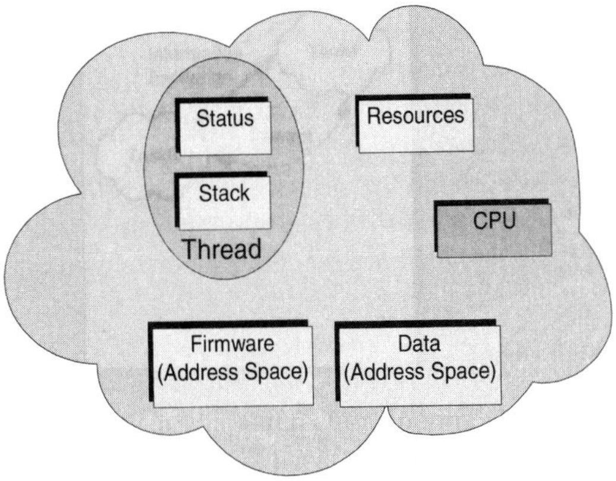

Figure 11.5 Single Process–Single Thread

running, blocked, ready, terminated *multiprocess–single thread*

When we state that the process is *running, blocked, ready,* or *terminated* in fact, we are describing the different states of the thread.

If the embedded design is intended to perform a wide variety of operations with minimal interaction, then it may be appropriate to allocate one process to each major function to be performed. Such systems are ideal for a *multiprocess–single thread* implementation.

11.4.2 Multiple Threads

Many embedded systems are intended to perform a single primary function. The operations to be performed by that function are all interrelated. During partitioning and functional decomposition, we should seek to identify which of those actions would benefit from parallel execution. We might consider allocating a subtask for each type of I/O.

The nature of an application executing as a single primary function suggests that the associated process should be decomposed into a number of subtasks executing in parallel. At runtime, the process can pass the CPU around to each of these subtasks, thereby enabling each to do its job.

single process–multithread design

We now see that each of the smaller jobs has its own thread of execution. Such a system is called a *single process–multithread design.* Unlike processes or tasks, threads are not independent of each other. They can access any address within the process, including other threads' stacks. Why is this important to note?

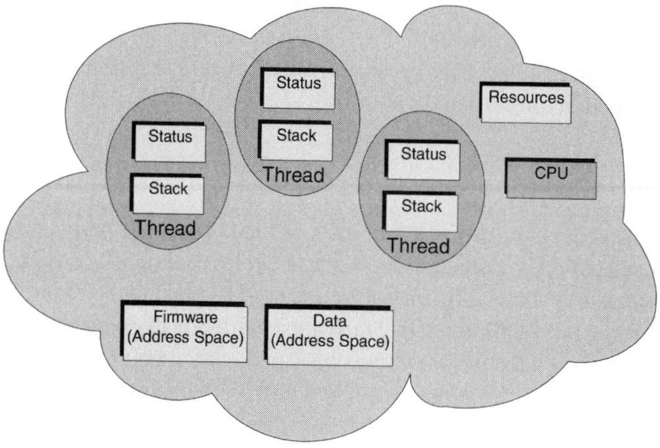

Figure 11.6 Single Process–Multiple Threads

Of significance is that a context switch between threads can be substantially simpler and therefore faster than between processes. When switching between threads, much less information must be saved and restored. Figure 11.6 illustrates one such task with multiple threads.

multithreaded operating system

An operating system that supports tasks with multiple threads is, naturally, referred to as a *multithreaded operating system.*

multiprocess–multithread design

We can easily extend the design of the application to support multiple processes. We can further decompose each process into multiple subtasks. Such a system is, as expected, called a *multiprocess–multithread design.*

11.5 SHARING RESOURCES

Based on the discussions up to this point, one can now identify four categories of multitasking operating system.

single process–single thread ***multiprocess–single thread*** ***single process–multiple threads*** ***multiprocess–multiple threads***

- *Single process–single thread,* as the name implies has only one process, and, in an embedded application, that process runs forever.
- A *multiprocess–single thread* supports multiple simultaneously executing processes; each process has only a single thread of control.
- A *single process–multiple threads* design supports only one process; within the process, it has multiple threads of control.
- A *multiprocess–multiple threads* implementation supports multiple processes, and within each process there is support for multiple threads of control.

The major distinguishing feature among each of these schemes is which resources the process and hence thread(s) is/are using and where the resources come from. First the resources. At a minimum, a process or task will need the following,

- The code or firmware, the instructions.

These are in memory and have addresses.

- The data that the code is manipulating.

The data starts out in memory and may be moved to registers. The data has addresses.

- The CPU and associated physical registers
- A stack
- Status information

These are reflected in each of the previous diagrams. The first three items are shared among member threads, and the last two are proprietary to each thread. Note that each thread does have a copy of the registers, however. There are often other necessary resources as well such as timers, measurement or signal-generation resources, and I/O ports.

11.5.1 Memory Resource Management

11.5.1.1 System-Level Management

Most microprocessor designs today are still based on the von Neumann architecture in which the program (instructions) is stored in memory in the same manner as any other piece of information (data). When a process is created by the operating system, it is given a portion of that physical memory in which to work. The set of addresses delimiting that code and data memory, proprietary to each process, is called its *address space*. That address space will typically not be shared with any other peer processes. However, when multiple processes are concurrently executing in memory, an errant pointer or stack error can easily result in memory owned by other processes being overwritten.

address space

The system software must restrict the range of addresses that are accessible to the executing process. A process (thread) trying to access memory outside its allowed range should be immediately stopped before it can inflict damage on memory belonging to other processes. One means by which such restrictions are enforced is through the concept of *privilege level.*

privilege level

Processes are segregated into those that have *supervisor mode* capability and those that have *user mode* capability. User mode limits the subset of instructions that a process can use. To be able to access the entire memory space requires supervisory mode access.

supervisory mode

user mode

Processes with a low (user mode) privilege level are simply not allowed to perform certain kinds of memory accesses or to execute certain instructions. When a process attempts to execute such restricted instructions, an interrupt is generated and a supervisory program with a higher privilege level decides how to respond. The higher (supervisor mode) privilege level is generally reserved for supervisory or administration types of tasks that one finds delegated to the operating system or other such software. Processes with such privilege have access to any firmware and can use any instructions within the microprocessor's instruction, set as we see in the diagram of the processor's firmware address space in Figure 11.7.

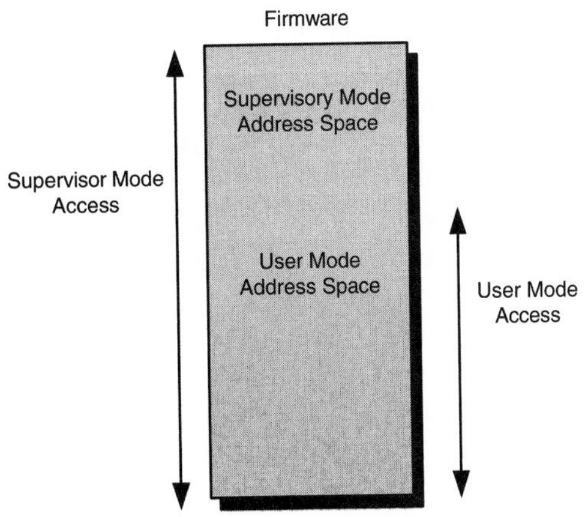

Figure 11.7 Address Space Access Privileges

11.5.2 Process-Level Management

child processes A process may create or spawn *child processes*. When doing so, that parent process may choose to give a subset of its resources to each of the children. The children are separate processes, and each has its own data address space, data, status, and stack. The code portion of the address space is shared.

multiple threads A process may create *multiple threads*. When doing so, that parent process shares most of its resources with each of the threads. These are not separate processes but separate threads of execution within the same process. Each thread will have its own stack and status information.

processes or tasks Figure 11.2 illustrates that in contrast to lightweight threads, *processes or tasks* exist in separate address spaces. Therefore, one must use some form of messaging or shared variable for intertask exchange. Processes have a stronger notion of encapsulation than threads since *thread* each *thread* has its own CPU state but shares the code section, data section, and task resources with peer threads. It is this sharing that gives threads a weaker notion of encapsulation.

11.5.3 Reentrant Code

Child processes and consequently their threads share the same firmware memory area. As a result, two different threads can be executing the same function at the same time. *reentrant* Functions using *only* local variables are inherently *reentrant*. That is, they can be simultaneously called and executed in two or more contexts.

Local variables are copied to the stack, and each invocation will get new copies. On the other hand, functions that use global variables, variables local to the process, variables passed by reference, or shared resources are not reentrant. One must be particularly careful to ensure that all accesses to any common resources are coordinated. When designing the application, one must make certain that one thread cannot corrupt the values of the variables in a second. Any shared functions must be designed to be reentrant.

Coding Style

It is good practice to make certain that all functions are reentrant. One never knows when a future modification to the design may need to share an existing function.

11.6 FOREGROUND/BACKGROUND SYSTEMS

foreground/background model, background tasks, foreground tasks The *foreground/background model* for managing task execution decomposes the set of tasks comprising the application into two subsets called *background tasks* and *foreground tasks*. The traditional view of such systems allocates tasks that interact with the user or other I/O devices to the foreground set and the remainder to the background set. The interpretation is slightly modified in the embedded world.

The foreground tasks are those initiated by interrupt or by a real-time constraint that must be met. They will be assigned the higher priority levels in the system. In contrast, background tasks are noninterrupt driven and are assigned the lower priorities. Once started, the background task will typically run to completion; however, they can be interrupted or preempted by any foreground task at any time. Often separate ready queues will be maintained for the two types of tasks. Schedules, scheduling, and priorities will be discussed in the next chapter.

The background tasks should include all those that do not have tight time constraints. Tasks that are designed to continuously monitor system integrity or involve heavy processing are good candidates.

11.7 THE OPERATING SYSTEM

operating system

An embedded *operating system* provides an environment within which the firmware pieces, the tasks that make up an embedded application, are executed. Perhaps the easiest way to first view an operating system is from the perspective of the services it can provide. Internally, operating systems vary greatly in both design and the strategy for delivering such services.

To begin, an operating system must provide or support three specific functions.

- Schedule task execution.
- Dispatch a task to run.
- Ensure communication and synchronization among tasks.

scheduler, dispatcher
intertask or interprocess communication
kernel

The *scheduler* determines which task will run and when it will do so. The *dispatcher* performs the necessary operations to start the task, and *intertask or interprocess communication* is the mechanism for exchanging data and information between tasks or processes on the same machine or on different ones. The *kernel* is the smallest portion of operating system that provides these functions.

In an embedded operating system, such functions are captured in the following types of services.

- Process or Task Management
  The central component of task management entails the creation and deletion of user and system processes as well as the suspension and resumption of such processes. How the task management responsibilities are handled determines, in large part, whether the OS can be defined as real-time. Additional responsibilities include the management of interprocess communication and of deadlocks. Deadlocks arise when two or more tasks need a resource that is held by some other task.
- Memory Management
  Among other responsibilities, memory management services include the tracking and control of which tasks are loaded into memory, monitoring which parts of memory are being used and by whom, administering dynamic memory if it is used, and managing caching schemes.
- I/O System Management
  Management of system input and output can include a wide range of responsibilities. An embedded application must interact with a great variety of different devices. In more complex systems, such interaction occurs through a special piece of software called a *device driver*. In a well-designed system, the internal side of that software has what is called a *common calling interface*—an *application programmer's interface* (API). The motivation in such an approach is to permit the application software to interact with each of the different devices in the same way. With UNIX™, for example, everything looks like a file. The operating system must manage the interaction between each of those devices and the users or tasks in the application. Also included in such interaction is the caching and buffering of all input and output transactions as necessary.

  device driver
  common calling interface, application programmer's interface
  API
- File System Management
  As the name suggests, file system management responsibilities are directed toward the creation, deletion, and management of files and directories. Recall the discussions about file management problems with the Mars rover *Spirit*. In that instance, the directory structure could not be created during boot because of available memory limitations.

Another task that falls under the auspices of the file management portion of the OS is that of working with nonvolatile storage if such capability is included in the system. Duties can include routine backup of any data that is to be saved as well as emergency backup either as power is failing or as some other catastrophic event is occurring to the system.

- System Protection
  As discussed earlier, ensuring the protection of data and resources in the context of concurrent processes is an important and essential duty for the operating system. Such a duty is more acute in the context of a von Neumann machine.
- Networking
  In the context of a distributed application, the operating system must also take on the responsibility of managing distributed intrasystem communication and the remote scheduling of tasks.
- Command Interpretation
  The operating system in machines such as the familiar desktop computers that directly interact with the user provides the interface to that user's application. In embedded applications that support provisions for user interaction, the task is implemented via a variety of software drivers supported by the OS that interact with the hardware I/O devices. As commands and directives come into the system, they must be parsed, checked for grammatical accuracy, and directed to the target task.

11.8 THE REAL-TIME OPERATING SYSTEM (RTOS)

real-time operating system (RTOS)

A *real-time operating system* (RTOS) is primarily an operating system. In addition to the responsibilities already enumerated, this special class of operating system ensures (among other things) that (rigid) time constraints can be met. The RTOS is commonly found in embedded applications because, as noted, in certain such applications, if such requirements are not met, the performance of the application is inaccurate or compromised in some way. Such systems are often interacting with the physical environment through sensors and various types of measurement devices. RTOS-based applications are frequently used in scientific experiments, control systems, or other applications where missed deadlines cannot be tolerated.

Often people misuse the term real-time to mean that the system responds quickly. Such an interpretation is only partially correct. The key characteristic of an RTOS is deterministic behavior. By this term we mean that given the same state and same set of inputs, the next state (and any associated outputs) will be the same each time the control algorithm utilized by the system is executed.

hard real-time, soft real-time

In earlier discussions, we identified the two extremes in real-time behavior: that which is termed *hard real-time* and that designated *soft real-time*. Behavior that falls into the first category is sufficiently characterized such that system delays are known or at least bounded. These systems are said to be operating correctly if they can return results within the specified timing bounds. Behavior classified as soft real-time ensures that critical tasks have priority over other tasks and retain that priority until complete. A real-time task cannot be kept waiting indefinitely. We will return to this discussion shortly.

11.9 OPERATING SYSTEM ARCHITECTURE

virtual machines

Most contemporary operating systems are designed and implemented as a hierarchy of what are called *virtual machines,* as illustrated in Figure 11.8. Organized like the onion model discussed earlier, the only real machine that the various pieces of functionality within the

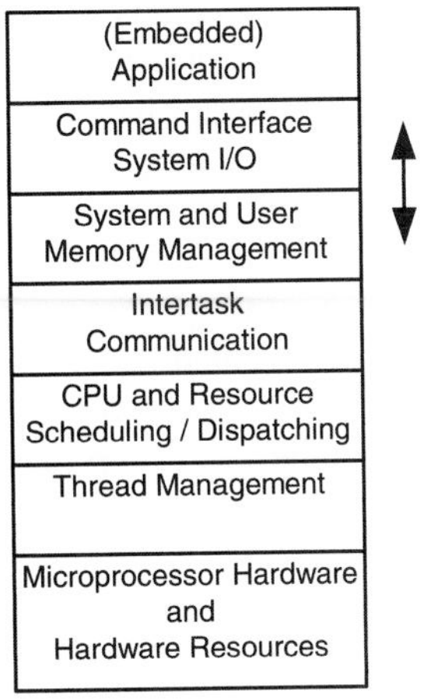

Figure 11.8 Operating System Virtual Machine Model

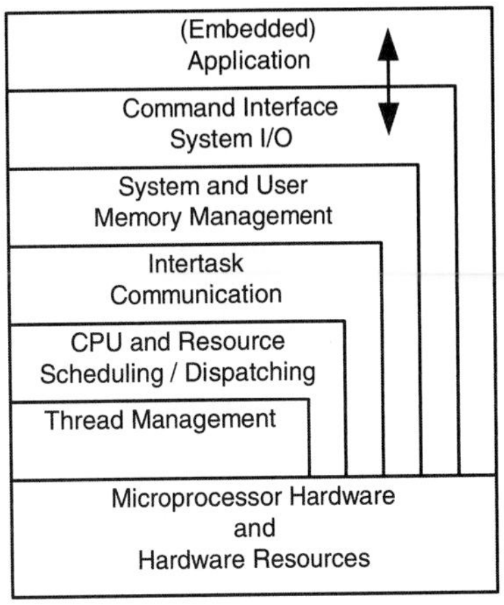

Figure 11.9 Typical High-Level Operating System Architecture

operating system see is the underlying physical microprocessor; specifically, the OS sees the CPU, the memory, and the concrete I/O devices. The hierarchy is designed such that each layer uses the functions/operations and services of lower layers. The primary advantage of such an approach is increased modularity.

A typical architecture for an operating system appears in Figure 11.9. In some architectures, the higher level layers have access to lower levels through system calls and hardware instructions. The existing calling interface between levels is retained while providing access to the physical hardware below.

With such capability, an interface can be made to appear as if it is a machine executing a specific set of instructions as defined by the API. The idea can be logically extended so as to create the illusion that the tasks at each level are running on its own machine. Each level in such a model is called a *virtual machine.*

virtual machine

With such an approach, one could run entirely different operating system as an application within the primary OS. Such a virtual machine implementation can be difficult to effect in general. There is not always a good match between the hardware on the real machine and that required by the emulated or virtual machine. The real machine may have two I/O ports, one serial and one parallel, for example, and the emulated machine may need three serial and two parallel ports. Clearly, one cannot create more physical ports than exist in reality; therefore, the remaining necessary ports must be virtual.

11.10 TASKS AND TASK CONTROL BLOCKS

A traditional or real-time operating system orchestrates the behavior of an application by executing each of the tasks that comprise the design according to a specified schedule. That schedule and its management in an RTOS can determine success or failure of the design. Each *task* or process is represented by a *task or process control block* (TCB).

task, task or process control block (TCB)

11.10.1 The Task

A task or process simply identifies a job that is to be done within an embedded application. More specifically, it is a set of software (firmware) instructions, collected together, that are designed and executed to accomplish that job. An embedded application is thus nothing more than a collection of such jobs. How and when each is executed is determined by the schedule and the dispatch algorithms; how and what data are acted upon by the task is specified by the intertask communication scheme. The performance of each of these three operations determines the robustness and quality of the design.

11.10.2 The Task Control Block

task control block (TCB), process control block

In a tasked-based approach, each process is represented in the operating system by a data structure called a *task control block* (TCB), also known as a *process control block*. The TCB contains all of the important information about the task. A typical TCB, which contains the following information, is illustrated in Figure 11.10.

- Pointer (for linking the TCB to various queues)
- Process ID and state
- Program counter
- CPU registers
- Scheduling information (priorities and pointers to scheduling queues)
- Memory management information (tag tables and cache information)
- Scheduling information (time limits or time and resources used)
- I/O status information (resources allocated or open files)

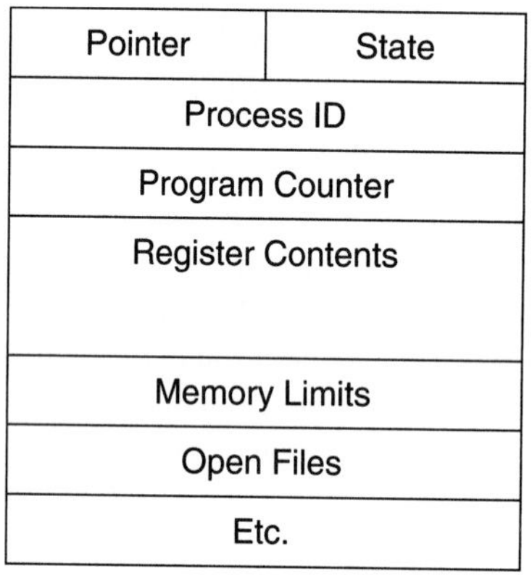

Figure 11.10 Task Control Block

ready, execute, dormant

TCB allocation may be static or dynamic. Static allocation is typically used in embedded systems with no memory management. There are a fixed number of task control blocks; the memory is allocated at system generation time and placed in a dormant or unused state. When a task is initiated, a TCB is created and the appropriate information is entered. The TCB is then placed into the *ready* state by the scheduler. From the ready state, it will be moved to the *execute* state by dispatcher. When a task terminates, the associated TCB is returned to the *dormant* state. With a fixed number of TCBs, no runtime memory management is necessary. One must be cautious, however, not to exhaust the supply of TCBs.

ready, execute

With dynamic allocation, a variable number of task control blocks can be allocated from the heap at runtime. When a task is created, as was done with a static allocation, the TCB is created, initialized, and placed into the *ready* state and scheduled by the scheduler. From the ready state, it will be moved to the *execute* state and given the CPU by dispatcher. When a task is terminated, the TCB memory is returned to heap storage. With a dynamic allocation, heap management must be supported. Dynamic allocation suggests an unlimited supply of TCBs. However, the typical embedded application has limited memory; allocating too many TCBs can exhaust the supply. A dynamic memory allocation scheme is generally too expensive for smaller embedded systems.

Entry Queue, Job Queue

When a task enters the system, it will typically be placed into a queue called the *Entry Queue* or *Job Queue*. The easiest and most flexible way to implement such a queue is to utilize a linked list as the underlying data structure. Thus, the last entries in the TCB hold the pointers to the preceding and succeeding TCBs in the queue. One certainly could use an array data type as well. However, some flexibility is compromised later in the implementation of the OS. Whether a queue, an array, or some other data type is used to hold the TCBs, the entries must all look alike. Such a requirement will impose some restrictions on how the TCB is implemented.

In C, the TCB is implemented as a struct containing pointers to all relevant information, as seen in the C code fragments in Figure 11.11. Because the data members of a struct must all be of the same type, the pointers are all void* pointers. The skeletal structure for a typical TCB identifying the essential elements, the task, and an example set of task data are given in the C declarations presented in Figure 11.11.

```
// The task control block
struct TCB
{
    void (*taskPtr)(void* taskDataPtr);
    void* taskDataPtr;
    void* stackPtr;
    unsigned short priority;
    struct TCB* nextPtr;
    struct TCB* prevPtr
};
```

```
// The task
void aTask(void* taskDataPtr)
{
    function body;
}
```

```
// The data passed into the task
struct taskData
{
    int taskData0;
    int taskData1;
    char taskData2
};
```

Figure 11.11 Task Control Block

taskPtr

The first entry in the TCB in the figure is a pointer to a function—*taskPtr*. That function embodies the functionality associated with the task. The function's parameter list comprises the single argument of type void*. Because we do not wish to place any restrictions on the kinds of information that is passed into the task and because we do not want to force each task to take the same kinds of data, we utilize a struct as the means through which to pass the data into the task. To satisfy the requirement that all TCBs must look alike and yet be able to retain flexibility on what data is passed into the task, the type information associated with the data struct is removed by referencing it through a void* pointer. Within the task itself, the pointer must be cast back to the original type before it can be dereferenced to get the data.

Each task will have its own stack. The third entry in the TCB is a pointer to that stack. The fourth entry gives the priority for the task. The fifth and sixth entries are pointers used to link the TCB to the next and previous TCBs in any of the aforementioned queues.

11.10.3 A Simple Kernel

Let's now develop a rudimentary operating system kernel through a progression of simple examples to see how all of these pieces might work together. We will assume that three simple jobs are to be scheduled and performed:

- Bring in some data.
- Perform a computation on the data.
- Display the data.

The initial example will be a simple queue of functions operating on shared data. In this example, an array will be used as the underlying data type of the queue. The system will run forever, and each task will be scheduled and executed in turn. An important characteristic of such an implementation is that each task will run to completion before another is allowed to run.

The second example will declare a TCB for each task. The TCB will contain the task (referenced through a pointer to the function implementing the task) and the data that will be passed into that task. The task queue will still be implemented using an array, and the scheduling and dispatching algorithm will be retained. As in the first example, each task runs to completion. Both designs are expressed in the data flow diagram in Figure 11.12.

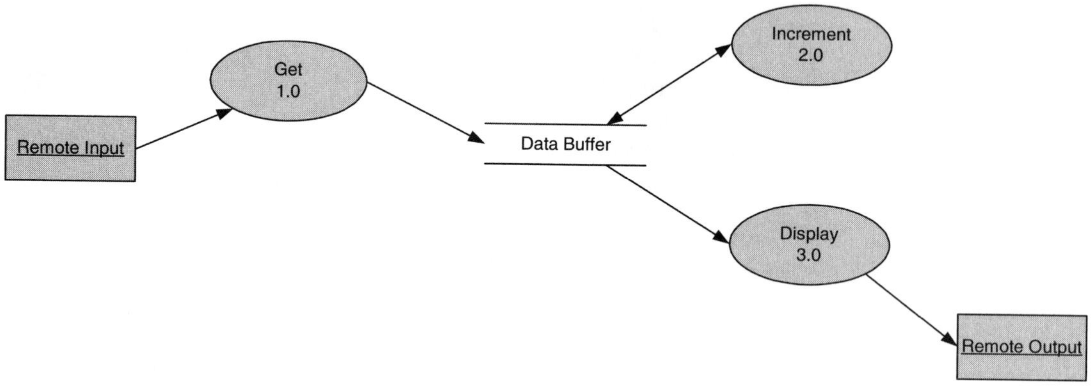

Figure 11.12 Three Asynchronous Tasks Sharing a Common Data Buffer

EXAMPLE 11.0

The software listing in Figure 11.13 gives a first cut at the design of a simple operating system kernel.

```
// Building a simple OS kernel - step 1
#include <stdio.h>
// Declare the prototypes for the tasks

void get (void* aNumber);              // input task
void increment (void* aNumber);        // computation task
void display (void* aNumber);          // output task
```

Figure 11.13 A Simple Operating System Kernel

```
void main(void)
{
    int i=0;                            // queue index
    int data;                           // declare a shared data
    int* aPtr = &data;                  // point to it

    void (*queue[3])(void*);            // declare queue as an array of pointers to
                                        // functions taking an arg of type void*
    queue[0] = get;                     // enter the tasks into the queue
    queue[1] = increment;
    queue[2] = display;

    while(1)
    {
        queue[i] ((void*) aPtr);        // dispatch each task in turn
        i = (i+1)%3;
    }
    return;
}
void get (void* aNumber)                // perform input operation
{
    printf ("Enter a number: 0..9 ");
    *(int*) aNumber = getchar();
    getchar();                          // discard cr
    *(int*) aNumber -= '0';             // convert to decimal from ascii
    return;
}

void increment (void* aNumber)          // perform computation
{
    int* aPtr = (int*) aNumber;
    (*aPtr)++;
    return;
}

void display (void* aNumber)            // perform output operation
{
    printf ("The result is: %d\n", *(int*)aNumber);
    return;
}
```

Figure 11.13 A Simple Operating System Kernel *(Cont.)*

EXAMPLE 11.1

The design in Example 11.0 is now modified in Figure 11.14 to utilize task control blocks.

```
// Building a simple OS kernel - step 2
#include <stdio.h>

// Declare the prototypes for the tasks
void get (void* aNumber);                    // input task
void increment (void* aNumber);              // computation task
void display (void* aNumber);                // output task

// Declare a TCB structure
typedef struct
{
    void* taskDataPtr;
    void (*taskPtr)(void*);
}
TCB;
void main(void)
{
    int i=0;                                 // queue index
    int data;                                // declare a shared data
    int* aPtr = &data;                       // point to it
    TCB* queue[3];                           // declare queue as an array of pointers to TCBs

    // Declare some TCBs
    TCB inTask;
    TCB compTask;
    TCB outTask;
    TCB* aTCBPtr;

    //  Initialize the TCBs
    inTask.taskDataPtr = (void*)&data;
    inTask.taskPtr = get;

    compTask.taskDataPtr = (void*)&data;
    compTask.taskPtr = increment;

    outTask.taskDataPtr = (void*)&data;
    outTask.taskPtr = display;

    // Initialize the task queue
    queue[0] = &inTask;
    queue[1] = &compTask;
    queue[2] = &outTask;

    // schedule and dispatch the tasks
    while(1)
    {
        aTCBPtr = queue[i];
        aTCBPtr->taskPtr( (aTCBPtr->taskDataPtr) );
        i = (i+1)%3;
    }
    return;
}
```

Figure 11.14 A Simple Operating System Kernel

```
void get (void* aNumber)                    // perform input operation
{
    printf ("Enter a number: 0..9 ");
    *(int*) aNumber = getchar();
    getchar();                              // discard cr
    *(int*) aNumber -= '0';                 // convert to decimal from ascii
    return;
}

void increment (void* aNumber)              // perform computation
{
    int* aPtr = (int*) aNumber;
    (*aPtr)++;
    return;
}

void display (void* aNumber)                // perform output operation
{
    printf ("The result is: %d\n", *(int*)aNumber);
    return;
}
```

Figure 11.14 A Simple Operating System Kernel *(Cont.)*

There are potentially two basic problems with the designs in the previous two examples. The first arises from the flow of control through the set of tasks. Because each task holds the CPU until it completes, if any of the tasks does not relinquish control, the system hangs forever. Case in point is the *get()* task, which depends on the user entering a piece of data. The second potential problem arises from how the intertask communication is affected. All of the tasks are sharing a common variable, *data*. In the present design, two of the tasks are reading the data and only one is writing the data. Moreover, since only one task can be active at any one time, there is no problem.

get()

data

The first problem can be addressed by using interrupts. Rather than waiting for data to be entered, the *get()* task can be decomposed into two pieces. The first task can prompt for data to be entered and then exit. The second, with invocation based on a keyboard interrupt, can read data when it is available.

To implement the design improvement, several modifications must be made. The *interrupt service routine* (ISR) must be written, and the ISR must be added to the vector table.

interrupt service routine

ISR

11.10.4 Interrupts Revisited

Since each processor and cross compiler manages interrupts using a proprietary protocol, we will illustrate the generic procedure by mixing pseudo code with the C routines. To that end, we will define the pseudo-code function *setVect()* as shown in Figure 11.15.

setVect()

When called, the function will enter the pointer to the ISR function into the designated slot in the interrupt vector table.

Each processor associates the supported interrupts with the corresponding hardware or software function or source. Interrupts may originate inside or outside of the processor and may be proprietary to the system or to the user.

Syntax

```
void setVect(unsigned int intNum, void(anISR*)(void));
intNum          interrupt number
anISR           the interrupt service routine
```

Figure 11.15 Specifying an Interrupt Service Routine

When defining and using interrupts, one must be certain that an ISR be written and assigned to every interrupt that is being used and to ensure that the routine is assigned to the proper interrupt. If an interrupt is used and no ISR is written or assigned, when the interrupt occurs, the (invalid) contents of the associated slot in the vector table will be interpreted as the address of the ISR. The processor will vector to that address in memory which has no meaningful code associated; the execution of subsequent instructions (or data for that matter) can potentially cause the system to crash.

Most microprocessors support several levels of control of the interrupt. In this context, control specifies the ability of the system (and ultimately the process) to accept or ignore interrupts. The highest level of control is provided by *enable* and *disable* instructions. As the names suggest, the *enable* instruction permits an interrupt to be recognized by the system. The *disable* instruction does the opposite.

enable, disable

masking

The second level of control is implemented through *masking*. Such capability permits one to selectively listen to or ignore individual interrupts. Typically, the microprocessor supports a mask register with 1 bit associated with each interrupt. If the mask bit is a logical 1, the associated interrupt will be recognized when it occurs. Similarly, when the bit is a logical 0, the interrupt will be ignored. If masking is supported, normally at least one of the interrupts will be designated as *nonmaskable*. That is, the interrupt must be listened to and responded to. Generally nonmaskable interrupts are associated with system-level functionality and are often disaster management tools.

nonmaskable

The third level of control assigns a priority to each interrupt. Higher priority interrupts can interrupt those with lower priority, but not vice versa. In most cases, the priority of each interrupt is set by the microprocessor manufacturer.

An interrupt can be viewed as an asynchronous function or a subroutine call. The mechanics of handling an interrupt (by the system) duplicate most of those we encountered with function calls. Like the function call, under interrupt, the system state information is held on the stack and restored on return. Consequently, as is also found with the function call, it is possible to overflow the stack. If, under a priority-based scheme, interrupts are permitted to interrupt an interrupt in its ISR at the same level, the potential for stack overflow exists and must be managed. The normal solution is to disable or mask the interrupts as appropriate to ensure that overflow cannot occur. When disabling or masking interrupts, bear in mind that the causative event still occurs; the system simply does not respond. Thus, when working with interrupts and ISRs, always keep the routine as simple and short as possible. An ISR with more than a dozen to 18 lines of code is probably too long. The objective is to respond to the interrupt, do the minimum amount of work that absolutely needs to be done, and then exit the ISR; further processing, if necessary, can be done in one of the tasks or foreground processes.

The following example illustrates the use of an interrupt to manage the asynchronous input to the system from the keyboard. In the design, all of the tasks now access the shared variable globally as illustrated in the data and control flow diagram in Figure 11.16.

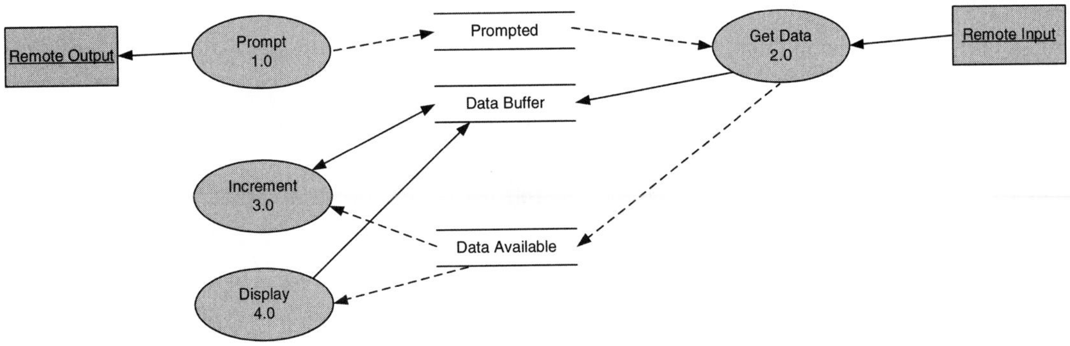

Figure 11.16 Using an Interrupt to Manage Asynchronous Keyboard Input

EXAMPLE 11.2 The design in Example 11.1 is now modified in Figure 11.17 to incorporate interrupts.

```
// Building a simple OS kernel - step 3

#include <stdio.h>
#define KBINT 0x3;                          // the kb will interrupt on interrupt 3

typedef enum aBool{FALSE, TRUE};            // create a boolean value
typedef unsigned char boolean;              // create a boolean type

// Declare the globals

boolean prompted = FALSE;                   // user data requested
boolean dataAvail = FALSE;                  // user data available

int data;                                   // declare a shared data

// Declare the prototypes for the tasks

void prompt(void);                          // prompt task
void increment (void);                      // computation task
void display (void);                        // output task

// Declare the prototype for the ISR

void getDataISR (void);                     // get data ISR

// Declare a TCB structure
typedef struct
{
   void (*taskPtr)(void);
}
TCB;
```

Figure 11.17 A Simple Operating System Kernel

```
void main(void)
{
    int i=0;                          // queue index
    TCB* queue[3];                    // declare queue as an array of pointers to TCBs

    // Declare some TCBs
    TCB promptTask;
    TCB compTask;
    TCB outTask;

    // Declare a working TCB pointer
    TCB* aTCBPtr;

    // Initialize the TCBs
    promptTask.taskPtr = prompt;
    compTask.taskPtr = increment;
    outTask.taskPtr = display;

    // Initialize the task queue
    queue[0] = &promptTask;
    queue[1] = &compTask;
    queue[2] = &outTask;

    // Enter the keyboard ISR into the interrupt vector table
    setVect(KBINT, getDataISR);

    //  Schedule and dispatch the tasks
    while(1)
    {
        aTCBPtr = queue[i];
        aTCBPtr->taskPtr();
        i = (i+1)%3;
    }
    return;
}

void prompt(void)                            // perform input operation
{
    if (!prompted)
    {
        printf ("Enter a number: 0..9 ");
        prompted = TRUE;
    }
    return;
}
```

Figure 11.17 A Simple Operating System Kernel *(Cont.)*

```
void increment (void)                              // perform computation
{
    if (dataAvail)
    {
        data++;
    }
    return;
}

void display (void)                                // perform output operation
{
    if (dataAvail)
    {
        printf ("The result is: %d\n", data);

        prompted = FALSE;
        dataAvail = FALSE;
    }
    return;
}

// keyboard ISR
void getDataISR(void)                              // perform input operation
{
    data = getchar();
    getchar();                                     // discard cr
    data -= '0';                                   // convert to decimal from ascii
    dataAvail = TRUE;
    return;
}
```

Figure 11.17 A Simple Operating System Kernel *(Cont.)*

Observe that each task checks one of the control variables to determine whether it should execute its body or simply return. Such a scheme is used to ensure a loosely coupled design. The knowledge of whether a specific task has enough information to execute is best kept with the task rather than with the scheduler. The negative aspect of such a decision is that the overhead of the function call will be incurred whether or not any real work gets done by the task.

In a tightly coupled design, tailored for a specific purpose, such knowledge could be moved to the scheduler. Under such circumstances, the overall flow of the system must be analyzed to confirm that the approach has a temporal advantage.

11.11 MEMORY MANAGEMENT REVISITED

The architecture of most contemporary embedded applications is built around multiple tasks/threads. If the design supports the ability to preempt or block a running task or thread and initiate another, there must be a switch to a new context. A context switch often involves

- Saving the existing context
- Switching to the new one
- Restoring the old one

These three steps can consume a significant amount of time. When operating under real-time constraints, the time required to affect the switch can be critical to the success or failure of the application.

The information that must be saved from an existing context may be as simple as the program counter and stack pointer for the original context or as complex as the state of the system at the time the switch occurs. The typical minimum includes

- The state of the CPU registers, including the CPU
- The values of local variables
- Status information

The saving of such information can be accomplished in several different ways.

Duplicate Hardware Context

- *Duplicate Hardware Context*
  Some microprocessor architectures significantly reduce the amount of information that must be saved and restored by simply switching to a duplicate or alternate context rather than devoting time to save the old, load a new one, and then restore the original on return.

Task Control Blocks

- *Task Control Blocks*
  These are best for systems ranging in complexity from those built around a simple kernel to those utilizing a more full-featured operating system.

Stack(s)

- *Stack(s)*
  These are best for interrupt only, foreground/background types of systems, or state machine-based systems.

In the later study of system performance, we will analyze the context switch in detail. Here, the study will examine several alternate methods for supporting such a switch. In any switch to a new context, some information must be saved.

11.11.1 Duplicate Hardware Context

The typical microprocessor has a limited number of general-purpose registers. When a context switch is necessary, the values contained therein must be saved prior to the switch and then restored on return. Some microprocessors provide some hardware support for a context switch by substantially increasing the number of available general-purpose registers.

At the software level, several different contexts can be defined and a subset of the registers allocated to each. For example, with 64 general-purpose registers, 4 different contexts, each with 16 general-purpose registers, can be defined. Thus, each context can have a set of registers called R0–R15 as illustrated in Figure 11.18. When the switch is to occur, rather than saving the contents of the current set of registers, the system simply switches to a new hardware context. An assembly language instruction of the form *add(R3, R1, R2)*, for example, can be executed in all contexts simultaneously without concern for data corruption.

Because the different contexts are a logical interpretation of the register set at the software level, there is nothing precluding overlapping contexts. That is, a subset of registers can be included in two adjacent contexts as depicted in Figure 11.19. In this illustration, the fourteenth and fifteenth registers appear as registers E and F in context 0 and as registers 0

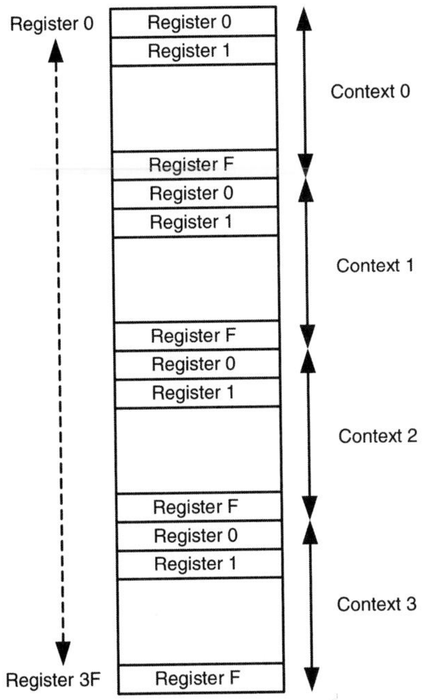

Figure 11.18 General-Purpose Registers Organized as Four Different Contexts

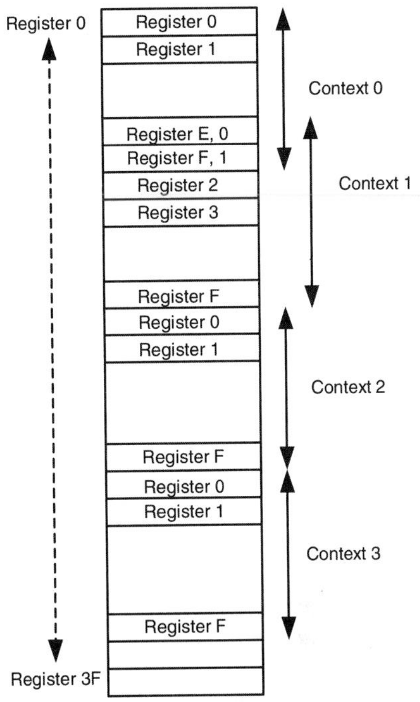

Figure 11.19 General-Purpose Registers Organized with Overlapping Contexts

and 1 in context 1. Using such a scheme, variables can easily be passed between contexts with no overhead.

11.11.2 Task Control Blocks

When a system is implemented using the task control block model, each TCB will contain all relevant information about the state of the task. To affect the context switch, necessary task state information is copied to the TCB. The TCB can then be inserted into the appropriate queue, and the status and state information for the new or resumed task can be entered into the system variables. If the running task has been preempted, the TCB will be linked into the *ready* queue waiting for the CPU to become available. Based on the scheduling algorithm, it may or may not be the next task to run. If the task has blocked, the TCB will be linked into the waiting queue for the required resource. When the resource becomes available, the task will move to the *ready* queue.

ready

11.11.3 Stacks

The stack is a rather simple data structure used for storing information associated with a task or thread. It is an area set aside in memory as part of system allocation. The information is held in a data structure similar to TCB called a *stack frame* or *activation record*. Typical information that must be stored is illustrated in Figure 11.20.

stack frame, activation record

When a stack is used, procedures must be written to manage the processes of saving, accessing, and removing information to or from the stack. Such procedures are initially invoked as part of a function call or by the interrupt handler prior to a context switch. In the

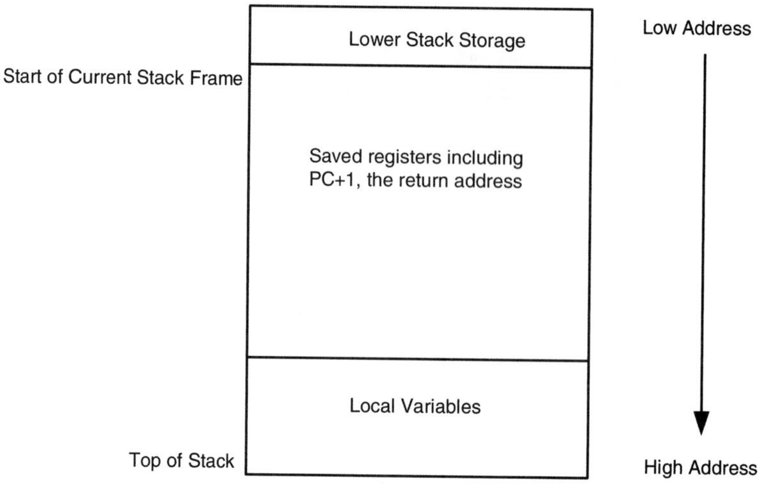

Figure 11.20 Information Stored in a Stack Frame

case of an interrupt, further interrupts are temporarily blocked to allow the mechanics of the switch to occur. The stack management procedures are also invoked when returning to the calling context to restore the original state.

stack pointer The current top of the stack is identified by a variable called the *stack pointer*. When an activation record is added to the stack, the stack pointer is advanced. Top of stack and stack pointer advanced have several different interpretations. Based on implementation, top ***empty*** of stack can be interpreted either as the next available *empty* location on the stack or as the location of the last valid entry. Figure 11.20 shows the stack growing from low to high memory. An alternate implementation grows the stack from high to low memory. Thus, it is important to always read the documentation for the particular implementation being used.

The stack data type generally supports the following operations:

Push—Add to the top of the stack.
Pop—Remove from the top of the stack.
Peek—Look at the top of the stack.

Three kinds of stack are identified:

- Runtime
- Application
- Multiprocessing

Runtime Stack

runtime stack In stack-based designs, the *runtime stack* is under system control and may be shared by other processes or threads. The stack size is known *a priori*, and there is usually no dynamic allocation, although one tries to build in some buffer space. This is known as defensive design.

Design Heuristic
As part of any design, always try to anticipate and accommodate the unexpected.

Thus, at runtime, one must ensure that not too many stack frames are pushed on to the stack; otherwise, there is potential for overflow, eventually leading to a system crash.

A difficulty with a single runtime stack in a TCB context arises from the access semantics of the stack, which permit access only to the top of the stack. Consider a simple system comprising two tasks, T0 and T1. If T0 is running and blocks on an I/O operation, for example, its state information is saved on the stack. T1 now starts and similarly blocks. In the meantime, the I/O operation, for T0 completes, and it is ready to resume. However, its state information is contained in the second entry on the stack.

The single runtime stack can work in a foreground/background model. Tasks in the background will generally run to completion. Real-time tasks, driven by interrupts, will push then pop stack frames onto the stack, thereby precluding the need to access an entry that is not at the top of the stack. Interrupts within interrupts do not present a problem as long as the stack size is not exceeded.

Application Stacks

This is an interesting approach. The single-stack model can be extended by incorporating several additional stacks as we see in Figure 11.21. The design is utilizing a runtime stack as well as multiple *application stacks* to simplify the management of multiple tasks in a preemptive environment.

application stacks

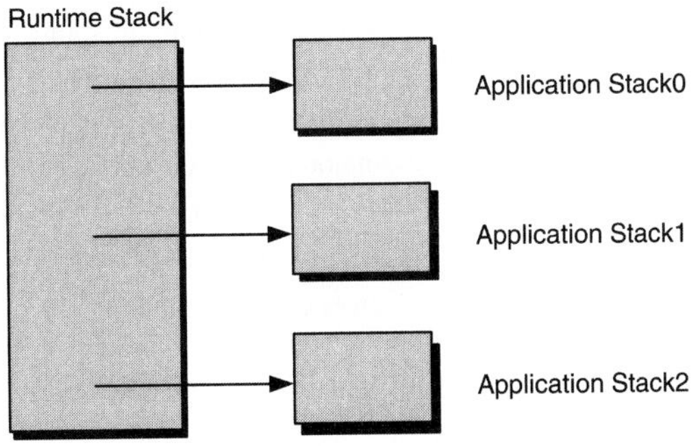

Figure 11.21 A Stack Architecture Using a Runtime Stack and Application Stacks

On interrupt, the runtime stack holds a pointer to the application stack associated with the initial or preempted task or thread. The preempting process now works with a new stack. If that task is subsequently preempted, the existing context is held on the preempted task's application stack, and a pointer to new application stack is placed on the runtime stack.

The save and restore interface functions must be modified to store/restore with respect to the current context as the runtime stack is unwound. Such a scheme can provide a very fast context switch.

Could such a design be applicable to multithreaded systems?

Multiprocessing Stacks

Multiprocessing in the current context refers to working with multiple processes rather than multiple processors. Multiprocessing stacks are similar to the main runtime stack. When a task is started, among other resources, it is allocated its own stack space. In contrast to application stacks, which are managed by the foreground task (assuming a foreground/background versus a TCB architecture), the process stack is managed by the owner process. It is allocated from heap when the process is created and returned to the heap when the process exits.

11.12 SUMMARY

In this chapter we began the first portion of our study of tasks, threads, multitasking, the operating system, and the real-time operating system. We elaborated on the central responsibilities of an operating system, examined the characteristics and capabilities that distinguish an RTOS, and then identified the core set of requirements of the OS as embodied in the kernel. We then illustrated such capabilities through the design of several versions of a primitive operating system kernel. We introduced some of the necessary terminology and examined the critical role of time in developing and deploying many embedded applications. Finally, we looked at different kinds of stacks and their role in managing context switches associated with task state changes, task preemption, or interrupts.

11.13 REVIEW QUESTIONS

Programs and Processes

11.1 What is the difference between a program and a process?

11.2 What is the difference between a task and a process?

11.3 What is execution time? persistence?

11.4 Explain what is meant by task or process concurrency.

11.5 Why do we say that most of the time concurrent execution is only an illusion?

11.6 What is a process or task schedule? scheduling strategy?

11.7 Identify the major states in which a task or process within an embedded application might exist.

Threads

11.8 What is a thread?

11.9 What is the difference between a task or process and a thread?

11.10 What is a lightweight thread? heavyweight thread?

Sharing Resources

11.11 Identify several of the primary system resources that a task or process might require and use.

11.12 Identify several of the major responsibilities associated with managing the memory resource in an embedded design.

11.13 What is supervisor mode in a memory management scheme? user mode?

11.14 Identify several major responsibilities associated with process management.

11.15 What is reentrant code?

Foreground/Background Systems

11.16 What is a foreground/background system?

11.17 What are some of the strengths of a foreground/background model?

11.18 What is the difference between a foreground and a background task?

Kernels and Operating Systems

11.19 What is an operating system?

11.20 Identify and explain the core responsibilities of an operating system.

11.21 What are the major components of an operating system? Briefly describe the responsibilities of each component.

11.22 What is a real-time operating system?

11.23 What are some of the major characteristics that distinguish a real-time operating system from one that is not real-time?

11.24 What is a task control block? What are some of the major components of a task control block?

11.25 What is an operating system kernel?

11.26 What is the difference between an operating system and an operating system kernel?

Interrupts

11.27 What is an interrupt? Why is it used?

11.28 What is an interrupt number? What is its purpose?

11.29 What is an interrupt service routine? What is its purpose?

11.30 What is an interrupt vector table? What is its purpose?

11.31 Describe the sequence of steps that are necessary to handle an interrupt once one has occurred.

11.32 In the context of managing interrupts, what do the enable and disable commands do?

11.33 What is an interrupt mask? What is it used for?

Changing Contexts

11.34 What is a context switch?

11.35 Identify several different kinds of stack that one might find in an embedded application.

11.14 THOUGHT QUESTIONS

Programs and Processes

11.1 Can an embedded application have more than one process? If so, give several examples when one might want to design such a system. Discuss the advantages and disadvantages of such a design.

11.2 The chapter identified three general scheduling strategies. What are these strategies, and what are their differences?

11.3 Give several examples of embedded applications when each of the scheduling strategies identified in question 11.2 might be used. Give several pros and cons for the choice of strategy for each application.

Threads

11.4 Can a task or process have more than one thread? If so, what is the advantage of such a design? Are there disadvantages?

11.5 When should we use a heavyweight thread? a lightweight thread?

Sharing Resources

11.6 Why is the supervisor mode necessary? When is it necessary? Under such circumstances, identify and elaborate on several problems that might occur if it is not used.

11.7 Are there embedded applications when the supervisor mode is not necessary? If so, give several examples and discuss why it is not necessary.

11.8 Why is it good practice to ensure that all functions are reentrant?

11.9 Give several examples of functions that are not reentrant.

Foreground/Background Systems

11.10 What kinds of embedded designs are best suited for implementation using a foreground/background model?

Kernels and Operating Systems

11.11 Discuss possible strengths and weaknesses of the architectural strategy used in most contemporary operating systems.

11.12 Identify some way in which an embedded operating system might be different from the one in your desktop computer? In what ways might they be the same?

11.13 When might one elect to use a foreground/background model in an embedded design? a basic kernel? a full-featured operating system?

11.14 Give several examples of when it would be necessary to incorporate real-time capabilities into the strategies discussed in Question 11.11.

Interrupts

11.15 Give several examples of where an interrupt mask might be used.

11.16 What is interrupt priority? Why is it used? What determines the priority of an interrupt?

Changing Contexts

11.17 Identify several cases when a context switch might be necessary in an embedded application.

11.18 Identify several events internal to an embedded system that might cause a context switch. Identify several events external to the system that might cause a context switch.

11.19 Identify and describe each of the major steps in a context switch when duplicate hardware is available; in a design using task control blocks; when a stack is used; in a foreground/background system.

11.20 Give several examples of embedded applications when each of the different kinds of stack discussed in this chapter might be used. Identify several pros and cons for your choice of stack in each application.

11.15 PROBLEMS

11.1 Give an example of an embedded application that has at least three tasks that run concurrently. Give a UML activity diagram expressing the behavior of these tasks.

11.2 Give a sequence diagram illustrating the context switch between the tasks in the system designed in Problem 11.1.

11.3 Give a UML class diagram for the single process illustrated in Figure 11.1.

11.4 If an embedded system has five processes with the following execution times, propose a schedule in which the average waiting time is the smallest: P1(9), P2(25), P3(4), P4(8), P5(12). Illustrate the schedule using a UML sequence diagram.

11.5 Present a UML activity diagram to illustrate the behavior of tasks in each of the following operating systems.

(a) Single process–single thread
(b) Multiple process–single thread
(c) Single process–multiple threads
(d) Multiple process–multiple threads

For each case, identify which resources each process or thread is using.

11.6 Give an example of a function that is not reentrant. Give an example of a function that is reentrant. How would you modify your first function to make it reentrant?

11.7 Consider implementing an embedded system to control a traffic light as a foreground/background system. Each direction supports a left turn (right turn if traffic normally drives on the left hand side) and pedestrian-activated crosswalk control.

(a) Which tasks are foreground tasks?

(b) Which tasks are background tasks?

(c) Give a UML state diagram illustrating the behavior of the system during a change from north-south green to east-west green. Be certain to consider the operation with and without a left (right) turn and with and without a pedestrian.

(d) Give a UML sequence diagram for the events in part (c).

11.8 Repeat Problem 11.7 for a microwave cooker.

11.9 Repeat Problem 11.7 for a washing machine.

11.10 Repeat Problem 11.7 for a video-on-demand entertainment system for a large hotel.

11.11 Consider implementing an embedded system to control a traffic light as an RTOS-based system. Each direction supports a left turn (right turn if traffic normally drives on the left-hand side) and pedestrian-activated crosswalk control.

(a) Which tasks are the major tasks?

(b) Give a UML state diagram illustrating the behavior of the system during a change from north-south green to east-west green. Be certain to consider the operation with and without a left (right) turn and with and without a pedestrian.

(c) Give a UML sequence diagram for the events in part (c).

11.12 Repeat Problem 11.11 for a microwave cooker.

11.13 Repeat Problem 11.11 for a washing machine.

11.14 Repeat Problem 11.11 for a video-on-demand entertainment system for a large hotel.

11.15 Provide a UML class diagram for a task control block (TCB). Implement the design using a C struct data structure.

11.16 Design a method that would enable the dynamic allocation and deallocation of TCBs as tasks are created or terminated.

11.17 Modify the design in Example 11.1 to support a dynamic number of tasks in the task queue without using malloc and free (C) or new and delete (C++) while retaining the array as the queue container.

11.18 Provide a UML class diagram for a task queue that supports the dynamic insertion and deletion of tasks.

11.19 Implement the task queue specified in Example 11.1 to use a doubly linked list as the underlying data type for the queue container.

11.20 Combine the subsystems in Problem 11.16 and Problem 11.19.

11.21 Modify the design of the TCB in Problem 11.15 to support a task priority number in the range of {0–9}. Assume 0 is the highest and 9 the lowest priority.

Incorporate the modified TCB design into the task queue design in Problem 11.19. Modify the access method to always return the highest priority task.

11.22 Modify the design of the TCB in Problem 11.15 to support the inclusion of an estimate of execution time number in the range of {0–99}.

Incorporate the modified TCB design into the task queue design in Problem 11.19. Modify the access method to always return the shortest task.

11.23 Give a high-level description of how the system in Figure P11.22 works. You should not need more than 10 lines.

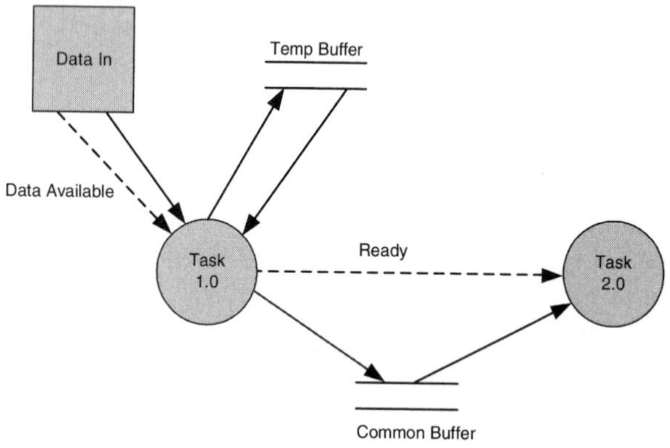

Figure P11.22

11.24 Write a C program to implement the design given in the data/control flow diagram in Problem 11.23.

Chapter 12

Tasks and Task Management

THINGS TO LOOK FOR . . .

- The role of time in embedded designs.
- The definitions of reactive and time-based systems.
- The differences between preemptive and nonpreemptive systems.
- The need for effectively scheduling the use of the system CPU(s).
- The criteria for making scheduling decisions.
- Common scheduling algorithms.
- Real-time scheduling considerations.
- How scheduling algorithms might be evaluated.
- Methods for intertask communication.
- The critical section problem and several solutions.
- Methods for task synchronization.

12.0 INTRODUCTION

In the previous chapter we introduced some of the basic concepts and methods involved in controlling multitasking systems. We learned that foreground / background systems can be effective under real-time constraints and that the basic responsibilities of the operating system comprise task scheduling, intertask communication, and task dispatch. In addition, we introduced some of the issues associated with the context switch in preemptable systems.

In this chapter, we will examine the scheduling problem and intertask communication in greater detail. The resource management aspects of task scheduling and dispatch will be covered in the following chapter. We will open by continuing the discussion of time and the critical role it plays in the design of embedded applications by introducing the concepts of *reactive* and *time-based systems*. We will present and discuss various metrics for specifying and assessing a task schedule. We will then investigate several different scheduling algorithms and analyze task synchronization and intertask communication in some detail. The focus will be primarily from the perspective of either a kernel-based or more complete operating system-based control strategy.

reactive, time-based systems

12.1 TIME, TIME-BASED SYSTEMS, AND REACTIVE SYSTEMS

12.1.1 Time

We have already briefly encountered time and the important role it plays in the design and execution of embedded applications. We will now explore that role in greater detail.

absolute, relative
interval
duration

We define two different measures of time: *absolute* and *relative,* based on what the measurement is referenced to. Absolute time is based on real-world time; relative time is measured with respect to some reference. Time is further qualified as either an *interval* or a *duration*; these are distinct. An *interval* is marked by specific start and end times; a *duration* is a relative time measure. Equal intervals must have the same start times and the same stop times; nonequal intervals can have the same duration. This difference is captured in Figure 12.0.

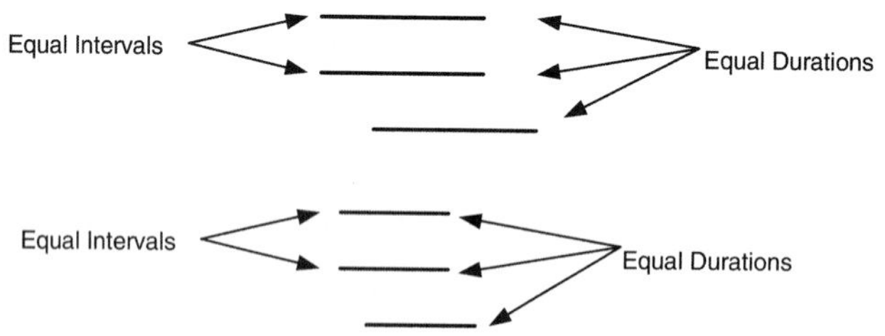

Figure 12.0 Equal Intervals and Equal Durations

12.1.2 Reactive and Time-Based Systems

reactive, time based

Embedded systems are classified into two broad categories: *reactive* and *time based. Reactive* systems, as the name suggests, contain tasks that are initiated by some event that may be either internal or external to the system. An internal event may be an elapsed time or a temporal bound on data that has been exceeded. An external event is the recognition of a switch that has been activated or an external response to an internally generated command, for example. Typically, the initiating events are asynchronous to the normal activity of the system. Foreground/background systems are a good example of those classed as *reactive.*

time-based systems
absolute, relative
following an interval

Time-based systems are those systems whose behavior is controlled by time. Such a relationship can be *absolute*—an action must occur at a specific time; *relative*—an action must occur after or before some reference; or *following an interval*—an action must occur at a specified time with respect to some reference. The behavior in time-based systems is generally synchronous with a timing element of one form or another. Time-shared systems are a good example of those classed as *time based.*

periodic
aperiodic, periodic
execution times

The relevance of time in embedded applications becomes clear when trying to schedule tasks and threads, that is, deciding when and how often each is executed. Tasks or threads that are initiated with repeating duration between invocations are called *periodic;* otherwise they are designated as *aperiodic.* A repeating duration is called the *period.* The time to complete a task is called the *execution time.*

jitter
delay

In a periodic system, variation in the evoking event is called *jitter.* The time between the evoking event and the intended action is called the *delay.* When designing a system, each context in which it is anticipated that the system will be operating must be examined to determine the significance of jitter and delay with respect to specified time constraints.

hard, hard deadline

An action that must occur by a specified time is defined as *hard* or is said to have a *hard deadline.* A missed deadline in such cases is considered to be a partial or total system fail-

hard real-time

ure. A system is defined as *hard real-time* if it contains one or more tasks containing such constraints. Such systems may have other tasks that do not have temporal deadlines. The major focus, however, is on the hard deadlines.

soft real-time

Systems with relaxed time constraints are defined as *soft real-time.* Such systems may meet their deadlines on average. Soft real-time systems may be soft in several ways:

- Relaxation of the constraint that missing the deadline constitutes system failure. Such a system may tolerate missing the specific deadline provided some other deadline or timeliness constraint is met—the average throughput, for example.
- Evaluating the correctness of timeliness as a gradation of values rather than pass or fail.

firm real-time

Systems with tasks that have some relaxed constraints as well as hard deadlines are defined as *firm real-time.*

predictability *when, how* *periodic*

Real-time systems are those in which correctness demands timeliness. Most such systems carefully manage resources with respect to maintaining the *predictability* of timeliness constraints. Such predictability gives us a measure of accuracy with which one can state in advance *when* and *how* an action will occur. We elaborate by annotating the durations, events, jitter, and actions. Figure 12.1 illustrates a *periodic* system typical of a time-based design.

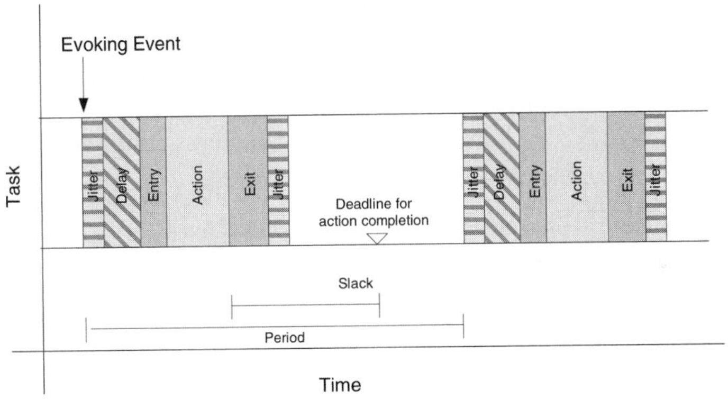

Figure 12.1 Task Activity in a Periodic Time-Based System

In the figure, the period of the recurrence of the tasks is defined. The evoking event occurs with respect to the start of the period. The first rectangle expresses the variation in the actual invocation with respect to the intended. Such jitter may arise from variations in the system's ability to respond to a timer expiring, for example. Once the event occurs, the second rectangle captures the delay in getting the task started. When the task begins to execute, the third rectangle accounts for any initialization or similar operations that must occur before the intended action takes place. The intended action occurs during the time indicated by the fourth rectangle. After the action completes, the fifth rectangle mirrors the entry actions with any necessary cleanup before the task completes. The sixth rectangle accounts for variation in exiting the task.

The diagram also marks the latest time at which the intended action could complete and still meet the time constraints on the period. The duration between the completion deadline and the start of the next cycle is equal to that between the end of the action and the end of the exit jitter.

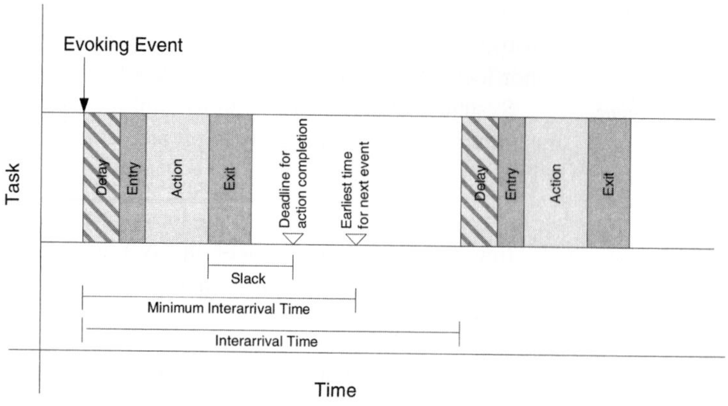

Figure 12.2 Task Activity in an Aperiodic Foreground/Background Design

aperiodic

Figure 12.2 illustrates an *aperiodic* system that is typical of a foreground/background design. Notice how the minimum and maximum times are specified.

interarrival time

The invocation of *aperiodic* tasks is not fixed in time—they are asynchronous to the operation of the core system. Thus, there can be no jitter because there is no expected time for the initiating event. The duration between such tasks is called *interarrival time.* Such a time is critical when one needs to determine how to schedule real-time tasks. Under such circumstances, the lower bound on interarrival time must be identified. Such things as the maximum number of events occurring within a given time interval may also need to be considered.

Table 12.0 captures timeliness constraints with respect to whether the task is soft or hard real-time.

Table 12.0 Hard and Soft Real-Time Timeliness Constraints

Property	Nonreal-time	Soft Real-time	Hard Real-time
Deterministic	No	Possibly	Yes
Predictable	No	Possibly	Yes
Consequences of late computation	No effect	Degraded performance	Failure
Critical reliability	No	Yes	Yes
Response dictated by external events	No	Yes	Yes
Timing analysis possible	No	Analytic (sometimes) stochastic simulation	Analytic, stochastic simulation

At this point, we should be sufficiently comfortable with some of the terminology that we can start to investigate the control of embedded systems in greater detail. We will begin with the problem of task scheduling.

12.2 TASK SCHEDULING

How efficiently and effectively a task moves through the various queues along the control path following its arrival and how effectively and efficiently the CPU is utilized during such a movement establish the quality of the embedded design. An essential component of that control strategy is the algorithm used to schedule the allocation of the CPU.

In a multitasking system, the main objective is to have some process using the CPU at all times. Such a scheme maximizes the usage of that resource. Which task is running at any specific time is based on a number of criteria. It is the scheduler's responsibility to ensure that the CPU is efficiently utilized and that the various jobs are executed in such an order as to meet any required constraints.

priority When working with a scheduling algorithm, one must also consider the *priority* of the task. Priority is assigned by the designer and is based on a variety of different criteria. We will examine these shortly. Such criteria are used to resolve which task to execute when more than one is waiting and ready to execute. Tasks with higher priority execute preferentially over those with lower priority.

schedulable ***deterministically schedulable*** In a real-time context, a task that can be determined to always meet its timeliness constraints is said to be *schedulable*. A task that can be guaranteed to always meet all deadlines is said to be *deterministically schedulable*. Such a situation occurs when an event's worst case response time is less than or equal to the task's deadline. When all tasks can be scheduled, the overall system can be scheduled.

Scheduling decisions must be made during the design phase of the system development since such decisions involve trade-offs that affect and optimize the overall performance of the system. When the system specification stipulates hard deadlines, one must ensure that the implementing tasks and their associated actions can meet every deadline. Soft deadlines naturally give more flexibility.

12.2.1 CPU Utilization

CPU Utilization In addition to satisfying time constraints, a goal in formulating a task schedule is to keep the CPU as busy as possible, ideally close to 100%, but with some margin for additional tasks. Such a metric is referred to as *CPU utilization*. In a practical system, utilization should range between 40% for a lightly loaded system and 90% for one that is heavily loaded.

For a single periodic task, CPU utilization is given as

$$u_i = e_i / p_i \tag{12.0}$$

u_I	fraction of time task keeps CPU busy
e_i	execution time
p_i	for periodic task is the period

One can express a similar relationship for aperiodic tasks.

CPU utilization information can be used in conjunction with a sequence diagram to aid in assessing when each of the tasks can and needs to run.

12.2.2 Scheduling Decisions

Two key elements of real-time design, repeatability and predictability, are absolutely essential in the context of hard deadlines. To ensure predictability, one must completely understand and define the timing characteristics of each task and properly schedule those tasks using a predictable scheduling algorithm. The first step in developing a robust schedule is knowing when a scheduling decision must be made.

Scheduling decisions are made under the following four conditions:

running, waiting ***running, ready*** ***waiting, ready***

1. A process switches from the *running* to the *waiting* state—initiated by an I/O request.
2. A process switches from the *running* to the *ready* state—when an interrupt occurs.
3. A process switches from the *waiting* to the *ready* state—the completion of I/O activity.
4. A process terminates.

nonpreemptive *preemptive* If only conditions 1 and 4 are used to make a scheduling decision, such scheduling is called *nonpreemptive.* Under such scheduling criteria, a process keeps the CPU until it decides to release, that is, when it terminates or switches to the waiting state. Otherwise, the schedule is called *preemptive.*

12.2.3 Scheduling Criteria

Today there are a great number of different scheduling algorithms. When making a choice, one must consider the properties of the various algorithms coupled with what is considered important or essential for the specific application. In the following sections, we identify several of the more common metrics. The list is, by no means, complete, nor is it universally applicable.

12.2.3.1 Priority

In a design that utilizes priority as a part of the scheduling criteria, the designer must critically assess each task in the system to establish the appropriate priority. The scheduler utilizes such information at several different times. If no task is running or if a task terminates, the highest priority task among the tasks that are ready will be selected to run next. Under a preemptive scheduling policy, if a lower priority task is executing when a higher priority task arrives, the arriving task preempts the executing task. The lower priority task is then suspended. The suspended task resumes when the higher priority task completes or blocks waiting for some resource. If no task with a higher priority ever arrives, the executing task runs to completion.

blocking Although a priority scheme seems to ensure that the most important tasks will always complete, such is not always the case. With preemption, the problem of *blocking* arises. Blocking occurs when a task needs a resource that is owned by another task.

Consider several examples.

Case 1

1. Task A has higher priority than Task B.
2. Task B starts and reserves Resource R1.
3. Task A preempts Task B.
4. Task A begins execution and becomes blocked at the point that Resource R1 is needed.
5. Task A must suspend and allow B to complete, thereby releasing R1.

priority inversion A second case introduces a problem called *priority inversion.* A problem of this nature occurred on one of the Mars missions. (Please see Chapter 8 on safety and reliability.)

Case 2

We have three tasks: Task A, Task B, and Task C.

Task A has the highest priority and Task C the lowest.

1. Task C starts and reserves Resource R1.
2. Task A enters and preempts Task C.
3. Task A begins execution and becomes blocked at the point that Resource R1 is needed.
4. Task A must suspend and allow C to continue, hopefully releasing R1.
5. Task B preempts Task C and does not need R1.
6. Task B completes and allows Task C to resume.

It is easy to create a situation in which the highest priority task is blocked forever. A high priority task that can be scheduled in isolation may fail in a multitasking context. In a hard real-time context, one must ensure a bound on priority inversion.

12.2.3.2 Turnaround Time

turnaround time

Turnaround time specifies the interval from the time of the submission of a task until its completion. Included is the time spent waiting to get into memory, the time waiting in the ready queue, and the time spent executing on the CPU or doing I/O.

12.2.3.3 Throughput

throughput

Coupled with turnaround time is *throughput*, the number of processes that are completed per unit of time. Throughput depends, of course, on the complexity of the task. One should be careful when working with a throughput metric. A system may exhibit a very high throughput, but if the turnaround time is excessive, we may not be able to meet our timeliness constraints.

12.2.3.4 Waiting Time

entry queue
ready queue

In embedded applications built around a kernel or full OS, the path a task takes through the system involves a number of different queues. When a user or system task initially enters the system, it is put into an *entry queue*. When all of its necessary conditions are satisfied such that it can run when the CPU is available, it is placed in a *ready queue*. Tasks may also arrive at the ready queue via other paths as well—for example, if they have been interrupted by a higher priority task or if they have blocked on an I/O operation that has completed. When a process is put into the ready queue, it waits until it is selected for execution. At such a time, it is dispatched—given the CPU to execute.

I/O queue
device queue

During execution, the process may issue an I/O request and be placed in an *I/O queue*, request a resource that may not be immediately available, or create new subprocess(es) and wait for their termination. Processes waiting for a particular resource may be placed in the queue for that resource. That queue is often called a *device queue*. When a process (is) terminated, it is removed from all queues. Its TCB and all resources are deallocated.

waiting time

Minimized *waiting time* as a criteria in scheduling algorithm execution and I/O time affects only time spent waiting in queues. Evaluation includes all time in waiting queues.

12.2.3.5 Response Time

response time
first response

Response time is yet another consideration. For an interactive system, turnaround time may not be the best measure. Instead, the time from submission to *first response* is considered. The time taken for the first response is not the time to the first output.

12.3 SCHEDULING ALGORITHMS

asynchronous interrupt
event driven, polled,
polled with a timing event

Although it is beyond the scope of this text to go into details of all the many scheduling algorithms, it is informative to look at a number of them. Several of the very simplest include *asynchronous interrupt event driven, polled,* and *polled with a timing event*. With such algorithms, the control strategy is architected to support one or a few tasks. Scheduling and dispatch are automatic. Intertask communication either does not exist or it relies on global variables. Though simple, such algorithms can be essential in cases with hard deadlines.

12.3.1 Asynchronous Interrupt Event Driven

One of the simplest scheduling schemes is asynchronous interrupt event driven. Certainly, the asynchronous nature of the scheme calls into question the use of the word "schedule." Under such an approach, the system is constrained to operate in a basic one-line infinite loop until an interrupting event occurs, as is illustrated in the code fragment shown in Figure 12.3. As such, the design is a special case of the foreground/background model. In this case, the design has no background tasks. The design can also be considered to be reactive.

```
global variable declarations

isr set up
function prototypes
void main (void)
{
    local variable declarations
    while(1);           // task loop
}
ISRs
function definitions
```

Figure 12.3 An Event-Driven Schedule Algorithm

When an interrupting event occurs, flow of control jumps to the associated ISR where the designated task is executed; flow then resumes in the infinite loop. Generally, the event originates from some external source. We will look at an extension to the event-driven approach in which the event derives from a system timer.

The overall behavior of such a system can be difficult to analyze because of the nondeterministic nature of asynchronous interrupts. However, it is rather straightforward to determine the postevent behavior for systems with a single interrupt or the behavior of the highest priority interrupt in systems with more than one interrupt.

12.3.2 Polled and Polled with a Timing Element

The basic polled algorithm is among the simplest and fastest algorithms. The system continually loops, waiting for an event to occur. The difference between the polled algorithm and the event driven is that the polled algorithm is continually testing the value of the polled signal looking for a state change. The interrupt-driven design, on the other hand, does nothing until the event occurs. Only then does it respond. Schematically, the algorithm is given as shown in Figure 12.4.

Such a scheme works well for a single task. It is completely deterministic. The time to respond to the event is computable and bounded. In the worst case, let's assume the event occurs immediately after the test instruction. Under such a circumstance, the response time is the length of the loop. Polled with a timing event is a simple extension. The scheme uses a timing element to ensure a delay action after a polled event is true. Such a technique deskews the incoming signals.

The polled model is also a special case of the foreground/background model. In contrast to the event-driven schedule, the polled model has no foreground tasks. The design implements a reactive system.

```
global variable declarations
function prototypes
void main (void)
{
     local variable declarations
     while(1)                 // task loop
     {         // test state of each signal in polled set
               if then construct
                    or
               switch statement
     }
}
function definitions
```

Figure 12.4 A Polling-Based Schedule Algorithm

12.3.3 State Based

The next approach implements the flow of control through the task set as a finite automaton or state machine. The two basic implementations of the finite-state machine (FSM), Mealy and Moore, are distinguished by the implementation of the output function: in Mealy the output is a function of the current state and the input, and in Moore the output is a function of the current state only. The basic machine can be expressed as illustrated in Figure 12.5.

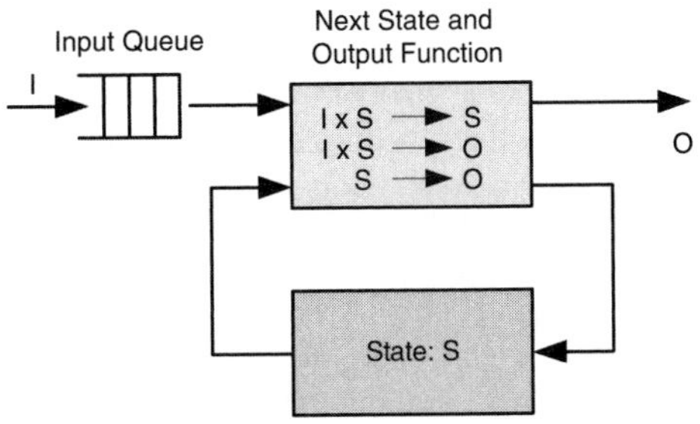

Figure 12.5 A Basic State Machine Model

The state machine can easily be implemented as either a set of case statements, as an if-then, or if-then-else construct.

Some of the limitations of such an approach begin with the theoretical limit on the computational power of the finite-state machine. Using states is not efficient, and the state space explosion for large problems makes the approach impractical for systems with large numbers of inputs. There is a rich set of variations on the basic FSM, however, some of which address the various limitations of the basic implementation. A state-based design is reactive in nature.

12.3.4 Synchronous Interrupt Event Driven

The next level of sophistication entails constraining the asynchronous event used in the opening algorithm to one that is synchronous, based on a timer. Such a system continually loops until interrupted by a *timing* signal (which is typically internally generated). The timing/interrupt event triggers a context switch to an ISR that manages it. A schedule based on

timing

a periodic event is defined as fixed rate. In contrast, an aperiodic schedule is defined as sporadic. Such a synchronous interrupt-based scheme can work with multiple tasks and is the basis for *time-sharing systems*. The design is an example of a time-based system, although it is reacting to a special interrupt.

time-sharing systems

12.3.5 Combined Interrupt Event Driven

A simple variation on the two interrupt event-driven designs is to permit both synchronous and asynchronous interrupts. In such a system, priority is used to select among tasks that are ready when the timing interrupt occurs. If multiple tasks are permitted to have the same priority, then selection from among ready tasks proceeds in a round robin fashion. Naturally, higher priority tasks will be given preference at any time.

12.3.6 Foreground–Background

foreground–background
foreground
background

A system utilizing a *foreground–background* flow of control strategy implements a combination of interrupt and noninterrupt-driven tasks. The former are designated the *foreground* tasks and the latter the *background* tasks. The background tasks can be interrupted at any time by any of the foreground tasks and are thus operating at the lowest priority. The interrupt-driven processes implement the real-time aspects of the application; the interrupt events may be either synchronous or asynchronous. All of the previous algorithms are special cases of foreground/background designs in which either the foreground (polled systems) or the background (interrupt based) component is missing.

12.3.7 Time-Shared Systems

In a time-shared system, tasks may or may not all be equally important. When all are given the same amount of time, the schedule is periodic, and when the allocation is based on priority, the schedule is aperiodic. Several of the more common algorithms are examined in the ensuing paragraphs.

12.3.7.1 First-Come First-Served

A very simple algorithm is first-come first-served and is easily managed with a FIFO queue. When a process enters the ready queue, the task control block is linked to the tail of the queue. When the CPU becomes free, it is allocated to the process at the head of the queue. The currently running process is removed from the queue. Such an approach is nonpreemptive and can be troublesome in a system with real-time constraints.

12.3.7.2 Shortest Job First

The shortest job first schedule assumes that the CPU is used in bursts of activity. Each task has associated with it an estimate of how much time the job will need when next given the CPU. The estimate is based on measured lengths of previous CPU usage. The algorithm can be either preemptive or nonpreemptive. With a preemptive schedule, the currently running process can be interrupted by one with a shorter remaining time to completion.

12.3.7.3 Round Robin

The round robin algorithm is designed especially for time-shared systems. It is similar to first-come first-served, with preemption added to switch between processes. A small unit of *time quantum, slice* time called *time quantum* or *slice* is defined, and the ready queue is treated as a circular queue. The scheduler walks the queue, allocating the CPU to each process for one time slice. If a process completes in less than its allocated time, it releases the CPU; otherwise, the process is interrupted when time expires and it's put at the end of queue. New processes are added to the tail of the queue. Observe that if the time slice is increased to infinity, round robin becomes a first-come first-served scheduler.

12.3.8 Priority Schedule

Shortest job first is a special case of the more general priority scheduling class of algorithms. A priority is associated with each process, and the CPU is allocated to the process with the highest priority. Equal priority jobs are scheduled first-come first-served or in round robin fashion. The major problem with a priority schedule is the potential for indefinite blocking or starving—priority inversion. The algorithms can be either preemptive or nonpreemptive.

12.3.8.1 Rate-Monotonic

With a preemptive schedule, the currently running process can be interrupted by any other task with a higher priority. A special class of priority-driven algorithms called *rate-monotonic* was initially developed in 1973 and has been updated over the years. In the basic algorithm, priority is assigned based on execution period; the shorter the period, the higher the priority.

rate-monotonic

Priorities that are determined and assigned at design time and then remain fixed during execution are said to use a *static* or *fixed* scheduling policy. The ability to schedule a set of tasks is computed as a bound on utilization of the CPU as shown in Eq. 12.1.

static, fixed

$$\sum_{i=0}^{n-1} \frac{e_i}{p_i} \leq n\left(2^{\frac{1}{n}} - 1\right) \tag{12.1}$$

e = Execution time of the task
p = Period of the task

This approach makes the following assumptions.

- The deadline for each task is equal to its period.
- Any task can be preempted at any time.

The expression on the right-hand side gives a bound on CPU utilization; the bound is extreme, that is, worst case. If it cannot be met, a more detailed analysis must be performed to prove whether or not the task can be scheduled. The above equation sets a CPU utilization bound at 69%. Practically, the bound could be relaxed to around 88%, and the tasks can still be scheduled.

The basic algorithm given above simplifies system analysis. Scheduling is static, and the worst case occurs when all the jobs must be started simultaneously. Formal analysis that is beyond the scope of this text leads us to the rate-monotonic schedule also known as the *critical zone theorem*.

critical zone theorem

> *Critical Zone Theorem*
> If the computed utilization is less than the utilization bound, then the system is guaranteed to meet all task deadlines in all task orderings.

It can be shown that rate-monotonic systems are the optimal fixed rate scheduling method. If a rate-monotonic schedule cannot be found, then no other fixed rate scheme will work. The algorithm is defined as *stable*, which means that as additional, lower priority tasks are added to the system, the higher priority tasks can still meet their deadlines even if lower priority tasks fail to do so. The initial algorithm bases assurance upon the assumption that there is no task blocking. The basic algorithm can be modified to include blocking as illustrated in Eq. 12.2.

stable

$$\sum_{i=0}^{n-1} \frac{e_i}{p_i} + \max\left(\frac{b_0}{p_0}, \ldots, \frac{b_{n-1}}{p_{n-1}}\right) \le n\left(2^{\frac{1}{n}} - 1\right) \tag{12.2}$$

The terms b_i give the maximum time task i can be blocked by a lower priority task

With a nonpreemptive schedule, a currently arriving higher priority process is placed at the head of the ready queue.

12.3.8.2 Earliest Deadline

earliest deadline

A dynamic variation on the rate-monotonic algorithm is called *earliest deadline*. The earliest deadline schedule uses a dynamic algorithm with priority assigned based on the task with the closest deadline. The schedule must be established and modified during runtime, for only then can the deadline(s) be assessed.

A set of tasks is considered schedulable if the sum of the task loading is less than 100%. It is considered *optimal* in the sense that if a task can be scheduled by other algorithms, then it can be scheduled by the earliest deadline.

The algorithm is not considered stable. If the runtime task load rises above 100%, some task may miss its deadline. Generally, it is not possible to predict which task will fail. This uncertainty adds greater runtime complexity. The scheduler must continually determine which task to execute next whenever such decisions must be made. Such analytical methods are more complex than fixed priority cases.

12.3.8.3 Least Laxity

least laxity

The *least laxity* algorithm is similar to the earliest deadline with slightly tighter constraints. In addition to the deadline, the time to execute the task is considered. Task priority is based on the following relationship. It should be clear that a task with negative laxity cannot meet its deadline.

$$\text{laxity} = \text{deadline} - \text{execution time} \tag{12.3}$$

The schedule is then based on the metric using ascending laxity. On paper it is a rather straightforward concept. However, it means that one must know the exact value of the execution time, or at least an upper bound on it. Furthermore, the values must be updated with each system change.

The least laxity algorithm can be utilized in systems with a mixture of hard and soft deadlines. Hard real-time tasks can be given priority over those with less rigid constraints. However, it has weaknesses similar to those found with the earliest deadline algorithm; that is, it is not stable. In addition, it has a greater runtime burden than the fixed schedule schemes. The algorithm tends to devote CPU cycles to tasks that are clearly going to be late and thereby causes more tasks to miss deadlines.

12.3.8.4 Maximum Urgency

maximum-urgency-first

criticality

critical, noncritical

The *maximum-urgency-first* algorithm includes features of both the rate-monotonic and the least laxity algorithms. As a first cut, it assigns priority according to the task's period, as is done with the rate-monotonic algorithm. Next, a binary *criticality* task parameter is added. The criticality parameter is used to decompose the tasks into two sets: *critical* and *noncritical*. Then the least laxity algorithm is applied to those in the critical set. The criticality parameter and the priority assignment are assessed at runtime.

If no critical tasks are waiting, then tasks from the noncritical set are scheduled. Because the critical set is based on the rate-monotonic algorithm, the schedule can be structured so that no critical task fails to meet its deadline.

The major advantage of the algorithm is the simplicity of the static priority component and reduced runtime burden compared with full least laxity. The algorithm, however, lacks some flexibility. The rate-monotonic component assumes unconstrained preemption. Typically, short deviations are well tolerated; longer deviations can lead to missed deadlines.

Maximum-urgency-first is best applied to tasks that are well understood and for which blocking constraints are easy to determine. The dynamic scheduling contribution from least laxity potentially can compensate by elevating a task's priority. The algorithm has some of the runtime complexity of pure least laxity and is best applied to tasks that can vary in their ability to miss deadlines. It can be thought of primarily as a rate-monotonic algorithm with some runtime checking to ensure that deadlines can be met.

12.4 REAL-TIME SCHEDULING CONSIDERATIONS

resource reservation

A real-time system may be hard or soft real-time, and the task scheduling may be static or dynamic. For a dynamic hard real-time schedule, the process is submitted along with a statement of the time required to compute and to do I/O. If, following assessment of the task's requirements, the scheduler accepts the task, it guarantees that the task will complete on time. Otherwise, it rejects the task as nonschedulable. Such a guarantee calls for *resource reservation* and requires the scheduler to know exactly how long each operating system function takes along with a completion time guarantee. Such a restriction is impossible for systems with secondary storage or using virtual memory algorithms.

A soft real-time schedule is less restrictive. Such a schedule does require that critical processes have priority over the less critical. Implementing a soft real-time system requires careful design of the scheduler and other related aspects of the operating system. There is a further requirement for priority scheduling. Real-time processes must have the highest priority, and that priority must not degrade over time. Such a constraint is relatively easy to ensure. Furthermore, the dispatch latency must be small; thus, system calls must be preemptable.

Such a requirement can be accomplished in several ways. One approach is to insert preemption points where the system can check to see if a high-priority process needs to be run. Alternatively, the entire kernel can be made preemptable. In such a case, all kernel data structures must be protected, and one must have synchronization methods.

conflict phase, dispatch phase

The preemption process has two components: a *conflict phase* and a *dispatch phase.* During the conflict phase, preemption of any process running in the kernel is permitted. The lower priority process must release needed resources. The next step is a context switch to the high-priority process. In the dispatch phase, the process moves from the ready state to the run state.

12.5 ALGORITHM EVALUATION

With the plethora of algorithms and each having its own parameters, selecting the proper and appropriate one can be difficult. To begin the evaluation, one must first establish assessment criteria. For example, CPU utilization, response time, or throughput may be the most critical factors in a design. Next, the candidate algorithms must be evaluated against the selection criteria. Once again, there are a variety of methods.

12.5.1 Deterministic Modeling

analytic evaluation

deterministic modeling

A major class of methods is called *analytic evaluation.* The approach uses the candidate algorithm and a representative system workload to produce a formula or number from which to evaluate the algorithm. One such method is called *deterministic modeling.* To see how this works, consider the following processes and workloads.

Process	Burst Time
P1	10
P2	20
P3	3
P4	7
P5	12

Figures 12.6a–c illustrate the results of evaluating the following scheduling algorithms against the example workload.

- First-come first-served
- Shortest job first
- Round robin

first-come first-served

Starting with the *first-come first-served*, each algorithm will be evaluated with the goal of achieving the shortest average wait time.

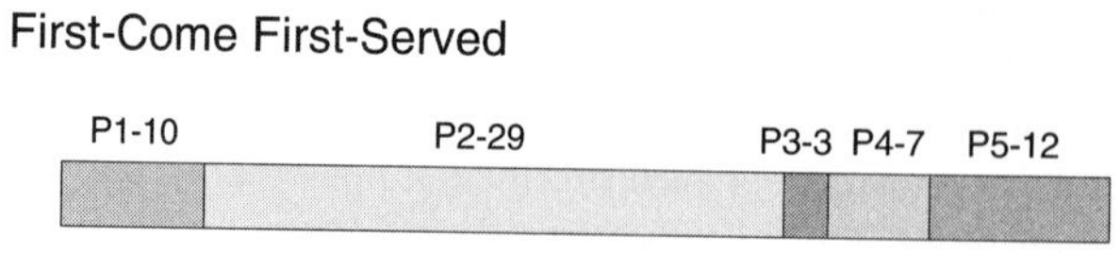

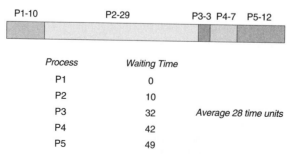

Process	*Waiting Time*
P1	0
P2	10
P3	32
P4	42
P5	49

Average 28 time units

Figure 12.6a The First-Come First-Served Algorithm

It is assumed that the jobs arrive into the system in the order shown. With this algorithm, the average wait time is computed to be 28 time units.

shortest job first

Next is the *shortest job first* schedule.

Shortest Job First

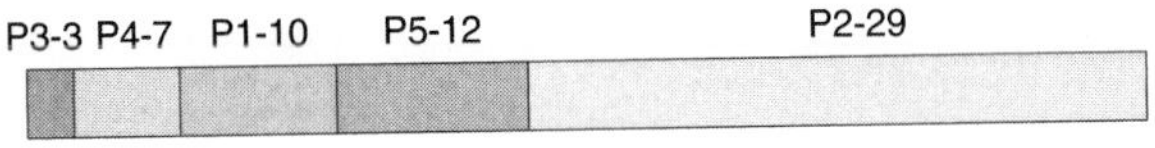

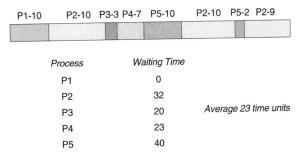

Process	*Waiting Time*	
P3	0	
P4	3	
P1	10	*Average 13 time units*
P5	20	
P2	32	

Figure 12.6b The Shortest Job First Algorithm

Now, the average wait is 13 time units. The algorithm achieves a two to one improvement over the FIFO schedule.

round robin

For, the *round robin* algorithm, the time slice is set to 10 time units. Under such a constraint, jobs P1, P3, and P4 will complete in their allotted time. P2 and P5 will have to be preempted and returned to the queue.

Round Robin

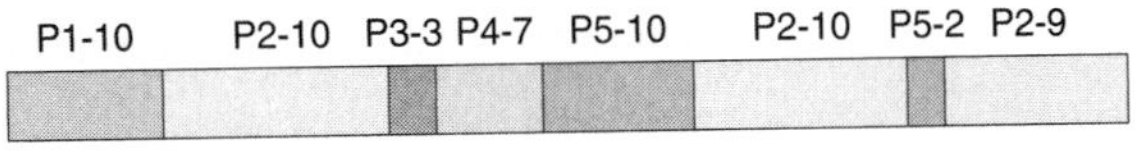

Process	*Waiting Time*	
P1	0	
P2	32	
P3	20	*Average 23 time units*
P4	23	
P5	40	

Figure 12.6c The Round Robin Algorithm

shortest job first

Now the average wait is 23 time units. In the above example, clearly the *shortest job first* algorithm should be the choice since it performs the best against the specified metric.

As can be seen, deterministic modeling is simple and fast, but it does require exact knowledge of the process times, which often can be difficult to establish. One obvious solution is to measure the process times over repeated executions. Such data collection can be done more easily in the embedded world than in the applications world because one generally knows the task mix in advance.

12.5.2 Queuing Models

If the system being designed is one in which the processes can vary from day to day, there may be no static set of processes and times that can be used in a deterministic model.

Statistical studies have shown that task execution generally consists of a cycle of CPU execution followed by I/O activity. The CPU and I/O bursts alternate until the job is finished. The frequency of the bursts tends to be fairly predictable and is typically independent of machine or process. As a first-order approximation, such behavior can be modeled as the exponential graph given in Figure 12.7. One can measure or compute the distribution of

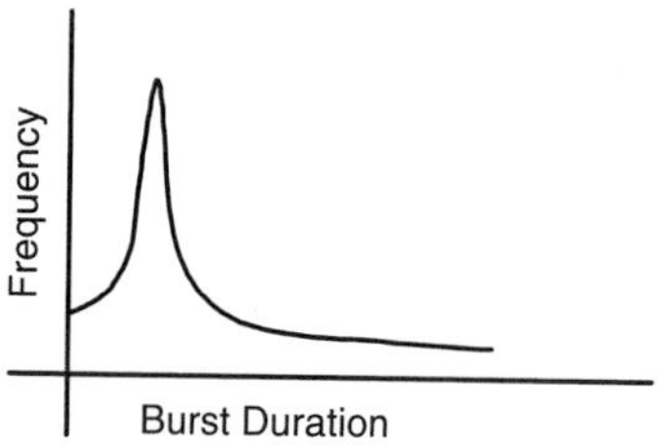

Figure 12.7 CPU or I/O Burst Duration vs. Frequency

CPU and I/O bursts over a collection of tasks and determine a similar distribution for process arrival times. Based on these two distributions, for most algorithms, it is possible to compute average throughput, utilization, waiting times, and so on.

The computer can be modeled as a collection or network of servers, with each server having an associated queue. Knowing the arrival and service rates, one can compute utilization, the average queue length–n, and the average wait time–w. The average arrival time is specified as λ. Thus, if the system is in steady state, the number of processes leaving a queue is equal to the number of processes arriving, and one can write,

$$n = \lambda \times W \tag{12.4}$$

Little's Formula

The expression relating the three variables is known as *Little's formula*. The approach is useful because it is valid for any scheduling algorithm. Knowing any two variables, one can compute the third. Though useful for comparing algorithms, it has limitations. The mathematics of complex algorithms and distributions is difficult to work with. The arrival and service distributions are complex, and the queuing models are only an approximation of the real system.

12.5.3 Simulation

To produce a more accurate evaluation of a scheduling algorithm, one can use simulations. Such an approach requires models of the computer system and the processes as well as appropriate data to drive the simulation. Often such data is collected from a trace of actual processes by recording the actual events on a real system. Simulation can be expensive, but it is growing in popularity and is becoming an increasingly powerful and effective tool.

12.5.4 Implementation

As another alternative, one can simply build and test the system. Certainly, this is the most accurate method. Once again, the difficulty is the cost.

12.6 TASKS, THREADS, AND COMMUNICATION

12.6.1 Getting Started

exchanging data
synchronizing,
sharing resources

A multitasking/multithreading system supports multiple tasks, and those tasks will have one or more threads. Important jobs in any multitasking system include *exchanging data* between tasks and between threads, *synchronizing* tasks and threads, and *sharing resources*.

In the not too recent past, such activities were limited primarily to tasks or threads within a single microprocessor. Today, one finds a growing use of FPGA-based designs utilizing devices that support the inclusion of multiple microprocessor cores within a single-gate array. Consequently, it is not uncommon for communication, synchronization, and sharing to involve tasks on multiple processors. We will find that certain assumptions can be made when tasks are localized that cannot be made when working with multiple distributed processors or other centers of computation.

12.6.2 Intertask/Interthread Communication

When tasks are operating independently, systems have few if any conflicts, chances for corruption, or contentions. Real systems, the interesting ones, must deal with the challenge of such problems. In real-world systems, resource sharing and intertask synchronization and communication must take place in a robust, safe, and reliable manner. Interaction between tasks may be direct or indirect and must be synchronized and coordinated. We want to prevent race conditions—conditions under which the outcome of a computation depends on the order in which tasks execute. Such an exchange is illustrated in Figure 12.8.

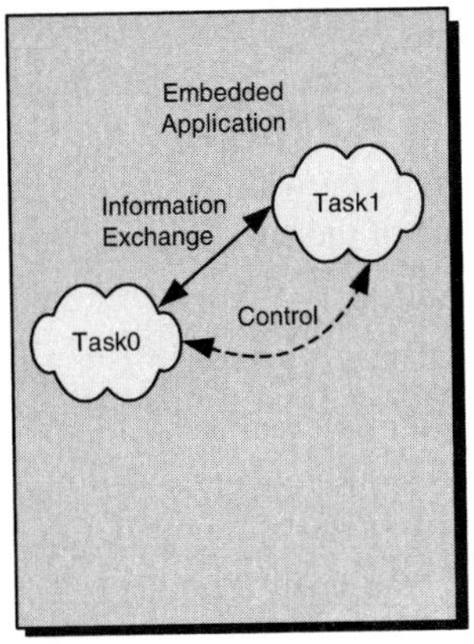

Figure 12.8 Intertask Communication

We see, then, that interaction and interchange among tasks requires three basic components: the information that is to be interchanged, the places where the information can be found, and where it is ultimately to be put, coupled with the conventions that govern the interaction and interchange. These requirements are captured in the following model of interprocess communication and synchronization.

information
place, places
control, synchronization

- The *information*—the data or signals being moved
- The *place* or *places* from which the information is moved to or from
- The *control* and *synchronization* of actions and the movement of the information

places

In such a model, the *places*—that is, the source and destination(s) for the exchange—are identified variously by named variables or by pointer variables holding memory addresses. Control and coordination comprises a number of different techniques ranging from flags or status bits to interrupts or managed access into critical areas under the control of semaphores or monitors. Information is moved either through *shared variables,* or *messages* on busses internal to the microprocessor that (except in rare circumstances) were of little immediate concern to us.

shared variables, messages

Let's begin our study of intertask communication and synchronization by looking at the shared information component. Such sharing can occur in a variety of ways. In subsequent chapters, we will extend the model to include centers of control outside of the core microprocessor.

12.6.3 Shared Variables

Such sharing can occur in a variety of ways. We will begin with the simplest model: shared global variables.

12.6.3.1 Global Variables

global variables

One fundamental solution for exchanging data among tasks is a shared memory environment. In such an environment, *global variables* can be a very effective mechanism for sharing information. Global variables have the obvious problems that arise when two or more tasks require the ability to read a piece of global data and potentially modify its value. The major advantage of globals is that they do not have to be copied to the stack during a context switch. By obviating the need for such copying, critical time in hard real-time systems can be saved. Properly managed, global variables can be an effective tool.

12.6.3.2 Shared Buffer

shared buffer
producer
consumer

A *shared buffer* is an exchange technique in which two processes share a common set of memory locations as seen in the data flow diagram in Figure 12.9. A *producer* of the data puts it into the buffer, and a *consumer* removes it. Once again, there are several obvious problems. If one process is faster than the other, the potential for overrun or underrun arises. Clearly, identifying the proper buffer size (for the application) and access protocol is critical to avoiding such problems. Even with the proper buffer size, the producer and consumer must always check the state of the buffer before inserting or removing an item.

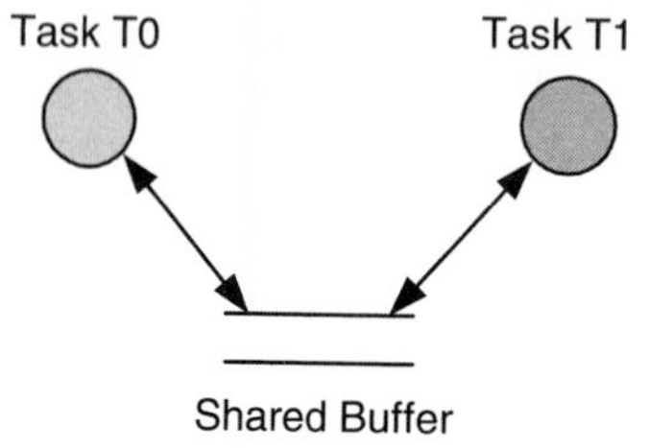

Figure 12.9 Intertask Communication Using a Shared Buffer

Good design practice recommends adding methods of the form

```
bool isFull() or bool isEmpty()
```

to the public interface of the container. Such methods should always be invoked prior to a read from or write to the buffer.

12.6.3.3 Shared Double Buffer—Ping-Pong Buffer

shared double buffer
ping-pong buffer

The *shared double buffer* model permits two tasks to share two (or more) common sets of memory locations. Shown in the data and control flow diagram in Figure 12.10, the configuration is also called a *ping-pong buffer*.

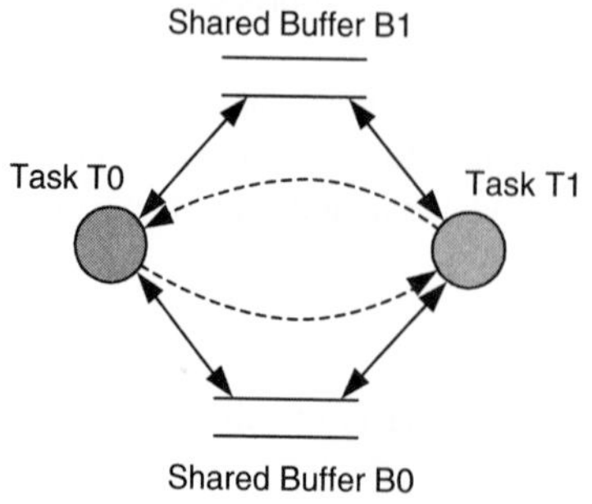

Figure 12.10 Intertask Communication Using a Shared Double Buffer

Several control schemes can be used with a ping-pong buffer. One implementation begins with both buffers being empty. T0 is designated as the producer and T1 as the consumer. During operation, task T0 will write to buffer B0 until it is full. In the meantime, T1 is blocked because there is no data available. Once B0 is filled, T0 will signal T1 and switch to writing to buffer B1.

T1 can now begin reading the data from B0. When T1 has removed all the data from B0, it signals T0 that the buffer is empty. If T0 has filled B1, T1 can begin reading from that buffer; otherwise it waits. Similarly, if T0 finishes writing to B1 before T1 has emptied B0, then it must block. The operation of the buffer scheme is illustrated in the two skeletal code fragments in Figure 12.11. Such an approach can be a very effective "buffer" between processes that are running at different rates. One buffer is being filled while the other is being emptied. Improved robustness requires that the consumer block on a lack of data and the producer must avoid overrunning the buffer; thus, it blocks on a full buffer.

```
Task T0                                  Task T1
while(1)                                 while(1)
    ...                                      ...
    if (B0 == EMPTY)                         if (B0 == FULL)
        repeat                                   repeat
            produce item in nextB0                   consume item in nextB0
        until (B0 == FULL)                       until (B0 == EMPTY)
        signal (T1, FULLB0)                      signal (T0, EMPTYB0)
    endif                                    endif
    if (B1 == EMPTY)                         if (B1 == FULL)
        repeat                                   repeat
            produce item in nextB1                   consume item in nextB1
        until (B1 == FULL)                       until (B1 == EMPTY)
        signal (T1, FULLB1)                      signal (T0, EMPTYB1)
    endif                                    endif
    ...                                      ...
end while                                end while
```

Figure 12.11 Two Tasks Exchanging Information Using a Shared Buffer

A second variant on the ping-pong buffer utilizes more than two buffers. Consider that we have two tasks, T0 and T1; the first task can produce data at a rate of 4 MHz, but the second can only consume at 1 MHz. To further complicate the problem, let's also assume that the buffer can only be written to at a 1 MHz rate. An implementation to solve the problem is given in the data and control flow diagram in Figure 12.12.

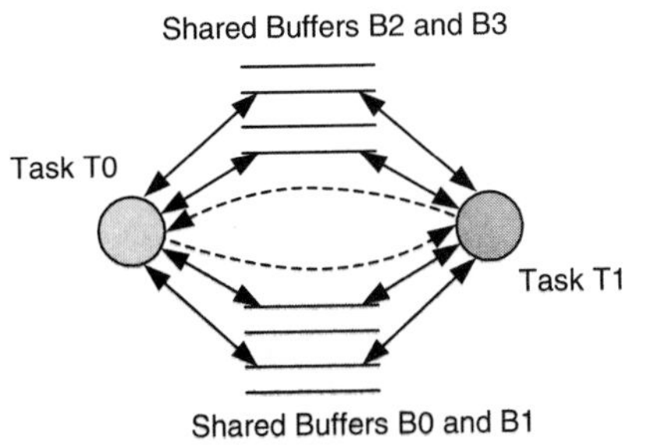

Figure 12.12 Information Sharing Between Tasks Executing at Different Speeds

The execution of the synchronization scheme is given in the pseudo-code fragments in Figure 12.13. Each buffer is written to at the 1-MHz rate. The buffers are filled in bursts in T0 and read at a more uniform rate in T1.

```
Task T0
while(1)
    ...
    if (B3 == EMPTY)
        repeat
            produce item in nextB0
            produce item in nextB1
            produce item in nextB2
            produce item in nextB3
        until (B3 == FULL)
        signal (T1, FULLB3)
    endif
    ...
end while
```

```
Task T1
while(1)
    ...
    if (B3 == FULL)
        repeat
            consume item in nextB0
            consume item in nextB1
            consume item in nextB2
            consume item in nextB3
        until (B3 == EMPTY)
        signal (T0, EMPTYB3)
    endif
    ...
end while
```

Figure 12.13 Information Sharing Between Tasks Executing at Different Speeds

12.6.3.4 Ring Buffer

ring buffer

A *ring buffer* scheme uses a FIFO structure as illustrated in the accompanying schematic representation in Figure 12.14. The structure permits simultaneous input and output using head and tail pointers. Task T0, the producer, adds data to the buffer, and task T1, the consumer, removes it. As with the other buffers, one must take precautions to properly manage overflow and underflow.

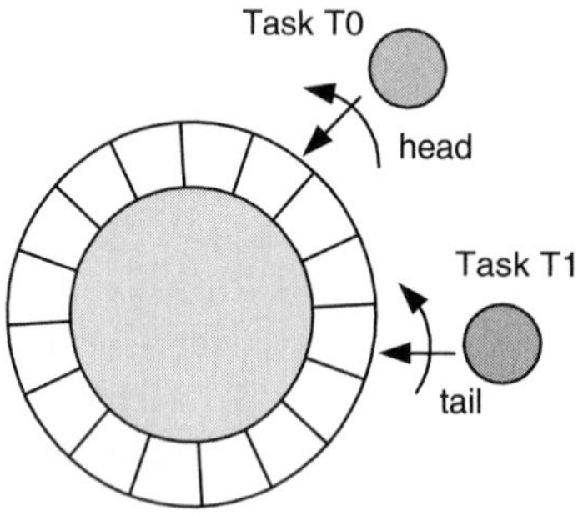

Figure 12.14 Information Sharing Using a Ring Buffer

12.6.3.5 Mailbox

mailbox

A *mailbox* is another data structure with access semantics that are similar to those used for the queue. Two or more tasks can use the mailbox to pass data or for synchronization. Generally, one finds mailboxes included in full-featured operating systems. Two operations on the data structure are defined: a write operation called *post* and a read operation called *pend*.

post, pend

When a task posts data to the mailbox, a flag associated with the mailbox is raised, indicating that data is available. A task that may be pending or waiting on that flag is alerted and can then read the data, resetting the flag.

The pend and post operations present the following public interface:

```
post (mailbox, data)        // post to mailbox
pend (mailbox, data)        // pend on mailbox
```

At first blush, the pend operation may appear to be the same as a poll because a poll task continually interrogates the polled variable (occupying the CPU) looking for a change in state of the signal. In contrast, however, the pending task is suspended (giving up the CPU), while there is no data available only to be awakened when data becomes available. Thus, in the case of a polling operation, the CPU is devoted to testing the state of the poll signal, whereas the pend operation frees the CPU to another task. A variety of things can be passed through a mailbox, a single bit or flag, a single data word, a pointer to a data buffer, or a more elaborate message.

The data and control flow diagram is given in Figure 12.15.

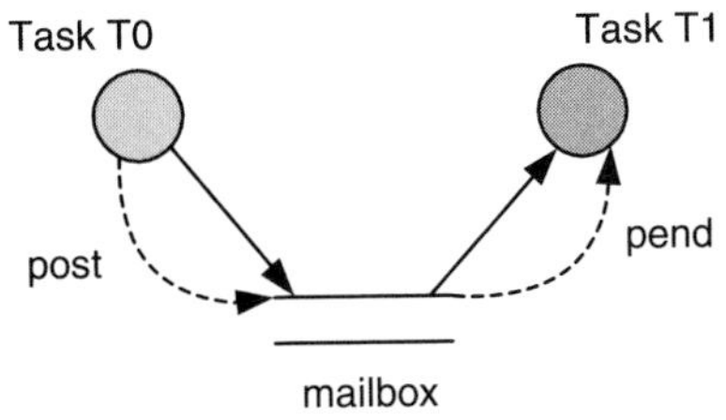

Figure 12.15 Information Sharing Using Messages and a Mailbox

One straightforward implementation of the mailbox data type utilizes a queue as the underlying container. In the basic implementation, the queue is of length one and thus, the post operation fills the mailbox precluding further posts until a pend operation takes place to empty the mailbox. If several tasks are pending on a flag, the enabled task resets the flag. Such a scheme blocks multiple accesses to the resource from a single flag. Other implementations extend the queue length, thereby supporting a queue of pending elements rather than a single entry. Such a scheme may be useful when there are multiple independent copies of a critical resource. Another variation on this latter design utilizes a priority queue and thence permits a priority to be assigned to each message. The associated pend operation will always read the highest priority message first.

12.6.4 Messages

The methods for intertask communication discussed up to this point have relied on a mutually agreed upon memory location to at least begin the exchange. Today's embedded applications are becoming increasingly distributed. With such an expansion, the need for synchronization and information interchange remains and, to some extent, increases.

To execute such an exchange, one can build on the concept of mailboxes. Using a mailbox-based approach, data—now the message—is sent to a named mailbox or destination. The named mailbox now becomes the address of the message destination. The message may or may not be buffered at the source of the message—a source mailbox or at the destination—a destination mailbox. Such a scheme, however, is not mutually exclusive with shared memory.

interprocess communication
send, receive, pend, post

A message-based approach, called an *interprocess communication* facility (IPC), supports two operations, *send* and *receive*. These are analogous to the *pend* and *post* operations used for mailboxes. Continuing the analogy, messages may be of fixed or variable size. If tasks T0 and T1 wish to use messages to exchange information, they must first establish a communication link and then proceed to send and receive the messages.

As noted earlier, with the increasing use of multiprocessor core FPGAs, the communication link can be between processors within the same gate array as well as between physically and geographically separated microprocessors.

As one begins to think about message exchange, several questions immediately arise,

- How is the link established?
- Can the link be associated with multiple tasks?
- How many links are there between a pair of tasks?
- What is the link capacity, and are there buffers?
- What is the message size?
- Are links unidirectional or bidirectional?

We will look at several of these questions but defer the last two to a later chapter in which we present a more in-depth discussion of networking and remote systems.

When considering implementation methods, one may choose

- Direct/indirect communication
- Symmetric/asymmetric addressing
- Auto or explicit buffering
- Send by copy or reference
- Fixed or variable message size

12.6.4.1 Communication

directly, indirectly

A message can be moved from one place to another, either *directly* or *indirectly,* via some intermediate point or points. Each way has advantages and disadvantages.

DIRECT

When using a direct communication scheme, each process must explicitly name the sender/receiver of the message. Messages are logically of the form

```
send (T1, message)        // send message to task T1
receive (T0, message)     // receive message from task T0
```

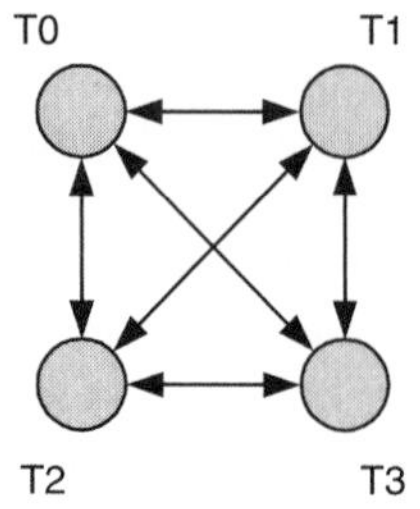

Figure 12.16 Four Fully Interconnected Tasks

The link is automatically established between every pair of processes or threads within a process. For a system with four different processes, the configuration in Figure 12.16 gives full, bidirectional interconnection among all of the processes. Several important points need to be considered with such an implementation:

- The individual tasks may or may not be physically collocated. On one extreme, they may be within the same FPGA. On the other, they could be in several different countries.
- Full interconnectivity is not efficient for larger numbers of tasks. A hierarchical scheme in which a smaller subset of the tasks is so interconnected may be more feasible to implement and manage. Consider the Internet as a good model.

Using a direct communication scheme, each task only needs to know each other's identity; that is, the link is associated with only two processes. The link may be unidirectional or bidirectional.

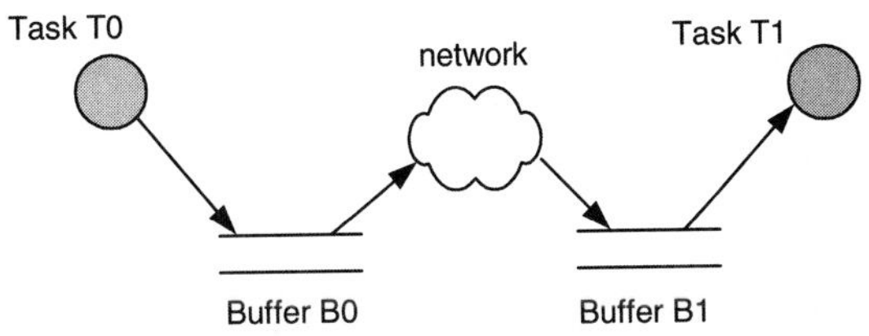

Figure 12.17 Information Exchange Between Two Tasks over a Network

The exchange can be expressed in a modified data flow diagram in Figure 12.17. Note that a buffer is associated with each process, although this may not be the case in all implementations. More specifically, the buffer will probably be attached with an I/O task.

EXAMPLE 12.0

Consider the skeletal structure between two tasks—a producer task, T0 and consumer task, T1. Task T0 produces the data and stores it in a buffer it shares with the send task. The send task takes the data from the buffer and formats it into a message that it sends as the payload in a message to task T1, the consumer task. T1 then reverses the process.

The activities by both tasks during the exchange are first expressed in the activity diagram in Figure 12.18 and then in the sequence diagram in Figure 12.19.

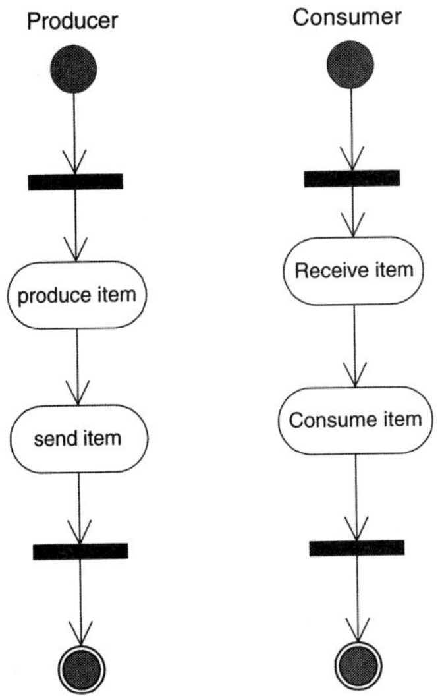

Figure 12.18 Activity Diagram Illustrating a Producer–Consumer Exchange

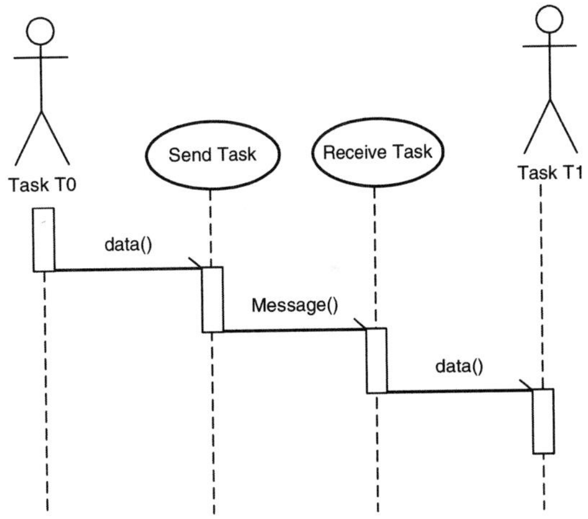

Figure 12.19 Sequence Diagram Illustrating a Producer–Consumer Exchange

Finally, the code fragment shown in Figure 12.20 reflects the operation of the two tasks.

```
while(1)                          while(1)
    ...                               ...
    produce item in nextB0            receive(T0, nextB1)
    ...                               ...
    send (T1, nextB0)                 consume item in nextB1
...                               ...
end while                         end while
```

Figure 12.20 Code Fragment Illustrating a Producer–Consumer Exchange

symmetrical addressing

Observe that the scheme uses *symmetrical addressing*; the sender and receiver must name each other. The disadvantage of such an approach is that it ties the process name to the implementation, thereby making future changes more difficult.

asymmetric addressing

If *asymmetric addressing* is used, the sender only names the recipient.

INDIRECT

With an indirect approach, messages are sent to or received from a shared variable, generally in the form of a mailbox. Thus,

```
send (M0, message)        // send message to mailbox M0
receive (M0, message)     // receive message from mailboxM0
```

The link is established only if the tasks/threads have a shared mailbox or similar container. The link may be associated with multiple processes, and there may be multiple links between processes. As with the direct scheme, the link may be unidirectional or bidirectional. The modified data flow diagram takes the form shown in Figure 12.21, in which two tasks are illustrated. The interconnecting links are shown as bidirectional.

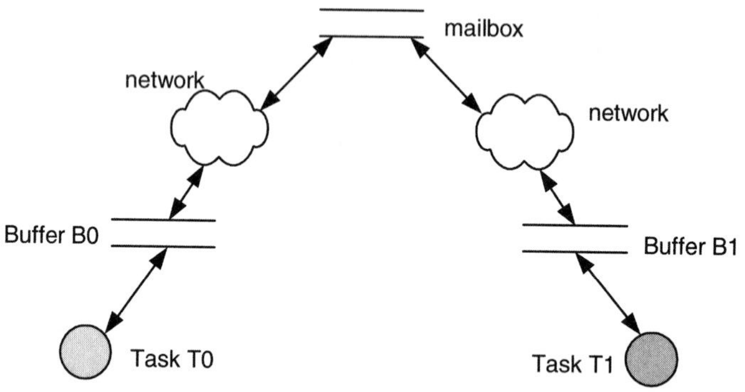

Figure 12.21 Indirect Information Exchange Between Two Tasks over a Network Using a Shared Mailbox

Now, consider three processes: T0, T1, and T2, all of which wish to exchange messages via the shared mailbox M0. Furthermore, let T0 send and T1 and T2 receive. The question of who gets the message, T1 or T2, arises.

One possible solution is to associate the link with at most two processes. Thus, only one process is allowed to receive at a time. As an alternative approach, the system could select a receiver. A third approach can be based on the owner of the mailbox.

If a task owns the mailbox, one can easily distinguish between the owner, who can only receive (there is no reason to send a message to ourselves other than as a built-in test), and the user, who can only send. Since each mailbox has a unique owner, there is no ambiguity. If the system owns the mailbox, then it exists independent of any process or thread.

12.6.4.2 Buffering

A buffer or buffers may be associated with the link. Error management aside, for the moment, buffering establishes the number of messages that can be safely sent out onto the link with the assurance that they will be received properly at the destination. If messages are sent too quickly, the receiver may not have sufficient time to accept and process one message before the next one arrives.

Three possible buffering schemes can be identified.

- The link has zero capacity.
  That is, the link cannot store messages. The sender must wait for the receiver to accept the message either by delaying or through a handshake. Such a scheme is called a *rendezvous* or an *Idle RQ protocol.*

rendezvous
Idle RQ protocol

- The link has bounded capacity.
  Associated with the link is a message queue of length n. If there is space remaining when the sender wishes to transmit, a message can be placed into the queue and the sender can continue. Otherwise the sender must wait for space.
- If the link has unbounded capacity, it can be viewed as having infinite length.
  The sender can post a message and continue. There is no wait. It is important to recognize that the criterion here is that the sender does not have to wait. If the receiver can remove the incoming data quickly enough, a buffer size of one will suffice and can still be called unbounded. Such a scheme is called a *Continuous RQ protocol.*

Continuous RQ protocol

All of the approaches to intertask communication that we have discussed are captured in Figure 12.22.

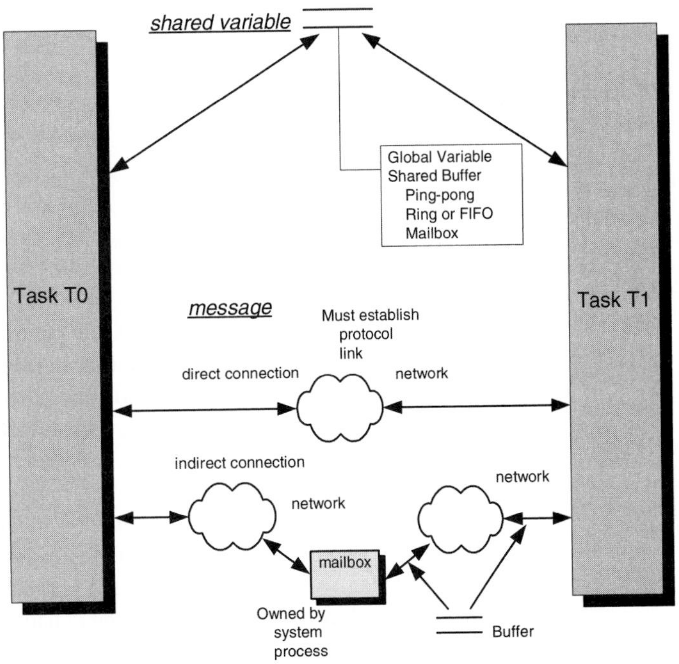

Figure 12.22 Alternative Approaches for Intertask Communication

12.7 TASK COOPERATION, SYNCHRONIZATION, AND SHARING

In addition to sharing information, the tasks in a multitasking system or the processors in a multiprocessor system are often charged with cooperating/synchronizing with each other as they execute the application. Cooperating tasks (and threads) or processors can affect or be affected by other tasks (and threads) or processors. They may directly share a logical address space (both code *and* data) or be allowed to share data only through any of the various shared variable models that have been discussed. Such concurrent access to common data can result in data inconsistency, aberrant or unexpected system behavior, and potentially complete system failure.

12.7.1 Critical Sections and Synchronization

Northern Scotland is beautiful, rugged, and lightly populated. There are few roads, with little traffic. Many of the roads are narrow, bucolic, single-lane driving challenges populated with passing places and sometimes even narrow bridges as seen in the accompanying simple drawing in Figure 12.23. As the two cars arrive, the bridge clearly presents a problem since it is only wide enough for a single car to cross at any time. Not having both vehicles simultaneously occupying this critical section of the road is most certainly beneficial to all concerned.

If each car is modeled as a process and the bridge as a shared resource, the problem is expressed using the data flow diagram in Figure 12.24.

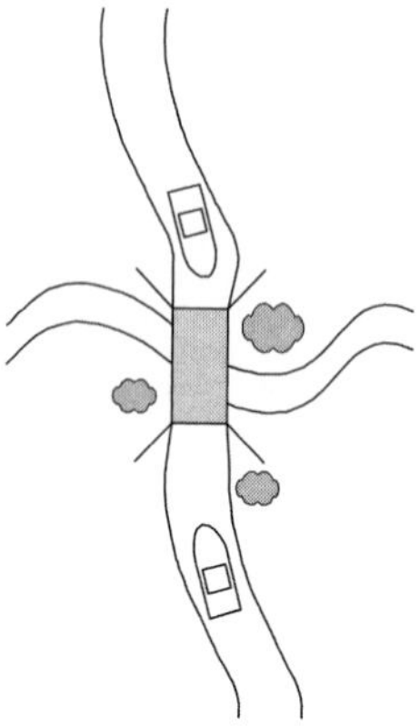

Figure 12.23 A Critical Section

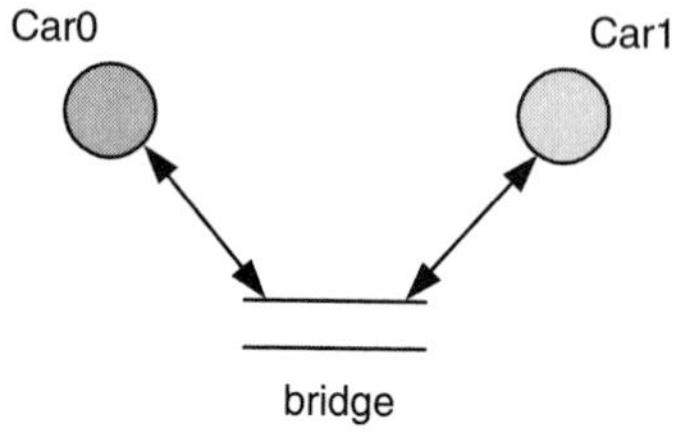

Figure 12.24 A Shared Variable Critical Section

One possible solution to the problem is to control access to the bridge by placing a rock on the edge of the bridge. When a car approaches the bridge and wants to cross, it must stop first, pick up the rock, drive across, and then put the rock back on the other side of the bridge. If the rock is not available, the car must wait.

Of course, it is necessary to make several underlying assumptions for the solution to be feasible. The first assumption is that no one decides to see how far they can throw the rock or forgets to return it. Second, two people don't arrive simultaneously and decide to fight over the rock. If two people do try to grab the rock at the same time (in the olden days we may have had clan warfare), today we have learned to play nice and share—after you; oh no, after you.The third assumption is that the musical group from England doesn't go rolling off with it as a souvenir.

The data flow diagram is extended and illustrated in Figure 12.25 in order to add control, and the design begins to look a bit like a mailbox.

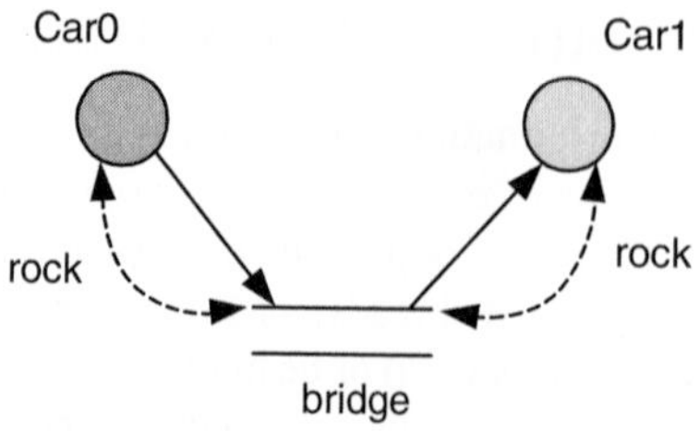

Figure 12.25 Adding Control to Manage a Critical Section

Let's examine how concurrent access to a shared resource can be manifest in a design. Consider the problem that subsequently arises in the accompanying pseudo-code and code fragments. Implemented is a simple data transfer between two tasks, one a producer and the other a consumer, via a shared buffer. The buffer has a limited capacity of n items. The transfer must be managed to ensure that the producer does not try to put data into the buffer when it is full and the consumer must not try to take data out when the buffer is empty. A variable *count* provides a measure of the number of items in the buffer. It is incremented when an item is added and decremented when one is removed. The data flow diagram for the shared buffer is given in Figure 12.26.

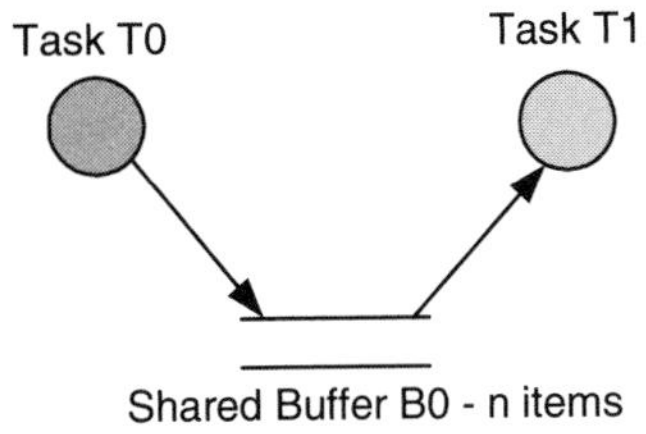

Figure 12.26 Producer–Consumer Exchange Through a Shared n Item Buffer

not full
not empty

The behavior of the system is first captured in the state chart in Figure 12.27. Observe that for the producer task, T0, the transition from idle to the write state is guarded by the *not full* condition on the buffers. Similarly, the transition into the read state is guarded by the *not empty* condition in the consumer diagram.

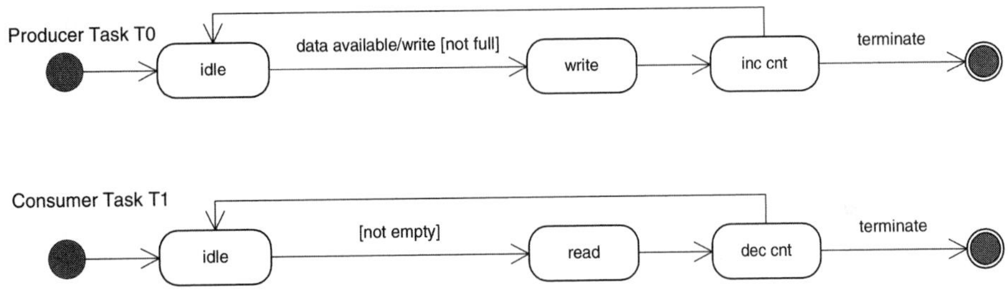

Figure 12.27 State Chart Diagram Modeling a Producer–Consumer Information Exchange

The problem is then expressed in pseudo code (see Figure 12.28).

```
Task T0 - Producer
    while(1)
        If not full
            add item
            increment count
        else
            wait for space
    end while
```

```
Task T1 - Consumer
    while(1)
        If not empty
            get item
            decrement count
        else
            wait for item
    end while
```

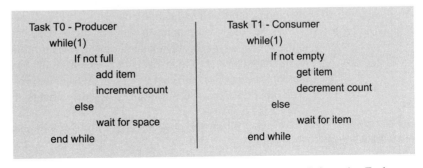

Figure 12.28 Pseudo-Code Modeling a Producer–Consumer Information Exchange

The C code fragments are given in Figure 12.29.

```
Task T0 - Producer                          Task T1 - Consumer
   int in = 0;                                 int out = 0;
   while(1)                                    while(1)
   {                                           {
       // produce an item nextT0                   while (count == 0);    // wait for item
       // wait for room                            nextT1 = B0[out];
       while (count == MAXSIZE);                   out = (out + 1) % MAXSIZE;
       B0[in] = nextT0;                            count--;
       in = (in + 1) % MAXSIZE;                    // consume an item nextT1
       count++;                                }
   }
```

Figure 12.29 C Code Fragment Modeling a Producer–Consumer Information Exchange

count

critical section

As with the attempts at simultaneous access to the bridge, there is a potential problem with simultaneous access to *count*. The value of the variable *count* depends on which task accesses it and in which order. Because the two tasks are running asynchronously, the variable may have any of three different values at any instant in time. Like the bridge, count represents a critical piece of data or *critical section* shared between the two processes, T0 and T1.

In general, a critical section is a resource that several tasks may be sharing such as an I/O port or a segment of memory in which they are reading *and* writing common variables. Such variables may be as simple as a single bit or as complex as a file or a table. As was the goal in crossing the Scottish bridge, while a task is working with a piece of data or some other resource in a critical section, we want to prevent access by all other processes. That is, one wants to ensure *mutually exclusive* access.

mutually exclusive

synchronization, mutual exclusion

synchronization, condition synchronization

The need to control access to a shared resource or to common data gives rise to one form of process or processor *synchronization* that is called *mutual exclusion synchronization*. A second form of synchronization is called *condition synchronization*. For the case of mutual exclusion synchronization, the objective is to make certain that two processes are not in their critical sections at the same time. Condition synchronization, on the other hand, requires that a process delay or block until a specified condition is true (or false).

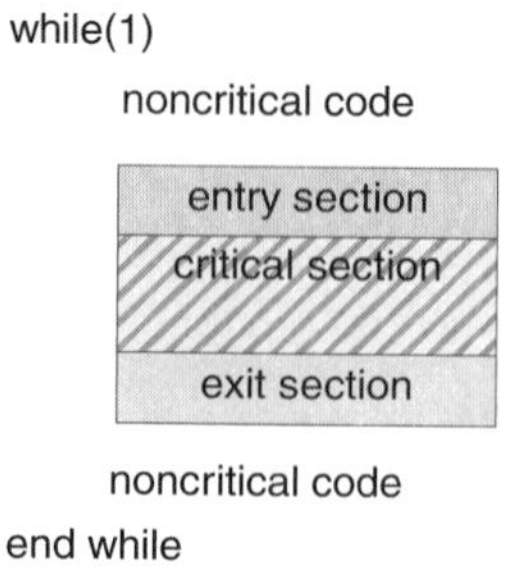
while(1)
noncritical code
entry section
critical section
exit section
noncritical code
end while

Figure 12.30 An Abstract Model of a Critical Section

The need to share and to coordinate access exists only if there is more than one task or processor that wishes to use a nonsharable resource or to modify common data at the same time. This is a key point. If the resource is sharable or if the tasks are executing read only operations, there will be no problem.

As we sought to accomplish with the simple bridge management schemes, the solution to the critical section problem requires a control algorithm or protocol that regulates access to the shared area. At a high level, the protocol should be such that a task wishing to access the critical section should check to see if anyone else is using the variable; if not, announce to all other tasks that it is now going to use the variable, do its work, and then tell everyone when it is finished.

An abstract model of the structure of a task with a critical section can be depicted as shown in Figure 12.30.

entry section

The code relevant to the critical section is enclosed in the three rectangles shown in the figure. The top rectangle, the *entry section*, acts as the gatekeeper controlling access to the

exit section

critical region. The bottom rectangle, the *exit section*, serves to tell the world that the task that had been using the critical variable is now finished.

Any solution to the critical section problem must satisfy the following requirements.

mutual exclusion

- It must ensure *mutual exclusion* in the critical region.
  If a task is in the critical section, no other task may be allowed in.

deadlock

- It must prevent *deadlock.*
  If two or more tasks are trying to enter the critical section, one must succeed.

progress

- It must ensure *progress* through the critical section.
  If no task is in the critical section and some other task wishes to enter, only tasks that are *not* in the exit section rectangle can affect which task enters the critical section next. Furthermore, a task wishing to enter cannot be prohibited from doing so indefinitely.

bounded waiting

- The solution must ensure *bounded waiting*.

  An upper limit must be set on the number of times a lower priority task can be blocked by one with a higher priority once it has made a request to enter.

atomic

Let's examine several possible solutions to the critical section problem. We will begin with a flag-based approach. Prior to doing so, however, we introduce the word *atomic* as a qualifier to an operation.

> *Atomic Operation*
>
> One that is guaranteed to terminate and is indivisible when applied to either examining a program variable or modifying the state of such a variable.

Indivisible simply means that, once started, the operation carries through to completion without interrupt. From a coarse-grained perspective, the operation appears as a single statement; from a fine-grained view, the operation may actually comprise several steps. The full sequence of steps must be guaranteed to complete and to do so uninterrupted.

12.7.2 Flags

To protect a critical section, the first goal is to ensure mutually exclusive access. This exclusion can be accomplished using flags embedded in an atomic operation. The method is illustrated using two flags and two processes. Expansion to a greater number of processes follows logically.

await

Define two processes, T0 and T1. Let them share a critical section. Define two Boolean flags, T0Flag and T1Flag, to mark which process is in the critical section. Finally, define the atomic operation, *await,* which is expressed in pseudo code as shown in Figure 12.31.

```
await( condition )
{
        statements
} variable.
```

Figure 12.31 Await Statement Pseudo-Code Model

condition
statements

Condition is a Boolean expression on which a task, thread, or processor waits until it evaluates to true. *Statements* comprise a set of actions that are to be performed when the condition evaluates to true. If the condition evaluates to true, execution proceeds through *await* *awaiting* the statements comprising the body of the *await* construct. An important assumption here is that when a process is *awaiting* a condition, other processes have the opportunity to run. Otherwise there is a deadlock.

Using the *await* operation, one can now reexamine the earlier shared buffer problem. The *await* statements are expressed, one for each task, as

```
await(!T1Flag) {T0Flag = true;}
await (!T0Flag){T1Flag = true;}
```

await *count* Next, the *await* statements are used to control access to the critical section—the variable *count*. First, we look at the producer (see Figure 12.32a).

```
Task T0 - Producer
    int in = 0;
    while(1)
    {
        // produce an item nextT0
        while (count == n);                          // wait for room
        B0[in] = nextT0;
        in = (in + 1) % n;
        await( !T1Flag ) {T0Flag = true;}            // entry section
        count++;                                     // critical section
        T0Flag = false;                              // exit section
    }
```

Figure 12.32a Managing a Critical Section Using the Await Statement—Producer Side

Then we look at the consumer (Figure 12.32b).

```
Task T1 - Consumer
    int out = 0;
    while(1)
    {
        while (count == 0);                          // wait for item
        nextT1 = B0[out];
        out = (out + 1) % n;
        await( !T0Flag ) {T1Flag = true;}            // entry section
            count--;                                 // critical section
        T1Flag = false;                              // exit section
        // consume an item nextT1
    }
```

Figure 12.32b Managing a Critical Section Using the Await Statement—Consumer Side

It is rather straightforward to show that this scheme satisfies the first three conditions for solving the critical section problem. Ensuring eventual access is a bit more involved and is contingent on the scheduling policy.

12.7.3 Token Passing

Another possible solution to the shared buffer problem is an extension of the rock-passing protocol developed for the Scottish bridge problem. We define a flag or token. To ensure sharing of the data, only one token is issued. The token is continuously passed from task to task; any task wishing to access the critical section can only do so when it has the token as illustrated in the state chart in Figure 12.33. The transition from state A to state B, from which the access to the shared variable occurs, is guarded by the requirement of possessing the token.

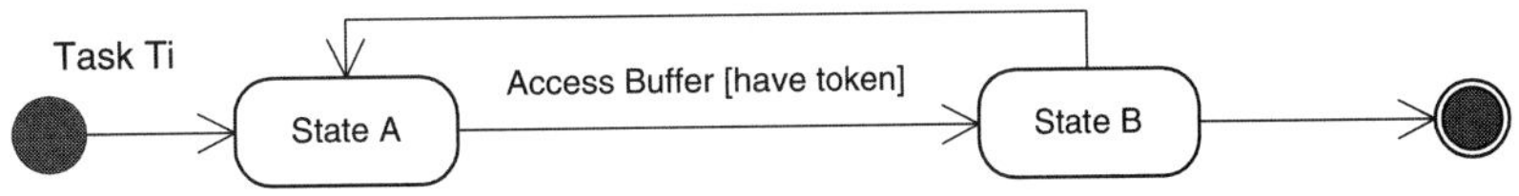

Figure 12.33 State Chart Modeling a Token Passing Protocol as a Solution to the Critical Section Problem

Although there is now controlled access to the critical section, several problems arise immediately:

1. A task or processor that does not want to share holds onto the token forever.
2. The task or processor with the token crashes for an extended time.
3. The token gets lost or corrupted because of noise.
4. The task or process with the token terminates or leaves the system without releasing the token.
5. How does one identify a new task or processor that gets added to the system?

One possible solution to all of these problems is to borrow an idea from our network colleagues. A system-level task, charged with managing the token, is added. The task includes a watchdog timer. Each time the token is released, the timer is reset. If the timer expires, a ping message is sent to all tasks or processors querying for the token. If no one responds, a new token is generated.

Borrowing again from the network people, each time a task or processor enters or leaves the system, it must register with the token management task. Alternatively, the system task could periodically query for new entries into the system.

It is evident that such a protocol satisfies all of the requirements stipulated above and thus does solve the critical section problem. The approach, however, adds a significant intra- and intersystem communication burden as well as extra overhead to each task.

12.7.4 Interrupts

Another approach to solving the buffer problem centers on managing interrupts. Since the problem only arises in a single-processor context when preemption is allowed, preventing preemption solves it. Disallowing all preemption is a bit too extreme in most cases. Taking a more surgical approach offers a more practical path.

Referring back to the earlier figure describing a task with a critical section, we should be able to solve the problem if interrupts are disabled when entering the rectangle labeled *entry* section and reenabled in the section labeled *exit* section.

entry

Using such an approach, one can encounter some of the same problems discovered with a token-based method. Specifically, if a task implements a long or infinite loop in its critical section, interrupts may be disabled for an extended period.

The problem can be solved with a variation on the solution developed for the token based scheme. Rather than disabling all interrupts, when the *entry* code segment is entered, all interrupts below a specified level are disabled or masked. A timer that can interrupt at a level above that set by the mask is enabled. If the timer expires, the system can preempt the offending task and handle it as is appropriate for the design.

entry

Once again, an interrupt-based approach meets the requirements for solving the critical section problem. The one caveat is that such an approach will not be effective in a multiprocessor approach utilizing shared memory since we only have the ability to manage interrupts on our own processor.

12.7.5 Semaphores

A protocol to protect a critical section was suggested by Professor Edsger Wybe Dijkstra, a distinguished computer science pioneer from Rotterdam, The Netherlands. Dr. Dijkstra has made significant contributions to almost every aspect of the field of computing science.

semaphore

atomic

As his solution to the critical section problem, he devised what is called a *semaphore.* In its simplest form, a semaphore is a Boolean variable or an integer– S that can be accessed only through two *atomic* operations:

```
wait - P(S)
signal - V(S)
```

proberen
to test, verhogen,
to increment

The letters P and V are the first letters of the Dutch words *proberen*, which means *to test*, and *verhogen*, which means *to increment.* At this point in the discussion, the value of a semaphore will reflect whether or not access to the critical variable is available. The word "atomic" qualifying the access operations for the semaphore is important, as was discussed earlier for the await operation.

wait
signal, test
set

The *wait* operation tests the value of the semaphore, and if it is false, sets it to true. The *signal* operation sets the value to false. The wait operation performs its job in two steps: *test,* then *set.* These steps must be seen from outside of the wait as a single, atomic operation.

wait, test, set

The sequence of events diagrammed in Figure 12.34 should not be possible. In the situation presented, the two tasks, T0 and T1, are executing. T0 currently has the CPU and needs to enter the critical section. It executes the *wait.* If the *test* and *set* operation is not atomic, T0 could complete the test portion and see that the resource is available. In the meantime, task T1, which has a higher priority, interrupts and also needs the resource. It,

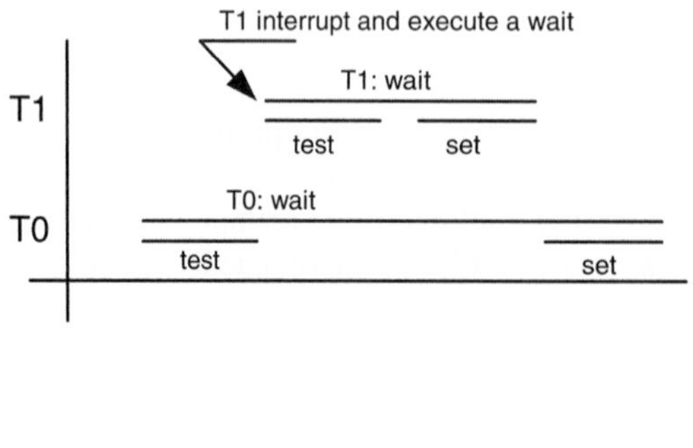

Figure 12.34 A Nonatomic Model of a Flag Used to Protect a Critical Section

wait

too, executes the *wait,* which it is allowed to complete. Task T1 then exits, and T0 resumes where it left off and sets the flag. Both processes now believe that they have mutually exclusive access to the critical area.

As long as neither task changes the value of the critical variable, everything will work as expected. However, a write operation by either task can potentially create a serious problem.

The operations may be defined by the code fragments presented in Figure 12.35. Observe the similarity with the await operation.

```
wait(s)
{
    while (s);
    s = TRUE;
}
s initialized to FALSE
```

```
signal(s)
{
    s = FALSE;
}
```

Figure 12.35 A Model of Semaphore Behavior

await

Bear in mind that, as with the *await* control statement, although shown as several steps, the wait must execute as a single, atomic operation. Lest the reader think that the semicolon following while is in error, it is not. Such a construct forces a task to block as long as the semaphore is set.

test, set

The *test* and *set* operation (abbreviated in various texts as *TS*, *TAS*, or *TNS*) is implemented as a hardware instruction on many processors.

The semaphore can now be used to protect a critical resource as demonstrated in the two code fragments presented in Figure 12.36.

```
Task T0
{
    ...
    wait(s)
    critical section
    signal(s)
    ...
}
```

```
Task T1
{
    ...
    wait(s)
    critical section
    signal(s)
    ...
}
```

Figure 12.36 Protecting a Critical Section with a Semaphore

The task that executes the wait(s) first will gain access to the critical section. The second task will block, waiting for the other task to execute the signal. Thereafter, it, too, can proceed.

12.7.6 Process Synchronization

One can use the semaphore in a slightly different way to force the execution order of several asynchronous tasks. For the basic case, consider an application with two such tasks, T0 and T1, which are cooperating on a portion of the application. Task T0 contains a function $f(s_0)$,

```
Task T0
{
    ...
    f(s1);
    signal(sync);        // signal
    ...
}
```

```
Task T1
{
    ...
    wait(sync);          // wait
    g(s2);
    ...
}
```

Figure 12.37 Using a Semaphore to Control the Order of Execution

and task T1 contains a function, $g(s_1)$. Their execution order is critical; the function $f(s_0)$ must be executed before $g(s_1)$. To achieve such a synchronization, we define the semaphore *sync* and initialize it to TRUE. The code fragments in Figure 12.37 illustrate the design.

Observe that because sync is initialized to TRUE, T1 will execute $g(s_2)$ only after T0 executes statement $f(s_1)$.

12.7.7 Spin Lock and Busy Waiting

wait ***busy waiting*** ***spin lock***

The one disadvantage of using semaphores for synchronization as we have described earlier is that when a *wait* for a shared resource or event, for example, is encountered, the encountering process is blocked and must loop continuously while waiting. Such a phenomenon is called *busy waiting.* Under such a condition, the waiting processes waste CPU cycles that other processes could use productively. The lock on the critical section is called a *spin lock* because the process spins while waiting for the lock to open. Of course, the advantage of such a lock is that there is no context switch which can take significant time. If the lock is expected to be held for only a short time, the spin lock can be particularly useful in time-critical situations.

12.7.8 Counting Semaphores

binary semaphores ***counting semaphores***

The semaphores we have looked at are called *binary semaphores*; they can take on either one of two values. The definition can be expanded slightly to permit the semaphore to take on a range of values from 0 to N-1; such semaphores are called *counting semaphores.*

wait ***block*** ***waiting*** ***signal*** ***ready***

Each such semaphore has an integer value and (potentially) a list of associated processes. When a process executes a *wait* operation and the semaphore is not available, rather than wait the process can *block* itself. Through the block operation, the process places itself in a waiting queue associated with the semaphore. The state of the process is changed to *waiting,* and control is transferred to the scheduler. The blocked process can be restarted when some other task executes a *signal* operation. The restart operation is initiated by a *wakeup* operation that places the task in the *ready* state and into the ready queue. Counting semaphores can be particularly useful when we must manage a pool of identical resources.

The definition of the semaphore operations is modified slightly, as seen in the code fragments in Figure 12.38. Nonetheless, the modeled operation of the semaphore remains atomic. The semaphore now defined as s is initialized to 0.

block, wakeup

Note that the *block* operation suspends the invoking process and the *wakeup* resumes execution of the blocked process. Both operations are provided by operating system calls. Observe that the waiting list can be implemented by a linked list and perhaps implement as FIFO or a priority queue.

```
wait(s)                                   signal(s)
{                                         {
    s = s+1;                                  s = s-1;
    if (s > 1)                                if (s >1)
    {                                         {
        add process to waiting queue;             remove process from waiting queue;
        block;                                    wakeup(p);
    }                                         }
}                                         }
```

Figure 12.38 A Code Fragment Modeling a Counting Semaphore

12.8 TALKING AND SHARING IN SPACE

So far, we have discussed the problems of sharing, cooperation, and synchronization among asynchronous tasks. Let's look at an application in which we can begin to use these concepts.

12.8.1 The Bounded Buffer Problem

First let's describe the objective. One of the major goals in designing embedded applications is to ensure that they perform in a highly robust manner that tolerates faults and misuse. Consider the following problem.

EXAMPLE 12.1

The application is to build the data management portion of an extensible digital imaging system to be used on the next generation Rovers that will engage in an ongoing exploration of Mars.

The goal of the mission is to conduct a series of detailed studies of the Martian surface and surrounding environment. The system is configured with several cameras that can continuously collect a variety of image data. The data may include infrared scans, atmospheric analysis, or topographic mapping.

The imaging system is mounted on the Rover. Data is collected in a buffer and then uploaded to an orbiting satellite that will subsequently transmit the image data to any one of a number of tracking stations on the Earth.

Because the objective is to map or sample as much of the environment as possible during each mission as data is collected, it is stored into any one of a set of N smaller buffers rather than one large one. With such a scheme, there is no waiting for the one buffer to be emptied before scanning can begin again, thereby maximizing the transfer on both sides. Thus, as each buffer is filled, image data is directed to the next free buffer. So as not to miss communication with one of the various Earth stations, the mother ship must upload the collected data as soon as it becomes available.

The block diagram in Figure 12.39 illustrates the system.

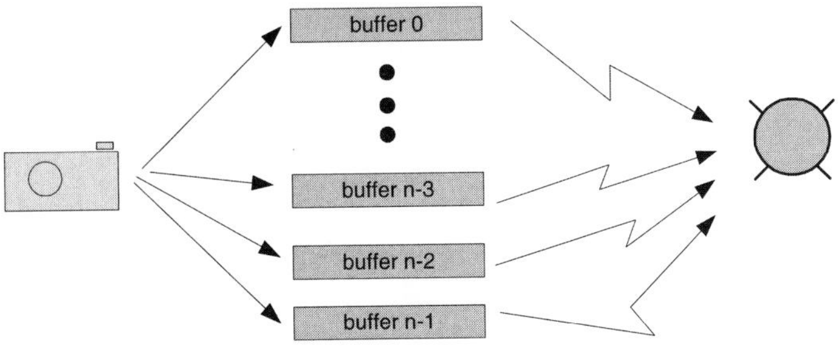

Figure 12.39 Information Sharing Utilizing an n Buffer Design

To solve the problem we first identify the essential requirements.

There are a couple of things that must be managed: the count of the number of free/full buffers and controlled access to a specific buffer for reading and writing the image data.

Next, we work on a solution.

The imaging system is a producer of data and the satellite is a consumer. We will use semaphores to manage access to the variables specifying the number of full or empty buffers and thence access to those buffers. To begin, we define the semaphores:

mutex Provides mutual exclusion for accesses to buffer pool—initialized to the value 1

empty Count number of empty buffers—initialized to n-1

full Count number of full buffers—initialized to 0

The algorithm works as follows.

The producer will check to see if there are empty buffers, if so, wait for exclusive access to the buffer pool. Once access is gained, the producer will add the data, then exit. On the consumer side, the consumer will see if any buffers have data available; if so, will wait for exclusive access. When the buffer pool is open, the consumer will retrieve the data and exit.

The producer code fragment is illustrated in Figure 12.40.

```
Task T0–Produce–Rover Side
   while(1)
        ...
        produce an item T0Item
        ...
        wait(empty);                    // wait for available buffer
            wait(mutex);                // buffer available
                                        // wait for exclusive access to buffer pool
            ...
                add T0Item to buffer;   // copy image data to buffer
            ...
            signal(mutex);              // signal buffer pool available
        signal(full);                   // signal data available
        ...
   end while
```

Figure 12.40 A Solution to the Bounded Buffer Problem: The Producer Side

The consumer code fragment is illustrated as shown in Figure 12.41.

```
Task T1–Consume–Satellite Side
   while(1)
        wait(full);                          // wait for data to become available
            wait(mutex);                     // wait for exclusive access to buffer pool
            ...
                remove T1Item from buffer;   // retrieve image data
            ...
            signal(mutex);                   // signal buffer pool available
        signal(empty);                       // signal date read
        ...
        consume item T1Item                  // use image data
        ...
   end while
```

Figure 12.41 A Solution to the Bounded Buffer Problem: The Consumer Side

Bounded Buffer problem

The problem just described is a classic synchronization problem known as the *Bounded Buffer Problem.*

12.8.2 The Readers and Writers Problem

A new engineer proposes that since there are a number of buffers, the imaging system can be enhanced by permitting data to be collected from several cameras at the same time and stored in one of the buffers. Also, data can be uploaded using several links and thereby speed up that process as well.

To demonstrate its operation, the engineer quickly puts together a simple model of the system. It works well most of the time, but occasionally data gets corrupted and he or she cannot understand why.

The proposed design exhibits one of the classic problems. We have a data object that must be shared among several concurrent processes. Some may want to upload (read) and others may want to store (write). The processes are referred to as *readers* and *writers.*

readers, writers

When operating, if multiple readers access the data simultaneously, there is no problem. If a writer and any other process access the shared data simultaneously, then there is the potential for a big problem. This problem is referred to as the *readers-writers* problem. There are several variations to the problem.

readers-writers

First Readers-Writers: No reader waits unless a writer has obtained access of shared variable.

Second Readers-Writers: Once a writer is ready, it performs the write as soon as possible. If a writer is waiting, no new reader started.

Let's see how the young engineer's problem can be solved. We will present a solution to the first readers-writers problem. To start, we define the following terms.

Semaphores
mutex, wrtSem, both initialized to 1

mutex
Used to ensure mutual exclusion when numReaders is updated

wrtSem
Used to ensure mutual exclusion for writer access

numReaders
Integer count of the number of readers currently accessing the shared buffer pool, initialize to 0

Each writer process must check for exclusive access to the buffer pool before writing. We ensure this by protecting the pool with the semaphore *wrtSem*. The code fragment for the writer is given in Figure 12.42.

wrtSem

As many readers as desired are permitted, provided that no other process is accessing the buffer pool to change the data. The code fragment for the reader is given in Figure 12.43.

Observe that in the entry section of the critical section, if the entering task is not the only reader, then, there must already be other readers. Such a condition implies there cannot be any writers. Otherwise, one must check to ensure that there are no writers before proceeding.

```
Writer Process
    wait(wrtSem);                          // wait for wrtSem == 1
                                           // wrtSem = 0
        ...
    // critical section

            perform writing;
        ...
    signal(wrtSem);                        // wrtSem = 1
    ...
```

Figure 12.42 The First Readers and Writers Problem: The Writer Side

```
Reader Process
    while(1)
        wait(mutex);                       // wait while mutex == 1
                                           // mutex = 0
            numReaders++;                  // inc number of readers
            if (numReaders ==1)            // if i'm the only reader
                wait(wrtSem);              // make sure no writers
                                           // wrtSem = 1
            end if
        signal(mutex);                     // mutex = 0

    // critical section
        ...
        Perform reading;
        ...

        wait(mutex);                       // wait for mutex == 1
                                           // mutex = 0
            numReaders--;                  // dec number of readers

            if (numReaders ==0)            // no readers
                signal(wrtSem);            // wrtSem = 0
            end if
        signal(mutex);                     // mutex = 0
        ...
    end while
```

Figure 12.43 The First Readers and Writers Problem: The Reader Side

wrtSem
mutex, signal(wrtSem)

If a writer is in the critical section, n readers are waiting, one reader is queued on *wrtSem*, n-1 readers are queued on *mutex,* and if a writer executes *signal(wrtSem)*, it may resume the waiting readers or one waiting writer. The decision is made by the scheduler.

The tacit assumption being made is that the buffers that are being written to or read from are managed to ensure that neither underflow nor overflow occurs.

12.9 MONITORS

monitor

The semaphores we have studied are a fundamental method for synchronism. However, they are a low-level mechanism, and it is easy to make errors with them. An alternate solution uses a data type called a *monitor*. Monitors are program modules that offer more structure than semaphores, with an implementation that can be as efficient.

condition variables

A monitor is a data abstraction mechanism that encapsulates a representation of an abstract object. The monitor provides a public interface as the only means by which internal data may be manipulated. Note that this is similar to a class in either C++ or Java. The monitor contains an internal (private) variable to store the object's state and procedures (methods or function members) that implement the operations on the object. Mutual exclusion is satisfied by ensuring that procedures in the same monitor cannot execute simultaneously. Conditional synchronization is provided through *condition variables.*

interface, body

A monitor is used to group a representation and implementation of a shared resource. It has an *interface* and a *body.* The (public) interface specifies those operations provided by the resource, while the body contains variables that represent the state of the resource. Internal procedures implement the operations specified in the interface. The monitor can be schematically illustrated as shown in Figure 12.44.

```
monitor monName
{
    initialization statements
    procedures
    permanent variables
}
```

Figure 12.44 The Monitor—A Typical Structure

The procedures implement the visible operations. All processes in the monitor share the permanent variables. They are denoted permanent because they retain their values on exit as long as the monitor exists. Such behavior occurs in C or C++ with static variables. The procedures may also have local variables.

By virtue of being an abstract data type (ADT), the monitor is a distinct scope. Only the procedure names are visible outside of the monitor—the public interface. Permanent variables can only be changed through one of the visible procedures. Statements within the monitor cannot affect variables outside the monitor, that is, those in a different scope. Permanent variables are initialized before any procedure is called. The initialization is accomplished by executing initialization procedures when the monitor instance is created.

mutual exclusion
synchronization

The major difference between the monitor and a class in C++ or Java is that the monitor is shared by multiple concurrently executing processes or threads. Consequently, the threads or processes using a monitor may require *mutual exclusion* to the monitor variables as well as *synchronization* to ensure that the monitor state is conducive to continued execution.

condition variables
active

Mutual exclusion is usually implicit; synchronization is implemented explicitly. Different processes require different forms of synchronization. The implementation of the necessary synchronization is accomplished through *condition variables*. An external task or thread calls a monitor procedure. The procedure is *active* if a thread or task is executing a statement in the procedure. At most one instance of a monitor procedure is *active* at any one time. The simultaneous invocation of two different procedures or two invocations of the same procedure is not permitted.

By definition, the procedures execute with mutual exclusion that is ensured by the language library and operating system. Mutual exclusion is generally implemented by using locks or semaphores and by inhibiting certain interrupts.

12.9.1 Condition Variables

Condition variables are used as part of the synchronization process and are intended to delay a task or thread that cannot safely continue until the monitor's state satisfies some Boolean condition. Note that condition variables are similar to the guard conditions in UML state charts. They are then used to awaken the delayed process once the condition becomes true.

cond A condition variable is an instance of a variable of type *cond*.

```
cond myCondVar;
```

The declaration can only occur inside the monitor. The value of the condition variable is a queue of delayed processes. Initially, the queue is empty. The value on the queue can only be accessed indirectly, for example, to test its state.

```
empty(myCondVar);
```

A thread can block on a condition variable:

```
wait(myCondVar);
```

wait Execution of the *wait* causes the task to move to the rear of the queue and to relinquish exclusive access to the monitor. A blocked process is awakened using

```
signal(myCondVar);
```

signal Execution of a *signal* causes the task at the head of the queue to awaken.

Observe that the execution of *signal* seems to cause a dilemma. Upon execution, two tasks have the potential to execute: the awakened task and the signaling task. Such a situation seems to contradict the requirement that only a single task or thread can be active in the monitor at any one time.

There are two possible paths for resolution:

Signal and Continue, nonpreemptive

- *Signal and Continue*—the signaling task continues, and the awakened task resumes at some later time. Such a scheme is considered *nonpreemptive;* the process executing the signal retains exclusive control of the monitor.

Signal and Wait, preemptive

- *Signal and Wait*—is considered to be *preemptive*. The task executing the signal relinquishes control and passes the lock to the awakened task. The awakened process preempts the signaling process.

The process is described in Figure 12.45.

calls, entry queue, return, wait

The operation/synchronization occurs as follows. A task *calls* a monitor procedure. If another task is executing in the monitor, the caller is placed into the *entry queue*. When the monitor becomes free, as a result of a *return* or *wait,* one task moves from the entry queue into the monitor.

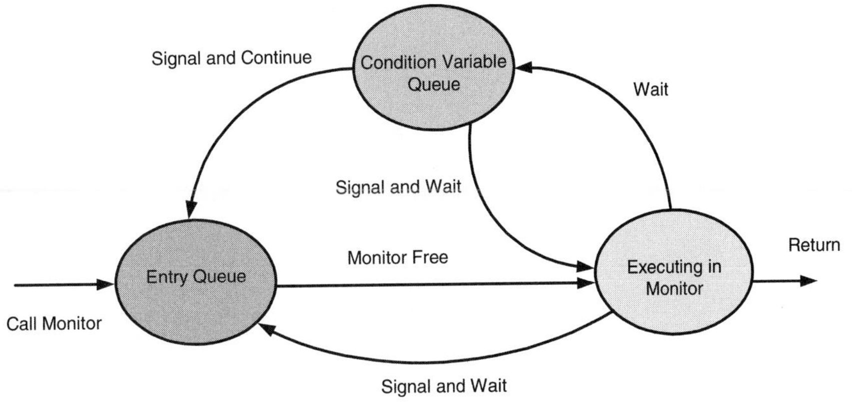

Figure 12.45 A State Diagram Model for a Monitor

If no other tasks are executing, the calling task passes through the entry queue and begins executing immediately. If the task executes *wait* on a condition variable while executing in the monitor, it enters the queue associated with that variable.

Signal and Continue

entry, Signal and Wait

When the task executes a *Signal and Continue* on a condition variable, the task at the head of the associated queue now moves to the *entry* queue. If a task executes a *Signal and Wait* on a condition variable, the task at the head of the associated queue moves to the monitor and the task executing in the monitor moves to the entry queue.

12.9.2 Bounded Buffer Problem with Monitor

Let's revisit the bounded buffer problem and implement the design with a monitor. As before, there is a pool of n buffers. We will assume that each can hold one item.

Define a monitor *boundedBuffer.*

Define the following condition variables:

notEmpty

Signaled when buffer count > 0

Tracks empty buffers, initialized to 0

notFull

Signaled when buffer count < n-1

Tracks full buffers, Initialized to 0

Define the procedures:

put(data)

Puts data into a buffer when space available

get(data)

Gets data from a buffer when data available

Define the protected entity:

bufferPool

The monitor can be implemented as shown in Figure 12.46.

```
monitor boundBuffer
    bufferPool;
    count = 0;
    cond notEmpty;                          // signaled when count > 0
    cond notFull;                           // signaled when count < n

    put(anItem)
    {
        while(count == n) wait (notFull);
        put anItem into a buffer
        signal (notEmpty);
    }

    get(anItem)
    {
        while(count == 0) wait (notEmpty);
        get anItem from a buffer
        signal (notFull);
    }
```

Figure 12.46 A Monitor Solution to the Bounded Buffer Problem

Code fragments for the implementation are illustrated in Figure 12.47.

Producer	Consumer
```while(1)```	```while(1)```

```
Producer                            | Consumer
    while(1)                        |     while(1)
        ...                         |         ...
        produce item anItem         |         boundBuffer.get(anItem)
        ...                         |         ...
        boundBuffer.put(anItem)     |         consume item anItem
        ...                         |         ...
    end while                       |     end while
```

Figure 12.47 Using the Monitor in the Producer and the Consumer to Solve the Bounded Buffer Problem

12.10 STARVATION

When working with semaphores and monitors, a potential problem called *starvation* exists. That is, one process is permanently prevented from running. Such a situation can occur when a process is waiting within a monitor or semaphore and other processes are added or removed in LIFO order.

12.11 DEADLOCKS

When working in a multitasking environment, one can create a second problem called a *deadlock*. A deadlock occurs when each process in a set of processes needs resources that are held by other processes in that set in order to continue. We will study the deadlock problem and examine several possible solutions in depth in the next chapter.

deadlock

12.12 SUMMARY

In this chapter we continued the discussion of time and the critical role it plays in the design of embedded applications by introducing the concepts of *reactive* and *time-based systems*. We have studied, in some detail, the basic responsibilities of task scheduling and intertask communication in the operating system. We have examined a number of different criteria for assessing scheduling algorithms; we learned the difference between static and dynamic scheduling, and we looked at several algorithms in each category.

We have looked at two categories of intertask communication—shared variables and message exchange—and at several ways by which we can implement those strategies. We have learned that a side effect of using shared data is the need for coordinated access by the tasks and threads comprising the system. We have seen that such a shared data, called a critical section, can be managed by several methods, including semaphores and monitors. Finally, we studied several classical models for shared data problems and how such problems can be solved using semaphores and monitors.

12.13 REVIEW QUESTIONS

Time, Time-Based Systems, Reactive Systems

12.1 What is the difference between an interval and a duration?

12.2 What is a time-based embedded system? a reactive embedded system?

12.3 What is the difference between a periodic and an aperiodic event or operation?

12.4 Explain what is meant by delay in an embedded application; by jitter.

12.5 What is meant by the expressions *hard* or *hard deadline* in a real-time embedded context?

12.6 What is firm real-time? soft real-time?

Scheduling

12.7 What is meant when a task is said to be schedulable? deterministically schedulable?

12.8 What is CPU utilization? Why is it important?

12.9 When are scheduling decisions made?

12.10 What is the difference between a preemptive and a nonpreemptive system?

12.11 Several scheduling criteria were outlined in the chapter. What are these?

12.12 What are the different scheduling algorithms identified in the chapter?

12.13 What is deterministic modeling? a queuing model?

12.14 What is simulation? emulation? What is the difference between them?

Intertask Communication

12.15 What are the three primary components that make up the intertask communication model introduced in this chapter?

12.16 One method introduced in the chapter for exchanging information between tasks was called shared variables. What does this mean?

12.17 Message exchange was introduced as another means by which information might be exchanged between tasks in an embedded application. What does this mean?

12.18 What is a rendezvous in a message exchange model?

12.19 What is a buffer in a message exchange model?

Task Cooperation, Synchronization, and Sharing

12.20 What is a critical section?

12.21 Describe what is meant by the entry and exit sections with respect to a critical section.

12.22 What requirements must be met in order to solve a critical section problem?

12.23 What is meant by the expression *atomic operation*?

12.24 What does the expression *test and set* mean?

12.25 What is a semaphore?

12.26 Discuss how a semaphore can be used to solve the critical section problem.

12.27 What is a spin lock?

12.28 What is a counting semaphore?

12.29 What is the bounded buffer problem?

12.30 What is the readers and writers problem?

12.31 What is a monitor?

12.32 How does a monitor meet the specified requirements for solving a critical section problem?

12.33 What is starvation?

12.34 What is a deadlock?

12.14 THOUGHT QUESTIONS

Time, Time-Based Systems, Reactive Systems

12.1 What is the difference between absolute time and relative time? Give two examples of each in an embedded application.

12.2 Give two examples of periodic and aperiodic events or operations in an embedded application.

Scheduling

12.3 Give an example of an embedded application for which each of the scheduling criteria discussed in the chapter might be best suited. Explain and justify your answer.

12.4 The chapter introduces several different scheduling algorithms. For each algorithm presented, give an example of an embedded application for which the algorithm might be best suited. Explain and justify your answer.

Intertask Communication

12.5 The chapter introduced several shared variable models. Identify each of these and explain how each works.

12.6 For each of the shared variable models, identify a strength and a weakness.

12.7 Give an example of an embedded application in which each of the shared variable models might be used. Explain and justify your choice.

12.8 Explain how message exchange as a means for exchanging information between tasks in an embedded application might work.

12.9 Discuss the advantages and disadvantages of message exchange versus shared variables in an embedded application.

12.10 Explain the difference between direct and indirect communication in a message exchange model? Give an example of each and explain the pros and cons of each approach in your selected applications.

12.11 Explain the difference between symmetric and asymmetric addressing in a message exchange model. Give an example of each and explain the pros and cons of each approach in your selected applications.

12.12 Several different buffering schemes were introduced. What were these? Give several advantages and disadvantages of each approach.

12.13 Give an example of an embedded application in which each of the buffering schemes might be used. Explain and justify your choice.

Task Cooperation, Synchronization, and Sharing

12.14 Give an example of a critical section in an embedded application and explain why it exists.

12.15 Why should a *test and set* operation be atomic?

12.16 The chapter presents several alternate solutions to the critical section problem. Describe each and discuss its advantages and disadvantages.

12.17 Discuss the advantages and disadvantages of using a counting versus binary semaphore in embedded applications.

12.18 Give several examples of embedded applications in which a binary or counting semaphore is used. Explain and justify your choice in each case.

12.19 What real-world problem is the bounded buffer problem modeling?

12.20 Give several examples of embedded applications containing a bounded buffer problem.

12.21 What real-world problem is the readers and writers problem modeling?

12.22 Give several examples of embedded applications containing a readers and writers problem.

12.23 How does a monitor differ from a binary semaphore? counting semaphore?

12.24 Explain the purpose of condition variables in a monitor.

12.15 PROBLEMS

12.1 Present a UML sequence diagram to illustrate the behavior of an embedded design comprising four tasks in the polled set.

12.2 Complete the design of the basic polled algorithm given in Figure 12.4 for a system with four tasks in the polled set. Model each task as a mod N_i counter that is incremented each time the task is polled.

12.3 You have a digital event, a positive transition on a signal line, that you must respond to within 40 μ sec. As the designer, you need to determine the best way to handle such a signal. You have two choices, polling or an interrupt. You are in a design review and must present a case justifying one or the other.

(a) Present the pros and cons of polling.

(b) Present the pros and cons of an interrupt-based scheme.

(c) For a polled scheme, give a detailed description of necessary steps prior to polling, during polling, and after the event occurs. Be specific.

(d) For an interrupt-based scheme, give a detailed description of necessary steps prior to the interrupt, during the interrupt, and after the interrupt has been handled. Be specific.

(e) What happens in both cases (polled and interrupt) if all interrupts are globally disabled?

(f) What happens in the interrupt case if no ISR is set up at the interrupt vector location?

12.4 You have a task that must respond to an external event at five different times during a cycle. For two of the times, t_2 and t_3, the response is considered hard real-time and for three of the times, t_0, t_1, t_4, the response is considered soft real-time as shown in Figure P12.48.

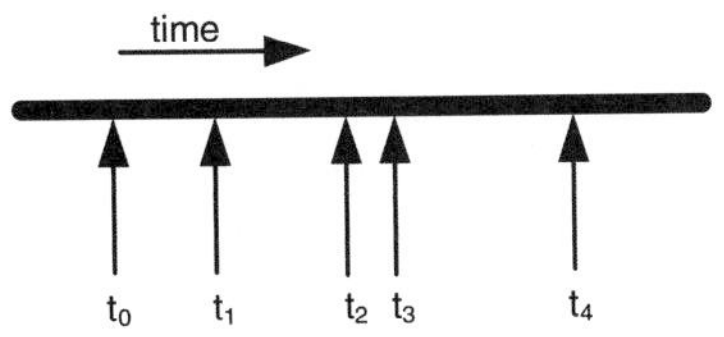

Figure P12.48

As the designer, you can choose only one of the following methods to accommodate the external event: polled, interrupt, or polling an interrupt. Discuss the advantages and disadvantages of each method.

12.5 Design an embedded system to control a traffic light utilizing a state-based schedule. Each direction supports a left turn (right turn if traffic normally drives on the left-hand side) and pedestrian-activated crosswalk control.

12.6 Design an embedded system to control a portable personal entertainment system utilizing a state-based schedule. The system must support the ability to: turn on / select a song to play, play the song, suspend playing, replay a song, turn off.

12.7 Implement a *first-come first-served* scheduling algorithm utilizing a doubly linked list based task queue.

12.8 Repeat Problem 12.7 for a *shortest job first* scheduling algorithm.

12.9 Repeat Problem 12.7 for a *round robin* scheduling algorithm.

12.10 An embedded system has three processes with the following execution times and periods: P1(4, 16), P2(3, 12), P3(2, 8).

(a) What is the CPU utilization for such a system?

(b) Can the set of tasks be scheduled using a rate-monotonic schedule?

(c) If the set of tasks can be scheduled, give the UML sequence diagram for the schedule.

12.11 An embedded system has three processes with the following execution times and periods: P1(4, 16), P2(3, 8), P3(2, 7).

(a) What is the CPU utilization for such a system?

(b) Can the set of tasks be scheduled using a rate-monotonic schedule?

(c) If not, what changes would have to be made to enable the set of tasks to be scheduled using a rate-monotonic schedule?

12.12 An embedded system has five processes with the following execution times and periods: P1(5, 40), P2(5, 60), P3(4, 16), P4(6, 48), P5(12, 96).

(a) What is the CPU utilization for such a system?

(b) Can the set of tasks be scheduled using a rate-monotonic schedule?

(c) If the set of tasks can be scheduled, give the UML sequence diagram for the schedule.

12.13 An embedded system has three processes with the following execution times and periods: P1(4, 16), P2(3, 8), P3(2, 7).

(a) What is the CPU utilization for such a system?

(b) Can the set of tasks be scheduled using an *earliest deadline* schedule?

(c) If the set of tasks can be scheduled, give the UML sequence diagram for the schedule.

12.14 Provide a C algorithm to schedule a set of three tasks using an *earliest deadline* schedule.

12.15 Repeat Problem 12.14 for a *least laxity* schedule.

12.16 An embedded system has the following three jobs, processes, and resources. Devise a schedule using the *shortest job first* algorithm that will achieve optimum utilization of resources and system throughput.

3 Jobs:	J1, J2, J3		
3 Resources:	A/D		
3 Processes:	Measure		M
	CPU	Compute	C
	I/O	Output	O

J1	Time Units	J2	Time Units	J3	Time Units
M1	1	M1	2	M1	3
C1	1	C1	3	C1	3
M2	2	M2	1	M2	2
C2	3	C2	2	C2	2
O1	3	M3	2	M3	3
M3	2	C3	3	C3	3
C3	1	O1	2	O1	2
O2	1				
Total	14		15		18

12.17 Repeat Problem 12.16 using a *rate-monotonic* schedule.

12.18 Repeat Problem 12.16 using an *earliest deadline* schedule.

12.19 An embedded application is designed as three tasks. The requirements for each are given in the following table.

Task	Priority	Period	Time Units
1	1	7	2
2	2	16	4
3	3	31	7

(a) Can the three tasks be scheduled using a nonpreemptive scheduling scheme? Why or why not? If so, show the schedule using a UML sequence diagram.

(b) Can the three tasks be scheduled using a preemptive scheduling scheme? Why or why not? If so, show the schedule using a UML sequence diagram.

(c) Can the three tasks be scheduled using a time slice scheduling scheme? Why or why not? If so, what is the value of the time slice to ensure minimum average wait time for all three tasks. Show the schedule using a UML sequence diagram.

12.20 Give a UML class diagram for a buffer that can be shared between two tasks.

12.21 Provide a C implementation of the buffer specified by the class diagram in Problem 12.20.

12.22 Provide a Verilog model of the buffer specified by the class diagram in Problem 12.20.

12.23 Give a UML class diagram for a ping-pong buffer that can be shared between two tasks.

12.24 Give a UML sequence diagram for the operation of a ping-pong buffer.

12.25 Provide a C implementation of the ping-pong buffer specified by the class diagram in Problem 12.24.

12.26 Provide a Verilog model of the ping-pong buffer specified by the class diagram in Problem 12.24.

12.27 Give a UML class diagram for a ring buffer that can be shared between two tasks.

12.28 Provide a C implementation of the ring buffer specified by the class diagram in Problem 12.27.

12.29 Provide a Verilog model of the ring buffer specified by the class diagram in Problem 12.27.

12.30 A shared memory scheme is to be used as a means of exchanging blocks of data between two tasks, T_0 and T_1. The number of blocks of data to be exchanged and their location is not fixed.

(a) Give a data/control flow diagram for the shared memory system.

(b) Explain how your memory system works using a UML sequence diagram and by describing a complete cycle that includes the following: Write by T_0—Read by T_1—Write by T_1—Read by T_0. Be certain to explain how each task knows when and how much to read or write.

(c) How would your design change if three tasks were involved in the exchange?

12.31 As the chief engineer for *Make Me Rich Consultancy*, you have been hired by a start-up embedded systems company *Inside Your Stuff, Ltd.* It seems that they have designed (in less than two weeks) a hard real-time control system for *Fastern Yours Processes, Etc.* The control system supports the following two operations on a collection of data items, $a_0, a_1, a_2 \ldots a_{n-1}$,

get (i)—Returns the value of a_i

put (i, aValue)—Assigns a Value to a_i

The control system has three asynchronous processes that must perform the following transactions:

```
p0: x = read (j); y = read (i); write (j, 52); write (i, 27);
p1: x = read (k); write (i, 43); y = read (j); write (k, 72);
p2: write (k, 25); x = read (i); y = read (j); write (i, 27);
```

Occasionally, the system produces incorrect results and *Fastern Yours Processes, Etc.* is threatening to return the system. It is now 3:30 in the morning and you are at the *Fastern Yours Processes* site with a not so happy customer and a system that is running pretty slowly.

(a) When *Inside Your Stuff, Ltd.* said they had designed a hard real-time system, what did they mean?

(b) Can you identify the problem and explain why it is occurring?

(c) Can you propose a fix? Explain why your solution will solve the problem?

12.32 A colleague has built a simulation of a portion of a telecommunications block. He explains that the system uses a shared buffer that accepts blocks of characters from a measurement process P1 and forward blocks of data to the output process, P2. He has written the following routines, one for P1 and one for P2.

```
full = 0
max = buffer size
p1Generate( )
{
   while (full < max)
   {
      buffer(head) = anItem;
      (head = head + 1) mod max;
      full++;
   }
}

full = 0
max = buffer size
p2Transmit( )
   {
   while (full > 0)
   {
      anItem = buffer(head);
      (head = head - 1) mod max;
      full--;
   }
}
```

Occasionally the system either loses data or forwards incorrect data.

(a) Can you explain why?

(b) Please propose (in detail) a way to fix the problem. Modify the existing code as necessary.

(c) Show how your design solves the problem.

12.33 In the pastry corner of the kitchen of a small restaurant, we find two world-class chefs, grumpy Pierre des Oeufs and Jean "la loupe" Farouche, who despise each other. Nonetheless, they must work in the same place and share the same resources. Each is responsible for a different kind of cookie. Here are the recipes:

Grumpy Pierre	***Jean la loupe***
Mix 1 cup of milk with	Preheat oven to 190 C
2 eggs	Mix 1 cup of water with
add 1 cup of sugar	1 cup of flour
add 1 cup of flour	add 1 cup of sugar
Bake in oven at 170 C for 10 minutes	add 1 egg
	Bake in oven for 5 minutes

In the kitchen, we have,

One giant carton of milk

One giant crate of eggs

Two large sugar bowls

One large container of flour

One cold water tap

One small oven that has space for one batch of cookies

The previous consultant who tried to schedule the work of Pierre and Jean had a sudden job change to Cinque Terre on the Italian Riviera where he now spends his days sun-drying porcini mushrooms.

Your predecessor was actually quite clever and modeled the two chefs as processes. You find the following bits of code (encrusted with cookie dough) and partially implemented chef processes. Please complete the design.

You have the following nonatomic (they can be interrupted) subroutines available:

```
getEggs( numEggs )            // retrieves numEggs from the crate
                              // of eggs
getFlour( numCups )           // retrieves numCups from the flour
                              // container
getMilk( numCups )            // retrieves and pours numCups from
                              // milk carton
getSugar( numCups )           // retrieves numCups from the
                              // sugar bowl
getWater( numCups )           // retrieves numCups from the tap
putIntoOven( numMinutes )//    puts cookie tray into oven for
                              // numMinutes
setOvenTemp( numDegrees )// sets oven temperature to
                              // numDegrees
```

Initialize the following semaphores:

```
Semaphore eggCrate =
Semaphore flourContainer =
Semaphore sugarBowl =
Semaphore waterTap =
Semaphore oven =
Semaphore milkCarton =
```

Complete the two chef processes:

```
process grumpyPierre( )
{
}
process jeanlaLoup( )
{
}
```

12.34 A now defunct engineering firm was hired to design the switching system in a small town railway station. Their final design appears as shown in Figure P12.49.

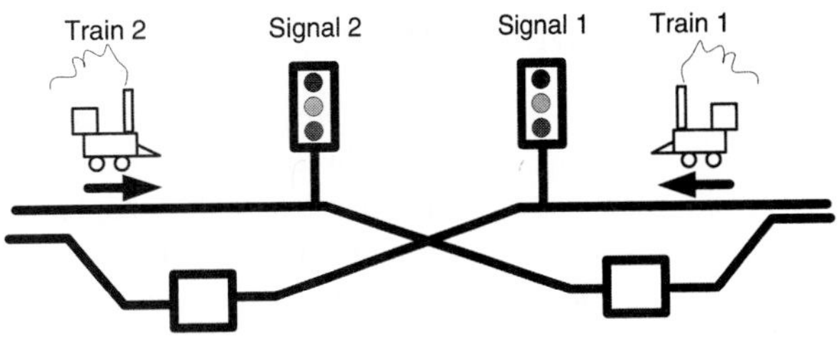

Figure P12.49

Signals 1 and 2 may be Red, Yellow, or Blue.

If Train 1 is approaching Platform 1, it must turn Signal 2, then Signal 1, to *Blue* before proceeding. Similarly, if Train 2 is approaching Station 2, it must turn Signal 1, then Signal 2 to *Red.*

A train may only change the signal (to *Red* or *Blue*) if the signal is in the *Yellow* state.

When Train 1 leaves Station 1, it must turn Signal 1, then Signal 2, to *Yellow*. Similarly, when Train 2 leaves Station 2, it must turn Signal 2, then Signal 1, to *Yellow.*

(a) Are there any problems with the scheme described above? If so, identify what they are.

(b) Will such a scheme prevent collisions? Justify your answer. If not, propose a solution that will.

(c) Will such a scheme prevent deadlocks? Justify your answer. If not, propose a solution that will.

Chapter 13

Deadlocks

THINGS TO LOOK FOR . . .

- Scheduling tasks and resource management.
- The problem of deadlock in a shared resource environment.
- The necessary and sufficient conditions for deadlock to occur.
- How to prevent, avoid, and detect deadlocks.
- How to recover from a deadlock state.

13.0 INTRODUCTION

In the previous two chapters, we have addressed several important aspects of task management in embedded systems; among these were scheduling task execution and intertask communication. In this chapter, we will examine aspects of the scheduling and dispatch of tasks with respect to managing task demands for resources. To that end, we will introduce the problem of *deadlock* in a shared-resource, multitasking environment. We will identify the necessary and sufficient conditions for deadlock to occur. First, we examine ways to prevent or avoid deadlock, and then we study methods for detecting a deadlock if, despite best efforts, a deadlock does occur. We conclude by presenting several techniques for recovering from a deadlock state.

deadlock

13.1 SHARING RESOURCES

A multitasking or multiprocessing embedded system has a finite number of resources such as timers, analog-to-digital converters, digital-to-analog converters, and I/O ports. Often several tasks may compete for those resources. When such a request is made and if the requested resources are not available, the task or processor blocks. The implementation of a semaphore or monitor with waiting queue, for example, can result in a situation in which two or more processes wait indefinitely. Such a situation is called a *deadlock.*

Consider the following simple problem in which there are two tasks, T0 and T1, and two resources, R1 and R2. Let each task have two counting semaphores, S0 and S1. Furthermore, let each need both resources to execute its job. Now, let

```
T0 set wait(S0)    // wait for R1 increment S0 (= 1)
T1 set wait(S1)    // wait for R2 increment S1 (= 1)
```

Now let

```
T0 set wait(S1)    // wait for R2 increment S1 (= 2)
T1 set wait(S0)    // wait for R1 increment S0 (= 2)
```

The system is now stuck; neither process can continue.

Today the problem of deadlocks is treated rather casually. As systems become more complex and the number of tasks and threads increases, the problem will have to be addressed.

13.2 SYSTEM MODEL

To begin, we formulate a model of the deadlock problem. Any embedded system has a limited number of resources. On one hand, if all systems were architected as a single task or if all the tasks in a multiple-task system have mutually exclusive resource demands, deadlocks cannot occur. On the other hand, for most designs, as tasks enter the system, they are going to need those resources. If the system is going to support preemptive multitasking, those resources will have to be shared. Making this same statement another way, one can say that from the perspective of a single task, a deadlock is not a problem. When analyzing deadlocks—their cause, prevention, detection, and correction—the problem must be considered from a system level. One must take into consideration *all* of the tasks in the system.

tasks
resources

A first high-level model decomposes the problem into two pieces: a set of *tasks* and a set of *resources*. Tasks are largely equivalent; resources are not. One can, therefore, form a coarse-grained partition on the set of resources. One possible partition decomposes the set into two groups—those that are identical and those that are not. Although such a decomposition seems reasonable, one must quantify what constitutes identical resources and what distinguishes them from those that are not. Unlike the factors that were considered when decomposing a problem statement into functional blocks, such a process for resources is a bit more straightforward.

identical resources
dissimilar resources

For the current model, *identical resources* are considered to be those for which multiple interchangeable copies of the same resource exist. For example, if the system has two analog-to-digital converters, two digital-to-analog converters, three serial I/O ports, or eight memory buffers, then one can consider instances of each type of resource to be interchangeable. Allocation of any one to a task may be sufficient. On the other hand, *dissimilar resources* are those that are unique for one reason or another. Of these, for example, there may be only a single copy such as the highest priority interrupt or a single serial I/O port. The current state of the model can be expressed graphically as in Figure 13.0.

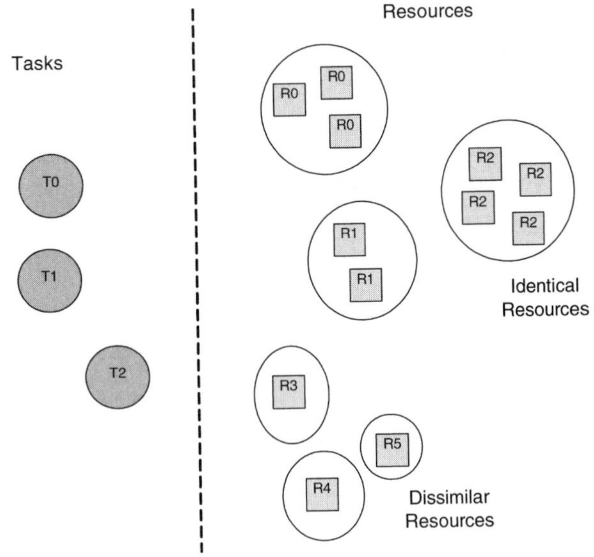

Figure 13.0 System State as a Collection of Tasks and Resources

To use a resource, a task must request the resource in advance. Such a situation is critical in tasks with hard real-time constraints. The task may request as many resources as it wishes but may not exceed the total number of available copies of the resource. Under normal operation, the task may only utilize resources according to the following protocol.

- Request
  If the resource is not available immediately, the requesting process must wait.
- Use
  The resource is allocated to the task that operates on or uses the resource.
- Release
  When the task or thread is finished with the resource, return it to the allocating task.

13.3 DEADLOCK MODEL

From the earlier discussion and empirical analysis, one can infer that a set of tasks is in a deadlock state if every member of the set is waiting for the event that can only originate with another member of the set. Looking at the resource utilization protocol, we see that such events arise from resource acquisition and release. Revisiting the earlier discussion of shared resources, we note that if all tasks cooperated, one would not have a deadlock. Furthermore, since the system is controlling resource allocation, then, it seems that herein lies the root cause of the problem. Restating, if the system can allocate resources in the "proper" way and if tasks would release them in the "proper" way, the deadlock problem can be solved.

That said, if one knows what constitutes an "improper" way, it can be avoided. First, however, it is necessary to identify under what conditions a deadlock may occur.

NECESSARY CONDITIONS

A deadlock is only possible if each of the following four conditions holds simultaneously. These conditions are necessary, not sufficient, and not independent.

- ***Mutual Exclusion***
  Once a resource has been allocated to a process, it has exclusive control over that resource. The resource is considered to be nonsharable mode.
- ***Hold and Wait***
  There must be tasks or threads holding a resource and requesting additional resources that are being held by other tasks or threads.
- ***No Preemption***
  Resources cannot be preempted.
- ***Circular Wait***
  A system state exists such that each process in a set of processes $\{T_0 ... T_{n-1}\}$ is holding a resource and requesting a resource that is held by another process, thus,

  T_0 waiting for resource held by T_1

  T_1 waiting for resource held by T_2

  ...

13.4 A GRAPH THEORETIC TOOL—THE RESOURCE ALLOCATION GRAPH

resource allocation graph

One can begin to understand and formally analyze a deadlock using a *resource allocation graph*. Such a graph is a formalized model of the earlier figure capturing the tasks and resources. It is a directed graph that contains a set of nodes or vertices, V, and a set of directed arcs or edges, E. The nodes represent both the set of system tasks and the set of available resources. Such an interpretation thus partitions the nodes into two subsets:

```
Set of processes {Pn}
Set of resources {Rm}
```

request, allocation

The edges may be partitioned similarly; one set contains edges directed from the task to the resource, and the second contains edges directed from the resource to the task. An edge directed from the task expresses a *request* for a resource and toward the task, an *allocation* of the requested resource. Thus, we have the two sets of edges:

```
{Pn} to {Rm}
{Rm} to {Pn}
```

A directed edge from P_i to R_j

$$P_i \rightarrow R_j$$

request edge

signifies that P_i has requested resource R_j and is currently waiting. Such an edge is called a *request edge*. A directed edge from R_j to P_i

$$R_j \rightarrow P_i$$

assignment edge

denotes that R_j has been allocated to P_i. Such an edge is called an *assignment edge*.

Let's again return to the earlier drawing. Each task is presented as a circle. A set of resources (a resource node in a resource allocation graph) is represented as a small rectangle. Each copy of a resource is indicated by a dot or small circle in the rectangle.

The earlier drawing can now be expressed formally as in Figure 13.1.

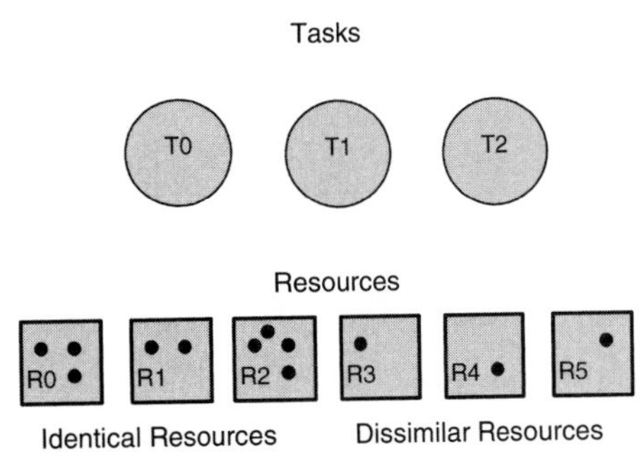

Figure 13.1 System State as a Collection of Tasks, Similar, and Dissimilar Resources

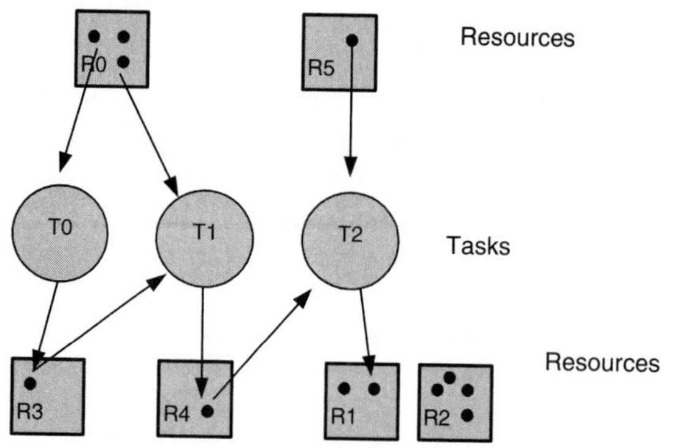

Figure 13.2 A Resource Allocation Graph Showing Resource Requests and Allocations

Consider the resource allocation graph drawn in Figure 13.2. The following situation exists.

Sets

Processes

$T = \{T_0, T_1, T_2\}$

Resources

$R = \{R_0, R_1, R_2, R_3, R_4, R_5\}$

Edges or allocations

$E = \{T_0 \rightarrow R_3, T_1 \rightarrow R_4, T_2 \rightarrow R_1, R_0 \rightarrow T_0, R_0 \rightarrow T_1, R_3 \rightarrow T_1, R_4 \rightarrow T_2, R_5 \rightarrow T_2\}$

Resource Instances

3 of R_0
2 of R_1
3 of R_1
1 of R_3
1 of R_4
4 of R_2

Process States

T_0
Holding 1 R_0
Waiting for R_3

T_1
Holding 1 R_0 and 1 R_3
Waiting for R_4

T_2
Holding 1 R_4 and 1 R_5
Waiting for R_1

Using techniques from graph theory, we can show that if the graph does not contain any cycles, then no process in the system will be deadlocked. If a cycle does exist, however, then the *potential* for deadlock exists; this does not guarantee that deadlock exists or will occur.

potential

necessary
sufficient
necessary, not sufficient

To understand why, consider the case in which there is only a single instance of each resource; a cycle implies that a deadlock has occurred. A cycle thus becomes a *necessary* and *sufficient* condition. But if there are multiple instances of the resource, a cycle does not necessarily imply deadlock. Now the cycle expresses a *necessary* but *not sufficient* condition.

The graph in Figure 13.2 does not have any cycles with the allocation and requests that currently exist. The system does not have a deadlock. Although the loop involving T_0, T_1, R_0, and R_3 appears to be a cycle, remember that this is a directed graph. For a cycle to exist, all the edges must flow in the same direction.

Let's look at two examples, the first, in Figure 13.3, has a cycle and a deadlock while the second, in Figure 13.4, has a cycle but no deadlock. In Figure 13.3, T_1 has been allocated one copy of R_5 and is requesting the use of R_1. However, one copy of R_1 has been allocated to T_0 and one to T_2. At the same time, T_2 is requesting to use R_5. Neither T_1 nor T_2 can advance. Furthermore, the second copy of R_1 has been allocated to T_0. Nonetheless, T_0 is blocked because it is waiting for R_3, which has been allocated to T_1. Hence, deadlock exists.

In the second case below, the same cycle involving T_1, R_1, T_2, and R_5 occurs; however, T_0 can be granted use of resource R_3. When it terminates, R_1 will be released and T_1 can continue.

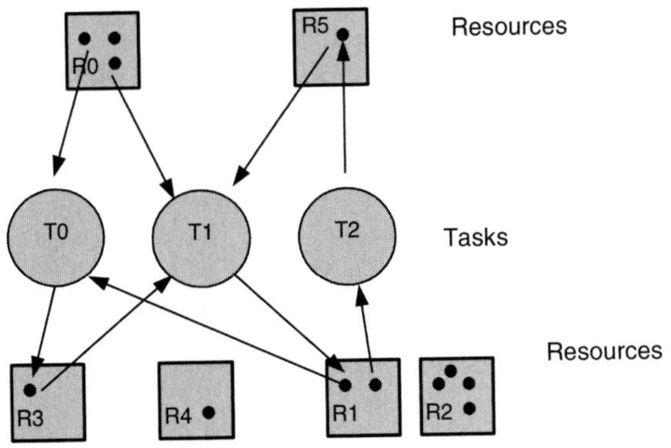

Figure 13.3 A Resource Allocation Graph with a Cycle (T1, R1, T2, R5) and a Deadlock

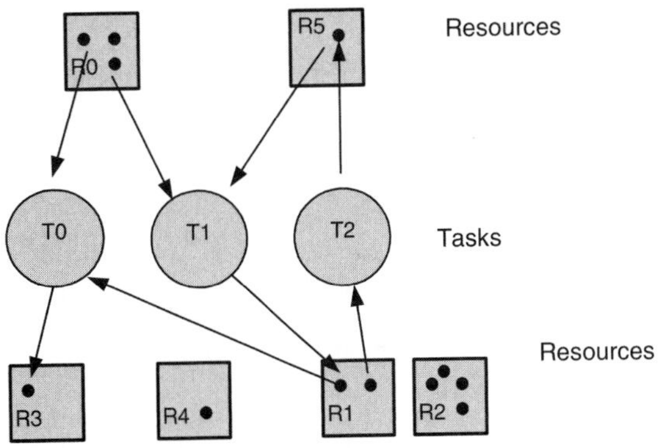

Figure 13.4 A Resource Allocation Graph with a Cycle (T1, R1, T2, R5) and no Deadlock

13.5 HANDLING DEADLOCKS

Three general philosophies can be used to manage the deadlock problem. In dealing with deadlocks, we follow a philosophy and approach that is similar to that used when designing safe and reliable systems. The initial objective is to try to design the system so that the problem does not happen. It is possible, however, that such an approach can add significant cost or complexity to the design. Depending on the system that is being designed, one may find that it is more efficient to simply let the problem occur than fix it if or when it does occur. This approach works well when the problem occurs very infrequently and is relatively easy to detect and correct. A third approach is simply to ignore the problem; assuming (or hoping) that it will not occur. This is not a good solution. Let's look at the first two.

We will start by examining ways to prevent a deadlock condition from occurring. In the opening discussion, four necessary conditions for deadlock were identified. One approach for addressing the problem is to ensure that one of the necessary conditions cannot occur.

deadlock prevention

Such a method is called *deadlock prevention*. If the operating system has sufficient knowledge about a process and the resources that the process will require, those requirements can be compared against what is and will be available were the task to run. Based on such foreknowledge, the operating system can decide to delay the task if the potential for deadlock exists. Such an approach is called *deadlock avoidance*. A hard real-time task or thread will have such information.

deadlock avoidance

13.6 DEADLOCK PREVENTION

Prevention is the easiest solution. James W. Havender of IBM suggested three ways of preventing one of the various necessary conditions from occurring. He did not address the first condition, that of mutual exclusion. Let's understand why.

13.6.1 Mutual Exclusion

When executing a design, one must ensure mutually exclusive access for each nonsharable resource in the system. Such resources include certain communication ports or any of the shared variables that support multiple writers. For sharable resources, one does not require such a restriction. Stored tables, input only ports, or similar external interfaces are examples of such resources. These can be accessed at any time by any process. In most cases, one cannot prevent deadlocks by denying mutual exclusion. Like those just identified, certain resources are naturally nonsharable.

13.6.2 Hold and Wait

The hold and wait situation arises when a process has resources and issues a request for additional ones. One can address the problem by stipulating that the task cannot ask for resources if it already has some. Two cases must be considered: a new task and one that has been running.

Case 1 A new task or thread must request and be granted all required resources before being allowed to run. Such a protocol is essential for a task or thread with a hard deadline.

The problem with such a solution is that if, for example, a task only uses a resource once just before it terminates, that resource will be unavailable to other tasks that could have used and released it long before it is needed. The disadvantage of this approach is a potentially low utilization of resources.

Case 2 If an executing task requests additional resources, it must give up those it already has. Thus, it is not holding any resources and can now complete the request and allocation. If some of the released resources are later required, they are re-requested.

Although the second approach addresses the problem of low resource utilization, it opens the possibility of starvation. A lower priority task that needs a resource that is in high demand may have to wait indefinitely.

13.6.3 No Preemption

To address the no preemption condition, it is stipulated that under certain conditions a task must voluntarily relinquish its resources. Such a requirement, once again, leads to two cases. They differ as to when the task must give up the resources.

Case 1 If a task is holding resources and needs additional ones that are not available, it must wait. Under such a condition, it must give up all resources it is currently holding. A list is then built identifying the resources it currently has plus any additional ones for which the task is requesting. The task is resumed when it can regain all of its original resources and the new ones it requested.

Case 2 If a task requires some additional resources, a two-step protocol is followed. First, determine if the requested resources are available. If so, allocate them and continue. Second, if they are not, check to see whether they are with another process that is also waiting for resources. If the requested resources are with another waiting process, require the waiting process to relinquish the resources and allocate them to the requesting process. Otherwise, simply block.

The disadvantage of either approach is that the task may have completed a significant part of its job. Those intermediate results may be lost. The advantage of the second approach over the first is that resources are not given up unless and until necessary. The resource may never be needed, and therefore the time and effort devoted to managing the resource will be wasted.

13.6.4 Circular Wait

hold and wait
total
linear order

The *circular wait* is a special case of the *hold and wait* condition. To prevent a circular wait, a *total* or *linear order* is placed on all resources. One such order is the $\leq$ (less than or equal); that order is a total order on the set of integers, for example. We observe that for *any* two integers, one of them will be less than or equal to the other. Next, a unique integer is assigned to each resource in the system, thereby producing the set $R = \{R_i\}$. Then the order is placed on the set of resource types $R = \{R_0, R_2, ...R_{m-1}\}$.

When a process requires a resource, the stipulation is made that it can only request resources in increasing order of enumeration. Once again there are two cases: a new task and a currently running task that needs additional resources.

Case 1 A new task may request any resources it wishes. This is similar to what we have already seen for addressing the hold and wait problem.

Case 2 A running task makes a request for any desired resources.

a. One approach is to constrain a task to request additional resources only in increasing order of enumeration. If multiple copies of a single resource are needed, they must be requested all at once.
b. An alternative approach stipulates that if additional resources are needed, for example, R_j, then the task must release any resources $\{R_i\}$ such that $i < j$.

The pros and cons of this approach are similar to those already mentioned for hold and wait.

13.7 DEADLOCK AVOIDANCE

Algorithms aimed at preventing deadlocks do so by managing requests for resources so as to ensure that at least one of the necessary conditions for deadlock cannot occur. Two of the major drawbacks of such a strategy are a possible reduction in system throughput (because of the burden of resource management) and low resource utilization. Algorithms that strive to avoid deadlocks require and utilize deeper information from the task about how and when resources are requested.

Consider a system with the following resources: a timer, R_0, and an A/D converter, R_1, and two tasks, T_0 and T_1. Now assume that each task requires the timer and the A/D. The resource allocation graph in Figure 13.5 has a cycle and a deadlock. On the other hand, if one knows in advance when, during a task's execution, each will need the resource, it is possible to establish a schedule that will ensure no deadlock.

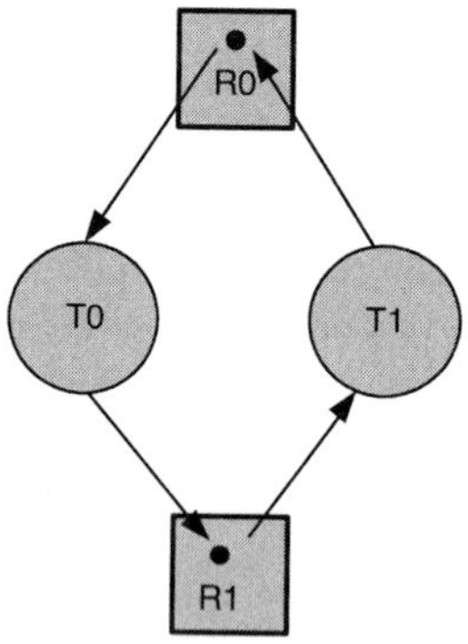

Figure 13.5 A Resource Allocation Graph with a Cycle and a Deadlock

There are a great many different avoidance algorithms, each of which requires different amounts of advance information. Let's analyze a simple one to see how the process might work.

13.7.1 Algorithms Based on the Resource Allocation Graph

In the boundary case of systems with one instance of each resource, one can use a simple extension to the resource allocation graph to avoid deadlocks. The intent of such an extension is, once again, to introduce additional information into the system that will enable anticipation of problems before they actually occur. To this end, we introduce an edge type called a *claim edge*. A claim edge $T_i \rightarrow R_j$ announces to the system that task T_i may require and thus claim the specific resource R_j. The edge has similar, yet relaxed, semantics to request edge. The direction of the edge is the same and is expressed as a dashed line in the allocation graph.

claim edge

The avoidance algorithms that utilize the additional edge require that advance notification for all anticipated resources be issued before the process starts executing. Thus, all claim and request edges will be reflected in the resource allocation graph. The restriction may be relaxed only if no resources have been allocated—that is, only if all other edges from the process are claim edges. Formalizing such requirements, we now develop the following protocol.

At the time that the task enters the system, all claim and request edges for the task are known and declared. Thereafter, when a task T_i requests a resource R_j, the corresponding *claim edge* is converted to a *request edge*. In a similar fashion, when a resource R_j is released by the task, that *request edge* is converted back into a *claim edge*. Thus, a deadlock can be avoided only if the conversion into a request edge does not result in a cycle. If a cycle does not exist, allocation and subsequent conversion will leave the system in a safe state.

claim edge, request edge

Consider the resource allocation graph in Figure 13.6. Observe that if T_1 requests and is allocated R_1, the allocation cannot be made, even though it is available since such an allocation will create a cycle and thus an unsafe state. Under such a circumstance, if T_0 requests R_1, there is a deadlock.

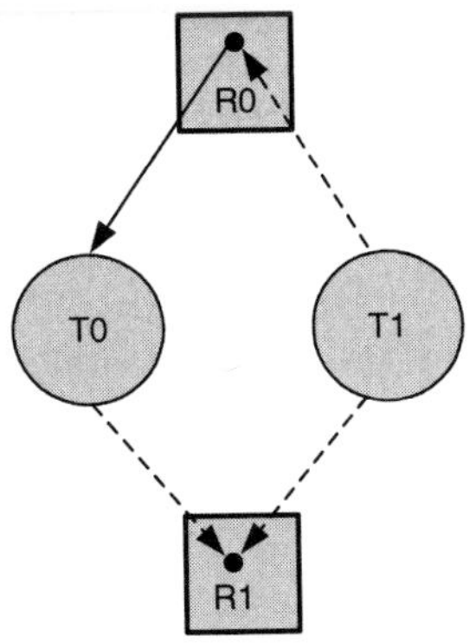

Figure 13.6 A Resource Allocation Graph with Three Claim Edges

13.7.2 Banker's Algorithm and Safe States

banker's algorithm

When designing a system with more than one instance of each resource, avoidance algorithms based on a resource graph will not work. The next algorithm that we will examine, the *banker's algorithm*, will work for such systems, albeit, somewhat less efficiently. The algorithm is the work of Dijkstra; the name derives from a banker who is working with a single source of money from which he makes loans and to which he adds the payments. When applying the algorithm to scheduling resources, the client is the process and the money is the resource.

According to the banker's algorithm, the lender has a certain amount of money that can be used for making loans. When a client enters the bank and asks for money, he or she must specify, in advance, the maximum amount of money needed. The client's request will be honored if the request does not exceed the total amount of money the banker has.

The client may have to wait to obtain the full amount requested; however, it will be available eventually as other clients return the money they have borrowed. Furthermore, if the client has been given a portion of that requested, an additional request does not require that the initial amount be repaid immediately. The understanding is that the total will eventually be repaid. Such an approach applies directly to the resource allocation problem for deadlock avoidance.

In the discussion of prevention schemes, it was proposed that the hold and wait or circular wait conditions could be avoided by simply giving each task all the resources it requested in advance. We now take a finer-grained, dynamic view of this approach based on Dijkstra's algorithm.

As a task enters the system, it is required that it declare in advance the maximum number of resources of each type it is going to need during execution. Using such knowledge, one can allocate resources if they are available and if a sequence of requests, allocations, and deallocations can be found so as to ensure that each process will eventually complete—even if each process requires its maximum number of resources. It is evident, then, that it should be possible to construct an algorithm, based on the banker's algorithm, that will ensure that the system will never enter a deadlock state. Such an understanding establishes a basis for deadlock avoidance with multiple copies of a resource. Let's see how this can work.

resource allocation state

Define a *resource allocation state* to be characterized by the following three measures:

- The number of available resources
- The number of allocated resources
- The maximum number of resources requested by the processes

safe
safe sequence

Any such state is valid or *safe* if resources can be allocated to each process in some order and avoid a deadlock. Such a sequence of allocations is called a *safe sequence*. Thus, one can declare that the system is in a safe state if, from that state, there exists a safe sequence.

Formally, a sequence of task executions $<T_0, T_1...T_{n-1}>$ is a safe sequence for the current allocation state if, for each T_i, the resources that T_i can still request can be satisfied by the currently available resources plus the resources held by all T_j such that $j < i$. Observe that if the needed resources are not available, T_i can simply wait until some subset of the T_j has finished. At such a time, one can then have the necessary resources. When T_i finishes, T_{i+1} can obtain the needed resources. If no such sequence exists, the system state is *unsafe*.

unsafe

The allocation states for the system are decomposed in the accompanying Venn diagram in Figure 13.7. Observe that a safe state cannot be a deadlock state. One can also see that a state that is not safe is not necessarily a deadlock state but that it can lead to one. Let's look at a simple example.

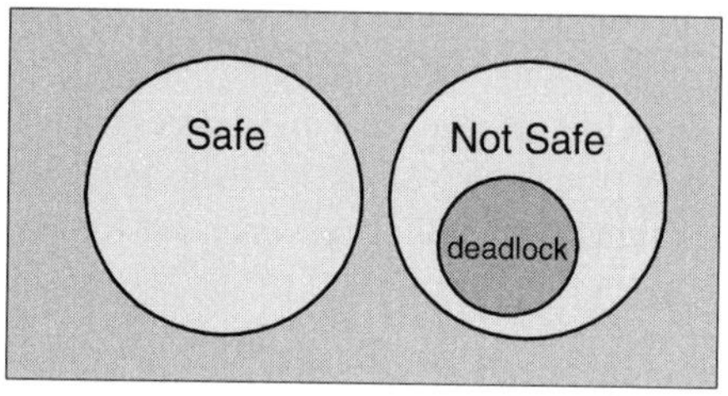

Figure 13.7 Venn Diagram Illustrating Safe, Not Safe, and Deadlocked Situations

EXAMPLE 13.0

We will look at a basic case first in which instances of a single resource are being allocated. Consider a system with an A/D that can accept and convert analog data from any one of 10 different inputs or channels. Using a multiplexer, we can connect signals from a number of different sources onto each input.

Figure 13.8 illustrates such a design for a four-channel A/D converter.

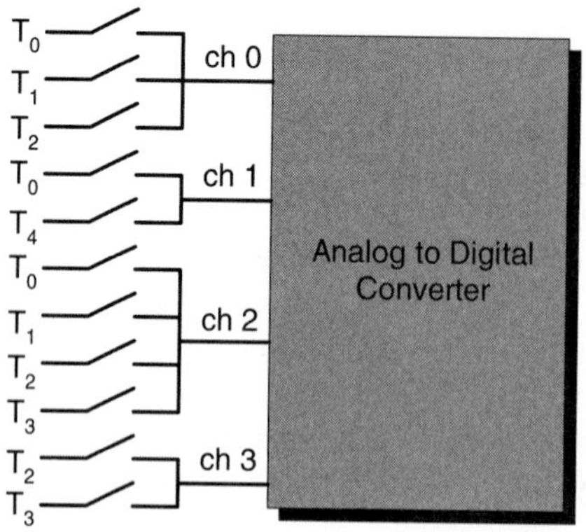

Figure 13.8 An A/D Converter as a Shared Resource

In the four channel design given, task T_0 requires a maximum of three channels, task T_1 requires two channels, task T_2 three channels, task T_3 two channels, and task T_4 one channel.

Returning to the ten channel system, three different tasks must use the A/D to make a number of different measurements. The tasks have the following requirements and have been allocated the resources (channels) indicated in Figure 13.9.

Task	A/D	
	Maximum	Current
T0	5	3
T1	4	1
T2	8	4
Total Allocated		8

Figure 13.9 Task Requirements and Allocations

The current state is safe. We have allocated eight of the channels and have two remaining. We can schedule the resources such that if we give the remaining two channels to T_0, it can run to completion, freeing up five. Four of those five can then be given to task T_2, allowing it to finish, and finally T_1 can complete. We see that all tasks will eventually finish.

EXAMPLE 13.1

Let's now look at how a poor allocation can lead to an unsafe state. We start at the same initial state (see Figure 13.10).

Task	A/D	
	Maximum	Current
T0	5	3
T1	4	1
T2	8	4
Total Allocated		8

Figure 13.10 Task Requirements and a Poor Allocation

Rather than permitting T_0 to run, a request from T_1 for two additional channels is honored. Such an allocation allows T_1 to continue for a short while. However, when it issues a request for the last resource that it needs, there are none available. Furthermore, the other two tasks are blocked as well, and a deadlock now exists.

Thus the allocation given in Figure 13.10 can lead to an unsafe state.

With the luxury of hindsight, these two examples show that a safe state is one in which there is at least one resource allocation sequence that will allow all tasks to finish eventually. One can also see that the existence of an unsafe state does not inherently lead to a deadlock. It does show that, with an improper allocation, such a condition can occur.

13.8 DEADLOCK DETECTION

If the system utilizes neither a prevention nor an avoidance algorithm, a deadlock may occur. In such an environment, the system must provide an algorithm to determine whether such a state has occurred as well as one to recover from the deadlock.

13.8.1 Detection in a Single-Instance Environment

wait-for graph

When designing a system in which there is a single instance of each resource, then, as was done earlier, one can begin with the resource allocation graph. From the resource allocation graph, a *wait-for graph* is developed by removing the nodes of type resource and then collapsing the edges as appropriate. The result of such a process is a graph with only processes; a deadlock then exists if and only if the reduced graph contains a cycle.

Starting with the resource allocation graph in the left-hand graph (in Figure 13.11), the set of resources $\{R_1..R_6\}$ is removed. Removal of those nodes results in the reduced graph in the right-hand figure.

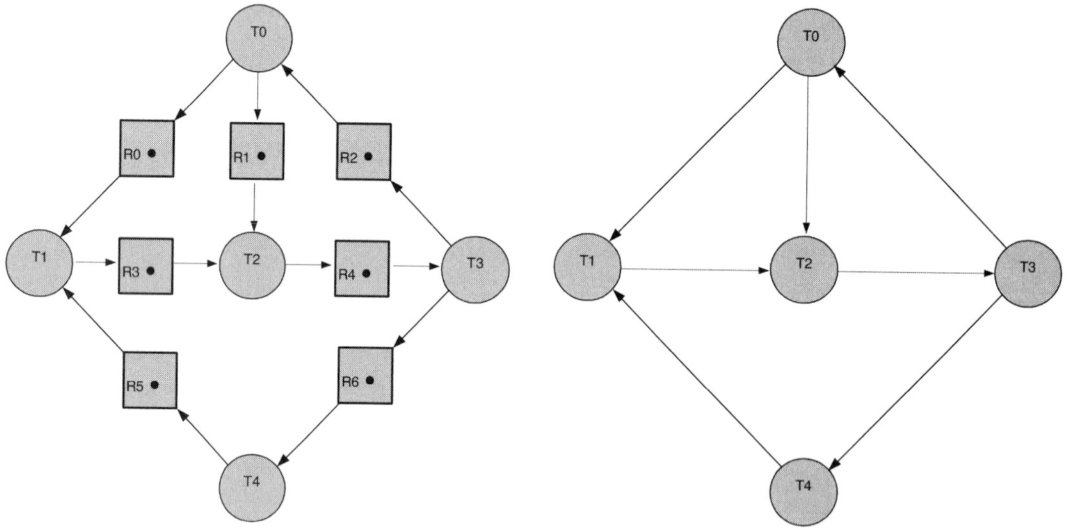

Figure 13.11 A Resource Allocation Graph and the Associated Wait-for Graph

It is immediately evident that the graph on the right has several cycles and thus has a number of processes in the deadlock state.

13.8.2 Deadlock Recovery

When it has been determined that a deadlock exists, the objective changes from detection to recovery. Several courses of action are open. Ignoring the deadlock is not one of the reasonable alternatives. One can always inform the users that such a situation exists and let them handle it. Such an approach is often difficult in an embedded system. Another possibility is to let the system recover automatically. Selecting automatic recovery leads to two general schemes: a termination signal can be sent to all deadlocked processes (one at a time), or the processes can be preempted one at a time and their resources temporarily taken.

13.8.2.1 Task Termination

The drastic approach of terminating all deadlocked processes will clearly have the desired effect, but at significant cost since the tasks may have been running for some time. Following such an action, it is most likely that all results may be lost. On the other hand, terminating processes, one at a time, until a deadlock cycle is eliminated involves considerable temporal overhead. As each process is aborted, the deadlock detection algorithm must be rerun.

Extreme care must be taken when terminating a task because doing so may leave a resource or the system in an unknown, unusable, or dangerous state. One must also determine which process to terminate. The problem is similar to that encountered when trying to schedule usage of the CPU. The objective is to terminate processes so as to do the least damage, incur minimal cost, and ensure an efficient recovery. Some things to consider include the following.

- Task priority
- The time since starting the task and the remaining runtime
- The resource mix and quantity
- The resource demand to complete
- The number of tasks/threads to be terminated

13.8.2.2 Resource Preemption

The process preemption alternative to termination entails successive preemption of the task and its resources and their subsequent allocation to other processes until the deadlock cycle is broken. If preemption is used, three issues must be considered.

1. Selection of a task to preempt.
   One must determine the order of preemption to minimize the cost. When making such a decision, the same factors are considered as when process termination is assessed.
2. Rollback.
   If a resource is preempted, what should be done with the preempted task? Certainly, it cannot continue from its current state. One alternative that can be used is the same as that used when developing software or writing long documents. A backup is saved periodically. Such a backup gives a snapshot of the state of the system called a *checkpoint*. When a process and its resources must be preempted, it can be restarted—*rolled back*—sometime in the future to the last checkpoint. All resources and the state of the process are restored to values at the last checkpoint.

   rolled back

   However, one may not be able to determine a completely safe internal state of the system or for external devices being controlled. It is rather tricky to roll back the temperature of a chemical process or the yeast in a fermenting batch of beer in a brewery and hold it for a little while. Such factors must be taken into consideration when deciding which processes to preempt. Generally, the simplest solution is a complete rollback, subject, of course, to the earlier considerations. That is, abort the task and restart it.

One can try to roll back as far as necessary to break the deadlock. Such a strategy entails maintaining information on all the running tasks and threads.

3. Starvation.

How does one ensure starvation will not occur? One strives to ensure that the resources are not always preempted from the same process.

13.9 SUMMARY

Deadlock occurs when two or more processes are waiting for an event that can only be caused by one of the waiting processes. There are three major methods for addressing the problem.

- Use a protocol to ensure that the system will never enter a deadlock state.
- Allow the system to enter a deadlock state and the recover.
- Ignore the problem.

Deadlock occurs if, and only if, four conditions (mutual exclusion, hold and wait, no preemption, and circular wait) occur simultaneously. We prevent deadlock by ensuring that one of the conditions will not occur.

If a system does not employ a protocol to ensure that deadlock does not occur, then a detection and recovery scheme of some form or another must be employed. If a deadlock is detected, we can recover by global or selective termination of tasks (threads) or resources.

13.10 REVIEW QUESTIONS

A Model of Tasks and Resources

13.1 What is a deadlock in an embedded application?

13.2 What is the typical protocol that a task will use for handling resources?

13.3 What is the difference between deadlock and starvation?

A Deadlock Model

13.4 What are the necessary conditions for a deadlock to occur?

13.5 Give a real-world example in which a deadlock can occur.

13.6 What is a *resource allocation graph*?

13.7 Within a resource allocation graph, what is a *request* edge? an *allocation* edge?

Deadlock Prevention

13.8 Describe the conditions under which the necessary condition *hold and wait* cannot occur.

13.9 Describe the conditions under which the necessary condition *no preemption* cannot occur.

13.10 Describe the conditions under which the necessary condition *circular wait* cannot occur.

Deadlock Avoidance

13.11 What strategy underlies most deadlock avoidance algorithms?

13.12 One strategy for avoiding deadlock utilizes a modified allocation graph. Describe that strategy.

13.13 In the context of the banker's algorithm, what is a *resource allocation state*?

13.14 Under what conditions is a resource allocation state defined as *safe*?

13.15 What is a *safe sequence*?

13.16 What is an *unsafe* state?

13.17 Can a safe state be a deadlock state?

13.18 Is an unsafe state guaranteed to be a deadlock state?

Deadlock Detection

13.19 What is a *wait-for* graph?

13.20 How is a wait-for graph developed? What does a cycle in a wait-for graph imply?

13.11 THOUGHT QUESTIONS

A Model of Tasks and Resources

13.1 What is the minimum number of tasks in an embedded system necessary for a deadlock to occur? Why?

13.2 Is an embedded system with two tasks guaranteed to eventually encounter a deadlock? Why or why not?

13.3 Resources within an embedded application can be collected into groups of resources that are considered identical and into groups that are considered dissimilar. When can a set of resources be considered to be identical? dissimilar?

13.4 Can tasks be partitioned into groups of identical and dissimilar tasks?

A Deadlock Model

13.5 Review Question 13.5 asks for a real-world example in which a deadlock can occur. Show that the four necessary conditions for deadlock hold for your example.

13.6 What are the conditions necessary for starvation to occur?

13.7 What does a cycle in a resource allocation graph imply?

13.8 Is a cycle in a resource allocation graph a necessary and sufficient condition for deadlock? Why or why not?

13.9 How can one ensure that a deadlock will not occur in an embedded system?

13.10 Would you consider the consequences of a deadlock to be more or less severe in an embedded system than a desktop computer? Why?

Deadlock Prevention

13.11 One approach to preventing deadlocks proposes ensuring that one of the necessary conditions cannot occur. Why can one not prevent deadlocks by enforcing mutually exclusive access to resources?

13.12 Discuss some of the problems that accompany the deadlock prevention strategy.

13.13 Can you think of ways to avoid many of the problems identified in Question 13.12 and yet be able to utilize the prevention strategy?

Deadlock Avoidance

13.14 What strategy underlies most deadlock avoidance algorithms?

13.15 One strategy for avoiding deadlock utilizes a modified allocation graph. What is the major limitation of such resource graph based algorithms?

13.16 Briefly describe how the *banker's algorithm* works for deadlock avoidance.

13.17 Can you think of how the *banker's algorithm* can be extended to multiple resources?

Deadlock Detection

13.18 If an embedded application does not prevent or avoid deadlocks, is it possible to determine whether deadlock has occurred? If so, how?

13.19 If a deadlock has occurred in an embedded system, is recovery possible? If so, how?

13.20 Task termination is proposed as one strategy for deadlock recovery. What are the major disadvantages of such a strategy?

13.21 When using a termination strategy, what things should be considered?

13.22 Resource preemption is proposed as an alternative to the task termination strategy. What are the major disadvantages of such a strategy?

13.23 When using a preemption strategy, what things should be considered?

13.12 PROBLEMS

13.1 The *dining philosophers* problem is one of the classic examples of a synchronization and, ultimately, a deadlock problem. As the story goes, Edsger Dijkstra posed a question on an exam in which five computers competed for the use of five different tape drives. Subsequently, Anthony Hoare, recast the problem as the *dining philosophers*.

Hoare's version of the problem places five philosophers sitting around a table alternately thinking or eating. In front of each philosopher is a plate filled with food; between each plate is a chop stick. To be able to eat, a philosopher must have two chopsticks. Each has taken a vow of silence and therefore can never speak to one another.

The result: possible deadlock.

(a) Model the problem and resources using a resource allocation graph. Does the graph contain a potential cycle?

(b) Based on the conditions necessary for deadlock discussed, why is there the possibility for deadlock?

(c) Propose a solution to the problem that avoids the deadlock. Give a pseudo-code implementation and describe why your solution avoids the problem.

(d) Propose a solution to the problem that prevents the deadlock. Give a pseudo-code implementation and describe why your solution avoids the problem.

13.2 A proposed design for an interchange in a mass transit system is shown in Figure P13.12.

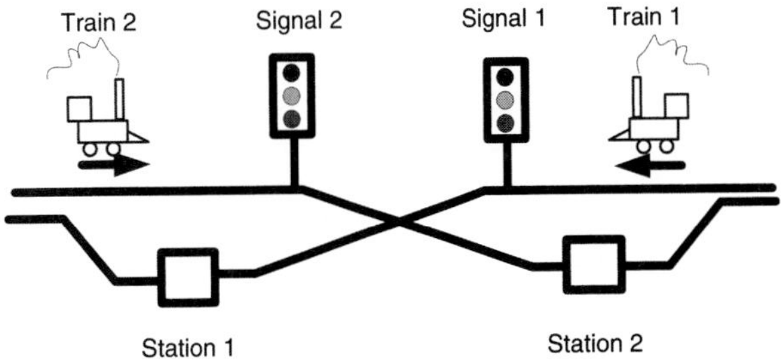

Figure P13.12

Signals 1 and 2 may be Red, Yellow, or Blue.

If Train 1 is approaching Station 1, it must turn Signal 2, then Signal 1, to *Blue* before proceeding. Similarly, if Train 2 is approaching Station 2, it must turn Signal 1, then Signal 2, to *Red*.

A train may only change a signal (to *Red* or *Blue*) if the signal is in the *Yellow* state.

When Train 1 leaves Station 1, it must turn Signal 1, then Signal 2, to *Yellow*. Similarly, when Train 2 leaves Station 2, it must turn Signal 2, then Signal 1, to *Yellow*.

(a) Are there any problems with the scheme described above? If so, identify what they are.

(b) Will such a scheme prevent collisions? Justify your answer. If not, propose a solution that will.

(c) Will such a scheme prevent deadlocks? Justify your answer. If not, propose a solution that will.

13.3 An embedded control system supports the following two operations on a collection of data items: a_0, a_1, $a_2 \ldots a_{n-1}$,

```
read(i)          Returns the value of a_i
write(i, aValue) Assigns aValue to a_i
```

The control system has three asynchronous processes that must perform the following transactions:

```
p0:   x = read (j);       y = read (i);
      write (j, y+13);    write (i, x-27);
p1:   x = read (k);       write (i, x-3);
      y = read (j);       write (k, x+y);
p2:   write (k, 25);      x = read (i);
      y = read (j);       write (i, x-y);
```

(a) Using a resource allocation graph, determine whether there is the possibility of deadlock for this system.

(b) Based on the conditions necessary for deadlock discussed, why is there the possibility for deadlock?

(c) Does a safe sequence for the execution of these tasks exist? If so, what is it?

13.4 Consider the following problem. Two tasks are sharing a FIFO queue. Either task can write to or read from the FIFO.

(a) Can you hypothesize a situation in which deadlock can occur?

(b) Use a resource allocation graph to illustrate your theory.

13.5 Earlier, we studied the bounded buffer problem. We have an embedded system, S1, that must exchange information with a second, similar system, S2, over a network. The network is designed to use the TCP/IP protocol. With such a protocol, when the connection is established, an input buffer and an output buffer are set up on each side of the connection.

When a message is to be sent over the network, it is first copied into the sender's output buffer. When the message is sent, the sender's buffer is cleared and the message is placed into the receiver's input buffer. When the receiver reads the message, the input buffer is cleared.

(a) Can you hypothesize a situation in which deadlock can occur? *Hint*: A task cannot be writing to a buffer and reading from a buffer at the same time.

(b) Can you propose a solution to the problem?

13.6 On holiday in Venezia—Venice—the city of canals, you book a quaint *pensione, Casa Rosa della Quercia*, a few miles upstream on the Canal San Marco and settle down for some rest and relaxation.

In the accompanying figure (Figure P13.13), we see a rough layout of the canals and surrounding area near your *pensione*. The shaded areas are land masses or islands, the black areas are points of tourist interest, and the rest is water.

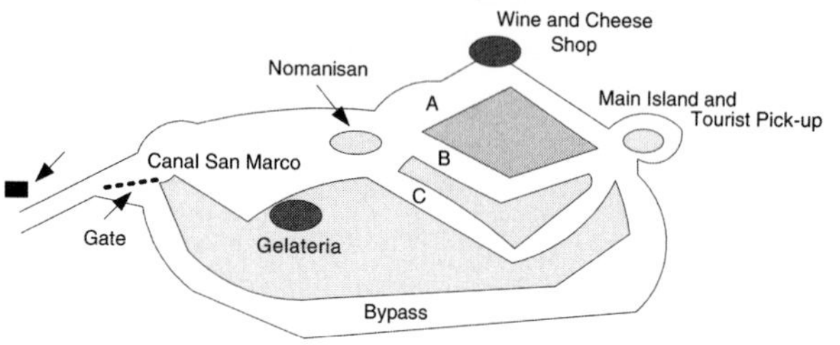

Figure P13.13

The small canals, A, B, and C, are rather narrow. It seems that there are two kinds of gondolas—the sports utility gondolas (SUGs) and the small racy ones, the fleeaht sports gondolas (FSGs). Several of the FSGs are easily able to pass each other. However, only one SUG is able to get through at any one time.

If the wrong kinds of gondolas enter a canal from the opposite directions, they will be unable to pass and one must back out causing great delays.

Over a friendly bottle of good Italian red wine, you and the great contemporary Italian inventor, Vito del Lampada, discuss how to solve the problem. Vito says that he can develop a light of some kind if that might help. He proposes to develop a remote-controlled two-color (Red and Green) light such as that shown in Figure P13.14.

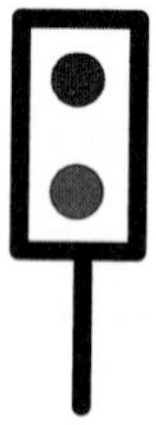

Figure P13.14

(a) Devise an algorithm that will prevent two SUGs or a SUG and an FSG from entering the canal at the same time. Explain in detail how your design works and how it will solve the problem. Be certain to identify the minimum number of lights you will need and where they will be placed.

(b) What features/capabilities are you going to ask Vito to put into the light/remote control system?

(c) Does your solution require any equipment other than your buddy's light? If so, what might that be?

13.7 Consider the traffic deadlock shown in Figure P13.15.

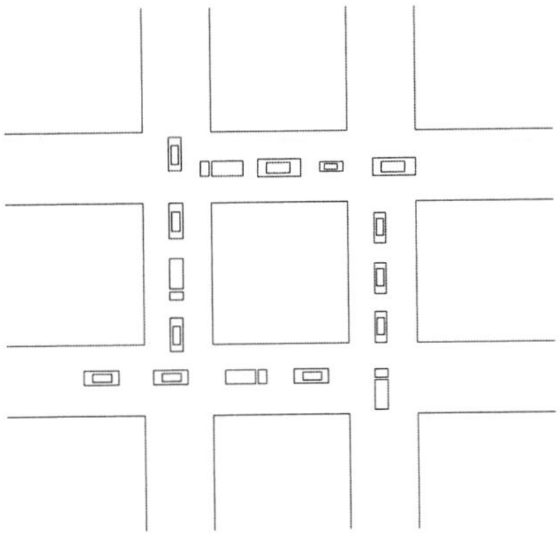

Figure P13.15

(a) For the system, what are the resources and what are the processes?

(b) Draw a resource allocation graph capturing the processes and resources.

(c) Does the graph contain a cycle?

(d) Show that the four necessary conditions for deadlock hold. Be precise.

(e) Give a simple rule that will avoid deadlocks in the system.

(f) Show how or why your scheme will avoid deadlocks.

13.8 We have an embedded system with four tasks, T0–T3, and three resources, R0–R2. The system has nine instances of R0, three instances of R1, and six instances of R2. After the system has been running for a while, we have the state shown in Figure P13.16.

Task	R0		R1		R2	
	Reqd.	Alloc.	Reqd.	Alloc.	Reqd.	Alloc.
T0	3	1	2	0	2	0
T1	6	5	1	1	1	1
T2	3	2	1	1	4	1
T3	4	0	2	0	2	2

Figure P13.16

(a) If task T1 requests and is allocated one additional instance of resources R0 and R2, will this lead to a safe state?

(b) If so, what is the proper sequence of task execution that will ensure no deadlock?

(c) Propose a resource request and allocation from the above state that would not lead to a safe state.

Chapter 14

Performance Analysis and Optimization

THINGS TO LOOK FOR . . .

- Why performance analysis and optimization is important in embedded applications.
- Some of the limits on analysis and improvement.
- The kinds of performance we focus on.
- The vocabulary of performance quantification.
- The levels at which we can evaluate performance and make trade-offs.
- The basic flow of control constructs at different levels of program.
- How to determine the execution times of such constructs at the assembler level.
- What the performance metrics time loading, response time, and memory loading are and how we measure them.
- Common mistakes made when analyzing performance and for improving performance in time, power, and memory access.

14.0 INTRODUCTION

The speed at which an embedded application operates is only one small aspect of its overall performance. As today's applications become increasingly ubiquitous, expectations are broadening. Delivery vehicles are becoming smaller and smaller; necessary features are becoming more complex and are expanding; battery technology is improving, albeit more slowly than demand. How well a design meets all of the often conflicting requirements is quantified by what we term the *performance* of the system.

performance

In this chapter, we will begin by introducing some of the relevant vocabulary and trying to capture a workable definition of performance. We will then examine several metrics by which we can begin to assess performance in embedded systems such as *response time, time loading,* and *memory loading.* As part of the study of time loading, we will discuss the basic flow of control constructs that comprise most contemporary software programs. We look at such constructs first from a C and then from an assembler level. The objective is to learn how to perform a detailed timing analysis by counting instruction times. Such an analysis is often necessary when hard real-time constraints must be understood and accommodated. We will conclude with an assessment of how utilizing cache can affect performance and with an introduction to power management, including several ways to reduce power consumption.

response, time, time loading

memory loading

14.1 GETTING STARTED

Is performance important? Yes! Faster, smaller, cheaper, lower power, are all definitely better; assuming, of course, that the design meets all the specified constraints. Such characteristics are all very important in embedded systems and are becoming more so every day. During design, one must often trade off speed, power, memory size, and cost to meet specified constraints; to be able to do so, one must have concrete numbers. Such techniques become more and more significant as the size and complexity of modern systems increase. Smaller systems and larger systems require different rules and different approaches.

When studying performance, we will follow the same approach that we have been using throughout this text. We will start at the top with an abstracted view of the problem and work down to the details.

14.2 PERFORMANCE OR EFFICIENCY MEASURES

14.2.1 Introduction

An embedded system comprises an aggregation of hardware and software components that, taken together, is intended to provide a desired service or behavior. The specification often stipulates that certain aspects of that behavior or those services meet a specified set of constraints. Working from the specification, the engineer will optimize the relevant portions of the design to meet or exceed those requirements.

optimization, performance

The words *optimization* and *performance* of a system mean many things to many people. Although one can say that these are all inherently good, at the end of the day, what do they really mean? What is being optimized? What kind of performance is being examined? What is performance? With any design, there are many aspects that one can optimize and there are many different measures of performance.

Performance or efficiency usually means "time" (to run) or "space" (memory used), "power" (consumed or battery life), and "cost" (to the customer). How does one measure efficiency? There are lots of ways. One could simply run the program, see how long it takes, see how much memory it uses, measure its power consumption, and add up the cost of the parts. The difficulty is the significant variability one encounters when running the program.

- What input data?
- What hardware platform?
- What compiler?
- What compiler options?

Just because one program is faster than another right now, will it always be faster? Any algorithm, method, or protocol has certain overhead. The choice of language or processor can have as much as a 100% effect on the results. Therefore, at first cut, these are not really significant. For the moment, they are details; one can usually wait for a faster machine and, presumably, the problem goes away. However, the choice of the fundamental algorithm can make a significant difference.

Let's begin to quantify. We can begin to focus on several major areas; we have already identified the following.

- Complexity
- Time
- Power consumption

- Memory size
- Cost
- Weight

Other considerations to think about include

- Development time
- Ease of maintenance
- Extensibility

In the course of our studies, we will examine several of these areas. For each such measure, one must consider:

- Best or Minimum Case
    - *time* When referring to *time*, the emphasis is on measuring the ability to complete a task. Such a measure is an essential quantity in many real-time scheduling algorithms.
    - *cost, power, weight* With respect to *cost, power,* or *weight*, the metric becomes a value below which one cannot remove any more parts.
    - *size* With respect to *size*, one is looking for the smallest amount needed.
- Average Case
    - Gives a typical measure; often, this is sufficient.
- Worst Case
    - *time* The largest or longest value of a particular measure. When we refer to *time*, we are looking at an upper or lower bound on a schedule.

14.2.2 The System

The scope of the analysis and optimization problem is restricted to the architecture and internal components of the system and how their behavior is manifest through the public interface to that system. The internal architecture of a typical embedded system comprises a root hardware platform and may also include a number of peripheral devices. Thus, from the embedded point of view, we consider *hardware* to comprise

hardware

- Computational and control elements
- Communication subsystem
- Memory

software (firmware)

We consider *software (firmware)* to be

- Algorithms and data structures
- Control and scheduling

To optimize the performance of the combined system, one must consider each hardware and software component. When optimizing or trading off different aspects or features of the system, the reference against which decisions are made must be the specification. Based on the specified requirements, the task becomes one of identifying the level at which performance is to be measured, deciding on the meaningful parameters at that level, and selecting reasonable and proper values for the things that are going to be measured or optimized. As designers, this is our job.

14.2.3 Some Limitations

Before addressing the problem of performance improvement/optimization, one must quantify limits of what can be done. From Amdahl's law one can write:

$$\frac{T_{total}}{T_{improved}} = \frac{T_{total}}{(T_{total} - T_{component}) + \frac{T_{component}}{n}}$$

T_{total} = System metric prior to improvement

$T_{improved}$ = System metric after improvement

$T_{component}$ = Contribution of the component to be improved to the system metric

n = the amount of the improvement

EXAMPLE 14.0

Consider a system with the following characteristics: The task to be analyzed and improved currently executes in 100 time units, and the goal is to reduce execution time to 80 time units. The algorithm under consideration in the task uses 40 time units.

$$\frac{100}{80} = \frac{100}{(100 - 40) + \frac{40}{n}}$$

Simplifying gives a value of 2 for n. The analysis shows that to meet the new performance goals, the algorithm execution speed will have to be decreased to 20 time units. Whether or not such a goal can be met is resolved by the designer; the analysis merely identifies the extent of the necessary improvement.

EXAMPLE 14.1

Consider a system with the following characteristics: The task to be analyzed and improved currently executes in 100 time units, and the goal is to reduce execution time to 50 time units. The algorithm to be improved uses 40 time units.

$$\frac{100}{50} = \frac{100}{(100 - 40) + \frac{40}{n}}$$

Simplifying gives a value of -4 for n. The algorithm speed will have to run in negative time to meet the new specification. Clearly this is a noncausal system.

With such restrictions in mind, we can now investigate the various performance measures beginning on the software side. The first metric will be the algorithm and program complexity.

14.3 COMPLEXITY ANALYSIS—A HIGH-LEVEL MEASURE

steps, time ticks, units

Complexity analysis provides a high-level or heuristic view of algorithms and system software. The intent is to abstract away effects of the hardware on the analysis. Specifically, time will be measured in *steps* of time or *time ticks,* and memory quantified in *units* of storage. Using such metrics, we will assume that each elementary operation will take one step and that each elementary object will occupy one unit of memory. Of course, it will be necessary to quantify what comprises an elementary operation.

Complexity analysis is used when one is looking for higher level measures for comparing the relative performance of different designs. The analysis is conducted at a very coarse-grained level, looking for orders of magnitude types of comparison and effects as the problem size increases. Nanosecond differences in execution time or microwatts of power consumption are not relevant at this early stage of analysis. The goal is to focus on the larger issues first.

When the analysis moves to the instruction level, the approach will be at a much finer grain. At that time, the analysis will focus on specific machines and limited blocks of code. At the lower level, the objective changes to optimizing a specific algorithm or identifying upper and lower bounds on a sequence through a piece of code.

EXAMPLE 14.2

Let's analyze a very simple algorithm that accepts as input an array of integers and the number of elements in the array (Figure 14.0). We have numbered each line of the algorithm for easier reference later.

```
1  int total (int myArray[], int n)
2  {
3      int sum = 0;
4      int i = 0;
5      for ( i = 0; i < n; i++ )
6      {
7          sum = sum + myArray[i];
8      }
9      return sum;
10 }
```

Figure 14.0 An Algorithm to Sum the Elements of an Array

Analysis of total

1. Describe the *size* of the input in terms of one or more parameters. The input to the algorithm is the array of integers, and the size of that array is given as n. The size of the problem is set to n.
2. Count how many steps are required to execute the algorithm for an input of that size. For the current analysis, a step is interpreted to be an elementary operation such as + or = or the subscripting operation.

We can analyze each line of the algorithm as follows.

Line 1: Two push onto the stack operations—this happens once.
2 operations

Line 3: One assignment operation—this happens once.
1 operation

Line 4: One assignment operation—this happens once.
1 operation

Line 5: Three operations—the initialization of i happens one time, the comparison against n happens n times, and the increment of i happens n times.
2 * n + 1 operations

Line 7: Three operations—the index operation, the sum calculation, and the assignment to sum. Each operation happens n times.
3 * n operations

Line 9:	One return operation—this happens 1 time.
	1 operation
Final:	5 * n + 6 operations

The expression for the number of operations in the code fragment in the last example can be interpreted as a function of n; that is, the number of operations to execute the algorithm depends directly on the size of the container. Thus, one can write a complexity function for the algorithm:

$$f(n) = 5n + 6$$

Now let's explore a bit with this expression to see how it behaves. Of particular interest is how the number of operations changes as the size of the original container is modified. Such an analysis is motivated by the observation that, through such a study, one can reach a reasonable estimate of the computational load of the algorithm for larger problems.

If one makes a couple of back-of-the-envelope calculations, the growth of the algorithm with input is evident:

```
n = 10 => 54 steps
n = 100 => 504 steps
n = 1,000 => 5,004 steps
n = 1,000,000 => 5,000,003 steps
```

linear proportion

Based on the simple calculations, several things become apparent: the number of operations seems to be growing in *linear proportion* to n, and the relative significance of the number 4 on the final answer is decreasing.

14.4 THE METHODOLOGY

Example 14.2 and the analysis that followed is typical of the approach one takes to gaining an understanding of the complexity of an application. Such a measure enables one to perform trade-off analyses early in the design cycle. Summarizing the approach:

1. Decompose the problem into a set of basic operations.
2. Count the total number of such operations.
3. Derive a formula, based in some parameter n that is the size of the problem.
4. Use order of magnitudes estimation to assess behavior.

For example, one may have one algorithm for which the number of operations increases linearly with increasing input size, as in the preceding example. An alternate algorithm might increase as the square of the size of the input. Yet another might behave as 2^n.

14.4.1 A Simple Experiment

Another simple order of magnitude experiment provides some interesting results. The experiment will study several familiar growth functions to see how each behaves as the size of the input is increased (see Table 14.0). The growth functions are:

- Linear
- Quadratic

- Logarithmic
- Exponential

Table 14.0 The Growth of Several Functions vs. Size of Input

N	10N	N^2	N^3	$\log_2 N$	$N\log_2 N$	2N
8	80	64	512	3	24	256
16	160	256	4096	4	64	65536
32	320	1024	32768	5	160	$\sim 4x10^9$
64	640	4096	26144	6	384	$\sim 16x10^{18}$
128	1280	16384	2097152	7	896	$\sim 256x10^{36}$
256	2560	65536	$\sim 16x10^6$	8	2048	$\sim 6x10^{76}$
512	5120	262144	$\sim 1x10^8$	9	4608	$\sim 2x10^{149}$
1024	10240	1048576	$\sim 1x10^9$	10	10240	$\sim 1x10^{200}$

With any analysis, one should always check boundary conditions. Relevant and necessary questions include: If this piece of code is completely eliminated, how fast would the program run? If the CPU is infinitely fast, how fast would the program run? If the cost of this part was \$0.00, how much would the system cost?

Such questions give a quick approximation for comparison. For the experiment conducted above, we assume that science and engineering make incredible breakthroughs far surpassing Moore's law, and within three years, CPU performance is one billion times faster than what is available today.

14.4.2 Working with Big Numbers

Now for the important question of the day: How much will that help if the algorithm grows as 2^N? Examining the results of the experiment, if we were able to achieve such a breakthrough, we find that performance on a problem with an input of size 1000 would improve from 10^{200} to 10^{191}. This sounds impressive, but what does it mean in real numbers? Let's return to the back-of-the-envelope.

Suppose there is an algorithm for which the number of operations is proportional to n!, that is, n factorial. Assume that for an input of size 10, the algorithm takes 1 ms to run. The execution time for an input of size 12 is 12! = 12 x 11 x 10!, which is 132 times longer than 1 ms: 132 ms. Not too bad, so where is the problem? Continuing, let's make n 14. For n = 14, the runtime is approximately 24 seconds. Continuing again, for n = 16, the runtime is about 1.6 hours; for n = 18, the runtime is about 1.4 years; and for n = 20, the runtime is about 500 years.

If the same algorithm is executed on a machine for which the performance has been improved from 10^{200} to 10^{191}, runtime will decrease from 10^{197} to 10^{188} seconds. One year is approximately 31 $x10^6$ seconds long.

14.4.3 Asymptotic Complexity

During the experiment assessing the complexity formula for the simple summing algorithm, it was observed that as the size of the input increased, the effect on the total of the least significant digit decreased. When we reexame that expression,

$$f(n) = 5n + 4$$

we find that not only does the effect of the 4 decrease, but the 5 is also inaccurate. The reason is that on most CISCs—complex instruction set computers—the operations <, [], +, =,

++ require varying amounts of time. As a result, for the calculations, one can safely ignore that multiplier. What is important is that the increase/decrease in the total number of operations is *linear* in n. As n gets large, one can concentrate on the *highest order* term and drop lower order terms such as +4 and the constant coefficient of the highest order term.

linear
highest order

From such recognition, one can state that for the expression 5n + 4 the bound on the number of operations *grows asymptotically* like n. Such an interpretation provides a means for approximating the complexity of an algorithm. Such an approximation is referred to as the *asymptotic complexity* of the algorithm. Although the method ignores many of the lower level details, it enables one to concentrate on the bigger picture.

grows asymptotically
asymptotic complexity

14.5 COMPARING ALGORITHMS

When comparing algorithms, typical questions that can be asked include:

- What is the worst case performance (upper bound) of a particular algorithm?
- What is the average case performance of a particular algorithm?
- What is the best possible performance (lower bound) for a particular type of problem?

Using complexity analysis, we can now (partially) answer the question, "Given algorithms A and B, which has better performance in time?" Such a question is equivalent to asking, "Which algorithm has the smaller asymptotic time bound?"

Specific values of n will probably lead to different (and generally uninformative) answers. However, conducting a boundary analysis enables one to compute and to compare the *growth rates* for arbitrarily large values of n, that is, the *asymptotic case*. Such an analysis provides a basis for comparison of the algorithms.

growth rates,
asymptotic case

> ***Caution:*** At the same time one must be careful not to forget the context in which the analysis is conducted. If it can be ensured that the input size remains small, the asymptotic growth rate is not the proper metric to be using.

The abstracted function that we have defined gives a bound on the complexity of an algorithm that is approached asymptotically. Thus, one can state that the complexity of an algorithm *approaches* that bound or is *on the order of* that bound.

approaches
on the order of

If such a function is expressed as a function of the problem size, N, and that function is called g(N), then one can say that (the complexity of) a function is on the order of g(N). That comparison can be written as

f(N) = O(g(N))	(14.0)
If there is a constant c such that f(N) < c g(N) for all sufficiently large N. read "f(N) is order g(N)" or "f(N) is big-O of g(N)"	

14.5.1 Big-O Notation

It is easiest to think of the expression f(N) = O(g(N)) as *f(N) grows at most like g(N)* or *f grows no faster than g*, ignoring constant factors for large N. Once again, g(N) gives an

f(N) grows at most like g(N)
f grows no faster than g

upper bound on the behavior of f(n). Of interest is the rate of change of a function, not a single value.

Remember that big-O is *not* a function; it is a notation. It is a means of describing something. We never read the symbol = in this context as *equals*!

equals

> ***Definition***
> Function f(N) is O(g(N)) if there is a constant C and a value N_0, such that f(N) is $\leq C*g(N)$, for $N \geq N_0$.

An earlier experiment examined how several different functions of N grew as the magnitude of N increased. That information can now be used to specify bounds on growth. Table 14.1 captures and compares several of the more common bounds.

Table 14.1 Common Bounds on Complexity vs. Input Size

O(k) = O(1)	Constant Time, complexity is independent of number of data items
$O(\log_b N)$ = O(log N)	Logarithmic Time
O(N)	Linear Time, complexity proportional to size
O(N log N)	
$O(N^2)$	Quadratic Time
$O(N^3)$	Cubic Time
...	
$O(k^N)$	Exponential Time
$N^{anyinteger}$	is called "polynomial" time

Once again, N specifies the input size.

In the table, complexity increases from top to bottom. The complexity ranking in the table reveals that as the size of the input grows, *any* algorithm of a smaller order will be more efficient than an algorithm of a larger order. As noted earlier, however, context is important, as is reflected in Figure 14.1.

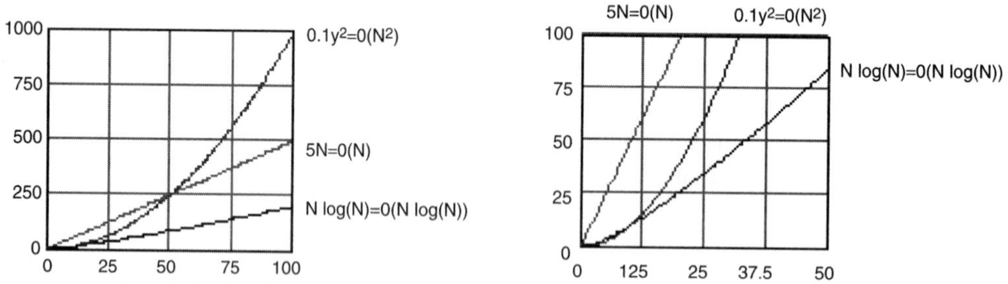

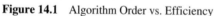

Figure 14.1 Algorithm Order vs. Efficiency

For an input size below 50, the time performance of an algorithm that is of $O(N^2)$ will be better than one that is of O(N). Beyond that value, the roles reverse. We also plot the behavior of an O(Nlog(N)) algorithm for comparison. Note that for values below approximately 12 the $O(N^2)$ still gives the best performance.

14.5.2 Big-O Arithmetic

Big-O arithmetic is based on the following simple rules.

- Order common functions from smallest to largest.

$$1, \log(N), N, N\log(N), N^2, N^3, ..., 2^N, 3^N, ...$$

- Ignore constant multipliers.

$$300\ N + 5N^4 + 6 \bullet 2^N = O(N + N^4 + 2^N)$$

- Ignore everything except the highest order term.

$$N + N^4 + 2^N = O(2^N)$$

Let's look at a couple of examples.

EXAMPLE 14.3

$$5N + 4 = O(N)$$

It is certainly also true: $5N + 3 = O(N^2)$.

That is—it grows no faster than N^2 or N! or 2^N for that matter.

The objective is to identify the tightest bound, the best indication of performance.

EXAMPLE 14.4

$$37N^5 + 7N^2 - 2N + 1$$

Starting with the smallest term, as N increases, the 1 becomes insignificant; the same holds first for the N and then for the N^2. The 37 N^5 remains.

The multiplicative constant is neglected; the expression is $O(N^5)$.

14.6 ANALYZING CODE

As one gains facility in analyzing and understanding the behavior of a system, it becomes evident rather quickly that even the most complex parts of a system are ultimately composed of fundamental modules. Most modules or pieces of the system are linear; consequently, one can take advantage of the benefits of superposition. The most immediate benefit is that an algorithm can be decomposed into its constituent pieces, analyzed, and the individual pieces summed. Such an ability, however, does not obviate the need to understand both the algorithm and the context.

flow of control constructs

Let's now analyze several of the basic *flow of control constructs* that are commonly found in many algorithms. The analysis at this stage will be conducted from the big-O perspective; shortly, the same constructs will be examined from the perspective of time performance.

14.6.1 Constant Time Statements

The execution of constant time statements, as their name suggests, is constant, independent of the size of the input. These are designated to be O(1), of order 1. Such statements include:

- Declarations and initializations of simple data types:

```
int x, y;
char myChar = 'a';
```

- Assignment statements of simple data types:

```
x = y;
```

- Arithmetic operations:

```
x = 5• y + 4• z;
```

- Array referencing:

```
A[j]
```

- Referencing/dereferencing pointers:

```
Cursor = Head -> Next;
```

- Most conditional tests:

```
if ( x < 12 ) …
```

14.6.2 Looping Constructs

Looping constructs are a common flow of control mechanism. From a complexity point of view, any loop analysis has two parts:

1. Determine the number of iterations to be performed.
2. Determine the number of steps per iteration.

For loops

The basic for loop is shown in Figure 14.2.

```
int sum = 0;
for (int j = 0; j < N; j++ )
    sum = sum + j ;
```

Figure 14.2 The Basic For Loop

- Number of iterations

  The loop executes N times (0–N-1),

- Number of steps per iteration

$$4 = O(1) \text{ steps per iteration}$$

1. The sum sum + j
2. The assignment sum =
3. The auto increment j++
4. The comparison j < N

Total time is $N \cdot O(1) = O(N \cdot 1) = O(N)$

The code fragment in Figure 14.3 is a variant on the basic for loop.

```
int sum = 0;
for (int j = 0; j < 100; j++ )
    sum = sum + j ;
```

Figure 14.3 A For Loop of Fixed Size

- Number of iterations

  The loop executes 100 times (0–99).

- Number of steps per iteration

$4 = O(1)$ steps per iteration

1. The sum — sum + j
2. The assignment — sum =
3. The auto increment — j++
4. The comparison — j < N

Total time is $100 \cdot O(1) = O(100 \cdot 1) = O(100)$

The complexity of this loop is constant.

That this loop is faster makes sense when N >> 100.

While Loops

```
bool done = false;
int result = 1
int n;       // n has some value
while ( !done )
{
    result = result * n;
    n--;
    if ( n <= 1 ) done = true;
}
```

Figure 14.4 The While Loop

Analysis of the while loop shown in Figure 14.4, duplicates that of the for loop.

- Number of iterations

  The loop terminates when done == true,

  which happens after n iterations.

- Number of steps per iteration

$3 = O(1)$ steps per iteration

1. The multiply — result • n
2. The assignment — result =
3. The auto decrement — n--

Total time is $N \cdot O(1) = O(N \cdot 1) = O(N)$

14.6.3 Sequences of Statements

For a sequence of statements, simply compute their individual complexity functions and add them up. If the two loops are executed in sequence, the result is as shown in Figure 14.5.

```
int j, k, sum = 0;
for ( j = 0; j < N; j++ )
    for ( k = 0; k < j; k++ )
        sum = sum + k * j;

for (i = 0; I < N; I++ )
    sum = sum - i;
```

Figure 14.5 Sequences of Statements

The complexity is given as

Total time is $N^3 + N = O(N^3)$

14.6.4 Conditional Statements

Conditional statements are no more difficult to analyze; one just has to consider all of the components. Starting with the simple branch statement, as shown in Figure 14.6:

```
if (condition)
    statement1;
else
    statement2;
```

Figure 14.6 Conditional Statements

assume that statement_1 has a time complexity that is $O(n^2)$ and that statement_2 has a complexity of O(n). With such a construct, some of the kinds of analysis that must be undertaken when designing real-time systems should be becoming clear. To understand the algorithm, one must consider *worst case complexity*. One must ask, for this algorithm and for all inputs of size n, what is the *maximum running time*?

worst case complexity

maximum running time

For this example, we conclude that the worst case time complexity is $O(n^2)$ based on the possibility of continually (or at least frequently) executing statement_1.

14.6.5 Function Calls

Function calls present the next level of complexity. Decomposing the problem, we see that the time complexity of a function call is made up of four components:

Cost = the call + passing the arguments + executing the function + returning a value

Let's examine each in turn.

- Making and returning from the call.

  The function call itself is independent of the size of the input. The complexity is O(1).

- Passing the arguments.

  The complexity of this component depends upon how they are passed.

  - Pass by value—the entire object must be copied and put onto the stack. This can be an expensive operation, particularly if dynamic memory allocation is supported.
  - Pass by reference—a reference to the object is put onto the stack. There is no copy of the object created. The time complexity should be constant.

- Determining the cost of execution.
  The complexity depends on the task being executed. We must decompose and analyze the components of the function body.

- Determining the cost of return.
  The complexity of the return depends on how the value is returned. The return can be either by value or by reference; the former is more expensive than the latter.

14.7 ANALYZING ALGORITHMS

Let's examine several searching and sorting algorithms and determine their complexity. We will start with search and then move to sort.

14.7.1 Analyzing Search

14.7.1.1 Linear Search

The linear search algorithm is given in Figure 14.7, and each line is numbered for reference.

```
// Return index of x if found, or -1 if not
1.  int find (int A[], int size, int x)
    {
2.      unsigned char gotIt = -1;
3.      unsigned int i;
4.      for ( i = 0; i < size && gotIt < 0; i++ )
        {
5.          if ( A[i] == x )
6.              gotIt = i;
        }
7.      return gotIt;
    }
```

Figure 14.7 Analyzing a Linear Search Algorithm

The worst case performance of the algorithm will be assessed first.

Line 1: Three push onto the stack operations—this happens once.
3 operations

Line 2: One assignment operation—this happens once.
1 operation

Line 3: One assignment operation—this happens once.
1 operation

Line 4: Five operations—the initialization of i happens one time, the comparison against size, the comparison against 0, the AND operation—these happen size times each, and the increment of i happens size times.

3 • size + 2 operations

Line 5: One comparison operation—this happens size times.

size operations

Line 6: One assignment operation—this happens once.

1 operation

Line 7: One return operation—this happens once.

1 operation

Final: 5 • size + 8 operations

The worst case complexity is O(N) when N is the size of the container. The best case performance is achieved when the target value is always the first entry in the container. Under such circumstances, the best case complexity is constant; that is, O(1). One can also argue convincingly that the number of operations, on average, will be (size/2). Nonetheless, this is still O(N), linear in the size of the container.

14.7.1.2 Binary Search

The binary search algorithm has a worst case complexity of $O(\log_2 N)$ where N is the size of the search range. Computing this value will be left as an exercise.

14.7.2 Analyzing Sort

14.7.2.1 Selection Sort

The code for the selection sort algorithm is given in Figure 14.8. The sort routine and the helper search routine are cooperating to execute the sort; both must be considered.

selectionSort

Starting with the function *selectionSort*, we see that it iterates N times where N is the sort range. Next, we can ask, how much work is done each time? For this algorithm, rather than look line by line, we will take a more expeditious path. Let's look at the pieces and estimate the complexity of each. In doing so, we neglect operations that are independent of the size of the input.

1. findSmallest()
   The number of for loop iterations within the function is given by

   ```
   N-1 + N-2 + N-3...1
   ```

   Since the search range decreases by one with each pass the total work can be computed as the sum of the first N numbers.

   $$N \bullet \frac{N-1}{2}$$

2. By the three lines comprising the swap operation

   ```
   N - 1 calls → N - 1 exchanges
   ```

3. By other statements

   ```
   Each exchange → 3 assignments
   ```

```
void selectionSort (int a[ ], int lower, int upper)
{
    // declare some working variables
    int low = 0;
    int smallest;
    int working;

    for (low = lower; low<upper; low++)
    {
        // find index of smallest element
        smallest = findSmallest(a, low, upper);

        // swap smallest with current top of container
        working = a[low];
        a[low] = a[smallest];
        a[smallest] = working;
    }
    return;
}
```

```
int findSmallest(int a[ ], int lower, int upper)
{
    int smallIndex = lower;
    int i = 0;
    for (i=lower+1; i<=upper; i++)
    {
        if (a[i] < a[smallIndex])
            smallIndex = i;
    }
    return smallIndex;
}
```

Figure 14.8 Analyzing a Selection Sort Algorithm

The final total is given as

$$\text{Total} = N \bullet \frac{N-1}{2} + 3 \bullet (N-1)$$

The complexity of selection sort thus reduces to

$$O\left(\frac{N^2}{2}\right) \Rightarrow O(N^2)$$

14.7.2.2 Quick Sort

The quick sort algorithm has a worst case complexity of $O(N \log_2 N)$. Computing this value will be left as an exercise.

14.8 ANALYZING DATA STRUCTURES

We will now examine two important containers: the array and the linked list. For each, we will look at the following fundamental operations.

- Insert/delete at the beginning
- Insert/delete at the end
- Insert/delete in the middle
- Access at the beginning, the end, and in the middle

For the analysis, it is assumed that each of the data structures is allocated at compile time and does not support runtime allocation.

14.8.1 Array

Two cases must be considered for each operation: whether the operation is to be executed as an overwrite or as an insert. The first case will not require moving data, whereas the second will.

- Insert/delete at the beginning
  In the overwrite mode, inserting an element is done in constant time. The complexity is O(1).
  In the insert mode, each element of the container must be moved to make room for the new element. Thus, the complexity is O(N), where N is the number of elements in the array.
  The complexity of the delete operation is the same as that for the insert mode, O(N). Each element in the container must be moved to fill the void.
- Insert/delete at the end
  The insert and delete operations at the end of the array in either mode are done in constant time. No elements need be moved; thus, the complexity is O(1).
- Insert/delete in the middle
  The operation comprises two pieces: finding the element then performing the insert or delete. The array supports random access; thus, finding the element is a constant time operation. In the overwrite mode, inserting an element is also done in constant time. The complexity is O(1).
  In the insert mode, all elements below (with higher index) must be moved to make room for the new element. For the two boundary cases, we only move a single element, or we move all elements but one. Thus, the complexity is, on average, O(N/2), or simply O(N), where N is the number of elements that need to be moved.
  The complexity of the delete operation is the same as that for the insert mode for both the boundary and typical cases, O(N).
- Access at the beginning, the end, and in the middle.
  These are all constant time operations since the array supports random access.

14.8.2 Linked List

- Insert/delete at the beginning
  Inserting or deleting a link at the head of a linked list involves the modification of a couple of addresses. These operations are independent of the size of the list; thus, the complexity is O(1).
- Insert/delete at the end
  For either of these operations, two cases must be considered. If a reference to the tail of the linked list is maintained, then either operation can be completed in constant time.
  On the other hand, if only the head reference is retained, then one must first find the tail of the list. Such an operation does depend on the number of elements in the list; thus, the complexity in such a case is O(N), where N is the size of the container.
- Insert/delete in the middle
  The operation comprises two pieces: finding the element and performing the insert or delete. The linked list does not support random access; thus, finding the element depends on the number of elements in the list. Like the delete at the end, the access is of order N, and the insert or delete is constant. Thus, either of these operations has complexity O(N).

- Access at the beginning, the end, and in the middle

  Like insert or delete in the beginning, the end, or the middle of the linked list, the time complexity is controlled by the amount of time to find the element. Thus, either of these operations will have complexity that is the same as the corresponding insert or delete operations.

14.9 INSTRUCTIONS IN DETAIL

We have looked at order of magnitude measures and comparisons for algorithms. Eventually, the code must be written, compiled, and run on the microprocessor. In real-time systems, this is where the interesting design issues and challenges arise. In a hard real-time system, a few nanoseconds can mean the difference between success and failure of a design.

We will now move inside of the algorithm to examine the temporal performance of each of the instructions in detail. As with any other tools and approaches that one is working with, the tools, the problem, and the context must be thoroughly understood. Analyzing individual instructions or sequences of instructions, which will be done shortly, is most definitely not appropriate for an entire program. Rather, the technique is used and applied to understand and to optimize a critical set of instructions.

flow of control constructs

Once again, it is assumed that a program or algorithm is made up of several common *flow of control constructs*. The basic constructs will be analyzed in detail; these components can be combined later as needed.

Several additional caveats are in order.

1. Single thread of execution is assumed.
2. The analysis is conducted at the assembly language level. Each different compiler is going to generate somewhat different assembly code, even for the same target. The analysis must be based on the compiler that is generating the final code for the microprocessor used in the design.
3. Compilers support different options for the compilation process. Such variations include the size of the target memory. Different code may be generated for a small memory model versus a large memory model.

Consistency is the key word. Always perform the analysis on the code that will ultimately be embedded in the system being designed.

14.9.1 Getting Started

After the high-level code to be analyzed is identified, the analysis is conducted on the assembly language listing. Most contemporary compilers will not generate such a listing automatically. However, the option to do so is generally available. Once one has a complete assembly listing, the specific instructions that are of interest can be identified.

From the processor vendor's assembly language manuals, one then determines the time for each instruction. This time can vary with any of the following.

- Addressing mode of instruction
- The piece of memory from which the instruction or data must be fetched:

  Immediate

  Register

  Primary

  Secondary

It may be necessary to use minimum, maximum, or average numbers depending upon the objective at hand. For example, is one looking for the longest path or the shortest? Is the objective to meet a deadline, or is to it ensure that a value doesn't change too quickly?

14.9.2 Flow of Control

As the design and implementation of increasingly complex embedded systems continue, it is not going to be possible to develop a solution based on executing a few lines of code. Rather, the designs are going to be implemented as collections of cooperating tasks and threads. Some of the tasks will be scheduled according to a predetermined algorithm, whereas others will be invoked asynchronously in response to internal or external events.

The invocation of each new task or thread will entail a change from a current context to a new one and may involve saving the current context and retrieving an old one. Depending on the tasks to be performed, such a series of operations will take varying amounts of time and can be critical in a real-time system. To be able to effectively design embedded systems, one must thoroughly understand the flow of control both inside and outside of the system. Essential to such an understanding is the ability to analyze, in time, the flow of control through the system.

The flow of control—the single-threaded path of execution—through most contemporary programs can be modeled and analyzed as a composite of four basic elements:

- Sequential
- Branch
- Loop
- Function call

big-O We have already analyzed each of these constructs from a *big-O* or order of magnitude perspective. We will now examine them, first from a C language level and then in greater detail at the assembler level.

Sequential

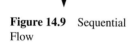

Figure 14.9 Sequential Flow

A sequential block is a set of instructions, each of which is executed in sequence—that is, in the order that the instructions appear in the program and ultimately in program memory, our firmware. Such a set of instructions may include declarations, definitions, or assignments. (See Figure 14.9.)

Branch

A branch is the simplest construct that allows the flow of a thread of execution through the program to be altered. One of several branches can be selected based on some condition. Graphically, this type of construct is seen in Figure 14.10 and appears in high-level code as statements such as

```
if else
switch or case
```

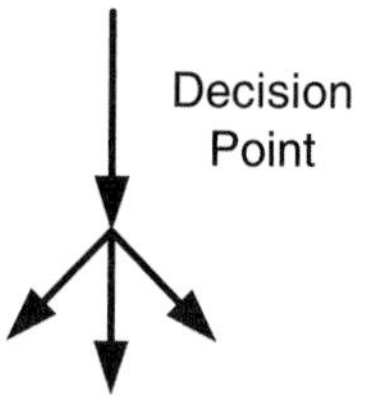

Figure 14.10 The Branch

In assembler, the branch will be implemented as a series of jump or branch instructions, depending on the assembler.

Loop

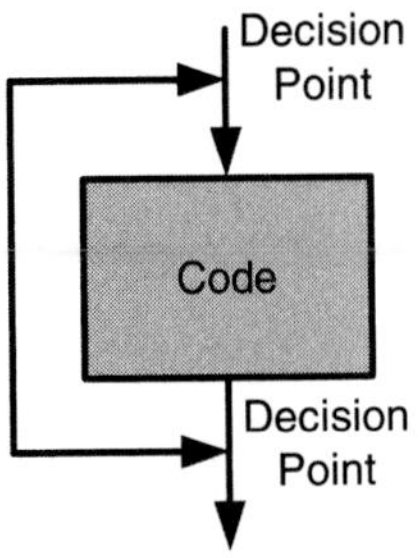

Figure 14.11 The Loop

The loop construct expresses a set of instructions that is repeatedly executed until some termination condition is met. As the diagram in Figure 14.11 illustrates, a decision about whether to execute the code block can be made before—the code may not be executed—or after the loop—the code is executed at least once.

A construct of this type is seen in high-level instructions of the form

```
do or repeat
while
for
```

and in assembler as a coordinated collection of jumps.

Function Call

The most complex flow of control component is the function call. In this component, the current context is exited, a set of instructions is executed in a new context, and then flow returns to the initial context. Such a construct can be found in a

```
Function, procedure or subroutine call
Interrupt handler and Interrupt Service Routine
Co-routine
```

Context is interpreted as the information that characterizes the current executing environment of the program and includes items such as

- Program counter
- Auto variables
- Register contents
- State of globals

The flow of control is illustrated in Figure 14.12.

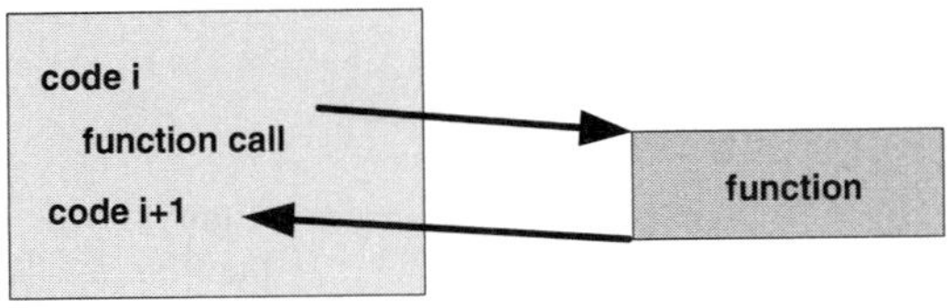

Figure 14.12 The Function Call

14.9.3 Analyzing the Flow of Control—Two Views

The major components that can be used to analyze the flow of control at the instruction level have now been identified. For each type, we begin with a high-level language program that embodies the construct, and then we present and analyze an assembly language implementation.

The essential point to remember is that the assembly language implementation is compiler and processor dependent. The analysis that follows should be used as a methodology for analyzing a system rather than a set of specific steps to be followed.

The C and assembly language-level implementation of each of the flow of control constructs will be presented. The assembler instructions are those of an Intel microcontroller; however, the process can be applied to any machine. Each instruction is annotated with its execution time. The processor on which these times are computed is running at 20 MHz. Such a clock rate is not unusual for an embedded microcontroller; it is sufficient for many smaller applications.

Sequential Flow

The code fragment given in Figure 14.13 represents a typical set of instructions that one might encounter in a C sequential flow.

```
// make a couple of declarations
int a = 10;
int b = 20;
// perform an arithmetic operation followed by an assignment
c = a + b;
```

Figure 14.13 Analyzing Sequential Flow—The C Level

The C fragment is now expressed in assembler in Figure 14.14. Each instruction is annotated with its execution time.

```
ldbse  R0,#0AH     // load 10 into a temp register                 400 ns
push   R0          // push the local variable onto the stack       600 ns
ldbse  R2,#14H     // load 20 into a temp register                 400 ns
push   R2          // push the local variable onto the stack       600 ns
add    R0,R2       // c ← a + b                                    400 ns
push   R0          // push the local variable onto the stack       600 ns
                                                          Total    3000 ns
```

Figure 14.14 Analyzing Sequential Flow—The Assembler Level

Branch

`if - else construct`

The code fragment in Figure 14.15 is a typical example of a branch construct.

```
if (a == b)
    c = d + e;
else
    c = d - e;
```

Figure 14.15 Analyzing the Branch—The C Level

The assembler code follows in Figure 14.16. It is assumed that the variables a–e have already been loaded into registers R1–R5.

```
     cmp   R1,R2      // compare R1 and R2                 400 ns
     jne   @0002      // if they are not equal branch to   800 ns for branch taken
                      // label @0002                       400 ns for branch not taken
     add   R3,R4,R5   // R3 <- R4 + R5                     500 ns
     br    @0003      // go to label @0003                 700 ns
@0002:
     sub   R3,R4,R5   // R3 <- R4 - R5                     500 ns
@0003:
                                               Total       1700–2000 ns
```

Figure 14.16 Analyzing the Branch—The Assembler Level

Observe that for the branch construct, there will be different execution times for the case when the branch is taken and when it is not. These numbers must be considered in context. If a hard real-time constraint is associated with this branch, then the worst case number, 2000, must be used. This is the best execution time that can be guaranteed. If only general performance is being assessed, however, one might consider averaging the two values.

Loop

A typical loop construct in C appears as in the next code fragment (see Figure 14.17).

```
while (myVar < 10)
{
        i = i + 2;
        myVar++;
}
```

Figure 14.17 Analyzing the Loop—The C Level

The basic loop leads to the assembler code fragment in Figure 14.18. It is assumed that myVar has been loaded into R1 and i into R0.

```
@0004:                // start of the while loop
    cmp   R0,#0AH     // compare myVar with 10            400 ns
    jge   @0004       // if greater than or equal to 10   800 ns for branch taken
                      // jump to label @0005               400 ns for branch not taken
    add   R0,#2       // increment I by 2                  500 ns
    inc   R1          // increment myVar                   300 ns
    br    @0004       // jump to start of while loop       700ns
@0005:
                                       Total                1200–2300 ns
```

Figure 14.18 Analyzing the Loop—The Assembler Level

As was done with the branch, one must consider the operating context when using the times from such a construct. Under a hard real-time constraint, one must use the worst case value. The numbers above are for a single pass through the loop.

Function Call

A procedure call, illustrated in the code fragment in Figure 14.19, is the most complex of the flow of control constructs. It is not particularly more difficult, but rather, a bit more

```
3000 Code
3053 Function Call F1()
3054 More Code
5000 F1
   Function Code
5053 Return
```

Figure 14.19 Analyzing the Function Call—The C Level

involved. The process is considered from a high level first. Assume that the program is loaded at address 0x3000 in code memory. Let the instructions be executed until flow reaches address 0x3053. At this time, a procedure is encountered.

The following steps are now executed.

1. Save the return address.
   - There are several important things to note
   - Address that is saved is 0x3054
   - The stack gets
     - Return address
     - Parameters
     - Local variables in both old and new contexts

   This step can be very time consuming. In a context with a hard real-time constraint, one may choose to implement the code in line, and perhaps in assembler, if the timing constraints warrant it.

   As an exercise, write a simple function call for your processor, and compile the program so that you get the assembly listing. Look at the instructions and associate a time with each. How long does the invocation take?
2. The address of the procedure, 0x5000 put into PC.
3. The instruction at 0x5000 begins executing.
4. Execution continues until we reach address 0x5053.

   The return is now encountered and we get a series of actions similar to those for the call.

   The stack gets

   Return values

   Stack loses

   Return address

   The return address is put into PC

   Additional steps may be necessary to delete the stack frame on return. How expensive is this?
5. Execution continues at 0x3057

A representative code fragment is given first in C (as might exist in main()), in Figure 14.20, then in assembler in Figure 14.21 for one possible implementation of the function call.

```
int myVar0 = 30;
int myVar1 = 40;
myVar1 = myFunction(myVar0);
```

Figure 14.20 Analyzing the Function Call—The C Level

A couple of variables are declared; one is passed to the function and the other is used to hold the return value. The code fragment in main() will be examined first, followed by that in the body of the function. It is assumed that myVar0 has already been stored in R0 and myVar1 has been stored in R1.

```
push    myVar0          // push myVar0 onto the stack                          600 ns
lcall   myFunction      // execute the function call                          1100 ns
                        // the call pushes the contents of the PC
                        // (the return address) onto the stack, adds
                        // the displacement between the current PC and
                        // the address of the function to the PC
add     SP,#2           // increment the stack pointer                         400 ns
ld      myVar1,Tmp0     // put the function return value into myVar1           400 ns
                                                                 Total        2500 ns
```

Figure 14.21 Analyzing the Function Call—The Assembler Level

The C code in the function body appears as shown in Figure 14.22.

```
int myFunction(int aVar)
{
    int localVar = 15;
    localVar = localVar + aVar;
    return localVar;
}
```

Figure 14.22 Analyzing the Function Call—The C Level

The assembler implementation is given in Figure 14.23. Had there been a second procedure call in procedure *myFunction()*, an identical process would have been initiated. The process can be repeated multiple times. However, one must be aware that the stack can overflow if too much is pushed on. Under such a circumstance, information, particularly the return address, gets lost.

```
push   Tmp01                   // pushes a temp variable onto the stack              600 ns
ld     Tmp01,SP                // puts the stack pointer into that local variable    400 ns
ldbse  localVar,#0FH           // load 15 into a temp register                       400 ns
add    localVar,aVar[Tmp01]    // use indexing into stack to get passed in arg       600 ns
ld     Tmp0, localVar          // use global temp to return local variable           400 ns
pop    Tmp01                   // pop the stack                                      800 ns
ret                            // return to calling function                        1100 ns
                               // puts top of stack into PC
                                                                       Total        4300 ns
```

Figure 14.23 Analyzing the Function Call—The Assembler Level

The function call has consumed almost 7 μs, 2500 ns to save the context and 4300 ns to execute the function and return.

Observe how the authors of the compiler for this processor handled the return value. From the times given above, the push and pop operations consume 1.4 μs in contrast to the load that requires 400 ns. By using a global temporary register rather than the stack, they improved performance by almost 300% on that sequence.

Co-routine

A co-routine is a special kind of procedure call in which there is a mutual call exchange between cooperating procedures—that is, two procedures sharing time. The mechanics are the same as the simple procedure call, and so is the time budget. The major difference is that a conventional procedure executes until the end unless it leaves under extraordinary circumstances. Co-routines exit and return throughout the body of the procedure. Usually, this is executed under the direction of a third process or procedure. Graphically, the process appears as shown in Figure 14.24.

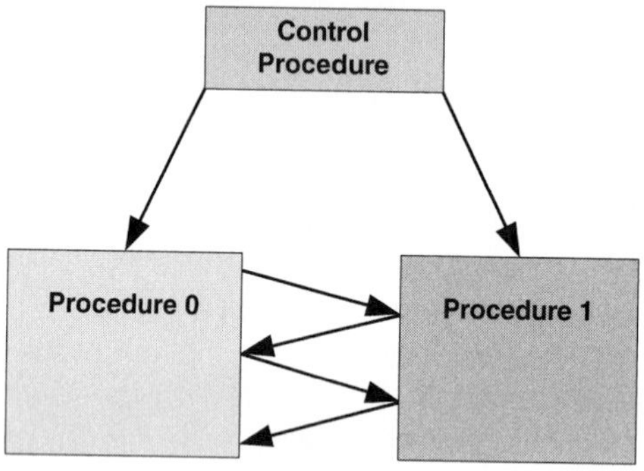

Figure 14.24 The Co-routine

The control procedure starts the process. Each context switch is determined by any of the following:

- Control procedure
- External event—a timing signal
- Internal event—a data value

The process continues until both procedures are completed. With each switch, the appropriate information from the current context must be saved. Such activities incur a significant time burden. If such a construct is used in a time-constrained context, then one must permit preemption as appropriate. The co-routine sequence is analyzed exactly as was done with the procedure call.

Interrupt Call

An interrupt is another special kind of procedure call. In this case, the initiator is some asynchronous internal or external event. As is illustrated in Figure 14.25, normal execution proceeds in the foreground task. When the interrupt occurs, control is first transferred to the interrupt handler and then the appropriate ISR.

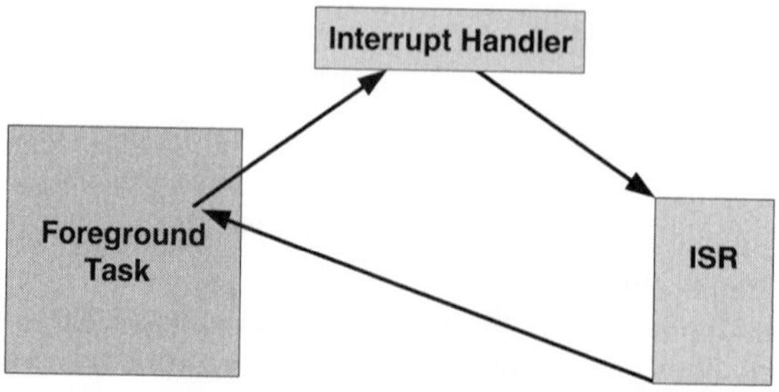

Figure 14.25 The Interrupt

The analysis of an interrupt follows that for the function call. Most processors complete the current instruction before initiating the context switch. Thus, since it is not generally known which instruction is being executed when the interrupt occurs, the longest is selected. Such a choice gives an upper bound. To this number, one must add the time for the context switch exactly as was done for the function call except that no variables are pushed onto the stack. Values cannot be passed into an ISR. The return from the ISR is the same as the function call except that, once again, there are no variables to return.

When working in a context with hard real-time constraints, one must analyze the code as has been done above to establish an exact or bounded execution time. Any program can be built from the basic constructs that have been studied above.

14.10 TIME, ETC.—A MORE DETAILED LOOK

As has been repeatedly stressed, time is one of the more critical constraints that must be considered when designing embedded systems. Up to this point, analysis has taken a coarse-grained view of system (software) performance using order of magnitude estimates on algorithm complexity. The time performance of the basic flow of control constructs at the assembler level has been studied as well. The next step is to move inside the individual hardware components and software tasks to learn where and how time affects their performance.

When looking at the time performance in embedded systems, one must consider both hardware and software timing. On the hardware side, one must consider the internal delays of the hardware components as well as delays through external elements or systems as appropriate. Software performance is affected by both the path through the program and the timing of individual instructions, as we have seen.

In examining time, we are interested in several things: exact times if computable, bounded times if exact times are not computable. We may also consider measuring the times over a large sample of units. The other important consideration is that the times be deterministic.

Time is an important factor in analyzing and specifying the performance of most embedded applications. It can be expressed in a number of different ways, as will be evident shortly. Its importance notwithstanding, time is not the only consideration. Several other factors should also be considered. Let's take a look at these.

METRICS

When discussing embedded system performance, several simple measures can be used. One of the more common ones is *response time*—the interval between the occurrence of an event and the completion of some associated action (typically the first useful action). Sometimes, this is also referred to as *execution time* or *throughput*. However, these terms are different. The former is the time to complete the entire task, whereas the latter is the number of tasks completed per unit time. In a pipelined system, once the pipe is full, the throughput could be very high, yet the execution time per task is much slower.

response time

execution time, throughput

Time loading is another important metric. This is the percentage of time that the CPU is doing useful work—that is, working on user rather than system jobs. There is no point in optimizing the performance of the application program to the nanosecond level if 90% of the CPU resources will be devoted to running the system tasks.

time loading

Memory loading is similar to time loading. This is the percentage of usable memory being used (by the application rather than the system). Most nonhard real-time applications are multitasking and use a virtual memory scheme of one form or another. In hard real-time applications, however, we generally avoid using such schemes. If the amount of memory allocated to the application is sufficiently small that the system is continually paging, then

memory loading

most likely, low performance lies with the system rather than the program. Nonetheless, one still must be conscious of the need to reduce the size of a program.

Let's take a more detailed look at each of these; we will start with response time.

14.11 RESPONSE TIME

Response time is the interval between an event and the completion of the associated action. For example, one might issue a command to an A/D to make reading and receive an event from the A/D signifying completion of the task. More accurately, however, response time is driven by the type of system involved—for example, the time between issuing a command to an A/D to make a reading and receiving the event from the A/D signifying completion of the task. In the following sections, we examine different control flow segments and the response time of each.

14.11.1 Polled Loops

Polled loops are the simplest and best understood. The response time consists of three components:

1. Hardware delays in the external device to set the signaling event
2. Time to test the flag
3. Time needed to respond to and process the event associated with the flag

1. External Hardware Device Delay
   Two cases must be considered:
   a. The response through the external system to a prior internal event
   b. An asynchronous external event

CASE 1

Figure 14.26 gives a graphical expression of the problem.

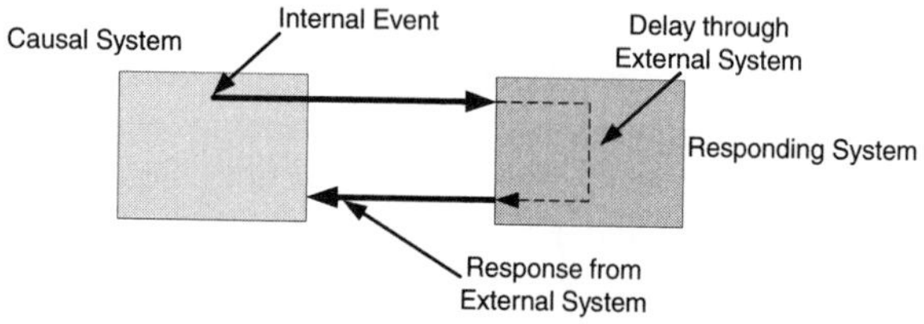

Figure 14.26 The Delay Path Through an External Device

In analyzing the behavior one must consider

a. The time to get to the polling loop from the internal causal event
b. The delay through the external device
c. The time to generate the response

The timing can be complicated to analyze, particularly if the triggering event takes several different paths through an external device. In fact, it may not be possible to calculate the exact value. Alternatively, one can place an upper bound on the time. Such a constraint sets a minimum limit on hard real-time behavior.

In time, the picture looks like that in Figure 14.27. We label the time through the external device τ_{ed1}.

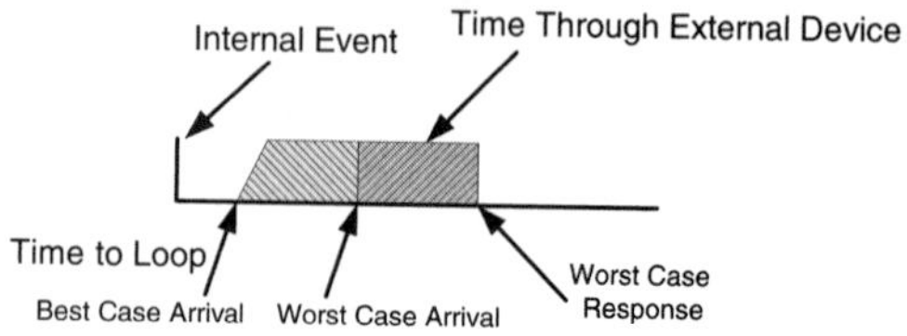

Figure 14.27 Analyzing the Delay Path Through an External Device

CASE 2

The problem now appears as illustrated in Figure 14.28.

In such a case, one cannot determine when the event will occur.

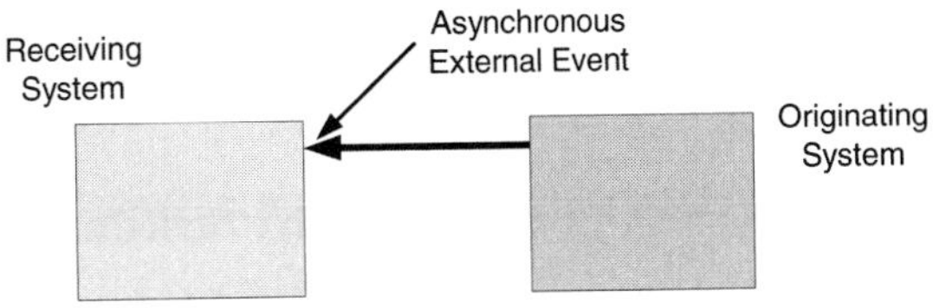

Figure 14.28 An Asynchronous Event from an External Device

2. Flag Time
   Flag time is determined from the execution time of the machine's bit test instruction. Label this time τ_f.
3. Processing Time
   Processing time is the time to perform the task associated with the triggering event. The triggering event may be either internal or external. This time must include the time to reach the flag from the current instruction. We make the assumption that we are in the polling loop and not at the test instruction. One must consider the best, worst, and average times. One must also include the time to reset the flag and to execute the task. We call this time τ_p.

   One can consider anticipating the event if it is necessary to meet a very high-speed requirement with a slow causative process or device. Anticipation is implemented by arming the system so that when an event occurs, everything is set up to go. One could use hardware as an implementing mechanism and consider a small window to respond to the event.

   In computing the processing time, one must consider two cases, the first event and the nth event. For the first event, the loop is unburdened. In such a case, one has the minimum time to execute. If the loop permits events to queue, for the nth event, time must be added to complete some subset of the n-1 previous events. Such a time can be bounded by n-1 times time to process a single event.

14.11.2 Co-routine

In a noninterrupt environment, the time for a co-routine may be computed directly or, more often, bounded, which we compute as the worst case path through each component.

14.11.3 Interrupt-Driven Environment

An interrupt-driven environment is the most complex of the calculations because one is dealing with asynchronous events that can be nondeterministic. Events probably will not occur in the same sequence each time the program is executed. One can set a bound on the complexity of the computation by assuming only one such event can occur.

Several affecting factors include interrupt latency, the time for the context switch, the schedule, and the task execution time. For the context switch, the following times must be considered:

- Context switch to the interrupt handler
- To acknowledge the interrupt

- Context switch to the processing routine
- Context switch back to the original context

The schedule may be nonpreemptive or preemptive. A preemptive schedule with fixed rate scheduling is the easiest to compute. Let's look at the pieces.

Preemptive Schedule

- Context Switch
  The time for the context switch can be computed directly by identifying the instructions at the assembler level and counting the time each takes.
- Task Execution
  When computing the time for the task execution, typically three values are considered: the minimum, average, and maximum times. These times can be computed, once again, by counting instruction times.
- Interrupt Latency
  When computing interrupt latency, two cases must be considered:
  1. Highest priority device
  2. Lower priority device

CASE 1 *Highest Priority Device*

Three factors are examined:

- The time from the leading edge of the interrupt in the external device until that edge is recognized inside the system.
- The time to complete the current instruction if interrupts are enabled. Most processors complete the current instruction before switching context. Some do permit an interrupt to be recognized at the microinstruction level. Thus, the time is going to be bounded by the longest instruction.
- The time to complete the current task if interrupts are disabled. This time will be bounded by the task size.

As a first cut, one can say that the time is bounded by the longer of the latter two factors.

CASE 2 *Lower Priority Device*

If one is working with a lower priority device, two cases must be considered. First, the interrupt occurs and is processed. In such a case, the time is computed as shown above. Second, the interrupt occurs and is interrupted. Unless interrupts are disabled, the situation is nondeterministic. In critical cases one may have to change the priority or place limits on the number of preemptions.

Nonpreemptive Schedule

Since preemption is not allowed, times are computed as in highest priority case above.

14.12 TIME LOADING

Time loading is the percentage of time that the CPU is doing useful work. By useful work we mean the execution of those tasks for which the embedded program has been designed. Analyzing time loading entails understanding the execution times of the constituent modules. These times are computed by finding the time spent in both the primary tasks and the support tasks. Then compute the ratio of

$$\frac{\text{Primary}}{\text{Primary} + \text{Secondary}}$$

To compute the times, three primary methods are used:

- Instruction counting
- Simulation
- Physical measurement

14.12.1 Instruction Counting

Instruction counting requires that the code actually be written. At the end of the day, this is the best method to determine the time loading due to the code execution time.

periodic

sporadic

For *periodic* systems, the total task execution time is computed and then divided by time for the individual module. This becomes the time loading for that task. For *sporadic* systems, the maximum task execution rates are used, and the percentages are combined over all of the tasks. This gives a total time loading. For example, if we have

Total time loading is T

T_i is cycle time for i^{th} task

A_i is execution time for i^{th} task

For n tasks,

$$T = \sum_{i=1}^{n} \frac{A_i}{T_i} \qquad (14.1)$$

Effective instruction counting requires an understanding of the basic flow of control through a piece of software. Often altering the flow of control involves context switch.

14.12.2 Simulation

Though essential in some cases, there are other cases for which instruction counting is of limited utility, particularly if one must analyze more than a handful of instructions. As noted earlier, there are many other factors in computing times such as memory accesses, addressing schemes, and loop iterations. To effectively use simulation as a design and development tool, one must have a complete understanding of the system and must have an accurate and representative workload against which to run the simulation. From such an understanding, one can then begin to develop an accurate model of the system. The model can include hardware, software, or both. Tools like VHDL or Verilog can be used to model the hardware, a variety of software modeling tools that are also available. System C is one such tool that will allow one to do both. Modeling can be done at a variety of levels based on the kind of information that is being sought.

It is beyond the scope of this text to present more than a brief introduction to simulation and models. However, lack of coverage here should in no way be interpreted as limiting their importance. For large systems, it is simply not practical to count all of the instructions; simulation and modeling are the only viable tools.

14.12.2.1 Models

behavioral, conceptual, structural, analytic

The two major categories of models are *behavioral* or *conceptual* and *structural* or *analytic*. The first category is usually based on symbols to represent qualitative aspects, whereas the second uses mathematical or logical relations to represent physical behavior.

We develop and apply models at a variety of levels and for a variety of reasons. The most common models are as follows.

SYSTEM-LEVEL MODEL
The system-level model is described by a hierarchical and structural model and is represented by a set of communicating functions or processes. Typically, the functions are specified using a behavioral model.

FUNCTIONAL MODEL
A functional model expresses the system as a collection of functions. Its structure is hierarchical and graphical, and it describes a system by a set of interacting functional elements. The behavior of each element is independent of any future hardware or software implementation.

PHYSICAL MODEL
The physical model describes the architectural structure of the system based on real components and their interactions.

STRUCTURAL MODEL
A structural model specifies the organization of the system based on the components in the system and the interconnections among them. It includes both functional and physical-level elements and the mapping between them. The model binds the functional to the physical and can be used at any level of abstraction.

BEHAVIORAL MODEL
There are a wide variety of models in this category. As noted earlier, such a model is usually based on symbols to represent qualitative aspects, and behavior is frequently expressed as a function of time.

DATA MODEL
A data model or entity-relation model represents the world in terms of entities and their attributes and the relations between/among them.

14.12.3 Timers

Timers can be associated with various busses or pieces of code in the system. One can then start the timer when entering the block of code to be timed and stop the timer on exit. Such an approach is best for timing blocks of code. The approach is not particularly effective for a long program.

14.12.4 Instrumentation

Another effective way of assessing the performance of a system is simply to measure it. Numerous instruments, such as the basic logic analyzer and code analyzer, permit a system to be instrumented and its performance to be measured qualitatively. Such instruments can measure maximum and minimum times, time loops, identify nonexecuted code, and capture rates of execution, among other things. They can also identify the most frequently used code so that it may be optimized in the future. The major caveat with any such measurements is that they are only as good as the input to the system. If you are not executing both typical and boundary condition applications, the quality of any measurements is suspect. Furthermore, it is very important to remember that the measurements are not predictive in the sense that one cannot say that the measured values guarantee performance of the system under all circumstances. Any such instruments should be used with caution; they can provide a significant amount of useful information, but we must keep what we learn in perspective.

14.13 MEMORY LOADING

Today, in many applications, memory is almost free. In many cases, however, it is not. The amount of memory available may be reduced to save weight in such applications as in aircraft or spacecraft. There may be severe cost constraints such as those found in very high-volume consumer products such as televisions or the automobile. There are also times when one must eliminate parts to reduce power, as is common in portable systems such as cell phones or the PDA. In such cases, one must optimize the use of what memory is available. As we learned earlier, memory has several different components: code space, data space, and system space. Recall once again that we optimize a design in order to focus most of the resources on getting the target application completed. Memory loading is defined as the percentage of usable memory being devoted to that application.

14.13.1 Memory Map

The memory map is a useful step for understanding the allocation and use of the available memory. For reference, a typical memory map is presented in Figure 14.29.

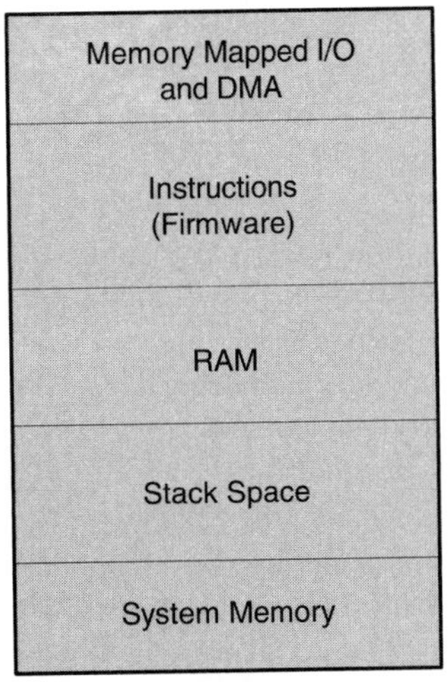

Figure 14.29 A Typical Memory Map

The total memory loading will be the sum of the individual loadings for Instructions, Stack, and RAM. The loading is given by

$$M_T = M_i \bullet P_i + M_R \bullet P_R + M_S \bullet P_S \tag{14.2}$$

The values M_i reflect the memory loading for each portion of memory. The values P_i represent the percentage of total memory allocated for the program. M_T will be expressed as a percentage.

EXAMPLE

Let system be implemented as follows

M_I–15 megabytes
M_R–100 kilobytes
M_S–150 kilobytes

P_I–55%
P_R–33%
P_S–10%

Giving a value for M_T of

$$M_T = 0.55 \bullet \frac{15}{15.25} + 0.33 \bullet \frac{0.1}{15.25} + 0.1 \bullet \frac{0.15}{15.25}$$

$$M_T = 54\%$$

Observe that memory mapped I/O and DMA space are not included in the calculation. These are fixed by the hardware design.

14.13.2 Designing a Memory Map

When designing a memory map, allocate the minimum amount of memory necessary for the instructions and the stack, but be sure to allow room for future growth. Leave the remaining amount of RAM for application program(s).

Instruction/Firmware Area

This portion of memory space is generally ROM of one form or another, hence its label firmware. The firmware contains the program that implements the application. Memory loading is computed by dividing the number of user locations by the maximum allowable. We get

$$M_I = \frac{U_I}{T_I} \tag{14.3}$$

RAM Area

This portion of memory space is generally used for storing program data. Such data also includes any global variables and what are called RAM registers in some CPU architectures. Occasionally, RAM may be used for storing instructions. This is done to improve the instruction fetch speed or to support modifiable instructions. Generally, however, we prefer to avoid such things. Once again the instructions are called firmware because they are not intended to be changed.

The size of the RAM area is determined at design time. Thus, loading can only be determined after the design is completed. Memory loading is computed by dividing the number of user locations by the maximum allowable RAM area. Doing so gives

$$M_R = \frac{U_R}{T_R} \tag{14.4}$$

Stack Area

The stack area is the portion of memory space used to store context information and auto variables. Depending on the design, one may have multiple stacks in this area of memory. From the point of view of the memory loading calculations, it is modeled as one single stack. The capacity is generally determined at design time, and the size is based on use at runtime. For the current calculations, one can establish a bound. Assume a maximum number of tasks and call that number t_{max}. Next assume a maximum allocation for each task. Call the allocation $s_{max.}$ From these, the maximum stack size can be computed as

$$U_S = S_{max} \bullet T_{max} \tag{14.5}$$

Memory loading is computed by dividing U_S by the maximum allocated stack area to yield

$$M_R = \frac{U_R}{T_R} \tag{14.6}$$

With memory allocation, remember, Occam's razor applies—never allocate more space than necessary. Most operating systems allow for user control over the stack size. Specify a size, based on your analysis, that is large enough to get the job done without being too large. Be certain to understand the problem, for stack overflow can be dangerous. If you are developing multithreaded to multitasking applications without a purchased kernel, carefully manage how the stack is allocated and deallocated.

14.14 EVALUATING PERFORMANCE

When analyzing and quantifying the performance of any system, we are interested in the best information available. Of course, exact times are preferred if they are computable or measurable: otherwise bounded times can be used if exact numbers are not available. This can be accomplished by using any of a variety of methods. In our discussion of time loading above, three techniques for acquiring performance information were identified: analytical modeling, simulation, and measurement.

The key consideration in deciding which of these to use is the stage in the development cycle that the system is in. Measurement is possible only if the system or one similar to the proposed system already exists. Otherwise, analytic modeling or simulation are the only alternatives. A set of criteria for selecting an evaluation technique is presented in Table 14.2.

One must remember that any performance measurement is valid only when it is considered in the context of the environment; it is the environment that establishes the system workload. Performance analysis cannot be delayed until the design is completed and the product is ready to ship. At that time it is too late and the cost of recovery may be too high.

Table 14.2 Evaluating Performance Methods, Stages, and Criterion

Criterion	Analytic Modeling	Simulation	Measurement
Stage	Any	Any	Post-prototype
Time Required	Small	Medium	Varies
Tools	Analysis	Computer Languages	Instrumentation
Accuracy	Low	Moderate	Varies
Trade-off Evaluation	Easy	Moderate	Difficult
Cost	Small	Medium	High
Scalability	Low	Medium	High

EARLY STAGES

During the early stages of a design, very often one is constrained to use modeling techniques. When developing that model, the following should be considered.

- The model should be hierarchical. In this way, a complex system can be modeled by decomposing it into simpler parts. Useful techniques include progressive refinement, abstraction, and the reuse of existing (known) components.
- The model should be able to express concurrent and temporal interdependencies among physical and modeled elements. With such an ability, one can begin to understand the dynamic performance of the system and the interactions among the constituent elements.
- Ideally, the model should be graphical; such a presentation makes interaction easier. This is not absolutely necessary, however.
- The model should have parameters that permit worst case and scenario analysis. Thus, boundary condition analyses can be performed.
- The model should support movement in time. That is, one should be able to (repeatedly) verify the performance of the system model forwards and backwards in time.

MIDSTAGES

During the midstages of the design, real components are becoming available. One can begin using prototype modules and integrating them into subsystems.

LATER STAGES

During the later stages of the development, one can begin integrating the pieces into larger and larger portions of the system. At this time, we are now prepared to begin exercising integrated subsystems.

14.15 THOUGHTS ON PERFORMANCE OPTIMIZATION

When investigating how to improve the performance of a system, one should think of a few obvious things. In this context, we will assume that performance means response time and time loading.

QUESTIONS TO ASK

When optimizing, it is important to think about

- What is being optimized?

  If this question cannot be answered, one should rethink the problem and the design.
- Why is it being optimized?

  What is the intended effect of the optimization?
- What will be the effect on the overall program if the module being optimized is eliminated from the program?

  Presume a module under study has zero execution time or requires no memory. If the effect on the performance of the system is minimal, then there is no point in spending the effort to reduce its execution time or memory requirements.
- Is the optimization appropriate to the operating context?

  Don't optimize for floating point performance if the system is intended to work only with integers.

14.16 PERFORMANCE OPTIMIZATION

Let's now look at a few ways by which one can begin to improve system performance. Once again, we will assume that performance means response time and time loading. We will look first at some of the more common mistakes that are often made when assessing and trying to improve performance.

COMMON MISTAKES

When working to improve or optimize the performance of a design, it is easy to be seduced by several common misconceptions. Here are a few.

- Expecting improvement in one aspect of the design to improve the overall performance proportional to improvement.

  The context in which one is working must be understood. A 100% improvement in an aspect of a design that contributes to only 1% of the overall performance is going to have minimal large-scale impact.
- Using hardware independent metrics to predict performance.

  A good example is code size. A large executable module does not necessarily imply a slower program; often, we trade off one parameter, such as size, for another, such as speed. Remember the difference between macros or inline definitions and subroutines.

  When we use a macro or inline function body, we are doing so for speed. We are making a conscious decision to trade off increased memory for additional speed. With an inline definition, the cost (in time) of the function call is eliminated—no stack frame to create or destroy, no copying of variables, and so on.
- Using peak performance.

  This is the classic "your mileage may vary" situation. Peak performance is just that; it's a boundary value. It is useful information and allows one to make limiting statements about a design. By knowing the peak performance of the system, one knows that over a wide range of contexts, one will not be able to do better. These values are approached asymptotically.

- Comparing performance based on a couple of metrics.

  Examples are clock rate, instruction per clock cycles, or instruction count. Higher clock rate or more instructions per cycle does not guarantee better performance. Recall the early Pentium processors. They were the last of the family optimized for 16-bit word size. As the succeeding generation was introduced, people found that a 16-bit program would actually execute faster on the older machines—with a lower clock rate—than on the new ones.

- Using synthetic benchmarks.

  Code can be optimized to excel on any benchmark; however, these are probably never encountered in the real world. This is standard practice. Be sure to read the fine print.

14.17 TRICKS OF THE TRADE

Response times and time loading can be reduced in a number of ways. Here are a couple of simple ones.

1. Perform measurements and computations at a rate and significance that is consistent with the rate of change and values of the data, the type of arithmetic, and the number of significant digits calculated. Often in embedded applications, we are interacting with the external world. Temperature, for example, is typically a very slowly changing entity. Measuring change at a sampling interval greater than 1 second is wasting CPU cycles.
2. Use lookup tables or combinational logic.

   Lookup is much faster than computing or making a measurement, scaling data, or converting from one form to another.
3. Certain arithmetic calculations can be implemented through shifting operations rather than using a standard mathematical computation. Scaling a value by a constant is a logical operation. Use table lookup. Multiplying two integers is also a combinational logic problem. Store the product in a ROM and look the answer up.
4. Learn from the compiler experts. Compiler writers commonly use many tricks to reduce code size and to improve speed performance. Be careful at the same time.

   Optimizing can also cause problems. For example, one may be unpleasantly surprised if a value is put into a register, assuming that it will be there and unchanged and not have to be reloaded, only to find out several instructions later that this is not so. The value of the variable may have been modified by some other routine. One has the same problem with shared variables. C++ has the volatile and const qualifiers to deal with such situations.
5. Loop Management

Loop-invariant optimization

Precalculate any values that will not change within a block of repeated code. Some good compilers will already do this. Use a precomputed value rather than recompute the value each time. Such a technique can be particularly significant if the operand requires an indirect memory access, for example. Another case occurs when working with several arrays in which the indices differ by integer value.

The code can easily be rewritten and simplified using pointers

```
int offset = 0;
for(i = 0; i < k; i++)
{
  for(j = 0; i < m; j++)
  {
        *(aPtr + offset) = *(bPtr + offset) + *(cPtr + offset);
        offset++;
  }
}
```

The code fragment assumes starting at index 0 for all arrays.

Unroll loops

Consider the following simple code fragment.

```
for(j = 0; j < 4; j++)
a[j] = a[j]*8;
```

The loop can be unrolled in several ways.

CASE 1

```
a[0] = a[0]*8;
a[1] = a[1]*8;
a[2] = a[2]*8;
a[3] = a[3]*8;
```

CASE 2

```
for(j = 0; j < 2; j++)
{
  a[j] = a[j]*8;
  a[j+1] = a[j+1]*8;
}
```

Loops and Arrays

Arrays are a commonly used data structure. A simple modification in how they are accessed can have large impact on performance. Consider the following code fragment.

```
for(j = 0; j < x + 3 ; j++)
{
  a[j] = b[j] + c[j];
}
```

Observe that the test parameter is computed with each iteration of the loop. For a large value of x, such an operation can accumulate substantial time. A good compiler should spot and optimize the computed value in test parameter.

Without relying on the compiler, move the computation outside of the context of loop.

```
int tempVar = x + 3;
for(j = 0; j < tempVar ; j++)
{
  a[j] = b[j] + c[j];
}
```

Now the value of tempVar is computed just a single time.

Nested Loops

Let's modify the preceding example into a nested loop on several multidimensional arrays.

```
for(i = 0; i < k; i++)
{
  for(j = 0; i < m; j++)
  {
       a[i][j] = b[i][j] + c[i][j];
  }
}
```

6. Flow of control optimization.

When using branches or switches, avoid repeated jumps or tests. Consider the following assembly code fragment.

```
Instead of…
je $2
$1: ...
$2:     jmp $3  ...
We write…
je $3
$1: ...
$2:     jmp $3  ...
```

For the following C code fragment, instead of the first fragment, we write the second. It may also be possible to set x to value before switch and only change if necessary.

```
switch (y)
{
case 0: x = x+1;
case 1: x = x+2;
case 2: x = x+1;
}

switch (y)
{
case 0:
case 2: x = x+1;
case 1: x = x+2;
}
```

In the next code fragment, the first implementation is replaced with the second.

```
while(1)
{
if (light==ON)
        light = OFF;
else
        light = ON;
}
while(1)
light = ~light;
```

7. Use registers and caches.
Languages such as C and C++ support register-type variables. It is usually advantageous to utilize such types. Register operations are faster than memory operations. When working with C or C++, register qualification on variable declaration requests that the compiler put the variable into the register. Although there is no guarantee that the compiler will comply, one can ensure that the variables are placed into registers by writing the code in assembler.
   Some processors support caching. Use caching to store frequently used variables. Access from the cache is more rapid than access from general-purpose memory.
8. Use only necessary values.
An early implementation of tracking mouse movement in X Windows entailed generating a series of interrupts as the mouse was moved from one place to another. Such a scheme was quickly replaced when the performance turned out to be reasonably glacial.
   As another example, consider moving a graphic image from one place on a screen to another. Rather than redrawing the complete image several dozen times, we only reflect a graphic wire frame during movement. A similar situation exists when slewing a variable from one value to a second. Typically, one is only concerned about the final value; the system can be designed with such a recognition.
9. Optimize a common path or frequently used code block. The most frequently used path or highly used code segment should be the most highly optimized.
10. Use page mode accesses.
For main memory accesses, set the row address and modify only the column address, in essence moving pages / blocks of data.
11. Know when to use recursion vs. iteration.
It is important to know when to use recursion. Some obvious places include processing recursive data structures or in divide and conquer algorithms. Such algorithms divide a problem into subproblems, solve each subproblem recursively, and combine the individual subproblem solutions.
   When should iteration be used instead? Such times include nonrecursive data structures, problems without an obvious recursive structure, and functions with a large "footprint," especially when many iterations are needed.
   In theory, any iteration can be rewritten using recursion, and vice versa (at least in theory). However, the rewrite is not always simple. Iteration is generally more efficient, faster, and takes less memory. As a compromise, if the problem is naturally recursive, first design the algorithm recursively and then convert to an iterative solution if needed for efficiency.

Suppose the last action of a function is to make a call back to itself. In a stack-based implementation, local variables are pushed onto the stack when the function (recursive) call is initiated. When the function terminates, the values for the local variables will be popped off the stack and restored. Doing this last step is pointless since the recursive call was the last operation of function. The values that just got restored are discarded.

When the last action of function is a recursive call to itself, it is not necessary to use the stack since no local variables need to be saved. Instead, on entering the function for the first time, declare and initialize a set of working variables to the values of the incoming parameters. After each pass through the repeated code, modify the working variables as appropriate and branch to the beginning of the function.

If the last executed statement of a function is a recursive call to the function itself, the call can be eliminated by assigning the calling parameters to the values specified in the recursive call and then repeating the whole function.

A recursive call is at the very end of the function known as *tail recursion*. It is easy for a smart compiler to automatically rewrite the function using iteration.

12. Macros and Inlining Functions

Each function call requires that a stack frame be built to store the necessary information about the current context so that it may be restored on return. Such a process can be very expensive, particularly in situations with tight time constraints.

The C language supports macros based on the #define directive. Such a directive allows the body of the function to be placed directly inline in the code, thereby avoiding the cost of a function call.

When used in such a way, the #define directive declares the macro and a formal parameter list. The parameterized macro is invoked by writing its name, a left parenthesis, one actual argument for each formal parameter, separated by commas, followed by a right parenthesis. If there are no formal parameters, one must include an empty argument list. White space may appear between the name and the left parenthesis.

EXAMPLE 14.5

```
#define sum(x,y) ((x) + (y))
// On expansion, the expression for sum in all cases
// will be replaced by the macro body (x + y)

x = sum(2•a, b) / sum (c,d); → (2•a + b) / (c + d)

x = sum(2•g(a,b), h(a,b)) / sum (c,d); → (2•g(a,b) + h(a,b)) / (c + d)
```

The #undef macro is the companion to #define. It is used to make the name of the macro, *myMacro*, for example, no longer defined. The #undef causes the preprocessor to forget the macro definition of *myMacro*. Once *myMacro* is undefined, it can be given a new definition using #define.

myMacro

inline

The C++ language supports a similar construct called *inline*. The motivation is the same—that is, to avoid the cost of a function call by replacing the function call with the function body. Like other optimization techniques, we always have a trade-off. Here, the trade-off is increased memory size for better speed performance.

14.18 HARDWARE ACCELERATORS

hardware accelerator

One technique that can be used to gain significant performance increase with respect to a software implementation is to move some of the functionality to hardware. Such a collection of components is called a *hardware accelerator.* The accelerator is often attached to the CPU bus. Communication with the CPU is accomplished through many of the same techniques that have already been discussed:

- Shared variables

  Implemented as data and control registers located in accelerator
- Shared memory locations

  We may use DMA

Using shared locations comes with all of the problems that we discussed earlier. The shared variables must be managed using semaphores, monitors, or some other scheme.

An accelerator is distinguished from a co-processor. The accelerator does not generally execute instructions; its interface appears as I/O. It is designed to perform a specific function and is generally implemented as an ASIC, FPGA, or CPLD. With increasing capabilities in today's arrayed logics, however, the distinction between the accelerator and a co-processor is diminishing. Typically, a co-processor is tightly integrated with the CPU and has the ability to execute instructions.

Hardware accelerators are used when there are functions whose operations do not map well onto the CPU. Possible examples include

- Bit and bit field operations
- Differing precisions of arithmetic calculations
- Very high-speed arithmetic
- FFT calculations
- Multiplies
- Very high-speed or associative search
- High-demand input or output operations, with tight timing constraints and high throughput
- Streaming applications including high-speed audio and video. With such applications, delays in the time domain translate directly to distortion in the frequency domain.

14.19 OPTIMIZING FOR POWER CONSUMPTION

Today more and more embedded applications are targeted toward small hand-held or other types of portable devices. A common thread through all such applications is the need for longer and longer battery life. This requirement translates to low power consumption and makes the job more interesting and challenging.

Advanced Configuration and Power Interface (ACPI)

Power consumption can be addressed in several ways. Certainly one hardware solution for devices with low power requirements is to turn portions of the system off. The *Advanced Configuration and Power Interface* (ACPI) is an international standard for such applications. Surprisingly there can be a software contribution to power reduction as well.

14.19.1 Software

A number of places can be examined from the software point of view. Some of the initial places to look include

- The algorithms that are used
- The location of the code (memory accesses can have significant impact on power consumption.)
- Use of software to control various subsystems

To be able to analyze and then control a particular aspect of performance, one must be able to measure that aspect both before and after the modification.

14.19.1.1 Measuring Power Consumption

For the moment, assume that the goal is to reduce power consumed by processor. To such an end, measuring power consumption is a two-step process.

Measure

1. Identify the portion of the code to be analyzed. Typically, this will be a loop of one form or another, but it does not need to be.
2. Measure the current consumed by the processor while the code is being exercised.
3. Modify the loop such that the code comprising the loop is disabled. Ensure that the compiler has not optimized the loop or section of code out.
4. Measure the current consumed by the processor.

Reduce

Once the amount of power consumed has been identified, the next step is to try to reduce it if appropriate or possible. Studies have identified several software factors that can contribute to processor power consumption.

Among the contributors are found

- The kind of instruction
- The collection or sequence of instructions executed
- The locations of the instructions and their operands

Memory systems and transfers in and out of main memory have been shown to be the most expensive operations (in terms of power) performed by the processor. This is typically the DRAM in the system. Using a simple addition operation as a reference, Catthoor et al. (Catthoor 1998) illustrate the relative power consumption for commercial operations. Their data is presented in Table 14.3.

Table 14.3 Relative Power Consumption for Common Processor Operations

Operation	Relative Power Consumption
16-Bit Add	1
16-Bit Multiply	3.6
8x128x16 SRAM Read	4.4
8x128x16 SRAM Write	9
I/O Access	10
16-Bit DRAM Memory Transfer	33

After examining the SRAM operations in the table, it is evident that using cache can have a significant effect on system power consumption. These numbers assume a cache hit; a cache miss requires main memory access. SRAM generally consumes more power than DRAM on a per-cell basis, and the cache is generally SRAM. The size of the cache should be optimized to reflect the minimum size that gives the required temporal performance. This almost becomes an empirical process.

Other optimizations include the following.

1. Power aware compilers.

   These take an instruction-level view of the problem and modify the schedule of bus activity.
2. Use registers efficiently.

   Bring a value into the register and leave it there for reuse.
3. Look for cache conflicts and eliminate them if possible.

   For instruction conflicts, rewrite the code if possible. It may be necessary to move the code. For scalar data conflicts, the data can be moved to different locations. Arrayed data can also be moved to an alternative location or the access pattern can be changed.
4. Unroll loops.

   One must be careful that the unrolled loop does not result in cache misses, however.
5. Eliminate recursive procedures where possible, thereby eliminating the overhead of a function call.

14.19.2 Hardware

Another technique for managing the power consumption in embedded applications draws from familiar schemes that are often used at home. Turn off the portions of the system that are not being used. Such a scheme has been used for years in the space program in both orbital and interplanetary satellites as well as the shuttle and the *Mercury, Gemini,* and *Apollo* capsules. Therein the hardware is battery powered. The batteries must be recharged, which is done via solar panels for such space-borne systems.

Today it is possible to fly from Seattle to Japan in 9 hours. A laptop computer or other such tools have a typical battery life of 3 to 5 hours. Absolutely, a laptop is still an embedded application. As engineers, we are in a continuous race between battery technology and the demand for more and more powerful features. All such features require power.

14.19.2.1 Power Management Schemes

To begin to address the problem as part of the design, one must formulate power management strategy at the outset. This is exactly the same approach taken when examining safety and reliability issues and when studying system test.

At one extreme, it is possible to simply turn power off. In such a state, power consumption is limited to leakage. As with other metrics, this sets a lower bound on consumption. The opposite extreme is to apply power to all parts of the system and make certain that all parts are operating. In such a state, power consumption approaches its maximum. Such a condition sets an upper bound, which is softer than the lower bound; to see why, refer back to the earlier discussion on the software effects on power. The goal is somewhere in the middle, governed, once again, by the requirements specification.

Based on such a goal, the system components can be segregated into two categories: those that must remain powered up and those that may be powered down. The first are referred to as *static components* and the second as *dynamic components*.

static, dynamic components

Such a scheme sounds simple, and it is at the high level. Like everything else being considered, certain trade-offs can be made. One must

1. Decide which portions of the system to power down. These may be all dynamic components or subgroups based on need.
2. Recognize that components cannot be shut down instantly.
3. Recognize that components cannot be powered up instantly.

These factors can be expressed with a simple first cut graphically as seen in Figure 14.30.

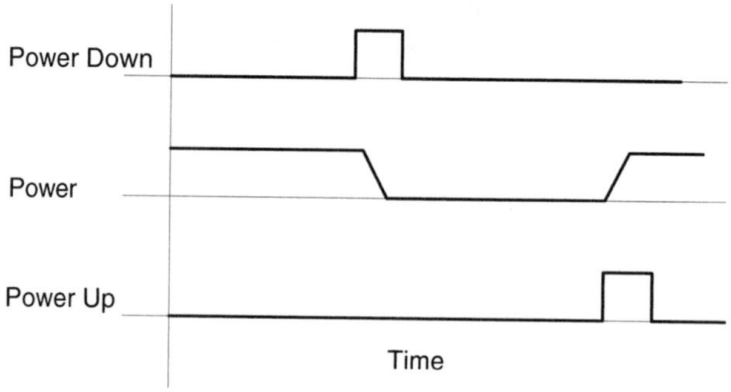

Figure 14.30 Basic for a System Power Down–Power Up Sequence

We use a topographic mapping satellite as the application. As the satellite is circling the Earth collecting data, data is sent to a ground station at known points in the orbit when the satellite is over the appropriate station. There is no reason to keep the transmitter powered up when it is not in a position to transmit. Furthermore, the timing of the orbit is known with sufficient resolution that one can know in advance when one will need to transmit. After passing the ground station, the transmitter is shut down and reenabled shortly before reaching the next download point. Such a fixed schedule scheme is among the simplest and can be very effective. Observe that it is similar to the round robin schedule with no preemption.

The next level of sophistication is to recognize that the schedule may not be fixed. The problem now moves from deterministic to probabilistic. Knowledge of the current history of the system and an understanding of the problem can be used to anticipate when to shut dynamic portions of the system down. Such an approach is denoted *predictive shutdown*. Observe that such a scheme is commonly used in branch prediction logic in an instruction prefetch pipeline. Use of such a scheme can involve premature shutdown or restart.

predictive shutdown

A related idea is to control the algorithm with an associated timer rather than a set schedule. The timer monitors the activities of devices to be dynamically controlled. If the timer expires, the device is powered down. The device is reactivated on demand. We have already used such a scheme in a watchdog timer. One can also find the scheme in personal computers, which, among other things, bring up a screen saver if no activity is detected for a while.

The next level of sophistication draws from basic queuing theory. Under such a scheme, a resource or *producer* and a *service* are provided by a system whose power is being controlled. There is also a *consumer*, the portion of the system that needs the service and a queue of service requests. A power manager monitors behavior of the system (the producer, the consumer, and the queue). The power manager can utilize a schedule based on

producer, service

consumer

Markov modeling, for example, which maximizes system computational performance while satisfying the specified power budget.

Let's look at an example of simple power management from Pedram (2001). A simple data/control flow diagram appears in Figure 14.31.

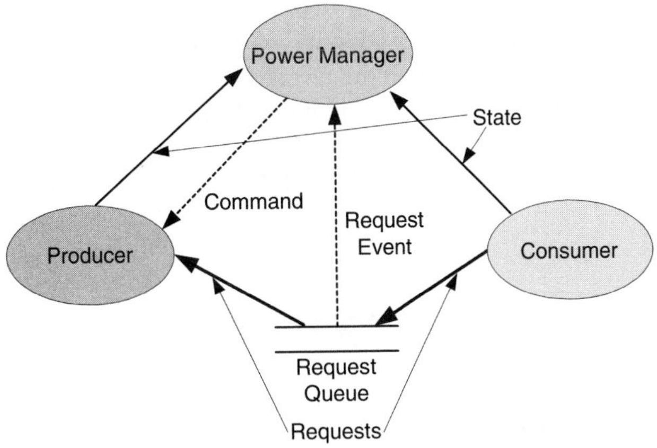

Figure 14.31 Data/Control Flow Diagram for a Queue-Based Power Management Model (Derived from Pedram 2001)

EXAMPLE 14.6

The operating system is responsible for dynamically controlling the power in a simple I/O subsystem. The dynamically controlled portion supports two modes, OFF and ON. The dynamic subcomponents consume 10 watts when on and 0 watts when off.

Switching takes 2 seconds and consumes 40 joules to switch from the OFF state to the ON state and 1 second and 10 joules to switch from ON to OFF. The request has a period of 25 seconds.

Graphically, three alternative schemes are illustrated in Figure 14.32,

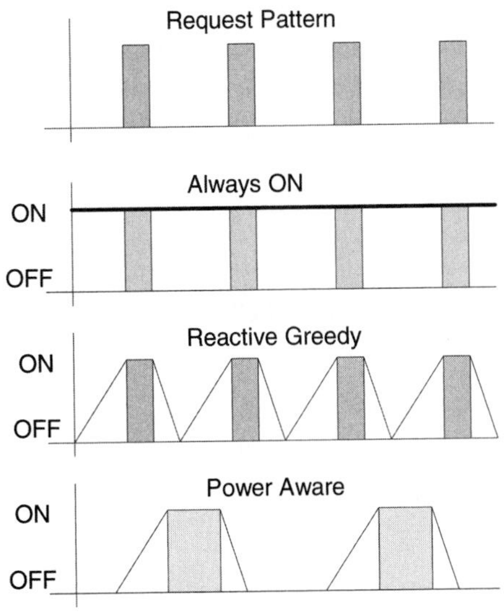

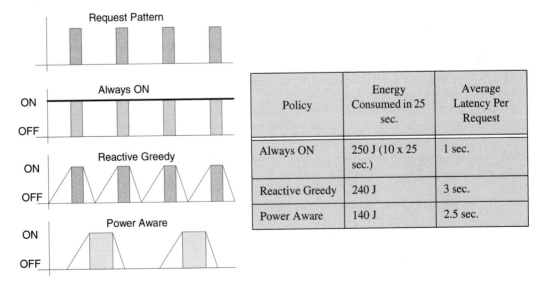

Policy	Energy Consumed in 25 sec.	Average Latency Per Request
Always ON	250 J (10 x 25 sec.)	1 sec.
Reactive Greedy	240 J	3 sec.
Power Aware	140 J	2.5 sec.

Figure 14.32 Three Alternative Schemes for Dynamic System Power Management © 2001 IEEE

Observe that we have the same average throughput, with substantially reduced power consumption.

14.19.2.2 Advanced Configuration and Power Interface—ACPI

The Advanced Configuration and Power Interface (ACPI) is an industry standard power management scheme that was initially applied to the PC and more specifically Windows™. In recent years, it has been targeted to an increasingly wider variety of operating systems.

The standard provides some basic power management facilities as well as an interface to the hardware. The software, more specifically the operating system, provides a power management module. It is the responsibility of the OS to specify the power management policy for the system. The operating system uses the ACPI module to send the required controls to the hardware and to monitor the state of the hardware as an input to the power manager. The behavior of the ACPI scheme is expressed in the state diagram in Figure 14.33.

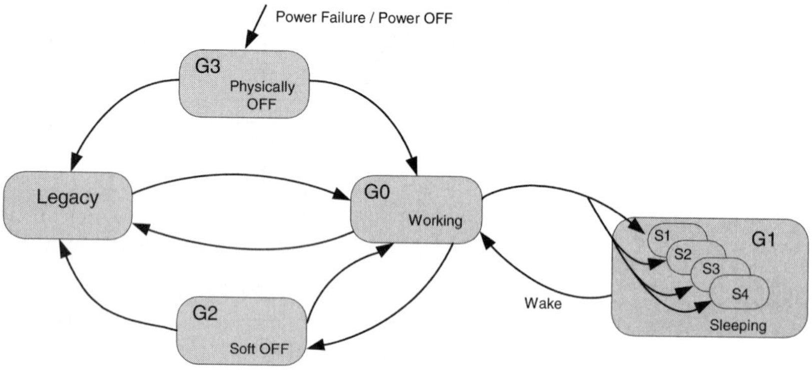

Figure 14.33 ACPI Standard Block Diagram (Drawing Adapted from ACPI standard)

The standard supports five global power states.

1. G3—hard off or full off.
   Defined as a physically off state—the system consumes no power.
2. G2—soft off requires full OS reboot to restore system to full operational condition.
3. G1—sleeping state—the system appears to be off. The time required to return to an operational condition is inversely proportional to power consumption.

   Substates

   S1—low wakeup latency—ensures no loss of system context.

   S2—low wakeup latency state—has loss of CPU and system cache state.

   S3—low wakeup latency state—all system state except for main memory is lost.

   S4—lowest power sleeping state—all devices are off.
4. G0—working state in which the system is fully usable.
5. Legacy state—the system does not comply with ACPI.

14.20 CACHES AND PERFORMANCE

Based on the locality of reference characteristic of most contemporary programs, one can use small amounts of high-speed memory to hold a subset of the instructions and data for immediate use. Such a scheme gives the illusion that the program has unlimited amounts of high-speed memory. In fact, the bulk of the instructions and data are held in memory with much longer cycle/access times than available in the system CPU.

One major problem in real-time embedded applications is that cache behavior is nondeterministic. It is difficult to predict when there will be a cache miss or hit. As a consequence, it is difficult to set reasonable upper bounds on execution times for tasks. In the extreme case, one can certainly assume that every access is a miss; this is overly pessimistic. One can also be the optimist and assume that every access is a hit; this is folly.

The problem is rooted in two sources: conditional branches and shared access with preemption. Today, there are a number of very good branch prediction algorithms. Nonetheless, one cannot know for certain, in advance, which branch will be taken—not even Robert Frost. Such knowledge is important because one path may be a cache hit and the other may cause a cache miss.

The path taken and a successful cache access may vary with iteration. The problem is exacerbated with pipelined architectures. Pipelining techniques are used to prefetch data and instructions while other activities are taking place. The selection of an alternate branch requires that the pipe be flushed and refilled. A side effect is the potential for a cache miss, thereby extending the time delay.

In a multitasking or interrupt context, one task may preempt another. In such a context, the preempting task may require different blocks of data or instruction, with the consequence that we may get a significant number of cache misses as tasks switch. A similar situation arises during the instruction cycle in a von Neumann machine. In such a machine, instructions and data share the same physical memory. With such an architecture, one may force cache misses based on instruction and data fetches.

Let's elaborate on the problem of shared access. Consider a direct mapping caching scheme. Recall that blocks or lines from main memory are mapped into cache modulo the cache size. If we have a 1K cache with blocks of 64 words, such blocks from main memory addresses 0, 1024, 2048, and so on, are all going to map to block 0 in cache.

Let's assume the following memory map. Instructions are loaded starting at location 1024, and data is loaded starting at location 8192. Consider the accompanying simple code fragment.

```
for (i = 0; i < 10; i++)
{
    a[i] = b[i] + 4;
}
```

On first access, the instruction access will miss and bring in the appropriate block from main memory. The instruction will execute and have to bring in data. The data access will miss and bring in the appropriate block from main memory. Because block 0 is occupied, the data block will overwrite the instructions in cache block 0. On the second access, the instruction access will again miss and bring in the appropriate block from main memory. The miss occurs because the instructions had been overwritten by the incoming data. The instruction will execute and have to bring in the data again. The data access will also miss again and bring in appropriate block from main memory again. Because block 0 is again occupied, the data block will overwrite block 0 again. The process will repeat, thereby causing serious performance degradation. In fact, performance is actually worse with cache. Not only do we now have the main memory accesses, but we also have the time burden of searching and managing the cache. The continued main memory accesses can also increase the power consumption of the system.

Possible solutions to the shared access problem under a cache-based design include the following.

1. Use a set associative rather than a direct mapping scheme, which can help to mitigate some of the effects of the direct mapping scheme.
2. Move to a Harvard or Aiken architecture.
3. Support an instruction cache and a data cache.

The advantage of the last-named approach is that one can support multiple accesses per clock cycle. The two caches can be designed to different criteria and also utilize different architectures, for example, direct and set associative.

Smart Memory Allocation for Real Time (SMART)

One scheme that may be used to address the preemption problem is to give each task its own portion of cache. Such a scheme is called a *Smart Memory Allocation for Real Time* (SMART) cache. Cache can be decomposed into restricted portions and a common portion. A critical task is assigned a restricted portion(s) on start-up. All cache accesses are restricted to those partitions and to the common area. The task retains exclusive rights to the restricted areas until it terminates or is aborted. Such a restriction includes preemption by other tasks. The method for assigning partitions remains an open problem. Various heuristic schemes have been explored and utilized.

14.21 TRADE-OFFS

Often, improved performance is an optimization issue that involves trading several contradictory requirements. Such requirements may include speed, memory size, cost, weight, or power. We must spend time at the start of a design to thoroughly understand the application and any associated constraints.

14.22 SUMMARY

In this chapter, we have studied several measures of performance in embedded systems. We began with the vocabulary we use to talk about performance and then introduced several common measures. Those measures started at a high level with big-O analysis and then moved to a lower level of detail when we examined the performance of common flow of control constructs. We looked at several metrics for assessing embedded performance such as response time, time loading, and memory loading. We concluded with an assessment of how a cache can affect performance and with an introduction to power management, including several ways to reduce power consumption.

14.23 REVIEW QUESTIONS

Performance

14.1 What is meant by the performance of an embedded application?

14.2 What is the difference between an optimization and a trade-off?

14.3 Does performance optimization apply equally to the hardware and software components comprising an embedded system?

14.4 What is Amdahl's law?

Complexity Analysis

14.5 What is meant by the expression "complexity analysis"?

14.6 What is the purpose of performing a complexity analysis on a software algorithm?

14.7 What are the basic steps that make up a complexity analysis?

14.8 What is big-O notation?

Analyzing Instructions

14.9 Identify the major factors that can affect the time performance of an instruction.

14.10 What is a reasonable scope for performing an instruction analysis within an embedded application?

Performance Metrics

14.11 In an embedded application, what is meant by the term *response time*? *throughput*? *memory loading*? *time loading*?

14.12 For each of the performance metrics identified in Question 14.11, suggest one means by which we can measure the value of the metric.

14.13 Identify and describe the three major components of a response time analysis of a polled loop.

14.14 Identify and describe the major components of a response time analysis of a preemptive schedule in an embedded application.

14.15 What is a memory map?

14.16 When should a performance analysis be conducted on an embedded application?

Performance Optimization Considerations

14.17 What are some of the important questions that one should ask both before and during a performance optimization analysis?

14.18 What are some of the common mistakes that might be made during a performance optimization analysis?

14.19 What is a hardware accelerator? How does it differ from a co-processor?

14.20 Why is power usage included in performance?

14.21 What are some of the effects that the embedded software can have on power usage?

14.22 How can we measure the effect that a software algorithm can have on power consumption?

14.23 What are some of the effects that the embedded software can have on power usage?

14.24 THOUGHT QUESTIONS

Performance

14.1 Identify the major criteria by which the performance of an embedded application may be measured. Do these criteria apply to all embedded applications?

14.2 Give an example of an embedded application in which one or more of the criteria listed in Question 14.1 would be considered important. For each identified application and criteria, why are the criteria considered to be important? What are the consequences for failure to meet the criteria?

14.3 Discuss the stages during the development process at which we should conduct a performance analysis? Explain why you have selected each stage of the development cycle. What are several criteria that should be used during the analysis?

14.4 What information do we gain when applying Amdahl's law to the problem of performance optimization?

Complexity Analysis

14.5 Explain the difference between linear, quadratic, logarithmic, and exponential growth with respect to a software algorithm.

14.6 What does the term *asymptotic complexity* mean? Give an example.

14.7 We use various types of containers in an embedded application to hold data. We can read, insert, or delete data from the top, bottom, or middle of a container. Discuss the effect on the performance of an algorithm when using each of the four major containers that we have studied.

14.8 What is a reasonable scope for performing a big-O analysis within an embedded application?

Analyzing Instructions

14.9 Big-O analysis gives a macro view of program performance; analysis of blocks of instructions gives a micro view. What kind of information are we trying to gain with respect to an embedded application from each type of analysis?

14.10 Should the time performance of a block of instructions be analyzed at the source code (e.g., C or C++. assembly) or object code level? Why?

Performance Metrics

14.11 Describe the methods by which we can perform a time loading analysis of an embedded application. Discuss the advantages and disadvantages of each.

14.12 The chapter presents several alternative models we may use in analyzing the performance of an embedded application. Describe each and elaborate on the kind of information we are trying to gain from each model.

14.13 How can one use a microprocessor's built-in timer to aid in a performance analysis?

14.14 A memory map is said to be useful in performing a memory loading analysis. How might this be done?

Performance Optimization Considerations

14.15 The chapter identified several "tricks of the trade" that might be utilized to help reduce time loading and response times. What are these? Discuss why such techniques might be useful.

14.16 When should one consider using a hardware accelerator in an embedded design? Give several examples and identify the benefit in each case.

14.17 Discuss the effects of caching and virtual memory schemes on the time performance of an embedded application.

14.18 Give several pros and cons of caching and virtual memory schemes in an embedded application.

14.19 Cite several examples of instances when caching might be useful and explain why.

14.20 Identify and discuss several schemes that we can use to optimize power usage in an embedded application. An Internet search might reveal some interesting answers.

14.21 What is the Advanced Configuration and Power Interface standard? Does or can it apply to embedded applications?

14.22 Can the embedded systems memory organization affect the performance of an embedded system? How?

14.25 PROBLEMS

14.1 Compute the time loading for the two independent nested loops given in the code fragment presented in Figure 14.34.

```
int j, k, sum = 0;
for ( j = 0; j < N; j++ )
     for ( k = N; k > 0; k-- )
          sum += k + j;
```

Figure P14.34

14.2 Repeat Problem 14.1 for the two interdependent nested loops given in Figure 14.35.

```
int j, k, sum = 0;
for ( j = 0; j < N; j++ )
     for ( k = 0; k < j; k++ )
          sum = sum + k * j;
```

Figure P14.35

14.3 Design and implement a recursive function that computes the factorial of N numbers. Implement the same function using an iterative design. Compare the time loading for N having the values 10, 100, and 1000.

14.4 The binary search algorithm has a worst case complexity of $O(\log_2 N)$ when N is the size of the search range. Provide the complexity analysis to show that this is correct.

14.5 The quick sort algorithm has a worst case complexity of $O(N \log_2 N)$ when N is the size of the search range. Provide the complexity analysis to show that this is correct.

14.6 Compute the time complexity for the following operations on the queue data structure.

- Insert/delete at the beginning
- Insert/delete at the end
- Insert/delete in the middle
- Access at the beginning, the end, and in the middle

14.7 Repeat Problem 14.6 for the stack data structure.

14.8 Examine and analyze an assembly language implementation of passing a single variable into a function via the stack. Compare the time loading for such an operation with accessing the same information using a global variable. Discuss the advantages and disadvantages of each approach.

14.9 A simple embedded application is using a schedule based on polling with a timing element. What is the smallest timing element that the system will support using one of the built-in timers? using a delay loop written as a series of assembly language instructions?

14.10 An embedded application utilizes an external interrupt to signal that an event has occurred. In response to the event, the application must perform an action following a delay.

(a) What is the smallest delay that can be accommodated if the delay is implemented as a series of assembly instructions? What is the worst case error?

(b) What is the smallest delay if a timer is used? What is the worst case error?

14.11 Distortion in the frequency domain in an FFT is determined, in part, by errors in sampling in the time domain. For your system, what is the best-case error, in time, if the analog-to digital converter readings are

(a) Scheduled using an interrupt from one of your system timers?

(b) Scheduled using a delay implemented as a series of assembly language instructions?

(c) Scheduled by polling the timer interrupt?

What are the advantages and disadvantages of each approach?

14.12 Design and build a linked list ADT. Compute the complexity to add/delete an element from the head, the tail, and the middle of the linked list. Perform the computation on a linked list of the following sizes: 10, 100, 1000.

14.13 Design and build a queue ADT using an array, a linked list, and a binary tree as the underlying data structure. Compute the complexity to add/delete an element from the tail or the head of the queue for each implementation. Perform the computations on a queue of the following sizes: 10, 100, 1000.

14.14 Design and build an array-based priority queue ADT using an array, a linked list, and a binary tree as the underlying data structure. Compute the complexity to add/delete an element from the tail or the head of the queue for each implementation. Perform the computations on a queue of the following sizes: 10, 100, 1000. How do the complexity and time change if the queue is sorted?

14.15 Design and build a priority queue ADT using a heap as the underlying data structure. Compute the complexity to add/delete an element from the tail or the head of the queue for each implementation. Perform the computations on a queue of the following sizes: 10, 100, 1000. How do the complexity and time change if the queue is sorted? Does the order in which the data is entered affect the time loading? If so, by how much?

14.16 Write an algorithm *min3* that uses a series of nested if statements to determine the smallest of three integer values that have been passed as parameters. Using your processor's assembly language manual, determine the execution time of the algorithm.

14.17 Write the *min3* algorithm in Problem 14.16 as a C macro and a C function. Design two versions of a program, one that uses *min3* as a macro to determine the smallest of three numbers and the other that uses it as a function. Using your processor's assembly language manual, determine the difference execution time between the two implementations.

What is the difference in memory loading between the two?

14.18 Compare the minimum, average, and maximum time performance between a C switch statement with 10 cases and a series of if-else statements to identify a target from a set of 10 alternative values.

14.19 Design and build a 1-millisecond delay block using C language instructions. Build the same loop using your microprocessor's assembly language instructions. What is the error for each implementation? What is the error in both cases if your delays are used to implement a 10-ms delay? a 100-ms delay?

14.20 Design and build a 1-millisecond delay block using one of your microprocessor's timer. What is the error in the implementation? What is the error if your delay is used to implement a 10-ms delay? a 100-ms delay?

14.21 What are the advantages and disadvantages of the alternative approaches for implementing a delay that were studied in Problems 14.19 and 14.20? Consider the behavior with respect to a hard real-time deadline.

14.22 Write a piece of code that toggles a bit on one of the output ports on your microprocessor each time it is executed. How can this code block be utilized to determine the execution time of a function?

14.23 A colleague has designed an embedded application that utilizes a timer that is supposed to interrupt every 5 ms. She is debugging the code and claims that she cannot determine whether the timer is working properly. Suggest a way she can instrument the code to enable her to determine whether the program is entering the interrupt service routine and, if so, at what interval.

14.24 As with most real-world sensing devices, the thermocouple is a nonlinear device. As a result, we approximate the temperature corresponding to its corresponding output voltage according to a power series equation given as

$$TM = c_0 + c_1V + c_2V^2 + \ldots + c_nV^n$$

where:

V = thermoelectric voltage (microvolts)
c_n = type-dependent polynomial coefficients
T = temperature (C)
n = order of the polynomial

The calculated thermoelectric voltage generated at TM is converted into an equivalent temperature value using such a power series polynomial along with type-dependent coefficient tables.

The National Institute of Standards and Technology (NIST) publishes several tables for each thermocouple type containing coefficients representing quadratic (second order), cubic (third order), or quartic (fourth order). Voltage-to-temperature conversion accuracy can be increased by using higher order coefficient tables, but at the cost of longer processing time to perform the calculations. Accuracy can be further enhanced by selecting tables representing the narrowest temperature range for the specific measurement application.

For a fourth-order polynomial for a J-type thermocouple 0 C to 760 C with error range -0.9°C to 0.7°C, we have the following coefficients.

Coefficients
$c_0 = 0.0$
$c_1 = 1.9323799\text{x}10^{-2}$
$c_2 = -1.0306020\text{x}10^{-7}$
$c_3 = 3.7084018\text{x}10^{-12}$
$c_4 = -5.1031937\text{x}10^{-17}$

The following table gives the output voltage, in microvolts, for the J-type thermocouple for the range 0 C–190 C.

	0	10	20	30	40	50	60	70	80	90
0	0	507	1.019	1.537	2.059	2.585	3.118	3.650	4.187	4.26
100	5.269	5.814	6.360	6.909	7.459	8.010	8.562	9.115	9.669	10.224

Derive a lookup table that converts a measured voltage to the corresponding temperature in one-degree steps. Design an algorithm that utilizes a lookup table to implement the conversion.

(a) Using the instruction times for your processor, compare the time to perform the conversion using the fourth-order equation with that for the lookup table.

(b) Compare the amount of memory required for each of the two alternate approaches.

14.25 Repeat Problem 14.24 using a linear curve fit (y = mx + b) between 10 degree increments. Rather than storing all of the precomputed temperatures, modify the design of the lookup table to hold only the values for m and b.

14.26 The chapter presented an analysis of the time behavior of a polled loop. Determine each value for the constituent times to poll a single event in your system. What are the minimum and maximum times for which you can respond to the event?

14.27 For your system, give a UML sequence diagram for all of the steps required to identify and respond to an external interrupt. What are the minimum and maximum times for which you can respond to the event? What effect will such variation have on a hard real-time schedule?

P14.28 An embedded application initiates the sequence of events illustrated in Figure P14.36.

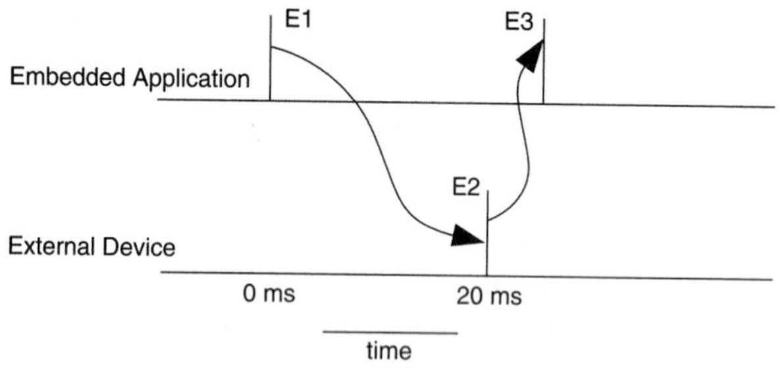

Figure P14.36

(a) For your processor, what are the minimum and maximum times to which you will be able to generate event E3 using polling? using interrupts?

(b) What are the advantages and disadvantages of each approach?

14.29 Using a C struct, design a probe data type that is inserted as a static variable into a function to count the number of times the function has been invoked. Demonstrate the probe on several different functions.

14.30 Extend the probe data type in Problem 14.29 to include two data members, *enter* and *exit*. In conjunction with one of your system timers, use the probe to measure the execution time of several different functions.

14.31 Design a simple application with three or four tasks. Repeat Problem 14.30 to measure the execution time of the different tasks in your design.

14.32 Design a simple application that implements the following:

1. Declares an array, *unsigned short anArray[10000]*.

2. Fills the array with arbitrary data.

3. Contains three functions. Each accesses the array elements via an index and then squares each element in the array, as follows:

(a) Function0, as a C for loop in which each iteration squares one element of the array

(b) Function1, as a C for loop in which each iteration squares two successive elements of the array

(c) Function2, as a C for loop in which each iteration squares four successive elements of the array

4. Contains three functions. Each accesses the array elements via pointer and offset and then squares each element in the array, as follows:

(a) Function3, as a C for loop in which each iteration squares one element of the array

(b) Function4, as a C for loop in which each iteration squares two successive elements of the array

(c) Function5, as a C for loop in which each iteration squares four successive elements of the array.

5. As each function is entered and exited, the function will toggle a bit on an output port on your microprocessor as markers that can be used to measure the length of time needed to perform each calculation.

Compare the results of each of the six test cases in 3a-c and 4a-c.

PART 4 INTERACTING WITH THE PHYSICAL WORLD

Chapter 15

Working Outside of the Processor I: A Model of Interprocess Communication

THINGS TO LOOK FOR . . .

- The extended model of interprocess communication.
- The meaning of information, control, and synchronization, addressing, and transport in the context of external world information exchange.
- Critical components of the shared variable interpretation of the communication model.
- Critical components of the message-based interpretation of the communication model.

15.0 COMMUNICATION AND SYNCHRONIZATION WITH THE OUTSIDE WORLD

A few years ago, an embedded system utilized a microprocessor as the main control element in various kinds of measurement or control systems. Today, in addition to those applications, we have expanded into nearly every corner of the modern world. Yesterday's systems with a processor and a few logic gates have become complex systems comprising potentially several processors, programmable logic devices, networks, communications systems, ASICs, and much more. In addition to the familiar control and measurement elements of yesterday, today we are interfacing to every kind of device imaginable.

In our earlier studies, the tasks, the processes with which we worked, were inside of the microprocessor. In today's distributed designs, some of these processes have migrated to the outside world. That world outside of the processor is a heterogeneous complex of hardware and software that we must understand, be able to talk about, and work with. The requirements for synchronization and for exchanging data and information among tasks inside of the microprocessor persist as we move to the outside. The unpredictability of the physical environment, coupled with the distributed nature and vagaries of the external hardware and software, make communication and synchronization a more interesting and challenging problem.

information, place
control and synchronization,
transport

In this chapter and the next, we will lay the foundation for how an embedded application can interact with the external world. We will begin by extending the internal interprocess and communication model developed earlier in Chapter 4. Our first step will be to introduce the model and to briefly discuss each of its four components: *information, place, control and synchronization,* and *transport*. We will then follow with a more in-depth analysis of each component as we learn the important fundamental aspects of that component and how it can be manifest, in general, in concrete applications.

In the next chapter, we will then subclass the model into two more specific models, one focusing on local devices and the other on remote devices. Each is then studied in two steps. First, the model is introduced, and its unique characteristics are examined. Next, a detailed discussion illustrates how it applies, in general, to real-world applications. Chapters 17 and 18 will illustrate the application of each model to specific real-world situations.

15.1 FIRST STEPS: UNDERSTANDING THE PROBLEM

Input
Output
I/O Subsystem
local
remote
Local Device Model
distributed tasks
Remote Device Model

We are now dealing with the portions of the von Neumann machine designated as *Input* and *Output*. We view the hardware and software world outside of the main microprocessor through a window that is collectively called the *I/O subsystem*. There ends the easy part of the problem. In an attempt to bring some order to the wide variety of interfaces and cacophony of exchange protocols with which the embedded designer must cope, we will place external world devices into two general categories—those that are *local* and those that are *remote*. Local devices *tend* to be in closer proximity (generally 1 to 3 meters or less) to the core system and typically have proprietary or specialized interfaces. Any tasks executing on such devices are usually associated with the function of the specific device and are not considered to be part of the embedded application proper. Interprocess communication and synchronization with such devices is based primarily on variations on the shared variable paradigm. Interaction with such devices will be characterized by a *Local Device Model*.

Interaction with remote external devices begins with the notion of *distributed tasks* executing on these devices and forms the basis for the *Remote Device Model*. Such tasks are now often considered to be an integral and contributing part of the main application. Interprocess communication and synchronization typically occur over a network using message exchange. Such devices *tend* to be located at a greater physical distance (3 to 5 meters or more). However, today, with the growth of systems and networks on a chip, the model has expanded to include external devices that are on the same die or within the same gate array.

A small sampling of such devices in both categories includes

- Analog-to-digital and digital converters
- A wide range of analog and digital sensors
- A variety of different kinds of (special-purpose) processors
- A vast collection of dedicated programmable logic devices or application-specific integrated circuits
- High-speed audio and video systems
- File systems and storage devices to allow us to read and write data
- Input devices to enable interaction with or control of other computers

- Scanning and sensing devices to capture and bring in information
- Display, recording, and printing devices to permit the display of a variety of data
- Networks and communications systems
- Remote applications

driver, device driver

Associated with each input or output device, is generally a software procedure called a *driver* or *device driver* that supports interaction with the device. When studying input and output interaction with the external world, several things must be considered, notably:

- The source or destination for any exchange
- The I/O ports on the microprocessor
- Local and global memory address space
- The nature of the exchange as an *event*, a *shared variable*, or a *message*.
- The I/O procedure invocation and any associated restrictions on that procedure
- The location of the I/O driver
- The protocol for the data exchange
- Timing requirements
- The physical medium of the exchange

event, shared variable, message

15.2 INTERPROCESS INTERACTION REVISITED

As part of earlier studies of interprocess communication and synchronization inside of the microprocessor, we formulated a model based on three questions:

- What are we communicating?
- With whom?
- How do we control the exchange?

We repeat that model here for reference.

information

places

control, synchronization

- The *information*—the data or signals being moved that convey our intent or our goals
- The place or *places* from which the information is moved to or from
- The *control* and *synchronization* of actions and the movement of the information

In such a model, the source and destination for the exchange were variously identified by named variables or by pointer variables holding memory addresses. Control and coordination comprised methods ranging from different flags or status bits to manage access to critical areas under the control of semaphores or monitors. Information moved either through shared variables or through messages on busses internal to the microprocessor that (except in rare circumstances) were of little concern to us.

As our studies expand to include interaction with the world outside of the core processor, the model of communication and synchronization similarly expands to include the physical means of moving the information. In addition, details of the exchange that previously fell within the purview of the microprocessor must now be considered and accommodated. The interprocess communication model developed earlier is now expanded to include the external world and also includes the answer to the question,

- How do we get the information to where it is going?

The fourth component of the model becomes the physical means by which the information is moved—the *transport mechanism.*

Our first formal view of the model begins as shown in Figure 15.0. The local and remote models are subclasses from a parent model that defines the essential and common components of each. Each subclassed model implements the specific components as appropriate for its context. Instances of either model implement the component as is appropriate to the application and device where it applied.

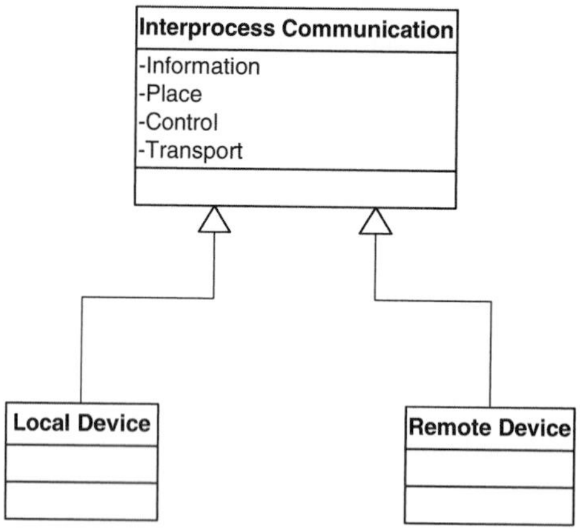

Figure 15.0 The Interprocess Communication Model

In summary, the components are given as

information *places* *control, synchronization* *transport mechanism*

- The *information*—the data or signals being moved that convey the intent or goals
- The place or *places* from which the information is moved to or from
- The *control* and *synchronization* of actions and the movement of the information
- The *transport mechanism*, the physical means by which it is moved

These four major elements of the interprocess communication model are reflected in Figure 15.1.

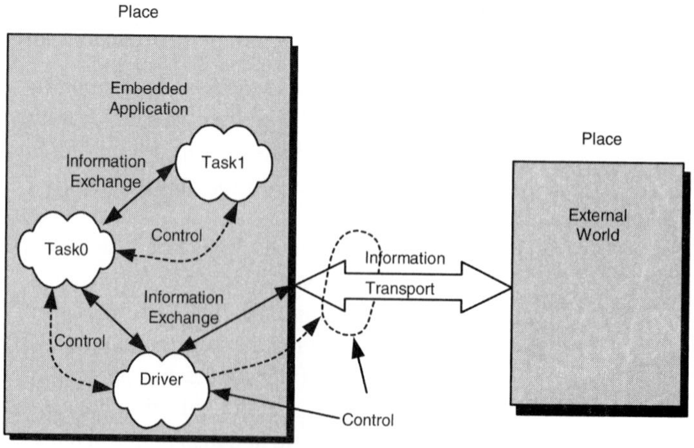

Figure 15.1 The Four Major Elements of the Task Interaction Model

15.3 THE MODEL

We will begin our study of the extended interprocess communication and synchronization model with an elaboration of each component. We will then study each of these components in some depth in the contexts of the local and remote device models.

15.3.1 Information

information, data or signals

The *information—data* or *signals* —will be expressed either directly as a voltage, a current, and an electromagnetic wave, or indirectly as a fundamental physical quantity such as pressure, strain, sonic, or temperature. In the latter case, the signal can be converted into an electrical signal using a device called a *transducer*. Once inside of the microprocessor, these physical quantities are abstracted either as primitive types such as integers or floats or as more complex data types such as collections of primitive types or aggregates manifest as structs or classes.

transducer

When data brought into or generated within the microprocessor is to be exchanged with an external device, several potential difficulties can arise. First, one must remember that not all processors or devices express the data same way; one must be concerned about different endianness and different word sizes. Such differences are evident in even simple types such as integers. Furthermore, to permit the exchange of information among such devices, one must ensure that more complex data types and values are expressed in (or converted to) an agreed upon form before being sent to another device.

The nature of the information that is exchanged is limited only by needs and imagination. Some of the exchanges will be *unidirectional*—either input or output only—whereas others may be *bidirectional*. In the collection of embedded applications classed as measurement and control devices, the outgoing information may be configuration data followed by subsequent commands to execute a measurement or series of measurements; that returned might be the results of those measurements. An analog-to-digital converter, or CCD or CMOS image scanner, would fit into this category. In the category of outgoing only types of devices, one may have to work with a digital-to-analog converter as part of a control system or with digital data transferred to an external storage device. For such applications, the information will often appear as shared variables in one form or another, as discussed earlier in our studies on intertask communication.

unidirectional

bidirectional

For larger, more complex applications, the system may be a component in a larger and more sophisticated networked application that may be serving video on demand to the passengers on a commercial airliner or production information around an automated manufacturing site. In such cases, the information will most likely be expressed in the form of messages that are exchanged using a standard protocol such as TCP/IP or I^2C.

15.3.2 Places

source, destination

In the expanded context, the *source* and *destination* for the exchange extends to locations outside of the local address space. The memory location that was previously reached by dereferencing a pointer may now be several meters away in a device that can only be reached by message exchange. Any local address is meaningless; moving outside of the processor means managing the remote access and exchange of information.

addresses

Nevertheless, we see that the source and destination of any exchanges are still identified by *addresses*. These addresses may be implicit—the destination device is directly connected to an output port or bus on the embedded processor or explicit; the source and destination have an associated name of one form or another by which they can be referred to by other devices in the system. The domain name as an alias for the actual IP address is a good example.

point to point The majority of the exchanges with which we will work are denoted *point to point*. In such cases, interaction is with a specific component, system, subsystem, or other piece of equipment. The exchange may command a measurement, alter the configuration of the component, direct it to perform a specific operation and return a value, set its output to a designated value, or simply request status information.

For most embedded applications there is a single source for any exchange that is the local system. The destination may include all of the subsystems comprising the application. ***broadcast*** Such an exchange is known as a *broadcast.* A broadcast message is used to send the same information to all components. The information may direct all member subsystems to a reset state, to initiate a self-test sequence, or to signal that the state of some system variable has changed and that an update is necessary.

On occasion, the information to be sent is intended for a reduced subset of the member ***multicast*** elements. The exchange, referred to as a *multicast,* transfers information only to those for whom it is relevant—a communications or imaging subsystem on a commercial aircraft for example. A firmware update to all imagers might be initiated with a broadcast message. If a specific package is to be sent only to all first-class passengers, however, a multicast might be used.

15.3.3 Control and Synchronization

control, synchronization The *control* and *synchronization* portion of the model is a combination of both hardware and software. The hardware portion comprises the overall structure and organization of the transport mechanism, any connected devices, and any necessary control signals. The soft- ***drivers*** ware component includes a special collection of routines called *drivers,* which are used to manage communication with individual devices or classes of devices.

The management of remote processes and information exchanges in the expanded model is complicated by intra-and intersystem delays, as well as by failures of the transport mechanism or of the remote devices themselves. The earlier model identified shared variables and messages as the principal means for executing the exchange. We now expand the scope of these concepts to include locations in remote address spaces.

The source or destination of a shared variable pair may now include an external device such as a register or set of registers in a peripheral device to which one must write initialization or configuration values, or perhaps data buffer on such a device. The message model will expand to include the invocation of methods or procedures on a remote external device.

15.3.4 Transport

transport mechanism The *transport mechanism,* the physical means by which the information is moved, can be implemented by any of a great variety of physical mediums and configurations. Included among the many choices are a simple piece of wire, a bundle of fiber-optic filaments, or the surrounding air. The target of the exchange can be local—within the same gate array—or it can be remote—across the office, the factory, the country, or the world.

The most common and most familiar means of transport today is the familiar copper connection, although this preference is rapidly changing to fiber, air, or wireless. In the most basic case, the transport medium is simply the necessary number of wires bundled together, carrying electrical signals from one place to another. Today, however, I/O speeds are beginning to track the increasing capabilities of the processing units. As the speed increases, so must the quality of the communication channel.

We may use a number of design approaches to enable us to begin to ensure the necessary increase in quality and reliability. Two of the main causes of electrical contamination are crosstalk between adjacent conducting paths and noise induced from external sources. Crosstalk can be addressed by alternating signal and ground conductors in the conducting path or by twisting ground and signal conductors together. External contamination can be attacked by using differential signals, shielding the entire cable or the individual twisted pairs, or both.

Fiber optics provides an increased level of robustness. Prior to transport, the information is converted into optical signals that move, without electrical interference, along thin, optically conductive channels. At the end of the day, the objective remains the same: to reliably move data and control information from one place to another. At the time of this writing, fiber is a somewhat more expensive alternative to standard copper wire for most applications. In addition to the cost of the material, the difficulty of making a connection with low-cost tools remains. The strength of fiber optics is its immunity to most of the electrical contamination that affects traditional wire. Both objections will change with time and continued advances in technology.

Wireless, in the form of radio waves, offers another alternative to copper. A wireless communication network is easy to install and works very well in areas where wire infrastructure is not in place or where a temporary connection is needed. It is cheaper and more flexible than a wire-based approach. However, it is typically slower than wire and more prone to errors from environmental interference.

The organization of the medium can range from a few signal lines with information flowing in serial to a larger number of signals simultaneously transporting greater amounts of the information. No matter which transport scheme is used, a solid understanding of all timing relationships, the strengths and limitations of the medium, and the transport protocol is required.

15.4 EXPLORING THE MODEL

With that overview, we will now study each component of the model in greater detail. The exchange can be characterized, analyzed, and designed from a number of different perspectives. As we explore, we will begin at a high level and work down to specific details. Earlier studies of interprocess communication and synchronization have provided a solid foundation upon which we can build. The transport mechanism introduces a new consideration into the designs. As a result, we will develop the extended model starting from this point. We will begin with the vocabulary and basic concepts; these will be examined in depth as the chapter unfolds. We will follow with some of the characteristics that distinguish the different kinds of I/O interfaces and that one must consider and can use as part of a design. These become important when making trade-offs during the early stages of a design.

15.4.1 The Transport Mechanism

physical level, interconnection architecture

The hierarchy given in Figure 15.2 identifies the two major elements of the transport mechanism: the *physical level* and the *interconnection architecture*.

We have already noted that the physical means by which information is moved can be implemented in a variety of ways. On top of the physical medium is the interconnection architecture or topology. The choice of interconnection topology and architecture can have a significant effect on the performance (generally in time), reliability, and economic cost of a system.

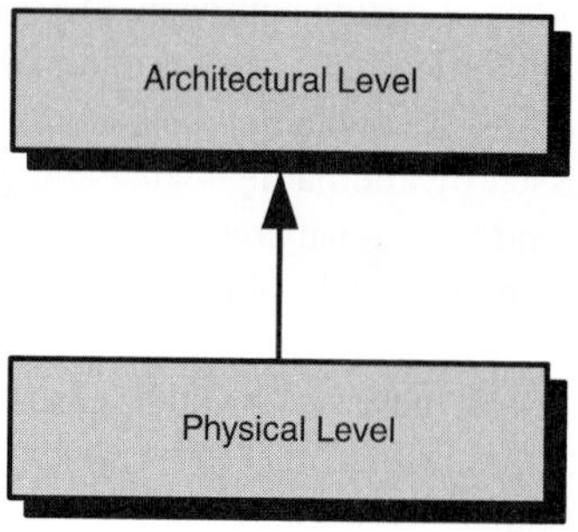

Figure 15.2 The Two Major Elements of the Transport Mechanism

15.4.1.1 The Interconnection Topology

An important consideration in the design of the physical medium is its organizational topology. In the local device model, such a medium implements an extension of one of the familiar *bus* architectures; in the remote device model, the medium is more often called a *network*. Whichever name is used, however, the intent is the same.

bus
network

Among the vast number of ways of configuring the interconnection, in general one finds three fundamental organizations. These are the *Star* illustrated in Figure 15.3, the *Ring*, given in Figure 15.4, and the simple *Parallel Bus,* shown later in Figure 15.7. The architecture of the transport mechanism in most contemporary embedded systems modifies or extends one or more of these in some way. We have already looked at different aspects of these bus topologies in other contexts. Some of the material presented here will repeat parts of those discussions.

Star
Ring, Parallel Bus

Each configuration has certain advantages and disadvantages. For all configurations, there are three kinds of messages:

- Those addressed to a single device (point to point)
- Those addrressed to a subset of the devices (multicast)
- Those sent to all devices (broadcast)

Each of these configurations can find application in a (wired) local context, such as a collection of microprocessors in a contemporary automobile, within a complex integrated circuit, or in a highly distributed wireless or networked system of Internet appliances. As we look at each of the three major topologies, we will present a high-level description of information flow and fault tolerance. We begin with the *star* configuration.

star

15.4.1.2 Star

The star configuration, illustrated in Figure 15.3, is a *master–slave* type of arrangement. Device-to-device communication must go through the master. The transmit and receive operations proceed as follows.

master–slave

TRANSMIT FROM MASTER TO SLAVE

The device designated as the *master* resides at the center of the system; this will typically be the local system. The slave units are any of a variety of peripheral devices. All communication, which typically follows a *command-response* protocol, must originate from the master, which initiates and directs all the activities within the system and coordinates any message exchange with other devices.

master
command-response

Transactions are typically *read* or *write* operations. A write operation sends information to the slave, and the read operation requests that information be returned.

read, write

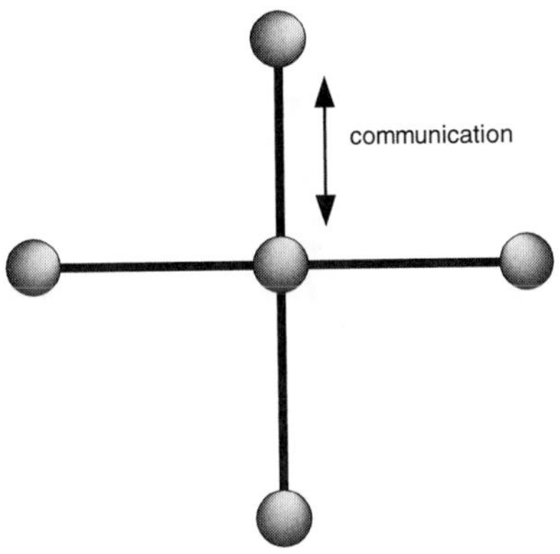

Figure 15.3 The Star Network Architecture

RECEIVE FROM SLAVE TO MASTER
The transaction is initiated by a request from the master through the issuance of a read command. That command may be used to request status information, perhaps the result of a self-test, or the retrieval of the results of some earlier requested operation.

TRANSMIT/RECEIVE FROM ONE SLAVE TO ANOTHER
Transmission from one slave device to others is somewhat uncommon in star configurations. The exchange can be executed in several ways. One approach requires that the master act as the intermediary. Information moves from the source device to the master and then from the master to the destination device. The shortcomings of such a scheme are pretty clear. An alternative approach requires that the master configure the exchange by designating one slave device as the source and the other(s) as the destination(s). Thence, the master authorizes the exchange to begin and waits until it completes.

FAILURE
If one device or link fails, communication with others can continue, although system performance may be/is degraded; the services of the failed slave device are lost, however. In contrast, loss of the master represents a potential single-point failure unless a replacement or backup scheme has been incorporated.

15.4.1.3 Ring

Variants on the ring are common in communication networks. We find it to be the basis for token ring networks, for networks of embedded processors in an automobile or aircraft, or within a system or network on a chip type of designs. Typically, there is no bus master, and all devices are considered equal. The basic configuration is presented in Figure 15.4. A more robust configuration utilizing two concentric rings is also presented.

Each device accepts all messages circulating in ring. If a device receiving a message is ***addressed*** the *addressed* device, the message is accepted; otherwise, the message is passed on to the next device on the ring.

TRANSMIT-RECEIVE
Because there is typically no bus master to control access to the bus and because all devices are considered equal, a protocol must be established and used to decide who is able to transmit messages and to use the bus.

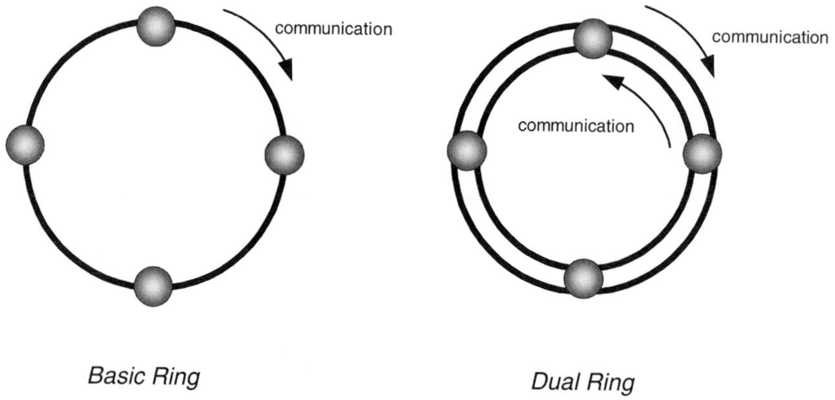

Figure 15.4 The Ring Network Architecture

Referring back to an earlier discussion of shared resources, the bus, in the ring, is a critical and shared resource. We learned from the *readers* and *writers* problem that we can permit multiple readers but only a single writer. Access to the ring bus is a readers and writers problem.

readers, writers

Any device can read—receive messages—from the bus. However, only one writer is permitted. One approach that is commonly used to ensure that there is only a single writer is to have a special message or packet called a *token* continually circulating in the ring. A device is only able to write when it has the token. When it finishes writing, it releases the token and the process continues.

token

Another approach that is used is to implement a collision detection/retransmit scheme. The underlying premise is that attempts at access are occurring randomly. Thus, when a device wants to transmit, it first checks for activity on the bus. If it does not see any activity, it puts its data onto the bus and looks for a collision (someone else may have had the same idea). If it detects a collision, it ceases transmission and waits (*backs off*) a random amount of time before repeating the process. With a lightly loaded bus or bursty transmissions, the probability of repeated collisions is small. We will see several alternative approaches for dealing with collisions when we study the I^2C and CAN busses in Chapter 16.

backs off

FAILURE

The ring can provide a very robust context for information exchange. Consider first the single ring given in Figure 15.5. If either of the failures shown in the accompanying drawing

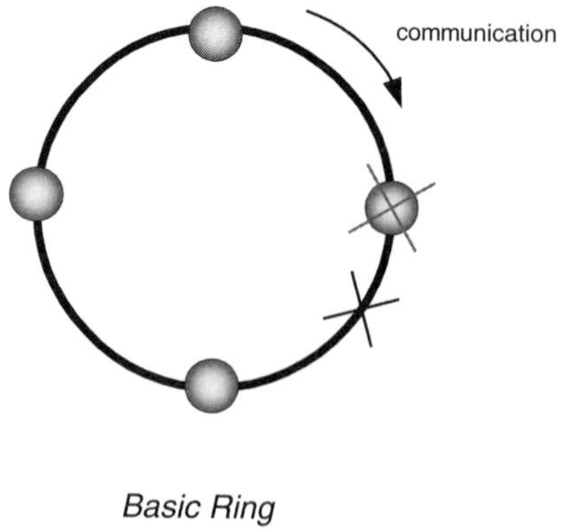

Figure 15.5 Basic Ring Architecture with a Single Failure

occurs, the system can reconfigure itself into a parallel bus that will be discussed next. In the event of a link failure (X on the link), full connectivity and communication with all devices on the network can be maintained. If a device (X on the node) is lost, the system has the same degraded performance encountered with the master–slave configuration.

When implemented as two concentric rings, as in Figure 15.6, there are several possible failure and recovery modes. If one link is lost, as shown with failures numbered as 1 or 2, the system can reconfigure to a fully operational single-link system. If two links are lost, as depicted with the failure numbered 3, once again, the system can reconfigure into a fully operational single-link topology. If a device is lost, as reflected with the failure designated 4, the remaining devices are still fully interconnected via a single-ring configuration.

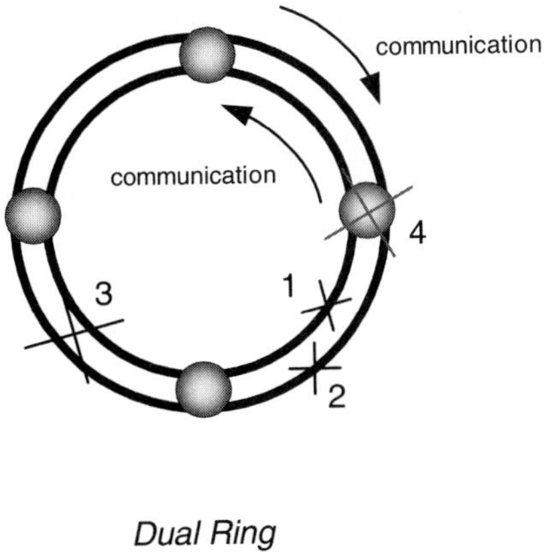

Figure 15.6 Dual-Ring Architecture with Multiple Failures

The double ring is also tolerant of second failures. Observe that failure 1 followed by 2 leaves a fully operational system. Other combinations follow with varying levels of degraded performance.

PARALLEL BUS

The traditional bus, shown in Figure 15.7, is a variation on the star architecture. There may or may not be a bus master. The SCSI (Small Computer Systems Interface) subsystem in the familiar PC is a design that uses a master device called a controller.

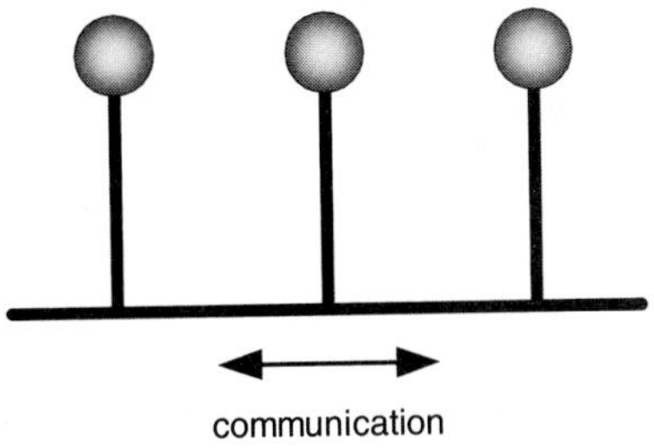

Figure 15.7 Parallel Bus Architecture

Such a simple bus is probably one of the more commonly used architectures. Device interconnection occurs in a variety of different ways. Generally, all devices can receive information whether it is data and commands or simply commands. The ability to transmit may be more restricted, with some devices being designated as receive only.

As encountered with the ring configuration, the problem of controlling access to the bus for transmit operations must be addressed. Alternatives range from those already discussed with the star topology—designating a bus master—to variants on the token schemes, to the implementation of a control bus to coordinate all transactions to the implementation of a request/grant protocol.

TRANSMIT-RECEIVE

If there is a bus master, the protocol follows the one discussed in a similar context earlier. The information exchange may be point to point, broadcast, multicast, or polled. All devices can listen for and act on a message.

FAILURE

Failure modes and effects follow those discussed for the star configuration. An individual device failure will not compromise the bus—assuming proper isolation. However, a severed bus can prevent communication beyond the damage.

15.4.2 Control and Synchronization

The control and synchronization aspects of the extended model of interprocess communication are characterized by

- The flow of information
- The I/O timing
- The software drivers that manage the exchange

The relationship among these is captured in Figure 15.8. Note that the control and synchronization component sits on top of the transport mechanism.

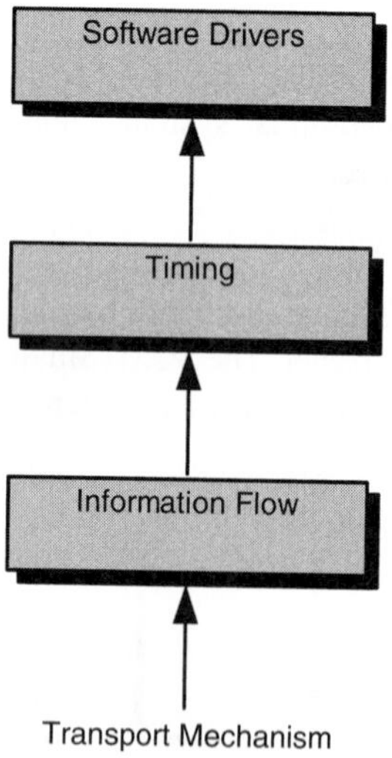

Figure 15.8 The Three Major Elements of the Control and Synchronization Mechanism

Shortly we will consider how local and remote exchanges can be expressed. At that point, we will see that the lower level aspects of control and synchronization will be unique to each type of exchange. For the moment, the analysis that follows applies to both.

15.4.3 Information Flow

Managing the movement of information includes controlling two aspects of the transport process: the direction of the flow and the magnitude of the flow. We will first consider flow direction.

15.4.3.1 Direction of Flow

If information is being sent in one direction only—sender to receiver or receiver to sender—the transport is called *simplex*. If information is permitted to flow in both directions, but in only one direction at a time, it is called *half duplex*. If the exchange supports flow in both directions, possibly simultaneously, it is designated as *full duplex*. Figure 15.9 shows each scheme.

simplex
half duplex
full duplex

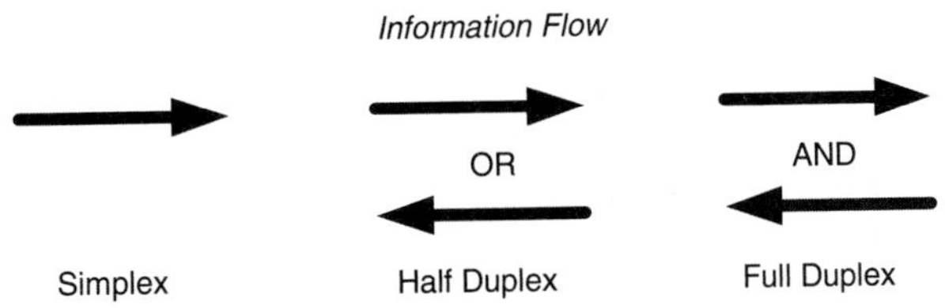

Figure 15.9 Types of Information Flow

15.4.3.2 Magnitude of the Flow

As with any other part of a design, the I/O subsystem design entails continual trade-offs. Here, one of the early decisions evaluates cost versus speed. As the transfer rate through the medium increases, so does the cost burden; at the same time, so does the amount of information that can be conveyed with each transaction.

Flow magnitude quantifies the amount of information that is moved during a single transaction. At the highest level, information can be sent in *serial* or in *parallel*. Information sent in serial utilizes a narrow channel (1 bit per transfer), while that sent in parallel utilizes a wider channel and can move n bits (the width of the channel) per transfer.

serial, parallel

On the one extreme, the lowest cost mechanism is serial by bit. With such a design, a lower flow rate is accepted in exchange for the simplicity and (typically) lower cost of the transport. If the unit of exchange expands to a character, the width of the transport path is increased and is accompanied by a corresponding increase in speed.

Serial by word (parallel by bit) once again increases the width of the transmission path. As with the previous case, such an exchange might also be seen as parallel by character with the proper encoding. In reality, we interpret parallel by character as the transmission of multiple characters at the same time. At the opposite extreme, parallel by word entails sending multiple words simultaneously.

Figure 15.10 tries to capture each of these ideas. In presenting the graphic, we will assume that a character comprises 8 bits and a word 32.

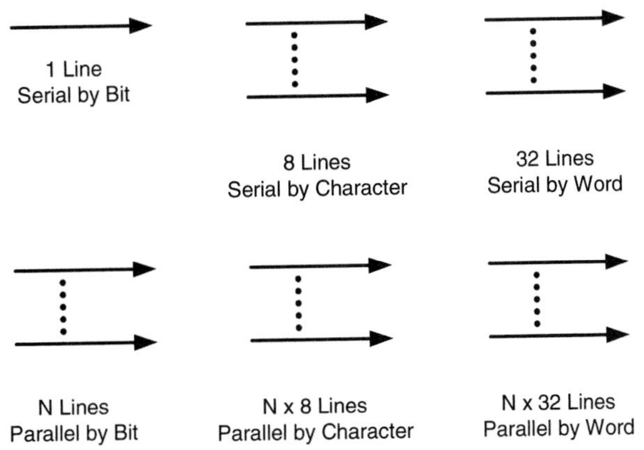

Figure 15.10 Information Flow vs. Transmission Path

It was noted earlier in the discussion of performance that measurements and computations should be performed at a rate and significance consistent with the rate of change and values of the data. The same heuristic applies to the movement of information. If a serial channel is adequate for the application, there is no need to incur the cost and added complexity of a high-throughput parallel channel.

15.4.3.3 I/O Timing

synchronous

The next important aspect of controlling and synchronizing the transport mechanism is the timing of the exchange. The exchange with the outside world may be *synchronous* based on some shared timing element or piece of information. The reference may be a common clock or similar timing signal. Alternately, the timing information may be encoded in the transmitted data. In such a case, the clock signal can be recovered or regenerated by the receiver of the data.

asynchronous

The exchange may also be *asynchronous*, in which case there is no shared timing information between sender and receiver. The start of any specific transaction and subsequent transactions are temporally independent. Synchronization is reestablished with each component of the transaction.

15.4.3.4 Software Device Drivers

The software device drivers provide a significant portion of the software side of the control and coordination of the outside world exchange. The sophistication and complexity of these device drivers vary greatly with the sophistication and complexity of the embedded design and of the devices themselves. The simple washing machine or microwave oven controller will frequently implement the control routines as a few function calls that directly provide and manage the control of and data exchange with any of the hardware.

On higher end, more powerful systems, these routines provide the interface between the system software and application tasks and the physical devices to which they need to communicate. One purpose of the device drivers is to provide a (common) high-level calling interface in support of the I/O operation, while at the same time separating the users of the devices from the low-level details of managing the physical hardware.

Whether ad hoc or more general purpose, the device driver will typically provide the following capabilities:

- Support for registering the device with the system
- Device initialization
- Support for moving data to and from the device
- Support for managing control events such as interrupts

The device driver may reside in the main system microprocessor or in a dedicated peripheral processor.

information
places

Whichever physical transport architecture or control and synchronization mechanism is chosen for the design, the remaining two components of the model (the *information* and the *places*) must be supported.

15.4.4 Places

local, remote

The *places* component in the model, at the very minimum, identifies the destination of any transfer. The means by which this information is acquired, represented, and conveyed differs between the *local* devices and the *remote* devices. For local devices, typically only a destination address is used. In contrast, remote devices will often include both the source and destination address.

In the model, local devices are assumed to be in close proximity to the core system, while remote devices are often at much greater distances and tend to be network based. In the next chapter, we will begin with the local device model followed by a similar study of the remote model.

15.5 SUMMARY

In this chapter, we have studied how an embedded application can communicate and coordinate with the external world. We extended the interprocess and communication model developed earlier by adding a transport mechanism component. We studied the meaning of information, control and synchronization, and addressing in the context of the external world.

In the next chapter, we will continue to refine the model by developing and examining the local and remote components in greater detail from the points of view of a shared variable and a message-based interpretation of the information exchange. The objective is to establish the basic infrastructure and various implementation architectures for both models. The subsequent two chapters will study several real-world examples of each rendering of the model.

15.6 REVIEW QUESTIONS

Communication with the Outside World

15.1 Identify the kinds of devices that an embedded application may be required to exchange information with.

15.2 What are some of the considerations that must be taken when designing and implementing an interface to an external world device?

15.3 In an earlier chapter, an intertask communication model was developed based on the answers to three questions. What are those questions, and why are they important?

15.4 How is the earlier model of information exchange inside of the processor extended to accommodate a similar information exchange with the outside world?

The Transport Mechanism

15.5 What are the three major kinds of message exchange with external world devices?

15.6 What are the major architectural topographies that may be utilized to effect an interconnection with external world devices?

Control, Synchronization, and Sharing

15.7 The control and synchronization of an external world exchange are characterized by what three aspects?

Information Flow

15.8 Identify the three kinds of information flow between the source and destination of an external world exchange.

15.9 Identify and discuss the differing amounts of information that may be moved during each segment of an exchange.

15.10 What is the purpose of a software algorithm called a device driver in the context of an external world exchange?

15.11 Where is the device driver typically located in an embedded application?

15.7 THOUGHT QUESTIONS

Communication with the Outside World

15.1 Identify and discuss possible problems that might arise when data or signals must be exchanged with the outside world compared to a similar exchange inside of the processor.

15.2 Identify and discuss how the source and destination of an exchange with the outside world might be recognized during an exchange with the outside world.

15.3 Identify and discuss how control and synchronization of the exchange between source and destination might be implemented to effect an exchange with the outside world.

The Transport Mechanism

15.4 Identify and discuss possible transport mechanisms that might be used during the exchange between source and destination.

15.5 What are the strengths and weaknesses of each interconnection topography that may be used for interconnection with the outside world. Discuss each from the perspectives of performance, reliability, and safety.

Control, Synchronization, and Sharing

15.6 What are some differences one might encounter when trying to control or to synchronize with external world devices that may not be encountered with internal processes? Discuss some of the consequences of these differences for the design of an embedded application.

15.7 Can a critical section exist in an exchange with an outside world device? If so, how should it be solved?

15.8 Can a semaphore be used to control access to shared information between internal and external processes? If so, how? If not, are there alternatives?

15.9 Does the notion of an atomic test and set have meaning in the context of synchronization with an external world device or process?

Information Flow

15.10 Three different kinds of information flow between the source and destination of an external world exchange are identified. Discuss the advantages and disadvantages of each form. Focus, in particular, on performance and reliability.

15.11 Differing amounts of information may be moved during each segment of an exchange. Discuss the advantages and disadvantages of each such piece of information. Focus, in particular, on performance and reliability.

15.12 A software device driver provides a significant portion of the control and coordination of an external world exchange. What capabilities does such a driver typically provide?

Chapter 16

Working Outside of the Processor I: Refining the Model of Interprocess Communication

THINGS TO LOOK FOR . . .

- Critical components of the shared variable interpretation of the communication model.
- Critical components of the message-based interpretation of the communication model.
- Various ways of implementing the shared variable and message-based interpretations of the model.

16.0 COMMUNICATION AND SYNCHRONIZATION WITH THE OUTSIDE WORLD

In the previous chapter, we established the foundation for how an embedded application can interact with the external world. We began by extending the internal interprocess and communication model developed in Chapter 4 by incorporating a transport component. That model is repeated here in Figure 16.0.

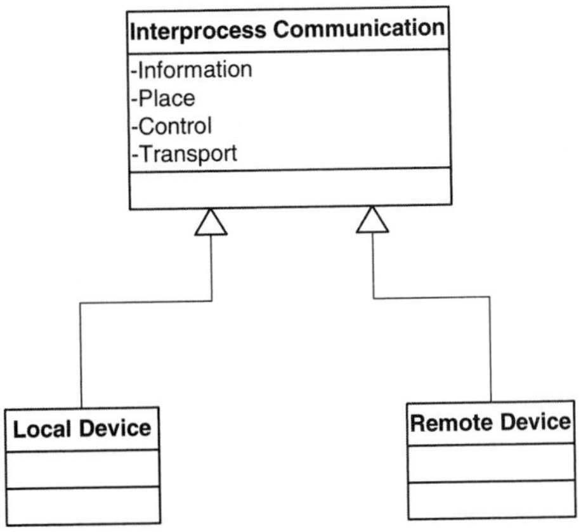

Figure 16.0 The Interprocess Communication Model

In this chapter, we will continue to refine that model by subclassing it into two more specific models, one focusing on local devices and the other on remote devices. Each will then be studied in two steps. First, the model is introduced and its unique characteristics are examined. Next, a detailed discussion illustrates how it applies, in general, to real-world situations. The following two chapters will illustrate the application of each to specific real-world situations.

In the model, local devices are assumed to be in close proximity to the core system, while remote devices are often at much greater distances and tend to be network based. The model does not distinguish between macro peripheral devices that are implemented as independent standalone units and micro devices that may be implemented within a single system or network on a chip. We will begin with the local device model followed by a similar study of the remote model.

16.1 THE LOCAL DEVICE MODEL

A high-level architecture of the local device model utilizing a local external bus is given in Figure 16.1. In the model, the information, the source and destination, and the control and synchronization over the local bus structure are supported through the following sets of signals:

- Address
- Data
- Control

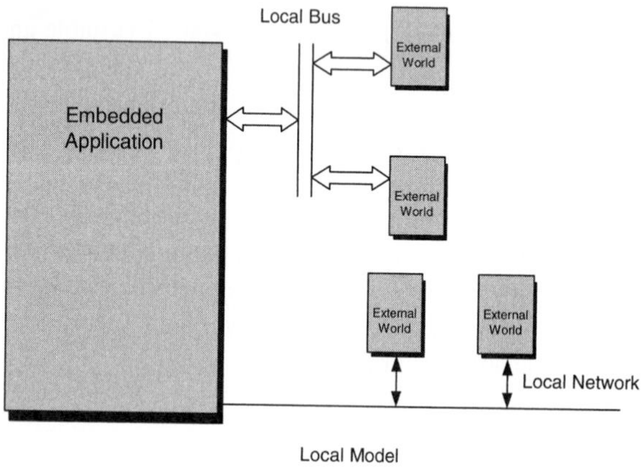

Figure 16.1 The Local Device Model Architecture

address, places, information data, control

The *address* information provides the means of identifying the *places* where the *information* or *data* is to be written to or read from in the model. The *control* signals implement the control and synchronization that is unique to the local device model and provide the physical means by which a transaction is directed and coordinated. Each of these can be implemented in a variety of ways depending on the nature and structure of the underlying I/O channel. It is not unusual for an embedded application even to support several different schemes.

16.1.1 Control, Synchronization, and Places

The number and structure of the control signals in a local device model is generally system-specific. Typical signals may include

- Read/Write signals
- Address/Data present or stable strobes

- Clock—where the clock comes from, either a separate line or encoded in the data
- Transmission direction
- Ready or active
- Synchronize
- Reset
- Power—may or may not be counted as a control signal

The means for identifying the places involved in the exchange must consider the initial set of devices that make up the system as well as any new devices that may be added during runtime. If the system configuration either never changes or changes infrequently, address assignment can be accomplished through a set of switches or a set of jumpers as is done on a SCSI device, or it can be permanently assigned at the time the device is built. Alternately, an approach that works very well for systems that may have a somewhat more transient configuration uses what is called *geographic addressing*. With such an approach, the system's management routine assigns an address to every module on the bus each time the system in powered ON or each time a new device is attached to the system and subsequently recognized. Such a process is sometimes called *enumeration*. A device may or may not have the same address each time the system is powered on.

geographic addressing

enumeration

How the address information is used to identify and support communication with a device involves the usual trade-offs, including familiar constraints such as cost and speed. Let's look at a serial implementation first.

16.1.1.1 A Serial Model

When a serial addressing scheme is used, the address and data bits are sent as a serial stream of 1's and 0's over the same physical transport medium. As illustrated in Figure 16.2, the address appears on the bus first to select the receiver and the data follows.

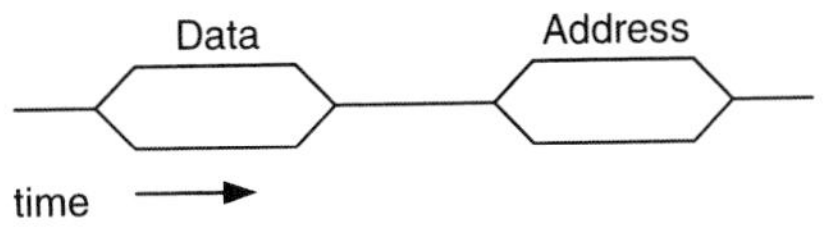

Figure 16.2
Information Transport over a Single Serial Bus

A higher level protocol must be used on top of the bit stream to distinguish between data and address information and to ensure that data cannot be incorrectly interpreted as an address, or vice versa. One approach is to have a common and specified message format that each participant in the exchange understands and abides by.

The advantage of a serial system is low cost. In some applications, the cost of the connection hardware and the physical transport mechanism is a major concern. For larger installations, spread out over a significant area, that cost can exceed that of the core system. The disadvantage, of course, is reduced communication speeds.

Today, high-throughput Universal Serial Bus, Firewire, and WIFI interfaces are providing quite respectable performances. The main difficulty with such schemes is that to achieve the same information transfer rates that are possible in a more parallel architecture, the transfer rate has to be increased significantly. With increasing speed comes the need for much more careful design of the physical transport mechanism. With such increasing speeds, one begins to move into the world of transmission lines and differential signaling. Analysis of signal integrity now requires the tools from electromagnetic field theory.

16.1.1.2 A Parallel Model

In a parallel system, the address transmission is commonly handled in either of two ways. One approach is to transmit the address and data over the same physical bus. As illustrated in Figure 16.3, the address precedes the data and operates much like the earlier serial method, only faster since the bits are transmitted in parallel. Again, the address must be tagged to distinguish it from data. Such a tag can be implemented either as part of the transmission (again as was done with the serial implementation) or with control lines. In the following graphic two control lines, the *address* and *data strobes* are used. The polarity of the two strobes is shown as low going. One could just as easily invert the polarity.

address, data strobes

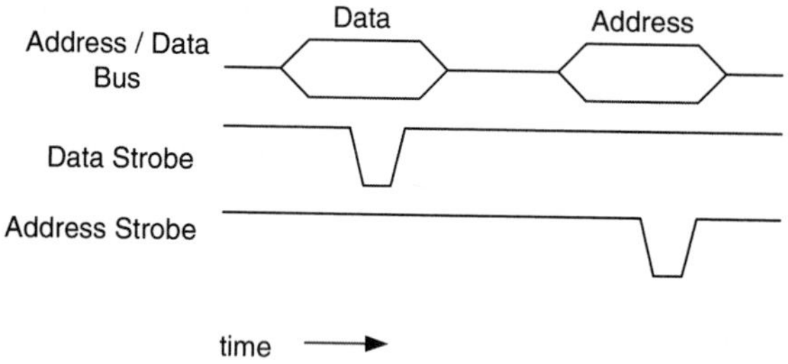

Figure 16.3 Information Transport over a Single Parallel Bus

The strobes provide two benefits: (1) they simplify distinguishing between the two sets of bits; and (2) they enable one to deskew the signals, that is, to evaluate the signals when they have had time to settle after being switched onto the bus. The address and data information can be captured and stored using either a register or a latch.

The capture can be executed on either edge of the strobe for the register or on either state for the latch as shown in the following portion of a logic diagram in Figure 16.4.

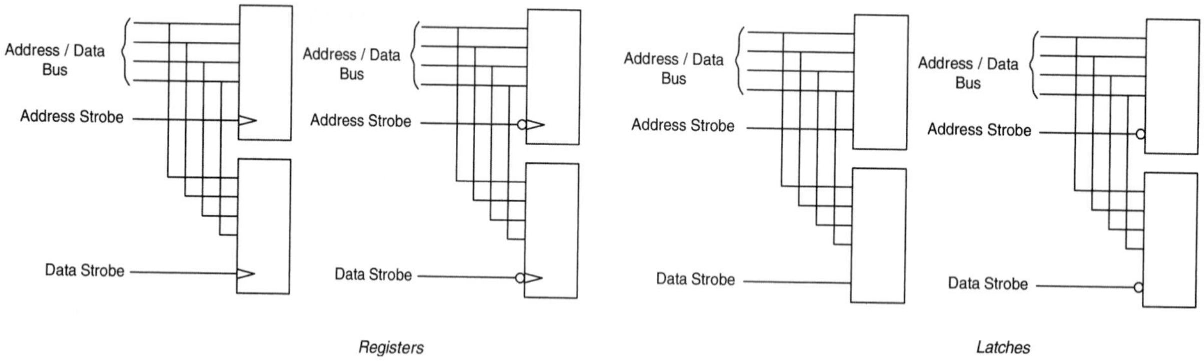

Figure 16.4 Address/Data Capture on a Single Parallel Bus

An alternative approach transmits the address and data over physically separate busses. In such a configuration, the address bus need not be the same width as that used for the data; the size depends on the architecture and requirements. The address and data are transmitted simultaneously as seen in Figure 16.5. With such a scheme come significant improvements in throughput.

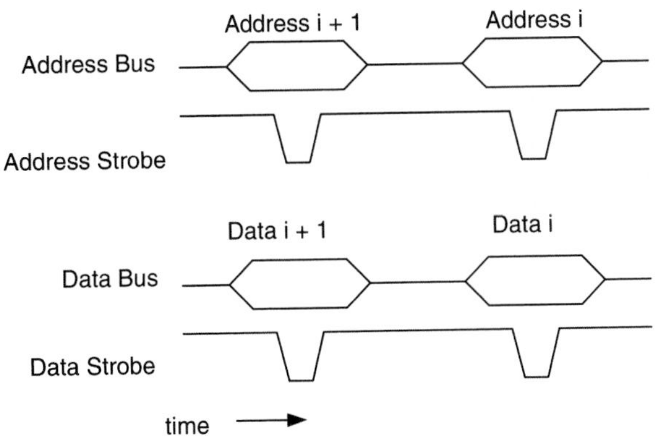

Figure 16.5 Information Transport over Separate Busses

In either case, the strobes are essential. Each identifies when the signals on a bus are stable and valid. Without a strobe, there is no way to properly interpret the values of the signals.

16.1.2 Information—Data

Whether realized as a serial or parallel bus, the data lines carry the information to be transmitted or received. When implemented in parallel, they will typically carry one word. For a system with 32-bit words, the data bus will be 32 bits wide and carry DB0–DB31. It is important to determine which bit is the MSB and which the LSB. It is also important to determine whether the data is positive or negative true.

16.1.3 Transport

The physical transport of the information between the system core and local external devices can utilize any of the schemas introduced earlier in Chapter 15. Most frequently, copper wire provides the means for interconnection.

16.2 IMPLEMENTING THE LOCAL DEVICE MODEL—A FIRST STEP

16.2.1 An Overview

memory address space, I/O ports, peripheral processor

We will now study three different implementations of the local device model for an I/O subsystem. The source of the data exchange with the external world may be either the system microprocessor or an external peripheral processor. An exchange originating with the main system microprocessor can be implemented as a series reads and writes to locations in the system processor's *memory address space* or through specifically designated *I/O ports*.

If a special *peripheral processor* is used, that device will interact with both the main processor and the peripheral devices. Communication with the main processor identifies what needs to be done, and with the devices directs them to execute those requirements. Figure 16.6 illustrates the interface from the microprocessor to the I/O ports and the memory address space.

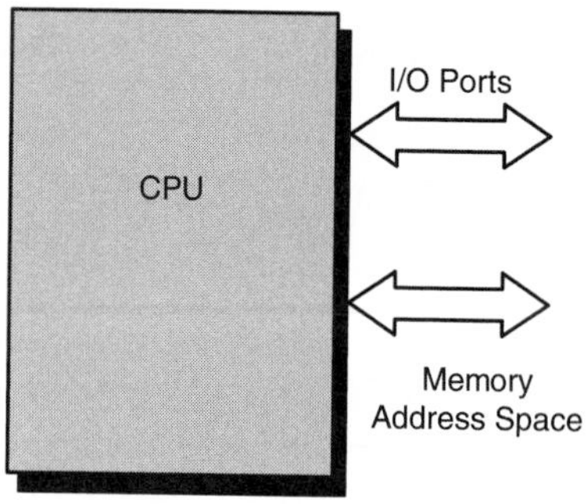

Figure 16.6 Local Bus Model I/O Ports and Memory Address Space

16.2.1.1 Main Memory Address Space

Most microprocessors or microcontrollers have limited on-board memory. To support more complex applications, external memory must be used. To support access to external memory, the CPU address and data busses are made available outside of the processor. Consequently, one can read data from or write data to any location that "appears" to be an address within the processor's primary memory address space, independent of whether that address is physically inside or outside of the processor. One can take advantage of such a capability to implement a simple interface to a peripheral device, provided that the device appears as just another memory location to the processor.

For example, if the storage buffer in a digital imager is placed at memory address location 0x3000 and a memory read from that address is executed, the stored data can be accessed as if it were being read from a traditional array in memory at that same address. Such a scheme is called *memory-mapped I/O*. The principal advantages of such a design are easy implementation and low cost; the disadvantage is the additional burden the scheme places on the CPU.

memory-mapped I/O

16.2.1.2 I/O Ports

On many microcontrollers or microcomputers there are a number of pins specifically dedicated to bringing data into or sending data out of the device. Collectively, they are referred to as *I/O Ports* and are different from the external memory bus.

I/O Ports

The lines may be designated as *Input, Output* (unidirectional), or *Input and Output* (bidirectional). Unidirectional lines tend to be static. The direction is established in hardware and is usually done during initialization. Bidirectional lines are dynamic; the direction is selected under program control based on the nature of the transaction. Usually, such signals are grouped in sets of four or eight lines, and the direction is set for an entire group.

Input, Output, Input and Output

An information exchange based on specifically designated I/O ports is called *program-controlled I/O*. Its advantages over memory-mapped I/O are that it does not use any of the main memory addresses and it eliminates the dual use of (and thus time burden on) the memory address and data busses. The disadvantage is that the control of any exchanges with peripheral devices remains under the auspices of the main CPU.

program-controlled I/O

16.2.1.3 Peripheral Processor

If we move outside of the main system processor and incorporate a special-purpose processor to handle the interface to the various peripheral devices in the extended system, we have yet another form of I/O. Such a processor is called a *peripheral processor*. The purpose of the device is to unburden the main processor from the details of the I/O operations and, gen-

peripheral processor

erally, to create a higher performance interface than might be possible with either of the previous two designs.

We will now examine each of these three approaches to supporting input and output operations in greater detail. We will start inside of the processor and then move to the outside.

16.2.2 Main Memory Address Space—Memory-Mapped I/O

memory-mapped I/O

The idea behind *memory-mapped I/O* is to have I/O share a portion of the system's memory address space. The I/O address space is mapped into a subset of memory addresses; the data path is common and shared. Thus, I/O reads and writes are done to the processor's memory address space exactly as one would any other memory access. The main advantage of memory-mapped I/O is that it is easy to implement and is low cost. The principal disadvantages are the lower I/O bandwidth and the extra burden placed on the CPU.

A memory-mapped I/O scheme is rather straightforward to implement. An address in memory address space is assigned to each input or output device as illustrated in the partial memory map presented in Figure 16.7. Here address 0xF000 is designated for the serial communication device, 0xF010 for the measurement device, and 0xF100 for the display. Such a mapping is also illustrated schematically in the block diagram in Figure 16.8.

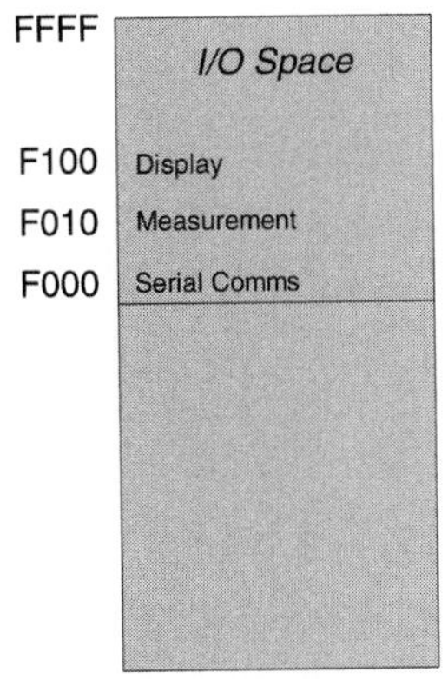

Figure 16.7 I/O Address Mapping to Memory Address Space

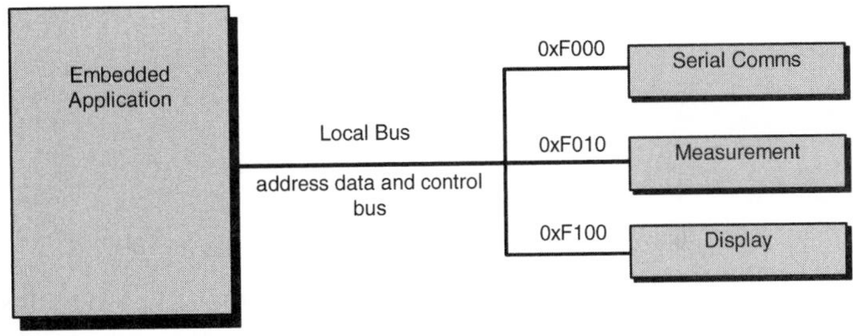

Figure 16.8 Physical Address Assignment to Memory Addresses

Some devices may have multiple addresses: one for read and one for write, for example. Typically, addresses are permanently fixed on the device or set using switches or jumpers.

The early PCs used such a scheme because it was low cost and simple to implement. As the PC proliferated, the increased development of a wide variety of peripherals led to address conflicts, IRQ (interrupt request) conflicts, and limited expansion capabilities. We will now walk through the design of a memory-mapped I/O scheme for a hypothetical processor. It is assumed that the external device is connected to the local system.

Address Bus

The address lines, A0–A15, come out of the core processor on the memory expansion ports: Ports 0 and 1. They will be valid during the address portion of an external bus cycle and are multiplexed with the data, as discussed earlier.

Data Bus

For the processor, D0–D16 appear on Ports 0 and 1 following the address.

Control Bus

There are a minimum of four control signals:

- *AS*—Address Strobe—asserted high, the trailing edge identifies valid address.
- *RD*—Read-asserted low, the trailing edge identifies that the data has been read.
- *WR*—Write-asserted low, the trailing edge identifies that data has been written.
- *Direction*—logical 0 bus out; logical 1 bus in.

To support a read and write operation, the bus must support bidirectional communication.
The timing diagrams in Figure 16.9 and Figure 16.11 illustrate the high-level timing for the read and write operations.

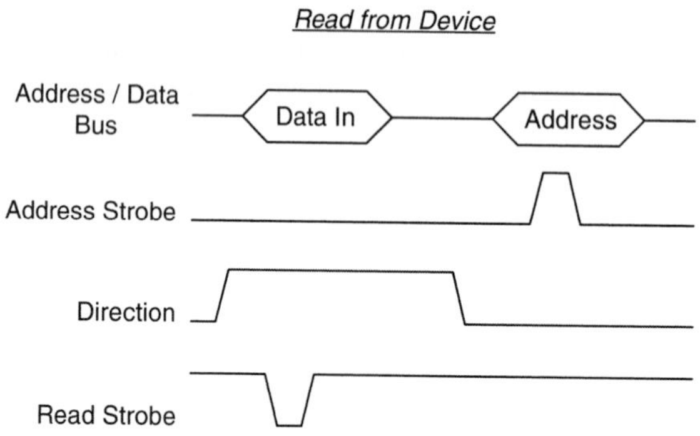

Figure 16.9 High–Level Timing for a Read Operation from an I/O Device

Read

For a read operation, the processor will set the direction of the bus to *out*, place the address to be read from onto the bus, and issue the address strobe (AS). The address lines are usually accepted from the bus and stored in buffer as seen in Figure 16.10. On the external device, after the address is received, it is decoded. If there are matches, the device then responds as appropriate for the control signals.

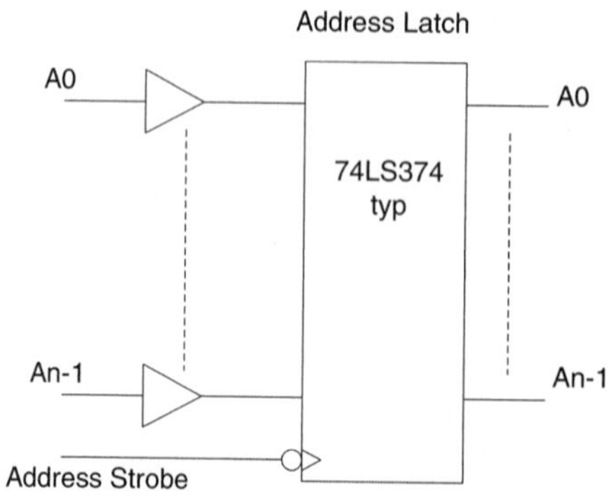

Figure 16.10 Address Storage on the I/O Device from the Bus

The operation continues as the processor sets the direction of the bus to *in* and the peripheral device places the data onto the bus accompanied by the read strobe to complete the cycle. In the event of a block transfer, successive words in the block would be placed onto the bus, each accompanied by a read strobe, until the transfer completed. Subsequent addresses would not be necessary, and the direction of the bus would remain set to *in* until all data was transferred.

Write

The write operation proceeds in a similar manner. The processor sets the direction of the bus to *out* and places the device address onto the bus accompanied by the address strobe. The addressed device accepts and decodes the address and waits for the incoming data. For each data word to be transferred, the processor places the data onto the bus and issues the write strobe. As with a block read operation, addresses for the remaining transfers are unnecessary.

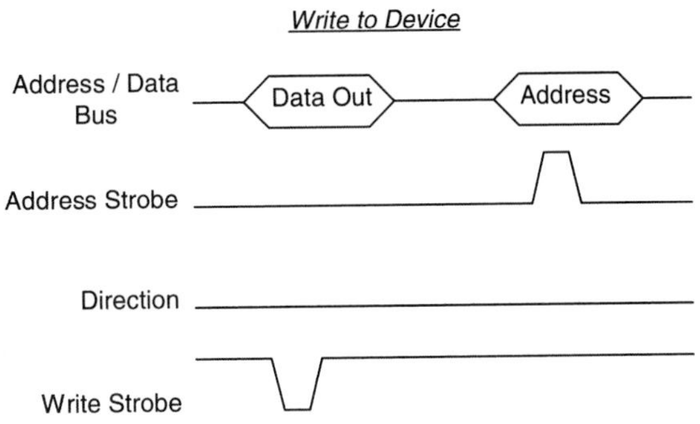

Figure 16.11 High–Level Timing for a Write Operation from an I/O Device

Bidirectional Bus

Higher speed systems with hard real-time constraints will often have two unidirectional busses, thereby eliminating the cost of turning the bus around. The design in Figure 16.12 illustrates a first attempt at a bidirectional bus.

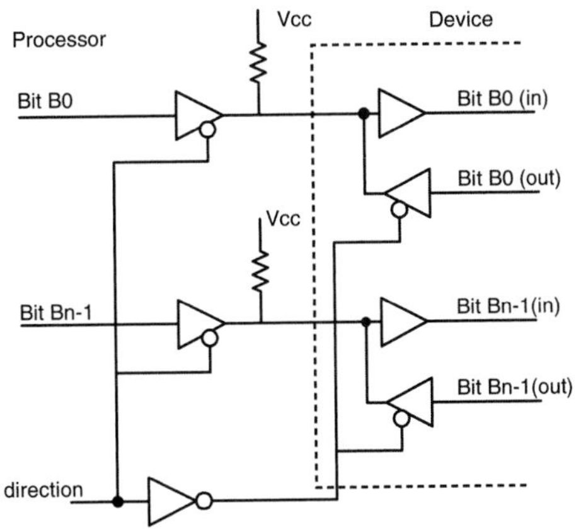

Figure 16.12 A Bidirectional I/O Bus—Design 1

Let's look at the pieces of this system. First, notice that the bus lines are buffered as they come off the bus into the device. This is done to ensure a known load on the bus. Next, each of the bus lines has a pull-up resistor to VCC to ensure that there is never a floating signal line.

This design uses a single control signal to select whether the processor or the device is driving the bus. Such a scheme can create several different problems.

Consider the following sequence of events.

direction

1. The state of the *direction* line is changed from logical 1 (device on the bus) to logical 0 (processor on the bus),
2. The state change will enable the tristate drivers on the processor and allow them to begin driving the bus.
3. Simultaneously, the state change on the *direction* line begins to propagate through the inverter to the tristate control on the drivers on the device. The delay through the inverter permits both sets of drivers to be on the bus for the length of the delay.

The consequences of having both sets of drivers on the bus simultaneously include

- Excessive current draw as the drivers are fighting, producing noise in the power and ground system
- Excessive power consumption in the system
- Potential damage to the drivers

break-before-make ***enable*** ***direction***

The proper design executes a *break-before-make* switch by using two control lines. Before turning the bus around, the first step is to direct all devices to release the bus. This is accomplished by placing the *enable* control line into the logical 0 state. Then the state of the *direction* control is changed. Finally, the devices are reenabled onto the bus by placing the *enable* control line into the logical 1 state. The design appears in Figure 16.13.

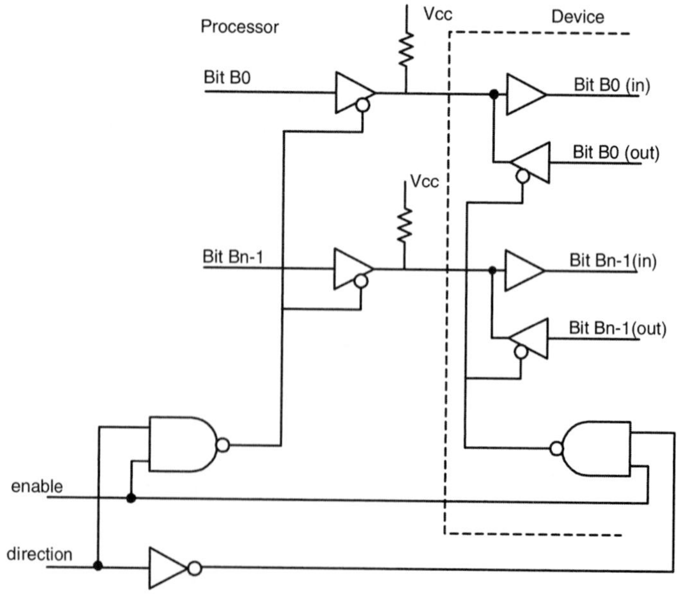

Figure 16.13 A Bidirectional I/O Bus—Design 2

From the preceding timing diagrams, it is evident that the CPU must be involved in each aspect of the exchange. Furthermore, the transfer rate for any such exchange is determined by the rate at which the device can read or write data. A slower device can place a significant burden on the CPU operation. It should be evident that utilizing the CPU in such an activity in higher performance systems is not the best use of the resource.

anAddress

On the software side of the picture, we have the following code fragments in Figure 16.14. In each case, *anAddress* is the address of the target device in I/O address space.

```
C
    *anAddress = aValue;        // Write to anAddress
    aValue = *anAddress;        // Read from anAddress

Assembler
    LD aReg, anAddress;         // Register ← anAddress
    ST anAddress, aReg;         // anAddress ← Register
```

Figure 16.14 C and Assembler Code Fragments for a Write and Read Operation to and from an I/O Device

16.2.3 I/O Ports—Program-Controlled I/O

On many microprocessors, there are instructions in the CPU instruction set to execute the transfer of data to and from the system.

The *IN*-type instructions are used to transfer data:

From

Specified memory location or I/O Port

To

Specified memory location or Register

The *OUT*-type instruction used to transfer data:

From

Specified memory location or Register

To

Specified memory location or I/O Port

The hardware implementation of the external infrastructure follows that utilized in the memory-mapped design. The major difference is that a dedicated I/O bus, rather than an external memory access bus, is used as the transport medium for the transfer.

The timing and instructions for utilizing the I/O ports are specified in the vendor's literature for each specific microcontroller or microcomputer. Its advantage over memory-mapped I/O is that the port I/O is separate from main memory address space and it eliminates the shared usage of the memory address and data busses. The disadvantage is that the control of any exchanges with peripheral devices remains under the auspices of the main CPU.

16.2.4 The Peripheral Processor

The memory-mapped or program-controlled I/O models require the CPU to be involved in all transactions, including managing any of the detailed timing, which can place a significant burden on CPU. In contrast, a peripheral processor scheme dedicates a (special-purpose) processor to handle all I/O tasks. The basic architecture appears as a peripheral

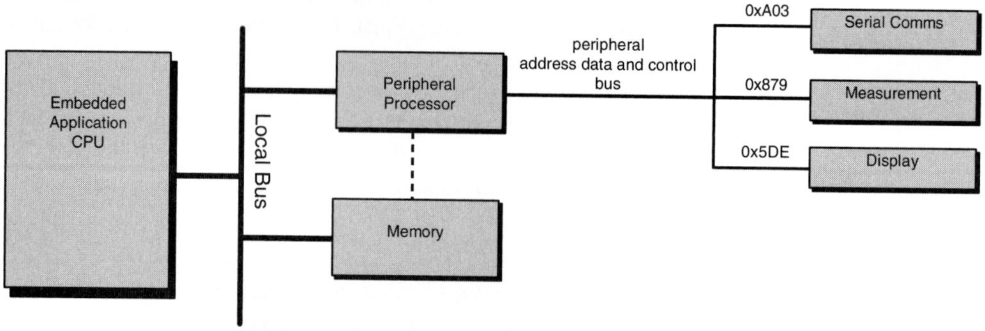

Figure 16.15 A High-Level Block Diagram for Managing I/O Devices Using a Peripheral Processor

processor that may or may not be connected to system memory. A high-level design is illustrated with a simple block diagram as shown in Figure 16.15.

Several different exchange algorithms, based on the various levels of involvement of the main system bus, the CPU, and any nonperipheral devices, are possible. The following alternative protocols are classified according to the level of the CPU involvement.

- The CPU must send to/receive from the peripheral processor while the peripheral processor manages all I/O. The peripheral processor uses the system bus in bursts during the exchange and signals the CPU when data is available.
- The CPU tells the peripheral processor where to find/put the data in memory. The peripheral processor exchanges data with the memory, manages all I/O, and signals the CPU when data is available. The peripheral processor uses the system bus in bursts during the exchange or, for the case of direct memory access (DMA), for the duration of the exchange. The scheme uses address passing and a shared buffer.
- The CPU enables a nonperipheral device and the peripheral processor to communicate. The peripheral processor exchanges data with the device, manages all I/O, and signals the device when data is available. It may signal the CPU when the transaction is complete. The peripheral processor uses the bus in bursts during exchange or for the duration of exchange.

The major advantage of using a peripheral processor is that the I/O speed and transactions can be independent of the CPU, thereby unburdening an expensive resource. The major disadvantages are the higher cost and complexity.

16.3 IMPLEMENTING THE LOCAL DEVICE MODEL—A SECOND STEP

We have now looked at three alternative architectures for executing the exchange with the external world using a local device model. Let's now take a more detailed look into the control and synchronization component of that exchange. While working inside of the processor, three types of interchange between tasks and threads were identified. Moving into the local context outside of the microprocessor, little changes. Three types of interchange remain possible: an *event*, a *shared variable*, and a *message*.

event, shared variable, message

Remember that these are abstractions of more varied concepts. Within each type, there are a wide variety of related signals. Thus, we see that the data exchange may be used with the outside world or between tasks within the processor. Let's revisit the three modes of exchange discussed earlier.

16.3.1 Information Interchange—An Event

An event is any change in the state of a signal of interest. Usually, the event is assumed to be a single signal that is asynchronous to the executing process. Every occurrence of the event simultaneously activates functions or procedures associated with tasks that are linked to the event. The occurrence of an event may or may not be stored in some way. This becomes an important issue in real-time systems.

polling, synchronous, asynchronous, interrupt

The event may be acquired in several ways. It can be sampled; one example is called *polling*. In such a case, recognition of the event is *synchronous* with normal program flow. In another form, it arrives *asynchronous* to the normal flow; one example is called an *interrupt*. The processor is not required to respond to such events.

The control flow model for an event is given in Figure 16.16.

Figure 16.16 Control Flow Diagram Event-Based Information Exchange with an I/O Device

16.3.2 Information Interchange—A Shared Variable

A shared variable may be read or written by multiple processors or I/O devices. It is typically used to exchange data between asynchronous processes. Because there are no interprocess timing constraints, the integrity of data must be respected. Such shared data represents a critical section; it is important that it be protected with a semaphore, a monitor, or some other means, as was done earlier for the case of shared data among tasks and threads. Ensuring such protection is more difficult as one moves outside of the processor.

Shared variable(s) may be global. Normally, the use of globals is discouraged in traditional programming; often, we will use such schemes in real-time designs to eliminate the cost (in time) of passing parameters via the stack. Here a global buffer area may be designated as a place into which data or a "pointer" to a buffer area may be held. The source of the transaction may then issue a control event indicating that new information is now available.

The direction of the transaction may be unidirectional or bidirectional and the operation a simple Read or a Read/Write. The destination of the transaction may be a word or buffer in a shared memory space or to one of several bits in I/O port space. For the more extensive containers, generally, a pointer to the container is exchanged if the processes cooperating in the exchange are working in the same address space. Pointer exchange will be infeasible or meaningless for devices that are not sharing a common memory address space. The data and control flow diagram in Figure 16.17 illustrates a shared variable exchange.

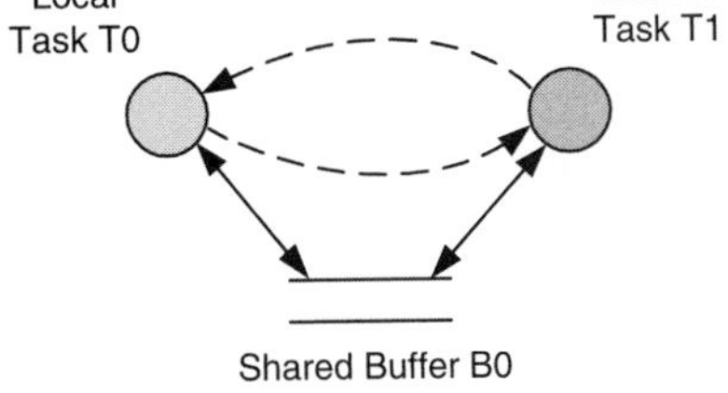

Figure 16.17 Control Flow Diagram: Shared Buffer Information Exchange with an I/O Device

16.3.3 Information Interchange—A Message

When a greater amount of information, coupled with a more sophisticated exchange protocol becomes necessary, the message model is preferred over the shared variable or the event. The exchange is typically over either a proprietary interface, a modified standard such as EIA 232, or a dedicated version of one of the standard channels such as USB or Firewire. The accompanying high-level diagram, in Figure 16.18, adds a simple network to the local model.

As with shared variables, the direction of the message exchange may be unidirectional or bidirectional, and the intent may be a simple Read or a Read/Write operation. A task wishing to send or receive a message from a local peripheral device will provide the address of a buffer to the I/O driver from which information is read or to which it is written by the driver.

A data and control flow diagram for one implementation of the message model of the local exchange is illustrated in Figure 16.18.

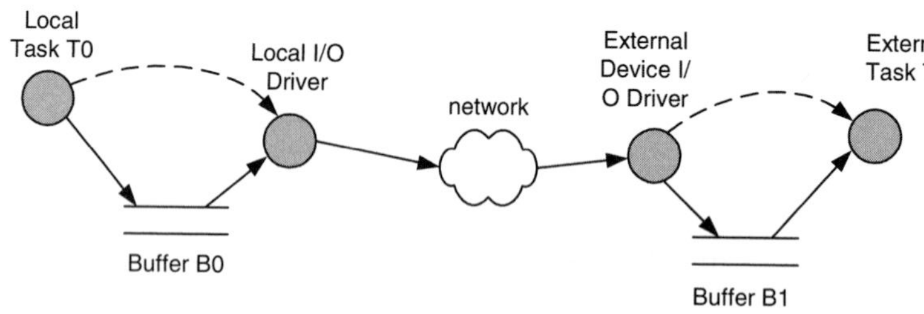

Figure 16.18 Control Flow Diagram Message-Based Information Exchange with an I/O Device

16.4 IMPLEMENTING AN EVENT-DRIVEN EXCHANGE—INTERRUPTS AND POLLING

An event-driven exchange of information with local devices is implemented in a variety of different ways based on the level of control and information that is necessary. Whether inside or outside of the processor, the necessary operations reduce to what we have already learned: polling operations and interrupts. We will now examine each in a context that moves beyond the bounds of the processor. Let's look first at polling as a means of completing an exchange.

16.4.1 Polling

With a polling scheme, a control device is required. Such a device can be either the main CPU or a peripheral processor. In the following discussions, we refer to either one as simply the CPU. For such a scheme, flow of control is generally implemented as a *polling loop*. In the polling loop, each external device that may require service or may have essential information is interrogated. Service may be necessary on several occasions:

polling loop

- During power up
- On demand
- As part of normal flow of control

During power up, one may be completing the task of confirming system integrity by requiring each local device or process to report its status. The event source may be a piece of hardware that is reporting the results of a self-test or an initialization sequence. It may also be the same information coming from a software process that is now up and running.

When needed, the application may request that a hardware or software module execute a self-test or an automatic calibration and return the results. The request may also be part of a system integrity check or routine updates to the system configuration.

Alternatively, as an integral part of the task being executed, the application may initiate some action such as a switch closure or signal activation and then continually test for results from such a request. Whatever the motivation, the algorithm precedes as follows.

1. Send device address followed by specific request.

2. Receive a response.

The response may consist of a single signal, a word, state information, or status. The result may be the state of the system or the result from a requested action.

As a result of the response, we may choose further action or continue polling.

3. If further response

if send operation

When the *device ready* received—as appropriate

Transfer to appropriate routine

Execute transfer

Return to polling loop to look for result

else if collect status, results, or receive operation

Collect or receive, then continue polling other devices

Status may include self-test results, a ready condition after power up, availability for additional transfer, data available, or completion of a requested operation.

The general polling operation is expressed in the following state diagram in Figure 16.19. Following each response, flow of control may be temporarily switched to an associated routine that handles the response.

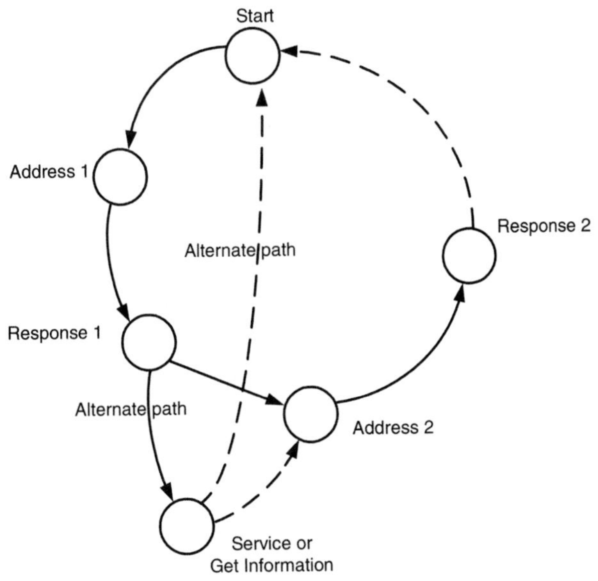

Figure 16.19 State Diagram Describing a Typical System Polling Algorithm

A limitation that one encounters with polling, as with the busy wait or spin lock studied earlier, is that the CPU can do nothing else while polling. The advantages, however, are that the process is deterministic and the time to complete the operation (or a specific phase of the operation) is predictable based on instruction counting or direct measurement, as we learned earlier. The worst case response will occur if the state of the signal being polled changes immediately after it was sampled and the remaining code in the polling loop must be executed prior to returning to the appropriate test. In real-time systems, with a hard deadline, being able to analyze and to quantify the flow of control is absolutely essential.

16.4.2 Interrupts

Whether one is working inside or outside of the processor, the goal of an interrupt-based exchange is the same as that of a polled approach. The major difference is that when using interrupts, the CPU is not dedicated to monitoring the state of a signal input; it can be engaged in other tasks. The source of the interrupt signals from outside of the processor is generally going to be in the hardware. A typical microprocessor-based I/O system may have one or more lines designated as *external interrupts*. Each such interrupt input may potentially be connected to one or to several devices.

external interrupts

We will first examine how a single external interrupt, originating outside of the processor, might be managed. As the name suggests, an interrupt signal interrupts a background activity (using a foreground/background model). As with internal interrupts, one must write an ISR to handle the event. The processor vendor will have designated a priority level and associated a source with each supported interrupt. The ISR is entered into the vector table in exactly the same way as was done earlier for internally based interrupts. Because of such a seamless structure between internal and external interrupts, the management scheme will differ little from the one we have already studied.

16.4.2.1 Single Interrupt Line with Single Device

The first task in managing an external interrupt is the same as that for the internal cousin: identify the source of the interrupt. Identifying the causative event and the device that initiated the event is easy with only a single device. When the interrupt occurs, two actions are possible: It can be ignored or responded to. We will discuss ignoring the interrupt and the consequences shortly.

Responding to an external interrupt is no different from responding to an internal one. It is not much more than a subroutine call.

The procedure is as follows.

1. Suspend the current process.
2. Save the current context.
3. Acknowledge the interrupt.
4. Branch to the ISR appropriate to interrupting device.
5. Execute the routine.
6. Restore the former context and resume the former process.

16.4.2.2 Single Interrupt Line with Multiple Devices

When dealing with multiple devices on a single interrupt line, the problem is only slightly more complicated than with a single device. Figure 16.20 illustrates one method of connecting to the interrupt line. Each source connects using an open collector/drain driver as shown in the figure.

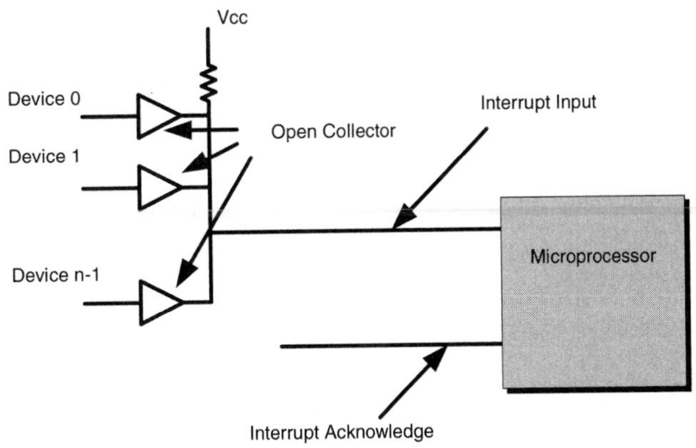

Figure 16.20 Block Diagram for a System Utilizing a Single External Interrupt to Support Multiple Devices

acknowledge

In responding to the event, the CPU issues an *acknowledge* informing the interrupting device that the interrupt has been recognized and the handling process will begin. The acknowledge can be managed in several different ways. One approach is illustrated with the block diagram in Figure 16.21.

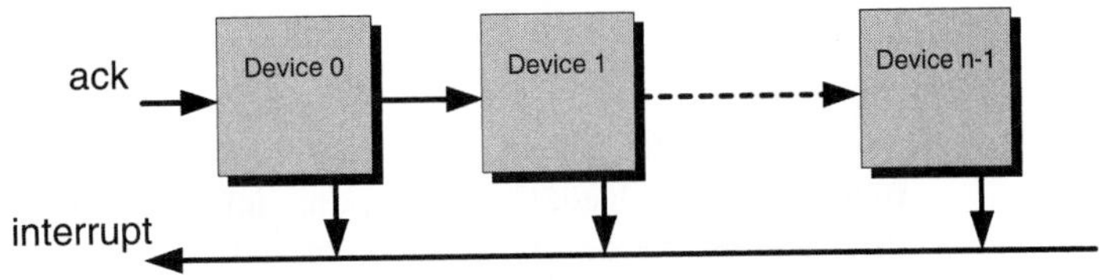

Figure 16.21 Block Diagram for a System Utilizing a Single Interrupt with a Chained Interrupt Acknowledge Scheme

In the design, the ACK is chained through the peripheral devices. Therefore, priority is based on physical proximity to the controller. The closest device has the highest priority. Each device in the chain must handle the ACK and pass it on or block the flow of the ACK and execute its ISR routine. The design is similar to that in the token ring for selecting writers.

An alternative acknowledgment scheme is coupled with the process of identifying the source of the interrupt as we will see next.

IDENTIFYING THE INTERRUPT SOURCE

When multiple sources use a single interrupt, the identity of the device requesting service must be determined and the possibility of multiple interrupts must be considered. We will address the problem of identification first. In addition, for the moment, it will be assumed that only a single interrupt has occurred.

SINGLE INTERRUPT

A polling or a vectoring scheme both offer a simple and effective means to identify the source of a single interrupt. We will look first at polling.

The polling operation begins when the interrupt occurs. At this point, the current task is suspended and the flow of control switches to an ISR. The ISR will query each device in turn. Once the source is identified, the interrupt will be acknowledged, and the flow of control will vector to the appropriate handler routine to manage the request and then return and resume the suspended task. The accompanying code fragment in Figure 16.22 illustrates a pseudo-code implementation for the ISR.

```
interrupt service routine
{
    repeat
        query device
        receive status
    until (status == interrupt)
    switch on device id
    {
        routine 0
            •
            •
            •
        routine n-1
    }
    return
}
```

Figure 16.22 Pseudo-Code Algorithm for Responding to an Interrupt in a System Utilizing a Single Interrupt with a Chained Interrupt Acknowledge Scheme

With a vector scheme, the device requesting service issues an interrupt. When the interrupt is acknowledged, the interrupting device returns an identifier of some sort. The identifier can be the device name or the address of the service routine, for example. The sequence to handle the interrupt then proceeds as with the polled alternative.

MULTIPLE INTERRUPTS

With several devices on the same line, one must consider the possibility of having multiple simultaneous and/or sequential interrupts. We will examine each of these cases next.

SIMULTANEOUS INTERRUPTS

The easiest solution for identifying the source is to handle each interrupt in turn in a round robin fashion. The pseudo code for an ISR to implement the search is given in Figure 16.23a. A priority-based scheme can be an effective alternative. Priorities can be assigned based on physical proximity to the CPU (closer is higher priority), on an assigned value, or on the time the interrupt occurred. In any case, the higher priority device gets serviced first. In the latter case, a tie can still occur. The easiest solution is to manage them on a first-identified first-served basis. Alternative approaches to resolving the tie are best left to the designer who has a good understanding of the system and the application.

A pseudo-code implementation for a round robin-based ISR is given in Figure 16.23a, and a priority based ISR is given in Figure 16.23b.

A third approach to resolving the interrupt source utilizes a vector-based scheme. The process begins when the device requesting service issues an interrupt. When the interrupt is acknowledged, the interrupting device returns an identifier. The identifier can be the device name or the address of the service routine, for example. The sequence to handle the interrupt

```
interrupt service routine
{
    repeat
        query device
        receive status
        if (status == interrupt)
        {
            switch on device id
            {
                routine 0
                    •
                    •
                    •
                routine n-1
            }
        }
    until no interrupting device identified
return
}
```

(a)

```
interrupt service routine
{
    for each device
        query device
        receive status
        if (status == interrupt)
        {
            add to list
        }
        end for
    repeat
    {
        select highest priority from list
        switch on device id
        {
            routine 0
                •
                •
                •
            routine n-1
        }
    }
    until list empty
    return
}
```

(b)

Figure 16.23 (a) Pseudo-Code Algorithm for First-Come First-Served Scheme for Servicing Multiple Simultaneous Interrupt. (b) Pseudo-Code Algorithm for a Priority Scheme for Servicing Multiple Simultaneous Interrupts

then proceeds as with the polled alternative. Acknowledge messages can be repeatedly issued until the interrupts are handled and the interrupt signal returns to the inactive state.

SEQUENTIAL INTERRUPTS

If a second interrupt can potentially occur while the first is being handled, one can either initially disable further interrupts and thereby ignore all that subsequently occurs until the current ISR exits or assign a priority to each device. If a newly interrupting device has higher priority than the one being handled, it is managed in the same way as is done when calling a subroutine from subroutine.

When incorporating a protocol that disables interrupts, it is important to thoroughly understand the consequences. Because an interrupt is generally a transient event, it may be gone by the time the system is ready to handle it. Under such a circumstance, one may elect to implement a queue in which the event and its source are stored. This approach will work well as long as the state of the context in which the interrupt occurred is not critical or transient.

16.4.2.3 Multiple Interrupt Lines

When working with a processor that supports multiple external interrupts, the analysis from the previous sections is easily extended. For each interrupt, one must consider the case of a single device on each interrupt line and that for multiple devices per line. We will start with a single device per line.

SINGLE DEVICE ON EACH LINE

For the case of a single device on each individual line, we treat that line as we did for a single line with single device. To manage the multiple lines, we follow the model that we established for the case of the single line with multiple sources. Thus, we can manage the interrupt handling on a round robin basis, or we can assign priority to each line.

A priority-based design can proceed in several ways by using

- External hardware
- Internal hardware
- Internal software

EXTERNAL HARDWARE

priority encoder To resolve priority-using external hardware, one can use a device called a *priority encoder* shown as a high-level block diagram in Figure 16.24. The circuit can be purchased as an MSI device, or one can opt for a proprietary design if commercially available components do not satisfy requirements.

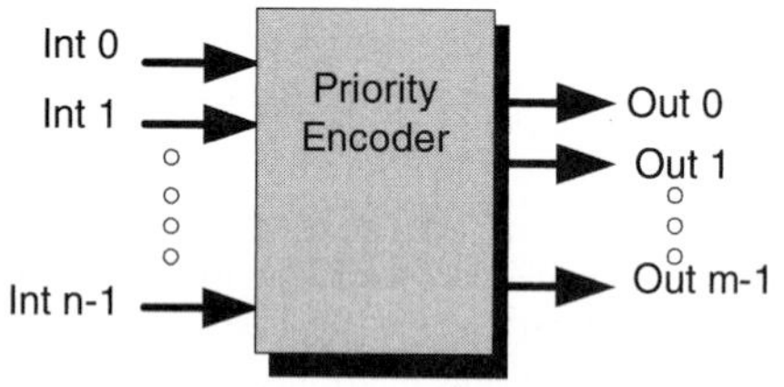

Figure 16.24 A Hardware Priority Scheme for Managing Multiple Simultaneous Interrupts

The high-level behavior for the priority encoder is to accept n inputs and to present a binary number corresponding to that input (based on its assigned and fixed priority) as an output. For the drawing in Figure 16.24, assume Int_0 has the highest priority as set by the design of the encoder. Under such an assumption, when Int_0 is asserted, the output set $[Out_0 .. Out_{m-1}]$ will contain the pattern binary 0. If Int_0 is not asserted and any other interrupt input, Int_i is asserted, the output set $[Out_0 .. Out_{m-1}]$ will present the binary number corresponding to Int_i. If later Int_0 is asserted or reasserted, then the output set $[Out_0 .. Out_{m-1}]$ will assert binary 0 since Int_0 has the highest priority. Processing of Int_i by the processor is suspended, and Int_0 processing commences.

The truth table in Figure 16.25 specifies an eight-line to three-line priority encoder. Int_0 ***Valid*** is assumed to have the highest priority. A *Valid* output is added to ensure support for the full eight priority levels. Without the valid output, one could not distinguish between interrupt, Int_7, and no interrupt active.

MANAGING WITH INTERNAL HARDWARE

The same scheme described earlier is implemented in hardware inside the processor or controller chip.

int0	int1	int2	int3	int4	int5	int6	int7	Out1	Out2	Out3	Valid
0								0	0	0	1
1	0							0	0	1	1
1	1	0						0	1	0	1
1	1	1	0					0	1	1	1
1	1	1	1	0				1	0	0	1
1	1	1	1	1	0			1	0	1	1
1	1	1	1	1	1	0		1	1	0	1
1	1	1	1	1	1	1	0	1	1	1	1
1	1	1	1	1	1	1	1	1	1	1	0

Figure 16.25 A Truth Table for an Eight Interrupt Priority Encoder

MANAGING WITH INTERNAL SOFTWARE

The same scheme described earlier is implemented in software inside the controller or processor chip.

MULTIPLE INTERRUPT LINES WITH MULTIPLE DEVICES ON EACH

When each interrupt line supports multiple devices, we begin with the same model we developed for the single-device case. Once an individual line is selected to be serviced, we follow the single interrupt–multiple devices model.

16.4.3 Masking Interrupts

Masking is the process of ignoring an interrupt by preventing it from propagating to the interrupt management hardware and software. As with other concepts we have looked at, the scheme can be implemented in software or hardware. Figure 16.26 gives a hardware implementation. A software design would be functionally equivalent.

mask register

To implement the scheme, a *mask register* is added to the system of interrupts. An interrupt is selectively enabled by placing a logical 1 on the corresponding position in the mask register and disabled by entering a logical 0. Microprocessors that support masking will provide instructions in support of managing the mask register. Observe that the interrupt can still happen; it is blocked, however, from initiating the internal interrupt signal. A priority scheme could easily be incorporated into the design as well. A general term is of the form

$$e_i \bullet i_i \bullet \bar{i}_{i+1} \bullet \bar{i}_{i+2} \bullet \ldots \quad (16.0)$$

as shown in the truth table in Figure 16.25. Higher priority interrupts are those to the right.

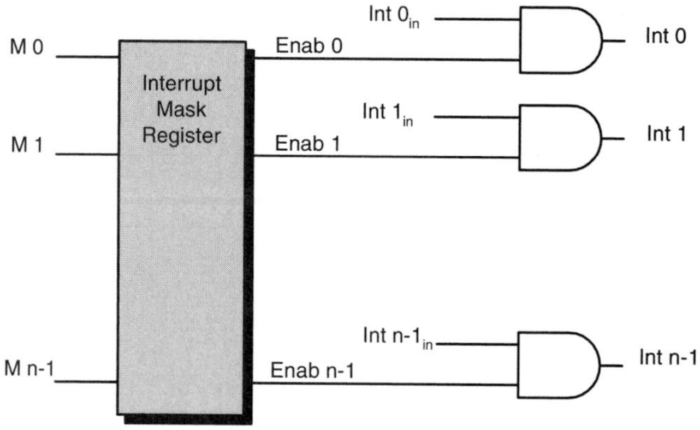

Figure 16.26 A Block Diagram for Masking Interrupts

When a processor supports a masking scheme, often a subset of the potential interrupts is designated as *nonmaskable*. These are usually interrupts associated with critical system functions, such as an illegal instruction trap, that must be handled.

nonmaskable

16.5 A MESSAGE

The diagram in Figure 16.27 adds basic network capability to the local model to support simple message-based exchanges.

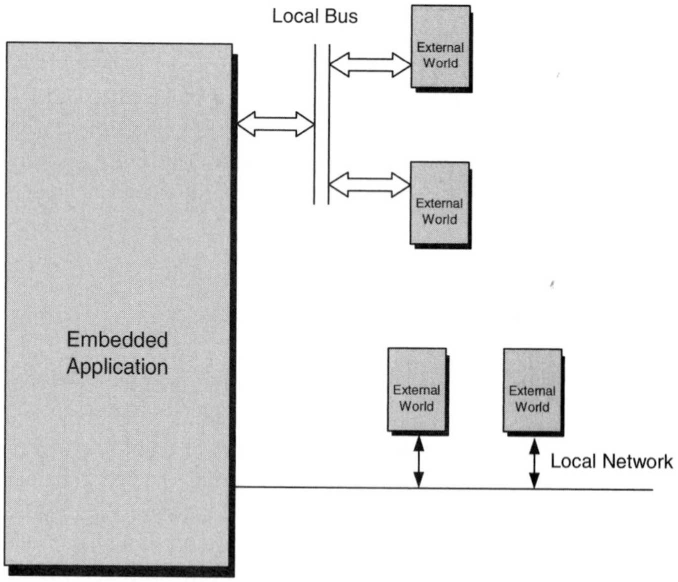

Figure 16.27 A Block Diagram for a System Utilizing Both a Local Bus and Local Network Architecture

When messages are exchanged within the local system or between the local system and connected peripheral devices, the receiving device must be able to accept the incoming stream of information and then to detect and identify the start and end of a bit, the start and end of a character, and the start and end of a message block or frame. These are known as *bit, character,* and *frame synchronization.*

bit, character, frame synchronization

asynchronous

synchronous

The different transmission modes give rise to two general categories of message exchange: *asynchronous* transmission in which the receiver resynchronizes at the start of each bit and *synchronous* transmission in which the receiver resynchronizes either continuously based on encoded clock edge transitions or at the start of each block or frame.

synchronous transmission

Asynchronous communication is characterized by irregular intervals between the transmitted data groups. The intercharacter spacing on the communication channel may vary widely. There may be bursts of activity followed by long periods of inactivity. In contrast, when blocks of regularly spaced data are transferred over a serial line, the transmitter and receiver can be synchronized to a common clock, thereby permitting character transfer at a much higher rate. Such a format is known as *synchronous transmission.* Generally, synchronous transfer requires less overhead and therefore is more efficient than an asynchronous design. Let's now look at asynchronous communication and timing in greater detail and then follow with a look at a synchronous approach.

16.5.1 Asynchronous Information Exchange

Because there is no inherent clock associated with an asynchronous exchange, coordination and synchronization are accomplished using a protocol that permits (re)synchronization of the data to the receiving system's internal clock. Both the protocols and the amount of data exchanged can vary tremendously.

Strobes

Let's look at several common design examples. The first is illustrated in Figure 16.28. In one of the simpler designs, the source will transmit data in parallel, by word, and associate a strobe with each outgoing word. The received data will not be acknowledged.

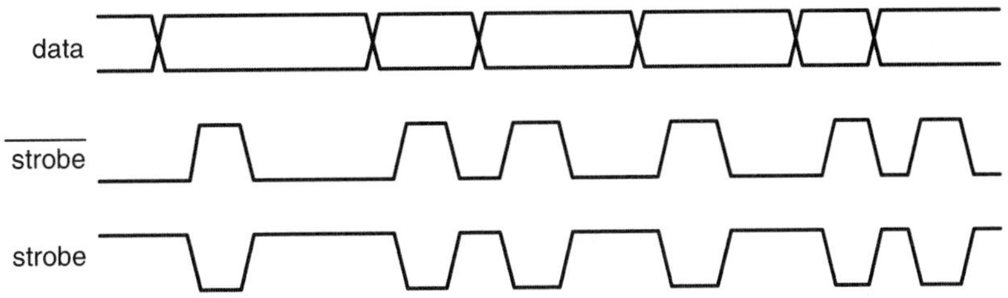

Figure 16.28 Using Positive Going or Negative Going Strobes to Deskew and Capture Asynchronous Data

Observe, as the timing diagram reflects, that the strobe can be of either polarity, the data sampled on either edge, and the data transmission is sporadic. We use such a scheme when speed is important and the probability of data corruption is low.

Strobe with Acknowledge

The next level of sophistication (and reliability) associates a strobe with each outgoing data word. Receipt of the word is acknowledged with a return strobe or acknowledge as we see in Figure 16.29. In the design, the sender blocks on receipt of the ACK.

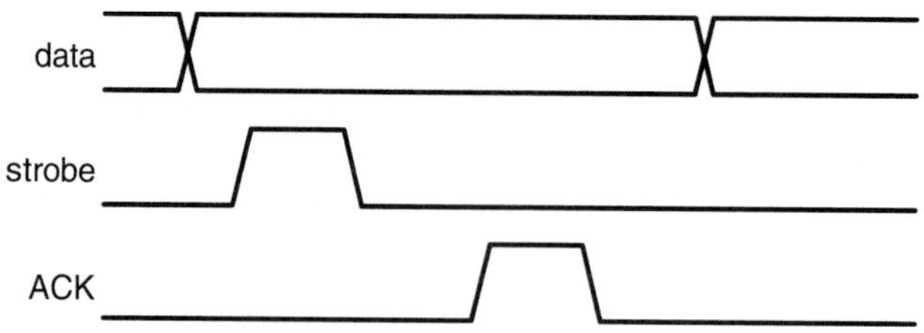

Figure 16.29 An Asynchronous Data Capture Scheme Utilizing a Strobe and Acknowledge

The strobe and acknowledge signals can be of either polarity.

Full Handshake

A full handshake confirms all phases of the exchange. As Figure 16.30 illustrates, the transaction begins at the receiver when it indicates that it is ready to accept data by placing its control line into the logical 0 state.

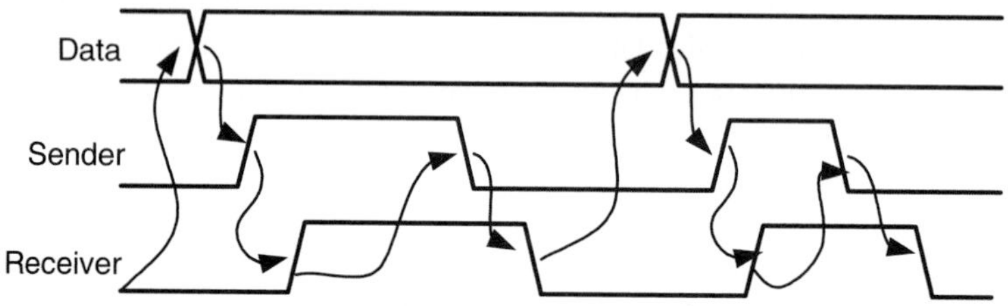

Figure 16.30 An Asynchronous Data Capture Scheme Utilizing a Full Handshake

That low state initially (or the trailing edge following a transaction) tells the sender that data may now be placed onto the bus. The sender responds by placing the new data onto the bus, followed sometime later by the rising edge of the control signal. That action informs the receiver that new data is on the bus and that it has settled and can be captured correctly.

In response, the receiver raises its control line to inform the sender that data has been received and that it may now be removed from the bus. The state change on the receiver side prompts the sender to lower its control line, thereby acknowledging the receiver's capture of the data. The receiver then lowers its strobe to complete the transaction. The trailing edge in the receiver control indicates to the sender that a new transaction may begin if data remains to be sent.

Resynchronization

Another form of synchronization protocol entails generating a sampling signal on the receiver side based on knowing the transfer rate and when the first data bit has arrived. Such an approach is known as *bit timing*.

bit timing

The approach works as follows. The transmitter and receiver are timed by independent clocks. To capture the incoming signal reliably, one must know the length or duration of a bit and when a transmission starts. In the ideal situation, the signal is sampled in the center, which gives the maximum tolerance for errors on either side of the signal.

Such an approach can be implemented as illustrated in Figure 16.31.

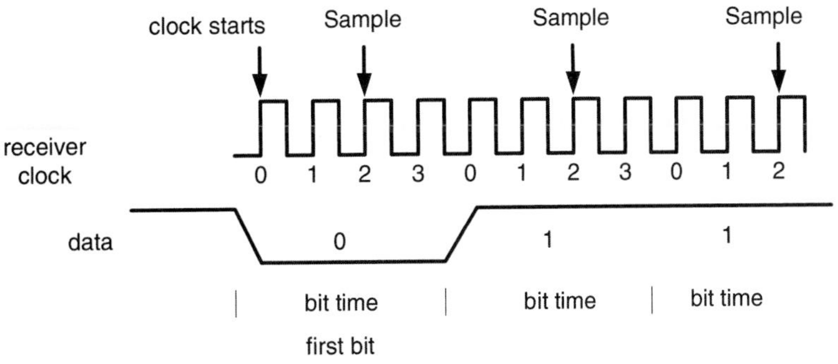

Figure 16.31 An Asynchronous Data Capture Scheme Utilizing Bit Sampling at the Receiver

The bit time and message length are agreed upon, in advance, by the sender and receiver. It is also agreed in advance that the idle state of the data line will be a logical 1 and that a transition from logical 1 to logical 0 will signify the start of a transmission. In the current design, we select a receiver clock with a period that is one-fourth of the bit time; that is, there are four receiver clocks during each bit time.

The start of a character is signaled by the transition of the data line from logical 1 to logical 0. In response, the receiver clock is started, and the number of receiver clocks is counted. Based on the agreed upon timing, it is known that the falling edge of the second clock will be in the center of the data bit. At this point, the incoming data bit can be stored. The falling edge of the sixth (two clocks + four clocks) clock pulse will occur in the center of the second data bit, which can now be stored. The process can be repeated until all data has been received. For the current example, the stored data would be read as 011.

The block diagram in Figure 16.32 illustrates the design.

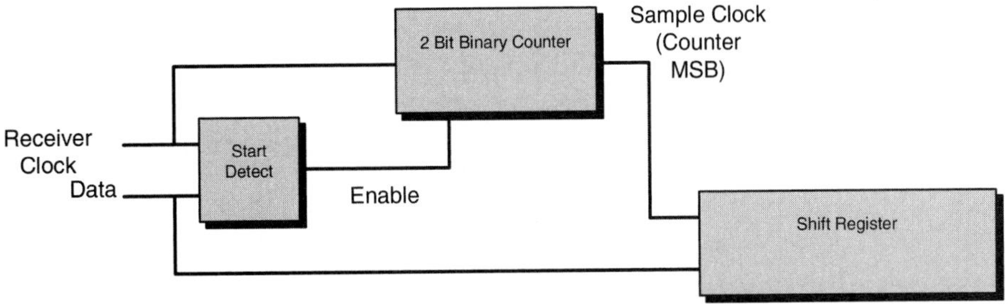

Figure 16.32 A High-Level Block Diagram for a System Utilizing Bit Sampling at the Receiver

Analysis

The potential problems with an asynchronous approach include the following.

- It is difficult to test.
- Clock noise is more difficult to filter out.
- The protocol to identify the start/end of transmission is potentially a bit more complex than a synchronous scheme.

At the same time, the asynchronous approach can offer several advantages.

- The devices within the system can run at different/differing speed.
- There will be no clock skew on long busses.

16.5.2 Synchronous Information Exchange

The asynchronous transmission schemes have several drawbacks, including the extra overhead of control bits and the bit clock synchronization scheme, which becomes less reliable at higher data rates. Such problems can be mitigated to a large extent with synchronous transmission. Nonetheless, it is still necessary to achieve bit, character, and frame synchronization. Frame synchronization is usually derived from bit or character synchronization. With synchronous transmission, exchanges between the sender and receiver are synchronized to the clock either directly or through signals encoded in the data.

16.5.2.1 Bit Synchronization

To achieve bit synchronization, a two-step process is typically used,

- Encode the clock in the data.
- Re-derive the clock from the data.

ENCODED CLOCK

To encode the clock in the data, three different methods or their variants are commonly used.

BIPOLAR ENCODING

When using bipolar encoding, binary 0's and 1's are represented by different polarity signals, as is shown in Figure 16.33. Each bit cell contains clocking information, as reflected by the transition in the center of the bit cell.

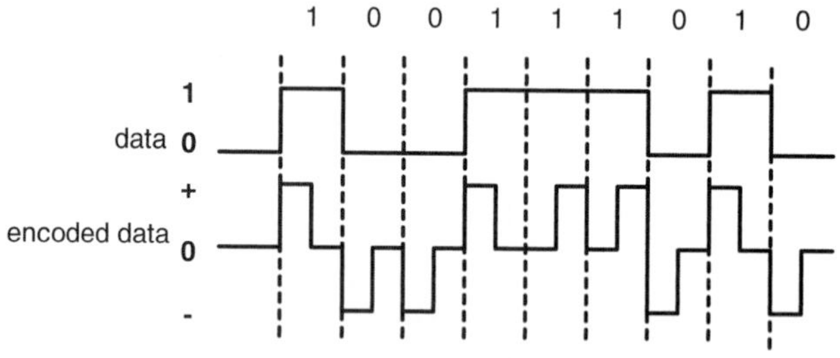

Figure 16.33 Clock Encoding Using Bipolar Encoding

return-to-zero (RZ)

Observe in the diagram in Figure 16.33 that the signal returns to zero level after each encoded bit. Such a scheme is referred to as *return-to-zero* (RZ) signaling. The approach requires three distinct signal levels.

MANCHESTER PHASE ENCODING

Manchester Phase Encoding

In a *Manchester Phase Encoding* scheme, a binary 0 is encoded as a high to low signal transition and a binary 1 as a low to high signal transition. The transition occurs in the center of each bit cell, which provides the clock information.

non-return-to-zero (NRZ)

Observe in Figure 16.34 that the signal does not return to zero level after each encoded bit. Such a scheme is referred to as a *non-return-to-zero* (NRZ) signaling.

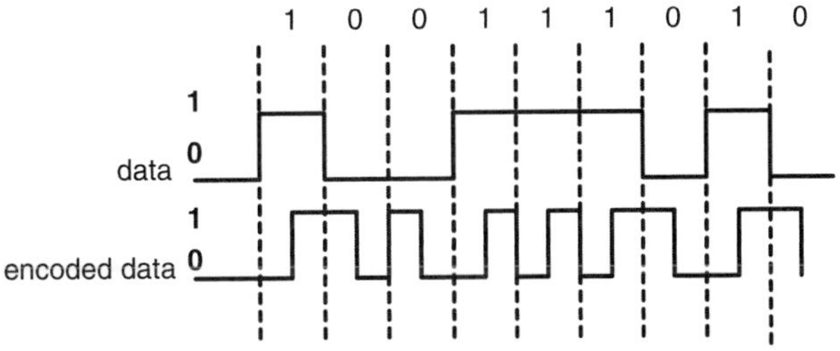

Figure 16.34 Clock Encoding Using Manchester NRZI Phase Encoding

MANCHESTER DIFFERENTIAL ENCODING

Manchester Differential Encoding
center
start

With *Manchester Differential Encoding*, illustrated in Figure 16.35, once again the transition occurs in the *center* of each bit cell and provides the clock information. We have a transition at the *start* of each bit cell only if the next bit to be encoded is a binary 0.

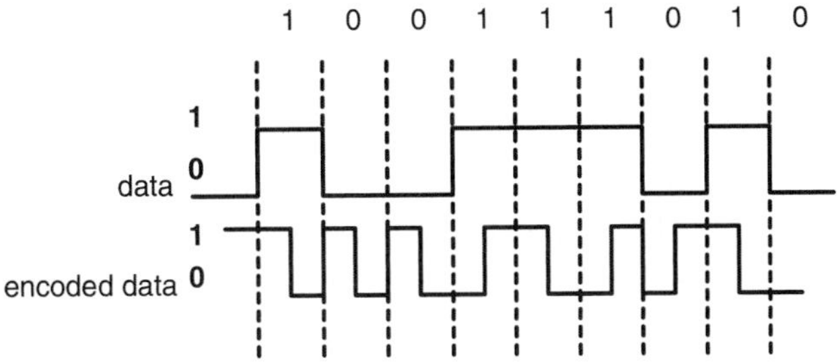

Figure 16.35 Clock Encoding Using Manchester NRZI Differential Encoding

RE-DERIVING THE CLOCK

phase lock loop (PLL)

To re-derive the clock from the data, the transmission begins with a preamble, including a synchronization sequence. A *phase locked loop* (PLL), based on a very stable receiver clock, is used to keep the sample clock locked to the signal transitions in the incoming signal. Data must be encoded to ensure a sufficient number of signal transitions to retain synchronization. At each transition, the sample timing is adjusted to ensure sampling in the center of a bit. The design will tolerate intervals without transitions, provided there is a stable fundamental clock.

The PLL is a conventional closed loop control system with some additions and modifications. The basic structure for a closed loop system is given in Figure 16.36.

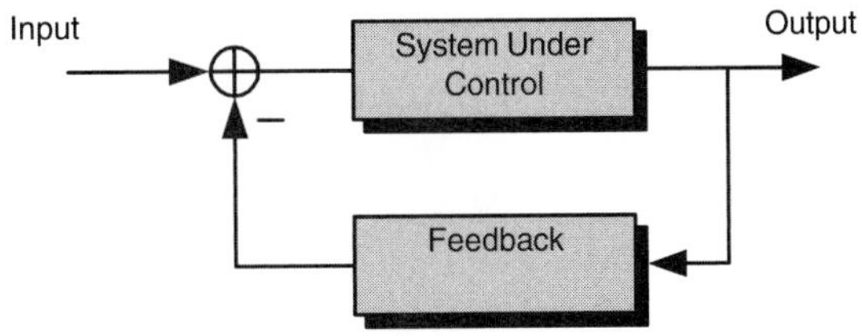

Figure 16.36 Basic Feedback Control System

For the traditional analog closed loop control system, the input is algebraically added to a signal that is modified and fed back from the output of the system. The result is an error signal that serves as an input to the system under control. The objective of the system is to drive the error signal to 0.

In the case of a phase locked loop, the objective is to control a frequency. The basic block diagram is presented in Figure 16.37.

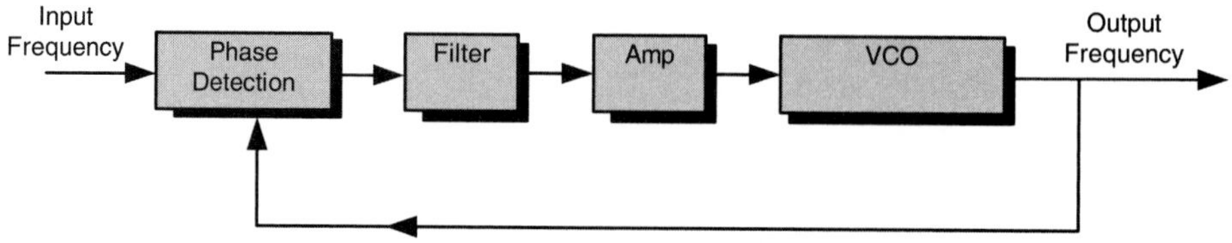

Figure 16.37 Implementing a Phase Locked Loop Utilizing a Basic Feedback Control System

The output of the PLL is generated using a voltage-controlled oscillator (VCO). The output of the VCO is fed back to a phase detector that compares the signal characteristics of the input signal with those of the one being fed back. When the frequency and phase difference between the input signal and the output of the VCO is 0, the system has *locked* onto the input frequency. A difference in frequency and phase appears as an error voltage that is filtered by the low pass filter shown, amplified, and provides an input voltage to the VCO. The output of the VCO can now serve as the clock to our system. The input signal to the PLL is of any of the encoded data streams we discussed earlier.

locked

ANALYSIS

As we learned with the asynchronous approach, potential problems are also associated with a synchronous design.

- All devices must run at the same speed.
- Because of (potentially) different loading on clock versus data lines, we can have different propagation delays along a bus.
- There is the possibility that the clock will arrive at the various destinations at different times with respect to the data as illustrated in in Figure 16.38. Thus, one can easily get clock skew (with respect to the data) on long busses, particularly at higher clocking frequencies.

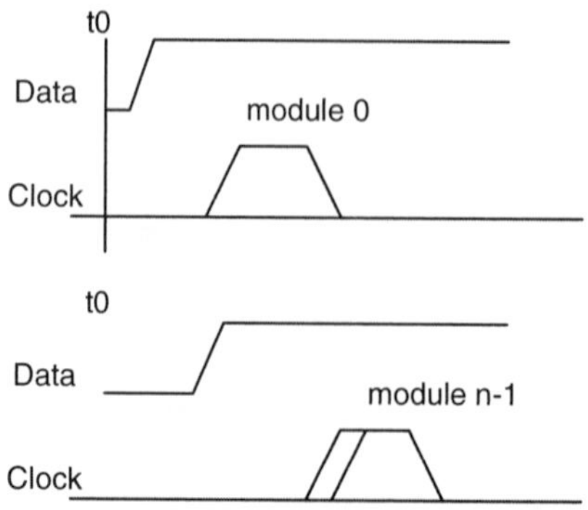

Figure 16.38 Clock Skew on a Long Bus in a Synchronous System

Some of the potential advantages of a synchronous design are as follows.

- It is easier to test.
- Generally, the protocol is simpler than an asynchronous approach.
- It is easier to stay in sync with the data than with an asynchronous approach.

16.6 THE REMOTE DEVICE MODEL

As the demands on embedded systems grow in sophistication, so does the complexity of their design. Heretofore the tasks doing the majority of the work in the application have been primarily found in the main processor. The local device model we have been studying has focused on and supported interaction with peripheral devices in close proximity to the local system. Any tasks executing on such devices have associated with the function of the specific device. Those tasks are generally not considered to be part of the application proper.

remote device model

distributed tasks

The other component of external world interaction introduces the *remote device model* and the notion of *distributed tasks* executing on such devices. These tasks are often considered to be a contributing part of the main application.

Figure 16.39 now adds remote capability to the expanding embedded system architecture.

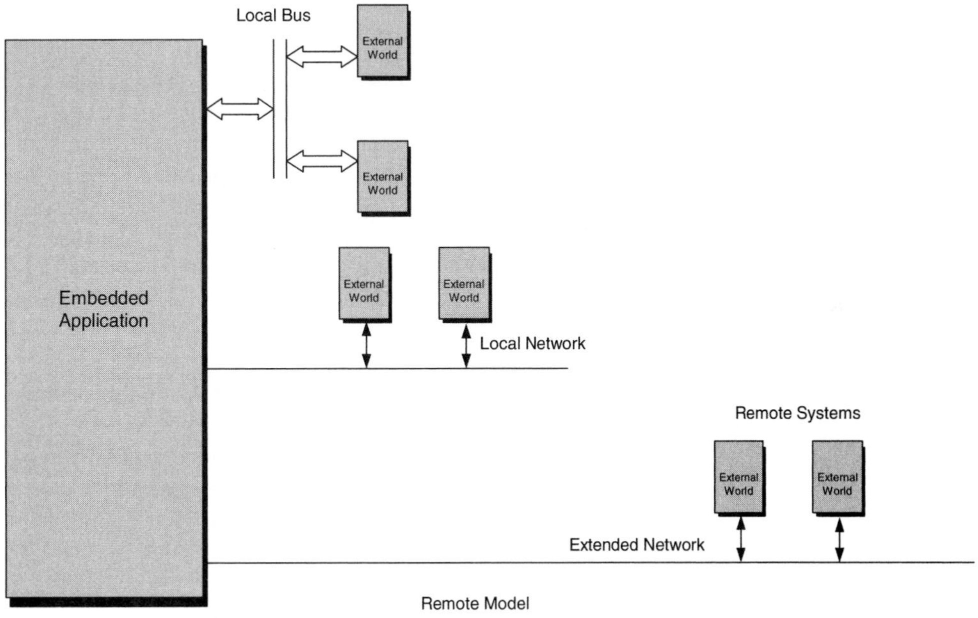

Figure 16.39 Extending the External Intrasystem Communication by Adding a Network

Up to this point, interprocess communication and synchronization has depended primarily on familiar semantics utilizing a number of variations on the shared variable paradigm. The local device model works well as long as the devices with which the system is interacting are within 3 to 5 meters of the controlling microprocessor. Frequently, the data movement is done in parallel. Although such communication is far more efficient at moving large numbers of bits than serial, it is not always as practical.

As we begin to expand to greater distances, our thinking shifts to a network-based approach in which tasks can exchange information through messages. The sending process transmits a set of data values, the *message*, through the specified communication medium where it is accepted by the receiving process. The medium may be a *channel* or *port*. The basic supporting operations are *Send* and *Receive*.

message

channel, port

Send, Receive

The major differences between the remote and local device models are reflected in the details of the transport mechanism and the control and synchronization of the information exchange. Most remote intra- and intersystem communications within a distributed embedded system take place over a standard network using a serial scheme—EIA-232, I^2C, Ethernet, USB, and so on.

Any modern automobile provides an excellent example of such a system. Processors throughout the vehicle manage everything from the fuel system to the passenger environment and entertainment systems. Internet and Internet appliances are further examples of contemporary distributed embedded applications.

As we move to networked systems, we introduce a new collection of opportunities and challenges. One of the basic goals is to ensure that the underlying architecture is invisible to the tasks comprising the application. That is, from any task's perspective, interaction with other tasks should not depend on where the tasks are physically located or on the computing engine on which each is executing. Furthermore, we want to be able to exchange information with any part of the system both easily and seamlessly. The notion of highly cohesive, loosely coupled modules that was introduced earlier continues now with movement outside of the processor.

Challenges arise because of the very nature of the distributed system. With such systems, the possibility of local failures now exists. The system can experience hardware or software failures on any of the distributed portions of the application while the remainder of the system continues to operate. The designs must be tolerant of such failures. The interprocess communication and synchronization problem is also exacerbated. As the application becomes increasingly distributed, the communication delays become longer and may become nondeterministic. The need to meet hard real-time constraints thus remains, increasing the complexity of any analysis and modeling of such problems.

16.6.1 Places and Information

places, information

Figure 16.39 gave a high-level architecture for the remote device model. In the model, the identity of the *places* where the *information* is to be written to or read from and the *information* itself are embodied in messages exchanged over the remote network structure. The format of the message can be implemented in a variety of ways depending on the nature and structure of the underlying protocol and supporting networks.

16.6.2 Control and Synchronization

control and synchronization

The *control and synchronization* strategy is incorporated into the protocol by which the messages are exchanged.

16.6.3 Transport

transport

The physical *transport* of the information between the system core and the remote external devices can utilize any of the models introduced earlier in this chapter. Today, copper wire remains the medium of choice; however, fiber and air are gaining widespread support. Within programmable logic devices or networks on a chip, it is a silicon path.

16.7 IMPLEMENTING THE REMOTE DEVICE MODEL—A FIRST STEP

We will now begin our study of the message exchange portion of the remote device model. Central to any such communications between electronic devices is the protocol for transmitting and receiving the information or message. We will start with the transport level. Message exchange in distributed embedded applications occurs either via a proprietary network or one implemented according to one of the many standards. Typically, the transport topology is serial, and information flow is full duplex. Whether it utilizes a proprietary or standard topology, the typical transport architecture comprises a hierarchy of virtual networks.

Above the physical portion of the transport mechanism will be a varying number of software layers or levels as illustrated in Figure 16.40. The function at each level or layer on one machine interacts with the corresponding function at the same level on the second machine.

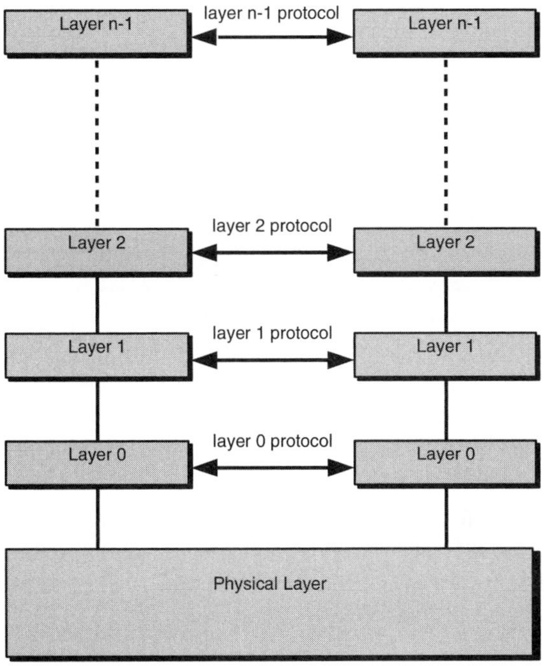

Figure 16.40 An N Layer Network Architecture

protocol

At each level, potentially a different language, referred to as a *protocol*, is spoken. The function at each level is to provide services for the level above. Thus, between levels, we have the relationship of a *service provider* and a *service consumer*. At each level, the protocols may be implemented in either hardware or software. Typically, the lower levels are done in hardware and the upper in software.

service provider, service consumer

network architecture

protocol stack, message

The entire collection is called a *network architecture*, and the set of protocols used is called a *protocol stack*. The information sent on each level is called a *message*. It is possible that a message on a higher level is composed of several lower level messages. Synchronization between or among distributed processes is accomplished through such a message exchange.

Today, a wide variety of protocol standards are available. Although a proprietary network and protocol must sometimes be used, given a choice one should opt for one of the standards. The general objective of each standard is to facilitate message exchange in a specific application context such as small computer networks (EIA-232 or USB), simple local area networks (Firewire, Bluetooth, I^2C), automotive networks (CAN bus), or manufacturing environments (CAMAC). Though unique to their particular context, most of these models trace their ancestry to two major protocol schemes or stacks, *OSI* and *TCP/IP*.

OSI, TCP/IP

16.7.1 The OSI and TCP/IP Protocol Stacks

Open Systems Interconnection Model (OSI) Transmission Control Protocol/Internet Protocol (TCP/IP), physical, data link, host to network

The *Open Systems Interconnection model* (OSI) was proposed and developed by the International Standards Organization (ISO). The OSI protocol specifies a seven-layer virtual machine. The *Transmission Control Protocol/Internet Protocol* (TCP/IP), comprises a five-layer virtual machine. We compare the two in Figure 16.41. The *physical* and *data link* layers of OSI are combined into the *host to network* layer in TCP/IP.

OSI	TCP / IP
Physical	Host to Network
Data Link	
Network	Internet
Transport	Transport
Session	Not Present
Presentation	Not Present
Application	Application

Figure 16.41 Layer in the Network Architectures for the OSI and TCO/IP Models

The following diagrams present and compare the hierarchical architecture and layers for the OSI and the TCP/IP models. Observe that at the network layer and below, the models are hardware based, and above that level, the model is expressed in software. Figure 16.42 gives the OSI and TCP/IP hierarchies.

OSI—Physical Layer

bits

The physical layer moves collections of *bits* (1's and 0's) over a communications channel. There is no meaning or structure to the collections. At this level, concern is for mechanical and electrical interfaces, the integrity of bits, and the physical characteristics of the bits. Such characteristics include the number of volts and the width (in time) of each bit. Control issues address how a connection is established and released.

OSI—Data Link Layer

frames, data frames, acknowledgment frame

The data link layer moves collections of bits aggregated as *frames*. The sender breaks the data stream into *data frames*. The receiver acknowledges reception via an *acknowledgment*

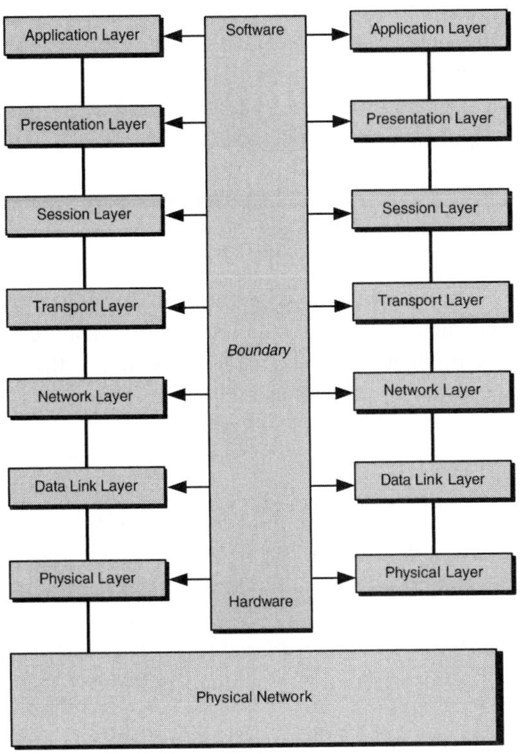

OSI Hierarchy

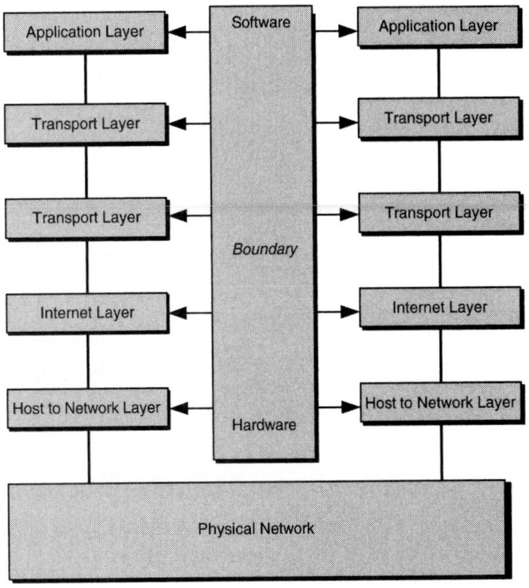

TCP/IP Hierarchy

Figure 16.42 The Network Architectures for the OSI and TCO/IP Models

frame. The data link layer must create and recognize frame boundaries, which is facilitated by surrounding a frame with delimiters. The data link layer also manages flow control and some error management.

TCP/IP—Host to Network

No significant requirements are specified at this level. The host system must simply be able to connect to the network and to transmit or receive IP (Internet protocol) packets.

network layer, Internet

The OSI *network layer* corresponds to the TCP/IP *Internet* layer.

OSI—Network Layer

network layer

In the OSI stack, the *network layer* manages the routing of a transmission from the source to the destination. As part of that task, it must accommodate the different characteristics between or among networks such as addressing, message size, and protocols.

Activities are directed toward managing the network and the physical movement of data; bits are collected into manageable packets. Above the network layer is a collection of virtual machines that have the responsibility for managing the session.

TCP/IP—Internet Layer

internet layer
IP, Internet Protocol

The *Internet layer* is the key element of the TCP/IP model. It defines the official packet format and protocol, the *IP* or *Internet Protocol*. The main task of the Internet layer is to move a message comprised of packets from point A to point B. No requirement is placed on the packet ordering during transmission or the route a packet may take. During an exchange, all packets may or may not take the same route from source to destination.

transport layer

Both the OSI and the TCP/IP models support a *transport layer*. The basic purpose of this layer in either model is to isolate the application from the underlying mechanics of managing the network below.

OSI—Transport Layer

transport layer, session layer, network layer

The tasks of the *transport layer* in the OSI model include accepting data from the *session layer* that is immediately above and then subdividing that data into packets that are compatible with the *network layer* below. The fundamental objective is to ensure that the transactions are implemented such that the hardware appears invisible to the higher layers.

TCP/IP—Transport Layer

transport layer, TCP, UDP, Transmission Control Protocol, UDP—User Datagram Protocol

The TCP/IP *transport layer* is equivalent to the OSI transport layer and has similar responsibilities. Two communication protocols are defined for the layer: *TCP* and *UDP*. The former, TCP—*Transmission Control Protocol*—is very reliable and ensures that a data stream originating on one machine is delivered to any other machine on the network.

The latter, *UDP—User Datagram Protocol*—is considered to be unreliable in the sense that message delivery is under a best effort constraint rather than guaranteed delivery, as is found with TCP. UDP is designed for hosts who want to implement their own packet sequencing and flow control. It finds application in *request-response* and *client-server* type applications in which speed is traded for accuracy.

request-response, client-server

OSI—Session Layer

session layer, must dos, offers to do

In the OSI model, the *session layer* permits users on different machines to communicate. Like the transport layer, it supports movement of data between machines. However, it offers a richer set of features and capabilities. At the session layer, we are moving from *must dos* to *offers to do*. The layer manages dialog control; for single-direction transmission, it tracks turns to send and manage tokens in token passing protocols. The session layer also synchronizes transactions and reassembles the message if necessary. Such cases occur if the transfer cannot be completed in a single session or if there is a major error such as a line drop or node crash.

OSI—Presentation Layer

presentation layer

The goal of the *presentation layer* is to offer a generic set of solutions to common problems. Potential services include mapping the information, including types, structures, and encoding, from the source computer representation to the network representation and then from the network representation to the destination representation. We will discuss this process in greater detail shortly.

session, presentation layers, application layer

The *session* and *presentation layers* in the OSI stack have no counterpart in the TCP/IP model. Both models support the top level, the *application layer*.

OSI—Application Layer

This level also deals with incompatibilities between systems at opposite ends of the network. Although there is some accommodation for hardware differences, the primary focus is on the software. Potential incompatibilities important to embedded applications include file systems and remote procedure execution. We will discuss remote procedures shortly.

TCP/IP—Application Layer

application layer

The *application layer* on the TCP/IP model duplicates most of the responsibilities that we have already identified in the OSI model.

In any distributed embedded design, understanding either of the base models facilitates the understanding of protocols derived therefrom. When one elects to communicate using any of the common standards, generally one integrates a commercially available protocol stack rather than choosing a proprietary design. It is also important to recognize that the OSI hierarchy is a model on which other protocols may be built. One typically does not find a specific implementation in practice.

16.7.2 The Models

client-server, peer-to-peer
group multicast

Most distributed embedded systems will implement a message-based exchange utilizing any of three patterns of communication and synchronization, *client-server*, *peer-to-peer*, and *group multicast*.

16.7.2.1 The Client-Server Model

client-server
producer-consumer, server
client, request-reply

The *client-server* model, shown in the state diagram in Figure 16.43, closely parallels the *producer-consumer* model we studied earlier. The model assumes that a *server* (or set of servers, analogous to the producer) exists that is able to provide some service required by some *client*. The client-server pattern involves the exchange of *request-reply* messages according to the following sequence.

1. Client: Transmit a request to the server process and block.
2. Server: Execute the request.
3. Server: Return the reply to the client.

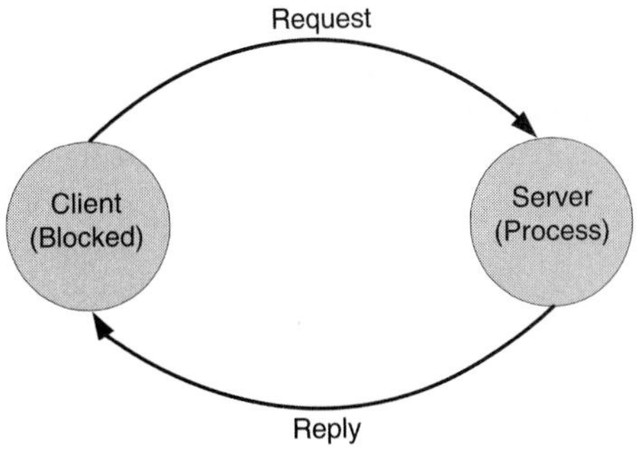

Figure 16.43 The Client-Server Model for Message-Based Exchange

remote procedure call

The server process, analogous to the producer process, is aware of the message as soon as it arrives. Activity in the sending process suspends or blocks until the reply is received, thereby providing a form of synchronization. The process is commonly represented at the language level as a *remote procedure call*, which thus hides the underlying communication operations—the invisibility of the infrastructure that was required earlier.

At the logical or functional level, the exchange appears to be directly between the client and the server processes. In reality, the interchange is managed by the local kernel. Signals move from or to the respective software drivers and to and from the physical network.

16.7.2.2 The Peer-to-Peer Model

peer-to-peer model The *peer-to-peer model* follows naturally from the client-server model. In the model, several (peer or equal) processes cooperate to solve a problem or to share information. The notion of a predesignated client or server does not exist; rather, any member of the network may request a service from or provide one to any of the others. Such an approach can remove a potential bottleneck that arises in the client-server model when a number of clients must interact with a single server at the same time. The peer-to-peer model permits several nodes to provide the requisite services. Synchronization is achieved through the message exchange as was done in the client-server model.

A portion of the architecture of such a system appears in Figure 16.44 as a minor modification of that for the client server.

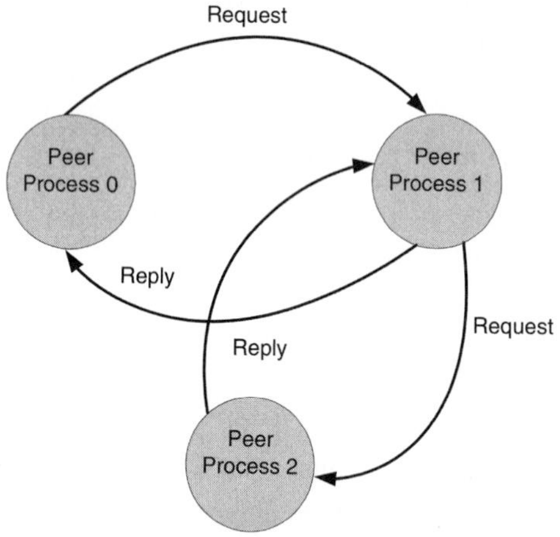

Figure 16.44 The Peer-to-Peer Model for Message-Based Exchange

16.7.2.3 The Group Multicast Model

group multicast The *group multicast* model, shown in Figure 16.45, comprises a single sender and multiple receivers. Such a scheme is used when it is necessary to pass information to all nodes within the network. We may use such a scheme to force all nodes into a known state, to initiate a

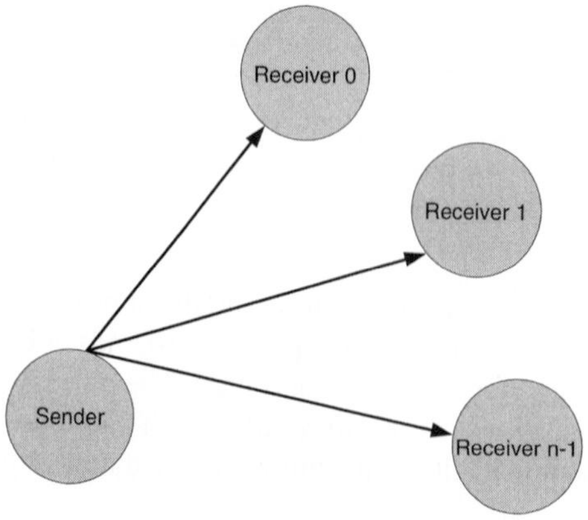

Figure 16.45 The Group Multicast Model for Message-Based Exchange

systemwide self-test, or to locate an object or service. In the last case, for example, the name of the desired resource or service might be multicast to a group of server processes, the one that holds the resource or that can provide the service responds. Similar ideas underlie Sun's Jini architecture. The USB uses a group multicast to require all nodes to "disconnect" from the network and to listen at a known address as an initial step in the enumeration process.

The approach can be inherently fault tolerant. The same task can be multicast to multiple servers; if one fails, the task can still continue. Multicast also works well if the same information is to be sent to a group of interested processes.

The multicast is not mutually exclusive with the other communication and synchronization patterns. In a peer-to-peer network, for example, a multicast might be used by a node entering the network to announce its presence and the services it can provide.

16.8 IMPLEMENTING THE REMOTE DEVICE MODEL—A SECOND STEP

We will now examine the client-server and group multicast communication schemes in greater detail. Peer to peer follows from client-server. We begin with the client-server model by taking a look at the fundamental components of such systems, including the underlying data structures and the messages.

16.8.1 The Messages

When designing and implementing distributed embedded systems, one quickly discovers that remote operations make up a substantial proportion of the interactions between processes. Such operations are initiated by one process sending a request message to another process. The receiving process responds with an acknowledgment or a reply indicating that the operation has been or will be carried out.

Viewed from the most abstract level, a message is simply a collection of bits, as we see in Figure 16.46, and the exchange is the movement of those bits from one place to another. To make the design of message-based communication tractable, rules are applied to the exchange and to the interpretation of the bits.

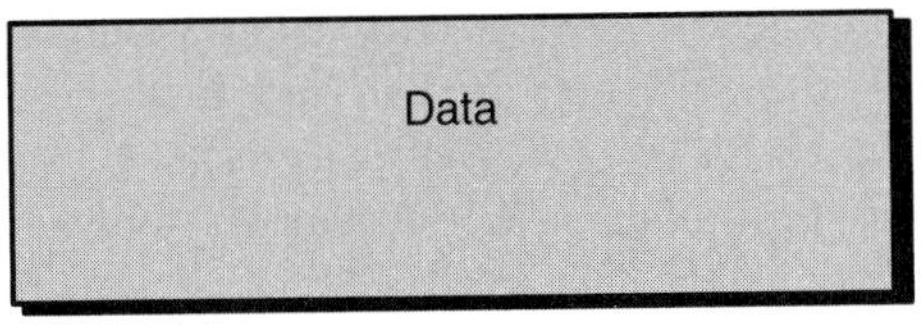

Figure 16.46 An Abstraction of the Basic Message

16.8.2 The Message Structure

data, payload, header
information
addressing
control and synchronization

One such interpretation views others of the bits as *data* or *payload* and others as *header* information. The payload is the *information* being transported. Moving the payload from one place to another is the ultimate objective of sending the message. The header information facilitates that job and is added by the communication driver to provide *addressing* and *control and synchronization* information. The message now appears as in Figure 16.47.

Not all messages are the same size. They may be simple, occupying only a few words of memory, or they can be complex, comprising a large number of blocks of data. The design of the exchange process is cleaner and more robust if the bits are organized to ensure that fixed sized groupings are always transferred. Such groupings are variously referred to

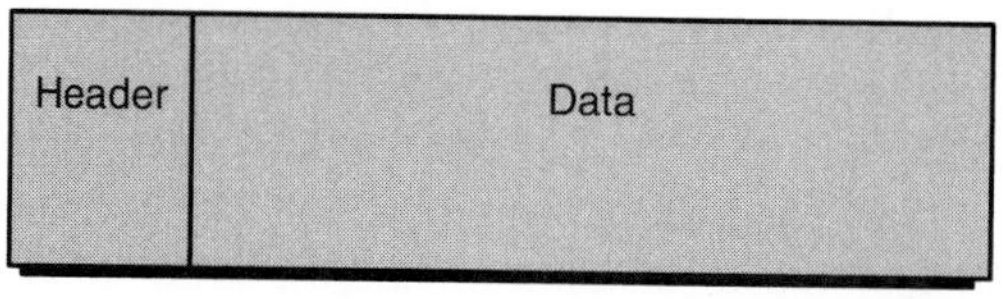

Figure 16.47 A Header Added to the Basic Message

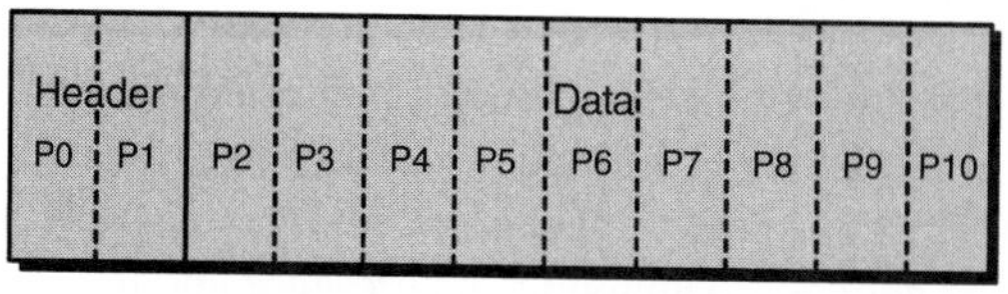

Figure 16.48 The Basic Message Decomposed into Packets

datagrams, packets

as *datagrams* or *packets*. There are times when padding or fill bits must be included to ensure that the packets are the proper size if there is insufficient data available to complete the packet. Figure 16.48 now gives a logical view of the message that has been divided into packets.

16.8.3 Message Control and Synchronization

There are actually two kinds of control and synchronization in a message-based exchange: the header information and the data transfer scheme.

16.8.3.1 The Header

start, end
start identifier, length field

The header information is overhead that is necessary for getting the data from one place to another. This information is added (at each level within the protocol stack) by the communication driver software based on the requirements of the exchange protocol (at that level). Potential header elements might include the destination address or message identifier information. At minimum, this field identifies the destination for the message. If one is working in a networked context, the header might also provide routing information and identify both the sender and receiver of the message. The header field may also provide an indication of the size of the message. This is done in several ways: there may be unique *start* and *end* identifiers, or a *start identifier* and a *length field*.

The header generally includes information about the message type or structure. It may be desirable to distinguish between data-type messages and command-type messages, for example.

As was discussed in the earlier chapter on safety, an important element of communication is ensuring that the data given to the user following reception contains no errors that may have occurred during transmission. Note that there is no guarantee that there will never be transmission errors; these happen. Rather, at the end of the day, the guarantee is that, if passed to a task, the data will be correct. As discussed earlier, this is accomplished through a variety of schemes: all begin with recognizing that a transmission error has occurred. Thus, to this end, in the header field one might elect to include error management information as well. Such information may support detection only, for example, simple parity, or detection and correction with the inclusion of a block check or a CRC sequence.

16.8.3.2 The Transfer Scheme

connection oriented, connectionless

The physical information transfer may follow a proprietary protocol or one of the standards or derivatives discussed earlier. Within such protocols, two kinds of services are identified: *connection oriented* and *connectionless*. A connection-oriented service establishes the connection between the source and destination prior to the exchange of any data. The exchange follows, and the connection is terminated. Messages enter one end and are extracted from the other end; ordering is preserved. The exchange is designated as *reliable* because the reply is effectively an acknowledgment. Such a scheme is referred to as *circuit switching*. Each packet in Figure 16.49 will be sent, in turn, through the same physical path.

reliable

circuit switching

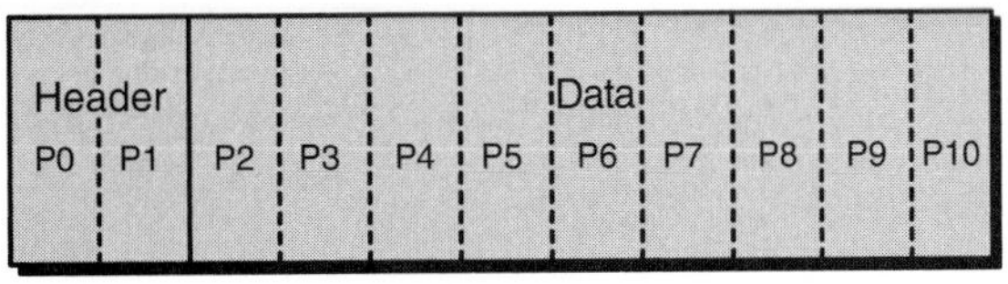

Figure 16.49 The Basic Message Decomposed into Packets

A connectionless service does not establish a specific connection prior to the start of the exchange. Each packet carries full address information; each may arrive at the destination through any of several different routes and may not arrive in the same order in which it was sent. Address information has been added to each packet shown in Figure 16.50. Such a scheme is referred to as *packet switching*. A connectionless exchange is designated as *best effort*.

packet switching, best effort

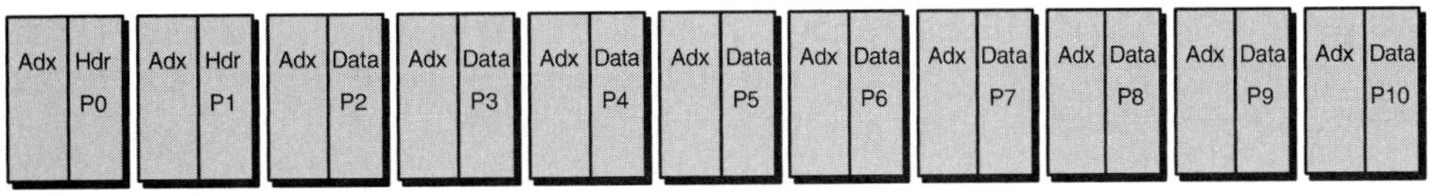

Figure 16.50 Address Information Added to Each Packet

Messages may be sent as a *datagram* service, in which the message is sent but the receiver does not acknowledge; as an *acknowledged datagram* service, in which the message is sent and the receiver acknowledges; or as a *request-reply* service, in which the sender transmits a datagram containing a request and the receiver returns a datagram containing the answer. This last-named scheme is often used in the client-server model.

datagram

acknowledged datagram

request-reply

16.9 WORKING WITH REMOTE TASKS

The next step in examining the inner workings of message-based aspects of the remote device model begins with the client-server model. With this model, the processes (whether local or remote) either provide a service or request one. The former are the *servers* and the latter the *clients*. Any process may play either or both roles.

servers

clients

16.9.1 Preliminary Thoughts on Working with Remote Tasks

Before proceeding with the development of remote functionality, it is important to be aware of several major differences between local and remote tasks. Starting at a high level, the initial view of distributed client-server interaction is presented in the block diagram in Figure 16.51.

The client and the server each assume direct communication with the other. The communication link proceeds through the local kernel (client or server side) to the network and then to the remote node (server or client side), where the message is interpreted and passed to that local process.

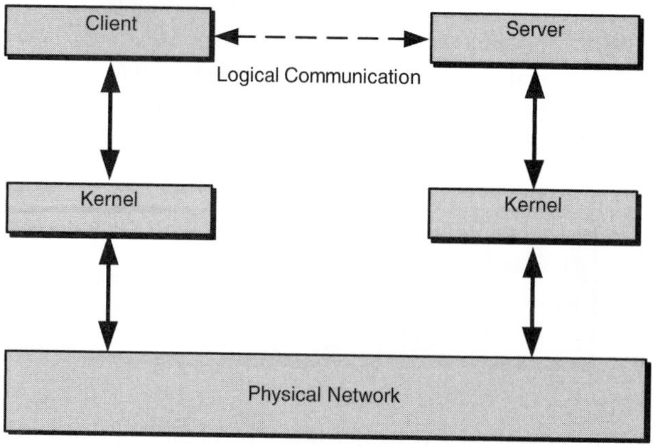

Figure 16.51 A High-Level View of a Client-Server Model

At this level, the implementation seems rather straightforward. Such is not always the case, however. Before taking the next step, let's anticipate some of the problems that might be encountered.

Local vs. Remote Addresses and Data

When working with distributed systems, one must remember that not all tasks are going to be using the same memory space or be on the same machine. The different addressing schemes and data formats must now be carefully considered. Data items in the programs are expressed as primitives such as arrays, structs, and classes, as well as richer, more complex structures built from these. In contrast, the information being exchanged in messages is (inherently) flat or sequential.

One must also remember that not all processors express data in the same way—different endianness or different word sizes are common. Such differences are evident in even simple elements such as integers. To permit the exchange of information among computers, one must ensure that at some level, the data values are expressed in an agreed upon common (external) form.

If all the components in an external system speak the same language, in the same way, there may be no need for conversion. More often, the outside world is made up of a heterogeneous collection of devices provided by a variety of different vendors. Under such conditions, communication and information interchange become more of a challenge. In such cases, part of establishing a connection may be negotiating a common language. Another alternative is to elect to communicate in some native form; such communication may have to include an architecture identifier.

Repeated Task Execution

When one is designing a distributed embedded application, one must consider the possibility that the request for an action or procedure invocation from a remote device may become corrupted and hence rejected. One must also address the possibility that the complete message may never be received. Consequently, the remote procedure may never be executed, be partially executed, or be completely executed.

Any of these alternatives may lead to serious safety problems. Although the complete execution of a requested remote procedure may seem innocuous, if confirmation that the task completed is not received or properly interpreted by the sender, additional requests may be issued. If the request is of the form, "decrease flow rate of an inhibitor or increase the temperature of a process," repeated requests may create serious safety problems. When designing the exchange, one must consider

- How to avoid such duplicate messages
- How to handle missed acknowledgments
- How to handle both the success and failure of an operation

at most once
atomic transactions

In an attempt to anticipate and manage such situations, contemporary distributed embedded applications incorporate what are called *at most once* semantics and *atomic transactions*. We will examine both of these shortly.

Node Failure, Link Failure, Message Loss

A distributed system is susceptible to a variety of failure modes not seen in the local model. One can generally detect failure, but often it is not possible to distinguish between a link failure, a node failure, or a message loss. Once a fault is detected, the appropriate action can be taken.

16.9.2 Procedures and Remote Procedures

procedure call
remote procedure call (RPC)
remote procedure invocation (RPI)
interface language processor
binding service
communication driver
request-reply protocol

With these preliminary caveats in mind, we continue with the discussion. In a traditional software application, perhaps the most commonly used means for encapsulating a set of software instructions is the procedure. A *procedure call* is executed on the main processor by writing the name of the procedure followed by the associated parameters enclosed in parentheses. When that procedure resides in a remote address space, we would still like to be able to use similar semantics. Such an invocation is known as a *remote procedure call* (RPC). One may also see the terminology *remote procedure invocation* (RPI) used.

Remote procedure calls are similar to, yet different from, the familiar local procedure calls. Support for the remote call generally includes an *interface language processor*, a *binding service*, and a *communication driver*. The invocation is most commonly based on a *request-reply protocol*. The client invokes a service by sending request messages to the server. The server performs the requested service and sends a reply back to the client. Generally, the client waits for a reply before proceeding, analogous to a local call.

16.9.2.1 Calling a Remote Procedure—RPC Semantics

The remote procedure call (RPC) paradigm combines the familiar (local) procedure call model with the client-server model. The goal of the RPC model is to have tasks interact with local and remote procedures seamlessly.

When a local procedure is called, parameters and any return value are usually passed into and returned from that procedure via a stack. Following the call, the calling procedure then blocks waiting for the return. Such an approach is not possible with a remote procedure. Nonetheless, it is desirable that the remote call appear as if it had been local.

The first step in creating such an illusion is to write stubs for the procedure that are then placed on the client and server. These stubs have the same public interface—the same procedure name, return type, and signature—as the full procedure. The public interface masks the behind-the-scenes magic.

When the server process is ready, it will execute a blocking receive. When the client performs the call, the input parameters are passed to the server as values to arguments in a

request message *request message*. To model local call semantics, following the call, the client blocks and awaits the return.

When the message arrives, the server retrieves the parameters and executes the procedure. Following execution, the output parameters are returned to the client in a *reply message*. The returned values replace the values of the corresponding variables in calling the context. Such a scheme is equivalent to *pass by value* semantics found in conventional procedures. *Pass by reference* semantics is more difficult to implement and requires additional information about the parameters used as input, output, or both.

reply message

pass by value

pass by reference

Because it is executed in a different context from the caller, the remote procedure cannot see global or other variables in the calling context. Passing memory addresses or the equivalent is meaningless. Arguments cannot directly include data structures or pointers to memory locations.

The block diagram in Figure 16.52 illustrates the structure and flow of the operation. As the diagram illustrates, when the client invokes a procedure that resides on a remote server, that call is intercepted by the *client stub*.

client stub

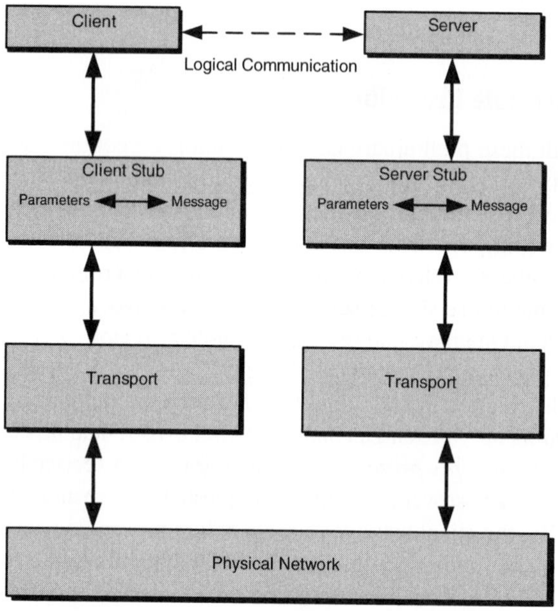

Figure 16.52 A Block Diagram View of a Remote Procedure Call

PASSING AND RETURNING PARAMETERS

The stub contains routines to put the parameters, return values, and any other data to be interchanged into a format that is compatible with the network and with the remote system. Such a conversion is called *marshalling*. The stub then builds a message containing that information and forwards that request message to the transport driver. The message is sent out over the network to the server node; there the process is reversed. Converting from a network-compatible format to the format of the remote device is called *unmarshalling*.

marshalling

unmarshalling

The response from the server, following the execution of the *requested* procedure, follows the same procedure to return the *reply* to the client. The remote procedure and associated operations have the same structure as a local version.

requested

reply

Marshalling begins with a collection of data types and then flattens or serializes those structures into a sequence of basic data items. The data items are then converted into a form that is suitable for transmission in an outgoing message. That is, they are translated into an

marshalling

unmarshalling

external representation. Marshalling can be "done by hand" in the sending program or generated automatically from a formal specification of the data items to be transmitted. A conversion "done by hand" means that the sending program explicitly converts each of the data items from their internal (local) representation to the agreed upon external (remote) representation. *Unmarshalling* is the process of reassembling the data to its equivalent form (may not be an identical form) on arrival at the remote node or at the local node when a response is returned.

16.9.2.2 The Transport

send, receive
receives
synchronous, asynchronous

Single-message transport is supported by two operations, *send* and *receive*, as seen in earlier chapters. To communicate, one process *sends* a message (a sequence of data items) to a destination. The destination process *receives* the message. Earlier, communication between the sending and receiving processes was identified as *synchronous* or *asynchronous* with respect to a common clock. In the current context, these words have slightly different meanings.

synchronous, send
receive
Idle RQ, Stop-and-Wait

A *synchronous* exchange is accomplished by requiring that when a *send* is issued, the client process blocks and waits until the corresponding *receive* is issued before sending out the next request. Similarly, the receiving process will block and await an incoming message. Such an exchange is called *Idle RQ* or *Stop-and-Wait*.

asynchronous
send

Significant improvements in performance can be gained if the constraints on receiving the reply are relaxed, thereby making the exchange *asynchronous*. Under such a scheme, rather than blocking following a *send*, the client process is allowed to proceed as soon as the outgoing message is copied into a local buffer.

Continuous RQ

If the client does not block, the client and the server are working in parallel. The client can send consecutive messages without waiting for a reply. Similarly, the server may queue up several reply messages while working on the next call. Such a scheme is similar to the pipelining techniques used to improve performance of the CPU instruction cycle or certain kinds of computations and is called *Continuous RQ*.

nonblocking
blocking

The *nonblocking* scheme can be used if the client tasks are computationally intense or if the client is working on a task that requires coordination with a number of servers. In the former (*blocking*) case, the client can proceed with the next computation while the server is working with the results of the first. In the latter (nonblocking) case, the client can send all the requests off and then collect the replies as they come in. Such might be the case when the client is in a master control console in an automated factory and the servers are at the various assembly lines. The client can send out status request messages to each of the distributed lines and then collect the results. Little is gained by forcing the client to wait for each reply before sending the next.

16.9.2.3 Message Source and Destination

send
mailbox

In the client-server model, there are a number of possible destinations for a message. The possibilities include a process, or group of processes, a port or group of ports, a socket, or an object. Thus, one of the arguments of a *send* operation is an identifier indicating the destination of the message. Most operating systems will use a process or port. A port is a message destination that has exactly one receiver but potentially many senders. On occasion, a port is also known as a *mailbox*. However, a mailbox always has a message queue, whereas a port may not.

In Internet protocols, the destination address is specified as a port number used by the process and the Internet address of the computer on which the receiving process is running. The problem that arises with such an approach is that the service must always be run on the same machine for the address to remain valid. Recall our earlier discussions on internal interprocess communication.

Ideally, one would like to have location transparency. To that end, location-independent identifiers are used. Such an identifier is mapped by network driver and router software into a lower level address to deliver the message. The approach naturally takes into account the current location of the service, thereby enabling message destinations and services to be changed without having to inform the clients of the new locations.

request-reply When working with a client-server implementation, communication is always in the form of *request-reply* pairs. Normally, the communication is synchronous. That is, the client process blocks until the reply is returned. However, one can elect to implement an asynchronous scheme when the client can afford to delay retrieval.

16.9.2.4 The Protocol

There are two primary ways by which a remote procedure call capability can be incorporated into a design. One approach is to utilize a programming language in which the mechanism is already built in. The advantage of such an approach is that the RPC requirements can be dealt with by language constructs similar to the way exceptions are handled in C++. An alternative is to use a special-purpose interface language. The advantage of this approach is that the design is not tied to a particular language or language environment.

The client-server protocol is often implemented as a trio of messages. Communications costs are low since only three system calls are required. The server reply message is interpreted as an acknowledgment. The exchange is presented in the state diagram in Figure 16.53.

DoOperation GetRequest SendReply

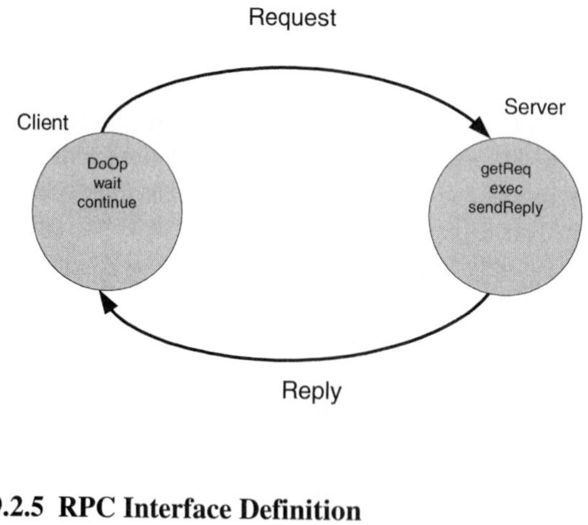

Figure 16.53 A State Diagram of a Client-Server Exchange

16.9.2.5 RPC Interface Definition

When writing a program in C or C++, the prototype for each function in the design is specified. The compiler uses that information to ensure the proper binding of the procedure call to the procedure body. An RPC interface definition provides the same information in a list of procedures and associated signatures. The list identifies the procedures, the variables types, and parameter types. For remote procedures we identify three basic parameter types:

input only

- *Input only*—such parameters are only permitted to pass information into a remote procedure.

output only

- *Output only*—parameters of this type can only send information from the server to the client. The same parameter cannot be used to send information back to the server.

input and output

- *Input and Output*—such a parameter can be used to send information to a server and then used by the server to return information to the client.

Such a list enables the RPC system to identify which values to marshal into request and reply messages.

Also included in the interface definition is similar information for those procedures offered by the server that are visible to clients. The clients and servers use the service name to refer each of the procedures.

16.9.3 Node Failure, Link Failure, Message Loss

The requirements in today's embedded systems are placing high demands on safety and reliability. An issue that is closely related to detecting and managing faults is managing the delivery of messages. When working in a distributed context, the problem of duplicate and lost messages is more acute than in a local context because there is greater opportunity for corruption.

16.9.3.1 Node Failure and Loss

I-am-up

request-reply-acknowledge

As an aid to the early identification of a link or node failure, one can use a handshaking protocol monitored by a watchdog timer. At periodic intervals, both sites send an *I-am-up* message. If the watchdog timer expires, the client is not be able to contact the server, or a time-out has occurred using a *request-reply-acknowledge* protocol because a failure has occurred, further action must be taken.

The client can respond by polling the server or source of the expected *I-am-up* message. If there is no response, no additional information has been gained. A second route can then be tried. If there is a response, it is known that the server is up and the link has failed. Otherwise, it is known that the server is down or the time-out is too short. If lengthening the time-out fails, a server failure can be assumed. Such reasoning presumes no double failure.

Suppose that the above detection protocol identifies a problem. When such exceptions occur, the client process must be able to report and manage them in a safe and robust way. For software exceptions, some languages such as C++ and Java provide constructs for handling them. When no such means exist within the implementation language, the procedure call can, at minimum, return an error code. For hardware exceptions, one can initiate a protocol to allow the system to reconfigure to continue operation.

If the direct link to the receiver has failed and been identified, the information must be rebroadcast to all other sites in the system, thereby allowing the routers to reconfigure. If the client believes the site has failed, every other site must be notified so that they will not attempt to use failed node.

When a failed site is repaired, it must be reintegrated into the system. Reintegration can be done by a handshaking procedure. Information to update routing tables also needs to be broadcast. Queued messages may then be delivered to the site.

16.9.3.2 Message Loss

The RPC semantics must specify what happens when a procedure call is repeated. In a distributed embedded application there is always a finite probability that an initial procedure call, a reply message, or a return value may be lost. Therefore, it must be assumed that a procedure call may be repeated.

Consider the following situation. An RPC is executed to increase the set point value on a boiler by a certain number of degrees. The call is received and executed, but the acknowledge is lost. The sender times out on the response and resends. Now, a potentially dangerous situation exists: *The set point should not be raised a second time.*

The exact implementation of such semantics depends on whether or not the receiver maintains state. For the case in which the server maintains state, the client holds state information in some data structure. Subsequent client calls to the receiver build on the stored information. However, a server crash can potentially lose that information unbeknownst to the client. When the server (and client) does not retain state information, each transaction stands alone.

Observe an analogous situation with MPEG-encoded data. The high data compression and throughput speed are achieved by transmitting only the differences from a reference frame. If the reference is lost, the subsequent differences are irrelevant.

Several of the more common RPC call semantics are expressed as follows.

MAYBE CALL

As the name suggests, under the following case, the execution of the call is uncertain. The request is sent and a timer is started. If the reply message is not received before the timer expires, the safe exit is taken with no retry. However, there is no way of knowing if the procedure call succeeded or if it was ever executed. The request message may have been lost or the server crashed; or the procedure may be executed and the reply message lost. Such semantics are unacceptable in an embedded application.

CALL AT LEAST ONCE

With such a scheme, unless the server has failed, it is known that the call has succeeded; however, what is not known is how many times. If a timely reply is not received from the server, the request message is retransmitted. Eventually, a reply is returned and received by the client, indicating that either the call succeeded or the server has failed. In the former case, the server may have received and executed the message more than once. If the server is designed to be *idempotent*—that is, an operation can be performed repeatedly with exactly the same effect as if it had been executed once—there is no problem and such semantics are acceptable. If all operations are idempotent, then there are no special needs for handling repeated requests.

idempotent

CALL AT MOST ONCE

at most once

At most once semantics requires that a request be executed either zero times or at most one time. If the transaction cannot be completed, the request is abandoned or the state of the system is rolled back to that preceding the requested procedure invocation. As a caveat, one must remember that it is not always possible to roll the state of a system back. As the old expression goes, "we can multiply by zero, but, we can't divide by zero."

To deal with the rollback problem, the server tracks duplicate messages, for example, by looking at a time tag associated with the message. Contemporary protocols are (easily) designed to recognize as duplicates successive messages from the same client with the same message identifier. These are filtered out. That is, if a duplicate message is received and has been acted upon, the reply is retransmitted, but the operation is not reexecuted. This scheme requires a guarantee from the server that it will not process a repeat invocation of the same call. The semantic is typically implemented on servers that retain state information.

16.10 GROUP MULTICAST REVISITED

multicast

An exchange used for communication from a single process to a group of processes is called *multicast*. A multicast message can be viewed as a broadcast message to a subset of all recipients. It is a useful tool for constructing distributed systems that must

- Be fault tolerant, that is, require replicated services.
- Locate distributed services or resources. Client requests can be multicast to members of group of servers.
- Work with replicated data.
- Support group update in the event of change.

discovery query
service announcement

When a process enters the system, it may wish to locate services or resources or announce those services it can provide. To locate services, the process will multicast a *discovery query*; to announce services, it will multicast a *service announcement*. Only the appropriate server responds to the discovery query. After the resource or service has been located, the information is cached to reduce the need for further multicast messages. With multicast, we can get improved performance through replicated data. Copies of data are cached locally, and thus access speed is increased. Multicast can be used to update all copies when data changes.

The multicast approaches used are described in the following sections.

ATOMIC MULTICAST

A message transmitted by atomic multicast must be received and acted upon by all tasks that are part of the group or by none. Such a requirement ensures that all receivers are in the same state after the operation. If one does not receive, then none receives. If a receiver dies, then it is removed from the group.

RELIABLE MULTICAST

A reliable multicast makes a best effort to deliver a message to all members of the group; however, there is no guarantee that all members will receive and act upon the message. An unreliable multicast transmits a message only once.

totally ordered multicast
causal ordering

An *atomic* transaction requires that the entire transaction be interpreted as a single, indivisible unit of information. If the full request is not available, it is not acted upon. For the atomic multicast, message ordering must be preserved. The ordering is implemented through FIFO buffering on the receivers. All receivers must execute commands in the same sequence. The strongest ordering is called a *totally ordered multicast*; a less restrictive ordering is called *casual ordering*. Causal ordering assumes that if two events occurred in the same process, they occurred in the order observed. For messages sent between processes, we assume that the event of sending a message occurred before the event of receiving it.

16.11 CONNECTING TO DISTRIBUTED PROCESSES—PIPES, SOCKETS, AND STREAMS

pipes, sockets, streams

Let's now look at how one might make a logical connection to a (remote) process. Three alternatives are identified: *pipes, sockets, and streams*.

16.11.1 Pipes

Pipes are the earliest and most elementary type of interprocess communication mechanism. They are simply an implementation of the classic producer-consumer model. Such a scheme allows two processes to communicate through a buffer of finite size. That buffer is implemented as a shared FIFO data type and thus supports only one-way communication. The pipe is created by a process using a system call. Analogous to the descriptors returned from a file access call, the system returns two pipe descriptors, one for reading and one for writing.

The data flow diagram in Figure 16.54 expresses such a relationship. The bidirectional flow illustrated in the figure is made up of two unidirectional flows.

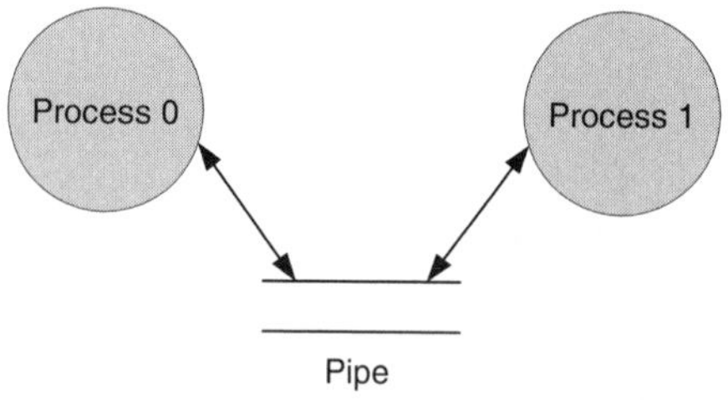

Figure 16.54 A Data Flow Diagram of an Information Exchange via a Pipe

The interchanged data is stored in FIFO order using standard read and write operations. The communication is one-to-one, and the pipe exists only as long as the processes do. However, one process could perform a write operation and terminate long before the consuming process.

named pipes

When the processes are on separate compute engines, the pipe is identified by the path to its location. Such pipes are referred to as *named pipes*. Named pipes are restricted to one domain and a single file system. Such a restriction is not particularly limiting for most distributed embedded applications.

16.11.2 Sockets

socket

The communication path between two processes can be modeled as a channel terminated on either side by an endpoint or *socket*. In such a model, interprocess communication operations are based on sending messages between socket pairs; one belongs to each of two communicating processes. Each socket is identified by an address that is made up of a local endpoint address (typically, a port number) and a global endpoint address, which is the host address on the network (typically, the Internet address of the machine on which the socket was created).

descriptor

Communication can be either bidirectional or unidirectional; the communicating tasks can be on the same or on different machines. Any process can create a socket for use in communicating with another process. Like the pipe, a socket is created by a system call, and also like the pipe, it has file I/O type semantics. The system call returns a *descriptor* that becomes a handle or logical endpoint by which the socket is referenced in future.

bind

Before the sockets can be used to communicate, the destination process must *bind* the descriptor to its socket address, which is the physical endpoint for communication. The sender must do so as well if a reply is required. A system call used to execute the binding requires a socket descriptor and a reference to a structure containing the socket address to which the socket is to be bound. Once bound, a socket address cannot be changed. As was found with the pipe or a file, a socket lasts until it is closed or until every process with the descriptor exits.

When communication begins, messages to be sent are queued at the sending socket until transmitted by the associated software driver. Similarly, they are queued in the receiving socket until they are accepted by the receiving process.

The pseudo-code fragments shown in Figure 16.55 illustrate setting up a client and server socket pair.

```
clientSocket = socket(aDomain, aType, aProtocol);
code
bind(clientSocket, clientAddress);
code
sendto(clientSocket, myMessage, serverAdderess);
code
```

```
serverSocket = socket(aDomain, aType, aProtocol);
code
bind(serverSocket, serverAddress);
code
recvFrom(serverSocket, myBuffer, clientAdderess);
code
```

Figure 16.55 Pseudo Code for Setting Up a Client-Server Socket Pair

domain ***type*** ***protocol***

The *domain* specifies the communication domain, which identifies the protocol family that will be used. The *type* identifies the semantics of the communication, a stream we will discuss next, for example. Finally, the *protocol* stipulates the protocol that will be used for the communication.

Today sockets are probably the most widely used interface for message-based interprocess communication.

16.11.3 Stream Communication

The notion of streams was developed by Dennis Ritchie of Bell Labs in the early 1980s. A stream is another means by which one can connect a process to the many devices that make up a distributed embedded application. Whereas pipes or sockets provide an interface to a connection between two processes, a stream forms a connection between a device (more specifically, the device driver) and an application process. Communication is byte-oriented and full duplex, and is characterized by a *stream head* (which interfaces to the application process), the *stream end* or *driver end*, which, naturally, connects to the driver software, and zero or more *stream modules* or *processing modules*.

stream head ***stream end, driver end*** ***stream modules, processing modules***

The stream modules provide a means of implementing and dynamically configuring device drivers. A module has an associated read queue for input and a write queue for output. The modules are pushed into the stream, and thereby the queues are connected together, much like a linked list, in FIFO order to form a data flow between the stream head and the driver end.

In addition, the modules can perform basic operations on the byte stream as it moves from the stream head to the driver end. For example, a module may read a line of data in, discard the line termination, and store the data in a character buffer. The major benefits of using such an approach are that it is modular and incremental. Once it is written, a module, like a class instance, can be used in many different streams.

To use the stream protocol, two processes must first establish a connection between their associated pair of sockets, as was illustrated in the previous section. This operation is implemented through a series of system calls. The sockets are opened, bound to their respective processes, and linked through another system call. The arrangement is asymmetrical because one socket is listening for a connection (the driver end), while the other is asking for a connection (the stream head). Once the connection is requested and accepted, the server forks a new process to communicate with the client. It creates a new socket, pairs that socket with the client socket, and resumes listening in original process and through the original socket.

The connection can now be used to communicate in either or both directions. Data is read immediately and in the order transmitted. The operation continues until the connection is closed.

16.12 SUMMARY

In the previous chapter, we studied how an embedded application can communicate and coordinate with the external world. We extended the interprocess and communication model developed earlier by adding a transport mechanism component.

In this chapter, we continued to refine the model by examining the local and remote components from the points of view of a shared variable and a message-based interpretation of the information exchange in greater detail. The objective has been to establish the basic infrastructure and various implementation architectures for both models. The subsequent two chapters will now study several real-world examples of each rendering of the model.

16.13 REVIEW QUESTIONS

The Local Device Model

16.1 What are the three sets of signals utilized to effect an information exchange in the local device model?

16.2 Give a list of signals that are typically included in the set of control signals in the local device model. Briefly describe the purpose of each.

16.3 Identify several different commercially available device interfaces that utilize a serial implementation of the local device model.

16.4 Identify several different commercially available device interfaces that utilize a parallel implementation of the local device model.

16.5 The chapter identifies three models by which a peripheral device may be connected to the local processor. What are these?

16.6 What is memory mapped I/O? an I/O port exchange? a peripheral processor?

16.7 With respect to a bidirectional bus, what does *break before make* mean?

Polling and Interrupts

16.8 What is polling?

16.9 What is an interrupt?

16.10 Give the sequence of steps to effect a polling operation.

16.11 Give the sequence of steps to effect an interrupt operation.

16.12 What is the meaning of "interrupt priority"?

Local Networks

16.13 The chapter identified asynchronous and synchronous communication modes as two different methods for exchanging information over a local network. What are the most significant differences between these two modes?

16.14 Three different asynchronous communication schemes were identified in the chapter. What were these?

16.15 Several different methods were identified in the chapter for encoding the clock information into the transmitted data stream. What were these?

The Remote Device Model

16.16 What is a virtual network? network architecture?

16.17 What is a service provider? service consumer?

16.18 What is a protocol stack, and what role does it play in the remote device model?

16.19 The chapter identified two major protocol schemes. What are these, and what are their major differences?

16.20 What are the three more commonly used patterns of communication and synchronization that one might find in embedded systems?

16.21 Describe the typical structure of a message that might be used in an exchange with a remote device. Explain the purpose of each component.

16.22 What is the difference between a connectionless and a connection-oriented service?

16.23 With respect to a procedure invocation, what is the difference between pass by value and pass by reference semantics?

16.24 Why do most remote procedure invocations use pass by value rather than pass by reference semantics?

16.25 Describe the steps involved in executing a remote procedure in an embedded application.

16.26 What does the term *marshalling* mean? *unmarshalling*?

16.27 Describe the remote procedure call interface and discuss its operation.

16.28 Discuss how failures and errors are managed in a remote device model.

16.29 What is an atomic multicast? reliable multicast?

16.30 What is a pipe? socket? stream?

16.14 THOUGHT QUESTIONS

The Local Device Model

16.1 Describe how address and data information are exchanged in the serial implementation of the local device model? What are the major advantages and disadvantages of such an implementation?

16.2 Why are strobes used to accompany an address or data exchange with a peripheral device? What would be the consequences on the design if such strobes were not used?

16.3 Describe how address and data information are exchanged in the parallel implementation of the local device model? What are the major advantages and disadvantages of such an implementation?

16.4 The chapter identifies three models by which a peripheral device may be connected to the local processor. Give several examples of real-world devices that utilize each model. Discuss why the interface model might have been chosen and the strengths and weaknesses of the approach.

16.5 For each device in Question 16.4, from a performance perspective, what would be the consequences of implementing the interface using one of the other two models?

16.6 Discuss the advantages and disadvantages of memory mapped I/O.

16.7 What are the strengths and weaknesses of memory mapped I/O? an I/O port exchange? a peripheral processor?

16.8 A bidirectional bus is commonly used to send data to and receive data from a peripheral device. Describe the sequence of steps that should be used to turn the bus around from sending to receiving, for example.

16.9 Why is a *break before make* scheme used on a bidirectional bus?

Polling and Interrupts

16.10 Polling and interrupts have been identified as two methods for managing the flow of information from sender to receiver. Discuss the advantages and disadvantages of each.

16.11 Give several real-world examples for which a polling scheme would be the best choice. Justify the choice, citing the effects of using an interrupt scheme.

16.12 Give several real-world examples for which an interrupt scheme would be the best choice. Justify the choice, citing the effects of using an polling scheme.

16.13 Describe how the source of an interrupt can be identified in each of the following configurations: single interrupt–single device, single interrupt–multiple devices, multiple interrupts–single device per line, and multiple interrupts–multiple devices per line.

16.14 Why would an interrupt priority scheme be used in an external device interface in an embedded application?

Local Networks

16.15 What are the respective advantages and disadvantages of the asynchronous and synchronous communications modes from a reliability perspective?

16.16 What are the respective advantages and disadvantages of the asynchronous and synchronous communications modes from a performance perspective?

16.17 Give several real-world examples of devices using either an asynchronous or a synchronous communications mode.

16.18 What are the advantages and disadvantages of the three different asynchronous communication schemes identified in the chapter from the perspective of reliability?

16.19 What are the advantages and disadvantages of the three different asynchronous communication schemes identified in the chapter from the perspective of time performance?

The Remote Device Model

16.20 What is one of the more significant contributions that the remote device model introduces into an embedded design?

16.21 How does the general format of the information exchange among devices change in the remote device model compared with that in the local model?

16.22 Give several examples of real-world networks that might interconnect and exchange information with an embedded system.

16.23 Give several examples of real-world systems that might utilize each of the models identified in Question 16.22. Identify when each may used in an embedded application.

16.24 What are the advantages and disadvantages of a connectionless and a connection oriented service?

16.25 Identify and discuss several of the problems that may arise in an information interchange in a remote device model that may not occur in a local model.

16.26 Identify and discuss several of the problems that may arise during a procedure invocation in a remote device model that may not occur in a local model.

16.15 PROBLEMS

16.1 Design the hardware and software driver that will implement a byte-wide data transfer from your processor to a peripheral device. Each transfer must be accompanied by a strobe to deskew the data. Draw the UML sequence diagram and the timing diagram reflecting the operation of your design.

16.2 Design the hardware and software driver that will implement a byte-wide bidirectional data transfer between your processor and a peripheral device. Each transfer must be accompanied by a strobe to deskew the data. Draw the UML sequence diagram and the timing diagram reflecting the operation of your design.

16.3 For the bus design in Problem 16.2, describe the process for turning the bus around from output from the processor to input to the processor and vice versa.

16.4 Design the hardware and software driver that will implement a byte-wide data transfer from your processor to a peripheral device using a 4-bit data bus. Each transfer must be accompanied by the appropriate control signals to deskew the data. Draw the UML sequence diagram and the timing diagram reflecting the operation of your design.

16.5 Design the hardware and software driver that will implement a byte-wide bidirectional data transfer between your processor and a peripheral device using a 4-bit data bus. Each transfer must be accompanied by the appropriate control signals to deskew the data. Draw the timing diagram reflecting the operation of your design.

16.6 Repeat Problem 16.1 using a full handshake.

16.7 Repeat Problem 16.2 using a full handshake.

16.8 There are a number of different methods by which an address is associated with a peripheral device. Several of the simpler ones are a set of jumpers or switches set to the desired bit pattern. Design the logic that will accept a bit pattern from a 4-bit address bus, compare the pattern against that set for the device, assert a match signal if the incoming address and the set pattern agree, and hold the match signal asserted until another address is received. Identify all necessary control signals. Draw the UML sequence diagram and the timing diagram reflecting the operation of your design.

16.9 Using jumpers or switches to specify the address for a peripheral device as suggested in Problem 16.8 has a number of drawbacks. Identify at least three. An alternative approach is called *geographic addressing*. With such an approach, each device is assigned an address by a bus master when the system is first powered on. Design the hardware and software driver(s) that will implement a geographic addressing scheme for a system that will support up to eight peripheral devices.

16.10 Design the Verilog model, hardware, and the software driver that will implement a byte-wide bidirectional data transfer between your processor and four different peripheral devices utilizing a star bus configuration. Each leg of the star supports separate address and data bus components. In addition to the address and data lines, identify all of the necessary control signals. Draw the timing diagram reflecting the operation of your design.

16.11 Repeat Problem 16.10 for a single ring bus configuration.

16.12 Repeat Problem 16.10 for a parallel bus configuration.

16.13 Design the Verilog model, hardware, and software driver that will transfer a 4-byte block of data from your processor. Data is to be transferred from the processor one byte at a time, converted to a serial data stream, and sent to a peripheral device. Each outgoing bit is to be accompanied by a data clock. There are to be no gaps in the data stream. Identify all of the necessary control signals. Draw the timing diagram reflecting the operation of your design.

16.14 Design the Verilog model, hardware, and software driver that will accept an incoming serial data stream. Data is to be accepted, one byte at a time, converted to parallel, and brought into the processor. Each incoming bit is to be accompanied by a data clock. Identify all of the necessary control signals. Draw the timing diagram reflecting the operation of your design.

16.15 Design a hardware block that will accept the serial data stream and clock described in Problem 16.13 and then output a Manchester phase encoded data stream.

16.16 Design a hardware block that will accept a Manchester phase encoded serial data stream and output a serial data stream with each bit accompanied by a data clock.

16.17 Repeat Problem 16.15 to produce a Manchester differential encoded data stream.

16.18 Repeat Problem 16.16 to accept a Manchester differential encoded data stream.

Chapter 17

Working Outside of the Processor II: Interfacing to Local Devices

THINGS TO LOOK FOR . . .

- Some of the commonly used architectures for local device interfaces.
- Some of the strengths and weaknesses of the different architectures.
- The different transport mechanisms.
- The control and synchronization schemes utilized for the different architectures.
- The implementation of device and subsystem addressing in each of the different designs.

17.0 SHARED VARIABLE I/O—INTERFACING TO PERIPHERAL DEVICES

In this chapter, we will continue to study the many ways that one can interact with the seemingly endless array of peripheral devices in the world outside of the local microprocessor. In the previous chapter, we studied network-based systems. The primary purpose of such remote systems is to move information from one point within the system to another or to utilize computational capability that may not be available in the local components.

In the embedded world, we also routinely work with a wide variety of analog and digital signals typically originating in or being sent to devices within the local proximity. As inputs to the application, such signals can originate either from the environment surrounding the application or from the myriad peripheral devices that may comprise the application. As outputs, they may be generated as control signals to a portion of the application or as captured data being sent somewhere for further processing. Such signals are dealt with more effectively utilizing a shared variable model.

Analog signals may arrive directly or indirectly (transduced) as inputs from physical world signals, or they may be produced as outputs from an internally generated digital data source. Digital signals may also arise as inputs from physical world signals originating in either the time or frequency domains or from a direct interface to a wide variety of peripheral devices that produce digital data. As outputs, they may function as control or configuration information for a peripheral device or information to be stored or displayed.

In this chapter, we will introduce and study several different ways of generating and working with analog and digital signals. The focus will be on producers and consumers rather than the senders and receivers of information. For each design, we will examine the transport mechanism, study how control and synchronism are affected, and investigate how producers and consumers are identified. We will open with an analysis of several different methods by which one can generate analog signals, and then look at how various physical world analog signals can be converted into a digital form that is more appropriate for use in the microprocessor. Three specific conversion algorithms—dual slope, successive approximation, and voltage to frequency—will be examined in some depth. Because the outputs of the various sensors and transducers are typically nonlinear, we examine how to deal with such nonlinearity.

We next move to generating digital signals as control inputs to several different kinds of small motors including stepper and servo motors and as information that must be displayed. We finally conclude by introducing and studying how time and frequency signals can be measured.

17.1 THE SHARED VARIABLE EXCHANGE

The world of digital I/O in a local device model is frequently built around shared variables. Events are used to signal a state change or to request an action; however, their ability to convey significant information is limited. Like the exchange through messages, the objective in the shared variable model is to move information from a source to a destination. That exchange, however, is somewhat less structured than that found in a message-based model.

Implementations range from a basic architecture in which the information comprises sets of commands directing a peripheral device to perform some operation to sophisticated data collection, measurement, or command and control systems. In contrast to message-based architectures, the shared variable model works well for one or two devices in relatively close proximity to the local core processor.

Control and synchronization in shared variable systems is generally supported in the driver firmware that is written specifically for the associated peripheral device or application. Any error management is generally a function of the particular application. The external interface is frequently implemented using either a memory mapped I/O, program-controlled I/O, or a separate peripheral processor.

The transport mechanism for the shared variable infrastructure tends toward a more parallel implementation than the message-based scheme and can potentially involve several tens of signals if wider address and data busses are considered.

17.2 GENERATING ANALOG SIGNALS

A great variety of applications require analog signals—for example, audio signals for a sound or music system or a reference voltage that can be used in an analog-to-digital converter. In many control systems, the stimulus or set point is often an analog level. In such cases, the necessary signals are generated from a digital word using a device known as a *digital-to-analog converter* or *D/A*.

digital-to-analog converter (D/A)

17.2.1 Binary Weighted Digital-to-Analog Converter

The quality of the analog signal produced from a digital-to-analog converter is a direct function of the number of bits in the digital word that is being used as the input to the device and the value or weight assigned to each bit. When weighted number systems were introduced earlier, it was noted that a number can be represented in an arbitrary base according to the formula, in Eq. 17.0.

$$N = \sum_{i=0}^{n-1} w^i S_i \tag{17.0}$$

w = the base or weight associated with each position
S = a symbol from the alphabet of symbols for the specific base
n = the number of positions in the number

For the input to a D/A, the symbols will be those from the binary system {0, 1}. The weight will be a specified voltage level. The value of n will be the number of bits in the digital word that is being converted to analog.

EXAMPLE 17.0

Working with a 4-bit word,

If the weight of the least significant bit is specified to have a value of 1 mv, the following binary words will correspond to the indicated voltages:

0000 – 0 mv
0001 – 1 mv
0101 – 5 mv
1010 – 10 mv
1111 – 15 mv

The resolution of the number is clearly 1 mv; that is, each increment or step is equivalent to 1 mv. The largest signal that expressed using such a weighted 4-bit number is 15 mv.

If the value of 1 µv is assigned to the weight of the least significant bit (LSB), the following binary words will now correspond to the indicated voltages:

0000 – 0 µv
0001 – 1 µv
0101 – 5 µv
1010 – 10 µv
1111 – 15 µv

The resolution now increases to 1 µv; however, the largest signal that can be expressed reduces to 15 µv.

EXAMPLE 17.1

Let's continue to work with a 4-bit word and examine the problem from a different perspective. If we wish to use such a word to synthesize a voltage with a maximum value of 150 mv, then the least significant bit must have a weight of 10 mv. This value also determines the best resolution that we can achieve in the design.

Figure 17.0 presents an ideal implementation of a 4-bit binary weighed digital-to-analog converter (DAC or D/A converter),

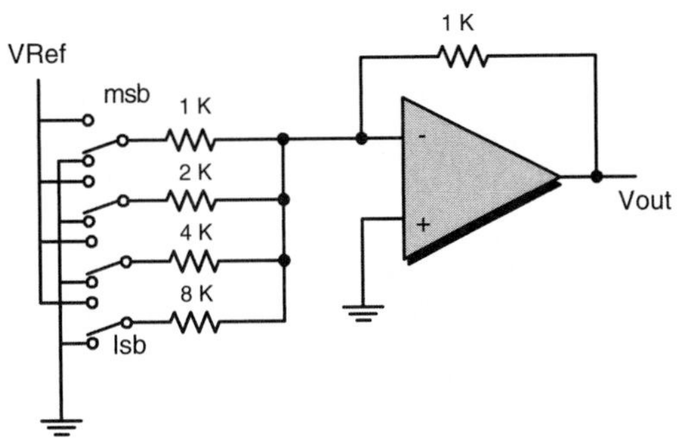

Figure 17.0 4-Bit Digital-to-Analog Converter

Observe that the resistors have been selected to have a binary weighting. If a switch connected to ground is defined as a logical 0 and one connected to the reference voltage as a logical 1, we can easily create the accompanying Table 17.0.

Table 17.0 Relationship Between Switch Closures and Output Voltage for an Ideal Binary Weighted D/A

msb			lsb	Vout
0	0	0	0	0
0	0	0	1	1VRef/8
0	0	1	0	2VRef/8
0	0	1	1	3VRef/8
0	1	0	0	4VRef/8
0	1	0	1	5VRef/8
0	1	1	0	6VRef/8
0	1	1	1	7VRef/8
1	0	0	0	8VRef/8
1	0	0	1	9VRef/8
1	0	1	0	10VRef/8
1	0	1	1	11VRef/8
1	1	0	0	12VRef/8
1	1	0	1	13VRef/8
1	1	1	0	14VRef/8
1	1	1	1	15VRef/8

By selecting VRef to be 8 VDC, in Example 17.1, then selecting the proper switch combination, the resolution will be 1 volt and we can theoretically produce any output value in the range of 0 to 15 volts.

To interact with such a device from a microprocessor, a register can be utilized as a shared variable as illustrated in Figure 17.1.

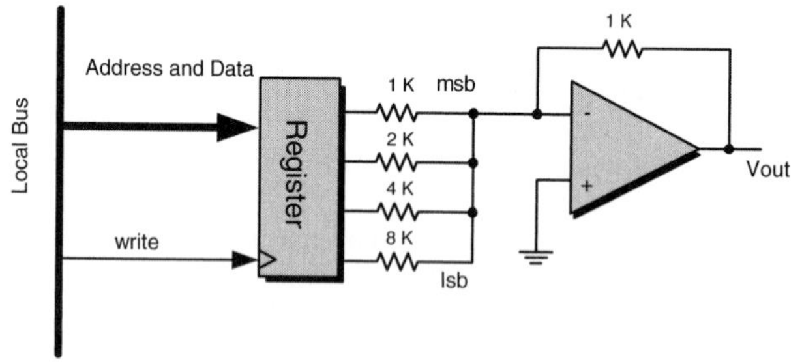

Figure 17.1 Basic Interface to a 4-Bit Digital-to-Analog Converter

The data word corresponding to the desired voltage is written from the microprocessor by the software driver to the register. If the design uses a CMOS register, the value of VRef for each input bit to the D/A will be 5.0 volts, the value of the output logical level of the register.

Such a theoretical model can serve as a good base for understanding how such devices operate; however, this design has several fundamental problems.

1. The value of 5.0 VDC was specified for VRef. The accuracy and precision of the reference voltage directly affects those same attributes of the analog output signal. For

a CMOS device, the typical vendor specification for VOH is 4.95 to 5.0 VDC at a load of 1 μA; for a TTLS device, VOH ranges from 2.4 to 3.6 VDC. Such an error is generally not acceptable.

The output of the register should be used to select between a voltage source that has been designed and calibrated to provide a reference voltage of the required accuracy and precision and a clean reference of 0 VDC. In addition, the connection should be through a switch (either mechanical in the form of a reed relay or electronic in the form of a FET) that has a very low ON impedance and very high (approaching infinity) OFF impedance.

Electronic Industries Association (EIA)

2. The tolerances on the resistors should be consistent with the accuracy and precision specified for the output analog signal. The best standard tolerances specified by the *Electronic Industries Association* (EIA) are ±0.1%.
3. The exact values specified for the resistors in the design are not available as standard values. Laser trimming to such values can be expensive. For the resistors used in the above design, standard 0.1% resistor values are specified as 1 K, 2 K, 4.02 K, and 8.06 K.

17.2.2 R/2R Ladder Digital-to-Analog Converter

A more practical and widely used design utilizes what is called an R/2R ladder network as given in Figure 17.2 for a 4-bit DAC.

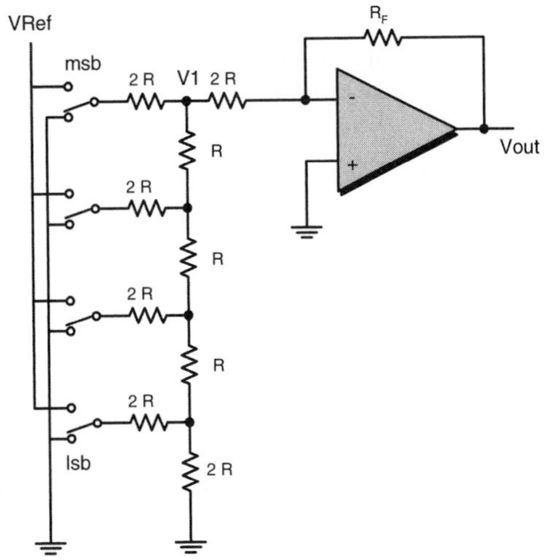

Figure 17.2 4-Bit Digital-to-Analog Converter Using an R/2R Ladder Input Network

If the switch for the MSB is connected to VRef and the others to ground, the analysis in Figure 17.3 will give the corresponding output signal.

From the last step in the network transformation,

$$\boxed{V_1 = \frac{V_{Ref}}{3}} \tag{17.1}$$

and for the op amp,

$$\boxed{V_{out} = -V_1 \bullet \frac{R_F}{2R}} \tag{17.2}$$

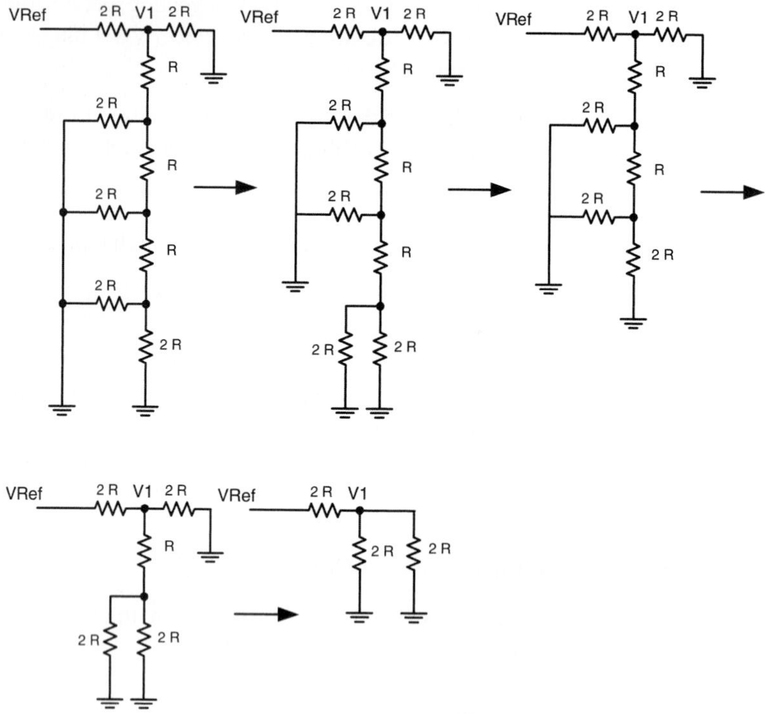

Figure 17.3 Analyzing the 4-Bit R/2R Ladder Digital-to-Analog Converter When the MSB Selected

Substituting Eq.17.1 into Eq.17.2 gives

$$V_{out} = -\frac{V_{Ref}}{6} \bullet \frac{R_F}{R} \tag{17.3}$$

Performing a similar analysis for each of the three remaining bits gives us Table 17.1.

Table 17.1 Relationship Between Switch Closures and Output Voltage for an R/2R Weighted D/A

Bit	Output
Msb 3	$-\frac{V_{Ref}}{6} \bullet \frac{R_F}{R}$
2	$-\frac{V_{Ref}}{12} \bullet \frac{R_F}{R}$
1	$-\frac{V_{Ref}}{24} \bullet \frac{R_F}{R}$
0	$-\frac{V_{Ref}}{48} \bullet \frac{R_F}{R}$

Note that the ratios among the outputs are 8,4,2,1.

Superposition can be applied to compute the output voltage for any of the 16 binary combinations. The bit pattern 0101, for example, will give,

$$
\begin{aligned}
V_{out} &= -\left(\frac{V_{Ref}}{12} \bullet \frac{R_F}{R} + \frac{V_{Ref}}{48} \bullet \frac{R_F}{R}\right) \\
&= -\frac{5V_{Ref}}{48(12)} \bullet \frac{R_F}{R}
\end{aligned}
\tag{17.4}
$$

The R/2R ladder DAC is preferred to the earlier model for several reasons.

1. The design uses only two resistor values independent of the number of bits in the conversion. More importantly, the absolute values of the resistors is not significant, only their ratio. In design and fabrication, it is easier to hold a ratio than specific values.
2. All resistors contribute equally to the output error in contrast to the varying contribution evident in the previous model.
3. Monolithic implementations of the ladder are readily available.

The interface to the R/2R-based DAC from a microprocessor can be the same as that in the earlier design. In such an implementation, care must still be taken to ensure that the reference voltage meets specified accuracy and precision requirements. The means for connecting the reference voltage or ground to each resistor is also still subject to the impedance constraints discussed earlier.

Let's now look at several common analog measurements that can be made.

17.3 COMMON MEASUREMENTS

Most physical world analog quantities such as pressure, temperature, strain, flow, or weight, can easily be converted into some other form such as resistance, current, or voltage using transducers or sensors. At the end of the day, capturing these signals reduces to making a voltage measurement. On the digital side, most physical world quantities will require measuring time or frequency.

17.3.1 Voltage

The ability to measure voltage is a fundamental part of electrical engineering. Most techniques generally involve comparing the unknown voltage to a known reference. One highly accurate method uses a bridge circuit; however, automatically nulling a bridge is not practical in embedded applications.

Early analog meters used the unknown voltage to deflect a meter movement against a calibrated dial. Calibration was accomplished by noting the extent of the deflection by a series of known reference values. Contemporary voltmeters implement the comparison using digital methods. We will examine several of those methods.

17.3.2 Current

Current can be measured in several ways. One approach is to use what is called a current shunt. Such a shunt is a precise resistor of known value inserted into the current path. Typical values range from 0.1Ω (or lower) to 1Ω. Then the voltage drop across the shunt is measured, and a bit of simple math and Ohm's law gives the current. The disadvantage of using a shunt is that the circuit must be broken to permit the shunt to be inserted.

An alternative approach that does not require interrupting the circuit entails wrapping a coil of wire around the conductor and measuring the induced voltage. In either case, it is voltage that is being measured.

17.3.3 Resistance

Resistance can be measured in several different ways. Like a voltage measurement, one very accurate method is to use a bridge-type circuit. Also, like a voltage measurement, using a bridge is typically not feasible in an embedded application. A second approach is to apply a known current to the resistor and measure the voltage drop. Ohm's law and some math provides the resistance value.

17.4 MEASURING VOLTAGE

analog-to-digital converter, A/D converter

Voltage is an analog signal. Measuring such a signal means converting the analog value into the equivalent digital value. The resulting binary value can then be used in subsequent computations and control algorithms, or for display. The circuit to implement the conversion is called an *analog-to-digital* or *A/D converter*. The quality of the conversion and thus the measurement is assessed at minimum by its accuracy, resolution, and repeatability. Both the accuracy and the resolution of the conversion are a direct function of the number of bits in the word containing the digital result.

Analog-to-digital converters appear as an integrated peripheral on various microcomputers or as an external peripheral device that is available from a number of different vendors. The objective in the next few pages is not to create expert A/D designers but to introduce several of the more common conversion methods that are used, identify the strengths and weaknesses of each, and understand how we can develop an interface to them.

17.4.1 Dual Slope Analog-to-Digital Conversion

The dual slope approach to A/D conversion begins with a basic analog integrator configured as presented in Figure 17.4.

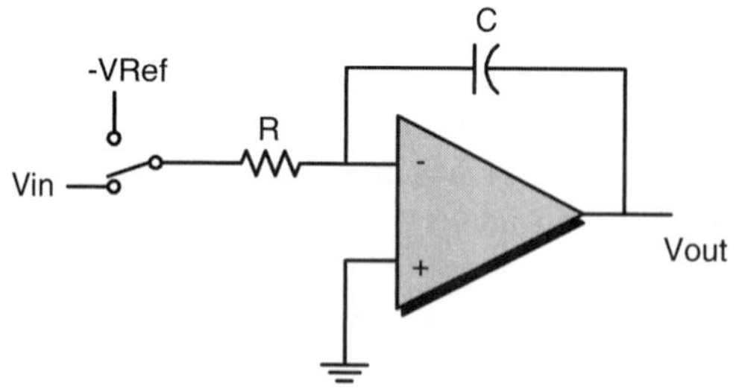

Figure 17.4 Analog Integrator

The transfer function for the circuit can be written as the equation:

$$V_{out}(t) = -\frac{1}{RC}\int V_{in}(t)dt \tag{17.5}$$

If $V_{in}(t)$ is a constant voltage, after an amount of time, t_0, the output of the integrator will reach a constant value of

$$V_{out}(t) = -\frac{V_{in} \bullet t_0}{RC} \qquad (17.6)$$

If the switch in the above circuit is then connected to a voltage of value VRef after some amount of time, t_1, the output of the integrator will decrease to a value of zero. If the value of VRef = Vin, then t_1 will equal t_0.

If the values for R and C are selected such that RC and t_0 are equal, the circuit will behave as is illustrated in Figure 17.5.

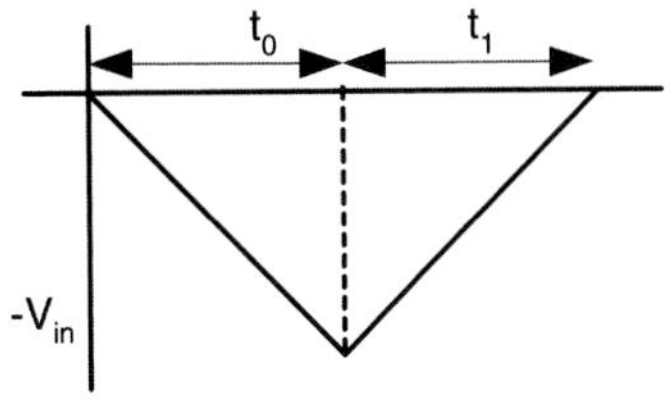

Figure 17.5 Output for an Analog Integrator When the Input Is Switched Between Equal but Opposite Voltages

Let VRef have a value of 10.0 VDC. It should be evident from the figure above that V_{in} can also be permitted to have a maximum value of 10.0 VDC and still preserve the behavior shown; that is, t_1 will equal t_0. It should also be evident that if Vin< VRef and t_0 remains fixed, then t_1 will be less than t_0. In particular, if V_{in} = 5.0 VDC, then t_1 will be ½ of t_0. Generalizing, one can easily show that

$$\frac{t_1}{t_0} = \frac{V_{in}}{V_{Ref}} \qquad (17.7)$$

Figure 17.6 illustrates the relationship for several values of Vin along with the resulting different values for t_1.

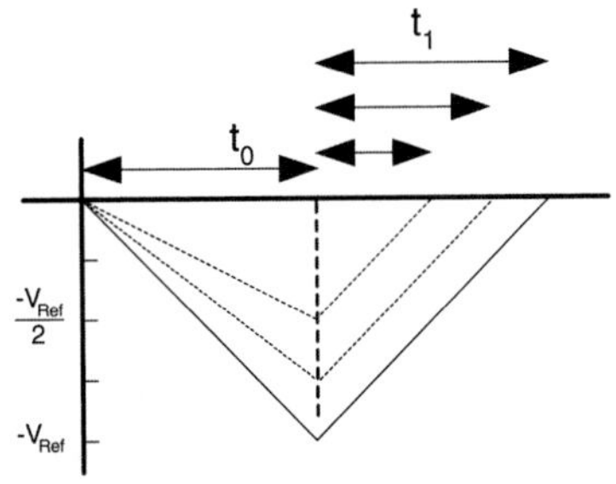

Figure 17.6 Output for an Analog Integrator Showing the Measure and Read Timing

Since the values of VRef and t_0 are known, if one can measure the time t_1, then the computation of V_{in} is rather straightforward.

Now, select t_0 to be 16 2/3 ms and design a timer that operates at 6 MHz in order to measure the t_1 time interval. These numbers may sound a bit arbitrary, but they are not. The first is selected because it is the period of a 60-Hz sine wave—the line frequency in many countries of the world. If we were in a country using 50-Hz power, we would select t_0 to be 20 ms and adjust the oscillator frequency accordingly.

What difference does this make? Recall from calculus that the integral of a sine wave over a full period is 0. Signals coupled in from the all power lines in the surrounding environment are one of the major contributors to the noise in electronic circuits and systems.

The closer that one can hold the duration of t_0 to 16 2/3 ms, the better the line-related noise rejection will be. In the limit, if the power company could hold the line frequency to exactly 60 Hz and if t_0 could be held to exactly 16 2/3 ms, then the A/D converter would have infinite line noise rejection.

The value of 6 MHz is selected because it accrues 100,000 cycles in 16 2/3 ms. Thus, if the value of the input voltage is 10.0 VDC, the duration for t_1 will be the same as the duration of 100,000 cycles of the 6-MHz oscillator. If the input voltage is 5.0 VDC, the duration for t_1 will be equal to that for 50,000 cycles; for 2.5 VDC, the duration of t_1 will be equal to that for 25,000 cycles and so on. By properly placing the decimal point, one can directly convert the duration measured for t_1 into the value of the input voltage, Vin.

integrate interval ***read interval***

In a dual slope A/D converter, the time t_0 is called the *integrate interval* and the time t_1 the *read interval*. The remaining necessary components can now be added to complete the design of the converter as shown in Figure 17.7.

integrate, read, autozero

The counter is implemented as a presettable, synchronous, binary, up counter with tristate outputs; it serves a triple purpose in this design. In addition to being used to time both the *integrate* and *read* intervals, it is used to time a third interval called *autozero*. We will see where this interval is used shortly. To ensure that it can accumulate 100,000 counts at a frequency of 6 MHz, in a 16 2/3 ms interval, the counter must be at least 17 bits.

Start ***Load***

To initiate a conversion, the microprocessor loads a value of $(2^{17} - 100{,}000)$ into the register and issues a *Start* command to the state machine. The state machine responds by issuing a *Load* signal to the counter, which thereby presets the counter to the value stored in the register.

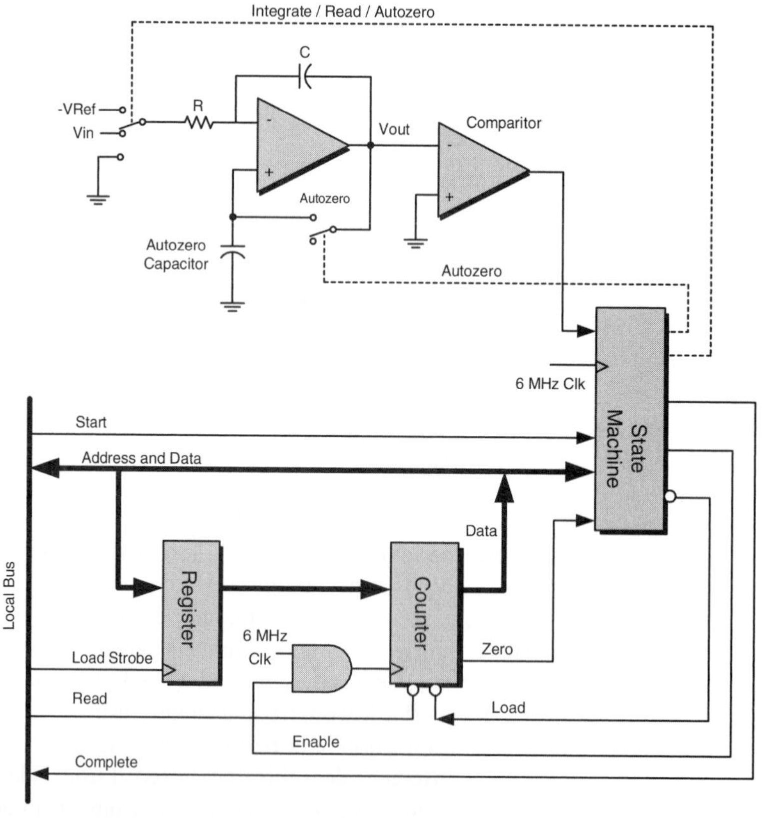

Figure 17.7 Block Diagram for a Basic Dual Slope Analog-to-Digital Converter

integrate

By setting such an initial value in the counter, after 100,000 counts or 16 2/3 ms, the counter will overflow from 1FFFF to 00000, signaling the end of the *integrate* interval. The zero value is easy to detect, and the counter can then immediately start timing the read interval—from the zero state. The zero value in the counter also tells the state machine to switch the input to the integrator from the unknown voltage to the reference voltage.

read

During the *read* interval, the integrator is integrating back toward zero from the unknown voltage that has been stored on the feedback capacitor, and the counter is incrementing from zero. When the integrator output reaches zero, the comparator changes state, thereby signaling the state machine that the conversion is complete. The counter now contains the digital equivalent of the input signal. The state machine in turn signals the microprocessor by asserting the *Complete* line.

Complete

autozero

To complete a measurement cycle, the A/D will execute what is called an *autozero* measurement. The motivation for such a measurement arises because any electronic circuitry and signals are subject to variations resulting from external or internal noise, temperature, or general drift in the behavior of the components as well as many other factors. Such variation can be partially compensated for by measuring the *bias* originating from such sources and then algebraically adding that value to the actual measured value.

bias

The bias is the value that is measured if the input to the system is connected to ground or a signal with a known zero value. The autozero interval is generally approximately half or the integrate interval. For this design, that will be approximately 8 ms or 50,000 counts.

Start

Thus, sometime after issuing the *Start* command, the microprocessor will preset the register with the value ($2^{17} - 50{,}000$). After it has read the converted value from the counter, the microprocessor will tell the state machine to execute the autozero measurement. In response, the state machine will transfer the value stored in the register to the counter, connect the input of the integrator to ground, and connect the output of the integrator to the autozero capacitor. When the counter reaches zero, the cycle is complete and the bias voltage will be stored on the autozero capacitor. That value will then be algebraically added to the next measurement.

The complete cycle is now given in Figure 17.8.

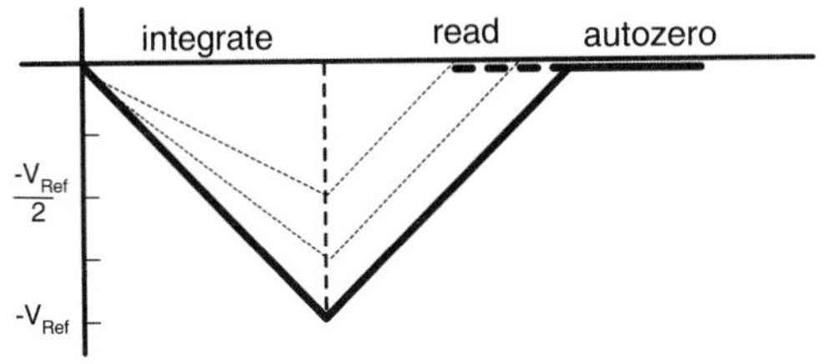

Figure 17.8 Complete Integrate, Read, and Zero Intervals for a Basic Dual Slope Analog-to-Digital Converter

integrate, autozero, register, Start, Read

A portion of the control of the measurement is implemented in software in the microprocessor, and a portion is managed by the state machine. Presetting initial values for the *integrate* and *autozero* intervals into the *register*, issuing the *Start* command (to initiate a read or autozero interval), and the *Read* command to read the contents of the counter following the conversion are relatively slow tasks that can easily be accomplished in software. These tasks are done by the driver software in the microprocessor. Switching the integrator input signal from the unknown voltage to the reference, responding to the change in state of the comparator output, and disabling the clock to the counter are all hard real-time critical operations that are best implemented in hardware. Let's examine in greater detail why such a decision was made.

These latter three tasks are the critical ones. A delay or other temporal error in switching from the unknown voltage to the reference voltage alters the length of the integration interval, producing two effects: a reduction in the power line-related noise rejection and potentially an incorrect value stored on the integration capacitor. Both will result in errors in the converted value. A similar delay or temporal error in responding to a state change on the comparator or in disabling the clock to the counter will alter the *read* interval and thus the number of accrued counts during that interval, thereby leading to an error in the measurement.

read

There are two ways by which the microprocessor can be made aware of external event information: interrupts and polling. For most microprocessors, the CPU will complete the current instruction before responding to an interrupt. Because the external interrupt is asynchronous to the internal activity of the microprocessor, one has no way of knowing which instruction is being executed. In a CISC architecture, different instructions require different numbers of clock cycles to complete. Thus, there is an inherent temporal uncertainty in any response to an external interrupt. At best, one can set an upper bound on response time; nonetheless, any uncertainty is reflected in errors in the conversion. Polling for an event change can reduce the ambiguity to the length of the polling loop, as was discussed earlier. However, the error remains.

> ***Design Heuristic***
>
> When making hardware—software trade-off decisions, utilize hardware speeds when necessary and take advantage of software strengths where speed is not critical.

The principal advantage of the dual slope A/D converter is its ability to reject line-related noise if the integrate interval is set to the duration of a line cycle. That strength is also one of its limitations. Each measurement requires one full power line cycle; the conversion method is not appropriate for high-speed measurements.

17.4.2 Successive Approximation Analog-to-Digital Conversion

If high speed A/D conversion is necessary, the successive approximation, S/A, approach can be very effective. The simple block diagram shown in Figure 17.9 illustrates the essence of the approach.

sample ***hold***

To make a measurement, the switch is placed in the *sample* position for some time, t_0, to allow the capacitor to charge to the unknown voltage. In the ideal case, t_0 will approach 0. The switch is then opened (placed in the *hold* position), and the reference voltage is adjusted until the output of the comparator is 0. That is, until the two input voltages are equal.

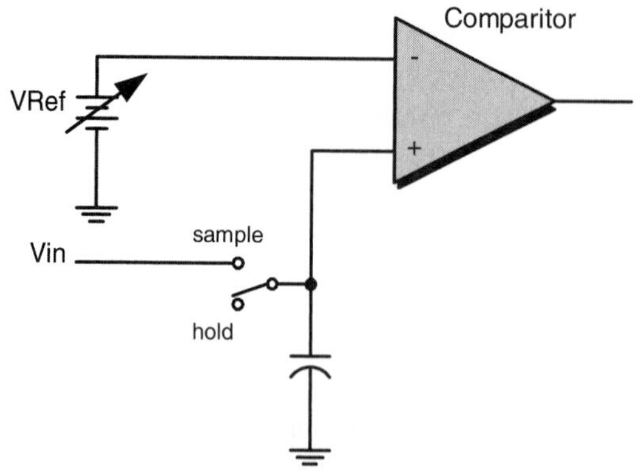

Figure 17.9 Schematic Diagram for a Basic Successive Approximation Analog-to-Digital Converter

Recall that the binary search algorithm locates the item of interest by starting in the middle of a sorted container and comparing the value stored there with the item being sought. Based on results of the comparison, the item has been found, or the upper or lower half of the container should be searched. The process is repeated until the item is found or the container has been exhausted. A slightly modified version of that algorithm is used in the successive approximation A/D.

At the start of the conversion, the reference voltage is set to one-half of the full-scale value and compared against the sampled value. If the reference is larger, its value is reduced by half; similarly, if the reference is too small, its value is increased by half. In either case, the algorithm is repeated until the proper value is found.

Clearly, the adjustable voltage reference is a key component in the S/A converter. The accuracy and resolution of the measured voltage are directly dependent on the accuracy and resolution of the voltage reference. In practice, the reference is derived from a digital-to-analog converter. We will use the R/2R DAC developed earlier for the present application.

We will set VRef as 5.0 VDC and the ratio RF/R as 6. Table 17.2 gives the corresponding output voltages for the DAC.

Table 17.2 Input Bit vs. Output Voltages for a 4-Bit R/2R Ladder DAC with 5.0 V Reference

Bit	Output
Msb 3	5.0
2	2.5
1	1.25
Lsb 0	0.625

The high-level diagram in Figure 17.10 brings all the pieces together.

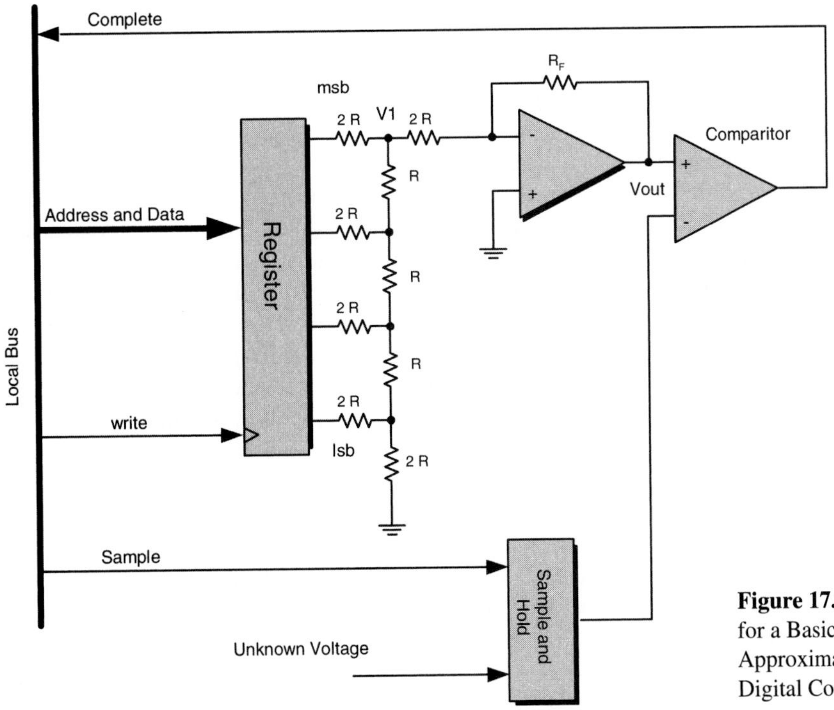

Figure 17.10 Block Diagram for a Basic Successive Approximation Analog-to-Digital Converter

Sample

A measurement is executed by initially entering the 4-bit binary word 1000 into the register and issuing the *Sample* command. Following the algorithm outlined earlier, successive values are entered into the register until either the DAC output equals the unknown voltage (based on the comparator output) or all possible DAC values are exhausted. The latter case comprises three subcases: the unknown voltage is too large or too small, or the best match within the resolution of the converter is reached. At that time, the state of the switches represents the digital equivalent of the unknown voltage.

Sample and Hold

sample and hold

The *sample and hold* circuit is an essential component of the S/A A/D. The schematic in Figure 17.11 gives a high-level diagram of one version implemented using two operational amplifiers configured as voltage followers.

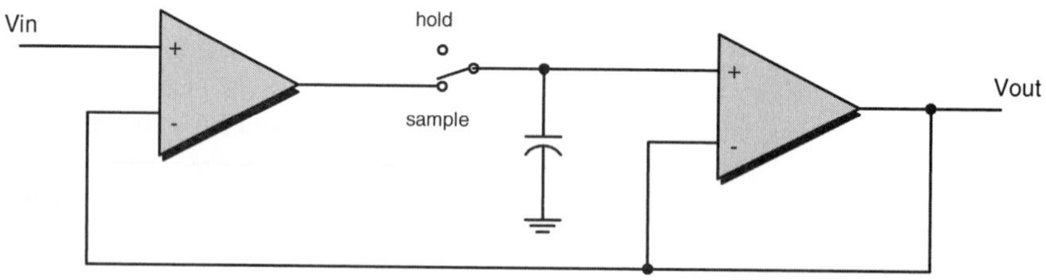

Figure 17.11 Sample and Hold Circuit

One must consider several factors in the design of a sample and hold circuit to ensure that the data is accurately sampled and that the sampled signal does not change during the subsequent A/D conversion. We will elaborate on each of these as we walk through a conversion.

sample
acquisition time, sample and hold
hold

At the start of a conversion, the switch above is placed into the *sample* position, and the hold capacitor begins to charge. The *acquisition time* of the *sample and hold* is the amount of time required for the value stored on the capacitor to reach the full value of sampled signal plus the time for output of circuit to reach the value of input. The output will follow the input until the circuit is put into the *hold* mode. The circuit must remain in the sample mode until the output has reached full value.

sample, hold
aperture time
aperture uncertainty

Following acquisition, the circuit switches from the *sample* to the *hold* mode. The state change cannot occur in zero time; the time to make that transition is called the *aperture time*. During this time, the output may change slightly, thereby losing an accurate representation of the unknown signal. Variation in the aperture time is called *aperture uncertainty*. A design objective is to make the aperture time as close to zero as possible.

droop rate

While the conversion is taking place, charge can leak off the hold capacitor, thereby decreasing the stored voltage. The rate of such a charge loss during hold time is called the *droop rate*. Clearly, one wishes to ensure very high-impedance paths for any connections to the capacitor.

dielectric absorption

If one is making repeated measurements and thus repeated samples, one must take into consideration a phenomenon called *dielectric absorption*. When a voltage is applied across a capacitor, charge is stored in the dielectric of the capacitor. That charge cannot be removed instantly, even if the capacitor is shorted. If a small signal is sampled after a large one, the stored value of the smaller signal may be inaccurate because of charge left from the larger one. Such a phenomenon affects the ability of the sample and hold circuit to respond quickly to a substantial change in the sampled signal.

Any time one is working with operational amplifiers, one must also be concerned about the usual offset and gain errors.

The main advantage of the successive approximation A/D when compared with the dual slope approach is speed. The conversion requires one cycle for each bit attempt. In a worst case scenario, a 16-bit converter will require eight cycles. Unlike the dual slope converter, the S/A approach does not have any inherent noise rejection. Appropriate filtering must be incorporated to handle any noise problems.

17.4.3 VCO Analog-to-Digital Conversion

A third alternative for implementing an A/D conversion is based on a voltage-controlled oscillator (VCO). A VCO is a circuit that produces a frequency proportional to an input voltage. If the VCO is designed to produce a frequency of 50 KHz in response to a 5.0-VDC signal, gating the frequency to a counter for 1 second will yield a value of 50,000 counts. Appropriate placement of the decimal point gives the digital equivalent of the analog voltage.

A high-level design for an A/D based on such a concept is given in Figure 17.12.

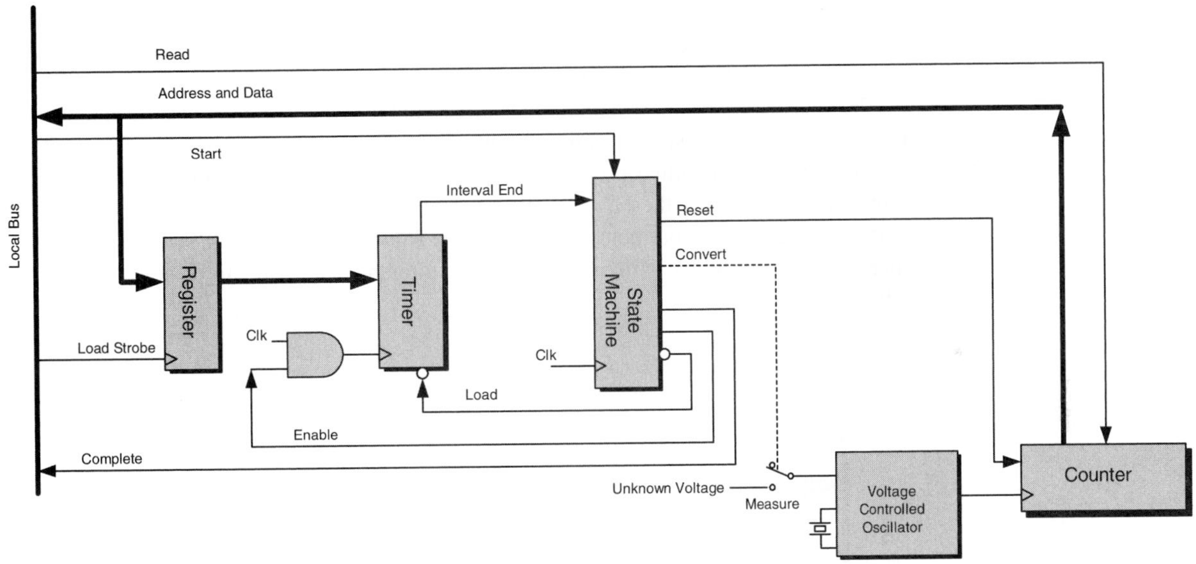

Figure 17.12 Block Diagram for a Voltage-Controlled Oscillator-Based A/D

Register
Start, state machine

A measurement begins when the microprocessor loads a value into the *Register* and issues a *Start* command. Following the *Start* command, the *state machine* issues the following commands:

Load, Register, Timer
Enable, Clk, Timer
Convert, unknown voltage

1. A *Load* command to transfer the contents of the *Register* into the *Timer*
2. An *Enable* to the gate controlling the *Clk* to the *Timer*
3. A *Convert* command to connect the *unknown voltage* to the input of the VCO

Interval End, State Machine
Complete
Read
Counter

After one second, the timer issues an *Interval End* to the *State Machine*, which responds by disconnecting the unknown signal from the VCO and issues a *Complete* event to the microprocessor. The microprocessor responds by asserting the *Read* signal to capture the state of the *Counter*.

timer

In the diagram, the *timer* is designed to time a one-second interval. As was done with the counter design used in the dual slope converter, the *timer* counts up from a preset value and signals when it overflows to the all-zero state. The number of bits in the timer and the frequency of its clock affect the resolution of the window gating the unknown signal into the VCO.

The hardware–software trade-offs in this design are similar to those in the dual slope design and so will not be repeated here.

17.5 MEASURING RESISTANCE

Let's now put the A/D to work. The need to measure resistance arises in many embedded applications. The target of the measurement may be the simple resistor, or the resistance may be the transduction of some other physical parameter such as strain—the "output" of a strain gauge or temperature—the output of a Resistance Temperature Device (RTD), for example. In any case, the solution to the problem derives from Ohm's law.

Like any other measurement, a great variety of methods can be used to measure resistance. One commonly used approach is to inject a known current through the resistor and measure the voltage drop across the resistor. The current should be sufficiently small that it does not damage the resistive element or cause it to dissipate significant power. A typical value is less than 100 mA with a preference for 1 mA or less.

Start

Complete

Read

The basic measurement technique is illustrated in Figure 17.13. The A/D can be any of those that have been discussed, although it is certainly not restricted to those. The measurement begins when the microprocessor issues a *Start* command. In response, the A/D closes both measure switches, thereby connecting the current source and the A/D to the unknown resistor. Once the measurement is complete, the A/D asserts the *Complete* signal back to the microprocessor, which can then issue a *Read* command at any time to retrieve the measured value.

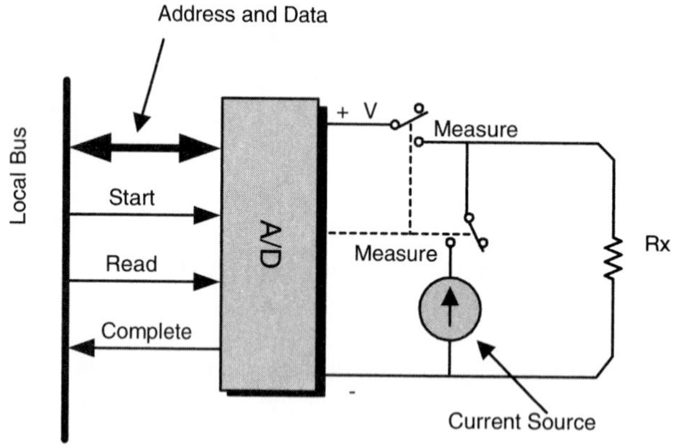

Figure 17.13 Measuring Resistance

The conversion from volts to ohms is typically made in the associated measurement driver. The motivation for doing so is to keep the measurement circuitry independent of the specific measurement. Moreover, the conversion from voltage to resistance can easily be performed at software speeds.

two-wire measurement

Such a measurement is called a *two-wire measurement* because the current source and the A/D are connected to the same points. A two-wire configuration gives rise to the problem illustrated in the modified version of the circuit shown in Figure 17.14.

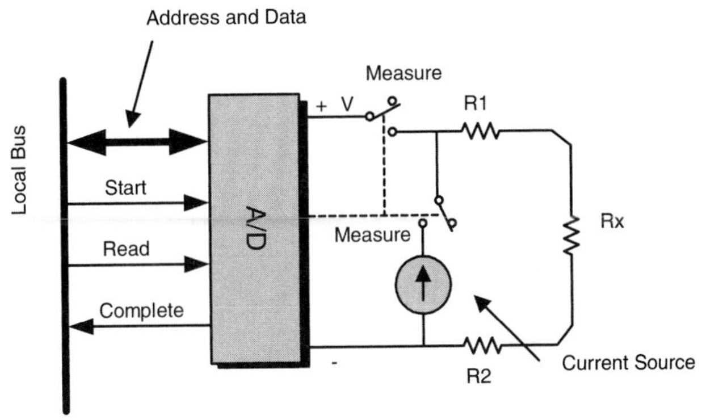

Figure 17.14 Parasitic Resistances in a Two-Wire Resistance Measurement

The measurement circuitry now includes the two parasitic resistors, R_1 and R_2. Both exist and are sources of error in any measurement. As can be seen, the measured voltage includes the drop across the unknown as well as that across the two parasitic components. Consequently, the computed value of the resistor will be in error by the series value of those two additional resistors.

To compensate for the additional resistance, the measurement circuitry can be modified slightly as illustrated in Figure 17.15.

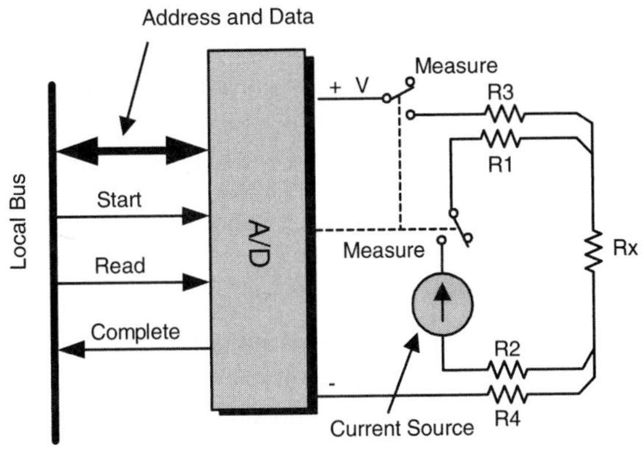

Figure 17.15 Using a Four Wire-Resistance Measurement to Compensate for Parasitic Resistances

Certainly the initial parasitic resistors R_1 and R_2 remain; initially, it appears that the problem has been compounded by the inclusion of two new ones, R_3 and R_4. The significant difference is that with the configuration shown above the current flowing through either R_3 or R_4 is close to zero because the Thévenin-equivalent impedance looking back into the A/D is designed to approach infinity. Thus, although the resistors may be there, the drop across them is small compared to the drop across the unknown. Such a scheme is called a *four-wire measurement*.

four-wire measurement

17.6 MEASURING CURRENT

A current measurement is similar to a resistance measurement. Once again, the measurement can be implemented in a number of ways. One common method is to reverse the roles of the current source and the resistance in the design for measuring resistance. The resistor now becomes a current shunt—a precision resistor with typical values of 0.1Ω to 1Ω inserted into the current path. The voltage across the shunt is measured and converted to the

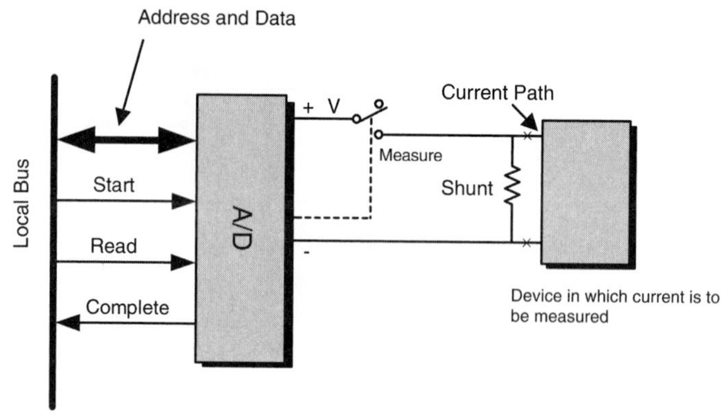

Figure 17.16 Measuring Current

equivalent current using Ohm's law and the known value for the shunt. Such a design is presented in Figure 17.16.

Start ***Complete*** ***Read***

As was done in the previous measurements, the process begins when the microprocessor issues a *Start* command. In response, the A/D closes both measure switches, thereby connecting the current source and the A/D to the unknown resistor. Once the measurement is complete, the A/D asserts the *Complete* signal back to the microprocessor which can then issue a *Read* command at any time to retrieve the measured value. The conversion from volts to amps will typically be done in the associated measurement driver.

The one drawback of using a shunt is the need to interrupt the current path to insert the shunt. An alternate scheme is to utilize a coil of wire wrapped around the conductor in which the current is to be measured and to measure the induced voltage. Basic physics provides the conversion to current.

17.7 MEASURING TEMPERATURE

Like the other measurements discussed to this point, a large number of approaches can be taken in making temperature measurements. One common and inexpensive technique is to use a sensing device called a thermocouple.

Seebeck Effect ***Seebeck thermal emf***

The phenomenon of thermoelectricity was discovered by a German physicist, Thomas Johann Seebeck, in 1821. He found that, when two wires made of dissimilar metals were connected to each other at two points and the two junctions held at different temperatures, a current will flow due to a phenomenon that is now called the *Seebeck Effect*. The force driving the current is known as the *Seebeck thermal emf*. The flow will continue as long as a temperature difference exists between the two junctions. This electromotive force (voltage) is the parameter measured in thermocouple thermometry.

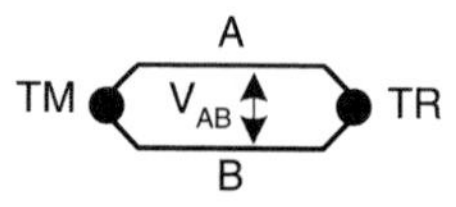

Figure 17.17 A Basic Thermocouple

When a circuit containing two dissimilar metals is completed (as seen in Figure 17.17), there will always be at least one additional thermocouple in the loop. The simple loop shown contains two dissimilar metals A and B and two junctions: TM—measurement—and TR—reference. The amount of current flowing is related to temperature difference.

17.7.1 Sensors

Generally thermocouples are alloys of several different kinds of metals, including, iron, copper, nickel, chromium, aluminum, platinum, tungsten, and rhenium. Several of the

Constantan, Chrommel, Alumel

alloys have become so common that their trade names have come into familiar usage. These include *Constantan* (Copper–Nickel), *Chrommel* (Chromium–Nickel), and *Alumel* (Aluminum–Nickel). Using these alloys conjoined with other metals leads to the more common thermocouple configurations, many of which have been given a letter designation.

They are presented in Table 17.3.

Table 17.3 Common Thermocouple Types

Type	Alloy	Range
J	Iron Constantan	–210 C to +1200 C –8 to 70 mV
K	Chrommel–Alumel	–270 C to +1372 C –6.5 to 54.8 mV
T	Copper–Constantan	–270 C to +400 C –6.3 to 28.9 mV
R and S	R–Platinum 13% Rhodium	–50 C to +1768 C –0.2 to 21.1 mV
	S–Platinum 10% Rhodium	–270 C to +400 C –6.3 to 18.7 mV

Another kind of temperature sensor (transducer) is a Resistance Temperature Detector or RTD. The RTD is based on the principle that conductivity of material changes in a predictable manner when the material is subjected to different temperatures. The device is constructed using a coil of fine gauge wire wrapped around ceramic core. The materials used include platinum, copper, nickel, or tungsten, but most frequently platinum. The device has a high operating range, linear characteristics, and long-term stability. Using such a device, the most accurate measurements are made using a four-wire resistance measurement.

17.7.2 Making the Measurement

For a system using the basic thermocouple as the sensing device, the voltage (thermal emf) is measured as shown in Figure 17.18. As noted, the materials comprising the thermocouple are typically alloys of several different metals; the connection from the thermocouple to the measurement device is frequently copper. Because copper is a different metal from the thermocouple alloys, by making a connection to the thermocouple, additional thermocouples are introduced as illustrated in the drawing. These additional thermocouples produce the voltages V_{JunctA} and V_{JunctB} as shown. Examining the circuit in the drawing, observe that the Voltage V_{AB} will equal the algebraic sum of the voltages V_{JunctA} and V_{JunctB}. If the thermocouple–copper junctions (JunctA and JunctB) are maintained at the same temperature, they will act as a single thermocouple (driven by TR). Under such a condition, when making the measurement, the voltage value that is read will be proportional to the difference between TR and TM.

Once the voltage measurement of the thermoelectric voltage (V_{AB}) is complete, the first operation in converting that value into an equivalent temperature value is the algebraic addition of the voltage measured at the reference junction terminals (V_{JuncA} and V_{JuncB})—this is TR. The resulting sum represents an approximation of the thermoelectric voltage generated at the temperature-sensing junction (TM in the figure).

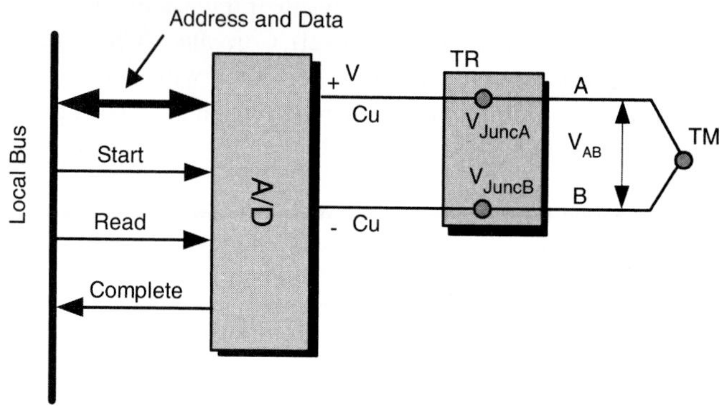

Figure 17.18 Measuring Temperature Using a Thermocouple

17.7.3 Working with Nonlinear Devices

National Institute of Standards and Technology (NIST)

Thermocouples, like many other real-world sensors and transducers, have a monotonic nonlinear relationship between the physical parameter and the electrical signal that is actually measured. In the United States, the *National Institute of Standards and Technology* (NIST) provides equations expressing such relationships. The equations are normally given in the form of a power series accompanied by tables of coefficients corresponding to the type of device and the ranges over which it is operated.

The mathematical operations for performing the conversion from the measured signal to the physical quantity are carried out in the software driver for the measurement device. The significant overhead in evaluating the power series for each measurement is an unreasonable burden in most applications. Thus, the series is often replaced by a linearized version of the polynomial. Such an approximation can be a linear fit ($y = mx + b$) or a higher order fit based on the degree of conformity required for the application.

In general, the approximation comprises a number of linearized segments. The length of each segment is determined by the required conformity to the actual curve for the measurement being made. To see this, consider the following curves in Figure 17.19 that are approximated by a linear curve fit.

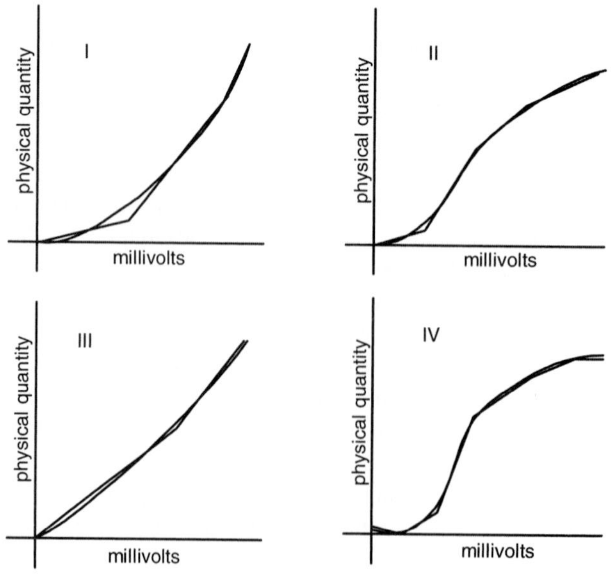

Figure 17.19 A Linear Approximation to a Nonlinear Curve

Curve III is more linear than curve I; potentially, it could be approximated by two straight-line segments, whereas curve I probably would require three. A similar phenomenon occurs in curves II and IV.

Once the segments have been computed, the reduced sets of coefficients for the linearizing equations are stored in a table in ROM. For the linear fit, for example, the values for each of the m and b pairs would be stored. To perform the conversion, the software driver uses the measured signal to compute an index into the table of coefficients. The appropriate set of coefficients is selected and used with the measured value to compute the corresponding value of the physical quantity.

For thermocouple measurements, the temperature corresponding to the device's output voltage is approximated according to a power series equation given as:

$$\boxed{TM = c_0 + c_1V + c_2V^2 + \ldots + c_nV^n} \tag{17.8}$$

where

V = thermoelectric voltage (microvolts)

c_n = thermocouple type-dependent polynomial coefficients

T = temperature (C)

n = order of the polynomial

The calculated thermoelectric voltage generated at TM is converted into an equivalent temperature value using the (linearized) power series polynomial along with thermocouple type-dependent coefficient tables.

NIST publishes several tables for each thermocouple type containing coefficients representing quadratic (second order), cubic (third order), or quartic (fourth order). Voltage-to-temperature conversion accuracy can be increased by using higher order coefficient tables, but at the cost of longer processing time to perform the calculations. Accuracy can be further enhanced by selecting tables representing the narrowest temperature range for the specific measurement application.

For a fourth-order polynomial for a J-type thermocouple (–200 C to 0 C with error range –0.4 C to 0.5 C and 0 C to 760 C with error range –0.9° C to 0.7° C), the coefficients are given in Table 17.4.

Table 17.4 Coefficients for a J-Type Thermocouple Polynomial

$c_0 = 0.0$	$c_0 = 0.0$
$c_1 = 1.8843850 \text{x} 10^{-2}$	$c_1 = 1.9323799 \text{x} 10^{-2}$
$c_2 = 1.2029733 \text{x} 10^{-6}$	$c_2 = -1.0306020 \text{x} 10^{-7}$
$c_3 = -2.5278593 \text{x} 10^{-10}$	$c_3 = 3.7084018 \text{x} 10^{-12}$
$c_4 = -2.5849263 \text{x} 10^{-14}$	$c_4 = -5.1031937 \text{x} 10^{-17}$

To perform a temperature measurement, the reference junction temperature (TR) and the microvolt output of the thermocouple circuit are recorded. Next, the circuit output voltage is corrected for any deviation from 0 C in the reference junction by multiplying the measured reference junction temperature by the appropriate Seebeck coefficient. For the type J thermocouple, the value is 51.71μV/C. If a more accurate conversion is required, the reference junction temperature can be converted into an equivalent thermoelectric voltage using a power series polynomial.

The calculated value of the reference junction voltage is then algebraically added to the thermocouple circuit output voltage measured at the reference junction. The new value represents an approximation of the thermoelectric voltage generated by the temperature-sensing junction (TM) of the thermocouple. The calculated voltage can now be converted into an equivalent temperature value as described earlier.

17.8 GENERATING DIGITAL SIGNALS

Several different kinds of digital signals may be required in an embedded application. These often come into play in applications that utilize and therefore need to control various kinds of motors. On other occasions, the interface to some form of display must be provided. At other times the embedded application is providing the control for a piece of equipment such as a printer, keyboard, CDROM, or video imager. The next several sections examine representative examples of several of the more common of these applications.

17.8.1 Motors and Motor Control

The ability to control different kinds of motors is important in a host of contemporary applications ranging from assembly robots to remotely controlled vehicles to the precision positioning of medical instruments. Motors that are typically found in such applications fall into three categories: DC motors, servo motors, and stepper motors.

17.8.2 DC Motors

DC motor

Figure 17.20 gives a high-level diagram of the basic components of a *DC motor*.

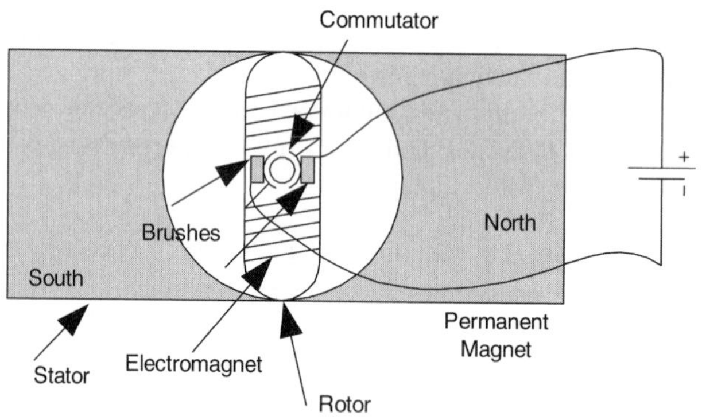

Figure 17.20 A Basic DC Motor

stator
rotor
brushes, commutator

These components comprise a stationary permanent magnet called a *stator*, a movable (rotating) electromagnetic called a *rotor*, and a system to connect power to the electromagnetic called *brushes* and a *commutator*.

Operation of the motor proceeds as follows. When a voltage is applied across the electromagnetic, the magnetic poles of the rotor are attracted to the opposite poles of the stator, thereby causing the rotor to turn. As the rotor turns, the electromagnet becomes polarized in the opposite direction and the poles of the rotor are now repelled by the nearer poles and are attracted to the opposite poles of the permanent magnet causing the rotor to turn once again.

Observe that the commutator is a split ring against which the brushes make physical contact. One portion of the commutator is connected to one end of the electromagnet, and the other portion is connected to the opposite end. Through the action of the commutator, the direction of the field in the electromagnet is continually switched, thus causing the rotor to continue to move.

The actions of the commutator, brushes, and electromagnet are illustrated through the simple model in Figure 17.21. The brushes are fixed. However, as the rotor rotates, the commutator (which is attached to the rotor) acts like a switch, connecting the voltage source first one way then the opposite way across the electromagnetic thereby changing its polarization.

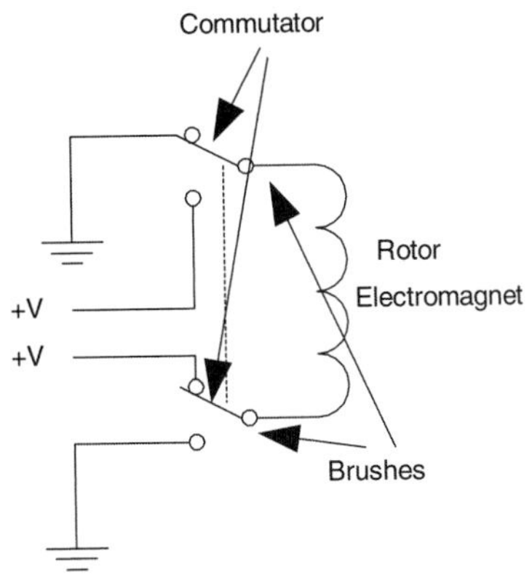

Figure 17.21 Schematic of the Commutator, Brushes, and Electromagnet in a DC Motor

As should be evident, the DC motor has the ability to turn through 360 degrees, continuously, in one direction, when power is applied. If the applied voltage is held constant, the speed of the motor is also held constant; increasing or decreasing the applied voltage will have a corresponding effect on the motor's speed.

pulse width modulation (PWM)

Using a scheme called *pulse width modulation* (PWM), the average magnitude of the applied voltage can effectively be controlled and so can the motor's speed. We will learn how to do this shortly. As the speed of the motor decreases, so does its torque.

If the polarity of the applied voltage is reversed, the motor will run in the opposite direction, as should be expected. We will use a circuit called an H bridge to manage the reversal. Generally, a DC motor is not used for positioning tasks unless it is incorporated into a control system that can provide position (and possibly velocity) feedback information.

17.8.3 Servo Motors

servo motor

A *servo motor* is a special case of a DC motor to which position or velocity feedback circuitry has been added to implement a closed loop control system. Like the DC motor, the servo motor can rotate in either direction; however, generally the range is less than 360 degrees. Also like the DC motor, the servo motor is controlled by a pulse width modulated signal; however, the signal is used to control position rather than speed. The servo motor finds common use in systems such as remotely controlled systems, robotics applications, numerically controlled machinery, plotters, or similar systems where starts and stops must be made quickly and accurate position is essential.

17.8.4 Stepper Motors

stepper motor

A *stepper motor* is different from, and yet similar to, both the DC and the servo motor. One major difference is that each of the latter motors moves in either the forward or reverse direction with a smooth and continuous motion; the stepper motor moves in a series of increments or steps. The accompanying diagram in Figure 17.22 presents a high-level view of the essential elements of a stepper motor.

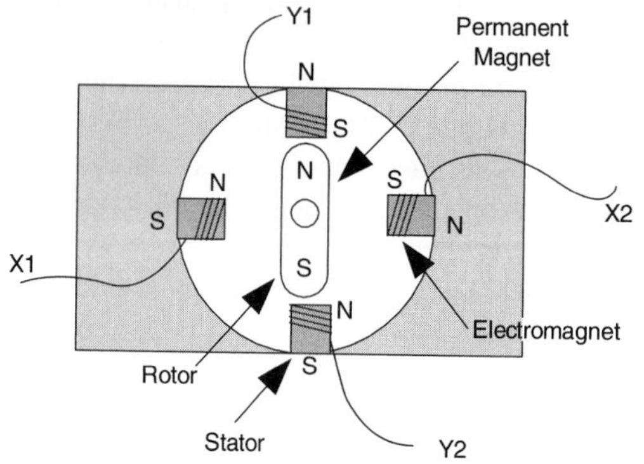

Figure 17.22 Basic Components of a Stepper Motor

The first point to observe is that the rotor is a permanent magnet rather than the stator as in the DC and servo motors. The rotor in the motor in Figure 17.22 has two teeth, and the stator has four poles and four electromagnets.

In a stepper motor, the size of each step is specified in degrees and varies with the design of the motor. The step size is selected based on the precision of the positioning required. The simple motor given above has a step angle of 90 degrees, based on the spacing of the poles. Connections are made to the electromagnets through the signals marked X1, X2, Y1, and Y2. Like the DC motor, the stepper can rotate through 360 degrees and in either direction. The speed of the motor is determined by the repetition rate of the steps.

17.9 CONTROLLING DC AND SERVO MOTORS

17.9.1 DC Motors

pulse width modulation (PWM), pulse

Both the DC motor and the servo motor require a pulse width modulated signal to control either speed or position. *Pulse width modulation* (PWM), as its name implies, is the process of using the width of a *pulse* to convey information in a digital signal. For example, suppose that we have the perfect square wave depicted in Figure 17.23.

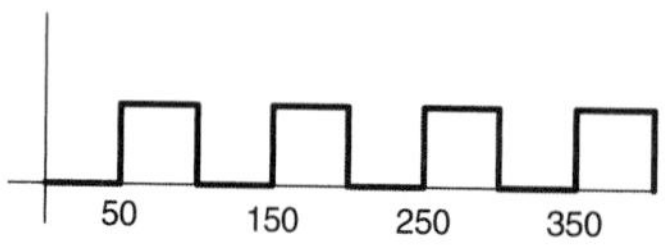

Figure 17.23 An Ideal Square Wave

50% duty-cycle

high

From this diagram, we can see that the period of the signal is fixed (in this case to 100 time units) and that the signal is in the high-state 50 time units out of 100 possible time units. Thus, the signal is ON for half of the period. The signal is said to have a *50% duty-cycle*, where the duty-cycle of a signal is defined as the percentage of time the digital signal is in the *high* state during the waveform's period. Using this definition, we can easily see that the signal in Figure 17.24a has a 25% duty-cycle and that Figure 17.24b has a 75% duty-cycle.

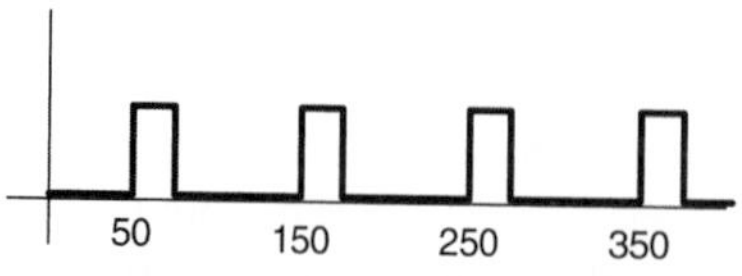

Figure 17.24a A Signal with 25% Duty-Cycle

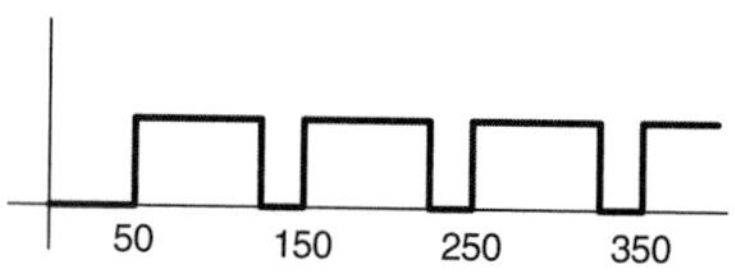

Figure 17.24b A Signal with 75% Duty-Cycle

Similarly, the next signal in Figure 17.25a has a 0% duty-cycle and finally that in Figure 17.25b has a 100% duty-cycle:

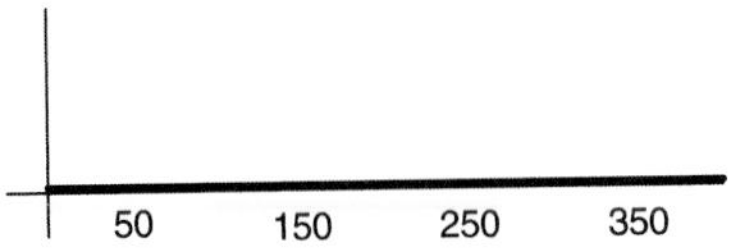

Figure 17.25a A Signal with 25% Duty-Cycle

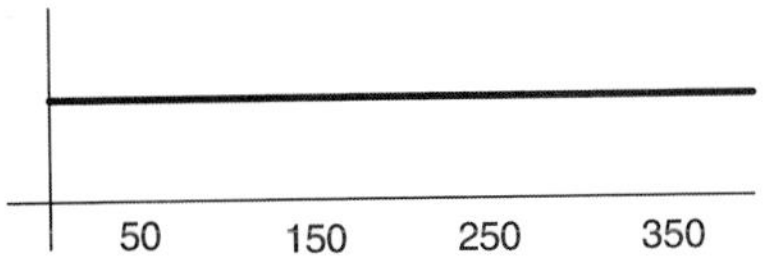

Figure 17.25b A Signal with 75% Duty-Cycle

Assume that a DC motor is driven by a voltage signal ranging from 0 to 12 V. To run the motor at full speed, a 12 V signal is applied; to run the motor at half speed a 6 V signal is applied; to run the motor at one-quarter speed a 3 V signal is applied; and so on.

Based on these timing diagrams, if a signal with a 100% duty-cycle is applied to the motor, one will expect it to run at full speed; similarly, if a signal with a 0% duty-cycle is applied, the motor should stop. If a signal with a 75% duty-cycle is applied, what should one expect? The average voltage applied to the motor during each period of the waveform is given by Eq. 17.9.

$$\begin{aligned} V_{ave} &= 0.75 \bullet 12VDC + 0.25 \bullet 0VDC \\ &= 9VDC \end{aligned} \tag{17.9}$$

average voltage

That is, one should expect the motor to run at 75% of full speed. By using such a pulse width modulated signal, the speed of a DC motor can be controlled because it is the *average voltage* that determines its speed.

Today, it is not uncommon to find PWM capability built in to the microprocessor or microcontroller. Under such circumstances, implementing the software side of the PWM capability reduces to programming the desired period and duty-cycle according to the device's data sheet. If PWM capability is not intrinsically supported and if the microprocessor or microcontroller has a built-in timer, generating a PWM signal to the output ports is rather straightforward.

For example, suppose that a PWM signal with a 75% duty-cycle is required and the signal's period has been set to 100 ms. The signal can be implemented as follows: configure a timer to time 75 ms, turn a digital output ON, and wait for the timer to expire. When the timer expires, turn the digital output OFF and time 25ms. The process can be executed repeatedly to generate the 75% duty-cycle PWM signal. Observe that the frequency of the signal is not changing, only its duty cycle.

In either case, the motor generally cannot be driven directly from the microprocessor's digital output ports. Rather, one must ensure that the hardware motor drivers can support the current requirements for the intended motor. Several alternate implementations will be discussed shortly.

17.9.2 Servo Motors

One can use a pulse width modulation (PWM) signal to control the position of a servo motor in the following way. Every servo motor has a neutral or base position. The servo is put into that position by applying a continuous train of pulses of a width specified by the manufacturer of the servo. An internal feedback control system holds the servo in the commanded position. To cause the servo to move in one direction, the width of the pulse is increased, and

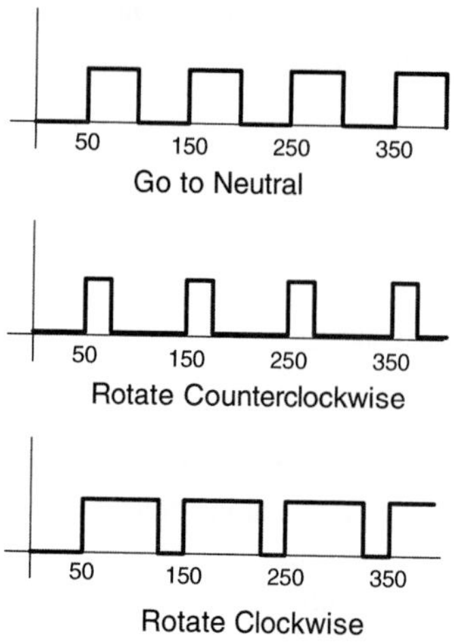

Figure 17.26 Using a PWM Signal to Control a Servo Motor

to effect movement in the opposite direction, the width of the pulse is decreased. The change in pulse width causes the movement; the repeated sequence holds the position. These actions are illustrated in Figure 17.26.

The design may place a number of requirements on the servo motor, including the ability to control the acceleration, velocity, and position to very tight tolerances. Slew rate, the time that it takes for the servo to change from one position to another, is often another critical parameter. As with so many other parts of the design, such constraints must be identified and included in the design specification, not during the prototype development.

Motors are mechanical devices and thus typically have much looser time constraints than one frequently finds in the control of their electronic counterparts. It is reasonable, therefore, to consider controlling them directly by command from the microprocessor unless there are other overriding considerations.

17.9.3 Controlling Stepper Motors

Controlling stepper motors is not that much more complicated than controlling DC motors, although it may seem a lot like juggling as one tries to keep all the signals straight. The earlier figure of the stepper motor is repeated here for reference. The polarization of the electromagnets as illustrated in Figure 17.27a requires that the indicated input signals are applied to X1, X2, Y1, and Y2: V to X1 and Y2 and 0 to X2 and Y1.

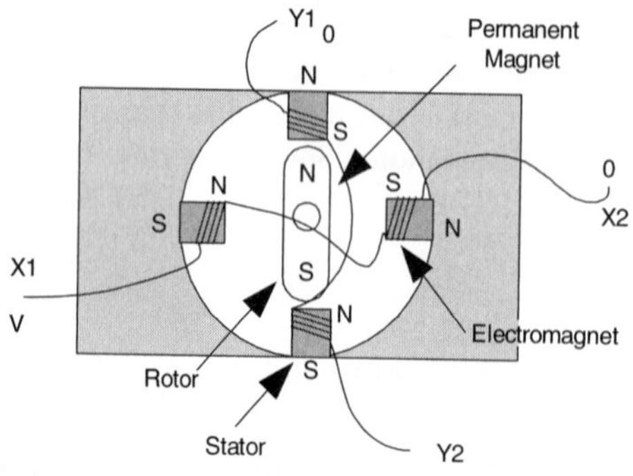

Figure 17.27a Controlling a Stepper Motor

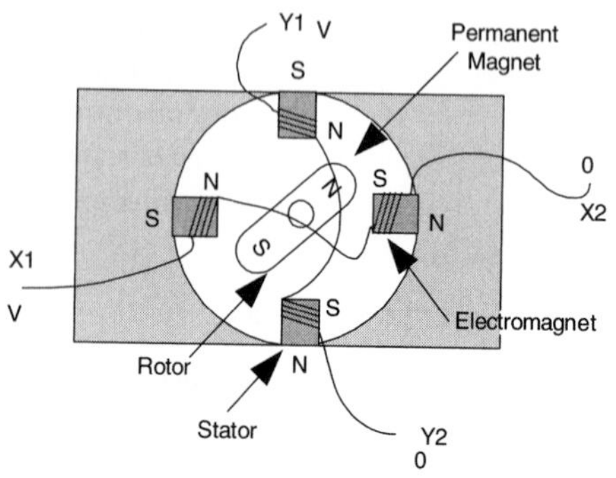

Figure 17.27b Controlling a Stepper Motor

If the input signals to V on X1 and Y1 and 0 to X2 and Y2 are now changed, the polarization on the electromagnets changes to that shown in Figure 17.27b. The two north poles at the top of the drawing will repel, and the north pole on the rotor will be attracted to the south pole on the right-hand side of the stator. The rotor will thus move 90° in the clockwise direction (see Figure 17.28).

X1	X2	Y1	Y2	Position
V	0	0	V	0°
V	0	V	0	90°
0	V	V	0	180°
0	V	0	V	270°

Figure 17.28 Stepper Motor with 90° per Step

Similarly, changes to the input signal levels shown in the accompanying table will produce the rotor movements shown in Figure 17.29.

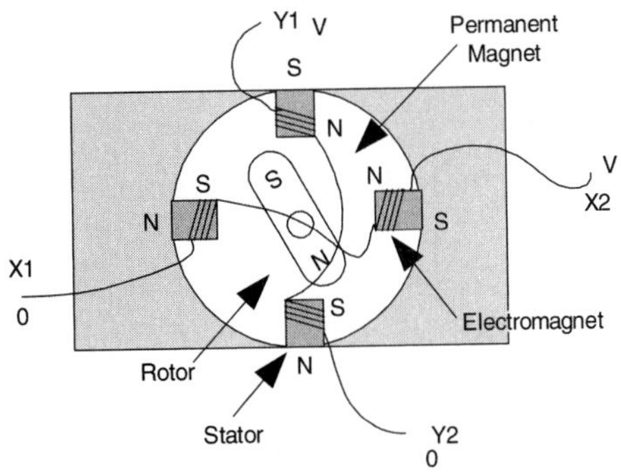

Figure 17.29a Controlling a Stepper Motor

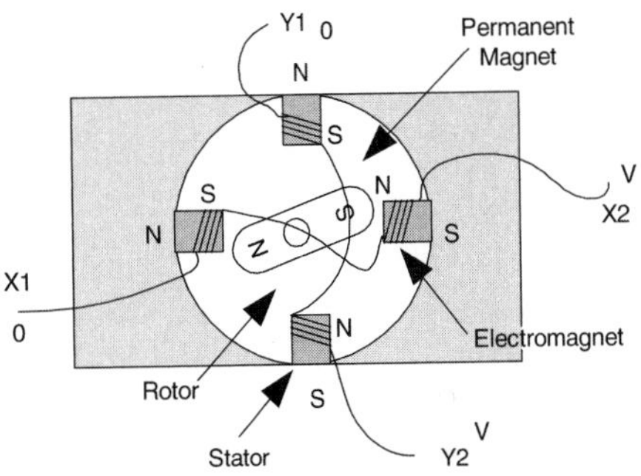

Figure 17.29b Controlling a Stepper Motor

Extending the design to motors with a greater number of poles or stator teeth is a straightforward application of the pattern illustrated. The variable will be the number of times that the pattern will have to be repeated to achieve a full rotation as the number of degrees per step will decrease.

The timing diagram for one cycle (not full rotation) is given in Figure 17.30.

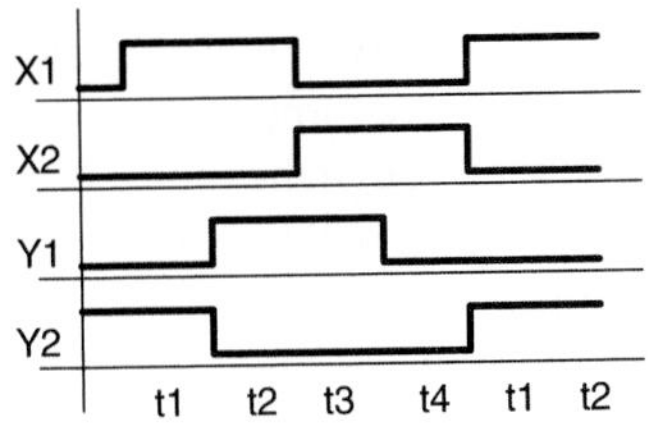

Figure 17.30 Stepper Motor Control Timing Diagram

Such a pattern can be generated in several ways, including the following.

1. Utilize four digital output lines from the microprocessor and base the signal timing on an internal timer.
2. Utilize two digital output lines from the microprocessor and an external decoder that will map the four possible combinations of the output lines to the necessary drive signals. The timing is based on an internal timer.
3. Implement an external up/down counter (for bidirectional rotation). The counter can be based on a four flip-flop design directly replicating the pattern in (1) above, thereby minimizing the combinational decoding. Alternately, the design can utilize two flip-flops and a decoding network, thereby replicating the design in (2).

17.9.4 Motor Drive Circuitry

in

Motors generally require more drive current than a typical microprocessor, TTL, or CMOS gate can provide. To provide that current, the control signals being discussed are connected to a driver circuit rather than directly to the motor. For unidirectional drive, any number of variations on the accompanying design in Figure 17.31 can be used. The drive transistor must be able to sink the required motor current. The buffer is an open collector driver. Thus, when the digital signal *in* is a logical 1, the base current for the transistor is supplied through the pull-up resistor rather than from the buffer. When the digital signal *in* is a logical 0, the buffer can sink more current than a standard gate.

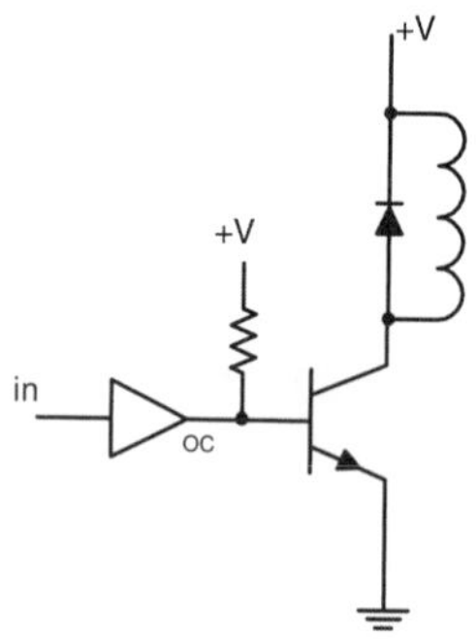

Figure 17.31 Unidirectional Motor Drive

The diode is used to suppress the flyback voltage that is generated by the collapsing field in the coil when the motor is switched OFF. If it is not included, the resulting voltage can damage other parts in the circuit.

H bridge, half H bridge

If the motor must support bidirectional rotation, one of the more commonly used driver designs is called an *H bridge* or a variant called a *half H bridge*. The circuit has acquired such an appellation because its topology resembles an upper case H. One such design for an H bridge is given in Figure 17.32.

in1

All four of the gates are open collector or open drain devices. Thus, for example, if input *in1* is in the logical 0 state, the output of the open collector device is floating and the base of Q3 is pulled to the supply voltage, thereby cutting it off.

If transistors Q2 and Q3 are turned ON and transistors Q1 and Q4 turned OFF, current will flow from left to right through the motor winding. Conversely, if the states of the four transistors are reversed, current will flow in the opposite direction and the motor will rotate in the opposite direction.

The four diodes are to suppress the flyback voltage that is generated by the collapsing field in the coil when the motor is switched OFF or the direction is changed.

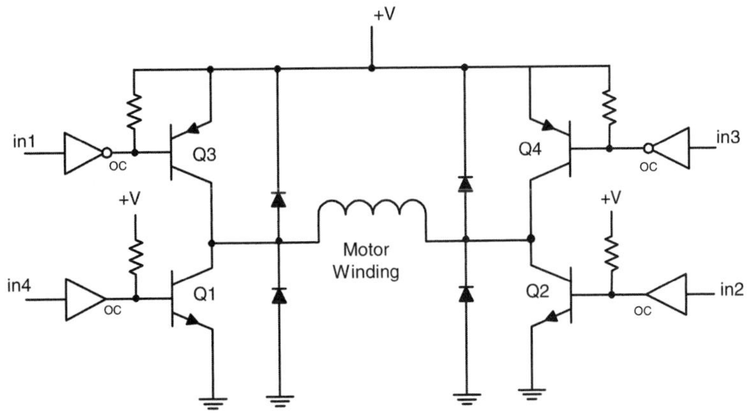

Figure 17.32 H Bridge Motor Drive

in1, in2

To control a DC or servo motor, the PWM signal is connected to one pair of the input signals, *in1* and *in2*, while the other input pair is connected to ground. To reverse the direction of rotation, the input connections are reversed. Connections for a stepper motor follow in a similar manner. For the stepper motor, one bridge will be required for each winding.

A design for a half H bridge is presented in Figure 17.33.

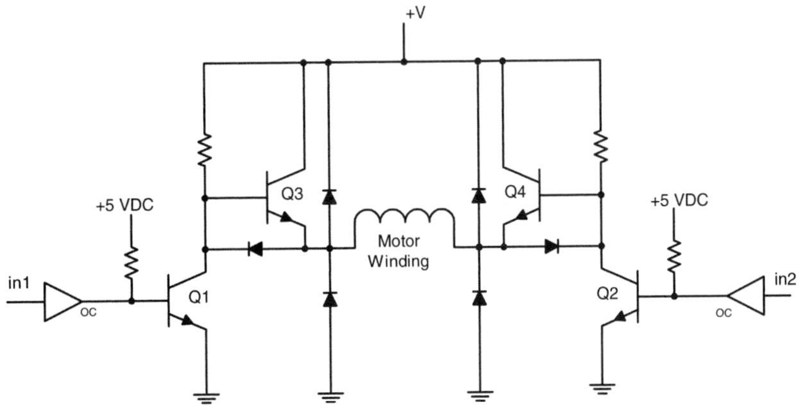

Figure 17.33 Half H Bridge Motor Drive

If the input signals, IN1 and IN2, to the half H bridge are at ground and 5.0 VDC, respectively, transistors Q1 and Q4 will be OFF while transistors Q2 and Q3 will be ON. Current will flow through the winding from left to right in the drawing. If the input signals are reversed, the states of the four transistors will be reversed and current will flow in the opposite direction through the winding.

To control a DC or servo motor, the PWM signal is connected to one of the input signals, IN1 or IN2, and the other input is connected to ground. To reverse the direction of rotation, the input connections are reversed. Connections for a stepper motor follow in a similar manner. For the stepper motor, one bridge will be required for each winding.

Today numerous vendors provide an excellent selection of H bridge, half H bridge, and other types of motor drive integrated circuits that should satisfy most design specifications.

17.9.5 Motor Drive Noise

Electric motors are notorious sources of noise in embedded applications. Such noise arises from the switching currents in the windings in the motor as one can readily see from the simple equation for the voltage drop across an inductor.

$$\boxed{V = L\frac{di}{dt}} \tag{17.10}$$

ground bounce

The large switching currents that are common in motors give rise to noise that eventually appears throughout the ground distribution system as a contributor to *ground bounce*—the movement of ground away from the reference 0.0 V.

One way to address such a problem is to put the motors onto a power and ground system that is physically separate from the rest of the logic and any precision analog circuitry. Any necessary control signals are optically coupled into the isolated subsystem. Such a scheme is illustrated in Figure 17.34.

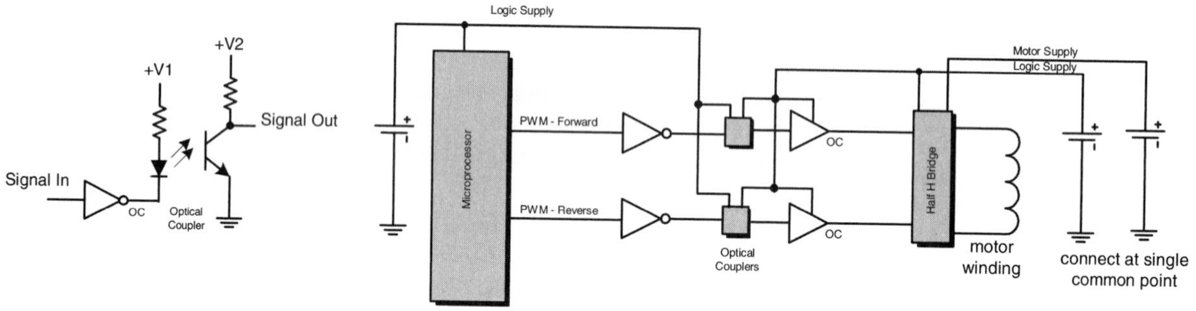

Figure 17.34 Using Optical Couplers to Isolate Motor Noise

17.10 LEDS AND LED DISPLAYS

Light-emitting diodes (LEDs), dot matrix, and multisegment LED displays are common in many embedded applications. The amount of external hardware that should be included in the design is determined by the current drive capabilities of the microprocessor output ports and by I/O space limitations in the design.

Assume that limited hardware support from the processor and therefore most of the design must be implemented outside of the processor. The designs can easily be migrated to software if the necessary resources are available.

17.10.1 Individual LEDs

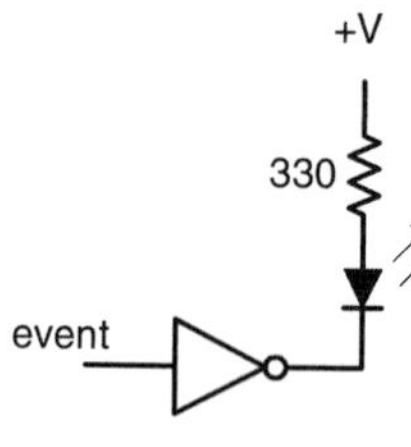

Figure 17.35 Controlling an LED Using Cathode Drive

Most TTL and CMOS devices sink current better than they source it. An open collector or open drain device works very well as a driver. Such devices are designed to sink substantially more current than the standard gates and are available as either inverting or noninverting drivers.

Assume that the application specifies that an annunciation be given when a certain event is TRUE. If we assume the event is an active HIGH or HIGH TRUE signal, then the inverting device should be selected. The schematic in Figure 17.35 illustrates the design of the annunciator. The resistor is incorporated to limit the current through the LED, which ranges from 20 to 60 mA. With LEDs, as the current level is increased, the brightness does as well.

17.10.2 Multi–LED Displays

The ubiquitous seven-segment or numeric display simply combines a number of individual LEDs into a package with an appropriate lens to enable the display of any of the 10 decimal digits (plus decimal points) when the proper LEDs are illuminated. A top view of the device and several possible digits is shown in Figure 17.36.

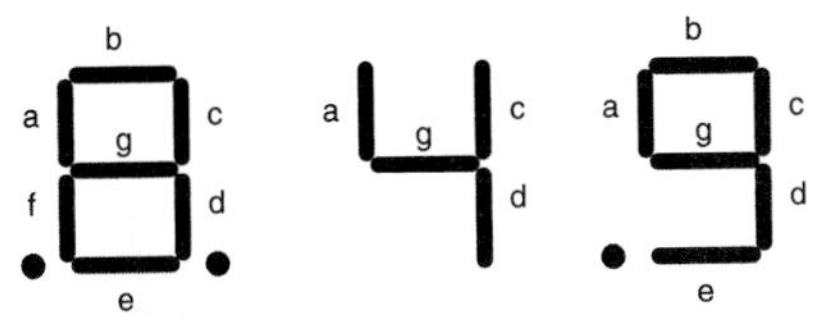

Figure 17.36 A Three-Digit LED Display

The LEDs within the display are connected in either a common anode or a common cathode configuration. Simply put, either all the anodes are connected together and the drive signal is applied to the individual cathodes or vice versa as depicted in Figure 17.37 (omitting the decimal points).

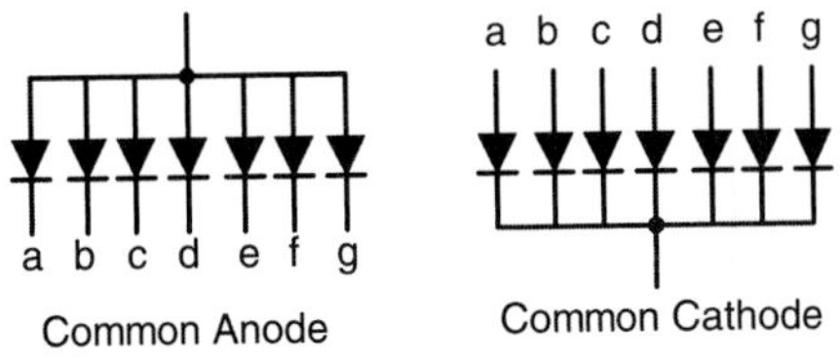

Figure 17.37 Seven-Segment LED Display Configurations

BCD to Seven-Segment Decoder

To drive the device, an MSI part called a *BCD to Seven-Segment Decoder* can be used. As the name suggests, the part takes four input signals, encoded as a BCD number, and produces seven output signals. If those signals are connected to a seven-segment display as shown in Figure 17.38, the proper LEDs will turn on to display the corresponding BCD number. The decimal points, if necessary, would be controlled separately.

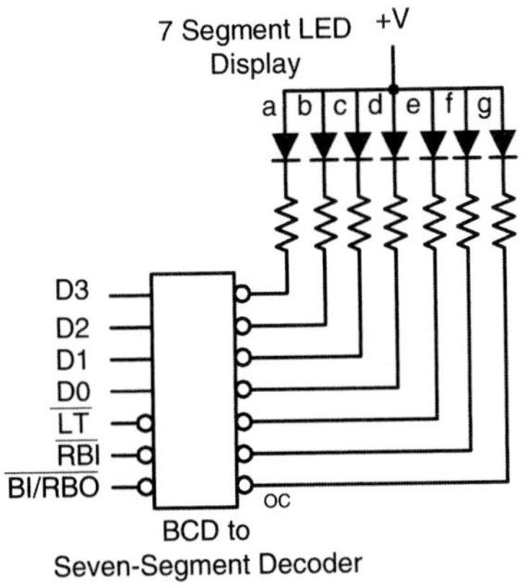

Figure 17.38 Using a Seven-Segment Decoder/Driver to Control a Common Anode LED Display

Lamp Test

Blank Input

The outputs on the decoder are implemented as open collector devices. In addition to the four data inputs, the decoder has three, active low, control inputs. The first, ~LT–*Lamp Test*, when active, turns all seven segments ON. The remaining two support leading zero suppression in multidigit displays. When enabled, the number 00789 would display as 789. When the signal ~BI–*Blank Input*, is active, all data outputs are OFF independent of the

Ripple Blank Input

input data. When the signal ~RBI–*Ripple Blank Input*, is active, all data inputs are low, all data outputs are OFF, and the signal ~RBO is active.

When implementing a multidigit display, to save power, weight, and the cost of parts, the decoder can be multiplexed among all of the display devices as illustrated in Figure 17.39.

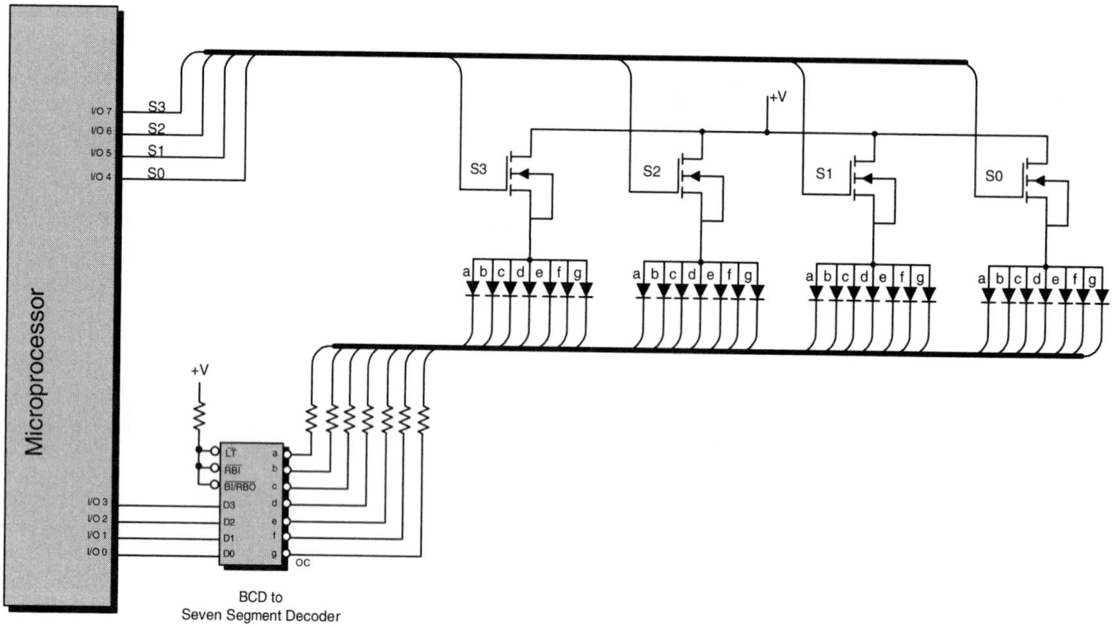

Figure 17.39 A Multiplexed Four-Digit LED Display

The design takes advantage of the fact that the human eye is able to integrate out short-term transients in an image so that it appears to be constant. The operation proceeds as shown in the timing diagram shown in Figure 17.40.

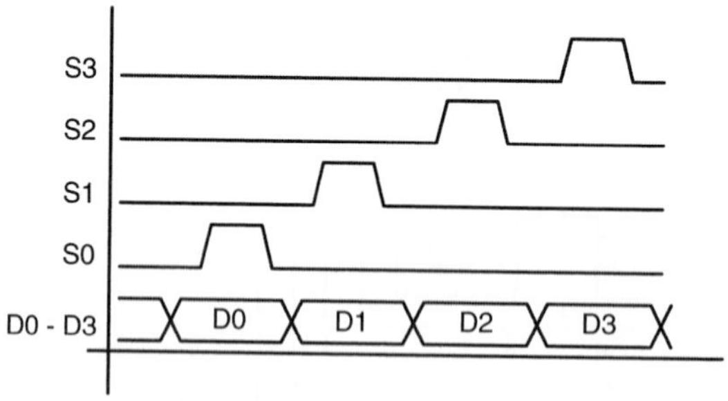

Figure 17.40 Timing for the Anode Drive in a Multiplexed Four-Digit LED Display

The data for each digit to be displayed is successively written to one of the microprocessor's I/O ports as the input to the BCD to seven-segment decoder. A short time later, a strobe is issued to turn ON the transistor in the corresponding display digit. The cycle is repeated for all digits in the display.

The update rate must be high enough that interdigit flicker is not perceivable. Because each digit is only enabled for (*1/number of digits*) of a display cycle, its average current will be correspondingly reduced. To ensure the same brightness as a nonstrobed implementation, the current limiting resistors will need to be modified.

17.11 MEASURING DIGITAL SIGNALS

The most common digital signals that are measured are those in the time and frequency domains. In the time domain, we measure any of the following.

1. The period of a periodic signal
2. The duration of a signal
3. The elapsed time between two events

In the frequency domain we measure

1. The frequency of a periodic signal
2. The number of events per time for a periodic or aperiodic signal

We now look at a portion of the detailed design of the counter that we began working with in an earlier chapter.

17.11.1 The Approach

To implement a time domain measurement, a known signal is measured for an unknown time, and for a frequency domain measurement, an unknown signal is measured for a known amount of time (see Figure 17.41).

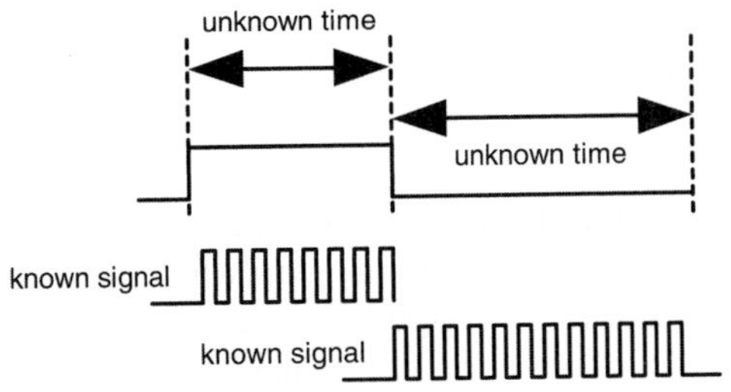

Figure 17.41 Measuring a Known Signal for an Unknown Time

unknown time

For the measurements illustrated in the figure, there is a signal of an unknown duration as reflected in the two regions marked as *unknown time*. If that signal is used to enable a second signal of known frequency (actually it is the period that is important) into a counter, the value in the counter at the end of the unknown time will provide a measure of the duration of the unknown signal. The resolution of the measurement is a direct function of the frequency of the clock to the counter.

If the frequency to the counter is 1 MHz, then, it is known that 1000 counts will occur during a 1-ms interval and that the resolution of the measurement will be 1 μsec. If at the end of the measurement, 654 counts have accrued, the duration must have been 654 μsec. The diagram presented in Figure 17.42 simply reverses what is known.

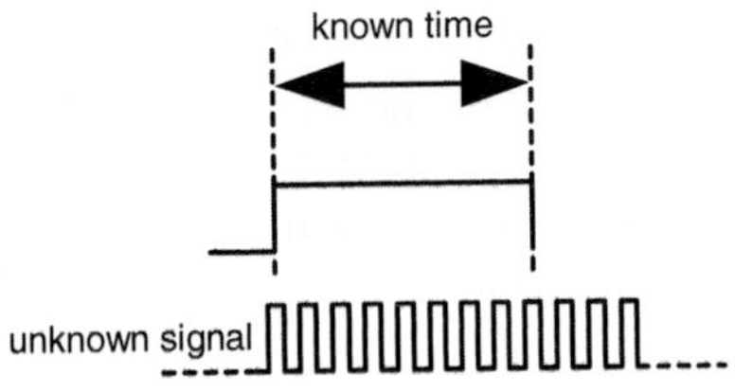

Figure 17.42 Measuring an Unknown Signal for a Known Time

Here, the time is known and the goal is to determine the frequency of the unknown signal. Thus, if the known duration is used as an enable to a counter, at the end of the time the counter will have accumulated a number of counts. That is, we have events per time or the frequency for a periodic signal. For an aperiodic signal, the count can be interpreted either as an average frequency or events per time.

17.11.2 Working with Asynchronous Signals

When working with digital signals coming into the system that are asynchronous to the internal clock, one must be aware of and properly manage metastable behavior. To that end, the objective is to synchronize such a signal to the internal clock prior to trying to do any significant work with it.

Many different approaches can be used to deal with the problem; one of the simpler ones is given in Figure 17.43.

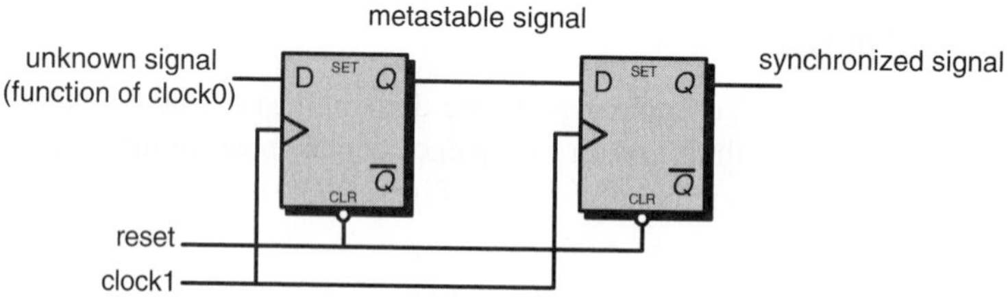

Figure 17.43 Synchronizing an Asynchronous External Signal to an Internal Clock

The unknown or incoming signal is a function of some clock outside of the system. Consequently, there is no way of knowing when a state change will occur with respect to the internal clock, clock1. As Figure 17.44 illustrates, the incoming signal may or may not violate the setup time for the flip-flop. If the setup time is violated, the output of the first flip-flop may enter a metastable state for some time.

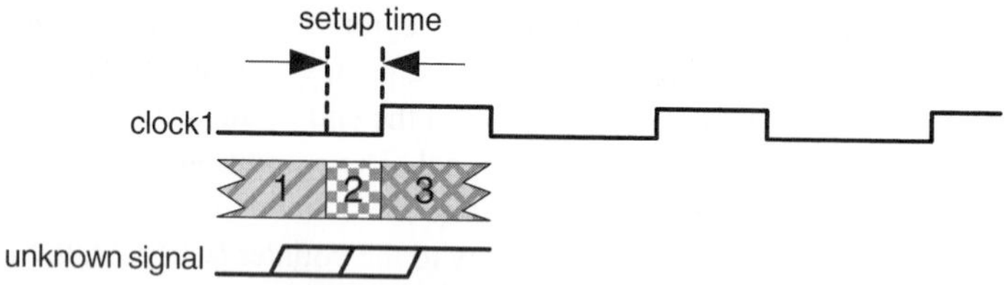

Figure 17.44 Setup Time for an Asynchronous External Signal vs. an Internal Clock

In Figure 17.44, if the unknown signal changes state in region 1, it will be recognized correctly by the first clock pulse. If it changes state in region 3, it will be missed by the first clock pulse but recognized by the second. A state change in region 2 creates a potential problem. In such a case, the first flip-flop can enter a metastable state.

The metastability will be "filtered out" by the synchronizer, and the unknown signal will be recognized and synchronized properly if the following two conditions hold:

1. The unknown signal persists longer than two cycles of the internal clock, in this case, clock1.
2. The metastable state is shorter than the period of clock1 minus the flip-flop setup time.

17.11.3 Buffering Input Signals

buffer In addition to having to deal with the asynchronous timing of external signals with respect to the internal clock, it is also necessary to accommodate signal levels that exceed traditional logical levels. To do so, we use a *buffer* of some form. A circuit such as that shown in Figure 17.45 will work well for signals with lower frequencies (less than 10 MHz). For higher frequencies, the buffer must be designed using parts that are appropriate to the frequencies being used. It is beyond the scope of this text to present analog design at that level.

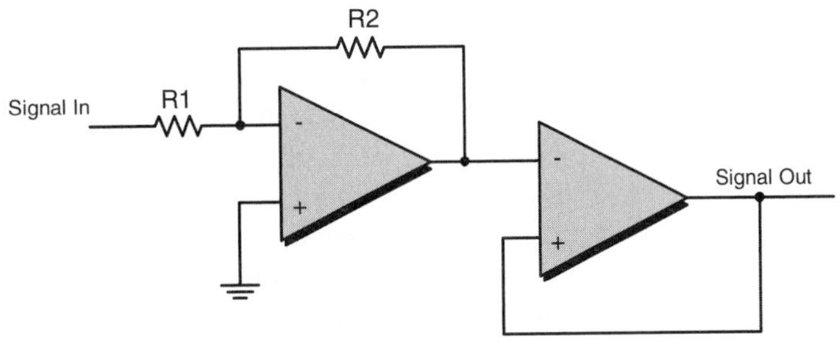

Figure 17.45 Buffering Input Signals

17.11.4 Inside vs. Outside

Many microprocessors have one or more built-in timers that can be utilized for making both time and frequency measurements. The decision as to whether to use one of the internal timers or build the measurement circuitry outside of the microprocessor is based on several factors. For systems with lower performance constraints but with more restricted cost constraints, utilizing as much of the internal circuitry as possible is the preferable alternative. Alternatively, when measuring signals with higher frequencies or shorter time durations combined with possible hard real-time constraints, a greater portion of the design will need to be implemented in hardware outside of the microprocessor.

A third alternative utilizes a combination of both external hardware and the internal timers. The hardware component manages the higher speed/shorter duration measurement, whereas the internal counter/timer deals with the slower portion.

17.11.5 Measuring Frequency and Time Interval

Consider an application that requires measuring the frequency of a signal in the range of 1 MHz. We will look at two of the several ways by which the measurement can be performed. One approach requires that the period of the signal be measured and then converted to frequency; this approach, of course, gives the period or interval measurement as well. A second approach requires gating the signal into a counter for a known interval. For each, we will examine an internal and an external implementation.

17.11.5.1 Measuring the Period—An Internal Implementation

When taking the first approach and implementing the design using an internal counter/timer, one will have to increment the counter at a rate that is much higher than the frequency of the unknown. This way, the frequency can be determined with adequate precision.

Figure 17.46 illustrates three different measurements that can be made using such a technique.

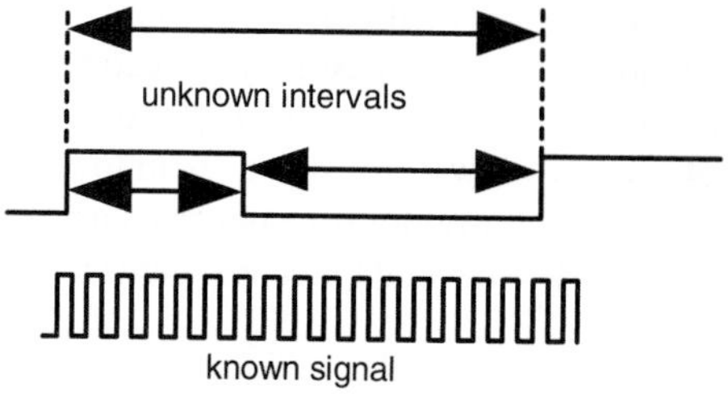

Figure 17.46
Measuring Time

In one case, the period of a periodic signal can be measured. The interval spanned by the rising and falling edges (or the falling and rising edges) of the signal can also be measured.

To measure the period, the unknown signal is used as an interrupt into the microprocessor. The interrupt is configured to trigger on a rising edge. When the interrupt occurs, the counter is started. At that point, the counter is incrementing at the known rate. When the second interrupt occurs, the counter is disabled. Its contents, combined with the frequency of the incrementing signal, provide sufficient information to compute the frequency of the unknown signal, thus,

$$\text{unknown frequency} = \left(\text{known period}\frac{\text{sec}}{\text{count}} \bullet \text{accumulated counts}\right)^{-1} \quad (17.11)$$

The difficulty with this approach arises from the fact that the frequency of the internal clock source to the counter may not be high enough to achieve the desired resolution.

17.11.5.2 Measuring the Period—An External Implementation

In contrast, if the measurement is implemented with external hardware, it is possible to achieve much greater accuracy and precision, and the microprocessor is unburdened—it does not have to directly participate in the measurement. One such implementation is shown in Figure 17.47.

Start The high-level timing diagram for the system is shown in Figure 17.48. The *Start* signal from the microprocessor initiates the measurement. In response, the state machine enables the synchronizer. The synchronizer serves a dual role. In addition to synchronizing the external signal to the internal clock, the second synchronizer flip-flop serves to delimit the measurement. One to two *clock1* pulses after the external signal makes a 0 to 1 transition, the *Enable* signal is asserted by the state machine, thereby starting the counter. On the second 0 to 1 transition by the external signal, the *Enable* is deasserted and the *Complete* event is sent to the microprocessor. The state of the counter, representing the period of the unknown signal, can be read at any time after that.

*(margin notes: **clock1**, **Enable**, **Complete**)*

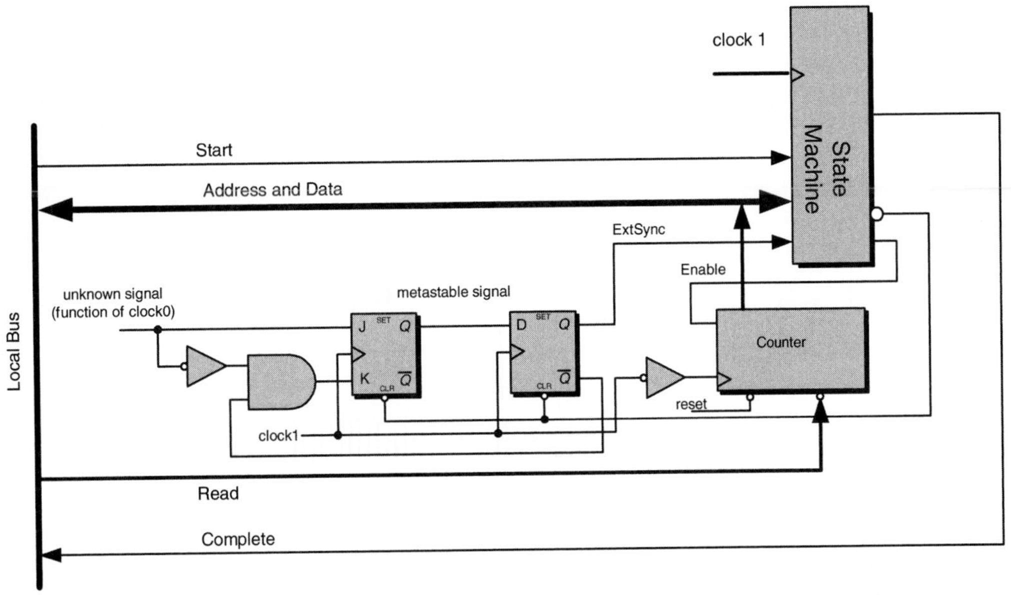

Figure 17.47 Block Diagram for System to Measure the Period of a Signal Based on a Hardware Implementation Outside of the Microprocessor

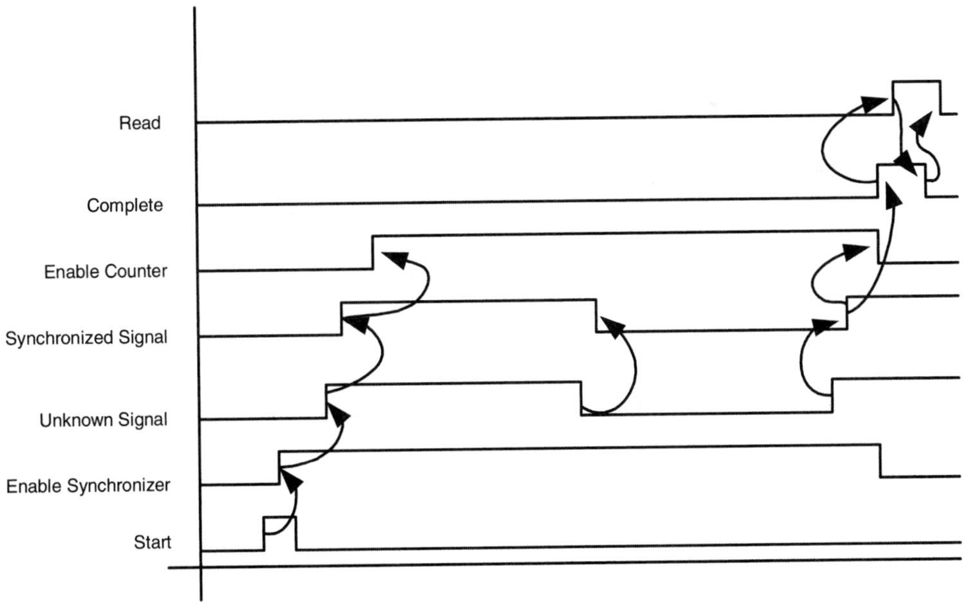

Figure 17.48 Timing Diagram for System to Measure the Period of a Signal Based on a Hardware Implementation Outside of the Microprocessor

17.11.5.3 Counting for a Known Interval—An Internal Implementation

The second approach reverses the roles of the gate and the signal being counted. In this case, the gate is opened for a known and specified interval, and the unknown signal is used to increment a counter. When the interval ends, the counter contains the frequency of the unknown signal. This relationship is illustrated in the timing diagram in Figure 17.49. For

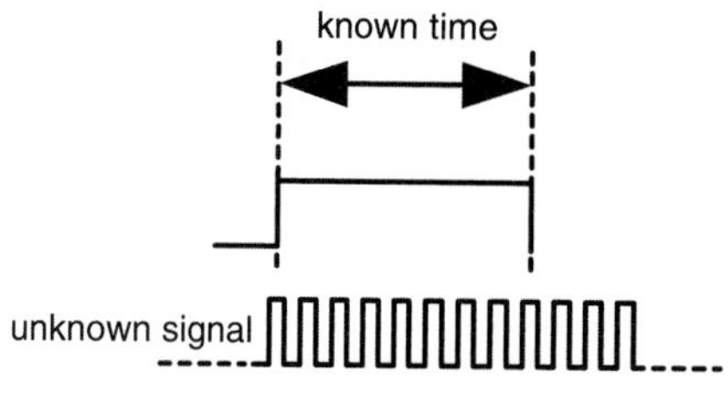

Figure 17.49 Measuring the Frequency of an Unknown Signal

example, if the frequency to be measured is in the range of 1 MHz and the desired precision is three digits, 1.000 MHz, then the window should be open for

$$\begin{aligned} \text{window} &= 1000 \text{ counts} \bullet \frac{1\,\mu\text{sec}}{\text{count}} \\ &= 1\,\text{ms} \end{aligned} \tag{17.12}$$

To implement the measurement, a timer and a counter are needed. The unknown signal is used as an interrupt into the microprocessor. When the first interrupt occurs, the timer is started and the counter is incremented. The counter is incremented for each subsequent interrupt until the timer expires. At that point, the external interrupt is disabled. The counter will now contain the number of accrued counts, which translates directly to the unknown frequency.

The difficulty with this approach is that for higher frequencies, the microprocessor is going to be heavily burdened with processing all of the interrupts. For a sufficiently high frequency, it may be possible to cause a stack overflow.

17.11.5.4 Counting for a Known Interval—An External Implementation

The measurement can also be implemented in hardware outside of the microprocessor. Such a design is presented in Figure 17.50.

The high level timing diagram is given in Figure 17.51. In this design, as in the previous external hardware designs for other measurements, the process commences when the microprocessor issues the *Start* command. In turn, the state machine enables the time base, the synchronizer, and the counter. The time base generates a window, *Enable Counter*, for a length of time consistent with the measurement being made. When the window duration has expired, the *Complete* signal is asserted to the microprocessor, which responds with a *Read* command to read the state of the counter.

Start
Enable Counter
Complete
Read

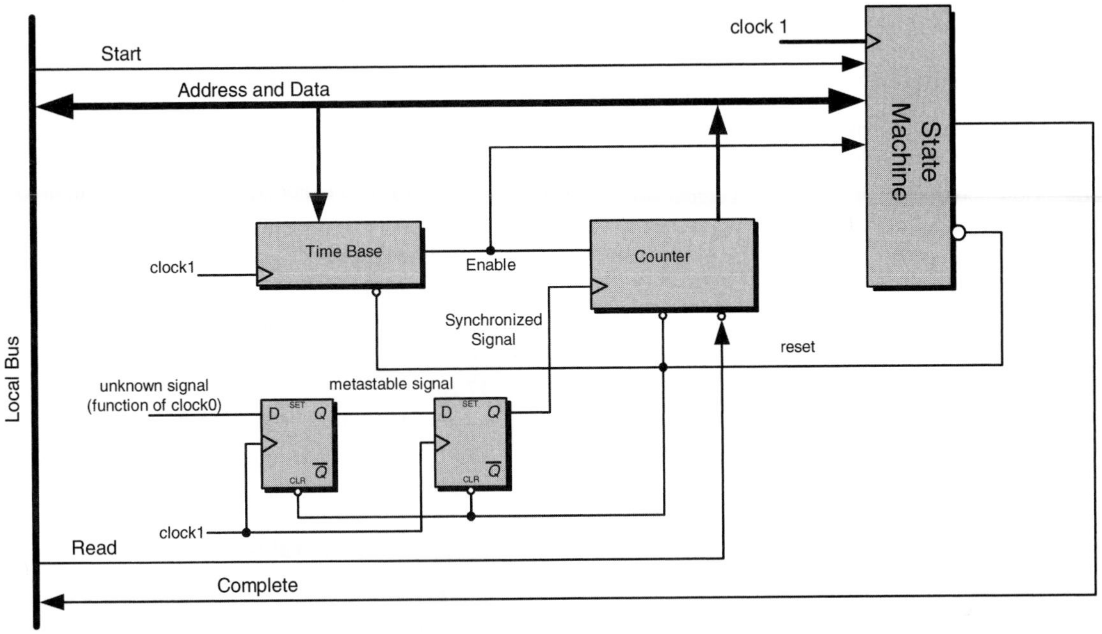

Figure 17.50 Block Diagram for System to Measure the Frequency of a Signal Based on a Hardware Implementation Outside of the Microprocessor

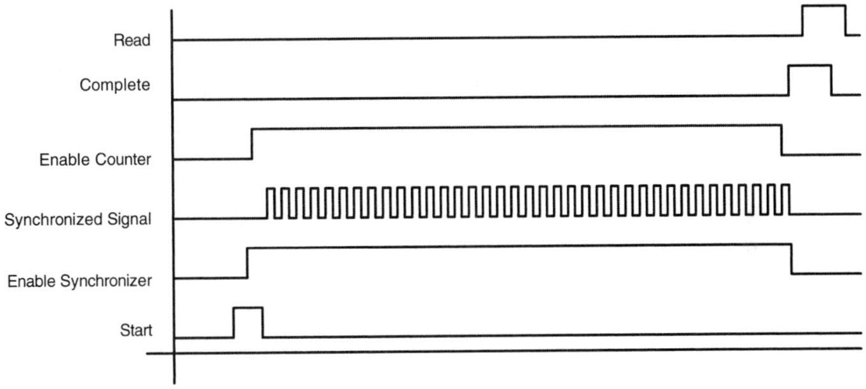

Figure 17.51 Timing Diagram for System to Measure the Frequency of a Signal Based on a Hardware Implementation Outside of the Microprocessor

17.12 SUMMARY

In this chapter, we have studied several different ways of generating and working with analog and digital signals utilizing the shared variable model. For each design, we examined the transport mechanism, studied how control and synchronism are implemented, and learned how producers and consumers can be identified. We opened with a discussion of how to generate analog signals, and then we studied various methods for converting physical world analog signals into digital form for use inside the microprocessor. Because of the nonlinear nature of the various transducer signals, we examined how to deal with such nonlinearity.

We then moved to the problem of generating digital signals as control inputs to several different kinds of small motors and as information that must be displayed. We finally concluded by introducing and studying how time and frequency signals can be measured.

17.13 REVIEW QUESTIONS

Generating Analog Signals

17.1 What is one of the main techniques that we use in a digital system to generate analog signals?

17.2 How does the number of bits in a digital word affect the quality of the output of a digital-to-analog converter?

17.3 What is an R/2R ladder, and what is it used for?

Making Analog Measurements

17.4 Please give three different ways by which we can measure voltage. Briefly explain the measurement technique used in each case.

17.5 What are the three major intervals in a dual slope analog-to-digital converter? Explain the purpose of each interval.

17.6 Briefly explain how a successive approximation analog-to-digital converter works.

17.7 What is the purpose of the sample and hold circuit in a successive approximation A/D?

17.8 How does the operation of the sample and hold circuit affect the accuracy of the conversion?

17.9 What are some sources of error in a sample and hold circuit?

17.10 How does analog-to-digital conversion using a voltage-controlled oscillator work?

17.11 What are some of the major sources of error in a voltage-controlled oscillator A/D converter?

17.12 Give several ways by which we can measure resistance.

17.13 Give several ways by which we can measure current.

17.14 Give several ways by which we can measure temperature.

17.15 When we say that a sensor output is nonlinear, what do we mean?

17.16 Give several ways by which we can correct for nonlinear signals.

Generating Digital Signals

17.17 Embedded systems will sometimes have to drive motors as part of an application. What are three of the more commonly used motor types in such applications?

17.18 What are the major differences between each type of motor identified in Question 17.17?

17.19 What technique is commonly used to control the speed or position of a DC or servo motor? Explain how the technique operates.

17.20 What technique is commonly used for controlling stepper motors? Explain how the technique operates.

17.21 What is an H bridge? What is it used for? Explain how it operates.

Measuring Digital Signals

17.22 What are some of the more common digital measurements that we might be required to make in an embedded application?

17.23 Describe how we might measure frequency.

17.24 Describe how we might measure time.

Working with Input Signals from External World Devices

17.25 When working with input signals, what is the difference between synchronous and asynchronous signals?

17.26 What is metastability?

17.27 What causes metastability?

17.28 Why do we buffer digital signals that are coming in from external world devices?

17.29 Why do we buffer analog signals that are coming in from external world devices?

17.14 THOUGHT QUESTIONS

Generating Analog Signals

17.1 Give several reasons why we might need to generate analog signals in an embedded application.

Making Analog Measurements

17.2 What are some of the more common analog measurements that we might be required to make in an embedded application?

17.3 Give several reasons why we might have to make analog measurements in an embedded application.

17.4 Give several examples of devices that produce analog signals that might serve as inputs to an embedded application. What kind of signal, voltage, current, or some other type might come from such devices? Briefly explain the measurement technique used in each case.

17.5 In the chapter, we identified three different ways by which we can measure voltage. Compare the advantages and disadvantages of each measurement method.

17.6 Three major intervals in a dual slope analog-to-digital converter were identified in the chapter. Do variations in the duration of each interval have an effect on the measurement? If so, what is the effect?

17.7 How does the operation of the sample and hold circuit affect the accuracy of the conversion?

17.8 Give several examples of when measuring resistance might be necessary in an embedded application.

17.9 Give several examples of when measuring current might be necessary in an embedded application.

17.10 Give several examples of when measuring temperature might be necessary in an embedded application.

Generating Digital Signals

17.11 What are the major differences between each type of motor identified in the chapter?

17.12 Give several examples of applications that would require one of the motor types identified in the chapter. Explain why the type you have identified is the best choice for the application.

Measuring Digital Signals

17.13 Give several reasons why we might have to make digital measurements in an embedded application.

17.14 Give several examples of devices that produce digital signals that might serve as inputs to an embedded application. What kind of signal might come from such devices?

17.15 If we can make only one measurement, time or frequency, how might we obtain the other one? What is the impact of such a method on the time performance of an embedded application?

Working with Input Signals from External World Devices

17.16 What are some of the problems one encounters when working with digital signals originating in external world devices?

17.17 How can we deal with the problem of metastability?

17.18 How can we synchronize to external world digital signals?

17.19 How do we accommodate signals from the external world that have levels that are outside of the valid range of digital logic signals (i.e., are either too high or too low)?

17.15 PROBLEMS

17.1 Design the Verilog model, hardware, and a software driver that can display the BCD digits 0–9 on a single-digit LED display. Build the BCD to seven-segment decoder in software.

17.2 Modify the design in Problem 17.1 to perform the BCD to seven-segment conversion using an external hardware decoder. Compare the costs and benefits of the two approaches.

17.3 Extend the design in Problem 17.1 to support a four-digit LED display. Multiplexing hardware may be added; however, the BCD to decimal decoding should still be implemented in software.

17.4 Extend the design in Problem 17.2 to support a four-digit LED display using only a single-hardware BCD to seven-segment decoder. Additional multiplexing hardware may be included as necessary.

17.5 An embedded system uses a processor that provides two hardware timers. The multitasking application comprises four tasks that require intervals of 1, 2, 6, and 10 μ seconds be timed and three tasks that intervals of 2, 5, 15, and 25 ms be timed.

Each timer is 16 bits, and each is clocked at 10 MHz. A 16-bit value can be loaded into a timer using a software load command.

Give the pseudo code for a time base that will support all of the tasks.

17.6 An embedded application must be able to enable or disable an aural alarm on any of eight different entrances to a secure building. Design a system that can set the state (enabled or disabled) of all alarms in a single transaction.

17.7 Extend the design in Problem 17.6 so that the state of all of the alarms can be read in a single transaction.

17.8 Design the Verilog model, hardware, and a software driver that can poll any of four different devices for status information. Status information is to be returned from the polled device as a single byte.

17.9 Design the Verilog model, hardware, and a software driver for a system that supports interrupts from any of four different devices connected to a single interrupt line. Be certain to address the problem of simultaneous interrupts.

17.10 Extend the design in Problem 17.9 to associate a priority with each device.

17.11 An embedded system has three Input/Output devices (A, B, and C). The processor has two input and two output lines available for control. Devices B and C have the same priority. A has higher priority than either B or C.

Design an I/O system for this computer that satisfies the following requirements. In each case, be sure to specify how the device requests service, how the service routine is invoked, and how simultaneous requests are handled.

(a) Show a block diagram and explain an I/O scheme using interrupts.

(b) Show a block diagram and explain an I/O system using polling.

(c) How are simultaneous requests for service handled in each case.

(d) Briefly discuss the advantages and disadvantages of each.

17.12 An embedded system is designed to control a home entertainment system. The processor must bring in data from any of four different sources: a CD player, a DVD player, a Tuner, and a Joystick. The CD and the DVD player transfer 16-bit data words, and the Tuner and Joystick transfer byte-wide data words. Each transfer comprises four data words.

Design the Verilog model, hardware interface, and software driver that will select any of these devices and transfer the data via the system bus to the processor.

17.13 An embedded system is designed to control a home entertainment system. The processor must send data to any of four different devices: a Digital-to-Analog Converter, a Digital Display, a Memory, and a Graphic coprocessor. The D/A converter and memory each support a 12-bit interface, the Graphic coprocessor requires 16-bit data words, and the Display requires 8-bit words. Each transfer comprises four data words.

Design the Verilog model, hardware interface, and software driver that will select any of these devices and transfer the data via the system bus from the processor to the device.

17.14 A peripheral device must receive a 16-bit data word in two 8-bit pieces—least significant byte, then most significant byte—according to the following sequence.

When a *Ready* signal from an external device is received:

- Generate a signal *E1* to output the lower 8 bits.
- Wait τ_d, then output the signal *dStrobe*.
- Wait $2\tau_d$, then terminate the signals *E1* and *dStrobe*
- Generate a signal *E2* to output the upper 8 bits.
- Wait τ_d, then output the signal *dStrobe*.
- Wait $2\tau_d$, then terminate the signals *E2* and *dStrobe*.

(a) Describe the required transfer using a UML state diagram.

(b) Design the software driver to execute the described data transfer.

17.15 The processor must accept a 10-bit serial data word peripheral communications device. Each input data bit has an accompanying clock as shown in Figure P17.52. Note, the clock is running continuously.

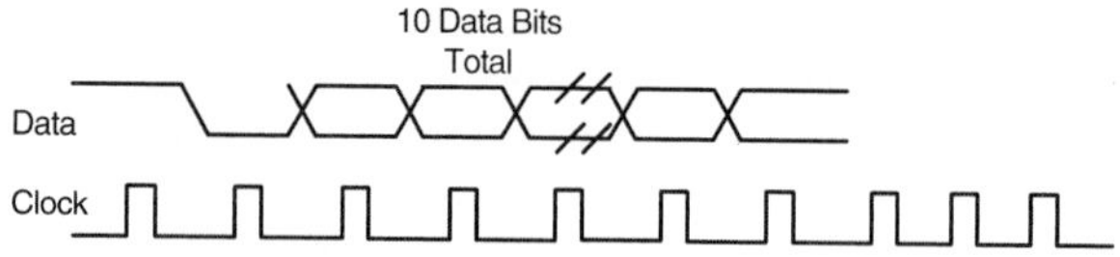

Figure P17.52

The device must operate as follows.

The serial data line is in a quiescent state of logical 1, and the input device is in the *ready* state.

- A logical 0 bit appears on the input.
- A counter is enabled to count incoming data bits.
- After 10 data bits have been received, a *recComplete* signal is generated.
- An error check circuit, which tests the incoming data for errors, has an *error* output signal to indicate if the received word contains an error. A logical 1 on the *error* signal indicates an error.
- In either case, the circuit is to signal the processor that data is available. If no error has occurred, the data is to be tagged a valid and transferred into the processor.

If the error check circuit indicates an *error* when the *recComplete* signal occurs, the device should mark the data as invalid and send an error status word to the processor during the transfer.

(a) Give a UML state diagram for the operation of the communications device.

(b) Give a timing diagram for the transfer from the communications device to the processor.

(c) Specify the format for the data and status words that will be returned from the peripheral device.

(d) Write the software driver to interface with the peripheral device.

17.16 Design a Verilog model, hardware interface, and software driver that supports read and write access to a 1024 x 8 SRAM over an 8-bit bus.

17.17 Design a Verilog model, hardware interface, and software driver that support read and write access to a 1024 x 8 SRAM using memory-mapped I/O. Assume a 16-bit external address bus and an 8-bit data bus.

17.18 Extend the design in Figure 17.17 to support an LCD display that accepts data in a character serial format in 16 character blocks.

17.19 A shared memory scheme is to be used as a means of exchanging blocks of data between two tasks, T_0 and T_1. One of the tasks is on the main processor, and the other is executing on an external device. The shared area occupies 2 K of memory in a 16K x 8 SRAM; however, the number of bytes written with each exchange is variable.

(a) Present a design for the shared memory system.

(b) Using a UML sequence diagram, explain how your memory system works by describing a complete cycle that includes the following: Write by T_0—Read by T_1—Write by T_1—Read by T_0.

(c) How does each task know when data is available and how much data is available?

(d) Are there any potential problems with your design?

(e) How would your design change if three tasks were involved in the exchange?

17.20 Create a lookup table containing sufficient "sampled" data to reconstruct the following sinusoidal function:

$$v(t) = 2\sin(\omega t) + 2$$

Let the frequency be 5 KHz and express each data sample as a byte.

(a) Design a Verilog model, hardware interface, and software driver to repeatedly write the data from the lookup table to a digital-to-analog converter.

(b) What is the value, in volts, of the least significant data bit?

(c) On your system, what is the highest frequency for the sine wave that can be supported?

(d) What limits the upper frequency?

(e) Why should the "sampling frequency" of your data be slightly greater than twice the highest frequency?

17.21 Repeat Problem 17.17 by first storing the "sampled" data in an external SRAM. What is the highest frequency sine wave that can be supported with your modified design?

17.22 Repeat Problem 17.20 with a lookup table containing sufficient "sampled" data to reconstruct the following sinusoidal functions:

$$v_1(t) = 2\sin(\omega t) + 2$$

followed in time by

$$v_2(t) = 3\sin(2\omega t) + 3$$

Let the frequency be 5 KHz and express data sample as a byte.

17.23 Repeat Problem 17.22 by first storing the "sampled" data in an external SRAM. What is the highest frequency sine wave that can be supported with your modified design?

17.24 Design a Verilog model, hardware interface, and software driver to an 8-bit successive approximation analog-to-digital converter. Assume that the analog input signal will be in the range of 0–5.0 VDC.

(a) What is the value, in volts, of the least significant data bit?

(b) What is the smallest full-scale error in a sample?

(c) Use your measurement subsystem to sample the following voltages: 0.0, 1.0, 2.0, 3.0, 4.0, 5.0. Compare your measured values with the input voltages. What are the errors in your readings?

(d) Write a simple software loop to repeat the measurements in part (c) ten times. Plot your samples and the minimum and maximum error for each cardinal point. Are the errors consistent across the range of values? If not, how do you explain the differences?

17.25 The basic measurement cycle for a dual slope analog-to-digital converter is comprised of three subintervals, *integrate* or *sample*, *read* or *convert*, and *autozero*, as discussed in the chapter.

Thus, the device can be in any one of three modes: *sampling* the unknown signal, *converting* it to a digital value, or *zeroing* out errors. Control signals sent to the A/D place it in one of the three modes.

The *integrate* and *autozero* intervals are fixed and known times. The *read* interval begins at the end of the *integrate* interval and ends when a compare event is received from the A/D. The length of the *read* interval corresponds to the magnitude of the unknown signal.

(a) Give a UML sequence diagram expressing the dual slope A/D measurement cycle.

(b) Give a UML state diagram describing the operation of the measurement cycle.

(c) Using pseudo code, write a task to perform a basic dual slope A/D converter measurement cycle for execution on your processor. Be sure to specify any data storage that might be needed and the minimum number of (A/D) control signals necessary, what they do, and where they come from.

(d) Do any portions of the measurement cycle have timing constraints that may be critical?

(e) Based on your pseudo code, write the software driver to control the conversion.

17.26 Design a Verilog model, hardware interface, and software driver to an 8-bit successive approximation analog-to-digital converter. Assume that the analog input signal will be in the range of 0–5.0 VDC.

(a) Use your measurement subsystem to sample the following sinusoidal function.

$$v(t) = 2\sin(\omega t) + 2$$

(b) Compare your measured values with the input voltages. What are the errors in your readings?

17.27 Design a software driver that will poll a periodic digital signal on an input port of your processor and, using a timer, determine the period of the signal on the port.

(a) What is the shortest period that your design will support, assuming that no other tasks are running?

(b) What is the worst case error in your measurement?

(c) What is the longest period that you can measure without timer overflow?

(d) How would you modify your design to accommodate timer overflow?

17.28 Design a software driver that will poll a periodic digital signal on an input port of your processor and, using a timer, determine the frequency of the signal on the port.

(a) What is the highest frequency that your design will support assuming that no other tasks are running?

(b) What is the worst case error in your measurement?

(c) What is the lowest frequency that you can measure without timer overflow?

(d) How would you modify your design to accommodate timer overflow?

17.29 Repeat Problem 17.27 by connecting the digital signal to your processor's external interrupt.

17.30 Repeat Problem 17.28 by connecting the digital signal to your processor's external interrupt.

17.31 Design the Verilog model, external hardware, and software driver to measure the period of a digital signal in the range of 0 to 100 μ seconds.

17.32 Design the Verilog model, external hardware, and software driver to measure the frequency of a digital signal in the range of 0 to 100 KHz.

17.33 Design the Verilog model, external hardware, and software driver to control the speed of a DC motor using a pulse width modulation scheme. The output waveform should support controlling the motor from full OFF to full ON based on the value of an 8-bit control word. The hexadecimal value 0 X 00 should correspond to a speed of 0 RPM, and 0xFF should correspond to full speed.

(a) What is the smallest change in motor speed that you can control?

(b) Based on your answer to part (a), what is the worst case error in motor speed control?

17.34 Design the external hardware and software driver to control the position of a stepper motor assuming changes only in the forward direction.

(a) What is the smallest change in motor position that you can command?

(b) Based on your answer to part (a), what is the worst case error in motor position?

17.35 Design the Verilog model, external hardware, and software driver to control the position of a stepper motor in both the forward and reverse directions.

(a) What is the smallest change in motor position that you can command?

(b) Based on your answer to part (a), what is the worst case error in motor position?

Chapter 18

Working Outside of the Processor III: Interfacing to Remote Devices

THINGS TO LOOK FOR . . .

- Some of the commonly used architectures for network-based interfaces.
- Some of the strengths and weaknesses of the different architectures.
- The different transport mechanisms.
- The control and synchronization schemes utilized for the different architectures.
- The implementation of device and subsystem addressing in each of the different designs.

18.0 COMMON NETWORK-BASED I/O ARCHITECTURES

We have been studying the many different ways that one can interact with and incorporate the world outside of the core microprocessor into an embedded design. That world includes devices that are local to the immediate context and those that may be substantially remote. Let's now look at some specific examples of how such techniques move from the textbook to the real world.

In this chapter, we will study four different, commonly used network-based input/output designs. For each design, we will briefly examine the problems that motivated designers to develop the interface, identify the contributions that each has introduced to the embedded world, and cite the strengths and weaknesses of each approach.

Following the model of intertask communication and synchronization developed in earlier chapters, for each scheme we will examine the transport mechanism, study how control and synchronism are affected, and investigate how message senders and receivers are identified.

We will open with an examination of the traditional RS-232, which is now the EIA-232 standard asynchronous serial interface. We will then explore a synchronous serial interface approach utilized by the Universal Serial Bus. The I^2C bus as a small local area network will be the next design that we will study. Finally, we will conclude with the CAN bus, another type of local area network commonly used in automotive applications.

These busses were selected because each represented a change in thinking about the way information was exchanged in the context in which the design was applied. The underlying architecture and control/synchronization mechanisms utilized in the busses that we will study here are representative of those found in most of the network-type busses in use today. In this way you will understand the key aspects, strengths, and weaknesses of each; you should try to identify what existing problem(s) the bus was intended to address, determine whether you think it succeeded, and learn if it created new ones.

18.1 NETWORK-BASED SYSTEMS

Information exchange through messages is a universally used technique in embedded applications. Implementations range from a basic simplex architecture for moving collected data to a remote site for storage or processing to sophisticated, robust, high-speed full-duplex networks. In contrast to local device model architectures, which tend to consist of several devices in relatively close proximity to the local application, network-based designs typically include a number of remote nodes or subsystems and are often geographically more widely distributed.

places, control and synchronization, information transport

The *places*, *control and synchronization*, and *information* in such systems is generally supported by the firmware in the device drivers on the local and remote machines. The device drivers will often incorporate a formal protocol that manages the addressing, flow of control, error management, and packaging of the payload. The *transport* mechanism for the network-based infrastructure is most often serial and involves only a limited number of signal paths. We will begin with one of the more common message-based serial communication schemes. The current embodiment has evolved from what started life as the RS-232 standard from the *Electronic Industries Association* (EIA).

Electronic Industries Association (EIA)

18.2 RS-232/EIA-232—ASYNCHRONOUS SERIAL COMMUNICATION

18.2.1 Introduction

One of the more familiar asynchronous network-based I/O schemes in use today has evolved from the RS-232 (now the EIA-232) standard model. The model, with its underlying standard, was initially developed in the early 1960s. At that time, a committee, the *EIA*, was formed to develop a standard interface between a piece of computing equipment and a piece of data communications equipment. At its inception, the RS-232 specification was not intended as a network specification.

POTS, plain old telephone system

Before the days of broadband, DSL, or cable modems, any data exchange between geographically separated sites was over the telephone lines—affectionately referred to as *POTS* or the *plain old telephone system.* The underlying infrastructure for the telephone system was analog, and the data to be sent was digital. To remedy the seeming conflict, the digital data was modulated on the sending side into a form that was compatible with the telephone system and then demodulated on the receiving side back into a form that was compatible with the digital devices there. The *modulator–demodulator* pair and controlling process became shortened into *mod demod* or further into *modem.*

modulator—demodulator mod demod, modem

data communications equipment (DCE), data circuit terminating equipment, data terminal equipment (DTE)

The modem, or other equipment performing a similar task, was designated to be a piece of *data communications equipment* (DCE). The current interpretation of the acronym is *data circuit terminating equipment*. The digital source on either end was similarly designated to be a piece of *data terminal equipment* (DTE).

The basic idea is rather simple and elegant. However, as we have learned, not everything is always quite so. The digital exchange over the analog channel afforded many opportunities for data corruption. As the importance of the data to be exchanged increased, so did the need for a more reliable means of affecting that exchange. In addition, as the telecommunications field started to grow, so did the number of vendors offering equipment—often with incompatible interfaces. As we will learn when we study the USB interface, these requirements and expectations drove the need for standardization. The standard that was adopted was the RS-232 interface. It specified signaling voltages, timing, and functions as well as a protocol for exchanging information, the physical connectors, and pin assignments for the equipment involved in the exchange. The specific equipment was a piece of DCE and a piece of DTE.

Since 1960, the standard has seen three modifications. In addition to the name change to EIA-232, several of the signals have been renamed and new ones have been added. The most current version of the standard is designated EIA-232E.

Its ease of use has led to such a plethora of variations that the original intent of the standard has become clouded or forgotten. Today these variations often appear under the name RS-232, but in use, they take a significant departure from the original intent. As a result, significant amounts of time, money, and frustration are often spent trying to sort all this out. Before we look at how RS-232 is typically misused, let's look at its initial intended purpose in a bit more detail.

18.2.2 The EIA-232 Standard

The EIA-232 standard specifies the signals and interconnecting lines between DTE and DCE devices. The full standard specifies that the DTE device uses a 25-pin DB25P (male) connector and the DCE end uses a mating 25 pin DB25S (female) connector. The standard specifies signals for 22 of the available pins. Today a subset of these appears on a wide variety of computing equipment, with cables terminating in DB9P and DB9S connectors. In either case, the original cabling is parallel, straight through—no crossover connections. The drawings in Figure 18.0 show the pin numbers on the DB-9 and DB-25 connectors as well as the EIA-232 inputs/outputs to which they correspond.

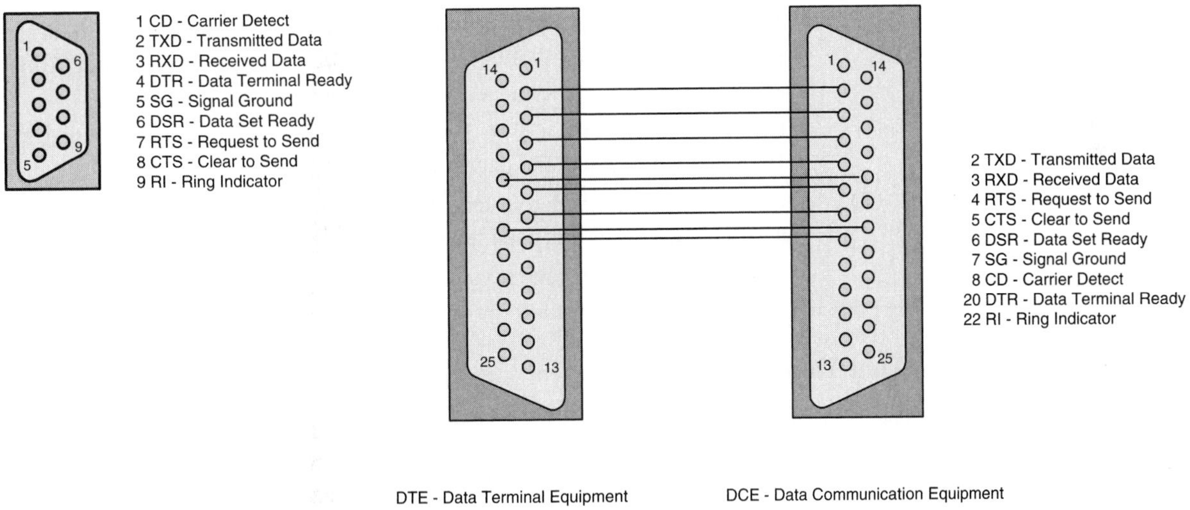

Figure 18.0 Pin Numbering for the DB-9 and DB-25 EIA-232 Connectors

Figure 18.1 gives a high-level picture of a representative early communications system. Note, once again, that the RS-232 interface was strictly defined between a piece of DTE, a computer of one form or another, and a piece of DCE, typically a modem.

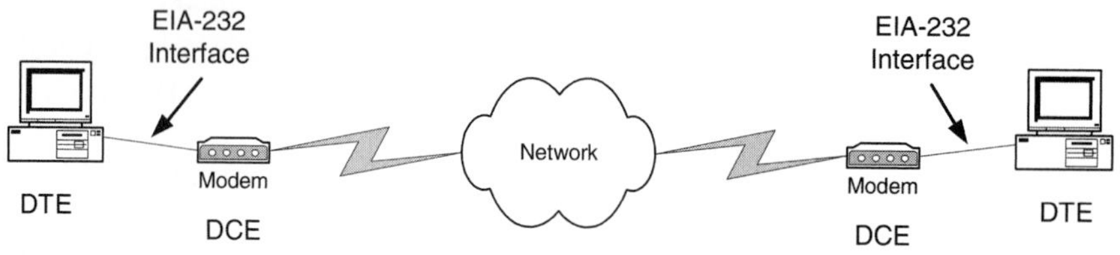

Figure 18.1 A High-Level Representation of an Early Communication System

What It Is . . .

In addition to the lines for exchanging data, the standard also specified a number of handshaking and status lines. The more familiar are identified in the following box, along with their initial intended purpose.

TXD	Data transmission line from DTE to DCE.
RXD	Data transmission line from DCE to DTE.
DSR	Data Set Ready from DCE to DTE—intended to inform the DTE that the data set has a valid connection, has completed whatever initialization might be necessary, and is ready to engage in a message exchange. If the connection drops during the exchange, this signal is deasserted.
DTR	Data Terminal Ready from DTE to DCE—intended to inform the DCE that the data terminal has completed whatever initialization might be necessary, is ready to engage in a message exchange, and would like to open a communication channel.
RTS	Request to Send from DTE to DCE—intended to inform the DCE that the DTE had data to send and for the DCE to do whatever was necessary (dial, ensure carrier, ensure a line, etc.) to effect the communication.
CTS	Clear to Send from DCE to DTE—intended to inform the DTE that the DCE had done its job and data could now be sent.
CD	Carrier detect—intended to indicate that a connection has been established and an answer tone has been received from the remote modem.
SG	Signal ground—the name says it.

What They Think it is . . .

The contemporary view of an EIA-232-based system appears more like that in Figure 18.2.

CTS, RTS, DTR, DSR

Observe that the original modems have been replaced by what is now known as a NULL modem. All too often today the *CTS, RTS, DTR*, and *DSR* lines are incorrectly used for handshaking. Why is this a problem? Why will data potentially be lost using such a scheme? Let's return to the original configuration and consider the actual flow of data.

CTS—Clear to Send, DSR—Data Set Ready

Handshaking, which is a type of flow control, is a way for one piece of DTE to synchronize actions or the exchange of data with another piece of DTE. For example, if data is sent to a printer at a rate higher than the printer can handle because of the speed of printing, it will send a signal to the sending device to stop until it catches up. In the EIA-232 specification, signals such as *CTS—Clear to Send* and *DSR—Data Set Ready* are sometimes (mis)used to serve that purpose.

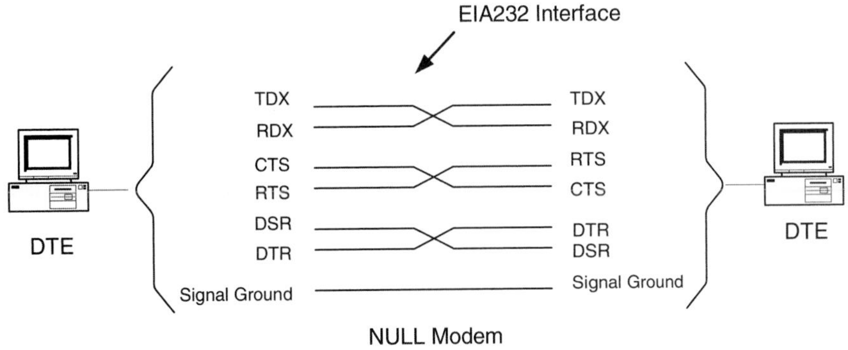

Figure 18.2 A Contemporary View of an EIA-232 Communication System

The original intent of an asserted signal on the DSR line was to inform the transmitting device that the communications device (typically the modem) was ready to send data, whereas a deasserted signal would indicate the opposite. The line should be asserted following power up (self-tests, other initialization, and establishing a connection) and should remain in that state until the system is powered down. The signal CTS was/is intended to indicate to the transmitting device that it is now OK to send data—that the physical line is intact, that a carrier has been detected, and so on.

Let's examine the exchange process a bit more closely to identify the problems that can arise from using the DSR and CTS signals as part of a handshake protocol. Most EIA-232-based systems use a *Universal Asynchronous Receiver/Transmitter* (UART) to manage the message interface. Typically, such devices are double buffered to help unburden the sending device. Similarly, on the receiving side, a UART is also used to manage incoming data. Once again, a double buffer is incorporated.

Universal Asynchronous Receiver Transmitter (UART)

Let's walk through the diagram in Figure 18.3 and count how many characters may be in transit at any time. Starting with the sender, there may be one in the local application that is ready to be sent, two in the transmitting UART's buffers, one in transit, and two in the receiver's buffers for a total of six characters.

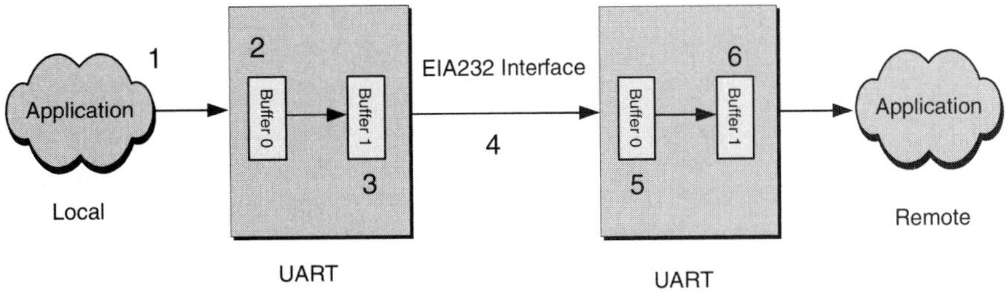

Figure 18.3 Data Flow Through an EIA-232 Communication System

If the receiving device's I/O driver (which is using the CTS/RTS pair for flow control) finds that data is coming in faster than it can be processed, the driver will deassert the CTS line. If the receiver's I/O driver immediately switches from the receive thread to the process thread to start working with some of the data, it may lose up to six characters that are in transit. A timer may help, but there is still no guarantee; why? To ensure the proper control of data flowing between the sender and the receiver, that control should be incorporated into the exchange protocol in the driver software.

18.2.3 EIA-232 Addressing

Because the original focus of the RS-232 interface was the exchange between a single piece of DTE and a single piece of DCE, addressing was unnecessary. Addressing at a higher level between systems connected through modems to the telephone system occurred naturally through the corresponding telephone numbers.

Today the vast majority of EIA-232 interfaces use neither a modem nor the telephone system. Consequently, source and destination addressing must be implemented as part of the message exchange protocol utilized by the specific application. The standard makes no provision for such addressing.

18.2.4 Asynchronous Serial Communication

The EIA-232 standard utilizes an asynchronous communication scheme. Asynchronous communication recognizes and accepts that there are irregular intervals between the sending of pieces data.

To help clarify the operation, suppose that a serial communication line is set up to transmit ASCII characters as typed by a person at a keyboard. The spacing between the transmissions of successive characters will naturally vary widely, and there may be long periods when no characters are typed or sent. In such a situation, the receiving device needs to determine when a character is being sent to prepare it to receive that character and sort out which part is data, which part is the error-checking field, and so on . . . or even if it is a legitimate piece of data rather than noise.

framing
start, stop

This is accomplished by a procedure known as *framing*. In the context of EIA-232 data exchange, each character is framed by a *start* and a *stop* bit as illustrated in Figure 18.4.

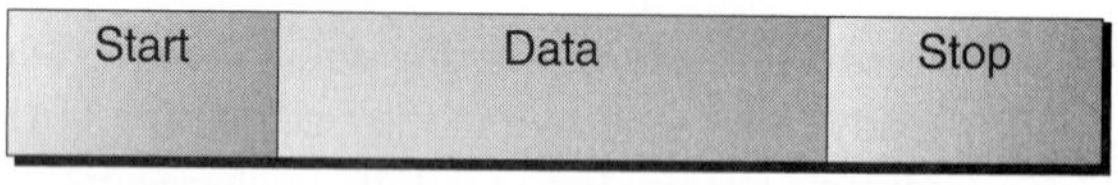

Figure 18.4 Data Character Framing in an EIA-232 Communication System

The *start* bit signals that a data character will follow and thereby enables the receiving device to temporarily synchronize with the transmitting device. The *stop* bit signals the end of the data character and provides time for the receiving device to get ready for the next one.

18.2.5 Configuring the Interface

US/ART—Universal Synchronous/Asynchronous Receiver Transmitter

Today the EIA-232 interface is implemented either as an integrated component within a microprocessor or microcomputer or externally using an LSI *US/ART—Universal Synchronous/Asynchronous Receiver Transmitter*. The external device may be a peripheral processor that is a component included in the microcomputer's supporting chip set or a general-purpose device that is provided by another vendor.

Whichever method is used, the device must still be configured to ensure that the sender and the receiver are speaking the same language. The typical minimum set of parameters that must be configured are given in the following list.

Baud Rate—A measure of the speed at which a modem transmits data. Often this is incorrectly assumed to be a measure of the number of bits that are transmitted each second. Baud rate is actually a measure of the number of signaling changes or events per second.

In the early days of digital communication one baud may have been 1 bit per second; today's technology permits a single event to encode more than 1 bit. Thus, for example, a modem that is configured to transmit at 9600 baud is actually communicating at 9600 bits per second by encoding 4 bits per signal event.

Bits per Character—A specification of the size of the character being sent. Typical values are 5, 6, 7, or 8 bits per character.

Parity—A specification of the parity over the character. Typical values are odd, even, or none.

Number of Stop Bits—A specification of the number of stop bits to include. Typical values are 1, 1½, or 2. Two stop bits are rarely used today. This value originated with the old teletypes that literally moved the carriage back to the start of each line. This mechanical operation took some time to complete.

18.2.6 Data Recovery and Timing

With an asynchronous transmission scheme, the transmitting and receiving devices are each operating on independent local clocks, which are usually designed to operate at 16X, 32X, or 64X the baud rate. Why do we do this?

start, stop
bit timer

EIA-232 data recovery is based on a bit-timing scheme. Such a scheme works as follows. Each character is framed by a *start* bit and a *stop* bit. Once the *start* bit is detected, a *bit timer* is enabled to begin incrementing at the selected clock rate. The *bit timer* is designed such that its period is given as:

$$\text{timer period} = \frac{\text{clock rate}}{\text{baud rate}} \tag{18.0}$$

For example, if the clock rate is 16X the baud rate, the period of the counter will be 16.

For 9600 baud, the clock rate should be 16 times that or 153.6 K Hz.

bit timer, start

Consequently, the *bit timer*, which has been enabled at the leading edge of the *start* bit, will reach a count of 8, at the center of the first data bit as illustrated in Figure 18.5. Furthermore, because the timer is incrementing modulo 16, it will again reach a count of 8 by the center of the second and succeeding data bits.

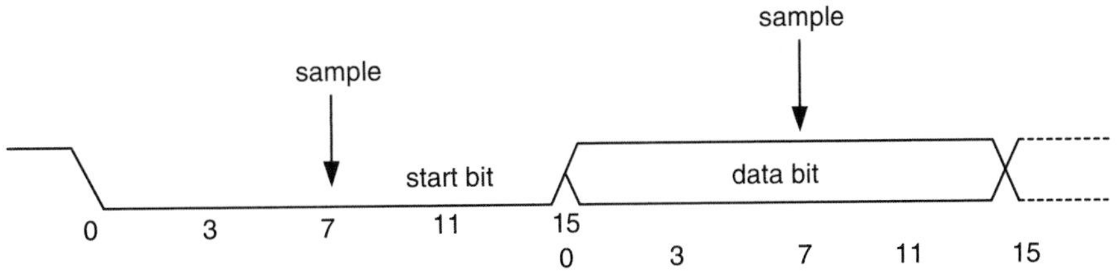

Figure 18.5 Data Bit Sampling

bit timer Observe that the Q output of the most significant bit of the *bit timer* makes a 0⟶1 transition when the count advances from 7 (0111) to 8 (1000). That transition can be used to clock the incoming data into a shift register. The same transition can be used to increment ***bit counter*** a second *bit counter* that counts the number of incoming data bits that have been stored. When the agreed upon (by the sender and receiver) number of bits have been stored, it is ***bit timer, bit counter*** known that a full character has been received. Both the *bit timer* and *bit counter* return to ***start*** the quiescent state awaiting the next *start* bit.

The following are key elements to the approach working properly.

1. The sender and receiver must be operating at the same baud rate.
2. The sender and receiver must agree on the number of bits comprising a character.
3. The quiescent state of the data lines is known. The EIA-232 standard specifies this to be the logical one state.
4. The sender must place the data line into the quiescent state for at least one bit time between characters. This time is known as the stop bit.

The major advantage of the technique is that the sampling signal does not have to be decoded from some counter state and thus cannot have any decoding spikes. Furthermore, by sampling in the center of each bit, the maximum tolerance for error in bit timing is designed into the receiver. Using such a scheme, we can resynchronize the receiver and transmitter with each character. Although the clocks in the sending and receiving devices are ideally operating at the same frequency, a difference of a percent or two in the frequencies should not result in transmission errors.

18.2.7 EIA-232 Interface Signals

The EIA-232 data and control signals along with their voltage levels are summarized in ***mark*** Table 18.0. A logical 1, known as a *mark*, corresponds to a voltage level between -3 and -15 ***space*** volts. A logical 0, or *space*, corresponds to a voltage level between +3 and +15 volts. Such values are intended to improve system noise immunity.

Table 18.0 EIA-232 Signal Levels

Notation	Interchange Voltage	
	Negative	Positive
Binary State	1	0
Signal Condition	Marking	Spacing
Function	OFF	ON

The internal logic levels in most contemporary embedded systems remain at the 5.0 VDC level. Consequently, outgoing and incoming EIA-232 signals must be buffered and/or level shifted from or to standard logical levels before they can be used. Finally, note that the data link remains in the marking state (< -3 V) until the start bit, a space (> +3 V), is sent.

18.2.8 An Implementation

The block diagram in Figure 18.6 gives a typical interface to the external UART-type device. From the microprocessor's point of view, the device can appear either as a memory mapped I/O device or as a special purpose peripheral processor.

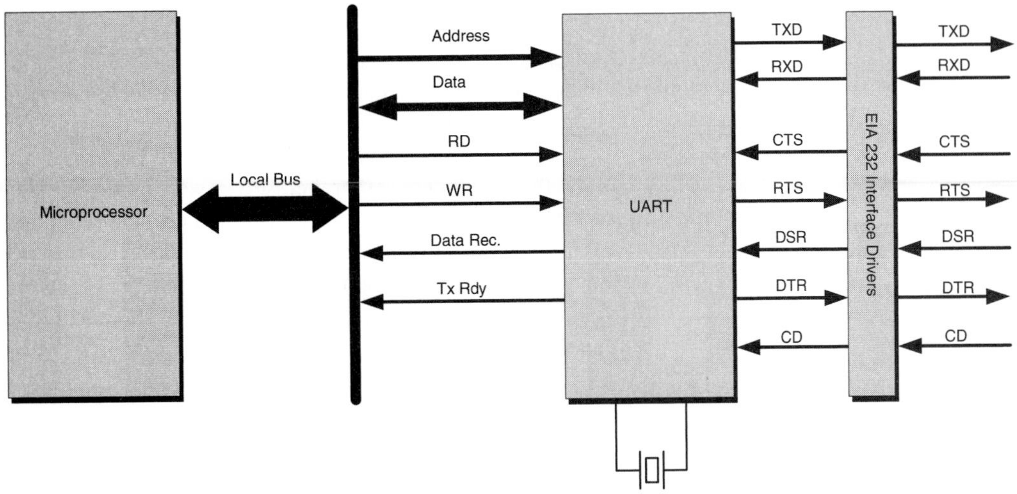

Figure 18.6 Block Diagram for a UART Type Device

In the block diagram, the UART is a peripheral device sitting on the microprocessor bus. The *address* lines serve the dual purpose of selecting the UART and identifying registers internal to the device that must be written to configure the device. The *data* lines are bidirectional and contain data that is to be transmitted from or received by the UART. Each exchange is accompanied by either an *RD* strobe to read a received character from the UART or a *WR* strobe to send one. The *Data Rec.* line can be either polled or used to generate an interrupt when a character has been received. The *Tx Rdy* line indicates that the UART's internal transmit buffer is empty and a new character can be transmitted. Like *Data Rec.*, the line can either be polled or used as an interrupt.

address ***data*** ***Data Rec.*** ***Tx Rdy***

18.3 THE UNIVERSAL SERIAL BUS—SYNCHRONOUS SERIAL COMMUNICATION

synchronous transmission

When it is necessary to rapidly transfer larger blocks of regularly spaced data over a significant distance, the overhead of resynchronizing the timing between sender and receiver with each character can become significant. An alternative approach is known as *synchronous transmission*.

Start and stop bits are no longer needed. Both the sender and receiver are working, directly or indirectly, from a common clock. That clock may exist as a separate signal on the communication channel, or it may be encoded in the data using any of the techniques discussed in the previous chapter.

Although synchronous transfer requires less overhead and therefore can be much more efficient, its uses are more limited than asynchronous data transfer. Thus, today, asynchronous implementations remain more widely used. This ratio is changing with some of the newer interfaces such as the Universal Serial Bus (USB) or Firewire.

The USB provides a good example of a typical synchronous interface. Like the EIA-232 interface, much of the low-level design work has been subsumed in a variety of LSI interface chips. In most cases, one can simply include such devices as part of a design. Nonetheless, it is still important to understand the motivation for the standard as well as the underlying signaling and protocols.

18.3.1 Background

The factors leading to the creation of the USB parallel many of the factors that preceded the development of the RS-232 standard. Among these are the cacophony of different interfaces and associated connection schemes, limitations on and conflicts with system I/O resources, and cost.

The goals that the developers set for themselves were rather mundane: any new system should overcome existing shortcomings, and it should provide room for growth and expansion. Such ideas are good to keep in mind at the start of each new design. More specifically, the designers identified the following needs:

- Single connector type
- Ability to attach many different peripherals to the same connector
- Method to ease resource conflicts
- Automatic detection and configuration of peripheral devices
- Low cost for system and peripheral implementers
- Enhanced performance capability
- Support for attaching new peripherals
- Support for legacy software and hardware
- Low power implementation—support for green systems

The ultimate solution did a very good job of addressing each of these needs. In particular, I/O resource limitations and conflicts, once all too common with legacy systems, no longer exist. Each device residing on the USB is assigned an address known only to the USB subsystem and therefore does not consume any of the primary system resources. While the upper bound of 127 addresses may pose a limit in some large systems, this should not be a problem in most distributed embedded applications. In addition to the 127 directly accessible addresses, each USB device supports the number of ports called endpoints that can be accessed indirectly.

18.3.2 The Universal Serial Bus Architecture

The design and implementation of the USB system follows the OSI and TCP/IP network architectures that we studied earlier. The USB uses a three-level hierarchy as shown in Figure 18.7.

Application

Host Controller

On the host side, the block labeled *Application* contains the software drivers that provide the application programmer's interface (API) to the USB-hosted device, as well as the means to communicate with the application interface on the client side via the *Host Controller*. On the client side, the *Application* block provides the drivers for the physical device and the interface to the USB level below. Observe that on the host side, the middle two layers are logically split into two components: one that provides the interface to the layer above and one that provides the interface to the layer below.

18.3.3 The Universal Serial Bus Protocol

All transactions in the USB system originate on the host side. The design does not support interrupts from client devices. On the host side, the USB client initiates an exchange when it calls the USB driver and requests a transfer. The client drivers supply a memory buffer

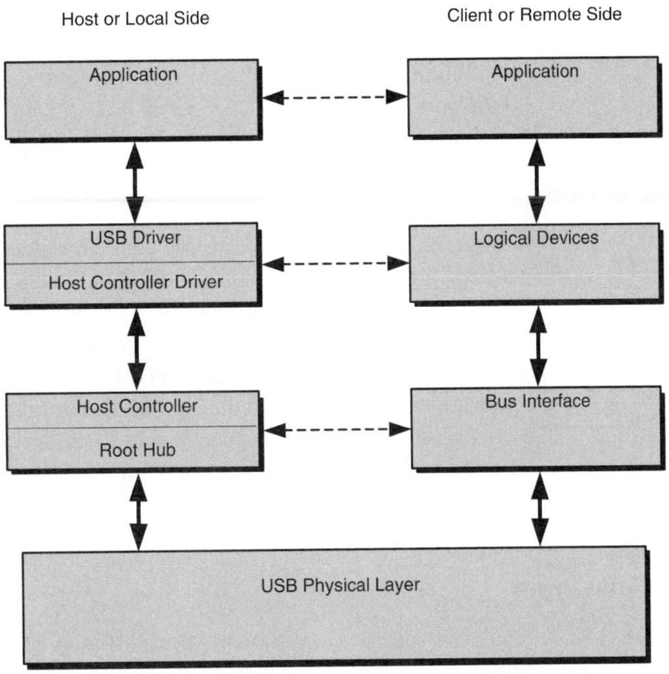

Figure 18.7 Universal Serial Bus Network Architecture

that is used to store data when sending to or receiving from the peripheral device. Each exchange between an endpoint on the client side and the client driver takes place via a *communication pipe* that is established by USB system software during device configuration. Such a pipe implements a connection-oriented communication scheme.

communication pipe

When the client driver wishes to perform a transfer to/from an endpoint, it invokes the *USB driver* to initiate the transfer by issuing an *IO Request Packet (IRP)*. When the IRP is received by the *USB driver*, it organizes the request into individual *transactions* that are executed during a series of 1-ms *frames*. The driver sets up the transactions based on knowledge of the target device's requirements, the needs of the client driver, and the limitations and capabilities of USB.

USB driver, IO Request Packet (IRP)
frames

The *host controller driver* then builds a linked list of data structures called *transfer descriptors*. The list defines the transactions scheduled to be performed during a given frame. The data structures contain all the information that the *host controller* needs to be able to generate the transactions. These include

host controller driver, transfer descriptors
host controller

- USB device address
- Type of transfer
- Direction of transfer
- Address of device driver's memory buffer

The list of *transfer descriptors* is passed to the *host controller,* which then performs the transactions necessary to satisfy the client's transfer request. Each transaction results in data being transferred from the client's buffer to the USB device or from the USB device to buffer. When the entire transfer has been completed, the USB system software notifies the client driver.

transfer descriptors, host controller

root hub The *root hub* provides the physical connection points for the various USB devices. In addition, it controls power to USB ports, enables and disables ports, recognizes when devices are attached to or removed from the ports, and maintains status information relevant to the port.

18.3.4 USB Devices

The USB supports two kinds of devices: those designated as high speed and those designated as low speed. The high speed see all transactions broadcast over USB and can be implemented as full-feature devices. They accept and send serial data at the maximum rate of 12 M bits/sec. The low-speed devices are limited to a maximum throughput of 1.5 M bits/sec. They see only those transactions that follow a special preamble packet. The low-speed ports are normally disabled during full-speed transactions.

The preamble packets specify that the following transaction will be broadcast at low speed. Hubs are thereby directed to enable low-speed ports; low-speed devices can now accept low-speed bus activity.

18.3.5 Transfer Types

isochronous, bulk, interrupt, control The USB specifies and supports four different transfer types: *isochronous, bulk, interrupt,* and *control*. High-speed devices support all four, whereas the low-speed devices only support the last two.

Isochronous transfers are those, such as high-speed audio or video, which must be completed in constant time. Bulk transfers are intended for moving large amounts of data. Although the USB does not support interrupts, one of the stated goals was the need to support legacy devices and many of those devices require interrupt support. Interrupt transfers accommodate those devices by ensuring that the transfers occur at such a rate that interrupts and associated information will not be lost. Finally, control transfers are designated for managing the USB.

18.3.6 Device Descriptors

In satisfying one of the stated goals of supporting new (as yet to be developed) devices, the USB developers devised a clever scheme for managing the network configuration. Each device that wishes to be attached to the USB describes itself to host software using a number of descriptors. Four of the descriptors are organized in a hierarchical tree-like structure as shown in Figure 18.8. The remaining two have broader scope.

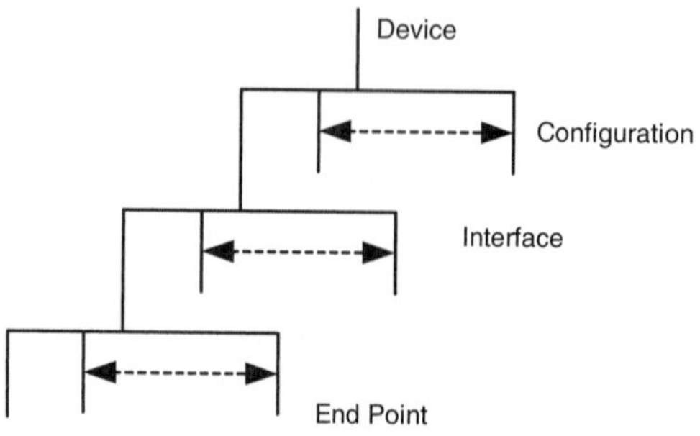

Figure 18.8 Universal Serial Bus Descriptor Hierarchy

The descriptors provide the following information

device descriptor

Device Descriptor Each device has one *device descriptor* that specifies the number of possible configurations supported by the device. In addition, it contains information about the default communication pipe to be used to the configure device and any other general information about the device.

configuration descriptor

Configuration Descriptor Each device has one *configuration descriptor* for each configuration that it supports. That descriptor provides relevant information about the configuration and specifies the number of interfaces, such as a CD/DVD ROM, supported by the device when using the named configuration.

interface descriptor

Interface Descriptor The *interface descriptor* contains information about the class of the device supported by the interface as well as general information about the specified interface and the number of endpoints it supports. A CD/DVD ROM may require several different drivers based on its supported capabilities. Different drivers may be necessary for audio, video, mass storage, or write capability, for example.

endpoint descriptor

Endpoint Descriptor Each device interface can support multiple endpoints or capabilities. Each endpoint defines a point of communication with the configuration. The descriptor provides information such as the transfer type that is supported by the endpoint or the maximum transfer rate supported.

In addition to the four named descriptors, two others are supported.

string descriptor

String Descriptors A human readable descriptor, called a *string descriptor*, can be defined to provide information for or about each device, a given configuration, or each interface supported by the device. The string descriptor expresses its information in Unicode format.

Class-specific descriptors

Class-Specific Descriptors *Class-specific descriptors* provide the means of developing descriptors that are not covered by the USB standard. These are analogous to pragma statements in C or C++, which give software vendors the ability to include product-specific information or requirements that may not be supported by the language in general into a compiler. At present the following device classes are defined:

- HID Device Class—Human Interface Devices
- Communication Device Class
- Monitor Device Class
- Mass Storage Device Class
- Audio Device Class

18.3.7 Network Configuration

enumeration

The host software is responsible for detecting and managing the configuration of all the devices connected to the root hub. In the context of the USB, the process is commonly referred to as USB device *enumeration*. The initial configuration process starts at the root hub when power is applied to the system. Following that process, devices can subsequently be added or removed incrementally.

reset

The enumeration process begins when the root hub, using a broadcast message, disables all ports and issues a *reset* command. Resetting a device forces it to respond to address zero as the default address and to enter a low-power configuration. Using such a scheme, the configuration software can read every device's descriptor at the same default address.

During configuration, each device will be assigned a unique address that the device will respond to thereafter. Through such a scheme, the designers of the protocol eliminated the possibility of address contention.

The host software then interrogates each device and reads the associated descriptors. Through such a process, the configuration software determines the endpoints associated with the device, if the demands of the endpoint can be accommodated based on remaining free bandwidth, and if bus power required by the device can be accommodated.

Devices may have multiple configurations, with each configuration descriptor representing a different set of resources that can be chosen. It is the responsibility of the host software to ensure that all required resource requests can be satisfied. If the requests cannot be met, then, the configuration must be refused. Recall the earlier discussions on deadlocks.

During configuration, the specification requires that each device consume no more than 100 mA of bus current. Thereafter, the maximum bus power that the device will need is determined from the configuration descriptor. The host software must verify that the bus power required by the device can be supplied by the hub port.

Each different configuration defines a set of endpoints, and each endpoint knows the amount of bandwidth it requires. Prior to admitting an endpoint to the bus, the host software must verify that the bandwidth requirement by the endpoint can be satisfied. If sufficient bandwidth is available, a link to the endpoint is set up and the required bandwidth is reserved. After successfully allocating bandwidth to each endpoint within the device, the device can be configured. If the bandwidth is not available, other configurations are checked. If all alternative configurations also exceed the available bandwidth, then the device is not configured.

Once a configuration has been accepted, the host software assigns a value corresponding to the chosen configuration. That value is given to the configuration software through the configuration descriptor. At this point, the device can be accessed by client software and consume the max amount of current and bandwidth specified in its configuration.

18.3.8 USB Transactions

A typical USB transaction comprises three phases:

1. Token packet phase
2. Data packet phase
3. Handshake phase

as shown in Figure 18.9.

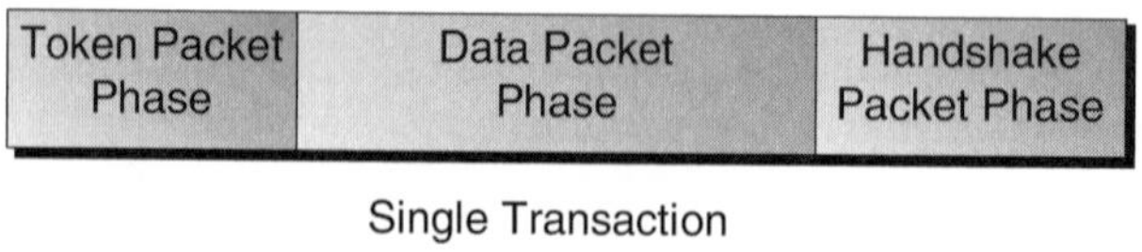

Figure 18.9 USB Bus Transaction Phases

token packet phase

Each transaction begins with a *token packet phase* that identifies the type of the transaction. When the transaction is intended for a specific device, its address is also included. The token can further indicate that the packet will not be followed by additional packets or that there may be two additional ones: the *data* and *handshake packets*.

data, handshake packets

The data packet phase carries the payload, which can be up to a maximum of 1023 bytes during each single transaction. The actual size of the payload is dependent on the type of transfer being performed.

Like the TCP protocol, all USB transfers (except the isochronous) are implemented to guarantee data delivery. Isochronous transfers are implemented to support best effort similar to the UDP transfers under the TCP/IP protocol. The isochronous transfers have no handshake phase. For all others, the handshake phase provides feedback to the sender of the data indicating whether or not the transaction occurred without errors. If errors have occurred, the error management scheme retries the transmission.

The format for all packets is given in Figure 18.10.

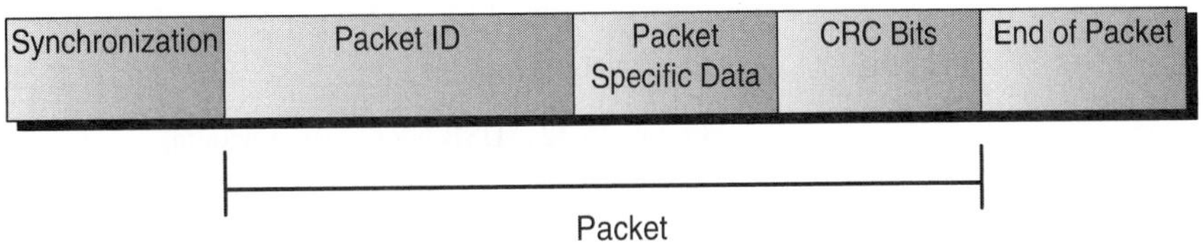

Figure 18.10 USB Packet Format

Unlike the EIA-232 transactions in which synchronization occurs for each character, the USB protocol resynchronizes for each packet. This task is accomplished through a special *synchronization sequence* shown in the packet diagram in the figure. The sequence, which consists of seven consecutive 0s followed by a single 1, is utilized by a local phase locked loop to resynthesize the data clock.

synchronization sequence

Packet identifiers specify the purpose and content of each packet. Identifiers are grouped into four major categories:

packet identifiers

- Token packets
- Data packets
- Handshake packets
- Special packets

The format and length of each packet depends on its type. Token packets require 4 bytes, bulk transfers are restricted to 64 bytes, and isochronous transfers are specified to be 1024 bytes.

18.3.9 USB Interface Signals

The USB implements a serial communications system. The signaling is differential, which helps to mitigate the effects of noise on the lines and to ensure data integrity. Observe that this is a different approach from that used by the EIA-232 standard. In that design, a signaling level far in excess of the noise helped to ensure integrity. The basic USB communication channel is configured as shown in Figure 18.11.

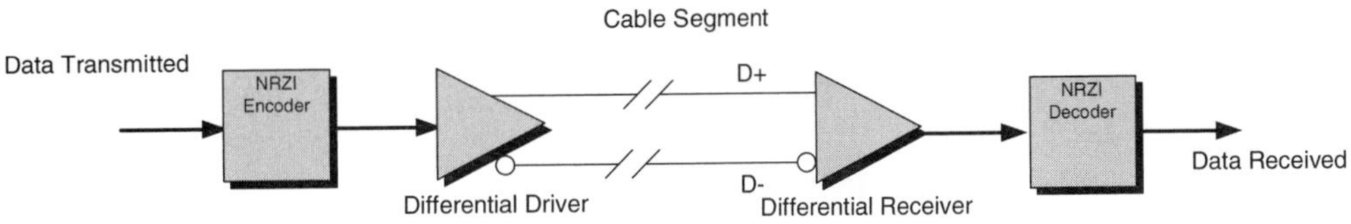

Figure 18.11 USB Communication Channel

The embedded system could be either the sender or the receiver of the data.

The USB implements a synchronous communication scheme. To provide timing information, the clock is incorporated into the transmitted data using an NRZI (Non-Return to Zero Inverted) encoding. The NRZI encoding scheme is as shown in Figure 18.12. Transitions in the data stream represent 0's and no transitions represent 1's. Observe that a transition occurs on the encoded data at the start of each 0 bit in the raw data.

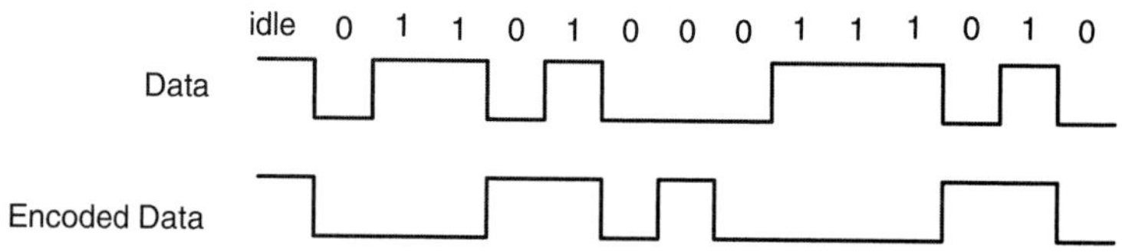

Figure 18.12 USB NRZI Data Encoding

The NRZI encoder must maintain synchronization with the incoming data stream to allow it to correctly sample the bits. The encoded data will be fed into a phase locked loop (PLL), which will sense the bit transitions and reconstruct a synchronized clock as we discussed earlier.

The data stream must be sampled within each data bit to determine whether a transition has occurred since the last bit time. This is implemented by the decoder. A transition represents a zero bit, and no state change indicates that a one bit was received. The transitions on the zero bits in the data stream permit the decoder to maintain sync with incoming data using the PLL. A long series of consecutive 1's will have no transitions, thus potentially resulting in a loss of sync. To solve this problem, a technique called *bit stuffing* is used.

bit stuffing

The USB implementation of bit stuffing in the transmitter forces a transition into an NRZI data stream whenever six consecutive 1's have been encountered. The added bits ensure that the receiver will detect a transition at least once every seventh bit time.

The extra zero bit will not cause confusion on decoding, even if the seventh bit is a legitimate zero. After six 1's, the receiver knows that the next bit received will be an inserted zero and so, on receipt, discards it. The real zero will be received following and interpreted correctly.

18.3.10 The Physical Environment

The USB connectors are designed to permit any USB peripheral device to be attached to any hub port. The USB subsystem supports two kinds of cables: low speed and high speed.

Low-speed Cables

subchannel cables

The low-speed cables, also referred to as *subchannel cables*, are intended only for 1.5M Byte/sec signaling. The maximum cable length cannot exceed 3 meters. The low-speed cables support differential pair signaling; the signal pair may be nontwisted 28 AWG stranded conductors. The low-speed cables do not require shielding.

High-speed Cables

The high-speed cables require twisted shielded pair (TWSP). The maximum cable length is extended to 5 meters as long as the propagation delay is less than 30 ns over the length of cable when operating in the range of 1–16 MHz. If such a constraint cannot be met, the cable must be shortened. Beyond the noted differences, the low-and high-speed cables are identical.

Cables and Cable Power

The USB cables support a limited amount of 5 VDC power that can be used by the peripheral devices. The system normally supports up to 500 ma, although it may be as little as 100 ma in certain implementations. The end view of the cable is given as illustrated in Figure 18.13.

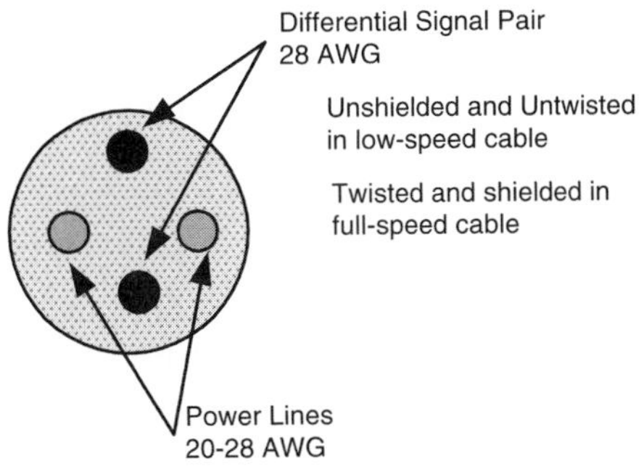

Figure 18.13 USB Cable Structure

18.3.11 Detecting Device Attachment and Speed

It is the responsibility of the root or other hubs and system software to automatically detect the presence or absence of the device both during initial configuration and later when a new device is attached or when one is removed from the bus. The same mechanism is used to determine the speed of each device.

Detection is accomplished by monitoring the differential data lines after cable power is applied to the port. The schematic in Figure 18.14 illustrates the device configured for full-speed operation. The channel from the device back to the host has been left off.

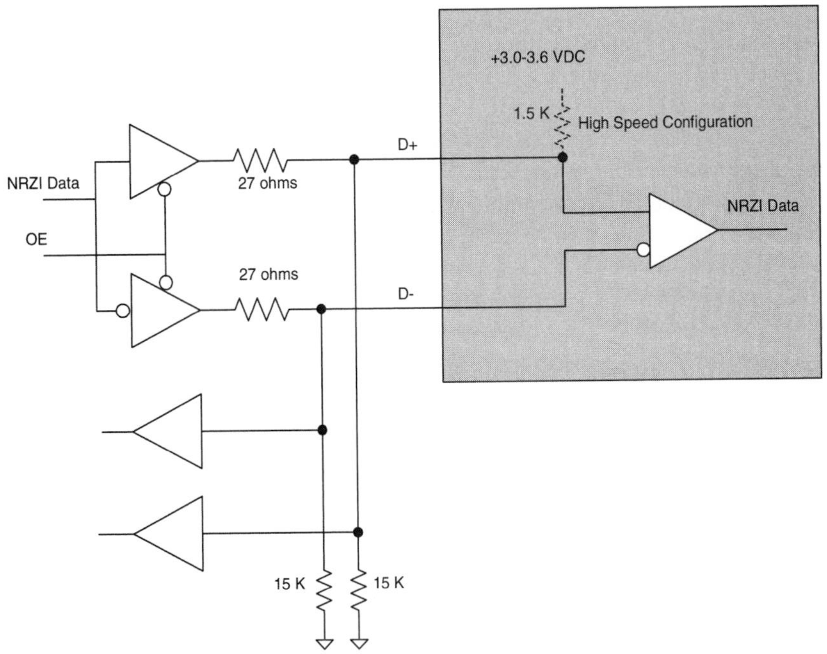

Figure 18.14 USB Communication Channel with High-Speed Device Attached

When no device is attached, the two pull-down resistors on D+ and D- ensure that the signal levels on both data lines coming into the single-ended receivers are close ground. When a device is connected to the network, it must provide a 1.5 KΩ pull-up resistor on either the D+ line for a full-speed device or on the D- for a low-speed device.

When a device is attached, the pull-up resistor increases the signal on the associated line through the voltage divider formed by the 15 KΩ and the 1.5 KΩ resistors. When the hub detects one of the data lines approaching VCC and the other near ground, it knows that a device is attached. By knowing which line is high, it can ascertain what kind of device has been attached. According to the specification, when either D+ or D- rises above 2.0 VDC for greater than 2.5 μsec, a device is detected as attached. When the device is removed and both lines fall below 0.8 VDC for greater than 2.5 μsec, the hub sets a status flag. The host software polls hub periodically to check for attachment or detachment.

18.3.12 Differential Pair Signaling

In Figure 18.14, we observe two things. First, the lines are terminated at the source using 27 Ω resistors; the drivers themselves have an output impedance of approximately 3 to 15 Ω. Second, differential signaling is used. Differential pair signaling is used to reduce the effects of noise that may be coupled into the signal path. Any noise coupled in will have an equal effect on both lines. When the bus signal is converted back to a single-ended form, the noise will be effectively canceled out.

Source or series termination is used to eliminate DC power consumption that is inherent in a parallel termination scheme. The one disadvantage of such a scheme is that one full round-trip is required before the signal reaches full amplitude.

The USB uses a half-duplex scheme. The device on either end can receive or transmit but in only one direction at a time. Such a design requires that the drivers be placed into the high-impedance state when not transmitting data.

18.3.13 Implementation

As with the EIA-232 interface, there are two principal means by which the USB interface and support can be implemented as part of a distributed embedded application: first as an integrated peripheral on the various microprocessor chips and second as an external chip set. Today a large number of USB chip set offerings are available. Most of these implement a general-purpose parallel I/O structure similar in architecture to that seen for the US/ART chips. Such a structure is compatible with the external CPU bus on most contemporary microprocessors.

18.4 I^{2}C—A LOCAL AREA NETWORK

I^{2}C bus—Inter Integrated Circuit Bus

The *I^{2}C bus—Inter Integrated Circuit Bus*—was developed in the 1980s by Philips Semiconductor as a means of supporting communication among a set of chips internal to a specific system. At its initial introduction, the bus was intended for small, lower speed systems. The initial bit rate of 100 K bits/sec has increased fourfold to 400 K bits/sec today. In addition to its low cost and ease of implementation, the I^{2}C bus offers several interesting features that we will expand on shortly.

18.4.1 The Architecture

multimaster–slave The I²C bus utilizes a simple serial two-wire *multimaster–slave* architecture as illustrated in the high-level block diagram in Figure 18.15.

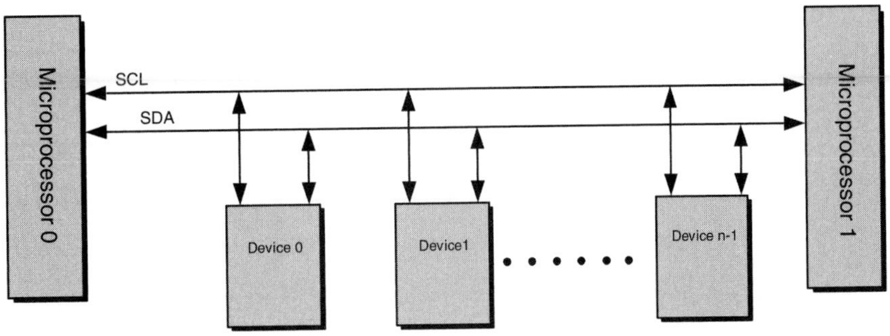

Figure 18.15 I²C Bus Architecture Block Diagram

Devices with bus master capability are typically microprocessors, but they need not be. Independent of bus master capabilities, any device on the bus has the potential to be a sender or receiver—source or destination—of a transaction. The bidirectional I²C bus implements what is known as *wired AND* signaling. Consequently, the only special interface circuitry that is required to connect a device onto the bus is two open-drain or open-collector devices that enable the device to pull either line to ground. Each device on the bus has a unique address independent of a physical device type, yet the device type is embedded into the address.

wired AND

serial clock (SCL) ***serial data (SCD)*** Physically, in addition to ground, the bus comprises two signal lines, *serial clock* (SCL) and *serial data* (SCD) as illustrated in Figure 18.16.

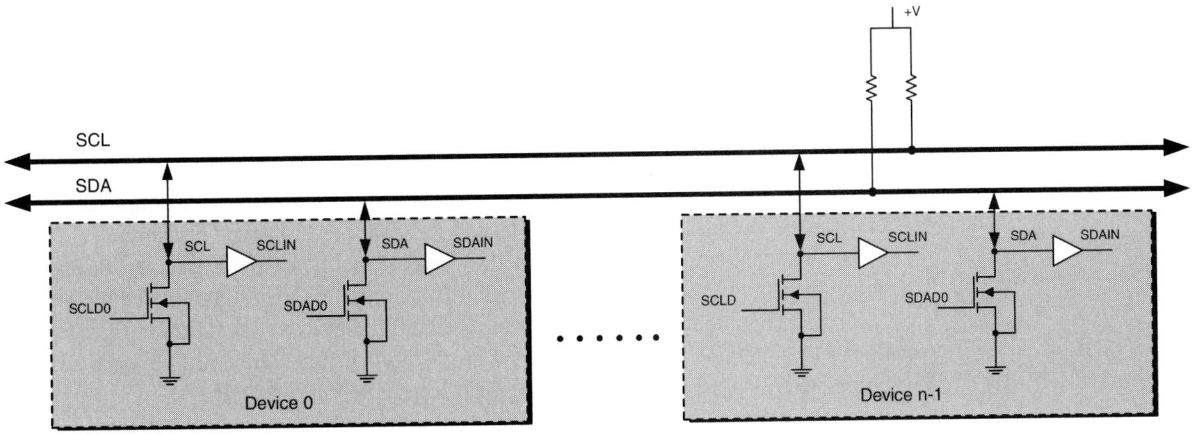

Figure 18.16 I²C Bus Serial Clock and Serial Data Signals

The drawing reflects the details of the bus and its connection to several devices.

18.4.2 Electrical Considerations

The design of the I^{2}C bus places no restrictions on the type of devices that may be connected to the bus. Thus, one can configure a system with a mixture of various TTL and CMOS

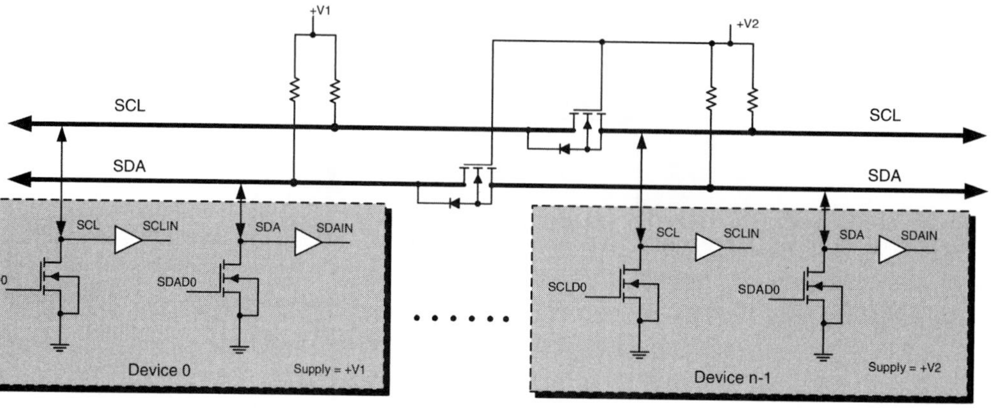

Figure 18.17 I^{2}C Bus Supporting Devices Operating

families, each with its own different supply voltage. To accommodate bidirectional communication with devices operating on less than 5.0 VDC, it is recommended that a simple buffering circuit be incorporated into the SCL and SDA signal paths as shown in Figure 18.17. The two subsystems, operating at different voltage levels, are now separated from one another. Today, the different voltage levels result from logic devices operating at either 5.0 V or 3.3 V.

To support the standard (100 K bits/sec) mode and fast mode (400 K bits/sec) transfer rates, the total bus capacitance must be less than 400 pf and the signal rise and fall times at 1000 ns and 300 ns, respectively. These are measured at the 30 and 70% points on the signal rather than the traditional 10 and 90% points. These constraints naturally place a limit on the number of devices that can be interconnected on the bus.

18.4.3 Basic Operation

Let's now take a look at the basic bus operation in a system comprising a single master and several slaves. We will look at both a master read and a master write operation.

The quiescent condition for both the SCL and SDA lines is the high state. A bus cycle begins with a *Start* condition and ends with a *Stop;* these are always generated by the master. A *Start* is signaled when the master causes a HIGH to Low transition on the SDA line while holding the SCL line in the HIGH state. A *Stop* is signaled by a LOW to HIGH transition on the SDA line while holding the SCL line in the HIGH state.

Stop
Start

An I^{2}C address comprises 7 bits. The four most significant bits (A7–A3) identify the category of the device being addressed. The three least significant (A2–A0) identify a programmable hardware address assigned to the device. Thus, up to eight instances of the same type of device can be included in the system. For example, if a system included eight serial EEPROMS, each would have the base address 1010 concatenated with one of the addresses 000–111.

Data is sent with the most significant bit first, with each bit accompanied by a clock signal. Data can only change when the SCL line is in the LOW state. Data is transferred as an

write, read

unrestricted number of bytes; each byte must be acknowledged by the receiver. A transaction may be a *write* operation—master to slave, a *read* operation—slave to master, or a combination in which there is a change in transmission direction during a transaction.

The contents of a complete data transfer cycle are given as follows:

```
Start

    Slave Address
    Read / Write
    Acknowledge
    Data - Acknowledge (the pair is repeated as necessary)

Stop
```

The message format is given in Figure 18.18.

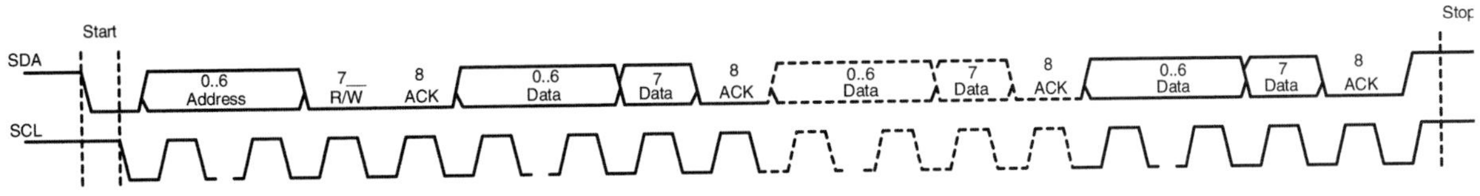

Figure 18.18 I²C Bus Message Format

read, Read/$\overline{Write}$
ACK
read

For a *read* operation, the *Read/$\overline{Write}$* bit will be a HIGH and for a Write, it will be a LOW. Following the *ACK* (which is generated by the slave and appears in bit 8), if the ensuing operation is to be a *read*, the master changes roles from transmitter to receiver and the slave from receiver to transmitter. Despite the reversed roles, the master still generates the *Stop* and manages the end of the transaction.

18.4.4 Flow of Control

The transaction protocol requires that each data byte be acknowledged. The clock pulse associated with the acknowledge (ACK*)* is generated by the master. During that clock time, the transmitter (which may not be the master) must release the SDA line, allowing it to float. The receiver must pull the SDA line LOW for the duration that the clock pulse on the SCL line is in the HIGH state.

Under normal circumstances, following the ACK bit time, the master will release the SCL line so that transmission may continue with the next byte. If, however, the receiver is temporarily unable to proceed, it will hold the SCL line LOW, thereby extending the ACK interval. When able to proceed again, the receiver will release the SCL line and transmission continues. The timing diagram in Figure 18.19 illustrates the ACK interval extension.

Stop
Start

Following the end of a communication session with one slave, the master typically will issue the *Stop* directive to end the session. If, however, it wishes to establish a connection with a different slave, rather than issue the *Stop*, the master will issue another *Start*, using the address of the new device.

18.4.5 Multiple Masters

arbitration, synchronization

Several problems can occur when a system has multiple masters. The first arises if two or more masters try to talk at the same time; the second results from having multiple clocks in the system. The first problem is resolved by *arbitration* and the second by *synchronization*.

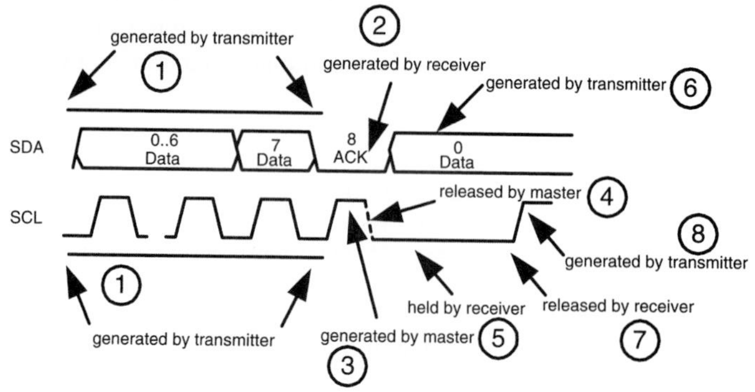

Figure 18.19 Acknowledge Extension

Arbitration

A master can initiate a transfer cycle only if the bus is not in use. As noted, such a cycle begins when the master places the SDA line in the LOW state while keeping the SCL line in the HIGH state. At this point, if multiple masters simultaneously issue a Start, there is no way to distinguish among them. Thus, arbitration can only begin at the most significant bit of the address.

Each device attempting to communicate on the bus drives the SDA line. The wired AND aspect of the bus inherently gives priority to a device, driving the SDA line to the LOW state. Each master is monitoring the SDA line, and each knows the state of the bit it has put onto the line. Therefore, if a master sees the SDA line in the LOW state, knowing that it has set a HIGH, it will disable its data drive capability and back off. The arbitration process can continue, bit by bit, for a number of SCL clock cycles until resolved.

If the losing master(s) also incorporates a slave function, the possibility exists that the winning master is trying to address that slave. The losing master(s) must immediately switch into the receiver mode.

Synchronization

Each master typically has its own internal clock, and each is responsible for generating the SCL clock for the bus. Since each master clock is asynchronous with respect to the others, for the arbitration scheme just described to work properly, the clocks must be synchronized. The operation takes advantage of the wired AND connection scheme utilized by the I^2C bus and proceeds as follows.

A HIGH to LOW transition on the SCL line (originating from any of the masters) directs each master to place its SCL driver in the LOW state and begins timing the LOW duration for its SCL clock. When that interval expires, on one of the masters, that device places its SCL driver in the HIGH state. However, the SCL line may not follow if some other master(s) is (are) still timing its LOW interval.

As each master completes timing the LOW SCL interval, it places its SCL driver in the HIGH state, enters a wait state until the last device releases the SCL line, and then enters the HIGH state. At that time, each master begins timing the HIGH duration for its SCL clock. In a similar manner, the last device to complete timing its HIGH duration will change the state of the SCL line to LOW.

Based on such a scheme, it is evident that for each master, the LOW intervals will be the same as will the HIGH intervals. The LOW intervals will be set by the device with the longest such interval, and the HIGH intervals will be set by the device with the shortest such interval.

18.4.6 Using the I²C Bus

Today a great variety of integrated circuit devices, including a plethora of different microprocessors and microcontrollers, support the I²C bus. Such devices range from displays and serial EEPROMS to analog-to-digital converters and video acquisition systems. The bus can provide a highly effective lower speed network for locally distributed embedded applications. The extent of the topographic distribution is subject to the 400 pf capacitive loading specification. Such a constraint suggests 20 to 30 devices and a maximum signal path of approximately 10 meters.

18.5 THE CONTROLLER AREA NETWORK—THE CAN BUS

CAN Bus, Controller Area Network

The automobiles of today are significantly different from those Henry Ford introduced almost one hundred years ago. The introduction of larger and larger numbers of increasingly sophisticated electronic systems into the modern automobile has led to a corresponding increase in the size and complexity of the wiring harness interconnecting all of the devices. To address the problem, Bosch, the German automotive manufacturer, developed a simple two-wire serial communications bus, the *CAN Bus* or *Controller Area Network*. Although its initial target was the automotive industry, the acceptance of the CAN bus has expanded well beyond that and is now supported by the International Standards Organization as the standard ISO 11898 as well.

18.5.1 The Architecture

The CAN network corresponds to the physical and data link layers of the ISO/OSI reference model. These layers are shown in the hierarchy in Figure 18.20 as reflected in the ISO standard, ISO 11898. The remaining layers of the model are managed by the microprocessor in software as appropriate.

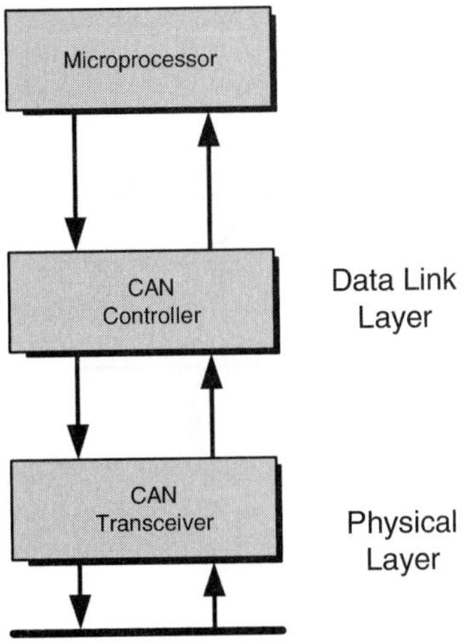

Figure 18.20 CAN Bus Network Hierarchy

On the hardware side, the physical layer utilizes a twisted pair multidrop cable. It includes the connectors and transceivers for getting onto and off of the bus as well. A basic system is configured as shown in the following high-level block diagram in Figure 18.21.

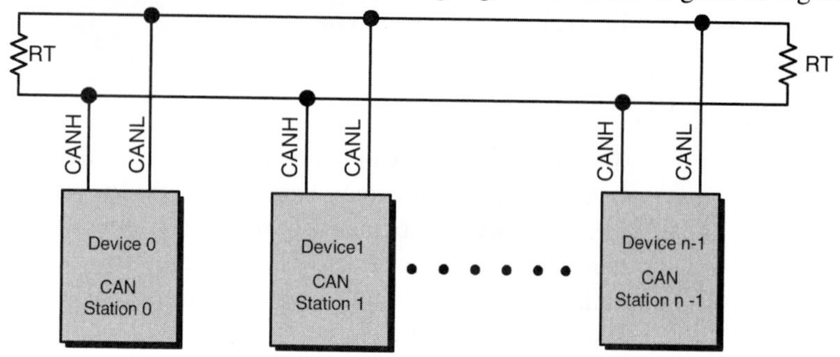

Figure 18.21 A Block Diagram for a Basic CAN Bus Network

Unlike the I^2C bus, the CAN bus does not require that one of the nodes is a master. Nodes can be added to the network at any time; it is not necessary to power the system down. The standard specifies that up to 30 nodes can be added to the bus.

18.5.2 Electrical Considerations

Electrically, the CAN bus utilizes balanced differential signaling similar to the approach used by the USB—the current in each signal line is equal and opposite. Such a scheme significantly enhances noise immunity, increases common mode noise rejection, and improves fault tolerance over single-ended drive models. All are essential for the automotive environment in which the Bus is designed to operate.

dominant, recessive

The two serial lines that make up the CAN Bus are designated CANH and CANL. The bus signaling protocol defines two states, *dominant* and *recessive*. Similar to the wired AND configuration in the I^2C bus, *dominant* will override *recessive*. When the transmitted data, TXD, is a logical 0, the bus is in the *dominate* state; the CANH signal line is taken to 3.5 V, and the CANL is taken to 1.5 V, giving a difference of 2.0 volts. When the transmitted data is a logical 1, the bus is in the recessive (quiescent) state, which is set to 2.5 V. The timing diagram in Figure 18.22 illustrates the two conditions.

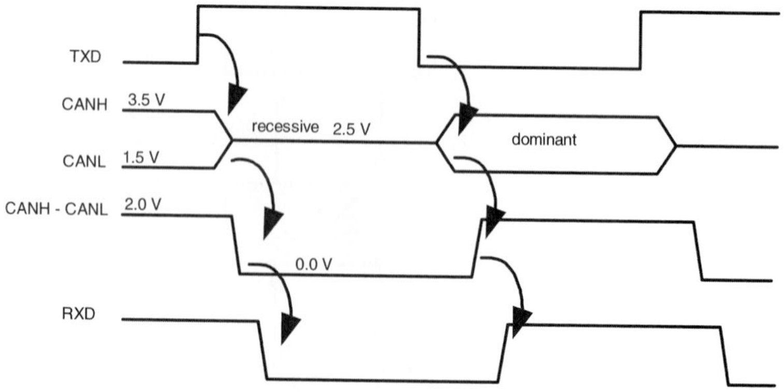

Figure 18.22 A Timing Diagram Illustrating Dominant and Recessive Signaling on the CAN Bus

The transmission rates on the bus range from 40 K bits/sec over a 1000 m cable to 1 M bit/sec over a 40 m cable. The standard further specifies the maximum stub length off the main bus to be 0.3 m.

The characteristic impedance of the cable is specified as 120 Ω, and it should be resistively terminated at both ends with 120 Ω.

18.5.3 Message Types

frames

data frame, remote frame, error frame, overload frame

The CAN standard refers to messages as *frames*. The protocol specifies support for four different kinds of frames. These include the *data frame*, the *remote frame*, the *error frame*, and the *overload frame*.

arbitration field, control field, data field, CRC field, acknowledgment field

Data Frame The data frame comprises the following fields: the *arbitration field*, *control field*, *data field*, *CRC field*, and *acknowledgment field*. The arbitration field, which will be explained shortly, contains an 11-bit identifier and the RTR bit, which identifies the operation as either transmit or receive. The control field contains information about the type of message being sent and its length. The data field contains the payload of up to 8 bytes. The CRC field contains a 16-bit checksum used for error management. At the end of a data frame, the transmitter examines the state of the acknowledgment field. If the bit is in the recessive state, the message is retransmitted.

Remote Frame The remote frame is charged with requesting data from another node. It mirrors the data frame with the exceptions that it contains no payload and the RTR bit is recessive.

Error Frame The error frame is transmitted when a node detects an error in a message. Such an action forces all other nodes in the network to send an error frame as well; the original transmitter then resends the message that led to the error.

Overload Frame The overload frame is used in support of flow control. It is used to force an extra delay between messages when a node is unable to process information quickly enough.

18.5.4 Message Format

The standard CAN message format is given in Figure 18.23.

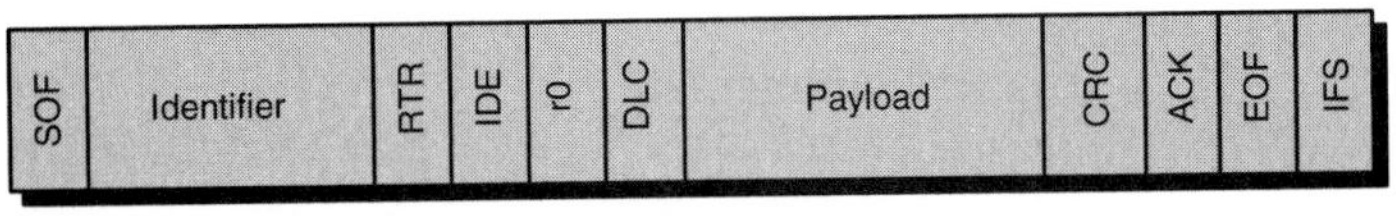

Figure 18.23 Standard CAN Bus Message Format

SOF (Start of Frame) Single dominant bit that marks the start of a message. It also serves to synchronize nodes following an idle period.

arbitration field

Identifier Identifier and RTR bit form the *arbitration field*. It identifies the destination and priority of the message. Higher priority messages have lower binary values.

RTR (Remote Transmission Request) Single bit, expressed as dominant when information is required from destination node. Returned data can be used by any node. Such a scheme helps to ensure data consistency across all nodes on the net.

control field

IDE Identifier Extension, r0, and the DLC bit form the *control field* for a standard message format, single dominant bit. It is used to indicate that the extended format is not being used.

r0 Reserved bit

DLC (Data Length Code) Four-bit field identifying the number of bytes of data contained in the message.

data field

Data The message payload comprising the *data field*. The payload can be up to 8 bytes.

CRC field

CRC (Cyclic Redundancy Check) CRC specifies the *CRC field*. This is a 15-bit field that contains a check sum over the payload data.

ACK field

ACK (Acknowledge bit, the *ACK field*) This is a single recessive bit in the originating message plus delimiter. If the message is received correctly, the receiver overwrites the bit with a dominant bit indicating that an error-free message has been sent. If the bit is left recessive, indicating an error, the receiver does not accept the message and the sender repeats the message.

EOF (End of Frame) EoF identifies the end of a CAN message frame.

IFS (Interframe Space) This is a 7-bit frame containing the amount of time for the controller to place the received frame into the buffer area.

18.5.5 Basic Operation

Synchronization

Data sent over the CAN network is transmitted in NRZ (Non-Return to Zero) format. Such a scheme enables the receiving node to synchronize with the sending node through clock edges that have been encoded into the data stream. To ensure that edge information is transmitted (in the event of long strings of 1's or 0's), a bit stuffing scheme is utilized. A string of five consecutive 1's or 0's prompts the sender to insert a bit of the opposite polarity into the data stream. Recall that a similar approach is utilized by the USB to ensure synchronization.

Error Management

Because of the stringent reliability requirements placed on the bus by the operating environment, the CAN protocol utilizes a three-pronged attack on errors. Each message uses a CRC check over the data payload. The CRC is recomputed by the receiver and compared against that which was sent. Any difference flags a *CRC error*.

CRC error

The format as well as the size of each received frame is checked against a known template for the frame. Should there be a disagreement, a *format error* is noted.

format error

Finally, each received frame must be acknowledged by a positive action—overwriting the ACK bit with a dominant bit. Lack of such an action prompts retransmission.

At the bit level, a transmitter monitors the state of the bus. Any disagreement between what was sent and the state of the bus indicates that an error has occurred.

Transmission and Arbitration

As noted earlier, the quiescent state of the CAN bus is recessive. Such a condition gives rise to an interesting bus arbitration and access protocol. Note first that the CAN bus is essentially a peer network. There is no bus master; thus, any node can potentially transmit on the bus and any time. The Ethernet utilizes a similar scheme. In the event of a collision on the Ethernet, both (all) nodes back off and retry at a (random) later time. Any information transmitted during the collision is lost. Such is not the case with the CAN bus.

The SOF signal is dominant; any device wishing to transmit will place a logical 0 onto the bus. At the same time, each node is monitoring the state of the bus similar to the I^2C bus. If four nodes had placed their SOF signal onto the bus, each would see such a state on the bus. The SOF signal on the bus is a valid bit—it has not been corrupted by the collision.

Following the SOF, each node assumes that it has the bus and will send its second bit—the first bit of the identifier field. Each node again tests the state of the bus. If the bus indicates dominant, any node that had set the bus state to recessive loses the arbitration and leaves its drivers in the recessive state for the duration of the transmission.

If all nodes have set the bus state to dominant, the process continues with the third bit. In any event, the state of the bus will be valid. No information has been lost. The process repeats until all nodes but one have lost the arbitration. The timing diagram in Figure 18.24 depicts the arbitration process for four nodes.

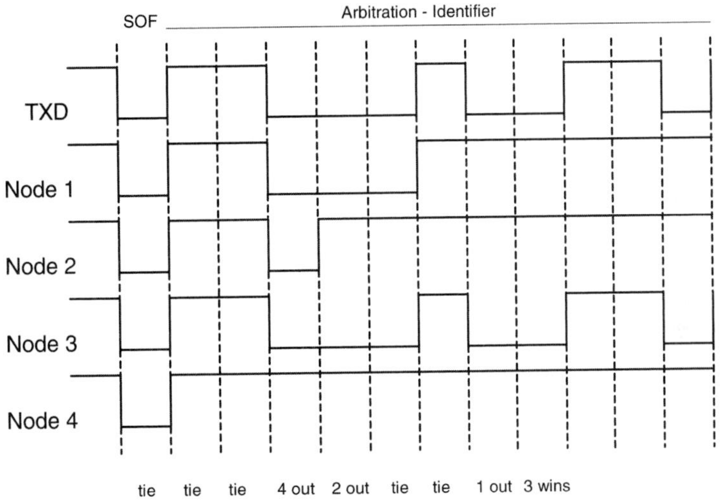

Figure 18.24 CAN Bus Arbitration for Four Nodes

Node 4 loses on the third arbitration bit, node 2 on the fourth, and node 1 on the seventh. Thus, node 3 is seen to ultimately win the arbitration. Observe that no information was ever lost or corrupted during the arbitration. The destination node will properly receive the complete transmission.

18.5.6 Using the CAN Bus

Today there is increasing support for and application of the CAN bus outside of the automotive industries. The bus and protocol are specified and controlled by the international ISO standard, ISO 11898. A number of semiconductor manufacturers offer integrated implementations of the CAN Transceiver and the Controller.

18.6 SUMMARY

In this chapter, we studied four different, commonly used network-based input/output designs. For each, we examined the problems that motivated designers to develop the interface, identified the contributions that each has brought about, and cited the strengths and weaknesses of each approach. For each architecture, we examined the transport mechanism, learned how control and synchronism are affected, and explored how message senders and receivers are identified. We began with the traditional EIA-232 standard asynchronous serial interface and then moved to the synchronous model utilized by the Universal Serial Bus. We concluded with the I^2C bus as a small local area network and the CAN bus, a LAN commonly used in automotive applications.

18.7 REVIEW QUESTIONS

Common Network-Based Architectures

18.1 The chapter introduces four common network-based architectures. What are they?

The EIA-232 Interface

18.2 What was the originally intended purpose of the RS-232 (now EIA-232) interface standard?

18.3 What are the primary signals that comprise the EIA-232 interface standard? Give a brief description of each and its function in a data exchange.

18.4 What do the acronyms DCE and DTE mean?

18.5 What is a null modem? Explain how such a device works.

18.6 What is the format of an EIA-232 character?

18.7 Why is information exchange over the EIA-232 network described as asynchronous?

18.8 In an EIA-232 exchange, what is the purpose of the *start* and *stop* bits in a data character?

18.9 What is meant by the term *baud rate*?

18.10 What are the signaling levels for a logical 0, logical 1, true or ON control signal, and a false or OFF control signal?

The Universal Serial Bus

18.11 What are some of the problems that the designers of the USB are trying to solve?

18.12 What are some of the major contributions of the USB?

18.13 Does the USB implement interrupts?

18.14 What are the major elements of the USB protocol stack? Briefly describe the function of each.

18.15 What is the purpose of the host controller? the root hub?

18.16 How is the address of a device made known to the USB software?

18.17 What is a transfer descriptor?

18.18 What kinds of data transfer does USB support?

18.19 What is a device descriptor? What is its purpose?

18.20 How many kinds of descriptors does the USB support? What is the purpose of each?

18.21 How many class descriptors does the USB support?

18.22 How many phases comprise a USB transaction? What are they?

18.23 Do all USB transactions support guaranteed delivery of data?

I^2C—A Local Area Network

18.24 What are the two primary signaling lines on the I^2C bus? What is the function of each?

18.25 What are some of the problems that the designers of the I^2C bus are trying to solve?

18.26 What are some of the major contributions of the I^2C?

18.27 How does the I^2C differ architecturally from the USB and EIA-232 busses?

18.28 What are the two primary signaling lines on the I^2C bus? What is the function of each?

18.29 Describe the steps involved in a bus master read operation on the I^2C bus.

18.30 Describe the steps involved in a bus master write operation on the I^2C bus.

18.31 Does the I^2C bus support multiple masters?

18.32 With multiple masters, how is a bus contention situation resolved?

The Controller Area Network—The CAN Bus

18.33 What are some of the more significant differences between the CAN bus and the I^2C, USB, and EIA-232 signaling?

18.34 What are some of the problems that the designers of the CAN bus were trying to solve?

18.35 What are some of the major contributions of the CAN bus?

18.36 What are the two primary signaling lines on the CAN bus? What is the function of each?

18.37 The CAN bus signaling protocol specifies two states, dominant and recessive. What do these terms mean in this context?

18.38 Describe the format for message that is sent over the CAN bus?

18.39 How are errors managed on the CAN bus?

18.8 THOUGHT QUESTIONS

Common Network-Based Architectures

18.1 What does each of the network architectures discussed in the chapter introduce and contribute to simplifying the problem of remote information interchange?

18.2 Compare and contrast the transport mechanisms used for the four bus architectures discussed in the chapter. What are the strengths and weaknesses of each?

The EIA-232 Interface

18.3 Why would one wish to use a null modem?

18.4 Why does the chapter advise not using the signals RTS, CTS, DSR, DTR as hardware handshake signals for flow control?

18.5 Describe how a character is transmitted and received over the EIA-232 network.

18.6 Propose a software protocol that could be used to control the flow of data in an EIA-232 exchange.

18.7 Describe the EIA-232 transport mechanism.

The Universal Serial Bus

18.8 What are some of the more significant differences between the USB and EIA-232 signaling?

18.9 Give examples of real-world devices that might utilize each of the USB transfer types identified in the chapter.

18.10 Describe the USB transport mechanism.

18.11 Why does the USB use differential signaling?

18.12 Because the USB is synchronous, the receiver must have knowledge of timing information from the source. How is this accomplished?

18.13 How does the USB determine when a device is attached to or removed from the bus?

18.14 What is the purpose of each of the different data transfer types that are implemented in the USB?

I^2C—A Local Area Network

18.15 What are some of the more significant differences between the I^2C and the USB and EIA-232 signaling?

18.16 What kinds of devices can be placed on the I^2C bus? Give some examples.

18.17 Describe the I^2C bus transport mechanism.

18.18 Why would one want to have a multiple master architecture on the I^2C bus?

18.19 How would the I^2C bus be utilized in an embedded context?

The Controller Area Network—The CAN Bus

18.20 What kinds of devices can be placed on the CAN bus? Give some examples.

18.21 Describe the CAN bus transport mechanism.

18.22 What kinds of message types can be exchanged over the CAN bus? Explain the purpose and meaning of each of the different types.

18.23 How are errors managed on the CAN bus? Compare the CAN strategy with that of the other three busses that we have studied in this chapter.

18.9 PROBLEMS

The EIA-232 Interface

18.1 The chapter discusses four different, commonly used, networked architectures. The Electronic Industries Association (EIA) specifies a number of others that can be found as part of various embedded applications. Three of these include the EIA-422, 423, and 485 architectures.

(a) How are these different from the four models discussed in this chapter?

(b) Where might such models be used in an embedded application?

18.2 Design a software flow control system for the EIA-232 network interface. Explain why your design prevents data characters from being lost.

18.3 Typically, a Universal Asynchronous Receiver Transmitter (UART) is used to manage data flow over an EIA-232 network. Without using a UART, design a logic block that will accept 7 data bit characters, in parallel, from your microprocessor, add an odd parity bit over the 7 bits, convert each to a 10-bit serial EIA-232 compatible character, and transmit the character over a 9600 baud bit stream.

The Universal Serial Bus

18.4 Without using a UART, design a logic block that will accept a serial EIA-232 compatible character from a 9600 baud bit stream, perform a parity check on the incoming data, convert the received data into a 7-bit word, signal the processor that data is available, and transfer the 7-bit characters into the processor and indicate a parity error, if appropriate.

18.5 The chapter discussed the USB 1 interface. What different features and capabilities have been incorporated into the USB 2 interface?

18.6 The USB 2 interface is intended to be backwards compatible with the USB 1 interface. How does the USB 2 design distinguish between and handle high speed, full speed, and low speed signaling?

18.7 How does the USB 2 interface differ from the Firewire interface? What are the advantages of each?

18.8 Design a Verilog model and hardware block that will accept the serial data stream and clock and output an NRZI-encoded data stream.

18.9 Design a Verilog model and hardware block that will accept an NRZI-encoded data stream and produce a serial data stream with accompanying clock.

18.10 When data is received over the USB, the decoder samples a data stream during each bit time to check for transitions. Such transitions permit the decoder to maintain synchronization with incoming data. However. if the data to be transmitted contains a long sequence of consecutive one bits, the output of the NRZI will contain no transitions. Consequently, the receiver will eventually lose sync. To remedy the problem, whenever six consecutive 1's are encountered, a 0 is automatically inserted into the data stream. Such a practice forces transitions into the NRZI data stream, thereby ensuring that the receiver detects a transition every seventh bit time. Such a practice is called *bit stuffing*.

Design and implement a software driver that will implement the described bit stuffing algorithm.

18.11 Design and implement a software driver that will accept a serial data stream such as would be produced in Problem 18.10 and remove any one bits that may have been inserted via a bit stuffing algorithm.

I²C—A Local Area Network

18.12 Design and implement a software driver that will enable a slave device to transfer a 256-byte block of data over the I²C bus to a master.

18.13 Design and implement a software driver that will enable a master device to request the transfer of a 256-byte block of data over the I²C bus from a master.

The Controller Area Network—The CAN Bus

18.14 Give a detailed block diagram for a CAN Bus-based network for a commercial aircraft passenger entertainment system.

18.15 Can the CAN bus support a streaming audio server? If so, what is the maximum number of clients that could be supported? Be certain to state any assumptions. If not, give a detailed timing analysis explaining why not.

18.16 Give a detailed block diagram for a CAN Bus-based network for a passenger environment management system for a standard automobile.

Other Busses and Networks

18.17 Research the USB-2 bus.

(a) Describe the operation of the bus.

(b) Compare and contrast the operation and performance of USB-2 with the USB-1 bus discussed in the chapter.

18.18 Research the Firewire bus.

(a) Describe the operation of the bus.

(b) Compare and contrast the operation and performance of Firewire with the USB-1 and USB-2 busses.

18.19 Research the PCI Express bus.

(a) Describe the operation of the bus.

(b) Discuss the pros and cons of using the PCI Express bus as a means of communicating with local peripheral devices in an embedded application.

(c) Discuss the pros and cons of using the PCI Express bus as a means of communicating with remote peripheral devices in an embedded application.

18.20 Research the SPI bus.

(a) Describe the operation of the bus.

(b) Discuss the pros and cons of using the SPI bus as a means of communicating with local peripheral devices in an embedded application.

(c) Discuss the pros and cons of using the SPI bus as a means of communicating with remote peripheral devices in an embedded application.

18.21 Compare the following busses: I²C bus, SPI bus, CAN bus, and PCI Express.

(a) Identify the major differences in architecture among each of these busses.

(b) Identify the major similarities in architecture among each of these busses.

(c) Identify the major strengths and weaknesses of each.

Chapter 19

Programmable Logic Devices

THINGS TO LOOK FOR . . .

- Why use programmable logic devices in embedded systems.
- How a programmable cell works.
- What is a programmable logic device (PLD)?
- What is a CPLD?
- What is an FPGA?
- What is an antifuse?
- The difference between a CPLD and an FPGA.
- The difference between SRAM and antifuse-based FPGAs.
- What is a programmable system on a chip?
- The PLD design process.

19.0 INTRODUCTION

Our hardware focus in previous chapters has been on the microprocessor, microcontroller, and microcomputer. The world of embedded systems is continually changing. Today we find an increasing number and variety of other components being designed into the applications to support the basic computing core. These devices are grouped as programmable logic devices (PLDs). With such devices, we begin to move into the world of large and very large-scale integrated devices. Today these devices play a supporting role; tomorrow they will provide a highly flexible hardware environment that will include, among other things, very high-speed logic, multiple microprocessor cores, and dynamically reconfigurable systems.

The key strengths of these devices lie in their small geometries and their ability to take advantage of the regularity in combinational logic and in certain kinds of memory elements. With such regularity, the chip designs and layouts can be highly optimized. Included in this category of devices we generally find (programmable) read only memories ((P)ROMs), programmable logic arrays (PLAs), field programmable gate arrays (FPGAs), application specific integrated circuits (ASICs), and full custom-designed integrated circuits.

ASICs offer the designer the support of libraries of components that might include logic gates, counters, arithmetic parts, and storage elements. These preexisting modules enable the designer to complete a new design very quickly. In addition to the supporting libraries, the component vendor will offer both *synthesis* and *place and route* tools to aid in the development process. A full custom-integrated circuit is going to be faster and denser than either the ASIC or PLD; however. the development cycle can be substantially longer.

synthesis, place and route

In this chapter, we will provide an introduction to programmable logic devices. Detailed design information is better found in the data sheets and application notes from the various device manufacturers. We will open with a brief discussion motivating the use of programmable logic devices in embedded systems and then examine the underlying logical concepts that have led to the development and widespread use of programmable logic devices (PLDs). We will next move to the basic building blocks of PLDs and show how these can be configured into useful tools. We will then look at the commonly used technologies for implementing programmable devices and how they are able to store information. We will present the basic structure of the devices, variations on I/O configurations, and the fundamental architectures for the CPLD and the FPGA, and then compare and contrast these architectures.

CPLD, Gate Array, Programmable System on a Chip

Next, we will introduce and study two of the more commonly used components: the *CPLD* and the *Gate Array*, as well as a more general-purpose device called a *Programmable System on a Chip*. We will conclude with a look at several applications.

19.1 WHY USE PROGRAMMABLE LOGIC DEVICES?

programmable logic device

Programmable logic device is a generic term that covers all subfamilies of programmable logic. Unfortunately, it also refers to a particular architecture. Hopefully, the discussion context will permit the reader to recognize when the term is being used in a general or a specific sense.

We utilize the devices in our designs because generally, they are faster, consume less power, and can support significantly more functionality in a much smaller package than SSI and MSI logics. There certainly will be far less work involved in the layout of system printed circuit boards. The design can be specified by a text file rather than on multiple pages of schematics. Certainly, some may consider this to be a disadvantage. A PLD-based design also facilitates the reuse core elements, thereby helping to get a new design to the market more quickly.

In the introductory chapter in this text, we observed that the contemporary world of embedded systems is expanding at an incredible pace. The systems in which our designs are embedded are growing smaller and smaller at probably the same or faster pace. Today, a programmable logic device can easily replace thousands of SSI and MSI gates and almost as many storage devices. A portable music player or cellular telephone implemented with an equivalent number of SSI devices would be enormous. Certainly, the reduction in size of our products alone would be reason enough for using these devices.

Today, PLDs can be programmed to incorporate several CPU cores. Now, in addition to the computing power of the main system processor, we can bring several support processors to bear on special portions of the application. We learned earlier that in a multitasking system we divide a problem into multiple cooperating tasks that appear to be running simultaneously. With multiple core PLDs, we can begin to achieve true multiprocessing both easily and economically. We can inexpensively offload some of the special-purpose tasks to the peripheral processor(s).

When we studied the design process, we learned that embedded systems are a mixture of hardware and software pieces. The developing field of co-design addresses the challenge of mapping a functional design onto the hardware and software components that make up the architecture of the system. With certain PLDs, the distinction between hardware and software is becoming increasingly fuzzy; we find that programmable logic devices can be dynamically reconfigured to accommodate or adapt to the problem being solved. Such capabilities give us, as engineers, much greater flexibility in developing our designs.

As our systems grow smaller in physical size, they are growing correspondingly larger in capabilities and complexity. To implement those capabilities, we turn to more sophisticated designs. We are putting an increasingly larger amount of circuitry into the same package. Several years ago, after we drew the logic diagram for our system, we built a breadboard of a prototype system. Although we had confidence in our designs, only the most exceptional among us knew that their prototype would work, the first time, as the theory had suggested. The problem was compounded by the physical realities of the real world. The parasitic effects on a 12- to 18-inch square breadboard are substantially different from those found on a production printed circuit board of the same circuit. As we learned in our earlier studies of parasitic effects, the associated problems become worse as the geometries get smaller. The problem is exacerbated as the operating frequency of today's designs continues to increase. A hardware-based breadboard cannot accurately reflect the true behavior of the design in the final product. PLD manufacturers have taken many of these issues into consideration with the architecture and designs of today's devices. In addition, they provide tools to aid in the analysis and solution of these problems.

Today much of our design can be implemented using programmable logic devices and are usually developed using Verilog, VHDL, or some other hardware design language (HDL). Designing using an HDL significantly simplifies the development process in comparison to a hardware-based breadboard approach. Because the development path entails significant modeling of the design and then repeated simulation and test (including real-world effects) of that model, by the time that the design is programmed into the PLD, the probability of it working properly the first time has been greatly increased. With a breadboard implementation of a circuit prototype, correcting any design errors can entail several days of rewiring (think about reprogramming the early computers). With the PLD and an HDL implementation of the design, the same modifications can be completed in substantially less time (programming in a high-level language beats requiring any day).

These last few paragraphs have summarized many of the reasons for utilizing PLDs as a design tool in our systems. In the sections ahead, we will examine these devices in greater detail.

19.2 BASIC CONCEPTS

The underlying strength of the PLD is its ability to represent combinational logic in a sum of products form, to build circuits as combinations of these (reduced) minterms, and to store (and utilize) the outputs of the combinational nets. They are typically configured as two-level AND-OR devices. The variables from which the logical equations can be built are available in true and negated form. The product terms are simply the logical AND of the variables, and the sum terms are built as the logical OR of the AND expressions.

The architecture of such a system is not difficult to visualize. It is made up of a uniform network of interconnections and set of variables to produce the desired logical expressions.

Consider the simple layout in Figure 19.0. Observe that we have the asserted and negated forms of each input variable. Each AND gate has available for input the true and negated form of each variable, and each OR gate has the output of each AND gate available as an input. In combination, we have an AND array followed by an OR array.

For the configuration above, with two input variables, call them A and B, we have four possible minterms:

$$\overline{A}\,\overline{B},\ \overline{A}\,B,\ A\,\overline{B},\ A\,B$$

and with the specified three outputs, we can express up to three different sums of product logic expressions based on which connections we choose to make (or break). In some

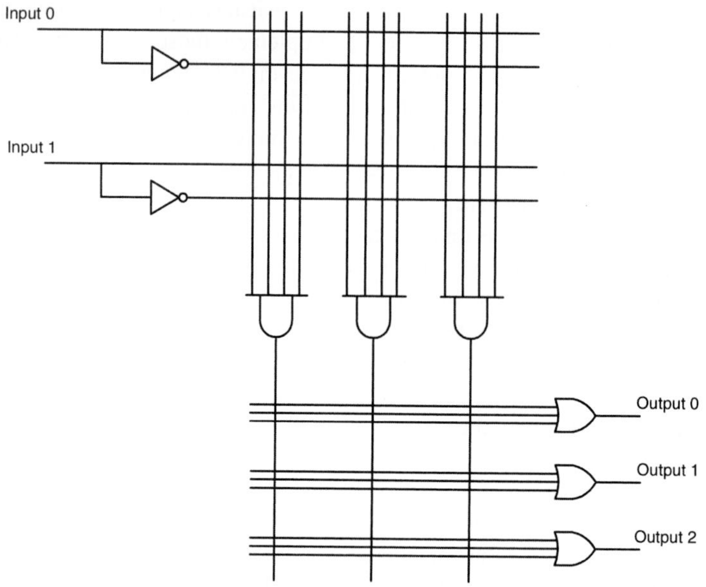

Figure 19.0 A Simple Combinational Logic Array

implementations, all of the connections are present (in others, they are absent). To implement a logic equation, we simply remove (or make) some of the connections.

EXAMPLE 19.0

Using the above device, we can implement the logical equation,

$$F = A\,\overline{B} + \overline{A}\,B$$

First AND

Make the A and $\overline{B}$ connections—these are indicated by small circles.

Second AND

Make the $\overline{A}$ and B connections—these are indicated by small circles.

First OR

Make connections to the first two legs and no connection to the third leg.

We can see that we have an AND array and an OR array as the final implementation in Figure 19.1.

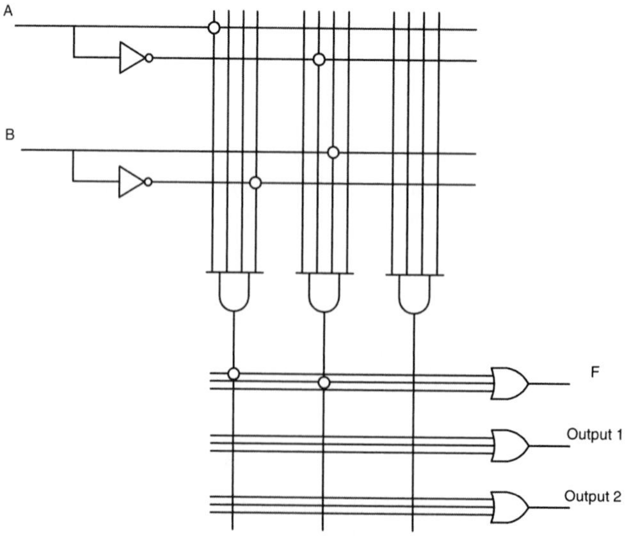

Figure 19.1 Implementing an Exclusive OR

Utilizing such an architecture, we can realize any sum of products expression. The only restriction we have is the size of the device, that is, the number of input and output pins and the number of product terms available.

To enhance both their usefulness and their flexibility, programmable logic devices are designed with a variety of output configurations. Typically, these include the standard unidirectional combinational output. This configuration may be extended to support bidirectional input and output (which may also be programmable) as well as tristate control. These outputs may also be invertible through a programmable XOR path. Latched or registered outputs support basic storage and permit the design and implementation of sequential logics. These are illustrated in the circuit fragments in the following figures.

Figure 19.2a depicts an input driver supporting the true and negated states of a signal. Figure 19.2b shows the tristate output driver, the state of that output being fed back into the array, and the bipolar input signal.

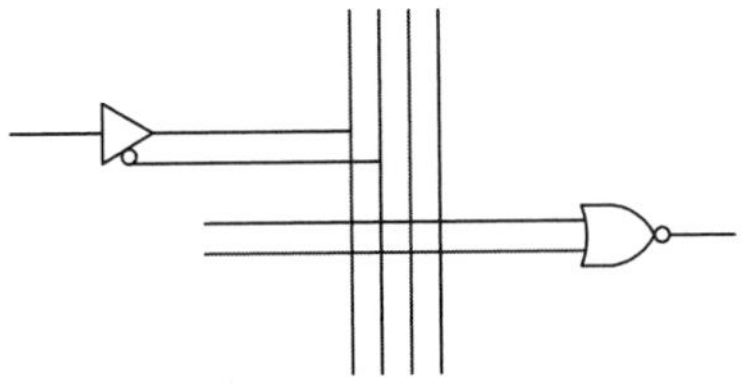

Figure 19.2a Input Driver with True and Negated States

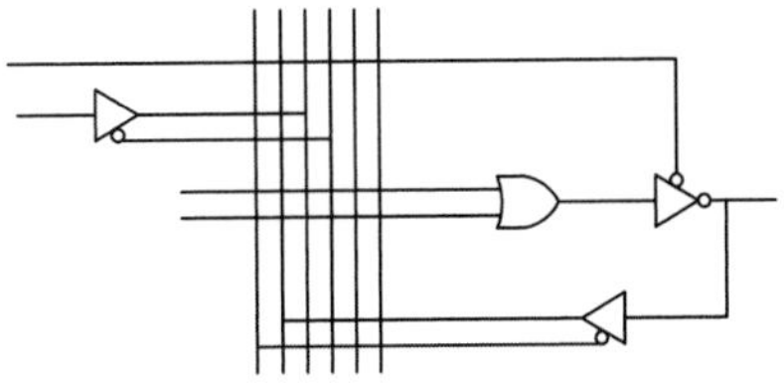

Figure 19.2b Output Driver with Tristate Output and Feedback into the Logic Array

The latched or registered tristate output is shown in Figure 19.3. The output of the storage element is fed back into the array from the $\overline{Q}$ output using a bipolar driver. Such an approach balances the loading on the outputs of the storage element. The polarity of the input to the storage element is controlled through the XOR device on the D input. The polarity of the output signal is controlled by selecting the state of the input signal.

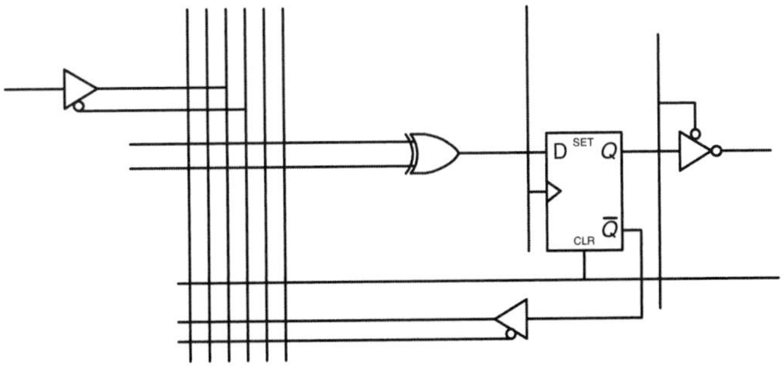

Figure 19.3 Simple Registered Output Configuration

The architecture of the device may require that all storage devices use the same clock and the same reset or clear signal. In the simpler devices, typically both the clock and the clear signal originate from outside the PLD device. More complex devices may also support a selection of internal or external clocking and reset sources.

19.3 BASIC CONFIGURATIONS

The core elements of programmable logics are found in four basic configurations:

- (P)ROM—(Programmable) Read Only Memory
- PAL—Programmable Array Logic
- PLA—Programmable Logic Array
- PLS—Programmable Logic Sequencer

19.3.1 The (P)ROM

The (programmable) read only memory device (P)ROM is the most general and flexible. All combinations of the input bits are programmable.

EXAMPLE 19.1

To use a ROM or PROM to implement the following logical expression,

$$F = \sum(2, 11, 12)$$

we need a 16 x 1 bit memory. Four address lines will enable each memory bit to be uniquely addressed. The equation is implemented by storing a logical 1 in addresses 2, 11, and 12 while storing a logical 0 in all remaining.

The device will have a logical 1 as an output only when those addresses (or minterms) appear on the device inputs. Each product term corresponds to 1 address.

A (P)ROM-based solution is generally appropriate only when a large number of product terms are required.

19.3.2 Programmable Array Logic—PAL

In the PAL or Programmable Array Logic device, the AND portion of the device is programmable and the OR portion is fixed. Such an architecture limits the number of product terms in the sum. Furthermore, the product terms are not reusable and must be duplicated if required. The implementation uses a fixed OR array. The output of each product term can be connected to only one OR gate. Typically, the device supports bidirectional I/O pins and tristate outputs with individual enables.

The structure of the device is shown in Figure 19.4. In the diagram, though drawn as only a single input to each device in the arrays, each supports multiple inputs. The open circles illustrate the programmable links.

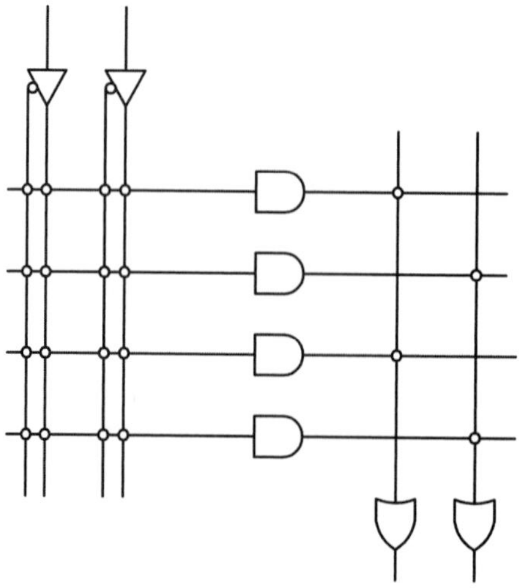

Figure 19.4 Basic Programmable Logic Array

19.3.3 Programmable Logic Array—PLA

In contrast to the PAL, in the PLA as shown in Figure 19.5, both the AND and the OR portions of the device are programmable. Consequently, the product terms are reusable.

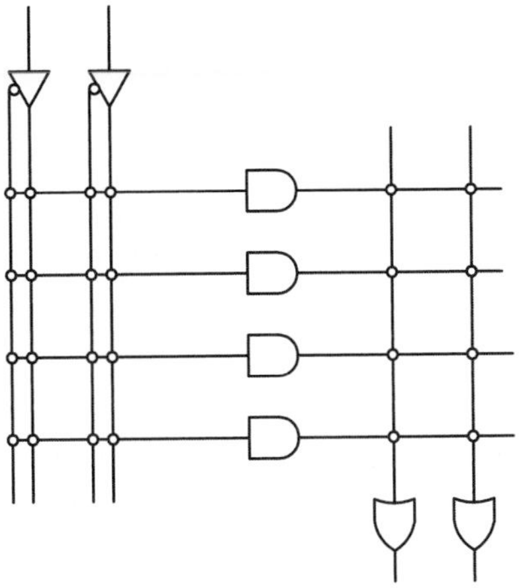

Figure 19.5 Basic Programmable Logic Array

19.3.4 Programmable Logic Sequencer—PLS

The programmable logic sequencer, which is also referred to as a registered device, is simply a PLA plus flip-flop storage elements. In most designs, the outputs of the storage elements are fed back to the logic array to support finite-state machine design. For these devices, both the AND and OR arrays are programmable. Once again, the product terms are reusable. A fragment of such a device is shown in Figure 19.6.

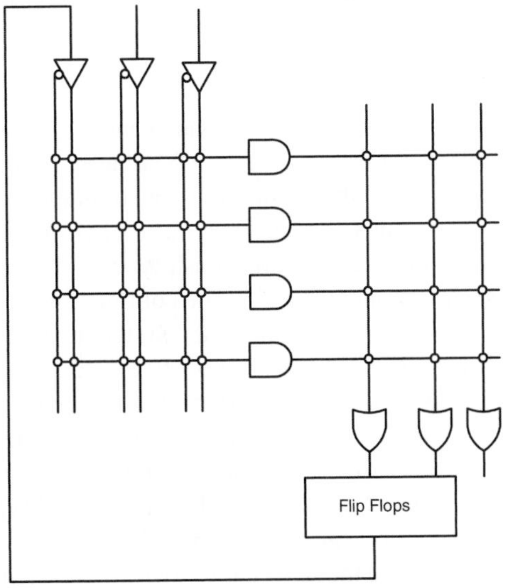

Figure 19.6 Basic Programmable Logic Sequencer

19.3.5 PLA vs. PAL vs. (P)ROM

A PAL is the opposite of a PROM. We can view the PROM as an AND-OR array with a fixed AND array and with all 2^n AND possibilities available. If a design needs a large number of AND combinations, the PROM is a good option. Some example applications include lookup tables, high-speed mathematics, or code translations.

If the design requires only a few AND combinations and not many of those are shared between outputs, the PAL with the fixed OR array is a good choice. If complete flexibility is necessary, the PLA with its programmable AND and OR arrays is more appropriate.

19.4 PROGRAMMABLE AND REPROGRAMMABLE TECHNOLOGIES

Programmable logic devices fall into two major categories: programmable and reprogrammable. Those in the first category can be programmed one time and those in the second multiple times.

19.4.1 Programmable Technologies

Devices that are one-time programmable are either built to order by the manufacturer of the device or utilize a technology that will permit the designer to enter the desired configuration one time. Devices built by a vendor mirror the technologies studied earlier for implementing ROM-type devices. Transistors are selectively included to produce the desired behavior.

antifuse

Devices that can be programmed once, in the field, are often based on a technology called the *antifuse*. In traditional electronics, a fuse is utilized in a circuit to protect against potentially damaging high currents by opening a conducting path when necessary. The antifuse is designed to do the opposite. When a sufficiently high voltage is applied across an amorphous silicon link between two metal conductors, a metal-crystalline alloy is formed to complete the conducting path. The newly formed conducting path(s) enable the interconnection of generic blocks of primitive logic components to form more complex logic circuits. Once the low-resistance path is formed, the process is irreversible.

19.4.2 Reprogrammable Technologies

Today's (re)programmable logic devices are generally either SRAM based or use variations on programmable ROM technologies. SRAM-based architectures are built around volatile Read/Write memory cells that control the state of intradevice connections. The device configuration and interconnection information are held in a companion nonvolatile storage medium such as a PROM or similar flash type of external boot device. One significant advantage of such an approach is that the configuration of the device can be dynamically changed at runtime, thereby permitting the system to adapt to the problem at hand.

floating gate

Programmable ROM technologies fall into three broad categories: EPROM, EEPROM, and FLASH. All of these devices are built on what are known as *floating gate* technologies. To introduce the concept, we will begin with the memory fragment in Figure 19.7, which gives a high-level view of a portion of a programmable AND array.

Each column in the AND array implements a NOR type AND, that is, an AND of low true signals. All transistors on a column must be OFF for the output to be logical 1. Each N type transistor comprising the AND has two gates. One of the gates is floating, that is, unconnected, and is surrounded by high-impedance insulating material as shown in Figure 19.8.

Initially, the floating gate has no charge on it and thus has no effect on circuit operation. All transistors are effectively connected. When a positive voltage is applied to the nonfloating gate, the transistor turns ON, and the output of the associated AND is logical 0.

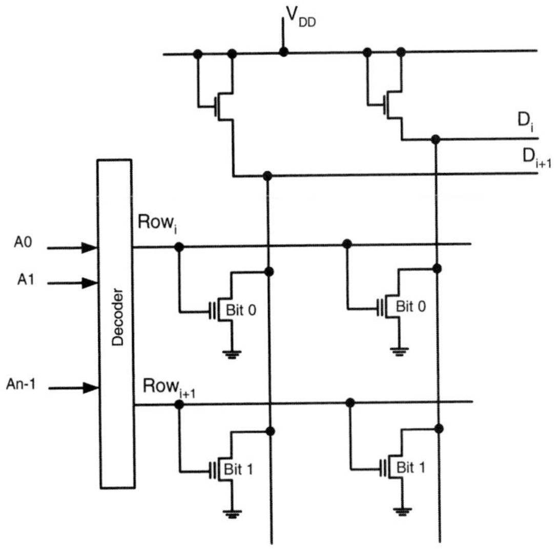

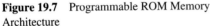

Figure 19.7 Programmable ROM Memory Architecture

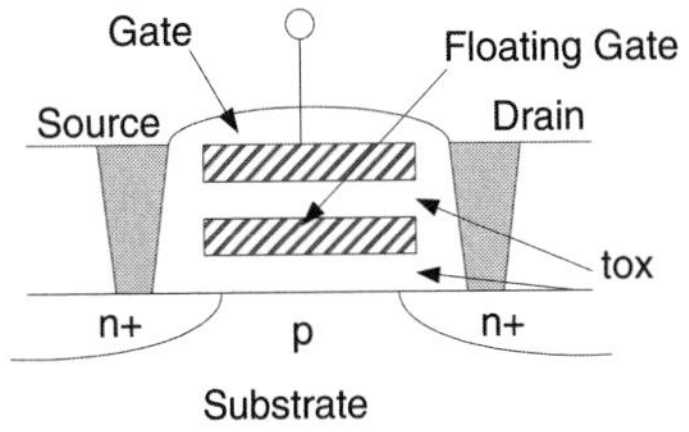

Figure 19.8 Dual Gate Programmable Memory Device

To program the device, a high voltage is applied to each location where a link is not wanted, as shown in the first diagram in Figure 19.9. Through avalanche injection, a negative charge collects on the floating gate. When the programming voltage is removed, a number of electrons are trapped on the floating gate as shown in the second graphic. The trapped electrons cause an increase in the threshold voltage of the transistor to approximately 7.0 V, which thereby prevents the transistor from turning ON when a normal logical 1 is applied to the nonfloating gate as illustrated in the final drawing. The transistor is effectively disconnected from the circuit. Tests have shown that the charge can be retained for up to 10 years.

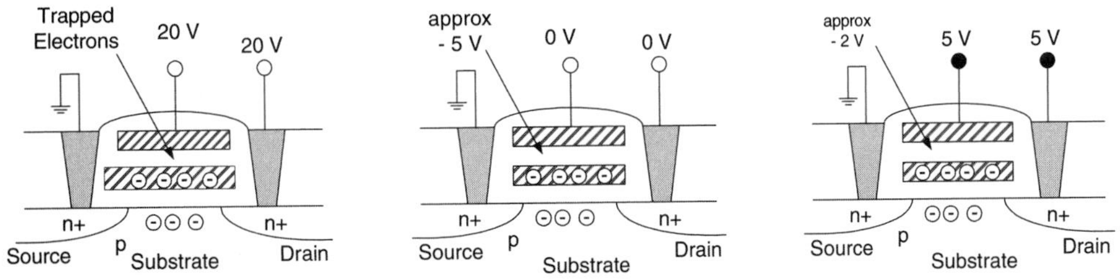

Figure 19.9 Programming a Dual Gate Programmable Memory Cell

In the early years, an ultraviolet light was used to erase the device. Under the ultraviolet light, the floating gate becomes slightly conductive. Charges trapped during programming are given enough energy to leak away. Such devices are known as EPROMs—erasable PROMs.

Today's devices are significantly improved from the early designs. The floating gate is surrounded by an ultra-thin insulating layer. Rather than using an avalanche injection scheme, charge is placed onto the floating gate using tunneling physics. The devices are also

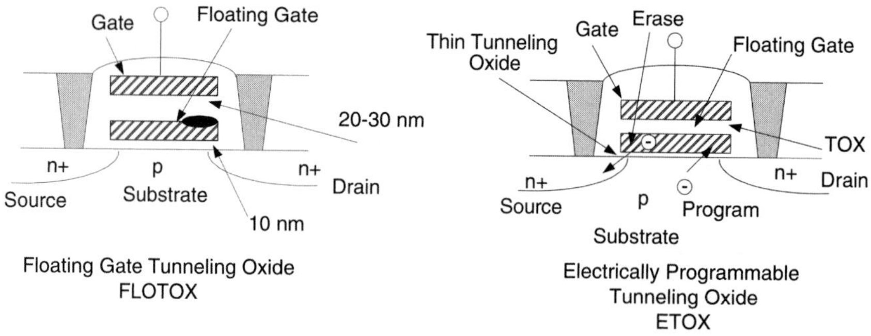

Figure 19.10 Electrically Erasable Dual Gate Programmable Memory Cells

electrically erasable. The device can be erased by applying a voltage of opposite polarity to the charging voltage on the nonfloating gate. Thus, we can use the same equipment as was used to program the device. A cross-sectional diagram of two contemporary types of programmable device are given in Figure 19.10. The diagram on the left illustrates what is called the electrically erasable device, EEPROM. That on the right is known as FLASH technology.

19.5 ARCHITECTURES

Independent of whether the programmable logic device appears as a PLD, CPLD, or FPGA, the architecture of the device comprises blocks of combinational logic and/or storage elements, the Input/Output logic, and the interconnections between these blocks of functionality. The size (or grain) and flexibility of the logic blocks and the speed and generality of the interconnection net determine the power and capabilities of the device.

The PLD and CPLD devices tend to be coarser grained. The building blocks are generally referred to as macrocells. They can be viewed as the programmable logic equivalent of MSI logic blocks. In contrast, the FPGA devices are usually finer grained with a very rich interconnection topology. The building blocks, often built as lookup tables (referred to as LUTs), tend to be the SSI logic equivalent.

Today, the devices range in capability from simple encoding or decoding networks to the ability to implement a full CPU core (refer back to Chapter 1) with accompanying peripheral devices. We will examine the architecture of these devices in greater detail beginning with the PLD.

19.5.1 PLDs

The simplest devices are known as PLDs, or programmable logic devices (distinguished from the general use of the term to describe the complete class of programmable devices). The basic devices are intended to replace collections of combinational logic circuitry implemented using SSI and MSI components. The devices are implemented as the AND array–OR array pair discussed earlier.

generic array logic

Lattice Semiconductor provided an early implementation of such a device called a *generic array logic,* or GAL16V8™ device. The GAL ™ supports 16 inputs and 8 outputs that are configured as 10 input only, 2 output only, and 6 that are bidirectional. Each output can accept up to seven product terms; each product term can have up to 32 inputs. The circuit fragment in Figure 19.11 illustrates an input and the two different output configurations. The programmable exclusive OR gate provides the ability to invert the sense of the output signal.

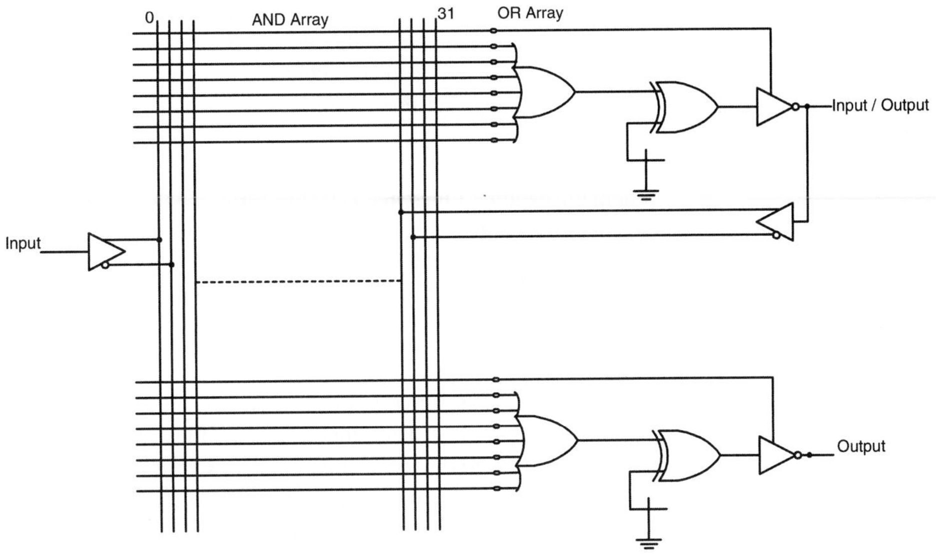

Figure 19.11 Output Configurations for a GAL 16V8 PLD

With the addition of storage devices, the capability of the GAL16V8™ is extended as the GAL22V10™ to support the design and implementation of basic sequential digital circuits. The device incorporates 10 D-type flip-flops with common clock and asynchronous reset and individual synchronous preset into a structure called a *macrocell*. Each macrocell can be configured as registered or nonregistered. Output product term support is organized in pairs: two support 8 product terms, two support 10, and so on, up to a maximum of 16.

macrocell

The circuit fragment in Figure 19.12 illustrates typical unregistered and registered output macrocells.

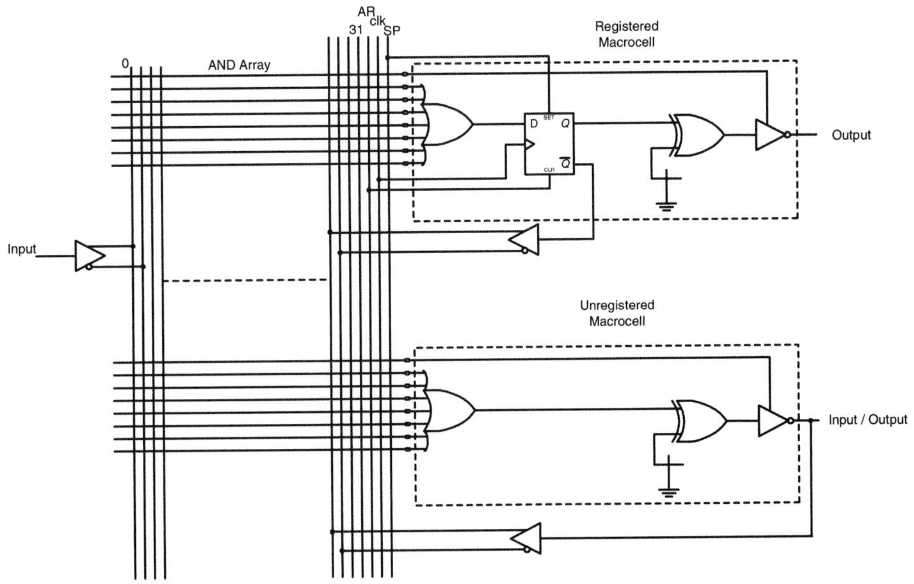

Figure 19.12 Registered and Unregistered Output Configurations for a GAL 22V10 PLD

The macrocell building block concept forms the basis on which the larger and more sophisticated CPLDs are built. The AND-OR array provides a fully interconnected mesh within the macrocell. Full interconnectivity means that any macrocell can communicate directly with any other macrocell.

Logic designs are developed either textually using any of a number of standard or proprietary hardware design languages (HDL) such as Verilog, VHDL, or ABEL or through schematic capture. Once in electronic form, the design can be synthesized (using a tool that is similar to, yet different from, a software compiler) into a form that is compatible with the tool used to program the device.

19.5.2 CPLD

The Complex Programmable Logic Device (CPLD) provides significantly greater capability than the basic PLD. The functionality of these devices ranges from what is found in the more powerful MSI devices to that in the low ends of the LSI units. The general architecture comprises a collection of logic blocks and an interconnection net. Each logic block contains an AND/OR array and a number of macrocells. The basic structure, shown in Figure 19.13, illustrates a device with six logic blocks, each containing eight macrocells.

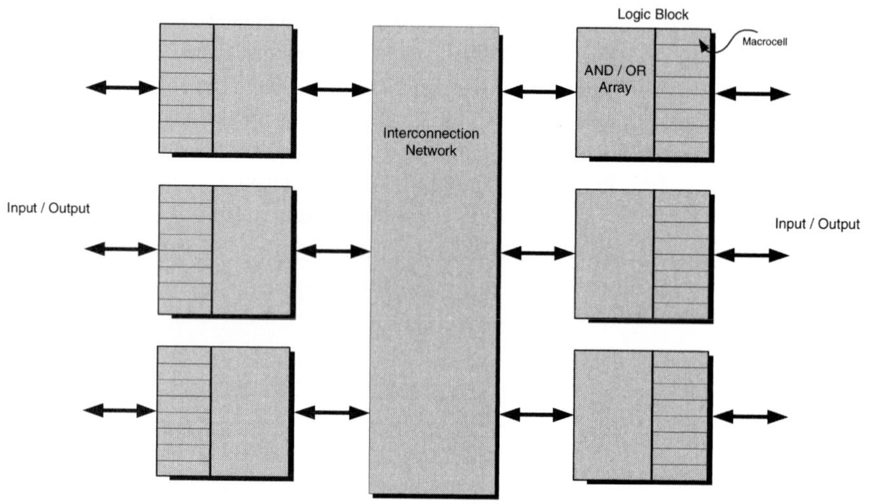

Figure 19.13 Basic Architecture for a CPLD

In addition to providing the means to route information from one logic block to another, the interconnection net will often contain a global system clock and signals supporting global set and reset controls for any sequential logic or memory elements.

Signal routing between logic blocks within the interconnection net will be supported on several different levels. In some cases, full interconnectivity is not supported. Some logic blocks may not be able to directly (or indirectly) exchange information with every other logic block. In other cases, the interconnectivity is qualified. Qualification includes direct connection to a limited subset of the logic blocks or connection to another block via routing through one or two other blocks along the path. Such routing restrictions may preclude fully utilizing all of the logic blocks or macrocells available in the device.

Each logic block will contain a number of macrocells. Depending on the vendor and the design of the part, within each logic block there will be a local interconnection mesh. When the source and destination of a transfer are within the same block, the rate of exchange can be significantly faster than between logic blocks.

Each macrocell will contain a rich and flexible set of logic functionality supporting both combinational and storage capability. Storage, which can be selectively bypassed, is generally implemented as either a D- or T-type flip-flop. The input to the flip-flop can be selected from a number of different sources either internal to the macrocell or from without. The flip-flop clock may be a global clock or built from product terms in the logic array.

Inputs, Outputs

The macrocell *Inputs* and *Outputs* can include a variety of selectable capabilities. From above, an output signal may originate from either the storage element or a combinational term from the AND/OR array. In what may seem unusual in today's world of increasing logic speeds, some devices support the capability to slow signal rise and fall times. A little reflection on the fact that rapidly changing voltages or currents coupled with the pandemic parasitic inductors and capacitors in our circuits are a significant source of noise explains the oddity.

Tristate capability on I/O lines enables external information to be brought into the logic equations implemented in the macrocells. Because the device may be interfacing with a bus, each I/O line may also include a weak pull-up that can easily be overdriven by an input signal but will define the state of the bus in an undriven or tristate mode.

19.5.3 FPGAs

The Field Programmable Logic Array (FPGA) provides capabilities on a par with the CPLD. As the technologies continue to evolve, the distinctions between the two devices are becoming increasingly blurred. As we saw earlier, the CPLD implements a coarse-grained architecture, built around logic blocks and macrocells. The FPGA utilizes a finer-grained structure based on smaller configurable logic blocks and a rich interconnection scheme. Each logic block in an FPGA is far simpler than that in the CLPD, typically comprising some basic combinational logic implemented via a lookup table, a storage device, and a large amount of internal I/O. The large number of flip-flops in the FPGA and rich interconnect capability make the device much more flexible for the designer of embedded systems than the CPLD.

The FPGA is architected either as a SRAM device or via electrically programmable antifuses. A SRAM-based design gives tremendous flexibility. At power ON, the configuration is downloaded to the device as a serial bit stream from an external PROM. Because it is a soft load, the configuration of the device can be dynamically changed at runtime in response to the type of problem being solved. The configuration of an FPGA utilizing an antifuse-based architecture is irreversibly set when the user of the device programs it.

A representative architecture for each type of device is given in the following figures. Figure 19.14 illustrates a segment of the general structure of a SRAM-based FPGA.

As is seen, the device is organized as an array of interconnected configurable logic blocks. The devices on the periphery of the array connect to I/O blocks. Interconnection is supported by a series of channels over which signals are routed using switch matrices. A portion of a typical switch matrix is implemented as shown in Figure 19.15. In the diagram, a signal on any row can be routed to any column simply by closing the switch at the desired intersection. A signal on any column can be routed to any row in a similar way.

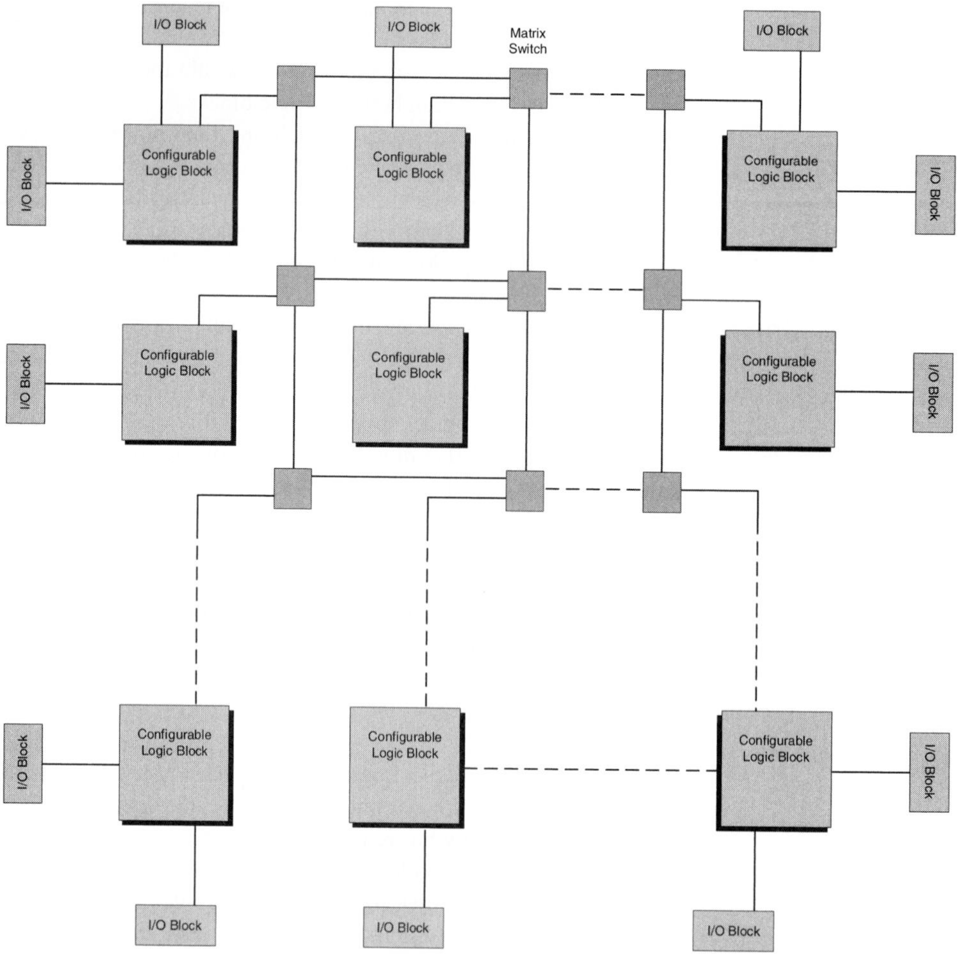

Figure 19.14 Basic Architecture for a SRAM-Based FPGA

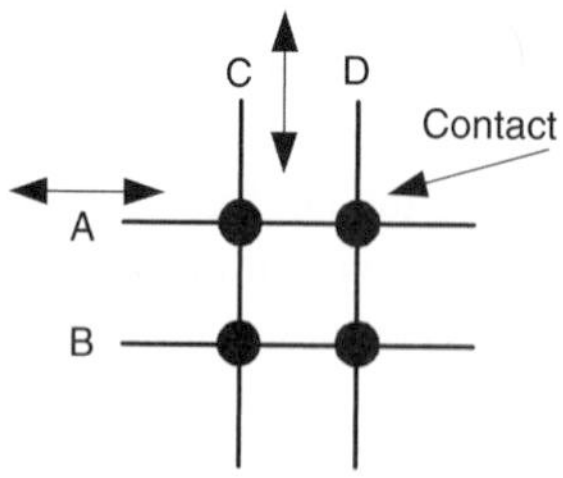

Figure 19.15 Segment of a Matrix Switch

Figure 19.16 shows a portion of an antifuse-based architecture. The device comprises columns or rows of configurable logic blocks separated by an interconnection channel. Connections are made from a logic block signal to a path in the channel by programming the antifuse at the desired connection point to the low-resistance state. The very small size of the antifuses permits the device to support a substantial number of interconnections.

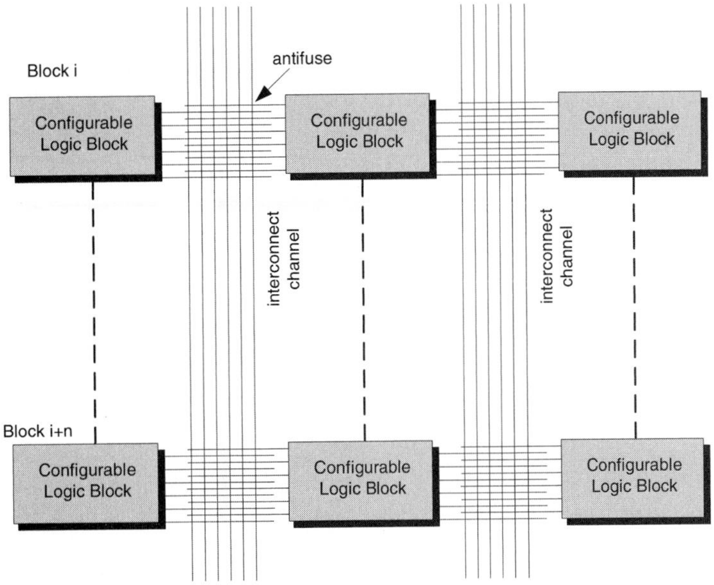

Figure 19.16 Basic Architecture for an Antifuse-Based FPGA

19.6 EXAMPLE PLD DEVICES

Let's now look at several commercially available programmable logic devices that are representative examples of the concepts we have been discussing. While not pushing the limits of the state of the art in programmable logic devices, they are very good choices for many midlevel embedded applications. We will first examine a Xilinx XC9500XL™ CPLD, then an Altera Flex 10K™ FPGA, and finally a Cypress PSOC™ (Programmable System on a Chip) mixed-signal array.

19.6.1 Xilinx XC 9500XL™ Family

The Xilinx XC9500XL™ family comprises four devices of increasing complexity and capability. Considered to be medium density, the devices support from 800 to 6400 usable gates and from 36 to 288 registers. The high-level functional block diagram for the device is given in Figure 19.17.

Function and Input/ Output Blocks

The architecture is based on fully interconnected *Function* and *Input/Output Blocks*; interconnection is accomplished via a switch matrix. Each Function Block has 54 true and complemented inputs, up to 18 outputs, and comprises up to 18 independent macrocells and a logic array. The logic array can be programmed to produce up to 90 product terms; each of the 90 can be allocated to each macrocell.

In addition to the data inputs, each *Function Block* also receives three global clocks, set and reset signals, and either two or four global output enable signals. The *Function Block* outputs and their associated output enable signals are sent to the I/O Block (shown in Figure 19.17 as two separate blocks). The 18 data output signals are also sent to the interconnect switch for routing to other *Function Blocks*.

Function Block

Each macrocell can be individually configured to implement either combinational or registered logic functions. The configuration of the macrocell is controlled by five local product terms derived from the AND array as well as by product terms from other

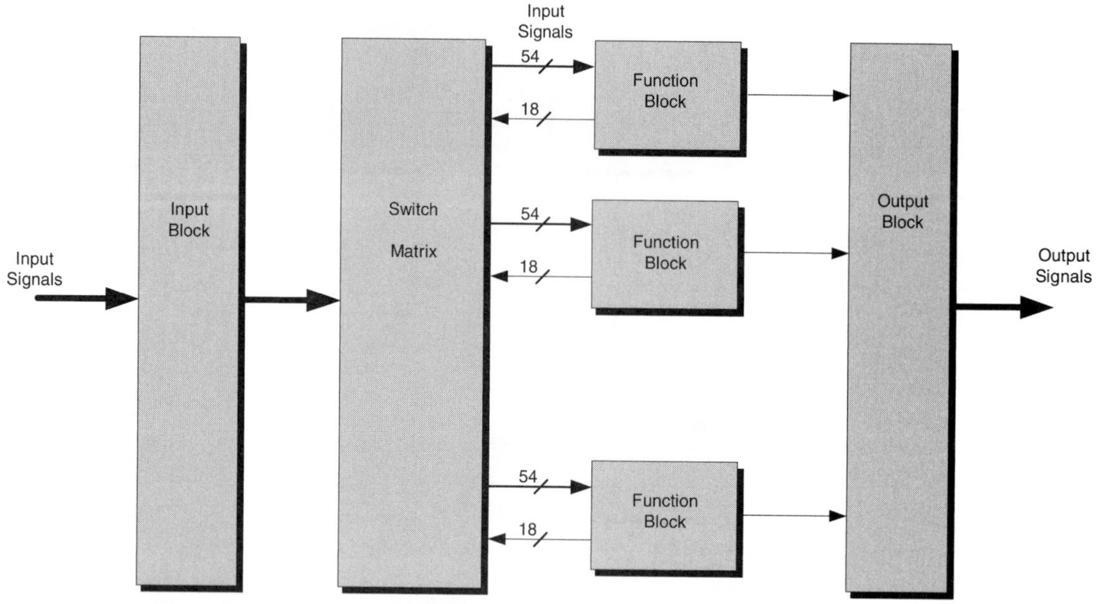

Figure 19.17 High-Level Functional Architecture for a Xilinx XC 9500 XL Family CPLD (Diagram adapted from the Xilinx XC 9500 XL data sheet)

macrocells. The register function implements either a D- or T-type with asynchronous set and reset operations.

The five local product terms provide the following local controls:

- Flip-Flop Set
- Flip-Flop Reset
- Flip-Flop Clock
- Flip-Flop Data Polarity
- Output Enable

These are illustrated in Figure 19.18.

Switch Matrix, Function Blocks, I/O Block

The *Switch Matrix* is used to connect signals to the *Function Block* inputs. As noted earlier, all *Function Block* outputs also drive the switch matrix. The *I/O Block* provides the means by which the internal logic connects to the device I/O pins. The block comprises a set of input and output buffers and the output enable selection. Output enable control can originate from any one of four different sources:

- A product term from the macrocell
- Any of the global OE signals
- Always enabled
- Always disabled

The I/O subsystem also supports programmable slew rate control for noise management and programmable ground pins. Additional ground pins also contribute to noise management by lowering the resistance of the ground path for the chip.

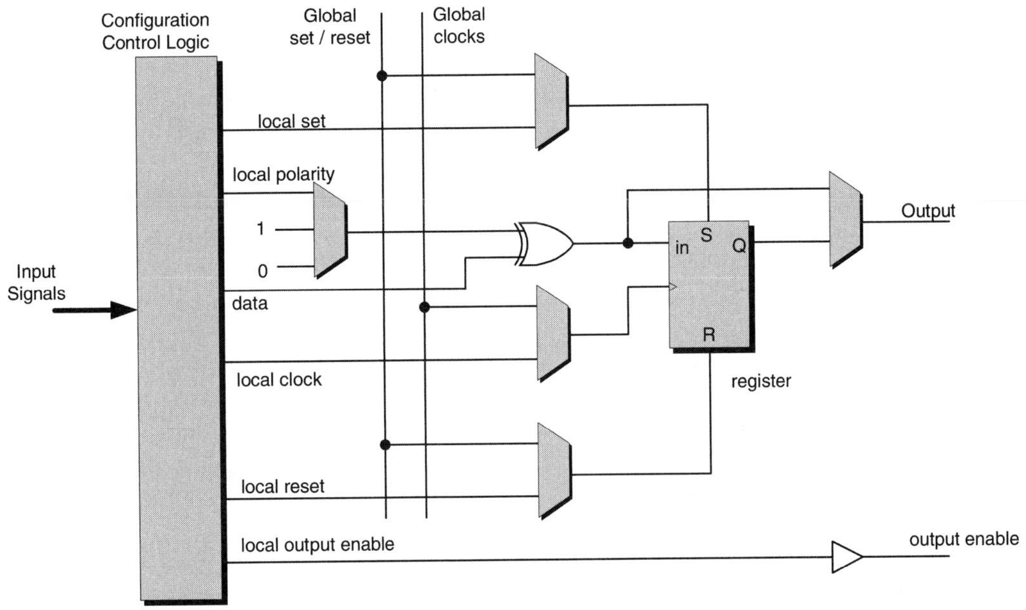

Figure 19.18 Functional Diagram for a Xilinx XC 9500 XL Family CPLD Macrocell (Diagram adapted from the Xilinx XC 9500 XL data sheet)

19.6.2 Altera Flex 10K™ FPGA

The Altera Flex 10K™ is a logic array plus embedded memory based on a high-density CMOS SRAM process. The device family supports up to a maximum of over 300,000 system gates and 41K bits of RAM with Read and Write cycle times of up to 84 MHz and 63 MHz, respectively.

As we have learned in our earlier studies, with the increasing internal and external data rates for devices that we are designing into our systems, coupled with the ever decreasing device geometries (and associated parasitic effects), the problems of clock management are becoming increasingly significant and increasingly challenging. Of particular importance in the Flex 10K is the ability to manage clock delay and/or skew within and across the device and the ability to multiply an input frequency up to provide finer-grained temporal resolution within the device. The Flex 10K supports both of these capabilities through its built-in low skew clock distribution trees and phase lock technologies used to manage clock synchronization across the device and to provide devicewide management of signals in time. Similar to earlier devices that we have discussed, the Flex 10K family supports slew rate control on output signals to help to control system noise. The I/O capability of the family (at close to 500 I/O pins) is on a par with many contemporary high-performance microprocessors. The high-level architecture for the device is given in the diagram in Figure 19.19.

embedded array, logic array

Each device contains two major blocks or subsystems, an *embedded array* that is used to build memory and specialized logic functions, and a *logic array* to implement more general logic.

19.6.2.1 Embedded Array

embedded array blocks

The embedded array comprises a series of *embedded array blocks* (EABs) as shown in Figure 19.20.

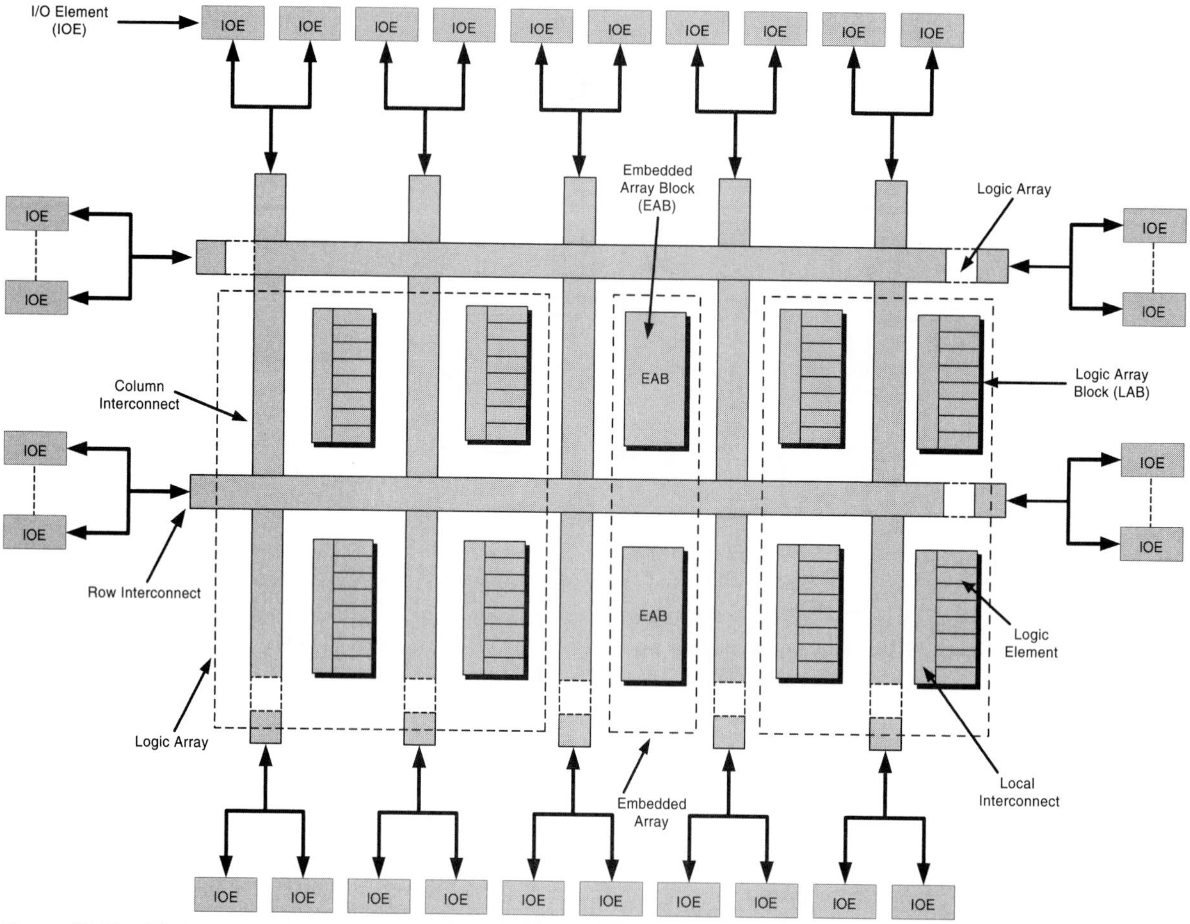

Figure 19.19 High-Level Architecture for an Altera Flex 10K FPGA (Diagram provided courtesy of the Altera Corporation)

memory When the EABs are used to implement *memory*, each provides up to 2 K bits that can be utilized to create ROM, RAM, dual-ported RAM, or FIFO functions. Alternately, when ***logic functions*** used to create *logic functions*, each EAB can implement from 100 to 600 gates that can be utilized to construct such expected logic functions as arithmetic circuits, microcontrollers, sequential circuits, or digital signal processing functions. The EABs can be used either independently or in concert to implement more complex logical functions.

An embedded array block is implemented as a block of RAM with registered input and output ports. In the registered configuration, the device can easily implement the underlying state machines utilized to implement error management in data telecommunication schemes or the computation and control blocks necessary for performing FFT computations.

To implement logic functions, each EAB is programmed with a read only pattern during configuration to create a large lookup table or LUT. As we discussed earlier in this chapter, combinatorial functions can easily be implemented by simply reading the memory at the appropriate address—where the results have been stored. As we learned, the major advantage of such an approach is that the design is much faster than building and propagating signals through a corresponding logic block. The LUT approach enables complex logic functions to be implemented with only a single level of delay, thereby eliminating routing

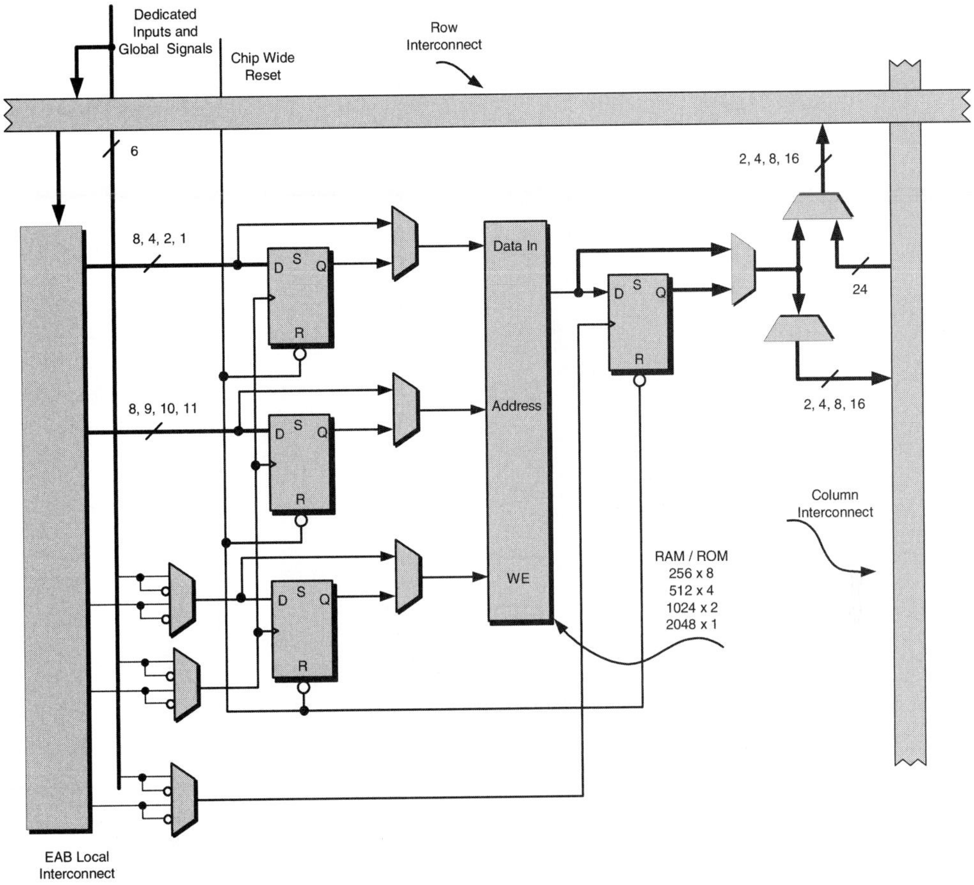

Figure 19.20 Altera Flex 10K FPGA Embedded Array Block (Diagram provided courtesy of the Altera Corporation)

delays inherent in an AND/OR array approach. As an example, using the lookup table approach, one can easily implement a high speed 4 x 4 multiply block.

The EABs can be utilized as a synchronous RAM (SDRAM). The synchronous RAM block in an EAB is self-timed based on a global clock; write signals are thence derived from that clock. Multiple EABs can be combined to produce larger RAM blocks, and all the EABs can be cascaded to form a single RAM block.

19.6.2.2 Logic Array

logic array blocks

The logic array is made up of a series of *logic array blocks* (LABs) as illustrated in Figure 19.21.

logic elements, local interconnect
lookup table
carry, cascade

Each LAB contains eight *logic elements* (LE) and a *local interconnect*. Each logic element contains a four-input *lookup table* (LUT), a programmable flip-flop, and specialized signal paths that support *carry* and *cascade* functionality. The logic elements can be used to create MSI scale logic blocks. Examples might include smaller counters, decoding logic, or simple finite-state machines. Similar to the EABs, multiple LABs can be combined to create larger and more complex logical functions. Each LAB is the equivalent of approximately 96 usable logic gates.

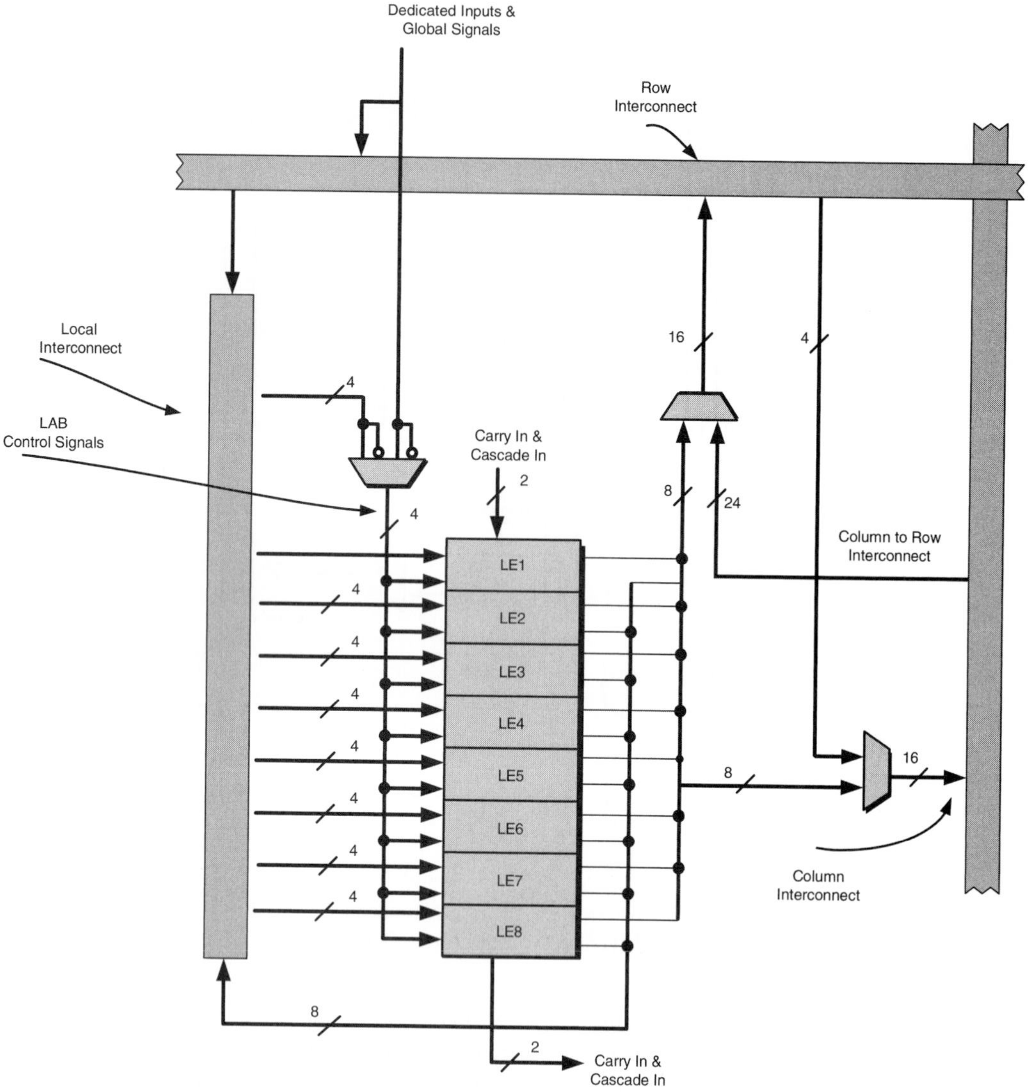

Figure 19.21 Altera Flex 10K FPGA Logic Array Block
(Diagram provided courtesy of the Altera Corporation)

As we saw with the Xilinx XC 9500XL™ family, each LAB provides four local control signals for configuring LAB functionality. Each supports programmable inversion; two of the control signals can be used as clocks and two can be used as clear/preset control for the local flip-flop. The clock source can originate either from a dedicated clock input pin or from the global clock.

logic element

The *logic element* is the smallest unit of logic in the device. Each contains a four-input lookup table and thus can compute any function of four variables. The local flip-flop can be configured as a D, T, JK, or SR-type device; each supports clock, clear, and preset. The clock source can originate either from a dedicated clock input pin or from the global clock. Similar to the XC 9500XL™ CPLD devices, the Preset/Clear can come from a global signal, an I/O signal, or a locally generated signal.

To support high-speed logical operations involving multiple adjacent logic elements, the device incorporates two dedicated data paths, a carry chain, and a cascade chain. These bypass the local interconnect net with its attendant delays.

FastTrack Interconnect

Each logic element provides two independently controlled outputs; one drives the local interconnect net, and the other drives either the row or column *FastTrack Interconnect.*

19.6.3 Input/Output and Internal Interconnection

FastTrack Interconnect

IOE

As Figure 19.19 illustrates, internal to the device, interconnection to and from the input and output device pins is achieved via a series of row and column channels, called *FastTrack Interconnect*, that run the length and width of the device. At the end of each row and column is an I/O element—*IOE.* A portion of the IOE is illustrated in Figure 19.22; observe that the I/O element contains a bidirectional buffer and flip-flop that can be used to provide general-purpose input output or as a bidirectional register.

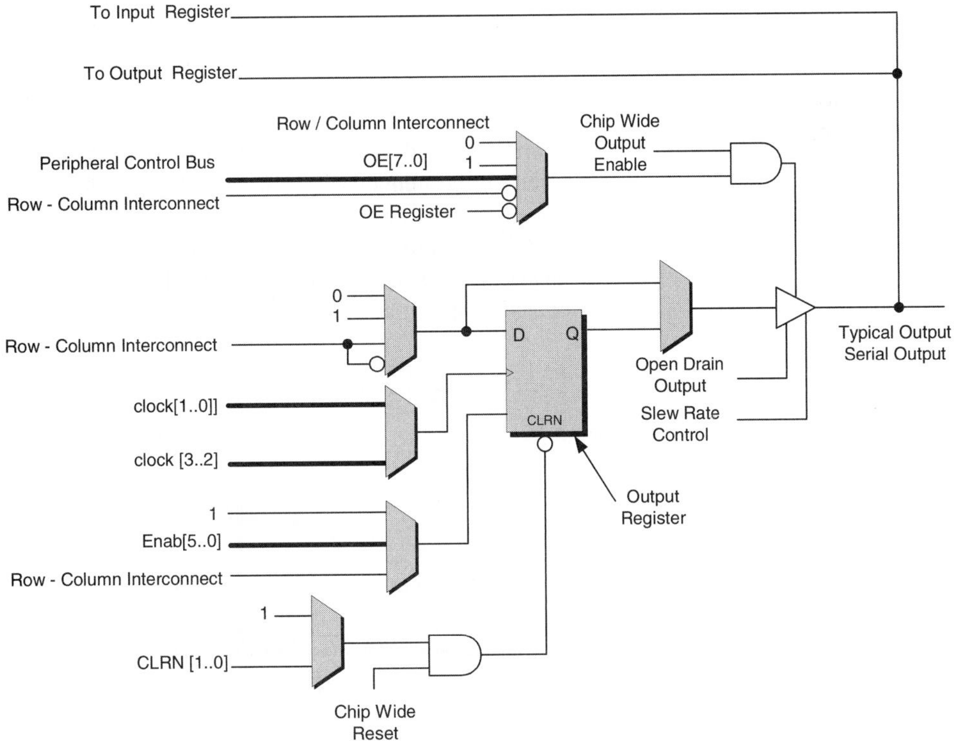

Figure 19.22 Altera Flex 10K FPGA I/O Element (Diagram provided courtesy of the Altera Corporation)

When configured into the registered mode and utilizing a dedicated clock, the input setup time, τ_{su}, can be as low as 3.7 ns with τ_{hold}, the hold time, at 0 ns. In the registered output mode, the propagation delays, τ_{HL} or τ_{LH}, from the clock are specified as 5.3 ns.

FastTrack Interconnect

The *FastTrack Interconnect* architecture provides connections between the logic elements (LE) and the device I/O pins. The signal path is implemented as a series of horizontal and vertical routing channels. Each row is served by a dedicated row interconnect that can drive I/O pins and feed other LABs. Each column interconnect routes signals between rows and can drive the I/O pins.

The I/O Element (IOE) implements a bidirectional I/O buffer and register. Similar to designs discussed earlier, each IOE selects clock, clear, clock enable, and output enable controls from an internal network called a *peripheral control bus.* The bus uses high-speed drivers so as to minimize signal skew across devices. The peripheral control signals can be allocated as

peripheral control bus

- Output enable signals
- Clock enable signals
- Clock signals
- Clear signals

19.6.4 Cypress CY8C21x23 PSOC™

In Chapter 1, we introduced the microprocessor, microcomputer, and microcontroller. We observed that in today's embedded systems, in addition to the core microprocessor, the design frequently includes a mix of analog and digital peripheral devices such as A/D or D/A converters, timers, or communications channels. The CPLD and FPGA devices that we have discussed in the previous two sections are strictly digital. They have grown to become essential components in the many contemporary designs. Although their role is becoming increasingly important today, they are still ancillary to the core design. Cypress Semiconductor, with their Programmable System on a Chip (PSOC) family, is taking a step toward offering a more general purpose solution.

The PSOC™ is built around a CPU core and then adds a digital, an analog, and resources subsystem as we see in Figure 19.23. The analog and digital blocks, I/O, and the system bus are all configurable.

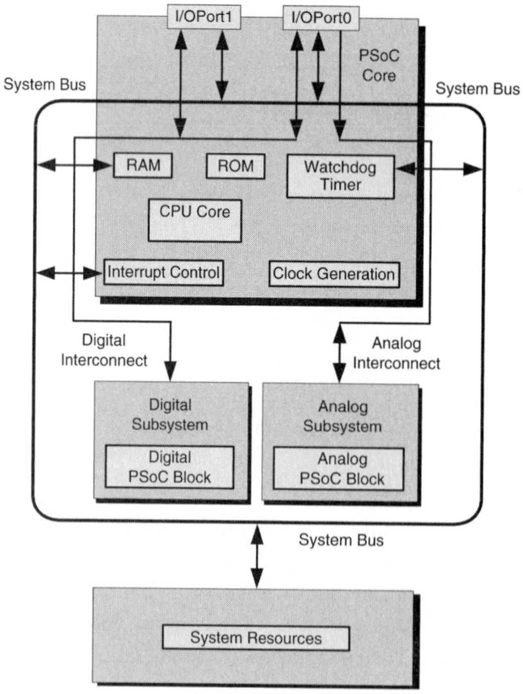

Figure 19.23 Functional Architecture for a Cypress CY8C21x23 Family PSoC (Diagram provided courtesy of Cypress semiconductor)

The CPU Core

The CPU core is built around an 8-bit Harvard architecture. Driven from a clock source of up to 24 MHz, the CPU performs at the four MIPS (million instructions per second) level. Supporting the CPU core are a Flash ROM for program store and an SRAM for data store. Completing the core is an interrupt controller, a sleep and watchdog timer, and clock source module. The components within the CPU core are connected to each other and to the system resources via a system bus.

The Digital Subsystem

Digital Subsystem

The *Digital Subsystem* is built around an array of four digital blocks. Each block is an 8-bit configurable resource that can be combined with other blocks, as we saw with the logic elements in the Altera Flex 10 FPGA, into more complex peripheral devices. Typical examples include:

Timing Peripherals
- Counters
- Timers
- PWMs

Telecommunications Devices
- UART
- SPI Master and Slave

Shift Register Based Devices
- CRC Generator/Checker
- PN Sequence Generation

Digital Interconnect Bus

Components within the *Digital Subsystem* are connected to each other and to any of the I/O ports through a *Digital Interconnect Bus*.

The Analog Subsystem

Analog Subsystem

Similar to the *Digital Subsystem*, the *Analog Subsystem* is built around four analog blocks. These blocks can be configured into a variety of different devices such as

Analog-to-Digital Conversion
- Single 8-bit Conversion
- Dual 8-bit Conversion

Comparison Devices
- Single-ended Comparison with Absolute Reference
- Single-ended Comparison with DAC Reference

Analog Interconnect Bus

Using a configuration scheme similar to that in the *Digital Subsystem*, the *Analog Subsystem* components are connected to each other and to any of the I/O ports through an *Analog Interconnect Bus*.

The System Resources

System Resources

In addition to the capabilities provided by the Analog and Digital Subsystems, the device provides further capabilities grouped as *System Resources*. These are accessed via the system bus. Among the capabilities supported by the block are

Digital

- Clock Dividers supporting three different frequencies
- I^2C Master, Multimaster, and Slave

Analog

- Low-Voltage Detection Interrupts and Power on Reset Support
- Fixed Voltage Reference
- Switch Mode Pump

19.7 THE DESIGN PROCESS

The design process for PLD-based systems differs little from what we have already discussed in earlier chapters. The development cycle is governed by the same cautions and precautions. As we learned earlier, the embedded system development cycle begins with identifying the requirements. For PLD-based designs, we are, more often than not, the customer. Thus, we know the requirements. These requirements need to be documented nonetheless. From the requirements, we write a formal design specification, quantifying all of the signals and all of the constraints with which we must deal. Our requirements and design specifications for the PLD naturally derive from those of the larger enclosing system.

A PLD-based design will, by and large, be developed using one of the many hardware design languages, such as Verilog or VHDL. Incorporating a programmable device into a system does not eliminate the need for a detailed timing analysis of the portions of the larger system that will be implemented in the PLD. Each device and device type is going to be different; thus, it is important to work with the manufacturer's data sheets and thoroughly understand the behavior of the device and of any critical timing paths. Although the following list is by no means exhaustive, some basic, yet important, timing specifications to be aware of include

τ_{PD} Propagation delay from input to output

τ_{CO} Propagation delay from clock(edge) to output

τ_{CF} Propagation delay from clock(edge) to internal flip-flop feedback

τ_{SU} Setup time from inputs to clock(edge)

τ_{H} Hold time from inputs to clock(edge)

Clock management, signal routing and management, the partitioning of the logic into appropriate blocks to maximize performance (including inter-and intrablock communication), and minimize power are essential parts of the design, modeling, and simulation of the design. Our earlier discussion of module coupling and cohesion definitely applies in the PLD context as well. Any device will ultimately be exchanging information with other external companion devices. Properly assigning input and output pins and associating these assignments with corresponding logic functions and their internal placement can have a significant effect on device performance. While focused on the design and development of a PLD-based subsystem, remember that at the end of the day it is part of a larger system. It must interact with and is subject to the same constraints as the containing system.

Working with the vendor's tools, the design is ultimately synthesized into an electronic interchange format that can be used either to program the CPLD or to build a SRAM set or antifuse pattern for an FPGA.

19.8 DESIGN EXAMPLES

We will now look at two embedded applications of PLD technology. These projects were developed as part of an advanced embedded systems class at the University of Washington. Both projects use the Xilinx Spartan-III™ FPGA. The first system is a lane departure detection system intended for use in a moving automobile; the second is the creation of a MicroBlaze™ softcore CPU-based system and the port of the uClinux operating system, custom-compiled for the MicroBlaze™ hardware environment.

19.8.1 Lane Departure Detection Implementation and Acceleration

The project was designed and developed by Aaron Severance of the University of Washington, Seattle, Washington, November 2005.

19.8.1.1 Introduction

A recent advance in safety technology in the automotive industry has been the design of lane departure detection systems. These systems are designed to alert an unaware driver that his or her vehicle has started to leave the designated lane. Such a system can be very useful in alerting tired or distracted drivers of their potentially harmful state.

In order to function properly, such a system must be able to handle different size, color, shape, and spacing of lane markings. One popular approach is to use a forward-looking camera, mounted in the windshield of the vehicle, to examine the road. This approach's utility lies in its ability to analyze a large field of information and to be easily adapted/upgraded, something that approaches utilizing specialized sensors lack.

Algorithmically, this can be accomplished using three main steps: edge detection, line finding, and image space conversion. Edge detection is the process of reducing the amount of information to be analyzed by selecting only portions of the image with a strong gradient. Line finding does a transformation on the image in order to detect predominant lines in the image, which should correspond to lane markings. Finally, image space conversion converts the positions of the lines found in the image to positions in a real-world coordinate system, relative to the position of the vehicle.

Implementation was done as a dual core processor system on a Xilinx Spartan-III™ FPGA. The hardware and software configurations were created using Xilinx Platform Studio 6.2i, which included the MicroBlaze™ soft processor core that was used in the design. In addition, Xilinx State CAD was used in order to design the custom hardware acceleration logic.

19.8.1.2 Requirements

The lane detection problem reduces to two tasks: edge detection followed by line finding.

EDGE DETECTION

To identify an edge within a visual field, a region of the input must be specified to be the region of interest (ROI). The edge detection routine must have an output that corresponds to convolving the image with a 3 x 3 Sobel vertical edge detection filter in the ROI. Any pixels in the image not in the ROI must be set to zero. The convolution must not be circular;

the outermost pixels of the image, where a full convolution cannot be performed, must be set to zero. Finally, a threshold input must be specified; pixels with edge strength below this threshold must be set to zero.

LINE FINDING

Line finding was implemented using the Hough Transform, with the output bin of angles equal in number to the input width of the image. Each of the left/right halves of the image must be searched for one lane marking, with at least $\pi/2$ angles scanned. A line finding algorithm must be able to identify the two peaks with the highest value in the output of the Hough Transform as probable lane markings. An inverse Hough Transform must be provided, which will allow for output to an image buffer of the lines identified as lane markings.

19.8.1.3 Design

The design of the system was implemented through a set of phased deliverables. First, a basic setup with the MicroBlaze™ processor was developed. Next, the code for edge detection and line finding were ported to the setup. A dual processor system was then implemented, and basic communication between the processors was established. The code was then parallelized, and functional, static, semidynamic, and dynamic approaches were examined. Finally, the Sobelerator hardware accelerator was designed and tested.

The baseline system was designed using Xilinx Platform Studio's Base System Builder™. This allowed for the creation of a basic design including a MicroBlaze™ processor, OPB SDRAM controller, and OPB timers. The necessary user constraint file was also generated to map I/O correctly to the prototyping board used.

All code was written in C. In order to minimize code size, lookup tables for the sin and cos functions used in the Hough Transform had to be precomputed rather than be generated upon initialization of the program.

Because Base System Builder does not allow for more than one microprocessor, the dual processor system had to be implemented in Platform Studio. Adding the hardware simply required manually connecting cores to the appropriate busses and allocating space for memory-mapped I/O appropriately. The two MicroBlaze™ processors share a common OPB bus for peripherals and external memory. The two processors could also be connected through Fast Simple Link (FSL) connections to examine the performance of message passing rather than shared memory.

Since there was only one external memory available, however, this message passing system would not have the distributed memory of a typical point-to-point network and therefore would be a poor model. Message passing was used through shared memory for command information, but all data was shared via pointers to buffers.

In addition, memory contention and critical sections had to be dealt with. For the sake of keeping the code small and simple, it was decided to use no operating system, and the MicroBlaze™ ISA does not provide test and set instructions for synchronization. A simple solution was to design the system as a master/slave setup rather than true symmetrical multiprocessing. Communication then became a matter of sending commands from the master and receiving acknowledgments from the slave. In order to implement this in an extensible manner, a FIFO was modeled in memory, using a circular buffer.

With the dual processor system in place, the code needed to be parallelized in order to take advantage of the second processor. The edge detection algorithm requires the same processing time for each pixel and has no interdependencies of data. It was therefore decided that a static, data parallel partitioning should be sufficient. Testing later showed that this assumption was correct. The runtime of the Hough Transform is dependent on the number of points that must be examined, which may change between frames and between different portions of a frame. A static partitioning then should not be optimal. Compared against the static partitioning baseline would be a semidynamic partitioning scheme where the amount of the image to be processed by each processor would be updated between frames, and a dynamic partitioning scheme where blocks of pixels would be dynamically assigned to each processor. A functional implementation would also be compared, where one processor did lane finding while the other did edge detection of the previous frame.

Finally, the Sobelerator hardware accelerator was designed. Its purpose was to implement in hardware the additions, subtractions, shifts, magnitude and rounding operations required to do edge detection. The FSL interface was chosen because of its simplicity and its low latency to the MicroBlaze™'s data path. The design was initially developed in the VHDL hardware description language. As the design progressed, Xilinx's StateCAD™ was used to generate the VDHL code for the Sobelerator from a specified state diagram. The Sobelerator was designed to take 32-bit words consisting of four 8-bit pixel values as input. This led to a shift-and-add design, allowing it to process a different pixel after each shift.

Separate code had to be written to take advantage of the Sobelerator. One change made to the code was to not write the output of the edge detection performed by the Sobelerator to a memory buffer, but perform the Hough Transform on it directly.

19.8.1.4 Results

The assembled system was tested to make sure all functions worked correctly. The board was able to receive and transmit images as bitmaps. The system was then tested on 16 input frames, taken from inside the front windshield of a Pontiac Sunfire outside of the University of Washington campus. Times for performing the Sobel transform varied less than 1% between frames. The combination of Sobel and Hough was able to identify lane markings for some test images, as shown in Figure 19.24.

Figure 19.24 Lane Marking Detection

19.8.1.5 Section Summary

Lane Departure Detection was successfully implemented on a Xilinx Spartan-III™ FPGA. The algorithms used were examined in a dual processor setup. Doubling the number of processors gave less than a doubling of speed. For the given algorithms, a simple static partitioning of the data gave the most consistent and generally fastest results. Using the Sobelerator hardware accelerator gave a large gain in speed in the edge detection algorithm; however, the line finding part of the algorithm dominated runtime.

19.8.2 Local Area Tracking System—LATS with uCLinux™ OS

The project was designed and developed by John Burnette and David Burnett of the University of Washington, Seattle, Washington, November 2004.

19.8.2.1 Introduction

Local Area Tracking System

As a component in a larger project, an ultra wideband *Local Area Tracking System* (LATS) control unit, a MicroBlaze™ softcore CPU-based system utilizing a Xilinx Spartan-III™ has been designed and developed. This CPU runs an implementation of uClinux™, custom-compiled for the MicroBlaze™ hardware environment.

We employ and test the functionality of not only the overarching uClinux system, but also the uClinux bootloader, UART communication systems, CPU data and instruction cache, and SRAM and flash memory as both storage devices and as file systems. The end result is a MicroBlaze™/uClinux-based standalone system with many paths for future development.

19.8.2.2 Requirements

The uClinux OS was required to control most peripherals on the Spartan III™ development board, including LEDs, UARTs, LCD, Flash memory, and SDRAM. The implementation of uClinux interacted with other PCs via RS232, accepted input, and provided output.

The OS had to be able to add new input and output paths to the maximum capacity of the development environment. The uClinux kernel and boot loader were required to reside on the Flash memory, thereby allowing the OS to boot from a local memory system (Flash) rather than relying on re-download of OS on power cycle.

The principal job of the OS was to mediate the interaction of all the components in the system (including user interface, display, networking, and communication components) and to orchestrate safe handling of shared memory resources.

19.8.2.3 System Description

The system configuration for the LATS is given in Figure 19.25.

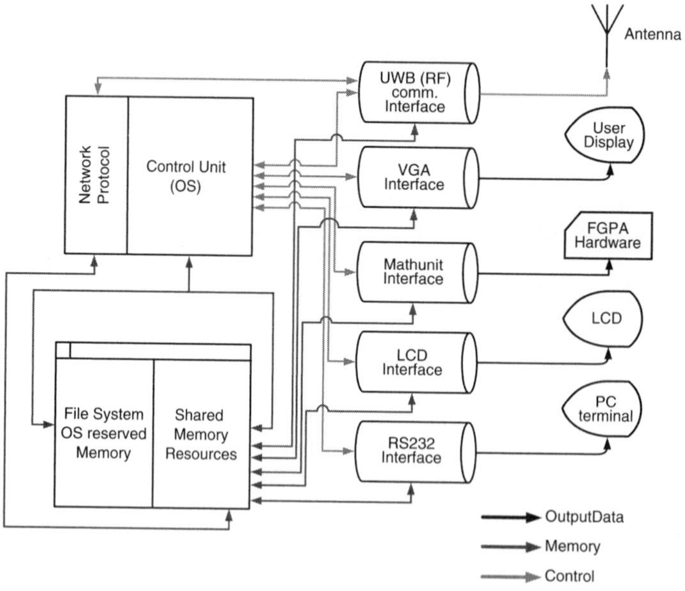

Figure 19.25 LATS System High-Level Architecture

The command and control center for the system is the uClinux^{TM} OS, which runs on a Xilinx Spartan III^{TM} FPGA. This OS mediates the interaction between the remaining system components, which include:

- UI interface
- VGA interface
- Network protocol
- UWB communication interface (RF for now)
- Math unit—for matrix manipulation
- LCD
- RS232 communication interface

19.8.2.4 Design Procedure

SOFTWARE—UCLINUX
An investigation of possible operating systems to control the LATS ultimately led to uClinux^{TM} as the preferred choice. A significant advantage of uClinux^{TM} was that a version was available; thus, the only necessary changes were those required for it to function with Spartan III^{TM} hardware. These changes included modifying the kernel configuration.

SOFTWARE—TEST APPLICATION
Design of the test application was very quick and straightforward; all that was needed was a function to demonstrate some measure of hardware interaction while inside the uClinux^{TM} system. From previous work, a basic test suite was available and thus simplified the task. The existing code was updated to work within Xilinx EDK 6.2 and integrated into the uClinux^{TM} image.

HARDWARE
The hardware for this project was set up using the Base System Builder and was modified to meet our needs. These modifications included bug fixes, cache enabling, and processor speedup.

The first step in the hardware development was to set up the hardware project using the board support package (BSB). Then, we started with the bootloader source that was provided in the *mbvanilla_net*^{TM} distribution and modified it to work with our board configuration.

mbvanilla_net^{TM}

Required changes included modifying the base addresses of system components and integrating a new flash driver. These source files were compiled to work on the Microblaze^{TM} soft-core processor and to function as the primary means of directing the processor to boot our kernel image and run our applications.

19.8.2.5 Test Plan

UCLINUX^{TM}
Testing uClinux's functionality consisted of a straightforward verification of the file system and responsiveness. After selecting the appropriate option from the bootloader, the system should boot through a suite of standard startup routines, expand the file system, print the uClinux logo, and present a console for interaction with the system. Typing alphanumeric characters should result in an echo back—this verifies basic UART input/output functionality of the system. Using the Linux^{TM} *cd* and *ls* commands verify the presence of those

applications compiled into the uClinux image in the /bin directory. Typing *ps -ef* at the command prompt ensures that Linux™ processes are running and the system is active.

TEST APPLICATION

Once the uClinux™ system booted to a command prompt, a test application was executed. In an ideal world, it should turn an LED on and off and print to the screen via the UART in response to a button on the development board. In addition, it should observe all the usual program politeness: not crash the system, exit with Ctrl+C, and respond to the "kill" command.

HARDWARE

One should download the hardware configuration bit stream to the target and run some diagnostic code to make sure everything is working. Diagnostics should include reading and writing to the SDRAM and Flash, printing to the LCD, writing text to the UART, which appears in a HyperTerminal™ session, and making the LEDs on the development board blink.

19.8.2.6 Section Summary

After a standard progression of research, investigation, design, prototyping, and debugging, the FPGA hardware and basic uClinux operating system work together. While the overall project was still some distance from completion, much was accomplished toward developing a basis for future work.

19.9 SUMMARY

In this chapter, we began by motivating the use of PLDs as an important tool and aid in developing contemporary embedded systems; we then examined the underlying logical concepts that have led to the development and widespread use of programmable logic devices (PLDs). We started with the basic building blocks of PLDs and how these are configured into useful tools. We then looked at the commonly used technologies for implementing programmable devices and how programmable devices are able to store information. We introduced the basic structure of the devices, examined variations on I/O configurations, and studied, compared, and contrasted the fundamental architectures for the CPLD and the FPGA.

We introduced two of the more commonly used components: the *CPLD* and the *Gate Array*, as well as a more general-purpose device called a *Programmable System on a Chip*. We briefly addressed the PLD design process and concluded with a look at several applications.

19.10 REVIEW QUESTIONS

Programmable Technology

19.1 Explain how a programmable cell works.

19.2 Are there different kinds of programmable cells? What are the differences?

19.3 What is an antifuse?

19.4 Can programmable cells be reprogrammed? How?

19.5 How long can a bit be stored in a programmable cell?

19.6 What is a matrix switch?

Programmable Logic Devices

19.7 Why might we wish to use PLDs in an embedded design?

19.8 What is a programmable logic device?

19.9 Explain how we can build logical functions using a PLD.

19.10 What is a CPLD?

19.11 What is an FPGA?

19.12 What is an antifuse device?

19.13 What is a lookup table, and what is it used for?

19.14 What is the difference between a CPLD and an FPGA?

19.15 What are the two major kinds of FPGA?

19.16 Explain how a SRAM-based FPGA works.

19.17 What is the difference between SRAM- and antifuse-based FPGAs.

19.18 What is a programmable system on a chip?

19.19 Identify and describe the output functionality commonly found in PLDs.

Design

19.20 How does the design cycle for PLDs differ from that for the standard embedded system in general?

19.21 How is the design cycle for PLDs similar to that for the standard embedded system in general?

19.11 THOUGHT QUESTIONS

Programmable Logic Devices

19.1 Can we implement a PLD device without using a specifically designed CPLD of FPGA? If so, how? If not, why not?

19.2 What are the advantages and disadvantages of using a CPLD device versus a software implementation of the function either in a microprocessor or in discrete hardware?

19.3 What are the advantages and disadvantages of using an FPGA device versus either a software implementation of the function in a microprocessor or in discrete hardware?

19.4 What are the advantages and disadvantages of using a SRAM FPGA device versus an antifuse-based device?

19.5 What are the advantages and disadvantages of using a CPLD device versus an FPGA device?

19.6 What are the advantages and disadvantages of using a PSoC such as the Cypress device discussed in the chapter versus a discrete implementation?

19.7 What are the advantages and disadvantages of a matrix switch?

19.8 What effect might using a PLD have on the noise in a low-speed embedded system? a high-speed embedded system?

19.9 Some PLDs provide the ability to decrease the output signal slew rate. Why is this done? Be specific in your analysis.

19.10 Why do some PLD vendors permit the user to define extra ground pins on the device? Be specific in your analysis.

19.11 When might one wish to use a PLD versus either an ASIC or full custom designed integrated circuit?

19.12 Discuss some of the potential problems that one might encounter in trying to implement a high-speed FPGA-based design. Be specific in your answer. Consider propagation delays, noise, path routing and lengths, and so forth.

19.13 How can one address the potential problem areas identified in Question 19.12?

19.14 Discuss the advantages and disadvantages of one-time versus reprogrammable devices.

19.15 When should we use a PROM, PAL, or PLA-type device in a design? Give several example applications where each type of device might be appropriate.

19.16 While a PLD-based design may support multiple processing cores, the programs that we develop today are generally sequential rather than parallel. Rewriting a sequential problem as a parallel implementation is challenging. Suggest some new ways that we might think about problems to take advantage of a multicore design.

Appendix A

Verilog Overview: The Verilog Hardware Description Language

THINGS TO LOOK FOR . . .

- The structure of a Verilog program.
- How to develop and use Verilog modules.
- The differences between gate-level, dataflow, and behavioral level models.
- How to develop combinational and sequential circuit models at all three levels.
- The types of assignment at each level of modeling.
- How to specify and model real-world delays in a circuit.
- How to monitor and display dynamic circuit behavior.
- How to build a tester and test bench to evaluate a model.

A.0 INTRODUCTION

The circuits and systems that we are developing today are growing in capability and complexity every day. Yesterday, a sketch on a piece of paper and a handful of parts were sufficient to try out a design idea. Today, that is no longer possible. Today, the idea is modeled using computer-based tools and languages, which are frequently synthesized into the desired hardware implementation. We use two key words here, *model* and *synthesize*.

model, synthesize

We first model the design, iterating until we are satisfied, and then we transform that design into an FPGA or ASIC. A number of languages permit such a design approach; Verilog and VHDL are two of the more common. SystemC for modeling both the hardware and software components is finding its way into an increasing number of designs in the embedded world. In this text, we will use Verilog.

Verilog is a hardware design language that provides a means of specifying a digital system at a wide range of levels of abstraction. The language supports the early conceptual stages of design with its *behavioral* level of abstraction and later implementation stages with its *structural* level of abstraction. The language provides hierarchical constructs that allow the designer to efficiently and effectively manage the complexity of contemporary designs.

behavioral
structural

This appendix will introduce the Verilog language and present the important features and capabilities used in this book. It does not purport to be a comprehensive study of the language. We will begin with the basic components and organization of a Verilog program, next examine the gate-level or structural, dataflow, and behavioral models for combinational logic circuits, and follow with similar models for sequential circuits.

Design is only one aspect of the product development; each design must also be tested to confirm that it meets specified requirements and the objectives of the modeling process. To that end, each section will also discuss how one can formulate test suites to verify the intended operation. The material on testing will lay the foundation for enabling the developer to build test cases that will support testing to the desired level. It is beyond the scope of this text to present a comprehensive treatise on testing.

A.1 AN OVERVIEW OF A VERILOG PROGRAM

The structure of a Verilog program replicates the traditional way of designing, testing, and debugging a module, subsystem, or system. As engineers, we design a circuit, we build the circuit, and we take the circuit to our bench where we test it. On our electronics test bench, we have test equipment. Such equipment consists of stimulus instruments, switches, function generators, sophisticated data, or pattern generators. We also have measurement equipment such as voltmeters—DVM or DMM, oscilloscopes, logic analyzers, and network analyzers. The circuit consists of electronic parts and wires. We build the modules by interconnecting the wires and electronic parts. Once the circuit is built, we connect the test equipment to the circuit with wires. We now have a picture that looks like that in Figure A.0. The circuit or module is called the unit or device under test—UUT or DUT. A Verilog source program follows this model. It comprises three major elements:

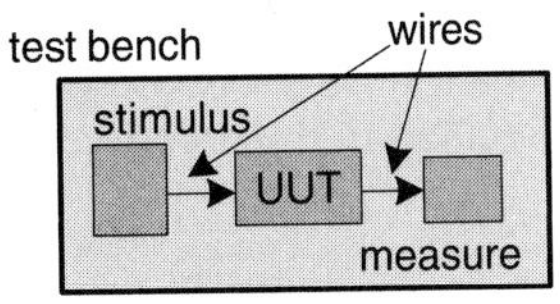

Figure A.0 The Structure of an Electronic Test System

- A test bench
- A collection of stimulus and measurement modules
- A circuit or system that is being modeled

That circuit or system is made up of a number of logical components. A logical component may be an atomic device such as a logic gate or a number of components or modules. Each may, in turn, also be made up of other logical devices. The stimulus module provides signals into the UUT; the measurement module acquires/measures the corresponding outputs of the UUT. A Verilog program, very much like the physical electronics bench, has stimulus and measurement equipment connected to the circuit or system being modeled. As is done on a physical bench, equipment is connected to the UUT using wires. On occasion in a Verilog program, the stimulus and measurement equipment may be in the same software module.

A.2 CREATING A VERILOG PROGRAM

In order to perform a digital circuit simulation using Verilog we need to

- Create a Verilog source file using a text editor
- Synthesize and simulate the source file
- Debug if necessary by looking at the simulation output

The goal in writing a traditional program in a language such as C, C++, or Java is to implement and run an application. In this case, the program is the final deliverable. In contrast, a Verilog program has an initial purpose of modeling a circuit design. Once the performance of the design is satisfactory, the program is used to synthesize a hardware circuit. The HDL program is an intermediate step.

A.2.1 Some Concepts in a Verilog Source File

Before continuing, one should learn several important points about the language.

Case-sensitivity Like C, C++, or Java, Verilog is case sensitive. If an error is encountered while compiling a Verilog source file, look for case-errors.

Identifier Names The rules for identifier names are similar to those found in C, C++, or Java. An identifier name may contain any digit or letter as well as the underscore and $ character. The first character must be a letter, and the identifier cannot be a Verilog keyword.

Annotation The Verilog language supports both the C style multiple-line comment and the C++ style single-line comment. The paired /* */ symbols state that all text inside the delimiter is to be interpreted as a comment. The symbol // specifies that all text on a line after the symbol is to be viewed as a comment.

White Space The white space characters "space" and "tab" are ignored by the Verilog compiler.

sequential block

Block Delimiters A *sequential block* comprises one or more statements that are intended to act together. In C, C++, or Java, a block of statements is delimited by a pair of curly braces, '{ }'. The Verilog language uses the Pascal-style statements *begin* and *end*. The statements in a sequential block are executed in the order that they are specified.

A.2.2 Modules

module, black box
black boxes, wires

The *module* is the basic building block of Verilog. One can think of a module as a *black box*. To make a system consisting of modules, we link up the individual *black boxes* with *wires*. One can also think of the modules as loosely analogous to the struct in C or as a class in C++ or Java. Bear in mind that modules are *not* classes.

Like each of these data types, the module represents a user-defined type. Once defined, instances of a module can be declared in the same manner as any of the intrinsic types. The concept of module permits one to build complex systems by composing or aggregating lower-level components. Like the C struct or the C++ or Java class, each module expresses a distinct local scope. All variables declared and defined therein are visible only in that scope.

The module provides a structure for the design process. As the number of modules that are defined increases, the more complex the design becomes. In such cases, it is convenient to be able to verify functionality module by module.

The code fragment in Figure A.1 gives the general syntax and structure for a Verilog module.

module, endmodule

Observe first that each line in a Verilog module, except the last, must be terminated with a semicolon. In C, C++, or Java, the scope of a block is delimited by curly brackets, { }. In Verilog, the scope of a module is delimited by the key words *module* and *endmodule*.

Module Name

Analogous to a struct or class declaration, the declaration of a Verilog module begins with the key word *module* as illustrated in the opening line of the code fragment.

```
module moduleName(outputsList, inputsList);
```

```
module moduleName(outputsList, inputsList);
   outputs          // outputs from the module
   inputs           // inputs to the module

   reg              // local storage in the module
   wire             // conduction paths in the module

   initial          // initialize variables in block
      block
   always           // always execute statements in block
      block

   code             // your code
      ...
      ...
endmodule
```

Figure A.1 The Structure of a Verilog Module

Following the module keyword is the name of the module. The module name can now be used as a type specifier.

> **Coding Style**
>
> Always try to select a module name that conveys the purpose or function of the module.

Inputs and Outputs Declarations

inputsList, outputsList

Following the module name, enclosed in parentheses, are the inputs and outputs to the module. The *inputsList* and the *outputsList* are optional; however, they will be used most of the time. The inputs and outputs can be specified in any order, even commingled (not a good idea, though).

> **Coding Style**
>
> The standard convention in Verilog is that the *outputsList* comes before the *inputsList.*
> Always try to select input and output names that convey the meaning of the variables

Consequently, when the module is declared, each item in the *inputsList* and the *outputsList* must be identified in an input or output declaration as follows.

> **Syntax**
> output *outputsList*;
> input *inputsList*

Nets and Variables

nets, variables

The Verilog language defines several different kinds of *nets* and *variables*. The net represents a class of primitive data types that are used to model a node or an electrical connection in a circuit. A net cannot be assigned to; it cannot hold a value. The value on a net results from being continuously driven by the output of some logical device. If a net is not driven, it takes on the default value of *z* meaning high impedance or floating. A Verilog variable, like a variable in C, C++, or Java, can be assigned a value and will hold that value until a subsequent assignment replaces the value.

wire A *wire* type is a kind of net and like real-world wires is used to connect the output of one logic element to the input(s) of other logical elements. Because it is a net, the value of a wire can only be changed as the result of a gate or a behavioral statement driving it.

reg A *reg* is a kind of variable. The value of a *reg* or register can be changed directly by an assignment. One should not confuse the Verilog *reg* with the hardware register. The *reg* is simply an entity that can hold a value. The default value of a *reg* data type is "***x***," or unknown.

reg, wire The syntax for the *reg* and *wire* declarations is given as:

Syntax
reg *regList;*
wire *wireList;*

Declaring Multi-Bit Signals

It is often necessary to represent multi-bit wires, for example, a 3-bit wire that can carry digital signals representing the values 0–7. The types *reg* and *wire* can also be formed into a bus such as:

Syntax
Big Endian
reg [msb:lsb] *regList*
wire [msb:lsb] *wireList;*

Little Endian
reg [lsb:msb] *regList*
wire [lsb:msb] *wireList;*

msb, lsb where *msb* is the bit index of the most significant bit and *lsb* is the bit index of the least significant bit. The value of the lsb index must be zero since bit position 0 conventionally denotes the least-significant bit. Such statements configure a set of individual wires so that they can now be treated as a group, for example,

```
wire [2:0] myWires;      // a 3-bit signal (a bus)
reg [15:0] aState;       // a 16-bit state holding value
```

Figure A.2 Declaring Multi Bit Signals

myWires The declaration, *myWires*, in Figure A.2 declares a 3-bit signal that has

MSB (the 2^2's place) as myWires[2]
Middle bit of myWires[1].
LSB (the 2^0's place) as myWires[0]

The individual signals can be used just like any other binary value in Verilog. For example, we could declare, as in Figure A.3,

```
and a1(myWires[2], myWires[0], C);
```

Figure A.3 Using a Multi-Bit Signal

This statement AND's together *C* and the LSB of *myWires* and puts the result in the MSB of *myWires*.

myWires

This bus specification can be extended to input and output lists as well; that is, multi-bit signals can also be passed together to a module (see Figure A.4).

```
module random(bus1, bus2);
    output [31:0]   bus1;
    input [19:0]    bus2;
    wire c;

    anotherRandom ar1(C, bus2, bus1);
endmodule
```

Figure A.4 Using Multi-Bit Input and Output

Subsets of Multi-Bit Expressions

On occasion, it is necessary to break apart multi-bit values. We can do that by selecting a subset of a value. For example, if we have, as in Figure A.5:

```
wire [31:0] myWires;
initial myWires[3:1] = 'b101;
```

Figure A.5 Accessing a Subset of a Multi-Bit Signal

This would set

```
myWires[3] = 1
myWires[2] = 0
myWires[1] = 1
```

myWires

All other bits of *myWires* will not be altered. One can also use the same form to take a subset of a multi-bit wire and pass it as an input to another module.

$display and $monitor statements

$display, $monitor

The *$display* and *$monitor* are standard system tasks that enable one to see the states of certain signals in text form. The output is typically directed to the screen (or window). The difference between the two statements is that *$display* is only evaluated when the directive is encountered during execution. The *$monitor* statement is evaluated every time *any* of the signals that is being monitored changes state.

The syntax for the two directives is given as

Syntax
$display (["formatrString"], variableList);
$monitor (["formatString"], variableList);

formatString
printf
variableList

The *formatString* is optional for both statements; both follow the C *printf* statement syntax. The *formatString* is a text string containing format variables that are to be instantiated, one-to-one, from the values specified in the *variableList*. The more commonly used format variables are given in Table A.0.

Table A.0 Verilog Format Variables

Format Variable	Display
%b	Binary
%d	Decimal
%h	Hexadecimal
%c	Character

high
$display, $monitor
initial, always

By convention, a logic *high* is denoted as a 1 and a logic *low* is denoted as a 0. An unknown state is denoted as an x. The *$display* and *$monitor* output statements must be placed within an *initial* or *always* block.

$stop and $finish Statements

$stop, $finish
$stop

The *$stop* and *$finish* statements are system tasks that are used to either stop or finish a simulation. The former directs the simulation to the interactive mode and the latter terminates the simulation. The *$stop* is used when the designer wishes to suspend the simulation prior to exit to examine the state of signal values.

The syntax for the two directives is given as

Syntax
$stop;
$finish;

$time Statement

$time

The *$time* statement is a system function that returns the current time. The syntax is given as,

Syntax
$time;

The statement can be included in a $display or $monitor statement as

```
$display ($time, ["formatrString"], variableList);
$monitor ($time, ["formatString"], variableList);
```

A.3 THREE MODELS—THE GATE LEVEL, THE DATAFLOW, AND THE BEHAVIORAL

gate-level
behavioral level
structural
dataflow level
behavior level

With this brief introduction to some elements of the Verilog language, we will next look at how the language supports the modeling process. The Verilog language supports the development of models at three different primary levels of abstraction. The *gate-level* model gives the most detailed expression and the *behavioral level* the most abstract. At the *gate level*, modules are implemented by interconnecting the various logic gates much as one would do when working with SSI and MSI components. This is also known as a *structural* model. At the *dataflow level*, the module is implemented by specifying the movement of the data among the comprising hardware registers. The dataflow model is analogous to the RTL (Register Transfer Level) level used in specifying a microprocessor architecture. At the *behavioral level*, modeling is based on an algorithmic description of the problem without regard for the underlying hardware.

The language does support modeling at the transistor level. However, work at that level will not be discussed in this text.

We will begin at the gate level and work up. The path that we will follow will be to use the three different levels at which the modeling process may be conducted as a means of introducing the core aspects of the language. Following the discussion of the different approaches, we will bring everything together with a discussion of developing a test module and then couple the test module with the UUT in a test bench. Because working at the gate level is the most familiar to many engineers, we will begin at that level and then move up to higher levels of abstraction.

We will utilize the same combinational and sequential designs to illustrate how a model is developed at each of the different levels. The combinational circuits will be a logic block using an AND and an OR gate, which are extended to implement a NAND and a NOR circuit. The sequential circuits will progress from a basic latch to a gated latch to a flip-flop, and ultimately, to a 2-bit binary counter.

A.3.1 The Structural/Gate-Level Model

buf	not
and	nand
or	nor
xor	xnor

Figure A.6 Basic Verilog Logic Gates

As the name suggests, at the gate level, we are working with the basic logic gates and flip-flops that one finds in any detailed digital logic diagram. These devices model the behavior of the parts that we can buy from any electronics store or that we might design into an ASIC or use in FPGA. Verilog supports the logic gates identified in Figure A.6 as predefined intrinsic modules.

The prototypes for each of the gates are given in Figure A.7.

```
buf <name> (OUT1, IN1);            // Sets output equal to input
not <name> (OUT1, IN1);            // Sets output to opposite of input
and <name> (OUT, IN1, IN2);        // Sets output to AND of inputs
or <name> (OUT, IN1, IN2);         // Sets output to OR of inputs
nand <name> (OUT, IN1, IN2);       // Sets to NAND of inputs
nor <name> (OUT, IN1, IN2);        // Sets output to NOR of inputs
xor <name> (OUT, IN1, IN2);        // Sets output to XOR of inputs
xnor <name> (OUT, IN1, IN2);       // Sets to XNOR of inputs
```

Figure A.7 Basic Verilog Logic Gate Prototypes

The device prototypes appear very much like those for a C or C++ function or procedure. The <name> for a gate instance must begin with a letter and thereafter can be any combination of letters, numbers, the underscore _, or the $. Gates with more than two inputs are created by simply including additional inputs in the declaration. Observe that the output list appears first, followed by the input list.

EXAMPLE A.0

A five-input and gate is declared as

```
and <name> (OUT, IN1, IN2, IN3, IN4, IN5);    // 5-input AND
```

A.3.1.1 Creating Modules

At the gate level, whether one is building a combinational or sequential logic circuit, a Verilog module really is a collection of logic gates. Each time we declare and define a module, we are creating that set of gates. We will look first at combinational logic models and follow with sequential circuits.

Combinational Logic

The structural or gate-level model of a combinational circuit reflects the physical gates used to implement the design. To illustrate the basic process of creating a Verilog program and modeling combinational logic at the gate level, we will begin with the following simple circuit.

An example of a simple module begins with the logic diagram in Figure A.8; the module requires a name, and we will call it *AndOr*.

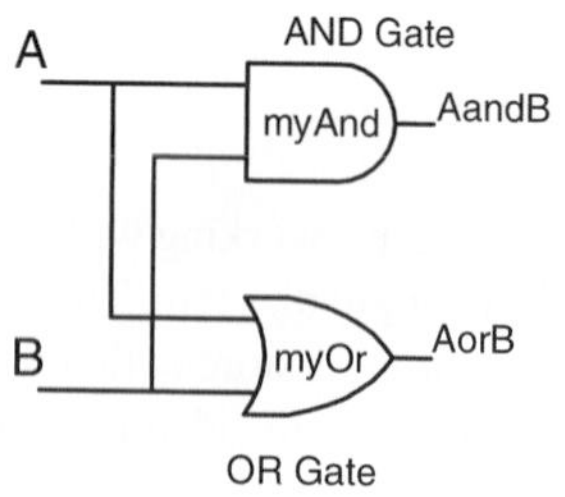


```
// Compute the logical AND and OR of inputs A and B.
module AndOr(AandB, AorB, A, B);
     output AandB, AorB;
     input A, B;

     and myAnd (AandB, A, B);
     or myOr (AorB, A, B);
endmodule
```

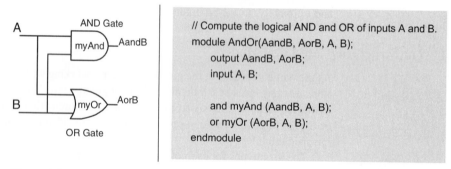

Figure A.8 A Combinational Logic Circuit with Corresponding Structural Verilog Module

We can analyze the module line by line.

```
// Compute the logical AND and OR of inputs A and B
```

The first line is a comment designated by the //. Everything on a line after a // is ignored. Comments can appear on separate lines or at the end of lines of code.

```
module AndOr(AandB, AorB, A, B);
    output AandB, AorB;
    input A, B;
```

module
AndOr
outputs
inputs

The top of a module begins with the keyword *module* indicating start of module, the name of the module, *AndOr*, and a list of signals connected to that module. Subsequent lines first declare that the first two binary values generated by this module are *outputs* from the module and the next two (A, B) are *inputs* to the module.

The next lines

```
and myAnd (AandB, A, B);
or myOr (AorB, A, B);
```

myAnd, AandB
myOr, orOut

create instances of two gates: an AND gate called *myAnd* with output *AandB* and inputs *A* and *B* and an OR gate called *myOr* with output *orOut* and inputs *A* and *B*.

We declare such intrinsic components the same as we did in C, C++, or Java with int, float, or char.

The final line declares the end of the module.

```
endmodule
```

endmodule

All modules must end with an *endmodule* statement. Observe that the *endmodule* statement is the only one that is not terminated by a semicolon.

A.3.1.2 Using Modules

We build up a complex traditional software program by having procedures call subprocedures or by combining classes into larger and more powerful class structures. Verilog builds up complex circuits and systems from modules using a design approach similar to composition or aggregation.

AndOr, NandNor

To illustrate the process, we will use the previous *AndOr* module to build a *NandNor* circuit. We begin with the logic diagram and Verilog module in Figure A.9.

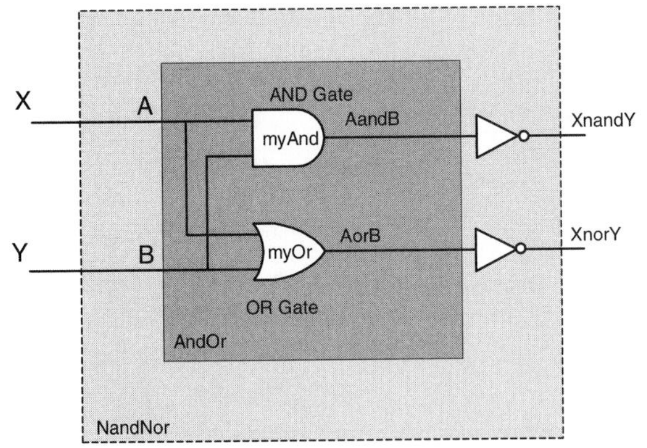


```
// Compute the logical AND and OR of inputs A and B.
module AndOr(AandB, AorB, A, B);
    output AandB, AorB;
    input A, B;
    and myAnd (AandB, A, B);
    or myOr (AorB, A, B);
endmodule

// Compute the logical NAND and NOR of inputs X and Y.
module NandNor (XnandY, XnorY, X, Y);
    output XnandY, XnorY;
    input X, Y;
    wire XandY, XorY;

    AndOr myAndOr (XandY, XorY, X, Y);
    not n1 (XnandY, XandY);
    not n2 (XnorY, XorY);
endmodule
```

Figure A.9 Defining and Using a Combinational Logic Circuit with Corresponding Structural Verilog Module

AndOr The *NandNor* module declares an instance of the *AndOr* module as it would any of the intrinsic types. One can declare multiple instances of a submodule. Another instance of the *AndOr* module could be added to the *NandNor* module. Each instance of the submodule creates a new set of gates. Three instances of *AndOr* would create a total of 2•3 = 6 gates.

wire The *wire* statement is used to connect the outputs of the *AndOr* module to the two not gates. These wires comprise a net that carries the signals from the output of the *AndOr* module to the inverters.

> **Syntax**
> wire XandY, XorY;

A.3.1.3 Delays

 # operator In a perfect world, parts are ideal and signals flow through wires and parts with no delay; in the real world, parts are not perfect. Signals are delayed by varying amounts. In Verilog, we can model how long signals take to propagate through the basic gates in a circuit using the *# operator*. The basic syntax is given as

> **Syntax**
> #delay device;

We modify the AndOr module in Figure A.10 to incorporate delays into the design to model real-world behavior.

```
// Compute the logical AND and OR of inputs A and B.
module AndOr(AandB, AorB, A, B);
    output AandB, AorB;
    input A, B;

    and #5 myAnd (AandB, A, B);
    or #10 myOr (AorB, A, B);
endmodule
```

Figure A.10 Modeling Gate Delays—First Attempt

The line

```
and #5 myAnd (AandB, A, B);
```

states that the AND gate takes 5 time units to propagate a change on the input to the output, while the OR gate is twice as slow, taking 10 time units.

```
or #10 myOr (AorB, A, B);
```

Note that the units of time can be whatever we want as long as we use consistent values.

In the perfect world, logic devices change state in zero time; in the real world we rarely encounter such ability. To support modeling the time required for a signal to rise or fall, Verilog also supports including device rise time and fall time. The syntax for all three parameters is given as

Syntax
(rise time, fall time, delay) device;

A.3.1.4 Defining Constants

magic, numbers

parameter

Although one can use what are called *magic numbers,* a more robust design will use named or symbolic constants, variables whose value is set in one place and then used throughout a piece of code. The symbolic constant in Verilog is called a *parameter.* A parameter is defined and initialized using the following syntax.

Syntax
parameter = aValue;

The following code fragment illustrates the inclusion of a delay of 2 time units in a part model.

```
parameter propagationDelay = 2;
not #propagationDelay myNot(sigOut, sigIn);
```

Let's modify the previous example to that in Figure A.11 to reflect a more professional approach and also incorporate the signal rise and fall times.

```
// Compute the logical AND and OR of inputs A and B.
module AndOr(AandB, AorB, A, B);
    output AandB, AorB;
    input A, B;

    parameter delay0 = 5;
    parameter delay1 = 10;
    parameter riseTime = 3;
    parameter fallTime = 4;

    and #(riseTime, fallTime, delay0) myAnd (AandB, A, B);
    or #(riseTime, fallTime, delay1) myOr (AorB, A, B);
endmodule
```

Figure A.11 Modeling Gate Delays—Second Attempt

The modified code sets the delay of the gates to delay0 and delay1, respectively, and the rise and fall times to the values specified by the remaining two parameters. To speed up either gate, one could simply change the value in the parameter lines to the desired values.

SEQUENTIAL LOGIC

Sequential logic is modeled at the gate level by first developing the appropriate flip-flop module and then implementing the design as a composition of instances of that module, the necessary gates, and interconnecting the components with wires. To illustrate the process we begin with the basic SR latch, which is given in the logic diagram and Verilog code fragment in Figure A.12.

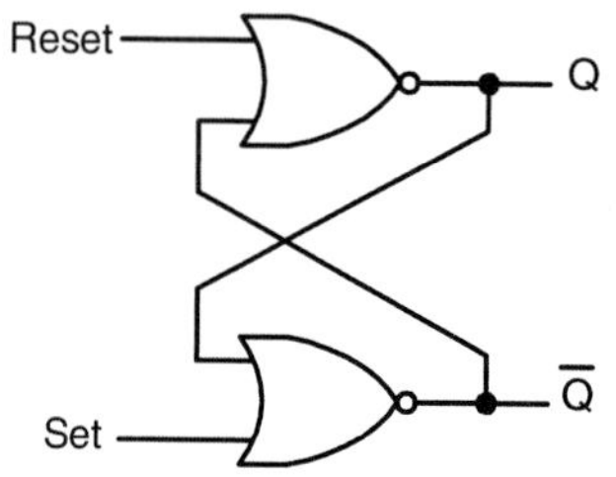

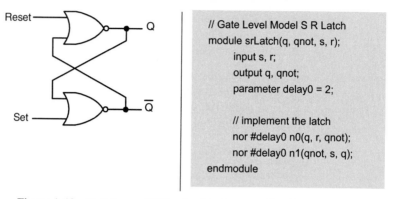

```
// Gate Level Model S R Latch
module srLatch(q, qnot, s, r);
    input s, r;
    output q, qnot;
    parameter delay0 = 2;

    // implement the latch
    nor #delay0 n0(q, r, qnot);
    nor #delay0 n1(qnot, s, q);
endmodule
```

Figure A.12 Defining an S R Latch with Corresponding Structural Verilog Module

The basic design can be extended to include an enable as an additional level of control.
srLatch The logic diagram and Verilog implementation, using the *srLatch,* are given in Figure A.13.

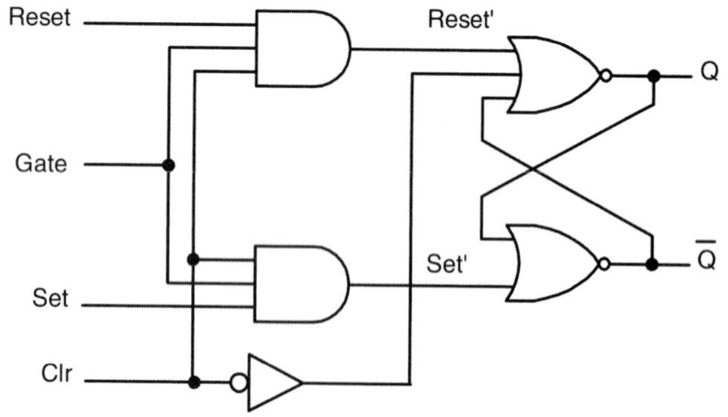

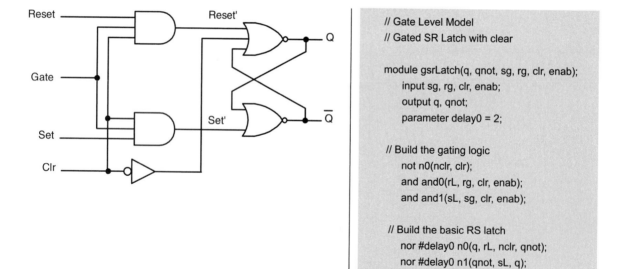

```
// Gate Level Model
// Gated SR Latch with clear

module gsrLatch(q, qnot, sg, rg, clr, enab);
    input sg, rg, clr, enab;
    output q, qnot;
    parameter delay0 = 2;

// Build the gating logic
    not n0(nclr, clr);
    and and0(rL, rg, clr, enab);
    and and1(sL, sg, clr, enab);

// Build the basic RS latch
    nor #delay0 n0(q, rL, nclr, qnot);
    nor #delay0 n1(qnot, sL, q);
endmodule
```

Figure A.13 Extending the S R Latch with Corresponding Structural Verilog Module

The master–slave implementation using the gated latch follows in Figure A.14.

We can now use the SR flip-flop to build a simple 2-bit synchronous binary up counter. The logic diagram and Verilog model follow in Figure A.15.

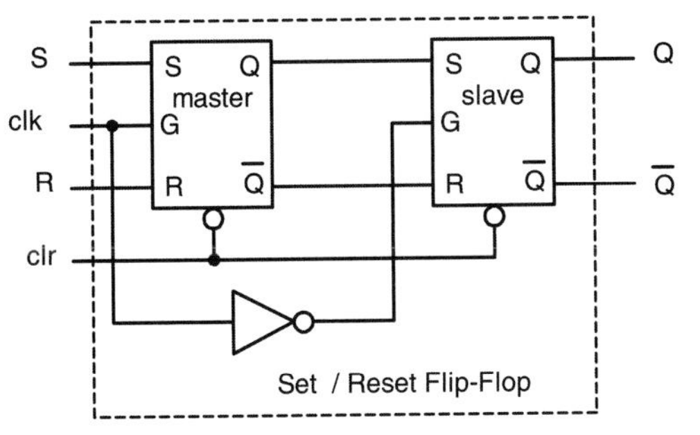

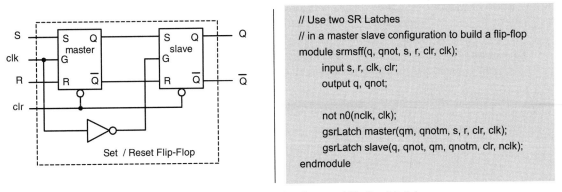

```
// Use two SR Latches
// in a master slave configuration to build a flip-flop
module srmsff(q, qnot, s, r, clr, clk);
    input s, r, clk, clr;
    output q, qnot;

    not n0(nclk, clk);
    gsrLatch master(qm, qnotm, s, r, clr, clk);
    gsrLatch slave(q, qnot, qm, qnotm, clr, nclk);
endmodule
```

Figure A.14 The Master–Slave S R Latch with Corresponding Structural Verilog Module

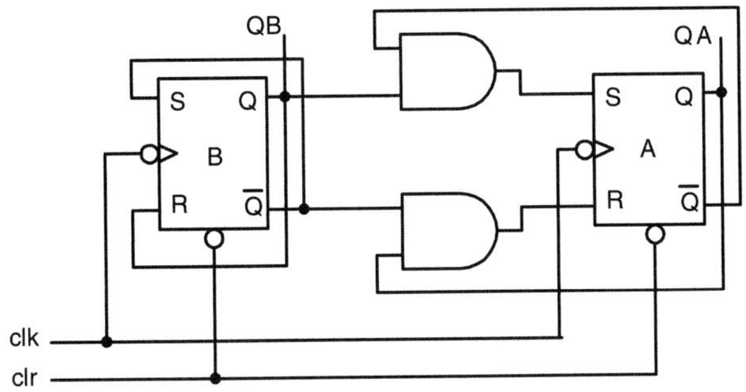

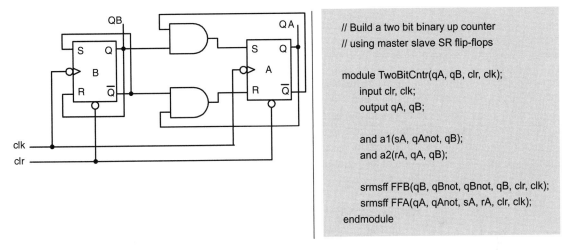

```
// Build a two bit binary up counter
// using master slave SR flip-flops

module TwoBitCntr(qA, qB, clr, clk);
    input clr, clk;
    output qA, qB;

    and a1(sA, qAnot, qB);
    and a2(rA, qA, qB);

    srmsff FFB(qB, qBnot, qBnot, qB, clr, clk);
    srmsff FFA(qA, qAnot, sA, rA, clr, clk);
endmodule
```

Figure A.15 A 2-Bit Binary Up Counter Using the Master–Slave S R Latch with Corresponding Structural Verilog Module

A.3.2 The Dataflow Model

Gate-level modeling is an effective approach for working with smaller problems. Such an approach directly follows the typical detailed logic diagram and thus simplifies moving from design to model and simulation. Embedded applications are continually increasing in complexity. The SSI and MSI modules of yesterday are being replaced by ASICs, FPGAs, and microprocessors. Developing a complete design at the gate level is no longer feasible. Working at the gate level is similar to trying to write sophisticated application in assembler. Although it can be done, such an approach is not practical.

Developing at a higher level is not without problems, however. The farther that one moves away from the low-level details and increases reliance on tools to produce those details, the greater the risk that the tools will produce a less than optimum design. The ability to push the limits of a design and a technology comes from years of experience and understanding of the problem. Tools can help us to solve the majority of the design problems. They are not sufficiently advanced to solve all autonomously.

dataflow modeling

RTL, register transfer level

logic synthesis

Dataflow modeling, as the name implies, views a design from the perspective of data moving through the system from source to destinations. In the digital world, such a view is often referred to as *RTL* or *register transfer level* design. Contemporary tools are able to accept a dataflow model as input and produce a low-level logic gate implementation through a process called *logic synthesis*.

A.3.2.1 Continuous Assignment

continuous assignment

At the dataflow level, the design is modeled as the movement of data from module to module in order to effect the application. That data moves over a net. Thus, a fundamental element of such modeling is the ability to drive a value from a source module onto the interconnecting net to the destination modules. In Verilog, such an ability is expressed by *continuous assignment*. The continuous assignment statement is specified using the following syntax.

Syntax
assign destination net = source net expression

The left-hand side of the continuous assignment must be either a scalar or vector (multiple lines) net. The right-hand side of the expression can be a net, register, or function call return and must be of the same size as the left-hand side. A scalar cannot be assigned to a vector and vice versa, for example.

A continuous assignment is always active. A change on the right-hand side forces evaluation of the left-hand side, with the resulting assignment of the right-hand side value to the left-hand side net.

COMBINATIONAL LOGIC

We illustrate a combinational dataflow model using the AndOr circuit designed earlier. That model, using the continuous assignment, is expressed in Figure A.16.

```
// continuous assignment
module AndOr(AandB, AorB, A, B);
        output AandB, AorB;
        input A, B;

        wire AandB, AorB;
        parameter delay0 = 10;

        assign AandB = A&B;
        assign AorB = A|B;
endmodule
```

Figure A.16 A Combinational Logic Module Using a Dataflow Verilog Model

The implementation of the function using the bitwise AND and OR operators should be familiar from earlier work with their C counterparts.

A.3.2.2 Delays

Moving up one level of abstraction from the gate level does not preclude the need to model real-world effects on circuit behavior. The Verilog model for delay at the dataflow level follows naturally from that at the gate level.

The syntax is given as

Syntax
assign #delay net

EXAMPLE A.1

The model for the AndOr circuit designed earlier can include delays as seen in Figure A.17.

```
// continuous assignment
module AndOr(AandB, AorB, A, B);
   output AandB, AorB;
   input A, B;

   wire AandB, AorB;
   parameter delay0 = 10;

   assign #delay0 AandB = A&B;
   assign #delay0 AorB = A|B;
endmodule
```

Figure A.17 A Combinational Logic Module with Gate Delays Using a Dataflow Verilog Model

The outputs of the system will now change 10 time units after either of the input signals changes, as illustrated in Figure A.18.

Time,	A,	B,	AandB,	AorB
0	1,	1,	x,	x
10	0,	1,	1,	1
20	0,	0,	0,	1
30	0,	1,	0,	0
40	0,	1,	0,	1

Figure A.18 System Output from the Circuit Module in Figure A.17

Rise and fall time delays are incorporated in a similar manner. The syntax for all three is given as

Syntax
assign # (rise time, fall time, delay) net;

EXAMPLE A.2

The model for the AndOr circuit designed earlier can include all three delays as seen in Figure A.19.

```
// Compute the logical AND and OR of inputs A and B.
module AndOr(AandB, AorB, A, B);
    output AandB, AorB;
    input A, B;

    wire AandB, AorB;
    parameter delay0 = 10;
    parameter rise = 5;
    parameter fall = 7;

    assign #(rise, fall,delay0) AandB = A&B;
    assign #(rise, fall,delay0) AorB = A|B;
endmodule
```

Figure A.19 A Combinational Logic Module with All Delays Using a Dataflow Verilog Model

The outputs of the system will now change 10 time units after either of the input signals changes and reflect the rise and fall times as well, as illustrated in Figure A.20.

```
Time,   A,   B,   AandB,   AorB
  0     1,   1,     x,      x
  5     1,   1,     1,      1
 10     0,   1,     1,      1
 17     0,   1,     0,      1
 20     0,   0,     0,      1
 30     0,   1,     0,      0
```

Figure A.20 System Output from the Circuit Module in Figure A.19

A.3.2.3 Operators

The syntax and operators used in Verilog at the dataflow level follow that of the C language very closely. Table A.1 gives the most commonly used operators.

Table A.1 Commonly Used Verilog Operators

<table>
<tr><th>Operator</th><th>Symbol</th><th>Operation</th><th>Operator</th><th>Symbol</th><th>Operation</th></tr>
<tr><td>Arithmetic</td><td>+</td><td>Add</td><td>Equality</td><td>==</td><td>Equal</td></tr>
<tr><td></td><td>-</td><td>Subtract</td><td></td><td>!=</td><td>Not Equal</td></tr>
<tr><td></td><td>/</td><td>Divide</td><td>Logical</td><td>!</td><td>Logical Negation</td></tr>
<tr><td></td><td>*</td><td>Multiply</td><td></td><td>&&</td><td>Logical AND</td></tr>
<tr><td></td><td>%</td><td>Modulus</td><td></td><td>||</td><td>Logical OR</td></tr>
<tr><td>Relational</td><td>></td><td>Greater Than</td><td>Bitwise</td><td>~</td><td>Bitwise Negation</td></tr>
<tr><td></td><td><</td><td>Less Than</td><td></td><td>&</td><td>Bitwise AND</td></tr>
<tr><td></td><td>>=</td><td>Greater Than or Equal</td><td></td><td>|</td><td>Bitwise OR</td></tr>
<tr><td></td><td><=</td><td>Less Than or Equal</td><td>Shift</td><td><<</td><td>Shift Left</td></tr>
<tr><td></td><td></td><td></td><td></td><td>>></td><td>Shift Right</td></tr>
</table>

SEQUENTIAL LOGIC

The following three code modules in Figure A.21 evolve the dataflow implementations of the gated SR latch, the master–slave SR flip-flop, and the 2-bit binary counter designed earlier at the gate level.

```
// Dataflow Level Model
// Gated SR Latch

module gsrLatch(q, qnot, sg, rg, clr, enab);
    input sg, rg, clr, enab;
    output q, qnot;

    wire rL, sL;
    wire q, qnot;

  // Build the gating logic
    assign rL = rg & clr & enab;
    assign sL = sg & clr & enab;

    // Build the basic RS latch
    assign q = ~(rL | ~clr | qnot);
    assign qnot = ~(sL | q);
endmodule
```

```
// Use two SR Latches in
// a master slave configuration to build a flip-flop

module srmsff(q, qnot, s, r, clk, clr);
    input s, r, clk, clr;
    output q, qnot;

    gsrLatch master(qm, qmnot, s, r, clr, clk);
    gsrLatch slave(q, qnot, qm, qmnot, clr, ~clk);
endmodule
```

```
// Build a synchronous two bit binary up counter
// using master slave SR flip-flops
module TwoBitCntr(qA, qB, clr, clk);
    input clr, clk;
    output qA, qB;
    wire sA, rA;
    wire qA, qAnot, qB;
    assign sA = qAnot & qB;
    assign rA = qA & qB;
    srmsff FFB(qB, qBnot, qBnot, qB, clk, clr);
    srmsff FFA(qA, qAnot, sA, rA, clk, clr);
endmodule
```

Figure A.21 Dataflow Models of the S R Latch, Master–Slave Flip-Flop, and 2-Bit Binary Up Counter

A.3.3 The Behavioral Model

The behavioral model increases the design abstraction by an additional level. Our thinking about the design now moves above considerations of the flow of data within the system to the algorithms that express the behavior of the system. At the behavioral level, the model begins to take on more of the guise of a C or C++ program than a digital circuit. Flow of control through the system is expressed in the familiar looping and branching constructs rather than in logic gates.

A.3.3.1 Program Structure

sequential
concurrent

At the behavioral level, one of the major differences between languages such as C or C++ becomes clear. Unlike either C or C++, in which flow of control is generally *sequential*, flow of control in Verilog is *concurrent*. Statements in C or C++ execute in series; those in Verilog execute in parallel.

ALWAYS AND INITIAL STATEMENTS

initial
always, separate flow of control

At the behavioral level, a Verilog program is structured as a collection of *initial* and/or *always* blocks. Each such block expresses a *separate flow of control,* and each will finish execution independent of any other block. A module may define multiple *initial* and/or *always* blocks; however, such blocks cannot be nested. Beyond the input, output statements, and parameter declarations, all behavioral statements must be included in either one of these blocks.

initial block, begin, end

The statements contained in an *initial block* (delimited by *begin* and *end*) are evaluated one time at the start of a simulation. The statements contained in an *always* block (delimited by *begin* and *end*) are evaluated continuously from the start of a simulation.

always, initial

The *always* and *initial* statements are two of the many keywords in Verilog that allow one to set stimuli to a module. The syntax for the initial statement is given as

Syntax
```
initial
    begin
        Initial statements
    end
```

The syntax for the always statement is as follows.

Syntax
```
always
    begin
        statements to always be executed
    end
```

A.3.3.2 Procedural Assignment

procedural assignment
continuous assignment

Assignment in the behavioral model differs from that in either the gate-level or dataflow model. In the behavioral model, *procedural assignment* statements are used to update the state circuit variables. In the dataflow model, the *continuous assignment* construct continually updates the value of the net on the left-hand side. In contrast, in the behavioral model, a value is only updated as the result of the execution of a procedural assignment statement.

blocking, nonblocking
sequential, parallel

Verilog supports two kinds of procedural assignment: *blocking* and *nonblocking* and two kinds of blocks: *sequential* and *parallel*. Statements in a *sequential* block, which is delimited by a *begin* and an *end*, are executed in sequence. Statements in a *parallel* block, which is delimited by a *fork* and a *join*, are executed in parallel.

fork, join

blocking assignment

same sequential block

nonblocking assignment

Blocking assignment statements are executed in the order in which they are written in a sequential block. They will block the execution of subsequent statements that appear in the *same sequential block*; they will not block the execution of statements that appear in a parallel block. A *nonblocking assignment* will not block subsequent statements in a sequential block.

Put another way, a *blocking assignment* will successively evaluate the *right-hand* side and then the *left-hand* side of each assignment statement in a *sequential* block. A *nonblocking assignment* will evaluate *all* of the *right-hand* sides, then *all* of the *left-hand* sides of each statement in a *sequential* block.

The syntax for the two types of assignment is as follows.

Syntax

```
Blocking
        aVariable = aValue;
Nonblocking
        aVariable <= aValue;
```

A.3.3.3 Delays

Delays may be incorporated on either side of the assignment statement according to the following syntax.

Syntax

```
Blocking
        aVariable = #d aValue;
        #d aVariable = aValue
Non-blocking
        aVariable <= #d aValue;
        #d aVariable <= aValue
```

How each is interpreted can be a bit confusing.

BLOCKING

The first statement says:

Evaluate *aValue*, then block for d time units before assigning *aValue* to *aVariable*. Any subsequent use of *aVariable* will get the new value.

The second statement says:

Block for d time units before evaluating *aVariable* = *aValue*. The variable *aVariable* will have the value *aValue* d time units in future.

NONBLOCKING

The first statement says:

Evaluate *aValue*. Schedule *aVariable* to be updated d time units later; however, continue processing other statements. Any other variables using the value of *aVariable* within the next d time units will be assigned the old value.

The second statement says:

Wait d time units before evaluating *aVariable = aValue*. The variable *aVariable* will have the value *aValue* d time units in future.

The following two examples in Figures A.22 and A.24 will illustrate the behavior for each of the four cases in the same and in separate initial blocks.

EXAMPLE A.3

From the execution of the code fragment in Figure A.22, we observe the output given in Figure A.23.

- The variables *a* and *g* from the two initial blocks change state at time 10. The variables (*b* and *c*) and (*h*, and *i*) follow similarly according to their specified delays or 2 and 4 time units after *a* and *g*, respectively.
- After the blocking statements have been evaluated, the nonblocking statements are evaluated.
- The variable *d* is assigned the value 1 10 time units after the blocking statements in the first initial block; the expression *j<=1* is evaluated 10 time units after the blocking statements in the second initial block.
- The variables *e* and *f* are evaluated 2 and 4 time units, respectively, after the blocking statements in the first initial block.
- Finally, the expressions *k <= 1* and *l <= 1* are evaluated 2 and 4 time units, respectively, after the blocking statements in the second initial block.

```
// Illustrate Procedural blocking and non-blocking assignment
// Separate initial block

module blockingNonblocking();
// declare temp registers
    reg a,b,c,d,e,f,g,h,i,j,k,l;

// initialize reg variables
    initial
        begin
            a = 0; b = 0; c = 0; d = 0; e = 0; f = 0;
            g = 0; h = 0; i = 0; j = 0; k = 0; l = 0;
        end

    initial
        begin
            // delay on right hand side
            // blocking
            a = #10 1;
            b = #2 1;
            c = #4 1;

            // non-blocking
            d <= #10 1;
            e <= #2 1;
            f <= #4 1;
        end
```

Figure A.22a Using Procedural Blocking and Nonblocking Assignment

```
// Illustrate Procedural blocking and non-blocking assignment
// Separate initial block

initial
    begin
    // delay on left hand side

    // blocking
    #10 g = 1;
    #2 h = 1;
    #4 i = 1;

    // non-blocking
    #10 j <= 1;
    #2 k <= 1;
    #4 l <= 1;
end

initial
    begin
        $display("\ttime, \ta, \tb, \tc, \td, \te, \tf, \tg, \th, \ti, \tj, \tk, \tl");
        $monitor($time, " \t%b, \t%b, \t%b, \t%b, \t%b, \t%b, \t%b, \t%b, \t%b, \t%b, \t%b,
                          \t%b",a,b,c,d,e,f,g,h,i,j,k,l);
        #50 $finish(1);
    end
endmodule
```

Figure A.22b Using Procedural Blocking and Nonblocking Assignment

time,	a,	b,	c,	d,	e,	f,	g,	h,	i,	j,	k,	l
0	0,	0,	0,	0,	0,	0,	0,	0,	0,	0,	0,	0
10	1,	0,	0,	0,	0,	0,	1,	0,	0,	0,	0,	0
12	1,	1,	0,	0,	0,	0,	1,	1,	0,	0,	0,	0
16	1,	1,	1,	0,	0,	0,	1,	1,	1,	0,	0,	0
18	1,	1,	1,	0,	1,	0,	1,	1,	1,	0,	0,	0
20	1,	1,	1,	0,	1,	1,	1,	1,	1,	0,	0,	0
26	1,	1,	1,	1,	1,	1,	1,	1,	1,	1,	0,	0
28	1,	1,	1,	1,	1,	1,	1,	1,	1,	1,	1,	0
32	1,	1,	1,	1,	1,	1,	1,	1,	1,	1,	1,	1

Figure A.23 System Output from the Module in Figure A.22

EXAMPLE A.4

```
// Illustrate Procedural blocking and non-blocking assignment
// Single initial block
module blockingNonblocking();
    // declare temp registers
    reg a,b,c,d,e,f,g,h,i,j,k,l;
    // initialize reg variables
    initial
    begin
        a = 0; b = 0; c = 0; d = 0; e = 0; f = 0;
        g = 0; h = 0; i = 0; j = 0; k = 0; l = 0;
    end
    initial
    begin
        // delay on right hand side
        // blocking
            a = #10 1;
            b = #2 1;
            c = #4 1;

        // non-blocking
            d <= #10 1;
            e <= #2 1;
            f <= #4 1;
        // delay on left hand side
        // blocking
            #10 g = 1;
            #2 h = 1;
            #4 i = 1;
        // non-blocking
            #10 j <= 1;
            #2 k <= 1;
            #4 l <= 1;
    end
    initial
        begin
            $display("\ttime, \ta, \tb, \tc, \td, \te, \tf, \tg, \th, \ti, \tj, \tk, \tl");
            $monitor($time, " \t%b, \t%b, \t%b, \t%b, \t%b, \t%b, \t%b, \t%b, \t%b, \t%b,
                            \t%b, \t%b",a,b,c,d,e,f,g,h,i,j,k,l);
            #50 $finish(1);
        end
endmodule
```

Figure A.24 Using Procedural Blocking and Nonblocking Assignment

The results following execution are given in Figure A.25.

time,	a,	b,	c,	d,	e,	f,	g,	h,	i,	j,	k,	l
0	0,	0,	0,	0,	0,	0,	0,	0,	0,	0,	0,	0
10	1,	0,	0,	0,	0,	0,	0,	0,	0,	0,	0,	0
12	1,	1,	0,	0,	0,	0,	0,	0,	0,	0,	0,	0
16	1,	1,	1,	0,	0,	0,	0,	0,	0,	0,	0,	0
18	1,	1,	1,	0,	1,	0,	0,	0,	0,	0,	0,	0
20	1,	1,	1,	0,	1,	1,	0,	0,	0,	0,	0,	0
26	1,	1,	1,	1,	1,	1,	1,	0,	0,	0,	0,	0
28	1,	1,	1,	1,	1,	1,	1,	1,	0,	0,	0,	0
32	1,	1,	1,	1,	1,	1,	1,	1,	1,	0,	0,	0
42	1,	1,	1,	1,	1,	1,	1,	1,	1,	1,	0,	0
44	1,	1,	1,	1,	1,	1,	1,	1,	1,	1,	1,	0
48	1,	1,	1,	1,	1,	1,	1,	1,	1,	1,	1,	1

Figure A.25 System Output from the Module in Figure A.24

The major differences between the two implementations are reflected in the evaluation times for the variables d, e, f, g, h, and i.

COMBINATIONAL LOGIC

The next example, in Figure A.26, implements the earlier NandNor combinational logic circuit using a behavioral model and utilizing both the blocking and nonblocking assignments with the right-and left-hand side delays.

EXAMPLE A.5

```
module blocking_nonblocking();
    reg a,b, AandB,AorB, AnandB,AnorB;
    reg e,f, EandF,EorF, EnandF,EnorF;

    // Blocking Assignment
    initial
    begin
        a = 1; b = 1;
        // Delay on the right hand side
        AandB = #10 a&b;
        AnandB = #11 ~AandB;

        // Delay on the left hand side
        #10 AorB = a|b;
        #11 AnorB = ~AorB;
    end

    // Non-blocking Assignment
    initial
    begin
        e = 1; f = 1;
         // Delay on the right hand side
        EandF <= #10 e&f;
        EnandF <= #11 ~EandF;

        // Delay on the left hand side
        #12 EorF <= e|f;
        #13 EnorF <= ~EorF;
    end

    initial
    begin
        $display("\t time\t a, \tb, \tAnandB, \tAnorB, \t\te, \tf, \tEnandF, \tEnorF");
        $monitor($time, "\t%b \t%b \t%b \t\t%b \t\t%b \t %b \t %b \t\t%b", a,b, AnandB,
                                               AnorB, e, f, EnandF, EnorF);
        #50 $finish(1);
    end
endmodule
```

Figure A.26 A Combinational Logic Module Using a Behavioral Verilog Model with Blocking and Nonblocking Assignment

The outputs of the circuits for each of the cases are given in Figure A.27.

time	a,	b,	AnandB,	AnorB,	e,	f,	EnandF,	EnorF
0	1	1	x	x	1	1	x	x
21	1	1	0	x	1	1	x	x
25	1	1	0	x	1	1	x	0
42	1	1	0	0	1	1	x	0

Figure A.27 System Output from the Module in Figure A.26

Observe that based on the order of evaluation of the nonblocking assignment, the NAND operand is never assigned a valid value.

A.3.3.4 Flow of Control

The behavioral Verilog model supports many of the familiar flow of control constructs such as branches, switches, and loops. In addition, the language provides support for event-based control.

EVENTS

event-based control

Verilog supports four different types of *event-based control.* These are given as

- Regular event
- Named event
- OR event
- Level

Each is identified by the event control symbol, @. Verilog interprets an *event* as a change in the value of either a net or a register. Such a change can be used to invoke the evaluation of either a single statement or a block of statements.

The syntax for each is given as follows.

Syntax

Regular Event
```
    @(signal) action
    variable = @( signal) action
    signal may be clock, posedge clock, negedge clock for example
```
Named Event
```
    event anEvent                    // event is a keyword
    always @(anEvent) action
```
OR Event
```
    always @( signal1 or signal2 or signal3 or...) action
```
Level
```
    always wait( signal) action      // wait is a keyword
```

BRANCHES

if, if else

Like the C and C++ languages, Verilog utilizes the *if* and *if else* constructs to select alternate paths of execution based on the value of a condition variable. Permitted combinations follow the C and C++ syntax.

Syntax

```
if (condition)
      statement;
if (condition)
      statement1;
else
      statement2;

if (condition1)
      statement1;
else if (condition2)
      statement2;
else
      statement 3;
```

If statement comprises a block of statements, the block must be delimited by the begin-end pair.

CASE STATEMENT

The *switch* or *case* statement in Verilog uses the Pascal rather than the C language syntax as shown

Syntax

```
case (expression)
      label0:          statement0;
      label1:          statement1;
        .
        .
      labeln-1:        statementn-1;
      default:         defaultStatement;
endcase
```

If statement comprises a block of statements, the block must be delimited by the begin-end pair.

Unlike the C switch, once a statement or block of statements is evaluated, flow of control leaves the case rather than continuing through the remaining alternatives.

LOOPS

The Verilog language supports the four common loop constructs:

- while
- repeat
- for
- forever

The first three should be familiar from the C or C++ languages; the forever is unique to Verilog. The syntax for each is given as follows.

Syntax

```
while(test)
begin
    loop body
end

repeat(repeatcount)
begin
    loop body
end

for(init; test; action)
begin
    loop body
end
```

init and action are usually assignments.

```
forever
begin
    loop body
end
```

SEQUENTIAL LOGIC

The following three code modules in Figure A.28 evolve the behavioral implementations of the gated SR latch, the master–slave SR flip-flop, and the 2-bit binary counter designed earlier at the gate and dataflow levels.

```
// Behavioral Level Model
// Gated SR Latch
module gsrLatch(q, qnot, s, r, clr, enab);
    input s, r, enab, clr;
    output q, qnot;

    reg q, qnot;

    always@ (~clr or enab)
    begin
        if(~clr)
        begin
            q = 1'b0;
            qnot = 1'b1;
        end

        else
        begin
            if (s & ~r)
            begin
                q <= s;
                qnot <= r;
            end
            else if (~s & r)
            begin
                q <= s;
                qnot <= r;
            end
        end
    end
endmodule
```

```
// Use two SR Latches in a master slave
// configuration to build a flip-flop

module srmsff(q, qnot, s, r, clk, clr);
    input s, r, clk, clr;
    output q, qnot;

    gsrLatch master(qm, qmnot, s, r, clr, clk);
    gsrLatch slave(q, qnot, qm, qmnot, clr, ~clk);
endmodule
```

```
// Build a synchronous two bit binary up counter
// using master slave SR flip-flops

module TwoBitCntr(qA, qB, clr, clk);
    input clr, clk;
    output qA, qB;

    reg sA, rA;
    wire qA, qAnot, qB;

    always@(posedge clk)
    begin
        sA = qAnot & qB;
        rA = qA & qB;
    end

    srmsff FFB(qB, qBnot, qBnot, qB, clk, clr);
    srmsff FFA(qA, qAnot, sA, rA, clk, clr);
endmodule
```

Figure A.28 Behavioral Models of the S R Latch, Master–Slave Flip-Flop, and 2-Bit Binary Up Counter

The next code module in Figure A.29 illustrates a more commonly used approach for modeling counting, timing, or registered types of designs. Rather than working with individual flip-flops, the design is approached algorithmically.

```
// Build a synchronous two bit binary up counter
module TwoBitCntr(state, clr, clk);
    input clr, clk;
    output[1:0] state;

    reg[1:0] state;

    // Name the states
    parameter state0 = 2'b00;
    parameter state1 = 2'b01;
    parameter state2 = 2'b10;
    parameter state3 = 2'b11;

    // Build a synchronous two bit binary up counter
    always@(~clr or negedge clk)
    begin
        if(~clr)
        begin
            state = state0;
        end

        else case(state)
            state0:
                state = state1;
            state1:
                state = state2;
            state2:
                state = state3;
            state3:
                state = state0;
        endcase
    end
endmodule
```

Figure A.29 A Behavioral Model of a 2-Bit Binary Up Counter Using a Case Statement

A.4 TESTING AND VERIFYING THE CIRCUIT

Once the circuit is designed and modeled in Verilog, we move into the next phase. We first need to verify that the model functions properly. The next step is to use it for its intended purpose. To that end, we perform any functional, parametric, and stress tests on the design, through the model, that we deem necessary to confirm the design before committing to hardware.

NandNor

test bench

We will illustrate the verification phase of the process using the *NandNor* circuit that was designed earlier. To do this we create a *test bench*. A test bench models the electronics workbench. It comprises the measurement and stimulus instruments and the circuit to be tested. The modules used for stimulus and measurement will go in a test module.

A high-level model for the test bench has the general structure shown in Figure A.30.

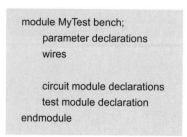

```
module MyTest bench;
    parameter declarations
    wires

    circuit module declarations
    test module declaration
endmodule
```

Figure A.30 A Model of a Verilog Test Bench

main()

The test bench plays the same role as does the *main()* function in C or C++ and the top-level class in Java. It acts as the outermost container in the program.

A.4.1 The Circuit Module

We will use the *NandNor* circuit that we developed earlier as the circuit module to be tested and verified. During test, we must confirm that each path through the logic circuit is functional and that it performs according to specification. The logic diagram for the circuit is repeated in Figure A.31 for reference.

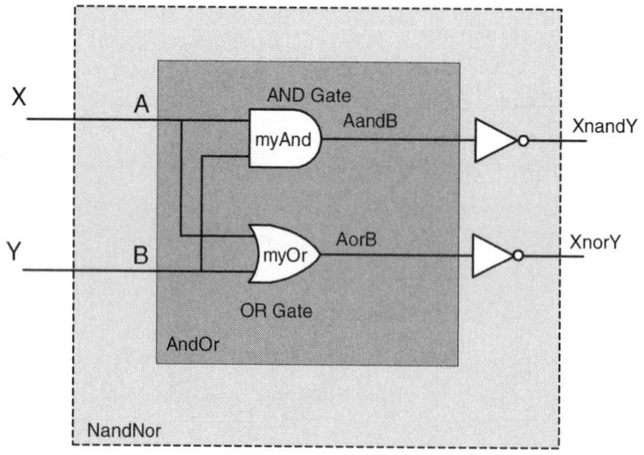

Figure A.31 A Simple Unit Under Test

A.4.2 The Test Module

As with other modules, the test module will have a set of inputs and a set of outputs. The inputs to the test module will be the outputs of the UUT and will model the measurement equipment. The outputs from the test module will be the inputs of the UUT. These will model the stimulus equipment.

NandNor

The tester module for the *NandNor* combinational logic is given in the code fragment in Figure A.32.

The opening lines of the test module identify the sets of inputs and outputs. These signals will come from the UUT and will send the stimulus vector to the UUT. The parameter, *stimDelay*, specifies the delay between the applications of successive test vectors. Next, the test vectors are defined and appear as successive statements.

```
module Tester (X, Y, XnandYin, XnorYin);
    input       XnandYin, XnorYin;
    output      X, Y;

    reg         X, Y;
    parameter   stimDelay = 10;

    initial                                  // Stimulus
    begin
        X = 1; Y = 1;
        #stimDelay    X = 0;
        #stimDelay    Y = 0;
        #stimDelay    X = 1;
    end

    initial
    begin                                    // Response
        display("\t Time, \t \tX, \t Y, \t XnandYin, \t XnorYin");
        monitor($time, "\t \t %b, \t %b, \t %b, \t \t%b", X, Y, XnandYin, XnorYin);
    end
endmodule
```

Figure A.32 A Tester Module for the Unit Under Test

Four different combinations of the signals X and Y are applied to the circuit input. A delay is specified between each stimulus application. The design of the *NandNor* circuit assumes ideal parts. Had the logic gates included a delay, the *stimDelay*, between the applications of successive vectors would have provided time for the signal to propagate through the logic block.

stimDelay

The test vectors are written as statements within an *initial* block. Thus, the test suite is applied one time during the simulation. The circuit output in response to the set of test vectors is presented using the *$display* and *$monitor* system tasks.

initial

$display, $monitor

The tester for the behavioral sequential *2-bit binary counter* module follows the same pattern with several additions and is presented in the code module in Figure A.33.

2-bit binary counter

```
// Test module for two bit binary up counter
module tester(clr, clk, qA, qB);
    input qA, qB;
    output clr, clk;

    reg clk, clr;

    parameter stimDelay = 15;
    parameter clkDelay = 5;

    initial
    begin
        clk = 0;
        clr = 0;
        #stimDelay clr = ~clr;

        repeat(16)
        #clkDelay clk = ~clk;
    end
    initial
    begin
        $display("\tTime, \t\tqA, \tqB, \tclr, \tclk");
        $monitor($time,"\t\t%b, \t%b, \t%b, \t%b", qA, qB, clr, clk);
    end

endmodule
```

Figure A.33 A Tester Module for a 2-Bit Binary Up Counter

Clocks and Resets

A synchronous sequential circuit will need a strobe, enable, or clock in order to operate. Good designs also include a reset or clear signal to establish the initial state of the circuit. Typically, these signals are supplied by the tester with a block of code such as the code fragment in Figure A.34.

```
reg clk, clr;

parameter stimDelay = 15;
parameter clkDelay = 5;

initial
begin
    clk = 0;
    clr = 0;
    #stimDelay clr = ~clr;

    always
        #halfPeriod clk = ~clk;
end
```

Figure A.34 Building a Clock

A.4.3 The Test Bench

We will now bring everything together with the test bench. In the test bench, we instantiate one copy of the NandNor gate—the UUT—and one copy of the tester. These are the stimulus and monitoring instruments. Finally, we connect them together using wires as illustrated in Figure A.35.

```
module MyTest bench;
    wire XnandY, XnorY, X, Y;
    NandNor aNandNor (XnandY, XnorY, X, Y);
    Tester aTester (X, Y, XnandY, XnorY);
endmodule
```

Figure A.35 Building a Test Bench

A.4.4 Performing the Simulation

If the simulation is now run, the test vectors are successively applied to the input of the UUT. As the simulation executes, the $monitor system task will display the state of the input and output signals and the system time at which the samples were taken. These appear in Figure A.36.

If the results are satisfactory, we can move on to the real work of confirming the design.

Time,	X,	Y,	XnandYin,	XnorYin
0	1,	1,	0,	0
10	0,	1,	1,	0
20	0,	0,	1,	1
30	1,	0,	1,	0

Figure A.36 Output from Running the Test Bench

A.5 SUMMARY

This appendix introduced the Verilog language and presented the important features and capabilities used in this book. It does not purport to be a comprehensive study of either the language or the kinds of testing necessary to confirm an embedded design.

We began with the basic components and organization of a Verilog program; then we examined gate-level or structural, dataflow, and behavioral models for combinational logic circuits, and followed with similar models for sequential circuits. Design is only one element of the product development. Each design must also be tested to confirm that it meets specified requirements. Then the model must be used for testing and verifying the original design. To that end, the appendix concludes with a short discussion on how one can formulate a test bench and test suites to verify the proper operation. The material on testing establishes a foundation to enable the developer to build test cases that will enable testing, verifying, and stressing to the desired level.

Verilog and other hardware design languages such as VHDL offer designers a rich and powerful set of tools to help to attack today's complex designs. It is beyond the scope of this text to present a comprehensive treatise on testing or modeling using a language like Verilog. The interested reader is strongly encouraged to consult the reference material cited in References.

References

Computer Architecture

Baer, J., *Computer Systems Architecture*, Computer Science Press, 1980.

Baron, R., & Higbie, L., *Computer Architecture*, Addison-Wesley, 1992.

Coulouris, G., Dollimore, J., & Kindberg, T., *Distributed Systems Concepts and Design*, 3rd ed., Addison-Wesley, 2001.

Hamacher, C., Vranesic, Z., & Zaky, S., *Computer Organization*, 2nd ed., McGraw-Hill, 1984.

Heuring, V., & Jordan, H., *Computer Systems Design and Architecture*, Addison-Wesley Longman, 1997.

Mano, M., & Kime, C., *Logic and Computer Fundamentals*, 3rd ed., Pearson Prentice-Hall, 2004.

Miller, G., *Microcomputer Engineering*, 2nd ed., Prentice-Hall, 1999.

Null, L., & Lobur, J., *The Essentials of Computer Organization and Architecture,* Jones and Bartlett Publishers, 2003.

Patterson, D., & Hennessy, J., *Computer Organization & Design: The Hardware/Software Interface*, 3rd ed., Morgan Kaufmann Publishers, 2004.

Patterson, D., & Hennessy, J., *Computer Architecture: A Quantitative Approach*, 3rd ed., Morgan Kaufmann Publishers, 2002.

Shen, J., & Lipasti, M., *Modern Processor Design Fundamentals of Superscalar Processors*, McGraw-Hill, 2005.

Shuey, R., Spooner, D., & Frieder, O., *The Architecture of Distributed Computer Systems*, Addison-Wesley Longman, 1997.

Sima, D., Fountain, T., & Kacsuk, P., *Advanced Computer Architectures: A Design Space Approach*, Addison-Wesley Longman, 1997.

Tanenbaum, A., *Structured Computer Organization*, 4th ed., Prentice-Hall, 1999.

Design

Abdi, S., & Gajski, D., *Formal Verification of System Partitioning*, *Technical Report CECS-03-06*, 6 March 2003, Center for Embedded Computer Systems, University of California, Irvine.

Boehm, B., *A Spiral Model of Software Development and Enhancement, Software Engineering Project Management*, 1987, pp. 128–142.

Budgen, D., *Software Design*, Pearson Addison-Wesley, 1993.

Guerrouat, A., & Richter, H., "A Component-Based Specification Approach for Embedded Systems Using FDTS," Proceedings of the 2005 Conference on Specification and Verification of Component-based Systems, 2005, Article No. 14.

Hardung, B., Kölzow, T., & Krüger, A., "Reuse of Software in Distributed Embedded Automotive Systems," Proceedings of the 4th ACM International Conference on Embedded Software, 2004, pp. 203–210.

Hyman, B., *Fundamentals of Engineering Design*, Prentice-Hall, 1998.

Jones, M., *The Thinkers Toolkit*, Three Rivers Press, 1998.

Kaplan, D., *Introduction to Scientific Computation and Programming,* Thomson Brooks/Cole, 2004.

Norman, D., *The Design of Everyday Things*, Doubleday, 1988.

Pop, P., Eles, P., Pop, T., & Peng, Z., "An Approach to Incremental Design of Distributed Embedded Systems," Proceedings of the 38th Conference on Design Automation, 2001, pp. 450–455.

Richter, K., & Ernst, R., *Event Model for Heterogeneous System Analysis*, Proceedings of the 2002 Design, Proceedings of the 2002 Design, Automation and Test in Europe Conference, and Exhibition.

Stankovic, J., "Strategic Directions in Real-Time and Embedded Systems," *ACM Computing Surveys*, 28(4):751–763, Special ACM 50th-anniversary issue: Strategic Directions in Computing Research, December 1996.

VanOech, R., *A Whack on the Side of the Head*, Warner Books, 1983.

Voland, G., *Engineering by Design*, Addison-Wesley Longman, 1999.

Hardware Design Languages

Arnold, M., *Verilog Digital Computer Design Algorithms into Hardware*, Prentice-Hall, 1999.

Bhaskar, J., *A Verilog HDL Primer*, Star Galaxy Publishing, 1997.

Bhaskar, J., *A VHDL Synthesis Primer*, 2nd ed., Star Galaxy Publishing, 1996.

Bhaskar, J., *VHDL Primer*, 3rd ed., Prentice-Hall, 1999.

Botros, N., *HDL Programming Fundamentals VHDL and Verilog*, Da Vinci Engineering Press, 2006.

Ciletti, M., *Modeling, Synthesis and Rapid Prototyping with Verilog HDL*, Prentice-Hall, 1999.

Dewey, A., *Analysis and Design of Digital Systems with VHDL*, PWS Publishing Company, 1997.

Palnitkar, S., *Verilog HDL: A Guide to Digital Design and Synthesis*, Prentice-Hall, 1996.

Roth, C., *Digital Systems Design Using VHDL*, PWS Publishing Company, 1998.

Skahill, K., *VHDL for Programmable Logic*, Addison-Wesley Longman, 1996.

Smith, D., & Franzon, P., *Verilog Styles for Synthesis of Digital Systems*, Prentice-Hall, 2000.

Thomas, D., & Moorby, P., *The Verilog Hardware Description Language*, 3rd ed., Kluwer Academic Publishers, 1996.

Yalamanchili, S., *Introductory VHDL: From Simulation to Synthesis*, Prentice-Hall, 2001.

UML and Structured Design

Armour, F., & Miller, G., *Advanced Use Case Modeling Software Systems*, Pearson Addison-Wesley, 2000.

Cheeseman, J., & Daniels, J., *UML Components: A Simple Process of Specifying Component-Based Software*, Addison-Wesley Longman, 2001.

Douglass, B., *Real-Time UML, Second Edition: Developing Efficient Objects for Embedded Systems*, Addison-Wesley Longman, 2001.

Eriksson, H., & Penker, M., *UML Toolkit*, John Wiley & Sons, 1998.

Fowler, M., *UML Distilled, Third Edition: A Brief Guide to the Standard Object Modeling Language*, Pearson Addison-Wesley, 2004.

Harmon, P., & Watson, M., *Understanding UML: The Developer's Guide*, Morgan Kaufmann Publishers, 1994.

Holt, R., Graham, G., Lazowska, E., & Scott, M., *Structured Concurrent Programming with Operating Systems Applications*, Addison-Wesley, 1978.

Larman, C., *Applying UML and Patterns: An Introduction to Object-Oriented Analysis and Design and the Unified Process*, 2nd ed., Prentice-Hall, 2002.

Lee, R., & Tepfenhart, W., *UML and C++: A Practical Guide to Object Oriented Development*, 2nd ed., Pearson Prentice-Hall, 2001.

Naiburg, E., Maksimchuk, R., *UML for Database Design*, Pearson Addison-Wesley, 2001.

Page-Jones, M., *The Practical Guide to Structured Systems Design*, 2nd ed., Prentice-Hall, 1988.

Richter, C., *Designing Flexible Object-Oriented Systems with UML*, McMillan Technical Publishing, 1999.

Rosenberg, D., & Scott, K., *Use Case Driven Object Modeling with UML: A Practical Approach*, Addison-Wesley Longman, 1999.

Scott, K., *UML Explained*, Pearson Addison-Wesley, 2001.

Stevens, P., & Pooley, R., *Using UML Software Engineering with Objects and Components*, Pearson Addison-Wesley, 2000.

Ward, P., & Mellor, S., *Structured Development for Real-Time Systems. Vol. I–III*, Yourdon Press, 1985.

Yourdon, E., & Constantine, L., *Structured Design*. Prentice-Hall, 1979.

Analog Design

Frerking, M., *Crystal Oscillator Design and Temperature Compensation*, Van Nostrand Reinhold Company, 1978.

Geiger, D., *Phaselock Loops for DC Motor Speed Control*, John Wiley & Sons, 1981.

Morrison, R., *Grounding and Shielding Techniques in Instrumentation*, 2nd ed., John Wiley & Sons, 1977.

Motchenbacher, C., & Fitchen, F., *Low Noise Electronic Design*, John Wiley & Sons, 1973.

Roberge, J., *Operational Amplifiers: Theory and Practice*, John Wiley & Sons, 1975.

Thomas, R., & Rosa, A., *The Analysis and Design of Linear Circuits*, 4th ed., John Wiley & Sons, 2004.

Digital Design

Balabanian, N., & Carlson, B., *Digital Logic Design Principles*, John Wiley & Sons, 2001.

Brown, S., & Vranesic, Z., *Fundamentals of Digital Logic with Verilog Design*, McGraw-Hill, 2003.

Cheung, J., & Bredeson, J., *Modern Digital Systems Design*, West Publishing Company, 1990.

Givonne, D., *Digital Principles and Design*, McGraw-Hill, 2003.

Katz, R., & Borriello, G., *Contemporary Logic Design*, 2nd ed., Pearson Prentice-Hall, 2005.

Mano, M., *Digital Design*, 3rd ed., Pearson Prentice-Hall, 2002.

Marcovitz, A., *Introduction to Logic Design*, 2nd ed., McGraw-Hill, 2005.

Nelson, V., Nagle, H., Carroll, B., & Irwin, J., *Digital Circuit Analysis & Design*, Prentice-Hall, 1995.

Roth, C., *Fundamentals of Logic Design*, 5th ed., Thomson Brooks/Cole, 2004.

Salcic, Z., & Smailaglic, A., *Digital Systems Design and Prototyping Using Field Programmable Logic*, Kluwer Academic Publishers, 1997.

Sandige, R., *Digital Design Essentials*, Prentice-Hall, 2002.

Shiva, S., *Introduction to Logic Design*, 2nd ed., Marcel Dekker, 1998

Tinder, R., *Engineering Digital Design*, 2nd ed., Academic Press, 2000.

Vahid, F., *Digital Design*, John Wiley & Sons, 2006.

Wakerly, J., *Digital Design Principles and Practices*, 4th ed., Pearson Prentice-Hall, 2006.

Coding Theory

Berlekamp, E., *Algebraic Coding Theory*, McGraw-Hill, 1968.

Lin, S., *An Introduction to Error-Correcting Codes*, Prentice-Hall, 1970.

Peterson, W., & Weldon, E., *Error Correcting Codes*, 2nd ed., 1972.

Sellers, Jr., F., Hsiao, M., & Bearnson, W., *Error Detecting Logic for Digital Computers*, McGraw-Hill, 1968.

C Language

Antonakos, J., & Mansfield, K., Jr., *Structured C for Engineering and Technology*, 4th ed., Prentice-Hall, 2001.

Austell-Wolfson, B., & Otieno, R., *Complete Book of C Programming*, Prentice-Hall, 2000.

Deitel, H., & Deitel, P., *C: How to Program*, 2nd ed., Prentice-Hall, 1994.

Hanly, J., & Koffman, E., *Problem Solving and Program Design in C*, Addison-Wesley, 1996.

Harbison, S., & Steele, G., Jr., *C: A Reference Manual*, 5th ed., Prentice-Hall, 2002.

Kernighan, B., & Ritchie, D., *The C Programming Language*, 2nd ed., Prentice-Hall, 1988.

Miller, L., & Quilici, A., *The Joy of C*, John Wiley & Sons, 1997.

Press, W., Teukolsky, S., Vetterling, W., & Flannery, B., *Numerical Recipes in C: The Art of Scientific Computing*, 2nd ed., Cambridge University Press, 1992.

Waite, M., & Prata, S., *C Primer Plus*, Sams Publishing, 1993.

Data Structures

Carrano, F., Helman, P., & Veroff, R., *Data Abstraction and Problem Solving with C++ Walls and Mirrors*, 2nd ed., Addison-Wesley Longman, 1998.

Dale, N., *C++ Plus Data Structures*, 3rd ed., Jones and Bartlett Publishers, 2003.

Dale, N., Joyce, D., & Weems, C., *Object Oriented Data Structures Using Java*, Jones and Bartlett Publishers, 2002.

Ford, W., & Topp, W., *Data Structures with C++*, Prentice-Hall, 1996.

Horowitz, E., & Sahni, S., *Fundamentals of Data Structures*, Computer Science Press, 1976.

Kruse, R., & Ryba, A., *Data Structures and Program Design in C++*, Prentice-Hall, 1999.

Murray, W., & Pappas, C., *Data Structures with STL*, Prentice-Hall, 2001.

Nyhoff, L., *C++: An Introduction to Data Structures*, Prentice-Hall, 1999.

Weiss, M., *Data Structures and Algorithm Analysis in C*, 2nd ed., Addison-Wesley Longman, 1997.

Software Engineering

Andrews, G., *Foundations of Multithreaded, Parallel, and Distributed Programming*, Addison-Wesley Longman, 2000.

Bryant, R., & O'Hallaron, D., *Computer Systems: A Programmer's Perspective*, Prentice-Hall, 2003.

Dorfman, M., & Thayer, R. editors, *Software Engineering*, IEEE Computer Society Press, 1997.

IEEE Standard for Microprocessor Assembly Language, Institute of Electrical and Electronic Engineers, 1985.

McConnell, S., *Rapid Development*, Microsoft Press, 1996.

Murphy, M., *C/C++ Software Quality Tools*, Prentice-Hall, 1996.

Savage, J., *Models of Computation: Exploring the Power of Computing*, Addison-Wesley, 1998.

Sommerville, I., *Software Engineering*, Addison-Wesley, 1996.

Embedded and Real-Time Systems

Auslander, D., Ridgely, J., & Ringgenberg, J., *Control Software for Mechanical Systems, Object Oriented Design in a Real-Time World*, Prentice-Hall, 2002.

Buhr, R., & Bailey, D., *An Introduction to Real-Time Systems: From Design to Networking with C/C++*, Prentice-Hall, 1999.

Burns, A., & Wellings, A., *Real-Time Systems and Programming Languages*, 2nd ed., Addison-Wesley Longman, 1996.

Buttazzo, G., *Hard Real-Time Computing Systems: Predictable Scheduling Algorithms and Applications*, 2nd ed., Springer Science+Business Media, 2004.

Calvez, J., *Embedded Real-Time Systems: A Specification and Design Methodology*, John Wiley & Sons, 1993.

Cheng, A., *Real-Time Systems Scheduling, Analysis, and Verification*, John Wiley & Sons, 2002.

Cooling, J., *Real-Time Software Systems*, PWS Publishing Company, 1997.

Douglass, B., *Doing Hard Time: Developing Real-Time Systems with UML, Objects, Frameworks, and Patterns*, Addison-Wesley, Longman, 1999.

Fisher, J., Faraboschi, P., & Young, C., *Embedded Computing: A VLIW Approach to Architecture, Compilers, and Tools*, Morgan Kaufmann Publishers, 2005.

Gajski, D., Vahid, F., Narayan, S., & Gong, J., *Specification and Design of Embedded Systems*, Prentice-Hall, 1994.

Grehan, R., Moote, R., & Cyliax, I., *Real-Time Programming: A Guide to 32-Bit Embedded Development*, Addison-Wesley, Longman, 1998.

Krishna, C., & Shin, K., *Real-Time Systems*, McGraw-Hill, 1997.

LaPlante, P., *Real-Time Systems Design and Analysis*, 3rd ed., John Wiley & Sons, 2004.

Lewis, D., *Fundamentals of Embedded Software: Where C and Assembly Meet*, Prentice-Hall, 2002.

Liu, J., *Real-Time Systems*, Prentice-Hall, 2000.

Mathai, J. editor, *Real-Time Systems Specification, Verification and Analysis*, Prentice-Hall, 1996.

Noergaard, T., *Embedded Systems Architecture: A Comprehensive Guide for Engineers and Programmers*, Elsevier, 2005.

Simon, D., *An Embedded Systems Primer,* Addison-Wesley, 1999.

Vahid, F., & Givargis, T., *Embedded System Design: A Unified Hardware / Software Introduction*, John Wiley & Sons, 2002.

Valvano, J., *Embedded Microcomputer Systems: Real Time Interfacing*, Brooks/Cole Thomson, 2000.

Wolf, W., *Computers as Components: Principles of Embedded Computing Design*, Morgan Kaufmann Publishers, 2001.

Microelectronics

Jaeger, R., *Microelectronic Circuit Design*, WCB/ McGraw-Hill, 1997.

Miller, G., *Microcomputer Engineering*, 2nd ed., Prentice-Hall, 1999.

Rabaey, J., *Digital Integrated Circuits, A Design Perspective*, Prentice-Hall, 1996.

Rabaey, J., Chandrakasan, A., & Nikolic, B., *Digital Integrated Circuits, A Design Perspective*, 2nd ed., Prentice-Hall, 2003.

Weste, N., & Harris, D., *CMOS VLSI Design, A Circuits and Systems Perspective*, 3rd ed., Pearson Addison-Wesley, 2005.

Wolf, Wayne, *Modern VLSI Design: Systems on Silicon*, 2nd ed., Prentice-Hall, 1998.

Programmable Logic Devices

Barr, Michael. "Programmable Logic: What's It to Ya?," Embedded Systems Programming, June 1999, pp. 75–84.

FLEX 10K Embedded Programmable Logic Device Family, Data Sheet, Altera Corp., January 2003, ver. 4.2.

Hamblen, J., & Furman, M., *Rapid Prototyping of Digital Systems, A Tutorial Approach*, 2nd ed., Kluwer Academic Publishers, 2001.

PSoC™ Mixed Signal Array, Final Data Sheet, CY8C21123, CY8C21223, CY8C21323, Cypress Semiconductor, Corp., February 25, 2005.

Salcic, Z., & Smailagic, A., *Digital Systems Design and Prototyping Usign Field Programmable Logic*, Kluwer Academic Publishers, 1997.

XC9500XL High-Performance CPLD Family Data Sheet, Xilinx, Inc., DS054 (v2.1), March 22, 2006.

Operating Systems

Bach, M. *The Design of the Unix Operating System*, Prentice-Hall, 1986.

Brinch Hanmsen, P., *Operating Systems Principles*, Prentice-Hall, 1973.

Chow, R., & Johnson, T., *Distributed Operating Systems & Algorithms*, Addison-Wesley Longman, 1997.

Cole, B., *The Emergence of Net-Centric Computing*, Prentice-Hall, 1999.

Comer, D., *Operating System Design: The XINU Approach*, Prentice-Hall, 1984.

Deitel, H., *An Introduction to Operating Systems*, 1st ed., Addison-Wesley, 1984.

Deitel, H., Deitel, P., & Choffnes, D., *Operating Systems,* 3rd ed., Pearson Prentice-Hall, 2004.

Finkel, R., *An Operating Systems Vade Mechum*, Prentice-Hall, 1986.

Galli, D., *Distributed Operating Systems*, Prentice-Hall, 2000.

Havender, J., "Avoiding Deadlock in Multitasking Systems," *IBM Systems Journal* 7(2):74–84 (1968).

Labrosse, J., *MicroC/OS-II: The Real-Time Kernel*, 2nd ed., CMP Books, 2002.

Mullender, S., *Distributed Systems*, Addison-Wesley, ACM Press, 1993.

Nutt, G., *Operating Systems*, 3rd ed., Pearson Education, 2004.

Peterson, J., & Silberschatz, A., *Operating System Concepts*, Addison-Wesley, 1983.

Silberschatz, A., Galvin, G., & Gagne, P., *Operating Systems Concepts*, 7th ed., John Wiley & Sons, 2005.

Tanenbaum, A., *Distributed Operating Systems*, Prentice-Hall, 1995.

Deadlock

Andrews, G., & Levin, G., "On-the-Fly Deadlock Prevention," Proceedings of the First ACM SIGACT-SIGOPS Symposium on Principles of Distributed Computing, 1982, pp. 165–172.

Chen, X., Davare, A., Hsieh, H., Sangiovanni-Vincentelli, A., & Watanabe, Y., "Simulation Based Deadlock Analysis for System Level Designs," Proceedings of the 42nd Annual Conference on Design Automation, 2005, pp. 260–265.

de Alfaro, L., Raman, V., Faella, M., & Majumdar, R., "Code Aware Resource Management," Proceedings of the 5th ACM

International Conference on Embedded Software, 2005, pp. 191–202.

Dijkstra, E., *Co-operating Sequential Processes,* In Programming languages: NATO Advanced Study Institute, F. Genuys, ed., Academic Press, London, 1968.

Felder, M., & Pezzè, M., "A Formal Design Notation for Real-Time Systems," *ACM Transactions on Software Engineering and Methodology* 11(2):149–190 (2002).

Fontao, R., "A Concurrent Algorithm for Avoiding Deadlocks in Multiprocess Multiple Resource Systems," *ACM SIGOPS Operating Systems Review* 6(1/2):72–79, SPECIAL ISSUE: Process Interactions and System Correctness (1972).

Frailey, D., "A Practical Approach to Managing Resources and Avoiding Deadlocks," *Communications of the ACM* 16(5):323–329 (2003).

Havender, J. "Avoiding Deadlock in Multitasking Systems," *IBM Systems Journal* 2:74–84 (1968).

Lee, J., & Mooney, V., III, "A Novel Deadlock Avoidance Algorithm and Its Hardware Implementation," Proceedings of the 2nd IEEE/ACM/IFIP International Conference on Hardware/Software Codesign and System Synthesis, 2004, pp. 200–205.

Lee, J., & Mooney, V., III, "A Novel O(N) Parallel Banker's Algorithm for System-On-A-Chip," Proceedings of the 2005 Conference on Asia South Pacific Design Automation, 2005, pp. 1305–1308.

Stepner, D., Rajan, N., & Hui, D., "Embedded Application Design Using a Real-Time OS," Proceedings of the 36th ACM/IEEE Conference on Design Automation, 1999, pp. 151–156.

Tanenbaum, A., & Renesse, R., "Distributed Operating Systems," *ACM Computing Surveys* 17(4):419–470 (1985).

Computer Networks

Anderson, D., *Universal Serial Bus System Architecture*, Addison-Wesley Longman, 2001.

Blahut, R., *Digital Transmission of Information*, Addison-Wesley, 1997.

Goldman, J., & Rawles, P., *Applied Data Communications: A Business-Oriented Approach*, 3rd ed., John Wiley & Sons, 2001.

Green, P., *Fiber Optic Networks*, Prentice-Hall, 1993.

Halsall, F., *Data Communications, Computer Networks and Open Systems*, 4th ed., Addison-Wesley, 1997.

Hyde, J., *USB Design by Example*, Intel University Press, John Wiley & Sons, 1999.

Keshav, S., *An Engineering Approach to Computer Networking*, Addison-Wesley Longman, 1997.

Kurose, J., & Ross, K., *Computer Networking, A Top-Down Approach Featuring the Internet*, 2nd ed. Addison-Wesley Longman, 2003.

Shankar, P., *Introduction to Wireless Systems*, John Wiley & Sons, 2002.

Tanenbaum, A., *Computer Networks*, 4th ed., Prentice-Hall, 2003.

Wilson, S., *Digital Modulation and Coding*, Prentice-Hall, 1996.

High-Speed Signals

Brooks, D., *Signal Integrity Issues and Printed Circuit Board Design,* Pearson Prentice-Hall, 2003.

Hall, S., Hall, G., & McCall, J., *High-Speed Digital System Design: A Handbook of Interconnect Theory and Design Practices*, John Wiley & Sons, 2000.

Johnson, H., & Graham, M., *High Speed Digital Design: A Handbook of Black Magic*, Prentice-Hall, 1993.

Johnson, H., & Graham, M., *High Speed Signal Propagation: Advanced Black Magic*, Pearson Prentice-Hall, 2003.

Performance, Safety, Reliability, and Test

Abramovici, M., Breuer, M., & Friedman, A., *Digital Systems Testing and Testable Design*, IEEE Press, 1990.

Ait-Ameur, Y., Bel, G., Boniol, F., Pairault, S., & Wiels, V., "Robustness Analysis of Avionics Embedded Systems," Proceedings of the 2003 ACM SIGPLAN Conference on Language, Compilers, and Tool for Embedded Systems, 2003, pp. 123–132.

Anantaraman, A., Seth, K., Patil, K., Rotenberg, E., & Mueller, F., "Virtual Simple Architecture (VISA): Exceeding the Complexity Limit in Safe Real-Time Systems," Proceedings of the 30th Annual International Symposium on Computer Architecture, 2003, pp. 350–361.

Asplund, L., & Lundqvist, K.,"Safety Critical Systems Based on Formal Models," *ACM SIGAda Ada Letters* 20(4), Special Issue on Presentations from SIGADA 2000, December 2000, pp. 32–39.

Bhansali, P., "Software Safety: Current Status and Future Direction," *ACM SIGSOFT Software Engineering Notes* 30(1), 2005, pp. 1–4.

Biswas, S., Simpson, M., & Barua, R., "Memory Overflow Protection for Embedded Systems Using Run-Time Checks, Reuse and Compression," Proceedings of the 2004 International Conference on Compilers, Architecture, and Synthesis for Embedded Systems, 2004, pp. 280–291.

Botaschanjan, J., Kof, L., Kühnel, C., & Spichkova, M., "Towards Verified Automotive Software," Proceedings of the 2nd International Workshop on Software Engineering for Automotive Systems, 2005, pp. 1–6.

Hilton, A., & Hall, J., "Developing Critical Systems with PLD Components," Proceedings of the 10th International Workshop on Formal Methods for Industrial Critical Systems, 2005, pp. 72–79.

Izosimov, V., Pop, P., Eles, P., & Peng, Z., "Design Optimization of Time-and Cost-Constrained Fault-Tolerant Distributed Embedded Systems," Proceedings of the Conference on Design, Automation and Test in Europe, Volume 2, 2005, pp. 864–869.

Jain, R., *The Art of Computer Systems Performance Analysis,* John Wiley & Sons, 1991.

Jhumka, A., Klaus, S., & Huss, S., "A Dependability-Driven System-Level Design Approach for Embedded Systems," Proceedings of the Conference on Design, Automation and Test in Europe, Volume 1, 2005, pp. 372–377.

Knight, J., "Safety Critical Systems: Challenges and Directions," Proceedings of the 24th International Conference on Software Engineering, 2002, pp. 547–550.

Leveson, N., "Evaluation of Software Safety," Proceedings of the 12th International Conference on Software Engineering, 1990, pp. 223–224.

Leveson, N., "Software Safety in Embedded Computer Systems," *Communications of the ACM* 34(2):34–46 (1991).

Leveson, N., & Weiss, K., "Making Embedded Software Reuse Practical and Safe," Proceedings of the 12th ACM SIGSOFT 12th International Symposium on Foundations of Software Engineering, 2004, pp. 171–178.

Lutz, R., "Targeting Safety-Related Errors During Software Requirements Analysis," Proceedings of the 1st ACM SIGSOFT Symposium on Foundations of Software Engineering, 1993, pp. 99–106.

Lutz, R., "Software Engineering for Safety: A Roadmap," Proceedings of the Conference on the Future of Software Engineering, 2000, pp. 213–226.

McCabe, T. *A Complexity Measure*, IEEE Transactions on Software Engineering, 2, 1976, pp. 308–320.

Marwedel, P., & Gebotys, C., "Secure and Safety-Critical vs. Insecure, Non Safety-Critical Embedded Systems: Do They Require Completely Different Design Approaches?", Proceedings of the 2nd IEEE/ACM/IFIP International Conference on Hardware/Software Codesign and System Synthesis, 2004, pp. 72–73.

Meyers, G., *Software Reliability*, John Wiley & Sons, 1976.

Perry, W., *Effective Methods for Software Testing*, John Wiley & Sons, 1995.

Siewiorek, D., & Swarz, R., *Reliable Computer Systems Design and Evaluation*, 2nd ed., Digital Press, 1992.

Stallings, W., *Computer Organization and Architecture Designing for Performance*, 4th ed., Prentice-Hall, 1996.

Steininger, A., "Testing and Built-In Self-Test—A Survey" (submitted), *Journal of System Architecture*, pp. 1–27, date unknown.

Vaishnavi, V., & Fraser, M., "A Validation Framework for a Maturity Measurement Model for Safety-Critical Software Systems," Proceedings of the 36th Annual Southeast Regional Conference, 1998, pp. 314–322.

Zhang, Y., & Krishnendu, C.,"Dynamic Adaptation for Fault Tolerance and Power Management in Embedded Real-Time Systems," *ACM Transactions on Embedded Computing Systems* 3(2):336–360 (2004).

Wu, W., & Kelly, T., "Failure Modeling in Software Architecture Design for Safety," Proceedings of the 2005 Workshop on Architecting Dependable Systems, 2005, pp. 1–7.

Power Management

Advanced Configuration and Power Interface Specification, Hewlett-Packard Corporation, Intel Corporation, Microsoft Corporation, Phoenix Technologies, Ltd., Toshiba Corporation, Revision 3.0b, October 10, 2006.

Bagherzadeh, N., Chou, P., & Li, D., "Mode Selection and Mode-Dependency Modeling for Power-Aware Embedded Systems," Proceedings of the 2002 Conference on Asia South Pacific Design Automation/VLSI Design, 2002, p. 697.

Benini, L., Macii, A., & Poncino, M., "Energy-Aware Design of Embedded Memories: A Survey of Technologies, Architectures, and Optimization Techniques," *ACM Transactions on Embedded Computing Systems* 2(1):5–32 (2003).

Cattheer, F., Wuytakk, S., DeGreef, E., Balasa, F., Nachtergaele, L., Vandecappelle, A., *Custom Memory Management Methodology: Exploration of Memory Organization for Embedded Multimedia System Design*, Kluwer Academic Publishers, 1998.

Chandar, S., Mehendale, M., & Govindarajan, R., "Area and Power Reduction of Embedded DSP Systems Using Instruction Compression and Re-Configurable Encoding," Proceedings of the 2001 IEEE/ACM International Conference on Computer-Aided Design, 2001, pp. 631–634.

Dutt, N., & Mamidipaka, M., "On-chip Stack Based Memory Organization for Low Power Embedded Architectures," Proceedings of the Conference on Design, Automation and Test in Europe, Volume 1, 2003, p. 11082–11089.

Gordon-Ross, A., Cotterell, S., & Vahid, F., "Tiny Instruction Caches for Low Power Embedded Systems," *ACM Transactions on Embedded Computing Systems* 2(4):449–481 (2003).

Hua, S., Qu, G., & Bhattacharyya, S., "Energy Reduction Techniques for Multimedia Applications with Tolerance to Deadline Misses," Proceedings of the 40th conference on Design Automation, 2003, pp. 131–136.

Joo, Y., Choi, Y., Shim, H., Lee, H., Kim, K., & Chang, N., "Energy Exploration and Reduction of SDRAM Memory Systems," Proceedings of the 39th Conference on Design Automation, 2002, pp. 892–897.

Mamidipaka, M., Dutt N., & Hirschberg, D. "Efficient Power Reduction Techniques for Time Multiplexed Address Buses," Proceedings of the 15th international symposium on System Synthesis, 2002, pp. 207–212.

Nachtergaele, L., Tiwari, V., & Dutt, N., "System and Architecture-Level Power Reduction of Microprocessor-Based Communication and Multi-Media Applications," Proceedings of the 2000 IEEE/ACM International Conference on Computer-Aided Design, 2000, pp. 569–574.

Niu, L., & Quan, G., "Reducing Both Dynamic and Leakage Energy Consumption for Hard Real-Time Systems," Proceedings of the 2004 International Conference on Compilers, Architecture, and Synthesis for Embedded Systems, 2004, pp. 140–148.

Pedram, M., "Power Optimization and Management in Embedded Systems," Proceedings of the 2001 Conference on Asia South Pacific Design Automation, 2001, pp. 239–244.

Shrivastava, A., Earlie, E., Dutt, N., & Nicolau, A., "Aggregating Processor Free Time for Energy Reduction," Proceedings of the 3rd IEEE/ACM/IFIP International Conference on Hardware/software Codesign and System Synthesis, 2005, pp. 154–159.

Tessier, R., Betz, V., Neto, D., & Gopalsamy, T., "Power-Aware RAM Mapping for FPGA Embedded Memory Blocks," Proceedings of the International Symposium on Field Programmable Gate Arrays, 2006, pp. 189–198.

Venkatachalam, V., & Franz, M., "Power Reduction Techniques for Microprocessor Systems," *ACM Computing Surveys* 37(3):195–237 (2005).

Zhang, Y., & Chakrabarty, K., "Dynamic Adaptation for Fault Tolerance and Power Management in Embedded Real-Time Systems," *ACM Transactions on Embedded Computing Systems* 3(2):336–360 (2004).

Microcontrollers, Microprocessors, and Microcomputers

Clements, A., *Microprocessor Systems Design, 68000 Hardware, Software, and Interfacing*, 3rd ed., PWS Publishing Company, 1997.

Haskell, R., *Design of Embedded Systems Using 68HC12/11 Microcontrollers*, Prentice-Hall, 2000.

Hellenbuyck, C., *Programming PIC Microcontrollers with PicBasic*, Elsevier Science, 2003.

Korneev, V., & Kiselev, A., *Modern Microprocessors*, 3rd ed., Charles River Media, 2004.

Lipovski, G., *Introduction to Microcontrollers Architecture, Programming, and Interfacing for the Motorola 68HC12*, Academic Press, 1999.

Peatman, J., *Design with PIC Microcontrollers,* Prentice-Hall, 1998.

Short, K., *Embedded Microprocessor Systems Design: An Introduction Using the INTEL 80C188EB*, Prentice-Hall, 1998.

Smith, D., *PIC in Practice*, D.W. Smith, 2002.

Uffenbeck, J., *The 80x86 Family*, Prentice-Hall, 2002.

Index

D

U

Directive	Definition
#define	Define a preprocessor macro
#undef	Undefine or remove a preprocessor macro
#include	Insert contents of another source file
#if	Conditionally include contents of another source file
#ifdef	Conditionally include contents of another source file if macro name is defined
#ifndef	Conditionally include contents of another source file if macro name is not defined
#elif	Conditionally include contents of another source file if macro name is defined and previous #if, #ifdef, #ifndef, or #elif failed
#else	Alternative action if preceding #if, #ifdef, #ifndef, or #elif directive fails
#endif	Closes #if, #ifdef, #ifndef, or #elif construct
#line	Return line number for compiler message
defined name defined(name)	Directive that returns 1 if name is defined as preprocessor macro and 0 otherwise
# operator	Directive to replace macro parameter with string constant containing parameter's value
## operator	Create single token from two adjacent tokens
#pragma	Specify proprietary information to the compiler
#error	Return a compile time error with associated message

C Preprocessor Directives